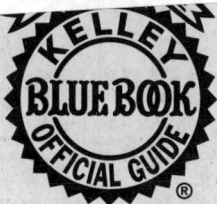

USED CAR GUIDE
Consumer Edition
1994 – 2008 Models

| Vol. 17 | July—September 2009 | No. 3 |

LES KELLEY - *Founder*
PAUL C. JOHNSON - - - - - - - - - - - - - - - - - *Publisher*
PATRICIA A. DEBACKER - - - - - - - - - - - *Editor-in-Chief*
LESA SPEROU - - - - - - - - - *Director, Data Configuration*
KELLY J. SALAZAR - - - - - - *Director, Strategic Initiatives*

Kelley Blue Book Used Car Guide, Consumer Edition is published four times per year in January, April, July and October for $9.95 per issue by Kelley Blue Book Co., P.O. Box 19691, Irvine, CA 92623. POSTMASTER: Send address changes to Kelley Blue Book Auto Market Report, P.O. Box 19691, Irvine, CA 92623.

This publication is distributed to the book trade by NBN (National Book Network), 4501 Forbes Blvd, Ste 200, Lanham, MD 20706.

Published at:

P.O. Box 19691, Irvine, California 92623

We assume no responsibility for errors or omissions.

Official Guidebooks Since 1926

ORDER YOUR BLUE BOOK NOW!

Kelley Blue Book
P.O. Box 19691
Irvine, California 92623

Please accept our order for _____ copies of the Kelley Blue Book Used Car Guide Consumer Edition, at $9.95 per copy, including shipping.

NAME _____

ADDRESS _____

CITY _____

STATE _____ ZIP _____

PHONE (_____)_____

VISA or MASTER CARD # _____

EXP. DATE _____ SIGNATURE _____

Visa ☐   MasterCard ☐   Check Enclosed ☐

California residents please add sales tax. Shipping outside U.S. extra.

INTRODUCTION

Since 1926, Kelley Blue Book has provided the automotive industry with used vehicle values. Today we are the trusted resource relied upon by both the automotive industry and consumers. This **Consumer Edition** has been prepared to provide values and information relevant to the different types of consumer transactions.

What is a guidebook?

A guidebook such as this one is just that, a guide. To produce the most timely, accurate and trusted used vehicle values, Kelley Blue Book's pricing analysts constantly collect and review new and used vehicle transaction data, as well as information on each vehicle's current supply and demand. They then meticulously determine and report used car values based on real market information.

This guidebook represents the educated opinion of Kelley Blue Book's staff and each value is determined after carefully studying information we deem complete and reliable. We assume no responsibility for errors or omissions.

Is this book the same as the Kelley Blue Book trade publication?

This book contains the trusted values you have come to expect from Kelley Blue Book. The values in the Consumer Guide represent transactions relevant to consumers including Trade-In, Private Party and used Retail Values.

What is the difference between Trade-In, Private Party and Retail Values?

Kelley Blue Book provides several different values representing different types of transactions.

Trade-In Value is what consumers can expect to receive from a dealer for a Trade-In vehicle assuming an accurate appraisal of condition. This value will likely be less than the Private Party Value because the dealer incurs the cost of safety inspections, reconditioning and other costs of doing business.

Kelley Blue Book factors the following into our Trade-In values:

Safety Inspections — The dealer will incur the cost of inspecting and repairing the vehicle to ensure that it meets government requirements for safety and smog emissions.

Reconditioning — Before reselling a vehicle a dealer can spend hundreds or even thousands of dollars performing repairs, routine maintenance and cosmetic detailing and touch up.

The dealer also hopes to make a fair profit for his efforts.

INTRODUCTION

Private Party Value is what a buyer can expect to pay when buying a used car from a private party. The Private Party Value assumes the vehicle is sold "As Is" and carries no warranty (other than the continuing factory warranty). The final sale price will vary depending on the vehicle's actual condition and local maket conditions. This value may also be used to derive Fair Market Value for insurance and vehicle donation purposes.

Suggested Retail Value is representative of dealers' asking prices and is the starting point for negotiation between a consumer and a dealer. This Suggested Retail Value assumes that the vehicle has been fully reconditioned and has a clean Title History. This value also takes into account the dealers' profit, costs for advertising, sales commissions and other costs of doing business. The final sale price will likely be less depending on the vehicle's actual condition, popularity, type of warranty offered and local market conditions.

How does Condition affect the value of the vehicle and what is the difference between "Fair," "Good," and "Excellent" ratings? There is never a single correct value for a used vehicle. The value of a vehicle depends on several factors, most importantly condition and overall appearance. Supply and demand for a particular vehicle, local market conditions and the economy also play a role in determining a car's value.

Kelley Blue Book provides additional values for used vehicles in each of the following conditions:

"Excellent" condition means that the vehicle looks new, is in excellent mechancial condition and needs no reconditioning. This vehicle has never had any body or paint work and is free of rust. The vehicle has a clean Title History and will pass a smog and safety inspection. The engine compartment is clean, with no fluid leaks and is free of visible defects. The vehicle also has complete and verifiable service and maintenance records. Less than 5% of all used vehicles fall into this category.

"Good" condition means that the vehicle is free of any major defects. This vehicle has a clean Title History, the paint, body and interior have only minor (if any) blemishes and there are no major mechanical problems. There should be little or no rust on this vehicle. The tires match and have substantial tread wear left. A "good" vehicle will need some reconditioning or routine servicing to be sold at retail. Most consumer owned vehicles fall into this catagory.

"Fair" condition means that the vehicle has some mechanical or cosmetic defects and needs servicing but is still in reasonable running condition. This vehicle has a clean Title History, the paint, body and/or interior need work performed by a professional. The tires may need to be replaced. There may be some repairable rust damage.

HOW TO USE THE BLUE BOOK

FINDING A VEHICLE

There are two sections in this book, the Automobile or Car section up front and the Truck & Van Section in the back. The Truck & Van section is marked by black tabs on each page. Within each section, the makes are listed alphabetically and models are listed by size within each make. Model years are listed oldest to newest.

EQUIPMENT ADJUSTMENTS

To get the most accurate value, you will need to add or deduct from the base value depending on the equipment. "Adds" and "Deducts" appear underneath individual vehicles and in separate Equipment Schedules. A value in parentheses represents a "Deduct." More generic equipment adjustments appear in the Equipment Schedules. Schedules for cars are at the front of the book. Equipment schedules for trucks and vans are at the back of the book.

You should always add or subtract for each item that is listed separately, even if it is part of a package that you have already added for or if it was considered original standard equipment. If an equipment item is listed both underneath the vehicle listing and in the Equipment Schedule, use the value underneath the vehicle listing because it is specific to that vehicle.

MILEAGE

Mileage must also be taken into consideration to derive the most accurate valuation of a used vehicle. On page 9 we have listed an "acceptable" range of mileage for each model year. The range does not represent the average mileage driven for the model year but the point of resistence where value can be affected. As a vehicle gets older, condition is more important than mileage. Vehicles with more miles may sometimes be worth more than lower mileage vehicles if its condition is better. It is important to note that the values we list are intended for vehicles within the acceptable mileage range.

HOW TO USE THE BLUE BOOK

ABBREVIATIONS USED IN THIS BOOK

VIN — Vehicle Identification Number. The VIN may vary depending on model, engine, transmission and option packages.

W.B. — Wheelbase. This is the distance from the center of the front wheel to the center of the rear wheel.

CID/L — Engine size displacement in cubic inches or liters.

List — This is the original suggested retail price of the vehicle when it was sold new, including destination charges and equipment as indicated on the equipment schedule.

Trucks — Trucks listed in this guide have a smooth exterior with the rear wheel wells inside the bed. Value adjustments for models with the rear wheel wells on the outside of the bed can be found on the Truck Equipment Schedules under the Stepside listing.

Premium Sound — This refers to an upgraded sound system (Bose, JBL, Infinity, etc.) not simply a CD changer, equalizer or an aftermarket receiver.

VEHICLE IDENTIFICATION NUMBERS (VINs)

If you are not sure of the year or model of a vehicle, you can often determine them from the Vehicle Identification Number or VIN. Using VINs can get a bit technical. If you already know the year and the model of the vehicle you can skip this information.

Under 1995 Lincoln, you will see the heading "1995 LINCOLN - 1LN(LM81W)-S-#." What this means is that all 1995 Lincolns have a VIN starting with 1LN and have an S in the 10th position. The fourth through eighth positions determine the specific Lincoln model and are marked by parentheses. The hyphens indicate positions which can be ignored and the # symbol represents the individual vehicle's serial number.

Please note that we do not have room in this guidebook to list all the VIN information. There are some VINs that you cannot decode using the information provided. Also there are some VINs that indicate two or more possible models. In these cases you must determine the particular model by inspecting the vehicle.

TIPS ON BUYING A USED CAR

DEALER vs PRIVATE PARTY

There are advantages and disadvantages to buying a car from a dealer vs a Private Party. With a dealer, you may get a warranty and some dealerships offer certification programs for late model vehicles that will extend the original factory warranty. While buying from a dealership provides security, buying from a Private Party can save you money. When buying from a private party, ask for all repair and maintenance records and contact information of the previous owner in case you have questions later.

TRADING-IN YOUR VEHICLE

If you are trading your vehicle to a dealer, be sure to check the Trade-In Value and the Private Party Value of your vehicle. You may find it to your benefit to sell the vehicle yourself.

CHECKING OUT A USED VEHICLE

If you are contacting a private party, be sure to ask why they are selling the vehicle. Ask them to describe the condition of the vehicle and how it was used (daily, as a second car, kids car). Ask if they have all of the repair and maintenance records for the vehicle. Ask if you can take the car to a mechanic for an inspection. This is extremely important as private party sales are "As Is" and once you have bought the vehicle, it's yours. If your state requires a smog certificate, insist that the vehicle pass a smog test before buying the car. Smog checks are the current owner's responsibility. Also be certain the vehicle's registration is current and paid to date. It can be costly to reinstate an expired registration. Registration fees vary from state to state, be sure to consult your state's Department of Motor Vehicles.

— Stand away from the vehicle and look at its body panels. Do they all match in color? Do they line up?

— Check the tires for wear. Uneven tire wear, balding on the sides or in the middle, could indicate the need for an alignment or a costly repair to the vehicle's suspension.

— Open the trunk, hood and doors. Look for paint specks or over spray, a sign that all or part of the vehicle has been repainted. If the vehicle has been repainted it is often a sign of some previous damage.

— Check the radiator fluid. If it is very dark or has oil droplets in it, there is a good chance the vehicle has a cracked head gasket meaning that coolant and oil are mixing together.

— Look at the condition of the rubber on each foot pedal and the leather on the steering wheel. Do they show heavy wear? Heavy wear in a low mileage vehicle may indicate that the vehicle has seen more mileage then the odometer indicates.

TIPS ON BUYING A USED CAR

— Spend as much time as you can inside the vehicle. Feel the seat, and we mean really feel it. Take a good long time to sit, because really, the seat is one of the most important parts of the vehicle.

— What about the steering wheel? Is it too high up or too close to the dash? When adjusted comfortably, does it cut off any or all the gauges? Look at the layout of the radio and heater controls. Can they be easily adjusted without taking your eyes off the road? Look over your shoulders, are there any blind spots that you cannot compensate for by using your mirrors? Climb into the seats, front and back. Is there enough legroom and headroom? Do the headrests come up far enough? Do they touch your head or are they raked back at an angle away from you? Does the seatbelt have an adjustable anchor or does it cut into your neck? Check to see how far the rear windows roll down. Some models have windows that only go down a few inches or are sealed in place and don't roll down at all. Take your time to explore all these areas.

— Then take it for a drive. How does it sound? A prolonged tapping could be the valves needing adjustment or a bad hydraulic lifter. Pump the brake pedal a few times and then press hard with your foot. If it slowly sinks all the way to the floor, there is either a leak in the line or the master cylinder/brake booster is dying. Shift into gear. If the vehicle is an automatic, the transmission should engage immediately and shifts should be crisp and quick. With your foot firmly on the brake, shift from drive to reverse; clunks or grinding noises could indicate a worn or broken engine/transmission mount, bad U-joints or differential wear.

— As you drive along, does the steering wheel shake or vibrate? It shouldn't. Vibration in the steering wheel can mean anything from an unbalanced wheel to a loose steering rack. Cars with ABS (anti-lock brakes) will have a slight pulsating action in the brake pedal when the brakes are applied with some force. Cars without ABS should not have a pulsating brake pedal.

— We also recommend that you contact your local Department of Motor Vehicles. Ask them what forms are required to transfer the vehicle title as well as any other required information. For example, some states require a smog certificate while others require the bill of sale from the current owner.

— Lastly, whatever you do, get it in WRITING. This means if you settle with a private party, write up a contract stating what you are paying for the vehicle and under what terms it is to be delivered. Likewise with a dealer, any work they promise to do or options they intend to add, get it in writing before you close the deal.

MILEAGE RANGES

ACCEPTABLE MILEAGE RANGES

The following are acceptable mileage ranges for each model year. They do **not** represent the average miles driven. Rather, they represent an accepted mileage range as demonstrated by market research. If a vehicle's mileage is outside of the accepted range, dollar adjustments may be necessary. Mileage higher than shown on the guidelines below can expect to encounter resistance from a buyer.

YEAR	ACCEPTABLE MILEAGE RANGE
1994 – 1996	96,000 – 101,000
1997	93,000 – 98,000
1998	90,000 – 95,000
1999	87,000 – 92,000
2000	84,000 – 89,000
2001	81,000 – 86,000
2002	79,000 – 84,000
2003	73,000 – 78,000
2004	67,000 – 72,000
2005	59,000 – 64,000
2006	47,000 – 52,000
2007	33,000 – 38,000
2008	19,000 – 24,000

PRIVATE PARTY & RETAIL EQUIPMENT VALUE CONVERSION

Use the chart below to convert Trade-In Equipment Values to Private Party and Retail Values. Simply find your total Trade-In Equipment Value under the Trade-In (TI) column then follow across to the Private Party and Retail (PP/R) column. This new figure will be your Private Party or Retail Equipment Value.

TI	PP/R	TI	PP/R	TI	PP/R	TI	PP/R	TI	PP/R
25	35	225	300	425	565	625	835	825	1100
50	65	250	335	450	600	650	865	850	1135
75	100	275	365	475	635	675	900	875	1165
100	135	300	400	500	665	700	935	900	1200
125	165	325	435	525	700	725	965	925	1235
150	200	350	465	550	735	750	1000	950	1265
175	235	375	500	575	765	775	1035	975	1300
200	265	400	535	600	800	800	1065	1000	1335

1994–1996 FACTORY EQUIP. TRADE-IN VALUES

Equipment	1	2	3	4	5	6
Automatic Trans	—	—	125	—	*	175
Power Steering	*	*	*	*	*	50
Air Conditioning	*	*	*	*	*	50
GROUP TOTAL	*	*	125	*	*	275
Cassette	*	*	*	50	25	25
Power Windows	*	*	*	25	25	25
Power Door Locks	*	*	25	25	25	25
Tilt Wheel	*	*	25	25	25	25
Cruise Control	*	*	25	25	25	25
BOTH GROUPS	*	*	200	150	125	400
CD (Single Disc)	100	100	100	100	100	100
CD (Multi Disc)	200	200	200	200	200	200
Leather	*	100	100	50	25	25
Sun Roof	*	50	50	50	50	25
Moon Roof	*	100	75	75	50	25
T-Bar Roof	—	—	225	225	—	100
Alloy Wheels	*	*	25	25	25	25
Premium Wheels	100	100	50	50	50	25
Third Seat (Wagon)	125	50	50	50	50	50
DEDUCT FOR:						
Manual Trans	—	(125)	—	(175)	(175)	*
w/o Power Steering	—	—	—	(50)	(50)	(50)
w/o Air Cond	(150)	(150)	(100)	(100)	(50)	(50)
w/o AM/FM Stereo	(25)	(25)	(25)	(25)	(25)	(25)

* — EQUIPMENT INCLUDED IN BASE PRICE

SEE PAGE 9 FOR PVT PARTY & RETAIL EQUIPMENT

1997 FACTORY EQUIPMENT TRADE-IN VALUES

Equipment	1	2	3	4	5	6
Automatic Trans	—	—	—	—	*	200
Power Steering	*	*	*	*	*	*
Air Conditioning	*	*	*	*	*	*
Power Windows	*	*	*	*	25	25
Power Door Locks	*	*	*	*	25	25
Tilt Wheel	*	*	*	*	25	25
Cruise Control	*	*	*	*	25	25
Cassette	*	*	*	*	25	25
GROUP TOTAL	*	*	*	*	125	325
Power Seat	*	*	25	25	25	25
Dual Power Seats	*	*	25	25	25	25
ABS (4 Wheel)	*	*	50	50	25	25
CD (Single Disc)	100	100	100	100	100	100
CD (Multi Disc)	200	200	200	200	200	200
Premium Sound	25	25	25	25	25	25
Navigation System	100	—	—	—	—	—
Leather	*	*	100	75	25	25
Sun Roof	*	50	50	50	50	25
Moon Roof	*	150	100	100	75	50
T-Bar Roof	—	—	—	250	—	—
Rear Spoiler	25	25	25	25	25	25
Alloy Wheels	*	*	25	25	25	25
Premium Wheels	150	150	100	100	50	25
Roof Rack (Wagon)	25	25	25	25	25	25
Third Seat (Wagon)	150	100	100	100	50	50
DEDUCT FOR:						
Manual Trans	—	—	—	—	(225)	*
w/o Power Steering	—	—	—	(50)	(50)	(50)
w/o Air Cond	(200)	(200)	(150)	(150)	(50)	(50)
w/o AM/FM Stereo	(25)	(25)	(25)	(25)	(25)	(25)
w/o Power Windows	—	(50)	—	(50)	—	—
w/o Pwr Door Locks	—	(25)	—	(25)	—	—
w/o Tilt Wheel	—	(50)	—	(50)	—	—
w/o Cruise Control	—	(25)	—	(25)	—	—
w/o Leather	(100)	(100)	—	—	—	—
w/o Sun/Moon Roof	(250)	—	—	—	—	—

* — EQUIPMENT INCLUDED IN BASE PRICE

1998 FACTORY EQUIPMENT TRADE-IN VALUES

Equipment	1	2	3	4	5	6
Automatic Trans	—	—	—	—	*	225
Power Steering	*	*	*	*	*	*
Air Conditioning	*	*	*	*	*	*
Power Windows	*	*	*	*	50	25
Power Door Locks	*	*	*	*	25	25
Tilt Wheel	*	*	*	*	25	25
Cruise Control	*	*	*	*	25	25
Cassette	*	*	*	*	25	25
GROUP TOTAL	*	*	*	*	150	350
Power Seat	*	*	25	25	25	25
Dual Power Seats	*	*	25	25	25	25
ABS (4 Wheel)	*	*	50	50	25	25
CD (Single Disc)	125	125	125	125	125	125
CD (Multi Disc)	225	225	225	225	225	225
Premium Sound	50	50	25	25	25	25
Navigation System	150	—	—	—	—	—
Leather	*	*	125	100	25	25
Sun Roof	*	75	50	50	50	25
Moon Roof	*	175	125	125	100	75
Rear Spoiler	25	25	25	25	25	25
Alloy Wheels	*	*	25	25	25	25
Premium Wheels	175	175	125	125	75	25
Roof Rack (Wagon)	25	25	25	25	25	25
Third Seat (Wagon)	200	125	125	125	75	75
DEDUCT FOR:						
Manual Trans	—	—	—	—	(275)	*
w/o Power Steering	—	—	—	(75)	(50)	(50)
w/o Air Cond	(225)	(225)	(175)	(175)	(75)	(75)
w/o AM/FM Stereo	(25)	(25)	(25)	(25)	(25)	(25)
w/o Power Windows	—	(75)	—	(75)	—	—
w/o Pwr Door Locks	—	(25)	—	(25)	—	—
w/o Tilt Wheel	—	(50)	—	(50)	—	—
w/o Cruise Control	—	(25)	—	(25)	—	—
w/o Leather	(100)	(125)	—	—	—	—
w/o Sun/Moon Roof	(300)	—	—	—	—	—

* — EQUIPMENT INCLUDED IN BASE PRICE

SEE PAGE 9 FOR PVT PARTY & RETAIL EQUIPMENT

1999 FACTORY EQUIPMENT TRADE-IN VALUES

Equipment	1	2	3	4	5	6
Automatic Trans	—	—	—	—	*	250
Power Steering	*	*	*	*	*	*
Air Conditioning	*	*	*	*	*	*
Power Windows	*	*	*	*	75	25
Power Door Locks	*	*	*	*	25	25
Tilt Wheel	*	*	*	*	50	25
Cruise Control	*	*	*	*	25	25
Cassette	*	*	*	*	25	25
GROUP TOTAL	*	*	*	*	200	375
Power Seat	*	*	25	25	25	25
Dual Power Seats	*	*	25	25	25	25
ABS (4 Wheel)	*	*	50	50	25	25
CD (Single Disc)	150	150	150	150	150	150
CD (Multi Disc)	250	250	250	250	250	250
Premium Sound	75	75	25	25	25	25
Navigation System	200	—	—	—	—	—
Leather	*	*	150	125	25	25
Sun Roof	*	100	75	75	50	25
Moon Roof	*	200	150	150	125	100
Rear Spoiler	25	25	25	25	25	25
Parking Sensors	150	—	—	—	—	—
Alloy Wheels	*	*	50	50	25	25
Premium Wheels	200	200	150	150	100	50
Roof Rack (Wagon)	25	25	25	25	25	25
Third Seat (Wagon)	250	150	150	150	100	100
DEDUCT FOR:						
Manual Trans	—	—	—	—	(325)	*
w/o Power Steering	—	—	—	(100)	(50)	(50)
w/o Air Cond.	(250)	(250)	(200)	(200)	(100)	(100)
w/o AM/FM Stereo	(25)	(25)	(25)	(25)	(25)	(25)
w/o Power Windows	—	(100)	—	(100)	—	—
w/o Pwr Door Locks	—	(25)	—	(25)	—	—
w/o Tilt Wheel	—	(75)	—	(75)	—	—
w/o Cruise Control	—	(25)	—	(25)	—	—
w/o Leather	(125)	(150)	—	—	—	—
w/o Sun/Moon Roof	(325)	—	—	—	—	—

* — EQUIPMENT INCLUDED IN BASE PRICE

2000 FACTORY EQUIPMENT TRADE-IN VALUES

Equipment	1	2	3	4	5	6
Automatic Trans	—	—	—	—	*	275
Power Steering	*	*	*	*	*	*
Air Conditioning	*	*	*	*	*	*
Power Windows	*	*	*	*	100	50
Power Door Locks	*	*	*	*	25	25
Tilt Wheel	*	*	*	*	75	25
Cruise Control	*	*	*	*	25	25
Cassette	*	*	*	*	50	25
GROUP TOTAL	*	*	*	*	275	425
Power Seat	*	*	25	25	25	25
Dual Power Seats	*	*	50	50	25	25
ABS (4 Wheel)	*	*	75	75	25	25
CD (Single Disc)	175	175	175	175	175	175
CD (Multi Disc)	275	275	275	275	275	275
Premium Sound	100	100	50	50	50	50
Navigation System	250	250	250	250	250	250
Leather	*	*	175	150	25	25
Sun Roof	*	125	100	100	75	50
Moon Roof	*	225	175	175	150	125
Rear Spoiler	25	25	25	25	25	25
Parking Sensors	175	125	—	—	—	—
Alloy Wheels	*	*	75	75	50	25
Premium Wheels	250	250	175	175	125	75
Roof Rack (Wagon)	25	25	25	25	25	25
Third Seat (Wagon)	300	175	175	175	125	125
DEDUCT FOR:						
Manual Trans	—	—	—	—	(375)	*
w/o Power Steering	—	—	—	(125)	(75)	(75)
w/o Air Cond	(275)	(275)	(225)	(225)	(125)	(125)
w/o AM/FM Stereo	(25)	(25)	(25)	(25)	(25)	(25)
w/o Power Windows	—	(125)	—	(125)	—	—
w/o Pwr Door Locks	—	(25)	—	(25)	—	—
w/o Tilt Wheel	—	(100)	—	(100)	—	—
w/o Cruise Control	—	(25)	—	(25)	—	—
w/o Leather	(150)	(175)	—	—	—	—
w/o Sun/Moon Roof	(350)	—	—	—	—	—

* — EQUIPMENT INCLUDED IN BASE PRICE

SEE PAGE 9 FOR PVT PARTY & RETAIL EQUIPMENT

2001 FACTORY EQUIPMENT TRADE-IN VALUES

Equipment	1	2	3	4	5	6
Automatic Trans	—	—	—	—	*	300
Power Steering	*	*	*	*	*	*
Air Conditioning	*	*	*	*	*	*
Power Windows	*	*	*	*	125	75
Power Door Locks	*	*	*	*	50	25
Tilt Wheel	*	*	*	*	100	50
Cruise Control	*	*	*	*	50	25
Cassette	*	*	*	*	75	50
GROUP TOTAL	*	*	*	*	400	525
Power Seat	*	*	50	50	25	25
Dual Power Seats	*	*	75	75	50	25
ABS (4 Wheel)	*	*	100	100	50	50
CD (Single Disc)	200	200	200	200	200	200
CD (Multi Disc)	300	300	300	300	300	300
MP3 (Single Disc)	200	200	200	200	200	200
MP3 (Multi Disc)	300	300	300	300	300	300
Premium Sound	125	125	75	75	75	75
Navigation System	300	300	300	300	300	300
Leather	*	*	200	175	50	25
Sun Roof	*	150	125	125	100	75
Moon Roof	*	250	200	200	175	150
Rear Spoiler	25	25	25	25	25	25
Sensing Cruise Ctrl	350	—	—	—	—	—
Parking Sensors	200	150	—	—	—	—
Alloy Wheels	*	*	100	100	75	50
Premium Wheels	300	300	200	200	150	100
Premium Whls 19"+	450	450	450	450	450	450
Roof Rack (Wagon)	25	25	25	25	25	25
Third Seat (Wagon)	350	200	200	200	150	150
DEDUCT FOR:						
Manual Trans	—	—	—	—	(400)	*
w/o Power Steering	—	—	—	(150)	(100)	(100)
w/o Air Cond	(300)	(300)	(250)	(250)	(150)	(150)
w/o AM/FM Stereo	(50)	(50)	(50)	(50)	(25)	(25)
w/o Power Windows	—	(150)	—	(150)	—	—
w/o Pwr Door Locks	—	(50)	—	(50)	—	—
w/o Tilt Wheel	—	(125)	—	(125)	—	—
w/o Cruise Control	—	(25)	—	(25)	—	—
w/o Leather	(175)	(200)	—	—	—	—
w/o Sun/Moon Roof	(375)	—	—	—	—	—

* — EQUIPMENT INCLUDED IN BASE PRICE

2002 FACTORY EQUIPMENT TRADE-IN VALUES

Equipment	1	2	3	4	5	6
Automatic Trans	—	—	—	—	*	300
Power Steering	*	*	*	*	*	*
Air Conditioning	*	*	*	*	*	*
Power Windows	*	*	*	*	125	75
Power Locks	*	*	*	*	50	25
Tilt Wheel	*	*	*	*	100	50
Cruise Control	*	*	*	*	50	25
Cassette	*	*	*	*	75	50
GROUP TOTAL	*	*	*	*	400	525
Power Seat	*	*	50	50	25	25
Dual Power Seats	*	*	100	100	50	25
ABS (4 Wheel)	*	*	100	100	50	50
CD (Single Disc)	200	200	200	200	200	200
CD (Multi Disc)	300	300	300	300	300	300
MP3 (Single Disc)	200	200	200	200	200	200
MP3 (Multi Disc)	300	300	300	300	300	300
Premium Sound	150	150	100	100	75	75
Navigation System	325	325	325	325	325	325
Leather	*	*	250	200	75	50
Sun Roof	*	200	150	150	125	100
Moon Roof	*	300	250	250	200	175
Rear Spoiler	50	50	50	50	50	50
Sensing Cruise Ctrl	375	—	—	—	—	—
Parking Sensors	225	150	100	—	—	—
Alloy Wheels	*	*	100	100	75	50
Premium Wheels	325	325	225	225	150	100
Premium Whls 19"+	500	500	500	500	500	500
Roof Rack (Wagon)	25	50	50	50	50	50
Third Seat (Wagon)	400	225	225	225	175	175
DEDUCT FOR:						
Manual Trans	—	—	—	—	(425)	*
w/o Power Steering	—	—	—	(175)	(125)	(100)
w/o Air Cond	(375)	(375)	(300)	(300)	(200)	(200)
w/o AM/FM Stereo	(50)	(50)	(50)	(50)	(25)	(25)
w/o Power Windows	—	(175)	—	(175)	—	—
w/o Power Locks	—	(50)	—	(50)	—	—
w/o Tilt Wheel	—	(150)	—	(150)	—	—
w/o Cruise Control	—	(50)	—	(50)	—	—
w/o Leather	(200)	(250)	—	—	—	—
w/o Sun/Moon Roof	(400)	—	—	—	—	—

* — EQUIPMENT INCLUDED IN BASE PRICE

SEE PAGE 9 FOR PVT PARTY & RETAIL EQUIPMENT

2003 FACTORY EQUIPMENT TRADE-IN VALUES

Equipment	1	2	3	4	5	6
Automatic Trans	—	—	—	—	*	350
Power Steering	*	*	*	*	*	*
Air Conditioning	*	*	*	*	*	*
Power Windows	*	*	*	*	150	75
Power Door Locks	*	*	*	*	50	25
Tilt Wheel	*	*	*	*	100	50
Cruise Control	*	*	*	*	50	25
Cassette	*	*	*	*	75	50
GROUP TOTAL	*	*	*	*	425	575
Power Seat	*	*	50	50	25	25
Dual Power Seats	*	*	125	125	50	25
ABS (4 Wheel)	*	*	100	100	50	50
CD (Single Disc)	200	200	200	200	200	200
CD (Multi Disc)	300	300	300	300	300	300
MP3 (Single Disc)	200	200	200	200	200	200
MP3 (Multi Disc)	300	300	300	300	300	300
Premium Sound	175	175	125	125	75	75
Video/DVD	300	300	300	300	300	300
Navigation System	350	350	350	350	350	350
Leather	*	*	300	225	100	75
Sun Roof	*	250	200	200	150	125
Moon Roof	*	375	300	300	250	200
Rear Spoiler	75	75	75	75	75	75
Sensing Cruise Ctrl	375	—	—	—	—	—
Parking Sensors	250	175	100	—	—	—
Alloy Wheels	*	*	100	100	75	50
Premium Wheels	350	350	250	250	175	100
Premium Whls 19"+	550	550	550	550	550	550
Roof Rack (Wagon)	50	75	75	75	50	50
Third Seat (Wagon)	425	250	250	250	200	200
DEDUCT FOR:						
Manual Trans	—	—	—	—	(450)	*
w/o Power Steering	—	—	—	(200)	(150)	(100)
w/o Air Cond	(450)	(450)	(350)	(350)	(250)	(250)
w/o AM/FM Stereo	(75)	(75)	(75)	(75)	(25)	(25)
w/o Power Windows	—	(200)	—	(200)	—	—
w/o Pwr Door Locks	—	(75)	—	(75)	—	—
w/o Tilt Wheel	—	(175)	—	(175)	—	—
w/o Cruise Control	—	(75)	—	(75)	—	—
w/o Leather	(250)	(300)	—	—	—	—
w/o Sun/Moon Roof	(475)	—	—	—	—	—

* — EQUIPMENT INCLUDED IN BASE PRICE

2004 FACTORY EQUIPMENT TRADE-IN VALUES

Equipment	1	2	3	4	5	6
Automatic Trans	—	—	—	—	*	400
Power Steering	*	*	*	*	*	*
Air Conditioning	*	*	*	*	*	*
Power Windows	*	*	*	*	175	75
Power Door Locks	*	*	*	*	50	25
Tilt Wheel	*	*	*	*	100	50
Cruise Control	*	*	*	*	50	25
Cassette	*	*	*	*	0	0
GROUP TOTAL	*	*	*	*	375	575
Power Seat	*	*	50	50	25	25
Dual Power Seats	*	*	150	150	50	25
ABS (4 Wheel)	*	*	100	100	50	50
CD (Single Disc)	200	200	200	200	200	200
CD (Multi Disc)	300	300	300	300	300	300
MP3 (Single Disc)	300	300	300	300	300	300
MP3 (Multi Disc)	400	400	400	400	400	400
Premium Sound	200	200	150	150	100	75
Video/DVD	350	350	350	350	350	350
Navigation System	400	400	400	400	400	400
Leather	*	*	350	250	125	100
Sun Roof	*	300	250	250	175	150
Moon Roof	*	450	350	350	300	250
Rear Spoiler	100	100	100	100	100	100
Sensing Cruise Ctrl	400	—	—	—	—	—
Parking Sensors	275	200	100	—	—	—
Alloy Wheels	*	*	100	100	75	50
Premium Wheels	400	400	275	275	200	100
Premium Whls 19"+	600	600	600	600	600	600
Roof Rack (Wagon)	75	100	100	100	50	50
Third Seat (Wagon)	450	275	275	275	225	225
DEDUCT FOR:						
Manual Trans	—	—	—	—	(475)	*
w/o Power Steering	—	—	—	(225)	(175)	(100)
w/o Air Cond	(525)	(525)	(400)	(400)	(300)	(300)
w/o AM/FM Stereo	(100)	(100)	(100)	(100)	(50)	(25)
w/o Power Windows	—	(225)	—	(225)	—	—
w/o Pwr Door Locks	—	(100)	—	(100)	—	—
w/o Tilt Wheel	—	(200)	—	(200)	—	—
w/o Cruise Control	—	(100)	—	(100)	—	—
w/o Leather	(300)	(350)	—	—	—	—
w/o Sun/Moon Roof	(550)	—	—	—	—	—

* — EQUIPMENT INCLUDED IN BASE PRICE

SEE PAGE 9 FOR PVT PARTY & RETAIL EQUIPMENT

2005 FACTORY EQUIPMENT TRADE-IN VALUES

Equipment	1	2	3	4	5	6
Automatic Trans	—	—	—	—	*	450
Power Steering	*	*	*	*	*	*
Air Conditioning	*	*	*	*	*	*
Power Windows	*	*	*	*	200	100
Power Door Locks	*	*	*	*	75	25
Tilt Wheel	*	*	*	*	100	75
Cruise Control	*	*	*	*	75	25
Cassette	*	*	*	*	0	0
GROUP TOTAL	*	*	*	*	450	675
Power Seat	*	*	75	75	25	25
Dual Power Seats	*	*	175	175	75	25
ABS (4 Wheel)	*	*	125	125	75	50
CD (Single Disc)	200	200	200	200	200	200
CD (Multi Disc)	300	300	300	300	300	300
MP3 (Single Disc)	300	300	300	300	300	300
MP3 (Multi Disc)	400	400	400	400	400	400
Premium Sound	225	225	175	175	125	75
Video/DVD	400	400	400	400	400	400
Navigation System	450	450	450	450	450	450
Leather	*	*	400	300	150	125
Sun Roof	*	350	300	300	200	175
Moon Roof	*	525	400	400	350	300
Rear Spoiler	100	100	100	100	100	100
Sensing Cruise Ctrl	425	425	425	—	—	—
Parking Sensors	300	225	100	—	—	—
Alloy Wheels	*	*	125	125	100	75
Premium Wheels	450	450	300	300	225	125
Premium Whls 19"+	675	675	675	675	675	675
Roof Rack (Wagon)	100	100	100	100	50	50
Third Seat (Wagon)	475	300	300	300	250	250
DEDUCT FOR:						
Manual Trans	—	—	—	—	(500)	*
w/o Power Steering	—	—	—	(250)	(200)	(125)
w/o Air Cond	(600)	(600)	(475)	(475)	(350)	(350)
w/o AM/FM Stereo	(125)	(125)	(125)	(125)	(75)	(25)
w/o Power Windows	—	(250)	—	(250)	—	—
w/o Pwr Door Locks	—	(125)	—	(125)	—	—
w/o Tilt Wheel	—	(250)	—	(225)	—	—
w/o Cruise Control	—	(125)	—	(125)	—	—
w/o Leather	(350)	(400)	—	—	—	—
w/o Sun/Moon Roof	(600)	—	—	—	—	—

* — EQUIPMENT INCLUDED IN BASE PRICE

2006 FACTORY EQUIPMENT TRADE-IN VALUES

Equipment	1	2	3	4	5	6
Automatic Trans	—	—	—	—	*	475
Power Steering	*	*	*	*	*	*
Air Conditioning	*	*	*	*	*	*
Power Windows	*	*	*	*	225	125
Power Door Locks	*	*	*	*	100	50
Tilt Wheel	*	*	*	*	125	100
Cruise Control	*	*	*	*	100	50
Cassette	*	*	*	*	*	*
GROUP TOTAL	*	*	*	*	550	800
Power Seat	*	*	100	100	50	25
Dual Power Seats	*	*	200	200	100	50
ABS (4 Wheel)	*	*	150	150	100	50
CD (Single Disc)	200	200	200	200	200	200
CD (Multi Disc)	300	300	300	300	300	300
MP3 (Single CD)	300	300	300	300	300	300
MP3 (Multi CD)	400	400	400	400	400	400
Premium Sound	250	250	200	200	150	100
Video/DVD	450	450	450	450	450	450
Navigation System	500	500	500	500	500	500
Leather	*	*	450	350	200	150
Sun Roof	*	400	350	350	250	200
Moon Roof	*	600	475	475	400	350
Rear Spoiler	100	100	100	100	100	100
Sensing Cruise Ctrl	450	450	450	—	—	—
Parking Sensors	325	250	125	—	—	—
Alloy Wheels	*	*	150	150	125	100
Premium Wheels	500	500	350	350	250	150
Premium Whls 19"+	750	750	750	750	750	750
Roof Rack (Wagon)	100	100	100	100	50	50
Third Seat (Wagon)	500	350	350	350	275	275
DEDUCT FOR:						
Manual Trans	—	—	—	—	(525)	*
w/o Power Steering	—	—	—	(275)	(225)	(150)
w/o Air Cond	(675)	(675)	(550)	(550)	(400)	(400)
w/o AM/FM Stereo	(150)	(150)	(150)	(150)	(100)	(50)
w/o Power Windows	—	(275)	—	(275)	—	—
w/o Pwr Door Locks	—	(150)	—	(150)	—	—
w/o Tilt Wheel	—	(300)	—	(250)	—	—
w/o Cruise Control	—	(150)	—	(150)	—	—
w/o Leather	(400)	(450)	—	—	—	—
w/o Sun/Moon Roof	(650)	—	—	—	—	—

* — EQUIPMENT INCLUDED IN BASE PRICE

SEE PAGE 9 FOR PVT PARTY & RETAIL EQUIPMENT   21

2007 FACTORY EQUIPMENT TRADE-IN VALUES

Equipment	1	2	3	4	5	6
Automatic Trans	—	—	—	—	*	500
Power Steering	*	*	*	*	*	*
Air Conditioning	*	*	*	*	*	*
Power Windows	*	*	*	*	250	150
Power Door Locks	*	*	*	*	125	75
Tilt Wheel	*	*	*	*	150	125
Cruise Control	*	*	*	*	125	75
Cassette	*	*	*	*	*	*
GROUP TOTAL	*	*	*	*	650	925
Power Seat	*	*	125	125	75	25
Dual Power Seats	*	*	225	225	125	75
ABS (4 Wheel)	*	*	175	175	125	75
CD (Single Disc)	200	200	200	200	200	200
CD (Multi Disc)	300	300	300	300	300	300
MP3 (Single CD)	300	300	300	300	300	300
MP3 (Multi CD)	400	400	400	400	400	400
Premium Sound	275	275	225	225	175	125
Video/DVD	500	500	500	500	500	500
Navigation System	550	550	550	550	550	550
Leather	*	*	525	400	250	175
Sun Roof	*	475	400	400	300	250
Moon Roof	*	675	550	550	450	400
Rear Spoiler	100	100	100	100	100	100
Sensing Cruise Ctrl	475	475	475	—	—	—
Parking Sensors	350	275	150	—	—	—
Alloy Wheels	*	*	175	175	150	125
Premium Wheels	550	550	400	400	275	175
Premium Whls 19"+	825	825	825	825	825	825
Roof Rack (Wagon)	100	100	100	100	50	50
Third Seat (Wagon)	525	400	400	400	300	300
DEDUCT FOR:						
Manual Trans	—	—	—	—	(550)	*
w/o Power Steering	—	—	—	(300)	(250)	(175)
w/o Air Cond	(750)	(750)	(625)	(625)	(450)	(450)
w/o AM/FM Stereo	(175)	(175)	(175)	(175)	(125)	(75)
w/o Power Windows	—	(300)	—	(300)	—	—
w/o Pwr Door Locks	—	(175)	—	(175)	—	—
w/o Tilt Wheel	—	(350)	—	(275)	—	—
w/o Cruise Control	—	(175)	—	(175)	—	—
w/o Leather	(450)	(525)	—	—	—	—
w/o Sun/Moon Roof	(700)	—	—	—	—	—

* — EQUIPMENT INCLUDED IN BASE PRICE

2008 FACTORY EQUIPMENT TRADE-IN VALUES

Equipment	1	2	3	4	5	6
Automatic Trans	—	—	—	—	*	525
Power Steering	*	*	*	*	*	*
Air Conditioning	*	*	*	*	*	*
Power Windows	*	*	*	*	275	175
Power Door Locks	*	*	*	*	150	100
Tilt Wheel	*	*	*	*	175	150
Cruise Control	*	*	*	*	150	100
Cassette	*	*	*	*	*	*
GROUP TOTAL	*	*	*	*	750	1050
Power Seat	*	*	150	150	100	50
Dual Power Seats	*	*	250	250	150	100
ABS (4 Wheel)	*	*	200	200	150	100
CD (Single Disc)	200	200	200	200	200	200
CD (Multi Disc)	300	300	300	300	300	300
MP3 (Single CD)	300	300	300	300	300	300
MP3 (Multi CD)	400	400	400	400	400	400
Premium Sound	325	325	275	275	200	150
Video/DVD	550	550	550	550	550	550
Navigation System	000	000	000	000	000	000
Leather	*	*	600	450	300	200
Sun Roof	*	550	450	450	350	300
Moon Roof	*	750	625	625	500	450
Rear Spoiler	100	100	100	100	100	100
Sensing Cruise Ctrl	500	500	500	—	—	—
Parking Sensors	400	300	175	—	—	—
Alloy Wheels	*	*	200	200	175	150
Premium Wheels	600	600	450	450	300	200
Premium Whls 19"+	900	900	900	900	900	900
Roof Rack (Wagon)	100	100	100	100	50	50
Third Seat (Wagon)	550	450	450	450	350	350
DEDUCT FOR:						
Manual Trans	—	—	—	—	(575)	*
w/o Power Steering	—	—	—	(325)	(275)	(200)
w/o Air Cond	(850)	(850)	(700)	(700)	(500)	(500)
w/o AM/FM Stereo	(200)	(200)	(200)	(200)	(150)	(100)
w/o Power Windows	—	(350)	—	(350)	—	—
w/o Pwr Door Locks	—	(200)	—	(200)	—	—
w/o Tilt Wheel	—	(400)	—	(300)	—	—
w/o Cruise Control	—	(200)	—	(200)	—	—
w/o Leather	(525)	(600)	—	—	—	—
w/o Sun/Moon Roof	(750)	—	—	—	—	—

* — EQUIPMENT INCLUDED IN BASE PRICE

SEE PAGE 9 FOR PVT PARTY & RETAIL EQUIPMENT

Body	Type	VIN	List	Trade-In Fair	Good	Pvt-Party Good	Retail Excellent

Automobile Section

ACURA

1994 ACURA — JH4(DB764)–R–#

INTEGRA—4-Cyl.—Equipment Schedule 3
W.B. 101.2", 103.1" (4D); 1.8 Liter.

RS Sedan 4D	DB764	16695	900	1275	2225	3725
RS Sport Coupe 2D	DC444	15935	925	1325	2375	4000
LS Sedan 4D	DB765	18565	1025	1450	2525	4175
LS Sport Coupe 2D	DC445	18565	1025	1450	2525	4175
GS-R Sedan 4D	DB858	20345	1150	1625	2775	4450
GS-R Sport Coupe 2D	DC238	20015	1225	1725	2875	4575
Manual Trans (Sedan)	3,5		(100)	(100)	(135)	(135)

VIGOR—5-Cyl.—Equipment Schedule 1
W.B. 110.4"; 2.5 Liter.

LS Sedan 4D	CC264	27485	1250	1725	2900	4600
GS Sedan 4D	CC266	29485	1450	1925	3125	4900
Manual Trans	5		(225)	(225)	(300)	(300)

LEGEND—V6—Equipment Schedule 1
W.B. 111.4", 114.6" (4D); 3.2 Liter.

L Sedan 4D	KA766	36485	1750	2250	3475	5325
L Coupe 2D	KA826	38085	1800	2300	3525	5375
LS Sedan 4D	KA767	38985	1875	2425	3675	5525
LS Coupe 2D	KA827	41885	1925	2475	3725	5575
GS Sedan 4D	KA768	41885	2025	2600	3875	5750
Manual Trans (Sedan)	1,5		(225)	(225)	(300)	(300)

NSX—V6—Equipment Schedule 2
W.B. 99.6"; 3.0 Liter.

Sport Coupe 2D	NA126	77200	22725	25375	29400	36500

1995 ACURA — JH4(DB764)–S–#

INTEGRA—4-Cyl.—Equipment Schedule 3
W.B. 101.2", 103.1" (4D); 1.8 Liter.

RS Sedan 4D	DB764	17390	1025	1450	2525	4175
RS Sport Coupe 2D	DC444	16630	1075	1500	2625	4275
LS Sedan 4D	DB765	20110	1175	1650	2800	4475
LS Sport Coupe 2D	DC445	19315	1175	1650	2800	4475
Special Ed Sedan 4D	DB766	21610	1200	1675	2825	4525
Special Ed Coupe 2D	DC446	21060	1225	1725	2875	4575
GS-R Sedan 4D	DB858	21100	1400	1850	3075	4800
GS-R Sport Coupe 2D	DC238	20770	1475	1950	3150	4925
Manual Trans (Sedan)	3,5		(100)	(100)	(135)	(135)

TL—5-Cyl.—Equipment Schedule 1
W.B. 111.8"; 2.5 Liter.

2.5 Sedan 4D	UA265	30370	1475	1950	3175	4975

LEGEND—V6—Equipment Schedule 1
W.B. 111.4", 114.6" (4D); 3.2 Liter.

L Sedan 4D	KA766	38220	2050	2625	3900	5800
L Coupe 2D	KA826	39820	2100	2675	3950	5875
SE Sedan 4D	KA769	39320	2125	2700	3975	5900
LS Sedan 4D	KA767	40120	2225	2825	4125	6075
LS Coupe 2D	KA827	43620	2275	2850	4175	6125
GS Sedan 4D	KA768	42420	2400	3000	4325	6325
Manual Trans (Sedan)	1,5		(225)	(225)	(300)	(300)

NSX-T—V6—Equipment Schedule 2
W.B. 99.6"; 3.0 Liter.

T-Targa 2D	NA128	85225	24200	26950	31200	38500

1996 ACURA — JH4(DB764)–T–#

INTEGRA—4-Cyl.—Equipment Schedule 3
W.B. 101.2", 103.1" (4D); 1.8 Liter.

RS Sedan 4D	DB764	18080	1200	1675	2825	4525
RS Sport Coupe 2D	DC444	17320	1250	1725	2925	4625
LS Sedan 4D	DB765	20870	1425	1900	3100	4875
LS Sport Coupe 2D	DC445	20070	1425	1900	3100	4875
Special Ed Sedan 4D	DB766	22370	1450	1925	3150	4925
Special Ed Coupe 2D	DC446	21820	1525	2000	3225	5025

1996 ACURA

Body Type	VIN	List	Trade-In Fair	Trade-In Good	Pvt-Party Good	Retail Excellent
GS-R Sedan 4D	DB858	21820	1700	2200	3450	5275
GS-R Sport Coupe 2D	DC238	21520	1800	2300	3550	5400
Manual Trans (Sedan)	3,5		(125)	(125)	(165)	(165)

TL—5-Cyl.—Equipment Schedule 1
W.B. 111.8"; 2.5 Liter.

Body Type	VIN	List	Trade-In Fair	Trade-In Good	Pvt-Party Good	Retail Excellent
2.5 Sedan 4D	UA265	30370	1775	2275	3525	5400

TL—V6—Equipment Schedule 1
W.B. 111.8"; 3.2 Liter.

Body Type	VIN	List	Trade-In Fair	Trade-In Good	Pvt-Party Good	Retail Excellent
3.2 Sedan 4D	UA365	35920	2250	2825	4150	6100

RL—V6—Equipment Schedule 1
W.B. 114.6"; 3.5 Liter.

Body Type	VIN	List	Trade-In Fair	Trade-In Good	Pvt-Party Good	Retail Excellent
3.5 Sedan 4D	KA964	41435	3025	3675	5100	7250
Traction Control	5,6		125	125	165	165

NSX—V6—Equipment Schedule 2
W.B. 99.6"; 3.0 Liter.

Body Type	VIN	List	Trade-In Fair	Trade-In Good	Pvt-Party Good	Retail Excellent
Sport Coupe 2D	NA126	83725	25275	28225	32400	40000
T-Targa 2D	NA128	87725	25775	28725	32900	40600

1997 ACURA — JH4(DC444)–V–#

INTEGRA—4-Cyl.—Equipment Schedule 3
W.B. 101.2", 103.1" (4D); 1.8 Liter.

Body Type	VIN	List	Trade-In Fair	Trade-In Good	Pvt-Party Good	Retail Excellent
RS Sport Coupe 2D	DC444	17335	1450	1925	3125	4925
LS Sedan 4D	DB765	20885	1650	2150	3375	5225
LS Sport Coupe 2D	DC445	20085	1675	2175	3400	5250
GS Sedan 4D	DB766	22235	1850	2375	3650	5525
GS Sport Coupe 2D	DC446	21835	1850	2375	3650	5525
GS-R Sedan 4D	DB858	21835	1925	2475	3750	5625
GS-R Sport Coupe 2D	DC238	21535	2025	2575	3850	5750
Type R Sport Cpe 2D	DC238	23535	****	****	****	10300
Manual Trans (Sedan)	3,5		(150)	(150)	(200)	(200)

CL—4-Cyl.—Equipment Schedule 1
W.B. 106.9"; 2.2 Liter.

Body Type	VIN	List	Trade-In Fair	Trade-In Good	Pvt-Party Good	Retail Excellent
2.2 Coupe 2D	YA125	24395	1725	2250	3500	5350
Manual Trans			(250)	(250)	(335)	(335)

CL—V6—Equipment Schedule 1
W.B. 106.9"; 3.0 Liter.

Body Type	VIN	List	Trade-In Fair	Trade-In Good	Pvt-Party Good	Retail Excellent
3.0 Coupe 2D	YA225	26895	2150	2725	4025	5950

TL—5-Cyl.—Equipment Schedule 1
W.B. 111.8"; 2.5 Liter.

Body Type	VIN	List	Trade-In Fair	Trade-In Good	Pvt-Party Good	Retail Excellent
2.5 Sedan 4D	UA265	30935	2100	2675	4000	5925

TL—V6—Equipment Schedule 1
W.B. 111.8"; 3.2 Liter.

Body Type	VIN	List	Trade-In Fair	Trade-In Good	Pvt-Party Good	Retail Excellent
3.2 Sedan 4D	UA365	33385	2700	3300	4650	6725
Traction Control			150	150	200	200

RL—V6—Equipment Schedule 1
W.B. 114.6"; 3.5 Liter.

Body Type	VIN	List	Trade-In Fair	Trade-In Good	Pvt-Party Good	Retail Excellent
3.5 Sedan 4D	KA964	41435	3400	4100	5550	7800
Traction Control			150	150	200	200

NSX—V6—Equipment Schedule 2
W.B. 99.6"; 3.0 Liter, 3.2 Liter.

Body Type	VIN	List	Trade-In Fair	Trade-In Good	Pvt-Party Good	Retail Excellent
Sport Coupe 2D	NA123	84725	27825	30975	35300	43000
T-Targa 2D	NA126	88725	28225	31350	35700	43500

1998 ACURA — JH4(DC444)–W–#

INTEGRA—4-Cyl.—Equipment Schedule 3
W.B. 101.2", 103.1" (4D); 1.8 Liter.

Body Type	VIN	List	Trade-In Fair	Trade-In Good	Pvt-Party Good	Retail Excellent
RS Sport Coupe 2D	DC444	17435	1725	2225	3475	5350
LS Sedan 4D	DB765	21235	1925	2475	3750	5625
LS Sport Coupe 2D	DC445	20435	1950	2525	3800	5700
GS Sedan 4D	DB766	22635	2175	2750	4075	6000
GS Sport Coupe 2D	DC446	22085	2175	2750	4075	6000
GS-R Sedan 4D	DB858	22035	2275	2850	4175	6125
GS-R Sport Coupe 2D	DC238	21735	2375	2950	4275	6250
Type R Sport Cpe 2D	DC231	23500	****	****	****	11000
Manual Trans (Sedan)	3,5		(175)	(175)	(235)	(235)

CL—4-Cyl.—Equipment Schedule 1
W.B. 106.9"; 2.3 Liter.

Body Type	VIN	List	Trade-In Fair	Trade-In Good	Pvt-Party Good	Retail Excellent
2.3 Coupe 2D	YA325	24595	2050	2625	3900	5825
Manual Trans	1		(300)	(300)	(400)	(400)

CL—V6—Equipment Schedule 1
W.B. 106.9"; 3.0 Liter.

Body Type	VIN	List	Trade-In Fair	Trade-In Good	Pvt-Party Good	Retail Excellent
3.0 Coupe 2D	YA225	27095	2550	3125	4475	6500

1998 ACURA

Body	Type	VIN	List	Trade-In Fair	Trade-In Good	Pvt-Party Good	Retail Excellent
TL—5-Cyl.—Equipment Schedule 1							
W.B. 111.8"; 2.5 Liter.							
2.5 Sedan 4D		UA265	31135	2575	3150	4500	6550
TL—V6—Equipment Schedule 1							
W.B. 111.8"; 3.2 Liter.							
3.2 Sedan 4D		UA364	33585	3175	3850	5275	7425
Traction Control				175	175	235	235
RL—V6—Equipment Schedule 1							
W.B. 114.6"; 3.5 Liter.							
3.5 Sedan 4D		KA964	41635	3875	4600	6100	8425
Traction Control				175	175	235	235
NSX—V6—Equipment Schedule 2							
W.B. 99.6"; 3.0 Liter, 3.2 Liter.							
Sport Coupe 2D		NA123	84725	30375	33800	38000	46100
T-Targa 2D		NA126	88725	30675	34100	38300	46400

1999 ACURA — (JH4or19U)(DB765)-X-#

Body	Type	VIN	List	Trade-In Fair	Trade-In Good	Pvt-Party Good	Retail Excellent
INTEGRA—4-Cyl.—Equipment Schedule 3							
W.B. 101.2", 103.1" (4D); 1.8 Liter.							
LS Sedan 4D		DB765	21255	2300	2900	4225	6175
LS Sport Coupe 2D		DC445	20375	2375	2975	4300	6275
GS Sedan 4D		DB766	22655	2600	3200	4525	6575
GS Sport Coupe 2D		DC446	21625	2625	3225	4550	6600
GS-R Sedan 4D		DB858	22855	2700	3325	4675	6725
GS-R Sport Coupe 2D		DC238	22555	2800	3400	4775	6825
Manual Trans (Sedan)		3,5		(200)	(200)	(265)	(265)
CL—4-Cyl.—Equipment Schedule 1							
W.B. 106.9"; 2.3 Liter.							
2.3 Coupe 2D		YA325	24355	2475	3075	4400	6425
Manual Trans				(350)	(350)	(465)	(465)
CL—V6—Equipment Schedule 1							
W.B. 106.9"; 3.0 Liter.							
3.0 Coupe 2D		YA225	26605	3000	3625	5025	7125
TL—V6—Equipment Schedule 1							
W.B. 108.1"; 3.2 Liter.							
3.2 Sedan 4D		UA564	28405	2925	3575	4950	7075
RL—V6—Equipment Schedule 1							
W.B. 114.6"; 3.5 Liter.							
3.5 Sedan 4D		KA964	42355	4450	5250	6775	9200
NSX—V6—Equipment Schedule 2							
W.B. 99.6"; 3.0 Liter, 3.2 Liter.							
Sport Coupe 2D		NA123	84745	32925	36550	40800	48900
T-Targa 2D		NA126	88745	33125	36850	41100	49300

2000 ACURA — (JH4or19U)(DB765)-Y-#

Body	Type	VIN	List	Trade-In Fair	Trade-In Good	Pvt-Party Good	Retail Excellent
INTEGRA—4-Cyl.—Equipment Schedule 3							
W.B. 101.2", 103.1" (4D); 1.8 Liter.							
LS Sedan 4D		DB765	21355	2800	3425	4775	6850
LS Sport Coupe 2D		DC445	20555	2875	3500	4875	6950
GS Sedan 4D		DB766	22755	3075	3750	5125	7250
GS Sport Coupe 2D		DC446	22205	3125	3800	5200	7325
GS-R Sedan 4D		DB859	22955	3200	3900	5275	7425
GS-R Sport Coupe 2D		DC239	22655	3300	4000	5400	7550
Type R Sport Cpe 2D		DC231	24805	****	****	****	12650
Manual Trans (Sedan)		3,5		(200)	(200)	(265)	(265)
TL—V6—Equipment Schedule 3							
W.B. 108.1"; 3.2 Liter.							
3.2 Sedan 4D		UA566	28855	3575	4275	5700	7950
RL—V6—Equipment Schedule 1							
W.B. 114.6"; 3.5 Liter.							
3.5 Sedan 4D		KA965	42455	5125	5975	7625	10450
NSX—V6—Equipment Schedule 2							
W.B. 99.6"; 3.0 Liter, 3.2 Liter.							
Sport Coupe 2D		NA123	84745	35475	39400	43500	51800
T-Targa 2D		NA126	88745	35775	39700	43800	52200

2001 ACURA — JH4or19U(DB765)-1-#

Body	Type	VIN	List	Trade-In Fair	Trade-In Good	Pvt-Party Good	Retail Excellent
INTEGRA—4-Cyl.—Equipment Schedule 3							
W.B. 101.2", 103.1" (4D); 1.8 Liter.							
LS Sedan 4D		DB765	21480	3400	4100	5500	7675
LS Sport Coupe 2D		DC445	20680	3475	4200	5575	7800
GS Sedan 4D		DB766	22880	3725	4425	5875	8100

2001 ACURA

Body	Type	VIN	List	Trade-In Fair	Trade-In Good	Pvt-Party Good	Retail Excellent
GS Sport Coupe 2D		DC446	22330	**3800**	**4500**	**5950**	**8175**
GS-R Sedan 4D		DB859	23080	**3850**	**4575**	**6025**	**8275**
GS-R Sport Coupe 2D		DC239	22780	**3975**	**4700**	**6150**	**8400**
Type R Sport Cpe 2D		DC231	24930	********	********	********	**13600**
Manual Trans (Sedan)		3,5		**(200)**	**(200)**	**(265)**	**(265)**

CL—V6—Equipment Schedule 1
W.B. 106.9"; 3.2 Liter.

Body	Type	VIN	List	Fair	Good	Good	Excellent
3.2 Coupe 2D		YA424	28460	**3850**	**4575**	**6025**	**8275**
3.2 Type S Coupe 2D		YA426	30810	**4750**	**5575**	**7100**	**9575**

TL—V6—Equipment Schedule 1
W.B. 108.1"; 3.2 Liter.

3.2 Sedan 4D		UA566	29030	**4325**	**5125**	**6625**	**8975**

RL—V6—Equipment Schedule 1
W.B. 114.6"; 3.5 Liter.

3.5 Sedan 4D		KA965	42630	**5900**	**6850**	**8500**	**11200**

NSX—V6—Equipment Schedule 2
W.B. 99.6"; 3.0 Liter, 3.2 Liter.

Sport Coupe 2D		NA123	84845	**36150**	**40175**	**44100**	**52200**
Targa 2D		NA126	88845	**36450**	**40475**	**44400**	**52500**

2002 ACURA — JH4or19U(DC548)-2-#

RSX—4-Cyl.—Equipment Schedule 3
W.B. 101.2"; 2.0 Liter.

Sport Coupe 2D		DC548	21330	**5325**	**6175**	**7900**	**10600**
Type S Sport Cpe 2D		DC530	23650	**6050**	**7000**	**8750**	**11550**

CL—V6—Equipment Schedule 1
W.B. 106.9"; 3.2 Liter.

3.2 Coupe 2D		YA424	28510	**4550**	**5375**	**7025**	**9600**
3.2 Type S Coupe 2D		YA426	30860	**5525**	**6425**	**8125**	**10900**

TL—V6—Equipment Schedule 1
W.B. 108.1"; 3.2 Liter.

3.2 Sedan 4D		UA566	29360	**5100**	**5950**	**7675**	**10400**
3.2 Type S Sedan 4D		UA568	31710	**5725**	**6675**	**8425**	**11200**

RL—V6—Equipment Schedule 1
W.B. 114.6"; 3.5 Liter.

3.5 Sedan 4D		KA965	43630	**6700**	**7700**	**9550**	**12550**

NSX—V6—Equipment Schedule 2
W.B. 99.6"; 3.0 Liter, 3.2 Liter.

Targa 2D		NA126	89745	**36750**	**40875**	**44600**	**52600**

2003 ACURA — JH4or19U(DC548)-3-#

RSX—V6—Equipment Schedule 3
W.B. 101.2"; 2.0 Liter.

Sport Coupe 2D		DC548	21375	**5875**	**6825**	**8550**	**11300**
Type S Sport Cpe 2D		DC530	23770	**6775**	**7825**	**9575**	**12500**

CL—V6—Equipment Schedule 1
W.B. 106.9"; 3.2 Liter.

3.2 Coupe 2D		YA424	28700	**5325**	**6200**	**7900**	**10600**
3.2 Type S Coupe 2D		YA426	31050	**6400**	**7375**	**9125**	**11950**

TL—V6—Equipment Schedule 1
W.B. 108.1"; 3.2 Liter.

3.2 Sedan 4D		UA566	29480	**5875**	**6825**	**8575**	**11350**
3.2 Type S Sedan 4D		UA568	31830	**6650**	**7650**	**9425**	**12350**

RL—V6—Equipment Schedule 1
W.B. 114.6"; 3.5 Liter.

3.5 Sedan 4D		KA965	43650	**7875**	**9000**	**10900**	**14050**

NSX—V6—Equipment Schedule 2
W.B. 99.6"; 3.0 Liter, 3.2 Liter.

Targa 2D		NA126	89765	**37625**	**41750**	**45400**	**53200**

2004 ACURA — (JH4or19U)(DC548)-4-#

RSX—4-Cyl.—Equipment Schedule 3
W.B. 101.2"; 2.0 Liter.

Sport Coupe 2D		DC548	21470	**6650**	**7650**	**9350**	**12200**
Type S Sport Cpe 2D		DC530	23865	**7725**	**8850**	**10600**	**13550**

TSX—4-Cyl.—Equipment Schedule 3
W.B. 105.1"; 2.4 Liter.

Sedan 4D		CL958	26990	**8150**	**9325**	**11150**	**14250**

TL—V6—Equipment Schedule 1
W.B. 107.9"; 3.2 Liter.

3.2 Sedan 4D		UA566	33195	**10350**	**11700**	**13650**	**17100**

2004 ACURA

Body	Type	VIN	List	Trade-In Fair	Trade-In Good	Pvt-Party Good	Retail Excellent
RL—V6—Equipment Schedule 1							
W.B. 114.6"; 3.5 Liter.							
3.5 Sedan 4D		KA965	46100	**9200**	**10475**	**12500**	**15900**
NSX—V6—Equipment Schedule 2							
W.B. 99.6"; 3.0 Liter, 3.2 Liter.							
Targa 2D		NA126	89765	**41650**	**46150**	**49600**	**57700**

2005 ACURA — (JH4or19U)(DC548)-5-#

Body	Type	VIN	List	Trade-In Fair	Trade-In Good	Pvt-Party Good	Retail Excellent
RSX—4-Cyl.—Equipment Schedule 3							
W.B. 101.2"; 2.0 Liter.							
Sport Coupe 2D		DC548	21745	**7600**	**8725**	**10450**	**13350**
Type S Sport Cpe 2D		DC530	24240	**8875**	**10100**	**11850**	**15000**
TSX—4-Cyl.—Equipment Schedule 3							
W.B. 105.1"; 2.4 Liter.							
Sedan 4D		CL958	27760	**9475**	**10775**	**12600**	**15850**
TL—V6—Equipment Schedule 1							
W.B. 107.9"; 3.2 Liter.							
3.2 Sedan 4D		UA662	33670	**11850**	**13425**	**15350**	**18900**
RL SH-AWD—V6—Equipment Schedule 1							
W.B. 110.2"; 3.5 Liter.							
3.5 Sedan 4D		KB165	49670	**13575**	**15300**	**17350**	**21300**
NSX—V6—Equipment Schedule 2							
W.B. 99.6"; 3.0 Liter, 3.2 Liter.							
Targa 2D		NA126	89765	**45875**	**50775**	**54100**	**62500**

2006 ACURA — (JH4or19U)(DC548)-6-#

Body	Type	VIN	List	Trade-In Fair	Trade-In Good	Pvt-Party Good	Retail Excellent
RSX—4-Cyl.—Equipment Schedule 3							
W.B. 101.2"; 2.0 Liter.							
Sport Coupe 2D		DC548	21840	**8825**	**10050**	**11800**	**14900**
Type S Sport Cpe 2D		DC530	24460	**10250**	**11625**	**13400**	**16650**
TSX—4-Cyl.—Equipment Schedule 3							
W.B. 105.1"; 2.4 Liter.							
Sedan 4D		CL958	28505	**10975**	**12450**	**14250**	**17600**
TL—V6—Equipment Schedule 1							
W.B. 107.9"; 3.2 Liter.							
3.2 Sedan 4D		UA662	33940	**13675**	**15425**	**17350**	**21100**
RL SH-AWD—V6—Equipment Schedule 1							
W.B. 110.2"; 3.5 Liter.							
3.5 Sedan 4D		KB165	49915	**15525**	**17450**	**19550**	**23600**

2007 ACURA — (JH4or19U)(CL958)-7-#

Body	Type	VIN	List	Trade-In Fair	Trade-In Good	Pvt-Party Good	Retail Excellent
TSX—4-Cyl.—Equipment Schedule 3							
W.B. 105.1"; 2.4 Liter.							
Sedan 4D		CL958	28760	**12750**	**14400**	**16050**	**19450**
TL—V6—Equipment Schedule 1							
W.B. 107.9"; 3.2 Liter, 3.5 Liter.							
3.2 Sedan 4D		UA662	34295	**16900**	**18975**	**20900**	**24800**
Type S Sedan 4D		UA755	38795	**18875**	**21075**	**22900**	**27100**
RL SH-AWD—V6—Equipment Schedule 1							
W.B. 110.2"; 3.5 Liter.							
3.5 Sedan 4D		KB165	46450	**19900**	**22250**	**24300**	**28700**

2008 ACURA — (JH4or19U)(CL958)-8-#

Body	Type	VIN	List	Trade-In Fair	Trade-In Good	Pvt-Party Good	Retail Excellent
TSX—4-Cyl.—Equipment Schedule 3							
W.B. 105.1"; 2.4 Liter.							
Sedan 4D		CL958	28905	**14800**	**16650**	**18350**	**21900**
TL—V6—Equipment Schedule 1							
W.B. 107.9"; 3.2 Liter, 3.5 Liter.							
3.2 Sedan 4D		UA662	34440	**19350**	**21650**	**23400**	**27500**
Type S Sedan 4D		UA755	38940	**21375**	**23825**	**25600**	**29900**
RL SH-AWD—V6—Equipment Schedule 1							
W.B. 110.2"; 3.5 Liter.							
3.5 Sedan 4D		KB165	46995	**22550**	**25175**	**27100**	**31700**

AUDI

1994 AUDI — WAU(BK88C)-R-#

Body	Type	VIN	List	Trade-In Fair	Trade-In Good	Pvt-Party Good	Retail Excellent
90—V6—Equipment Schedule 3							
W.B. 102.8", 102.2" (Quattro); 2.8 Liter.							
S Sedan 4D		BK88C	28265	**1100**	**1525**	**2650**	**4300**

Body Type	VIN	List	Trade-In Fair	Trade-In Good	Pvt-Party Good	Retail Excellent
CS Sedan 4D	DK88C	31215	1200	1675	2825	4525
CS Quattro Sedan 4D	EK88C	34865	1875	2425	3675	5525
Manual Trans			(125)	(125)	(165)	(165)

100—V6—Equipment Schedule 3
W.B. 105.8", 106.0" (Quattro); 2.8 Liter.

Body Type	VIN	List	Trade-In Fair	Trade-In Good	Pvt-Party Good	Retail Excellent
S Sedan 4D	BK84A	35565	1150	1625	2775	4450
S Wagon 4D	CK84A	38515	1550	2025	3225	5025
CS Sedan 4D	DK84A	41015	1450	1925	3125	4900
CS Quattro Sedan 4D	EK84A	43465	1775	2275	3500	5350
CS Quattro Wagon 4D	FK84A	47465	2275	2850	4150	6100
Manual Trans			(125)	(125)	(165)	(165)

CABRIOLET—V6—Equipment Schedule 1
W.B. 100.6"; 2.8 Liter.

Body Type	VIN	List	Trade-In Fair	Trade-In Good	Pvt-Party Good	Retail Excellent
Convertible 2D	BL88G	39395	2400	3000	4300	6300

S4—5-Cyl. Turbo—Equipment Schedule 1
W.B. 106.0"; 2.2 Liter.

Body Type	VIN	List	Trade-In Fair	Trade-In Good	Pvt-Party Good	Retail Excellent
Quattro Sedan 4D	HR84A	51615	3600	4300	5825	8125

QUATTRO—V8—Equipment Schedule 1
W.B. 106.4"; 4.2 Liter.

Body Type	VIN	List	Trade-In Fair	Trade-In Good	Pvt-Party Good	Retail Excellent
Sedan 4D	BW84C	59145	4500	5325	6875	9350

1995 AUDI — WAU(BK88C)-S-#

90—V6—Equipment Schedule 3
W.B. 102.8", 102.2" (Quattro); 2.8 Liter.

Body Type	VIN	List	Trade-In Fair	Trade-In Good	Pvt-Party Good	Retail Excellent
Sedan 4D	BK88C	26115	1300	1775	2975	4700
Sport Sedan 4D	DK88C	26515	1500	1975	3200	5000
Quattro AWD	C,E		1200	1200	1600	1600
Manual Trans			(125)	(125)	(165)	(165)

A6—V6—Equipment Schedule 3
W.B. 105.8", 106.0" (Quattro); 2.8 Liter.

Body Type	VIN	List	Trade-In Fair	Trade-In Good	Pvt-Party Good	Retail Excellent
Sedan 4D	FA84A	31045	1425	1900	3125	4900
Wagon 4D	HA84A	33615	1850	2400	3675	5525
Quattro AWD	G,J		1200	1200	1600	1600
Manual Trans			(125)	(125)	(165)	(165)

CABRIOLET—V6—Equipment Schedule 1
W.B. 100.6"; 2.8 Liter.

Body Type	VIN	List	Trade-In Fair	Trade-In Good	Pvt-Party Good	Retail Excellent
Convertible 2D	BL88G	36345	2875	3500	4900	7000

S6—5-Cyl. Turbo—Equipment Schedule 1
W.B. 106.0"; 2.2 Liter.

Body Type	VIN	List	Trade-In Fair	Trade-In Good	Pvt-Party Good	Retail Excellent
Quattro Sedan 4D	KA84A	45715	4225	4975	6550	8975
Quattro Wagon 4D	LA84A	48385	4925	5750	7475	10150

1996 AUDI — WAU(DA88D)-T-#

A4—V6—Equipment Schedule 3
W.B. 103.0"; 2.8 Liter.

Body Type	VIN	List	Trade-In Fair	Trade-In Good	Pvt-Party Good	Retail Excellent
Sedan 4D	DA88D	26975	1800	2300	3575	5450
Quattro AWD	E		1250	1250	1665	1665
Manual Trans			(125)	(125)	(165)	(165)

A6—V6—Equipment Schedule 3
W.B. 105.8", 2.8 Liter.

Body Type	VIN	List	Trade-In Fair	Trade-In Good	Pvt-Party Good	Retail Excellent
Sedan 4D	FA84A	32775	1775	2275	3550	5425
Wagon 4D	HA84A	34475	2250	2850	4175	6125
Quattro AWD	G,J		1250	1250	1665	1665

CABRIOLET—V6—Equipment Schedule 1
W.B. 100.6"; 2.8 Liter.

Body Type	VIN	List	Trade-In Fair	Trade-In Good	Pvt-Party Good	Retail Excellent
Convertible 2D	AA88G	37275	3425	4125	5550	7800

1997 AUDI — WAU(DA88A)-V-#

A4—V6—Equipment Schedule 3
W.B. 103.0"; 2.8 Liter.

Body Type	VIN	List	Trade-In Fair	Trade-In Good	Pvt-Party Good	Retail Excellent
Sedan 4D	DA88A	28905	2200	2775	4100	6050
Quattro AWD	C,E		1275	1275	1700	1700
Manual Trans			(150)	(150)	(200)	(200)
4-Cyl. 1.8L Turbo	B		(650)	(650)	(865)	(865)

A6—V6—Equipment Schedule 3
W.B. 105.8"; 2.8 Liter.

Body Type	VIN	List	Trade-In Fair	Trade-In Good	Pvt-Party Good	Retail Excellent
Sedan 4D	FA84A	33100	2200	2775	4100	6050
Wagon 4D	HA84A	34900	2775	3375	4750	6825
Quattro AWD	G,J		1275	1275	1700	1700

A8—V8—Equipment Schedule 1
W.B. 113.0"; 3.7 Liter, 4.2 Liter.

Body Type	VIN	List	Trade-In Fair	Trade-In Good	Pvt-Party Good	Retail Excellent
Sedan 4D	AF84D	57400	2150	2725	4050	6000

Body	Type	VIN	List	Trade-In Fair	Good	Pvt-Party Good	Retail Excellent
Quattro AWD Sed 4D		AG84D	65000	3625	4325	5825	8100
CABRIOLET—V6—Equipment Schedule 1							
W.B. 100.6"; 2.8 Liter.							
Convertible 2D		AA88G	38800	4075	4825	6350	8725

1998 AUDI — WAU(DD68D)-W-#

A4—V6—Equipment Schedule 3
W.B. 103.0"; 2.8 Liter.

Body	Type	VIN	List	Fair	Good	Good	Excellent
Sedan 4D		DD68D	29965	2700	3300	4700	6775
Avant Wagon 4D		FD68D	30965	3050	3700	5125	7275
Quattro AWD		G,C,E		1300	1300	1735	1735
Manual Trans				(175)	(175)	(235)	(235)
4-Cyl. 1.8L Turbo		B		(725)	(725)	(965)	(965)

A6—V6—Equipment Schedule 3
W.B. 105.8", 108.7" (Sed); 2.8 Liter.

Sedan 4D		AA74B	34250	2225	2800	4150	6125
Wagon 4D		JA84A	38050	2850	3475	4875	7000
Quattro AWD		B,J		1300	1300	1735	1735

A8—V8—Equipment Schedule 1
W.B. 113.0"; 3.7 Liter, 4.2 Liter.

| Sedan 4D | | AF74D | 57900 | 1975 | 2525 | 3850 | 5800 |
| Quattro AWD Sed 4D | | BG74D | 65500 | 3650 | 4350 | 5825 | 8125 |

CABRIOLET—V6—Equipment Schedule 1
W.B. 100.6"; 2.8 Liter.

| Convertible 2D | | AA88G | 38800 | 4800 | 5600 | 7250 | 9800 |

1999 AUDI — WAU(DD38D)-X-#

A4—V6—Equipment Schedule 3
W.B. 103.0"; 2.8 Liter.

Sedan 4D		DD38D	28890	3300	4000	5450	7650
Quattro AWD		C,E		1325	1325	1765	1765
Manual Trans				(200)	(200)	(265)	(265)
4-Cyl. 1.8L Turbo		B		(800)	(800)	(1065)	(1065)

A4 AVANT QUATTRO AWD—V6—Equipment Schedule 3
W.B. 102.6"; 2.8 Liter.

Wagon 4D		GD38D	31540	4075	4825	6325	8675
Manual Trans				(200)	(200)	(265)	(265)
4-Cyl. 1.8L Turbo		B		(800)	(800)	(1065)	(1065)

A6—V6—Equipment Schedule 3
W.B. 108.7"; 2.8 Liter.

| Sedan 4D | | AA24B | 34250 | 2800 | 3425 | 4825 | 6925 |
| Quattro AWD | | B | | 1325 | 1325 | 1765 | 1765 |

A6 AVANT QUATTRO AWD—V6—Equipment Schedule 3
W.B. 108.6"; 2.8 Liter.

| Wagon 4D | | DA24B | 37100 | 3575 | 4275 | 5725 | 7975 |

A8—V8—Equipment Schedule 1
W.B. 113.0"; 3.7 Liter, 4.2 Liter.

| Sedan 4D | | AF34D | 57900 | 2025 | 2600 | 3925 | 5900 |
| Quattro AWD Sed 4D | | BG34D | 65500 | 3900 | 4625 | 6150 | 8475 |

2000 AUDI — (WAUorTRU)(AH28D)-Y-#

A4—V6—Equipment Schedule 3
W.B. 103.0"; 2.8 Liter.

Sedan 4D		AH28D	30390	4025	4775	6275	8625
Quattro AWD		D		1350	1350	1800	1800
Manual Trans				(200)	(200)	(265)	(265)
4-Cyl. 1.8L Turbo		C		(875)	(875)	(1165)	(1165)

A4 AVANT QUATTRO AWD—V6—Equipment Schedule 3
W.B. 102.6"; 2.8 Liter.

Wagon 4D		KH28D	33140	4850	5675	7300	9850
Manual Trans				(200)	(200)	(265)	(265)
4-Cyl. 1.8L Turbo		C		(875)	(875)	(1165)	(1165)

S4 QUATTRO AWD—V6 Turbo—Equipment Schedule 3
W.B. 102.6"; 2.7 Liter.

| 2.7T Sedan 4D | | DD68D | 39625 | 5425 | 6300 | 8050 | 10850 |

A6—V6—Equipment Schedule 3
W.B. 108.7"; 2.8 Liter.

| Sedan 4D | | BH24B | 34475 | 3450 | 4175 | 5600 | 7875 |
| Quattro AWD | | G,J | | 1350 | 1350 | 1800 | 1800 |

A6 AVANT QUATTRO AWD—V6—Equipment Schedule 3
W.B. 108.6"; 2.8 Liter.

| Wagon 4D | | LH24B | 37425 | 4325 | 5125 | 6650 | 9050 |

Body Type	VIN	List	Trade-In Fair	Trade-In Good	Pvt-Party Good	Retail Excellent
A6 QUATTRO AWD—V6 Turbo—Equipment Schedule 3						
W.B. 108.7"; 2.7 Liter.						
2.7T Sedan 4D ED24B	39075	**5100**	**5950**	**7600**	**10200**	
A6 QUATTRO AWD—V8—Equipment Schedule 3						
W.B. 108.6"; 4.2 Liter.						
4.2 Sedan 4D ZL54B	49425	**7175**	**8250**	**10050**	**13000**	
A8 QUATTRO AWD—V8—Equipment Schedule 1						
W.B. 113.4", 118.5" (L); 4.2 Liter.						
Sedan 4D FL54D	62525	**4400**	**5200**	**6750**	**9175**	
L Sedan 4D FL54D	68425	**5900**	**6850**	**8550**	**11300**	
TT—4-Cyl. Turbo—Equipment Schedule 2						
W.B. 95.4", 95.6"; 1.8 Liter.						
Coupe 2D TC28N	31025	**4375**	**5175**	**6700**	**9125**	
Quattro AWD .... U		**1350**	**1350**	**1800**	**1800**	

Body Type	VIN	List	Trade-In Fair	Trade-In Good	Pvt-Party Good	Retail Excellent
A4—V6—Equipment Schedule 3						
W.B. 103.0"; 2.8 Liter.						
Sedan 4D AH68D	30890	**4850**	**5675**	**7300**	**9850**	
Quattro AWD .... D		**1375**	**1375**	**1835**	**1835**	
Manual Trans		**(200)**	**(200)**	**(265)**	**(265)**	
4-Cyl. 1.8L Turbo C		**(950)**	**(950)**	**(1265)**	**(1265)**	
A4 AVANT QUATTRO AWD—V6—Equipment Schedule 3						
W.B. 102.6"; 2.8 Liter.						
Wagon 4D KH68D	33640	**5750**	**6700**	**8325**	**11050**	
Manual Trans		**(200)**	**(200)**	**(265)**	**(265)**	
4-Cyl. 1.8L Turbo C		**(950)**	**(950)**	**(1265)**	**(1265)**	
S4 QUATTRO AWD—V6 Turbo—Equipment Schedule 3						
W.B. 102.6"; 2.7 Liter.						
2.7T Sedan 4D RD58D	39450	**6350**	**7325**	**9200**	**12150**	
2.7T Avant Wagon 4D XD68D	41050	**7150**	**8200**	**10150**	**13300**	
A6—V6—Equipment Schedule 3						
W.B. 108.7"; 2.8 Liter.						
Sedan 4D BH54B	34950	**4275**	**5050**	**6575**	**8950**	
Quattro AWD .... E		**1375**	**1375**	**1835**	**1835**	
A6 AVANT QUATTRO AWD—V6—Equipment Schedule 3						
W.B. 108.6"; 2.8 Liter.						
Wagon 4D LH54B	37900	**5225**	**6075**	**7700**	**10300**	
A6 QUATTRO AWD—V6 Turbo—Equipment Schedule 3						
W.B. 108.7"; 2.7 Liter.						
2.7T Sedan 4D ED54B	40050	**6025**	**6975**	**8650**	**11350**	
Sport Pkg		**350**	**350**	**465**	**465**	
ALLROAD QUATTRO AWD—V6 Turbo—Equipment Sch 1						
W.B. 108.5"; 2.7 Liter.						
2.7T Wagon 4D YP54B	43450	**6700**	**7725**	**9375**	**12200**	
A6 QUATTRO AWD—V8—Equipment Schedule 3						
W.B. 108.6"; 4.2 Liter.						
4.2 Sedan 4D ZL54B	49950	**8250**	**9425**	**11250**	**14450**	
Sport Pkg		**350**	**350**	**465**	**465**	
A8 QUATTRO AWD—V8—Equipment Schedule 1						
W.B. 113.4", 118.5" (L); 4.2 Liter.						
Sedan 4D FL54D	62750	**5250**	**6125**	**7775**	**10400**	
L Sedan 4D ML54D	68450	**6850**	**7900**	**9650**	**12550**	
S8 QUATTRO AWD—V8—Equipment Schedule 1						
W.B. 113.4"; 4.2 Liter.						
Sedan 4D GU54D	73050	**9200**	**10475**	**12550**	**15950**	
TT—4-Cyl. Turbo—Equipment Schedule 2						
W.B. 95.4"; 1.8 Liter.						
Coupe 2D SC28N	31750	**5225**	**6100**	**7750**	**10350**	
Roadster 2D TC28N	33750	**6175**	**7125**	**8825**	**11550**	
Power Folding Roof		**375**	**375**	**500**	**500**	
Quattro AWD		**1375**	**1375**	**1835**	**1835**	
TT QUATTRO AWD—4-Cyl. HO Turbo—Equipment Schedule 2						
W.B. 95.4"; 1.8 Liter.						
Coupe 2D WT28N	36650	**6750**	**7800**	**9500**	**12350**	
Roadster 2D UT28N	39450	**7575**	**8675**	**10450**	**13450**	

Body Type	VIN	List	Trade-In Fair	Trade-In Good	Pvt-Party Good	Retail Excellent
A4—V6—Equipment Schedule 3						
W.B. 104.3"; 3.0 Liter.						
Sedan 4D JC58E	31965	**5725**	**6650**	**8525**	**11450**	
Sport Pkg		**200**	**200**	**265**	**265**	

Body	Type	VIN	List	Trade-In Fair	Good	Pvt-Party Good	Retail Excellent
Quattro AWD		L	......	**1400**	**1400**	**1865**	**1865**
5-Spd Manual Trans				(200)	(200)	(265)	(265)
4-Cyl. 1.8L Turbo		C		(1000)	(1000)	(1335)	(1335)
A4 AVANT QUATTRO AWD—V6—Equipment Schedule 3							
W.B. 104.3"; 3.0 Liter.							
Wagon 4D		VC58E	34715	**6675**	**7700**	**9625**	**12750**
Sport Pkg				200	200	265	265
5-Spd Manual Trans				(200)	(200)	(265)	(265)
4-Cyl. 1.8L Turbo		C		(1000)	(1000)	(1335)	(1335)
S4 QUATTRO AWD—V6 Turbo—Equipment Schedule 3							
W.B. 102.6"; 2.7 Liter.							
2.TT Sedan 4D		RD68D	39475	**7325**	**8400**	**10500**	**13800**
2.TT Avant Wagon 4D		XD68D	41075	**8150**	**9325**	**11500**	**15100**
A6—V6—Equipment Schedule 3							
W.B. 108.7"; 3.0 Liter.							
Sedan 4D		JT54B	35975	**5075**	**5925**	**7800**	**10650**
Quattro AWD		L		1400	1400	1865	1865
A6 AVANT QUATTRO AWD—V6—Equipment Schedule 3							
W.B. 108.6"; 3.0 Liter.							
Wagon 4D		VT54B	38925	**6125**	**7075**	**9000**	**12000**
A6 QUATTRO AWD—V6 Turbo—Equipment Schedule 3							
W.B. 108.7"; 2.7 Liter.							
2.TT Sedan 4D		LD54B	40325	**6950**	**8000**	**10000**	**13200**
Sport Pkg				350	350	465	465
ALLROAD QUATTRO AWD—V6 Turbo—Equipment Sch 1							
W.B. 108.5"; 2.7 Liter.							
2.TT Wagon 4D		YD54B	43325	**7575**	**8700**	**10550**	**13600**
A6 AVANT QUATTRO AWD—V8—Equipment Schedule 3							
W.B. 108.6"; 4.2 Liter.							
4.2 Sedan 4D		ML54B	50225	**9375**	**10675**	**12800**	**16350**
Sport Pkg				350	350	465	465
S6 AVANT QUATTRO AWD—V8—Equipment Schedule 1							
W.B. 108.6"; 4.2 Liter.							
Wagon 4D		XU54B	61375	**13175**	**14850**	**17150**	**21300**
A8 QUATTRO AWD—V8—Equipment Schedule 1							
W.B. 113.4", 118.5" (L); 4.2 Liter.							
Sedan 4D		FL44D	62775	**6400**	**7375**	**9225**	**12200**
L Sedan 4D		ML44D	67775	**8100**	**9275**	**11300**	**14650**
S8 QUATTRO AWD—V8—Equipment Schedule 1							
W.B. 113.4"; 4.2 Liter.							
Sedan 4D		GU44D	74775	**10675**	**12100**	**14300**	**18150**
TT—4-Cyl. Turbo—Equipment Schedule 3							
W.B. 95.4"; 1.8 Liter.							
Coupe 2D		2A	31775	**6125**	**7075**	**9000**	**12000**
Roadster 2D		TC28N	33775	**7100**	**8150**	**10150**	**13350**
Power Folding Roof				400	400	535	535
TT QUATTRO AWD—4-Cyl. Turbo—Equipment Schedule 2							
W.B. 95.4"; 1.8 Liter.							
180 Coupe 2D		WC28N	33595	**6950**	**8000**	**10000**	**13200**
TT QUATTRO AWD—4-Cyl. HO Turbo—Equipment Schedule 2							
W.B. 95.6"; 1.8 Liter.							
225 Coupe 2D		WT28N	36675	**7775**	**8900**	**10900**	**14150**
225 Roadster 2D		UT28N	39475	**8600**	**9800**	**11900**	**15400**
225 ALMS Comm Cpe		WT28N	40245	**9375**	**10675**	**12800**	**16350**

2003 AUDI — (WAU,WUA,WA1orTRU)(JT58E)-3-#

Body	Type	VIN	List	Trade-In Fair	Good	Pvt-Party Good	Retail Excellent
A4—V6—Equipment Schedule 3							
W.B. 104.3", 104.5" (Cab); 3.0 Liter.							
Sedan 4D		JT58E	32250	**6750**	**7775**	**9725**	**12850**
Cabriolet 2D		AT28H	42160	**9625**	**10925**	**13100**	**16650**
Sport Pkg				250	250	335	335
Quattro AWD		L		1450	1450	1935	1935
5-Spd Manual Trans				(225)	(225)	(300)	(300)
4-Cyl. 1.8L Turbo		C		(1150)	(1150)	(1535)	(1535)
A4 AVANT QUATTRO AWD—V6—Equipment Schedule 3							
W.B. 104.3"; 3.0 Liter.							
Wagon 4D		VT58E	35000	**7850**	**8975**	**11050**	**14400**
Sport Pkg				250	250	335	335
5-Spd Manual Trans				(225)	(225)	(300)	(300)
4-Cyl. 1.8L Turbo		C		(1150)	(1150)	(1535)	(1535)
A6—V6—Equipment Schedule 3							
W.B. 108.7"; 3.0 Liter.							
Sedan 4D		JT54B	36360	**6050**	**7000**	**8950**	**11950**

2003 AUDI

Body	Type	VIN	List	Trade-In Fair	Trade-In Good	Pvt-Party Good	Retail Excellent
Quattro AWD		L	....	**1450**	**1450**	**1935**	**1935**

A6 QUATTRO AWD—V6—Equipment Schedule 3
W.B. 108.6"; 3.0 Liter.

Wagon 4D	VT54B	39310	**7325**	**8400**	**10400**	**13600**

A6 QUATTRO AWD—V6 Turbo—Equipment Schedule 3
W.B. 108.7"; 2.7 Liter.

2.7T Sedan 4D	LD54B	41510	**8250**	**9425**	**11500**	**14900**

ALLROAD QUATTRO AWD—V6 Turbo—Equipment Schedule 1
W.B. 108.5"; 2.7 Liter.

2.7T Wagon 4D	YD54B	45110	**8950**	**10200**	**12100**	**15450**

A6 QUATTRO AWD—V8—Equipment Schedule 3
W.B. 108.6"; 4.2 Liter.

4.2 Sedan 4D	ML54B	48460	**11025**	**12500**	**14650**	**18450**
Sport Pkg			**375**	**375**	**500**	**500**

S6 AVANT QUATTRO AWD—V8—Equipment Schedule 1
W.B. 108.6"; 4.2 Liter.

Wagon 4D	XU54B	61060	**15325**	**17250**	**19550**	**23900**

RS6 QUATTRO AWD—V8 Bi Turbo—Equipment Schedule 1
W.B. 108.6"; 4.2 Liter.

Sedan 4D	PV54B	84660	**19200**	**21450**	**24100**	**29200**

A8 QUATTRO AWD—V8—Equipment Schedule 1
W.B. 113.4", 118.5" (L); 4.2 Liter.

Sedan 4D	FL44D	62860	**8700**	**9900**	**11900**	**15300**
L Sedan 4D	ML44D	67860	**10625**	**12050**	**14150**	**17800**

S8 QUATTRO AWD—V8—Equipment Schedule 1
W.B. 113.4"; 4.2 Liter.

Sedan 4D	GU44D	74460	**13475**	**15200**	**17550**	**21800**

TT—4-Cyl. Turbo—Equipment Schedule 2
W.B. 95.4"; 1.8 Liter.

Coupe 2D	SC28N	33145	**7275**	**8350**	**10350**	**13550**
Roadster 2D	TC28N	35145	**8425**	**9625**	**11700**	**15150**
Power Folding Roof			**400**	**400**	**535**	**535**

TT QUATTRO AWD—4-Cyl. HO Turbo—Equipment Schedule 2
W.B. 95.4"; 1.8 Liter.

Coupe 2D	WT28N	36845	**9200**	**10475**	**12600**	**16100**
Roadster 2D	UT28N	39645	**10200**	**11575**	**13700**	**17400**

2004 AUDI — (WAU,WA1orTRU)(JT58E)-4-#

A4—V6—Equipment Schedule 3
W.B. 104.3", 104.5" (Cab); 3.0 Liter.

Sedan 4D	JT58E	31840	**7950**	**9100**	**11150**	**14550**
Cabriolet 2D	AT48H	42490	**11175**	**12650**	**14850**	**18650**
Sport Pkg			**275**	**275**	**365**	**365**
Ultra Sport Pkg			**1000**	**1000**	**1335**	**1335**
Quattro AWD	D,L		**1475**	**1475**	**1965**	**1965**
5-Spd Manual Trans			**(250)**	**(250)**	**(335)**	**(335)**
4-Cyl. 1.8L Turbo	C		**(1300)**	**(1300)**	**(1735)**	**(1735)**

A4 AVANT QUATTRO AWD—V6—Equipment Schedule 3
W.B. 104.3"; 3.0 Liter.

Wagon 4D	VT58E	35480	**9200**	**10475**	**12600**	**16100**
Sport Pkg			**275**	**275**	**365**	**365**
Ultra Sport Pkg			**1000**	**1000**	**1335**	**1335**
4-Cyl. 1.8L Turbo	C		**(1300)**	**(1300)**	**(1735)**	**(1735)**

S4 QUATTRO AWD—V8—Equipment Schedule 1
W.B. 104.3", 104.5" (Cab); 4.2 Liter.

Sedan 4D	PL58E	47490	**12850**	**14450**	**16900**	**21200**
Cabriolet 2D	RL48H	55720	**15925**	**17875**	**20400**	**25100**

S4 AVANT QUATTRO AWD—V8—Equipment Schedule 1
W.B. 104.3"; 4.2 Liter.

Wagon 4D	XL68E	48490	**13825**	**15575**	**18050**	**22400**

A6—V6—Equipment Schedule 3
W.B. 108.7"; 3.0 Liter.

Sedan 4D	JT54B	36640	**7225**	**8300**	**10350**	**13550**
Quattro AWD	L		**1475**	**1475**	**1965**	**1965**

A6 AVANT QUATTRO AWD—V6—Equipment Schedule 3
W.B. 108.6"; 3.0 Liter.

Wagon 4D	VT54B	40840	**8725**	**9950**	**12050**	**15550**

A6 QUATTRO AWD—V6 Turbo—Equipment Schedule 3
W.B. 108.7"; 2.7 Liter.

2.7T Sedan 4D	LD54B	42840	**9675**	**10975**	**13150**	**16700**
2.7T S-Line Sedan 4D	CD64B	43870	**10300**	**11650**	**13800**	**17500**

ALLROAD QUATTRO AWD—V6 Turbo—Equipment Schedule 1
W.B. 108.5"; 2.7 Liter.

2004 AUDI

Body	Type	VIN	List	Trade-In Fair	Trade-In Good	Pvt-Party Good	Retail Excellent
2.7T Wagon 4D		YD54B	40640	**10425**	**11850**	**13800**	**17300**
ALLROAD QUATTRO AWD—V8—Equipment Schedule 1							
W.B. 108.5"; 4.2 Liter.							
4.2 Wagon 4D		YL64B	47640	**12850**	**14450**	**16500**	**20300**
A6 QUATTRO AWD—V8—Equipment Schedule 3							
W.B. 108.6"; 4.2 Liter.							
4.2 Sedan 4D		ML54B	49690	**12800**	**14450**	**16650**	**20700**
Sport Pkg				400	400	535	535
A8 QUATTRO AWD—V8—Equipment Schedule 1							
W.B. 121.1"; 4.2 Liter.							
L Sedan 4D		ML44E	69190	**13875**	**15625**	**17800**	**21900**
TT—4-Cyl. Turbo—Equipment Schedule 2							
W.B. 95.4"; 1.8 Liter.							
Coupe 2D		SC28N	33940	**8650**	**9850**	**11950**	**15450**
Roadster 2D		TC28N	35940	**9950**	**11275**	**13450**	**17050**
Power Folding Roof				400	400	535	535
TT QUATTRO AWD—4-Cyl. HO Turbo—Equipment Schedule 2							
W.B. 95.6"; 1.8 Liter.							
Coupe 2D		WT28N	37390	**10825**	**12300**	**14450**	**18250**
Roadster 2D		UT28N	40190	**11950**	**13525**	**15750**	**19600**
TT QUATTRO AWD—V6—Equipment Schedule 2							
W.B. 95.6"; 3.2 Liter.							
Coupe 2D		WF28N	40590	**12000**	**13575**	**15800**	**19700**
Roadster 2D		UF28N	43590	**13075**	**14750**	**17000**	**21100**

2005 AUDI — (WAU, WA1 or TRU)(JT58E)-5-#

Body	Type	VIN	List	Trade-In Fair	Trade-In Good	Pvt-Party Good	Retail Excellent
A4—V6—Equipment Schedule 3							
W.B. 104.3", 104.5" (Cab); 3.0 Liter.							
Sedan 4D		JT58E	32670	**9350**	**10625**	**12800**	**16400**
Cabriolet 2D		AT48H	43020	**12975**	**14650**	**16850**	**20900**
Sport Pkg				300	300	400	400
Ultra Sport Pkg				1000	1000	1335	1335
S-Line Pkg				800	800	1065	1065
Quattro AWD		D,L		1500	1500	2000	2000
5-Spd Manual Trans				(275)	(275)	(365)	(365)
4-Cyl. 1.8L Turbo		C		(1450)	(1450)	(1935)	(1935)
A4 AVANT QUATTRO AWD—V6—Equipment Schedule 3							
W.B. 104.3"; 3.0 Liter.							
Wagon 4D		VT58E	36510	**10775**	**12200**	**14350**	**18150**
Sport Pkg				300	300	400	400
Ultra Sport Pkg				1000	1000	1335	1335
4-Cyl. 1.8L Turbo		C		(1450)	(1450)	(1935)	(1935)
A4 (2005.5)—4-Cyl. Turbo—Equipment Schedule 3							
W.B. 104.3"; 2.0 Liter.							
2.0T Sedan 4D		AF78E	29270	**9625**	**10925**	**13100**	**16700**
Sport Pkg				300	300	400	400
Quattro AWD				1500	1500	2000	2000
A4 AVANT QUATTRO AWD (2005.5)—4-Cyl. Turbo—Equip Sch 3							
W.B. 104.3"; 2.0 Liter.							
2.0T Wagon 4D		KF78E	32370	**11275**	**12750**	**14950**	**18750**
Sport Pkg				300	300	400	400
A4 QUATTRO AWD (2005.5)—V6—Equipment Schedule 3							
W.B. 104.3"; 3.2 Liter.							
3.2 Sedan 4D		DG78E	36120	**11700**	**13225**	**15450**	**19300**
Sport Pkg				300	300	400	400
A4 AVANT QUATTRO AWD (2005.5)—V6—Equipment Sch 3							
W.B. 104.3"; 3.2 Liter.							
3.2 Wagon 4D		KG78E	37120	**12850**	**14450**	**16650**	**20700**
Sport Pkg				300	300	400	400
S4 QUATTRO AWD—V8—Equipment Schedule 1							
W.B. 104.3", 104.5" (Cab); 4.2 Liter.							
Sedan 4D		PL58E	47770	**14850**	**16700**	**19200**	**23700**
Cabriolet 2D		RL48H	55870	**18325**	**20475**	**23100**	**28100**
S4 AVANT QUATTRO AWD—V8—Equipment Schedule 1							
W.B. 104.3"; 4.2 Liter.							
Wagon 4D		XL58E	48770	**15975**	**17925**	**20500**	**25100**
S4 QUATTRO AWD (2005.5)—V8—Equipment Schedule 1							
W.B. 104.3"; 4.2 Liter.							
Sedan 4D		GL68E	49320	**16850**	**18875**	**21500**	**26300**
S4 AVANT QUATTRO AWD (2005.5)—V8— Equipment Sch 1							
W.B. 104.3"; 4.2 Liter.							
Wagon 4D		UL58E	50320	**17450**	**19550**	**22100**	**27000**

Body	Type	VIN	List	Trade-In Fair	Good	Pvt-Party Good	Retail Excellent

A6 QUATTRO AWD—V6—Equipment Schedule 3
W.B. 111.9"; 3.2 Liter.

Body	Type	VIN	List	Fair	Good	Good	Excellent
Sedan 4D		DG54F	41620	13175	14850	17100	21200
Sport Pkg				425	425	565	565

A6 QUATTRO AWD—V8—Equipment Schedule 3
W.B. 111.9"; 4.2 Liter.

4.2 Sedan 4D		DL54F	51220	17100	19150	21600	26100
Sport Pkg				425	425	565	565
S-Line Pkg		E		800	800	1065	1065

ALLROAD QUATTRO AWD—V6—Equipment Schedule 1
W.B. 108.5"; 2.7 Liter.

2.7T Wagon 4D		YD54B	44570	14550	16375	18400	22200

ALLROAD QUATTRO AWD—V8—Equipment Schedule 1
W.B. 108.5"; 4.2 Liter.

4.2 Wagon 4D		YL54B	47970	17200	19250	21400	25700

A8 QUATTRO AWD—V8—Equipment Schedule 1
W.B. 115.9", 121.0" (L); 4.2 Liter.

Sedan 4D		LL44E	67310	17300	19350	21700	26100
L Sedan 4D		ML44E	70620	19700	22050	24400	29100

A8 QUATTRO AWD—W12—Equipment Schedule 1
W.B. 121.0"; 6.0 Liter.

L Sedan 4D		MR44E	118120	39000	43325	46100	53100

TT—4-Cyl. Turbo—Equipment Schedule 2
W.B. 95.4"; 1.8 Liter.

Coupe 2D		SC28N	34220	10250	11625	13750	17500
Roadster 2D		TC28N	36220	11700	13225	15450	19300
Power Folding Roof				400	400	535	535

TT QUATTRO AWD—4-Cyl. HO Turbo—Equipment Schedule 2
W.B. 95.4", 95.6" (Cpe); 1.8 Liter.

Coupe 2D		WT28N	37620	12750	14400	16600	20600
Roadster 2D		UT28N	40420	13975	15725	18000	22100

TT QUATTRO AWD—V6—Equipment Schedule 2
W.B. 95.6"; 3.2 Liter.

Coupe 2D		WF28N	40870	13975	15725	18000	22100
Roadster 2D		UF28N	43870	15200	17100	19350	23600

2006 AUDI — (WAU,WUAorTRU)(HF68P)-6-#

A3—4-Cyl. Turbo—Equipment Schedule 3
W.B. 101.5"; 2.0 Liter.

2.0T Wagon 4D		HF68P	26940	10825	12250	14300	18000
Dual Moon Roofs				550	550	735	735
Sport Pkg		M		325	325	435	435

A3 QUATTRO AWD—V6—Equipment Schedule 3
W.B. 101.5"; 3.2 Liter.

3.2 S-Line Wagon 4D		KD78P	34700	15725	17650	19800	24000
Dual Moon Roofs				550	550	735	735

A4—4-Cyl. Turbo—Equipment Schedule 3
W.B. 104.3", 104.5" (Cab); 1.8 Liter, 2.0 Liter.

2.0T Sedan 4D		AF78E	29560	10875	12350	14500	18300
1.8T Cabriolet 2D		AC48H	38060	14550	16375	18600	22800
S-Line Pkg		B,E		800	800	1065	1065
Quattro AWD		D,E		1525	1525	2035	2035

A4—V6—Equipment Schedule 3
W.B. 104.3"; 3.2 Liter.

3.2 Sedan 4D		AH78E	34660	13125	14800	17000	21100
S-Line Pkg				800	800	1065	1065
Quattro AWD		D		1525	1525	2035	2035

A4 QUATTRO AWD—V6—Equipment Schedule 1
W.B. 104.5"; 3.0 Liter.

3.0 Cabriolet 2D		DT48H	46210	17700	19900	22100	26800
S-Line Pkg		E		800	800	1065	1065

A4 AVANT QUATTRO AWD—4-Cyl. Turbo—Equipment Sch 3
W.B. 104.3"; 2.0 Liter.

2.0T Wagon 4D		KF78E	32660	12650	14300	16500	20500
S-Line Pkg		S		800	800	1065	1065

A4 AVANT QUATTRO AWD—V6—Equipment Schedule 3
W.B. 104.3"; 3.2 Liter.

3.2 Wagon 4D		KH78E	37760	14400	16175	18400	22500
S-Line Pkg		S		800	800	1065	1065

S4 QUATTRO AWD—V8—Equipment Schedule 1
W.B. 104.3", 104.5" (Cab); 4.2 Liter.

Sedan 4D		GL78E	49620	19300	21550	24200	29400
Special Ed Sedan 4D		GL78E	60970	24800	27625	30400	36100

Body	Type	VIN	List	Trade-In Fair	Trade-In Good	Pvt-Party Good	Retail Excellent
	Cabriolet 2D	RL48H	57860	23900	26650	29400	35000

S4 AVANT QUATTRO AWD—V8—Equipment Schedule 1
W.B. 104.3"; 4.2 Liter.

Body	Type	VIN	List	Trade-In Fair	Trade-In Good	Pvt-Party Good	Retail Excellent
	Wagon 4D	UL78E	50620	20000	22350	25100	30300

A6—V6—Equipment Schedule 3
W.B. 111.9"; 3.2 Liter.

	3.2 Sedan 4D	AH74F	41540	13275	14950	17150	21200
	S-Line Pkg	B		800	800	1065	1065

A6 QUATTRO AWD—V6—Equipment Schedule 3
W.B. 111.9"; 3.2 Liter.

	3.2 Sedan 4D	DG74F	44690	16075	18025	20300	24600
	S-Line Pkg	E		800	800	1065	1065

A6 AVANT QUATTRO AWD—V6—Equipment Schedule 3
W.B. 111.9"; 3.2 Liter.

	3.2 Wagon 4D	KG74F	47590	17200	19250	21600	26100

A6 QUATTRO AWD—V8—Equipment Schedule 3
W.B. 111.9"; 4.2 Liter.

	4.2 Sedan 4D	DL74F	54490	19600	21950	24300	29100
	S-Line Pkg	E		800	800	1065	1065

A8 QUATTRO AWD—V8—Equipment Schedule 1
W.B. 115.9", 121.0" (L); 4.2 Liter.

	Sedan 4D	LL44E	68850	22550	25100	27300	32200
	L Sedan 4D	ML44E	72810	25175	28025	30400	35700
	Sport Pkg			800	800	1065	1065

A8 QUATTRO AWD—W12—Equipment Schedule 1
W.B. 121.0"; 6.0 Liter.

	L Sedan 4D	MR44E	120610	46350	51350	53900	61500

TT—4-Cyl. Turbo—Equipment Schedule 2
W.B. 95.4"; 1.8 Liter.

	Coupe 2D	SC28N	34710	12000	13575	15800	19700
	Roadster 2D	TC28N	36710	13625	15325	17550	21700
	Power Folding Roof			400	400	535	535

TT QUATTRO AWD—4-Cyl. HO Turbo—Equipment Schedule 2
W.B. 95.6"; 1.8 Liter.

	Coupe 2D	WT28N	38110	14750	16600	18800	23000
	Roadster 2D	UT28N	40910	16125	18075	20400	24700

TT QUATTRO AWD—V6—Equipment Schedule 2
W.B. 95.6"; 3.2 Liter.

	Coupe 2D	WD28N	41360	16125	18075	20400	24700
	Special Ed Coupe 2D	PD28N	44259	17350	19450	21800	26400
	Roadster 2D	UD28N	44360	17450	19550	21900	26500
	Special Ed Roadster 2D	RD28N	47259	18675	20875	23200	27900

2007 AUDI — (WAU,WUAorTRU)(HF78P)-7-#

A3—4-Cyl. Turbo—Equipment Schedule 3
W.B. 101.5"; 2.0 Liter.

	2.0T Wagon 4D	HF78P	27540	12700	14350	16350	20200
	Dual Moon Roofs			650	650	865	865
	S-Line Pkg			800	800	1065	1065

A3 QUATTRO AWD—V6—Equipment Schedule 3
W.B. 101.5"; 3.2 Liter.

	3.2 S-Line Wagon 4D	KD78P	34700	18075	20200	22400	26900
	Dual Moon Roofs			650	650	865	865

A4—4-Cyl. Turbo—Equipment Schedule 3
W.B. 104.3"; 2.0 Liter.

	2.0T Sedan 4D	AF78E	30160	12800	14450	16600	20600
	2.0T Cabriolet 2D	AF48H	39820	16850	18875	21200	25700
	S-Line Pkg			800	800	1065	1065
	Quattro AWD	D		1550	1550	2065	2065

A4—V6—Equipment Schedule 3
W.B. 104.3"; 3.2 Liter.

	3.2 Sedan 4D	AH78E	36260	15250	17150	19350	23600
	S-Line Pkg			800	800	1065	1065
	Quattro AWD	D		1550	1550	2065	2065

A4 QUATTRO AWD—V6—Equipment Schedule 3
W.B. 104.3"; 3.2 Liter.

	3.2 Cabriolet 2D	DH48H	47670	20275	22725	25100	29900
	S-Line Pkg			800	800	1065	1065

A4 AVANT QUATTRO AWD—4-Cyl. Turbo—Equipment Sch 3
W.B. 104.3"; 2.0 Liter.

	2.0T Wagon 4D	KF78E	33260	14750	16550	18800	23000
	S-Line Pkg			800	800	1065	1065

Body	Type	VIN	List	Trade-In Fair	Trade-In Good	Pvt-Party Good	Retail Excellent
A4 AVANT QUATTRO AWD—V6—Equipment Schedule 3							
W.B. 104.3"; 3.2 Liter.							
3.2 Wagon 4D		KH78E	39360	**16650**	**18725**	**21000**	**25500**
S-Line Pkg				800	800	1065	1065
RS 4 QUATTRO AWD—V8—Equipment Schedule 1							
W.B. 104.3"; 4.2 Liter.							
Sedan 4D		RU78E	68820	**35575**	**39500**	**42200**	**49000**
S4 QUATTRO AWD—V8—Equipment Schedule 1							
W.B. 104.3", 104.5" (Cab); 4.2 Liter.							
Sedan 4D		GL78E	50720	**21950**	**24500**	**27200**	**32600**
Cabriolet 2D		RL48H	58920	**27050**	**30075**	**32800**	**38800**
S4 AVANT QUATTRO AWD—V8—Equipment Schedule 1							
W.B. 104.3"; 4.2 Liter.							
Wagon 4D		UL78E	51720	**22725**	**25375**	**28100**	**33600**
A6—V6—Equipment Schedule 3							
W.B. 111.9"; 3.2 Liter.							
3.2 Sedan 4D		AH74F	42670	**15375**	**17300**	**19500**	**23800**
S-Line Pkg				800	800	1065	1065
A6 QUATTRO AWD—V6—Equipment Schedule 3							
W.B. 111.9"; 3.2 Liter.							
3.2 Sedan 4D		DH74F	45820	**18525**	**20675**	**23000**	**27700**
S-Line Pkg				800	800	1065	1065
A6 AVANT QUATTRO AWD—V6—Equipment Schedule 3							
W.B. 111.9"; 3.2 Liter.							
3.2 Wagon 4D		KH94F	48720	**19600**	**21950**	**24300**	**29000**
S-Line Pkg				800	800	1065	1065
A6 QUATTRO AWD—V8—Equipment Schedule 3							
W.B. 111.9"; 4.2 Liter.							
4.2 Sedan 4D		DV74F	56020	**22350**	**24900**	**27200**	**32200**
S-Line Pkg		B		800	800	1065	1065
S6 QUATTRO AWD—V10—Equipment Schedule 1							
W.B. 112.1"; 5.2 Liter.							
Sedan 4D		GN74F	72720	**38025**	**42250**	**44400**	**50700**
A8 QUATTRO AWD—V8—Equipment Schedule 1							
W.B. 115.9"; 121.0" (L); 4.2 Liter.							
Sedan 4D		LV44E	69620	**27825**	**30975**	**33100**	**38400**
L Sedan 4D		MV44E	73620	**30775**	**34200**	**36400**	**41900**
Sport Pkg				800	800	1065	1065
A8 QUATTRO AWD—W12—Equipment Schedule 1							
W.B. 121.0"; 6.0 Liter.							
L Sedan 4D		MR44E	121770	**53800**	**59575**	**61700**	**69600**
S8 QUATTRO AWD—V10—Equipment Schedule 1							
W.B. 115.9"; 5.2 Liter.							
Sedan 4D		PN44E	92720	**48325**	**53600**	**56100**	**63800**

2008 AUDI — (WAUorWUA)(HF78P)-8-#

Body	Type	VIN	List	Trade-In Fair	Trade-In Good	Pvt-Party Good	Retail Excellent
A3—4-Cyl. Turbo—Equipment Schedule 3							
W.B. 101.5"; 2.0 Liter.							
2.0T Wagon 4D		HF78P	28185	**14850**	**16700**	**18750**	**22800**
Dual Moon Roofs				750	750	1000	1000
S-Line Pkg				800	800	1065	1065
A3 QUATTRO AWD—V6—Equipment Schedule 3							
W.B. 101.5"; 3.2 Liter.							
3.2 S-Line Wagon 4D		KD78P	35690	**20675**	**23125**	**25200**	**29800**
Dual Moon Roofs				750	750	1000	1000
A4—4-Cyl. Turbo—Equipment Schedule 3							
W.B. 104.3"; 2.0 Liter.							
2.0T Sedan 4D		AF78E	30975	**15000**	**16850**	**19100**	**23400**
2.0T Cabriolet 2D		AF48H	40525	**19350**	**21650**	**24000**	**28700**
S-Line Pkg		B		800	800	1065	1065
Quattro AWD				1575	1575	2100	2100
A4 AVANT QUATTRO AWD—4-Cyl. Turbo—Equipment Sch 3							
W.B. 104.3"; 2.0 Liter.							
2.0T Wagon 4D		KF78E	34075	**17100**	**19150**	**21600**	**26100**
S-Line Pkg		S		800	800	1065	1065
A4—V6—Equipment Schedule 3							
W.B. 104.3"; 3.2 Liter.							
3.2 Sedan 4D		AH78E	37075	**17650**	**19800**	**22100**	**26700**
S-Line Pkg		B		800	800	1065	1065
Quattro AWD		D		1575	1575	2100	2100
A4 QUATTRO AWD—V6—Equipment Schedule 3							
W.B. 104.3"; 3.2 Liter.							
3.2 Cabriolet 2D		DH48H	48675	**23125**	**25775**	**28000**	**33000**

2008 AUDI

Body	Type	VIN	List	Trade-In Fair	Good	Pvt-Party Good	Retail Excellent
S-Line Pkg		E		800	800	1065	1065
A4 AVANT QUATTRO AWD—V6—Equipment Schedule 3							
W.B. 104.3"; 3.2 Liter.							
3.2 Wagon 4D		KH78E	40175	19200	21450	23700	28400
S-Line Pkg		S		800	800	1065	1065
RS 4 QUATTRO AWD—V8—Equipment Schedule 1							
W.B. 104.3"; 4.2 Liter.							
Sedan 4D		RU78E	69785	40375	44775	47300	54400
Cabriolet 2D		YU78E	84775				
S4 QUATTRO AWD—V8—Equipment Schedule 1							
W.B. 104.5"; 4.2 Liter.							
Cabriolet 2D		RL48H	60050	30375	33800	36600	42700
A5 QUATTRO AWD—V6—Equipment Schedule 1							
W.B. 108.3"; 3.2 Liter.							
Coupe 2D		DH78T	41975	30000	33325	36100	42200
S-Line Pkg		E		800	800	1065	1065
S5 QUATTRO AWD—V8—Equipment Schedule 1							
W.B. 108.3"; 4.2 Liter.							
Coupe 2D		RV78T	54325	37250	41350	44000	50800
A6—V6—Equipment Schedule 3							
W.B. 111.9"; 3.2 Liter.							
3.2 Sedan 4D		AH74F	43725	17775	20000	22200	26900
S-Line Pkg		B		800	800	1065	1065
A6 QUATTRO AWD—V6—Equipment Schedule 3							
W.B. 111.9"; 3.2 Liter.							
3.2 Sedan 4D		DH74F	46875	21075	23625	25900	30700
S-Line Pkg		E,S		800	800	1065	1065
A6 AVANT QUATTRO AWD—V6—Equipment Schedule 3							
W.B. 111.9"; 3.2 Liter.							
3.2 Wagon 4D		KH94F	49775	22450	25000	27200	32200
S-Line Pkg		E,S		800	800	1065	1065
A6 QUATTRO AWD—V8—Equipment Schedule 3							
W.B. 111.9"; 4.2 Liter.							
4.2 Sedan 4D		DV74F	57075	25275	28125	30500	35700
S-Line Pkg		B		800	800	1065	1065
S6 QUATTRO AWD—V10—Equipment Schedule 1							
W.B. 112.1"; 5.2 Liter.							
Sedan 4D		DN74F	74425				
A8 QUATTRO AWD—V8—Equipment Schedule 1							
W.B. 115.9"; 121.0" (L); 4.2 Liter.							
Sedan 4D		LV44E	71465				
L Sedan 4D		MV44E	75465				
Sport Pkg							
A8 QUATTRO AWD—W12—Equipment Schedule 1							
W.B. 121.0"; 6.0 Liter.							
L Sedan 4D		MR44E	122575				
R8 QUATTRO AWD—V8—Equipment Schedule 1							
W.B. 104.3"; 4.2 Liter.							
Coupe 2D		AV342	124200				
S8 QUATTRO AWD—V10—Equipment Schedule 1							
W.B. 115.9"; 5.2 Liter.							
Sedan 4D		PN44E	96175				
TT—4-Cyl. Turbo—Equipment Schedule 2							
W.B. 97.2"; 2.0 Liter.							
Coupe 2D		AF38J	35575	18675	20875	23200	27800
Roadster 2D		MF38J	37575	20575	23025	25300	30100
Power Folding Roof				400	400	535	535
S-Line Pkg				800	800	1065	1065
TT QUATTRO AWD—V6—Equipment Schedule 2							
W.B. 97.2"; 3.2 Liter.							
3.2 Coupe 2D		DD38J	43675	23525	26275	28500	33500
3.2 Roadster 2D		RD38J	46675	25175	28025	30400	35600
S-Line Pkg				800	800	1065	1065

BMW

1994 BMW — WB(AorS)(CA632)-R-#

Body	Type	VIN	List	Trade-In Fair	Good	Pvt-Party Good	Retail Excellent
3 SERIES—4-Cyl.—Equipment Schedule 1							
W.B. 106.3"; 1.8 Liter.							
318i Sedan 4D		CA632	26720	1750	2250	3500	5350
318is Coupe 2D		BE632	27845	1800	2325	3575	5450

1994 BMW

Body Type	VIN	List	Trade-In Fair	Trade-In Good	Pvt-Party Good	Retail Excellent
318i Convertible 2D BK632		31945	**2650**	**3250**	**4600**	**6675**
Hard Top (Conv)	....		300	300	400	400
Rollover Pkg (Conv)	....		100	100	135	135
Manual Trans (Sedan)	....		(300)	(300)	(400)	(400)
3 SERIES—6-Cyl.—Equipment Schedule 1						
W.B. 106.3"; 2.5 Liter.						
325i Sedan 4D	CB432	33350	**2550**	**3125**	**4475**	**6525**
325is Coupe 2D	BF432	33550	**2500**	**3075**	**4425**	**6450**
325i Convertible 2D	BJ632	40150	**3975**	**4700**	**6225**	**8600**
Hard Top (Conv)	....		300	300	400	400
Rollover Pkg (Conv)	....		100	100	135	135
Traction Control	....		100	100	135	135
Manual Trans (Sedan)	....		(300)	(300)	(400)	(400)
5 SERIES—6-Cyl.—Equipment Schedule 1						
W.B. 108.7"; 2.5 Liter.						
525i Sedan 4D	HD632	39775	**2800**	**3425**	**4800**	**6875**
525i Touring Wagon 4D	HJ632	41050	**2750**	**3350**	**4725**	**6775**
Traction Control	....		100	100	135	135
w/o Premium Pkg	....		(200)	(200)	(265)	(265)
Manual Trans	....		(350)	(350)	(465)	(465)
5 SERIES—V8—Equipment Schedule 1						
W.B. 108.7"; 3.0 Liter, 4.0 Liter.						
530i Sedan 4D	HE232	43050	**3450**	**4175**	**5600**	**7875**
530i Touring Wagon 4D	HK232	46250	**3200**	**3875**	**5300**	**7500**
540i Sedan 4D	HE632	48950	**3975**	**4700**	**6225**	**8600**
Traction Control (Sedan)	....		100	100	135	135
7 SERIES—V8—Equipment Schedule 1						
W.B. 111.5", 116.0" (iL); 4.0 Liter.						
740i Sedan 4D	GD432	57400	**3075**	**3725**	**5150**	**7300**
740iL Sedan 4D	GD832	61400	**3325**	**4025**	**5475**	**7700**
Traction Control	....		100	100	135	135
7 SERIES—V12—Equipment Schedule 1						
W.B. 116.0"; 5.0 Liter.						
750iL Sedan 4D	GC832	87400	**3600**	**4300**	**5800**	**8075**
8 SERIES—V8—Equipment Schedule 1						
W.B. 105.7"; 4.0 Liter.						
840Ci Coupe 2D	EF632	69850	**9125**	**10400**	**12650**	**16350**
8 SERIES—V12—Equipment Schedule 1						
W.B. 105.7"; 5.0 Liter, 5.6 Liter.						
850i Coupe 2D	EG232	88500	**10350**	**11700**	**14100**	**18150**
850CSi Coupe 2D	EG932	101500	********	********	********	**37300**

1995 BMW — WB(AorS)(CG632)-S-#

Body Type	VIN	List	Trade-In Fair	Trade-In Good	Pvt-Party Good	Retail Excellent
3 SERIES—4-Cyl.—Equipment Schedule 1						
W.B. 106.3"; 1.8 Liter.						
318ti H'Back Coupe 2D	CG632	25295	**1250**	**1725**	**2925**	**4650**
318i Sedan 4D	CA632	27645	**2000**	**2575**	**3875**	**5775**
318is Coupe 2D	BE632	29690	**2075**	**2650**	**3950**	**5875**
318i Convertible 2D	BK632	33965	**3025**	**3675**	**5075**	**7225**
Sport Pkg	....		175	175	235	235
Hard Top (Conv)	....		300	300	400	400
Rollover Pkg (Conv)	....		100	100	135	135
Manual Trans (Sedan)	....		(300)	(300)	(400)	(400)
3 SERIES—6-Cyl.—Equipment Schedule 1						
W.B. 106.3"; 2.5 Liter.						
325i Sedan 4D	CB432	34120	**2925**	**3550**	**4950**	**7075**
325is Coupe 2D	BF432	34220	**2875**	**3500**	**4900**	**7000**
325i Convertible 2D	BJ632	40970	**4500**	**5325**	**6900**	**9400**
Sport Pkg	....		175	175	235	235
Hard Top (Conv)	....		300	300	400	400
Rollover Pkg (Conv)	....		100	100	135	135
Traction Control	....		100	100	135	135
Manual Trans (Sedan)	....		(300)	(300)	(400)	(400)
M3—6-Cyl.—Equipment Schedule 1						
W.B. 106.7"; 3.0 Liter.						
Sedan 2D	BF932	38845	**4675**	**5500**	**7125**	**9700**
5 SERIES—6-Cyl.—Equipment Schedule 1						
W.B. 108.7"; 2.5 Liter.						
525i Sedan 4D	HD632	40195	**3175**	**3850**	**5300**	**7500**
525i Touring Wagon 4D	HJ632	42795	**3075**	**3750**	**5200**	**7375**
Traction Control	....		100	100	135	135
w/o Premium Pkg	....		(200)	(200)	(265)	(265)
Manual Trans	....		(350)	(350)	(465)	(465)

0709   **EQUIPMENT & MILEAGE PAGE 9 TO 23**   39

1995 BMW

Body	Type	VIN	List	Trade-In Fair	Trade-In Good	Pvt-Party Good	Retail Excellent
5 SERIES—V8—Equipment Schedule 1							
W.B. 108.7"; 3.0 Liter, 4.0 Liter.							
530i Sedan 4D		HE232	44320	**3950**	**4675**	**6225**	**8600**
530i Touring Wagon 4D		HK232	47520	**3625**	**4325**	**5850**	**8150**
540i Sedan 4D		HE632	48420	**4475**	**5300**	**6875**	**9375**
Traction Control		-------		**100**	**100**	**135**	**135**
7 SERIES—V8—Equipment Schedule 1							
W.B. 115.4", 120.9" (iL); 4.0 Liter.							
740i Sedan 4D		GF632	59370	**4525**	**5375**	**6950**	**9475**
740iL Sedan 4D		GJ632	61470	**4875**	**5700**	**7425**	**10100**
Traction Control		-------		**100**	**100**	**135**	**135**
7 SERIES—V12—Equipment Schedule 1							
W.B. 120.9"; 5.4 Liter.							
750iL Sedan 4D		GK232	89770	**6050**	**7000**	**8875**	**11800**
8 SERIES—V8—Equipment Schedule 1							
W.B. 105.7"; 4.0 Liter.							
840Ci Coupe 2D		EF632	71670	**10250**	**11625**	**14000**	**18050**
8 SERIES—V12—Equipment Schedule 1							
W.B. 105.7"; 5.4 Liter, 5.6 Liter.							
850Ci Coupe 2D		EG432	90150	**10875**	**12350**	**14850**	**18950**
850CSi Coupe 2D		EG932	104650	********	********	********	**41600**

1996 BMW — WBA(CG732)-T-#

Body	Type	VIN	List	Trade-In Fair	Trade-In Good	Pvt-Party Good	Retail Excellent
3 SERIES—4-Cyl.—Equipment Schedule 1							
W.B. 106.3"; 1.9 Liter.							
318ti H'Back Coupe 2D		CG732	26180	**1475**	**1950**	**3200**	**5025**
318i Sedan 4D		CD732	30120	**2325**	**2925**	**4275**	**6275**
318is Coupe 2D		BE732	30995	**2400**	**3000**	**4325**	**6350**
318i Convertible 2D		BH732	35745	**3450**	**4150**	**5600**	**7900**
Sport Pkg		-------		**200**	**200**	**265**	**265**
Hard Top (Conv)		-------		**350**	**350**	**465**	**465**
Rollover Pkg (Conv)		-------		**150**	**150**	**200**	**200**
Traction Control		-------		**125**	**125**	**165**	**165**
Manual Trans (Sedan)		-------		**(325)**	**(325)**	**(435)**	**(435)**
3 SERIES—6-Cyl.—Equipment Schedule 1							
W.B. 106.3"; 2.8 Liter.							
328i Sedan 4D		CD132	36410	**3325**	**4000**	**5475**	**7700**
328is Coupe 2D		BG132	36500	**3275**	**3950**	**5425**	**7650**
328i Convertible 2D		BK832	42875	**5125**	**5975**	**7700**	**10400**
Sport Pkg		-------		**200**	**200**	**265**	**265**
Hard Top (Conv)		-------		**350**	**350**	**465**	**465**
Rollover Pkg (Conv)		-------		**150**	**150**	**200**	**200**
Traction Control		-------		**125**	**125**	**165**	**165**
Manual Trans (Sedan)		-------		**(325)**	**(325)**	**(435)**	**(435)**
M3—6-Cyl.—Equipment Schedule 1							
W.B. 106.7"; 3.2 Liter.							
Coupe 2D		BG932	41205	**5325**	**6200**	**7950**	**10700**
Z3—4-Cyl.—Equipment Schedule 1							
W.B. 96.3"; 1.9 Liter.							
Roadster 2D		CH732	31445	**2725**	**3350**	**4700**	**6750**
Hard Top		-------		**350**	**350**	**465**	**465**
Traction Control		-------		**125**	**125**	**165**	**165**
7 SERIES—V8—Equipment Schedule 1							
W.B. 120.9"; 4.4 Liter.							
740iL Sedan 4D		GJ832	63060	**5525**	**6450**	**8225**	**11050**
7 SERIES—V12—Equipment Schedule 1							
W.B. 120.9"; 5.4 Liter.							
750iL Sedan 4D		GK232	92630	**6850**	**7900**	**9850**	**12950**
8 SERIES—V8—Equipment Schedule 1							
W.B. 105.7"; 4.4 Liter.							
840Ci Coupe 2D		EF832	76670	**11525**	**13025**	**15600**	**19800**
8 SERIES—V12—Equipment Schedule 1							
W.B. 105.7"; 5.4 Liter.							
850Ci Coupe 2D		EG432	95460	**12250**	**13875**	**16450**	**20900**

1997 BMW — WBA(CG732)-V-#

Body	Type	VIN	List	Trade-In Fair	Trade-In Good	Pvt-Party Good	Retail Excellent
3 SERIES—4-Cyl.—Equipment Schedule 1							
W.B. 106.3"; 1.9 Liter.							
318ti H'Back Coupe 2D		CG732	26535	**1750**	**2250**	**3525**	**5425**
318i Sedan 4D		CC932	30745	**2750**	**3350**	**4750**	**6825**
318is Coupe 2D		BE732	31645	**2750**	**3375**	**4750**	**6850**
318i Convertible 2D		BH732	36145	**3975**	**4725**	**6250**	**8625**

Body Type	VIN	List	Trade-In Fair	Trade-In Good	Pvt-Party Good	Retail Excellent
w/o Leather			0	0	0	0
Sport Pkg			225	225	300	300
Hard Top (Conv)			375	375	500	500
Rollover Pkg (Conv)			200	200	265	265
Manual Trans (Sedan)			(350)	(350)	(465)	(465)

3 SERIES—6-Cyl.—Equipment Schedule 1
W.B. 106.3"; 2.8 Liter.

Body Type	VIN	List	Trade-In Fair	Trade-In Good	Pvt-Party Good	Retail Excellent
328i Sedan 4D	CD332	36845	3825	4550	6075	8400
328is Coupe 2D	BG132	36935	3775	4500	6025	8350
328i Convertible 2D	BK832	42935	5850	6775	8550	11350
Sport Pkg			225	225	300	300
Hard Top (Conv)			375	375	500	500
Rollover Pkg (Conv)			200	200	265	265
Manual Trans (Sedan)			(350)	(350)	(465)	(465)

M3—6-Cyl.—Equipment Schedule 1
W.B. 106.3"; 3.2 Liter.

Body Type	VIN	List	Trade-In Fair	Trade-In Good	Pvt-Party Good	Retail Excellent
Sedan 4D	CD932	45400	6400	7375	9225	12200
Coupe 2D	BG932	44200	6075	7025	8850	11750

Z3—4-Cyl.—Equipment Schedule 1
W.B. 96.3"; 1.9 Liter.

Body Type	VIN	List	Trade-In Fair	Trade-In Good	Pvt-Party Good	Retail Excellent
Roadster 2D	CH732	31695	3125	3800	5200	7350
Hard Top			375	375	500	500

Z3—6-Cyl.—Equipment Schedule 1
W.B. 96.3"; 2.8 Liter.

Body Type	VIN	List	Trade-In Fair	Trade-In Good	Pvt-Party Good	Retail Excellent
Roadster 2D	CJ332	37445	4200	4975	6500	8875
Hard Top			375	375	500	500

5 SERIES—6-Cyl.—Equipment Schedule 1
W.B. 111.4"; 2.8 Liter.

Body Type	VIN	List	Trade-In Fair	Trade-In Good	Pvt-Party Good	Retail Excellent
528i Sedan 4D	DD532	43895	4150	4900	6500	8975
w/o Premium Pkg			(400)	(400)	(535)	(535)
Manual Trans			(450)	(450)	(600)	(600)

5 SERIES—V8—Equipment Schedule 1
W.B. 111.4"; 4.4 Liter.

Body Type	VIN	List	Trade-In Fair	Trade-In Good	Pvt-Party Good	Retail Excellent
540i Sedan 4D	DE632	50470	5825	6750	8525	11350

7 SERIES—V8—Equipment Schedule 1
W.B. 115.4"; 120.9"; 4.4 Liter.

Body Type	VIN	List	Trade-In Fair	Trade-In Good	Pvt-Party Good	Retail Excellent
740i Sedan 4D	GF832	61420	5850	6775	8575	11400
740iL Sedan 4D	GJ832	65370	6350	7325	9175	12100

7 SERIES—V12—Equipment Schedule 1
W.B. 120.9"; 5.4 Liter.

Body Type	VIN	List	Trade-In Fair	Trade-In Good	Pvt-Party Good	Retail Excellent
750iL Sedan 4D	GK232	93370	7825	8950	10950	14150

8 SERIES—V8—Equipment Schedule 1
W.B. 105.7"; 4.4 Liter.

Body Type	VIN	List	Trade-In Fair	Trade-In Good	Pvt-Party Good	Retail Excellent
840Ci Coupe 2D	EF832	77970	13025	14700	17300	21800

8 SERIES—V12—Equipment Schedule 1
W.B. 105.7"; 5.4 Liter.

Body Type	VIN	List	Trade-In Fair	Trade-In Good	Pvt-Party Good	Retail Excellent
850Ci Coupe 2D	EG432	96800	14075	15825	18500	23200

1998 BMW — WBA(CG832)–W–#

3 SERIES—4-Cyl.—Equipment Schedule 1
W.B. 106.3"; 1.9 Liter.

Body Type	VIN	List	Trade-In Fair	Trade-In Good	Pvt-Party Good	Retail Excellent
318ti H'Back Coupe 2D	CG832	26685	2025	2600	3925	5875
318i Sedan 4D	CC032	31045	3150	3825	5275	7450
w/o Leather			0	0	0	0
Sport Pkg			250	250	335	335
Manual Trans (Sedan)			(375)	(375)	(500)	(500)

3 SERIES—6-Cyl.—Equipment Schedule 1
W.B. 106.3"; 2.5 Liter, 2.8 Liter.

Body Type	VIN	List	Trade-In Fair	Trade-In Good	Pvt-Party Good	Retail Excellent
323is Coupe 2D	BF832	32370	3325	4025	5475	7700
323i Convertible 2D	BJ832	38995	5450	6325	8000	10750
328i Sedan 4D	CD432	36770	4375	5175	6725	9175
328is Coupe 2D	BG232	36870	4325	5125	6675	9100
328i Convertible 2D	BK832	44495	6625	7625	9425	12400
Sport Pkg			250	250	335	335
Hard Top (Conv)			400	400	535	535
Rollover Pkg (Conv)			250	250	335	335
Manual Trans (Sedan)			(375)	(375)	(500)	(500)

M3—6-Cyl.—Equipment Schedule 1
W.B. 106.7"; 3.2 Liter.

Body Type	VIN	List	Trade-In Fair	Trade-In Good	Pvt-Party Good	Retail Excellent
Sedan 4D	CD032	43840	7250	8325	10250	13400
Coupe 2D	BG932	42640	6875	7925	9800	12850
Convertible 2D	BK033	46470	7925	9075	11050	14300
Hard Top (Conv)			400	400	535	535

1998 BMW

Body	Type	VIN	List	Trade-In Fair	Good	Pvt-Party Good	Retail Excellent
Z3—4-Cyl.—Equipment Schedule 1							
W.B. 96.3"; 1.9 Liter.							
Roadster 2D		CH732	32120	3600	4300	5750	8000
Hard Top				400	400	535	535
Z3—6-Cyl.—Equipment Schedule 1							
W.B. 96.3", 96.8" (M); 2.8 Liter, 3.2 Liter.							
Roadster 2D		CJ332	37445	4750	5575	7175	9725
M Roadster 2D		CK932	42770	6150	7100	8850	11650
Hard Top				400	400	535	535
5 SERIES—6-Cyl.—Equipment Schedule 1							
W.B. 111.4"; 2.8 Liter.							
528i Sedan 4D		DD632	43895	4700	5525	7150	9725
w/o Premium Pkg				(500)	(500)	(665)	(665)
Sport Pkg				450	450	600	600
Manual Trans		5		(500)	(500)	(665)	(665)
5 SERIES—V8—Equipment Schedule 1							
W.B. 111.4"; 4.4 Liter.							
540i Sedan 4D		DE632	51070	6600	7600	9400	12350
Sport Pkg				450	450	600	600
7 SERIES—V8—Equipment Schedule 1							
W.B. 115.4", 120.9" (iL); 4.4 Liter.							
740i Sedan 4D		GF832	62070	6650	7650	9500	12500
740iL Sedan 4D		GJ832	66070	7150	8225	10150	13250
7 SERIES—V12—Equipment Schedule 1							
W.B. 120.9"; 5.4 Liter.							
750iL Sedan 4D		GK232	92670	8825	10050	12150	15700

1999 BMW — (4UorWB)(SorA)(CG833)–X–#

Body	Type	VIN	List	Trade-In Fair	Good	Pvt-Party Good	Retail Excellent
3 SERIES—4-Cyl.—Equipment Schedule 1							
W.B. 96.3"; 1.9 Liter.							
318ti H'Back Coupe 2D		CG833	26270	2425	3025	4375	6450
w/o Leather				0	0	0	0
3 SERIES—6-Cyl.—Equipment Schedule 1							
W.B. 106.3", 107.3" (Sedan); 2.5 Liter, 2.8 Liter.							
323i Sedan 4D		AM332	30670	4500	5300	6850	9300
323is Coupe 2D		BF833	32645	3850	4575	6075	8400
323i Convertible 2D		BJ833	37695	6175	7125	8875	11700
328i Sedan 4D		AM633	37670	5600	6525	8200	10950
328is Coupe 2D		BG233	37145	4950	5775	7450	10050
328i Convertible 2D		BK833	43045	7450	8550	10450	13500
Sport Pkg				275	275	365	365
Hard Top (Conv)				425	425	565	565
Rollover Pkg (Conv)				275	275	365	365
Manual Trans (ex 2D)				(400)	(400)	(535)	(535)
M3—6-Cyl.—Equipment Schedule 1							
W.B. 106.3", 106.7" (Coupe); 3.2 Liter.							
Coupe 2D		BG933	41695	7750	8875	10800	13950
Convertible 2D		BK033	48145	8875	10100	12150	15650
Hard Top (Conv)				425	425	565	565
Z3—6-Cyl.—Equipment Schedule 1							
W.B. 96.3", 96.8" (M); 2.5 Liter, 2.8 Liter, 3.2 Liter.							
Coupe 2D		CK533	38045	5125	5975	7600	10200
2.3 Roadster 2D		CH933	33120	3625	4325	5775	8025
2.8 Roadster 2D		CH333	37745	5425	6300	7925	10550
M Coupe 2D		CM933	42670	6400	7400	9100	11900
M Roadster 2D		CK933	43270	6900	7975	9725	12650
Hard Top (Roadster)				425	425	565	565
5 SERIES—6-Cyl.—Equipment Schedule 1							
W.B. 111.4"; 2.8 Liter.							
528i Sedan 4D		DM633	42945	5350	6225	7925	10600
528iT Wagon 4D		DP633	44745	4800	5600	7250	9800
w/o Premium Pkg				(575)	(575)	(765)	(765)
Sport Pkg				500	500	665	665
Manual Trans				(550)	(550)	(735)	(735)
5 SERIES—V8—Equipment Schedule 1							
W.B. 111.4"; 4.4 Liter.							
540i Sedan 4D		DN633	51670	7425	8500	10450	13550
540iT Wagon 4D		DR633	54050	6800	7850	9700	12750
Sport Pkg				500	500	665	665
7 SERIES—V8—Equipment Schedule 1							
W.B. 115.4", 120.9" (iL); 4.4 Liter.							
740i Sedan 4D		GG833	62970	7500	8600	10500	13600
740iL Sedan 4D		GH833	66970	8025	9200	11150	14500

1999 BMW

Body	Type	VIN	List	Trade-In Fair	Trade-In Good	Pvt-Party Good	Retail Excellent
Sport Pkg			....	500	500	665	665
7 SERIES—V12—Equipment Schedule 1							
W.B. 120.9"; 5.4 Liter.							
750iL Sedan 4D		GJ033	92670	9850	11175	13350	17000

2000 BMW — (4UorWB)(SorA)(AM334)–Y–#

Body	Type	VIN	List	Trade-In Fair	Trade-In Good	Pvt-Party Good	Retail Excellent
3 SERIES—6-Cyl.—Equipment Schedule 1							
W.B. 107.3"; 2.5 Liter, 2.8 Liter.							
323i Sedan 4D		AM334	32680	5175	6025	7700	10350
323i Wagon 4D		AR334	32985	5075	5925	7600	10250
323Ci Coupe 2D		BM334	35065	5650	6600	8275	11050
323Ci Convertible 2D		BR334	38285	7650	8775	10650	13700
328i Sedan 4D		AM534	37670	6375	7350	9100	11950
328Ci Coupe 2D		BM534	38335	6825	7875	9650	12600
Hard Top (Conv)				450	450	600	600
Premium Pkg				275	275	365	365
Sport Pkg				300	300	400	400
Sport Premium Pkg				350	350	465	465
Manual Trans (ex 2D)				(425)	(425)	(565)	(565)
Z3—6-Cyl.—Equipment Schedule 1							
W.B. 96.3"; 2.5 Liter, 2.8 Liter.							
Coupe 2D		CK534	38395	5825	6775	8400	11050
2.3 Roadster 2D		CH933	34470	4250	5025	6500	8850
2.8 Roadster 2D		CH334	38445	6150	7100	8775	11500
Hard Top (Roadster)				450	450	600	600
M—6-Cyl.—Equipment Schedule 1							
W.B. 96.8"; 3.2 Liter.							
Coupe 2D		CM934	42670	7250	8300	10200	13300
Roadster 2D		CK934	43270	7800	8925	10850	14000
Hard Top (Roadster)				450	450	600	600
Z8—V8—Equipment Schedule 1							
W.B. 98.9"; 5.0 Liter.							
Roadster 2D		EJ134	130670	****	****	****	61000
5 SERIES—6-Cyl.—Equipment Schedule 1							
W.B. 111.4"; 2.8 Liter.							
528i Sedan 4D		DM634	44595	6075	7025	8800	11600
528iT Wagon 4D		DP634	46545	5475	6375	8050	10800
w/o Premium Pkg				(650)	(650)	(865)	(865)
Sport Pkg				550	550	735	735
Manual Trans				(600)	(600)	(800)	(800)
5 SERIES—V8—Equipment Schedule 1							
W.B. 111.4"; 4.4 Liter.							
540i Sedan 4D		DN634	52970	8325	9500	11450	14750
540iT Wagon 4D		DR634	55350	7700	8800	10750	13850
Sport Pkg				550	550	735	735
M5—V8—Equipment Schedule 1							
W.B. 111.4"; 5.0 Liter.							
Sedan 4D		DE934	72070	13825	15525	18000	22300
7 SERIES—V8—Equipment Schedule 1							
W.B. 115.4", 120.9" (iL); 4.4 Liter.							
740i Sedan 4D		GG834	64670	8775	10000	12050	15500
740iL Sedan 4D		GH834	66970	9375	10675	12750	16250
Sport Pkg				550	550	735	735
7 SERIES—V12—Equipment Schedule 1							
W.B. 120.9"; 5.4 Liter.							
750iL Sedan 4D		GJ034	95270	11375	12875	15100	18950

2001 BMW — WBAorWBS(AV334)–1–#

Body	Type	VIN	List	Trade-In Fair	Trade-In Good	Pvt-Party Good	Retail Excellent
3 SERIES—6-Cyl.—Equipment Schedule 1							
W.B. 107.3"; 2.5 Liter, 3.0 Liter.							
325i Sedan 4D		AV334	30060	5950	6875	8600	11350
325xi AWD Sedan 4D		AV334	31810	6450	7450	9175	12000
325Ci Coupe 2D		BN334	32060	6500	7500	9200	12050
325Cic Convertible 2D		BS334	38010	8650	9850	11800	15100
325iT Wagon 4D		AW334	32470	5850	6800	8475	11200
325xiT AWD Wagon 4D		AW334	34220	6625	7625	9375	12250
330i Sedan 4D		AV534	39280	7225	8300	10050	13050
330xi AWD Sedan 4D		AV534	41030	7675	8775	10600	13650
330Ci Coupe 2D		BN534	39335	7750	8875	10700	13750
330Cic Convertible 2D		BS534	44245	9425	10725	12700	16100
Hard Top (Conv)				475	475	635	635
Premium Pkg				300	300	400	400

EQUIPMENT & MILEAGE PAGE 9 TO 23   43

2001 BMW

Body	Type	VIN	List	Trade-In Fair	Trade-In Good	Pvt-Party Good	Retail Excellent
	Sport Pkg		....	325	325	435	435
	Manual Trans (ex 2D)		....	(425)	(425)	(565)	(565)
M3—6-Cyl.—Equipment Schedule 1							
W.B. 107.5"; 3.2 Liter.							
Coupe 2D		BL934	46045	11475	12975	15150	19000
Convertible 2D		BR934	54045	13125	14800	17100	21300
	Hard Top (Conv)		....	475	475	635	635
Z3—6-Cyl.—Equipment Schedule 1							
W.B. 96.8"; 2.5 Liter, 3.0 Liter.							
2.5i Roadster 2D		CN334	34295	4950	5775	7375	9900
3.0i Coupe 2D		CK734	39845	6675	7675	9350	12150
3.0i Roadster 2D		CN534	39745	6975	8025	9725	12600
	Hard Top (Roadster)		....	475	475	635	635
M—6-Cyl.—Equipment Schedule 1							
W.B. 96.8"; 3.2 Liter.							
Coupe 2D		CN934	45635	8225	9400	11350	14600
Roadster 2D		CL934	46635	8775	10000	12050	15450
	Hard Top (Roadster)		....	475	475	635	635
Z8—V8—Equipment Schedule 1							
W.B. 98.6"; 5.0 Liter.							
Roadster 2D		EJ134	130745	****	****	****	65600
5 SERIES—6-Cyl.—Equipment Schedule 1							
W.B. 111.4"; 2.5 Liter, 3.0 Liter.							
525i Sedan 4D		DT334	40195	6925	7975	9750	12700
525iT Wagon 4D		DS334	41995	6300	7275	9000	11800
530i Sedan 4D		DT534	44345	8250	9450	11300	14450
	w/o Premium Pkg		....	(725)	(725)	(965)	(965)
	Sport Pkg		....	575	575	765	765
	Manual Trans		....	(650)	(650)	(865)	(865)
5 SERIES—V8—Equipment Schedule 1							
W.B. 111.4"; 4.4 Liter.							
540i Sedan 4D		DN634	51670	9375	10675	12650	16050
540iT Wagon 4D		DR634	54050	8700	9900	11850	15150
	Sport Pkg		....	575	575	765	765
M5—V8—Equipment Schedule 1							
W.B. 111.4"; 5.0 Liter.							
Sedan 4D		DE934	69970	15300	17200	19600	24100
7 SERIES—V8—Equipment Schedule 1							
W.B. 115.4", 120.9" (iL); 4.4 Liter.							
740i Sedan 4D		GG834	63470	9850	11175	13250	16800
740iL Sedan 4D		GH834	67470	10475	11900	14000	17700
	Sport Pkg		....	575	575	765	765
7 SERIES—V12—Equipment Schedule 1							
W.B. 120.9"; 5.4 Liter.							
750iL Sedan 4D		GJ034	92670	12650	14300	16550	20600
	Sport Pkg		....	200	200	265	265

2002 BMW — WBA,WBS,4USor5UM(ET374)-2-#

Body	Type	VIN	List	Trade-In Fair	Trade-In Good	Pvt-Party Good	Retail Excellent
3 SERIES—6-Cyl.—Equipment Schedule 1							
W.B. 107.3"; 2.5 Liter, 3.0 Liter.							
325i Sedan 4D		ET374	32465	6750	7775	9775	12950
325xi AWD Sedan 4D		EU334	34215	7275	8350	10400	13600
325Ci Coupe 2D		BN334	34465	7300	8400	10450	13650
325Cic Convertible 2D		BS334	39470	9600	10925	13150	16800
325iT Wagon 4D		EN334	34865	6675	7675	9675	12850
325xiT AWD Wagon 4D		EP334	36615	7450	8525	10550	13800
330i Sedan 4D		EV534	38410	8075	9225	11350	14800
330xi AWD Sedan 4D		EW534	40160	8550	9775	11900	15450
330Ci Coupe 2D		BN534	39410	8650	9850	12000	15550
330Cic Convertible 2D		BS534	46820	10425	11850	14100	17950
	Hard Top (Conv)		....	500	500	665	665
	Premium Pkg		....	300	300	400	400
	Sport Pkg		....	350	350	465	465
	Manual Trans (ex 2D)		....	(425)	(425)	(565)	(565)
M3—6-Cyl.—Equipment Schedule 1							
W.B. 107.5"; 3.2 Liter.							
Coupe 2D		BL934	49745	12650	14250	16600	20800
Convertible 2D		BR934	55545	14450	16225	18700	23200
	Hard Top (Conv)		....	500	500	665	665
Z3—6-Cyl.—Equipment Schedule 1							
W.B. 96.3"; 2.5 Liter, 3.0 Liter.							
2.5i Roadster 2D		CN334	34370	5650	6600	8325	11100
3.0i Coupe 2D		CK734	39920	7500	8575	10450	13500

Body Type	VIN	List	Trade-In Fair	Good	Pvt-Party Good	Retail Excellent
3.0i Roadster 2D	CN534	39820	7850	8975	10850	13950
Hard Top (Roadster)			500	500	665	665
Sport Pkg			200	200	265	265
M—6-Cyl.—Equipment Schedule 1						
W.B. 96.8"; 3.2 Liter.						
Coupe 2D	CN934	45635	9125	10400	12600	16200
Roadster 2D	CL934	46635	9725	11075	13300	17000
Hard Top (Roadster)			500	500	665	665
Z8—V8—Equipment Schedule 1						
W.B. 98.6"; 5.0 Liter.						
Roadster 2D	EJ134	132745	****	****	****	65900
5 SERIES—6-Cyl.—Equipment Schedule 1						
W.B. 111.4"; 2.5 Liter, 3.0 Liter.						
525i Sedan 4D	DT434	41070	7800	8925	11000	14300
525iT Wagon 4D	DS334	42870	7100	8150	10150	13400
530i Sedan 4D	DT634	44670	9175	10425	12600	16200
w/o Premium Pkg			(800)	(800)	(1065)	(1065)
Sport Pkg			600	600	800	800
Manual Trans			(700)	(700)	(935)	(935)
5 SERIES—V8—Equipment Schedule 1						
W.B. 111.4"; 4.4 Liter.						
540i Sedan 4D	DN634	53145	10400	11750	14000	17800
540iT Wagon 4D	DR634	55545	9650	10975	13200	16850
Sport Pkg			600	600	800	800
M5—V8—Equipment Schedule 1						
W.B. 111.4"; 5.0 Liter.						
Sedan 4D	DE934	72645	16750	18825	21500	26300
7 SERIES—V8—Equipment Schedule 1						
W.B. 117.7", 123.2" (Li); 4.4 Liter.						
745i Sedan 4D	GL634	68495	10350	11750	14050	18000
745Li Sedan 4D	GN634	72495	11025	12500	14850	18850
Sport Pkg			600	600	800	800

2003 BMW — WBA,WBSor4US(EV334)-3-#

Body Type	VIN	List	Trade-In Fair	Good	Pvt-Party Good	Retail Excellent
3 SERIES—6-Cyl.—Equipment Schedule 1						
W.B. 107.3"; 2.5 Liter, 3.0 Liter.						
325i Sedan 4D	EV334	32270	7450	8550	10650	13900
325xi AWD Sedan 4D	EU334	34020	8075	9225	11350	14800
325Ci Coupe 2D	BN334	34070	8100	9275	11400	14850
325Cic Convertible 2D	BS334	40120	10200	11575	13750	17500
325iT Wagon 4D	EN334	33820	7375	8450	10500	13750
325xiT AWD Wagon 4D	EP334	35570	8275	9475	11550	15050
330i Sedan 4D	EV534	39070	9050	10300	12450	16000
330xi AWD Sedan 4D	EW534	40820	9525	10825	13050	16650
330Ci Coupe 2D	BN534	40070	9675	10975	13200	16850
330Cic Convertible 2D	BS534	44870	11425	12875	15150	19050
Hard Top (Conv)			525	525	700	700
Premium Pkg			350	350	465	465
Sport Pkg			250	250	335	335
Performance Pkg			500	500	665	665
5-Spd Manual (ex 2D)			(475)	(475)	(635)	(635)
M3—6-Cyl.—Equipment Schedule 1						
W.B. 107.5"; 3.2 Liter.						
Coupe 2D	BL934	49345	14200	15975	18400	22800
Convertible 2D	BR934	55195	15050	16900	19400	23900
Hard Top (Conv)			525	525	700	700
Z4—6-Cyl.—Equipment Schedule 1						
W.B. 98.2"; 2.5 Liter, 3.0 Liter.						
2.5i Roadster 2D	BT334	37690	7750	8875	10900	14150
3.0i Roadster 2D	BT534	43215	9350	10625	12750	16200
Premium Pkg			350	350	465	465
Sport Pkg			250	250	335	335
Z8—V8—Equipment Schedule 1						
W.B. 98.6"; 4.8 Liter, 5.0 Liter.						
Roadster 2D	EJ134	134295	****	****	****	73800
Alpina Roadster 2D	EJ134	139295	****	****	****	90000
5 SERIES—6-Cyl.—Equipment Schedule 1						
W.B. 111.4"; 2.5 Liter, 3.0 Liter.						
525i Sedan 4D	DT334	41770	7950	9100	11150	14600
525iT Wagon 4D	DS334	43470	7150	8225	10250	13500
530i Sedan 4D	DT534	45370	9525	10825	13050	16650
w/o Premium Pkg			(850)	(850)	(1135)	(1135)
Sport Pkg			700	700	935	935

2003 BMW

Body	Type	VIN	List	Trade-In Fair	Trade-In Good	Pvt-Party Good	Retail Excellent
	Manual Trans	....		**(550)**	**(550)**	**(735)**	**(735)**

5 SERIES—V8—Equipment Schedule 1
W.B. 111.4"; 4.4 Liter.

Body	Type	VIN	List	Fair	Good	Good	Excellent
	540i Sedan 4D	DN634	52495	**10925**	**12350**	**14600**	**18450**
	540iT Wagon 4D	DR634	56085	**10150**	**11525**	**13700**	**17450**
	Sport Pkg			**700**	**700**	**935**	**935**

M5—V8—Equipment Schedule 1
W.B. 111.4"; 5.0 Liter.

| | Sedan 4D | DE934 | 73195 | **18225** | **20375** | **23100** | **28100** |

7 SERIES—V8—Equipment Schedule 1
W.B. 117.7, 123.2" (Li); 4.4 Liter.

	745i Sedan 4D	GL634	70895	**12000**	**13525**	**15950**	**20100**
	745Li Sedan 4D	GN634	73195	**12925**	**14600**	**17000**	**21300**
	Sport Pkg			**700**	**700**	**935**	**935**

7 SERIES—V12—Equipment Schedule 1
W.B. 123.2"; 6.0 Liter.

| | 760Li Sedan 4D | GN834 | 118195 | **28325** | **31550** | **34700** | **41300** |

2004 BMW — WBA,WBSor4US(EV334)-4-#

3 SERIES—6-Cyl.—Equipment Schedule 1
W.B. 107.3"; 2.5 Liter, 3.0 Liter.

	325i Sedan 4D	EV334	33265	**8725**	**9950**	**12100**	**15700**
	325xi AWD Sedan 4D	EU334	35015	**9400**	**10675**	**12900**	**16550**
	325Ci Coupe 2D	BD334	34570	**9450**	**10725**	**12950**	**16600**
	325Cic Convertible 2D	BW334	40720	**11425**	**12875**	**15200**	**19100**
	325iT Wagon 4D	EN334	34815	**8650**	**9850**	**12000**	**15600**
	325xiT AWD Wagon 4D	EP334	36565	**9675**	**10975**	**13200**	**16900**
	330i Sedan 4D	EV334	39270	**10475**	**11900**	**14100**	**17950**
	330xi AWD Sedan 4D	EW334	41020	**11075**	**12550**	**14850**	**18700**
	330Ci Coupe 2D	BD334	40770	**11225**	**12700**	**14950**	**18850**
	330Cic Convertible 2D	BW534	45570	**12875**	**14550**	**16850**	**21000**
	Hard Top (Conv)			**550**	**550**	**735**	**735**
	Premium Pkg			**400**	**400**	**535**	**535**
	Sport Pkg			**275**	**275**	**365**	**365**
	Performance Pkg			**500**	**500**	**665**	**665**
	5-Spd Manual (ex 2D)			**(500)**	**(500)**	**(665)**	**(665)**

M3—6-Cyl.—Equipment Schedule 1
W.B. 107.5"; 3.2 Liter.

	Coupe 2D	BL934	51340	**16325**	**18325**	**20900**	**25600**
	Convertible 2D	BR934	56595	**17100**	**19150**	**21800**	**26600**
	Hard Top (Conv)			**550**	**550**	**735**	**735**

Z4—6-Cyl.—Equipment Schedule 1
W.B. 98.2"; 2.5 Liter, 3.0 Liter.

	2.5i Roadster 2D	BT334	37790	**9100**	**10350**	**12400**	**15900**
	3.0i Roadster 2D	BT534	43315	**10825**	**12250**	**14400**	**18100**
	Premium Pkg			**400**	**400**	**535**	**535**
	Sport Pkg			**275**	**275**	**365**	**365**

5 SERIES—6-Cyl.—Equipment Schedule 1
W.B. 113.7"; 2.5 Liter, 3.0 Liter.

	525i Sedan 4D	NA535	43670	**11625**	**13125**	**15400**	**19350**
	530i Sedan 4D	NA735	48670	**13425**	**15150**	**17450**	**21700**
	w/o Premium Pkg			**(875)**	**(875)**	**(1165)**	**(1165)**
	Sport Pkg			**800**	**800**	**1065**	**1065**
	Manual Trans			**(600)**	**(600)**	**(800)**	**(800)**

5 SERIES—V8—Equipment Schedule 1
W.B. 113.7"; 4.4 Liter.

| | 545i Sedan 4D | NB335 | 54995 | **13875** | **15625** | **18000** | **22200** |
| | Sport Pkg | | | **800** | **800** | **1065** | **1065** |

6 SERIES—V8—Equipment Schedule 1
W.B. 109.4"; 4.4 Liter.

	645Ci Coupe 2D	EH734	69995	**19600**	**21950**	**24600**	**29800**
	645Cic Convertible 2D	EK734	76995	**23025**	**25675**	**28400**	**34000**
	Sport Pkg			**800**	**800**	**1065**	**1065**

7 SERIES—V8—Equipment Schedule 1
W.B. 117.7", 123.2" (Li); 4.4 Liter.

	745i Sedan 4D	GL634	69195	**13875**	**15575**	**18100**	**22400**
	745Li Sedan 4D	GN634	73195	**15050**	**16900**	**19400**	**24000**
	Sport Pkg			**800**	**800**	**1065**	**1065**

7 SERIES—V12—Equipment Schedule 1
W.B. 117.7", 123.2" (Li); 6.0 Liter.

| | 760i Sedan 4D | GL834 | 111795 | **30575** | **34000** | **37100** | **43800** |
| | 760Li Sedan 4D | GN834 | 117795 | **32250** | **35875** | **39000** | **45900** |

2005 BMW

Body	Type	VIN	List	Trade-In Fair	Trade-In Good	Pvt-Party Good	Retail Excellent

2005 BMW — WBA,WBSor4US(EV334)-5-#

3 SERIES—6-Cyl.—Equipment Schedule 1
W.B. 107.3"; 2.5 Liter, 3.0 Liter.

Body Type	VIN	List	Fair	Good	Good	Excellent
325i Sedan 4D	EV334	33715	10250	11625	13850	17650
325xi AWD Sedan 4D	EU334	35465	11025	12450	14750	18600
325Ci Coupe 2D	BD334	36115	11025	12500	14800	18650
325Ci Convertible 2D	BW334	42420	12800	14400	16700	20800
325i Wagon 4D	EN334	35615	10150	11525	13750	17550
325xi AWD Wagon 4D	EP334	37365	11325	12800	15050	18950
330i Sedan 4D	EV534	39120	12250	13825	16050	20100
330xi AWD Sedan 4D	EW534	40870	12875	14500	16800	20900
330Ci Coupe 2D	BD534	40720	13025	14700	17000	21200
330Ci Convertible 2D	BW534	46470	14600	16425	18700	23000
Hard Top (Conv)		......	575	575	765	765
Premium Pkg		......	450	450	600	600
Sport Pkg		......	300	300	400	400
Performance Pkg		......	500	500	665	665
5-Spd Manual (ex 2D)		......	(525)	(525)	(700)	(700)

M3—6-Cyl.—Equipment Schedule 1
W.B. 107.5"; 3.2 Liter.

Body Type	VIN	List	Fair	Good	Good	Excellent
Coupe 2D	BL934	51140	18675	20875	23400	28400
Convertible 2D	BR934	56495	19350	21650	24300	29300
Hard Top (Conv)		......	575	575	765	765
Club Sport Pkg		......	1100	1100	1465	1465
Competition Pkg		......	1100	1100	1465	1465

Z4—6-Cyl.—Equipment Schedule 1
W.B. 98.2"; 2.5 Liter, 3.0 Liter.

Body Type	VIN	List	Fair	Good	Good	Excellent
2.5i Roadster 2D	BT335	38415	10625	12050	14100	17750
3.0i Roadster 2D	BT535	44265	12500	14100	16200	20100
Premium Pkg		......	450	450	600	600
Sport Pkg		......	300	300	400	400

5 SERIES—6-Cyl.—Equipment Schedule 1
W.B. 113.7"; 2.5 Liter, 3.0 Liter.

Body Type	VIN	List	Fair	Good	Good	Excellent
525i Sedan 4D	NA535	44720	13475	15200	17500	21700
530i Sedan 4D	NA735	48820	15475	17350	19700	24100
w/o Premium Pkg		......	(900)	(900)	(1200)	(1200)
Sport Pkg		......	900	900	1200	1200

5 SERIES—V8—Equipment Schedule 1
W.B. 113.7"; 4.4 Liter.

Body Type	VIN	List	Fair	Good	Good	Excellent
545i Sedan 4D	NB335	56495	15975	17925	20400	24900
Sport Pkg		......	900	900	1200	1200

6 SERIES—V8—Equipment Schedule 1
W.B. 109.4"; 4.4 Liter.

Body Type	VIN	List	Fair	Good	Good	Excellent
645Ci Coupe 2D	EH734	70595	22450	25000	27700	33100
645Cic Convertible 2D	EK734	78895	26275	29200	32000	37900
Sport Pkg		......	900	900	1200	1200

7 SERIES—V8—Equipment Schedule 1
W.B. 117.7", 123.2" (Li); 4.4 Liter.

Body Type	VIN	List	Fair	Good	Good	Excellent
745i Sedan 4D	GL635	70595	15925	17875	20500	25200
745Li Sedan 4D	GN635	74595	17350	19450	22100	27000
Sport Pkg		......	900	900	1200	1200

7 SERIES—V12—Equipment Schedule 1
W.B. 117.7", 123.2" (Li); 6.0 Liter.

Body Type	VIN	List	Fair	Good	Good	Excellent
760i Sedan 4D	GL835	111895	34600	38425	41400	48300
760Li Sedan 4D	GN835	119295	36450	40475	43500	50700

2006 BMW — WBA,WBSor4US(VB135)-6-#

3 SERIES—6-Cyl.—Equipment Schedule 1
W.B. 107.3", 108.7" (Sed & Wag); 2.5 Liter, 3.0 Liter.

Body Type	VIN	List	Fair	Good	Good	Excellent
325i Sedan 4D	VB135	35315	13675	15425	17750	22000
325xi AWD Sedan 4D	VD135	37215	14800	16650	19000	23300
325Ci Coupe 2D	BD334	36715	14400	16225	18550	22900
325Ci Convertible 2D	BW334	43020	15975	17925	20300	24700
325xi AWD Wagon 4D	VT135	39015	14700	16525	18800	23100
330i Sedan 4D	VB335	40020	15875	17825	20200	24600
330xi AWD Sedan 4D	VD335	41920	17000	19050	21500	26100
330Ci Coupe 2D	BD534	41520	16550	18625	21000	25600
330Ci Convertible 2D	BW534	46870	18075	20200	22600	27300
Hard Top (Conv)		......	600	600	800	800
Premium Pkg		......	500	500	665	665
Sport Pkg		......	325	325	435	435

Body	Type	VIN	List	Trade-In Fair	Trade-In Good	Pvt-Party Good	Retail Excellent
	Performance Pkg			500	500	665	665
M3—6-Cyl.—Equipment Schedule 1							
W.B. 107.5"; 3.2 Liter.							
Coupe 2D		BL934	52640	22350	24900	27400	32700
Convertible 2D		BR934	58295	22825	25475	28000	33400
	Hard Top (Conv)			600	600	800	800
	Competition Pkg			1200	1200	1600	1600
Z4—6-Cyl.—Equipment Schedule 1							
W.B. 98.2"; 3.0 Liter.							
3.0i Roadster 2D		BU335	39135	13675	15375	17500	21500
3.0si Coupe 2D		DU534	40795	14400	16175	18350	22300
3.0si Roadster 2D		BU535	44485	15425	17350	19450	23600
	Premium Pkg			500	500	665	665
	Sport Pkg			325	325	435	435
Z4 M SERIES—6-Cyl.—Equipment Schedule 1							
W.B. 98.3"; 3.2 Liter.							
Coupe 2D		DU934	49995	19200	21450	24000	29000
Roadster 2D		BT935	51995	20100	22450	25000	30000
	Premium Pkg			500	500	665	665
5 SERIES—6-Cyl.—Equipment Schedule 1							
W.B. 113.7", 113.6" (Wagon); 3.0 Liter.							
525i Sedan 4D		NE535	43195	15575	17500	19900	24400
525xi AWD Sedan 4D		NF335	45395	16275	18275	20700	25300
530i Sedan 4D		NE735	47495	17775	20000	22300	27000
530xi AWD Sedan 4D		NF735	49695	18575	20775	23200	28000
530xi AWD Wagon 4D		NN735	52095	19000	21275	23700	28500
	w/o Premium Pkg			(925)	(925)	(1235)	(1235)
	Sport Pkg			975	975	1300	1300
5 SERIES—V8—Equipment Schedule 1							
W.B. 113.7"; 4.8 Liter.							
550i Sedan 4D		NB535	58095	20100	22550	25000	29900
	Sport Pkg			975	975	1300	1300
M5—V10—Equipment Schedule 1							
W.B. 113.7"; 5.0 Liter.							
Sedan 4D		NB935	84895	33525	37250	40000	46600
6 SERIES—V8—Equipment Schedule 1							
W.B. 109.4"; 4.8 Liter.							
650i Coupe 2D		EH134	72495	25475	28325	31000	36700
650i Convertible 2D		EK134	79495	29700	33025	35800	41800
	Sport Pkg			975	975	1300	1300
M6—V10—Equipment Schedule 1							
W.B. 109.5"; 5.0 Liter.							
Coupe 2D		EH934	96795	38525	42725	45500	52500
7 SERIES—V8—Equipment Schedule 1							
W.B. 117.7", 123.2" (Li); 4.8 Liter.							
750i Sedan 4D		HL835	72495	26550	29600	32400	38400
750Li Sedan 4D		HN835	76495	28225	31450	34200	40400
	Sport Pkg			975	975	1300	1300
7 SERIES—V12—Equipment Schedule 1							
W.B. 117.7", 123.2" (Li); 6.0 Liter.							
760i Sedan 4D		HL035	113895	46950	52050	55100	63300
760Li Sedan 4D		HN035	121295	49000	54400	57400	65900

2007 BMW — WBA,WBSor4US(VA335)-7-#

Body	Type	VIN	List	Trade-In Fair	Trade-In Good	Pvt-Party Good	Retail Excellent
3 SERIES—6-Cyl.—Equipment Schedule 1							
W.B. 108.7"; 3.0 Liter.							
328i Sedan 4D		VA335	36815	18775	20975	23400	28200
328xi AWD Sedan 4D		VC935	38715	20000	22350	24800	29700
328i Coupe 2D		WB335	39715	19550	21850	24300	29100
328xi AWD Coupe 2D		WC335	41515	20675	23125	25500	30500
328i Convertible 2D		WL135	43975	24100	26950	29300	34600
328i Wagon 4D		VS135	38615	18875	21075	23500	28300
328xi AWD Wagon 4D		VT735	40515	19900	22250	24700	29600
	Premium Pkg			550	550	735	735
	Sport Pkg			350	350	465	465
3 SERIES—6-Cyl. Twin Turbo—Equipment Schedule 1							
W.B. 108.7"; 3.0 Liter.							
335i Sedan 4D		VB735	39675	21175	23725	26100	31100
335xi AWD Sedan 4D		VD535	41575	22350	24900	27300	32400
335i Coupe 2D		WB735	44020	23325	26075	28500	33700
335i Convertible 2D		WL735	49875	28625	31850	34300	40100
	Premium Pkg			550	550	735	735
	Sport Pkg			350	350	465	465

Body	Type	VIN	List	Trade-In Fair	Trade-In Good	Pvt-Party Good	Retail Excellent
Z4—6-Cyl.—Equipment Schedule 1							
W.B. 98.2"; 3.0 Liter.							
3.0i Roadster 2D		BU335	37095	18575	20775	22900	27400
3.0si Coupe 2D		DU535	41095	20000	22350	24500	29100
3.0si Roadster 2D		BU535	43095	20975	23525	25700	30400
Premium Pkg				550	550	735	735
Sport Pkg				350	350	465	465
Z4 M SERIES—6-Cyl.—Equipment Schedule 1							
W.B. 98.3"; 3.2 Liter.							
Coupe 2D		DU934	50795	25175	28025	30700	36300
Roadster 2D		BT935	52795	26175	29100	31800	37400
Premium Pkg				550	550	735	735
5 SERIES—6-Cyl.—Equipment Schedule 1							
W.B. 113.7", 113.6" (Wagon); 3.0 Liter.							
525i Sedan 4D		NE535	46920	18075	20200	22600	27300
525xi AWD Sedan 4D		NF535	49120	18875	21075	23500	28300
530i Sedan 4D		NE735	50920	20475	22925	25300	30300
530xi AWD Sedan 4D		NF735	53120	21375	23825	26300	31400
530xi AWD Wagon 4D		NN735	55520	21750	24300	26800	31900
w/o Premium Pkg				(950)	(950)	(1265)	(1265)
Sport Pkg				1050	1050	1400	1400
5 SERIES—V8—Equipment Schedule 1							
W.B. 113.7"; 4.8 Liter.							
550i Sedan 4D		NB535	60485	23025	25675	28100	33300
Sport Pkg				1050	1050	1400	1400
M5—V10—Equipment Schedule 1							
W.B. 113.7"; 5.0 Liter.							
Sedan 4D		NB935	86195	37925	42050	44700	51500
6 SERIES—V8—Equipment Schedule 1							
W.B. 109.4"; 4.8 Liter.							
650i Coupe 2D		EH135	74595	29000	32350	34900	40900
650i Convertible 2D		EK135	81595	33525	37250	39900	46300
Sport Pkg				1050	1050	1400	1400
M6—V10—Equipment Schedule 1							
W.B. 109.5"; 5.0 Liter.							
Coupe 2D		EH935	101995	43125	47825	50600	58000
Convertible 2D		EK935	108695	49200	54575	57200	65300
7 SERIES—V8—Equipment Schedule 1							
W.B. 117.7", 123.1" (Li); 4.8 Liter.							
750i Sedan 4D		HL835	75695	30575	34000	36800	43000
750Li Sedan 4D		HN835	78795	32450	36075	38700	45200
Sport Pkg				1050	1050	1400	1400
7 SERIES—V12—Equipment Schedule 1							
W.B. 123.1"; 6.0 Liter.							
760Li Sedan 4D		HN035	123795	55075	60950	63800	72400

2008 BMW — WBA,WBS(UP735)-8-#

Body	Type	VIN	List	Trade-In Fair	Trade-In Good	Pvt-Party Good	Retail Excellent
1 SERIES—6-Cyl.—Equipment Schedule 1							
W.B. 104.7"; 3.0 Liter.							
128i Coupe 2D		UP735	33095	21450	23900	26400	31500
128i Convertible 2D		UL735	33875	24700	27550	29900	35200
Premium Pkg				575	575	765	765
Sport Pkg				375	375	500	500
1 SERIES—6-Cyl. Twin Turbo—Equipment Schedule 1							
W.B. 104.7"; 3.0 Liter.							
135i Coupe 2D		UC735	39395	25475	28425	30900	36400
135i Convertible 2D		UN935	39875	28725	32050	34400	40100
Premium Pkg				575	575	765	765
Sport Pkg				375	375	500	500
3 SERIES—6-Cyl.—Equipment Schedule 1							
W.B. 108.7"; 3.0 Liter.							
328i Sedan 4D		VA335	36895	21750	24200	26700	31800
328xi AWD Sedan 4D		VC935	38795	23025	25675	28000	33200
328i Coupe 2D		WB335	39795	22550	25175	27600	32700
328xi AWD Coupe 2D		WC335	41595	23825	26550	28900	34200
328i Convertible 2D		WL135	46800	30000	33325	35800	41600
328i Wagon 4D		VS135	38695	21850	24400	26900	31900
328xi AWD Wagon 4D		VT735	40595	22925	25575	27900	33100
Premium Pkg				575	575	765	765
Sport Pkg				375	375	500	500
3 SERIES—6-Cyl. Twin Turbo—Equipment Schedule 1							
W.B. 108.7"; 3.0 Liter.							
335i Sedan 4D		VB735	42400	24300	27150	29500	34800

Body	Type	VIN	List	Trade-In Fair	Trade-In Good	Pvt-Party Good	Retail Excellent
	335xi AWD Sedan 4D	VD535	44300	25575	28525	31000	36500
	335i Coupe 2D	WB735	44300	26750	29800	32200	37700
	335xi AWD Coupe 2D	WC735	46100	27550	30675	33000	38600
	335i Convertible 2D	WL735	51150	34900	38700	41100	47200
	Premium Pkg			575	575	765	765
	Sport Pkg			375	375	500	500
M3—V8—Equipment Schedule 1							
W.B. 108.7"; 4.0 Liter.							
	Sedan 4D	VA935	56650	38525	42725	45200	51900
	Coupe 2D	WD935	59350	40375	44775	47100	54000
	Convertible 2D	WL935	68200	46850	51950	54400	61800
	Premium Pkg			575	575	765	765
Z4—6-Cyl.—Equipment Schedule 1							
W.B. 98.2"; 3.0 Liter.							
	3.0i Roadster 2D	BU335	40595	21450	23900	26100	30700
	3.0si Coupe 2D	DU535	43445	23525	26275	28300	33100
	3.0si Roadster 2D	BU535	45445	24400	27250	29300	34200
	Premium Pkg			575	575	765	765
	Sport Pkg			375	375	500	500
Z4 M SERIES—6-Cyl.—Equipment Schedule 1							
W.B. 98.3"; 3.2 Liter.							
	Coupe 2D	DU935	52870	29100	32450	35000	40900
	Roadster 2D	BT935	54870	30075	33425	36000	42000
	Premium Pkg			575	575	765	765
5 SERIES—6-Cyl.—Equipment Schedule 1							
W.B. 113.7"; 3.0 Liter.							
	528i Sedan 4D	NU535	46525	27550	30675	33000	38600
	528xi AWD Sedan 4D	NV135	48725	28425	31650	34000	39700
	w/o Premium Pkg			(975)	(975)	(1300)	(1300)
	Sport Pkg			1125	1125	1500	1500
5 SERIES—6-Cyl. Twin Turbo—Equipment Schedule 1							
W.B. 113.7", 113.6" (Wagon); 3.0 Liter.							
	535i Sedan 4D	NW135	51625	30175	33525	36000	41700
	535xi AWD Sedan 4D	NV935	53825	31075	34500	36800	42700
	535xi AWD Wagon 4D	PT735	56225	31650	35175	37500	43400
	w/o Premium Pkg			(975)	(975)	(1300)	(1300)
	Sport Pkg			1125	1125	1500	1500
5 SERIES—V8—Equipment Schedule 1							
W.B. 113.7"; 4.8 Liter.							
	550i Sedan 4D	NW535	61075	32925	36550	38900	45000
	Sport Pkg			1125	1125	1500	1500
M5—V10—Equipment Schedule 1							
W.B. 113.7"; 5.0 Liter.							
	Sedan 4D	NB935	86675	49100	54500	56800	64500
6 SERIES—V8—Equipment Schedule 1							
W.B. 109.4"; 4.8 Liter.							
	650i Coupe 2D	EA535	76375	42150	46750	49300	56400
	650i Convertible 2D	EB535	84775	47150	52225	54700	62200
	Sport Pkg			1125	1125	1500	1500
M6—V10—Equipment Schedule 1							
W.B. 109.5"; 5.0 Liter.							
	Coupe 2D	EH935	103075	57525	63700	66000	74300
	Convertible 2D	EK935	108875	64300	71150	73300	82200
7 SERIES—V8—Equipment Schedule 1							
W.B. 117.7", 123.2" (Li); 4.8 Liter.							
	750i Sedan 4D	HL835	76575	41950	46450	49000	56200
	750Li Sedan 4D	HN835	79675	43900	48700	51400	58800
	Sport Pkg			1125	1125	1500	1500
7 SERIES—V12—Equipment Schedule 1							
W.B. 123.2"; 6.0 Liter.							
	760Li Sedan 4D	HN035	125075	68500	75750	78100	87500
ALPINA B7—V8 Supercharged—Equipment Schedule 1							
W.B. 117.7"; 4.4 Liter.							
	Sedan 4D	HL835	117075				

BUICK

1994 BUICK — 1G4(NV553)-R-#

SKYLARK—4-Cyl.—Equipment Schedule 5
W.B. 103.4"; 2.3 Liter.

Body	Type	VIN	List	Fair	Good	Good	Excellent
	Custom Sedan 4D	NV553	14914	350	500	1075	2000

1994 BUICK

Body	Type	VIN	List	Trade-In Fair	Trade-In Good	Pvt-Party Good	Retail Excellent
Custom Coupe 2D		NV153	14914	350	500	1075	2000
Limited Sedan 4D		NJ553	16684	400	550	1150	2100
V6 3.1 Liter		M		125	125	165	165
SKYLARK—V6—Equipment Schedule 5							
W.B. 103.4"; 3.1 Liter.							
Gran Sport Sedan 4D		NM55M	18784	500	675	1350	2400
Gran Sport Coupe 2D		NM15M	18784	500	675	1350	2400
CENTURY—V6—Equipment Schedule 4							
W.B. 104.9"; 3.1 Liter.							
Special Sedan 4D		AG55M	17325	525	700	1425	2575
Special Wagon 4D		AG85M	18175	525	700	1425	2575
Custom Sedan 4D		AH55M	19686	525	700	1425	2575
4-Cyl. 2.2 Liter		4		(150)	(150)	(200)	(200)
REGAL—V6—Equipment Schedule 4							
W.B. 107.5"; 3.1 Liter.							
Custom Sedan 4D		WB55M	19672	750	1050	1900	3250
Custom Coupe 2D		WB15M	19372	625	825	1625	2875
Limited Sedan 4D		WD55L	21242	700	1000	1850	3150
Gran Sport Sedan 4D		WF55L	21724	825	1150	2050	3475
Gran Sport Coupe 2D		WF15L	21442	750	1050	1900	3250
Gran Touring Pkg				50	50	65	65
V6 3.8 Liter		L		150	150	200	200
LeSABRE—V6—Equipment Schedule 4							
W.B. 110.8"; 3.8 Liter.							
Custom Sedan 4D		HP52L	22541	625	875	1675	2975
Limited Sedan 4D		HR52L	24995	1050	1475	2575	4225
Gran Touring Pkg				50	50	65	65
PARK AVENUE—V6—Equipment Schedule 4							
W.B. 110.8"; 3.8 Liter.							
Sedan 4D		CW52L	27624	950	1325	2400	4000
Gran Touring Pkg				50	50	65	65
PARK AVENUE—V6 Supercharged—Equipment Schedule 4							
W.B. 110.8"; 3.8 Liter.							
Ultra Sedan 4D		CU521	32324	1175	1650	2800	4450
Gran Touring Pkg				50	50	65	65
ROADMASTER—V8—Equipment Schedule 2							
W.B. 115.9"; 5.7 Liter.							
Sedan 4D		BN52P	27224	1100	1550	2700	4350
Limited Sedan 4D		BT52P	27734	1200	1700	2850	4550
Estate Wagon 4D		BR82P	29078	2050	2625	3900	5775

1995 BUICK — (1or2)G4(NV55D)-S-#

Body	Type	VIN	List	Trade-In Fair	Trade-In Good	Pvt-Party Good	Retail Excellent
SKYLARK—4-Cyl.—Equipment Schedule 5							
W.B. 103.4"; 2.3 Liter.							
Custom Sedan 4D		NV55D	16070	425	600	1225	2225
Custom Coupe 2D		NV15D	16070	425	600	1225	2225
Gran Sport Pkg				50	50	65	65
V6 3.1 Liter		M		125	125	165	165
CENTURY—V6—Equipment Schedule 4							
W.B. 104.9"; 3.1 Liter.							
Special Sedan 4D		AG55M	19171	625	875	1675	2975
Special Wagon 4D		AG85M	19989	625	875	1675	2975
Custom Sedan 4D		AH55M	18865	625	875	1675	2975
4-Cyl. 2.2 Liter		4		(150)	(150)	(200)	(200)
REGAL—V6—Equipment Schedule 4							
W.B. 107.5"; 3.1 Liter.							
Custom Sedan 4D		WB52M	20650	850	1200	2125	3600
Custom Coupe 2D		WB12M	20333	675	950	1775	3075
Limited Sedan 4D		WD52L	22243	800	1125	2050	3475
Gran Sport Sedan 4D		WF52L	22878	925	1325	2375	4000
Gran Sport Coupe 2D		WF12L	19995	850	1175	2100	3550
Gran Touring Pkg				50	50	65	65
V6 3.8 Liter		L		150	150	200	200
LeSABRE—V6—Equipment Schedule 4							
W.B. 110.8"; 3.8 Liter.							
Custom Sedan 4D		HP52L	23481	750	1075	1925	3325
Limited Sedan 4D		HR52L	26050	1200	1700	2850	4550
Gran Touring Pkg				50	50	65	65
PARK AVENUE—V6—Equipment Schedule 4							
W.B. 110.8"; 3.8 Liter.							
Sedan 4D		CW52K	28879	1100	1550	2675	4325
Gran Touring Pkg				50	50	65	65

1995 BUICK

Body	Type	VIN	List	Trade-In Fair	Trade-In Good	Pvt-Party Good	Retail Excellent
PARK AVENUE—V6 Supercharged—Equipment Schedule 4							
W.B. 110.8"; 3.8 Liter.							
Ultra Sedan 4D		CU521	33719	**1425**	**1900**	**3100**	**4875**
Gran Touring Pkg				**50**	**50**	**65**	**65**
ROADMASTER—V8—Equipment Schedule 2							
W.B. 115.9"; 5.7 Liter.							
Sedan 4D		BN52P	28425	**1400**	**1875**	**3075**	**4825**
Limited Sedan 4D		BT52P	29930	**1550**	**2025**	**3225**	**5025**
Estate Wagon 4D		BR82P	30365	**2450**	**3050**	**4350**	**6350**
RIVIERA—V6—Equipment Schedule 2							
W.B. 113.8"; 3.8 Liter.							
Coupe 2D		GD12K	28857	**950**	**1325**	**2400**	**4025**
V6 3.8L Supercharged		1		**175**	**175**	**235**	**235**

1996 BUICK — (1,2or3)G4(NJ52T)–T–#

Body	Type	VIN	List	Trade-In Fair	Trade-In Good	Pvt-Party Good	Retail Excellent
SKYLARK—4-Cyl.—Equipment Schedule 5							
W.B. 103.4"; 2.4 Liter.							
Custom Sedan 4D		NJ52T	15995	**525**	**700**	**1450**	**2650**
Custom Coupe 2D		NJ12T	15995	**525**	**700**	**1450**	**2650**
Gran Sport Pkg				**75**	**75**	**100**	**100**
V6 3.1 Liter		M		**150**	**150**	**200**	**200**
CENTURY—V6—Equipment Schedule 4							
W.B. 104.9"; 3.1 Liter.							
Sedan 4D		AG55M	18235	**725**	**1025**	**1875**	**3250**
Wagon 4D		AG85M	19040	**725**	**1025**	**1875**	**3250**
4-Cyl. 2.2 Liter		4		**(175)**	**(175)**	**(235)**	**(235)**
REGAL—V6—Equipment Schedule 4							
W.B. 107.5"; 3.1 Liter.							
Custom Sedan 4D		WB52M	20280	**975**	**1375**	**2475**	**4125**
Custom Coupe 2D		WB12M	19985	**775**	**1075**	**2000**	**3425**
Limited Sedan 4D		WD52K	21735	**925**	**1300**	**2400**	**4025**
Gran Sport Sedan 4D		WF52K	22340	**1075**	**1500**	**2625**	**4300**
Gran Sport Coupe 2D		WF12K	21495	**950**	**1350**	**2450**	**4075**
Gran Touring Pkg				**75**	**75**	**100**	**100**
V6 3.8 Liter		K		**175**	**175**	**235**	**235**
LeSABRE—V6—Equipment Schedule 4							
W.B. 110.8"; 3.8 Liter.							
Custom Sedan 4D		HP52K	22345	**900**	**1250**	**2325**	**3950**
Limited Sedan 4D		HR52K	25975	**1500**	**1975**	**3175**	**4975**
Gran Touring Pkg				**75**	**75**	**100**	**100**
PARK AVENUE—V6—Equipment Schedule 4							
W.B. 110.8"; 3.8 Liter.							
Sedan 4D		CW52K	28845	**1325**	**1825**	**3000**	**4725**
Gran Touring Pkg				**75**	**75**	**100**	**100**
PARK AVENUE—V6 Supercharged—Equipment Schedule 4							
W.B. 110.8"; 3.8 Liter.							
Ultra Sedan 4D		CU521	33460	**1775**	**2275**	**3525**	**5375**
Gran Touring Pkg				**75**	**75**	**100**	**100**
ROADMASTER—V8—Equipment Schedule 2							
W.B. 115.9"; 5.7 Liter.							
Sedan 4D		BN52P	28590	**1725**	**2225**	**3475**	**5325**
Limited Sedan 4D		BT52P	30125	**1875**	**2425**	**3700**	**5575**
Estate Wagon 4D		BR82P	30230	**2900**	**3525**	**4900**	**7000**
RIVIERA—V6—Equipment Schedule 2							
W.B. 113.8"; 3.8 Liter.							
Coupe 2D		GD12K	30715	**1100**	**1550**	**2675**	**4350**
V6 3.8L Supercharged		1		**200**	**200**	**265**	**265**

1997 BUICK — (1,2or3)G4(NJ52T)–V–#

Body	Type	VIN	List	Trade-In Fair	Trade-In Good	Pvt-Party Good	Retail Excellent
SKYLARK—4-Cyl.—Equipment Schedule 5							
W.B. 103.4"; 2.4 Liter.							
Custom Sedan 4D		NJ52T	16495	**625**	**875**	**1725**	**3050**
Custom Coupe 2D		NJ12T	16495	**625**	**875**	**1725**	**3050**
Gran Sport Pkg				**100**	**100**	**135**	**135**
V6 3.1 Liter		M		**175**	**175**	**235**	**235**
CENTURY—V6—Equipment Schedule 4							
W.B. 109.0"; 3.1 Liter.							
Custom Sedan 4D		WS52M	18590	**800**	**1125**	**2025**	**3475**
Limited Sedan 4D		WY52M	19965	**1025**	**1450**	**2550**	**4200**
REGAL—V6—Equipment Schedule 4							
W.B. 109.0"; 3.8 Liter.							
LS Sedan 4D		WB52K	21095	**1250**	**1725**	**2900**	**4625**

Body	Type	VIN	List	Trade-In Fair	Trade-In Good	Pvt-Party Good	Retail Excellent
	Gran Touring Pkg			100	100	135	135
REGAL—V6 Supercharged—Equipment Schedule 4							
W.B. 109.0"; 3.8 Liter.							
GS Sedan 4D		WF521	23495	1950	2500	3775	5625
LeSABRE—V6—Equipment Schedule 4							
W.B. 110.8"; 3.8 Liter.							
Custom Sedan 4D		HP52K	23040	1050	1475	2625	4300
Limited Sedan 4D		HR52K	26170	1800	2325	3600	5475
	Gran Touring Pkg			100	100	135	135
PARK AVENUE—V6—Equipment Schedule 4							
W.B. 113.8"; 3.8 Liter.							
Sedan 4D		CW52K	30660	1800	2325	3575	5425
	Gran Touring Pkg			100	100	135	135
PARK AVENUE—V6 Supercharged—Equipment Schedule 4							
W.B. 113.8"; 3.8 Liter.							
Ultra Sedan 4D		CU521	35660	2300	2875	4175	6125
	Gran Touring Pkg			100	100	135	135
RIVIERA—V6—Equipment Schedule 2							
W.B. 113.8"; 3.8 Liter.							
Coupe 2D		GD22K	31375	1275	1775	2975	4725
	V6 3.8L Supercharged		1	225	225	300	300

1998 BUICK — (1,2or3)G4(NJ52M)—W-#

Body	Type	VIN	List	Trade-In Fair	Trade-In Good	Pvt-Party Good	Retail Excellent
SKYLARK—V6—Equipment Schedule 5							
W.B. 103.4"; 3.1 Liter.							
Custom Sedan 4D		NJ52M	16755	725	1025	1950	3375
CENTURY—V6—Equipment Schedule 4							
W.B. 109.0"; 3.1 Liter.							
Custom Sedan 4D		WS52M	19185	975	1375	2450	4100
Limited Sedan 4D		WY52M	20545	1250	1750	2925	4650
REGAL—V6—Equipment Schedule 4							
W.B. 109.0"; 3.8 Liter.							
LS Sedan 4D		WB52K	21495	1475	1950	3175	4975
	Gran Touring Pkg			100	100	135	135
REGAL—V6 Supercharged—Equipment Schedule 4							
W.B. 109.0"; 3.8 Liter.							
GS Sedan 4D		WF521	24240	2225	2800	4100	6025
LeSABRE—V6—Equipment Schedule 4							
W.B. 110.8"; 3.8 Liter.							
Custom Sedan 4D		HP52K	23265	1250	1725	2950	4700
Limited Sedan 4D		HR52K	26395	2125	2675	3975	5900
	Gran Touring Pkg			100	100	135	135
PARK AVENUE—V6—Equipment Schedule 4							
W.B. 113.8"; 3.8 Liter.							
Sedan 4D		CW52K	31340	2125	2675	3975	5875
	Gran Touring Pkg			100	100	135	135
PARK AVENUE—V6 Supercharged—Equipment Schedule 4							
W.B. 113.8"; 3.8 Liter.							
Ultra Sedan 4D		CU521	36215	2700	3300	4625	6675
	Gran Touring Pkg			100	100	135	135
RIVIERA—V6 Supercharged—Equipment Schedule 2							
W.B. 113.8"; 3.8 Liter.							
Coupe 2D		GD221	33165	1575	2075	3300	5125

1999 BUICK — (1,2or3)G4(WS52M)—X-#

Body	Type	VIN	List	Trade-In Fair	Trade-In Good	Pvt-Party Good	Retail Excellent
CENTURY—V6—Equipment Schedule 4							
W.B. 109.0"; 3.1 Liter.							
Custom Sedan 4D		WS52M	19755	1175	1650	2850	4575
Limited		Y		500	500	665	665
REGAL—V6—Equipment Schedule 4							
W.B. 109.0"; 3.8 Liter.							
LS Sedan 4D		WB52K	22255	1725	2225	3475	5325
	Gran Touring Pkg			100	100	135	135
REGAL—V6 Supercharged—Equipment Schedule 4							
W.B. 109.0"; 3.8 Liter.							
GS Sedan 4D		WF521	24955	2550	3125	4450	6450
LeSABRE—V6—Equipment Schedule 4							
W.B. 110.8"; 3.8 Liter.							
Custom Sedan 4D		HP52K	23535	1550	2050	3325	5175
Limited Sedan 4D		HR52K	26605	2500	3075	4425	6450
	Gran Touring Pkg			100	100	135	135

1999 BUICK

Body	Type	VIN	List	Trade-In Fair	Trade-In Good	Pvt-Party Good	Retail Excellent
PARK AVENUE—V6—Equipment Schedule 4							
W.B. 113.8"; 3.8 Liter.							
Sedan 4D		CW52K	31800	2500	3075	4400	6400
	Gran Touring Pkg			100	100	135	135
PARK AVENUE—V6 Supercharged—Equipment Schedule 4							
W.B. 113.8"; 3.8 Liter.							
Ultra Sedan 4D		CU521	36695	3075	3750	5125	7225
	Gran Touring Pkg			100	100	135	135
RIVIERA—V6 Supercharged—Equipment Schedule 2							
W.B. 113.8"; 3.8 Liter.							
Coupe 2D		GD221	35830	1950	2500	3775	5675

2000 BUICK — (1,2or3)G4(WS52J)–Y–#

Body	Type	VIN	List	Trade-In Fair	Trade-In Good	Pvt-Party Good	Retail Excellent
CENTURY—V6—Equipment Schedule 4							
W.B. 109.0"; 3.1 Liter.							
Custom Sedan 4D		WS52J	20592	1550	2025	3250	5075
	Century 2000 Pkg			250	250	335	335
	Limited	Y		550	550	735	735
REGAL—V6—Equipment Schedule 4							
W.B. 109.0"; 3.8 Liter.							
LS Sedan 4D		WB52K	22780	2000	2575	3850	5750
	Gran Touring Pkg			100	100	135	135
REGAL—V6 Supercharged—Equipment Schedule 4							
W.B. 109.0"; 3.8 Liter.							
GS Sedan 4D		WF521	25625	2900	3525	4875	6950
LeSABRE—V6—Equipment Schedule 4							
W.B. 112.2"; 3.8 Liter.							
Custom Sedan 4D		HP54K	24115	1925	2475	3775	5700
Limited Sedan 4D		HR54K	27310	2925	3550	4950	7050
	Gran Touring Pkg			100	100	135	135
PARK AVENUE—V6—Equipment Schedule 4							
W.B. 113.8"; 3.8 Liter.							
Sedan 4D		CW52K	32395	2900	3525	4875	6950
	Gran Touring Pkg			100	100	135	135
PARK AVENUE—V6 Supercharged—Equipment Schedule 4							
W.B. 113.8"; 3.8 Liter.							
Ultra Sedan 4D		CU521	37470	3550	4275	5650	7850
	Gran Touring Pkg			100	100	135	135

2001 BUICK — (1or2)G4(WS52J)–2–#

Body	Type	VIN	List	Trade-In Fair	Trade-In Good	Pvt-Party Good	Retail Excellent
CENTURY—V6—Equipment Schedule 4							
W.B. 109.0"; 3.1 Liter.							
Custom Sedan 4D		WS52J	20870	1925	2475	3750	5600
	Limited	Y		600	600	800	800
REGAL—V6—Equipment Schedule 4							
W.B. 109.0"; 3.8 Liter.							
LS Sedan 4D		WB52K	23445	2050	2625	3900	5825
	Abboud Pkg			100	100	135	135
	Gran Touring Pkg			100	100	135	135
REGAL—V6 Supercharged—Equipment Schedule 4							
W.B. 109.0"; 3.8 Liter.							
GS Sedan 4D		WF521	26695	3025	3650	5000	7075
	Abboud Pkg			100	100	135	135
LeSABRE—V6—Equipment Schedule 4							
W.B. 112.2"; 3.8 Liter.							
Custom Sedan 4D		HP54K	24762	2350	2950	4275	6275
Limited Sedan 4D		HR54K	29451	3400	4100	5525	7700
	Gran Touring Pkg			100	100	135	135
PARK AVENUE—V6—Equipment Schedule 4							
W.B. 113.8"; 3.8 Liter.							
Sedan 4D		CW52K	33700	3375	4075	5450	7575
	Gran Touring Pkg			100	100	135	135
PARK AVENUE—V6 Supercharged—Equipment Schedule 4							
W.B. 113.8"; 3.8 Liter.							
Ultra Sedan 4D		CU521	38210	4075	4825	6250	8500
	Gran Touring Pkg			100	100	135	135

2002 BUICK — (1or2)G4(WS52J)–2–#

Body	Type	VIN	List	Trade-In Fair	Trade-In Good	Pvt-Party Good	Retail Excellent
CENTURY—V6—Equipment Schedule 4							
W.B. 109.0"; 3.1 Liter.							
Custom Sedan 4D		WS52J	21325	2250	2850	4300	6400
	Limited	Y		650	650	865	865

2002 BUICK

Body	Type	VIN	List	Trade-In Fair	Trade-In Good	Pvt-Party Good	Retail Excellent
REGAL—V6—Equipment Schedule 4							
W.B. 109.0"; 3.8 Liter.							
LS Sedan 4D		WB52K	23840	**2175**	**2775**	**4225**	**6350**
Abboud Pkg				100	100	135	135
Gran Touring Pkg				100	100	135	135
REGAL—V6 Supercharged—Equipment Schedule 4							
W.B. 109.0"; 3.8 Liter.							
GS Sedan 4D		WF521	27895	**3175**	**3850**	**5375**	**7675**
Abboud Pkg				100	100	135	135
LeSABRE—V6—Equipment Schedule 4							
W.B. 112.2"; 3.8 Liter.							
Custom Sedan 4D		HP54K	24975	**2700**	**3300**	**4850**	**7100**
Limited Sedan 4D		HR54K	30675	**3800**	**4525**	**6125**	**8575**
PARK AVENUE—V6—Equipment Schedule 4							
W.B. 113.8"; 3.8 Liter.							
Sedan 4D		CW52K	34165	**3900**	**4625**	**6200**	**8600**
Gran Touring Pkg				100	100	135	135
PARK AVENUE—V6 Supercharged—Equipment Schedule 4							
W.B. 113.8"; 3.8 Liter.							
Ultra Sedan 4D		CU521	38675	**4600**	**5425**	**7075**	**9650**
Gran Touring Pkg				100	100	135	135

2003 BUICK — (1or2)G4(WS52J)-3-#

Body	Type	VIN	List	Trade-In Fair	Trade-In Good	Pvt-Party Good	Retail Excellent
CENTURY—V6—Equipment Schedule 4							
W.B. 109.0"; 3.1 Liter.							
Sedan 4D		WS52J	21685	**2575**	**3150**	**4625**	**6775**
Limited		Y		750	750	1000	1000
REGAL—V6—Equipment Schedule 4							
W.B. 109.0"; 3.8 Liter.							
LS Sedan 4D		WB52K	24230	**2700**	**3300**	**4800**	**7000**
Abboud Pkg				125	125	165	165
Gran Touring Pkg				125	125	165	165
REGAL—V6 Supercharged—Equipment Schedule 4							
W.B. 109.0"; 3.8 Liter.							
GS Sedan 4D		WF521	28175	**3850**	**4550**	**6100**	**8475**
Abboud Pkg				125	125	165	165
LeSABRE—V6—Equipment Schedule 4							
W.B. 112.2"; 3.8 Liter.							
Custom Sedan 4D		HP52K	25730	**3350**	**4050**	**5625**	**8000**
Limited Sedan 4D		HR54K	31360	**4600**	**5425**	**7100**	**9700**
Celebration Edition				500	500	665	665
PARK AVENUE—V6—Equipment Schedule 4							
W.B. 113.8"; 3.8 Liter.							
Sedan 4D		CW54K	34615	**4750**	**5575**	**7225**	**9800**
Gran Touring Pkg				125	125	165	165
PARK AVENUE—V6 Supercharged—Equipment Schedule 4							
W.B. 113.8"; 3.8 Liter.							
Ultra Sedan 4D		CU541	39915	**5700**	**6625**	**8275**	**11000**

2004 BUICK — (1or2)G4(WS52J)-4-#

Body	Type	VIN	List	Trade-In Fair	Trade-In Good	Pvt-Party Good	Retail Excellent
CENTURY—V6—Equipment Schedule 4							
W.B. 109.0"; 3.1 Liter.							
Sedan 4D		WS52J	22415	**3025**	**3650**	**5150**	**7375**
Limited				350	350	465	465
Special Edition				850	850	1135	1135
REGAL—V6—Equipment Schedule 4							
W.B. 109.0"; 3.8 Liter.							
LS Sedan 4D		WB52K	24895	**3325**	**4025**	**5525**	**7875**
Abboud Pkg				150	150	200	200
Gran Touring Pkg				150	150	200	200
REGAL—V6 Supercharged—Equipment Schedule 4							
W.B. 109.0"; 3.8 Liter.							
GS Sedan 4D		WF521	28345	**4625**	**5450**	**7050**	**9575**
Abboud Pkg				150	150	200	200
LeSABRE—V6—Equipment Schedule 4							
W.B. 112.2"; 3.8 Liter.							
Custom Sedan 4D		HP54K	26470	**4150**	**4900**	**6525**	**9025**
Limited Sedan 4D		HR54K	32245	**5500**	**6400**	**8100**	**10850**
Celebration Edition				500	500	665	665
PARK AVENUE—V6—Equipment Schedule 4							
W.B. 113.8"; 3.8 Liter.							
Sedan 4D		CW52K	35545	**5750**	**6700**	**8325**	**11050**

2004 BUICK

Body	Type	VIN	List	Trade-In Fair	Trade-In Good	Pvt-Party Good	Retail Excellent
	Gran Touring Pkg			150	150	200	200
PARK AVENUE—V6 Supercharged—Equipment Schedule 4							
W.B. 113.8"; 3.8 Liter.							
	Ultra Sedan 4D	CU521	40720	6850	7925	9600	12450

2005 BUICK — (1or2)G4(WS52J)-5-#

CENTURY—V6—Equipment Schedule 4							
W.B. 109.0". 3.1 Liter.							
	Sedan 4D	WS52J	22950	3525	4250	5725	8000
	Limited			350	350	465	465
	Special Edition			950	950	1265	1265
LACROSSE—V6—Equipment Schedule 4							
W.B. 110.5"; 3.6 Liter, 3.8 Liter.							
	CX Sedan 4D	WC532	23495	5875	6800	8450	11100
	CXL Sedan 4D	WD532	25995	6650	7650	9275	12050
	CXS Sedan 4D	WE537	28995	7425	8525	10200	13050
LESABRE—V6—Equipment Schedule 4							
W.B. 112.2"; 3.8 Liter.							
	Custom Sedan 4D	HP52K	27270	5025	5875	7575	10250
	Limited Sedan 4D	HR54K	32930	6500	7500	9200	12050
	Celebration Edition			500	500	665	665
PARK AVENUE—V6—Equipment Schedule 4							
W.B. 113.8"; 3.8 Liter.							
	Sedan 4D	CW54K	36350	6850	7900	9550	12350
PARK AVENUE—V6 Supercharged—Equipment Schedule 4							
W.B. 113.8"; 3.8 Liter.							
	Special Ed Ultra 4D	CU541	41525	8150	9325	11050	14100

2006 BUICK — (1or2)G4(WC582)-6-#

LACROSSE—V6—Equipment Schedule 4							
W.B. 110.5"; 3.6 Liter, 3.8 Liter.							
	CX Sedan 4D	WC582	23595	6725	7750	9350	12100
	CXL Sedan 4D	WD582	26095	7575	8675	10300	13150
	CXS Sedan 4D	WE587	29095	8425	9625	11250	14250
LUCERNE—V6—Equipment Schedule 4							
W.B. 115.6"; 3.8 Liter.							
	CX Sedan 4D	HP572	26990	8100	9275	11050	14150
	CXL Sedan 4D	HD572	28990	9600	10925	12750	15950
	V8 4.6 Liter	Y		800	800	1065	1065
LUCERNE—V8—Equipment Schedule 4							
W.B. 115.6"; 4.6 Liter.							
	CXS Sedan 4D	HE57Y	35990	12400	13975	15850	19350

2007 BUICK — (1or2)G4(WC582)-7-#

LACROSSE—V6—Equipment Schedule 4							
W.B. 110.5"; 3.6 Liter, 3.8 Liter.							
	CX Sedan 4D	WC582	22915	7675	8800	10350	13050
	CXL Sedan 4D	WD582	25330	8550	9775	11300	14200
	CXS Sedan 4D	WE587	27545	9500	10825	12400	15400
LUCERNE—V6—Equipment Schedule 4							
W.B. 115.6"; 3.8 Liter.							
	CX Sedan 4D	HP572	26265	9550	10875	12600	15700
	CXL Sedan 4D	HD572	29280	11375	12875	14600	17950
	V8 4.6 Liter	Y		800	800	1065	1065
LUCERNE—V8—Equipment Schedule 4							
W.B. 115.6"; 4.6 Liter.							
	CXS Sedan 4D	HE57Y	35295	14200	15975	17750	21400

2008 BUICK — (1or2)G4(WC582)-8-#

LACROSSE—V6—Equipment Schedule 4							
W.B. 110.5"; 3.6 Liter, 3.8 Liter.							
	CX Sedan 4D	WC582	23995	9675	10975	12550	15500
	CXL Sedan 4D	WD582	25995	10625	12050	13600	16650
	CXS Sedan 4D	WE587	27995	11650	13175	14800	18000
LACROSSE—V8—Equipment Schedule 4							
W.B. 110.5"; 5.3 Liter.							
	Super Sedan 4D	WN58C	31995	13275	15000	16550	19900
LUCERNE—V6—Equipment Schedule 4							
W.B. 115.6"; 3.8 Liter.							
	CX Sedan 4D	HP572	26995	11225	12750	14450	17750
	CXL Sedan 4D	HD572	29595	13375	15100	16800	20300
	CXL Special Ed 4D	HR572	32150	15325	17250	18900	22500

56   DEDUCT FOR RECONDITIONING

0709

Body	Type	VIN	List	Trade-In Fair	Trade-In Good	Pvt-Party Good	Retail Excellent
LUCERNE—V8—Equipment Schedule 4							
W.B. 115.6"; 4.6 Liter.							
CXL Special Ed 4D		HR57Y	33850	**15975**	**17925**	**19700**	**23400**
CXS Sedan 4D		HE57Y	36595	**16275**	**18225**	**20000**	**23700**
Super Sedan 4D		HF579	39395	**19600**	**21950**	**23700**	**27700**

CADILLAC

1994 CADILLAC — 1G6(EL12Y)-R-#

ELDORADO—V8—Equipment Schedule 2							
W.B. 108.0"; 4.6 Liter.							
Coupe 2D		EL12Y	38565	**1625**	**2125**	**3350**	**5150**
Touring Coupe 2D		ET129	41215	**1925**	**2475**	**3725**	**5575**
SEVILLE—V8—Equipment Schedule 2							
W.B. 111.0"; 4.6 Liter.							
SLS Sedan 4D		KS52Y	42265	**2075**	**2650**	**3900**	**5800**
STS Touring Sedan 4D		KY529	45515	**2625**	**3225**	**4575**	**6625**
DeVILLE—V8—Equipment Schedule 2							
W.B. 113.8"; 4.6 Liter, 4.9 Liter.							
Sedan 4D		KD52B	34400	**1400**	**1850**	**3075**	**4800**
Concours Sedan 4D		KF52Y	37215	**1950**	**2500**	**3750**	**5625**
FLEETWOOD—V8—Equipment Schedule 2							
W.B. 121.5"; 5.7 Liter.							
Sedan 4D		DW52P	35185	**2550**	**3125**	**4450**	**6475**
Brougham Pkg				**200**	**200**	**265**	**265**

1995 CADILLAC — 1G6(EL12Y)-S-#

ELDORADO—V8—Equipment Schedule 2							
W.B. 108.0"; 4.6 Liter.							
Coupe 2D		EL12Y	39505	**1950**	**2500**	**3775**	**5650**
Touring Coupe 2D		ET129	42170	**2300**	**2875**	**4200**	**6175**
SEVILLE—V8—Equipment Schedule 2							
W.B. 111.0"; 4.6 Liter.							
SLS Sedan 4D		KS52Y	43220	**2475**	**3075**	**4400**	**6425**
STS Touring Sedan 4D		KY529	46570	**3075**	**3725**	**5150**	**7300**
DeVILLE—V8—Equipment Schedule 2							
W.B. 113.8"; 4.6 Liter, 4.9 Liter.							
Sedan 4D		KD52B	36320	**1700**	**2200**	**3450**	**5275**
Concours Sedan 4D		KF52Y	40035	**2375**	**2950**	**4275**	**6250**
FLEETWOOD—V8—Equipment Schedule 2							
W.B. 121.5"; 5.7 Liter.							
Sedan 4D		DW52P	37015	**3025**	**3650**	**5050**	**7200**
Brougham Pkg				**200**	**200**	**265**	**265**

1996 CADILLAC — 1G6(EL12Y)-T-#

ELDORADO—V8—Equipment Schedule 2							
W.B. 108.0"; 4.6 Liter.							
Coupe 2D		EL12Y	41020	**2300**	**2900**	**4200**	**6175**
Touring Coupe 2D		ET129	43635	**2700**	**3300**	**4675**	**6750**
SEVILLE—V8—Equipment Schedule 2							
W.B. 111.0"; 4.6 Liter.							
SLS Sedan 4D		KS52Y	44420	**2900**	**3525**	**4925**	**7025**
STS Touring Sedan 4D		KY529	48135	**3600**	**4300**	**5750**	**8025**
DeVILLE—V8—Equipment Schedule 2							
W.B. 113.8"; 4.6 Liter.							
Sedan 4D		KD52Y	37420	**2050**	**2625**	**3925**	**5850**
Concours Sedan 4D		KF529	41135	**2825**	**3425**	**4850**	**6950**
FLEETWOOD—V8—Equipment Schedule 2							
W.B. 121.5"; 5.7 Liter.							
Sedan 4D		DW52P	38420	**3600**	**4300**	**5750**	**8025**
Brougham Pkg				**250**	**250**	**335**	**335**

1997 CADILLAC — (Wor1)(GorO)6(VR52R)-V-#

CATERA—V6—Equipment Schedule 2							
W.B. 107.4"; 3.0 Liter.							
Sedan 4D		VR52R	33635	**850**	**1200**	**2200**	**3725**
ELDORADO—V8—Equipment Schedule 2							
W.B. 108.0"; 4.6 Liter.							
Coupe 2D		EL12Y	39883	**2700**	**3300**	**4650**	**6725**
Touring Coupe 2D		ET129	42060	**3150**	**3825**	**5250**	**7400**

1997 CADILLAC

Body	Type	VIN	List	Trade-In Fair	Trade-In Good	Pvt-Party Good	Retail Excellent
SEVILLE—V8—Equipment Schedule 2							
W.B. 111.0"; 4.6 Liter.							
SLS Sedan 4D		KS52Y	41883	**2900**	**3525**	**4925**	**7025**
STS Touring Sedan 4D		KY529	45660	**3700**	**4425**	**5875**	**8150**
DeVILLE—V8—Equipment Schedule 2							
W.B. 113.8"; 4.6 Liter.							
Sedan 4D		KD54Y	38445	**2425**	**3025**	**4350**	**6375**
d'Elegance Sedan 4D		KE54Y	40660	**3050**	**3700**	**5125**	**7275**
Concours Sedan 4D		KF549	42660	**3325**	**4000**	**5450**	**7675**

1998 CADILLAC — (Wor1)(GorO)6(VR52R)-W-#

Body	Type	VIN	List	Trade-In Fair	Trade-In Good	Pvt-Party Good	Retail Excellent
CATERA—V6—Equipment Schedule 2							
W.B. 107.4"; 3.0 Liter.							
Sedan 4D		VR52R	34250	**950**	**1350**	**2475**	**4175**
ELDORADO—V8—Equipment Schedule 2							
W.B. 108.0"; 4.6 Liter.							
Coupe 2D		EL12Y	39945	**3150**	**3825**	**5225**	**7375**
Touring Coupe 2D		ET129	43360	**3725**	**4425**	**5900**	**8150**
SEVILLE—V8—Equipment Schedule 2							
W.B. 112.2"; 4.6 Liter.							
SLS Sedan 4D		KS52Y	43160	**3000**	**3650**	**5025**	**7150**
STS Touring Sedan 4D		KY529	47660	**3925**	**4650**	**6125**	**8425**
DeVILLE—V8—Equipment Schedule 2							
W.B. 113.8"; 4.6 Liter.							
Sedan 4D		KD54Y	39145	**2850**	**3475**	**4875**	**7000**
d'Elegance Sedan 4D		KE54Y	41960	**3550**	**4275**	**5725**	**8000**
Concours Sedan 4D		KF549	42960	**3925**	**4650**	**6150**	**8475**

1999 CADILLAC — (Wor1)(Gor0)6(VR52R)-X-#

Body	Type	VIN	List	Trade-In Fair	Trade-In Good	Pvt-Party Good	Retail Excellent
CATERA—V6—Equipment Schedule 2							
W.B. 107.5"; 3.0 Liter.							
Sedan 4D		VR52R	34820	**1125**	**1575**	**2800**	**4550**
Sport				**300**	**300**	**400**	**400**
ELDORADO—V8—Equipment Schedule 2							
W.B. 108.0"; 4.6 Liter.							
Coupe 2D		EL12Y	40690	**3700**	**4425**	**5875**	**8150**
Touring Coupe 2D		ET129	44165	**4350**	**5150**	**6675**	**9050**
SEVILLE—V8—Equipment Schedule 2							
W.B. 112.2"; 4.6 Liter.							
SLS Sedan 4D		KS52Y	44025	**3200**	**3875**	**5300**	**7475**
STS Touring Sedan 4D		KY529	48520	**4225**	**4975**	**6475**	**8825**
DeVILLE—V8—Equipment Schedule 2							
W.B. 113.8"; 4.6 Liter.							
Sedan 4D		KD54Y	40085	**3375**	**4075**	**5525**	**7775**
d'Elegance Sedan 4D		KE54Y	43400	**4175**	**4925**	**6450**	**8825**
Concours Sedan 4D		KF549	43900	**4575**	**5400**	**6975**	**9500**

2000 CADILLAC — (Wor1)(Gor0)6(VR52R)-Y-#

Body	Type	VIN	List	Trade-In Fair	Trade-In Good	Pvt-Party Good	Retail Excellent
CATERA—V6—Equipment Schedule 2							
W.B. 107.5"; 3.0 Liter.							
Sedan 4D		VR52R	31500	**1125**	**1575**	**2825**	**4575**
Sport				**300**	**300**	**400**	**400**
ELDORADO—V8—Equipment Schedule 2							
W.B. 108.0"; 4.6 Liter.							
ESC Coupe 2D		EL12Y	39790	**4375**	**5175**	**6675**	**9025**
ETC Coupe 2D		ET129	43365	**5100**	**5975**	**7550**	**10100**
SEVILLE—V8—Equipment Schedule 2							
W.B. 112.2"; 4.6 Liter.							
SLS Sedan 4D		KS52Y	44550	**3525**	**4250**	**5650**	**7875**
STS Touring Sedan 4D		KY529	49150	**4600**	**5425**	**6950**	**9425**
DeVILLE—V8—Equipment Schedule 2							
W.B. 115.3"; 4.6 Liter.							
Sedan 4D		KD54Y	40955	**2925**	**3550**	**4975**	**7100**
DHS Sedan 4D		KE54Y	45370	**4275**	**5025**	**6550**	**8925**
DTS Sedan 4D		KF549	45370	**4375**	**5175**	**6700**	**9125**

2001 CADILLAC — (Wor1)(Gor0)6(VR52R)-1-#

Body	Type	VIN	List	Trade-In Fair	Trade-In Good	Pvt-Party Good	Retail Excellent
CATERA—V6—Equipment Schedule 2							
W.B. 107.4"; 3.0 Liter.							
Sedan 4D		VR52R	31945	**1675**	**2150**	**3475**	**5400**
Sport Pkg				**300**	**300**	**400**	**400**

2001 CADILLAC

Body	Type	VIN	List	Trade-In Fair	Good	Pvt-Party Good	Retail Excellent
ELDORADO—V8—Equipment Schedule 2							
W.B. 108.0"; 4.6 Liter.							
ESC Coupe 2D		EL12Y	40756	**4275**	**5025**	**6500**	**8850**
ETC Coupe 2D		ET129	44331	**5050**	**5900**	**7475**	**10000**
SEVILLE—V8—Equipment Schedule 2							
W.B. 112.2"; 4.6 Liter.							
SLS Sedan 4D		KS52Y	42655	**3725**	**4450**	**5900**	**8150**
STS Touring Sedan 4D		KY529	48765	**4875**	**5700**	**7275**	**9775**
DeVILLE—V8—Equipment Schedule 2							
W.B. 115.3"; 4.6 Liter.							
Sedan 4D		KD54Y	42000	**3400**	**4125**	**5550**	**7825**
DHS Sedan 4D		KE54Y	46987	**4850**	**5675**	**7225**	**9700**
DTS Sedan 4D		KF549	46987	**5000**	**5850**	**7400**	**9900**

2002 CADILLAC — 1G6(EL12Y)-2-#

Body	Type	VIN	List	Trade-In Fair	Good	Pvt-Party Good	Retail Excellent
ELDORADO—V8—Equipment Schedule 2							
W.B. 108.0"; 4.6 Liter.							
ESC Coupe 2D		EL12Y	42610	**5000**	**5850**	**7650**	**10400**
ETC Coupe 2D		ET129	45745	**5875**	**6800**	**8625**	**11500**
ECS Coupe 2D		ET129	48405	**6150**	**7100**	**8975**	**11900**
SEVILLE—V8—Equipment Schedule 2							
W.B. 112.2"; 4.6 Liter.							
SLS Sedan 4D		KS52Y	44269	**3625**	**4325**	**6000**	**8475**
STS Touring Sedan 4D		KY529	49825	**4825**	**5650**	**7425**	**10150**
DeVILLE—V8—Equipment Schedule 2							
W.B. 115.3"; 4.6 Liter.							
Sedan 4D		KD54Y	43070	**4025**	**4775**	**6525**	**9175**
DHS Sedan 4D		KE54Y	48000	**5525**	**6425**	**8225**	**11050**
DTS Sedan 4D		KF549	48000	**5700**	**6625**	**8500**	**11450**

2003 CADILLAC — 1G6(DM57N)-3-#

Body	Type	VIN	List	Trade-In Fair	Good	Pvt-Party Good	Retail Excellent
CTS—V6—Equipment Schedule 2							
W.B. 113.4"; 3.2 Liter.							
Sedan 4D		DM57N	29990	**5825**	**6750**	**8675**	**11650**
Luxury Sport Pkg				**475**	**475**	**635**	**635**
SEVILLE—V8—Equipment Schedule 2							
W.B. 112.2"; 4.6 Liter.							
SLS Sedan 4D		KS54Y	45270	**4075**	**4825**	**6525**	**9100**
STS Touring Sedan 4D		KY549	51175	**5500**	**6375**	**8150**	**11000**
DeVILLE—V8—Equipment Schedule 2							
W.B. 115.3"; 4.6 Liter.							
Sedan 4D		KD54Y	43995	**4750**	**5550**	**7400**	**10200**
DHS Sedan 4D		KE54Y	48825	**6575**	**7575**	**9525**	**12650**
DTS Sedan 4D		KF549	48825	**6775**	**7825**	**9750**	**12900**

2004 CADILLAC — 1G6(DM57N)-4-#

Body	Type	VIN	List	Trade-In Fair	Good	Pvt-Party Good	Retail Excellent
CTS—V6—Equipment Schedule 2							
W.B. 113.4"; 3.2 Liter.							
Sedan 4D		DM57N	33155	**7650**	**8750**	**10850**	**14150**
Luxury Sport Pkg				**550**	**550**	**735**	**735**
V6 3.6 Liter		7		**600**	**600**	**800**	**800**
CTS-V—V8—Equipment Schedule 2							
W.B. 113.4"; 5.7 Liter.							
Sedan 4D		DN57S	49995	**10925**	**12350**	**14750**	**18750**
SEVILLE—V8—Equipment Schedule 2							
W.B. 112.2"; 4.6 Liter.							
SLS Sedan 4D		KS52Y	47955	**4800**	**5600**	**7400**	**10150**
DEVILLE—V8—Equipment Schedule 2							
W.B. 115.3"; 4.6 Liter.							
Sedan 4D		KD54Y	45445	**5850**	**6775**	**8725**	**11750**
DHS Sedan 4D		KE54Y	50595	**8000**	**9175**	**11150**	**14500**
DTS Sedan 4D		KF549	50595	**8250**	**9425**	**11500**	**14950**
XLR—V8—Equipment Schedule 1							
W.B. 105.7"; 4.6 Liter.							
Hardtop Conv 2D		YV34A	76200	**16550**	**18625**	**21300**	**26100**

2005 CADILLAC — 1G6(DM56T)-5-#

Body	Type	VIN	List	Trade-In Fair	Good	Pvt-Party Good	Retail Excellent
CTS—V6—Equipment Schedule 2							
W.B. 113.4"; 2.8 Liter.							
Sedan 4D		DM56T	33745	**8950**	**10200**	**12350**	**15900**
Luxury Pkg				**600**	**600**	**800**	**800**
V6 3.6 Liter		7		**600**	**600**	**800**	**800**

2005 CADILLAC

Body Type	VIN	List	Trade-In Fair	Good	Pvt-Party Good	Retail Excellent
CTS-V—V8—Equipment Schedule 2						
W.B. 113.4"; 5.7 Liter.						
Sedan 4D	DN56S	49995	13175	14850	17300	21700
STS—V6—Equipment Schedule 2						
W.B. 116.6"; 3.6 Liter.						
Sedan 4D	DW677	40995	10050	11425	13550	17250
STS—V8—Equipment Schedule 2						
W.B. 116.6"; 4.6 Liter.						
Sedan 4D	DC67A	47495	11375	12850	15050	18850
AWD			2000	2000	2665	2665
DEVILLE—V8—Equipment Schedule 2						
W.B. 115.3"; 4.6 Liter.						
Sedan 4D	KD54Y	46490	7400	8475	10550	13800
DHS Sedan 4D	KE54Y	52045	9850	11225	13400	17000
DTS Sedan 4D	KF549	52045	10100	11475	13600	17300
XLR—V8—Equipment Schedule 1						
W.B. 105.7"; 4.6 Liter.						
Hardtop Conv 2D	YV34A	76650	19300	21550	24200	29300

2006 CADILLAC — 1G6(DM57T)-6-#

Body Type	VIN	List	Trade-In Fair	Good	Pvt-Party Good	Retail Excellent
CTS—V6—Equipment Schedule 2						
W.B. 113.4"; 2.8 Liter.						
Sedan 4D	DM57T	32435	10875	12350	14500	18300
Luxury Pkg			650	650	865	865
V6 3.6 Liter	7		600	600	800	800
CTS-V—V8—Equipment Schedule 2						
W.B. 113.4"; 6.0 Liter.						
Sedan 4D	DN57U	51395	16075	18025	20700	25500
STS—V6—Equipment Schedule 2						
W.B. 116.4"; 3.6 Liter.						
Sedan 4D	DW677	41740	12350	13975	16150	20100
AWD			2000	2000	2665	2665
STS—V8—Equipment Schedule 2						
W.B. 116.4"; 4.6 Liter.						
Sedan 4D	DC67A	49240	13925	15675	17900	22000
AWD			2000	2000	2665	2665
STS-V—V8 Supercharged—Equipment Schedule 2						
W.B. 116.4"; 4.4 Liter.						
Sedan 4D	DX67D	77090	23325	26075	28500	33800
DTS—V8—Equipment Schedule 2						
W.B. 115.6"; 4.6 Liter.						
Sedan 4D	KD57Y	41990	11575	13075	15300	19150
Luxury Pkg			800	800	1065	1065
Performance Pkg			1500	1500	2000	2000
XLR—V8—Equipment Schedule 1						
W.B. 105.7"; 4.6 Liter.						
Hardtop Conv 2D	YV36A	77295	22350	24900	27600	33100
Star Black Ltd Conv 2D	YV36A	79795	23025	25675	28400	33900
XLR-V—V8 Supercharged—Equipment Schedule 1						
W.B. 105.7"; 4.4 Liter.						
Convertible 2D	YX36D	98300	28125	31350	34100	40300

2007 CADILLAC — 1G6(DM57T)-7-#

Body Type	VIN	List	Trade-In Fair	Good	Pvt-Party Good	Retail Excellent
CTS—V6—Equipment Schedule 2						
W.B. 113.4"; 2.8 Liter.						
Sedan 4D	DM57T	32905	13525	15250	17450	21600
Luxury Pkg			700	700	935	935
V6 3.6 Liter	7		600	600	800	800
CTS-V—V8—Equipment Schedule 2						
W.B. 113.4"; 6.0 Liter.						
Sedan 4D	DN57U	53205	19600	21950	24700	29900
STS—V6—Equipment Schedule 2						
W.B. 116.4"; 3.6 Liter.						
Sedan 4D	DW677	42765	15150	17050	19250	23500
Platinum Edition			1500	1500	2000	2000
4-AWD			2000	2000	2665	2665
STS—V8—Equipment Schedule 2						
W.B. 116.4"; 4.6 Liter.						
Sedan 4D	DC67A	53485	17875	20000	22300	27000
Platinum Edition			1500	1500	2000	2000
4-AWD			2000	2000	2665	2665

Body	Type	VIN	List	Trade-In Fair	Trade-In Good	Pvt-Party Good	Retail Excellent
STS-V—V8 Supercharged—Equipment Schedule 2							
W.B. 116.4"; 4.4 Liter.							
Sedan 4D		DX67D	77485	**27150**	**30275**	**32700**	**38400**
DTS—V8—Equipment Schedule 2							
W.B 115.6"; 4.6 Liter.							
Sedan 4D		KD57Y	41990	**13975**	**15725**	**17950**	**22100**
Luxury Pkg				**800**	**800**	**1065**	**1065**
Performance Pkg				**1500**	**1500**	**2000**	**2000**
XLR—V8—Equipment Schedule 1							
W.B. 105.7"; 4.6 Liter.							
Hardtop Conv 2D		YV36A	78495	**25875**	**28800**	**31600**	**37400**
Platinum Edition				**1500**	**1500**	**2000**	**2000**
XLR-V—V8 Supercharged—Equipment Schedule 1							
W.B. 105.7"; 4.4 Liter.							
Convertible 2D		YX36D	100000	**32250**	**35875**	**38500**	**45000**
2008 CADILLAC — 1G6(DM577)-8-#							
CTS—V6—Equipment Schedule 2							
W.B. 113.4"; 3.6 Liter.							
Sedan 4D		DM577	34290	**21075**	**23625**	**25900**	**30700**
Luxury Pkg				**750**	**750**	**1000**	**1000**
4-AWD		G,H,S,T		**2000**	**2000**	**2665**	**2665**
V6 3.6 Liter DI		V		**1500**	**1500**	**2000**	**2000**
STS—V6—Equipment Schedule 2							
W.B. 116.4"; 3.6 Liter.							
Sedan 4D		DW67V	43135	**18675**	**20875**	**23200**	**27800**
Platinum Edition				**1500**	**1500**	**2000**	**2000**
4-AWD		A,D,B,L		**2000**	**2000**	**2665**	**2665**
STS—V8—Equipment Schedule 2							
W.B. 116.4"; 4.6 Liter.							
Sedan 4D		DC67A	53855	**21650**	**24100**	**26500**	**31400**
Platinum Edition				**1500**	**1500**	**2000**	**2000**
4-AWD		A,D,B,L		**2000**	**2000**	**2665**	**2665**
STS-V—V8 Supercharged—Equipment Schedule 2							
W.B. 116.4"; 4.4 Liter.							
Sedan 4D		DX67D	79000	**31850**	**35375**	**37700**	**43600**
DTS—V8—Equipment Schedule 2							
W.B. 115.6"; 4.6 Liter.							
Sedan 4D		KD57Y	42590	**19600**	**21950**	**24300**	**29000**
Luxury Pkg				**800**	**800**	**1065**	**1065**
Performance Pkg				**1500**	**1500**	**2000**	**2000**
Platinum Edition				**1500**	**1500**	**2000**	**2000**
XLR—V8—Equipment Schedule 1							
W.B. 105.7"; 4.6 Liter.							
Hardtop Conv 2D		YV36A	79600				
Platinum Edition							
XLR-V—V8 Supercharged—Equipment Schedule 1							
W.B. 105.7"; 4.4 Liter.							
Convertible 2D		YX36D	100000				

CHEVROLET

Body	Type	VIN	List	Trade-In Fair	Trade-In Good	Pvt-Party Good	Retail Excellent
1994 CHEVROLET — 1G1(JC544)-R-#							
CAVALIER—4-Cyl.—Equipment Schedule 5							
W.B. 101.3"; 2.2 Liter.							
VL Sedan 4D		JC544	11082	**250**	**350**	**875**	**1725**
VL Coupe 2D		JC144	10932	**250**	**350**	**875**	**1725**
Wagon 4D		JC844	12375	**275**	**400**	**925**	**1800**
RS Sedan 4D		JC544	11790	**275**	**400**	**925**	**1800**
RS Coupe 2D		JC144	11685	**275**	**375**	**900**	**1775**
RS Convertible 2D		JC344	17470	**575**	**775**	**1550**	**2750**
V6 3.1 Liter		T		**100**	**100**	**135**	**135**
CAVALIER—V6—Equipment Schedule 5							
W.B. 101.3"; 3.1 Liter.							
Z24 Coupe 2D		JF14T	14965	**475**	**625**	**1350**	**2450**
Z24 Convertible 2D		JF34T	20965	**675**	**950**	**1775**	**3075**
CORSICA—4-Cyl.—Equipment Schedule 5							
W.B. 103.4"; 2.2 Liter.							
LT Sedan 4D		LD554	13630	**350**	**475**	**1050**	**1950**
V6 3.1 Liter		M		**125**	**125**	**165**	**165**

1994 CHEVROLET

Body	Type	VIN	List	Trade-In Fair	Trade-In Good	Pvt-Party Good	Retail Excellent
BERETTA—4-Cyl.—Equipment Schedule 5							
W.B. 103.4"; 2.2 Liter.							
Coupe 2D		LV154	13455	375	525	1100	2050
V6 3.1 Liter		M		125	125	165	165
BERETTA—4-Cyl. Quad 4—Equipment Schedule 5							
W.B. 103.4"; 2.3 Liter.							
Z26 Coupe 2D		LW15A	15795	550	750	1475	2650
Manual Trans				0	0	0	0
V6 3.1 Liter		M		125	125	165	165
LUMINA—V6—Equipment Schedule 4							
W.B. 107.5"; 3.1 Liter.							
Sedan 4D		WL54T	16645	325	450	1025	1950
Euro Sedan 4D		WN54T	17815	500	675	1350	2450
Euro Coupe 2D		WN14T	17625	500	675	1350	2450
Z34 Coupe 2D		WP14X	19835	675	950	1775	3075
V6 3.4 Liter		X		150	150	200	200
CAMARO—V6—Equipment Schedule 4							
W.B. 101.1"; 3.4 Liter.							
Coupe 2D		FP22S	16250	1600	2100	3325	5125
Convertible 2D		FP32S	22021	2425	3025	4325	6325
Manual Trans				(150)	(150)	(200)	(200)
CAMARO—V8—Equipment Schedule 4							
W.B. 101.1"; 5.7 Liter.							
Z28 Coupe 2D		FP22P	19900	2175	2750	4025	5950
Z28 Convertible 2D		FP32P	25351	3250	3950	5375	7550
CAPRICE CLASSIC—V8—Equipment Schedule 4							
W.B. 115.9"; 4.3 Liter.							
Sedan 4D		BL52W	20698	625	850	1650	2925
LS Sedan 4D		BN52W	22010	775	1100	1975	3375
Wagon 4D		BL82P	22703	1325	1800	3000	4700
V8 5.7 Liter		P		100	100	135	135
IMPALA SS—V8—Equipment Schedule 2							
W.B. 115.9"; 5.7 Liter.							
Sedan 4D		BN52P	23355	4050	4800	6325	8700
CORVETTE—V8—Equipment Schedule 2							
W.B. 96.2"; 5.7 Liter.							
Coupe 2D		YY22P	37345	6650	7650	9550	12600
Convertible 2D		YY32P	44120	7675	8775	10850	14100
ZR1 Coupe 2D		YZ22J	67993	22450	25100	29100	36100
Glass Roof Panel				250	250	335	335
Dual Roof Panels				300	300	400	400
Hard Top (Convertible)				200	200	265	265
Suspension Pkg				200	200	265	265
6-Spd Manual Trans				150	150	200	200

1995 CHEVROLET — (1or2)G1(JC524)–S–#

Body	Type	VIN	List	Trade-In Fair	Trade-In Good	Pvt-Party Good	Retail Excellent
CAVALIER—4-Cyl.—Equipment Schedule 5							
W.B. 104.1"; 2.2 Liter, 2.3 Liter.							
Sedan 4D		JC524	12030	425	600	1225	2225
Coupe 2D		JC124	11825	400	550	1150	2125
LS Sedan 4D		JF524	12950	475	650	1375	2525
LS Convertible 2D		JF324	17695	975	1350	2425	4050
Z24 Coupe 2D		JF12D	14295	600	800	1575	2825
CORSICA—4-Cyl.—Equipment Schedule 5							
W.B. 103.4"; 2.2 Liter.							
Sedan 4D		LD554	14385	425	600	1225	2225
V6 3.1 Liter		M		125	125	165	165
BERETTA—4-Cyl.—Equipment Schedule 5							
W.B. 103.4"; 2.2 Liter.							
Coupe 2D		LV154	14045	450	625	1275	2300
V6 3.1 Liter		M		125	125	165	165
BERETTA—V6—Equipment Schedule 5							
W.B. 103.4"; 3.1 Liter.							
Z26 Coupe 2D		LW15M	16790	650	925	1725	3050
LUMINA—V6—Equipment Schedule 4							
W.B. 107.5"; 3.1 Liter.							
Sedan 4D		WL52M	16837	325	450	1025	1950
LS Sedan 4D		WN52M	17712	475	650	1325	2400
V6 3.4 Liter		X		150	150	200	200
MONTE CARLO—V6—Equipment Schedule 4							
W.B. 107.5"; 3.1 Liter, 3.4 Liter.							
LS Coupe 2D		WW12M	17512	450	600	1250	2275
Z34 Coupe 2D		WX12X	19495	600	825	1625	2875

Body	Type	VIN	List	Trade-In Fair	Good	Pvt-Party Good	Retail Excellent
CAMARO—V6—Equipment Schedule 4							
W.B. 101.1"; 3.4 Liter.							
Coupe 2D		FP22S	17536	1625	2125	3350	5150
Convertible 2D		FP32S	22781	2450	3050	4350	6350
V6 3.8 Liter		K		100	100	135	135
CAMARO—V8—Equipment Schedule 4							
W.B. 101.1"; 5.7 Liter.							
Z28 Coupe 2D		FP22P	21236	2175	2775	4050	5975
Z28 Convertible 2D		FP32P	26388	3300	4000	5425	7625
CAPRICE CLASSIC—V8—Equipment Schedule 4							
W.B. 115.9"; 4.3 Liter.							
Sedan 4D		BL52W	21798	725	1025	1875	3250
Wagon 4D		BL82P	24373	1650	2150	3375	5200
V8 5.7 Liter		P		100	100	135	135
IMPALA SS—V8—Equipment Schedule 2							
W.B. 115.9"; 5.7 Liter.							
Sedan 4D		BL52P	24385	4850	5675	7375	10000
CORVETTE—V8—Equipment Schedule 2							
W.B. 96.2"; 5.7 Liter.							
Coupe 2D		YY22P	37955	7050	8125	10100	13300
Convertible 2D		YY32P	44835	8100	9275	11450	15000
ZR1 Coupe 2D		YZ22J	68603	23825	26550	30800	38000
Glass Roof Panel				250	250	335	335
Dual Roof Panels				300	300	400	400
Hard Top (Convertible)				200	200	265	265
Suspension Pkg				200	200	265	265
6-Spd Manual Trans				150	150	200	200

1996 CHEVROLET — (1,2or4)G1(JC524)-T-#

Body	Type	VIN	List	Trade-In Fair	Good	Pvt-Party Good	Retail Excellent
CAVALIER—4-Cyl.—Equipment Schedule 5							
W.B. 104.1"; 2.2 Liter, 2.4 Liter.							
Sedan 4D		JC524	12872	525	700	1450	2650
Coupe 2D		JC124	12672	500	675	1400	2575
LS Sedan 4D		JF524	13524	600	825	1600	2875
LS Convertible 2D		JF324	17995	1175	1650	2825	4500
Z24 Coupe 2D		JF12T	15490	725	1025	1875	3250
CORSICA—4-Cyl.—Equipment Schedule 5							
W.B. 103.4"; 2.2 Liter.							
Sedan 4D		LD554	14885	500	675	1375	2475
V6 3.1 Liter		M		150	150	200	200
BERETTA—4-Cyl.—Equipment Schedule 5							
W.B. 103.4"; 2.2 Liter.							
Coupe 2D		LV154	14545	575	775	1550	2800
V6 3.1 Liter		M		150	150	200	200
BERETTA—V6—Equipment Schedule 5							
W.B. 103.4"; 3.1 Liter.							
Z26 Coupe 2D		LW15M	17190	825	1150	2050	3500
LUMINA—V6—Equipment Schedule 4							
W.B. 107.5"; 3.1 Liter.							
Sedan 4D		WL52M	17863	400	550	1200	2225
LS Sedan 4D		WN52M	18812	550	750	1550	2800
V6 3.4 Liter		X		175	175	235	235
MONTE CARLO—V6—Equipment Schedule 4							
W.B. 107.5"; 3.1 Liter, 3.4 Liter.							
LS Coupe 2D		WW12M	18012	500	700	1450	2650
Z34 Coupe 2D		WX12X	19995	675	950	1825	3150
CAMARO—V6—Equipment Schedule 4							
W.B. 101.1"; 3.8 Liter.							
Coupe 2D		FP22K	18411	1925	2475	3725	5600
Convertible 2D		FP32K	23796	2875	3500	4875	6950
RS Coupe 2D		FP22K	20911	2200	2775	4050	5975
RS Convertible 2D		FP32K	25246	3100	3775	5175	7325
Manual Trans				(200)	(200)	(265)	(265)
CAMARO—V8—Equipment Schedule 4							
W.B. 101.1"; 5.7 Liter.							
Z28 Coupe 2D		FP22P	21951	2600	3175	4525	6550
Z28 Convertible 2D		FP32P	27016	3825	4550	6050	8350
SS Pkg				875	875	1165	1165
CAPRICE CLASSIC—V8—Equipment Schedule 4							
W.B. 115.9"; 4.3 Liter.							
Sedan 4D		BL52W	21495	850	1225	2175	3675
Wagon 4D		BL82P	22995	1975	2525	3800	5700
V8 5.7 Liter		P		125	125	165	165

1996 CHEVROLET

Body	Type	VIN	List	Trade-In Fair	Trade-In Good	Pvt-Party Good	Retail Excellent
IMPALA SS—V8—Equipment Schedule 2							
W.B. 115.9"; 5.7 Liter.							
Sedan 4D		BL52P	24995	**5725**	**6675**	**8425**	**11200**
CORVETTE—V8—Equipment Schedule 2							
W.B. 96.2"; 5.7 Liter.							
Coupe 2D		YY22P	38400	**7550**	**8675**	**10700**	**13900**
Convertible 2D		YY32P	46235	**8700**	**9900**	**12050**	**15650**
Grand Sport Coupe 2D		YY225	42373	********	********	********	**34300**
Grand Sport Conv 2D		YY325	49838	********	********	********	**43600**
Collector Edition			------	**2875**	**2875**	**3830**	**3830**
Glass Roof Panel			------	**250**	**250**	**335**	**335**
Dual Roof Panels			------	**300**	**300**	**400**	**400**
Hard Top (Convertible)			------	**250**	**250**	**335**	**335**
Suspension Pkg			------	**200**	**200**	**265**	**265**
6-Spd Manual Trans			------	**150**	**150**	**200**	**200**
V8 5.7 Liter (LT4) (Base)		5	------	**1100**	**1100**	**1465**	**1465**

1997 CHEVROLET — (1,2or4)G1(JC524)–V–#

Body	Type	VIN	List	Trade-In Fair	Trade-In Good	Pvt-Party Good	Retail Excellent
CAVALIER—4-Cyl.—Equipment Schedule 5							
W.B. 104.1"; 2.2 Liter, 2.4 Liter.							
Sedan 4D		JC524	13357	**650**	**900**	**1750**	**3075**
Coupe 2D		JC124	13157	**625**	**850**	**1650**	**2975**
RS Coupe 2D		JC124	14070	**750**	**1050**	**1925**	**3325**
LS Sedan 4D		JF524	13880	**725**	**1025**	**1900**	**3300**
LS Convertible 2D		JF324	18265	**1500**	**1975**	**3175**	**4975**
Z24 Coupe 2D		JF12T	15760	**875**	**1250**	**2225**	**3725**
MALIBU—V6—Equipment Schedule 5							
W.B. 107.0"; 3.1 Liter.							
Sedan 4D		ND52M	16390	**575**	**775**	**1600**	**2875**
LS Sedan 4D		NE52M	18715	**700**	**1000**	**1875**	**3300**
4-Cyl. 2.4 Liter		T		**(150)**	**(150)**	**(200)**	**(200)**
LUMINA—V6—Equipment Schedule 4							
W.B. 107.5"; 3.1 Liter.							
Sedan 4D		WL52M	18485	**425**	**575**	**1250**	**2300**
LS Sedan 4D		WL52M	19695	**575**	**775**	**1575**	**2875**
LTZ Sedan 4D		WN52M	20200	**575**	**800**	**1625**	**2925**
V6 3.4 Liter		X		**200**	**200**	**265**	**265**
MONTE CARLO—V6—Equipment Schedule 4							
W.B. 107.5"; 3.1 Liter, 3.4 Liter.							
LS Coupe 2D		WW12M	18220	**525**	**700**	**1500**	**2750**
Z34 Coupe 2D		WX12X	20495	**700**	**1000**	**1875**	**3300**
CAMARO—V6—Equipment Schedule 4							
W.B. 101.1"; 3.8 Liter.							
Coupe 2D		FP22K	18786	**1950**	**2500**	**3750**	**5625**
Convertible 2D		FP32K	24341	**2975**	**3600**	**4975**	**7050**
RS Coupe 2D		FP22K	20541	**2300**	**2900**	**4175**	**6125**
RS Convertible 2D		FP32K	25741	**3275**	**3975**	**5375**	**7550**
Manual Trans				**(250)**	**(250)**	**(335)**	**(335)**
CAMARO—V8—Equipment Schedule 4							
W.B. 101.1"; 5.7 Liter.							
Z28 Coupe 2D		FP22P	22721	**2775**	**3375**	**4725**	**6775**
Z28 Convertible 2D		FP32P	28091	**4225**	**4975**	**6475**	**8850**
SS Pkg				**1000**	**1000**	**1335**	**1335**
CORVETTE—V8—Equipment Schedule 2							
W.B. 104.5"; 5.7 Liter.							
Coupe 2D		YY22G	38365	**9000**	**10250**	**12400**	**15950**
Glass Roof Panel			------	**250**	**250**	**335**	**335**
Dual Roof Panels			------	**300**	**300**	**400**	**400**
Suspension Pkg			------	**200**	**200**	**265**	**265**
6-Spd Manual Trans			------	**150**	**150**	**200**	**200**

1998 CHEVROLET–(1,2or4)(C,GorY)1(MR226)–W–

Body	Type	VIN	List	Trade-In Fair	Trade-In Good	Pvt-Party Good	Retail Excellent
METRO—3-Cyl.—Equipment Schedule 6							
W.B. 93.1"; 1.0 Liter.							
Coupe 2D		MR226	10110	**400**	**575**	**1225**	**2275**
METRO—4-Cyl.—Equipment Schedule 6							
W.B. 93.1"; 1.3 Liter.							
LSi Sedan 4D		MR522	11800	**650**	**900**	**1750**	**3075**
LSi Coupe 2D		MR222	10910	**625**	**825**	**1650**	**2975**
PRIZM—4-Cyl.—Equipment Schedule 6							
W.B. 97.0"; 1.8 Liter.							
Sedan 4D		SK528	15248	**1100**	**1550**	**2700**	**4375**

1998 CHEVROLET

Body	Type	VIN	List	Trade-In Fair	Trade-In Good	Pvt-Party Good	Retail Excellent
LSi Sedan 4D		SK528	16208	**1225**	**1700**	**2900**	**4600**

CAVALIER—4-Cyl.—Equipment Schedule 5
W.B. 104.1"; 2.2 Liter, 2.4 Liter.

Sedan 4D		JC524	13705	800	1125	2075	3550
Coupe 2D		JC124	13505	750	1050	1975	3425
RS Coupe 2D		JC124	14945	900	1275	2375	4025
LS Sedan 4D		JF524	14750	900	1250	2350	3975
LS Convertible 2D		JF324		1625	2100	3350	5175
Z24 Coupe 2D		JF12T	16990	1050	1500	2625	4300
Z24 Convertible 2D		JF32T	20690	1850	2350	3600	5475

MALIBU—V6—Equipment Schedule 5
W.B. 107.0"; 3.1 Liter.

Sedan 4D		ND52M	16690	650	925	1825	3200
LS Sedan 4D		NE52M	18995	825	1175	2150	3675
4-Cyl. 2.4 Liter		T		(175)	(175)	(235)	(235)

LUMINA—V6—Equipment Schedule 4
W.B. 107.5"; 3.1 Liter.

Sedan 4D		WL52M	18785	450	625	1325	2450
LS Sedan 4D		WL52M	20020	625	850	1700	3050
LTZ Sedan 4D		WN52M	20520	625	875	1725	3075
V6 3.8 Liter		K		225	225	300	300

MONTE CARLO—V6—Equipment Schedule 4
W.B. 107.5"; 3.1 Liter, 3.8 Liter.

LS Coupe 2D		WW12M	18570	575	775	1600	2925
Z34 Coupe 2D		WX12K	20845	775	1075	2025	3500

CAMARO—V6—Equipment Schedule 4
W.B. 101.1"; 3.8 Liter.

Coupe 2D		FP22K	19196	2025	2575	3850	5750
Convertible 2D		FP32K	24771	3075	3725	5125	7250
T-Bar Roof				275	275	365	365
Manual Trans				(300)	(300)	(400)	(400)

CAMARO—V8—Equipment Schedule 4
W.B. 101.1"; 5.7 Liter.

Z28 Coupe 2D		FP22G	22571	2975	3600	5000	7100
Z28 Convertible 2D		FP32G	27975	4625	5450	6950	9375
T-Bar Roof				275	275	365	365
SS Pkg				1100	1100	1465	1465

CORVETTE—V8—Equipment Schedule 2
W.B. 104.5"; 5.7 Liter.

Coupe 2D		YY22G	38365	9750	11075	13300	17000
Convertible 2D		YY32G	45295	11650	13175	15550	19600
Glass Roof Panel				250	250	335	335
Dual Roof Panels				300	300	400	400
Suspension Pkg				200	200	265	265
6-Spd Manual Trans				150	150	200	200

1999 CHEVROLET — (1,2or3)(C,GorY)1(MR226)–X–

METRO—3-Cyl.—Equipment Schedule 6
W.B. 93.1"; 1.0 Liter.

Coupe 2D		MR226	10488	500	675	1400	2575

METRO—4-Cyl.—Equipment Schedule 6
W.B. 93.1"; 1.3 Liter.

LSi Sedan 4D		MR522	12187	775	1100	2050	3550
LSi Coupe 2D		MR222	11285	725	1025	1925	3375

PRIZM—4-Cyl.—Equipment Schedule 6
W.B. 97.1"; 1.8 Liter.

Sedan 4D		SK528	13828	1300	1775	3000	4750
LSi Sedan 4D		SK528	15269	1475	1950	3200	5000

CAVALIER—4-Cyl.—Equipment Schedule 5
W.B. 104.1"; 2.2 Liter, 2.4 Liter.

Sedan 4D		JC524	13876	1000	1400	2525	4200
Coupe 2D		JC124	13776	950	1325	2425	4100
RS Coupe 2D		JC124	15216	1100	1550	2725	4425
LS Sedan 4D		JF524	14921	1100	1550	2700	4375
Z24 Coupe 2D		JF12T	17261	1300	1800	3000	4750
Z24 Convertible 2D		JF32T	20861	2225	2800	4075	6000

MALIBU—V6—Equipment Schedule 5
W.B. 107.5"; 3.1 Liter.

Sedan 4D		ND52M,J	17080	775	1100	2075	3600
LS Sedan 4D		NE52M,J	19445	975	1375	2500	4200
4-Cyl. 2.4 Liter		T		(200)	(200)	(265)	(265)

LUMINA—V6—Equipment Schedule 4
W.B. 107.5"; 3.1 Liter, 3.8 Liter.

Body	Type	VIN	List	Trade-In Fair	Good	Pvt-Party Good	Retail Excellent
Sedan 4D		WL52M	18982	525	700	1525	2825
LS Sedan 4D		WL52M	20480	675	975	1875	3325
LTZ Sedan 4D		WN52K	20920	700	975	1900	3375
MONTE CARLO—V6—Equipment Schedule 4							
W.B. 107.5"; 3.1 Liter, 3.8 Liter.							
LS Coupe 2D		WW12M	19070	625	900	1800	3200
Z34 Coupe 2D		WX12K	21095	875	1225	2350	4025
CAMARO—V6—Equipment Schedule 4							
W.B. 101.1"; 3.8 Liter.							
Coupe 2D		FP22K	19221	2125	2700	4000	5900
Convertible 2D		FP32K	24796	3250	3925	5325	7475
T-Bar Roof			------	300	300	400	400
Manual Trans			------	(350)	(350)	(465)	(465)
CAMARO—V8—Equipment Schedule 4							
W.B. 101.1"; 5.7 Liter.							
Z28 Coupe 2D		FP22G	22996	3225	3900	5300	7425
Z28 Convertible 2D		FP32G	28385	5075	5925	7500	10050
T-Bar Roof			------	300	300	400	400
SS Pkg			------	1200	1200	1600	1600
CORVETTE—V8—Equipment Schedule 2							
W.B. 104.5"; 5.7 Liter.							
Hard Top 2D		YY12G	39082	9475	10775	12900	16400
Coupe 2D		YY22G	39476	10625	12050	14250	18050
Convertible 2D		YY32G	45884	12700	14350	16700	20900
Glass Roof Panel			------	250	250	335	335
Dual Roof Panels			------	300	300	400	400
Suspension Pkg			------	200	200	265	265
6-Spd Manual Trans			------	150	150	200	200

2000 CHEVROLET — (1,2or3)(C,GorY)1(MR226)–Y–

Body	Type	VIN	List	Trade-In Fair	Good	Pvt-Party Good	Retail Excellent
METRO—3-Cyl.—Equipment Schedule 6							
W.B. 93.1"; 1.0 Liter.							
Coupe 2D		MR226	10680	625	850	1725	3075
METRO—4-Cyl.—Equipment Schedule 6							
W.B. 93.1"; 1.3 Liter.							
LSi Sedan 4D		MR522	12395	975	1375	2500	4200
LSi Coupe 2D		MR222	11530	900	1250	2375	4050
PRIZM—4-Cyl.—Equipment Schedule 6							
W.B. 97.1"; 1.8 Liter.							
Sedan 4D		SK528	14246	1600	2100	3350	5175
LSi Sedan 4D		SK528	16272	1775	2300	3550	5425
CAVALIER—4-Cyl.—Equipment Schedule 5							
W.B. 104.1"; 2.2 Liter, 2.4 Liter.							
Sedan 4D		JC524	14275	1025	1450	2625	4325
Coupe 2D		JC124	14175	1000	1400	2550	4250
LS Sedan 4D		JF524	15220	1150	1625	2825	4550
Z24 Coupe 2D		JF12T	17425	1425	1900	3125	4950
Z24 Convertible 2D		JF32T	21025	2425	3025	4300	6300
MALIBU—V6—Equipment Schedule 5							
W.B. 107.0"; 3.1 Liter.							
Sedan 4D		ND52J	16995	950	1325	2475	4200
LS Sedan 4D		NE52J	19625	1150	1625	2825	4550
LUMINA—V6—Equipment Schedule 4							
W.B. 107.5"; 3.1 Liter.							
Sedan 4D		WL52J	19350	625	850	1775	3200
IMPALA—V6—Equipment Schedule 4							
W.B. 110.5"; 3.4 Liter, 3.8 Liter.							
Sedan 4D		WF52E	19787	1275	1750	3000	4775
LS Sedan 4D		WH52K	22925	2025	2575	3875	5800
MONTE CARLO—V6—Equipment Schedule 4							
W.B. 110.5"; 3.4 Liter, 3.8 Liter.							
LS Coupe 2D		WW12E	20090	1575	2050	3325	5175
SS Coupe 2D		WX12K	22295	2675	3275	4625	6675
CAMARO—V6—Equipment Schedule 4							
W.B. 101.1"; 3.8 Liter.							
Coupe 2D		FP22K	19360	2300	2900	4225	6175
Convertible 2D		FP32K	25490	3500	4200	5600	7800
T-Bar Roof			------	325	325	435	435
Manual Trans			------	(400)	(400)	(535)	(535)
CAMARO—V8—Equipment Schedule 4							
W.B. 101.1"; 5.7 Liter.							
Z28 Coupe 2D		FP22G	23515	3550	4275	5650	7875
Z28 Convertible 2D		FP32G	28900	5575	6500	8100	10750

2000 CHEVROLET

Body	Type	VIN	List	Trade-In Fair	Trade-In Good	Pvt-Party Good	Retail Excellent
T-Bar Roof				325	325	435	435
SS Pkg				1300	1300	1735	1735

CORVETTE—V8—Equipment Schedule 2
W.B. 104.5"; 5.7 Liter.

Body	Type	VIN	List	Fair	Good	Good	Excellent
Hard Top 2D		YY12G	39205	9675	11025	13100	16600
Coupe 2D		YY22G	40085	10975	12450	14600	18400
Convertible 2D		YY32G	46510	13225	14900	17250	21500
Glass Roof Panel				250	250	335	335
Dual Roof Panels				300	300	400	400
Suspension Pkg				200	200	265	265
6-Spd Manual Trans				150	150	200	200

2001 CHEVROLET — (1or2)(C,GorY)(MR522)–1–#

METRO—4-Cyl.—Equipment Schedule 6
W.B. 93.1"; 1.3 Liter.

Body	Type	VIN	List	Fair	Good	Good	Excellent
LSi Sedan 4D		MR522	12915	1225	1700	2925	4675

PRIZM—4-Cyl.—Equipment Schedule 6
W.B. 97.0"; 1.8 Liter.

Sedan 4D		SK528	14460	1950	2500	3775	5650
LSi Sedan 4D		SK528	16525	2125	2700	3975	5875

CAVALIER—4-Cyl.—Equipment Schedule 5
W.B. 104.1"; 2.2 Liter, 2.4 Liter.

Sedan 4D		JC524	14480	1125	1600	2800	4525
Coupe 2D		JC124	14380	1075	1525	2700	4425
LS Sedan 4D		JF524	15375	1275	1750	2975	4750
Z24 Coupe 2D		JF12T	17665	1600	2100	3350	5200

MALIBU—V6—Equipment Schedule 5
W.B. 107.0"; 3.1 Liter.

Sedan 4D		ND52J	17595	1150	1600	2825	4575
LS Sedan 4D		NE52J	19875	1425	1900	3150	5000

LUMINA—V6—Equipment Schedule 4
W.B. 107.5"; 3.1 Liter.

Sedan 4D		WL52J	19490	750	1075	2125	3725

IMPALA—V6—Equipment Schedule 4
W.B. 110.5"; 3.4 Liter, 3.8 Liter.

Sedan 4D		WF52E	20271	1700	2200	3500	5375
LS Sedan 4D		WH52K	23825	2525	3125	4425	6450

MONTE CARLO—V6—Equipment Schedule 4
W.B. 110.5"; 3.4 Liter, 3.8 Liter.

LS Coupe 2D		WW12E	20410	1850	2400	3700	5600
SS Coupe 2D		WX15K	23000	3075	3725	5100	7225

CAMARO—V6—Equipment Schedule 4
W.B. 101.1"; 3.8 Liter.

Coupe 2D		FP22K	19635	2550	3150	4500	6525
Convertible 2D		FP32K	25760	3800	4525	5950	8175
T-Bar Roof				350	350	465	465
RS				200	200	265	265
Manual Trans				(425)	(425)	(565)	(565)

CAMARO—V8—Equipment Schedule 4
W.B. 101.1"; 5.7 Liter.

Z28 Coupe 2D		FP22G	23935	3950	4700	6125	8375
Z28 Convertible 2D		FP32G	29325	6175	7150	8750	11400
T-Bar Roof				350	350	465	465
SS Pkg				1400	1400	1865	1865

CORVETTE—V8—Equipment Schedule 2
W.B. 104.5"; 5.7 Liter.

Coupe 2D		YY22G	40475	11900	13475	15700	19550
Z06 Hard Top 2D		YY12G	47500	13575	15300	17650	21900
Convertible 2D		YY32G	47000	14350	16125	18450	22700
Glass Roof Panel				250	250	335	335
Dual Roof Panels				300	300	400	400
Suspension Pkg				200	200	265	265
Z51 Handling				200	200	265	265
6-Spd Manual Trans				150	150	200	200

2002 CHEVROLET — (1or2)(GorY)1(SK528)–2–#

PRIZM—4-Cyl.—Equipment Schedule 6
W.B. 97.0"; 1.8 Liter.

Sedan 4D		SK528	14815	2225	2800	4275	6400
LSi Sedan 4D		SK528	16880	2400	3000	4450	6625

CAVALIER—4-Cyl.—Equipment Schedule 5
W.B. 104.1"; 2.2 Liter, 2.4 Liter.

Body	Type	VIN	List	Trade-In Fair	Trade-In Good	Pvt-Party Good	Retail Excellent
Sedan 4D		JC524	15280	1225	1700	3100	5075
Coupe 2D		JC124	15180	1175	1650	3050	5000
LS Sedan 4D		JF524	16330	1400	1875	3300	5325
LS Coupe 2D		JS124	16230	1425	1900	3325	5350
LS Sport Sedan 4D		JF52F	17700	1700	2200	3625	5675
LS Sport Coupe 2D		JS12F	17600	1600	2100	3525	5550
Z24 Sedan 4D		JH52T	17900	1850	2375	3825	5875
Z24 Coupe 2D		JF12T	17800	1775	2275	3700	5750
MALIBU—V6—Equipment Schedule 5							
W.B. 107.0"; 3.1 Liter.							
Sedan 4D		ND52J	18120	1300	1775	3200	5225
LS Sedan 4D		NE52J	20325	1625	2125	3600	5650
IMPALA—V6—Equipment Schedule 4							
W.B. 110.5"; 3.4 Liter, 3.8 Liter.							
Sedan 4D		WF52E	20820	2050	2625	4100	6225
LS Sedan 4D		WH52K	24270	2925	3550	5075	7350
MONTE CARLO—V6—Equipment Schedule 4							
W.B. 110.5"; 3.4 Liter, 3.8 Liter.							
LS Coupe 2D		WW12E	20920	2125	2700	4200	6350
SS Coupe 2D		WX12K	23470	3425	4150	5700	8075
CAMARO—V6—Equipment Schedule 4							
W.B. 101.1"; 3.8 Liter.							
Coupe 2D		FP22K	20640	2750	3350	4900	7200
Convertible 2D		FP32K	26650	4075	4825	6450	8950
T-Bar Roof				400	400	535	535
RS				200	200	265	265
Manual Trans				(450)	(450)	(600)	(600)
CAMARO—V8—Equipment Schedule 4							
W.B. 101.1"; 5.7 Liter.							
Z28 Coupe 2D		FP22G	24770	4300	5075	6725	9225
Z28 Convertible 2D		FP32G	30165	6725	7750	9525	12500
35th Annv Coupe 2D		FP22G	27270	5900	6825	8600	11400
35th Annv Conv 2D		FP32G	32665	7775	8900	10700	13750
T-Bar Roof				400	400	535	535
SS Pkg				1500	1500	2000	2000
CORVETTE—V8—Equipment Schedule 2							
W.B. 104.5"; 5.7 Liter.							
Coupe 2D		YY22G	41650	12875	14500	16950	21200
Z06 Hard Top 2D		YY12G	50350	14600	16425	18950	23500
Convertible 2D		YY32G	48175	15475	17350	19900	24600
Glass Roof Panel				250	250	335	335
Dual Roof Panels				300	300	400	400
Suspension Pkg				200	200	265	265
Z51 Handling				200	200	265	265
6-Spd Manual Trans				150	150	200	200

2003 CHEVROLET — (1or2)G1(JC52F)-3-#

Body	Type	VIN	List	Trade-In Fair	Trade-In Good	Pvt-Party Good	Retail Excellent
CAVALIER—4-Cyl.—Equipment Schedule 5							
W.B. 104.1"; 2.2 Liter.							
Sedan 4D		JC52F	15520	1525	2025	3450	5500
Coupe 2D		JC12F	15370	1475	1950	3375	5400
LS Sedan 4D		JF52F	16920	1775	2275	3725	5775
LS Coupe 2D		JF12F	16770	1800	2300	3750	5800
LS Sport Sedan 4D		JH52F	18120	2075	2650	4100	6200
LS Sport Coupe 2D		JH12F	17970	1975	2525	3975	6075
MALIBU—V6—Equipment Schedule 5							
W.B. 107.0"; 3.1 Liter.							
Sedan 4D		ND52J	18290	1500	1975	3450	5525
LS Sedan 4D		NE52J	20575	1850	2400	3900	6000
IMPALA—V6—Equipment Schedule 4							
W.B. 110.5"; 3.4 Liter, 3.8 Liter.							
Sedan 4D		WF52E	21350	2550	3125	4650	6875
LS Sedan 4D		WH52K	24460	3475	4200	5725	8100
MONTE CARLO—V6—Equipment Schedule 4							
W.B. 110.5"; 3.4 Liter, 3.8 Liter.							
LS Coupe 2D		WW12E	21350	2675	3275	4825	7100
SS Coupe 2D		WX12K	23665	4100	4850	6475	8950
CORVETTE—V8—Equipment Schedule 2							
W.B. 104.5"; 5.7 Liter.							
Coupe 2D		YY22G	43895	13575	15300	17700	22000
Z06 Hard Top 2D		YY12S	51155	15525	17450	20000	24600
Convertible 2D		YY32G	50370	16525	18525	21100	25900
50th Anniversary				3000	3000	4000	4000

2003 CHEVROLET

Body Type	VIN	List	Trade-In Fair	Good	Pvt-Party Good	Retail Excellent
Glass Roof Panel			275	275	365	365
Dual Roof Panels			350	350	465	465
Suspension Pkg			250	250	335	335
Z51 Handling			250	250	335	335
6-Spd Manual Trans			175	175	235	235

2004 CHEVROLET — (1,2orK)(GorL)1(TD526)–4–#

AVEO—4-Cyl.—Equipment Schedule 6
W.B. 97.6"; 1.6 Liter.
SVM Sedan 4D	TD526	9995	1250	1725	3200	5275
SVM Hatchback 4D	TD626	9995	1300	1775	3250	5325
Sedan 4D	TD526	11690	1750	2250	3750	5850
Hatchback 4D	TD626	11690	1775	2300	3800	5925
LS Sedan 4D	TJ526	12585	2025	2575	4100	6250
LS Hatchback 4D	TJ626	12585	2050	2600	4125	6275

CAVALIER—4-Cyl.—Equipment Schedule 5
W.B. 104.1"; 2.2 Liter.
Sedan 4D	JC52F	15995	1850	2400	3875	5975
Coupe 2D	JC12F	15810	1825	2325	3800	5875
LS Sedan 4D	JF52F	17230	2175	2750	4225	6350
LS Coupe 2D	JF12F	17030	2200	2775	4250	6400
LS Sport Sedan 4D	JH52F	18635	2550	3150	4625	6800
LS Sport Coupe 2D	JH12F	18435	2425	3025	4475	6675

CLASSIC—4-Cyl.—Equipment Schedule 5
W.B. 107.0" 2.2 Liter.
| Sedan 4D | ND52F | 19380 | 1600 | 2100 | 3575 | 5675 |

MALIBU—4-Cyl.—Equipment Schedule 5
W.B. 106.3"; 2.2 Liter.
| Sedan 4D | ZS52F | 18995 | 2975 | 3600 | 5150 | 7425 |
| V6 3.5 Liter | 8 | | 500 | 500 | 665 | 665 |

MALIBU—V6—Equipment Schedule 5
W.B. 106.3", 112.3" (MAXX); 3.5 Liter.
MAXX Hatchback 4D	ZS638	21725	3425	4150	5675	8025
LS Sedan 4D	ZT528	20995	3550	4250	5800	8150
LS MAXX H'Back 4D	ZT638	22225	3600	4300	5875	8250
LT Sedan 4D	ZU528	23495	3825	4550	6125	8525
LT MAXX H'Back 4D	ZU668	24725	3925	4650	6225	8625

IMPALA—V6—Equipment Schedule 4
W.B. 110.5"; 3.4 Liter, 3.8 Liter.
| Sedan 4D | WF52E | 22150 | 3075 | 3725 | 5275 | 7575 |
| LS Sedan 4D | WH52K | 25000 | 4125 | 4875 | 6450 | 8875 |

IMPALA—V6 Supercharged—Equipment Schedule 4
W.B. 110.5"; 3.8 Liter.
| SS Sedan 4D | WP521 | 27995 | 6525 | 7525 | 9200 | 12000 |

MONTE CARLO—V6—Equipment Schedule 4
W.B. 110.5"; 3.4 Liter, 3.8 Liter.
| LS Coupe 2D | WW12K | 22075 | 3350 | 4050 | 5625 | 8000 |
| SS Coupe 2D | WX12K | 24225 | 4900 | 5725 | 7400 | 10050 |

MONTE CARLO—V6 Supercharged—Equipment Schedule 4
W.B. 110.5"; 3.8 Liter.
| SS Coupe 2D | WZ121 | 27795 | 5975 | 6925 | 8650 | 11400 |

CORVETTE—V8—Equipment Schedule 2
W.B. 104.5"; 5.7 Liter.
Coupe 2D	YY22G	44535	14950	16800	19250	23700
Z06 Hard Top 2D	YY12S	52385	17200	19250	22000	26900
Convertible 2D	YY32G	51535	18225	20375	23000	28000
Commemorative Ed			600	600	800	800
Glass Roof Panel			300	300	400	400
Dual Roof Panels			400	400	535	535
Suspension Pkg			275	275	365	365
Z51 Handling			275	275	365	365
6-Spd Manual Trans			200	200	265	265

2005 CHEVROLET—(1,2orK)(GorL)1(TD526)–5–#

AVEO—4-Cyl.—Equipment Schedule 6
W.B. 97.6"; 1.6 Liter.
SVM Sedan 4D	TD526	9995	1875	2425	3950	6100
SVM Hatchback 4D	TD626	9995	1925	2475	4000	6150
LS Sedan 4D	TD526	11840	2750	3350	4900	7175
LS Hatchback 4D	TD626	11840	2775	3375	4925	7200
LT Sedan 4D	TG526	13110	3075	3725	5275	7575
LT Hatchback 4D	TG626	13335	3100	3775	5325	7650

0709　　**EQUIPMENT & MILEAGE PAGE 9 TO 23**　　69

Body Type	VIN	List	Trade-In Fair	Good	Pvt-Party Good	Retail Excellent
COBALT—4-Cyl.—Equipment Schedule 5						
W.B. 103.3"; 2.2 Liter.						
Sedan 4D	AJ52F	15040	3100	3750	5300	7600
Coupe 2D	AJ12F	15040	2850	3475	5000	7275
LS Sedan 4D	AL52F	17335	3750	4475	6025	8400
LS Coupe 2D	AL12F	17335	3675	4375	5925	8300
LT Sedan 4D	AM52F	18760	4425	5225	6825	9350
COBALT—4-Cyl. Supercharged—Equipment Schedule 5						
W.B. 103.3"; 2.0 Liter.						
SS Coupe 2D	AP12P	21995	6200	7175	8850	11550
Manual Trans		-------	0	0	0	0
CAVALIER—4-Cyl.—Equipment Schedule 5						
W.B. 104.1"; 2.2 Liter.						
Sedan 4D	JC52F	16025	2300	2900	4375	6550
Coupe 2D	JC12F	15825	2225	2800	4275	6425
LS Sedan 4D	JF52F	17705	2675	3275	4750	6950
LS Coupe 2D	JF12F	17505	2700	3300	4775	6975
LS Sport Sedan 4D	JH52F	19125	3050	3675	5200	7450
LS Sport Coupe 2D	JH12F	18925	2925	3550	5050	7275
CLASSIC—4-Cyl.—Equipment Schedule 5						
W.B. 107.0"; 2.2 Liter.						
Sedan 4D	ND52F	20130	1900	2450	3950	6100
MALIBU—4-Cyl.—Equipment Schedule 5						
W.B. 106.3"; 2.2 Liter.						
Sedan 4D	ZS528	19710	3450	4150	5700	8050
V6 3.5 Liter	8	-------	500	500	665	665
MALIBU—V6—Equipment Schedule 5						
W.B. 106.3", 112.3" (MAXX); 3.5 Liter.						
MAXX Hatchback 4D	ZS628	21475	4000	4725	6325	8750
LS Sedan 4D	ZT528	21775	4075	4825	6425	8850
LS MAXX H'Back 4D	ZT628	21975	4150	4900	6475	8925
LT Sedan 4D	ZU548	24570	4375	5175	6750	9200
LT MAXX H'Back 4D	ZU648	25120	4500	5300	6900	9450
IMPALA—V6—Equipment Schedule 4						
W.B. 110.5"; 3.4 Liter, 3.8 Liter.						
Sedan 4D	WF52E	23130	3700	4425	5975	8375
LS Sedan 4D	WH52K	25990	4825	5650	7275	9850
IMPALA—V6 Supercharged—Equipment Schedule 4						
W.B. 110.5"; 3.8 Liter.						
SS Sedan 4D	WP521	29085	7600	8700	10400	13300
MONTE CARLO—V6—Equipment Schedule 4						
W.B. 110.5"; 3.4 Liter, 3.8 Liter.						
LS Coupe 2D	WW12E	23060	4275	5025	6650	9150
LT Coupe 2D	WX12K	25220	5175	6025	7725	10400
MONTE CARLO—V6 Supercharged—Equipment Schedule 4						
W.B. 110.5"; 3.8 Liter.						
SS Coupe 2D	WZ121	28885	7150	8225	9950	12850
CORVETTE—V8—Equipment Schedule 2						
W.B. 105.8"; 6.0 Liter.						
Coupe 2D	YY22U	44245	17875	20000	22500	27400
Convertible 2D	YY34U	52245	21450	23900	26600	31900
Glass Roof Panel		-------	325	325	435	435
Dual Roof Panels		-------	450	450	600	600
Suspension Pkg		-------	300	300	400	400
Z51 Handling		-------	300	300	400	400
6-Spd Manual Trans		-------	225	225	300	300

2006 CHEVY—(1,2,3orK)(GorL)(1orN)(TD526)–6–#

Body Type	VIN	List	Trade-In Fair	Good	Pvt-Party Good	Retail Excellent
AVEO—4-Cyl.—Equipment Schedule 6						
W.B. 97.6"; 1.6 Liter.						
SVM Sedan 4D	TD526	9995	2725	3325	4900	7200
SVM Hatchback 4D	TD626	9995	2750	3375	4950	7250
LS Sedan 4D	TD526	12110	3650	4350	5925	8325
LS Hatchback 4D	TD626	12110	3700	4400	5975	8375
LT Sedan 4D	TG526	13530	4025	4775	6350	8775
LT Hatchback 4D	TG626	13775	4075	4825	6400	8850
COBALT—4-Cyl.—Equipment Schedule 5						
W.B. 103.3"; 2.2 Liter, 2.4 Liter.						
LS Sedan 4D	AK55F	15340	3850	4550	6125	8525
LS Coupe 2D	AK15F	15340	3550	4275	5800	8175
LT Sedan 4D	AL55F	17640	4525	5350	6925	9450
LT Coupe 2D	AL15F	17640	4425	5225	6825	9325
LTZ Sedan 4D	AZ55F	18990	5300	6175	7800	10400

Body	Type	VIN	List	Trade-In Fair	Good	Pvt-Party Good	Retail Excellent
SS Sedan 4D		AM55B	19640	5400	6275	7900	10500
SS Sedan 4D		AM15B	19640	5625	6550	8150	10800
COBALT—4-Cyl. Supercharged—Equipment Schedule 5							
W.B. 103.3"; 2.0 Liter.							
SS Coupe 2D		AP15P	21990	7250	8325	9950	12800
Manual Trans				0	0	0	0
HHR—4-Cyl.—Equipment Schedule 5							
W.B. 103.3"; 2.2 Liter.							
LS Sport Wagon 4D		A13D	16990	4750	5550	7175	9700
LT Sport Wagon 4D		A23D	17990	5325	6200	7800	10400
4-Cyl. 2.4 Liter		P		350	350	465	465
MALIBU—4-Cyl.—Equipment Schedule 5							
W.B. 106.3"; 2.2 Liter.							
LS Sedan 4D		ZS55F	19990	4350	5150	6750	9200
LT Sedan 4D		ZT55F	19990	4825	5650	7275	9850
V6 3.5 Liter		8		500	500	665	665
MALIBU—V6—Equipment Schedule 5							
W.B. 106.3", 112.3" (MAXX); 3.5 Liter, 3.9 Liter.							
LS MAXX H'Back 4D		ZS658	20835	4750	5550	7200	9750
LT MAXX H'Back 4D		ZT658	21650	5175	6025	7650	10250
SS Sedan 4D		ZW571	24490	5750	6675	8300	11000
SS MAXX H'Back 4D		ZW671	24690	5850	6775	8425	11100
LTZ Sedan 4D		ZU578	24830	6350	7325	8975	11700
LTZ MAXX H'Back 4D		ZU678	25380	6425	7400	9075	11800
IMPALA—V6—Equipment Schedule 4							
W.B. 110.5"; 3.5 Liter, 3.9 Liter.							
LS Sedan 4D		WB55K	21990	5625	6550	8175	10850
LT Sedan 4D		WC551	22520	5975	6925	8575	11300
LTZ Sedan 4D		WU551	27530	7550	8650	10300	13200
IMPALA—V8—Equipment Schedule 4							
W.B. 110.5"; 5.3 Liter.							
SS Sedan 4D		WD55C	27790	8725	9950	11650	14700
MONTE CARLO—V6—Equipment Schedule 4							
W.B. 110.5"; 3.5 Liter, 3.9 Liter.							
LS Coupe 2D		WJ15K	21990	5075	5925	7600	10250
LT Coupe 2D		WK15K	22520	5950	6900	8575	11300
LTZ Coupe 2D		WN151	26635	6650	7650	9325	12150
MONTE CARLO—V8—Equipment Schedule 4							
W.B. 110.5"; 5.3 Liter.							
SS Coupe 2D		WL15C	27790	8425	9625	11400	14500
CORVETTE—V8—Equipment Schedule 2							
W.B. 105.7"; 6.0 Liter, 7.0 Liter.							
Coupe 2D		YY22U	47345	20100	22450	25000	30000
Convertible 2D		YY32U	53585	24000	26750	29300	34800
Z06 Coupe 2D		YY25E	65800	32625	36250	39100	45700
Glass Roof Panel				350	350	465	465
Dual Roof Panels				500	500	665	665
Suspension Pkg				325	325	435	435
Z51 Handling				325	325	435	435
6-Spd Manual Trans				250	250	335	335

2007 CHEVY—(1,2,3orK)(GorL)(1orN)(TD566)-7-#

Body	Type	VIN	List	Trade-In Fair	Good	Pvt-Party Good	Retail Excellent
AVEO—4-Cyl.—Equipment Schedule 6							
W.B. 97.6"; 1.6 Liter.							
LS Sedan 4D		TD566	12365	4600	5425	6900	9300
LT Sedan 4D		TG566	14015	5025	5850	7350	9800
AVEO5—4-Cyl.—Equipment Schedule 6							
W.B. 97.6"; 1.6 Liter.							
SVM Hatchback 4D		TD666	10045	3650	4350	5825	8075
LS Hatchback 4D		TD666	12515	4650	5475	6950	9350
COBALT—4-Cyl.—Equipment Schedule 5							
W.B. 103.3"; 2.2 Liter, 2.4 Liter.							
LS Sedan 4D		AK55F	14515	4600	5450	6925	9350
LS Coupe 2D		AK15F	14515	4325	5125	6575	8900
LT Sedan 4D		AL55F	15635	5425	6300	7800	10300
LT Coupe 2D		AL15F	15635	5275	6150	7675	10150
LTZ Sedan 4D		AZ55F	18790	6225	7175	8725	11300
SS Sedan 4D		AM52B	19920	6400	7375	8925	11500
SS Coupe 2D		AM15B	19920	6575	7575	9100	11700
COBALT—4-Cyl. Supercharged—Equipment Schedule 5							
W.B. 103.3"; 2.0 Liter.							
SS Coupe 2D		AP18P	21465	8325	9525	11100	14000
Manual Trans				0	0	0	0

Body	Type	VIN	List	Trade-In Fair	Good	Pvt-Party Good	Retail Excellent
HHR—4-Cyl.—Equipment Schedule 5							
W.B. 103.5"; 2.2 Liter.							
LS Sport Wagon 4D	A13D	17470	5775	6700	8175	10700
LS Panel Sport Wag 2D	A15D	17750	6450	7450	8975	11550
LT Sport Wagon 4D	A23D	18470	6375	7350	8875	11450
LT Panel Sport Wag 2D	A25P	19595	7050	8100	9625	12300
4-Cyl. 2.4 Liter	P	------	350	350	465	465
MALIBU—4-Cyl.—Equipment Schedule 5							
W.B. 106.3"; 2.2 Liter.							
LS Sedan 4D	ZS58F	17710	5175	6025	7550	10050
LT Sedan 4D	ZT58N	18930	5725	6650	8175	10750
V6 3.5 Liter	N	------	500	500	665	665
MALIBU—V6—Equipment Schedule 5							
W.B. 106.3", 112.3" (MAXX); 3.5 Liter, 3.9 Liter.							
LS MAXX H'Back 4D	ZS68N	20385	5550	6475	7975	10550
LT MAXX H'Back 4D	ZT68N	21130	6025	6975	8525	11100
SS Sedan 4D	ZW571	23965	6675	7700	9225	11900
SS MAXX H'Back 4D	ZW671	24265	6800	7850	9375	12050
LTZ Sedan 4D	ZU57N	24170	7350	8425	10000	12750
LTZ MAXX H'Back 4D	ZU67N	24470	7425	8500	10050	12800
IMPALA—V6—Equipment Schedule 4							
W.B. 110.5"; 3.5 Liter, 3.9 Liter.							
LS Sedan 4D	WB55K	21515	6550	7550	9100	11700
LT Sedan 4D	WT55K	22125	6925	7975	9525	12200
LTZ Sedan 4D	WU551	26935	8600	9800	11400	14350
IMPALA—V8—Equipment Schedule 4							
W.B. 110.5"; 5.3 Liter.							
SS Sedan 4D	WD55C	28540	9950	11275	12950	16000
MONTE CARLO—V6—Equipment Schedule 4							
W.B. 110.5"; 3.5 Liter.							
LS Coupe 2D	WJ15K	21515	6525	7500	9125	11800
LT Coupe 2D	WK15K	23125	7600	8700	10350	13200
MONTE CARLO—V8—Equipment Schedule 4							
W.B. 110.5"; 5.3 Liter.							
SS Coupe 2D	WL15C	28240	10200	11575	13300	16450
CORVETTE—V8—Equipment Schedule 2							
W.B. 105.7"; 6.0 Liter, 7.0 Liter.							
Coupe 2D	YY25U	46245	22725	25375	27900	33300
Convertible 2D	YY36U	54320	27050	30075	32700	38500
Z06 Coupe 2D	YY25E	70000	36450	40475	43100	50000
Glass Roof Panel		------	375	375	500	500
Dual Roof Panels		------	550	550	735	735
Suspension Pkg		------	350	350	465	465
Z51 Handling		------	350	350	465	465
6-Spd Manual Trans		------	275	275	365	365

2008 CHEVY — (1,2,3orK)(GorL)(1orN)(TD566)-8-#

Body	Type	VIN	List	Trade-In Fair	Good	Pvt-Party Good	Retail Excellent
AVEO—4-Cyl.—Equipment Schedule 6							
W.B. 97.6"; 1.6 Liter.							
LS Sedan 4D	TD566	12695	5575	6500	7825	10100
LT Sedan 4D	TG566	14330	6050	7000	8300	10650
AVEO5—4-Cyl.—Equipment Schedule 6							
W.B. 97.6"; 1.6 Liter.							
SVM Hatchback 4D	TD666	10610	4550	5375	6675	8825
LS Hatchback 4D	TD666	12545	5625	6550	7875	10150
COBALT—4-Cyl.—Equipment Schedule 5							
W.B. 103.3"; 2.2 Liter, 2.4 Liter.							
LS Sedan 4D	AK58N	15215	6100	7050	8450	10900
LS Coupe 2D	AK18F	15215	5775	6725	8075	10450
LT Sedan 4D	AL58F	15915	6925	7975	9375	11900
LT Coupe 2D	AL18F	15915	6775	7825	9200	11700
Sport Sedan 4D	AM58B	20540	8025	9200	10700	13400
Sport Coupe 2D	AM18B	20540	8150	9325	10850	13550
COBALT—4-Cyl. Turbo—Equipment Schedule 5							
W.B. 103.3"; 2.0 Liter.							
SS Coupe 2D	AP18X	22995	11175	12650	14150	17200
Manual Trans		------	0	0	0	0
HHR—4-Cyl.—Equipment Schedule 5							
W.B. 103.5"; 2.2 Liter.							
LS Sport Wagon 4D	A13D	17795	7000	8050	9450	11950
LS Panel Sport Wag 2D	A15D	18095	7775	8900	10300	12900
LT Sport Wagon 4D	A23D	18795	7675	8800	10200	12800
LT Panel Sport Wag 2D	A25D	19095	8425	9625	11100	13850

2008 CHEVROLET

Body	Type	VIN	List	Trade-In Fair	Trade-In Good	Pvt-Party Good	Retail Excellent
4-Cyl. 2.4 Liter		P	.....	350	350	465	465

HHR—4-Cyl. Turbo—Equipment Schedule 5
W.B. 103.5"; 2.0 Liter.

| SS Sport Wagon 4D | | A83X | 22995 | 10525 | 11950 | 13500 | 16550 |

MALIBU CLASSIC—4-Cyl.—Equipment Schedule 5
W.B. 106.3"; 2.2 Liter.

| LS Sedan 4D | | ZS58F | 18495 | 6925 | 7975 | 9400 | 11950 |
| V6 3.5 Liter | | N | ..... | 500 | 500 | 665 | 665 |

MALIBU CLASSIC—V6—Equipment Schedule 5
W.B. 106.3"; 3.5 Liter.

| LT Sedan 4D | | ZT58N | 20880 | 7600 | 8700 | 10150 | 12800 |

MALIBU—4-Cyl. Hybrid—Equipment Schedule 4
W.B. 112.3"; 2.4 Liter.

| Sedan 4D | | ZF585 | 22790 | | | | |

MALIBU—4-Cyl.—Equipment Schedule 4
W.B. 112.3"; 2.4 Liter

LS Sedan 4D		ZG58B	19995	10050	11425	13000	16000
LT Sedan 4D		ZH58B	20955	11275	12800	14350	17550
V6 3.5 Liter		N	.....	500	500	665	665
V6 3.6 Liter		7	.....	1000	1000	1335	1335

MALIBU—V6—Equipment Schedule 4
W.B. 112.3"; 3.6 Liter.

| LTZ Sedan 4D | | ZK587 | 26995 | 13125 | 14800 | 16400 | 19800 |

IMPALA—V6—Equipment Schedule 4
W.B. 110.5"; 3.5 Liter, 3.9 Liter.

LS Sedan 4D		WB55K	21940	8475	9675	11200	14000
LT Sedan 4D		W55K	22550	8900	10150	11700	14550
LT 50th Anniv Ed Sed		WV55K	25995	10000	11325	12900	15900
LTZ Sedan 4D		WU553	27515	10725	12150	13700	16800

IMPALA—V8—Equipment Schedule 4
W.B. 110.5"; 5.3 Liter.

| SS Sedan 4D | | WD55C | 28920 | 12250 | 13825 | 15450 | 18650 |

CORVETTE—V8—Equipment Schedule 2
W.B. 105.7"; 6.2 Liter, 7.0 Liter.

Coupe 2D		YY25W	47895	25975	28900	31600	37200
Convertible 2D		YY36W	55585	30575	34000	36600	42600
Z06 Coupe 2D		YY25E	71000	40775	45275	47800	54900
Glass Roof Panel			.....	400	400	535	535
Dual Roof Panels			.....	575	575	765	765
Suspension Pkg			.....	375	375	500	500
Z51 Handling			.....	375	375	500	500
6-Spd Manual Trans			.....	300	300	400	400

CHRYSLER

1994 CHRYSLER — (1or3)C3-(A363)-R-#

LeBARON—V6—Equipment Schedule 4
W.B. 100.6", 103.5" (Sed); 3.0 Liter.

LE Sedan 4D		A363	17226	625	900	1700	3000
Landau Sedan 4D		A563	18438	700	975	1825	3150
GTC/LX Convertible 2D		U453	18239	750	1075	1925	3325
4-Cyl. 2.5 Liter		K	.....	(150)	(150)	(200)	(200)

CONCORDE—V6—Equipment Schedule 4
W.B. 113.0"; 3.3 Liter.

| Sedan 4D | | L56T | 21017 | 450 | 625 | 1275 | 2300 |
| V6 3.5 Liter | | F | ..... | 175 | 175 | 235 | 235 |

NEW YORKER—V6—Equipment Schedule 2
W.B. 113.0"; 3.5 Liter.

| Sedan 4D | | D46F | 26126 | 825 | 1150 | 2075 | 3500 |

LHS—V6—Equipment Schedule 2
W.B. 113.0"; 3.5 Liter.

| Sedan 4D | | D56F | 30868 | 1025 | 1450 | 2525 | 4175 |

1995 CHRYSLER — (1,2or4)C3-(U42Y)-S-#

SEBRING—4-Cyl.—Equipment Schedule 4
W.B. 103.7"; 2.0 Liter.

| LX Coupe 2D | | U42Y | 17636 | 350 | 475 | 1075 | 2000 |
| V6 2.5 Liter | | H,N | ..... | 100 | 100 | 135 | 135 |

SEBRING—V6—Equipment Schedule 4
W.B. 103.7"; 2.5 Liter.

| LXi Coupe 2D | | U52H,N | 20548 | 525 | 725 | 1475 | 2650 |

Body Type	VIN	List	Trade-In Fair	Good	Pvt-Party Good	Retail Excellent
CIRRUS—V6—Equipment Schedule 4						
W.B. 108.0"; 2.5 Liter.						
LX Sedan 4D	J56H,N	17970	875	1250	2200	3675
LXi		------	50	50	65	65
4-Cyl. 2.4 Liter	X	------	(175)	(175)	(235)	(235)
LeBARON—V6—Equipment Schedule 4						
W.B. 100.6"; 3.0 Liter.						
GTC/LX Convertible 2D	U453	18709	925	1300	2375	4000
CONCORDE—V6—Equipment Schedule 4						
W.B. 113.0"; 3.3 Liter.						
Sedan 4D	D56T	21085	550	750	1450	2575
V6 3.5 Liter	F	------	175	175	235	235
NEW YORKER—V6—Equipment Schedule 2						
W.B. 113.0"; 3.5 Liter.						
Sedan 4D	C46F	26191	975	1375	2475	4125
LHS—V6—Equipment Schedule 2						
W.B. 113.0"; 3.5 Liter.						
Sedan 4D	C56F	30190	1200	1700	2850	4550

1996 CHRYSLER — (1,2or4)C3-(U42Y)-T-#

Body Type	VIN	List	Trade-In Fair	Good	Pvt-Party Good	Retail Excellent
SEBRING—4-Cyl.—Equipment Schedule 4						
W.B. 103.7", 106.0" (Conv); 2.0 Liter, 2.4 Liter.						
LX Coupe 2D	U42Y	18418	425	575	1225	2275
JX Convertible 2D	L45X	19995	775	1100	2025	3475
Manual Trans		------	(200)	(200)	(265)	(265)
V6 2.5 Liter	H,N	------	150	150	200	200
SEBRING—V6—Equipment Schedule 4						
W.B. 103.7", 106.0" (Conv); 2.5 Liter.						
LXi Coupe 2D	U52N	20685	625	875	1675	3000
JXi Convertible 2D	L55H	25210	1025	1450	2575	4250
CIRRUS—V6—Equipment Schedule 4						
W.B. 108.0"; 2.5 Liter.						
LX Sedan 4D	J56H	18895	950	1350	2425	4050
LXi		------	75	75	100	100
4-Cyl. 2.4 Liter	X	------	(200)	(200)	(265)	(265)
CONCORDE—V6—Equipment Schedule 4						
W.B. 113.0"; 3.3 Liter.						
LX Sedan 4D	D56T	19995	650	900	1750	3075
LXi		------	75	75	100	100
V6 3.5 Liter	F	------	225	225	300	300
NEW YORKER—V6—Equipment Schedule 2						
W.B. 113.0"; 3.5 Liter.						
Sedan 4D	C46F	27895	1175	1625	2800	4500
LHS—V6—Equipment Schedule 2						
W.B. 113.0"; 3.5 Liter.						
Sedan 4D	C56F	30850	1525	2025	3250	5050

1997 CHRYSLER — (1,2,3or4)C3-(U42Y)-V-#

Body Type	VIN	List	Trade-In Fair	Good	Pvt-Party Good	Retail Excellent
SEBRING—4-Cyl.—Equipment Schedule 4						
W.B. 103.7", 106.0" (Conv); 2.0 Liter, 2.4 Liter.						
LX Coupe 2D	U42Y	18541	500	675	1400	2525
JX Convertible 2D	L45X	21560	950	1325	2425	4075
JXi Convertible 2D	L55X	25195	1075	1525	2675	4350
Manual Trans		------	(250)	(250)	(335)	(335)
V6 2.5 Liter	H,N	------	200	200	265	265
SEBRING—V6—Equipment Schedule 4						
W.B. 103.7"; 2.5 Liter.						
LXi Coupe 2D	U52N	21555	700	1000	1875	3300
CIRRUS—V6—Equipment Schedule 4						
W.B. 108.0"; 2.5 Liter.						
LX Sedan 4D	J56H	19265	1050	1475	2600	4275
LXi		------	100	100	135	135
4-Cyl. 2.4 Liter	X	------	(225)	(225)	(300)	(300)
CONCORDE—V6—Equipment Schedule 4						
W.B. 113.0"; 3.5 Liter.						
LX Sedan 4D	D56F	20985	725	1025	1900	3325
LXi		------	100	100	135	135
LHS—V6—Equipment Schedule 2						
W.B. 113.0"; 3.5 Liter.						
Sedan 4D	C56F	30850	1850	2400	3650	5525

Body	Type	VIN	List	Trade-In Fair	Trade-In Good	Pvt-Party Good	Retail Excellent
1998 CHRYSLER — (1,2,3or4)C3–(U49Y)–W–#							
SEBRING—4-Cyl.—Equipment Schedule 4							
W.B. 103.7", 106.0" (Conv); 2.0 Liter, 2.4 Liter.							
LX Coupe 2D		U49Y	18850	575	800	1625	2925
JX Convertible 2D		L45X	21985	1100	1550	2725	4400
JXi Convertible 2D		L55X	25575	1250	1750	2950	4675
Limited				275	275	365	365
Manual Trans				(300)	(300)	(400)	(400)
V6 2.5 Liter		H,N		250	250	335	335
SEBRING—V6—Equipment Schedule 4							
W.B. 103.7"; 2.5 Liter.							
LXi Coupe 2D		U59N	21310	825	1175	2150	3650
CIRRUS—V6—Equipment Schedule 4							
W.B. 108.0"; 2.5 Liter.							
LXi Sedan 4D		J56H	19995	1300	1800	3000	4725
CONCORDE—V6—Equipment Schedule 4							
W.B. 113.0"; 2.7 Liter.							
LX Sedan 4D		D46R	21855	850	1175	2175	3725
LXi				100	100	135	135
V6 3.2 Liter		J		300	300	400	400
1999 CHRYSLER — (1,2,3or4)C3–(U42Y)–X–#							
SEBRING—4-Cyl.—Equipment Schedule 4							
W.B. 103.7"; 2.0 Liter.							
LX Coupe 2D		U42Y	19390	675	950	1850	3300
Manual Trans				(350)	(350)	(465)	(465)
V6 2.5 Liter		N		225	225	300	300
SEBRING—V6—Equipment Schedule 4							
W.B. 103.7", 106.0" (Conv); 2.5 Liter.							
LXi Coupe 2D		U52N	21860	975	1375	2500	4200
JX Convertible 2D		L45H	24505	1175	1625	2850	4575
JXi Convertible 2D		L55H	26820	1675	2175	3425	5275
Limited				300	300	400	400
CIRRUS—V6—Equipment Schedule 4							
W.B. 108.0"; 2.5 Liter.							
LXi Sedan 4D		J56H	19995	1500	2000	3225	5050
CONCORDE—V6—Equipment Schedule 4							
W.B. 113.0"; 2.7 Liter.							
LX Sedan 4D		D46R	22115	1000	1400	2550	4250
LXi				100	100	135	135
V6 3.2 Liter		J		325	325	435	435
300M—V6—Equipment Schedule 2							
W.B. 113.0"; 3.5 Liter.							
Sedan 4D		E66G	29445	2100	2650	3950	5875
LHS—V6—Equipment Schedule 2							
W.B. 113.0"; 3.5 Liter.							
Sedan 4D		C56G	29445	1575	2075	3325	5175
2000 CHRYSLER — (1,2,3or4)C3–(U42N)–Y–#							
SEBRING—V6—Equipment Schedule 4							
W.B. 103.7", 106.0" (Conv); 2.5 Liter.							
LX Coupe 2D		U42N	19635	950	1325	2475	4175
LXi Coupe 2D		U52N	22015	1150	1625	2825	4550
JX Convertible 2D		L45H	24790	1450	1925	3150	4975
JXi Convertible 2D		L55H	27105	1950	2500	3800	5675
Limited				300	300	400	400
CIRRUS—4-Cyl.—Equipment Schedule 4							
W.B. 108.0"; 2.0 Liter, 2.4 Liter.							
LX Sedan 4D		J46B	17675	1050	1450	2625	4325
Manual Trans				(375)	(375)	(500)	(500)
CIRRUS—V6—Equipment Schedule 4							
W.B. 108.0"; 2.5 Liter.							
LXi Sedan 4D		J56H	20480	1750	2250	3500	5375
CONCORDE—V6—Equipment Schedule 4							
W.B. 113.0"; 2.7 Liter, 3.2 Liter.							
LX Sedan 4D		D46R	22550	1175	1650	2875	4625
LXi Sedan 4D		D36J	26480	1450	1925	3175	5025
300M—V6—Equipment Schedule 2							
W.B. 113.0"; 3.5 Liter.							
Sedan 4D		E66G	29690	2475	3075	4400	6425

2000 CHRYSLER

Body	Type	VIN	List	Trade-In Fair	Trade-In Good	Pvt-Party Good	Retail Excellent
LHS—V6—Equipment Schedule 2							
W.B. 113.0"; 3.5 Liter.							
Sedan 4D		C56G	28695	**1900**	**2450**	**3750**	**5650**

2001 CHRYSLER — 1C(4or8)–(Y4BB)–1–#

Body	Type	VIN	List	Fair	Good	Good	Excellent
PT CRUISER—4-Cyl.—Equipment Schedule 4							
W.B. 103.0"; 2.4 Liter.							
Sport Wagon 4D		Y4BB	18325	**2175**	**2750**	**4050**	**5975**
Limited Sport Wag 4D		Y4BB	20685	**2375**	**2950**	**4275**	**6225**
Touring				**200**	**200**	**265**	**265**
SEBRING—4-Cyl.—Equipment Schedule 4							
W.B. 103.7", 108.0" (Sed); 2.4 Liter.							
LX Sedan 4D		L46G	18520	**1225**	**1700**	**2925**	**4700**
LX Coupe 2D		G42G	20495	**1175**	**1650**	**2875**	**4625**
V6 2.7/3.0 Liter		R,H		**375**	**375**	**500**	**500**
SEBRING—V6—Equipment Schedule 4							
W.B. 103.7", 106.0" (Conv), 108.0" (Sed); 2.7 Liter, 3.0 Liter.							
LXi Sedan 4D		L66R	21405	**2025**	**2575**	**3850**	**5750**
LXi Coupe 2D		G62H	22885	**1675**	**2175**	**3425**	**5300**
LX Convertible 2D		L55U	24945	**1975**	**2525**	**3825**	**5725**
LXi Convertible 2D		L65U	27405	**2525**	**3125**	**4450**	**6450**
Limited Convertible 2D		L65J	29490	**3100**	**3775**	**5125**	**7225**
CONCORDE—V6—Equipment Schedule 4							
W.B. 113.0"; 2.7 Liter, 3.2 Liter.							
LX Sedan 4D		D46R	22995	**1425**	**1900**	**3175**	**5025**
LXi Sedan 4D		D36J	27240	**1775**	**2275**	**3575**	**5500**
300M—V6—Equipment Schedule 2							
W.B. 113.0"; 3.5 Liter.							
Sedan 4D		E66G	30170	**2900**	**3525**	**4900**	**6975**
LHS—V6—Equipment Schedule 2							
W.B. 113.0"; 3.5 Liter.							
Sedan 4D		C56G	29210	**2300**	**2900**	**4225**	**6200**
PROWLER—V6—Equipment Schedule 1							
W.B. 113.3"; 3.5 Liter.							
Roadster 2D		W65G	45400	**18475**	**20675**	**23200**	**28200**

2002 CHRYSLER–(1,2,3or4)C(3,4or8)–(Y48B)–2–#

Body	Type	VIN	List	Fair	Good	Good	Excellent
PT CRUISER—4-Cyl.—Equipment Schedule 4							
W.B. 103.0"; 2.4 Liter.							
Sport Wagon 4D		Y48B	18535	**2175**	**2750**	**4225**	**6350**
Touring Sport Wag 4D		Y58B	19540	**2225**	**2800**	**4275**	**6425**
Limited Sport Wag 4D		Y68B	21655	**2400**	**3000**	**4450**	**6650**
Dream Cruiser Wag 4D		Y68B	23395	**2875**	**3500**	**5000**	**7250**
Woodie Edition				**200**	**200**	**265**	**265**
SEBRING—4-Cyl.—Equipment Schedule 4							
W.B. 103.7", 106.0" (Conv), 108.0" (Sed); 2.4 Liter.							
LX Sedan 4D		L46X	18535	**1400**	**1850**	**3300**	**5325**
LX Coupe 2D		G42G	20615	**1150**	**1600**	**3000**	**4975**
LX Convertible 2D		L55G	23905	**2000**	**2575**	**4025**	**6125**
V6 2.7/3.0 Liter		R,H		**400**	**400**	**535**	**535**
SEBRING—V6—Equipment Schedule 4							
W.B. 103.7", 106.0" (Conv), 108.0" (Sed); 3.0 Liter.							
LXi Sedan 4D		L56R	20875	**2225**	**2825**	**4300**	**6425**
LXi Coupe 2D		G52H	23130	**1675**	**2175**	**3625**	**5675**
LXi Convertible 2D		L55R	26755	**2575**	**3175**	**4675**	**6850**
GTC Convertible 2D		L75R	25875	**2325**	**2900**	**4350**	**6525**
Limited Convertible 2D		L65R	29390	**3200**	**3900**	**5425**	**7725**
CONCORDE—V6—Equipment Schedule 4							
W.B. 113.0"; 2.7 Liter, 3.5 Liter.							
LX Sedan 4D		D46R	22995	**1400**	**1850**	**3350**	**5450**
LXi Sedan 4D		D36M	25600	**1800**	**2300**	**3825**	**5950**
Limited Sedan 4D		D56G	28495	**2200**	**2800**	**4300**	**6525**
300M—V6—Equipment Schedule 2							
W.B. 113.0"; 3.5 Liter.							
Sedan 4D		E66G	28995	**3675**	**4375**	**5975**	**8375**
Special Sedan 4D		E76K	32595	**3900**	**4625**	**6225**	**8650**
PROWLER—V6—Equipment Schedule 1							
W.B. 113.3"; 3.5 Liter.							
Roadster 2D		W65G	45400	**19900**	**22250**	**24900**	**30100**

Body	Type	VIN	List	Trade-In Fair	Trade-In Good	Pvt-Party Good	Retail Excellent
2003 CHRYSLER–(1,2,3or4)C(3,4or8)–(Y48B)–3–#							
PT CRUISER—4-Cyl.—Equipment Schedule 4							
W.B. 103.0"; 2.4 Liter.							
Sport Wagon 4D	Y48B	18815	2550	3125	4625	6800
Touring Sport Wag 4D	Y58B	19940	2600	3175	4675	6875
Limited Sport Wag 4D	Y68B	22180	2800	3400	4925	7150
Woodie Edition			225	225	300	300
PT CRUISER—4-Cyl. HO Turbo—Equipment Schedule 4							
W.B. 103.0"; 2.4 Liter.							
GT Sport Wagon 4D	Y78G	23170	4025	4750	6325	8725
Dream Cruiser			600	600	800	800
SEBRING—4-Cyl.—Equipment Schedule 4							
W.B. 103.7", 106.0" (Conv), 108.0" (Sed); 2.4 Liter.							
LX Sedan 4D	L46X	19930	1675	2175	3650	5725
LX Coupe 2D	G42G	21560	1325	1825	3250	5300
LX Convertible 2D	L45X	24560	2375	2975	4425	6625
V6 2.7/3.0 Liter	U.R		475	475	635	635
SEBRING—V6—Equipment Schedule 4							
W.B. 103.7", 106.0" (Conv), 108.0" (Sed); 2.7 Liter, 3.0 Liter.							
LXi Sedan 4D	L56R	21295	2625	3200	4725	6925
LXi Coupe 2D	G52H	23835	2050	2600	4075	6200
GTC Convertible 2D	L75R	26160	2700	3325	4825	7050
LXi Convertible 2D	L55T	27410	3050	3675	5225	7500
Limited Convertible 2D	L65R	30045	3775	4500	6050	8425
CONCORDE—V6—Equipment Schedule 4							
W.B. 113.0"; 2.7 Liter, 3.5 Liter.							
LX Sedan 4D	D46R	23510	1650	2150	3700	5875
LXi Sedan 4D	D36M	26240	2150	2725	4300	6525
Limited Sedan 4D	D56G	29135	2600	3175	4775	7050
300M—V6—Equipment Schedule 2							
W.B. 113.0"; 3.5 Liter.							
Sedan 4D	E66G	29245	4400	5200	6775	9275
Special Sedan 4D	E76K	32895	4625	5450	7100	9675
2004 CHRYSLER–(1,2,3or4)C(3,4or8)–(Y48B)–4–#							
PT CRUISER—4-Cyl.—Equipment Schedule 4							
W.B. 103.0"; 2.4 Liter.							
Sport Wagon 4D	Y48B	19515	3000	3650	5150	7425
Touring Sport Wag 4D	Y58B	20585	3050	3700	5200	7475
Limited Sport Wag 4D	Y68B	22825	3300	3975	5525	7825
4-Cyl. 2.4L Turbo	8		650	650	865	865
PT CRUISER—4-Cyl. HO Turbo—Equipment Schedule 4							
W.B. 103.0"; 2.4 Liter.							
GT Sport Wagon 4D	Y78G	26245	4675	5500	7100	9650
SEBRING—4-Cyl.—Equipment Schedule 4							
W.B. 103.7", 106.0" (Conv), 108.0" (Sed); 2.4 Liter.							
Sedan 4D	L66R	19360	1975	2525	4025	6150
Coupe 2D	G42G	22305	1600	2075	3550	5625
Convertible 2D	L45J	25570	2675	3275	4775	6975
LX Sedan 4D	L46X	19500	2000	2575	4050	6200
LX Convertible 2D	L45X	25215	2775	3400	4900	7150
V6 2.7 Liter	T		550	550	735	735
SEBRING—V6—Equipment Schedule 4							
W.B. 103.7", 106.0" (Conv), 108.0" (Sed); 2.7 Liter, 3.0 Liter.							
LXi Sedan 4D	L56R	21840	3025	3675	5200	7475
LXi Convertible 2D	L55T	28140	3525	4250	5775	8100
GTC Convertible 2D	L75R	27045	3150	3825	5350	7650
Touring Sedan 4D	L56R	21200	3000	3625	5150	7425
Touring Convertible 2D	L55T	28370	3650	4350	5900	8250
Limited Sedan 4D	L66R	23490	3300	4000	5525	7850
Limited Coupe 2D	G52H	24580	2875	3500	5000	7250
Limited Convertible 2D	L65R	31180	4375	5175	6750	9200
CONCORDE—V6—Equipment Schedule 4							
W.B. 113.0"; 2.7 Liter, 3.5 Liter.							
LX Sedan 4D	D46R	24130	2075	2650	4250	6500
LXi Sedan 4D	D36M	26860	2700	3300	4925	7250
Limited Sedan 4D	D56G	29755	3100	3775	5425	7825
300M—V6—Equipment Schedule 2							
W.B. 113.0"; 3.5 Liter.							
Sedan 4D	E66G	29865	5225	6100	7750	10400
Special Sedan 4D	E76K	33295	5500	6400	8050	10750

Body	Type	VIN	List	Trade-In Fair	Good	Pvt-Party Good	Retail Excellent
CROSSFIRE—V6—Equipment Schedule 1							
W.B. 94.5"; 3.2 Liter.							
Coupe 2D		N69L	35570	5550	6475	8200	11000

2005 CHRYSLER — (1,2,3or4)C(4or8)–(Y48B)–5

Body	Type	VIN	List	Fair	Good	Good	Excellent
PT CRUISER—4-Cyl.—Equipment Schedule 4							
W.B. 103.0"; 2.4 Liter.							
Sport Wagon 4D		Y48B	15820	3300	3975	5525	7825
Convertible 2D		Y45X	20820	4275	5025	6600	9025
Touring Sport Wag 4D		Y58B	17070	3325	4025	5550	7875
Touring Convertible 2D		Y55X	24490	5025	5875	7475	10050
Limited Sport Wag 4D		Y68B	18730	3650	4350	5900	8250
4-Cyl. 2.4L Turbo		E		725	725	965	965
PT CRUISER—4-Cyl. HO Turbo—Equipment Schedule 4							
W.B. 103.0"; 2.4 Liter.							
GT Sport Wagon 4D		Y78S	23935	5200	6075	7700	10300
GT Convertible 2D		Y75S	28860	6675	7675	9325	12100
SEBRING—4-Cyl.—Equipment Schedule 4							
W.B. 103.7", 106.0" (Conv), 108.0" (Sed); 2.4 Liter.							
Sedan 4D		L46X	19975	2375	2975	4450	6675
Coupe 2D		G42G	12770	1925	2475	3975	6125
Convertible 2D		L45X	26035	3150	3825	5375	7675
V6 2.7 Liter		R		600	600	800	800
SEBRING—V6—Equipment Schedule 4							
W.B. 103.7", 106.0" (Conv), 108.0" (Sed); 2.7 Liter, 3.0 Liter.							
GTC Convertible 2D		L75R	27510	3725	4425	5975	8325
Touring Sedan 4D		L56R	20695	3625	4325	5875	8225
Touring Convertible 2D		L55T	28835	4250	5000	6550	8975
Limited Sedan 4D		L66R	22985	3900	4625	6200	8575
Limited Coupe 2D		G52H	25045	3350	4050	5575	7925
Limited Convertible 2D		L65R	31645	5075	5925	7525	10100
TSi Sedan 4D		L56R	24455	4775	5600	7200	9750
300—V6—Equipment Schedule 2							
W.B. 120.0"; 2.7 Liter, 3.5 Liter.							
Sedan 4D		A43R	24695	7800	8950	10750	13750
Touring Sedan 4D		A53G	27720	7875	9000	10850	13950
Touring AWD Sedan 4D		K53G	29995	9325	10625	12550	15850
Signature Series				400	400	535	535
Limited				1000	1000	1335	1335
300C—V8 HEMI—Equipment Schedule 2							
W.B. 120.0"; 5.7 Liter, 6.1 Liter.							
Sedan 4D		A63H	33495	9750	11075	13000	16350
AWD Sedan 4D		K63H	34820	11375	12850	14800	18350
SRT8 Sedan 4D		A73W	39995	12750	14400	16350	20100
CROSSFIRE—V6—Equipment Schedule 1							
W.B. 94.5"; 3.2 Liter.							
Coupe 2D		N69L	29920	6850	7925	9675	12600
Roadster 2D		N65L	34960	8375	9575	11400	14550
Limited Coupe 2D		N69L	35695	7475	8575	10350	13350
Limited Roadster 2D		N65L	39995	10200	11575	13500	16850
CROSSFIRE—V6 Supercharged—Equipment Schedule 1							
W.B. 94.5"; 3.2 Liter.							
SRT-6 Coupe 2D		N79N	45695	11225	12750	14650	18150
SRT-6 Roadster 2D		N75N	49995	12200	13775	15700	19300

2006 CHRYSLER — (1,2,3or4)C(4or8)–(Y48B)–6

Body	Type	VIN	List	Fair	Good	Good	Excellent
PT CRUISER—4-Cyl.—Equipment Schedule 4							
W.B. 103.0"; 2.4 Liter.							
Sport Wagon 4D		Y48B	16925	4025	4775	6325	8725
Convertible 2D		Y45X	21355	5075	5925	7525	10100
Touring Sport Wag 4D		Y58B	17995	4100	4850	6400	8825
Limited Sport Wag 4D		Y68B	20160	4400	5225	6800	9300
Route 66 Edition				300	300	400	400
Signature Series				250	250	335	335
4-Cyl. 2.4L Turbo		E,8		800	800	1065	1065
PT CRUISER—4-Cyl. Turbo—Equipment Schedule 4							
W.B. 103.0"; 2.4 Liter.							
Touring Convertible 2D		Y55X	24870	5975	6900	8525	11150
GT Sport Wagon 4D		Y78G	24635	6150	7100	8725	11400
GT Convertible 2D		Y75S	30050	7800	8925	10550	13400
SEBRING—4-Cyl.—Equipment Schedule 4							
W.B. 106.0", 108.0" (Sed); 2.4 Liter.							

Body Type	VIN	List	Trade-In Fair	Trade-In Good	Pvt-Party Good	Retail Excellent
Sedan 4D	L46X	20380	2875	3500	5050	7325
Convertible 2D	L45X	26440	3750	4475	6000	8375
V6 2.7 Liter	T		650	650	865	865
SEBRING—V6—Equipment Schedule 4						
W.B. 106.0", 108.0" (Sed); 2.7 Liter.						
TSi Sedan 4D	L36R	24665	5525	6450	8050	10700
GTC Convertible 2D	L75R	27915	4325	5125	6675	9100
Touring Sedan 4D	L56R	21100	4350	5150	6725	9175
Touring Convertible 2D	L55R	29240	4875	5725	7325	9850
Limited Sedan 4D	L66R	23390	4575	5400	7000	9525
Limited Convertible 2D	L65R	32050	5850	6775	8375	11050
300—V6—Equipment Schedule 2						
W.B. 120.0"; 2.7 Liter, 3.5 Liter.						
Sedan 4D	A43R	24200	9125	10400	12200	15450
Touring Sedan 4D	A53G	25800	9275	10575	12400	15650
Touring AWD Sedan 4D	K53G	30200	10925	12400	14250	17650
Signature Series			400	400	535	535
Limited			1000	1000	1335	1335
300C—V8 HEMI—Equipment Schedule 2						
W.B. 120.0"; 5.7 Liter, 6.1 Liter.						
Sedan 4D	A63H	34100	11700	13225	15150	18650
AWD Sedan 4D	K63H	35425	13175	14850	16750	20500
SRT8 Sedan 4D	A73W	42695	14550	16375	18400	22200
CROSSFIRE—V6—Equipment Schedule 1						
W.B. 94.5"; 3.2 Liter.						
Coupe 2D	N59L	30070	8025	9200	11050	14100
Roadster 2D	N55L	35110	9650	10975	12800	16050
Limited Coupe 2D	N69L	35120	8700	9900	11700	14900
Limited Roadster 2D	N65L	39470	11575	13075	15000	18450
CROSSFIRE—V6 Supercharged—Equipment Schedule 1						
W.B. 94.5"; 3.2 Liter.						
SRT-6 Coupe 2D	N79N	46085	12400	14450	16300	19900
SRT-6 Roadster 2D	N75N	50395	13825	15575	17450	21200

Body Type	VIN	List	Trade-In Fair	Trade-In Good	Pvt-Party Good	Retail Excellent
PT CRUISER—4-Cyl.—Equipment Schedule 4						
W.B. 103.0"; 2.4 Liter.						
Sport Wagon 4D	Y48B	16950	4900	5725	7225	9650
Convertible 2D	Y45X	21355	6075	7025	8525	11050
Touring Sport Wag 4D	Y58B	18545	5000	5825	7325	9750
Limited Sport Wag 4D	Y68B	21740	5400	6275	7775	10250
Signature Series			250	250	335	335
Street Cruiser PCH			400	400	535	535
4-Cyl. 2.4L Turbo	8,E		875	875	1165	1165
PT CRUISER—4-Cyl. Turbo—Equipment Schedule 4						
W.B. 103.0"; 2.4 Liter.						
Touring Convertible 2D	Y55X	26350	7050	8100	9625	12300
GT Sport Wagon 4D	Y78G	24835	7275	8350	9900	12600
GT Convertible 2D	Y75S	30220	9050	10300	11850	14800
SEBRING—4-Cyl.—Equipment Schedule 4						
W.B. 108.9"; 2.4 Liter.						
Sedan 4D	C46K	18995	5600	6550	8000	10500
Touring Sedan 4D	C56K	20195	5975	6900	8400	10950
Limited Sedan 4D	C66K	23995	8100	9275	10900	13650
V6 2.7L Flex Fuel	R		700	700	935	935
V6 3.5 Liter HO	M		750	750	1000	1000
300—V6—Equipment Schedule 2						
W.B. 120.0"; 2.7 Liter, 3.5 Liter.						
Sedan 4D	A43R	24480	10675	12100	13900	17250
Touring Sedan 4D	A53G	29290	10925	12400	14200	17550
Touring AWD Sedan 4D	K53G	31290	12750	14400	16200	19800
Signature Series			400	400	535	535
Limited			1000	1000	1335	1335
300C—V8 HEMI—Equipment Schedule 2						
W.B. 120.0"; 5.7 Liter, 6.1 Liter.						
Sedan 4D	A63H	34935	13825	15575	17450	21200
AWD Sedan 4D	K63H	36260	15250	17150	19050	22900
SRT8 Sedan 4D	A73W	40970	16550	18625	20600	24700
CROSSFIRE—V6—Equipment Schedule 1						
W.B. 94.5"; 3.2 Liter.						
Coupe 2D	N59L	30435	9325	10625	12400	15550
Roadster 2D	N55L	36535	11125	12600	14350	17700
Limited Coupe 2D	N69L	36560	10050	11425	13250	16450

Body	Type	VIN	List	Trade-In Fair	Good	Pvt-Party Good	Retail Excellent
Limited Roadster 2D		N65L	40955	**13175**	**14850**	**16650**	**20300**

2008 CHRYSLER — (1,2,3or4)C(4or8)(Y48B)-8-#

PT CRUISER—4-Cyl.—Equipment Schedule 4
W.B. 103.0"; 2.4 Liter.

Sport Wagon 4D		Y48B	17480	6025	6975	8350	10750
Convertible 2D		Y55X	19170	7300	8375	9775	12300
Touring Sport Wag 4D		Y58B	19570	6125	7075	8450	10850
Signature Series				250	250	335	335
4-Cyl. 2.4L Turbo		E		950	950	1265	1265

PT CRUISER—4-Cyl. Turbo—Equipment Schedule 4
W.B. 103.0"; 2.4 Liter.

Limited Sport Wag 4D		Y688	23300	6550	7550	8925	11350

SEBRING—4-Cyl.—Equipment Schedule 4
W.B. 108.9"; 2.4 Liter.

LX Sedan 4D		C46K	19365	7450	8525	9900	12450
LX Convertible 2D		C45K	26515	8425	9625	11100	13850
Touring Sedan 4D		C56K	20540	7900	9050	10500	13150
Limited Sedan 4D		C66K	24190	10150	11525	13050	15950
Signature Series				400	400	535	535
V6 3.5 Liter HO		M		750	750	1000	1000

SEBRING—V6—Equipment Schedule 4
W.B. 108.9"; 2.7 Liter, 3.5 Liter.

Touring Convertible 2D		C55R	29115	9750	11075	12650	15600
Limited AWD Sedan 4D		D66M	28190	11275	12800	14350	17500
Limited Convertible 2D		C65M	32730	10150	11525	13050	15950
Power Hard Top				800	800	1065	1065

300—V6—Equipment Schedule 2
W.B. 120.0"; 2.7 Liter, 3.5 Liter.

Sedan 4D		A43R	25270	**12500**	**14100**	**15950**	**19400**
Touring Sedan 4D		A53G	29265	**12850**	**14450**	**16250**	**19800**
Touring AWD Sedan 4D		K53G	32120	**14800**	**16650**	**18400**	**22100**
Limited Sedan 4D		A33G	32295	**15300**	**17200**	**18900**	**22600**
Limited AWD Sedan 4D		K33G	34490	**16375**	**18375**	**20200**	**24000**
Signature Series				400	400	535	535

300C—V8 HEMI—Equipment Schedule 2
W.B. 120.0"; 5.7 Liter, 6.1 Liter.

Sedan 4D		A63H	36070	**16275**	**18225**	**20100**	**23900**
AWD Sedan 4D		K63H	38170	**17550**	**19700**	**21500**	**25500**
SRT8 Sedan 4D		A73W	44223	**18925**	**21175**	**23000**	**27200**

CROSSFIRE—V6—Equipment Schedule 1
W.B. 94.5"; 3.2 Liter.

Limited Coupe 2D		N69L	35610	**11625**	**13125**	**14900**	**18300**
Limited Roadster 2D		N65L	40055	**14900**	**16750**	**18500**	**22100**

DODGE

1994 DODGE — (1,3orJ)B3-(A11A)-R-#

COLT—4-Cyl.—Equipment Schedule 6
W.B. 96.1", 98.4" (4D); 1.5 Liter, 1.8 Liter.

Sedan 2D		A11A	10779	450	625	1250	2275
Sedan 4D		A36C	13248	550	750	1500	2700
ES Sedan 2D		A21A	11876	500	675	1375	2450
ES Sedan 4D		A46C	13824	600	800	1575	2800

SHADOW—4-Cyl.—Equipment Schedule 5
W.B. 97.2"; 2.2 Liter, 2.5 Liter.

Hatchback Sedan 4D		P28D	11452	300	425	950	1850
Hatchback 2D		P24D	11052	275	375	900	1775
ES H'Back Sedan 4D		P68K	12614	375	525	1100	2050
ES Hatchback 2D		P64K	12214	350	500	1075	2000
V6 3.0 Liter		3		100	100	135	135

SPIRIT—4-Cyl.—Equipment Schedule 5
W.B. 103.5"; 2.5 Liter.

Sedan 4D		A46K	14154	350	500	1100	2050
V6 3.0 Liter		3		150	150	200	200

INTREPID—V6—Equipment Schedule 4
W.B. 113.0"; 3.3 Liter.

Sedan 4D		D46T	19106	300	425	1000	1925
ES Sedan 4D		D56T	21423	450	625	1275	2300
V6 3.5 Liter		F		175	175	235	235

1994 DODGE

Body	Type	VIN	List	Trade-In Fair	Good	Pvt-Party Good	Retail Excellent
STEALTH—V6—Equipment Schedule 4							
W.B. 97.2"; 3.0 Liter.							
Coupe 2D		M44H	23659	**1450**	**1925**	**3125**	**4875**
R/T Coupe 2D		M64J	26404	**1625**	**2125**	**3350**	**5150**
Auto Trans				**125**	**125**	**165**	**165**
STEALTH—V6 Twin Turbo—Equipment Schedule 2							
W.B. 97.2"; 3.0 Liter.							
R/T AWD Coupe 2D		N74K	38785	**3100**	**3775**	**5175**	**7300**
VIPER—V10—Equipment Schedule 2							
W.B. 96.2"; 8.0 Liter.							
RT/10 Roadster 2D		R65E	58500	**18025**	**20200**	**23600**	**29600**

1995 DODGE — (1,4orJ)B3–(S27C)–S–#

Body	Type	VIN	List	Trade-In Fair	Good	Pvt-Party Good	Retail Excellent
NEON—4-Cyl.—Equipment Schedule 6							
W.B. 104.0"; 2.0 Liter.							
Sedan 4D		S27C	12195	**275**	**375**	**925**	**1800**
Highline Sedan 4D		S47C	12443	**350**	**475**	**1075**	**2000**
Highline Coupe 2D		S41C	12443	**300**	**425**	**1000**	**1925**
Sport Sedan 4D		S67C	14393	**450**	**600**	**1250**	**2275**
Sport Coupe 2D		S61C	14693	**525**	**700**	**1450**	**2625**
Competition Pkg				**0**	**0**	**0**	**0**
AVENGER—4-Cyl.—Equipment Schedule 4							
W.B. 103.7"; 2.0 Liter.							
Coupe 2D		U42Y	16309	**225**	**325**	**875**	**1725**
AVENGER—V6—Equipment Schedule 4							
W.B. 103.7"; 2.5 Liter.							
ES Coupe 2D		U52H,N	18260	**525**	**700**	**1375**	**2475**
SPIRIT—4-Cyl.—Equipment Schedule 5							
W.B. 103.5"; 2.5 Liter.							
Sedan 4D		A46K	14828	**450**	**625**	**1275**	**2350**
V6 3.0 Liter		3		**150**	**150**	**200**	**200**
STRATUS—4-Cyl.—Equipment Schedule 5							
W.B. 108.0"; 2.0 Liter, 2.4 Liter.							
Sedan 4D		J46C	15230	**675**	**950**	**1800**	**3125**
STRATUS—V6—Equipment Schedule 4							
W.B. 108.0"; 2.5 Liter.							
ES Sedan 4D		J56H,N	17800	**975**	**1375**	**2450**	**4075**
4-Cyl. 2.0L/2.4 Liter		C,X		**(175)**	**(175)**	**(235)**	**(235)**
INTREPID—V6—Equipment Schedule 4							
W.B. 113.0"; 3.3 Liter.							
Sedan 4D		D46T	19232	**375**	**525**	**1125**	**2100**
ES Sedan 4D		D56T	21379	**550**	**750**	**1450**	**2575**
V6 3.5 Liter		F		**175**	**175**	**235**	**235**
STEALTH—V6—Equipment Schedule 4							
W.B. 97.2"; 3.0 Liter.							
Hatchback 2D		M84H	24572	**1700**	**2200**	**3425**	**5275**
R/T Hatchback 2D		M44J	27756	**1900**	**2425**	**3700**	**5575**
Auto Trans				**125**	**125**	**165**	**165**
STEALTH—V6 Turbo—Equipment Schedule 2							
W.B. 97.2"; 3.0 Liter.							
R/T AWD H'Back 2D		N74K	39178	**3575**	**4300**	**5775**	**8050**
VIPER—V10—Equipment Schedule 2							
W.B. 96.2"; 8.0 Liter.							
RT/10 Roadster 2D		R65E	60500	**18925**	**21175**	**24700**	**30900**

1996 DODGE — (1,4orJ)B3–(S27C)–T–#

Body	Type	VIN	List	Trade-In Fair	Good	Pvt-Party Good	Retail Excellent
NEON—4-Cyl.—Equipment Schedule 4							
W.B. 104.0"; 2.0 Liter.							
Sedan 4D		S27C	11730	**300**	**425**	**1000**	**1925**
Coupe 2D		S22C	11230	**300**	**400**	**975**	**1875**
Highline Sedan 4D		S47C	12735	**400**	**550**	**1175**	**2175**
Highline Coupe 2D		S42C	12535	**375**	**525**	**1125**	**2100**
Sport Sedan 4D		S67C	14165	**500**	**700**	**1375**	**2475**
Sport Coupe 2D		S62C	13965	**600**	**800**	**1575**	**2825**
AVENGER—4-Cyl.—Equipment Schedule 4							
W.B. 103.7"; 2.0 Liter.							
Coupe 2D		U41B	17008	**300**	**400**	**1000**	**1925**
Manual Trans				**(200)**	**(200)**	**(265)**	**(265)**
AVENGER—V6—Equipment Schedule 4							
W.B. 103.7"; 2.5 Liter.							
ES Coupe 2D		U51H,N	19190	**625**	**850**	**1650**	**2975**
Manual Trans				**(200)**	**(200)**	**(265)**	**(265)**

1996 DODGE

Body	Type	VIN	List	Trade-In Fair	Trade-In Good	Pvt-Party Good	Retail Excellent
4-Cyl. 2.0 Liter		B		(150)	(150)	(200)	(200)

STRATUS—4-Cyl.—Equipment Schedule 5
W.B. 108.0"; 2.0 Liter, 2.4 Liter.

Body	Type	VIN	List	Fair	Good	Good	Excellent
Sedan 4D		J46C	15820	725	1025	1900	3300

STRATUS—V6—Equipment Schedule 4
W.B. 108.0"; 2.5 Liter.

ES Sedan 4D		J56H,N	18720	1075	1500	2625	4275
Manual Trans				(200)	(200)	(265)	(265)
4-Cyl. 2.0L/2.4 Liter		C,X		(200)	(200)	(265)	(265)

INTREPID—V6—Equipment Schedule 4
W.B. 113.0"; 3.3 Liter.

Sedan 4D		D46T	18995	475	650	1350	2450
ES Sedan 4D		D56F	22810	650	900	1750	3075
V6 3.5 Liter		F		225	225	300	300

STEALTH—V6—Equipment Schedule 4
W.B. 97.2"; 3.0 Liter.

Hatchback 2D		M84J	25651	1925	2475	3775	5650
R/T Hatchback 2D		M54J	29207	2200	2775	4100	6050
Auto Trans				125	125	165	165

STEALTH—V6 Twin Turbo—Equipment Schedule 2
W.B. 97.2"; 3.0 Liter.

| R/T AWD H'Back 2D | | N74K | 35355 | 4150 | 4900 | 6450 | 8850 |

VIPER—V10—Equipment Schedule 2
W.B. 96.2"; 8.0 Liter.

| RT/10 Roadster 2D | | R65E | 63100 | 20100 | 22450 | 26100 | 32300 |
| GTS Coupe 2D | | R69E | 66700 | 21550 | 24100 | 27800 | 34500 |

1997 DODGE — (1or4)B3-(S27C)-V-#

NEON—4-Cyl.—Equipment Schedule 6
W.B. 104.0"; 2.0 Liter.

Body	Type	VIN	List	Fair	Good	Good	Excellent
Sedan 4D		S27C	12430	350	500	1125	2100
Coupe 2D		S22C	12230	350	475	1075	2050
Highline Sedan 4D		S47C	13170	475	625	1325	2400
Highline Coupe 2D		S42C	12970	425	600	1250	2300

AVENGER—V6—Equipment Schedule 4
W.B. 103.7"; 2.5 Liter.

Coupe 2D		U42N	18857	625	875	1750	3075
ES Coupe 2D		U52N	19971	700	1000	1875	3300
Manual Trans				(250)	(250)	(335)	(335)
4-Cyl. 2.0 Liter		Y		(175)	(175)	(235)	(235)

STRATUS—4-Cyl.—Equipment Schedule 5
W.B. 108.0"; 2.0 Liter, 2.4 Liter.

| Sedan 4D | | J46C | 16545 | 775 | 1100 | 2000 | 3425 |

STRATUS—V6—Equipment Schedule 4
W.B. 108.0"; 2.5 Liter.

ES Sedan 4D		J56H	19390	1125	1575	2725	4400
Manual Trans				(250)	(250)	(335)	(335)
4-Cyl. 2.0L/2.4 Liter		C		(225)	(225)	(300)	(300)

INTREPID—V6—Equipment Schedule 4
W.B. 113.0"; 3.3 Liter.

Sedan 4D		D46T	19955	550	750	1475	2650
ES Sedan 4D		D56F	23460	725	1025	1900	3325
V6 3.5 Liter		F		275	275	365	365

VIPER—V10—Equipment Schedule 2
W.B. 96.2"; 8.0 Liter.

| GTS Coupe 2D | | R69E | 69300 | 21950 | 24500 | 28000 | 34500 |

1998 DODGE — (1,2or4)B3-(S47C)-W-#

NEON—4-Cyl.—Equipment Schedule 6
W.B. 104.0"; 2.0 Liter.

Body	Type	VIN	List	Fair	Good	Good	Excellent
Highline Sedan 4D		S47C	12855	550	750	1500	2700
Highline Coupe 2D		S42C	12655	525	700	1450	2625
Competition Sedan 4D		S27C	14660	800	1125	2075	3550
Competition Coupe 2D		S22Y	14480	775	1100	2025	3500

AVENGER—V6—Equipment Schedule 4
W.B. 103.7"; 2.5 Liter.

Coupe 2D		U42N	18685	725	1025	1950	3375
ES Coupe 2D		U52N	20525	825	1175	2150	3650
Manual Trans				(300)	(300)	(400)	(400)
4-Cyl. 2.0 Liter		Y		(200)	(200)	(265)	(265)

STRATUS—4-Cyl.—Equipment Schedule 5
W.B. 108.0"; 2.0 Liter, 2.4 Liter.

Body Type	VIN	List	Trade-In Fair	Good	Pvt-Party Good	Retail Excellent
Sedan 4D	J46C	16425	850	1175	2150	3650
STRATUS—V6—Equipment Schedule 4						
W.B. 108.0"; 2.5 Liter.						
ES Sedan 4D	J56H	19000	1250	1725	2900	4600
4-Cyl. 2.4 Liter	X		(250)	(250)	(335)	(335)
INTREPID—V6—Equipment Schedule 4						
W.B. 113.0"; 2.7 Liter, 3.2 Liter.						
Sedan 4D	D46R	20235	625	875	1750	3125
ES Sedan 4D	D56J	23015	850	1175	2175	3725
VIPER—V10—Equipment Schedule 2						
W.B. 96.2"; 8.0 Liter.						
RT/10 Roadster 2D	R65E	64700	20475	22925	26300	32200
GTS Coupe 2D	R69E	67900	22350	25000	28400	34800

1999 DODGE — (1,2or4)B3–(S47C)–X–#

Body Type	VIN	List	Trade-In Fair	Good	Pvt-Party Good	Retail Excellent
NEON—4-Cyl.—Equipment Schedule 6						
W.B. 104.0"; 2.0 Liter.						
Highline Sedan 4D	S47C	13320	650	925	1800	3150
Highline Coupe 2D	S42C	13120	625	875	1725	3075
Competition Sedan 4D	S27C	14985	950	1325	2450	4100
Competition Coupe 2D	S22Y	14805	925	1300	2400	4050
AVENGER—V6—Equipment Schedule 4						
W.B. 103.7"; 2.5 Liter.						
Coupe 2D	U42N	19665	850	1225	2325	3975
ES Coupe 2D	U52N	20975	975	1375	2500	4200
Manual Trans			(350)	(350)	(465)	(465)
4-Cyl. 2.0 Liter	Y		(225)	(225)	(300)	(300)
STRATUS—4-Cyl.—Equipment Schedule 5						
W.B. 108.0"; 2.0 Liter, 2.4 Liter.						
Sedan 4D	J46C	16865	950	1325	2425	4100
STRATUS—V6—Equipment Schedule 4						
W.B. 108.0"; 2.5 Liter.						
ES Sedan 4D	J56H	19495	1425	1900	3125	4900
INTREPID—V6—Equipment Schedule 4						
W.B. 113.0"; 2.7 Liter, 3.2 Liter.						
Sedan 4D	D46R	20495	750	1050	2025	3550
ES Sedan 4D	D56J	23340	1000	1400	2550	4250
VIPER—V10—Equipment Schedule 2						
W.B. 96.2"; 8.0 Liter.						
RT/10 Roadster 2D	R65E	66425	20775	23225	26400	32200
GTS Coupe 2D	R69E	68925	22825	25475	28800	35000
Competition Group			1600	1600	2135	2135

2000 DODGE — (1,2or4)B3–(S46C)–Y–#

Body Type	VIN	List	Trade-In Fair	Good	Pvt-Party Good	Retail Excellent
NEON—4-Cyl.—Equipment Schedule 6						
W.B. 105.0"; 2.0 Liter.						
Highline Sedan 4D	S46C	13890	800	1100	2075	3600
ES Sedan 4D	S56C	14680	1075	1525	2700	4375
AVENGER—V6—Equipment Schedule 4						
W.B. 103.7"; 2.5 Liter.						
Coupe 2D	U42N	18840	1025	1450	2625	4325
ES Coupe 2D	U52N	21130	1150	1625	2825	4550
STRATUS—4-Cyl.—Equipment Schedule 5						
W.B. 108.0"; 2.0 Liter, 2.4 Liter.						
SE Sedan 4D	J46C	17525	1075	1500	2675	4350
STRATUS—V6—Equipment Schedule 4						
W.B. 108.0"; 2.5 Liter.						
ES Sedan 4D	J56H	20655	1650	2150	3400	5225
INTREPID—V6—Equipment Schedule 4						
W.B. 113.0"; 2.7 Liter, 3.2 Liter, 3.5 Liter.						
Sedan 4D	D46R	20950	900	1275	2425	4125
ES Sedan 4D	D56J	22530	1175	1650	2875	4625
R/T Sedan 4D	D76V	24995	2100-	2650	3975	5900
VIPER—V10—Equipment Schedule 2						
W.B. 96.2"; 8.0 Liter.						
RT/10 Roadster 2D	R65E	70925	21275	23725	26800	32500
GTS Coupe 2D	R69E	73425	23425	26175	29300	35500
Competition Group			1750	1750	2335	2335

2001 DODGE — (1,2or4)B3–(S46C)–1–#

NEON—4-Cyl.—Equipment Schedule 6
W.B. 105.0"; 2.0 Liter.

Body	Type	VIN	List	Trade-In Fair	Trade-In Good	Pvt-Party Good	Retail Excellent
	Highline Sedan 4D	S46C	14275	**975**	**1375**	**2550**	**4250**
	ES Sedan 4D	S46C	15095	**1325**	**1800**	**3050**	**4800**
	Competition Sedan 4D	S66C	15155	**1350**	**1825**	**3075**	**4850**
	R/T Sedan 4D	S66F	16845	**1625**	**2125**	**3375**	**5225**
STRATUS—4-Cyl.—Equipment Schedule 4							
W.B. 103.7", 108.0" (Sed); 2.4 Liter.							
	SE Sedan 4D	J46X	18425	**1250**	**1750**	**2975**	**4725**
	SE Coupe 2D	G42X	19230	**1175**	**1650**	**2875**	**4625**
	Manual Trans			**(425)**	**(425)**	**(565)**	**(565)**
	V6 2.7/3.0 Liter	U,H		**375**	**375**	**500**	**500**
STRATUS—V6—Equipment Schedule 4							
W.B. 103.7", 108.0" (Sed); 2.7 Liter, 3.0 Liter.							
	ES Sedan 4D	J56U	21010	**1925**	**2475**	**3750**	**5600**
	R/T Coupe 2D	G52H	22115	**2225**	**2800**	**4075**	**6000**
INTREPID—V6—Equipment Schedule 4							
W.B. 113.0"; 2.7 Liter, 3.2 Liter, 3.5 Liter.							
	SE Sedan 4D	D46R	21395	**1075**	**1525**	**2750**	**4500**
	ES Sedan 4D	D56J	23090	**1450**	**1925**	**3200**	**5050**
	R/T Sedan 4D	D66V	25460	**2475**	**3075**	**4400**	**6425**
VIPER—V10—Equipment Schedule 2							
W.B. 96.2"; 8.0 Liter.							
	RT/10 Roadster 2D	R65E	67950	**21750**	**24300**	**27200**	**32900**
	GTS Coupe 2D	R69E	70450	**24100**	**26850**	**30000**	**36100**
	Competition Group			**1875**	**1875**	**2500**	**2500**

2002 DODGE — (1,2or4)B3–(S26C)–2–#

Body	Type	VIN	List	Trade-In Fair	Trade-In Good	Pvt-Party Good	Retail Excellent
NEON—4-Cyl.—Equipment Schedule 6							
W.B. 105.0"; 2.0 Liter.							
	S Sedan 4D	S26C	10570	**950**	**1325**	**2650**	**4525**
	Sedan 4D	S26C	13805	**1000**	**1425**	**2750**	**4650**
	SXT Sedan 4D	S66C	14130	**1150**	**1625**	**3000**	**4950**
	ACR Sedan 4D	S66F	14795	**1275**	**1750**	**3125**	**5125**
	SE Sedan 4D	S46C	15330	**1175**	**1650**	**3050**	**5000**
	ES Sedan 4D	S56C	15860	**1375**	**1850**	**3250**	**5250**
	R/T Sedan 4D	S76F	16680	**1725**	**2225**	**3650**	**5675**
STRATUS—4-Cyl.—Equipment Schedule 4							
W.B. 103.7", 108.0" (Sed); 2.4 Liter.							
	SE Sedan 4D	L46X	18290	**1425**	**1875**	**3300**	**5300**
	SE Coupe 2D	G42X	19340	**1150**	**1600**	**3000**	**4975**
	SXT Sedan 4D	L66X	19345	**1600**	**2075**	**3500**	**5525**
	SXT Coupe 2D	G42G	19695	**1450**	**1925**	**3350**	**5350**
	Manual Trans			**(450)**	**(450)**	**(600)**	**(600)**
	V6 2.7/3.0 Liter	R,H		**400**	**400**	**535**	**535**
STRATUS—V6—Equipment Schedule 4							
W.B. 103.7", 108.0" (Sed); 2.7 Liter, 3.0 Liter.							
	ES Sedan 4D	J56R	21255	**2150**	**2725**	**4150**	**6250**
	R/T Sedan 4D	L76R	22150	**3025**	**3650**	**5150**	**7375**
	R/T Coupe 2D	G52H	22360	**2275**	**2850**	**4300**	**6425**
INTREPID—V6—Equipment Schedule 4							
W.B. 113.0"; 2.7 Liter, 3.5 Liter.							
	SE Sedan 4D	D46R	21230	**1050**	**1475**	**2900**	**4900**
	ES Sedan 4D	D56J	23155	**1425**	**1875**	**3375**	**5500**
	SXT Sedan 4D	D66G	24170	**1675**	**2175**	**3675**	**5800**
	R/T Sedan 4D	D66V	27240	**2575**	**3150**	**4725**	**6975**
VIPER—V10—Equipment Schedule 2							
W.B. 96.2"; 8.0 Liter.							
	RT/10 Roadster 2D	R65E	75500	**22250**	**24800**	**27800**	**33600**
	GTS Coupe 2D	R69E	76000	**24800**	**27625**	**30800**	**36900**
	Competition Group			**2000**	**2000**	**2665**	**2665**

2003 DODGE — (1,2or4)B3–(S46C)–3–#

Body	Type	VIN	List	Trade-In Fair	Trade-In Good	Pvt-Party Good	Retail Excellent
NEON—4-Cyl.—Equipment Schedule 6							
W.B. 105.0"; 2.0 Liter.							
	SE Sedan 4D	S46C	14100	**1525**	**2000**	**3425**	**5475**
	SXT Sedan 4D	S66C	14295	**1500**	**1975**	**3400**	**5425**
	R/T Sedan 4D	S76F	17250	**2125**	**2700**	**4125**	**6225**
NEON—4-Cyl. Turbo—Equipment Schedule 6							
W.B. 105.0"; 2.4 Liter.							
	SRT-4 Sedan 4D	S66S	19965	**5575**	**6500**	**8150**	**10850**
STRATUS—4-Cyl.—Equipment Schedule 4							
W.B. 103.7", 108.0" (Sed); 2.4 Liter.							
	SE Sedan 4D	L46X	18470	**1700**	**2200**	**3650**	**5675**

Body	Type	VIN	List	Trade-In Fair	Trade-In Good	Pvt-Party Good	Retail Excellent
SE Coupe 2D		G42G	20680	1325	1825	3250	5300
SXT Sedan 4D		L46X	18340	1875	2425	3875	5925
SXT Coupe 2D		G42GX	20680	1725	2225	3675	5700
Manual Trans				(500)	(500)	(665)	(665)
V6 2.7/3.0 Liter		R,H		475	475	635	635
STRATUS—V6—Equipment Schedule 4							
W.B. 103.7", 108.0" (Sed); 2.7 Liter, 3.0 Liter.							
ES Sedan 4D		J56U	21980	2600	3175	4650	6800
R/T Sedan 4D		L76R	22340	3425	4125	5600	7925
R/T Coupe 2D		G52H	23175	2675	3275	4725	6900
INTREPID—V6—Equipment Schedule 4							
W.B. 113.0"; 2.7 Liter, 3.5 Liter.							
SE Sedan 4D		D46R	21720	1175	1650	3150	5275
ES Sedan 4D		D56J	25515	1675	2175	3725	5900
SXT Sedan 4D		D66G	24335	1975	2525	4100	6300
VIPER—V10—Equipment Schedule 2							
W.B. 98.8"; 8.3 Liter.							
SRT-10 Roadster 2D		R65Z	83795	26450	29500	32600	38900

2004 DODGE — (1,2or4)B3–(S46C)–4–#

Body	Type	VIN	List	Fair	Good	Good	Excellent
NEON—4-Cyl.—Equipment Schedule 6							
W.B. 105.0"; 2.0 Liter.							
SE Sedan 4D		S46C	14745	1950	2500	3950	6025
SXT Sedan 4D		S66C	15115	1950	2500	3950	6025
R/T Sedan 4D		S76F	17895	2650	3250	4700	6875
NEON—4-Cyl. HO Turbo—Equipment Schedule 6							
W.B. 105.0"; 2.4 Liter.							
SRT-4 Sedan 4D		S66S	20995	6525	7525	9200	11950
STRATUS—4-Cyl.—Equipment Schedule 4							
W.B. 103.7", 108.0" (Sed); 2.4 Liter.							
SXT Sedan 4D		L66X	19155	2250	2825	4300	6425
SXT Coupe 2D		G42G	20535	2050	2600	4050	6150
SE Sedan 4D		L46X	20315	2025	2600	4050	6150
Manual Trans				(525)	(525)	(700)	(700)
V6 2.7 Liter		T		550	550	735	735
STRATUS—V6—Equipment Schedule 4							
W.B. 103.7", 108.0" (Sed); 2.7 Liter, 3.0 Liter.							
ES Sedan 4D		J56R	22600	3075	3725	5225	7450
R/T Sedan 4D		L76R	23135	3900	4625	6150	8500
R/T Coupe 2D		G52H	23030	3075	3725	5225	7450
INTREPID—V6—Equipment Schedule 4							
W.B. 113.0"; 2.7 Liter, 3.5 Liter.							
SE Sedan 4D		D46R	22270	1550	2025	3600	5800
ES Sedan 4D		D56J	26065	2100	2675	4250	6525
SXT Sedan 4D		D66G	24485	2450	3050	4650	6950
VIPER—V10—Equipment Schedule 2							
W.B. 98.8"; 8.3 Liter.							
SRT-10 Roadster 2D		R65Z	84795	29500	32725	35800	42300

2005 DODGE — (1,2or4)B3–(S26C)–5–#

Body	Type	VIN	List	Fair	Good	Good	Excellent
NEON—4-Cyl.—Equipment Schedule 6							
W.B. 105.0"; 2.0 Liter.							
SE Sedan 4D		S26C	15160	2525	3125	4575	6750
SXT Sedan 4D		S56C	15530	2525	3125	4575	6750
Special Edition				100	100	135	135
NEON—4-Cyl. HO Turbo—Equipment Schedule 6							
W.B. 105.0"; 2.4 Liter.							
SRT-4 Sedan 4D		S66S	21195	7575	8700	10350	13250
STRATUS—4-Cyl.—Equipment Schedule 4							
W.B. 103.7", 108.0" (Sed); 2.4 Liter.							
SXT Sedan 4D		L46J	19770	2675	3300	4775	6950
SXT Coupe 2D		G42G	21825	2475	3075	4525	6700
Special Edition				200	200	265	265
Manual Trans				(550)	(550)	(735)	(735)
V6 2.7 Liter		R		600	600	800	800
STRATUS—V6—Equipment Schedule 4							
W.B. 103.7", 108.0" (Sed); 2.7 Liter, 3.0 Liter.							
R/T Sedan 4D		L76T	22250	4300	5100	6600	8975
R/T Coupe 2D		G52H	24320	3600	4300	5800	8100
MAGNUM—V6—Equipment Schedule 4							
W.B. 120.0"; 2.7 Liter, 3.5 Liter.							
SE Sport Wagon 4D		V48T	22495	5775	6725	8450	11200

Body	Type	VIN	List	Trade-In Fair	Trade-In Good	Pvt-Party Good	Retail Excellent
SXT Sport Wagon 4D		V48T	26145	5875	6800	8550	11300
SXT AWD Sport Wagon		Z48V	28525	6450	7450	9200	12050
Special Edition Pkg				200	200	265	265
MAGNUM—V8 HEMI—Equipment Schedule 4							
W.B. 120.0"; 5.7 Liter.							
RT Sport Wagon 4D		V582	29995	8950	10200	12050	15300
RT AWD Sport Wagon		Z582	31995	9325	10625	12500	15800
VIPER—V10—Equipment Schedule 2							
W.B. 98.8"; 8.3 Liter.							
SRT-10 Roadster 2D		R65H	85395	32825	36550	39500	46300

2006 DODGE — (1,2or4)B3–(L46X)–6–#

Body	Type	VIN	List	Trade-In Fair	Trade-In Good	Pvt-Party Good	Retail Excellent
STRATUS—4-Cyl.—Equipment Schedule 4							
W.B. 108.0"; 2.4 Liter.							
SXT Sedan 4D		L46X	20140	3225	3925	5400	7650
V6 2.7 Liter		R	....	750	750	1000	1000
STRATUS—V6—Equipment Schedule 4							
W.B. 108.0"; 2.7 Liter.							
R/T Sedan 4D		L76R	24120	4975	5825	7375	9850
MAGNUM—V6—Equipment Schedule 4							
W.B. 120.0"; 2.7 Liter, 3.5 Liter.							
Sport Wagon 4D		V47T	22995	6850	7925	9650	12550
SXT Sport Wagon 4D		V47T	25935	6950	8000	9750	12650
SXT AWD Sport Wagon		Z47V	29465	7775	8900	10750	13750
V8 5.7 Liter HEMI		2	....	1725	1725	2300	2300
MAGNUM—V8 HEMI—Equipment Schedule 4							
W.B. 120.0"; 5.7 Liter, 6.1 Liter.							
R/T Sport Wagon 4D		V572	30910	10400	11750	13600	16950
R/T AWD Sport Wagon		Z572	32910	10775	12200	14050	17450
SRT8 Sport Wagon 4D		V773	37995	13425	15150	17050	20800
CHARGER—V6—Equipment Schedule 4							
W.B. 120.0"; 2.7 Liter, 3.5 Liter.							
Sedan 4D		A43G	22295	8500	9725	11550	14700
SXT Sedan 4D		A43G	23245	8700	9900	11700	14900
V8 5.7 Liter HEMI		H	....	1725	1725	2300	2300
CHARGER—V8 HEMI—Equipment Schedule 4							
W.B. 120.0"; 5.7 Liter, 6.1 Liter.							
R/T Sedan 4D		A53H	29995	11475	12925	14850	18350
SRT8 Sedan 4D		A73W	38095	15475	17350	19350	23300
Daytona Edition				700	700	935	935
Performance Group				800	800	1065	1065
VIPER—V10—Equipment Schedule 2							
W.B. 98.8"; 8.3 Liter.							
SRT-10 Coupe 2D		R65H	86995	37925	42050	45000	52100
SRT-10 Convertible 2D		R65H	85745	36450	40575	43400	50500
First Edition Group				1000	1000	1335	1335

2007 DODGE — (1,2or4)B3–(B28C)–7–#

Body	Type	VIN	List	Trade-In Fair	Trade-In Good	Pvt-Party Good	Retail Excellent
CALIBER—4-Cyl.—Equipment Schedule 6							
W.B. 103.7"; 1.8 Liter, 2.0 Liter, 2.4 Liter.							
Sport Wagon 4D		B28C	16085	5975	6925	8425	10950
SXT Sport Wagon 4D		B48C	17085	6225	7175	8675	11200
R/T Sport Wagon 4D		B78K	19135	6975	8025	9525	12150
R/T AWD Sport Wagon		E78K	19985	7375	8450	9950	12650
MAGNUM—V6—Equipment Schedule 4							
W.B. 120.0"; 2.7 Liter, 3.5 Liter.							
Sport Wagon 4D		V47T	23545	8150	9325	11050	14100
SXT Sport Wagon 4D		V47V	27405	8250	9425	11150	14200
SXT AWD Sport Wagon		Z47V	29835	9275	10575	12350	15500
V8 5.7 Liter HEMI		2	....	1850	1850	2465	2465
MAGNUM—V8 HEMI—Equipment Schedule 4							
W.B. 120.0"; 5.7 Liter, 6.1 Liter.							
R/T Sport Wagon 4D		V572	31590	11950	13525	15350	18750
R/T AWD Sport Wagon		Z572	33590	12400	14025	15850	19300
SRT8 Sport Wagon 4D		V773	38220	15325	17250	19150	23000
CHARGER—V6—Equipment Schedule 4							
W.B. 120.0"; 2.7 Liter, 3.5 Liter.							
SE Sedan 4D		A43R	23475	10000	11375	13200	16400
SE AWD Sedan 4D		K43G	26440	10425	11800	13550	16850
SXT Sedan 4D		A43G	26580	10475	11900	13700	17000
SXT AWD Sedan 4D		K43G	28830	11850	13425	15250	18650
V6 3.5L HO (SE RWD)		V	....	350	350	465	465

Body	Type	VIN	List	Trade-In Fair	Trade-In Good	Pvt-Party Good	Retail Excellent
	V8 5.7 Liter HEMI	H		1850	1850	2465	2465

CHARGER—V8 HEMI—Equipment Schedule 4
W.B. 120.0"; 5.7 Liter, 6.1 Liter.

Body	Type	VIN	List	Fair	Good	Good	Excellent
	R/T Sedan 4D	A53H	30890	13225	14900	16750	20400
	R/T AWD Sedan 4D	K53H	32890	14350	16125	18050	21800
	SRT8 Sedan 4D	A73W	38695	18125	20275	22200	26500
	Performance Group			800	800	1065	1065
	Super Bee Special Ed			250	250	335	335
	Daytona Edition			800	800	1065	1065

2008 DODGE — (1,2or3)B3—(B28C)—8—#

CALIBER—4-Cyl.—Equipment Schedule 6
W.B. 103.7"; 1.8 Liter, 2.0 Liter, 2.4 Liter.

Body	Type	VIN	List	Fair	Good	Good	Excellent
	SE Sport Wagon 4D	B28C	14580	7250	8325	9625	12050
	SXT Sport Wagon 4D	B48C	17200	7525	8625	9950	12400
	R/T Sport Wagon 4D	B78K	18975	8275	9475	10900	13500
	R/T AWD Sport Wagon	E78K	21075	8725	9950	11350	14050

CALIBER—4-Cyl. Turbo—Equipment Schedule 6
W.B. 103.7"; 2.4 Liter.

Body	Type	VIN	List	Fair	Good	Good	Excellent
	SRT4 Sport Wagon 4D	B68F	23015	10350	11700	13150	16000

AVENGER—4-Cyl.—Equipment Schedule 4
W.B. 108.9"; 2.4 Liter.

Body	Type	VIN	List	Fair	Good	Good	Excellent
	SE Sedan 4D	C46K	19265	7325	8400	9800	12350
	SXT Sedan 4D	C56K	20195	7900	9050	10550	13250
	V6 2.7 Liter	R		750	750	1000	1000

AVENGER—V6—Equipment Schedule 4
W.B. 108.9"; 3.5 Liter.

Body	Type	VIN	List	Fair	Good	Good	Excellent
	R/T Sedan 4D	C76M	23945	9675	10975	12550	15500
	R/T AWD Sedan 4D	D76M	25945	10250	11625	13200	16150

MAGNUM—V6—Equipment Schedule 4
W.B. 120.0"; 2.7 Liter, 3.5 Liter.

Body	Type	VIN	List	Fair	Good	Good	Excellent
	Sport Wagon 4D	V47T	24095	9675	10975	12700	15850
	SXT Sport Wagon 4D	V37V	27900	9750	11075	12850	15950
	SXT AWD Sport Wagon	Z37V	30530	11075	12550	14300	17600
	V8 5.7 Liter HEMI	2		1975	1975	2635	2635

MAGNUM—V8 HEMI—Equipment Schedule 4
W.B. 120.0"; 5.7 Liter, 6.1 Liter.

Body	Type	VIN	List	Fair	Good	Good	Excellent
	R/T Sport Wagon 4D	V572	32455	13825	15575	17300	20900
	R/T AWD Sport Wagon	Z572	34555	14300	16075	17850	21500
	SRT8 Sport Wagon 4D	V773	38580	17450	19550	21400	25400

CHARGER—V6—Equipment Schedule 4
W.B. 120.0"; 2.7 Liter, 3.5 Liter.

Body	Type	VIN	List	Fair	Good	Good	Excellent
	Sedan 4D	A43R	22350	11750	13275	15050	18400
	AWD Sedan 4D	K43G	26615	12250	13825	15600	19000
	SXT Sedan 4D	A33G	26360	12400	14200	15950	19450
	SXT AWD Sedan 4D	K33G	28710	13775	15525	17350	21000
	V8 5.7 Liter HEMI	H		1975	1975	2635	2635

CHARGER—V8 HEMI—Equipment Schedule 4
W.B. 120.0"; 5.7 Liter, 6.1 Liter.

Body	Type	VIN	List	Fair	Good	Good	Excellent
	R/T Sedan 4D	A53H	31430	15200	17100	18850	22600
	R/T AWD Sedan 4D	K53H	33530	16475	18475	20300	24200
	SRT8 Sedan 4D	A73W	38993	21075	23625	25400	29800
	Performance Group			800	800	1065	1065
	Super Bee Special Ed			250	250	335	335
	Daytona Edition			800	800	1065	1065

CHALLENGER—V8 HEMI—Equipment Schedule 4
W.B. 98.8"; 6.1 Liter.

Body	Type	VIN	List	Fair	Good	Good	Excellent
	SRT8 Coupe 2D	J74W	40158	31075	34600	36600	41900

VIPER—V10—Equipment Schedule 2
W.B. 98.8"; 8.4 Liter.

Body	Type	VIN	List	Fair	Good	Good	Excellent
	SRT-10 Coupe 2D	Z69Z	86496	46850	51950	54600	62300
	SRT-10 Convertible 2D	Z65Z	85746	45275	50175	52900	60500

EAGLE

1994 EAGLE — (1,4orJ)E3—(A11A)—R—#

SUMMIT—4-Cyl.—Equipment Schedule 6
W.B. 96.1", 98.4" (Sed), 99.2" (Wag); 1.5 Liter, 1.8 Liter, 2.4 Liter.

Body	Type	VIN	List	Fair	Good	Good	Excellent
	DL Coupe 2D	A11A	10779	500	675	1325	2400
	LX Sedan 4D	A36C	13248	625	850	1625	2875
	ES Sedan 4D	A46C	13824	625	850	1650	2925

Body	Type	VIN	List	Trade-In Fair	Trade-In Good	Pvt-Party Good	Retail Excellent
ES Coupe 2D		A21A	11876	550	750	1500	2700
ESi Sedan 4D		A46C	14607	675	950	1775	3075
ESi Coupe 2D		A31C	12324	600	800	1575	2800
DL Wagon 3D		B30C	14565	1000	1400	2450	4075
LX Wagon 3D		B50G	16233	1025	1425	2525	4150
AWD Wagon 3D		C40G	16285	1175	1625	2775	4450

VISION—V6—Equipment Schedule 4
W.B. 113.0"; 3.3 Liter, 3.5 Liter.

ESi Sedan 4D		D56T	20272	300	425	950	1850
TSi Sedan 4D		D66F	23737	325	450	1025	1925

TALON—4-Cyl.—Equipment Schedule 4
W.B. 97.2"; 1.8 Liter, 2.0 Liter.

DL Coupe 2D		F34B	14080	575	775	1550	2800
ES Coupe 2D		F44E	16438	575	775	1550	2800
Auto Trans				125	125	165	165

TALON—4-Cyl. Turbo—Equipment Schedule 4
W.B. 97.2"; 2.0 Liter.

TSi Coupe 2D		F54F	18479	750	1050	1900	3300
TSi AWD Coupe 2D		G64F	20270	900	1275	2225	3725
Auto Trans				125	125	165	165

1995 EAGLE — (1,4orJ)E3—(A11A)—S—#

SUMMIT—4-Cyl.—Equipment Schedule 6
W.B. 96.1", 98.4" (Sed), 99.2" (Wag); 1.5 Liter, 1.8 Liter, 2.4 Liter.

DL Coupe 2D		A11A	11878	600	825	1600	2875
LX Sedan 4D		A36C	13553	700	1000	1850	3200
ESi Sedan 4D		A46C	15497	800	1125	2025	3475
ESi Coupe 2D		A31C	13257	675	950	1800	3125
DL Wagon 3D		B30C	15799	1125	1575	2700	4375
LX Wagon 3D		B50G	17305	1150	1600	2775	4450
AWD Wagon 3D		C50G	18461	1375	1850	3075	4800

VISION—V6—Equipment Schedule 4
W.B. 113.0"; 3.3 Liter.

ESi Sedan 4D		D56T	20232	300	425	1000	1925
TSi Sedan 4D		D66F	23406	400	575	1175	2175
V6 3.5 Liter		F		175	175	235	235

TALON—4-Cyl.—Equipment Schedule 4
W.B. 98.8"; 2.0 Liter.

ESi Coupe 2D		K44Y	16927	700	975	1850	3200
Auto Trans				125	125	165	165

TALON—4-Cyl. Turbo—Equipment Schedule 4
W.B. 98.8"; 2.0 Liter.

TSi Coupe 2D		K54F	19270	925	1300	2375	4000
TSi AWD Coupe 2D		L54F	20758	1100	1550	2700	4350
Auto Trans				125	125	165	165

1996 EAGLE — (J,2or4)E3—(A31A)—T—#

SUMMIT—4-Cyl.—Equipment Schedule 6
W.B. 96.1", 98.4" (Sed), 99.2" (Wag); 1.5 Liter, 1.8 Liter, 2.4 Liter.

DL Coupe 2D		A31A	12271	675	950	1800	3150
LX Sedan 4D		A56C	14474	825	1175	2125	3600
ESi Sedan 4D		A46C	16411	925	1325	2400	4050
ESi Coupe 2D		A41A	13759	800	1125	2050	3500
DL Wagon 3D		B30C	16347	1300	1800	3000	4725
LX Wagon 3D		B50G	17873	1400	1875	3075	4850
AWD Wagon 3D		C60G	19009	1650	2150	3400	5225

VISION—V6—Equipment Schedule 4
W.B. 113.0"; 3.3 Liter.

ESi Sedan 4D		D56T	19795	400	550	1175	2175
TSi Sedan 4D		D66F	24385	500	650	1350	2450
V6 3.5 Liter		F		225	225	300	300

TALON—4-Cyl.—Equipment Schedule 4
W.B. 98.8"; 2.0 Liter.

Hatchback 2D		K24Y	15954	775	1100	2025	3475
ESi Hatchback 2D		K44Y	17563	800	1125	2050	3500
Auto Trans				125	125	165	165

TALON—4-Cyl. Turbo—Equipment Schedule 4
W.B. 98.8"; 2.0 Liter.

TSi Hatchback 2D		K54F	20140	1075	1500	2625	4300
TSi AWD H'Back 2D		L54F	21695	1300	1800	3000	4725
Auto Trans				125	125	165	165

Body	Type	VIN	List	Trade-In Fair	Good	Pvt-Party Good	Retail Excellent

1997 EAGLE — (2or4)E3–(D56F)–V–#

VISION—V6—Equipment Schedule 4
W.B. 113.0"; 3.5 Liter.

ESi Sedan 4D		D56F	20855	425	600	1275	2350
TSi Sedan 4D		D66F	25035	600	800	1575	2800

TALON—4-Cyl.—Equipment Schedule 4
W.B. 98.8"; 2.0 Liter.

Hatchback 2D		K24Y	16701	875	1250	2350	4000
ESi Hatchback 2D		K44Y	17587	925	1300	2400	4050
Auto Trans				150	150	200	200

TALON—4-Cyl. Turbo—Equipment Schedule 4
W.B. 98.8"; 2.0 Liter.

TSi Hatchback 2D		K54F	20164	1225	1725	2925	4650
TSi AWD H'Back 2D		L54F	21666	1600	2075	3325	5150
Auto Trans				150	150	200	200

1998 EAGLE — 4E3–(K24Y)–W–#

TALON—4-Cyl.—Equipment Schedule 4
W.B. 98.8"; 2.0 Liter.

Hatchback 2D		K24Y	16400	1050	1475	2625	4300
ESi Hatchback 2D		K44Y	18550	1100	1525	2700	4400
Auto Trans				175	175	235	235

TALON—4-Cyl. Turbo—Equipment Schedule 4
W.B. 98.8"; 2.0 Liter.

TSi Hatchback 2D		K54F	21000	1550	2025	3275	5100
TSi AWD H'Back 2D		L54F	22110	1925	2475	3750	5625
Auto Trans				175	175	235	235

FORD

1994 FORD — (1FA,KNJor1ZV)–(T05H)–R–#

ASPIRE—4-Cyl.—Equipment Schedule 6
W.B. 90.7", 93.9" (4D); 1.3 Liter.

Hatchback 2D		T05H	9660	225	325	850	1675
Hatchback 4D		T06H	10525	300	425	1000	1875
SE Hatchback 2D		T07H	10315	300	425	1000	1875

ESCORT—4-Cyl.—Equipment Schedule 6
W.B. 98.4"; 1.8 Liter, 1.9 Liter.

Hatchback 2D		P10J	10510	250	325	875	1725
LX Sedan 4D		P13J	11885	275	400	925	1800
LX Hatchback 2D		P11J	11225	275	375	900	1775
LX Hatchback 4D		P14J	11660	275	400	925	1800
LX Wagon 4D		P15J	12215	350	500	1075	2000
GT Hatchback 2D		P128	12675	325	450	1025	1925

TEMPO—4-Cyl.—Equipment Schedule 5
W.B. 99.9"; 2.3 Liter.

GL Sedan 2D		P31X	12065	250	350	875	1725
GL Sedan 4D		P36X	12065	250	350	875	1725
LX Sedan 4D		P37X	13350	275	375	900	1775
V6 3.0 Liter		U		100	100	135	135

MUSTANG—V6—Equipment Schedule 4
W.B. 101.3"; 3.8 Liter.

Coupe 2D		P404	16455	1025	1450	2525	4175
Convertible 2D		P444	22840	1600	2075	3300	5100
Manual Trans				(150)	(150)	(200)	(200)

MUSTANG—V8—Equipment Schedule 4
W.B. 101.3"; 5.0 Liter.

GT Coupe 2D		P42T	19950	1600	2100	3325	5125
GT Convertible 2D		P45T	24640	2150	2725	4000	5900
Cobra Coupe 2D		P42D	22425	2875	3500	4875	6975
Cobra Convertible 2D		P45D	26845	3450	4175	5600	7850

PROBE—4-Cyl.—Equipment Schedule 5
W.B. 102.8"; 2.0 Liter.

Hatchback 2D		T20A	15975	650	925	1725	3050
SE Pkg				50	50	65	65

PROBE—V6—Equipment Schedule 5
W.B. 102.8"; 2.5 Liter.

GT Hatchback 2D		T22B	19105	875	1250	2200	3675
GT Plus Pkg				50	50	65	65

1994 FORD

Body	Type	VIN	List	Trade-In Fair	Trade-In Good	Pvt-Party Good	Retail Excellent
TAURUS—V6—Equipment Schedule 4							
W.B. 106.0"; 3.0 Liter, 3.2 Liter.							
GL Sedan 4D		P52U	18280	300	425	1000	1925
GL Wagon 4D		P57U	19360	500	675	1350	2450
LX Sedan 4D		P53U	19825	450	600	1250	2275
LX Wagon 4D		P584	21630	600	825	1625	2875
SHO Sedan 4D		P54Y	25240	725	1025	1875	3250
Manual Trans				(200)	(200)	(265)	(265)
V6 3.8 Liter		4		100	100	135	135
THUNDERBIRD—V6—Equipment Schedule 4							
W.B. 113.0"; 3.8 Liter.							
LX Coupe 2D		P624	17325	525	700	1450	2625
V8 4.6 Liter		W		250	250	335	335
THUNDERBIRD—V6 Supercharged—Equipment Schedule 4							
W.B. 113.0"; 3.8 Liter.							
Super Coupe 2D		P64R	23525	950	1325	2400	4025
CROWN VICTORIA—V8—Equipment Schedule 4							
W.B. 114.4"; 4.6 Liter.							
Sedan 4D		P73W	19345	675	950	1800	3125
LX Sedan 4D		P74W	20995	850	1200	2125	3600

1995 FORD — (K,1,2,3or4)(FA,NJorZV)—(T05H)—S—#

Body	Type	VIN	List	Trade-In Fair	Trade-In Good	Pvt-Party Good	Retail Excellent
ASPIRE—4-Cyl.—Equipment Schedule 6							
W.B. 90.7", 93.9" (4D); 1.3 Liter.							
Hatchback 2D		T05H	9860	275	400	950	1850
Hatchback 4D		T06H	10425	350	500	1100	2050
SE Hatchback 2D		T07H	10535	350	500	1100	2050
ESCORT—4-Cyl.—Equipment Schedule 6							
W.B. 98.4"; 1.8 Liter, 1.9 Liter.							
Hatchback 2D		P10J	11115	275	400	950	1850
LX Sedan 4D		P13J	12390	325	450	1025	1950
LX Hatchback 2D		P11J	11785	300	425	975	1875
LX Hatchback 4D		P14J	12220	325	450	1025	1950
LX Wagon 4D		P15J	12775	400	575	1175	2175
GT Hatchback 2D		P128	13530	375	525	1125	2100
CONTOUR—4-Cyl.—Equipment Schedule 5							
W.B. 106.5"; 2.0 Liter.							
GL Sedan 4D		P653	15470	400	550	1150	2125
LX Sedan 4D		P663	16655	425	600	1225	2225
V6 2.5 Liter		L		100	100	135	135
CONTOUR—V6—Equipment Schedule 5							
W.B. 106.5"; 2.5 Liter.							
SE Sedan 4D		P67L	18355	575	775	1550	2800
MUSTANG—V6—Equipment Schedule 4							
W.B. 101.3"; 3.8 Liter.							
Coupe 2D		P404	17550	1175	1650	2800	4475
Convertible 2D		P444	23610	1875	2425	3675	5525
Hard Top (Conv)				500	500	665	665
MUSTANG—V8—Equipment Schedule 4							
W.B. 101.3"; 5.0 Liter.							
GTS Coupe 2D		P42T	19080	1500	1975	3200	4975
GT Coupe 2D		P42T	20710	1900	2450	3700	5550
GT Convertible 2D		P45T	25400	2550	3125	4450	6475
Cobra Coupe 2D		P42D	23060	3350	4050	5500	7700
Cobra Convertible 2D		P45D	27365	4025	4775	6300	8675
Hard Top (Conv)				500	500	665	665
PROBE—4-Cyl.—Equipment Schedule 5							
W.B. 102.8"; 2.0 Liter.							
Hatchback 2D		T20A	15890	775	1100	2000	3425
SE Pkg				50	50	65	65
PROBE—V6—Equipment Schedule 5							
W.B. 102.8"; 2.5 Liter.							
GT Hatchback 2D		T22B	19485	1025	1450	2575	4225
TAURUS—V6—Equipment Schedule 4							
W.B. 106.0"; 3.0 Liter, 3.2 Liter.							
GL Sedan 4D		P52U	18295	425	600	1225	2225
GL Wagon 4D		P57U	19390	625	850	1650	2925
SE Sedan 4D		P52U	19165	450	625	1275	2300
LX Sedan 4D		P53U	20290	550	750	1500	2700
LX Wagon 4D		P584	22090	750	1050	1900	3300
SHO Sedan 4D		P54Y	26465	925	1300	2350	3950
V6 3.8 Liter		4		100	100	135	135

Body Type	VIN	List	Trade-In Fair	Good	Pvt-Party Good	Retail Excellent
THUNDERBIRD—V6—Equipment Schedule 4						
W.B. 113.0"; 3.8 Liter.						
LX Coupe 2D	P624	17895	575	775	1550	2800
V8 4.6 Liter	W		250	250	335	335
THUNDERBIRD—V6 Supercharged—Equipment Schedule 4						
W.B. 113.0"; 3.8 Liter.						
Super Coupe 2D	P64R	24195	1050	1500	2600	4250
CROWN VICTORIA—V8—Equipment Schedule 4						
W.B. 114.4"; 4.6 Liter.						
Sedan 4D	P73W	21315	800	1125	2050	3475
LX Sedan 4D	P74W	23365	1000	1400	2500	4125

1996 FORD — (K,1,2or3)(NJ,FAorZV)–(T05H)–T–#

Body Type	VIN	List	Trade-In Fair	Good	Pvt-Party Good	Retail Excellent
ASPIRE—4-Cyl.—Equipment Schedule 6						
W.B. 90.7", 93.9" (4D); 1.3 Liter.						
Hatchback 2D	T05H	10225	350	475	1100	2050
Hatchback 4D	T06H	11090	450	625	1300	2350
ESCORT—4-Cyl.—Equipment Schedule 6						
W.B. 98.4"; 1.8 Liter, 1.9 Liter.						
Hatchback 2D	P10J	11615	275	375	950	1850
LX Sedan 4D	P13J	12890	350	500	1100	2050
LX Hatchback 2D	P11J	12335	325	450	1025	1950
LX Hatchback 4D	P14J	12720	350	500	1100	2050
LX Wagon 4D	P15J	13275	425	600	1250	2275
GT Hatchback 2D	P12J	14040	400	550	1175	2175
CONTOUR—4-Cyl.—Equipment Schedule 5						
W.B. 106.5"; 2.0 Liter.						
GL Sedan 4D	P653	15980	450	625	1250	2300
LX Sedan 4D	P663	16995	500	650	1350	2450
V6 2.5 Liter	L		125	125	165	165
CONTOUR—V6—Equipment Schedule 5						
W.B. 106.5"; 2.5 Liter.						
SE Sedan 4D	P67L	18865	650	900	1725	3050
MUSTANG—V6—Equipment Schedule 4						
W.B. 101.3"; 3.8 Liter.						
Coupe 2D	P404	18485	1425	1900	3100	4875
Convertible 2D	P444	23935	2125	2700	3975	5875
Manual Trans			(200)	(200)	(265)	(265)
MUSTANG—V8—Equipment Schedule 4						
W.B. 101.3"; 4.6 Liter.						
GT Coupe 2D	P42X	21740	2275	2850	4150	6100
GT Convertible 2D	P45X	26430	3000	3625	5025	7125
Cobra Coupe 2D	P47V	26645	3950	4675	6175	8500
Cobra Convertible 2D	P46V	29415	4675	5525	7125	9700
PROBE—4-Cyl.—Equipment Schedule 5						
W.B. 102.8"; 2.0 Liter.						
SE Hatchback 2D	T20A	16240	900	1275	2375	4000
PROBE—V6—Equipment Schedule 5						
W.B. 102.8"; 2.5 Liter.						
GT Hatchback 2D	T22B	19545	1200	1675	2850	4575
TAURUS—V6—Equipment Schedule 4						
W.B. 108.5"; 3.0 Liter.						
G Sedan 4D	P51U	18545	400	550	1200	2225
GL Sedan 4D	P52U	19390	425	600	1250	2300
GL Wagon 4D	P57U	20470	625	875	1725	3050
LX Sedan 4D	P53S	21680	575	775	1575	2825
LX Wagon 4D	P58S	22700	775	1075	1975	3425
TAURUS—V8—Equipment Schedule 4						
W.B. 108.5"; 3.4 Liter.						
SHO Sedan 4D	P54N	27805	1400	1875	3075	4850
THUNDERBIRD—V6—Equipment Schedule 4						
W.B. 113.0"; 3.8 Liter.						
LX Coupe 2D	P624	17995	650	900	1750	3075
V8 4.6 Liter	W		275	275	365	365
CROWN VICTORIA—V8—Equipment Schedule 4						
W.B. 114.4"; 4.6 Liter.						
Sedan 4D	P73W	21780	900	1275	2375	4000
LX Sedan 4D	P74W	23895	1125	1575	2725	4400

1997 FORD — (K,1,2or3)(NJ,FAorZV)–(T05H)–V–#

ASPIRE—4-Cyl.—Equipment Schedule 6
W.B. 90.7", 93.9" (4D); 1.3 Liter.

Body Type	VIN	List	Trade-In Fair	Trade-In Good	Pvt-Party Good	Retail Excellent
Hatchback 2D	T05H	10655	400	575	1225	2275
Hatchback 4D	T06H	11285	550	750	1550	2800
ESCORT—4-Cyl.—Equipment Schedule 6						
W.B. 98.4"; 2.0 Liter.						
Sedan 4D	P10P	12225	300	400	1000	1925
LX Sedan 4D	P13P	12975	375	525	1125	2125
LX Wagon 4D	P15P	13630	475	625	1325	2400
CONTOUR—4-Cyl.—Equipment Schedule 5						
W.B. 106.5"; 2.0 Liter.						
Sedan 4D	P653	16015	450	625	1300	2400
GL Sedan 4D	P653	16945	550	750	1475	2650
LX Sedan 4D	P663	17480	600	800	1625	2925
V6 2.5 Liter	L		150	150	200	200
CONTOUR—V6—Equipment Schedule 5						
W.B. 106.5"; 2.5 Liter.						
SE Sedan 4D	P67L	19350	775	1100	2025	3475
MUSTANG—V6—Equipment Schedule 4						
W.B. 101.3"; 3.8 Liter.						
Coupe 2D	P404	18810	1725	2225	3475	5350
Convertible 2D	P444	23710	2425	3000	4325	6325
Manual Trans			(250)	(250)	(335)	(335)
MUSTANG—V8—Equipment Schedule 4						
W.B. 101.3"; 4.6 Liter.						
GT Coupe 2D	P42X	20790	2675	3275	4625	6700
GT Convertible 2D	P45X	27010	3450	4150	5550	7800
Cobra Coupe 2D	P47V	27195	4500	5325	6850	9275
Cobra Convertible 2D	P46V	29995	5375	6250	7950	10650
PROBE—4-Cyl.—Equipment Schedule 5						
W.B. 102.8"; 2.0 Liter.						
Hatchback 2D	T20A	16235	1050	1500	2625	4300
PROBE—V6—Equipment Schedule 5						
W.B. 102.8"; 2.5 Liter.						
GT Hatchback 2D	T22B	18735	1475	1950	3200	5000
GTS Pkg			100	100	135	135
TAURUS—V6—Equipment Schedule 4						
W.B. 108.5"; 3.0 Liter.						
G Sedan 4D	P51U	19005	425	600	1275	2350
GL Sedan 4D	P52U	19785	500	675	1400	2525
GL Wagon 4D	P57U	20995	725	1025	1900	3325
LX Sedan 4D	P53S	22880	625	900	1750	3075
LX Wagon 4D	P58S	23985	875	1250	2325	3950
TAURUS—V8—Equipment Schedule 4						
W.B. 108.5"; 3.4 Liter.						
SHO Sedan 4D	P54N	28220	1675	2175	3425	5250
THUNDERBIRD—V6—Equipment Schedule 4						
W.B. 113.0"; 3.8 Liter.						
LX Coupe 2D	P624	18395	700	1000	1875	3300
V8 4.6 Liter	W		300	300	400	400
CROWN VICTORIA—V8—Equipment Schedule 4						
W.B. 114.4"; 4.6 Liter.						
Sedan 4D	P73W	21425	1050	1450	2600	4275
LX Sedan 4D	P74W	23440	1325	1800	3000	4750

1998 FORD — (1,2or3)FA-(P10P)-W-#

Body Type	VIN	List	Trade-In Fair	Trade-In Good	Pvt-Party Good	Retail Excellent
ESCORT—4-Cyl.—Equipment Schedule 6						
W.B. 98.4"; 2.0 Liter.						
LX Sedan 4D	P10P	12490	325	475	1100	2100
SE Sedan 4D	P13P	12995	425	600	1275	2350
SE Wagon 4D	P15P	14195	550	725	1475	2650
ZX2 Coupe 2D	P113	14325	625	850	1675	3000
CONTOUR—4-Cyl.—Equipment Schedule 5						
W.B. 106.5"; 2.0 Liter.						
Sedan 4D	P653	15980	575	775	1525	2750
GL Sedan 4D	P653	17305	650	900	1775	3125
LX Sedan 4D	P653	17760	700	1000	1875	3300
SE Sedan 4D	P663	19475	775	1075	2000	3475
V6 2.5 Liter	L		175	175	235	235
CONTOUR—V6—Equipment Schedule 5						
W.B. 106.5"; 2.5 Liter.						
SVT Sedan 4D	P68G	22900	1775	2275	3525	5375
Manual Trans			0	0	0	0
MUSTANG—V6—Equipment Schedule 4						
W.B. 101.3"; 3.8 Liter.						

Body	Type	VIN	List	Trade-In Fair	Good	Pvt-Party Good	Retail Excellent
Coupe 2D		P404	17805	2025	2600	3900	5800
Convertible 2D		P444	22305	2750	3350	4700	6750
Manual Trans				(300)	(300)	(400)	(400)
MUSTANG—V8—Equipment Schedule 4							
W.B. 101.3"; 4.6 Liter.							
GT Coupe 2D		P42X	21605	3075	3725	5125	7250
GT Convertible 2D		P45X	25605	3950	4675	6150	8450
Cobra Coupe 2D		P47V	26155	5100	5950	7600	10200
Cobra Convertible 2D		P46V	28955	6075	7025	8725	11500
TAURUS—V6—Equipment Schedule 4							
W.B. 108.5"; 3.0 Liter.							
LX Sedan 4D		P52U	19255	625	825	1700	3050
SE Sedan 4D		P52U	19995	750	1050	2000	3475
SE Wagon 4D		P57U	21655	1050	1475	2625	4300
V6 3.0 Liter 24V		S		175	175	235	235
TAURUS—V8—Equipment Schedule 4							
W.B. 108.5"; 3.4 Liter.							
SHO Sedan 4D		P54N	29470	2000	2550	3825	5725
CROWN VICTORIA—V8—Equipment Schedule 4							
W.B. 114.7"; 4.6 Liter.							
Sedan 4D		P73W	21725	1175	1675	2850	4575
LX Sedan 4D		P74W	23740	1575	2075	3300	5125

1999 FORD — (1,2or3)FA-(P10P)-X-#

Body	Type	VIN	List	Trade-In Fair	Good	Pvt-Party Good	Retail Excellent
ESCORT—4-Cyl.—Equipment Schedule 6							
W.B. 98.4"; 2.0 Liter.							
LX Sedan 4D		P10P	12665	400	575	1225	2300
SE Sedan 4D		P13P	13350	525	700	1450	2625
SE Wagon 4D		P15P	14550	625	875	1725	3075
ZX2 Coupe 2D		P113	13705	700	975	1875	3300
S/R Performance Pkg				200	200	265	265
CONTOUR—4-Cyl.—Equipment Schedule 5							
W.B. 106.5"; 2.0 Liter.							
LX Sedan 4D		P653	15810	675	950	1850	3300
SE Sedan 4D		P663	17305	775	1075	2050	3550
V6 2.5 Liter		L		200	200	265	265
CONTOUR—V6—Equipment Schedule 5							
W.B. 106.5"; 2.5 Liter.							
SVT Sedan 4D		P68G	23200	2075	2625	3925	5825
Manual Trans				0	0	0	0
MUSTANG—V6—Equipment Schedule 4							
W.B. 101.3"; 3.8 Liter.							
Coupe 2D		P404	18360	1975	2525	3825	5725
Convertible 2D		P444	22960	2700	3300	4650	6700
Manual Trans				(350)	(350)	(465)	(465)
MUSTANG—V8—Equipment Schedule 4							
W.B. 101.3"; 4.6 Liter.							
GT Coupe 2D		P42X	22760	3100	3750	5150	7275
GT Convertible 2D		P45X	26760	4075	4825	6300	8600
Cobra Coupe 2D		P47V	27995	5350	6225	7850	10450
Cobra Convertible 2D		P46V	31995	6375	7350	9075	11850
TAURUS—V6—Equipment Schedule 4							
W.B. 108.5"; 3.0 Liter.							
LX Sedan 4D		P52U	18670	725	1050	2000	3475
SE Sedan 4D		P53U	18995	900	1250	2375	4050
SE Wagon 4D		P58U	19995	1250	1725	2950	4700
V6 3.0 Liter 24V		S		200	200	265	265
TAURUS—V8—Equipment Schedule 4							
W.B. 108.5"; 3.4 Liter.							
SHO Sedan 4D		P54N	29550	2375	2975	4275	6250
CROWN VICTORIA—V8—Equipment Schedule 4							
W.B. 114.7"; 4.6 Liter.							
Sedan 4D		P73W	22510	1450	1925	3150	4975
LX Sedan 4D		P74W	24530	1875	2425	3675	5550

2000 FORD — (1,2or3)FA-(P33P)-Y-#

Body	Type	VIN	List	Trade-In Fair	Good	Pvt-Party Good	Retail Excellent
FOCUS—4-Cyl.—Equipment Schedule 6							
W.B. 103.0"; 2.0 Liter.							
LX Sedan 4D		P33P	13335	950	1325	2475	4175
SE Sedan 4D		P34P	13980	1125	1575	2775	4500
SE Wagon 4D		P36P	15795	1325	1800	3025	4800
Sony Special Edition				50	50	65	65

2000 FORD

Body	Type	VIN	List	Trade-In Fair	Good	Pvt-Party Good	Retail Excellent
	4-Cyl. 2.0 Liter 16V	3		100	100	135	135
FOCUS—4-Cyl. 16V—Equipment Schedule 6							
W.B. 103.0"; 2.0 Liter.							
ZX3 Hatchback 2D		P313	13075	1325	1800	3025	4800
ZTS Sedan 4D		P383	15580	1325	1800	3025	4800
Kona Limited Edition				50	50	65	65
ESCORT—4-Cyl.—Equipment Schedule 6							
W.B. 98.4"; 2.0 Liter.							
Sedan 4D		P13P	12440	625	900	1775	3150
ZX2 Coupe 2D		P113	12970	850	1200	2300	3950
S/R Performance Pkg				200	200	265	265
CONTOUR—V6—Equipment Schedule 5							
W.B. 106.5"; 2.5 Liter.							
SE Sedan 4D		P66L	17265	825	1175	2275	3950
SE Sport Sedan 4D		P66L	18195	1325	1800	3025	4775
SVT Sedan 4D		P68G	23250	2425	3025	4300	6300
Manual Trans (SVT)				0	0	0	0
4-Cyl. 2.0 Liter		Z,3		(200)	(200)	(265)	(265)
MUSTANG—V6—Equipment Schedule 4							
W.B. 101.3"; 3.8 Liter.							
Coupe 2D		P404	18410	2150	2725	4025	5975
Convertible 2D		P444	23260	2850	3475	4825	6900
Manual Trans				(400)	(400)	(535)	(535)
MUSTANG—V8—Equipment Schedule 4							
W.B. 101.3"; 4.6 Liter.							
GT Coupe 2D		P42X	22905	3350	4050	5450	7625
GT Convertible 2D		P45X	27160	4400	5200	6675	9025
TAURUS—V6—Equipment Schedule 4							
W.B. 108.5"; 3.0 Liter.							
LX Sedan 4D		P52U	18995	750	1075	2050	3600
SE Sedan 4D		P53U	19295	925	1275	2425	4125
SE Wagon 4D		P58U	20450	1325	1800	3050	4825
SES Sedan 4D		P55U	20290	1025	1450	2625	4325
SES Wagon 4D		P55U	20870	1325	1800	3050	4825
SEL Sedan 4D		P56U	21565	1125	1575	2775	4500
V6 3.0 Liter 24V		S		200	200	265	265
CROWN VICTORIA—V8—Equipment Schedule 4							
W.B. 114.7"; 4.6 Liter.							
Sedan 4D		P73W	22610	1775	2275	3550	5425
LX Sedan 4D		P74W	24725	2225	2825	4125	6050

2001 FORD — (1,2or3)FA—(P33P)—1-#

Body	Type	VIN	List	Trade-In Fair	Good	Pvt-Party Good	Retail Excellent
FOCUS—4-Cyl.—Equipment Schedule 6							
W.B. 103.0"; 2.0 Liter.							
LX Sedan 4D		P33P	13645	1100	1550	2750	4500
SE Sedan 4D		P34P	14505	1350	1825	3075	4875
Street Edition				100	100	135	135
4-Cyl. 2.0 Liter 16V		3		100	100	135	135
FOCUS—4-Cyl. 16V—Equipment Schedule 6							
W.B. 103.0"; 2.0 Liter.							
ZX3 Hatchback 2D		P313	13385	1575	2050	3325	5175
ZTS Sedan 4D		P383	15725	1600	2075	3350	5200
SE Wagon 4D		P363	16700	1575	2050	3325	5175
Street Edition				100	100	135	135
S2 Feature Car				100	100	135	135
ZTW				225	225	300	300
Traction Control				200	200	265	265
ESCORT—4-Cyl.—Equipment Schedule 6							
W.B. 98.4"; 2.0 Liter.							
Sedan 4D		P13P	14230	800	1150	2150	3725
ZX2—4-Cyl.—Equipment Schedule 6							
W.B. 98.4"; 2.0 Liter.							
Coupe 2D		P113	13310	1050	1475	2650	4350
MUSTANG—V6—Equipment Schedule 4							
W.B. 101.3"; 3.8 Liter.							
Coupe 2D		P404	18195	2400	3000	4300	6325
Convertible 2D		P444	23610	3075	3750	5125	7225
Manual Trans				(425)	(425)	(565)	(565)
MUSTANG—V8—Equipment Schedule 4							
W.B. 101.3"; 4.6 Liter.							
GT Coupe 2D		P42X	23830	3700	4400	5825	8025
GT Convertible 2D		P45X	28085	4775	5600	7150	9600
Bullitt Coupe 2D		P42X	26830	4675	5500	7025	9450

0709

Body	Type	VIN	List	Trade-In Fair	Trade-In Good	Pvt-Party Good	Retail Excellent
Cobra Coupe 2D		P47V	29205	6275	7250	8875	11550
Cobra Convertible 2D		P46V	33205	7525	8625	10350	13300
TAURUS—V6—Equipment Schedule 4							
W.B. 108.5"; 3.0 Liter.							
LX Sedan 4D		P52U	19455	925	1300	2475	4200
SE Sedan 4D		P53U	19635	1075	1525	2725	4450
SE Wagon 4D		P58U	20790	1600	2075	3350	5225
SES Sedan 4D		P55U	20650	1200	1675	2925	4700
SES Wagon 4D		P55S	21225	1600	2075	3350	5225
SEL Sedan 4D		P56U	22135	1350	1850	3075	4900
V6 3.0 Liter 24V		S		200	200	265	265
CROWN VICTORIA—V8—Equipment Schedule 4							
W.B. 114.7"; 4.6 Liter.							
Sedan 4D		P73W	22620	2125	2700	4000	5925
LX Sedan 4D		P74W	24735	2625	3225	4575	6600

2002 FORD — (1,2or3)FA-(P33P)-2-#

Body	Type	VIN	List	Trade-In Fair	Trade-In Good	Pvt-Party Good	Retail Excellent
FOCUS—4-Cyl.—Equipment Schedule 6							
W.B. 103.0"; 2.0 Liter.							
LX Sedan 4D		P33P	13220	1050	1475	2850	4800
SE Sedan 4D		P34P	14810	1300	1775	3175	5200
SE Wagon 4D		P36P	17015	1525	2000	3450	5500
4-Cyl. 2.0 Liter 16V		3		100	100	135	135
FOCUS—4-Cyl. 16V—Equipment Schedule 6							
W.B. 103.0"; 2.0 Liter.							
ZX3 Hatchback 2D		P313	13700	1525	2000	3450	5500
ZTS Sedan 4D		P383	15730	1550	2050	3500	5525
ZX5 Hatchback 4D		P373	16105	1825	2350	3800	5875
SVT Hatchback 2D		P395	17995	2075	2625	4100	6225
ZTW Wagon 4D		P383	18195	1625	2125	3550	5600
ESCORT—4-Cyl.—Equipment Schedule 6							
W.B. 98.4"; 2.0 Liter.							
Sedan 4D		P13P	14450	950	1325	2650	4525
ZX2—4-Cyl.—Equipment Schedule 6							
W.B. 98.4"; 2.0 Liter.							
Coupe 2D		P113	13655	1175	1650	3050	5000
MUSTANG—V6—Equipment Schedule 4							
W.B. 101.3"; 3.8 Liter.							
Coupe 2D		P404	18635	2600	3200	4700	6925
Convertible 2D		P444	23955	3275	3950	5525	7850
Manual Trans				(450)	(450)	(600)	(600)
MUSTANG—V8—Equipment Schedule 4							
W.B. 101.3"; 4.6 Liter.							
GT Coupe 2D		P42X	24175	3975	4725	6300	8750
GT Convertible 2D		P45X	28430	5150	6000	7675	10350
TAURUS—V6—Equipment Schedule 4							
W.B. 108.5"; 3.0 Liter.							
LX Sedan 4D		P52U	19445	1025	1425	2825	4775
SE Sedan 4D		P53U	20070	1175	1650	3075	5050
SE Wagon 4D		P58U	22005	1800	2300	3775	5850
SES Sedan 4D		P55U	21085	1300	1775	3200	5225
SEL Sedan 4D		P56S	22995	1700	2200	3650	5725
SEL Wagon 4D		P59S	23265	1900	2450	3925	6025
V6 3.0 Liter 24V		S		200	200	265	265
CROWN VICTORIA—V8—Equipment Schedule 4							
W.B. 114.7"; 4.6 Liter.							
Sedan 4D		P73W	23435	2475	3075	4575	6775
LX Sedan 4D		P74W	27025	2975	3625	5175	7475
LX Sport Sedan 4D		P74W	28840	3275	3975	5525	7875
THUNDERBIRD—V8—Equipment Schedule 2							
W.B. 107.2"; 3.9 Liter.							
Soft Top Conv 2D		P60A	35495	9325	10625	12650	16050
Hard Top				550	550	735	735

2003 FORD — (1,2or3)FA-(P33P)-3-#

Body	Type	VIN	List	Trade-In Fair	Trade-In Good	Pvt-Party Good	Retail Excellent
FOCUS—4-Cyl.—Equipment Schedule 6							
W.B. 103.0"; 2.0 Liter, 2.3 Liter.							
LX Sedan 4D		P33P	13505	1325	1825	3225	5275
SE Sedan 4D		P34P	15175	1700	2200	3650	5725
SE Wagon 4D		P36P	17525	1925	2475	3925	6025
4-Cyl. 2.3 Liter 16V		Z		125	125	165	165

Body	Type	VIN	List	Trade-In Fair	Good	Pvt-Party Good	Retail Excellent
FOCUS—4-Cyl. 16V—Equipment Schedule 6							
W.B. 103.0"; 2.0 Liter, 2.3 Liter.							
ZX3 Hatchback 2D	P313	13990	1925	2475	3925	6025
ZX5 Hatchback 4D	P373	15900	2275	2875	4325	6500
ZTS Sedan 4D	P383	16095	1975	2525	4000	6100
ZTW Wagon 4D	P363	17870	2150	2725	4200	6325
ZX3 SVT Hatchback 2D	P395	19100	2600	3175	4675	6875
ZX5 SVT Hatchback 4D	P375	19600	3375	4075	5575	7925
ZX2—4-Cyl.—Equipment Schedule 6							
W.B. 98.4"; 2.0 Liter.							
Coupe 2D	P113	14250	1400	1850	3275	5300
MUSTANG—V6—Equipment Schedule 4							
W.B. 101.3"; 3.8 Liter.							
Coupe 2D	P404	18915	3100	3775	5325	7625
Convertible 2D	P444	24585	3925	4650	6225	8650
Manual Trans			(500)	(500)	(665)	(665)
MUSTANG—V8—Equipment Schedule 4							
W.B. 101.3"; 4.6 Liter.							
GT Coupe 2D	P42X	24785	4700	5525	7175	9775
GT Convertible 2D	P45X	29060	6025	6950	8650	11400
Mach 1 Coupe 2D	P42R	29810	6725	7750	9500	12400
MUSTANG—V8 Supercharged—Equipment Schedule 4							
W.B. 101.3"; 4.6 Liter.							
Cobra Coupe 2D	P48Y	33750	10300	11650	13600	17050
Cobra Convertible 2D	P49Y	37995	11850	13375	15400	19050
10th Anniversary Edition			300	300	400	400
TAURUS—V6—Equipment Schedule 4							
W.B. 108.5"; 3.0 Liter.							
LX Sedan 4D	P52U	20230	1450	1925	3400	5475
SE Sedan 4D	P53U	20345	1750	2250	3725	5825
SE Wagon 4D	P58U	21995	2400	3000	4475	6700
SES Sedan 4D	P55U	21670	1850	2375	3875	5975
SEL Sedan 4D	P56S	23570	2275	2875	4350	6550
SEL Wagon 4D	P59U	23820	2650	3225	4750	6975
V6 3.0 Liter 24V	S		250	250	335	335
CROWN VICTORIA—V8—Equipment Schedule 4							
W.B. 114.7"; 4.6 Liter.							
Sedan 4D	P73W	24510	3075	3700	5275	7575
LX Sedan 4D	P74W	27780	3675	4375	5950	8350
LX Sport Sedan 4D	P74W	29600	4025	4750	6350	8800
THUNDERBIRD—V8—Equipment Schedule 2							
W.B. 107.2"; 3.9 Liter.							
Soft Top Conv 2D	P60A	36895	10975	12450	14450	18050
007 Hard Top Conv 2D	P62A	43995	****	****	****	28500
Hard Top			625	625	835	835

2004 FORD — (1,2or3)FA–(P333)–4–#

Body	Type	VIN	List	Trade-In Fair	Good	Pvt-Party Good	Retail Excellent
FOCUS—4-Cyl.—Equipment Schedule 6							
W.B. 103.0"; 2.0 Liter.							
LX Sedan 4D	P333	14640	1775	2300	3750	5850
SE Wagon 4D	P363	17675	2475	3075	4550	6750
4-Cyl. 2.0/2.3L 16V	PZ		150	150	200	200
FOCUS—4-Cyl. 16V—Equipment Schedule 6							
W.B. 103.0"; 2.0 Liter, 2.3 Liter.							
ZX3 Hatchback 2D	P313	14180	2475	3075	4550	6750
ZX5 Hatchback 4D	P373	15580	2850	3475	4975	7225
SE Sedan 4D	P342	15460	2175	2750	4250	6400
ZTS Sedan 4D	P38Z	16080	2500	3100	4600	6775
ZTW Wagon 4D	P35Z	18290	2775	3400	4925	7150
SVT Hatchback 2D	P395	19375	3175	3850	5375	7675
SVT Hatchback 4D	P375	19630	4125	4875	6425	8825
MUSTANG—V6—Equipment Schedule 4							
W.B. 101.3"; 3.8 Liter, 3.9 Liter.							
Coupe 2D	P404	19160	3750	4475	6050	8475
Convertible 2D	P444	24895	4650	5475	7125	9700
Manual Trans			(525)	(525)	(700)	(700)
MUSTANG—V8—Equipment Schedule 4							
W.B. 101.3"; 4.6 Liter.							
GT Coupe 2D	P42X	24685	5525	6450	8125	10850
GT Convertible 2D	P45X	29025	6975	8025	9750	12650
Mach 1 Coupe 2D	P42R	30260	8025	9200	11050	14100
MUSTANG—V8 Supercharged—Equipment Schedule 4							
W.B. 101.3"; 4.6 Liter.							

Body	Type	VIN	List	Trade-In Fair	Trade-In Good	Pvt-Party Good	Retail Excellent
Cobra Coupe 2D		P48Y	35200	12200	13775	15750	19350
Cobra Convertible 2D		P49Y	39575	13925	15675	17700	21600

TAURUS—V6—Equipment Schedule 4
W.B. 108.5"; 3.0 Liter.

Body	Type	VIN	List	Fair	Good	Good	Excellent
LX Sedan 4D		P52U	20720	1975	2550	4050	6200
SE Sedan 4D		P53U	20855	2375	2950	4450	6675
SE Wagon 4D		P58S	22290	3075	3725	5275	7575
SES Sedan 4D		P55S	22040	2475	3075	4575	6775
SEL Sedan 4D		P56S	23965	2950	3575	5125	7400
SEL Wagon 4D		P59U	24115	3325	4025	5550	7900
V6 3.0 Liter 24V		S		275	275	365	365

CROWN VICTORIA—V8—Equipment Schedule 4
W.B. 114.7"; 4.6 Liter.

Body	Type	VIN	List	Fair	Good	Good	Excellent
Sedan 4D		P73W	24345	3775	4475	6075	8475
LX Sedan 4D		P74W	27370	4425	5250	6875	9425
LX Sport Sedan 4D		P74W	30890	4825	5650	7300	9900

THUNDERBIRD—V8—Equipment Schedule 4
W.B. 107.2"; 3.9 Liter.

Body	Type	VIN	List	Fair	Good	Good	Excellent
Soft Top Conv 2D		P60A	37530	12700	14350	16300	20100
Pacific Coast Conv 2D		P63A	43995	****	****	****	22400
Hard Top				700	700	935	935

2005 FORD — (1,2or3)(FAorZV)–(P31N)–5

FOCUS—4-Cyl.—Equipment Schedule 6
W.B. 102.9"; 2.0 Liter, 2.3 Liter.

Body	Type	VIN	List	Fair	Good	Good	Excellent
ZX3 S Hatchback 2D		P31N	14545	3300	3975	5525	7825
ZX3 SE Hatchback 2D		P31N	15135	3300	3975	5525	7825
ZX3 SES Hatchback 2D		P31N	16235	3475	4175	5700	8025
ZX4 S Sedan 4D		P34N	15145	2950	3575	5125	7400
ZX4 SE Sedan 4D		P34N	15735	2975	3600	5150	7425
ZX4 SES Sedan 4D		P34N	16835	3150	3825	5375	7675
ZX4 ST Sedan 4D		P38Z	18335	3725	4450	6000	8350
ZX5 S Hatchback 4D		P38N	15845	3725	4450	6000	8350
ZX5 SE Hatchback 4D		P37N	16435	3725	4450	6000	8350
ZX5 SES H'Back 4D		P37N	17535	3825	4550	6100	8475
ZXW SE Wagon 4D		P36N	17435	3300	3975	5525	7825
ZXW SES Wagon 4D		P33N	18535	3475	4175	5700	8025

MUSTANG—V6—Equipment Schedule 4
W.B. 107.1"; 4.0 Liter.

Body	Type	VIN	List	Fair	Good	Good	Excellent
Coupe 2D		T80N	20405	6150	7100	8800	11550
Convertible 2D		T84N	24495	7175	8225	10000	12900
Manual Trans				(550)	(550)	(735)	(735)

MUSTANG—V8—Equipment Schedule 4
W.B. 107.1"; 4.6 Liter.

Body	Type	VIN	List	Fair	Good	Good	Excellent
GT Coupe 2D		T82H	25990	9750	11075	12950	16200
GT Convertible 2D		T85H	29995	10625	12050	13950	17400

TAURUS—V6—Equipment Schedule 4
W.B. 108.5"; 3.0 Liter.

Body	Type	VIN	List	Fair	Good	Good	Excellent
SE Sedan 4D		P53U	21145	3075	3700	5275	7575
SE Wagon 4D		P58U	23015	3850	4575	6150	8550
SEL Sedan 4D		P56U	23055	3675	4400	5975	8350
SEL Wagon 4D		P59U	24005	4125	4875	6450	8900
V6 3.0 Liter 24V		S		300	300	400	400

FIVE HUNDRED—V6—Equipment Schedule 4
W.B. 112.9"; 3.0 Liter.

Body	Type	VIN	List	Fair	Good	Good	Excellent
SE Sedan 4D		P231	22795	4025	4700	6350	8775
SE AWD Sedan 4D		P261	24495	4725	5550	7175	9750
SEL Sedan 4D		P241	24795	4700	5525	7125	9700
SEL AWD Sedan 4D		P271	26495	5450	6325	7975	10650
Limited Sedan 4D		P251	26795	5525	6425	8050	10750
Limited AWD Sedan 4D		P281	28495	6225	7200	8875	11600

CROWN VICTORIA—V8—Equipment Schedule 4
W.B. 114.7"; 4.6 Liter.

Body	Type	VIN	List	Fair	Good	Good	Excellent
Sedan 4D		P73W	24810	4575	5400	7050	9625
LX Sedan 4D		P74W	27945	5375	6275	7925	10600
LX Sport Sedan 4D		P74W	31270	5800	6750	8400	11100

THUNDERBIRD—V8—Equipment Schedule 2
W.B. 107.2"; 3.9 Liter.

Body	Type	VIN	List	Fair	Good	Good	Excellent
Soft Top Conv 2D		P60A	38065	14700	16525	18450	22300
50th Anniv Conv 2D		P69A	44430	17700	19900	22000	26300
Hard Top				775	775	1035	1035

GT—V8 Supercharged—Equipment Schedule 2
W.B. 106.7"; 5.4 Liter.

Body	Type	VIN	List	Trade-In Fair	Trade-In Good	Pvt-Party Good	Retail Excellent
Coupe 2D		P90S	143345	****	****	****	137200

2006 FORD—(1,2or3)(F7,FAorZV)–(P31N)–6

FOCUS—4-Cyl.—Equipment Schedule 6
W.B. 102.9"; 2.0 Liter, 2.3 Liter.

ZX3 S Hatchback 2D		P31N	14905	4200	4975	6525	8950
ZX3 SE Hatchback 2D		P31N	15260	4225	5000	6550	8975
ZX3 SES Hatchback 2D		P31N	16020	4440	5200	6750	9200
ZX4 S Sedan 4D		P34N	15205	3825	4550	6100	8500
ZX4 SE Sedan 4D		P34N	15560	3850	4575	6125	8525
ZX4 SES Sedan 4D		P34N	16240	4075	4825	6375	8775
ZX4 ST Sedan 4D		P38Z	17585	4650	5475	7075	9600
ZX5 S Hatchback 4D		P37N	15905	4650	5475	7075	9600
ZX5 SE Hatchback 4D		P37N	16265	4675	5500	7100	9625
ZX5 SES Hatchback 4D		P37N	17030	4775	5575	7200	9725
ZXW SE Wagon 4D		P36N	17280	4200	4975	6525	8950
ZXW SES Wagon 4D		P36N	18040	4400	5200	6750	9200

FUSION—4-Cyl.—Equipment Schedule 4
W.B. 107.4"; 2.3 Liter.

S Sedan 4D		P06Z	18620	4975	5825	7475	10050
SE Sedan 4D		P07Z	19375	5575	6525	8125	10800
SEL Sedan 4D		P08Z	20460	5925	6850	8500	11150
Manual Trans				(575)	(575)	(765)	(765)
V6 3.0 Liter		1		750	750	1000	1000

MUSTANG—V6—Equipment Schedule 4
W.B. 107.1"; 4.0 Liter.

Coupe 2D		T80N	20830	7225	8300	10000	12850
Convertible 2D		T84N	24660	8325	9525	11300	14450
Manual Trans				(575)	(575)	(765)	(765)

MUSTANG—V8—Equipment Schedule 4
W.B. 107.1"; 4.6 Liter.

GT Coupe 2D		T82H	26855	11225	12700	14500	17950
GT Convertible 2D		T85H	31680	12200	13775	15650	19200

TAURUS—6-Cyl.—Equipment Schedule 4
W.B. 108.5"; 3.0 Liter.

SE Sedan 4D		P53U	21515	3850	4575	6150	8575
SEL Sedan 4D		P56U	23665	4500	5325	6925	9450

FIVE HUNDRED—V6—Equipment Schedule 4
W.B. 112.9"; 3.0 Liter.

SE Sedan 4D		P231	22930	4675	5500	7125	9675
SE AWD Sedan 4D		P261	24780	5500	6400	8025	10700
SEL Sedan 4D		P241	24930	5450	6350	7975	10600
SEL AWD Sedan 4D		P271	26780	6225	7200	8850	11550
Limited Sedan 4D		P251	27080	6325	7300	8975	11700
Limited AWD Sedan 4D		P281	28930	7125	8175	9850	12650

CROWN VICTORIA—V8—Equipment Schedule 4
W.B. 114.7"; 4.6 Liter.

Sedan 4D		P73W	25285	5575	6500	8150	10850
LX Sedan 4D		P74W	28830	6425	7400	9100	11850
LX Sport Sedan 4D		P74W	31605	6875	7950	9625	12450

GT—V8 Supercharged—Equipment Schedule 2
W.B. 106.7"; 5.4 Liter.

Coupe 2D		P90S	153345	****	****	****	148800

2007 FORD — (1,2or3)(F7,FAorZV)–(P31N)–7

FOCUS—4-Cyl.—Equipment Schedule 6
W.B. 102.9"; 2.0 Liter, 2.3 Liter.

S Hatchback 2D		P31N	14985	5250	6125	7600	10050
S Hatchback 4D		P37N	15985	5775	6700	8175	10700
S Sedan 4D		P34N	15310	4850	5675	7175	9600
SE Hatchback 2D		P31N	15365	5275	6150	7650	10100
SE Hatchback 4D		P37N	16370	5775	6725	8225	10750
SE Sedan 4D		P34N	15665	4875	5700	7200	9625
SE Wagon 4D		P36N	17385	5250	6125	7600	10050
ST Sedan 4D		P38Z	17690	5775	6700	8175	10700
SES Hatchback 2D		P31N	16125	5525	6425	7925	10400
SES Hatchback 4D		P37N	17135	5900	6825	8350	10900
SES Sedan 4D		P34N	16425	5125	5975	7475	9900
SES Wagon 4D		P36N	18145	5525	6425	7925	10400

FUSION—4-Cyl.—Equipment Schedule 4
W.B. 107.4"; 2.3 Liter.

S Sedan 4D		P06Z	18845	5775	6725	8250	10850

Body Type	VIN	List	Trade-In Fair	Trade-In Good	Pvt-Party Good	Retail Excellent
SE Sedan 4D	P07Z	19705	6425	7425	8975	11600
SEL Sedan 4D	P08Z	20800	6800	7850	9375	12050
Manual Trans			(600)	(600)	(800)	(800)
V6 3.0 Liter	1		750	750	1000	1000
FUSION—V6—Equipment Schedule 4						
W.B. 107.4"; 3.0 Liter.						
SE AWD Sedan 4D	P011	23430	7200	8275	9850	12600
SEL AWD Sedan 4D	P021	24525	7600	8700	10250	13000
MUSTANG—V6—Equipment Schedule 4						
W.B. 107.1"; 4.0 Liter.						
Coupe 2D	T80N	20990	8475	9675	11350	14350
Convertible 2D	T84N	25815	9675	10975	12750	15900
Pony Pkg			200	200	265	265
Manual Trans			(600)	(600)	(800)	(800)
MUSTANG—V8—Equipment Schedule 4						
W.B. 107.1"; 4.6 Liter.						
GT Coupe 2D	T82H	27015	12800	14450	16100	19550
GT Convertible 2D	T85H	28195	14550	16375	18150	21800
Shelby Pkg			1150	1150	1535	1535
MUSTANG—V8 Supercharged—Equipment Schedule 4						
W.B. 107.1"; 5.4 Liter.						
Shelby GT500 Cobra Cpe	T88S	42975	****	****	****	39800
Shelby GT500 Cobra Cnv	T89S	47800	****	****	****	43300
TAURUS—6-Cyl.—Equipment Schedule 4						
W.B. 108.5"; 3.0 Liter.						
SE Sedan 4D	P53U	21745	4725	5525	7050	9500
SEL Sedan 4D	P56U	23895	5450	6350	7875	10400
FIVE HUNDRED—V6—Equipment Schedule 4						
W.B. 112.9"; 3.0 Liter.						
SEL Sedan 4D	P241	23420	6275	7250	8800	11400
SEL AWD Sedan 4D	P271	25270	7150	8200	9775	12500
Limited Sedan 4D	P251	26995	7225	8300	9850	12600
Limited AWD Sedan 4D	P281	28845	8100	9275	10950	13800
CROWN VICTORIA—V8—Equipment Schedule 4						
W.B. 114.6"; 4.6 Liter.						
Sedan 4D	P73W	25390	6825	7900	9450	12150
LX Sedan 4D	P74W	28385	7775	8900	10500	13300

2008 FORD — (1,2or3)(F7,FAorZV)-(P32N)-8-#

Body Type	VIN	List	Trade-In Fair	Trade-In Good	Pvt-Party Good	Retail Excellent
FOCUS—4-Cyl.—Equipment Schedule 6						
W.B. 102.9"; 2.0 Liter.						
S Coupe 2D	P32N	14695	6875	7925	9300	11800
S Sedan 4D	P34N	14995	7050	8100	9525	12050
SE Coupe 2D	P33N	15695	7100	8150	9575	12100
SE Sedan 4D	P35N	15995	7150	8200	9525	11950
SES Coupe 2D	P33N	16695	7225	8300	9700	12250
SES Sedan 4D	P35N	16995	7350	8425	9800	12350
FUSION—4-Cyl.—Equipment Schedule 4						
W.B. 107.4"; 2.3 Liter.						
S Sedan 4D	P06Z	19370	7650	8750	10200	12850
SE Sedan 4D	P07Z	20295	8275	9475	11000	13750
SEL Sedan 4D	P08Z	21000	8725	9950	11450	14300
Manual Trans			(625)	(625)	(835)	(835)
V6 3.0 Liter	1		750	750	1000	1000
FUSION—V6—Equipment Schedule 4						
W.B. 107.4"; 3.0 Liter.						
SE AWD Sedan 4D	P011	24020	9175	10425	11950	14850
SEL AWD Sedan 4D	P021	24725	9550	10875	12400	15350
MUSTANG—V6—Equipment Schedule 4						
W.B. 107.1"; 4.0 Liter.						
Coupe 2D	T80N	20990	9850	11175	12900	16000
Convertible 2D	T84N	25815	11175	12650	14350	17650
Pony Pkg			200	200	265	265
Manual Trans			(625)	(625)	(835)	(835)
MUSTANG—V8—Equipment Schedule 4						
W.B. 107.1"; 4.6 Liter.						
GT Coupe 2D	T82H	27230	14500	16325	18050	21600
GT Convertible 2D	T85H	32055	16475	18475	20200	24000
Bullitt Pkg			1125	1125	1500	1500
Shelby Pkg			1225	1225	1635	1635
MUSTANG—V8 Supercharged—Equipment Schedule 4						
W.B. 107.1"; 5.4 Liter.						
Shelby GT500 Cobra Cpe	T88S	43975	****	****	****	43100

Body	Type	VIN	List	Trade-In Fair	Good	Pvt-Party Good	Retail Excellent
Shelby GT500 Cobra Cnv	....	T89S	48800	****	****	****	**46900**

TAURUS—V6—Equipment Schedule 4
W.B. 112.9"; 3.5 Liter.

Body	Type	VIN	List	Fair	Good	Good	Excellent
SEL Sedan 4D		P24W	23995	9550	10875	12400	15350
SEL AWD Sedan 4D		P27W	25845	11225	12700	14300	17450
Limited Sedan 4D		P25W	27980	10675	12100	13650	16750
Limited AWD Sedan 4D		P28W	29830	12450	14075	15700	18950

CROWN VICTORIA—V8—Equipment Schedule 4
W.B. 114.7"; 4.6 Liter.

Body	Type	VIN	List	Fair	Good	Good	Excellent
Sedan 4D		P73V	26150	8250	9425	11000	13800
LX Sedan 4D		P74V	29145	9250	10525	12150	15100

GEO

1994 GEO — (1Y,JGorJ8)1(MS246)-R-#

METRO—3-Cyl.—Equipment Schedule 6
W.B. 89.2", 93.1" (4D); 1.0 Liter.

Type	VIN	List	Fair	Good	Good	Excellent
XFi Hatchback 2D	MS246	7791	325	450	1025	1925
Hatchback 2D	MR246	8511	325	450	1000	1875
Hatchback 4D	MR646	9011	325	450	1025	1925

PRIZM—4-Cyl.—Equipment Schedule 6
W.B. 97.1"; 1.6 Liter, 1.8 Liter.

Type	VIN	List	Fair	Good	Good	Excellent
Sedan 4D	SK536	12480	575	775	1500	2700
LSi Sedan 4D	SK536	13410	625	900	1700	2975

1995 GEO — (JG,2Cor1Y)1(MR226)-S-#

METRO—3-Cyl.—Equipment Schedule 6
W.B. 93.1"; 1.0 Liter.

Type	VIN	List	Fair	Good	Good	Excellent
Hatchback 2D	MR226	9481	325	450	1025	1950
LSi Hatchback 2D	MR226	9781	375	525	1125	2100
4-Cyl. 1.3 Liter	9	------	50	50	65	65

METRO—4-Cyl.—Equipment Schedule 6
W.B. 93.1"; 1.3 Liter.

Type	VIN	List	Fair	Good	Good	Excellent
Sedan 4D	MR529	10741	375	525	1125	2100
LSi Sedan 4D	MR529	11141	375	525	1125	2100

PRIZM—4-Cyl.—Equipment Schedule 6
W.B. 97.1"; 1.6 Liter, 1.8 Liter.

Type	VIN	List	Fair	Good	Good	Excellent
Sedan 4D	SK526	13435	650	925	1725	3050
LSi Sedan 4D	SK526	14260	750	1050	1900	3300

1996 GEO — (1Yor2C)1(MR226)-T-#

METRO—3-Cyl.—Equipment Schedule 6
W.B. 93.1"; 1.0 Liter.

Type	VIN	List	Fair	Good	Good	Excellent
Coupe 2D	MR226	9988	350	475	1075	2050
LSi Coupe 2D	MR226	10271	450	625	1275	2350
4-Cyl. 1.3 Liter	9	------	75	75	100	100

METRO—3-Cyl.—Equipment Schedule 6
W.B. 93.1"; 1.3 Liter.

Type	VIN	List	Fair	Good	Good	Excellent
Sedan 4D	MR529	11026	450	625	1275	2350
LSi Sedan 4D	MR529	11426	475	625	1325	2400

PRIZM—4-Cyl.—Equipment Schedule 6
W.B. 97.1"; 1.6 Liter, 1.8 Liter.

Type	VIN	List	Fair	Good	Good	Excellent
Sedan 4D	SK526	14300	775	1075	1975	3375
LSi Sedan 4D	SK526	15010	875	1225	2200	3675

1997 GEO — (1Yor2C)1(MR226)-V-#

METRO—3-Cyl.—Equipment Schedule 6
W.B. 93.1"; 1.0 Liter.

Type	VIN	List	Fair	Good	Good	Excellent
Coupe 2D	MR226	10185	375	550	1175	2175

METRO—4-Cyl.—Equipment Schedule 6
W.B. 93.1"; 1.3 Liter.

Type	VIN	List	Fair	Good	Good	Excellent
LSi Sedan 4D	MR529	11546	575	775	1575	2825
LSi Coupe 2D	MR229	10606	550	725	1525	2750

PRIZM—4-Cyl.—Equipment Schedule 6
W.B. 97.1"; 1.6 Liter, 1.8 Liter.

Type	VIN	List	Fair	Good	Good	Excellent
Sedan 4D	SK526	14375	900	1250	2325	3950
LSi Sedan 4D	SK526	15020	1025	1425	2550	4200

1994 HONDA

Body	Type	VIN	List	Trade-In Fair	Trade-In Good	Pvt-Party Good	Retail Excellent

HONDA

1994 HONDA — (1HGorJHM)(EH235)–R–#

CIVIC—4-Cyl.—Equipment Schedule 6
W.B. 101.3", 103.2" (Sed, Cpe); 1.5 Liter, 1.6 Liter.

Body Type	VIN	List	Fair	Good	Pvt-Party Good	Retail Excellent
CX Hatchback 2D	EH235	9750	700	1000	1850	3200
DX Sedan 4D	EG854	12100	1000	1425	2500	4150
DX Coupe 2D	EJ212	11570	900	1275	2225	3725
DX Hatchback 2D	EH236	11150	825	1175	2100	3550
VX Hatchback 2D	EH237	11850	950	1350	2425	4050
Si Hatchback 2D	EH338	13520	1075	1500	2625	4275
LX Sedan 4D	EG855	13300	1050	1450	2575	4225
EX Sedan 4D	EH950	16090	1100	1550	2700	4350
EX Coupe 2D	EJ112	13950	1100	1550	2675	4325

del SOL—4-Cyl.—Equipment Schedule 6
W.B. 93.3"; 1.5 Liter, 1.6 Liter.

Body Type	VIN	List	Fair	Good	Pvt-Party Good	Retail Excellent
S Coupe 2D	EG114	14450	1225	1725	2875	4575
Si Coupe 2D	EH616	16450	1400	1875	3075	4825
VTEC Coupe 2D	EG217	17850	1550	2025	3225	5025

ACCORD—4-Cyl.—Equipment Schedule 3
W.B. 106.9"; 2.2 Liter.

Body Type	VIN	List	Fair	Good	Pvt-Party Good	Retail Excellent
DX Sedan 4D	CD562	15430	1075	1500	2625	4275
DX Coupe 2D	CD722	15230	1100	1550	2675	4325
LX Sedan 4D	CD563	18330	1225	1725	2875	4575
LX Coupe 2D	CD723	18130	1350	1825	3025	4750
LX Wagon 4D	CE182	19280	1275	1750	2950	4650
EX Sedan 4D	CD565	20850	1275	1750	2950	4650
EX Coupe 2D	CD725	20650	1400	1850	3075	4800
EX Wagon 4D	CE189	21850	1575	2050	3250	5050
Manual Trans			(200)	(200)	(265)	(265)

PRELUDE—4-Cyl.—Equipment Schedule 3
W.B. 100.4"; 2.2 Liter, 2.3 Liter.

Body Type	VIN	List	Fair	Good	Pvt-Party Good	Retail Excellent
S Coupe 2D	BA814	18450	1850	2400	3650	5525
Si Coupe 2D	BB215	21750	2025	2600	3875	5750
4WS Coupe 2D	BB216	24510	2050	2625	3900	5775
VTEC Coupe 2D	BB117	24850	2275	2850	4150	6100
Auto Trans			125	125	165	165

1995 HONDA — (1HGorJHM)(EH235)–S–#

CIVIC—4-Cyl.—Equipment Schedule 6
W.B. 101.3", 103.2" (Sed, Cpe); 1.5 Liter, 1.6 Liter.

Body Type	VIN	List	Fair	Good	Pvt-Party Good	Retail Excellent
CX Hatchback 2D	EH235	10130	850	1200	2125	3600
DX Sedan 4D	EG854	12360	1175	1625	2800	4475
DX Coupe 2D	EJ212	11970	1175	1500	2625	4300
DX Hatchback 2D	EH236	11480	1000	1425	2500	4150
VX Hatchback 2D	EH237	12180	1125	1575	2700	4375
Si Hatchback 2D	EH338	13920	1250	1725	2900	4600
LX Sedan 4D	EG855	13700	1200	1675	2850	4550
EX Sedan 4D	EH959	16580	1375	1850	3050	4800
EX Coupe 2D	EJ112	14410	1350	1825	3025	4775

del SOL—4-Cyl.—Equipment Schedule 6
W.B. 93.3"; 1.5 Liter, 1.6 Liter.

Body Type	VIN	List	Fair	Good	Pvt-Party Good	Retail Excellent
S Coupe 2D	EG114	15160	1500	1975	3200	4975
Si Coupe 2D	EH616	17330	1725	2225	3450	5275
VTEC Coupe 2D	EG217	19580	1850	2375	3625	5475

ACCORD—4-Cyl.—Equipment Schedule 3
W.B. 106.9"; 2.2 Liter.

Body Type	VIN	List	Fair	Good	Pvt-Party Good	Retail Excellent
DX Sedan 4D	CD562	15930	1225	1725	2900	4600
LX Sedan 4D	CD563	18880	1475	1950	3175	4975
LX Coupe 2D	CD723	18680	1600	2075	3300	5125
LX Wagon 4D	CE182	19840	1525	2000	3225	5025
EX Sedan 4D	CD565	21440	1525	2000	3225	5025
EX Coupe 2D	CD725	21240	1625	2125	3375	5200
EX Wagon 4D	CE189	22470	1850	2375	3650	5525
Manual Trans			(200)	(200)	(265)	(265)
V6 2.7 Liter			100	100	135	135

PRELUDE—4-Cyl.—Equipment Schedule 3
W.B. 100.4"; 2.2 Liter, 2.3 Liter.

Body Type	VIN	List	Fair	Good	Pvt-Party Good	Retail Excellent
S Coupe 2D	BA814	19930	2200	2775	4075	6000
Si Coupe 2D	BB215	22580	2375	2975	4275	6250

Body	Type	VIN	List	Trade-In Fair	Trade-In Good	Pvt-Party Good	Retail Excellent
SE Coupe 2D		BB217	23780	2375	2975	4300	6300
VTEC Coupe 2D		BB117	25730	2650	3250	4600	6675
Auto Trans				125	125	165	165

1996 HONDA — (1HG,2HGorJHM)(EJ632)–T-#

CIVIC—4-Cyl.—Equipment Schedule 6
W.B. 103.2"; 1.6 Liter.

Body	Type	VIN	List	Fair	Good	Good	Excellent
CX Hatchback 2D		EJ632	10360	975	1350	2475	4125
DX Sedan 4D		EJ652	12630	1425	1875	3100	4875
DX Coupe 2D		EJ612	12225	1225	1725	2900	4625
DX Hatchback 2D		EJ634	11630	1150	1600	2775	4475
HX Coupe 2D		EJ712	13480	1450	1925	3150	4950
LX Sedan 4D		EJ650	13980	1475	1950	3175	4975
EX Sedan 4D		EJ854	16660	1625	2125	3375	5200
EX Coupe 2D		EJ814	15530	1625	2100	3350	5175

del SOL—4-Cyl.—Equipment Schedule 6
W.B. 93.3"; 1.6 Liter.

Body	Type	VIN	List	Fair	Good	Good	Excellent
S Coupe 2D		EH614	15475	1825	2325	3575	5450
Si Coupe 2D		EH616	17695	2025	2600	3875	5775
VTEC Coupe 2D		EG217	19995	2200	2775	4075	6000

ACCORD—4-Cyl.—Equipment Schedule 3
W.B. 106.9"; 2.2 Liter.

Body	Type	VIN	List	Fair	Good	Good	Excellent
DX Sedan 4D		CD562	16280	1475	1975	3175	4975
Anniversary Ed Sed 4D		CD568	17390	1675	2175	3425	5275
LX Sedan 4D		CD563	19270	1850	2350	3625	5500
LX Coupe 2D		C723	19070	1925	2475	3750	5625
LX Wagon 4D		CE182	20170	1850	2400	3675	5525
EX Sedan 4D		CD565	21780	1900	2450	3725	5600
EX Coupe 2D		CD725	21580	2050	2600	3875	5775
EX Wagon 4D		CE189	22810	2200	2775	4075	6000
Manual Trans		1,5,7		(200)	(200)	(265)	(265)
V6 2.7 Liter				175	175	235	235

PRELUDE—4-Cyl.—Equipment Schedule 3
W.B. 100.4"; 2.2 Liter, 2.3 Liter.

Body	Type	VIN	List	Fair	Good	Good	Excellent
S Coupe 2D		BA814	20340	2625	3200	4575	6625
Si Coupe 2D		BB215	23035	2825	3425	4825	6900
VTEC Coupe 2D		BB117	26260	3100	3775	5200	7350
Auto Trans				125	125	165	165

1997 HONDA — (1HG,2HGorJHM)(EJ632)–V-#

CIVIC—4-Cyl.—Equipment Schedule 6
W.B. 103.2"; 1.6 Liter.

Body	Type	VIN	List	Fair	Good	Good	Excellent
CX Hatchback 2D		EJ632	10945	1125	1575	2725	4400
DX Sedan 4D		EJ652	13030	1725	2225	3450	5300
DX Coupe 2D		EJ612	12675	1525	2000	3225	5025
DX Hatchback 2D		EJ634	12195	1375	1850	3075	4850
HX Coupe 2D		EJ712	13795	1750	2275	3525	5375
LX Sedan 4D		EJ657	15045	1800	2325	3575	5425
EX Sedan 4D		EJ854	16875	1975	2525	3825	5700
EX Coupe 2D		EJ814	15645	1925	2500	3750	5625

del SOL—4-Cyl.—Equipment Schedule 6
W.B. 93.3"; 1.6 Liter.

Body	Type	VIN	List	Fair	Good	Good	Excellent
S Coupe 2D		EH614	15475	2100	2675	3975	5875
Si Coupe 2D		EH616	17695	2375	2975	4275	6250
VTEC Coupe 2D		EG217	19995	2575	3175	4500	6550

ACCORD—4-Cyl.—Equipment Schedule 3
W.B. 106.9"; 2.2 Liter.

Body	Type	VIN	List	Fair	Good	Good	Excellent
DX Sedan 4D		CD562	16295	1700	2200	3450	5300
LX Sedan 4D		CD563	19085	2100	2675	3950	5875
LX Coupe 2D		CD723	19185	2225	2825	4125	6075
LX Wagon 4D		CE182	20285	2175	2750	4050	5975
Special Edition 4D		CD560	20795	2100	2675	3950	5875
Special Edition 2D		CD720	20595	2225	2825	4125	6075
EX Sedan 4D		CD565	21895	2250	2850	4150	6100
EX Coupe 2D		CD725	21695	2400	3000	4325	6325
EX Wagon 4D		CE189	22925	2525	3100	4450	6475
Manual Trans		1,5,7		(250)	(250)	(335)	(335)
V6 2.7 Liter				250	250	335	335

PRELUDE—4-Cyl.—Equipment Schedule 3
W.B. 101.8"; 2.2 Liter.

Body	Type	VIN	List	Fair	Good	Good	Excellent
Coupe 2D		BB614	23595	3400	4100	5525	7750
Type SH Coupe 2D		BB615	26095	3750	4450	5950	8225

Body	Type	VIN	List	Trade-In Fair	Trade-In Good	Pvt-Party Good	Retail Excellent
Auto Trans			....	**150**	**150**	**200**	**200**

1998 HONDA — (1HG,2HGorJHM)(EJ632)-W-#

CIVIC—4-Cyl.—Equipment Schedule 6
W.B. 103.2"; 1.6 Liter.

Body	Type	VIN	List	Fair	Good	Good	Excellent
CX Hatchback 2D		EJ632	11045	**1325**	**1800**	**3050**	**4800**
DX Sedan 4D		EJ652	13130	**2000**	**2575**	**3850**	**5750**
DX Coupe 2D		EJ612	12975	**1825**	**2350**	**3625**	**5500**
DX Hatchback 2D		EJ634	12495	**1675**	**2175**	**3450**	**5300**
HX Coupe 2D		EJ712	13795	**2075**	**2650**	**3950**	**5850**
LX Sedan 4D		EJ657	15145	**2125**	**2700**	**3975**	**5900**
EX Sedan 4D		EJ854	16875	**2400**	**3000**	**4300**	**6275**
EX Coupe 2D		EJ814	15645	**2325**	**2925**	**4225**	**6200**

ACCORD—4-Cyl.—Equipment Schedule 3
W.B. 105.1", 106.9" (Sed); 2.3 Liter.

Body	Type	VIN	List	Fair	Good	Good	Excellent
DX Sedan 4D		CF864	16295	**1900**	**2450**	**3725**	**5600**
LX Sedan 4D		CG564	19485	**2400**	**3000**	**4300**	**6275**
LX Coupe 2D		CG324	19485	**2550**	**3150**	**4475**	**6500**
EX Sedan 4D		CG565	21995	**2625**	**3200**	**4550**	**6600**
EX Coupe 2D		CG325	21995	**2800**	**3400**	**4775**	**6825**
Manual Trans		1,3,5,7	....	**(300)**	**(300)**	**(400)**	**(400)**
V6 3.0 Liter VTEC			....	**300**	**300**	**400**	**400**

PRELUDE—4-Cyl.—Equipment Schedule 3
W.B. 101.8"; 2.2 Liter.

Body	Type	VIN	List	Fair	Good	Good	Excellent
Coupe 2D		BB614	23695	**3875**	**4600**	**6075**	**8350**
Type SH Coupe 2D		BB615	26195	**4275**	**5050**	**6550**	**8925**
Auto Trans			....	**175**	**175**	**235**	**235**

1999 HONDA — (1HG,2HGorJHM)(EJ632)-X-#

CIVIC—4-Cyl.—Equipment Schedule 6
W.B. 103.2"; 1.6 Liter.

Body	Type	VIN	List	Fair	Good	Good	Excellent
CX Hatchback 2D		EJ632	11065	**1650**	**2125**	**3400**	**5275**
DX Sedan 4D		EJ652	13200	**2400**	**3000**	**4300**	**6300**
DX Coupe 2D		EJ612	12995	**2200**	**2775**	**4075**	**6025**
DX Hatchback 2D		EJ634	12515	**2025**	**2575**	**3875**	**5800**
VP Sedan 4D		EJ661	15045	**2400**	**3000**	**4300**	**6300**
HX Coupe 2D		EJ712	13815	**2475**	**3075**	**4400**	**6425**
LX Sedan 4D		EJ657	15245	**2525**	**3125**	**4450**	**6475**
EX Sedan 4D		EJ854	17145	**2850**	**3475**	**4850**	**6925**
EX Coupe 2D		EJ814	15865	**2775**	**3375**	**4750**	**6800**
Si Coupe 2D		EM115	17860	**4100**	**4825**	**6300**	**8625**

ACCORD—4-Cyl.—Equipment Schedule 3
W.B. 105.1", 106.9" (Sed); 2.3 Liter.

Body	Type	VIN	List	Fair	Good	Good	Excellent
DX Sedan 4D		CF864	16415	**2200**	**2775**	**4075**	**6025**
LX Sedan 4D		CG564	19605	**2750**	**3350**	**4725**	**6775**
LX Coupe 2D		CG324	19605	**2925**	**3550**	**4925**	**7000**
EX Sedan 4D		CG565	22115	**3025**	**3650**	**5050**	**7150**
EX Coupe 2D		CG325	22115	**3175**	**3850**	**5250**	**7400**
Manual Trans		1,3,5	....	**(350)**	**(350)**	**(465)**	**(465)**
V6 3.0 Liter VTEC			....	**350**	**350**	**465**	**465**

PRELUDE—4-Cyl.—Equipment Schedule 3
W.B. 101.8"; 2.2 Liter.

Body	Type	VIN	List	Fair	Good	Good	Excellent
Coupe 2D		BB614	23865	**4375**	**5200**	**6700**	**9075**
Type SH Coupe 2D		BB615	26365	**4825**	**5625**	**7225**	**9750**
Auto Trans			....	**200**	**200**	**265**	**265**

2000 HONDA — (1HG,2HGorJHM)(ZE137)-Y-#

INSIGHT—3-Cyl. Hybrid—Equipment Schedule 3
W.B. 94.5"; 1.0 Liter.

Body	Type	VIN	List	Fair	Good	Good	Excellent
Hatchback 2D		ZE137	20495	**4325**	**5125**	**6600**	**8925**

CIVIC—4-Cyl.—Equipment Schedule 6
W.B. 103.2"; 1.6 Liter.

Body	Type	VIN	List	Fair	Good	Good	Excellent
CX Hatchback 2D		EJ632	11165	**2000**	**2550**	**3850**	**5750**
DX Sedan 4D		EJ652	13300	**2825**	**3425**	**4800**	**6850**
DX Coupe 2D		EJ612	13095	**2625**	**3225**	**4550**	**6600**
DX Hatchback 2D		EJ634	12615	**2425**	**3025**	**4325**	**6325**
VP Sedan 4D		EJ661	15145	**2825**	**3450**	**4800**	**6875**
HX Coupe 2D		EJ712	13915	**2925**	**3550**	**4925**	**7000**
LX Sedan 4D		EJ657	15345	**2950**	**3575**	**4950**	**7050**
EX Sedan 4D		EJ854	17245	**3300**	**4000**	**5400**	**7550**
EX Coupe 2D		EJ814	15965	**3225**	**3900**	**5300**	**7425**
Si Coupe 2D		EM115	17960	**4625**	**5450**	**6975**	**9425**

2000 HONDA

Body	Type	VIN	List	Trade-In Fair	Good	Pvt-Party Good	Retail Excellent
ACCORD—4-Cyl.—Equipment Schedule 3							
W.B. 105.1", 106.9" (Sed); 2.3 Liter.							
DX Sedan 4D		CF864	16565	2575	3150	4500	6525
LX Sedan 4D		CG564	19755	3150	3825	5225	7350
LX Coupe 2D		CG324	19755	3325	4025	5425	7575
SE Sedan 4D		CG567	20905	3375	4075	5475	7650
EX Sedan 4D		CG565	22265	3500	4200	5600	7825
EX Coupe 2D		CG325	22265	3675	4375	5825	8050
Manual Trans				(400)	(400)	(535)	(535)
V6 3.0 Liter VTEC				400	400	535	535
PRELUDE—4-Cyl.—Equipment Schedule 3							
W.B. 101.8"; 2.2 Liter.							
Coupe 2D		BB614	23915	4950	5800	7375	9900
Type SH Coupe 2D		BB615	26415	5450	6325	7950	10550
Auto Trans				200	200	265	265
S2000—4-Cyl.—Equipment Schedule 2							
W.B. 94.5"; 2.0 Liter.							
Convertible 2D		AP114	32415	6625	7650	9350	12200
Hard Top				625	625	835	835

2001 HONDA — (1HGorJHM)(ZE135)-1-#

Body	Type	VIN	List	Trade-In Fair	Good	Pvt-Party Good	Retail Excellent
INSIGHT—3-Cyl. Hybrid—Equipment Schedule 3							
W.B. 94.5"; 1.0 Liter.							
Hatchback 2D		ZE135	20620	4925	5750	7300	9775
CIVIC—4-Cyl.—Equipment Schedule 6							
W.B. 103.1"; 1.7 Liter.							
DX Sedan 4D		ES152	13400	3250	3925	5325	7475
DX Coupe 2D		EM212	13200	3075	3700	5100	7200
HX Coupe 2D		EM217	14000	3375	4075	5475	7650
LX Sedan 4D		ES155	15450	3425	4125	5525	7700
LX Coupe 2D		EM215	15250	3350	4050	5450	7625
EX Sedan 4D		ES257	17350	3850	4575	6000	8225
EX Coupe 2D		EM219	16850	3750	4475	5900	8125
GX Sedan 4D		EN264	20670	3400	4100	5500	7675
ACCORD—4-Cyl.—Equipment Schedule 3							
W.B. 105.1", 106.9" (Sed); 2.3 Liter.							
DX Sedan 4D		CF864	16640	3025	3650	5050	7150
VP Sedan 4D		CF866	17640	3225	3900	5300	7425
LX Sedan 4D		CG564	20030	3675	4400	5800	8025
LX Coupe 2D		CG324	20030	3850	4575	6025	8275
EX Sedan 4D		CG565	22640	4100	4850	6300	8600
EX Coupe 2D		CG325	22640	4275	5050	6500	8825
Manual Trans		1,5		(425)	(425)	(565)	(565)
V6 3.0 Liter VTEC				450	450	600	600
PRELUDE—4-Cyl.—Equipment Schedule 3							
W.B. 101.8"; 2.2 Liter.							
Coupe 2D		BB614	24040	5575	6500	8075	10700
Type SH Coupe 2D		BB615	26540	6075	7025	8675	11350
Auto Trans				200	200	265	265
S2000—4-Cyl.—Equipment Schedule 2							
W.B. 94.5"; 2.0 Liter.							
Convertible 2D		AP114	32740	7325	8425	10200	13150
Hard Top				650	650	865	865

2002 HONDA — (1HG,SHHorJHM)(ZE135)-2-#

Body	Type	VIN	List	Trade-In Fair	Good	Pvt-Party Good	Retail Excellent
INSIGHT—3-Cyl. Hybrid—Equipment Schedule 3							
W.B. 94.5"; 1.0 Liter.							
Hatchback 2D		ZE135	21720	5400	6275	7975	10700
CIVIC—4-Cyl.—Equipment Schedule 6							
W.B. 101.2", 103.1" (Sed & Cpe); 1.7 Liter, 2.0 Liter.							
DX Sedan 4D		ES151	13450	3625	4325	5900	8300
DX Coupe 2D		EM212	13250	3425	4125	5675	8050
HX Coupe 2D		EM217	14050	3750	4475	6050	8475
LX Sedan 4D		ES155	15550	3825	4550	6150	8575
LX Coupe 2D		EM215	15350	3750	4475	6050	8475
EX Sedan 4D		ES257	17450	4300	5050	6675	9175
EX Coupe 2D		EM219	16950	4200	4950	6575	9050
Si Hatchback 2D		EP335	19440	4575	5400	7075	9675
ACCORD—4-Cyl.—Equipment Schedule 3							
W.B. 105.1", 106.9" (Sed); 2.3 Liter.							
DX Sedan 4D		CF864	16740	3425	4125	5675	8050
VP Sedan 4D		CF866	17740	3650	4350	5925	8325

2002 HONDA

Body	Type	VIN	List	Trade-In Fair	Trade-In Good	Pvt-Party Good	Retail Excellent
LX Sedan 4D		CG564	20130	4175	4950	6550	9025
LX Coupe 2D		CG324	20130	4350	5150	6750	9225
SE Sedan 4D		CG567	21290	4400	5225	6875	9450
SE Coupe 2D		CG320	21290	4575	5400	7050	9650
EX Sedan 4D		CG566	22740	4625	5450	7125	9725
EX Coupe 2D		CG325	22740	4800	5625	7325	9950
Manual Trans		1,5		(450)	(450)	(600)	(600)
V6 3.0 Liter VTEC				500	500	665	665

S2000—4-Cyl.—Equipment Schedule 2
W.B. 94.5"; 2.0 Liter.

Body	Type	VIN	List	Trade-In Fair	Trade-In Good	Pvt-Party Good	Retail Excellent
Convertible 2D		AP114	32840	8000	9175	11050	14300
Hard Top				650	650	865	865

2003 HONDA — (1HG,SHHorJHM)(ZE135)-3-#

INSIGHT—3-Cyl. Hybrid—Equipment Schedule 3
W.B. 94.5"; 1.0 Liter.

Body	Type	VIN	List	Trade-In Fair	Trade-In Good	Pvt-Party Good	Retail Excellent
Hatchback 2D		ZE135	21740	6175	7150	8900	11700

CIVIC—4-Cyl.—Equipment Schedule 6
W.B. 101.2", 103.1" (Sed & Cpe); 1.7 Liter, 2.0 Liter.

Body	Type	VIN	List	Trade-In Fair	Trade-In Good	Pvt-Party Good	Retail Excellent
DX Sedan 4D		ES151	13470	4075	4825	6400	8850
DX Coupe 2D		EM212	13270	3900	4625	6200	8625
HX Coupe 2D		EM217	14170	4250	5000	6600	9075
LX Sedan 4D		ES155	15670	4375	5175	6750	9250
LX Coupe 2D		EM215	15470	4300	5075	6700	9175
EX Sedan 4D		ES257	17520	4900	5725	7400	10050
EX Coupe 2D		EM219	17270	4750	5575	7250	9850
Si Hatchback 2D		EP335	19460	5225	6100	7775	10450

CIVIC—4-Cyl. Hybrid—Equipment Schedule 6
W.B. 103.2"; 1.3 Liter.

Body	Type	VIN	List	Trade-In Fair	Trade-In Good	Pvt-Party Good	Retail Excellent
Sedan 4D		ES956	19990	5700	6625	8325	11050

ACCORD—4-Cyl.—Equipment Schedule 3
W.B. 105.1", 107.9" (Sed); 2.4 Liter.

Body	Type	VIN	List	Trade-In Fair	Trade-In Good	Pvt-Party Good	Retail Excellent
DX Sedan 4D		CM551	17060	3800	4525	6125	8550
LX Sedan 4D		CM564	20460	4825	5650	7325	9950
LX Coupe 2D		CM712	20560	4975	5825	7500	10150
EX Sedan 4D		CM556	22960	5375	6250	7975	10700
EX Coupe 2D		CM716	22960	5525	6450	8150	10900
5-Spd Manual Trans		1,5		(500)	(500)	(665)	(665)
V6 3.0 Liter VTEC				575	575	765	765

S2000—4-Cyl.—Equipment Schedule 2
W.B. 94.5"; 2.0 Liter.

Body	Type	VIN	List	Trade-In Fair	Trade-In Good	Pvt-Party Good	Retail Excellent
Convertible 2D		AP114	33060	8900	10150	12100	15500
Hard Top				675	675	900	900

2004 HONDA — (1HG,SHHorJHM)(ZE135)-4-#

INSIGHT—3-Cyl. Hybrid—Equipment Schedule 3
W.B. 94.5"; 1.0 Liter.

Body	Type	VIN	List	Trade-In Fair	Trade-In Good	Pvt-Party Good	Retail Excellent
Hatchback 2D		ZE135	21870	7025	8075	9850	12750

CIVIC—4-Cyl.—Equipment Schedule 6
W.B. 101.2", 103.1" (Sed & Cpe); 1.7 Liter, 2.0 Liter.

Body	Type	VIN	List	Trade-In Fair	Trade-In Good	Pvt-Party Good	Retail Excellent
DX Sedan 4D		ES151	13500	4525	5325	6975	9550
Value Sedan 4D		ES163	14900	4775	5600	7275	9900
Value Coupe 2D		EM221	13900	4375	5175	6775	9275
HX Coupe 2D		EM217	14200	4750	5550	7225	9850
LX Sedan 4D		ES155	15850	4950	5800	7475	10100
LX Coupe 2D		EM215	15650	4875	5700	7375	10000
EX Sedan 4D		ES257	17750	5550	6475	8150	10900
EX Coupe 2D		EM219	17350	5400	6300	7975	10650
Si Hatchback 2D		EP335	19560	5900	6825	8525	11250
GX Sedan 4D		EN264	21250	5075	5925	7600	10250

CIVIC—4-Cyl. Hybrid—Equipment Schedule 6
W.B. 103.1"; 1.3 Liter.

Body	Type	VIN	List	Trade-In Fair	Trade-In Good	Pvt-Party Good	Retail Excellent
Sedan 4D		ES956	20140	6375	7350	9075	11900

ACCORD—4-Cyl.—Equipment Schedule 3
W.B. 105.1", 107.9" (Sed); 2.4 Liter.

Body	Type	VIN	List	Trade-In Fair	Trade-In Good	Pvt-Party Good	Retail Excellent
DX Sedan 4D		CM551	17190	4275	5050	6650	9150
LX Sedan 4D		CM553	20590	5575	6525	8200	10950
LX Coupe 2D		CM712	20690	5750	6675	8375	11100
EX Sedan 4D		CM556	22990	6225	7175	8900	11700
EX Coupe 2D		CM716	23090	6400	7375	9125	11950
5-Spd Manual Trans		1,5		(525)	(525)	(700)	(700)
V6 3.0 Liter VTEC				650	650	865	865

EQUIPMENT & MILEAGE PAGE 9 TO 23

2004 HONDA

Body	Type	VIN	List	Trade-In Fair	Trade-In Good	Pvt-Party Good	Retail Excellent

S2000—4-Cyl.—Equipment Schedule 2
W.B. 94.5"; 2.2 Liter.

| | Convertible 2D | AP214 | 33290 | 9950 | 11275 | 13300 | 16700 |
| | Hard Top | | | 700 | 700 | 935 | 935 |

2005 HONDA — (1HG,SHHorJHM)(ZE137)-5-#

INSIGHT—3-Cyl. Hybrid—Equipment Schedule 3
W.B. 94.5"; 1.0 Liter.

| | Hatchback 2D | ZE137 | 22045 | 7900 | 9050 | 10800 | 13800 |

CIVIC—4-Cyl.—Equipment Schedule 6
W.B. 101.2", 103.1" (Sed & Cpe); 1.7 Liter, 2.0 Liter.

	DX Sedan 4D	ES151	13675	5075	5925	7575	10200
	Value Sedan 4D	ES163	15075	5400	6275	7975	10650
	Value Coupe 2D	EM221	14075	4925	5775	7425	10050
	HX Coupe 2D	EM217	14375	5325	6200	7875	10550
	LX Sedan 4D	ES155	16025	5600	6525	8175	10900
	LX Coupe 2D	EM215	15825	5525	6425	8075	10800
	LX Special Ed Sed 4D	ES155	16775	5875	6800	8500	11200
	LX Special Ed Cpe 2D	EM215	16575	5775	6725	8400	11100
	EX Sedan 4D	ES257	17925	6300	7275	8975	11750
	EX Coupe 2D	EM219	17025	6100	7050	8725	11450
	EX Special Ed Sed 4D	ES257	18375	6575	7575	9250	12050
	EX Special Ed Cpe 2D	EM219	17975	6425	7425	9125	11900
	Si Hatchback 2D	EP335	19735	6600	7625	9275	12100
	GX Sedan 4D	EN264		5850	6775	8450	11150

CIVIC—4-Cyl. Hybrid—Equipment Schedule 6
W.B. 103.1"; 1.3 Liter.

| | Sedan 4D | ES956 | 20315 | 7100 | 8150 | 9850 | 12750 |

ACCORD—4-Cyl.—Equipment Schedule 3
W.B. 105.1", 107.9" (Sed); 2.4 Liter.

	DX Sedan 4D	CM561	17510	4900	5725	7400	10050
	LX Sedan 4D	CM564	20990	6525	7525	9225	12050
	LX Coupe 2D	CM723	21090	6675	7675	9400	12250
	LX Special Ed Cpe 2D	CM723	25065	7225	8300	10000	12900
	EX Sedan 4D	CM567	23415	7225	8300	10000	12900
	EX Coupe 2D	CM726	23515	7400	8500	10200	13150
	5-Spd Manual Trans			(550)	(550)	(735)	(735)
	V6 3.0 Liter VTEC			725	725	965	965

ACCORD—V6 Hybrid—Equipment Schedule 3
W.B. 107.9"; 3.0 Liter.

| | Sedan 4D | CN364 | 30655 | 10150 | 11525 | 13350 | 16650 |

S2000—4-Cyl.—Equipment Schedule 2
W.B. 94.5"; 2.2 Liter.

| | Convertible 2D | AP214 | 33465 | 11175 | 12650 | 14600 | 18200 |
| | Hard Top | | | 725 | 725 | 965 | 965 |

2006 HONDA — (1HG,SHHorJHM)(ZE137)-6-#

INSIGHT—3-Cyl. Hybrid—Equipment Schedule 3
W.B. 94.5"; 1.0 Liter.

| | Hatchback 2D | ZE137 | 22080 | 8875 | 10100 | 11850 | 14950 |

CIVIC—4-Cyl.—Equipment Schedule 6
W.B. 104.3", 106.3" (Sed); 1.8 Liter, 2.0 Liter.

	DX Sedan 4D	FA152	15110	6575	7575	9250	12050
	DX Coupe 2D	FG112	14910	6475	7450	9150	11900
	LX Sedan 4D	FA155	17060	7625	8725	10450	13350
	LX Coupe 2D	FG116	16860	7500	8600	10350	13250
	EX Sedan 4D	FA158	18810	8375	9575	11300	14400
	EX Coupe 2D	FG118	18810	8100	9275	11050	14050
	Si Coupe 2D	FG215	20600	9250	10525	12300	15450
	GX Sedan 4D	FA465	24990	10000	11325	13100	16300

CIVIC—4-Cyl. Hybrid—Equipment Schedule 6
W.B. 106.3"; 1.3 Liter.

| | Sedan 4D | FA362 | 22400 | 10000 | 11375 | 13200 | 16400 |

ACCORD—4-Cyl.—Equipment Schedule 3
W.B. 105.1", 107.9" (Sed); 2.4 Liter.

	VP Sedan 4D	CM561	19575	5700	6650	8300	11050
	LX Sedan 4D	CM564	21375	7650	8775	10500	13400
	LX Coupe 2D	CM723	21725	7775	8900	10600	13500
	SE Sedan 4D	CM563	22075	7975	9150	10950	13950
	EX Sedan 4D	CM567	23800	8375	9575	11350	14450
	EX Coupe 2D	CM726	23900	8550	9775	11550	14650
	5-Spd Manual Trans			(575)	(575)	(765)	(765)

2006 HONDA

Body	Type	VIN	List	Trade-In Fair	Trade-In Good	Pvt-Party Good	Retail Excellent
V6 3.0 Liter VTEC				800	800	1065	1065

ACCORD—V6 Hybrid—Equipment Schedule 3
W.B. 107.9"; 3.0 Liter.

Body	Type	VIN	List	Fair	Good	Good	Excellent
Sedan 4D		CN364	31540	11575	13075	14900	18350

S2000—4-Cyl.—Equipment Schedule 2
W.B. 94.5"; 2.2 Liter.

Body	Type	VIN	List	Fair	Good	Good	Excellent
Convertible 2D		AP214	34600	12650	14300	16250	20000
Hard Top				750	750	1000	1000

2007 HONDA — (1HG,SHHorJHM)(GD374)–7–#

FIT—4-Cyl.—Equipment Schedule 6
W.B. 96.5"; 1.5 Liter.

Body	Type	VIN	List	Fair	Good	Good	Excellent
Hatchback 4D		GD374	14445	7250	8325	9900	12650
Sport Hatchback 4D		GD376	15765	7975	9150	10800	13600

CIVIC—4-Cyl.—Equipment Schedule 6
W.B. 104.3", 106.3" (Sed); 1.8 Liter, 2.0 Liter.

Body	Type	VIN	List	Fair	Good	Good	Excellent
DX Sedan 4D		FA152	15605	7300	8375	9950	12700
DX Coupe 2D		FG112	15405	7150	8225	9775	12500
LX Sedan 4D		FA155	17555	8425	9625	11250	14200
LX Coupe 2D		FG116	17355	8275	9475	11100	14050
EX Sedan 4D		FA158	19305	9250	10525	12200	15200
EX Coupe 2D		FG118	19305	9000	10250	11900	14900
Si Sedan 4D		FA555	21885	10350	11700	13400	16500
Si Coupe 2D		FG215	21685	10200	11575	13250	16350
GX Sedan 4D		FA465	25185	11025	12500	14150	17400

CIVIC—4-Cyl. Hybrid—Equipment Schedule 6
W.B. 106.3"; 1.3 Liter.

Body	Type	VIN	List	Fair	Good	Good	Excellent
Sedan 4D		FA362	23195	10975	12450	14100	17300

ACCORD—4-Cyl.—Equipment Schedule 3
W.B. 105.1", 107.9" (Sed); 2.4 Liter.

Body	Type	VIN	List	Fair	Good	Good	Excellent
VP Sedan 4D		CM561	20020	6725	7750	9325	12050
LX Sedan 4D		CM564	21520	9000	10250	11900	14900
LX Coupe 2D		CM723	21870	9100	10350	12000	15000
SE Sedan 4D		CM563	22220	9275	10575	12200	15250
EX Sedan 4D		CM567	23945	9800	11125	12800	15900
EX Coupe 2D		CM726	24045	10000	11325	13000	16050
5-Spd Manual Trans				(600)	(600)	(800)	(800)
V6 3.0 Liter VTEC				875	875	1165	1165

ACCORD—V6 Hybrid—Equipment Schedule 3
W.B. 107.9"; 3.0 Liter.

Body	Type	VIN	List	Fair	Good	Good	Excellent
Sedan 4D		CN364	33585	13275	14950	16650	20100

S2000—4-Cyl.—Equipment Schedule 2
W.B. 94.5"; 2.2 Liter.

Body	Type	VIN	List	Fair	Good	Good	Excellent
Convertible 2D		AP214	34845	14450	16225	18150	22000
Hard Top				775	775	1035	1035

2008 HONDA — (1HG,SHHorJHM)(GD374)–8–#

FIT—4-Cyl.—Equipment Schedule 6
W.B. 96.5"; 1.5 Liter.

Body	Type	VIN	List	Fair	Good	Good	Excellent
Hatchback 4D		GD374	14585	8375	9575	11050	13750
Sport Hatchback 4D		GD376	15905	9200	10475	11950	14800

CIVIC—4-Cyl.—Equipment Schedule 6
W.B. 104.3", 106.3" (Sed); 1.8 Liter, 2.0 Liter.

Body	Type	VIN	List	Fair	Good	Good	Excellent
DX Sedan 4D		FA152	15645	8200	9375	10900	13550
DX Coupe 2D		FG112	15445	8075	9225	10700	13400
LX Sedan 4D		FA155	17595	9475	10775	12250	15100
LX Coupe 2D		FG116	17395	9325	10625	12100	14950
EX Sedan 4D		FA158	19345	10400	11750	13300	16200
EX Coupe 2D		FG118	19345	10050	11425	12950	15900
Si Sedan 4D		FA555	21925	11475	12975	14550	17650
Si Coupe 2D		FG215	21725	11375	12850	14400	17500
Si Mugen Sedan 4D		FA555	30135				
GX Sedan 4D		FA465	25225	12300	13925	15550	18800

CIVIC—4-Cyl. Hybrid—Equipment Schedule 6
W.B. 106.3"; 1.3 Liter.

Body	Type	VIN	List	Fair	Good	Good	Excellent
Sedan 4D		FA362	23235	12200	13775	15300	18450

ACCORD—4-Cyl.—Equipment Schedule 3.
W.B. 107.9", 110.2" (Sed); 2.4 Liter.

Body	Type	VIN	List	Fair	Good	Good	Excellent
LX Sedan 4D		CP253	21795	12800	14450	16000	19300
LX-S Coupe 2D		CS113	23295	12975	14600	16300	19700
EX Sedan 4D		CP257	24495	13675	15375	17000	20400
EX Coupe 2D		CS117	24594	13825	15575	17200	20600

EQUIPMENT & MILEAGE PAGE 9 TO 23

Body	Type	VIN	List	Trade-In Fair	Good	Pvt-Party Good	Retail Excellent
	5-Spd Manual Trans		-------	(625)	(625)	(835)	(835)
	6-Spd Manual Trans		-------	0	0	0	0
	V6 3.5 Liter VTEC		-------	950	950	1265	1265
S2000—4-Cyl.—Equipment Schedule 2							
W.B. 94.5"; 2.2 Liter.							
Convertible 2D		AP214	34935	16475	18475	20400	24300
CR Convertible 2D		AP212	37935	18075	20200	22100	26400
	Hard Top		-------	800	800	1065	1065

HYUNDAI

1994 HYUNDAI — (KMHor2HM)(VD12J)–R–#

EXCEL—4-Cyl.—Equipment Schedule 6
W.B. 93.8"; 1.5 Liter.

Body	Type	VIN	List	Fair	Good	Good	Excellent
Hatchback 2D		VD12J	9140	175	250	750	1550
GL Sedan 4D		VF22J	9659	275	400	925	1800
GS Hatchback 2D		VD32J	9659	250	350	875	1725

SCOUPE—4-Cyl.—Equipment Schedule 6
W.B. 93.8"; 1.5 Liter.

Coupe 2D		VE22N	11409	350	475	1050	1950
LS Coupe 2D		VE32N	11889	500	675	1350	2400

SCOUPE—4-Cyl. Turbo—Equipment Schedule 6
W.B. 93.8"; 1.5 Liter.

Coupe 2D		VE32N	13189	600	800	1575	2800

ELANTRA—4-Cyl.—Equipment Schedule 5
W.B. 98.4"; 1.6 Liter, 1.8 Liter.

Sedan 4D		JF22R	12674	225	325	875	1725
GLS Sedan 4D		JF32M	13392	325	450	1025	1950

SONATA—4-Cyl.—Equipment Schedule 5
W.B. 104.3"; 2.0 Liter.

Sedan 4D		BF22F	13984	275	400	950	1850
GLS Sedan 4D		BF32F	15384	350	475	1075	2000
V6 3.0 Liter		T		100	100	135	135

1995 HYUNDAI — KMH(VD14N)–S–#

ACCENT—4-Cyl.—Equipment Schedule 6
W.B. 94.5"; 1.5 Liter.

L Hatchback 2D		VD14N	9674	175	250	750	1550
Hatchback 2D		VD14N	10310	225	325	875	1725
Sedan 4D		VF14N	10834	275	400	950	1850

SCOUPE—4-Cyl.—Equipment Schedule 6
W.B. 93.8"; 1.5 Liter.

Coupe 2D		VE12N	11905	400	575	1175	2175
LS Coupe 2D		VE32N	12735	575	775	1525	2750

SCOUPE—4-Cyl. Turbo—Equipment Schedule 6
W.B. 93.8"; 1.5 Liter.

Coupe 2D		VE32N	14045	675	950	1775	3075

ELANTRA—4-Cyl.—Equipment Schedule 5
W.B. 98.4"; 1.6 Liter, 1.8 Liter.

Sedan 4D		JF13M	13149	275	400	950	1850
SE Sedan 4D		JF23M	13848	275	400	950	1850
GLS Sedan 4D		JF33M	14032	375	525	1125	2100

SONATA—4-Cyl.—Equipment Schedule 5
W.B. 106.3"; 2.0 Liter.

Sedan 4D		CF14F	14614	300	425	1000	1925
GL Sedan 4D		CF24F	15334	350	475	1075	2000
V6 3.0 Liter		T		100	100	135	135

SONATA—V6—Equipment Schedule 5
W.B. 106.3"; 3.0 Liter.

GLS Sedan 4D		CF34T	17804	575	775	1550	2800

1996 HYUNDAI — KMH(VD14N)–T–#

ACCENT—4-Cyl.—Equipment Schedule 6
W.B. 94.5"; 1.5 Liter.

L Hatchback 2D		VD14N	8690	175	250	800	1625
Hatchback 2D		VD14N	10770	275	400	975	1875
Sedan 4D		VF14N	11270	350	475	1075	2050
GT Hatchback 2D		VD34N	11679	425	600	1250	2300

ELANTRA—4-Cyl.—Equipment Schedule 5
W.B. 100.4"; 1.8 Liter.

Sedan 4D		JF24M	13434	400	550	1175	2175

1996 HYUNDAI

Body	Type	VIN	List	Trade-In Fair	Good	Pvt-Party Good	Retail Excellent
Wagon 4D		JW24M	14334	575	775	1575	2825
GLS Sedan 4D		JF34M	14679	500	675	1375	2475
GLS Wagon 4D		JW34M	15329	625	900	1725	3050
SONATA—4-Cyl.—Equipment Schedule 5							
W.B. 106.3"; 2.0 Liter.							
Sedan 4D		CF14F	15204	325	475	1075	2050
GL Sedan 4D		CF24F	16104	375	525	1175	2175
V6 3.0 Liter		T		175	175	235	235
SONATA—V6—Equipment Schedule 5							
W.B. 106.3"; 3.0 Liter.							
GLS Sedan 4D		CF34T	18404	600	825	1575	2800

1997 HYUNDAI — KMH(VD14N)–V–#

ACCENT—4-Cyl.—Equipment Schedule 6
W.B. 94.5"; 1.5 Liter.

Body	Type	VIN	List	Trade-In Fair	Good	Pvt-Party Good	Retail Excellent
L Hatchback 2D		VD14N	9014	225	325	900	1800
GS Hatchback 2D		VD34N	11419	350	475	1100	2100
GL Sedan 4D		VF24N	11819	425	575	1250	2300
GT Hatchback 2D		VD34N	12139	525	725	1450	2625
ELANTRA—4-Cyl.—Equipment Schedule 5							
W.B. 100.4"; 1.8 Liter.							
Sedan 4D		JF24M	13659	475	650	1350	2475
Wagon 4D		JW24M	14559	675	950	1850	3200
GLS Sedan 4D		JF34M	14879	600	825	1650	2975
GLS Wagon 4D		JW34M	15529	775	1100	2025	3475
TIBURON—4-Cyl.—Equipment Schedule 5							
W.B. 97.4"; 1.8 Liter, 2.0 Liter.							
Coupe 2D		JG24M	15609	850	1175	2150	3675
FX Coupe 2D		JG34F	17539	1025	1425	2550	4250
SONATA—4-Cyl.—Equipment Schedule 5							
W.B. 106.3"; 2.0 Liter.							
Sedan 4D		CF24F	15964	375	525	1175	2225
GL Sedan 4D		CF24F	16764	450	625	1300	2400
V6 3.0 Liter		T		250	250	335	335
SONATA—V6—Equipment Schedule 5							
W.B. 106.3"; 3.0 Liter.							
GLS Sedan 4D		CF34T	18964	675	950	1825	3200

1998 HYUNDAI — KMH(VD14N)–W–#

ACCENT—4-Cyl.—Equipment Schedule 6
W.B. 94.5"; 1.5 Liter.

Body	Type	VIN	List	Trade-In Fair	Good	Pvt-Party Good	Retail Excellent
L Hatchback 2D		VD14N	9534	300	425	1050	2050
GS Hatchback 2D		VD34N	11328	425	600	1300	2400
GL Sedan 4D		VF24N	11728	525	700	1450	2650
GSi Hatchback 2D		VD34N	12573	625	850	1725	3075
ELANTRA—4-Cyl.—Equipment Schedule 5							
W.B. 100.4"; 1.8 Liter.							
Sedan 4D		JF24M	13728	600	825	1650	3000
Wagon 4D		JW24M	14628	825	1175	2150	3675
GLS Sedan 4D		JF34M	15023	725	1000	1925	3375
GLS Wagon 4D		JW34M	15673	925	1325	2425	4100
TIBURON—4-Cyl.—Equipment Schedule 5							
W.B. 97.4"; 2.0 Liter.							
Coupe 2D		JG24F	16217	1000	1425	2575	4275
FX Coupe 2D		JG34F	17717	1175	1675	2875	4600
SE Pkg				100	100	135	135
SONATA—4-Cyl.—Equipment Schedule 5							
W.B. 106.3"; 2.0 Liter.							
Sedan 4D		CF24F	15984	450	625	1350	2475
GL Sedan 4D		CF24F	16784	525	725	1500	2700
V6 3.0 Liter		T		300	300	400	400
SONATA—V6—Equipment Schedule 5							
W.B. 106.3"; 3.0 Liter.							
GLS Sedan 4D		CF34T	18984	800	1125	2100	3600

1999 HYUNDAI — KMH(VD14N)–X–#

ACCENT—4-Cyl.—Equipment Schedule 6
W.B. 94.5"; 1.5 Liter.

Body	Type	VIN	List	Trade-In Fair	Good	Pvt-Party Good	Retail Excellent
L Hatchback 2D		VD14N	9434	400	550	1250	2350
GS Hatchback 2D		VD34N	12129	550	725	1575	2875
GL Sedan 4D		VF24N	12129	625	900	1775	3150
Sport Pkg				150	150	200	200

Body	Type	VIN	List	Trade-In Fair	Good	Pvt-Party Good	Retail Excellent
ELANTRA—4-Cyl.—Equipment Schedule 5							
W.B. 100.4"; 2.0 Liter.							
GL Sedan 4D		JF24F	12734	650	900	1825	3200
GL Wagon 4D		JW24F	13634	925	1275	2400	4075
GLS Sedan 4D		JF34F	13934	800	1125	2125	3650
GLS Wagon 4D		JW34F	14434	1050	1475	2650	4325
TIBURON—4-Cyl.—Equipment Schedule 5							
W.B. 97.4"; 2.0 Liter.							
Coupe 2D		JG24F	16229	1200	1700	2900	4650
FX Coupe 2D		JG34F	17729	1500	1975	3225	5050
SONATA—4-Cyl.—Equipment Schedule 5							
W.B. 106.3"; 2.4 Liter.							
Sedan 4D		WF24S	16234	575	800	1675	3050
V6 2.5 Liter		V		350	350	465	465
SONATA—V6—Equipment Schedule 5							
W.B. 106.3"; 2.5 Liter.							
GLS Sedan 4D		WF34V	18234	900	1250	2375	4075
2000 HYUNDAI — KMH(CF35G)-Y-#							
ACCENT—4-Cyl.—Equipment Schedule 6							
W.B. 96.1"; 1.5 Liter.							
L Hatchback 2D		CF35G	9434	475	650	1425	2650
GS Hatchback 2D		CG35G	10784	625	875	1800	3200
GL Sedan 4D		CG45G	10884	725	1025	2000	3500
ELANTRA—4-Cyl.—Equipment Schedule 5							
W.B. 100.4"; 2.0 Liter.							
GLS Sedan 4D		JF34F	12984	1000	1425	2600	4300
GLS Wagon 4D		JW34F	13684	1300	1775	3025	4800
TIBURON—4-Cyl.—Equipment Schedule 5							
W.B. 97.4"; 2.0 Liter.							
Coupe 2D		JG24F	15184	1725	2225	3500	5400
SONATA—4-Cyl.—Equipment Schedule 5							
W.B. 106.3"; 2.4 Liter.							
Sedan 4D		WF14S	15934	700	975	1950	3475
SONATA—V6—Equipment Schedule 5							
W.B. 106.3"; 2.5 Liter.							
GLS Sedan 4D		WF34V	17934	1050	1475	2675	4400
2001 HYUNDAI — KMH(CF35G)-1-#							
ACCENT—4-Cyl.—Equipment Schedule 6							
W.B. 96.1"; 1.5 Liter, 1.6 Liter.							
L Hatchback 2D		CF35G	10184	650	900	1875	3375
GS Hatchback 2D		CH35C	10584	825	1150	2300	4025
GL Sedan 4D		CG45C	10684	925	1300	2475	4225
ELANTRA—4-Cyl.—Equipment Schedule 5							
W.B. 102.7"; 2.0 Liter.							
GLS Sedan 4D		JF35D	13734	1275	1750	3000	4800
GT Hatchback 4D		JF35D	15234	1675	2175	3450	5350
TIBURON—4-Cyl.—Equipment Schedule 5							
W.B. 97.4"; 2.0 Liter.							
Coupe 2D		JG25D	15734	2100	2650	3975	5900
SONATA—4-Cyl.—Equipment Schedule 5							
W.B. 106.3"; 2.4 Liter.							
Sedan 4D		WF15S	15934	900	1250	2425	4150
SONATA—V6—Equipment Schedule 5							
W.B. 106.3"; 2.5 Liter.							
GLS Sedan 4D		WF35V	17934	1300	1800	3050	4875
XG300—V6—Equipment Schedule 3							
W.B. 108.3"; 3.0 Liter.							
Sedan 4D		FU45D	23934	1500	2000	3275	5125
L Sedan 4D		FU45D	25434	1700	2175	3475	5375
2002 HYUNDAI — KMH(CF35G)-2-#							
ACCENT—4-Cyl.—Equipment Schedule 6							
W.B. 96.1"; 1.5 Liter, 1.6 Liter.							
L Hatchback 2D		CF35G	10244	825	1150	2500	4400
GS Hatchback 2D		CH35C	10744	1000	1425	2800	4750
GL Sedan 4D		CG45C	11144	1100	1550	2975	4950
ELANTRA—4-Cyl.—Equipment Schedule 5							
W.B. 102.7"; 2.0 Liter.							
GLS Sedan 4D		DN45D	13794	1550	2050	3500	5550
GT Hatchback 4D		DN55D	15294	1975	2525	4000	6125

2002 HYUNDAI

Body Type	VIN	List	Trade-In Fair	Good	Pvt-Party Good	Retail Excellent
SONATA—4-Cyl.—Equipment Schedule 5						
W.B. 106.3"; 2.4 Liter.						
Sedan 4D	WF15S	16494	1050	1475	2875	4850
V6 2.7 Liter	H		400	400	535	535
SONATA—V6—Equipment Schedule 5						
W.B. 106.3"; 2.7 Liter.						
GLS Sedan 4D	WF35H	17994	1575	2075	3550	5600
LX Sedan 4D	WF35H	19319	1825	2350	3825	5925
XG350—V6—Equipment Schedule 3						
W.B. 108.3"; 3.5 Liter.						
Sedan 4D	FU45E	24494	2700	3300	4800	7025
L Sedan 4D	FU45E	26094	2875	3500	5025	7250

2003 HYUNDAI — KMH(CF35C)-3-#

Body Type	VIN	List	Trade-In Fair	Good	Pvt-Party Good	Retail Excellent
ACCENT—4-Cyl.—Equipment Schedule 6						
W.B. 96.1"; 1.6 Liter.						
Hatchback 2D	CF35C	10745	1050	1475	2900	4900
GL Hatchback 2D	CG35C	11144	1325	1800	3250	5300
GL Sedan 4D	CG45C	11544	1550	2050	3500	5575
GT Hatchback 2D	CG45C	11544	1750	2275	3725	5825
ELANTRA—4-Cyl.—Equipment Schedule 5						
W.B. 102.7"; 2.0 Liter.						
GLS Sedan 4D	DN45D	13794	1975	2525	4025	6150
GT Sedan 4D	DN55D	15444	2350	2950	4425	6625
GT Hatchback 4D	DN55D	15444	2450	3050	4525	6750
TIBURON—4-Cyl.—Equipment Schedule 3						
W.B. 99.6"; 2.0 Liter.						
Coupe 2D	HM65D	16494	3525	4225	5775	8150
5-Spd Manual Trans			(450)	(450)	(600)	(600)
TIBURON—V6—Equipment Schedule 3						
W.B. 99.6"; 2.7 Liter.						
GT Coupe 2D	HN65F	19244	4075	4825	6400	8850
5-Spd Manual Trans			(450)	(450)	(600)	(600)
SONATA—4-Cyl.—Equipment Schedule 5						
W.B. 106.3"; 2.4 Liter.						
Sedan 4D	WF15S	16494	1275	1775	3225	5325
V6 2.7 Liter	H		475	475	635	635
SONATA—V6—Equipment Schedule 5						
W.B. 106.3"; 2.7 Liter.						
GLS Sedan 4D	WF35H	18094	1900	2450	3975	6125
LX Sedan 4D	WF35H	19319	2200	2775	4300	6500
XG350—V6—Equipment Schedule 3						
W.B. 108.3"; 3.5 Liter.						
Sedan 4D	FU45E	24494	2900	3525	5075	7325
L Sedan 4D	FU45E	26094	3100	3775	5300	7600

2004 HYUNDAI — KMH(CF35C)-4-#

Body Type	VIN	List	Trade-In Fair	Good	Pvt-Party Good	Retail Excellent
ACCENT—4-Cyl.—Equipment Schedule 6						
W.B. 96.1"; 1.6 Liter.						
Hatchback 2D	CF35C	11289	1500	1975	3475	5550
GL Hatchback 2D	CG35C	11439	1850	2375	3875	6000
GL Sedan 4D	CG45C	11839	2150	2725	4250	6425
GT Hatchback 2D	CG45C	11939	2325	2925	4425	6650
ELANTRA—4-Cyl.—Equipment Schedule 5						
W.B. 102.7"; 2.0 Liter.						
GLS Sedan 4D	DN45D	14639	2550	3150	4675	6900
GT Sedan 4D	DN55D	16189	2950	3575	5125	7400
GT Hatchback 4D	DN55D	16189	3025	3675	5200	7500
TIBURON—4-Cyl.—Equipment Schedule 3						
W.B. 99.6"; 2.0 Liter.						
Coupe 2D	HM65D	18439	4125	4875	6450	8900
5-Spd Manual Trans			(475)	(475)	(635)	(635)
TIBURON—V6—Equipment Schedule 3						
W.B. 99.6"; 2.7 Liter.						
GT Coupe 2D	HN65F	19639	4700	5525	7175	9750
GT Special Ed Cpe 2D	HN65F	20987	5350	6225	7900	10550
5-Spd Manual Trans			(475)	(475)	(635)	(635)
SONATA—4-Cyl.—Equipment Schedule 5						
W.B. 106.3"; 2.4 Liter.						
Sedan 4D	WF15S	17339	1700	2200	3725	5875
V6 2.7 Liter	H		550	550	735	735

Body	Type	VIN	List	Trade-In Fair	Trade-In Good	Pvt-Party Good	Retail Excellent
SONATA—V6—Equipment Schedule 5							
W.B. 106.3"; 2.7 Liter.							
GLS Sedan 4D		WF35H	19339	2375	2975	4500	6750
LX Sedan 4D		WF35H	20339	2700	3300	4875	7175
XG350—V6—Equipment Schedule 5							
W.B. 108.3"; 3.5 Liter.							
Sedan 4D		FU45E	24589	3175	3850	5375	7675
L Sedan 4D		FU45E	26189	3425	4125	5625	7975

2005 HYUNDAI — KMH(CG35C)-5-#

Body	Type	VIN	List	Trade-In Fair	Trade-In Good	Pvt-Party Good	Retail Excellent
ACCENT—4-Cyl.—Equipment Schedule 6							
W.B. 96.1"; 1.6 Liter.							
GLS Hatchback 2D		CG35C	11339	2525	3100	4650	6875
GLS Sedan 4D		CG45C	11839	2925	3550	5100	7400
GT Hatchback 2D		CG35C	11939	3075	3725	5275	7575
ELANTRA—4-Cyl.—Equipment Schedule 5							
W.B. 102.7"; 2.0 Liter.							
GLS Sedan 4D		DN46D	14644	3250	3950	5500	7825
GLS Hatchback 4D		DN56D	14944	3425	4125	5675	8025
GT Sedan 4D		DN46D	16194	3675	4375	5950	8325
GT Hatchback 4D		DN56D	16194	3775	4475	6050	8425
TIBURON—4-Cyl.—Equipment Schedule 3							
W.B. 99.6"; 2.0 Liter.							
GS Coupe 2D		HM65D	17494	4800	5625	7275	9850
5-Spd Manual Trans				(500)	(500)	(665)	(665)
TIBURON—V6—Equipment Schedule 3							
W.B. 99.6"; 2.0 Liter.							
GT Coupe 2D		HN65F	19494	5500	6375	8025	10700
SE Coupe 2D		HN65F	20594	6100	7050	8725	11450
5-Spd Manual Trans				(500)	(500)	(665)	(665)
SONATA—4-Cyl.—Equipment Schedule 5							
W.B. 106.3"; 2.4 Liter.							
GL Sedan 4D		WF25S	17394	2225	2825	4375	6650
V6 2.7 Liter		H		600	600	800	800
SONATA—V6—Equipment Schedule 3							
W.B. 106.3"; 2.7 Liter.							
GLS Sedan 4D		WF35H	19394	3000	3625	5225	7575
LX Sedan 4D		WF35H	20394	3350	4050	5625	8025
XG350—V6—Equipment Schedule 3							
W.B. 108.3"; 3.5 Liter.							
Sedan 4D		FU45E	24994	3600	4300	5850	8200
L Sedan 4D		FU45E	26594	3875	4600	6150	8525

2006 HYUNDAI — KMH(CN46C)-6-#

Body	Type	VIN	List	Trade-In Fair	Trade-In Good	Pvt-Party Good	Retail Excellent
ACCENT—4-Cyl.—Equipment Schedule 6							
W.B. 98.4"; 1.6 Liter.							
GLS Sedan 4D		CN46C	12995	3950	4675	6250	8675
ELANTRA—4-Cyl.—Equipment Schedule 5							
W.B. 102.7"; 2.0 Liter.							
GLS Sedan 4D		DN46D	15095	4175	4950	6525	8975
GLS Hatchback 4D		DN56D	15495	4325	5125	6725	9200
Limited Sedan 4D		DN46D	16045	4625	5450	7075	9625
GT Hatchback 4D		DN56D	16415	4675	5500	7125	9675
TIBURON—4-Cyl.—Equipment Schedule 3							
W.B. 99.6"; 2.0 Liter.							
GS Coupe 2D		HM65D	17595	5625	6550	8200	10900
5-Spd Manual Trans				(525)	(525)	(700)	(700)
TIBURON—V6—Equipment Schedule 3							
W.B. 99.6"; 2.7 Liter.							
GT Coupe 2D		HN65F	19995	6350	7350	9025	11750
GT Limited Coupe 2D		HN65F	21995	7125	8175	9850	12700
SE Coupe 2D		HN65F	21595	7050	8100	9800	12650
5-Spd Manual Trans				(525)	(525)	(700)	(700)
SONATA—4-Cyl.—Equipment Schedule 5							
W.B. 107.4"; 2.4 Liter.							
GL Sedan 4D		ET46C	19395	4275	5050	6675	9200
GLS Sedan 4D		EU46C	19995	5075	5925	7675	10400
V6 3.3 Liter		F		650	650	865	865
SONATA—V6—Equipment Schedule 5							
W.B. 107.4"; 3.3 Liter.							
LX Sedan 4D		EU46F	23495	5475	6375	8075	10850

2006 HYUNDAI

Body Type	VIN	List	Trade-In Fair	Good	Pvt-Party Good	Retail Excellent

AZERA—V6—Equipment Schedule 3
W.B. 109.4"; 3.8 Liter.

SE Sedan 4D	FC46F	24995	6050	7000	8700	11450
Limited Sedan 4D	FC46F	27495	7425	8525	10250	13250

2007 HYUNDAI — KMH(CM36C)-7-#

ACCENT—4-Cyl.—Equipment Schedule 6
W.B. 98.4"; 1.6 Liter.

GS Hatchback 2D	CM36C	11945	4400	5200	6700	9075
GLS Sedan 4D	CN46C	13145	4850	5675	7175	9600
SE Hatchback 2D	CN36C	14495	5100	5950	7450	9900

ELANTRA—4-Cyl.—Equipment Schedule 5
W.B. 104.3"; 2.0 Liter.

GLS Sedan 4D	DU46D	16495	6375	7350	8875	11450
SE Sedan 4D	DU46D	17295	6600	7600	9125	11700
Limited Sedan 4D	DU46D	18295	6875	7950	9450	12100

TIBURON—4-Cyl.—Equipment Schedule 3
W.B. 99.6"; 2.0 Liter.

GS Coupe 2D	HM65D	18295	7025	8075	9650	12350
5-Spd Manual Trans			(550)	(550)	(735)	(735)

TIBURON—V6—Equipment Schedule 3
W.B. 99.6"; 2.7 Liter.

GT Coupe 2D	HN66F	20995	7825	8950	10600	13500
GT Limited Coupe 2D	HN66F	23295	8650	9850	11500	14500
SE Coupe 2D	HN66F	22595	8600	9800	11450	14450
5-Spd Manual Trans			(550)	(550)	(735)	(735)

SONATA—4-Cyl.—Equipment Schedule 5
W.B. 107.4"; 2.4 Liter.

GLS Sedan 4D	ET46C	18895	5725	6675	8300	11000

SONATA—V6—Equipment Schedule 5
W.B. 107.4"; 3.3 Liter.

SE Sedan 4D	EU46D	21595	6600	7600	9250	12050
Limited Sedan 4D	EU46D	23595	7025	8075	9750	12600

AZERA—V6—Equipment Schedule 3
W.B. 109.4"; 3.3 Liter, 3.8 Liter.

GLS Sedan 4D	FC46D	24895	6475	7475	9100	11800
SE Sedan 4D	FC46F	25195	7225	8300	9950	12750
Limited Sedan 4D	FC46F	27795	8725	9950	11650	14650

2008 HYUNDAI — (KMHOR5NP)(CM36C)-8-#

ACCENT—4-Cyl.—Equipment Schedule 6
W.B. 98.4"; 1.6 Liter.

GS Hatchback 2D	CM36C	11395	5375	6250	7550	9800
GLS Sedan 4D	CN46C	13545	5775	6725	8025	10350
SE Hatchback 2D	CN36C	15195	6100	7075	8375	10750

ELANTRA—4-Cyl.—Equipment Schedule 5
W.B. 104.3"; 2.0 Liter.

GLS Sedan 4D	DU46D	15145	7500	8600	10000	12500
SE Sedan 4D	DU46D	17845	7725	8850	10200	12750

TIBURON—4-Cyl.—Equipment Schedule 3
W.B. 99.6"; 2.0 Liter.

GS Coupe 2D	HM65D	18595	8425	9625	11200	14050
5-Spd Manual Trans			(575)	(575)	(765)	(765)

TIBURON—V6—Equipment Schedule 3
W.B. 99.6"; 2.7 Liter.

GT Coupe 2D	HN66F	21495	9275	10575	12150	15150
GT Limited Coupe 2D	HN66F	22995	10150	11525	13150	16200
SE Coupe 2D	HN66F	22845	10100	11475	13100	16150
5-Spd Manual Trans			(575)	(575)	(765)	(765)
6-Spd Manual Trans			0	0	0	0

SONATA—V6—Equipment Schedule 5
W.B. 107.4"; 3.3 Liter.

GLS Sedan 4D	ET46F	21645	8200	9375	11050	14000
SE Sedan 4D	EU46F	22745	8275	9475	11150	14100
Limited Sedan 4D	EU46F	24695	8775	10000	11700	14700
4-Cyl. 2.4 Liter	C		(750)	(750)	(1000)	(1000)

AZERA—V6—Equipment Schedule 3
W.B. 109.4"; 3.3 Liter, 3.8 Liter.

GLS Sedan 4D	FC46D	25295	8550	9775	11350	14250
Limited Sedan 4D	FC46F	29245	11025	12500	14150	17350

Body	Type	VIN	List	Trade-In Fair	Trade-In Good	Pvt-Party Good	Retail Excellent

INFINITI

1994 INFINITI — JNK(CP01D)-R-#

G20—4-Cyl.—Equipment Schedule 1
W.B. 100.4"; 2.0 Liter.

Body	Type	VIN	List	Fair	Good	Good	Excellent
Sedan 4D		CP01D	25625	900	1275	2225	3725
Touring				100	100	135	135
Manual Trans				(225)	(225)	(300)	(300)

J30—V6—Equipment Schedule 1
W.B. 108.7"; 3.0 Liter.

| Sedan 4D | | AY21D | 37400 | 1375 | 1850 | 3050 | 4775 |
| Touring | | | | 100 | 100 | 135 | 135 |

Q45—V8—Equipment Schedule 1
W.B. 113.2"; 4.5 Liter.

Sedan 4D		NG01D	50900	825	1150	2100	3550
Active Suspension				200	200	265	265
Touring				100	100	135	135
Traction Control				100	100	135	135

1995 INFINITI — JNK(CP01D)-S-#

G20—4-Cyl.—Equipment Schedule 1
W.B. 100.4"; 2.0 Liter.

Sedan 4D		CP01D	26625	1050	1475	2575	4225
Touring				100	100	135	135
Manual Trans				(225)	(225)	(300)	(300)

J30—V6—Equipment Schedule 1
W.B. 108.7"; 3.0 Liter.

| Sedan 4D | | AY21D | 39000 | 1625 | 2125 | 3375 | 5200 |
| Touring | | | | 100 | 100 | 135 | 135 |

Q45—V8—Equipment Schedule 1
W.B. 113.4"; 4.5 Liter.

Sedan 4D		NG01D	52850	1050	1475	2600	4275
Active Suspension				200	200	265	265
Touring				100	100	135	135
Traction Control				100	100	135	135

1996 INFINITI — JNK(CP01D)-T-#

G20—4-Cyl.—Equipment Schedule 1
W.B. 100.4"; 2.0 Liter.

Sedan 4D		CP01D	27630	1200	1675	2825	4525
Touring				125	125	165	165
Manual Trans				(225)	(225)	(300)	(300)

I30—V6—Equipment Schedule 1
W.B. 106.3"; 3.0 Liter.

Sedan 4D		CA21D	32000	1800	2325	3575	5450
Touring				150	150	200	200
Manual Trans				(225)	(225)	(300)	(300)

J30—V6—Equipment Schedule 1
W.B. 108.7"; 3.0 Liter.

| Sedan 4D | | AY21D | 40400 | 1950 | 2500 | 3775 | 5650 |
| Touring | | | | 150 | 150 | 200 | 200 |

Q45—V8—Equipment Schedule 1
W.B. 113.4"; 4.5 Liter.

Sedan 4D		NG01D	54000	1150	1625	2800	4500
Touring				150	150	200	200
Traction Control				125	125	165	165

1997 INFINITI — JNK(CA21D)-V-#

I30—V6—Equipment Schedule 1
W.B. 106.3"; 3.0 Liter.

Sedan 4D		CA21D	30395	2000	2550	3850	5750
Touring				200	200	265	265
Manual Trans				(275)	(275)	(365)	(365)

J30—V6—Equipment Schedule 1
W.B. 108.7"; 3.0 Liter.

| Sedan 4D | | AY21D | 36245 | 2125 | 2700 | 4025 | 5950 |
| Touring | | | | 200 | 200 | 265 | 265 |

Q45—V8—Equipment Schedule 1
W.B. 111.4"; 4.1 Liter.

1997 INFINITI

Body	Type	VIN	List	Trade-In Fair	Good	Pvt-Party Good	Retail Excellent
Sedan 4D		BY31D	48395	**2975**	**3600**	**5000**	**7150**
	Touring			**200**	**200**	**265**	**265**

1998 INFINITI — JNK(CA21D)-W-#

I30—V6—Equipment Schedule 1
W.B. 106.3"; 3.0 Liter.

Body	Type	VIN	List	Trade-In Fair	Good	Pvt-Party Good	Retail Excellent
Sedan 4D		CA21D	30695	**2500**	**3075**	**4425**	**6475**
	Touring			**250**	**250**	**335**	**335**
	Manual Trans			**(325)**	**(325)**	**(435)**	**(435)**

Q45—V8—Equipment Schedule 1
W.B. 111.4"; 4.1 Liter.

Body	Type	VIN	List	Trade-In Fair	Good	Pvt-Party Good	Retail Excellent
Sedan 4D		BY31D	48395	**3100**	**3775**	**5225**	**7400**
	Touring			**250**	**250**	**335**	**335**

1999 INFINITI — JNK(CP11A)-X-#

G20—4-Cyl.—Equipment Schedule 1
W.B. 102.4"; 2.0 Liter.

Body	Type	VIN	List	Trade-In Fair	Good	Pvt-Party Good	Retail Excellent
Sedan 4D		CP11A	23820	**2475**	**3075**	**4375**	**6375**
	Touring			**200**	**200**	**265**	**265**
	Manual Trans			**(375)**	**(375)**	**(500)**	**(500)**

I30—V6—Equipment Schedule 1
W.B. 106.3"; 3.0 Liter.

Body	Type	VIN	List	Trade-In Fair	Good	Pvt-Party Good	Retail Excellent
Sedan 4D		CA21A	30725	**2925**	**3575**	**4950**	**7075**
Limited Sedan 4D		CA21A	31625	**2975**	**3625**	**5000**	**7125**
	Touring			**300**	**300**	**400**	**400**
	Manual Trans			**(375)**	**(375)**	**(500)**	**(500)**

Q45—V8—Equipment Schedule 1
W.B. 111.4"; 4.1 Liter.

Body	Type	VIN	List	Trade-In Fair	Good	Pvt-Party Good	Retail Excellent
Sedan 4D		BY31A	48725	**3500**	**4200**	**5675**	**7950**
	Touring			**300**	**300**	**400**	**400**

2000 INFINITI — JNK(CP11A)-Y-#

G20—4-Cyl.—Equipment Schedule 1
W.B. 102.4"; 2.0 Liter.

Body	Type	VIN	List	Trade-In Fair	Good	Pvt-Party Good	Retail Excellent
Sedan 4D		CP11A	24220	**2800**	**3425**	**4775**	**6800**
	Touring			**200**	**200**	**265**	**265**
	Manual Trans			**(425)**	**(425)**	**(565)**	**(565)**

I30—V6—Equipment Schedule 1
W.B. 108.3"; 3.0 Liter.

Body	Type	VIN	List	Trade-In Fair	Good	Pvt-Party Good	Retail Excellent
Sedan 4D		CA21A	29990	**3725**	**4425**	**5875**	**8125**
	Touring			**350**	**350**	**465**	**465**

Q45—V8—Equipment Schedule 1
W.B. 111.4"; 4.1 Liter.

Body	Type	VIN	List	Trade-In Fair	Good	Pvt-Party Good	Retail Excellent
Sedan 4D		BY31A	49420	**4175**	**4925**	**6450**	**8850**
	Touring			**350**	**350**	**465**	**465**
	Anniversary Edition			**300**	**300**	**400**	**400**

2001 INFINITI — JNK(CP11A)-1-#

G20—4-Cyl.—Equipment Schedule 1
W.B. 102.4"; 2.0 Liter.

Body	Type	VIN	List	Trade-In Fair	Good	Pvt-Party Good	Retail Excellent
Sedan 4D		CP11A	24220	**3250**	**3950**	**5325**	**7475**
	Touring			**200**	**200**	**265**	**265**
	Manual Trans			**(475)**	**(475)**	**(635)**	**(635)**

I30—V6—Equipment Schedule 1
W.B. 108.3"; 3.0 Liter.

Body	Type	VIN	List	Trade-In Fair	Good	Pvt-Party Good	Retail Excellent
Sedan 4D		CA31A	29990	**4450**	**5275**	**6750**	**9150**
	Touring			**375**	**375**	**500**	**500**

Q45—V8—Equipment Schedule 1
W.B. 111.4"; 4.1 Liter.

Body	Type	VIN	List	Trade-In Fair	Good	Pvt-Party Good	Retail Excellent
Sedan 4D		BY31A	49420	**5175**	**6025**	**7650**	**10250**
	Touring			**375**	**375**	**500**	**500**

2002 INFINITI — JNK(CP11A)-2-#

G20—4-Cyl.—Equipment Schedule 1
W.B. 102.4"; 2.0 Liter.

Body	Type	VIN	List	Trade-In Fair	Good	Pvt-Party Good	Retail Excellent
Sedan 4D		CP11A	24340	**3750**	**4475**	**6025**	**8425**
	Sport Pkg			**200**	**200**	**265**	**265**
	Manual Trans			**(500)**	**(500)**	**(665)**	**(665)**

I35—V6—Equipment Schedule 1
W.B. 108.3"; 3.5 Liter.

Body	Type	VIN	List	Trade-In Fair	Good	Pvt-Party Good	Retail Excellent
Sedan 4D		DA31A	29295	**4525**	**5325**	**6975**	**9575**

Body	Type	VIN	List	Trade-In Fair	Good	Pvt-Party Good	Retail Excellent
Sport Pkg				400	400	535	535
Q45—V8—Equipment Schedule 1							
W.B. 113.0"; 4.5 Liter.							
Sedan 4D		BF01A	51045	6025	6975	8825	11750
Sport Pkg				400	400	535	535
Premium Pkg				1000	1000	1335	1335

2003 INFINITI — JNK(CV51E)-3-#

Body	Type	VIN	List	Fair	Good	Good	Excellent
G35—V6—Equipment Schedule 1							
W.B. 112.2"; 3.5 Liter.							
Sedan 4D		CV51E	29495	7550	8650	10500	13500
Coupe 2D		CV54E	32945	9250	10525	12500	15850
I35—V6—Equipment Schedule 1							
W.B. 108.3"; 3.5 Liter.							
Sedan 4D		DA31A	30995	6275	7250	8975	11800
Sport Pkg				475	475	635	635
M45—V8—Equipment Schedule 1							
W.B. 110.2"; 4.5 Liter.							
Sedan 4D		AY41E	43845	7850	8975	10950	14100
Q45—V8—Equipment Schedule 1							
W.B. 113.0"; 4.5 Liter.							
Sedan 4D		BF01A	52545	7500	8600	10500	13600
Premium Sedan 4D		BF01A	62145	10000	11375	13450	17000

2004 INFINITI — JNK(CV51E)-4-#

Body	Type	VIN	List	Fair	Good	Good	Excellent
G35—V6—Equipment Schedule 1							
W.B. 112.2"; 3.5 Liter.							
Sedan 4D		CV51E	31690	8900	10150	12050	15300
AWD Sedan 4D		CV51F	33490	9625	10925	12850	16200
Coupe 2D		CV54E	33140	10675	12100	14050	17550
I35—V6—Equipment Schedule 1							
W.B. 108.3"; 3.5 Liter.							
Sedan 4D		DA31A	31190	7300	8375	10150	13150
M45—V8—Equipment Schedule 1							
W.B. 110.2"; 4.5 Liter.							
Sedan 4D		AY41E	44840	9100	10350	12400	15900
Q45—V8—Equipment Schedule 1							
W.B. 113.0"; 4.5 Liter.							
Sedan 4D		BF01A	52990	9675	10975	13050	16500
Premium Sedan 4D		BF01A	62190	12550	14150	16250	20100
Journey Pkg				1300	1300	1735	1735

2005 INFINITI — JNK(CV51E)-5-#

Body	Type	VIN	List	Fair	Good	Good	Excellent
G35—V6—Equipment Schedule 1							
W.B. 112.2"; 3.5 Liter.							
Sedan 4D		CV51E	32460	10425	11800	13700	17100
x AWD Sedan 4D		CV51F	34160	11225	12750	14650	18150
Coupe 2D		CV54E	34160	12250	13875	15800	19400
Q45—V8—Equipment Schedule 1							
W.B. 113.0"; 4.5 Liter.							
Sedan 4D		BF01A	56810	12500	14100	16150	20000
Premium Pkg				1450	1450	1935	1935

2006 INFINITI — JNK(CV51E)-6-#

Body	Type	VIN	List	Fair	Good	Good	Excellent
G35—V6—Equipment Schedule 1							
W.B. 112.2"; 3.5 Liter.							
Sedan 4D		CV51E	32910	12200	13775	15650	19200
x AWD Sedan 4D		CV51F	34710	13075	14750	16600	20300
Coupe 2D		CV54E	34850	14075	15875	17800	21600
M35—V6—Equipment Schedule 1							
W.B. 114.2"; 3.5 Liter.							
Sedan 4D		AY01E	41250	15625	17550	19450	23300
AWD Sedan 4D		AY01F	43750	16225	18175	20100	24100
Sport Sedan 4D		AY01E	44050	16125	18075	20000	24000
Premium Pkg				800	800	1065	1065
M45—V8—Equipment Schedule 1							
W.B. 114.2"; 4.5 Liter.							
Sedan 4D		BY01E	47560	16650	18725	20900	25300
Sport Sedan 4D		BY01E	50360	17350	19450	21700	26100
Premium Pkg				800	800	1065	1065
Q45—V8—Equipment Schedule 1							
W.B. 113.0"; 4.5 Liter.							

Body	Type	VIN	List	Trade-In Fair	Trade-In Good	Pvt-Party Good	Retail Excellent
Sport Sedan 4D		BF01A	58750	16850	18875	21100	25400
Premium Pkg			....	**1600**	**1600**	**2135**	**2135**

2007 INFINITI — JNK(BV61E)-7-#

G35—V6—Equipment Schedule 1
W.B. 112.2"; 3.5 Liter.

Body	Type	VIN	List	Trade-In Fair	Trade-In Good	Pvt-Party Good	Retail Excellent
Sedan 4D		BV61E	34500	16650	18725	20600	24500
Journey Sedan 4D		BV61E	34950	16850	18875	20800	24700
Sport Sedan 4D		BV61E	36500	17450	19550	21500	25500
x AWD Sedan 4D		BV61F	36800	17700	19900	21800	25800
Coupe 2D		CV54E	37000	16225	18175	20000	23800

M35—V6—Equipment Schedule 1
W.B. 114.2"; 3.5 Liter.

Sedan 4D		AY01E	42150	17775	20000	21900	26000
AWD Sedan 4D		AY01F	45250	18425	20575	22500	26700
Sport Sedan 4D		AY01E	44950	18325	20475	22400	26600
Premium Pkg				**800**	**800**	**1065**	**1065**

M45—V8—Equipment Schedule 1
W.B. 114.2"; 4.5 Liter.

Sedan 4D		BY01E	49800	20975	23525	25700	30400
Sport Sedan 4D		BY01E	51200	21750	24200	26500	31300
Premium Pkg				**800**	**800**	**1065**	**1065**

2008 INFINITI — JNK(BV61E)-8-#

G35—V6—Equipment Schedule 1
W.B. 112.2"; 3.5 Liter.

Sedan 4D		BV61E	32315	19100	21375	23100	27200
Journey Sedan 4D		BV61E	32765	19300	21550	23300	27400
Sport Sedan 4D		BV61E	33115	20000	22350	24100	28200
x AWD Sedan 4D		BV61F	34815	20200	22550	24300	28400

G37—V6—Equipment Schedule 1
W.B. 112.2"; 3.7 Liter.

Coupe 2D		CV64E	34965	24000	26750	28400	32900
Journey Coupe 2D		CV64E	35715	24100	26950	28600	33100
Sport Coupe 2D		CV64E	36265	24600	27450	29100	33700

M35—V6—Equipment Schedule 1
W.B. 114.2"; 3.5 Liter.

Sedan 4D		AY01E	43765	20275	22725	24500	28700
x AWD Sedan 4D		AY01F	45515	20975	23525	25300	29500
Premium Pkg				**800**	**800**	**1065**	**1065**

M45—V8—Equipment Schedule 1
W.B. 114.2"; 4.5 Liter.

Sedan 4D		BY01E	50065	23825	26550	28600	33400
AWD Sedan 4D		BY01F	52565	24600	27450	29500	34400
Premium Pkg				**800**	**800**	**1065**	**1065**

JAGUAR

1994 JAGUAR — SAJ(HX174)-R-#

XJ6—6-Cyl.—Equipment Schedule 1
W.B. 113.0"; 4.0 Liter.

Sedan 4D		HX174	52330	2175	2750	4050	5975
Vanden Plas Sedan 4D		KX174	59980	2375	2950	4275	6250

XJS—6-Cyl.—Equipment Schedule 2
W.B. 102.0"; 4.0 Liter.

Coupe 2D		NX574	52530	3600	4300	5775	8050
2+2 Convertible 2D		NX474	60530	5150	6000	7725	10450
Manual Trans				**(225)**	**(225)**	**(300)**	**(300)**

XJS—V12—Equipment Schedule 2
W.B. 102.0"; 6.0 Liter.

Coupe 2D		NX534	70530	4750	5575	7250	9850
2+2 Convertible 2D		NX234	80530	5825	6775	8600	11450

XJ12—V12—Equipment Schedule 1
W.B. 113.0"; 6.0 Liter.

Sedan 4D		MX134	72330	2400	3000	4325	6325

1995 JAGUAR — SAJ(HX174)-S-#

XJ6—6-Cyl.—Equipment Schedule 1
W.B. 113.0"; 4.0 Liter.

Sedan 4D		HX174	54030	2200	2800	4125	6075

1995 JAGUAR

Body	Type	VIN	List	Trade-In Fair	Good	Pvt-Party Good	Retail Excellent
Vanden Plas Sedan 4D		KX174	62780	2850	3475	4875	7000
Traction Control				100	100	135	135

XJR—6-Cyl. Supercharged—Equipment Schedule 1
W.B. 113.0"; 4.0 Liter.

| Sedan 4D | | PX114 | 65580 | 3700 | 4400 | 5925 | 8250 |

XJS—6-Cyl.—Equipment Schedule 2
W.B. 102.0"; 4.0 Liter.

| Coupe 2D | | NX574 | 53980 | 4125 | 4875 | 6425 | 8850 |
| 2+2 Convertible 2D | | NX274 | 62130 | 5825 | 6775 | 8600 | 11450 |

XJS—V12—Equipment Schedule 2
W.B. 102.0"; 6.0 Liter.

| Coupe 2D | | NX534 | 72930 | 5425 | 6300 | 8050 | 10850 |
| 2+2 Convertible 2D | | NX234 | 83130 | 6625 | 7625 | 9525 | 12600 |

XJ12—V12—Equipment Schedule 1
W.B. 113.0"; 6.0 Liter.

| Sedan 4D | | MX134 | 77830 | 2450 | 3050 | 4375 | 6425 |

1996 JAGUAR — SAJ(HX174)–T–#

XJ6—6-Cyl.—Equipment Schedule 1
W.B. 113.0", 117.9" (Vanden Plas); 4.0 Liter.

Sedan 4D		HX174	56900	2575	3175	4550	6625
Vanden Plas Sedan 4D		KX674	65000	4025	4750	6300	8700
Traction Control				125	125	165	165

XJR—6-Cyl. Supercharged—Equipment Schedule 1
W.B. 113.0"; 4.0 Liter.

| Sedan 4D | | PX114 | 66850 | 4250 | 5000 | 6575 | 9025 |

XJS—6-Cyl.—Equipment Schedule 2
W.B. 102.0"; 4.0 Liter.

| 2+2 Convertible 2D | | NX274 | 62150 | 6675 | 7675 | 9575 | 12650 |

XJ12—V12—Equipment Schedule 1
W.B. 117.9"; 6.0 Liter.

| Sedan 4D | | MX634 | 79950 | 4625 | 5450 | 7100 | 9700 |

1997 JAGUAR — SAJ(HX124)–V–#

XJ6—6-Cyl.—Equipment Schedule 1
W.B. 113.0", 117.9" (L & Vanden Plas); 4.0 Liter.

Sedan 4D		HX124	54980	3075	3725	5150	7325
L Sedan 4D		HX624	59980	3275	3975	5425	7650
Vanden Plas Sedan 4D		KX624	64380	4575	5400	7025	9575
Traction Control				150	150	200	200

XJR—6-Cyl. Supercharged—Equipment Schedule 1
W.B. 113.0"; 4.0 Liter.

| Sedan 4D | | PX114 | 67980 | 4975 | 5800 | 7500 | 10150 |

XK8—V8—Equipment Schedule 2
W.B. 101.9"; 4.0 Liter.

Coupe 2D		GX574	65480	5400	6275	7975	10750
Convertible 2D		GX274	70480	5075	5925	7625	10300
Traction Control				150	150	200	200

1998 JAGUAR — SAJ(HX124)–W–#

XJ8—V8—Equipment Schedule 1
W.B. 113.0", 117.9" (L & Vanden Plas); 4.0 Liter.

Sedan 4D		HX124	55330	4875	5700	7350	9950
L Sedan 4D		HX624	60330	4950	5800	7475	10100
Vanden Plas Sedan 4D		KX624	64380	5300	6175	7900	10600
Traction Control				175	175	235	235

XJR—V8 Supercharged—Equipment Schedule 1
W.B. 113.0"; 4.0 Liter.

| Sedan 4D | | PX184 | 67980 | 6575 | 7575 | 9400 | 12400 |

XK8—V8—Equipment Schedule 2
W.B. 101.9"; 4.0 Liter.

Coupe 2D		GX524	65480	6150	7125	8900	11750
Convertible 2D		GX224	70480	5800	6750	8475	11250
Traction Control				175	175	235	235

1999 JAGUAR — SAJ(HX104)–X–#

XJ8—V8—Equipment Schedule 1
W.B. 113.0", 117.9" (L & Vanden Plas); 4.0 Liter.

Sedan 4D		HX104	55780	5000	5850	7525	10150
L Sedan 4D		HX604	60830	5075	5925	7600	10250
Vanden Plas Sedan 4D		KX604	64880	5475	6350	8050	10800
Traction Control				200	200	265	265

Body	Type	VIN	List	Trade-In Fair	Trade-In Good	Pvt-Party Good	Retail Excellent
XJR—V8 Supercharged—Equipment Schedule 1							
W.B. 113.0'; 4.0 Liter.							
Sedan 4D		PX184	69030	**6725**	**7750**	**9575**	**12550**
XK8—V8—Equipment Schedule 2							
W.B. 101.9'; 4.0 Liter.							
Coupe 2D		GX504	66330	**7000**	**8050**	**9900**	**12900**
Convertible 2D		GX204	71330	**6650**	**7650**	**9450**	**12400**
Traction Control				**200**	**200**	**265**	**265**

2000 JAGUAR — SAJ(DorJ)(A01C)-Y-#

Body	Type	VIN	List	Trade-In Fair	Trade-In Good	Pvt-Party Good	Retail Excellent
S-TYPE—V6—Equipment Schedule 1							
W.B. 114.5'; 3.0 Liter.							
Sedan 4D		A01C	44980	**3300**	**3975**	**5425**	**7625**
Sport Pkg				**150**	**150**	**200**	**200**
S-TYPE—V8—Equipment Schedule 1							
W.B. 114.5'; 4.0 Liter.							
Sedan 4D		A01D	48580	**3600**	**4300**	**5750**	**8000**
Sport Pkg				**150**	**150**	**200**	**200**
XJ8—V8—Equipment Schedule 1							
W.B. 113.0', 117.9' (L & Vanden Plas); 4.0 Liter.							
Sedan 4D		A14C	56245	**5300**	**6175**	**7850**	**10450**
L Sedan 4D		A23C	61295	**5350**	**6225**	**7900**	**10600**
Vanden Plas Sedan 4D		A24C	65345	**5750**	**6700**	**8400**	**11150**
XJR—V8 Supercharged—Equipment Schedule 1							
W.B. 113.0'; 4.0 Liter.							
Sedan 4D		A15B	69145	**7000**	**8050**	**9900**	**12950**
XJ8—V8 Supercharged—Equipment Schedule 1							
W.B. 117.9'; 4.0 Liter.							
Vanden Plas Sedan 4D		A14B	81245	**10775**	**12200**	**14300**	**18050**
XK8—V8—Equipment Schedule 2							
W.B. 101.9'; 4.0 Liter.							
Coupe 2D		A41C	66795	**7975**	**9150**	**11050**	**14300**
Convertible 2D		A42C	71795	**7625**	**8750**	**10600**	**13700**
XKR—V8 Supercharged—Equipment Schedule 2							
W.B. 101.9'; 4.0 Liter.							
Coupe 2D		A41B	77395	**9675**	**11025**	**13150**	**16700**
Convertible 2D		A42B	82395	**9675**	**11025**	**13150**	**16700**

2001 JAGUAR — SAJD(A01C)-1-#

Body	Type	VIN	List	Trade-In Fair	Trade-In Good	Pvt-Party Good	Retail Excellent
S-TYPE—V6—Equipment Schedule 1							
W.B. 114.5'; 3.0 Liter.							
Sedan 4D		A01C	46250	**4225**	**5000**	**6500**	**8850**
Sport Pkg				**150**	**150**	**200**	**200**
S-TYPE—V8—Equipment Schedule 1							
W.B. 114.5'; 4.0 Liter.							
Sedan 4D		A01D	49950	**4525**	**5350**	**6850**	**9275**
Sport Pkg				**150**	**150**	**200**	**200**
XJ8—V8—Equipment Schedule 1							
W.B. 113.0', 117.9' (L & Vanden Plas); 4.0 Liter.							
Sedan 4D		A14C	56950	**5750**	**6700**	**8400**	**11150**
L Sedan 4D		A23C	62950	**5775**	**6725**	**8425**	**11150**
Vanden Plas Sedan 4D		A24C	68250	**6250**	**7225**	**8975**	**11800**
XJR—V8 Supercharged—Equipment Schedule 1							
W.B. 113.0'; 4.0 Liter.							
Sedan 4D		A15B	69930	**7500**	**8600**	**10450**	**13500**
XJ8—V8 Supercharged—Equipment Schedule 1							
W.B. 117.9'; 4.0 Liter.							
Vanden Plas Sedan 4D		A25B	83950	**11700**	**13225**	**15400**	**19200**
XK8—V8—Equipment Schedule 2							
W.B. 101.9'; 4.0 Liter.							
Coupe 2D		A41C	69750	**9200**	**10475**	**12450**	**15850**
Convertible 2D		A42C	74750	**8775**	**10000**	**11950**	**15300**
XKR—V8 Supercharged—Equipment Schedule 2							
W.B. 101.9'; 4.0 Liter.							
Coupe 2D		A41B	80750	**11075**	**12550**	**14700**	**18500**
Convertible 2D		A42B	85750	**11075**	**12550**	**14700**	**18500**

2002 JAGUAR — SAJ-(A51D)-2-#

Body	Type	VIN	List	Trade-In Fair	Trade-In Good	Pvt-Party Good	Retail Excellent
X-TYPE AWD—V6—Equipment Schedule 2							
W.B. 106.7'; 2.5 Liter, 3.0 Liter.							
2.5L Sedan 4D		A51D	34370	**3600**	**4300**	**5900**	**8300**
2.5L Sport Sedan 4D		A53D	36370	**3775**	**4475**	**6100**	**8550**

Body	Type	VIN	List	Trade-In Fair	Trade-In Good	Pvt-Party Good	Retail Excellent
3.0L Sedan 4D		A51C	39095	3625	4325	5975	8450
3.0L Sport Sedan 4D		A53C	41095	3600	4300	5925	8400
Manual Trans				(500)	(500)	(665)	(665)
S-TYPE—V6—Equipment Schedule 1							
W.B. 114.5"; 3.0 Liter.							
Sedan 4D		A01C	46320	5250	6100	7925	10750
Sport				1000	1000	1335	1335
Manual Trans				(500)	(500)	(665)	(665)
S-TYPE—V8—Equipment Schedule 1							
W.B. 114.5"; 4.0 Liter.							
Sedan 4D		A01D	49975	5575	6500	8300	11150
Sport				1000	1000	1335	1335
XJ8—V8—Equipment Schedule 1							
W.B. 113.0"; 4.0 Liter.							
Sedan 4D		A14C	56975	6350	7325	9225	12250
XJ SPORT—V8—Equipment Schedule 1							
W.B. 113.0"; 4.0 Liter.							
Sedan 4D		A14C	59975	5575	6500	8400	11350
VANDEN PLAS—V8—Equipment Schedule 1							
W.B. 117.9"; 4.0 Liter.							
Sedan 4D		A24C	68975	6850	7925	9850	12950
XJR—V8 Supercharged—Equipment Schedule 1							
W.B. 113.0"; 4.0 Liter.							
Sedan 4D		A15B	72475	8700	9900	12050	15550
100 Sedan 4D		A15B		11750	13275	15600	19550
XJ SUPER—V8 Supercharged—Equipment Schedule 1							
W.B. 117.9"; 4.0 Liter.							
Sedan 4D		A25B	79975	12800	14450	16850	21100
XK8—V8—Equipment Schedule 1							
W.B. 101.9"; 4.0 Liter.							
Coupe 2D		A41C	69975	10475	11900	14100	17900
Convertible 2D		A42C	74975	10050	11425	13600	17300
XKR—V8 Supercharged—Equipment Schedule 2							
W.B. 101.9"; 4.0 Liter.							
Coupe 2D		A41B	82975	12600	14200	16600	20800
Convertible 2D		A42B	87975	12600	14200	16600	20800
100 Coupe 2D		A41B	84000	****	****	****	34300
100 Convertible 2D		A42B	86975	****	****	****	37000

2003 JAGUAR — SAJ-(A51D)-3-#

Body	Type	VIN	List	Trade-In Fair	Trade-In Good	Pvt-Party Good	Retail Excellent
X-TYPE AWD—V6—Equipment Schedule 2							
W.B. 106.7"; 2.5 Liter, 3.0 Liter.							
2.5L Sedan 4D		A51D	29950	4500	5300	6975	9600
3.0L Sedan 4D		A51C	36950	4550	5375	7100	9775
Sport Pkg				875	875	1165	1165
Manual Trans				(575)	(575)	(765)	(765)
S-TYPE—V6—Equipment Schedule 1							
W.B. 114.5"; 3.0 Liter.							
Sedan 4D		A01T	44975	5600	6525	8350	11200
Sport Pkg				1000	1000	1335	1335
Manual Trans				(575)	(575)	(765)	(765)
S-TYPE—V8—Equipment Schedule 1							
W.B. 114.5"; 4.2 Liter.							
Sedan 4D		A01U	49975	6025	6975	8825	11750
Sport Pkg				1000	1000	1335	1335
S-TYPE R—V8 Supercharged—Equipment Schedule 1							
W.B. 114.5"; 4.2 Liter.							
Sedan 4D		A03V	62400	9550	10875	13050	16650
XJ8—V8—Equipment Schedule 1							
W.B. 113.0"; 4.0 Liter.							
Sedan 4D		A14C	56975	7350	8450	10550	13900
XJ SPORT—V8—Equipment Schedule 1							
W.B. 113.0"; 4.0 Liter.							
Sedan 4D		A12C	59975	6900	7950	9950	13150
VANDEN PLAS—V8—Equipment Schedule 1							
W.B. 117.9"; 4.0 Liter.							
Sedan 4D		A24C	68975	8950	10200	12300	15850
XJR—V8 Supercharged—Equipment Schedule 1							
W.B. 113.0"; 4.0 Liter.							
Sedan 4D		A15B	72475	10350	11700	13900	17650
XJ SUPER—V8 Supercharged—Equipment Schedule 1							
W.B. 117.9"; 4.0 Liter.							
Sedan 4D		A25B	79975	15525	17450	19900	24500

2003 JAGUAR

Body Type	VIN	List	Trade-In Fair	Good	Pvt-Party Good	Retail Excellent
XK8—V8—Equipment Schedule 2						
W.B. 101.9"; 4.2 Liter.						
Coupe 2D	A41U	69975	12600	14200	16450	20500
Convertible 2D	A42U	74975	11800	13325	15550	19450
XKR—V8 Supercharged—Equipment Schedule 2						
W.B. 101.9"; 4.2 Liter.						
Coupe 2D	A41V	81975	14700	16525	18950	23400
Convertible 2D	A42V	86975	14700	16525	18950	23400
Handling Pkg			2000	2000	2665	2665

2004 JAGUAR — SAJ-(A51D)-4-#

Body Type	VIN	List	Trade-In Fair	Good	Pvt-Party Good	Retail Excellent
X-TYPE AWD—V6—Equipment Schedule 2						
W.B. 106.7"; 2.5 Liter, 3.0 Liter.						
2.5L Sedan 4D	A51D	30520	5800	6750	8525	11350
3.0L Sedan 4D	A51C	33995	5900	6825	8625	11450
Sport Pkg			975	975	1300	1300
Manual Trans			(650)	(650)	(865)	(865)
S-TYPE—V6—Equipment Schedule 1						
W.B. 114.5"; 3.0 Liter.						
Sedan 4D	A01T	44995	7075	8125	10050	13150
Sport Pkg			1000	1000	1335	1335
Manual Trans			(650)	(650)	(865)	(865)
S-TYPE—V8—Equipment Schedule 1						
W.B. 114.5"; 4.2 Liter.						
Sedan 4D	A01U	49995	7575	8675	10600	13700
Sport Pkg			1000	1000	1335	1335
S-TYPE R—V8 Supercharged—Equipment Schedule 1						
W.B. 114.5"; 4.2 Liter.						
Sedan 4D	A03V	63120	11575	13025	15350	19250
XJ8—V8—Equipment Schedule 1						
W.B. 119.4"; 4.2 Liter.						
Sedan 4D	A71C	59995	8725	9950	12200	15900
VANDEN PLAS—V8—Equipment Schedule 1						
W.B. 119.4"; 4.2 Liter.						
Sedan 4D	A74C	68995	11375	12850	15050	18900
XJR—V8 Supercharged—Equipment Schedule 1						
W.B. 119.4"; 4.2 Liter.						
Sedan 4D	A73B	74995	12350	13975	16200	20200
XK8—V8—Equipment Schedule 2						
W.B. 101.9"; 4.2 Liter.						
Coupe 2D	A41C	69995	14950	16800	19050	23300
Convertible 2D	A42C	74995	13825	15575	17850	22000
XKR—V8 Supercharged—Equipment Schedule 2						
W.B. 101.9"; 4.2 Liter.						
Coupe 2D	A41B	82995	17200	19250	21900	26700
Convertible 2D	A42B	87995	17200	19250	21900	26700
Handling Pkg			2000	2000	2665	2665

2005 JAGUAR — SAJD(A51D)-5-#

Body Type	VIN	List	Trade-In Fair	Good	Pvt-Party Good	Retail Excellent
X-TYPE AWD—V6—Equipment Schedule 2						
W.B. 106.7"; 2.5 Liter, 3.0 Liter.						
2.5L Sedan 4D	A51D	32245	7500	8600	10350	13350
3.0L Sedan 4D	A51C	34995	7625	8750	10600	13650
3.0L Wagon 4D	A54C	36995	8825	10050	11950	15250
Sport Pkg			1075	1075	1435	1435
VDP Edition			1500	1500	2000	2000
Manual Trans			(725)	(725)	(965)	(965)
S-TYPE—V6—Equipment Schedule 1						
W.B. 114.5"; 3.0 Liter.						
Sedan 4D	A01T	45995	8950	10200	12150	15550
Sport Pkg			1000	1000	1335	1335
S-TYPE—V8—Equipment Schedule 1						
W.B. 114.5"; 4.2 Liter.						
Sedan 4D	A01U	51995	9475	10775	12850	16300
VDP Edition			1500	1500	2000	2000
Sport Pkg			1000	1000	1335	1335
S-TYPE R—V8 Supercharged—Equipment Schedule 1						
W.B. 114.5"; 4.2 Liter.						
Sedan 4D	A03V	58995	13925	15675	18050	22300
XJ8—V8—Equipment Schedule 1						
W.B. 119.4", 124.4" (L); 4.2 Liter.						
Sedan 4D	A71C	61495	10525	11950	14300	18300

Body	Type	VIN	List	Trade-In Fair	Trade-In Good	Pvt-Party Good	Retail Excellent
L Sedan 4D		A79C	63495	10975	12450	14800	18800
VANDEN PLAS—V8—Equipment Schedule 1							
W.B. 124.4"; 4.2 Liter.							
Sedan 4D		A82C	70995	16275	18275	20500	24900
XJR—V8 Supercharged—Equipment Schedule 1							
W.B. 119.4"; 4.2 Liter.							
Sedan 4D		A73B	75995	14800	16650	18950	23200
XJ SUPER—V8 Supercharged—Equipment Schedule 1							
W.B. 124.4"; 4.2 Liter.							
Sedan 4D		A86B	89995	22350	24900	27500	32900
XK8—V8—Equipment Schedule 2							
W.B. 101.9"; 4.2 Liter.							
Coupe 2D		A41C	70495	17700	19900	22200	26900
Convertible 2D		A42C	75495	16275	18275	20500	24900
XKR—V8 Supercharged—Equipment Schedule 2							
W.B. 101.9"; 4.2 Liter.							
Coupe 2D		A41B	82995	20100	22450	25100	30200
Convertible 2D		A42B	87995	20100	22450	25100	30200
Handling Pkg				2000	2000	2665	2665

2006 JAGUAR — SAJ—(A51A)—6—#

Body	Type	VIN	List	Trade-In Fair	Trade-In Good	Pvt-Party Good	Retail Excellent
X-TYPE AWD—V6—Equipment Schedule 2							
W.B. 106.7"; 3.0 Liter.							
3.0L Sedan 4D		A51A	32995	9800	11125	13050	16400
3.0L Wagon 4D		A54A	36995	11175	12650	14550	18050
Sport Pkg				1175	1175	1565	1565
VDP Edition				1500	1500	2000	2000
S-TYPE—V6—Equipment Schedule 1							
W.B. 114.5"; 3.0 Liter.							
Sedan 4D		A01A	45995	11225	12750	14700	18350
S-TYPE—V8—Equipment Schedule 1							
W.B. 114.5"; 4.2 Liter.							
Sedan 4D		A01B	52495	11800	13325	15450	19200
VDP Edition				1500	1500	2000	2000
S-TYPE R—V8 Supercharged—Equipment Schedule 1							
W.B. 114.5"; 4.2 Liter.							
Sedan 4D		A03C	63995	16650	18725	21200	25900
XJ8—V8—Equipment Schedule 1							
W.B. 119.4", 124.4" (L); 4.2 Liter.							
Sedan 4D		A71B	62495	16125	18125	20700	25400
L Sedan 4D		A79B	64995	17200	19250	21900	26700
VANDEN PLAS—V8—Equipment Schedule 1							
W.B. 124.4"; 4.2 Liter.							
Sedan 4D		A82B	74995	21750	24200	26600	31500
XJR—V8 Supercharged—Equipment Schedule 1							
W.B. 119.4"; 4.2 Liter.							
Sedan 4D		A73C	79995	21075	23625	26000	31000
XJ SUPER—V8 Supercharged—Equipment Schedule 1							
W.B. 124.4"; 4.2 Liter.							
Sedan 4D		A82C	91995	29800	33125	35900	41900
Portfolio Sedan 4D		A86C	115995	41950	46450	49200	56400
XK8—V8—Equipment Schedule 2							
W.B. 101.9"; 4.2 Liter.							
Coupe 2D		A41C	70495	21075	23525	25800	30700
Convertible 2D		A42C	75495	19200	21450	23700	28400
XKR—V8 Supercharged—Equipment Schedule 2							
W.B. 101.9"; 4.2 Liter.							
Coupe 2D		A41B	82995	23325	26075	28600	34000
Convertible 2D		A42B	87995	23325	26075	28600	34000
Handling Pkg				2000	2000	2665	2665

2007 JAGUAR — SAJ—(A51A)—7—#

Body	Type	VIN	List	Trade-In Fair	Trade-In Good	Pvt-Party Good	Retail Excellent
X-TYPE AWD—V6—Equipment Schedule 2							
W.B. 106.7"; 3.0 Liter.							
3.0L Sedan 4D		A51A	34995	12500	14100	15950	19550
3.0L Wagon 4D		A54A	39995	13925	15675	17550	21300
S-TYPE—V6—Equipment Schedule 1							
W.B. 114.5"; 3.0 Liter.							
Sedan 4D		A01A	49000	14075	15875	17900	21800
S-TYPE—V8—Equipment Schedule 1							
W.B. 114.5"; 4.2 Liter.							
Sedan 4D		A01B	56000	18225	20375	22800	27500

2007 JAGUAR

Body Type	VIN	List	Trade-In Fair	Trade-In Good	Pvt-Party Good	Retail Excellent
S-TYPE R—V8 Supercharged—Equipment Schedule 1						
W.B. 114.5"; 4.2 Liter.						
Sedan 4D	A03C	64000	25000	27925	30300	35700
XJ8—V8—Equipment Schedule 1						
W.B. 119.4", 124.4" (L); 4.2 Liter.						
Sedan 4D	A71B	64250	23225	25875	28500	33900
L Sedan 4D	A79B	67750	24900	27725	30300	35900
VANDEN PLAS—V8—Equipment Schedule 1						
W.B. 124.4"; 4.2 Liter.						
Sedan 4D	A82B	75500	30275	33625	36100	41900
XJR—V8 Supercharged—Equipment Schedule 1						
W.B. 119.4"; 4.2 Liter.						
Sedan 4D	A73C	81500	28800	32150	34600	40400
XJ SUPER—V8 Supercharged—Equipment Schedule 1						
W.B. 124.4"; 4.2 Liter.						
Sedan 4D	A82C	92000	38600	42825	45400	52200
XK—V8—Equipment Schedule 2						
W.B. 108.3"; 4.2 Liter.						
Coupe 2D	A43B	75500	32625	36250	38500	44400
Convertible 2D	A44B	81500	36350	40375	42600	48900
XKR—V8 Supercharged—Equipment Schedule 2						
W.B. 108.3"; 4.2 Liter.						
Coupe 2D	A43C	86500	37350	41450	44100	50900
Convertible 2D	A44C	92500	40975	45475	48000	55100

2008 JAGUAR — SAJ-(A51A)-8-#

Body Type	VIN	List	Trade-In Fair	Trade-In Good	Pvt-Party Good	Retail Excellent
X-TYPE AWD—V6—Equipment Schedule 2						
W.B. 106.7"; 3.0 Liter.						
3.0L Sedan 4D	A51A	35725	15875	17775	19700	23500
3.0L Wagon 4D	A54A	39995	17350	19450	21400	25400
S-TYPE—V6—Equipment Schedule 1						
W.B. 114.5"; 3.0 Liter.						
Sedan 4D	A01A	50000	17550	19700	21800	26000
Satin Edition			1500	1500	2000	2000
S-TYPE—V8—Equipment Schedule 1						
W.B. 114.5"; 4.2 Liter.						
Sedan 4D	A01A	57500	22050	24600	27000	32100
Satin Edition			1500	1500	2000	2000
S-TYPE R—V8 Supercharged—Equipment Schedule 1						
W.B. 114.5"; 4.2 Liter.						
Sedan 4D	A03C	66000	29300	32525	35000	40700
XJ8—V8—Equipment Schedule 1						
W.B. 119.4", 124.4" (L); 4.2 Liter.						
Sedan 4D	A71B	65500	27625	30775	33400	39300
L Sedan 4D	A79B	69000	29900	33225	35900	41900
VANDEN PLAS—V8—Equipment Schedule 1						
W.B. 124.4"; 4.2 Liter.						
Sedan 4D	A82B	77750	36075	40075	42200	48400
XJR—V8 Supercharged—Equipment Schedule 1						
W.B. 119.4"; 4.2 Liter.						
Sedan 4D	A73C	85250	34000	37725	40100	46200
XJ SUPER—V8 Supercharged—Equipment Schedule 1						
W.B. 124.4"; 4.2 Liter.						
Sedan 4D	A86C	95750	44775	49675	52100	59400
XK—V8—Equipment Schedule 2						
W.B. 108.3"; 4.2 Liter.						
Coupe 2D	A43B	76500	37625	41750	43800	50000
Convertible 2D	A44B	82500	41650	46150	48300	55000
XKR—V8 Supercharged—Equipment Schedule 2						
W.B. 108.3"; 4.2 Liter.						
Coupe 2D	A43C	87700				
Portfolio Coupe 2D	A45C	99700				
Convertible 2D	A44C	93700				
Portfolio Conv 2D	A46C	104800				

KIA

1994 KIA — KNA(FA121)-R-#

Body Type	VIN	List	Trade-In Fair	Trade-In Good	Pvt-Party Good	Retail Excellent
SEPHIA—4-Cyl.—Equipment Schedule 6						
W.B. 98.4"; 1.6 Liter.						
RS Sedan 4D	FA121	10130	200	275	775	1600

1994 KIA

Body	Type	VIN	List	Trade-In Fair	Good	Pvt-Party Good	Retail Excellent
LS Sedan 4D		FA121	10674	225	325	875	1725
GS Sedan 4D		FA121	11420	325	450	1025	1925

1995 KIA — KNA(FA121)–S–#

SEPHIA—4-Cyl.—Equipment Schedule 6
W.B. 98.4"; 1.6 Liter, 1.8 Liter.

RS Sedan 4D		FA121	10140	250	325	900	1775
LS Sedan 4D		FA121	10730	300	400	975	1875
GS Sedan 4D		FA121	11630	375	525	1125	2100

1996 KIA — KNA(FA125)–T–#

SEPHIA—4-Cyl.—Equipment Schedule 6
W.B. 98.4"; 1.6 Liter, 1.8 Liter.

RS Sedan 4D		FA125	11040	275	375	950	1850
LS Sedan 4D		FA125	11980	325	450	1050	2000
GS Sedan 4D		FA125	12880	425	600	1225	2275

1997 KIA — KNA(FA125)–V–#

SEPHIA—4-Cyl.—Equipment Schedule 6
W.B. 98.4"; 1.6 Liter, 1.8 Liter.

RS Sedan 4D		FA125	11350	300	425	1050	2000
LS Sedan 4D		FA125	12190	375	550	1200	2225
GS Sedan 4D		FA125	13250	475	650	1350	2475

1998 KIA — KNA(FB121)–W–#

SEPHIA—4-Cyl.—Equipment Schedule 6
W.B. 100.8"; 1.8 Liter.

Sedan 4D		FB121	11605	375	525	1175	2225
LS Sedan 4D		FB121	12345	475	625	1350	2475

1999 KIA — KNA(FB121)–X–#

SEPHIA—4-Cyl.—Equipment Schedule 6
W.B. 100.8"; 1.8 Liter.

Sedan 4D		FB121	11605	475	650	1400	2575
LS Sedan 4D		FB121	12345	575	775	1625	2975

2000 KIA — KNA(FA121)–Y–#

SEPHIA—4-Cyl.—Equipment Schedule 6
W.B. 100.8"; 1.8 Liter.

Sedan 4D		FA121	11605	625	875	1775	3150
LS Sedan 4D		FA121	12345	700	1000	1950	3425

SPECTRA—4-Cyl.—Equipment Schedule 6
W.B. 100.8"; 1.8 Liter.

GS Sedan 4D		FB161	11245	675	950	1900	3375
GSX Sedan 4D		FB161	13445	825	1175	2300	3975

2001 KIA — KNA(DC123)–1–#

RIO—4-Cyl.—Equipment Schedule 6
W.B. 94.9"; 1.5 Liter.

Sedan 4D		DC123	10175	600	800	1725	3150

SEPHIA—4-Cyl.—Equipment Schedule 6
W.B. 100.8"; 1.8 Liter.

Sedan 4D		FB121	11945	825	1150	2275	3975
LS Sedan 4D		FB121	12645	925	1275	2450	4150

SPECTRA—4-Cyl.—Equipment Schedule 6
W.B. 100.8"; 1.8 Liter.

GS Hatchback 4D		FB161	12345	875	1250	2400	4125
GSX Hatchback 4D		FB161	13645	1050	1450	2675	4400

OPTIMA—4-Cyl.—Equipment Schedule 6
W.B. 106.3"; 2.4 Liter.

LX Sedan 4D		GD126	16599	625	900	1850	3325
SE Sedan 4D		GD126	18899	1025	1450	2650	4375
V6 2.5 Liter		4		450	450	600	600

2002 KIA — KNA(DC123)–2–#

RIO—4-Cyl.—Equipment Schedule 6
W.B. 94.9"; 1.5 Liter.

Sedan 4D		DC123	10660	750	1050	2375	4275
Cinco Wagon 4D		DC163	11630	950	1350	2725	4650

Body Type	VIN	List	Trade-In Fair	Trade-In Good	Pvt-Party Good	Retail Excellent
SPECTRA—4-Cyl.—Equipment Schedule 6						
W.B. 100.8"; 1.8 Liter.						
Sedan 4D	FB121	12450	975	1375	2750	4675
GS Hatchback 4D	FB161	12850	1050	1475	2875	4825
LS Sedan 4D	FB121	13090	1100	1550	2975	4950
GSX Hatchback 4D	FB161	14090	1200	1675	3100	5125
OPTIMA—4-Cyl.—Equipment Schedule 5						
W.B. 106.3"; 2.4 Liter.						
LX Sedan 4D	GD126	16244	850	1200	2550	4450
SE Sedan 4D	GD126	17894	1275	1750	3175	5200
V6 2.7 Liter	8	....	500	500	665	665

2003 KIA — KNA(DC125)-3-#

Body Type	VIN	List	Trade-In Fair	Trade-In Good	Pvt-Party Good	Retail Excellent
RIO—4-Cyl.—Equipment Schedule 6						
W.B. 94.9"; 1.6 Liter.						
Sedan 4D	DC125	10495	975	1375	2775	4725
Cinco Wagon 4D	DC165	11995	1250	1725	3150	5200
SPECTRA—4-Cyl.—Equipment Schedule 6						
W.B. 100.8"; 1.8 Liter.						
Sedan 4D	FB121	12715	1225	1700	3125	5175
GS Hatchback 4D	FB161	13140	1350	1850	3275	5350
LS Sedan 4D	FB121	13320	1475	1950	3425	5500
GSX Hatchback 4D	FB161	14360	1625	2125	3600	5675
OPTIMA—4-Cyl.—Equipment Schedule 5						
W.B. 106.3"; 2.4 Liter.						
LX Sedan 4D	GD126	16915	975	1375	2775	4750
SE Sedan 4D	GD126	18590	1550	2050	3500	5575
V6 2.7 Liter	8	....	575	575	765	765

2004 KIA — KNA(DC125)-4-#

Body Type	VIN	List	Trade-In Fair	Trade-In Good	Pvt-Party Good	Retail Excellent
RIO—4-Cyl.—Equipment Schedule 6						
W.B. 94.9"; 1.6 Liter.						
Sedan 4D	DC125	11030	1350	1825	3300	5375
Cinco Wagon 4D	DC165	12655	1775	2300	3800	5925
SPECTRA—4-Cyl.—Equipment Schedule 6						
W.B. 100.8", 102.8" (LX & EX); 1.8 Liter, 2.0 Liter.						
Sedan 4D	FB121	13320	1725	2225	3725	5825
GS Hatchback 4D	FB161	13580	1850	2400	3900	6025
LS Sedan 4D	FB121	13590	1975	2525	4050	6200
LX Sedan 4D	FB121	14120	2025	2575	4100	6250
EX Sedan 4D	FB121	14290	2100	2650	4175	6325
GSX Hatchback 4D	FB161	14630	2150	2725	4250	6425
OPTIMA—4-Cyl.—Equipment Schedule 5						
W.B. 106.3"; 2.4 Liter.						
LX Sedan 4D	GD126	16960	1200	1675	3150	5225
EX Sedan 4D	GD126	18635	1950	2500	4000	6150
V6 2.7 Liter	8	....	650	650	865	865
AMANTI—V6—Equipment Schedule 3						
W.B. 110.2"; 3.5 Liter.						
Sedan 4D	LD124	25535	4975	5800	7475	10100

2005 KIA — KNA(DC125)-5-#

Body Type	VIN	List	Trade-In Fair	Trade-In Good	Pvt-Party Good	Retail Excellent
RIO—4-Cyl.—Equipment Schedule 6						
W.B. 94.9"; 1.6 Liter.						
Sedan 4D	DC125	11080	1950	2500	4000	6175
Cinco Wagon 4D	DC165	12705	2450	3050	4550	6775
SPECTRA—4-Cyl.—Equipment Schedule 6						
W.B. 102.8"; 2.0 Liter.						
LX Sedan 4D	FB121	14120	2775	3375	4925	7200
EX Sedan 4D	FB121	14290	2825	3450	5000	7275
SX Sedan 4D	FB121	15535	3175	3875	5425	7750
SPECTRA5—4-Cyl.—Equipment Schedule 6						
W.B. 102.8"; 2.0 Liter.						
Hatchback 4D	FE161	15535	3250	3950	5500	7825
OPTIMA—4-Cyl.—Equipment Schedule 5						
W.B. 106.3"; 2.4 Liter.						
LX Sedan 4D	GD126	17740	1700	2200	3725	5875
EX Sedan 4D	GD126	19190	2525	3100	4650	6900
V6 2.7 Liter	8	....	725	725	965	965
AMANTI—V6—Equipment Schedule 3						
W.B. 110.2"; 3.5 Liter.						
Sedan 4D	LD124	25840	5725	6650	8300	11050

Body	Type	VIN	List	Trade-In Fair	Trade-In Good	Pvt-Party Good	Retail Excellent
2006 KIA — KNA(DE123)-6-#							
RIO—4-Cyl.—Equipment Schedule 6							
W.B. 98.4"; 1.6 Liter.							
Sedan 4D		DE123	11110	3050	3700	5275	7600
LX Sedan 4D		DE123	12985	3475	4175	5725	8100
RIO5—4-Cyl.—Equipment Schedule 6							
W.B. 98.4"; 1.6 Liter.							
SX Hatchback 4D		DE163	14040	3750	4450	6025	8425
SPECTRA—4-Cyl.—Equipment Schedule 6							
W.B. 102.8"; 2.0 Liter.							
LX Sedan 4D		FE121	13475	3625	4325	5900	8300
EX Sedan 4D		FE121	14840	3700	4400	5975	8375
SX Sedan 4D		FE121	16140	4125	4875	6450	8900
SPECTRA5—4-Cyl.—Equipment Schedule 6							
W.B. 102.8"; 2.0 Liter.							
Hatchback 4D		FE161	16140	4200	4975	6550	9000
OPTIMA—4-Cyl.—Equipment Schedule 5							
W.B. 106.3"; 2.4 Liter.							
LX Sedan 4D		GD126	18040	2375	2950	4475	6750
EX Sedan 4D		GD126	19490	3250	3950	5525	7875
V6 2.7 Liter		8		800	800	1065	1065
OPTIMA (2006.5)—4-Cyl.—Equipment Schedule 5							
W.B. 107.1"; 2.4 Liter.							
LX Sedan 4D		GE123	18250	4000	4725	6300	8725
EX Sedan 4D		GE123	19995	4775	5575	7225	9775
V6 2.7 Liter		4		800	800	1065	1065
AMANTI—V6—Equipment Schedule 3							
W.B. 110.2"; 3.5 Liter.							
Sedan 4D		LD124	28435	6625	7625	9325	12150
2007 KIA — KNA(DE123)-7-#							
RIO—4-Cyl.—Equipment Schedule 6							
W.B. 98.4"; 1.6 Liter.							
Sedan 4D		DE123	11350	3950	4675	6150	8425
LX Sedan 4D		DE123	13275	4400	5200	6700	9075
SX Sedan 4D		DE123	14075	4625	5450	6925	9325
RIO5—4-Cyl.—Equipment Schedule 6							
W.B. 98.4"; 1.6 Liter.							
SX Hatchback 4D		DE163	14330	4675	5525	7000	9400
SPECTRA—4-Cyl.—Equipment Schedule 6							
W.B. 102.8"; 2.0 Liter.							
LX Sedan 4D		FE121	13495	4525	5350	6850	9275
EX Sedan 4D		FE121	15495	4600	5425	6925	9350
SX Sedan 4D		FE121	16595	5050	5900	7425	9900
SPECTRA5—4-Cyl.—Equipment Schedule 6							
W.B. 102.8"; 2.0 Liter.							
SX Hatchback 4D		FE161	16595	5175	6025	7575	10050
RONDO—V6—Equipment Schedule 4							
W.B. 106.3"; 2.7 Liter.							
LX Wagon 4D		FG526	19495	5675	6625	8125	10700
EX Wagon 4D		FG526	20795	6200	7175	8725	11300
4-Cyl. 2.4 Liter		5		(400)	(400)	(535)	(535)
OPTIMA—4-Cyl.—Equipment Schedule 5							
W.B. 107.1"; 2.4 Liter.							
LX Sedan 4D		GE123	18250	5000	5850	7375	9850
EX Sedan 4D		GE123	19995	5875	6800	8325	10900
V6 2.7 Liter		4		875	875	1165	1165
AMANTI—V6—Equipment Schedule 3							
W.B. 110.2"; 3.8 Liter.							
Sedan 4D		LD125	26175	7950	9100	10800	13650
2008 KIA — KNA(DE123)-8-#							
RIO—4-Cyl.—Equipment Schedule 6							
W.B. 98.4"; 1.6 Liter.							
Sedan 4D		DE123	11515	4850	5675	6975	9175
LX Sedan 4D		DE123	13440	5350	6225	7525	9775
SX Sedan 4D		DE123	14240	5575	6500	7825	10100
RIO5—4-Cyl.—Equipment Schedule 6							
W.B. 98.4"; 1.6 Liter.							
LX Hatchback 4D		DE163	13540	5500	6400	7700	9950
SX Hatchback 4D		DE163	14495	5650	6600	7925	10200

Body	Type	VIN	List	Trade-In Fair	Trade-In Good	Pvt-Party Good	Retail Excellent
SPECTRA—4-Cyl.—Equipment Schedule 6							
W.B. 102.8"; 2.0 Liter.							
LX Sedan 4D		FE121	13520	**5475**	**6375**	**7750**	**10100**
EX Sedan 4D		FE121	15520	**5525**	**6450**	**7850**	**10200**
SX Sedan 4D		FE121	16620	**6050**	**7000**	**8375**	**10800**
SPECTRA5—4-Cyl.—Equipment Schedule 6							
W.B. 102.8"; 2.0 Liter.							
SX Hatchback 4D		FE161	16620	**6150**	**7125**	**8525**	**11000**
RONDO—V6—Equipment Schedule 4							
W.B. 106.3"; 2.7 Liter.							
LX Wagon 4D		FG526	19495	**6925**	**7975**	**9375**	**11900**
EX Wagon 4D		FG526	20795	**7500**	**8600**	**10050**	**12650**
4-Cyl. 2.4 Liter		5		**(450)**	**(450)**	**(600)**	**(600)**
OPTIMA—4-Cyl.—Equipment Schedule 5							
W.B. 107.1"; 2.4 Liter.							
LX Sedan 4D		GE123	18390	**6425**	**7425**	**8850**	**11300**
EX Sedan 4D		GE123	20135	**7375**	**8450**	**9900**	**12450**
V6 2.7 Liter		4		**950**	**950**	**1265**	**1265**
AMANTI—V6—Equipment Schedule 3							
W.B. 110.2"; 3.8 Liter.							
Sedan 4D		LD125	26195	**10775**	**12200**	**13850**	**17050**

LEXUS

1994 LEXUS — JT8(GK13T)–R–#

Body	Type	VIN	List	Trade-In Fair	Trade-In Good	Pvt-Party Good	Retail Excellent
ES 300—V6—Equipment Schedule 1							
W.B. 103.1"; 3.0 Liter.							
Sedan 4D		GK13T	31070	**1900**	**2450**	**3700**	**5550**
GS 300—6-Cyl.—Equipment Schedule 1							
W.B. 109.4"; 3.0 Liter.							
Sedan 4D		JS47E	40370	**2750**	**3350**	**4700**	**6750**
Traction Control				**100**	**100**	**135**	**135**
SC 300—6-Cyl.—Equipment Schedule 1							
W.B. 105.9"; 3.0 Liter.							
Sport Coupe 2D		JZ31C	39370	**4325**	**5125**	**6675**	**9125**
Traction Control				**100**	**100**	**135**	**135**
SC 400—V8—Equipment Schedule 1							
W.B. 105.9"; 4.0 Liter.							
Sport Coupe 2D		UZ30C	45570	**4975**	**5800**	**7500**	**10150**
Traction Control				**100**	**100**	**135**	**135**
LS 400—V8—Equipment Schedule 1							
W.B. 110.8"; 4.0 Liter.							
Sedan 4D		UF11E	50370	**3575**	**4275**	**5750**	**8025**
Traction Control				**100**	**100**	**135**	**135**

1995 LEXUS — JT8(GK13T)–S–#

Body	Type	VIN	List	Trade-In Fair	Trade-In Good	Pvt-Party Good	Retail Excellent
ES 300—V6—Equipment Schedule 1							
W.B. 103.1"; 3.0 Liter.							
Sedan 4D		GK13T	34180	**2250**	**2825**	**4150**	**6100**
GS 300—6-Cyl.—Equipment Schedule 1							
W.B. 109.4"; 3.0 Liter.							
Sedan 4D		JS47E	45380	**3175**	**3850**	**5275**	**7450**
Traction Control				**100**	**100**	**135**	**135**
SC 300—6-Cyl.—Equipment Schedule 1							
W.B. 105.9"; 3.0 Liter.							
Sport Coupe 2D		JZ31C	44980	**4600**	**5425**	**7050**	**9625**
Traction Control				**100**	**100**	**135**	**135**
SC 400—V8—Equipment Schedule 1							
W.B. 105.9"; 4.0 Liter.							
Sport Coupe 2D		UZ30C	49780	**5300**	**6175**	**7925**	**10650**
Traction Control				**100**	**100**	**135**	**135**
LS 400—V8—Equipment Schedule 1							
W.B. 112.2"; 4.0 Liter.							
Sedan 4D		UF22E	52680	**4100**	**4850**	**6400**	**8825**
Traction Control				**100**	**100**	**135**	**135**

1996 LEXUS — JT8(BF12G)–T–#

Body	Type	VIN	List	Trade-In Fair	Trade-In Good	Pvt-Party Good	Retail Excellent
ES 300—V6—Equipment Schedule 1							
W.B. 103.1"; 3.0 Liter.							
Sedan 4D		BF12G	34895	**2675**	**3275**	**4625**	**6700**

1996 LEXUS

Body Type	VIN	List	Trade-In Fair	Trade-In Good	Pvt-Party Good	Retail Excellent
GS 300—6-Cyl.—Equipment Schedule 1						
W.B. 109.4"; 3.0 Liter.						
Sedan 4D	BD42S	48445	3725	4425	5925	8225
Traction Control			125	125	165	165
SC 300—6-Cyl.—Equipment Schedule 1						
W.B. 105.9"; 3.0 Liter.						
Sport Coupe 2D	CD32Z	47695	4925	5775	7425	10050
Traction Control			125	125	165	165
SC 400—V8—Equipment Schedule 1						
W.B. 105.9"; 4.0 Liter.						
Sport Coupe 2D	CH32Y	53845	5675	6600	8325	11100
Traction Control			125	125	165	165
LS 400—V8—Equipment Schedule 1						
W.B. 112.2"; 4.0 Liter.						
Sedan 4D	BH33F	54445	4425	5225	6800	9275
Traction Control			125	125	165	165

1997 LEXUS — JT8(BF22G)-V-#

Body Type	VIN	List	Trade-In Fair	Trade-In Good	Pvt-Party Good	Retail Excellent
ES 300—V6—Equipment Schedule 1						
W.B. 105.1"; 3.0 Liter.						
Sedan 4D	BF22G	33045	3150	3825	5250	7425
GS 300—6-Cyl.—Equipment Schedule 1						
W.B. 109.4"; 3.0 Liter.						
Sedan 4D	BD42S	48595	4325	5100	6650	9050
Traction Control			150	150	200	200
SC 300—6-Cyl.—Equipment Schedule 1						
W.B. 105.9"; 3.0 Liter.						
Sport Coupe 2D	CD32Z	43445	5750	6700	8425	11200
Traction Control			150	150	200	200
SC 400—V8—Equipment Schedule 1						
W.B. 105.9"; 4.0 Liter.						
Sport Coupe 2D	CH32Y	52295	6600	7600	9400	12350
Traction Control			150	150	200	200
LS 400—V8—Equipment Schedule 1						
W.B. 112.2"; 4.0 Liter.						
Sedan 4D	BH28F	54495	4875	5700	7375	10000
Traction Control			150	150	200	200

1998 LEXUS — JT8(BF28G)-W-#

Body Type	VIN	List	Trade-In Fair	Trade-In Good	Pvt-Party Good	Retail Excellent
ES 300—V6—Equipment Schedule 1						
W.B. 105.1"; 3.0 Liter.						
Sedan 4D	BF28G	33935	3725	4425	5900	8175
GS 300—6-Cyl.—Equipment Schedule 1						
W.B. 110.2"; 3.0 Liter.						
Sedan 4D	BD68S	40025	4100	4850	6350	8700
GS 400—V8—Equipment Schedule 1						
W.B. 110.2"; 4.0 Liter.						
Sedan 4D	BH68X	46315	4850	5675	7325	9900
SC 300—6-Cyl.—Equipment Schedule 1						
W.B. 105.9"; 3.0 Liter.						
Sport Coupe 2D	CD32Z	44565	6650	7675	9425	12350
Traction Control			175	175	235	235
SC 400—V8—Equipment Schedule 1						
W.B. 105.9"; 4.0 Liter.						
Sport Coupe 2D	CH32Y	54315	7575	8675	10550	13650
Traction Control			175	175	235	235
LS 400—V8—Equipment Schedule 1						
W.B. 112.2"; 4.0 Liter.						
Sedan 4D	BH28F	54515	5525	6425	8100	10850

1999 LEXUS — JT8(BF28G)-X-#

Body Type	VIN	List	Trade-In Fair	Trade-In Good	Pvt-Party Good	Retail Excellent
ES 300—V6—Equipment Schedule 1						
W.B. 105.1"; 3.0 Liter.						
Sedan 4D	BF28G	34235	4350	5150	6675	9050
Coach Edition			200	200	265	265
GS 300—6-Cyl.—Equipment Schedule 1						
W.B. 110.2"; 3.0 Liter.						
Sedan 4D	BD68S	40580	4750	5575	7175	9700
GS 400—V8—Equipment Schedule 1						
W.B. 110.2"; 4.0 Liter.						
Sedan 4D	BH68X	47020	5600	6525	8175	10900

Body	Type	VIN	List	Trade-In Fair	Good	Pvt-Party Good	Retail Excellent
SC 300—6-Cyl.—Equipment Schedule 1							
W.B. 105.9"; 3.0 Liter.							
Sport Coupe 2D		CD32Z	46640	7625	8725	10550	13600
Traction Control				200	200	265	265
SC 400—V8—Equipment Schedule 1							
W.B. 105.9"; 4.0 Liter.							
Sport Coupe 2D		CH32Y	56830	8600	9800	11750	15100
Traction Control				200	200	265	265
LS 400—V8—Equipment Schedule 1							
W.B. 112.2"; 4.0 Liter.							
Sedan 4D		BH28F	55220	6375	7350	9125	12000

2000 LEXUS — JT8(BF28G)-Y-#

Body	Type	VIN	List	Trade-In Fair	Good	Pvt-Party Good	Retail Excellent
ES 300—V6—Equipment Schedule 1							
W.B. 105.1"; 3.0 Liter.							
Sedan 4D		BF28G	34785	5125	5975	7575	10150
Platinum Series				250	250	335	335
GS 300—6-Cyl.—Equipment Schedule 1							
W.B. 110.2"; 3.0 Liter.							
Sedan 4D		BD68S	40880	5550	6475	8075	10750
Platinum Series				250	250	335	335
GS 400—V8—Equipment Schedule 1							
W.B. 110.2"; 4.0 Liter.							
Sedan 4D		BH68X	47520	6475	7450	9175	11950
Platinum Series				250	250	335	335
SC 300—6-Cyl.—Equipment Schedule 1							
W.B. 105.9"; 3.0 Liter.							
Sport Coupe 2D		CD32Z	47140	8600	9800	11700	15000
Traction Control				225	225	300	300
SC 400—V8—Equipment Schedule 1							
W.B. 105.9"; 4.0 Liter.							
Sport Coupe 2D		CH32Y	57530	9675	11025	13000	16450
Traction Control				225	225	300	300
LS 400—V8—Equipment Schedule 1							
W.B. 112.2"; 4.0 Liter.							
Sedan 4D		BH28F	55420	7525	8625	10450	13500
Platinum Series				250	250	335	335

2001 LEXUS — JT(8orH)(BF28G)-1-#

Body	Type	VIN	List	Trade-In Fair	Good	Pvt-Party Good	Retail Excellent
ES 300—V6—Equipment Schedule 1							
W.B. 105.1"; 3.0 Liter.							
Sedan 4D		BF28G	34935	6025	6950	8625	11300
Coach Edition				200	200	265	265
IS 300—6-Cyl.—Equipment Schedule 1							
W.B. 105.1"; 3.0 Liter.							
Sedan 4D		BD182	34055	5975	6900	8550	11200
GS 300—6-Cyl.—Equipment Schedule 1							
W.B. 110.2"; 3.0 Liter.							
Sedan 4D		BD68S	41780	6475	7450	9150	11900
GS 430—V8—Equipment Schedule 1							
W.B. 110.2"; 4.3 Liter.							
Sedan 4D		BN68X	50580	7450	8525	10250	13200
LS 430—V8—Equipment Schedule 1							
W.B. 115.2"; 4.3 Liter.							
Sedan 4D		BN30F	54550	8500	9725	11600	14800
Ultra Luxury Pkg				2450	2450	3265	3265

2002 LEXUS — JT(8orH)(BF30G)-2-#

Body	Type	VIN	List	Trade-In Fair	Good	Pvt-Party Good	Retail Excellent
ES 300—V6—Equipment Schedule 1							
W.B. 107.1"; 3.0 Liter.							
Sedan 4D		BF30G	33640	7250	8325	10200	13250
IS 300—6-Cyl.—Equipment Schedule 1							
W.B. 105.1"; 3.0 Liter.							
Sedan 4D		BD192	33655	6850	7900	9700	12700
Sport Cross H'Back 4D		ED192	35195	6925	7975	9850	12850
Manual Trans				(500)	(500)	(665)	(665)
GS 300—6-Cyl.—Equipment Schedule 1							
W.B. 110.2"; 3.0 Liter.							
Sedan 4D		BD69S	41840	7375	8475	10350	13400
SportDesign				500	500	665	665
GS 430—V8—Equipment Schedule 1							
W.B. 110.2"; 4.3 Liter.							

2002 LEXUS

Body	Type	VIN	List	Trade-In Fair	Trade-In Good	Pvt-Party Good	Retail Excellent
Sedan 4D		BL69S	48980	8425	9625	11550	14850
LS 430—V8—Equipment Schedule 1							
W.B. 115.2"; 4.3 Liter.							
Sedan 4D		BN30F	56080	10350	11700	13800	17450
Ultra Luxury Pkg		------		2500	2500	3335	3335
SC 430—V8—Equipment Schedule 1							
W.B. 103.1"; 4.3 Liter.							
Convertible 2D		FN48Y	59030	11850	13375	15650	19600

2003 LEXUS — JT(8orH)(BF30G)-3-#

Body	Type	VIN	List	Trade-In Fair	Trade-In Good	Pvt-Party Good	Retail Excellent
ES 300—V6—Equipment Schedule 1							
W.B. 107.1"; 3.0 Liter.							
Sedan 4D		BF30G	33780	8425	9625	11550	14800
IS 300—6-Cyl.—Equipment Schedule 1							
W.B. 105.1"; 3.0 Liter.							
Sedan 4D		BD192	32485	7950	9100	11000	14150
Sport Cross H'Back 4D		ED192	32525	8075	9225	11150	14350
SportDesign				800	800	1065	1065
Manual Trans				(500)	(500)	(665)	(665)
GS 300—6-Cyl.—Equipment Schedule 1							
W.B. 110.2"; 3.0 Liter.							
Sedan 4D		BD69S	40960	8500	9725	11650	14900
SportDesign				575	575	765	765
GS 430—V8—Equipment Schedule 1							
W.B. 110.2"; 4.3 Liter.							
Sedan 4D		BL69S	48400	9725	11025	13050	16450
LS 430—V8—Equipment Schedule 1							
W.B. 115.2"; 4.3 Liter.							
Sedan 4D		BN30F	56600	11750	13275	15400	19200
Ultra Luxury Pkg		------		2600	2600	3465	3465
SC 430—V8—Equipment Schedule 1							
W.B. 103.1"; 4.3 Liter.							
Convertible 2D		FN48Y	62600	14450	16275	18600	22900

2004 LEXUS — JT(8orH)(BA30G)-4-#

Body	Type	VIN	List	Trade-In Fair	Trade-In Good	Pvt-Party Good	Retail Excellent
ES 330—V6—Equipment Schedule 1							
W.B. 107.1"; 3.3 Liter.							
Sedan 4D		BA30G	32350	9750	11075	13050	16400
IS 300—6-Cyl.—Equipment Schedule 1							
W.B. 105.1"; 3.0 Liter.							
Sedan 4D		BD192	32815	9200	10475	12400	15700
Sport Cross H'Back 4D		ED192	32855	9325	10625	12550	15900
Manual Trans				(500)	(500)	(665)	(665)
GS 300—6-Cyl.—Equipment Schedule 1							
W.B. 110.2"; 3.0 Liter.							
Sedan 4D		BD68S	41010	9850	11175	13150	16500
GS 430—V8—Equipment Schedule 1							
W.B. 110.2"; 4.3 Liter.							
Sedan 4D		BL69S	48450	11225	12750	14700	18300
LS 430—V8—Equipment Schedule 1							
W.B. 115.2"; 4.3 Liter.							
Sedan 4D		BN30F	55750	13925	15675	17850	21900
Ultra Luxury Pkg		------		2700	2700	3600	3600
SC 430—V8—Equipment Schedule 1							
W.B. 103.1"; 4.3 Liter.							
Convertible 2D		FN48Y	63200	17200	19250	21700	26400

2005 LEXUS — JT(8orH)(BA30G)-5-#

Body	Type	VIN	List	Trade-In Fair	Trade-In Good	Pvt-Party Good	Retail Excellent
ES 330—V6—Equipment Schedule 1							
W.B. 107.1"; 3.3 Liter.							
Sedan 4D		BA30G	32600	11275	12800	14700	18200
IS 300—6-Cyl.—Equipment Schedule 1							
W.B. 105.1"; 3.0 Liter.							
Sedan 4D		BD192	34315	10625	12050	13950	17400
Sport Cross H'Back 4D		ED192	34355	10825	12250	14150	17600
Manual Trans				(500)	(500)	(665)	(665)
GS 300—6-Cyl.—Equipment Schedule 1							
W.B. 110.2"; 3.0 Liter.							
Sedan 4D		BD69S	41160	11375	12850	14750	18300
GS 430—V8—Equipment Schedule 1							
W.B. 110.2"; 4.3 Liter.							
Sedan 4D		BL69S	48600	12925	14550	16500	20200

Body Type	VIN	List	Trade-In Fair	Trade-In Good	Pvt-Party Good	Retail Excellent
LS 430—V8—Equipment Schedule 1						
W.B. 115.2"; 4.3 Liter.						
Sedan 4D	BN36F	56300	**16650**	**18725**	**20900**	**25200**
Ultra Luxury Pkg			**2775**	**2775**	**3700**	**3700**
SC 430—V8—Equipment Schedule 1						
W.B. 103.1"; 4.3 Liter.						
Convertible 2D	FN48Y	63800	**20200**	**22550**	**25000**	**29900**

2006 LEXUS — JT(8orH)(BA30G)-6-#

Body Type	VIN	List	Trade-In Fair	Trade-In Good	Pvt-Party Good	Retail Excellent
ES 330—V6—Equipment Schedule 1						
W.B. 107.1"; 3.3 Liter.						
Sedan 4D	BA30G	32950	**13025**	**14700**	**16600**	**20300**
IS 250—V6—Equipment Schedule 1						
W.B. 107.5"; 2.5 Liter.						
Sedan 4D	BK262	31750	**15575**	**17500**	**19400**	**23300**
AWD Sedan 4D	CK262	34875	**17000**	**19050**	**21100**	**25200**
IS 350—V6—Equipment Schedule 1						
W.B. 107.5"; 3.5 Liter.						
Sedan 4D	BE262	36030	**17700**	**19900**	**21800**	**26000**
GS 300—V6—Equipment Schedule 1						
W.B. 112.2"; 3.0 Liter.						
Sedan 4D	BH96S	44800	**17650**	**19800**	**21800**	**25900**
AWD Sedan 4D	CH96S	46750	**18325**	**20475**	**22500**	**26800**
GS 430—V8—Equipment Schedule 1						
W.B. 112.2"; 4.3 Liter.						
Sedan 4D	BN96S	53025	**19350**	**21650**	**23600**	**28000**
LS 430—V8—Equipment Schedule 1						
W.B. 115.2"; 4.3 Liter.						
Sedan 4D	BN36F	57175	**20275**	**22725**	**24900**	**29500**
Ultra Luxury Pkg			**2850**	**2850**	**3800**	**3800**
SC 430—V8—Equipment Schedule 1						
W.B. 103.1"; 4.3 Liter.						
Convertible 2D	FN48Y	66005	**23525**	**26275**	**28600**	**33700**
Pebble Beach Special Ed			**400**	**400**	**535**	**535**

2007 LEXUS — JT(8orH)(BJ46G)-7-#

Body Type	VIN	List	Trade-In Fair	Trade-In Good	Pvt-Party Good	Retail Excellent
ES 350—V6—Equipment Schedule 1						
W.B. 109.3"; 3.5 Liter.						
Sedan 4D	BJ46G	35145	**19300**	**21550**	**23400**	**27600**
Ultra Luxury Pkg			**2925**	**2925**	**3900**	**3900**
IS 250—V6—Equipment Schedule 1						
W.B. 107.5"; 2.5 Liter.						
Sedan 4D	BK262	32015	**17875**	**20000**	**21900**	**26000**
AWD Sedan 4D	CK262	34875	**19450**	**21750**	**23600**	**27800**
IS 350—V6—Equipment Schedule 1						
W.B. 107.5"; 3.5 Liter.						
Sedan 4D	BE262	36295	**20275**	**22650**	**24500**	**28800**
GS 350—V6—Equipment Schedule 1						
W.B. 112.2"; 3.5 Liter.						
Sedan 4D	BE96S	44845	**23525**	**26275**	**28100**	**32700**
AWD Sedan 4D	CE96S	46795	**24300**	**27150**	**29000**	**33700**
GS 430—V8—Equipment Schedule 1						
W.B. 112.2"; 4.3 Liter.						
Sedan 4D	BN96S	53070	**25475**	**28325**	**30300**	**35200**
GS 450h—V6 Hybrid—Equipment Schedule 1						
W.B. 112.2"; 3.5 Liter.						
Sedan 4D	BC96S	55595	**30275**	**33700**	**35700**	**41000**
LS 460—V8—Equipment Schedule 1						
W.B. 116.9", 121.7" (L); 4.6 Liter.						
Sedan 4D	BL46F	61715	**34300**	**38125**	**40300**	**46200**
L Sedan 4D	GL46F	71715	**41850**	**46350**	**48500**	**55100**
Executive Pkg			**3000**	**3000**	**4000**	**4000**
Luxury Pkg			**500**	**500**	**665**	**665**
Touring Pkg			**600**	**600**	**800**	**800**
SC 430—V8—Equipment Schedule 1						
W.B. 103.1"; 4.3 Liter.						
Convertible 2D	FN45Y	66150	**27350**	**30475**	**32700**	**38100**
Pebble Beach Special Ed			**400**	**400**	**535**	**535**

2008 LEXUS — JT(8orH)(BJ46G)-8-#

ES 350—V6—Equipment Schedule 1
W.B. 109.3"; 3.5 Liter.

Body	Type	VIN	List	Trade-In Fair	Good	Pvt-Party Good	Retail Excellent
Sedan 4D		BJ46G	34485	21950	24500	26300	30600
Ultra Luxury Pkg				3000	3000	4000	4000

IS 250—V6—Equipment Schedule 1
W.B. 107.5"; 2.5 Liter.

Body	Type	VIN	List	Trade-In Fair	Good	Pvt-Party Good	Retail Excellent
Sedan 4D		BK262	32390	20375	22825	24600	28800
AWD Sedan 4D		CK262	34850	22150	24700	26500	30800

IS 350—V6—Equipment Schedule 1
W.B. 107.5"; 3.5 Liter.

Body	Type	VIN	List	Trade-In Fair	Good	Pvt-Party Good	Retail Excellent
Sedan 4D		BE262	36670	22925	25575	27300	31800

IS F—V8—Equipment Schedule 1
W.B. 107.5"; 5.0 Liter.

Body	Type	VIN	List	Trade-In Fair	Good	Pvt-Party Good	Retail Excellent
Sedan 4D		BP262	56765	36250	40275	42300	48500

GS 350—V6—Equipment Schedule 1
W.B. 112.2"; 3.5 Liter.

Body	Type	VIN	List	Trade-In Fair	Good	Pvt-Party Good	Retail Excellent
Sedan 4D		BE96S	44915	26550	29600	31400	36100
AWD Sedan 4D		CE96S	46865	27450	30575	32300	37100

GS 450h—V6 Hybrid—Equipment Schedule 1
W.B. 112.2"; 3.5 Liter.

Body	Type	VIN	List	Trade-In Fair	Good	Pvt-Party Good	Retail Excellent
Sedan 4D		BC96S	55665	33900	37625	39300	44700

GS 460—V8—Equipment Schedule 1
W.B. 112.2"; 4.6 Liter.

Body	Type	VIN	List	Trade-In Fair	Good	Pvt-Party Good	Retail Excellent
Sedan 4D		BN96S	53385	31950	35575	37200	42400

LS 460—V8—Equipment Schedule 1
W.B. 116.9", 121.7" (L); 4.6 Liter.

Body	Type	VIN	List	Trade-In Fair	Good	Pvt-Party Good	Retail Excellent
Sedan 4D		BL46F	62265	37050	41050	42900	48800
L Sedan 4D		GL46F	72265	44975	49875	51700	58400
Executive Pkg				3000	3000	4000	4000
Luxury Pkg				500	500	665	665
Touring Pkg				600	600	800	800

LS 600h—V8 Hybrid—Equipment Schedule 1
W.B. 121.7"; 5.0 Liter.

Body	Type	VIN	List	Trade-In Fair	Good	Pvt-Party Good	Retail Excellent
L Sedan 4D		DU46F	104765	67625	74775	76600	85500
Executive Pkg				3000	3000	4000	4000

SC 430—V8—Equipment Schedule 1
W.B. 103.1"; 4.3 Liter.

Body	Type	VIN	List	Trade-In Fair	Good	Pvt-Party Good	Retail Excellent
Convertible 2D		FN45Y	66220	31850	35375	37400	43100
Pebble Beach Special Ed				400	400	535	535

LINCOLN

1994 LINCOLN — 1LN(LM81W)–R–#

TOWN CAR—V8—Equipment Schedule 2
W.B. 117.4"; 4.6 Liter.

Body	Type	VIN	List	Fair	Good	Good	Excellent
Executive Sedan 4D		LM81W	35930	1400	1875	3075	4825
Signature Sedan 4D		LM82W	37230	1525	2000	3225	5000
Cartier Dsgnr Sed 4D		LM83W	38725	1600	2075	3300	5100

CONTINENTAL—V6—Equipment Schedule 2
W.B. 109.0"; 3.8 Liter.

Body	Type	VIN	List	Fair	Good	Good	Excellent
Executive Sedan 4D		LM974	34375	1125	1575	2700	4350
Signature Sedan 4D		LM984	36225	1175	1650	2800	4450

MARK VIII—V8—Equipment Schedule 2
W.B. 113.0"; 4.6 Liter.

Body	Type	VIN	List	Fair	Good	Good	Excellent
Coupe 2D		LM91V	38675	1150	1600	2750	4425

1995 LINCOLN — 1LN(LM81W)–S–#

TOWN CAR—V8—Equipment Schedule 2
W.B. 117.4"; 4.6 Liter.

Body	Type	VIN	List	Fair	Good	Good	Excellent
Executive Sedan 4D		LM81W	37595	1725	2225	3475	5325
Signature Sedan 4D		LM82W	39695	1850	2375	3650	5525
Cartier Sedan 4D		LM83W	41825	1900	2450	3700	5575
Spinnaker Edition				50	50	65	65

CONTINENTAL—V8—Equipment Schedule 2
W.B. 109.0"; 4.6 Liter.

Body	Type	VIN	List	Fair	Good	Good	Excellent
Sedan 4D		LM97V	41375	1150	1600	2750	4425

MARK VIII—V8—Equipment Schedule 2
W.B. 113.0"; 4.6 Liter.

Body	Type	VIN	List	Fair	Good	Good	Excellent
Coupe 2D		LM91V	39425	1375	1850	3050	4775
LSC				100	100	135	135

Body	Type	VIN	List	Trade-In Fair	Trade-In Good	Pvt-Party Good	Retail Excellent

1996 LINCOLN — 1LN(LM81W)-T-#

TOWN CAR—V8—Equipment Schedule 2
W.B. 117.4"; 4.6 Liter.

Body	Type	VIN	List	Fair	Good	Pvt Good	Excellent
Executive Sedan 4D		LM81W	38120	2075	2650	3950	5850
Signature Sedan 4D		LM82W	40170	2225	2825	4125	6075
Cartier Sedan 4D		LM83W	42600	2325	2925	4225	6200

CONTINENTAL—V8—Equipment Schedule 2
W.B. 109.0"; 4.6 Liter.

Sedan 4D		LM97V	42440	1425	1875	3075	4850

MARK VIII—V8—Equipment Schedule 2
W.B. 113.0"; 4.6 Liter.

Coupe 2D		LM91V	40290	1650	2150	3375	5200
LSC				125	125	165	165

1997 LINCOLN — 1LN(LM81W)-V-#

TOWN CAR—V8—Equipment Schedule 2
W.B. 117.4"; 4.6 Liter.

Executive Sedan 4D		LM81W	38720	2525	3125	4450	6500
Signature Sedan 4D		LM82W	41080	2750	3350	4725	6800
Cartier Sedan 4D		LM83W	43870	2875	3500	4875	6975

CONTINENTAL—V8—Equipment Schedule 2
W.B. 109.0"; 4.6 Liter.

Sedan 4D		LM97V	37850	1750	2275	3500	5350

MARK VIII—V8—Equipment Schedule 2
W.B. 113.0"; 4.6 Liter.

Coupe 2D		LM91V	36950	1700	2200	3450	5300
LSC				150	150	200	200

1998 LINCOLN — 1LN(LM81W)-W-#

TOWN CAR—V8—Equipment Schedule 2
W.B. 117.7"; 4.6 Liter.

Executive Sedan 4D		LM81W	38330	2650	3250	4600	6675
Signature Sedan 4D		LM82W	40150	2925	3550	4925	7025
Cartier Sedan 4D		LM83W	42500	3100	3775	5175	7300

CONTINENTAL—V8—Equipment Schedule 2
W.B. 109.0"; 4.6 Liter.

Sedan 4D		LM97V	38500	2150	2725	4025	5950

MARK VIII—V8—Equipment Schedule 2
W.B. 113.0"; 4.6 Liter.

Coupe 2D		LM91V	37500	1825	2350	3600	5475
LSC				175	175	235	235

1999 LINCOLN — 1LN(LM81W)-X-#

TOWN CAR—V8—Equipment Schedule 2
W.B. 117.7"; 4.6 Liter.

Executive Sedan 4D		LM81W	38995	3025	3650	5075	7200
Signature Sedan 4D		LM82W	40995	3300	4000	5425	7625
Cartier Sedan 4D		LM83W	43495	3575	4300	5725	7975

CONTINENTAL—V8—Equipment Schedule 2
W.B. 109.0"; 4.6 Liter.

Sedan 4D		LM97V	38995	2675	3275	4625	6675

2000 LINCOLN — 1LN(HM81W)-Y-#

TOWN CAR—V8—Equipment Schedule 2
W.B. 117.7", 123.7" (L Pkg); 4.6 Liter.

Executive Sedan 4D		HM81W	39300	3500	4225	5625	7875
Signature Sedan 4D		HM82W	41300	3875	4600	6050	8350
Cartier Sedan 4D		HM83W	43800	4200	4950	6450	8775
L Pkg				1450	1450	1935	1935
Touring Pkg				100	100	135	135

CONTINENTAL—V8—Equipment Schedule 2
W.B. 117.7"; 4.6 Liter.

Sedan 4D		HM97V	39550	2625	3225	4550	6575

LS—V6—Equipment Schedule 2
W.B. 114.5"; 3.0 Liter.

Sedan 4D		HM86S	31450	1550	2025	3350	5250
Sport Pkg				100	100	135	135
Manual Trans				(425)	(425)	(565)	(565)

LS—V8—Equipment Schedule 2
W.B. 114.5"; 3.9 Liter.

Body Type	VIN	List	Trade-In Fair	Good	Pvt-Party Good	Retail Excellent
Sedan 4D	HM87A	35225	2875	3500	4925	7050
Sport Pkg			100	100	135	135

2001 LINCOLN — 1LN(HM81W)-1-#

TOWN CAR—V8—Equipment Schedule 2
W.B. 117.7", 123.7" (L); 4.6 Liter.

Executive Sedan 4D	HM81W	39865	4200	4950	6400	8725
Executive L Sed 4D	HM84W	44225	5900	6825	8450	11100
Signature Sedan 4D	HM82W	42035	4550	5375	6875	9325
Signature Touring 4D	HM82W	42745	4700	5525	7075	9525
Cartier Sedan 4D	HM83W	44420	4950	5775	7350	9850
Cartier L Sedan 4D	HM85W	49230	7400	8475	10200	13150

CONTINENTAL—V8—Equipment Schedule 2
W.B. 109.0"; 4.6 Liter.

Sedan 4D	HM97V	40100	3275	3975	5350	7475

LS—V6—Equipment Schedule 2
W.B. 114.5"; 3.0 Liter.

Sedan 4D	HM86S	32250	2100	2675	4050	6050
Sport Pkg		-------	100	100	135	135
Manual Trans		-------	(475)	(475)	(635)	(635)

LS—V8—Equipment Schedule 2
W.B. 114.5"; 3.9 Liter.

Sedan 4D	HM87A	36280	3525	4250	5700	7975
Sport Pkg		-------	100	100	135	135

2002 LINCOLN — 1LN(HM81W)-2-#

TOWN CAR—V8—Equipment Schedule 2
W.B. 117.7", 123.7" (L); 4.6 Liter.

Executive Sedan 4D	HM81W	40540	3900	4625	6225	8700
Executive L Sed 4D	HM84W	44600	5725	6675	8425	11200
Signature Sedan 4D	HM82W	42710	4300	5075	6750	9350
Signature Touring 4D	HM82W	43420	4475	5275	6950	9575
Cartier Sedan 4D	HM83W	45095	4725	5550	7275	9950
Cartier L Sedan 4D	HM85W	49605	7350	8425	10300	13350

CONTINENTAL—V8—Equipment Schedule 2
W.B. 109.0"; 4.6 Liter.

Sedan 4D	HM97V	38555	4075	4800	6400	8825

LS—V6—Equipment Schedule 2
W.B. 114.5"; 3.0 Liter.

Sedan 4D	HM86S	33455	2725	3325	4925	7250
LSE		-------	1500	1500	2000	2000
Manual Trans		-------	(500)	(500)	(665)	(665)

LS—V8—Equipment Schedule 2
W.B. 114.5"; 3.9 Liter.

Sedan 4D	HM87A	37630	4250	5025	6700	9225
LSE		-------	1500	1500	2000	2000

2003 LINCOLN — 1LN(HM81W)-3-#

TOWN CAR—V8—Equipment Schedule 2
W.B. 117.7", 123.7" (L); 4.6 Liter.

Executive Sedan 4D	HM81W	41140	4550	5375	7025	9650
Executive L Sed 4D	HM84W	45115	6675	7700	9475	12400
Signature Sedan 4D	HM82W	43600	5075	5925	7650	10350
Cartier Sedan 4D	HM83W	46110	5800	6725	8475	11250
Cartier L Sedan 4D	HM85W	51570	8500	9725	11650	14900
Limited Edition		-------	500	500	665	665

LS—V6—Equipment Schedule 2
W.B. 114.5"; 3.0 Liter.

Sedan 4D	HM86S	34495	3475	4200	5850	8325

LS—V8—Equipment Schedule 2
W.B. 114.5"; 3.9 Liter.

Sedan 4D	HM87A	40695	5225	6075	7875	10650

2004 LINCOLN — 1LN(HM81W)-4-#

TOWN CAR—V8—Equipment Schedule 2
W.B. 117.7", 123.7" (L); 4.6 Liter.

Executive Sedan 4D	HM81W	42810	5600	6525	8225	11000
Executive L Sed 4D	HM84W	45790	7975	9150	11050	14150
Signature Sedan 4D	HM81W	41815	6200	7175	8925	11750
Ultimate Sedan 4D	HM83W	44925	7200	8275	10050	13050
Ultimate L Sedan 4D	HM85W	50470	10100	11475	13450	16850

Body	Type	VIN	List	Trade-In Fair	Trade-In Good	Pvt-Party Good	Retail Excellent
LS—V6—Equipment Schedule 2							
W.B. 114.5"; 3.0 Liter.							
Sedan 4D		HM86S	32495	**4125**	**4875**	**6575**	**9150**
LS—V8—Equipment Schedule 2							
W.B. 114.5"; 3.9 Liter.							
Sedan 4D		HM87A	40095	**6050**	**7000**	**8825**	**11700**
LSE			-------	**1500**	**1500**	**2000**	**2000**

2005 LINCOLN — 1LN(ForH)(M81W)-5-#

Body	Type	VIN	List	Trade-In Fair	Trade-In Good	Pvt-Party Good	Retail Excellent
TOWN CAR—V8—Equipment Schedule 2							
W.B. 117.7", 123.7" (L); 4.6 Liter.							
Signature Sedan 4D		M81W	42470	**7775**	**8925**	**10700**	**13700**
Signature Ltd Sed		M83W	45310	**9050**	**10300**	**12150**	**15400**
Signature L Sedan		M85W	50915	**12100**	**13675**	**15600**	**19200**
Executive L Sedan		M84W	46445	**9725**	**11025**	**12900**	**16200**
Limited Edition				**300**	**300**	**400**	**400**
LS—V6—Equipment Schedule 2							
W.B. 114.5"; 3.0 Liter.							
Sedan 4D		M86S	32965	**5475**	**6350**	**8150**	**11000**
LS—V8—Equipment Schedule 2							
W.B. 114.5"; 3.9 Liter.							
Sedan 4D		M87A	40515	**7625**	**8725**	**10600**	**13650**
LSE			-------	**1500**	**1500**	**2000**	**2000**

2006 LINCOLN — (1or3)LN(ForH)(M261)-6

Body	Type	VIN	List	Trade-In Fair	Trade-In Good	Pvt-Party Good	Retail Excellent
ZEPHYR—V6—Equipment Schedule 2							
W.B. 107.4"; 3.0 Liter.							
Sedan 4D		M261	29660	**10000**	**11375**	**13250**	**16550**
TOWN CAR—V8—Equipment Schedule 2							
W.B. 117.7", 123.7" (L); 4.6 Liter.							
Signature Sedan 4D		M81W	42875	**8825**	**10050**	**11900**	**15100**
Signature Ltd Sed		M82W	45740	**10000**	**11325**	**13200**	**16500**
Designer Sedan 4D		M83W	46735	**12400**	**14025**	**15900**	**19450**
Signature L Sedan		M85W	51345	**13675**	**15375**	**17250**	**21000**
Executive L Sedan		M84W	46990	**12125**	**12500**	**14350**	**17800**
LS—V8—Equipment Schedule 2							
W.B. 114.5"; 3.9 Liter.							
Sedan 4D		M87A	39945	**9575**	**10875**	**12850**	**16150**

2007 LINCOLN — (1or3)LN-(M26T)-7-#

Body	Type	VIN	List	Trade-In Fair	Trade-In Good	Pvt-Party Good	Retail Excellent
MKZ—V6—Equipment Schedule 2							
W.B. 107.4"; 3.5 Liter.							
Sedan 4D		M26T	29890	**13125**	**14800**	**16600**	**20200**
AWD Sedan 4D		M28T	31765	**14200**	**15975**	**17750**	**21400**
TOWN CAR—V8—Equipment Schedule 2							
W.B. 117.7", 123.7" (L); 4.6 Liter.							
Signature Sedan 4D		M81W	42985	**11650**	**13175**	**15000**	**18400**
Signature Ltd Sed		M82W	45850	**13025**	**14700**	**16500**	**20100**
Designer Sedan 4D		M83W	48110	**15475**	**17400**	**19200**	**23000**
Signature L Sedan		M85W	51455	**16850**	**18875**	**20800**	**24800**
Executive L Sedan		M84W	47160	**13975**	**15725**	**17550**	**21200**

2008 LINCOLN — (1or3)LN-(M26T)-8-#

Body	Type	VIN	List	Trade-In Fair	Trade-In Good	Pvt-Party Good	Retail Excellent
MKZ—V6—Equipment Schedule 2							
W.B. 107.4"; 3.5 Liter.							
Sedan 4D		M26T	30915	**16275**	**18275**	**20000**	**23800**
AWD Sedan 4D		M28T	32785	**17350**	**19450**	**21300**	**25200**
TOWN CAR—V8—Equipment Schedule 2							
W.B. 117.7", 123.7" (L); 4.6 Liter.							
Signature Ltd Sed 4D		M82W	45910	**17100**	**19150**	**21000**	**24900**
Signature L Sedan 4D		M85W	51515	**21075**	**23625**	**25300**	**29600**

MAZDA

1994 MAZDA — (JM1or1YV)(BG232)-R-#

Body	Type	VIN	List	Trade-In Fair	Trade-In Good	Pvt-Party Good	Retail Excellent
323—4-Cyl.—Equipment Schedule 6							
W.B. 96.5"; 1.6 Liter.							
Hatchback 2D		BG232	10220	**575**	**775**	**1525**	**2750**
MX-3—4-Cyl.—Equipment Schedule 6							
W.B. 96.3"; 1.6 Liter.							

1994 MAZDA

Body	Type	VIN	List	Trade-In Fair	Trade-In Good	Pvt-Party Good	Retail Excellent
Hatchback 2D		EC435	14840	900	1250	2200	3675
MX-3—V6—Equipment Schedule 6							
W.B. 96.3"; 1.8 Liter.							
GS Hatchback 2D		EC436	17340	1125	1575	2675	4325
PROTEGE'—4-Cyl.—Equipment Schedule 6							
W.B. 98.4"; 1.8 Liter.							
Sedan 4D		BG224	10570	600	825	1575	2825
DX Sedan 4D		BG224	13070	650	900	1700	3000
LX Sedan 4D		BG226	14770	700	1000	1825	3150
626—4-Cyl.—Equipment Schedule 4							
W.B. 102.8"; 2.0 Liter.							
DX Sedan 4D		GE22C	15450	600	825	1600	2825
LX Sedan 4D		GE22C	17735	625	900	1700	2975
V6 2.5 Liter		D		100	100	135	135
626—V6—Equipment Schedule 4							
W.B. 102.8"; 2.5 Liter.							
ES Sedan 4D		GE22D	22740	900	1275	2200	3675
MX-6—4-Cyl.—Equipment Schedule 4							
W.B. 102.8"; 2.0 Liter.							
Coupe 2D		GE31C	19540	650	925	1725	3050
MX-6—V6—Equipment Schedule 4							
W.B. 102.8"; 2.5 Liter.							
LS Coupe 2D		GE31D	22690	650	925	1725	3050
MX-5 MIATA—4-Cyl.—Equipment Schedule 6							
W.B. 89.2"; 1.8 Liter.							
MX-5 Convertible 2D		NA353	17045	1275	1750	2950	4650
MX-5 M-Ed Conv 2D		NA353	21645	1775	2275	3500	5350
Auto Trans				0	0	0	0
Hard Top				300	300	400	400
RX-7—Rotary Turbo—Equipment Schedule 3							
W.B. 95.5"; 1.3 Liter.							
Coupe 2D		FD333	36395	9325	10625	12950	16700
Auto Trans				0	0	0	0
929—V6—Equipment Schedule 4							
W.B. 112.2"; 3.0 Liter.							
Sedan 4D		HD461	31895	1125	1575	2700	4350

1995 MAZDA — (JM1or1YV)(EC435)-S-#

Body	Type	VIN	List	Trade-In Fair	Trade-In Good	Pvt-Party Good	Retail Excellent
MX-3—4-Cyl.—Equipment Schedule 6							
W.B. 96.3"; 1.6 Liter.							
Hatchback 2D		EC435	15780	1000	1400	2500	4150
PROTEGE'—4-Cyl.—Equipment Schedule 6							
W.B. 102.6"; 1.5 Liter, 1.8 Liter.							
DX Sedan 4D		BA141	14010	675	950	1775	3075
LX Sedan 4D		BA141	14980	725	1025	1875	3250
ES Sedan 4D		BA142	16585	850	1200	2125	3600
626—4-Cyl.—Equipment Schedule 4							
W.B. 102.8"; 2.0 Liter.							
DX Sedan 4D		GE22C	17630	700	975	1825	3150
LX Sedan 4D		GE22C	18635	750	1050	1900	3300
V6 2.5 Liter		D		100	100	135	135
626—V6—Equipment Schedule 4							
W.B. 102.8"; 2.5 Liter.							
ES Sedan 4D		GE22D	23935	1050	1500	2600	4250
MX-6—4-Cyl.—Equipment Schedule 4							
W.B. 102.8"; 2.0 Liter.							
Coupe 2D		GE31C	20713	750	1075	1950	3375
MX-6—V6—Equipment Schedule 4							
W.B. 102.8"; 2.5 Liter.							
LS Coupe 2D		GE31D	22888	750	1075	1950	3375
MX-5 MIATA—4-Cyl.—Equipment Schedule 6							
W.B. 89.2"; 1.8 Liter.							
MX-5 Convertible 2D		NA353	17940	1575	2050	3275	5100
MX-5 M-Ed Conv 2D		NA353	23970	2075	2650	3925	5850
Auto Trans				0	0	0	0
Hard Top				300	300	400	400
RX-7—Rotary Turbo—Equipment Schedule 3							
W.B. 95.5"; 1.3 Liter.							
Coupe 2D		FD333	37950	10350	11700	14100	18150
Auto Trans				0	0	0	0
MILLENIA—V6—Equipment Schedule 2							
W.B. 108.3"; 2.5 Liter.							
Sedan 4D		TA221	29335	1075	1500	2625	4300

1995 MAZDA

Body Type	VIN	List	Trade-In Fair	Trade-In Good	Pvt-Party Good	Retail Excellent
MILLENIA—V6 Supercharged—Equipment Schedule 2						
W.B. 108.3"; 2.3 Liter.						
S Sedan 4D	TA222	32435	1750	2250	3500	5350
929—V6—Equipment Schedule 4						
W.B. 112.2"; 3.0 Liter.						
Sedan 4D	HD461	36235	1275	1750	2950	4650

1996 MAZDA — JM1(BB141)–T–#

Body Type	VIN	List	Trade-In Fair	Trade-In Good	Pvt-Party Good	Retail Excellent
PROTEGE'—4-Cyl.—Equipment Schedule 5						
W.B. 102.6"; 1.5 Liter, 1.8 Liter.						
DX Sedan 4D	BB141	13720	775	1100	2000	3425
LX Sedan 4D	BB141	14590	850	1225	2175	3650
ES Sedan 4D	BB142	15145	1000	1400	2500	4150
626—4-Cyl.—Equipment Schedule 4						
W.B. 102.8"; 2.0 Liter.						
DX Sedan 4D	GE22C	17960	800	1125	2025	3475
LX Sedan 4D	GE22C	18945	850	1200	2125	3600
Manual Trans			(200)	(200)	(265)	(265)
V6 2.5 Liter	D		150	150	200	200
626—V6—Equipment Schedule 4						
W.B. 102.8"; 2.5 Liter.						
ES Sedan 4D	GE22D	24045	1200	1675	2850	4525
Manual Trans			(200)	(200)	(265)	(265)
MX-6—4-Cyl.—Equipment Schedule 4						
W.B. 102.8"; 2.0 Liter.						
Coupe 2D	GE31C	21745	900	1250	2325	3950
Manual Trans			(200)	(200)	(265)	(265)
MX-6—V6—Equipment Schedule 4						
W.B. 102.8"; 2.5 Liter.						
LS Coupe 2D	GE31D	24100	975	1375	2500	4150
M-Edition Coupe 2D	GE31D	27600	1025	1450	2575	4250
Manual Trans			(200)	(200)	(265)	(265)
MX-5 MIATA—4-Cyl.—Equipment Schedule 6						
W.B. 89.2"; 1.8 Liter.						
MX-5 Convertible 2D	NA353	18900	1850	2400	3675	5525
MX-5 M-Ed Conv 2D	NA353	25210	2450	3075	4375	6400
Auto Trans			0	0	0	0
Hard Top			350	350	465	465
MILLENIA—V6—Equipment Schedule 2						
W.B. 108.3"; 2.5 Liter.						
Sedan 4D	TA221	28445	1150	1600	2800	4500
L Sedan 4D	TA221	31845	1200	1675	2875	4600
MILLENIA—V6 Supercharged—Equipment Schedule 2						
W.B. 108.3"; 2.3 Liter.						
S Sedan 4D	TA222	34845	1975	2525	3825	5725

1997 MAZDA — JM1(BC141)–V–#

Body Type	VIN	List	Trade-In Fair	Trade-In Good	Pvt-Party Good	Retail Excellent
PROTEGE'—4-Cyl.—Equipment Schedule 6						
W.B. 102.6"; 1.5 Liter, 1.8 Liter.						
DX Sedan 4D	BC141	14170	850	1175	2150	3650
LX Sedan 4D	BC141	15140	925	1325	2400	4050
ES Sedan 4D	BC142	15745	1100	1525	2675	4350
626—4-Cyl.—Equipment Schedule 4						
W.B. 102.8"; 2.0 Liter.						
DX Sedan 4D	GE22C	18160	900	1275	2350	4000
LX Sedan 4D	GE22C	19145	950	1325	2425	4075
Manual Trans			(250)	(250)	(335)	(335)
V6 2.5 Liter	D		200	200	265	265
626—V6—Equipment Schedule 4						
W.B. 102.8"; 2.5 Liter.						
ES Sedan 4D	GE22D	24245	1425	1900	3125	4900
Manual Trans			(250)	(250)	(335)	(335)
MX-6—4-Cyl.—Equipment Schedule 4						
W.B. 102.8"; 2.0 Liter.						
Coupe 2D	GE31C	22345	1025	1450	2575	4275
Manual Trans			(250)	(250)	(335)	(335)
MX-6—V6—Equipment Schedule 4						
W.B. 102.8"; 2.5 Liter.						
LS Coupe 2D	GE31D	25200	1200	1700	2900	4625
Manual Trans			(250)	(250)	(335)	(335)
MX-5 MIATA—4-Cyl.—Equipment Schedule 6						
W.B. 89.2"; 1.8 Liter.						

1997 MAZDA

Body Type	VIN	List	Trade-In Fair	Trade-In Good	Pvt-Party Good	Retail Excellent
MX-5 Convertible 2D	NA353	20775	2200	2775	4100	6050
MX-5 STO-Ed Conv 2D	NA353	22970	2625	3225	4600	6675
MX-5 M-Ed Conv 2D	NA353	24935	2850	3450	4850	6950
Auto Trans			0	0	0	0
Hard Top			375	375	500	500

MILLENIA—V6—Equipment Schedule 2
W.B. 108.3"; 2.5 Liter.

Body Type	VIN	List	Trade-In Fair	Trade-In Good	Pvt-Party Good	Retail Excellent
Sedan 4D	TA221	29445	1300	1800	3025	4800
L Sedan 4D	TA221	33445	1400	1875	3100	4925

MILLENIA—V6 Supercharged—Equipment Schedule 2
W.B. 108.3"; 2.3 Liter.

Body Type	VIN	List	Trade-In Fair	Trade-In Good	Pvt-Party Good	Retail Excellent
S Sedan 4D	TA222	37045	2250	2850	4200	6175

1998 MAZDA — JM1(BB141)-W-#

PROTEGE'—4-Cyl.—Equipment Schedule 6
W.B. 102.6"; 1.5 Liter, 1.8 Liter.

Body Type	VIN	List	Trade-In Fair	Trade-In Good	Pvt-Party Good	Retail Excellent
DX Sedan 4D	BB141	14170	925	1300	2400	4050
LX Sedan 4D	BB141	15140	1025	1450	2600	4275
ES Sedan 4D	BB142	15745	1200	1675	2875	4575

626—4-Cyl.—Equipment Schedule 4
W.B. 105.1"; 2.0 Liter.

Body Type	VIN	List	Trade-In Fair	Trade-In Good	Pvt-Party Good	Retail Excellent
DX Sedan 4D	GE22C	18690	850	1200	2200	3725
LX Sedan 4D	GE22C	19395	925	1300	2400	4050
Manual Trans			(300)	(300)	(400)	(400)
V6 2.5 Liter	D		250	250	335	335

626—V6—Equipment Schedule 4
W.B. 105.1"; 2.5 Liter.

Body Type	VIN	List	Trade-In Fair	Trade-In Good	Pvt-Party Good	Retail Excellent
ES Sedan 4D	GE22D	25495	1450	1950	3150	4950
Manual Trans			(300)	(300)	(400)	(400)

MILLENIA—V6—Equipment Schedule 2
W.B. 108.3"; 2.5 Liter.

Body Type	VIN	List	Trade-In Fair	Trade-In Good	Pvt-Party Good	Retail Excellent
Sedan 4D	TA221	33445	1650	2125	3425	5300

MILLENIA—V6 Supercharged—Equipment Schedule 2
W.B. 108.3"; 2.3 Liter.

Body Type	VIN	List	Trade-In Fair	Trade-In Good	Pvt-Party Good	Retail Excellent
S Sedan 4D	TA222	37045	2600	3175	4550	6625

1999 MAZDA — (Jor1)(M1orYV)(BJ222)-X-#

PROTEGE'—4-Cyl.—Equipment Schedule 6
W.B. 102.8"; 1.6 Liter, 1.8 Liter.

Body Type	VIN	List	Trade-In Fair	Trade-In Good	Pvt-Party Good	Retail Excellent
DX Sedan 4D	BJ222	13995	1200	1675	2875	4600
LX Sedan 4D	BJ222	14725	1375	1850	3075	4850
ES Sedan 4D	BJ221	15375	1625	2125	3375	5200

626—4-Cyl.—Equipment Schedule 4
W.B. 105.1"; 2.0 Liter.

Body Type	VIN	List	Trade-In Fair	Trade-In Good	Pvt-Party Good	Retail Excellent
LX Sedan 4D	GF22C	19165	1100	1550	2700	4375
ES Sedan 4D	GF22C	20245	1475	1975	3200	5000
Manual Trans			(350)	(350)	(465)	(465)
V6 2.5 Liter	D		300	300	400	400

MX-5 MIATA—4-Cyl.—Equipment Schedule 6
W.B. 89.2"; 1.8 Liter.

Body Type	VIN	List	Trade-In Fair	Trade-In Good	Pvt-Party Good	Retail Excellent
Convertible 2D	NB353	21420	3200	3875	5300	7475
10th Anniversary Conv	NB353	27325	4900	5725	7350	9900
Auto Trans			0	0	0	0
Hard Top			425	425	565	565

MILLENIA—V6—Equipment Schedule 2
W.B. 108.3"; 2.5 Liter.

Body Type	VIN	List	Trade-In Fair	Trade-In Good	Pvt-Party Good	Retail Excellent
Sedan 4D	TA221	28995	1975	2525	3875	5825

MILLENIA—V6 Supercharged—Equipment Schedule 2
W.B. 108.3"; 2.3 Liter.

Body Type	VIN	List	Trade-In Fair	Trade-In Good	Pvt-Party Good	Retail Excellent
S Sedan 4D	TA222	31495	3025	3650	5100	7250

2000 MAZDA — (Jor1)(M1orYV)(BJ222)-Y-#

PROTEGE'—4-Cyl.—Equipment Schedule 6
W.B. 102.8"; 1.6 Liter, 1.8 Liter.

Body Type	VIN	List	Trade-In Fair	Trade-In Good	Pvt-Party Good	Retail Excellent
DX Sedan 4D	BJ222	13995	1450	1925	3175	4975
LX Sedan 4D	BJ222	14840	1650	2150	3400	5250
ES Sedan 4D	BJ221	15490	1925	2475	3725	5600

626—4-Cyl.—Equipment Schedule 4
W.B. 105.1"; 2.0 Liter.

Body Type	VIN	List	Trade-In Fair	Trade-In Good	Pvt-Party Good	Retail Excellent
LX Sedan 4D	GF22C	19695	1375	1850	3075	4850
ES Sedan 4D	GF22C	21095	1825	2350	3600	5475
Manual Trans			(400)	(400)	(535)	(535)

2000 MAZDA

Body	Type	VIN	List	Trade-In Fair	Good	Pvt-Party Good	Retail Excellent
V6 2.5 Liter		D		350	350	465	465

MX-5 MIATA—4-Cyl.—Equipment Schedule 6
W.B. 89.2"; 1.8 Liter.

		VIN	List	Fair	Good	Good	Excellent
Convertible 2D		NB353	22595	3700	4425	5875	8125
LS Convertible 2D		NB353	25345	4350	5150	6650	9025
Special Ed Conv 2D		NB353	25505	4450	5275	6750	9175
Auto Trans				0	0	0	0
Hard Top				450	450	600	600

MILLENNIA—V6—Equipment Schedule 2
W.B. 108.3"; 2.5 Liter.

		VIN	List	Fair	Good	Good	Excellent
Sedan 4D		TA221	25445	2325	2900	4300	6325

MILLENIA—V6 Supercharged—Equipment Schedule 2
W.B. 108.3"; 2.3 Liter.

		VIN	List	Fair	Good	Good	Excellent
S Sedan 4D		TA222	30445	3425	4150	5575	7850
Millennium Edition				150	150	200	200

2001 MAZDA — (Jor1)(M1orYV)(BJ222)-1-#

PROTEGE'—4-Cyl.—Equipment Schedule 6
W.B. 102.8"; 1.6 Liter, 2.0 Liter.

		VIN	List	Fair	Good	Good	Excellent
DX Sedan 4D		BJ222	14095	1775	2275	3525	5400
LX Sedan 4D		BJ222	14895	1950	2525	3800	5675
ES Sedan 4D		BJ225	16015	2250	2825	4125	6050
MP3 Sedan 4D		BJ227	18500	3400	4125	5500	7625

626—4-Cyl.—Equipment Schedule 4
W.B. 105.1"; 2.0 Liter.

		VIN	List	Fair	Good	Good	Excellent
LX Sedan 4D		GF22C	20015	1375	1850	3075	4875
ES Sedan 4D		GF22C	21415	1850	2375	3650	5525
Manual Trans				(425)	(425)	(565)	(565)
V6 2.5 Liter		D		375	375	500	500

MX-5 MIATA—4-Cyl.—Equipment Schedule 6
W.B. 89.2"; 1.8 Liter.

		VIN	List	Fair	Good	Good	Excellent
Convertible 2D		NB353	21660	4275	5050	6525	8875
LS Convertible 2D		NB353	24410	4925	5750	7325	9850
SE Convertible 2D		NB353	26195	5075	5925	7525	10050
Auto Trans				0	0	0	0
Hard Top				475	475	635	635

MILLENIA—V6—Equipment Schedule 2
W.B. 108.3"; 2.5 Liter.

		VIN	List	Fair	Good	Good	Excellent
Sedan 4D		TA221	28505	2725	3350	4750	6875

MILLENIA—V6 Supercharged—Equipment Schedule 2
W.B. 108.3"; 2.3 Liter.

		VIN	List	Fair	Good	Good	Excellent
S Sedan 4D		TA222	31505	3925	4675	6175	8500

2002 MAZDA — (Jor1)(M1orYV)(BJ222)-2-#

PROTEGE'—4-Cyl.—Equipment Schedule 6
W.B. 102.8"; 2.0 Liter.

		VIN	List	Fair	Good	Good	Excellent
DX Sedan 4D		BJ222	14530	1975	2525	4000	6075
LX Sedan 4D		BJ222	15335	2200	2775	4250	6350
ES Sedan 4D		BJ221	16060	2525	3100	4575	6750

PROTEGE'5—4-Cyl.—Equipment Schedule 6
W.B. 102.8"; 2.0 Liter.

		VIN	List	Fair	Good	Good	Excellent
Hatchback 4D		BJ245	16815	3475	4175	5700	8025

626—4-Cyl.—Equipment Schedule 4
W.B. 105.1"; 2.0 Liter.

		VIN	List	Fair	Good	Good	Excellent
LX Sedan 4D		GF22C	20015	1700	2200	3625	5650
ES Sedan 4D		GF22C	22915	2175	2750	4200	6300
Manual Trans				(450)	(450)	(600)	(600)
V6 2.5 Liter		D		400	400	535	535

MX-5 MIATA—4-Cyl.—Equipment Schedule 6
W.B. 89.2"; 1.8 Liter.

		VIN	List	Fair	Good	Good	Excellent
Convertible 2D		NB353	21660	4725	5550	7275	9950
LS Convertible 2D		NB353	24410	5450	6325	8075	10900
SE Convertible 2D		NB353	26275	5600	6525	8275	11050
Auto Trans				0	0	0	0
Hard Top				500	500	665	665

MILLENIA—V6—Equipment Schedule 2
W.B. 108.3"; 2.5 Liter.

		VIN	List	Fair	Good	Good	Excellent
Sedan 4D		TA221	28505	3050	3700	5325	7725

MILLENIA—V6 Supercharged—Equipment Schedule 2
W.B. 108.3"; 2.3 Liter.

		VIN	List	Fair	Good	Good	Excellent
S Sedan 4D		TA222	31505	4350	5150	6800	9400

EQUIPMENT & MILEAGE PAGE 9 TO 23

Body	Type	VIN	List	Trade-In Fair	Good	Pvt-Party Good	Retail Excellent

2003 MAZDA — (Jor1)(M1orYV)(BJ225)-3-#

PROTEGE'—4-Cyl.—Equipment Schedule 6
W.B. 102.8"; 2.0 Liter.

DX Sedan 4D	BJ225	14690	2350	2950	4400	6575
LX Sedan 4D	BJ225	15575	2625	3225	4700	6900
ES Sedan 4D	BJ225	16300	2950	3600	5100	7350

PROTEGE'5—4-Cyl.—Equipment Schedule 6
W.B. 102.8"; 2.0 Liter.

Hatchback 4D	BJ245	17055	4100	4825	6400	8800

PROTEGE'—4-Cyl. Turbo—Equipment Schedule 6
W.B. 102.8"; 2.0 Liter.

Mazdaspeed Sedan 4D	BJ227	20500	5350	6225	7875	10500

6—4-Cyl.—Equipment Schedule 4
W.B. 105.3"; 2.3 Liter.

i Sedan 4D	FP80C	19900	4000	4725	6350	8800
Sport Pkg			300	300	400	400
Manual Trans			(500)	(500)	(665)	(665)

6—V6—Equipment Schedule 4
W.B. 105.3"; 3.0 Liter.

s Sedan 4D	FP80D	22520	4325	5125	6750	9225
Sport Pkg			300	300	400	400
Manual Trans			(500)	(500)	(665)	(665)

MX-5 MIATA—4-Cyl.—Equipment Schedule 6
W.B. 89.2"; 1.8 Liter.

Club Sport Conv 2D	NB353	20000				
Convertible 2D	NB353	22125	5350	6225	7975	10750
Shinsen Conv 2D	NB353	23625	5950	6900	8675	11500
LS Convertible 2D	NB353	24905	6075	7025	8850	11700
SE Convertible 2D	NB353	26550	6525	7525	9325	12250
Auto Trans			0	0	0	0
Hard Top			525	525	700	700

2004 MAZDA — (Jor1)(M1orYV)(BK12F)-4-#

MAZDA3—4-Cyl.—Equipment Schedule 6
W.B. 103.9"; 2.0 Liter, 2.3 Liter.

i Sedan 4D	BK12F	14200	5250	6125	7800	10450
s Sedan 4D	BK123	16925	5750	6900	8575	11300
s Hatchback 4D	BK143	17415	6125	7100	8800	11550

MAZDA6—4-Cyl.—Equipment Schedule 4
W.B. 105.3"; 2.3 Liter.

i Sedan 4D	FP80C	20120	4600	5450	7100	9700
i Hatchback 4D	FP84C	22165	5100	5950	7650	10300
Sport Pkg			300	300	400	400
Manual Trans			(525)	(525)	(700)	(700)

MAZDA6—V6—Equipment Schedule 4
W.B. 105.3"; 3.0 Liter.

s Sedan 4D	FP80D	22765	5000	5850	7550	10200
s Hatchback 4D	FP84D	24315	5575	6500	8150	10900
s Wagon 4D	FP82D	23645	5375	6250	7950	10650
Sport Pkg			300	300	400	400
Manual Trans			(525)	(525)	(700)	(700)

MX-5 MIATA—4-Cyl.—Equipment Schedule 4
W.B. 89.2"; 1.8 Liter.

Convertible 2D	NB353	22388	6000	6925	8725	11550
LS Convertible 2D	NB353	25193	6800	7875	9650	12600
Auto Trans			0	0	0	0
Hard Top			550	550	735	735

MX-5 MIATA—4-Cyl. Turbo—Equipment Schedule 6
W.B. 89.2"; 1.8 Liter.

Mazdaspeed Conv	NB354	26020	7425	8525	10350	13350

RX-8—Rotary—Equipment Schedule 3
W.B. 106.4"; 1.3 Liter.

Coupe 4D	FE173	25700	6400	7375	9200	12150
Sport Pkg			500	500	665	665
Touring Pkg			700	700	935	935
Grand Touring Pkg			1000	1000	1335	1335

2005 MAZDA — (Jor1)(M1orYV)-(K12F)-5-#

MAZDA3—4-Cyl.—Equipment Schedule 6
W.B. 103.9"; 2.0 Liter, 2.3 Liter.

i Sedan 4D	K12F	15075	6050	7000	8675	11400

Body	Type	VIN	List	Trade-In Fair	Good	Pvt-Party Good	Retail Excellent
s Sedan 4D		K123	17160	6825	7900	9575	12400
s Hatchback 4D		K143	17650	7025	8075	9775	12650
sp Sedan 4D		K323	19245	7375	8450	10200	13100
sp Hatchback 4D		K343	19245	7550	8650	10350	13300

MAZDA6—4-Cyl.—Equipment Schedule 4
W.B. 105.3"; 2.3 Liter.

Body	Type	VIN	List	Fair	Good	Good	Excellent
i Sedan 4D		P80C	20590	5425	6300	7975	10700
i Sport Sedan 4D		P80C	23090	5925	6875	8575	11300
i Sport Hatchback 4D		P84C	23620	6175	7150	8875	11650
i Grand Touring Sed		P80C	24940	6425	7425	9150	11950
Manual Trans				(550)	(550)	(735)	(735)

MAZDA6—V6—Equipment Schedule 4
W.B. 105.3"; 3.0 Liter.

Body	Type	VIN	List	Fair	Good	Good	Excellent
s Sedan 4D		P80D	24590	5850	6775	8475	11200
s Hatchback 4D		P84D	25690	6475	7450	9200	12000
s Base Sport Wag 4D		P82D	24590	6225	7200	8925	11700
s Sport Wagon 4D		P82D	25720	6625	7625	9350	12200
s Grand Touring Sed		P80D	26870	6675	7675	9400	12250
s Grand Touring Wag		P82D	27540	7050	8100	9800	12700
Manual Trans				(550)	(550)	(735)	(735)

MX-5 MIATA—4-Cyl.—Equipment Schedule 6
W.B. 89.2"; 1.8 Liter.

Body	Type	VIN	List	Fair	Good	Good	Excellent
Convertible 2D		B353	22643	6750	7800	9575	12500
LS Convertible 2D		B353	25448	7650	8775	10650	13700
Auto Trans				0	0	0	0
Hard Top				575	575	765	765

MX-5 MIATA—4-Cyl. Turbo—Equipment Schedule 6
W.B. 89.2"; 1.8 Liter.

Body	Type	VIN	List	Fair	Good	Good	Excellent
Mazdaspeed Conv 2D		B354	26325	8325	9525	11350	14550

RX-8—Rotary—Equipment Schedule 3
W.B. 106.4"; 1.3 Liter.

Body	Type	VIN	List	Fair	Good	Good	Excellent
Coupe 4D		E173	26120	7375	8450	10300	13400
Shinka Special Ed 4D		E173	32220	8100	9275	11150	14400
Sport Pkg				500	500	665	665
Touring Pkg				700	700	935	935
Grand Touring Pkg				1000	1000	1335	1335

2006 MAZDA — (Jor1)(M1orYV)-(K12F)-6-#

MAZDA3—4-Cyl.—Equipment Schedule 6
W.B. 103.9"; 2.0 Liter, 2.3 Liter.

Body	Type	VIN	List	Fair	Good	Good	Excellent
i Sedan 4D		K12F	15150	6950	8000	9700	12550
i Touring Sedan 4D		K12F	16550	7350	8450	10150	13050
s Sedan 4D		K123	17440	7850	8975	10650	13550
s Hatchback 4D		K143	17930	8025	9200	10950	13950
s Touring Sedan 4D		K123	18175	8100	9275	11050	14050
s Touring Hatchback 4D		K143	18175	8325	9525	11250	14300
s Grand Touring Sedan		K123	19725	8425	9625	11350	14450
s Grand Touring H'Bck		K143	19725	8600	9800	11550	14650

MAZDA6—4-Cyl.—Equipment Schedule 4
W.B. 105.3"; 2.3 Liter.

Body	Type	VIN	List	Fair	Good	Good	Excellent
i Sedan 4D		P80C	20570	6375	7350	9075	11850
i Sport Sedan 4D		P80C	23270	6925	7975	9675	12550
i Sport Hatchback 4D		P84C	23670	7225	8275	10000	12850
i Grand Touring Sed		P80C	25270	7500	8600	10300	13250
i Grand Sport Sedan 4D		P80C	25770	7825	8950	10650	13550
Manual Trans				(575)	(575)	(765)	(765)

MAZDA6—V6—Equipment Schedule 4
W.B. 105.3"; 3.0 Liter.

Body	Type	VIN	List	Fair	Good	Good	Excellent
s Sedan 4D		P80D	24520	6850	7900	9600	12450
s Wagon 4D		P82D	25120	7275	8350	10050	12950
s Sport Sedan 4D		P80D	25420	7325	8400	10150	13050
s Sport Hatchback 4D		P84D	26020	7550	8650	10350	13300
s Sport Wagon 4D		P82D	26120	7700	8825	10550	13450
s Grand Touring Sedan		P80D	27820	7775	8900	10600	13500
s Grand Touring Wagon		P82D	27720	8150	9325	11100	14150
s Grand Sport Sedan		P80D	28620	7825	8950	10650	13550
s Grand Sport H'Back 4D		P84D	29220	7975	9150	10950	13950
s Grand Sport Wag 4D		P82D	29420	8200	9375	11150	14200
Manual Trans				(575)	(575)	(765)	(765)

MAZDASPEED6 AWD—4-Cyl. Turbo—Equipment Schedule 4
W.B. 105.3"; 2.3 Liter.

Body	Type	VIN	List	Fair	Good	Good	Excellent
Sport Sedan 4D		G12L	28555	10300	11650	13550	16950
Grand Touring Sed 4D		G12L	30485	11025	12500	14400	17900

Body	Type	VIN	List	Trade-In Fair	Trade-In Good	Pvt-Party Good	Retail Excellent

MX-5 MIATA—4-Cyl.—Equipment Schedule 6
W.B. 91.7"; 2.0 Liter.

Body	Type	VIN	List	Fair	Good	Good	Excellent
	Club Spec Conv 2D	C25F	20995	7675	8775	10650	13700
	Convertible 2D	C25F	21995	8025	9200	11050	14150
	Touring Convertible 2D	C25F	22995	8725	9950	11800	15000
	Sport Convertible 2D	C25F	23495	9100	10350	12200	15450
	Grand Touring Conv	C25F	24995	9750	11075	12950	16250
	3rd Generation Ltd Cnv	C25F	27260	10825	12250	14100	17550
	Auto Trans	------		0	0	0	0
	Hard Top	------		600	600	800	800

RX-8—Rotary—Equipment Schedule 3
W.B. 106.4"; 1.3 Liter.

Body	Type	VIN	List	Fair	Good	Good	Excellent
	Coupe 4D	E173	26995	8600	9800	11700	15000
	Shinka Spcl Ed 4D	E173	33880	9475	10775	12700	16050
	Sport Pkg	------		500	500	665	665
	Touring Pkg	------		700	700	935	935
	Grand Touring Pkg	------		1000	1000	1335	1335

2007 MAZDA — (Jor1)(M1orYV)-(K12F)-7-#

MAZDA3—4-Cyl.—Equipment Schedule 6
W.B. 103.9"; 2.0 Liter, 2.3 Liter.

Body	Type	VIN	List	Fair	Good	Good	Excellent
i	Sport Sedan 4D	K12F	15235	7975	9150	10800	13600
i	Touring Sedan 4D	K12F	16715	8425	9625	11250	14150
s	Sport Sedan 4D	K123	17650	8950	10200	11800	14800
s	Sport Hatchback 4D	K143	18140	9175	10425	12050	15050
s	Touring Sedan 4D	K123	18885	9275	10575	12200	15200
s	Touring Hatchback 4D	K143	18885	9500	10825	12450	15500
s	Grand Touring Sedan	K123	20355	9575	10875	12550	15600
s	Grand Touring H'Bck	K143	20355	9800	11125	12800	15850

MAZDASPEED3—4-Cyl. Turbo—Equipment Schedule 6
W.B. 103.9"; 2.3 Liter.

Body	Type	VIN	List	Fair	Good	Good	Excellent
	Sport Hatchback 4D	K14L	22800	10625	12050	13750	16950
	Grand Touring H'Back	K14L	24515	11325	12800	14500	17800

MAZDA6—4-Cyl.—Equipment Schedule 4
W.B. 105.3"; 2.3 Liter.

Body	Type	VIN	List	Fair	Good	Good	Excellent
i	Sport Sedan 4D	P80C	20425	7550	8650	10300	13150
i	Sport Value Ed Sed	P80C	20925	7650	8750	10350	13150
i	Spt Value Ed H'Back	P84C	21925	8475	9675	11300	14300
i	Touring Sedan 4D	P80C	23015	8275	9475	11100	14050
i	Touring Hatchback 4D	P84C	24015	8600	9800	11450	14400
i	Grand Touring Sed	P80C	24585	8775	10000	11700	14700
i	Grand Touring H'Back	P84C	25335	8900	10150	11800	14800
	Manual Trans	------		(600)	(600)	(800)	(800)

MAZDA6—V6—Equipment Schedule 4
W.B. 105.3"; 3.0 Liter.

Body	Type	VIN	List	Fair	Good	Good	Excellent
s	Sport Value Sedan 4D	P80D	23635	8075	9225	10950	13850
s	Spt Value Ed H'Back	P84D	24635	8825	10050	11750	14750
s	Spt Value Ed Wag 4D	P82D	24685	8550	9775	11450	14450
s	Touring Sedan 4D	P80D	25725	8600	9800	11500	14500
s	Touring H'Back 4D	P84D	26725	9125	10400	12100	15150
s	Touring Wagon 4D	P82D	26775	9100	10825	12000	15050
s	Grand Touring Sedan	P80D	27595	9100	10350	12000	15050
s	Grand Touring H'Back	P84D	28345	9325	10625	12300	15400
s	Grand Touring Wag	P82D	28395	9575	10875	12600	15700
	Manual Trans	------		(600)	(600)	(800)	(800)

MAZDASPEED6 AWD—4-Cyl. Turbo—Equipment Schedule 4
W.B. 105.3"; 2.3 Liter.

Body	Type	VIN	List	Fair	Good	Good	Excellent
	Sport Sedan 4D	G12L	28590	11850	13375	15250	18750
	Grand Touring Sed 4D	G12L	30520	12650	14250	16100	19700

MX-5 MIATA—4-Cyl.—Equipment Schedule 6
W.B. 91.7"; 2.0 Liter.

Body	Type	VIN	List	Fair	Good	Good	Excellent
	SV Convertible 2D	C25F	20995	8775	10000	11750	14850
	Sport Conv 2D	C25F	21995	9175	10425	12200	15300
	Sport Conv Hard Top	C26F	24945	10925	12400	14150	17450
	Touring Convertible 2D	C25F	23800	9950	11275	13050	16250
	Touring Conv Hard Top	C26F	24789	11075	12550	14350	17700
	Grand Touring Conv	C25F	25060	11025	12450	14250	17600
	Grand Touring HT 2D	C26F	28055	12150	13725	15500	18900
	Auto Trans	------		0	0	0	0

RX-8—Rotary—Equipment Schedule 3
W.B. 106.4"; 1.3 Liter.

Body	Type	VIN	List	Fair	Good	Good	Excellent
	Sport Coupe 4D	E173	27030	10150	11525	13400	16750
	Touring Coupe 4D	E173	30930	10925	12400	14250	17750

Body Type	VIN	List	Trade-In Fair	Trade-In Good	Pvt-Party Good	Retail Excellent
Grand Touring Coupe	E173	32365	11475	12975	14900	18400
Performance Pkg			500	500	665	665

2008 MAZDA — (Jor1)(M1orYV)–(K12F)–8–#

MAZDA3—4-Cyl.—Equipment Schedule 6
W.B. 103.9"; 2.0 Liter, 2.3 Liter.

Body Type	VIN	List	Trade-In Fair	Trade-In Good	Pvt-Party Good	Retail Excellent
i Sport Sedan 4D	K12F	15370	9200	10475	11950	14800
i Touring Sedan 4D	K12F	16850	9625	10925	12450	15350
i Touring Value Sed 4D	K12F	17230	9725	11025	12550	15450
s Sport Sedan 4D	K123	18030	10200	11575	13100	16000
s Sport Hatchback 4D	K143	18520	10425	11800	13350	16300
s Touring Sedan 4D	K123	19020	10525	11950	13500	16450
s Touring Hatchback 4D	K143	19020	10625	12250	13750	16750
s Grand Touring Sedan	K123	20490	10875	12350	13850	16900
s Grand Touring H'Bck	K143	20490	11125	12600	14100	17150

MAZDASPEED3—4-Cyl. Turbo—Equipment Schedule 6
W.B. 103.9"; 2.3 Liter.

Body Type	VIN	List	Trade-In Fair	Trade-In Good	Pvt-Party Good	Retail Excellent
Sport Hatchback 4D	K14L	22935	12000	13575	15200	18400
Grand Touring H'Back	K14L	24650	12750	14400	16000	19350

MAZDA6—4-Cyl.—Equipment Schedule 4
W.B. 105.3"; 2.3 Liter.

Body Type	VIN	List	Trade-In Fair	Trade-In Good	Pvt-Party Good	Retail Excellent
i Sport Sedan 4D	P80C	19585	8900	10150	11750	14700
i Sport Value Sedan 4D	P80C	21245	9000	11750	11750	14600
i Spt Value Ed H'Back	P84C	22245	9900	11225	12900	15950
i Touring Sedan 4D	P80C	22835	9725	11025	12550	15500
i Touring Hatchback 4D	P84C	23835	10000	11375	12950	15900
i Grand Touring Sed	P80C	24685	10100	11575	13250	16300
i Grand Touring H'Back	P84C	25435	10400	11750	13350	16300
Manual Trans			(625)	(625)	(835)	(835)

MAZDA6—V6—Equipment Schedule 4
W.B. 105.3"; 3.0 Liter.

Body Type	VIN	List	Trade-In Fair	Trade-In Good	Pvt-Party Good	Retail Excellent
s Sport Value Sedan 4D	P80D	23755	9475	10775	12400	15400
s Spt Value Ed H'Back	P84D	24755	10300	11650	13350	16450
s Touring Sedan 4D	P80D	25445	10000	11375	13050	16100
s Touring H'Back 4D	P84D	26445	10575	12000	13650	16800
s Grand Touring Sedan	P80D	27595	10525	11950	13600	16750
s Grand Touring H'Back	P84D	28345	10825	12300	13950	17150
Manual Trans			(625)	(625)	(835)	(835)

MX-5 MIATA—4-Cyl.—Equipment Schedule 6
W.B. 91.7"; 2.0 Liter.

Body Type	VIN	List	Trade-In Fair	Trade-In Good	Pvt-Party Good	Retail Excellent
SV Convertible 2D	C25F	21180	10350	11700	13400	16500
Sport Conv 2D	C25F	22180	10725	12150	13800	17000
Sport Conv Hard Top	C26F	24995	12650	14250	15950	19350
Touring Convertible 2D	C25F	24225	11525	13025	14750	18050
Touring Conv Hard Top	C26F	26095	12800	14450	16150	19600
Grand Touring Conv	C25F	25485	12750	14350	16050	19500
Grand Touring HT 2D	C26F	27355	13975	15725	17450	21000
Special Ed Conv 2D	C26F	27225	13525	15250	16950	20500
Auto Trans			0	0	0	0

RX-8—Rotary—Equipment Schedule 3
W.B 106.4"; 1.3 Liter.

Body Type	VIN	List	Trade-In Fair	Trade-In Good	Pvt-Party Good	Retail Excellent
Sport Coupe 4D	E173	27030	11900	13475	15400	18900
Touring Coupe 4D	E173	30930	12750	14400	16250	19900
Grand Touring Coupe	E173	32365	13375	15100	17050	20800
40th Anniv Cpe 4D	E173	32705	13575	15300	17200	21000
Performance Pkg			500	500	665	665

MERCEDES-BENZ

1994 MERCEDES-BENZ — WDB(HA22E)–R–#

C-CLASS—4-Cyl.—Equipment Schedule 1
W.B. 105.9"; 2.2 Liter.

Body Type	VIN	List	Trade-In Fair	Trade-In Good	Pvt-Party Good	Retail Excellent
C220 Sedan 4D	HA22E	31085	1950	2500	3775	5650

C-CLASS—6-Cyl.—Equipment Schedule 1
W.B. 105.9"; 2.8 Liter.

Body Type	VIN	List	Trade-In Fair	Trade-In Good	Pvt-Party Good	Retail Excellent
C280 Sedan 4D	HA28E	37105	2100	2675	3950	5875
Slip Control			100	100	135	135

E-CLASS—6-Cyl.—Equipment Schedule 1
W.B. 106.9", 110.2" (4D); 3.2 Liter.

Body Type	VIN	List	Trade-In Fair	Trade-In Good	Pvt-Party Good	Retail Excellent
E320 Sedan 4D	EA32E	42975	2175	2775	4075	6000
E320 Coupe 2D	EA52E	62075	3025	3650	5050	7200

1994 MERCEDES-BENZ

Body	Type	VIN	List	Trade-In Fair	Trade-In Good	Pvt-Party Good	Retail Excellent
E320 Cabriolet 2D		EA66E	77775	**6900**	**7975**	**9900**	**13050**
E320 Wagon 4D		EA92E	46675	**3200**	**3900**	**5325**	**7525**
Slip Control				**100**	**100**	**135**	**135**
Sport Pkg				**200**	**200**	**265**	**265**
E-CLASS—V8—Equipment Schedule 1							
W.B. 110.2"; 4.2 Liter.							
E420 Sedan 4D		EA34E	51475	**2475**	**3075**	**4400**	**6450**
E500 Sedan 4D		EA36E	82975	**10825**	**12250**	**14700**	**18800**
Slip Control				**100**	**100**	**135**	**135**
S-CLASS—6-Cyl.—Equipment Schedule 1							
W.B. 119.7"; 3.2 Liter.							
S320 Sedan 4D		GA32E	71075	**3975**	**4700**	**6225**	**8600**
Slip Control				**100**	**100**	**135**	**135**
S-CLASS—6-Cyl. Turbo Diesel—Equipment Schedule 1							
W.B. 119.7"; 3.5 Liter.							
S350D Sedan 4D		GB34E	71075	**5750**	**6700**	**8475**	**11300**
S-CLASS—V8—Equipment Schedule 1							
W.B. 115.9", 123.6" (S420, S500 4D); 4.2 Liter, 5.0 Liter.							
S420 Sedan 4D		GA43E	81675	**4725**	**5550**	**7225**	**9850**
S500 Sedan 4D		GA51E	97875	**5325**	**6200**	**7950**	**10700**
S500 Coupe 2D		GA70E	102375	**7100**	**8175**	**10150**	**13350**
Slip Control				**100**	**100**	**135**	**135**
S-CLASS—V12—Equipment Schedule 1							
W.B. 123.6", 123.6" (4D); 6.0 Liter.							
S600 Sedan 4D		GA57E	134475	**3575**	**4275**	**5750**	**8025**
S600 Coupe 2D		GA76E	136775	**4650**	**5500**	**7125**	**9725**
SL-CLASS—6-Cyl.—Equipment Schedule 1							
W.B. 99.0"; 3.2 Liter.							
SL320 Roadster 2D		FA63E	85675	**7250**	**8325**	**10300**	**13500**
Slip Control				**100**	**100**	**135**	**135**
SL-CLASS—V8—Equipment Schedule 1							
W.B. 99.0"; 5.0 Liter.							
SL500 Roadster 2D		FA67E	101275	**8600**	**9800**	**12000**	**15650**
SL-CLASS—V12—Equipment Schedule 1							
W.B. 99.0"; 6.0 Liter.							
SL600 Roadster 2D		FA76E	123575	**8875**	**10100**	**12350**	**15950**

1995 MERCEDES-BENZ — WDB(HA22E)-S-#

Body	Type	VIN	List	Trade-In Fair	Trade-In Good	Pvt-Party Good	Retail Excellent
C-CLASS—4-Cyl.—Equipment Schedule 1							
W.B. 105.9"; 2.2 Liter.							
C220 Sedan 4D		HA22E	32000	**2325**	**2900**	**4250**	**6250**
Traction Control				**100**	**100**	**135**	**135**
C-CLASS—6-Cyl.—Equipment Schedule 1							
W.B. 105.9"; 2.8 Liter, 3.6 Liter.							
C280 Sedan 4D		HA28E	38400	**2475**	**3075**	**4425**	**6475**
C36 Sedan 4D		HM36E	50500	**4025**	**4750**	**6325**	**8725**
Slip Control				**100**	**100**	**135**	**135**
E-CLASS—6-Cyl.—Equipment Schedule 1							
W.B. 106.9", 110.2" (4D); 3.2 Liter.							
E320 Sedan 4D		EA32E	43975	**2575**	**3150**	**4525**	**6575**
E320 Coupe 2D		EA52E	63475	**3500**	**4225**	**5675**	**7975**
E320 Cabriolet 2D		EA66E	79475	**7950**	**9100**	**11200**	**14650**
E320 Wagon 4D		EA92E	49600	**3775**	**4475**	**6000**	**8350**
Slip Control				**100**	**100**	**135**	**135**
Sport Pkg				**200**	**200**	**265**	**265**
E-CLASS—6-Cyl. Diesel—Equipment Schedule 1							
W.B. 110.2"; 3.0 Liter.							
E300D Sedan 4D		EB31E	43100	**3450**	**4175**	**5625**	**7925**
E-CLASS—V8—Equipment Schedule 1							
W.B. 110.2"; 4.2 Liter.							
E420 Sedan 4D		EA34E	52975	**2800**	**3400**	**4825**	**6925**
Slip Control				**100**	**100**	**135**	**135**
S-CLASS—6-Cyl.—Equipment Schedule 1							
W.B. 119.7", 123.6" (LWB); 3.2 Liter.							
S320 SWB Sedan 4D		GA32E	63175	**3775**	**4475**	**6075**	**8500**
S320 LWB Sedan 4D		GA33E	66375	**4100**	**4850**	**6475**	**8975**
Slip Control				**100**	**100**	**135**	**135**
S-CLASS—6-Cyl. Turbo Diesel—Equipment Schedule 1							
W.B. 119.7"; 3.5 Liter.							
S350D Sedan 4D		GB34E	66375	**6675**	**7675**	**9600**	**12700**
S-CLASS—V8—Equipment Schedule 1							
W.B. 115.9", 123.6" (4D); 4.2 Liter, 5.0 Liter.							
S420 Sedan 4D		GA43E	76075	**4500**	**5325**	**6975**	**9575**

Body	Type	VIN	List	Trade-In Fair	Good	Pvt-Party Good	Retail Excellent
S500 Sedan 4D		GA51E	89675	**5075**	**5925**	**7700**	**10450**
S500 Coupe 2D		GA70E	94075	**6775**	**7825**	**9850**	**13050**
S-CLASS—V12—Equipment Schedule 1							
W.B. 115.9", 123.6" (4D); 6.0 Liter.							
S600 Sedan 4D		GA57E	133775	**4100**	**4850**	**6475**	**8975**
S600 Coupe 2D		GA76E	136775	**5350**	**6225**	**8000**	**10850**
SL-CLASS—6-Cyl.—Equipment Schedule 1							
W.B. 99.0"; 3.2 Liter.							
SL320 Roadster 2D		FA63E	78775	**8250**	**9425**	**11600**	**15200**
Slip Control				**100**	**100**	**135**	**135**
SL-CLASS—V8—Equipment Schedule 1							
W.B. 99.0"; 5.0 Liter.							
SL500 Roadster 2D		FA67E	91675	**9500**	**10775**	**13150**	**17000**
SL-CLASS—V12—Equipment Schedule 1							
W.B. 99.0"; 6.0 Liter.							
SL600 Roadster 2D		FA76E	123175	**10050**	**11425**	**13850**	**17850**

Body	Type	VIN	List	Trade-In Fair	Good	Pvt-Party Good	Retail Excellent
C-CLASS—4-Cyl.—Equipment Schedule 1							
W.B. 105.9"; 2.2 Liter.							
C220 Sedan 4D		HA22E	33055	**2750**	**3350**	**4750**	**6850**
Traction Control				**125**	**125**	**165**	**165**
C-CLASS—6-Cyl.—Equipment Schedule 1							
W.B. 105.9"; 2.8 Liter, 3.6 Liter.							
C280 Sedan 4D		HA28E	37815	**2825**	**3450**	**4875**	**7000**
C36 Sedan 4D		HM36E	51595	**3875**	**4600**	**6150**	**8500**
Slip Control				**125**	**125**	**165**	**165**
Sport Pkg				**250**	**250**	**335**	**335**
E-CLASS—6-Cyl.—Equipment Schedule 1							
W.B. 111.5"; 3.2 Liter.							
E320 Sedan 4D		JF55F	45165	**3250**	**3950**	**5400**	**7600**
Slip Control				**125**	**125**	**165**	**165**
E-CLASS—6-Cyl. Diesel—Equipment Schedule 1							
W.B. 111.5"; 3.0 Liter.							
E300D Sedan 4D		JF20F	42465	**4675**	**5525**	**7150**	**9750**
S-CLASS—6-Cyl.—Equipment Schedule 1							
W.B. 119.7", 123.6" (LWB); 3.2 Liter.							
S320 SWB Sedan 4D		GA32E	63295	**4650**	**5475**	**7125**	**9725**
S320 LWB Sedan 4D		GA33E	66495	**4825**	**5650**	**7350**	**10000**
Slip Control				**125**	**125**	**165**	**165**
S-CLASS—V8—Equipment Schedule 1							
W.B. 115.9", 123.6" (4D); 4.2 Liter, 5.0 Liter.							
S420 Sedan 4D		GA43E	74495	**5225**	**6100**	**7850**	**10600**
S500 Sedan 4D		GA51E	88095	**5875**	**6800**	**8625**	**11500**
S500 Coupe 2D		GA70E	92495	**7850**	**8975**	**11050**	**14450**
S-CLASS—V12—Equipment Schedule 1							
W.B. 115.9", 123.6" (4D); 6.0 Liter.							
S600 Sedan 4D		GA57E	130895	**4775**	**5575**	**7275**	**9900**
S600 Coupe 2D		GA76E	133895	**6200**	**7150**	**9025**	**11950**
SL-CLASS—6-Cyl.—Equipment Schedule 1							
W.B. 99.0"; 3.2 Liter.							
SL320 Roadster 2D		FA63F	78895	**9100**	**10350**	**12600**	**16250**
Slip Control				**125**	**125**	**165**	**165**
Sport Pkg				**925**	**925**	**1235**	**1235**
SL-CLASS—V8—Equipment Schedule 1							
W.B. 99.0"; 5.0 Liter.							
SL500 Roadster 2D		FA67F	90495	**10425**	**11850**	**14250**	**18300**
Sport Pkg				**925**	**925**	**1235**	**1235**
SL-CLASS—V12—Equipment Schedule 1							
W.B. 99.0"; 6.0 Liter.							
SL600 Roadster 2D		FA76F	122595	**11075**	**12550**	**15000**	**19150**
Sport Pkg				**925**	**925**	**1235**	**1235**

Body	Type	VIN	List	Trade-In Fair	Good	Pvt-Party Good	Retail Excellent
C-CLASS—4-Cyl.—Equipment Schedule 1							
W.B. 105.9"; 2.3 Liter.							
C230 Sedan 4D		HA23E	33235	**2475**	**3075**	**4450**	**6550**
Traction Control				**150**	**150**	**200**	**200**
C-CLASS—6-Cyl.—Equipment Schedule 1							
W.B. 105.9"; 2.8 Liter, 3.6 Liter.							
C280 Sedan 4D		HA28E	37985	**3000**	**3625**	**5075**	**7275**
C36 Sedan 4D		HM36E	52520	**4650**	**5475**	**7125**	**9725**

Body Type	VIN	List	Trade-In Fair	Good	Pvt-Party Good	Retail Excellent
Slip Control	....	......	150	150	200	200
Sport Pkg	....	......	275	275	365	365
E-CLASS—6-Cyl.—Equipment Schedule 1						
W.B. 111.5"; 3.2 Liter.						
E320 Sedan 4D	JF55F	46485	3850	4575	6100	8425
Slip Control	....	......	150	150	200	200
E-CLASS—6-Cyl. Diesel—Equipment Schedule 1						
W.B. 111.5"; 3.0 Liter.						
E300D Sedan 4D	JF20F	42475	5475	6350	8050	10800
E-CLASS—V8—Equipment Schedule 1						
W.B. 111.5"; 4.2 Liter.						
E420 Sedan 4D	JF72F	51585	4200	4950	6550	9025
Sport Pkg	....	......	625	625	835	835
S-CLASS—6-Cyl.—Equipment Schedule 1						
W.B. 119.7", 123.6" (LWB); 3.2 Liter.						
S320 SWB Sedan 4D	GA32G	63895	5475	6350	8100	10900
S320 LWB Sedan 4D	GA33G	67195	5650	6575	8325	11100
Slip Control	....	......	150	150	200	200
S-CLASS—V8—Equipment Schedule 1						
W.B. 119.9", 123.6" (4D); 4.2 Liter, 5.0 Liter.						
S420 Sedan 4D	GA43G	75795	5825	6750	8550	11400
S500 Sedan 4D	GA51G	89795	6450	7425	9350	12450
S500 Coupe 2D	GA70G	93795	8625	9850	12000	15550
S-CLASS—V12—Equipment Schedule 1						
W.B. 115.9", 123.6" (4D); 6.0 Liter.						
S600 Sedan 4D	GA57G	133895	5600	6525	8300	11100
S600 Coupe 2D	GA76G	136495	7225	8300	10300	13500
SL-CLASS—6-Cyl.—Equipment Schedule 1						
W.B. 99.0"; 3.2 Liter.						
SL320 Roadster 2D	FA63F	80195	8550	9775	11900	15450
Slip Control	....	......	150	150	200	200
Sport Pkg	....	......	1000	1000	1335	1335
Panorama Roof	....	......	750	750	1000	1000
SL-CLASS—V8—Equipment Schedule 1						
W.B. 99.0"; 5.0 Liter.						
SL500 Roadster 2D	FA67F	91795	10675	12100	14450	18400
Sport Pkg	....	......	625	625	835	835
Panorama Roof	....	......	750	750	1000	1000
SL-CLASS—V12—Equipment Schedule 1						
W.B. 99.0"; 6.0 Liter.						
SL600 Roadster 2D	FA76F	125895	11325	12800	15250	19350
Sport Pkg	....	......	1050	1050	1400	1400
Panorama Roof	....	......	750	750	1000	1000

1998 MERCEDES-BENZ — WDB(KK47F)–W–#

Body Type	VIN	List	Trade-In Fair	Good	Pvt-Party Good	Retail Excellent
SLK-CLASS—4-Cyl. Supercharged—Equipment Schedule 1						
W.B. 94.5"; 2.3 Liter.						
SLK230 Roadster 2D	KK47F	40295	4625	5475	7100	9700
C-CLASS—4-Cyl.—Equipment Schedule 1						
W.B. 105.9" 2.3 Liter.						
C230 Sedan 4D	HA23G	33235	3000	3625	5075	7275
Slip Control	....	......	175	175	235	235
C-CLASS—V6—Equipment Schedule 1						
W.B. 105.9"; 2.8 Liter.						
C280 Sedan 4D	HA29G	37985	3225	3925	5400	7650
Sport Pkg	....	......	300	300	400	400
C-CLASS—V8—Equipment Schedule 1						
W.B. 105.9"; 4.3 Liter.						
C43 Sedan 4D	HA33G	53345	5675	6600	8350	11150
CLK-CLASS—V6—Equipment Schedule 1						
W.B. 105.9"; 3.2 Liter.						
CLK320 Coupe 2D	LJ65G	41555	3850	4575	6100	8475
E-CLASS—V6—Equipment Schedule 1						
W.B. 111.5"; 3.2 Liter.						
E320 Sedan 4D	JF65F	47205	4550	5350	6900	9375
E320 4Matic Sedan 4D	JF82F	49955	4750	5550	7225	9800
E320 Wagon 4D	JH65F	49900	4325	5125	6675	9100
E320 4Matic Wagon 4D	JH82F	52650	4750	5550	7225	9800
E-CLASS—6-Cyl. Turbo Diesel—Equipment Schedule 1						
W.B. 111.5"; 3.0 Liter.						
E300TD Sedan 4D	JF25F	45200	7500	8600	10500	13600
E-CLASS—V8—Equipment Schedule 1						
W.B. 111.5"; 4.3 Liter.						

1998 MERCEDES-BENZ

Body	Type	VIN	List	Trade-In Fair	Good	Pvt-Party Good	Retail Excellent
E430 Sedan 4D		JF70F	52305	**5700**	**6650**	**8375**	**11150**
Sport Pkg			....	**625**	**625**	**835**	**835**
CL-CLASS—V8—Equipment Schedule 1							
W.B. 115.9"; 5.0 Liter.							
CL500 Coupe 2D		GA70G	92495	**9600**	**10925**	**13150**	**16850**
CL-CLASS—V12—Equipment Schedule 1							
W.B. 115.9"; 6.0 Liter.							
CL600 Coupe 2D		GA76G	135895	**8450**	**9650**	**11750**	**15250**
S-CLASS—6-Cyl.—Equipment Schedule 1							
W.B. 119.7", 123.6" (LWB); 3.2 Liter.							
S320 SWB Sedan 4D		GA32G	64595	**6350**	**7325**	**9175**	**12100**
S320 LWB Sedan 4D		GA33G	67895	**6575**	**7575**	**9400**	**12400**
S-CLASS—V8—Equipment Schedule 1							
W.B. 123.6"; 4.2 Liter, 5.0 Liter.							
S420 Sedan 4D		GA43G	75795	**6600**	**7600**	**9525**	**12600**
S500 Sedan 4D		GA51G	89795	**7200**	**8275**	**10250**	**13450**
S-CLASS—V12—Equipment Schedule 1							
W.B. 123.6"; 6.0 Liter.							
S600 Sedan 4D		GA57G	135845	**6650**	**7650**	**9575**	**12650**
SL-CLASS—V8—Equipment Schedule 1							
W.B. 99.0"; 5.0 Liter.							
SL500 Roadster 2D		FA67F	81495	**11025**	**12500**	**14850**	**18800**
Sport Pkg			....	**1175**	**1175**	**1565**	**1565**
Panorama Roof			....	**775**	**775**	**1035**	**1035**
SL-CLASS—V12—Equipment Schedule 1							
W.B. 99.0"; 6.0 Liter.							
SL600 Roadster 2D		FA76F	127695	**11750**	**13275**	**15700**	**19800**
Sport Pkg			....	**1175**	**1175**	**1565**	**1565**
Panorama Roof			....	**775**	**775**	**1035**	**1035**

1999 MERCEDES-BENZ — WDB(KK47F)-X-#

Body	Type	VIN	List	Trade-In Fair	Good	Pvt-Party Good	Retail Excellent
SLK-CLASS—4-Cyl. Supercharged—Equipment Schedule 1							
W.B. 94.5"; 2.3 Liter.							
SLK230 Roadster 2D		KK47F	41495	**5200**	**6050**	**7750**	**10450**
Sport Pkg			....	**625**	**625**	**835**	**835**
Manual Trans			....	**(425)**	**(425)**	**(565)**	**(565)**
C-CLASS—4-Cyl. Supercharged—Equipment Schedule 1							
W.B. 105.9"; 2.3 Liter.							
C230 Sedan 4D		HA24G	34795	**3425**	**4150**	**5625**	**7950**
Sport Pkg			....	**325**	**325**	**435**	**435**
C-CLASS—V6—Equipment Schedule 1							
W.B. 105.9"; 2.8 Liter.							
C280 Sedan 4D		HA29G	38630	**3625**	**4325**	**5875**	**8200**
Sport Pkg			....	**325**	**325**	**435**	**435**
C-CLASS—V8—Equipment Schedule 1							
W.B. 105.9"; 4.3 Liter.							
C43 Sedan 4D		HA33G	53595	**6225**	**7175**	**8975**	**11850**
CLK-CLASS—V6—Equipment Schedule 1							
W.B. 105.9"; 3.2 Liter.							
CLK320 Coupe 2D		LJ65G	42485	**4550**	**5375**	**7000**	**9575**
CLK320 Cabriolet 2D		LK65G	47795	**6450**	**7450**	**9250**	**12200**
CLK-CLASS—V8—Equipment Schedule 1							
W.B. 105.9"; 4.3 Liter.							
CLK430 Coupe 2D		LJ70G	49785	**5250**	**6100**	**7825**	**10550**
E-CLASS—V6—Equipment Schedule 1							
W.B. 111.5"; 3.2 Liter.							
E320 Sedan 4D		JF65F	47905	**5350**	**6225**	**7925**	**10600**
E320 AWD Sedan 4D		JF82F	50695	**5625**	**6575**	**8275**	**11050**
E320 Wagon 4D		JH65F	48905	**5200**	**6050**	**7725**	**10400**
E320 AWD Wagon 4D		JH82F	51695	**5650**	**6600**	**8275**	**11050**
E-CLASS—6-Cyl. Turbo Diesel—Equipment Schedule 1							
W.B. 111.5"; 3.0 Liter.							
E300TD Sedan 4D		JF25F	45430	**8550**	**9775**	**11750**	**15100**
E-CLASS—V8—Equipment Schedule 1							
W.B. 111.5"; 4.3 Liter, 5.5 Liter.							
E430 Sedan 4D		JF70F	53005	**6625**	**7625**	**9475**	**12500**
E55 Sedan 4D		JF744	69695	**10200**	**11575**	**13700**	**17400**
Sport Pkg (E430)			....	**625**	**625**	**835**	**835**
CL-CLASS—V8—Equipment Schedule 1							
W.B. 115.9"; 5.0 Liter.							
CL500 Coupe 2D		GA70G	93795	**10875**	**12300**	**14600**	**18500**
CL-CLASS—V12—Equipment Schedule 1							
W.B. 115.9"; 6.0 Liter.							

Body	Type	VIN	List	Trade-In Fair	Trade-In Good	Pvt-Party Good	Retail Excellent
CL600 Coupe 2D		GA76G	140495	9900	11275	13500	17200

S-CLASS—6-Cyl.—Equipment Schedule 1
W.B. 119.7", 123.6" (LWB); 3.2 Liter.

S320 SWB Sedan 4D		GA32G	65345	7375	8450	10350	13450
S320 LWB Sedan 4D		GA33G	68595	7625	8725	10650	13800

S-CLASS—V8—Equipment Schedule 1
W.B. 123.6"; 4.2 Liter, 5.0 Liter.

S420 Sedan 4D		GA43G	75795	7625	8725	10700	13900
S500 Sedan 4D		GA51G	89795	8175	9350	11400	14750
Grand Edition (S500)				200	200	265	265

S-CLASS—V12—Equipment Schedule 1
W.B. 123.6"; 6.0 Liter.

S600 Sedan 4D		GA57G	137845	7950	9100	11100	14400

SL-CLASS—V8—Equipment Schedule 1
W.B. 99.0"; 5.0 Liter.

SL500 Roadster 2D		FA68F	82695	11625	13125	15450	19450
Sport Pkg				1300	1300	1735	1735
Panorama Roof				800	800	1065	1065

SL-CLASS—V12—Equipment Schedule 1
W.B. 99.0"; 6.0 Liter.

SL600 Roadster 2D		FA76F	130095	12450	14075	16400	20600
Sport Pkg				1300	1300	1735	1735
Panorama Roof				800	800	1065	1065

2000 MERCEDES-BENZ — WDB(KK47F)-Y-#

SLK-CLASS—4-Cyl. Supercharged—Equipment Schedule 1
W.B. 94.5"; 2.3 Liter.

SLK230 Roadster 2D		KK47F	42495	6000	6950	8750	11600
Sport Pkg				625	625	835	835
designo Edition				700	700	935	935
Manual Trans				(450)	(450)	(600)	(600)

C-CLASS—4-Cyl. Supercharged—Equipment Schedule 1
W.B. 105.9"; 2.3 Liter.

C230 Sedan 4D		HA24G	34820	4225	4975	6575	9050
Sport Pkg				350	350	465	465

C-CLASS—V6—Equipment Schedule 1
W.B. 105.9"; 2.8 Liter.

C280 Sedan 4D		HA29G	39020	4175	4925	6525	9000
Sport Pkg				350	350	465	465

C-CLASS—V8—Equipment Schedule 1
W.B. 105.9"; 4.3 Liter.

C43 Sedan 4D		HA33G	53595	6850	7925	9750	12750

CLK-CLASS—V6—Equipment Schedule 1
W.B. 105.9"; 3.2 Liter.

CLK320 Coupe 2D		LJ65G	43505	5425	6325	8025	10800
CLK320 Cabriolet 2D		LK65G	48695	7675	8800	10700	13800
designo Edition				700	700	935	935

CLK-CLASS—V8—Equipment Schedule 1
W.B. 105.9"; 4.3 Liter.

CLK430 Coupe 2D		LJ70G	51005	6075	7050	8825	11650
CLK430 Cabriolet 2D		LK70G	56195	9850	11175	13300	16900
designo Edition				700	700	935	935

E-CLASS—V6—Equipment Schedule 1
W.B. 111.5"; 3.2 Liter.

E320 Sedan 4D		JF65G	48825	6275	7250	9000	11800
E320 AWD Sedan 4D		JF82G	51695	6675	7700	9450	12350
E320 Wagon 4D		JH65F	49675	6200	7175	8900	11700
E320 AWD Wagon 4D		JH82F	52475	6725	7750	9500	12400
designo Edition				700	700	935	935

E-CLASS—V8—Equipment Schedule 1
W.B. 111.5"; 4.3 Liter, 5.5 Liter.

E430 Sedan 4D		JF70G	54175	7675	8775	10650	13700
E430 AWD Sedan 4D		JF83G	56975	8300	9500	11350	14600
E55 Sedan 4D		JF74G	71395	11525	13025	15200	19000
Sport Pkg (E430)				625	625	835	835
designo Edition				700	700	935	935

CL-CLASS—V8—Equipment Schedule 1
W.B. 113.6"; 5.0 Liter.

CL500 Coupe 2D		PJ75J	87145	10775	12200	14400	18250

S-CLASS—V8—Equipment Schedule 1
W.B. 121.5"; 4.3 Liter, 5.0 Liter.

S430 Sedan 4D		NG70J	70295	7400	8475	10400	13500
S500 Sedan 4D		NG75J	79445	8550	9775	11800	15200

2000 MERCEDES-BENZ

Body Type	VIN	List	Trade-In Fair	Trade-In Good	Pvt-Party Good	Retail Excellent
Sport Pkg			1425	1425	1900	1900
designo Edition			700	700	935	935
Distronic Cruise Control			325	325	435	435
SL-CLASS—V8—Equipment Schedule 1						
W.B. 99.0"; 5.0 Liter.						
SL500 Roadster 2D	FA68F	84195	12500	14100	16400	20500
Sport Pkg			1425	1425	1900	1900
designo Edition			700	700	935	935
Panorama Roof			850	850	1135	1135
SL-CLASS—V12—Equipment Schedule 1						
W.B. 99.0"; 6.0 Liter.						
SL600 Roadster 2D	FA76F	132145	13375	15100	17500	21800
Sport Pkg			1425	1425	1900	1900
designo Edition			700	700	935	935
Panorama Roof			850	850	1135	1135

2001 MERCEDES-BENZ — WDB(KK49F)-1-#

Body Type	VIN	List	Trade-In Fair	Trade-In Good	Pvt-Party Good	Retail Excellent
SLK-CLASS—4-Cyl. Supercharged—Equipment Schedule 1						
W.B. 94.5"; 2.3 Liter.						
SLK230 Roadster 2D	KK49F	40495	7025	8075	9900	12950
Sport Pkg			625	625	835	835
designo Edition			750	750	1000	1000
Manual Trans			(475)	(475)	(635)	(635)
SLK-CLASS—V6—Equipment Schedule 1						
W.B. 94.5"; 3.2 Liter.						
SLK320 Roadster 2D	KK65F	45495	7975	9150	11050	14150
Sport Pkg			625	625	835	835
designo Edition			750	750	1000	1000
Manual Trans			(475)	(475)	(635)	(635)
C-CLASS—V6—Equipment Schedule 1						
W.B. 106.9"; 2.6 Liter, 3.2 Liter.						
C240 Sedan 4D	RF61G	34610	4625	5450	7125	9750
C320 Sedan 4D	RF64G	40310	5600	6525	8250	11050
Sport Pkg			375	375	500	500
Manual Trans			(475)	(475)	(635)	(635)
CLK-CLASS—V6—Equipment Schedule 1						
W.B. 105.9"; 3.2 Liter.						
CLK320 Coupe 2D	LJ65G	42595	6475	7450	9250	12200
CLK320 Cabriolet 2D	LK65G	49545	9050	10300	12300	15750
designo Edition			750	750	1000	1000
CLK-CLASS—V8—Equipment Schedule 1						
W.B. 105.9"; 4.3 Liter, 5.5 Liter.						
CLK430 Coupe 2D	LJ70G	50295	7275	8350	10250	13300
CLK430 Cabriolet 2D	LK70G	57145	11225	12700	14850	18600
CLK55 Coupe 2D	LJ74G	68045	9350	10625	12750	16200
designo Edition			750	750	1000	1000
E-CLASS—V6—Equipment Schedule 1						
W.B. 111.5"; 3.2 Liter.						
E320 Sedan 4D	JF65F	48495	7425	8500	10300	13350
E320 AWD Sedan 4D	JF82F	51345	7875	9025	10900	13950
E320 Wagon 4D	JH65F	49295	7400	8475	10300	13350
E320 AWD Wagon 4D	JH82F	52145	7975	9125	10950	14050
Sport Pkg (ex AWD)			625	625	835	835
designo Edition (ex AWD)			750	750	1000	1000
E-CLASS—V8—Equipment Schedule 1						
W.B. 111.5"; 4.3 Liter, 5.5 Liter.						
E430 Sedan 4D	JF70F	53845	9050	10300	12250	15650
E430 AWD Sedan 4D	JF83G	56695	9725	11075	13100	16550
E55 Sedan 4D	JF744	70945	13175	14850	17100	21200
Sport Pkg (ex AWD)			625	625	835	835
designo Ed (E430 RWD)			750	750	1000	1000
CL-CLASS—V8—Equipment Schedule 1						
W.B. 113.6"; 5.0 Liter, 5.5 Liter.						
CL500 Coupe 2D	PJ75J	89145	12400	14025	16300	20400
CL55 Coupe 2D	PJ73J	100145	17925	20100	22800	27900
Sport Pkg (CL500)			1550	1550	2065	2065
designo Edition			750	750	1000	1000
CL-CLASS—V12—Equipment Schedule 1						
W.B. 113.6"; 5.8 Liter.						
CL600 Coupe 2D	PJ78J	119145	16425	18425	21000	25800
Sport Pkg			1550	1550	2065	2065
designo Edition			750	750	1000	1000

2001 MERCEDES-BENZ

Body	Type	VIN	List	Trade-In Fair	Good	Pvt-Party Good	Retail Excellent
S-CLASS—V8—Equipment Schedule 1							
W.B. 121.5"; 4.3 Liter, 5.0 Liter, 5.5 Liter.							
S430 Sedan 4D		NG70J	71445	**8725**	**9950**	**11950**	**15350**
S500 Sedan 4D		NG75J	80595	**10000**	**11375**	**13500**	**17050**
S55 Sedan 4D		NG73J	98645	**15050**	**16900**	**19300**	**23700**
Sport Pkg (S430,S500)			------	**1550**	**1550**	**2065**	**2065**
designo Edition			------	**750**	**750**	**1000**	**1000**
S-CLASS—V12—Equipment Schedule 1							
W.B. 121.5"; 6.0 Liter.							
S600 Sedan 4D		NG78J	115985	**12700**	**14350**	**16600**	**20700**
Sport Pkg			------	**1550**	**1550**	**2065**	**2065**
designo Edition			------	**750**	**750**	**1000**	**1000**
SL-CLASS—V8—Equipment Schedule 1							
W.B. 99.0"; 5.0 Liter.							
SL500 Roadster 2D		FA68F	84445	**13675**	**15425**	**17800**	**22100**
designo Edition			------	**750**	**750**	**1000**	**1000**
Panorama Roof			------	**900**	**900**	**1200**	**1200**
SL-CLASS—V12—Equipment Schedule 1							
W.B. 99.0"; 6.0 Liter.							
SL600 Roadster 2D		FA76F	129595	**14650**	**16475**	**18900**	**23300**
designo Edition			------	**750**	**750**	**1000**	**1000**
Panorama Roof			------	**900**	**900**	**1200**	**1200**

2002 MERCEDES-BENZ — WDB(KK49F)-2-#

Body	Type	VIN	List	Trade-In Fair	Good	Pvt-Party Good	Retail Excellent
SLK-CLASS—4-Cyl. Supercharged—Equipment Schedule 1							
W.B. 94.5"; 2.3 Liter.							
SLK230 Roadster 2D		KK49F	41345	**8100**	**9275**	**11400**	**14850**
Sport Pkg			------	**625**	**625**	**835**	**835**
designo Edition			------	**800**	**800**	**1065**	**1065**
Manual Trans			------	**(500)**	**(500)**	**(665)**	**(665)**
SLK-CLASS—V6—Equipment Schedule 1							
W.B. 94.5"; 3.2 Liter.							
SLK320 Roadster 2D		KK65F	46745	**9275**	**10575**	**12750**	**16350**
Sport Pkg			------	**625**	**625**	**835**	**835**
designo Edition			------	**800**	**800**	**1065**	**1065**
Manual Trans			------	**(500)**	**(500)**	**(665)**	**(665)**
SLK-CLASS—V6 Supercharged—Equipment Schedule 1							
W.B. 94.5"; 3.2 Liter.							
SLK32 Roadster 2D		KK66F	55545	**11650**	**13175**	**15500**	**19500**
designo Edition			------	**800**	**800**	**1065**	**1065**
C-CLASS—4-Cyl. Supercharged—Equipment Schedule 1							
W.B. 106.9"; 2.3 Liter.							
C230 Sport Coupe 2D		RN47J	29490	**4550**	**5375**	**7225**	**10050**
Manual Trans			------	**(500)**	**(500)**	**(665)**	**(665)**
C-CLASS—V6—Equipment Schedule 1							
W.B. 106.9"; 2.6 Liter, 3.2 Liter.							
C240 Sedan 4D		RF61J	33680	**5700**	**6650**	**8575**	**11550**
C320 Sedan 4D		RF64J	38780	**6750**	**7775**	**9750**	**12950**
C320 Wagon 4D		RH64J	40280	**7125**	**8200**	**10200**	**13450**
Sport Pkg			------	**400**	**400**	**535**	**535**
Manual Trans			------	**(500)**	**(500)**	**(665)**	**(665)**
C-CLASS—V6 Supercharged—Equipment Schedule 1							
W.B. 106.9"; 3.2 Liter.							
C32 Sedan 4D		RF65J	50545	**9500**	**10825**	**13000**	**16650**
CLK-CLASS—V6—Equipment Schedule 1							
W.B. 105.9"; 3.2 Liter.							
CLK320 Coupe 2D		LJ65G	44565	**7625**	**8725**	**10800**	**14050**
CLK320 Cabriolet 2D		LK65G	50245	**10475**	**11900**	**14150**	**18000**
Sport Pkg			------	**625**	**625**	**835**	**835**
designo Edition			------	**800**	**800**	**1065**	**1065**
CLK-CLASS—V8—Equipment Schedule 1							
W.B. 106.9"; 4.3 Liter, 5.5 Liter.							
CLK430 Coupe 2D		LJ70G	52265	**8725**	**9950**	**12100**	**15650**
CLK430 Cabriolet 2D		LK70G	57945	**12750**	**14400**	**16700**	**20900**
CLK55 Coupe 2D		LJ74G	69095	**11025**	**12450**	**14750**	**18650**
CLK55 Cabriolet 2D		LK74G	79645	**13975**	**15725**	**18200**	**22500**
designo Edition			------	**800**	**800**	**1065**	**1065**
E-CLASS—V6—Equipment Schedule 1							
W.B. 111.5"; 3.2 Liter.							
E320 Sedan 4D		JF65J	50280	**8650**	**9850**	**12000**	**15550**
E320 AWD Sedan 4D		JF82J	53130	**9175**	**10425**	**12600**	**16200**
E320 Wagon 4D		JH65J	51080	**8700**	**9900**	**12050**	**15600**
E320 AWD Wagon 4D		JH82J	53130	**9275**	**10575**	**12750**	**16350**

2002 MERCEDES-BENZ

Body	Type	VIN	List	Trade-In Fair	Good	Pvt-Party Good	Retail Excellent
	Sport Pkg (ex AWD)			625	625	835	835
	designo Edition (ex AWD)			800	800	1065	1065
E-CLASS—V8—Equipment Schedule 1							
W.B. 111.5"; 4.3 Liter, 5.5 Liter.							
E430 Sedan 4D		JF70J	55680	10625	12050	14400	18350
E430 AWD Sedan 4D		JF83J	58530	11375	12875	15250	19250
E55 Sedan 4D		JF74J	71995	15150	17000	19600	24200
	Sport Pkg (E430 RWD)			625	625	835	835
	designo Edition			800	800	1065	1065
CL-CLASS—V8—Equipment Schedule 1							
W.B. 113.6"; 5.0 Liter, 5.5 Liter.							
CL500 Coupe 2D		PJ75J	92395	14250	16025	18550	23000
CL55 Coupe 2D		PJ73J	105145	20275	22650	25500	31000
	Sport Pkg (CL500)			1650	1650	2200	2200
	designo Edition			800	800	1065	1065
CL-CLASS—V12—Equipment Schedule 1							
W.B. 113.6"; 5.8 Liter.							
CL600 Coupe 2D		PJ78J	120895	18925	21175	24000	29300
	Sport Pkg			1650	1650	2200	2200
	designo Edition			800	800	1065	1065
S-CLASS—V8—Equipment Schedule 1							
W.B. 121.5"; 4.3 Liter, 5.0 Liter, 5.5 Liter.							
S430 Sedan 4D		NG70J	72495	10350	11700	14050	17950
S500 Sedan 4D		NG75J	81845	11750	13275	15700	19800
S55 Sedan 4D		NG73J	101145	17100	19150	22000	27000
	Sport Pkg (S430,S500)			1650	1650	2200	2200
	designo Edition			800	800	1065	1065
S-CLASS—V12—Equipment Schedule 1							
W.B. 121.5"; 5.8 Liter.							
S600 Sedan 4D		NG78J	117545	14900	16750	19300	23900
	Sport Pkg			1650	1650	2200	2200
	designo Edition			800	800	1065	1065
SL-CLASS—V8—Equipment Schedule 1							
W.B. 99.0"; 5.0 Liter.							
SL500 Roadster 2D		FA68F	85445	15100	17000	19550	24200
	Sport Pkg			1650	1650	2200	2200
	Panorama Roof			950	950	1265	1265
	Silver Arrow Edition			1450	1450	1935	1935
SL-CLASS—V12—Equipment Schedule 1							
W.B. 99.0"; 6.0 Liter.							
SL600 Roadster 2D		FA76F	132195	16175	18125	20800	25600
	Panorama Roof			950	950	1265	1265
	Silver Arrow Edition			1450	1450	1935	1935

2003 MERCEDES-BENZ — WDB(KK49F)-3-#

Body	Type	VIN	List	Trade-In Fair	Good	Pvt-Party Good	Retail Excellent
SLK-CLASS—4-Cyl. Supercharged—Equipment Schedule 1							
W.B. 94.5"; 2.3 Liter.							
SLK230 Roadster 2D		KK49F	40265	9450	10725	12950	16550
	Sport Pkg			700	700	935	935
	designo Edition			825	825	1100	1100
	Manual Trans			(500)	(500)	(665)	(665)
SLK-CLASS—V6—Equipment Schedule 1							
W.B. 94.5"; 3.2 Liter.							
SLK320 Roadster 2D		KK65F	45715	10475	11900	14100	17900
	Sport Pkg			700	700	935	935
	designo Edition			825	825	1100	1100
	Manual Trans			(500)	(500)	(665)	(665)
SLK-CLASS—V6 Supercharged—Equipment Schedule 1							
W.B. 94.5"; 3.2 Liter.							
SLK32 Roadster 2D		KK66F	56115	13475	15200	17550	21800
	designo Edition			825	825	1100	1100
C-CLASS—4-Cyl. Supercharged—Equipment Schedule 1							
W.B. 106.9"; 1.8 Liter.							
C230 Sport Sedan 4D		RF40J	30310	6900	7975	9950	13200
C230 Sport Coupe 2D		RN40J	28270	5450	6325	8275	11250
	Manual Trans			(500)	(500)	(665)	(665)
C-CLASS—V6—Equipment Schedule 1							
W.B. 106.9"; 2.6 Liter, 3.2 Liter.							
C240 Sedan 4D		RF61J	32165	6750	7775	9750	12950
C240 4Matic Sedan 4D		RF81J	33965	7250	8325	10350	13600
C240 Wagon 4D		RH61J	33544	6800	7850	9850	13050
C240 4Matic Wagon 4D		RH81J	35344	7550	8650	10700	14000
C320 Sedan 4D		RF64J	38790	7950	9100	11150	14600

Body	Type	VIN	List	Trade-In Fair	Good	Pvt-Party Good	Retail Excellent
C320 4Matic Sedan 4D	RF84J	40590	8425	9625	11750	15250
C320 Coupe 2D	RN64J	30620	5175	6025	7975	10950
C320 Wagon 4D	RH64J	38840	8375	9575	11700	15200
C320 4Matic Wagon 4D	RH84J	40640	8900	10150	12300	15850
Sport (C320 Sed & Cpe)			700	700	935	935
Manual Trans			(500)	(500)	(665)	(665)
C-CLASS—V6 Supercharged—Equipment Schedule 1						
W.B. 106.9"; 3.2 Liter.						
C32 Sedan 4D	RF65J	52065	11125	12600	14800	18650
CLK-CLASS—V6—Equipment Schedule 1						
W.B. 105.9", 106.9" (Coupe); 3.2 Liter.						
CLK320 Coupe 2D	TJ65J	44565	8475	9675	11800	15300
CLK320 Cabriolet 2D	LK65G	50615	12250	13875	16150	20200
Sport Pkg (Cabriolet)			700	700	935	935
designo Edition			825	825	1100	1100
CLK-CLASS—V8—Equipment Schedule 1						
W.B. 105.9", 106.9" (Coupe); 4.3 Liter, 5.0 Liter, 5.5 Liter.						
CLK430 Cabriolet 2D	LK70G	58315	13675	15425	17800	22100
CLK500 Coupe 2D	TJ75J	52865	9500	10775	13000	16600
CLK55 Coupe 2D	TJ76H	69470	12150	13725	16000	20100
designo Edition			825	825	1100	1100
E-CLASS—V6—Equipment Schedule 1						
W.B. 111.5", 112.4" (Sed); 3.2 Liter.						
E320 Sedan 4D	UF65J	49165	9800	11125	13350	17000
E320 Wagon 4D	JH65J	55415	10200	11575	13750	17500
E320 4Matic Wagon 4D	JH82J	55415	10825	12300	14500	18350
Sport Pkg (Sedan)			700	700	935	935
Panorama Roof			950	950	1265	1265
E-CLASS—V8—Equipment Schedule 1						
W.B. 112.4"; 5.0 Liter.						
E500 Sedan 4D	UF70J	57065	10825	12250	14550	18500
Sport Pkg			700	700	935	935
Panorama Roof			950	950	1265	1265
E-CLASS—V8 Supercharged—Equipment Schedule 1						
W.B. 112.4"; 5.5 Liter.						
E55 Sedan 4D	UF72J	76720	17000	19050	21800	26700
Panorama Roof			950	950	1265	1265
CL-CLASS—V8—Equipment Schedule 1						
W.B. 113.6"; 5.0 Liter.						
CL500 Coupe 2D	PJ75J	93315	15875	17775	20400	25100
Sport Pkg			1700	1700	2265	2265
designo Edition			825	825	1100	1100
CL-CLASS—V8 Supercharged—Equipment Schedule 1						
W.B. 113.6"; 5.5 Liter.						
CL55 Coupe 2D	PJ74J	115265	20975	23525	26300	31800
designo Edition			825	825	1100	1100
CL-CLASS—V12 Twin Turbo—Equipment Schedule 1						
W.B. 113.6"; 5.5 Liter.						
CL600 Coupe 2D	PJ76J	127265	21950	24500	27400	33000
Sport Pkg			1700	1700	2265	2265
designo Edition			825	825	1100	1100
S-CLASS—V8—Equipment Schedule 1						
W.B. 121.5"; 4.3 Liter, 5.0 Liter.						
S430 Sedan 4D	NG70J	73265	11375	12850	15250	19250
S430 4Matic Sedan 4D	NG83J	76165	12100	13675	16050	20200
S500 Sedan 4D	NG75J	82665	12975	14650	17100	21400
S500 4Matic Sedan 4D	NG84J	85565	14250	16025	18500	22900
Sport Pkg			1700	1700	2265	2265
designo Edition			825	825	1100	1100
S-CLASS—V8 Supercharged—Equipment Schedule 1						
W.B. 121.5"; 5.5 Liter.						
S55 Sedan 4D	NG74J	107165	18925	21175	23900	29100
designo Edition			825	825	1100	1100
S-CLASS—V12—Equipment Schedule 1						
W.B. 121.5"; 5.8 Liter.						
S600 Sedan 4D	NG76J	121205	17350	19450	22100	27000
Sport Pkg			1700	1700	2265	2265
designo Edition			825	825	1100	1100
SL-CLASS—V8—Equipment Schedule 1						
W.B. 100.8"; 5.0 Liter.						
SL500 Roadster 2D	SK75F	87655	20100	22550	25300	30700
Sport Pkg			1700	1700	2265	2265
designo Edition			825	825	1100	1100

2003 MERCEDES-BENZ

Body	Type	VIN	List	Trade-In Fair	Trade-In Good	Pvt-Party Good	Retail Excellent
	Panorama Roof		....	950	950	1265	1265
	Launch Edition		....	2000	2000	2665	2665
SL-CLASS—V8 Supercharged—Equipment Schedule 1							
W.B. 100.8"; 5.5 Liter.							
	SL55 Roadster 2D	SK74F	114915	25875	28800	31900	38100
	designo Edition		....	825	825	1100	1100
	Panorama Roof		....	950	950	1265	1265

2004 MERCEDES BENZ — WDB(KK49F)–4–#

Body	Type	VIN	List	Trade-In Fair	Trade-In Good	Pvt-Party Good	Retail Excellent
SLK-CLASS—4-Cyl. Supercharged—Equipment Schedule 1							
W.B. 94.5"; 2.3 Liter.							
	SLK230 Roadster 2D	KK49F	40320	11075	12550	14850	18700
	Sport Pkg		....	775	775	1035	1035
	designo Edition		....	850	850	1135	1135
	Manual Trans		....	(500)	(500)	(665)	(665)
SLK-CLASS—V6—Equipment Schedule 1							
W.B. 94.5"; 3.2 Liter.							
	SLK320 Roadster 2D	KK65F	47330	12150	13725	15950	20000
	Sport Pkg		....	775	775	1035	1035
	designo Edition		....	850	850	1135	1135
	Manual Trans		....	(500)	(500)	(665)	(665)
SLK-CLASS—V6 Supercharged—Equipment Schedule 1							
W.B. 94.5"; 3.2 Liter.							
	SLK32 Roadster 2D	KK66F	56170	15675	17600	20000	24500
	designo Edition		....	850	850	1135	1135
C-CLASS—4-Cyl. Supercharged—Equipment Schedule 1							
W.B. 106.9"; 1.8 Liter.							
	C230 Sport Sedan 4D	RF40J	33180	8250	9425	11550	15100
	C230 Sport Coupe 2D	RN47J	30090	6625	7625	9675	12900
	Manual Trans		....	(500)	(500)	(665)	(665)
C-CLASS—V6—Equipment Schedule 1							
W.B. 106.9"; 2.6 Liter, 3.2 Liter.							
	C240 Sedan 4D	RF61J	33920	8250	9425	11550	15100
	C240 4Matic Sedan 4D	RF81J	35120	8775	10000	12150	15750
	C240 Wagon 4D	RH61J	35350	8275	9475	11600	15150
	C240 4Matic Wagon 4D	RH81J	36490	9125	10400	12550	16150
	C320 Sedan 4D	RF64J	39270	9550	10875	13050	16700
	C320 4Matic Sedan 4D	RF84J	40470	10100	11475	13650	17450
	C320 Coupe 2D	RN64J	29610	6450	7425	9475	12700
	C320 Wagon 4D	RH64J	40640	10050	11425	13650	17400
	C320 4Matic Wagon 4D	RH84J	41840	10625	12050	14250	18100
	Sport (C320 Sed & Cpe)		....	775	775	1035	1035
	Manual Trans		....	(500)	(500)	(665)	(665)
C-CLASS—V6 Supercharged—Equipment Schedule 1							
W.B. 106.9"; 3.2 Liter.							
	C32 Sedan 4D	RF65J	53120	13125	14800	17100	21300
CLK-CLASS—V6—Equipment Schedule 1							
W.B. 106.9"; 3.2 Liter.							
	CLK320 Coupe 2D	TJ65J	46480	10100	11475	13650	17450
	CLK320 Cabriolet 2D	LK65G	52120	13225	14900	17200	21400
	designo Edition		....	850	850	1135	1135
CLK-CLASS—V8—Equipment Schedule 1							
W.B. 106.9"; 5.0 Liter, 5.5 Liter.							
	CLK500 Coupe 2D	TJ75J	54520	11850	13375	15650	19600
	CLK500 Cabriolet 2D	TK75G	61570	16225	18225	20700	25300
	CLK55 Coupe 2D	TJ76H	70240	13875	15575	18000	22200
	CLK55 Cabriolet 2D	LJ74G	80220	17650	19800	22220	27000
	designo Edition		....	850	850	1135	1135
E-CLASS—V6—Equipment Schedule 1							
W.B. 112.4"; 3.2 Liter.							
	E320 Sedan 4D	UF65J	49410	11425	12875	15200	19100
	E320 4Matic Sedan 4D	UF82J	51910	12250	13875	16000	19900
	E320 Wagon 4D	UH65J	51910	12200	13775	16050	20100
	E320 4Matic Wagon 4D	UH82J	54410	12850	14450	16650	20600
	Sport/Appearance Pkg		....	775	775	1035	1035
	designo Edition		....	850	850	1135	1135
	Panorama Roof		....	950	950	1265	1265
E-CLASS—V8—Equipment Schedule 1							
W.B. 112.4"; 5.0 Liter.							
	E500 Sedan 4D	UF70J	58510	12300	13925	16300	20500
	E500 4Matic Sedan 4D	UF83J	60545	13275	15000	17450	21800
	E500 4Matic Wagon 4D	UH83J	63210	13475	15200	17650	22000
	Sport/Appearance Pkg		....	775	775	1035	1035

2004 MERCEDES-BENZ

Body	Type	VIN	List	Trade-In Fair	Good	Pvt-Party Good	Retail Excellent
	designo Edition			850	850	1135	1135
	Panorama Roof			950	950	1265	1265

E-CLASS—V8 Supercharged—Equipment Schedule 1
W.B. 112.4"; 5.5 Liter.

E55 Sedan 4D		UF76J	80070	19900	22250	25000	30200
	designo Edition			850	850	1135	1135
	Panorama Roof			950	950	1265	1265

CL-CLASS—V8—Equipment Schedule 1
W.B. 113.6"; 5.0 Liter.

CL500 Coupe 2D		PJ75J	94520	18075	20200	22900	27900
	Sport Pkg			1750	1750	2335	2335
	designo Edition			850	850	1135	1135

CL-CLASS—V8 Supercharged—Equipment Schedule 1
W.B. 113.6"; 5.5 Liter.

CL55 Coupe 2D		PJ74J	119520	23900	26650	29500	35300
	designo Edition			850	850	1135	1135

CL-CLASS—V12 Twin Turbo—Equipment Schedule 1
W.B. 113.6"; 5.5 Liter.

CL600 Coupe 2D		PJ76J	129320	26175	29100	32000	38200
	Sport Pkg			1750	1750	2335	2335
	designo Edition			850	850	1135	1135

S-CLASS—V8—Equipment Schedule 1
W.B. 121.5"; 4.3 Liter, 5.0 Liter.

S430 Sedan 4D		NG70J	74320	12925	14600	17050	21400
S430 4Matic Sedan 4D		NG83J	78220	13825	15575	18050	22400
S500 Sedan 4D		NG75J	83770	14800	16650	19100	23600
S500 4Matic Sedan 4D		NG84J	86970	16175	18175	20800	25500
	Sport Pkg			1750	1750	2335	2335
	designo Edition			850	850	1135	1135

S-CLASS—V8 Supercharged—Equipment Schedule 1
W.B. 121.5"; 5.5 Liter.

S55 Sedan 4D		NG74J	111870	21375	23825	26700	32000
	designo Edition			850	850	1135	1135

S-CLASS—V12 Bi-Turbo—Equipment Schedule 1
W.B. 121.5"; 5.5 Liter.

S600 Sedan 4D		NG76J	124260	24300	27150	30000	35800
	Sport Pkg			1750	1750	2335	2335
	designo Edition			850	850	1135	1135

SL-CLASS—V8—Equipment Schedule 1
W.B. 100.8"; 5.0 Liter.

SL500 Roadster 2D		SK75F	89800	21650	24100	27000	32400
	Sport Pkg			1750	1750	2335	2335
	designo Edition			850	850	1135	1135
	Panorama Roof			950	950	1265	1265

SL-CLASS—V8 Supercharged—Equipment Schedule 1
W.B. 100.8"; 5.5 Liter.

SL55 Roadster 2D		SK74F	121450	30075	33425	36600	43100
	designo Edition			850	850	1135	1135
	Panorama Roof			950	950	1265	1265

SL-CLASS—V12 Twin Turbo—Equipment Schedule 1
W.B. 100.8"; 5.5 Liter.

SL600 Roadster 2D		SK76F	128550	30575	34000	37100	43800
	Sport Pkg			1750	1750	2335	2335
	designo Edition			850	850	1135	1135
	Panorama Roof			950	950	1265	1265

2005 MERCEDES-BENZ — WDBorWDD(WK56F)-5

SLK-CLASS—V6—Equipment Schedule 1
W.B. 95.7"; 3.5 Liter.

SLK350 Roadster 2D		WK56F	47610	16275	18275	20700	25200
	Sport Pkg			850	850	1135	1135
	designo Edition			875	875	1165	1165
	Manual Trans			(500)	(500)	(665)	(665)

SLK-CLASS—V8—Equipment Schedule 1
W.B. 95.7"; 5.5 Liter.

SLK55 Roadster 2D		WK73F	61220	19100	21375	23900	28800
	designo Edition			875	875	1165	1165

C-CLASS—4-Cyl. Supercharged—Equipment Schedule 1
W.B. 106.9"; 1.8 Liter.

C230 Sedan 4D		RF40J	34650	9850	11175	13450	17150
C230 Sport Coupe 2D		RN40J	30850	8075	9225	11400	14950
	Manual Trans			(500)	(500)	(665)	(665)

2005 MERCEDES-BENZ

Body	Type	VIN	List	Trade-In Fair	Trade-In Good	Pvt-Party Good	Retail Excellent
C-CLASS—V6—Equipment Schedule 1							
W.B. 106.9"; 2.6 Liter, 3.2 Liter.							
C240 Sedan 4D	RF61J	36660	**10000**	**11325**	**13550**	**17300**
C240 4Matic Sedan 4D	RF81J	37860	**10575**	**12000**	**14250**	**18100**
C240 Wagon 4D	RH61J	38030	**10050**	**11425**	**13650**	**17450**
C240 4Matic Wagon 4D	RH81J	39230	**10975**	**12450**	**14700**	**18550**
C320 Sedan 4D	RF64J	41960	**11475**	**12925**	**15250**	**19150**
C320 4Matic Sedan 4D	RF84J	43160	**12050**	**13625**	**15900**	**19900**
C320 Coupe 2D	RN64J	33250	**7975**	**9150**	**11300**	**14850**
Sport (C320 Sed & Cpe)			**850**	**850**	**1135**	**1135**
Manual Trans			**(500)**	**(500)**	**(665)**	**(665)**
C-CLASS—V8—Equipment Schedule 1							
W.B. 106.9"; 5.5 Liter.							
C55 Sedan 4D	RF76J	54620	**16750**	**18775**	**21300**	**25900**
CLK-CLASS—V6—Equipment Schedule 1							
W.B. 106.9"; 3.2 Liter.							
CLK320 Coupe 2D	TJ65G	47410	**12050**	**13625**	**15900**	**19900**
CLK320 Cabriolet 2D	TK65G	53420	**15925**	**17875**	**20300**	**24800**
designo Edition			**875**	**875**	**1165**	**1165**
CLK-CLASS—V8—Equipment Schedule 1							
W.B. 106.9"; 5.0 Liter, 5.5 Liter.							
CLK500 Coupe 2D	TJ75G	55910	**13825**	**15575**	**17900**	**22100**
CLK500 Cabriolet 2D	TK75G	61920	**18875**	**21075**	**23500**	**28400**
CLK55 Coupe 2D	TJ76G	71620	**16125**	**18075**	**20500**	**25100**
CLK55 Cabriolet 2D	TK76G	82870	**20275**	**22725**	**25200**	**30300**
designo Edition			**875**	**875**	**1165**	**1165**
E-CLASS—6-Cyl. Turbo Diesel—Equipment Schedule 1							
W.B. 112.4"; 3.2 Liter.							
E320 CDI Sedan 4D	UF26J	52855	**17775**	**20000**	**22400**	**27100**
designo Edition			**875**	**875**	**1165**	**1165**
Panorama Roof			**950**	**950**	**1265**	**1265**
E-CLASS—V6—Equipment Schedule 1							
W.B. 112.4"; 3.2 Liter.							
E320 Sedan 4D	UF65J	52280	**13275**	**14950**	**17250**	**21400**
E320 4Matic Sedan 4D	UF82J	54770	**13925**	**15675**	**18000**	**22200**
E320 Wagon 4D	UH65J	54400	**14400**	**16175**	**18500**	**22800**
E320 4Matic Wagon 4D	UH82J	56900	**15100**	**16950**	**19300**	**23700**
Sport/Appearance Pkg			**850**	**850**	**1135**	**1135**
designo Edition			**875**	**875**	**1165**	**1165**
Panorama Roof			**950**	**950**	**1265**	**1265**
E-CLASS—V8—Equipment Schedule 1							
W.B. 112.4"; 5.0 Liter.							
E500 Sedan 4D	UF70J	60480	**14400**	**16175**	**18700**	**23200**
E500 4Matic Sedan 4D	UF83J	61420	**15475**	**17350**	**19900**	**24500**
E500 4Matic Wagon 4D	UH83J	63950	**15675**	**17600**	**20200**	**24800**
Sport/Appearance Pkg			**850**	**850**	**1135**	**1135**
designo Edition			**875**	**875**	**1165**	**1165**
Panorama Roof			**950**	**950**	**1265**	**1265**
E-CLASS—V8 Supercharged—Equipment Schedule 1							
W.B. 112.4"; 5.5 Liter.							
E55 Sedan 4D	UF76J	81920	**23325**	**26075**	**28800**	**34400**
E55 Wagon 4D	UF86J	83220	**24900**	**27825**	**30500**	**36300**
designo Edition			**875**	**875**	**1165**	**1165**
Panorama Roof			**950**	**950**	**1265**	**1265**
CL-CLASS—V8—Equipment Schedule 1							
W.B. 113.6"; 5.0 Liter.							
CL500 Coupe 2D	PJ75J	94620	**20775**	**23225**	**25900**	**31200**
Sport Pkg			**1800**	**1800**	**2400**	**2400**
designo Edition			**875**	**875**	**1165**	**1165**
CL-CLASS—V8 Supercharged—Equipment Schedule 1							
W.B. 113.6"; 5.5 Liter.							
CL55 Coupe 2D	PJ74J	119620	**27150**	**30275**	**33100**	**39200**
designo Edition			**875**	**875**	**1165**	**1165**
CL-CLASS—V12 Twin Turbo—Equipment Schedule 1							
W.B. 113.6"; 5.5 Liter, 6.0 Liter.							
CL600 Coupe 2D	PJ76J	128620	**30275**	**33700**	**36700**	**43100**
CL65 Coupe 2D	PJ79J	178220	**48125**	**53300**	**56600**	**65400**
Sport Pkg			**1800**	**1800**	**2400**	**2400**
designo Edition			**875**	**875**	**1165**	**1165**
S-CLASS—V8—Equipment Schedule 1							
W.B. 121.5"; 4.3 Liter, 5.0 Liter.							
S430 Sedan 4D	NG70J	76020	**15100**	**16950**	**19450**	**24000**
S430 4Matic Sedan 4D	NG83J	76020	**16075**	**18025**	**20600**	**25400**

2005 MERCEDES-BENZ

Body	Type	VIN	List	Trade-In Fair	Good	Pvt-Party Good	Retail Excellent
	S500 Sedan 4D	NG75J	84620	**17200**	**19250**	**21900**	**26800**
	S500 4Matic Sedan 4D	NG84J	84620	**18675**	**20875**	**23500**	**28500**
	Sport Pkg			**725**	**725**	**965**	**965**
	designo Edition			**875**	**875**	**1165**	**1165**

S-CLASS—V8 Supercharged—Equipment Schedule 1
W.B. 121.5"; 5.5 Liter.

| | S55 Sedan 4D | NG74J | 112620 | **24200** | **27050** | **29800** | **35500** |
| | designo Edition | | | **875** | **875** | **1165** | **1165** |

S-CLASS—V12 Twin Turbo—Equipment Schedule 1
W.B. 121.5"; 5.5 Liter.

	S600 Sedan 4D	NG76J	125470	**28225**	**31450**	**34300**	**40500**
	Sport Pkg			**1800**	**1800**	**2400**	**2400**
	designo Edition			**875**	**875**	**1165**	**1165**

SL-CLASS—V8—Equipment Schedule 1
W.B. 100.8"; 5.0 Liter.

	SL500 Roadster 2D	SK75F	91920	**25475**	**28425**	**31300**	**37100**
	Sport Pkg			**1800**	**1800**	**2400**	**2400**
	designo Edition			**875**	**875**	**1165**	**1165**
	Panorama Roof			**950**	**950**	**1265**	**1265**

SL-CLASS—V8 Supercharged—Equipment Schedule 1
W.B. 100.8"; 5.5 Liter.

	SL55 Roadster 2D	SK74F	120120	**34900**	**38700**	**41700**	**48700**
	designo Edition			**875**	**875**	**1165**	**1165**
	Panorama Roof			**950**	**950**	**1265**	**1265**

SL-CLASS—V12 Twin Turbo—Equipment Schedule 1
W.B. 100.8"; 5.5 Liter, 6.0 Liter.

	SL600 Roadster 2D	SK76F	125620	**35475**	**39400**	**42300**	**49400**
	SL65 Roadster 2D	SK79F	182720	**50575**	**56050**	**59500**	**68500**
	Sport Pkg (SL600)			**1800**	**1800**	**2400**	**2400**
	designo Edition			**875**	**875**	**1165**	**1165**
	Panorama Roof			**950**	**950**	**1265**	**1265**

2006 MERCEDES-BENZ — WDBorWDD(WK54F)-6

SLK-CLASS—V6—Equipment Schedule 1
W.B. 95.7"; 3.0 Liter, 3.5 Liter.

	SLK280 Roadster 2D	WK54F	45085	**17100**	**19150**	**21600**	**26300**
	SLK350 Roadster 2D	WK56F	49135	**19000**	**21275**	**23700**	**28500**
	Sport Pkg			**925**	**925**	**1235**	**1235**
	designo Edition			**900**	**900**	**1200**	**1200**
	Manual Trans			**(500)**	**(500)**	**(665)**	**(665)**

SLK-CLASS—V8—Equipment Schedule 1
W.B. 95.7"; 5.5 Liter.

| | SLK55 Roadster 2D | WK73F | 63575 | **22450** | **25000** | **27400** | **32600** |
| | designo Edition | | | **900** | **900** | **1200** | **1200** |

C-CLASS—V6—Equipment Schedule 1
W.B. 106.9"; 2.5 Liter, 3.0 Liter, 3.5 Liter.

	C230 Sport Sedan 4D	RF52J	33155	**11475**	**12975**	**15300**	**19300**
	C280 Sedan 4D	RF54J	35515	**12100**	**13675**	**15950**	**20000**
	C280 4Matic Sedan 4D	RF92J	37315	**12750**	**14400**	**16700**	**20900**
	C350 Sedan 4D	RF56J	40715	**13675**	**15375**	**17750**	**22000**
	C350 4Matic Sedan 4D	RF87J	42515	**14400**	**16175**	**18500**	**22800**
	Manual Trans			**(500)**	**(500)**	**(665)**	**(665)**

C-CLASS—V8—Equipment Schedule 1
W.B. 106.9"; 5.5 Liter.

| | C55 Sedan 4D | RF76J | 56225 | **19800** | **22150** | **24600** | **29500** |

CLK-CLASS—V6—Equipment Schedule 1
W.B. 106.9"; 3.5 Liter.

	CLK350 Coupe 2D	TJ56J	49025	**14400**	**16175**	**18500**	**22800**
	CLK350 Cabriolet 2D	TK56G	55975	**19000**	**21275**	**23700**	**28500**
	designo Edition			**900**	**900**	**1200**	**1200**

CLK-CLASS—V8—Equipment Schedule 1
W.B. 106.9"; 5.0 Liter, 5.5 Liter.

	CLK500 Coupe 2D	TJ57J	57325	**16550**	**18625**	**21000**	**25600**
	CLK500 Cabriolet 2D	TK75G	64275	**22250**	**24800**	**27200**	**32400**
	CLK55 Cabriolet 2D	TK76G	84275	**23825**	**26550**	**29000**	**34400**
	designo Edition			**900**	**900**	**1200**	**1200**

E-CLASS—6-Cyl. Turbo Diesel—Equipment Schedule 1
W.B. 112.4"; 3.2 Liter.

| | E320 CDI Sedan 4D | UF26J | 54845 | **20675** | **23125** | **25600** | **30600** |
| | designo Edition | | | **900** | **900** | **1200** | **1200** |

E-CLASS—V6—Equipment Schedule 1
W.B. 112.4"; 3.5 Liter.

| | E350 Sedan 4D | UF56J | 52325 | **16750** | **18825** | **21200** | **25700** |

Body	Type	VIN	List	Trade-In Fair	Good	Pvt-Party Good	Retail Excellent
	E350 4Matic Sedan 4D	UF87J	54825	**17975**	**20100**	**22500**	**27200**
	E350 Wagon 4D	UH56J	54505	**16650**	**18725**	**21100**	**25700**
	E350 4Matic Wagon 4D	UH87J	57005	**19800**	**22150**	**24600**	**29500**
	Sport/Appearance Pkg			**925**	**925**	**1235**	**1235**
	designo Edition			**900**	**900**	**1200**	**1200**
	Panorama Roof			**975**	**975**	**1300**	**1300**

E-CLASS—V8—Equipment Schedule 1
W.B. 112.4"; 5.0 Liter.

Body	Type	VIN	List	Trade-In Fair	Good	Pvt-Party Good	Retail Excellent
	E500 Sedan 4D	UF70J	60675	**17200**	**19250**	**22000**	**26900**
	E500 4Matic Sedan 4D	UF83J	64475	**18425**	**20575**	**23300**	**28300**
	E500 4Matic Wagon 4D	UH83J	65505	**18675**	**20875**	**23500**	**28600**
	Sport/Appearance Pkg			**925**	**925**	**1235**	**1235**
	designo Edition			**900**	**900**	**1200**	**1200**
	Panorama Roof			**975**	**975**	**1300**	**1300**

E-CLASS—V8 Supercharged—Equipment Schedule 1
W.B. 112.4"; 5.5 Liter.

Body	Type	VIN	List	Trade-In Fair	Good	Pvt-Party Good	Retail Excellent
	E55 Sedan 4D	UF76J	84275	**27550**	**30675**	**33400**	**39500**
	E55 Wagon 4D	UH76J	83375	**28800**	**32150**	**34900**	**41200**
	designo Edition			**900**	**900**	**1200**	**1200**
	Panorama Roof			**975**	**975**	**1300**	**1300**

CL-CLASS—V8—Equipment Schedule 1
W.B. 113.6"; 5.0 Liter.

Body	Type	VIN	List	Trade-In Fair	Good	Pvt-Party Good	Retail Excellent
	CL500 Coupe 2D	PJ75J	97275	**24200**	**27050**	**29700**	**35400**
	designo Edition			**900**	**900**	**1200**	**1200**

CL-CLASS—V8 Supercharged—Equipment Schedule 1
W.B. 113.6"; 5.5 Liter.

Body	Type	VIN	List	Trade-In Fair	Good	Pvt-Party Good	Retail Excellent
	CL55 Coupe 2D	PJ74J	122975	**31350**	**34900**	**37700**	**44200**
	designo Edition			**900**	**900**	**1200**	**1200**

CL-CLASS—V12 Twin Turbo—Equipment Schedule 1
W.B. 113.6"; 5.5 Liter, 6.0 Liter.

Body	Type	VIN	List	Trade-In Fair	Good	Pvt-Party Good	Retail Excellent
	CL600 Coupe 2D	PJ76J	132875	**35175**	**39100**	**41900**	**48800**
	CL65 Coupe 2D	PJ79J	182975	**54775**	**60650**	**63800**	**72800**
	designo Edition			**900**	**900**	**1200**	**1200**

CLS-CLASS—V8—Equipment Schedule 1
W.B. 112.4"; 5.0 Liter.

Body	Type	VIN	List	Trade-In Fair	Good	Pvt-Party Good	Retail Excellent
	CLS500 Coupe 4D	DJ75X	66975	**23025**	**25675**	**28400**	**33900**
	Sport Pkg			**1850**	**1850**	**2465**	**2465**
	designo Edition			**900**	**900**	**1200**	**1200**

CLS-CLASS—V8 Supercharged—Equipment Schedule 1
W.B. 112.4"; 5.5 Liter.

Body	Type	VIN	List	Trade-In Fair	Good	Pvt-Party Good	Retail Excellent
	CLS55 Coupe 4D	DJ76X	89075	**34500**	**38325**	**41200**	**48000**
	designo Edition			**900**	**900**	**1200**	**1200**

S-CLASS—V6—Equipment Schedule 1
W.B. 121.5"; 3.7 Liter.

Body	Type	VIN	List	Trade-In Fair	Good	Pvt-Party Good	Retail Excellent
	S350 Sedan 4D	NF67J	65675	**16850**	**18875**	**21600**	**26500**

S-CLASS—V8—Equipment Schedule 1
W.B. 121.5"; 4.3 Liter, 5.0 Liter.

Body	Type	VIN	List	Trade-In Fair	Good	Pvt-Party Good	Retail Excellent
	S430 Sedan 4D	NG70J	78025	**17975**	**20100**	**22800**	**27800**
	S430 4Matic Sedan 4D	NG83J	79025	**19100**	**21375**	**24100**	**29200**
	S500 Sedan 4D	NG75J	87825	**20275**	**22725**	**25400**	**30700**
	S500 4Matic Sedan 4D	NG84J	88125	**21950**	**24500**	**27200**	**32600**
	Sport Pkg			**800**	**800**	**1065**	**1065**
	designo Edition			**900**	**900**	**1200**	**1200**

S-CLASS—V8 Supercharged—Equipment Schedule 1
W.B. 121.5"; 5.5 Liter.

Body	Type	VIN	List	Trade-In Fair	Good	Pvt-Party Good	Retail Excellent
	S55 Sedan 4D	NG74J	116625	**27925**	**31175**	**33900**	**40100**
	designo Edition			**900**	**900**	**1200**	**1200**

S-CLASS—V12 Twin Turbo—Equipment Schedule 1
W.B. 121.5"; 5.5 Liter, 6.0 Liter.

Body	Type	VIN	List	Trade-In Fair	Good	Pvt-Party Good	Retail Excellent
	S600 Sedan 4D	NG76J	131725	**32925**	**36650**	**39400**	**46100**
	S65 Sedan 4D	NG79J	169775	**44775**	**49675**	**52700**	**60700**
	Sport Pkg (S600)			**1850**	**1850**	**2465**	**2465**
	designo Edition			**900**	**900**	**1200**	**1200**

SL-CLASS—V8—Equipment Schedule 1
W.B. 100.8"; 5.0 Liter.

Body	Type	VIN	List	Trade-In Fair	Good	Pvt-Party Good	Retail Excellent
	SL500 Roadster 2D	SK75F	94675	**30175**	**33525**	**36400**	**42700**
	Sport Pkg			**1850**	**1850**	**2465**	**2465**
	designo Edition			**900**	**900**	**1200**	**1200**
	Panorama Roof			**975**	**975**	**1300**	**1300**

SL-CLASS—V8 Supercharged—Equipment Schedule 1
W.B. 100.8"; 5.5 Liter.

Body	Type	VIN	List	Trade-In Fair	Good	Pvt-Party Good	Retail Excellent
	SL55 Roadster 2D	SK74F	127875	**40375**	**44875**	**47700**	**55200**
	designo Edition			**900**	**900**	**1200**	**1200**

2006 MERCEDES-BENZ

Body	Type	VIN	List	Trade-In Fair	Good	Pvt-Party Good	Retail Excellent
	Panorama Roof			975	975	1300	1300
SL-CLASS—V12 Twin Turbo—Equipment Schedule 1							
W.B. 100.8"; 5.5 Liter, 6.0 Liter.							
	SL600 Roadster 2D	SK76F	134275	41150	45675	48500	56100
	SL65 Roadster 2D	SK79F	188375	61650	68200	71300	81000
	Sport Pkg (SL600)			1850	1850	2465	2465
	designo Edition			900	900	1200	1200
	Panorama Roof			975	975	1300	1300

2007 MERCEDES-BENZ — WDBorWDD(WK54F)-7

Body	Type	VIN	List	Trade-In Fair	Good	Pvt-Party Good	Retail Excellent
SLK-CLASS—V6—Equipment Schedule 1							
W.B. 95.7"; 3.0 Liter, 3.5 Liter.							
	SLK280 Roadster 2D	WK54F	45555	20100	22450	24900	29800
	SLK350 Roadster 2D	WK56F	49605	22150	24700	27100	32200
	Sport Pkg			1000	1000	1335	1335
	designo Edition			900	900	1200	1200
	Manual Trans			(500)	(500)	(665)	(665)
SLK-CLASS—V8—Equipment Schedule 1							
W.B. 95.7"; 5.5 Liter.							
	SLK55 Roadster 2D	WK73F	64575	30575	34000	36500	42400
	designo Edition			900	900	1200	1200
C-CLASS—V6—Equipment Schedule 1							
W.B. 106.9"; 2.5 Liter, 3.0 Liter, 3.5 Liter.							
	C230 Sport Sedan 4D	RF52J	34205	13775	15525	17900	22100
	C280 Sedan 4D	RF54J	35965	14550	16375	18750	23100
	C280 4Matic Sedan 4D	RF92J	37765	15300	17200	19500	23900
	C350 Sedan 4D	RF56J	41165	16275	18275	20700	25200
	C350 4Matic Sedan 4D	RF87J	42965	17100	19150	21600	26300
	Manual Trans			(500)	(500)	(665)	(665)
CLK-CLASS—V6—Equipment Schedule 1							
W.B. 106.9"; 3.5 Liter.							
	CLK350 Coupe 2D	TJ56J	49505	17100	19150	21600	26300
	CLK350 Cabriolet 2D	TK56F	54975	22550	25100	27500	32600
	designo Edition			900	900	1200	1200
CLK-CLASS—V8—Equipment Schedule 1							
W.B. 106.9"; 5.5 Liter, 6.3 Liter.							
	CLK550 Coupe 2D	TJ72H	58205	21750	24300	26800	31900
	CLK550 Cabriolet 2D	TK72F	63675	27450	30575	33000	38700
	CLK63 Cabriolet 2D	TK77G	92575	33900	37625	40100	46400
	designo Edition			900	900	1200	1200
E-CLASS—V6 Turbo Diesel—Equipment Schedule 1							
W.B. 112.4"; 3.0 Liter.							
	E320 BLUETEC Sed	UF22X	52325	26350	29400	31900	37400
	designo Edition			900	900	1200	1200
	Panorama Roof			1000	1000	1335	1335
E-CLASS—V6—Equipment Schedule 1							
W.B. 112.4"; 3.5 Liter.							
	E350 Sedan 4D	UF56X	51325	20575	23025	25400	30400
	E350 4Matic Sedan	UF87X	56475	21950	24500	27000	32000
	E350 4Matic Wagon	UH87X	53825	23900	26650	29000	34300
	Sport Pkg (Sedan)			1000	1000	1335	1335
	designo Edition			900	900	1200	1200
	Panorama Roof			1000	1000	1335	1335
E-CLASS—V8—Equipment Schedule 1							
W.B. 112.4"; 5.5 Liter, 6.3 Liter.							
	E550 Sedan 4D	UF72X	59775	25575	28525	31300	37100
	E550 4Matic Sedan 4D	UF90X	62275	26350	29400	32100	38000
	E63 Sedan 4D	UF77X	85375	39975	44400	47100	54300
	E63 Wagon 4D	UH77X	86115	40775	45275	47900	55200
	Sport Pkg (E550)			1000	1000	1335	1335
	designo Edition			900	900	1200	1200
	Panorama Roof			1000	1000	1335	1335
CL-CLASS—V8—Equipment Schedule 1							
W.B. 116.3"; 5.5 Liter.							
	CL550 Coupe 2D	EJ71X	100675	53400	59200	61900	70500
	Sport Pkg			1000	1000	1335	1335
	designo Edition			900	900	1200	1200
CL-CLASS—V12 Twin Turbo—Equipment Schedule 1							
W.B. 116.3"; 5.5 Liter.							
	CL600 Coupe 2D	EJ76X	144975	63900	70650	73400	82900
	designo Edition			900	900	1200	1200
CLS-CLASS—V8—Equipment Schedule 1							
W.B. 112.4"; 5.5 Liter, 6.3 Liter.							

2007 MERCEDES-BENZ

Body	Type	VIN	List	Trade-In Fair	Trade-In Good	Pvt-Party Good	Retail Excellent
CLS550 Coupe 4D		DJ72X	68975	29800	33125	35900	42100
CLS63 Coupe 4D		DJ77X	92975	45475	50375	53200	61000
	Sport Pkg (CLS550)			1900	1900	2535	2535
	designo Edition			900	900	1200	1200

S-CLASS—V8—Equipment Schedule 1
W.B. 124.6"; 5.5 Liter.

Body	Type	VIN	List	Fair	Good	Pvt Good	Excellent
S550 Sedan 4D		NG71X	87175	43500	48325	51100	58700
S550 4Matic Sedan 4D		NG86X	89525	44600	49500	52200	60000
	Sport Pkg			1000	1000	1335	1335
	designo Edition			900	900	1200	1200
	Panorama Roof			1000	1000	1335	1335

S-CLASS—V12 Twin Turbo—Equipment Schedule 1
W.B. 124.6"; 5.5 Liter, 6.0 Liter.

Body	Type	VIN	List	Fair	Good	Pvt Good	Excellent
S600 Sedan 4D		NG76X	143675	61450	68000	70800	80000
S65 Sedan 4D		NG79X	184875	90550	100050	102800	114800
	designo Edition			900	900	1200	1200
	Panorama Roof			1000	1000	1335	1335

SL-CLASS—V8—Equipment Schedule 1
W.B. 100.8"; 5.5 Liter.

Body	Type	VIN	List	Fair	Good	Pvt Good	Excellent
SL550 Roadster 2D		SK71F	97275	40375	44775	47500	54700
	Sport Pkg			1900	1900	2535	2535
	designo Edition			900	900	1200	1200
	Panorama Roof			1000	1000	1335	1335

SL-CLASS—V8 Supercharged—Equipment Schedule 1
W.B. 100.8"; 5.5 Liter.

Body	Type	VIN	List	Fair	Good	Pvt Good	Excellent
SL55 Roadster 2D		SK72F	132175	51450	57025	59900	68200
	designo Edition			900	900	1200	1200
	Panorama Roof			1000	1000	1335	1335

SL-CLASS—V12 Twin Turbo—Equipment Schedule 1
W.B. 100.8"; 5.5 Liter, 6.0 Liter.

Body	Type	VIN	List	Fair	Good	Pvt Good	Excellent
SL600 Roadster 2D		SK77F	135375	55275	61150	63900	72600
SL65 Roadster 2D		SK79F	189375	80250	88700	91400	102400
	Sport Pkg (SL600)			1900	1900	2535	2535
	designo Edition			900	900	1200	1200
	Panorama Roof			1000	1000	1335	1335

2008 MERCEDES-BENZ — WDBorWDD(WK54F)-8

SLK-CLASS—V6—Equipment Schedule 1
W.B. 95.7"; 3.0 Liter, 3.5 Liter.

Body	Type	VIN	List	Fair	Good	Pvt Good	Excellent
SLK280 Roadster 2D		WK54F	46115	23325	26075	28500	33700
SLK280 Edition Rdstr		WK54F	51100				
SLK350 Roadster 2D		WK56F	49975	25675	28625	31000	36400
SLK350 Edition Rdstr		WK56F	56800				
	Sport Pkg			1050	1050	1400	1400
	designo Edition			900	900	1200	1200
	Manual Trans			(500)	(500)	(665)	(665)

SLK-CLASS—V8—Equipment Schedule 1
W.B. 95.7"; 5.5 Liter.

Body	Type	VIN	List	Fair	Good	Pvt Good	Excellent
SLK55 Roadster 2D		WK73F	65025	38025	42250	44500	51000
	designo Edition			900	900	1200	1200

C-CLASS—V6—Equipment Schedule 1
W.B. 108.7"; 3.0 Liter, 3.5 Liter.

Body	Type	VIN	List	Fair	Good	Pvt Good	Excellent
C300 Sport Sed 4D		GF54X	34915	22250	24800	27200	32300
C300 Sport 4Matic Sed 4D		GF81X	36715	22825	25475	27800	33000
C300 Luxury Sedan 4D		GF54X	35175	22050	24700	27000	32100
C300 Luxury 4Matic		GF81X	35925	22925	25575	27900	33100
C350 Sport Sedan 4D		GF56X	38775	23900	26650	29000	34300
	Panorama Roof			1025	1025	1365	1365
	Manual Trans			(500)	(500)	(665)	(665)

C-CLASS—V8—Equipment Schedule 1
W.B. 108.7"; 6.3 Liter.

Body	Type	VIN	List	Fair	Good	Pvt Good	Excellent
C63 AMG Sedan 4D		GF77X	54625	39000	43325	45600	52100
	Panorama Roof			1025	1025	1365	1365

CLK-CLASS—V6—Equipment Schedule 1
W.B. 106.9"; 3.5 Liter.

Body	Type	VIN	List	Fair	Good	Pvt Good	Excellent
CLK350 Coupe 2D		TJ56H	46975	20200	22550	25000	29900
CLK350 Cabriolet 2D		TK56F	54975	26275	29300	31800	37200
	designo Edition			900	900	1200	1200

CLK-CLASS—V8—Equipment Schedule 1
W.B. 106.9"; 6.3 Liter.

Body	Type	VIN	List	Fair	Good	Pvt Good	Excellent
CLK550 Coupe 2D		TJ72H	56675	28625	31850	34200	39900
CLK550 Cabriolet 2D		TK72F	64675	34700	38525	40900	47000
CLK63 Cabriolet 2D		TK77G	89975				

2008 MERCEDES-BENZ

Body	Type	VIN	List	Trade-In Fair	Trade-In Good	Pvt-Party Good	Retail Excellent
CLK63 Black Series		TJ77H	135775				
designo Edition				900	900	1200	1200

E-CLASS—V6 Turbo Diesel—Equipment Schedule 1
W.B. 112.4"; 3.0 Liter.

Body	Type	VIN	List	Fair	Good	Good	Excellent
E320 BLUETEC Sed		UF22X	52675	30275	33625	36000	41800
designo Edition				900	900	1200	1200
Panorama Roof				1025	1025	1365	1365

E-CLASS—V6—Equipment Schedule 1
W.B. 112.4"; 3.5 Liter.

Body	Type	VIN	List	Fair	Good	Good	Excellent
E350 Sedan 4D		UF56X	51675	24800	27625	30000	35300
E350 4Matic Sedan 4D		UF87X	53175	26275	29200	31600	37000
E350 4Matic Wagon		UH87X	56475	28425	31650	34000	39700
Sport Pkg (Sedan)				1050	1050	1400	1400
designo Edition				900	900	1200	1200
Panorama Roof				1025	1025	1365	1365

E-CLASS—V8—Equipment Schedule 1
W.B. 112.4"; 5.5 Liter, 6.3 Liter.

Body	Type	VIN	List	Fair	Good	Good	Excellent
E550 Sedan 4D		UF72X	61875	32725	36450	39100	45500
E550 4Matic Sedan 4D		UF90X	63375	33525	37250	39900	46400
E63 Sedan 4D		UF77X	85775	48225	53500	56100	63900
E63 Wagon 4D		UH77X	86575	49000	54400	56900	64900
AMG Sport Pkg				1050	1050	1400	1400
designo Edition				900	900	1200	1200
Panorama Roof				1025	1025	1365	1365

CL-CLASS—V8—Equipment Schedule 1
W.B. 116.3"; 5.5 Liter, 6.2 Liter.

Body	Type	VIN	List	Fair	Good	Good	Excellent
CL550 Coupe 2D		EJ71X	103875	62825	69475	71900	80900
CL63 Coupe 2D		EJ77X	137775	78200	86425	88700	98900
Sport Pkg				1050	1050	1400	1400
designo Edition				900	900	1200	1200

CL-CLASS—V12 Twin Turbo—Equipment Schedule 1
W.B. 116.3"; 5.5 Liter, 6.0 Liter.

Body	Type	VIN	List	Fair	Good	Good	Excellent
CL600 Coupe 2D		EJ76X	147675				
CL65 Coupe 2D		EJ79X	197775				
designo Edition							

CLS-CLASS—V8—Equipment Schedule 1
W.B. 112.4"; 5.5 Liter, 6.3 Liter.

Body	Type	VIN	List	Fair	Good	Good	Excellent
CLS550 Coupe 4D		DJ72X	69675	37425	41550	44200	51000
CLS63 Coupe 4D		DJ77X	96575	54200	59975	62500	70900
Sport Pkg (CLS550)				1950	1950	2600	2600
designo Edition				900	900	1200	1200

S-CLASS—V8—Equipment Schedule 1
W.B. 124.6"; 5.5 Liter, 6.3 Liter.

Body	Type	VIN	List	Fair	Good	Good	Excellent
S550 Sedan 4D		NG71X	88775	52625	58300	60900	69000
S550 4Matic Sedan 4D		NG86X	91775	54000	59775	62300	70700
S63 Sedan 4D		NG77X	127775	80650	89075	91300	101700
Sport Pkg				1050	1050	1400	1400
designo Edition				900	900	1200	1200
Panorama Roof				1025	1025	1365	1365

S-CLASS—V12 Twin Turbo—Equipment Schedule 1
W.B. 124.6"; 5.5 Liter, 6.0 Liter.

Body	Type	VIN	List	Fair	Good	Good	Excellent
S600 Sedan 4D		NG76X	147975				
S65 Sedan 4D		NG79X	186575				
designo Edition							

SL-CLASS—V8—Equipment Schedule 1
W.B. 100.8"; 5.5 Liter.

Body	Type	VIN	List	Fair	Good	Good	Excellent
SL550 Roadster 2D		SK71F	97375	48500	53800	56400	64200
Sport Pkg				1950	1950	2600	2600
designo Edition				900	900	1200	1200
Panorama Roof				1025	1025	1365	1365

SL-CLASS—V8 Supercharged—Equipment Schedule 1
W.B. 100.8"; 5.5 Liter.

Body	Type	VIN	List	Fair	Good	Good	Excellent
SL55 Roadster 2D		SK72F	132675				
designo Edition							
Panorama Roof							

SL-CLASS—V12 Twin Turbo—Equipment Schedule 1
W.B. 100.8"; 5.5 Liter, 6.0 Liter.

Body	Type	VIN	List	Fair	Good	Good	Excellent
SL600 Roadster 2D		SK77F	133975				
SL65 Roadster 2D		SK79F	187975				
Sport Pkg (SL600)							
designo Edition							
Panorama Roof							

Body	Type	VIN	List	Trade-In Fair	Trade-In Good	Pvt-Party Good	Retail Excellent

MERCURY

1994 MERCURY — (1,3or6)M(E,AorP)(PM10J)–R–#

TRACER—4-Cyl.—Equipment Schedule 6
W.B. 98.4"; 1.8 Liter, 1.9 Liter.

Sedan 4D		PM10J	11350	275	400	925	1800
Wagon 4D		PM15J	11620	350	475	1050	1950
LTS Notchback 4D		PM148	13660	375	525	1100	2050

CAPRI—4-Cyl.—Equipment Schedule 6
W.B. 94.7"; 1.6 Liter.

Convertible 2D		CT01Z	13565	700	975	1825	3150

CAPRI—4-Cyl. Turbo—Equipment Schedule 6
W.B. 94.7"; 1.6 Liter.

XR2 Convertible 2D		CT036	15275	825	1150	2075	3500

TOPAZ—4-Cyl.—Equipment Schedule 6
W.B. 99.9"; 2.3 Liter.

GS Sedan 2D		PM31X	12585	250	350	875	1725
GS Sedan 4D		PM36X	12625	250	350	875	1725
V6 3.0 Liter		U		100	100	135	135

SABLE—V6—Equipment Schedule 4
W.B. 106.0"; 3.0 Liter.

GS Sedan 4D		LM50U	19230	375	525	1125	2100
GS Wagon 4D		LM55U	20390	550	750	1500	2700
LS Sedan 4D		LM53U	21625	475	625	1300	2350
LS Wagon 4D		LM58U	22735	625	900	1700	3000
LTS Pkg				50	50	65	65
V6 3.8 Liter		4		100	100	135	135

COUGAR—V8—Equipment Schedule 5
W.B. 113.0"; 4.6 Liter.

XR-7 Coupe 2D		LM62W	18360	650	925	1725	3000
V6 3.8 Liter		4		(75)	(75)	(100)	(100)

GRAND MARQUIS—V8—Equipment Schedule 4
W.B. 114.4"; 4.6 Liter.

GS Sedan 4D		LM74W	21130	600	825	1625	2875
LS Sedan 4D		LM75W	23130	725	1025	1875	3250

1995 MERCURY — (1ME,2MEor3MA)(SM10J)–S–#

TRACER—4-Cyl.—Equipment Schedule 6
W.B. 98.4"; 1.8 Liter, 1.9 Liter.

Sedan 4D		SM10J	12040	325	450	1025	1950
Wagon 4D		SM15J	12310	400	550	1150	2125
LTS Notchback 4D		SM148	14445	450	600	1250	2275

MYSTIQUE—4-Cyl.—Equipment Schedule 5
W.B. 106.5"; 2.0 Liter.

GS Sedan 4D		LM653	16060	350	475	1075	2000
LS Sedan 4D		LM663	17920	450	600	1250	2275
Young America Edition				100	100	135	135
V6 2.5 Liter		L		100	100	135	135

SABLE—V6—Equipment Schedule 4
W.B. 106.0"; 3.0 Liter.

GS Sedan 4D		LM50U	19710	475	650	1325	2400
GS Wagon 4D		LM55U	20860	675	950	1775	3075
LS Sedan 4D		LM53U	21450	600	800	1575	2825
LS Wagon 4D		LM58U	22550	800	1125	2050	3475
LTS Pkg				50	50	65	65
V6 3.8 Liter		4		100	100	135	135

COUGAR—V8—Equipment Schedule 4
W.B. 113.0"; 4.6 Liter.

XR-7 Coupe 2D		LM62W	18960	750	1050	1900	3300
V6 3.8 Liter		4		(75)	(75)	(100)	(100)

GRAND MARQUIS—V8—Equipment Schedule 4
W.B. 114.4"; 4.6 Liter.

GS Sedan 4D		LM74W	22130	700	1000	1850	3200
LS Sedan 4D		LM75W	24335	875	1225	2175	3650

1996 MERCURY — (1,2or3)M(EorA)–(M10J)–T–#

TRACER—4-Cyl.—Equipment Schedule 6
W.B. 98.4"; 1.8 Liter, 1.9 Liter.

Sedan 4D		M10J	12540	375	525	1150	2125
Wagon 4D		M15J	12810	475	625	1300	2350

Body	Type	VIN	List	Trade-In Fair	Trade-In Good	Pvt-Party Good	Retail Excellent
LTS Notchback 4D		M148	14945	500	700	1375	2475

MYSTIQUE—4-Cyl.—Equipment Schedule 5
W.B. 106.5"; 2.0 Liter.

Body	Type	VIN	List	Fair	Good	Good	Excellent
GS Sedan 4D		M653	16570	400	550	1175	2175
LS Sedan 4D		M663	19280	500	675	1375	2475
V6 2.5 Liter		L		125	125	165	165

SABLE—V6—Equipment Schedule 4
W.B. 108.5"; 3.0 Liter.

Body	Type	VIN	List	Fair	Good	Good	Excellent
G Sedan 4D		M51U	18910	425	600	1250	2300
GS Sedan 4D		M50U	19755	500	650	1375	2475
GS Wagon 4D		M55U	20775	675	975	1850	3200
LS Sedan 4D		M53S	21995	625	825	1650	2975
LS Wagon 4D		M58S	23055	825	1175	2125	3600

COUGAR—V8—Equipment Schedule 4
W.B. 113.0"; 4.6 Liter.

Body	Type	VIN	List	Fair	Good	Good	Excellent
XR-7 Coupe 2D		M62W	18445	850	1200	2125	3600
V6 3.8 Liter		4		(100)	(100)	(135)	(135)

GRAND MARQUIS—V8—Equipment Schedule 4
W.B. 114.4"; 4.6 Liter.

Body	Type	VIN	List	Fair	Good	Good	Excellent
GS Sedan 4D		M74W	22595	850	1200	2150	3650
LS Sedan 4D		M75W	24785	1025	1450	2575	4250

1997 MERCURY — (1,2or3)ME-(M10P)-V-#

TRACER—4-Cyl.—Equipment Schedule 6
W.B. 98.4"; 2.0 Liter.

Body	Type	VIN	List	Fair	Good	Good	Excellent
GS Sedan 4D		M10P	12355	300	400	1000	1925
LS Sedan 4D		M13P	13200	400	575	1200	2225
LS Wagon 4D		M15P	13855	575	775	1575	2825

MYSTIQUE—4-Cyl.—Equipment Schedule 5
W.B. 106.5"; 2.0 Liter.

Body	Type	VIN	List	Fair	Good	Good	Excellent
Sedan 4D		M653	16105	400	575	1225	2275
GS Sedan 4D		M653	17605	475	650	1350	2475
LS Sedan 4D		M663	19920	600	825	1650	2975
V6 2.5 Liter		L		150	150	200	200

SABLE—V6—Equipment Schedule 4
W.B. 108.5"; 3.0 Liter.

Body	Type	VIN	List	Fair	Good	Good	Excellent
GS Sedan 4D		M50U	20295	575	775	1600	2875
GS Wagon 4D		M55U	20295	800	1125	2050	3500
LS Sedan 4D		M53S	23350	700	975	1850	3250
LS Wagon 4D		M58S	23350	975	1375	2500	4150

COUGAR—V8—Equipment Schedule 4
W.B. 113.0"; 4.6 Liter.

Body	Type	VIN	List	Fair	Good	Good	Excellent
XR-7 Sedan 2D		M62W	19685	950	1350	2425	4075
V6 3.8 Liter		4		(125)	(125)	(165)	(165)

GRAND MARQUIS—V8—Equipment Schedule 4
W.B. 114.4"; 4.6 Liter.

Body	Type	VIN	List	Fair	Good	Good	Excellent
GS Sedan 4D		M74W	23140	975	1375	2475	4150
LS Sedan 4D		M75W	25330	1175	1675	2850	4550

1998 MERCURY — (1,2or3)ME-(M10P)-W-#

TRACER—4-Cyl.—Equipment Schedule 6
W.B. 98.4"; 2.0 Liter.

Body	Type	VIN	List	Fair	Good	Good	Excellent
GS Sedan 4D		M10P	12565	350	500	1125	2125
LS Sedan 4D		M13P	13125	475	650	1350	2475
LS Wagon 4D		M15P	14620	650	900	1775	3125

MYSTIQUE—4-Cyl.—Equipment Schedule 5
W.B. 106.5"; 2.0 Liter.

Body	Type	VIN	List	Fair	Good	Good	Excellent
Sedan 4D		M653	16105	500	675	1425	2575
GS Sedan 4D		M653	18230	600	825	1575	2825

MYSTIQUE—V6—Equipment Schedule 5
W.B. 106.5"; 2.5 Liter.

Body	Type	VIN	List	Fair	Good	Good	Excellent
LS Sedan 4D		M66L	19295	800	1125	2075	3550

SABLE—V6—Equipment Schedule 4
W.B. 108.5"; 3.0 Liter.

Body	Type	VIN	List	Fair	Good	Good	Excellent
GS Sedan 4D		M50U	19995	675	975	1875	3300
LS Sedan 4D		M53U	20995	850	1175	2175	3725
LS Wagon 4D		M58U	22835	1150	1625	2825	4550
V6 3.0 Liter 24V		S		175	175	235	235

GRAND MARQUIS—V8—Equipment Schedule 4
W.B. 114.7"; 4.6 Liter.

Body	Type	VIN	List	Fair	Good	Good	Excellent
GS Sedan 4D		M74W	22495	1125	1575	2750	4450
LS Sedan 4D		M75W	24395	1450	1925	3150	4950

1999 MERCURY

Body	Type	VIN	List	Trade-In Fair	Trade-In Good	Pvt-Party Good	Retail Excellent

1999 MERCURY — (1,2or3)(MEorZW)-(M10P)-X-#

TRACER—4-Cyl.—Equipment Schedule 6
W.B. 98.4"; 2.0 Liter.

GS Sedan 4D		M10P	12740	450	625	1325	2450
LS Sedan 4D		M13P	13485	575	775	1625	2975
LS Wagon 4D		M15P	14690	750	1075	2025	3500

MYSTIQUE—4-Cyl.—Equipment Schedule 5
W.B. 106.5"; 2.0 Liter.

GS Sedan 4D		M653	17740	700	1000	1925	3375

MYSTIQUE—V6—Equipment Schedule 5
W.B. 106.5"; 2.5 Liter.

LS Sedan 4D		M66L	19095	950	1325	2450	4150

SABLE—V6—Equipment Schedule 4
W.B. 108.5"; 3.0 Liter.

GS Sedan 4D		M50U	18995	850	1200	2300	3950
LS Sedan 4D		M53U	20095	1025	1425	2600	4300
LS Wagon 4D		M58U	21195	1475	1950	3175	5000
V6 3.0 Liter 24V		S		200	200	265	265

COUGAR—V6—Equipment Schedule 4
W.B. 106.4"; 2.5 Liter.

Coupe 2D		T61L	18630	1625	2125	3350	5175
Manual Trans				(200)	(200)	(265)	(265)
4-Cyl. 2.0 Liter		3		(325)	(325)	(435)	(435)

GRAND MARQUIS—V8—Equipment Schedule 4
W.B. 114.7"; 4.6 Liter.

GS Sedan 4D		M74W	22825	1350	1850	3075	4875
LS Sedan 4D		M75W	24725	1725	2300	3525	5400

2000 MERCURY — (1,2or3)(MEorZW)-(M653)-Y-#

MYSTIQUE—4-Cyl.—Equipment Schedule 5
W.B. 106.5"; 2.0 Liter.

GS Sedan 4D		M653	17495	875	1225	2350	4025

MYSTIQUE—V6—Equipment Schedule 5
W.B. 106.5"; 2.5 Liter.

LS Sedan 4D		M66L	18795	1125	1575	2750	4475

SABLE—V6—Equipment Schedule 4
W.B. 108.5"; 3.0 Liter.

GS Sedan 4D		M50U	19395	875	1250	2375	4075
GS Wagon 4D		M58U	21195	1150	1625	2825	4575
LS Sedan 4D		M53U	20495	1075	1500	2700	4400
V6 3.0 Liter 24V		S		200	200	265	265

SABLE—V6 24V—Equipment Schedule 4
W.B. 108.5"; 3.0 Liter.

LS Premium Sedan 4D		M55S	21795	1350	1850	3075	4875
LS Premium Wagon 4D		M59S	22895	1750	2275	3550	5425

COUGAR—V6—Equipment Schedule 4
W.B. 106.4"; 2.5 Liter.

Coupe 2D		T61L	18880	1975	2525	3800	5675
Manual Trans				(225)	(225)	(300)	(300)
4-Cyl. 2.0 Liter		3		(350)	(350)	(465)	(465)

GRAND MARQUIS—V8—Equipment Schedule 4
W.B. 114.7"; 4.6 Liter.

GS Sedan 4D		M74W	23020	1675	2175	3450	5325
LS Sedan 4D		M75W	24920	2050	2625	3925	5850

2001 MERCURY — (1or2)(MEorZW)-(M50U)-1-#

SABLE—V6—Equipment Schedule 4
W.B. 108.5"; 3.0 Liter.

GS Sedan 4D		M50U	19785	1050	1475	2675	4400
GS Wagon 4D		M58U	21585	1425	1900	3150	5000
LS Sedan 4D		M53U	20885	1250	1750	3000	4775
V6 3.0 Liter 24V		S		200	200	265	265

SABLE—V6 24V—Equipment Schedule 4
W.B. 108.5"; 3.0 Liter.

LS Premium Sedan 4D		M55S	22185	1650	2150	3425	5300
LS Premium Wagon 4D		M59S	23285	2050	2625	3925	5850

COUGAR—V6—Equipment Schedule 4
W.B. 106.4"; 2.5 Liter.

Coupe 2D		T61L	18545	2400	3000	4300	6250
C2 Coupe 2D		T61L	20660	2800	3425	4775	6800
Zn Coupe 2D		T61L	21645	2975	3600	4950	7000

Body	Type	VIN	List	Trade-In Fair	Trade-In Good	Pvt-Party Good	Retail Excellent
Manual Trans							
4-Cyl. 2.0 Liter		3	......	(250)	(250)	(335)	(335)
GRAND MARQUIS—V8—Equipment Schedule 4				(375)	(375)	(500)	(500)
W.B. 114.7"; 4.6 Liter.							
GS Sedan 4D		M74W	23460	2025	2600	3925	5850
LS Sedan 4D		M75W	25360	2450	3050	4375	6400

2002 MERCURY — (1or2)(MEorZW)-(M50U)-2-#

SABLE—V6—Equipment Schedule 4							
W.B. 108.5"; 3.0 Liter.							
GS Sedan 4D		M50U	20255	1150	1600	3025	5000
GS Wagon 4D		M58U	21665	1625	2100	3550	5600
SABLE—V6 24V—Equipment Schedule 4							
W.B. 108.5"; 3.0 Liter.							
LS Premium Sedan 4D		M55S	22680	1850	2400	3850	5950
LS Premium Wagon 4D		M59S	23845	2300	2900	4350	6525
COUGAR—V6—Equipment Schedule 4							
W.B. 106.4"; 2.5 Liter.							
Coupe 2D		M61L	18490	2750	3350	4850	7050
Sport Coupe 2D		M62L	18990	3075	3750	5250	7525
C2 Coupe 2D		M62L	19505	3175	3850	5375	7650
Xr Coupe 2D		M62L	19940	3350	4050	5550	7875
Manual Trans							
4-Cyl. 2.0 Liter		3	......	(250)	(250)	(335)	(335)
				(400)	(400)	(535)	(535)
35th Anniversary Ed				150	150	200	200
GRAND MARQUIS—V8—Equipment Schedule 4							
W.B. 114.7"; 4.6 Liter.							
GS Sedan 4D		M74W	24325	2375	2975	4450	6675
LS Sedan 4D		M75W	27800	2800	3425	4950	7225
LSE Sedan 4D		M75W	29305	3225	3925	5475	7800

2003 MERCURY — (1or2)ME-(M50U)-3-#

SABLE—V6—Equipment Schedule 4							
W.B. 108.5"; 3.0 Liter.							
GS Sedan 4D		M50U	20770	1700	2200	3675	5775
GS Wagon 4D		M58U	22180	2250	2850	4325	6525
SABLE—V6 24V—Equipment Schedule 4							
W.B. 108.5"; 3.0 Liter.							
LS Premium Sedan 4D		M55S	23145	2475	3075	4575	6775
LS Premium Wagon 4D		M59S	24310	3050	3675	5225	7525
GRAND MARQUIS—V8—Equipment Schedule 4							
W.B. 114.7"; 4.6 Liter.							
GS Sedan 4D		M74W	24875	3000	3625	5200	7500
LS Sedan 4D		M75W	28605	3550	4275	5825	8200
LSE Sedan 4D		M75W	30110	4000	4725	6325	8775
Limited Edition				500	500	665	665
MARAUDER—V8—Equipment Schedule 2							
W.B. 114.7"; 4.6 Liter.							
Sedan 4D		M75V	34495	7325	8400	10150	13150

2004 MERCURY — (1or2)ME-(M50U)-4-#

SABLE—V6—Equipment Schedule 4							
W.B. 108.5"; 3.0 Liter.							
GS Sedan 4D		M50U	21595	2350	2925	4425	6650
GS Wagon 4D		M58U	22595	3000	3625	5175	7450
SABLE—V6 24V—Equipment Schedule 4							
W.B. 108.5"; 3.0 Liter.							
LS Premium Sedan 4D		M55S	23895	3150	3825	5375	7675
LS Premium Wagon 4D		M59S	24795	3850	4575	6150	8550
GRAND MARQUIS—V8—Equipment Schedule 4							
W.B. 114.7"; 4.6 Liter.							
GS Sedan 4D		M74W	24695	3725	4425	6000	8400
LS Sedan 4D		M75W	29595	4375	5175	6800	9325
Limited Edition				500	500	665	665
MARAUDER—V8—Equipment Schedule 2							
W.B. 114.7"; 4.6 Liter.							
Sedan 4D		M79V	34495	8250	9425	11200	14350

2005 MERCURY — (1or2)ME-(M50U)-5-#

SABLE—V6—Equipment Schedule 4							
W.B. 108.5"; 3.0 Liter.							
GS Sedan 4D		M50U	21525	3075	3700	5275	7575

2005 MERCURY

Body	Type	VIN	List	Trade-In Fair	Trade-In Good	Pvt-Party Good	Retail Excellent
SABLE—V6 24V—Equipment Schedule 4							
W.B. 108.5"; 3.0 Liter.							
LS Sedan 4D	M55S	24490	3925	4650	6225	8650
LS Wagon 4D	M59S	25800	4725	5550	7175	9750
MONTEGO—V6—Equipment Schedule 4							
W.B. 112.9"; 3.0 Liter.							
Luxury Sedan 4D	M401	24995	4700	5525	7125	9700
Luxury AWD Sedan 4D	M411	26695	5450	6325	7975	10650
Premier Sedan 4D	M421	27195	5525	6425	8050	10750
Premier AWD Sedan 4D	M431	28895	6225	7200	8875	11600
GRAND MARQUIS—V8—Equipment Schedule 4							
W.B. 114.7"; 4.6 Liter.							
GS Sedan 4D	M74W	25095	4575	5375	7025	9600
LS Sedan 4D	M75W	30150	5375	6250	7925	10600
LSE Sedan 4D	M75W	30620	5375	6250	7925	10600

2006 MERCURY — (1,2or3)ME—(M07Z)–6–#

Body	Type	VIN	List	Trade-In Fair	Trade-In Good	Pvt-Party Good	Retail Excellent
MILAN—4-Cyl.—Equipment Schedule 4							
W.B. 107.4"; 2.3 Liter.							
Sedan 4D	M07Z	19820	5575	6500	8125	10800
Premier Sedan 4D	M08Z	21715	6300	7275	8925	11650
Manual Trans			(575)	(575)	(765)	(765)
V6 3.0 Liter	1		750	750	1000	1000
MONTEGO—V6—Equipment Schedule 4							
W.B. 112.9"; 3.0 Liter.							
Luxury Sedan 4D	M401	25130	5450	6350	7975	10600
Luxury AWD Sedan 4D	M411	26980	6225	7200	8850	11550
Premier Sedan 4D	M421	27500	6325	7300	8975	11700
Premier AWD Sedan 4D	M431	29430	7125	8175	9850	12650
GRAND MARQUIS—V8—Equipment Schedule 4							
W.B. 114.7"; 4.6 Liter.							
GS Sedan 4D	M74W	25555	5600	6525	8150	10850
LS Sedan 4D	M75V	30840	6475	7475	9150	11900
Limited Edition			500	500	665	665

2007 MERCURY—(1,2or3)ME–(M07Z)–7–#

Body	Type	VIN	List	Trade-In Fair	Trade-In Good	Pvt-Party Good	Retail Excellent
MILAN—4-Cyl.—Equipment Schedule 4							
W.B. 107.4"; 2.3 Liter.							
Sedan 4D	M07Z	22465	6425	7400	8950	11550
Premier Sedan 4D	M08Z	23995	7200	8275	9850	12600
Manual Trans			(600)	(600)	(800)	(800)
V6 3.0 Liter	1		750	750	1000	1000
MILAN—V6—Equipment Schedule 4							
W.B. 107.4"; 3.0 Liter.							
AWD Sedan 4D	M011	24315	7650	8775	10350	13150
Premier AWD Sedan 4D	M021	25845	8025	9200	10850	13650
MONTEGO—V6—Equipment Schedule 4							
W.B. 112.9"; 3.0 Liter.							
Luxury Sedan 4D	M401	24220	6275	7250	8800	11400
Premier Sedan 4D	M421	27995	7225	8300	9850	12600
Premier AWD Sedan 4D	M431	29845	8100	9275	10950	13800
GRAND MARQUIS—V8—Equipment Schedule 4							
W.B. 114.6"; 4.6 Liter.							
GS Sedan 4D	M74V	25660	7150	8200	9800	12550
LS Sedan 4D	M75V	30320	8100	9275	10950	13850
Palm Beach Edition			500	500	665	665

2008 MERCURY — (1,2or3)ME–(M07Z)–8–#

Body	Type	VIN	List	Trade-In Fair	Trade-In Good	Pvt-Party Good	Retail Excellent
MILAN—4-Cyl.—Equipment Schedule 4							
W.B. 107.4"; 2.3 Liter.							
Sedan 4D	M07Z	20325	8275	9475	11000	13750
Premier Sedan 4D	M08Z	22020	9175	10425	11950	14850
Manual Trans			(625)	(625)	(835)	(835)
V6 3.0 Liter	1		750	750	1000	1000
MILAN—V6—Equipment Schedule 4							
W.B. 107.4"; 3.0 Liter.							
AWD Sedan 4D	M011	24550	9625	10925	12550	15500
Premier AWD Sed 4D	M021	25870	10000	11375	13000	15950
SABLE—V6—Equipment Schedule 4							
W.B. 112.9"; 3.5 Liter.							
Sedan 4D	M40W	24290	9550	10875	12400	15350
AWD Sedan 4D	M41W	26140	11025	12500	14050	17200

Body	Type	VIN	List	Trade-In Fair	Good	Pvt-Party Good	Retail Excellent
Premier Sedan 4D		M42W	28080	**10675**	**12100**	**13650**	**16750**
Premier AWD Sed 4D		M43W	29930	**12450**	**14075**	**15700**	**18950**
GRAND MARQUIS—V8—Equipment Schedule 4							
W.B. 114.6"; 4.6 Liter.							
GS Sedan 4D		M74V	25830	**8600**	**9800**	**11350**	**14250**
LS Sedan 4D		M75V	28720	**9725**	**11025**	**12650**	**15700**
Palm Beach Edition				**500**	**500**	**665**	**665**

MINI

2003 MINI — WMW(RC334)-3-#

COOPER—4-Cyl.—Equipment Schedule 3
W.B. 97.1"; 1.6 Liter.

Body	Type	VIN	List	Trade-In Fair	Good	Pvt-Party Good	Retail Excellent
Hatchback 2D		RC334	18575	**7350**	**8425**	**10250**	**13300**
Sport Pkg				**400**	**400**	**535**	**535**
COOPER S—4-Cyl. Supercharged—Equipment Schedule 3							
W.B. 97.1"; 1.6 Liter.							
Hatchback 2D		RE334	20325	**8825**	**10050**	**12000**	**15300**
Sport Pkg				**400**	**400**	**535**	**535**
John Cooper Works Kit				**2000**	**2000**	**2665**	**2665**

2004 MINI — WMW(RC334)-4-#

COOPER—4-Cyl.—Equipment Schedule 3
W.B. 97.1"; 1.6 Liter.

Body	Type	VIN	List	Trade-In Fair	Good	Pvt-Party Good	Retail Excellent
Hatchback 2D		RC334	18299	**8325**	**9525**	**11400**	**14600**
Sport Pkg				**450**	**450**	**600**	**600**
COOPER S—4-Cyl. Supercharged—Equipment Schedule 3							
W.B. 97.1"; 1.6 Liter.							
Hatchback 2D		RE334	19999	**10000**	**11375**	**13350**	**16700**
Sport Pkg				**450**	**450**	**600**	**600**
MC40 Pkg				**2500**	**2500**	**3335**	**3335**
John Cooper Works Kit				**2000**	**2000**	**2665**	**2665**

2005 MINI — WMW(RC334)-5-#

COOPER—4-Cyl.—Equipment Schedule 3
W.B. 97.1"; 1.6 Liter.

Body	Type	VIN	List	Trade-In Fair	Good	Pvt-Party Good	Retail Excellent
Hatchback 2D		RC334	18299	**9375**	**10675**	**12550**	**15850**
Convertible 2D		RF334	22800	**10925**	**12400**	**14250**	**17750**
Sport Pkg				**500**	**500**	**665**	**665**
COOPER S—4-Cyl. Supercharged—Equipment Schedule 3							
W.B. 97.1"; 1.6 Liter.							
Hatchback 2D		RE334	20449	**11275**	**12800**	**14700**	**18200**
Convertible 2D		RH334	24950	**12750**	**14400**	**16300**	**20000**
Sport Pkg				**500**	**500**	**665**	**665**
John Cooper Works Kit				**2000**	**2000**	**2665**	**2665**

2006 MINI — WMW(RC335)-6-#

COOPER—4-Cyl.—Equipment Schedule 3
W.B. 97.1"; 1.6 Liter.

Body	Type	VIN	List	Trade-In Fair	Good	Pvt-Party Good	Retail Excellent
Hatchback 2D		RC335	18800	**10425**	**11850**	**13700**	**17100**
Convertible 2D		RF335	23300	**12200**	**13775**	**15650**	**19200**
Sport Pkg				**550**	**550**	**735**	**735**
Checkmate Pkg				**650**	**650**	**865**	**865**
COOPER S—4-Cyl. Supercharged—Equipment Schedule 3							
W.B. 97.1"; 1.6 Liter.							
Hatchback 2D		RE335	22500	**12550**	**14150**	**16000**	**19600**
Convertible 2D		RH335	26800	**14150**	**15925**	**17900**	**21700**
Sport Pkg				**550**	**550**	**735**	**735**
Checkmate Pkg				**650**	**650**	**865**	**865**
John Cooper Works (ex GP)				**4000**	**4000**	**5330**	**5330**

2007 MINI — WMW(MF335)-7-#

COOPER—4-Cyl.—Equipment Schedule 3
W.B. 97.1"; 1.6 Liter.

Body	Type	VIN	List	Trade-In Fair	Good	Pvt-Party Good	Retail Excellent
Hatchback 2D		MF335	20050	**12350**	**13975**	**15750**	**19150**
Convertible 2D		RF335	23900	**14200**	**15975**	**17750**	**21400**
Sport Pkg				**600**	**600**	**800**	**800**
COOPER S—4-Cyl. Turbocharged—Equipment Schedule 3							
W.B. 97.1"; 1.6 Liter.							
Hatchback 2D		MF735	23200	**14600**	**16425**	**18200**	**21900**

Body	Type	VIN	List	Trade-In Fair	Trade-In Good	Pvt-Party Good	Retail Excellent
Convertible 2D		RH335	27400	16375	18375	20200	24100
Sport Pkg				600	600	800	800
John Cooper Works Kit				4000	4000	5330	5330

2008 MINI — WMW(MF335)-8-#

COOPER—4-Cyl.—Equipment Schedule 3
W.B. 97.1", 100.4" (Clubman); 1.6 Liter.

Body	Type	VIN	List	Trade-In Fair	Trade-In Good	Pvt-Party Good	Retail Excellent
Hatchback 2D		MF335	19950	13675	15425	17150	20700
Convertible 2D		RF335	23850	15725	17650	19400	23100
Clubman H'Back 2D		ML335	21850	14500	16325	18100	21700
Sport Pkg				650	650	865	865

COOPER S—4-Cyl. Turbocharged—Equipment Schedule 3
W.B. 97.1", 100.4" (Clubman); 1.6 Liter.

Body	Type	VIN	List	Trade-In Fair	Trade-In Good	Pvt-Party Good	Retail Excellent
Hatchback 2D		MF735	23100	16125	18075	19800	23600
Convertible 2D		RH335	25920	18075	20200	22100	26100
S Clubman H'Back 2D		MM335	25350	17450	19550	21400	25300
Sport Pkg				650	650	865	865
John Cooper Works Kit				4000	4000	5330	5330

MITSUBISHI

1994 MITSUBISHI — (JA3,4A3orKPH)(VD12J)-R-#

PRECIS—4-Cyl.—Equipment Schedule 6
W.B. 93.8"; 1.5 Liter.

Body	Type	VIN	List	Trade-In Fair	Trade-In Good	Pvt-Party Good	Retail Excellent
Hatchback 2D		VD12J		175	250	750	1550

MIRAGE—4-Cyl.—Equipment Schedule 6
W.B. 96.1", 98.4" (Sed); 1.5 Liter, 1.8 Liter.

Body	Type	VIN	List	Trade-In Fair	Trade-In Good	Pvt-Party Good	Retail Excellent
S Sedan 4D		EA26A	12928	500	650	1325	2400
S Coupe 2D		EA11A	10548	375	525	1125	2100
ES Sedan 4D		EA36C	13488	400	575	1175	2175
ES Coupe 2D		EA21A	11918	400	575	1175	2175
LS Sedan 4D		EA46C	15754	400	575	1175	2175
LS Coupe 2D		EA31C	13104	400	575	1175	2175

EXPO—4-Cyl.—Equipment Schedule 6
W.B. 99.2" (LRV), 107.1"; 1.8 Liter, 2.4 Liter.

Body	Type	VIN	List	Trade-In Fair	Trade-In Good	Pvt-Party Good	Retail Excellent
LRV Wagon 3D		EB30C	14627	1025	1425	2525	4150
LRV Sport Wagon 3D		EB40G	17244	1075	1525	2625	4275
Wagon 4D		ED59G	17429	1200	1675	2850	4525
AWD Wagon 4D		EE59G	18869	1550	2050	3250	5025

ECLIPSE—4-Cyl.—Equipment Schedule 4
W.B. 97.2"; 1.8 Liter, 2.0 Liter.

Body	Type	VIN	List	Trade-In Fair	Trade-In Good	Pvt-Party Good	Retail Excellent
Coupe 2D		CF34B	13686	575	775	1550	2800
GS Coupe 2D		CF44B	16037	625	875	1675	2975
GS 16V DOHC Cpe 2D		CF44E	16711	700	975	1825	3150
Auto Trans				125	125	165	165

ECLIPSE—4-Cyl. Turbo—Equipment Schedule 4
W.B. 97.2"; 2.0 Liter.

Body	Type	VIN	List	Trade-In Fair	Trade-In Good	Pvt-Party Good	Retail Excellent
GS DOHC Coupe 2D		CF54F	18949	825	1150	2075	3500
GSX AWD Coupe 2D		CG64F	21689	1125	1575	2700	4350
Auto Trans				125	125	165	165

GALANT—4-Cyl.—Equipment Schedule 4
W.B. 103.7"; 2.4 Liter.

Body	Type	VIN	List	Trade-In Fair	Trade-In Good	Pvt-Party Good	Retail Excellent
S Sedan 4D		AJ46G	16204	500	675	1425	2575
ES Sedan 4D		AJ56G	17165	625	850	1650	2925
LS Sport Sedan 4D		AJ56G	18635	750	1075	1925	3325
GS DOHC Sedan 4D		AJ56L	21697	775	1100	1975	3375
Manual Trans				(200)	(200)	(265)	(265)

3000GT—V6—Equipment Schedule 4
W.B. 97.2"; 3.0 Liter.

Body	Type	VIN	List	Trade-In Fair	Trade-In Good	Pvt-Party Good	Retail Excellent
Coupe 2D		AM54J	27645	2500	3075	4400	6425
SL Coupe 2D		AM64J	32120	2925	3550	4925	7000
Auto Trans				125	125	165	165

3000GT—V6 Turbo—Equipment Schedule 2
W.B. 97.2"; 3.0 Liter.

Body	Type	VIN	List	Trade-In Fair	Trade-In Good	Pvt-Party Good	Retail Excellent
VR-4 Coupe 2D		BN74K	41370	4825	5650	7275	9850

DIAMANTE—V6—Equipment Schedule 4
W.B. 107.1", 107.2" (Wag); 3.0 Liter.

Body	Type	VIN	List	Trade-In Fair	Trade-In Good	Pvt-Party Good	Retail Excellent
ES Luxury Sedan 4D		AP47H	25995	925	1325	2350	3950
LS Luxury Sedan 4D		AP57J	32970	1200	1700	2850	4525
Wagon 4D		AC49S	26320	850	1175	2075	3500
Traction Control				100	100	135	135

1995 MITSUBISHI

Body	Type	VIN	List	Trade-In Fair	Good	Pvt-Party Good	Retail Excellent

1995 MITSUBISHI — (J,4or6)(A3orMM)A(A26A)-S-

MIRAGE—4-Cyl.—Equipment Schedule 6
W.B. 96.1", 98.4" (Sed); 1.5 Liter, 1.8 Liter.

Body	Type	VIN	List	Fair	Good	Good	Excellent
S Sedan 4D		A26A	13707	625	850	1650	2925
S Coupe 2D		A11A	11563	500	700	1375	2475
ES Sedan 4D		A36C	14627	550	725	1500	2700
ES Coupe 2D		A21A	13367	550	725	1500	2700
LS Coupe 2D		A31C	14696	550	725	1500	2700

EXPO—4-Cyl.—Equipment Schedule 6
W.B. 107.1"; 2.4 Liter.

Wagon 4D		D59G	17894	1425	1900	3100	4875
AWD Wagon 4D		E59G	19364	1850	2350	3600	5475

ECLIPSE—4-Cyl.—Equipment Schedule 4
W.B. 98.8"; 2.0 Liter.

RS Coupe 2D		K34Y	15891	700	975	1850	3200
GS Coupe 2D		K44Y	18544	850	1200	2150	3650
Auto Trans				125	125	165	165

ECLIPSE—4-Cyl. Turbo—Equipment Schedule 4
W.B. 98.8"; 2.0 Liter.

GS-T Coupe 2D		K54F	20419	975	1375	2475	4125
GSX Coupe 2D		L54F	23349	1375	1850	3050	4800
Auto Trans				125	125	165	165

GALANT—4-Cyl.—Equipment Schedule 4
W.B. 103.7"; 2.4 Liter.

S Sedan 4D		J46G	17017	575	775	1550	2800
ES Sedan 4D		J56G	19089	675	950	1800	3125
LS Sedan 4D		J56G	20689	825	1150	2075	3500

3000GT—V6—Equipment Schedule 4
W.B. 97.2"; 3.0 Liter.

Coupe 2D		M84J	28920	2850	3475	4850	6950
SL Coupe 2D		M54J	34220	3275	3950	5400	7625
SL Spyder Conv 2D		V65J	57969	6425	7400	9250	12250
Auto Trans				125	125	165	165

3000GT—V6 Turbo—Equipment Schedule 2
W.B. 97.2"; 3.0 Liter.

VR-4 Coupe 2D		N74K	43520	5325	6200	7950	10700
VR-4 Spyder Conv 2D		W75K	64919	8175	9350	11400	14850

DIAMANTE—V6—Equipment Schedule 4
W.B. 107.1", 107.2" (Wag); 3.0 Liter.

ES Luxury Sedan 4D		P47H	28370	1050	1500	2600	4250
LS Luxury Sedan 4D		P57J	35720	1425	1900	3100	4875
Wagon 4D		P49H	28720	950	1325	2400	4025
Traction Control				100	100	135	135

1996 MITSUBISHI — (Jor4)A3A(A26A)-T-#

MIRAGE—4-Cyl.—Equipment Schedule 6
W.B. 96.1", 98.4" (Sed); 1.5 Liter, 1.8 Liter.

S Sedan 4D		A26A	14834	650	925	1775	3075
S Coupe 2D		A11A	12422	550	725	1500	2700
LS Coupe 2D		A31C	14924	625	850	1650	2925

ECLIPSE—4-Cyl.—Equipment Schedule 4
W.B. 98.8"; 2.0 Liter, 2.4 Liter.

Coupe 2D		K34Y	15135	625	875	1725	3050
RS Coupe 2D		K34Y	16281	800	1150	2075	3550
GS Coupe 2D		K44Y	19310	1025	1450	2575	4250
GS Spyder Conv 2+2		X35G	21227	1525	2000	3250	5050
Auto Trans				125	125	165	165

ECLIPSE—4-Cyl. Turbo—Equipment Schedule 4
W.B. 98.8"; 2.0 Liter.

GS-T Coupe 2D		K54F	21360	1150	1625	2800	4500
GS-T Spyder Conv 2+2		X55F	25410	2025	2600	3875	5775
GSX Coupe 2D		L54F	24330	1650	2150	3400	5225
Auto Trans				125	125	165	165

GALANT—4-Cyl.—Equipment Schedule 4
W.B. 103.7"; 2.4 Liter.

S Sedan 4D		J46G	18535	675	975	1850	3200
ES Sedan 4D		J56G	20210	800	1150	2075	3550
LS Sedan 4D		J56G	23280	950	1350	2425	4075
Manual Trans				(200)	(200)	(265)	(265)

3000GT—V6—Equipment Schedule 4
W.B. 97.2"; 3.0 Liter.

1996 MITSUBISHI

Body	Type	VIN	List	Trade-In Fair	Good	Pvt-Party Good	Retail Excellent
Coupe 2D		M84J	31110	3350	4050	5500	7725
SL Coupe 2D		M54J	36250	3925	4675	6200	8550
SL Spyder Conv 2D		V65J	58600	7500	8600	10550	13750
Auto Trans				125	125	165	165

3000GT—V6 Turbo—Equipment Schedule 2
W.B. 97.2"; 3.0 Liter.

Body	Type	VIN	List	Trade-In Fair	Good	Pvt-Party Good	Retail Excellent
VR-4 Coupe 2D		N74K	46878	6225	7200	9025	11950
VR-4 Spyder Conv 2D		W75K	65740	9500	10825	13100	16850

DIAMANTE—V6—Equipment Schedule 4
W.B. 107.1"; 3.0 Liter.

Body	Type	VIN	List	Trade-In Fair	Good	Pvt-Party Good	Retail Excellent
ES Luxury Sedan 4D		P47H	27540	1250	1725	2900	4600

1997 MITSUBISHI—(J,4or6)(A3orMM)A(Y26A)–V–#

MIRAGE—4-Cyl.—Equipment Schedule 6
W.B. 95.1", 98.4" (Sed); 1.5 Liter, 1.8 Liter.

Body	Type	VIN	List	Trade-In Fair	Good	Pvt-Party Good	Retail Excellent
DE Sedan 4D		Y26A	13390	625	900	1750	3075
DE Coupe 2D		Y11A	11962	500	650	1350	2475
LS Sedan 4D		Y36C	14907	625	850	1675	3000
LS Coupe 2D		Y31C	14547	625	825	1650	2975

ECLIPSE—4-Cyl.—Equipment Schedule 4
W.B. 98.8"; 2.0 Liter, 2.4 Liter.

Body	Type	VIN	List	Trade-In Fair	Good	Pvt-Party Good	Retail Excellent
Coupe 2D		K24Y	15821	750	1050	1975	3425
RS Coupe 2D		K34Y	18219	950	1325	2450	4125
GS Coupe 2D		K44Y	20623	1225	1725	2925	4650
GS Spyder Conv 2D		X35G	22411	1850	2375	3650	5525
Auto Trans				150	150	200	200

ECLIPSE—4-Cyl. Turbo—Equipment Schedule 4
W.B. 98.8"; 2.0 Liter.

Body	Type	VIN	List	Trade-In Fair	Good	Pvt-Party Good	Retail Excellent
GS-T Coupe 2D		K54F	22440	1425	1900	3125	4925
GS-T Spyder Conv 2D		X55F	26800	2425	3025	4350	6350
GSX Coupe 2D		L54F	24490	1975	2525	3800	5700
Auto Trans				150	150	200	200

GALANT—4-Cyl.—Equipment Schedule 4
W.B. 103.7"; 2.4 Liter.

Body	Type	VIN	List	Trade-In Fair	Good	Pvt-Party Good	Retail Excellent
DE Sedan 4D		J46G	17964	775	1100	2025	3475
ES Sedan 4D		J56G	18535	900	1275	2350	4000
LS Sedan 4D		J56G	24400	1075	1500	2650	4300
Manual Trans				(250)	(250)	(335)	(335)

3000GT—V6—Equipment Schedule 4
W.B. 97.2"; 3.0 Liter.

Body	Type	VIN	List	Trade-In Fair	Good	Pvt-Party Good	Retail Excellent
Coupe 2D		M44H	28400	3925	4675	6175	8500
SL Coupe 2D		M84J	34460	4575	5400	6950	9400
Auto Trans				150	150	200	200

3000GT—V6 Turbo—Equipment Schedule 2
W.B. 97.2"; 3.0 Liter.

Body	Type	VIN	List	Trade-In Fair	Good	Pvt-Party Good	Retail Excellent
VR-4 Coupe 2D		N74K	45060	7150	8200	10100	13200

DIAMANTE—V6—Equipment Schedule 4
W.B. 107.1"; 3.5 Liter.

Body	Type	VIN	List	Trade-In Fair	Good	Pvt-Party Good	Retail Excellent
ES Luxury Sedan 4D		P37P	26370	1250	1725	2900	4600
LS Luxury Sedan 4D		P47P	30460	1825	2325	3550	5400

1998 MITSUBISHI—(J,4or6)(A3orMM)A(Y26A)–W–#

MIRAGE—4-Cyl.—Equipment Schedule 6
W.B. 95.1", 98.4" (Sed); 1.5 Liter, 1.8 Liter.

Body	Type	VIN	List	Trade-In Fair	Good	Pvt-Party Good	Retail Excellent
DE Sedan 4D		Y26A	13660	700	1000	1875	3300
DE Coupe 2D		Y11A	12130	550	725	1525	2800
LS Sedan 4D		Y36C	15320	700	975	1850	3250
LS Coupe 2D		Y31C	14750	675	950	1850	3200

ECLIPSE—4-Cyl.—Equipment Schedule 4
W.B. 98.8"; 2.0 Liter, 2.4 Liter.

Body	Type	VIN	List	Trade-In Fair	Good	Pvt-Party Good	Retail Excellent
RS Coupe 2D		K24Y	17775	1125	1575	2775	4475
GS Coupe 2D		K44Y	20171	1575	2050	3300	5125
GS Spyder Conv 2D		X35G	22311	2225	2800	4125	6075
Auto Trans				175	175	235	235

ECLIPSE—4-Cyl. Turbo—Equipment Schedule 4
W.B. 98.8"; 2.0 Liter.

Body	Type	VIN	List	Trade-In Fair	Good	Pvt-Party Good	Retail Excellent
GS-T Coupe 2D		K54F	22380	1800	2300	3575	5450
GS-T Spyder Conv 2D		X55F	27080	2875	3500	4875	6975
GSX Coupe 2D		L54F	25740	2375	2950	4275	6250
Auto Trans				175	175	235	235

GALANT—4-Cyl.—Equipment Schedule 4
W.B. 103.7"; 2.4 Liter.

1998 MITSUBISHI

Body	Type	VIN	List	Trade-In Fair	Trade-In Good	Pvt-Party Good	Retail Excellent
DE Sedan 4D		J46G	18222	900	1275	2375	4050
ES Sedan 4D		J56G	18870	1025	1450	2600	4300
LS Sedan 4D		J56G	25730	1250	1725	2925	4675
Manual Trans				(300)	(300)	(400)	(400)

3000GT—V6—Equipment Schedule 4
W.B. 97.2"; 3.0 Liter.

Coupe 2D		M44H	28240	4550	5375	6875	9325
SL Coupe 2D		M84J	35660	5275	6150	7800	10450
Auto Trans				175	175	235	235

3000GT—V6 Turbo—Equipment Schedule 2
W.B. 97.2"; 3.0 Liter.

VR-4 Coupe 2D		N74K	46700	8075	9250	11150	14400

DIAMANTE—V6—Equipment Schedule 4
W.B. 107.1"; 3.5 Liter.

ES Luxury Sedan 4D		P37P	28120	1375	1850	3075	4800
LS Luxury Sedan 4D		P47P	33520	2000	2550	3800	5675

1999 MITSUBISHI — (J,4or6)(A3orMM)A(Y26A)–X–

MIRAGE—4-Cyl.—Equipment Schedule 6
W.B. 95.1", 98.4" (Sed); 1.5 Liter, 1.8 Liter.

DE Sedan 4D		Y26A	14405	800	1150	2125	3650
DE Coupe 2D		Y11A	12455	625	850	1725	3075
LS Sedan 4D		Y36C	15432	800	1150	2125	3650
LS Coupe 2D		Y31C	15025	800	1125	2100	3600

ECLIPSE—4-Cyl.—Equipment Schedule 4
W.B. 98.8"; 2.0 Liter, 2.4 Liter.

RS Coupe 2D		K34Y	18474	1400	1875	3125	4925
GS Coupe 2D		K44Y	20214	1925	2475	3750	5625
GS Spyder Conv 2D		X35G	22836	2650	3250	4600	6650
Auto Trans				200	200	265	265

ECLIPSE—4-Cyl. Turbo—Equipment Schedule 4
W.B. 98.8"; 2.0 Liter.

GS-T Coupe 2D		K54F	23645	2175	2725	4050	5975
GS-T Spyder Conv 2D		X55F	27395	3350	4050	5450	7625
GSX Coupe 2D		L54F	26985	2800	3400	4775	6825
Auto Trans				200	200	265	265

GALANT—4-Cyl.—Equipment Schedule 4
W.B. 103.7"; 2.4 Liter.

DE Sedan 4D		A36G	17425	950	1350	2475	4175
ES Sedan 4D		A46G	18425	1075	1525	2675	4375
V6 3.0 Liter		L		350	350	465	465

GALANT—V6—Equipment Schedule 4
W.B. 103.7"; 3.0 Liter.

LS Sedan 4D		A56L	24685	1975	2525	3800	5700
GTZ Sedan 4D		A46L	24785	2025	2575	3850	5750

3000GT—V6—Equipment Schedule 4
W.B. 97.2"; 3.0 Liter.

Coupe 2D		M44H	25920	4600	5400	6925	9350
SL Coupe 2D		M84J	33870	6025	6950	8650	11400
Auto Trans				200	200	265	265

3000GT—V6 Turbo—Equipment Schedule 2
W.B. 97.2"; 3.0 Liter.

VR-4 Coupe 2D		N74K	45070	9100	10350	12350	15800

DIAMANTE—V6—Equipment Schedule 4
W.B. 107.1"; 3.5 Liter.

Luxury Sedan 4D		P37P	27669	1550	2050	3250	5050
Traction Control				175	175	235	235

2000 MITSUBISHI — (J,4or6)(A3orMM)A(Y26A)–Y–

MIRAGE—4-Cyl.—Equipment Schedule 6
W.B. 95.1", 98.4" (Sed); 1.5 Liter, 1.8 Liter.

DE Sedan 4D		Y26A	14412	950	1325	2475	4175
DE Coupe 2D		Y11A	13062	725	1025	1975	3475
LS Sedan 4D		Y36C	17372	950	1350	2500	4200
LS Coupe 2D		Y31C	15032	950	1325	2475	4175

ECLIPSE—4-Cyl.—Equipment Schedule 4
W.B. 100.8"; 2.4 Liter.

RS Coupe 2D		C34G	18932	1700	2200	3475	5375
GS Coupe 2D		C44G	20482	2275	2875	4175	6150
Auto Trans				200	200	265	265

ECLIPSE—V6—Equipment Schedule 4
W.B. 100.8"; 3.0 Liter.

2000 MITSUBISHI

Body	Type	VIN	List	Trade-In Fair	Good	Pvt-Party Good	Retail Excellent
	GT Coupe 2D	C84L	21622	2925	3550	4925	7025
	Traction Control			200	200	265	265
	Auto Trans			200	200	265	265
GALANT—4-Cyl.—Equipment Schedule 4							
W.B. 103.7"; 2.4 Liter.							
	DE Sedan 4D	A36G	17792	1175	1675	2875	4625
	ES Sedan 4D	A46G	18692	1350	1825	3075	4850
	V6 3.0 Liter	L		400	400	535	535
GALANT—V6—Equipment Schedule 4							
W.B. 103.7"; 3.0 Liter.							
	LS Sedan 4D	A56L	24092	2375	2975	4300	6275
	GTZ Sedan 4D	A46L	24192	2425	3025	4325	6325
DIAMANTE—V6—Equipment Schedule 4							
W.B. 107.1"; 3.5 Liter.							
	ES Sedan 4D	P57P	25467	1825	2325	3575	5425
	LS Sedan 4D	P67P	28367	2575	3150	4450	6450

2001 MITSUBISHI–(J,4or6)(A3orMM)A(Y11A)–1–#

Body	Type	VIN	List	Trade-In Fair	Good	Pvt-Party Good	Retail Excellent
MIRAGE—4-Cyl.—Equipment Schedule 6							
W.B. 95.1", 98.4" (Sed); 1.5 Liter, 1.8 Liter.							
	DE Coupe 2D	Y11A	13277	875	1250	2375	4075
	ES Sedan 4D	Y26C	14147	1100	1550	2725	4450
	LS Sedan 4D	Y36C	14997	1150	1600	2800	4550
	LS Coupe 2D	Y31C	15237	1125	1575	2775	4525
ECLIPSE—4-Cyl.—Equipment Schedule 4							
W.B. 100.8"; 2.4 Liter.							
	RS Coupe 2D	C31G	18507	2075	2625	3950	5900
	GS Coupe 2D	C41G	19317	2725	3325	4700	6750
	GS Spyder Conv 2D	E35G	23927	3475	4175	5575	7800
	Auto Trans			200	200	265	265
ECLIPSE—V6—Equipment Schedule 4							
W.B. 100.8"; 3.0 Liter.							
	GT Coupe 2D	C81H	21467	3400	4100	5525	7700
	GT Spyder Conv 2D	E55H	25927	4450	5275	6775	9200
	Auto Trans			200	200	265	265
	Traction Control			225	225	300	300
GALANT—4-Cyl.—Equipment Schedule 4							
W.B. 103.7"; 2.4 Liter.							
	DE Sedan 4D	A36G	18077	1575	2050	3325	5200
	ES Sedan 4D	A46G	18927	1750	2250	3525	5425
	V6 3.0 Liter	H		450	450	600	600
GALANT—V6—Equipment Schedule 4							
W.B. 103.7"; 3.0 Liter.							
	LS Sedan 4D	A56H	24427	2875	3500	4850	6900
	GTZ Sedan 4D	A46H	24527	2925	3550	4900	6975
DIAMANTE—V6—Equipment Schedule 4							
W.B. 107.1"; 3.5 Liter.							
	ES Sedan 4D	P57P	25907	2100	2675	3950	5850
	LS Sedan 4D	P67P	28927	2925	3575	4900	6925

2002 MITSUBISHI–(J,4or6)(A3orMM)A(Y11A)–2–#

Body	Type	VIN	List	Trade-In Fair	Good	Pvt-Party Good	Retail Excellent
MIRAGE—4-Cyl.—Equipment Schedule 6							
W.B. 95.1"; 1.5 Liter, 1.8 Liter.							
	DE Coupe 2D	Y11A	13362	1000	1400	2750	4650
	LS Coupe 2D	Y31C	15332	1300	1775	3175	5175
LANCER—4-Cyl.—Equipment Schedule 6							
W.B. 102.4"; 2.0 Liter.							
	ES Sedan 4D	J26E	15242	2125	2675	4175	6325
	LS Sedan 4D	J36E	16442	2300	2875	4375	6575
	OZ Rally Sedan 4D	J86E	16832	2775	3375	4925	7175
ECLIPSE—4-Cyl.—Equipment Schedule 4							
W.B. 100.8"; 2.4 Liter.							
	RS Coupe 2D	C31G	18642	2400	3000	4500	6750
	GS Coupe 2D	C41G	19512	3100	3775	5350	7675
	GS Spyder Conv 2D	E35G	24172	3925	4650	6250	8700
	Auto Trans			200	200	265	265
ECLIPSE—V6—Equipment Schedule 4							
W.B. 100.8"; 3.0 Liter.							
	GT Coupe 2D	C81H	21702	3825	4550	6150	8600
	GT Spyder Conv 2D	E55H	26152	4975	5800	7525	10200
	Auto Trans			200	200	265	265
	Traction Control			250	250	335	335

Body	Type	VIN	List	Trade-In Fair	Trade-In Good	Pvt-Party Good	Retail Excellent
GALANT—4-Cyl.—Equipment Schedule 4							
W.B. 103.7"; 2.4 Liter.							
DE Sedan 4D	A36G	18262	**1925**	**2475**	**3950**	**6050**
ES Sedan 4D	A46G	19072	**2100**	**2650**	**4150**	**6275**
LS Sedan 4D	A46G	21672	**2525**	**3125**	**4625**	**6825**
V6 3.0 Liter	L		**500**	**500**	**665**	**665**
GALANT—V6—Equipment Schedule 4							
W.B. 103.7"; 3.0 Liter.							
GTZ Sedan 4D	A46H	24712	**3350**	**4025**	**5575**	**7925**
DIAMANTE—V6—Equipment Schedule 4							
W.B. 107.1"; 3.5 Liter.							
ES Sedan 4D	P57P	26247	**2375**	**2950**	**4375**	**6525**
VR-X Sedan 4D	P67P	27557	**2800**	**3400**	**4900**	**7100**
LS Sedan 4D	P67P	29007	**3225**	**3900**	**5400**	**7675**

2003 MITSUBISHI — (J,4or6)(A3orMM)A(J26E)-3-#

Body	Type	VIN	List	Trade-In Fair	Trade-In Good	Pvt-Party Good	Retail Excellent
LANCER—4-Cyl.—Equipment Schedule 6							
W.B. 102.4"; 2.0 Liter.							
ES Sedan 4D	J26E	14587	**2575**	**3175**	**4700**	**6925**
LS Sedan 4D	J36E	16617	**2775**	**3400**	**4925**	**7200**
OZ Rally Sedan 4D	J86E	16317	**3300**	**4000**	**5550**	**7925**
LANCER AWD—4-Cyl. Turbo—Equipment Schedule 4							
W.B. 103.3"; 2.0 Liter.							
Evolution Sedan 4D	H86F	29582	**10775**	**12200**	**14200**	**17800**
ECLIPSE—4-Cyl.—Equipment Schedule 4							
W.B. 100.8"; 2.4 Liter.							
RS Coupe 2D	C34G	18717	**2775**	**3375**	**4925**	**7200**
GS Coupe 2D	C44G	19617	**3600**	**4300**	**5875**	**8250**
GS Spyder Conv 2D	E45G	24397	**4450**	**5275**	**6900**	**9475**
Auto Trans			**225**	**225**	**300**	**300**
ECLIPSE—V6—Equipment Schedule 4							
W.B. 100.8"; 3.0 Liter.							
GT Coupe 2D	C84H	21807	**4350**	**5150**	**6800**	**9350**
GT Spyder Conv 2D	E85H	26477	**5675**	**6625**	**8325**	**11050**
GTS Coupe 2D	C74H	24777	**5525**	**6450**	**8150**	**10900**
GTS Spyder Conv 2D	E75H	28847	**6250**	**7225**	**8975**	**11800**
Auto Trans			**225**	**225**	**300**	**300**
Traction Control			**275**	**275**	**365**	**365**
GALANT—4-Cyl.—Equipment Schedule 4							
W.B. 103.7"; 2.4 Liter.							
DE Sedan 4D	A36G	18347	**2250**	**2825**	**4300**	**6500**
ES Sedan 4D	A46G	19157	**2475**	**3075**	**4550**	**6750**
LS Sedan 4D	A46G	21757	**2925**	**3550**	**5100**	**7375**
V6 3.0 Liter	H		**575**	**575**	**765**	**765**
GALANT—V6—Equipment Schedule 4							
W.B. 103.7"; 3.0 Liter.							
GTZ Sedan 4D	A46H	25047	**3875**	**4600**	**6175**	**8575**
DIAMANTE—V6—Equipment Schedule 4							
W.B. 107.1"; 3.5 Liter.							
ES Sedan 4D	P57P	26557	**2600**	**3175**	**4650**	**6800**
VR-X Sedan 4D	P87P	27677	**3075**	**3725**	**5225**	**7450**
LS Sedan 4D	P67P	29027	**3575**	**4300**	**5775**	**8100**

2004 MITSUBISHI — (J,4or6)(A3)A(J26E)-4-#

Body	Type	VIN	List	Trade-In Fair	Trade-In Good	Pvt-Party Good	Retail Excellent
LANCER—4-Cyl.—Equipment Schedule 4							
W.B. 102.4"; 2.0 Liter, 2.4 Liter.							
ES Sedan 4D	J26E	14172	**3075**	**3725**	**5300**	**7625**
LS Sedan 4D	J36E	16572	**3300**	**4000**	**5550**	**7925**
LS Wagon 4D	D29F	17172	**3550**	**4275**	**5825**	**8200**
OZ Rally Sedan 4D	J86E	16372	**3950**	**4700**	**6275**	**8725**
Ralliart Sedan 4D	J66F	18572	**4750**	**5575**	**7250**	**9850**
Ralliart Wagon 4D	D69F	19772	**5325**	**6225**	**7875**	**10550**
LANCER AWD—4-Cyl. Turbo—Equipment Schedule 4							
W.B. 103.3"; 2.0 Liter.							
Evolution RS Sedan 4D	H36D	27374	**11225**	**12700**	**14650**	**18250**
Evolution Sedan 4D	H86D	30574	**12300**	**13925**	**15900**	**19600**
ECLIPSE—4-Cyl.—Equipment Schedule 4							
W.B. 100.8"; 2.4 Liter.							
RS Coupe 2D	C34G	18892	**3175**	**3850**	**5450**	**7800**
GS Coupe 2D	C44G	19892	**4150**	**4900**	**6500**	**8975**
GS Spyder Conv 2D	E45G	24892	**5100**	**5950**	**7650**	**10300**
Auto Trans			**250**	**250**	**335**	**335**

2004 MITSUBISHI

Body	Type	VIN	List	Trade-In Fair	Good	Pvt-Party Good	Retail Excellent
ECLIPSE—V6—Equipment Schedule 4							
W.B. 100.8"; 3.0 Liter.							
GT Coupe 2D		C84H	22092	**4950**	**5775**	**7450**	**10100**
GT Spyder Conv 2D		E85H	26992	**6450**	**7450**	**9175**	**12000**
GTS Coupe 2D		C74H	25092	**6250**	**7225**	**8950**	**11750**
GTS Spyder Conv 2D		E75H	29372	**7100**	**8150**	**9900**	**12850**
Auto Trans				**250**	**250**	**335**	**335**
GALANT—4-Cyl.—Equipment Schedule 4							
W.B. 108.3"; 2.4 Liter.							
DE Sedan 4D		A36G	18592	**3475**	**4175**	**5725**	**8075**
ES Sedan 4D		A46G	19592	**3775**	**4475**	**6050**	**8425**
V6 3.8 Liter		S		**650**	**650**	**865**	**865**
GALANT—V6—Equipment Schedule 4							
W.B. 108.3"; 3.8 Liter.							
LS Sedan 4D		A46H	21592	**5025**	**5875**	**7525**	**10150**
GTS Sedan 4D		A46H	26292	**5325**	**6200**	**7850**	**10500**
DIAMANTE—V6—Equipment Schedule 4							
W.B. 107.2"; 3.5 Liter.							
ES Sedan 4D		P57P	25594	**2900**	**3525**	**5000**	**7200**
VR-X Sedan 4D		P87P	27414	**3450**	**4150**	**5625**	**7925**
LS Sedan 4D		P67P	28214	**4025**	**4775**	**6275**	**8625**

2005 MITSUBISHI — (J,4or6)(A3)A(J26E)-5-#

Body	Type	VIN	List	Trade-In Fair	Good	Pvt-Party Good	Retail Excellent
LANCER—4-Cyl.—Equipment Schedule 6							
W.B. 102.4"; 2.0 Liter, 2.4 Liter.							
ES Sedan 4D		J26E	14574	**3700**	**4400**	**6000**	**8400**
OZ Rally Sedan 4D		J86E	16974	**4625**	**5450**	**7100**	**9675**
Ralliart Sedan 4D		J66F	18774	**5575**	**6500**	**8150**	**10850**
LANCER AWD—4-Cyl. Turbo—Equipment Schedule 4							
W.B. 103.3"; 2.0 Liter.							
Evolution RS Sedan 4D		H36D	28774	**12650**	**14300**	**16250**	**20000**
Evolution VIII Sedan		H76D	31074	**13925**	**15675**	**17700**	**21600**
Evolution MR Ed Sedan		H86D	35574	**15150**	**17050**	**19050**	**23000**
ECLIPSE—4-Cyl.—Equipment Schedule 4							
W.B. 100.8"; 2.4 Liter.							
GS Coupe 2D		C44G	20044	**4775**	**5600**	**7275**	**9900**
GS Spyder Conv 2D		E45G	25494	**5825**	**6750**	**8450**	**11150**
Auto Trans				**275**	**275**	**365**	**365**
ECLIPSE—V6—Equipment Schedule 4							
W.B. 100.8"; 3.0 Liter.							
GT Coupe 2D		C84H	23494	**5650**	**6575**	**8250**	**11000**
GT Spyder Conv 2D		E55H	27694	**7325**	**8425**	**10150**	**13100**
GTS Coupe 2D		C74H	25244	**7100**	**8175**	**9900**	**12800**
GTS Spyder Conv 2D		E75H	30094	**8075**	**9225**	**11050**	**14100**
Auto Trans				**275**	**275**	**365**	**365**
GALANT—4-Cyl.—Equipment Schedule 4							
W.B. 108.3"; 2.4 Liter.							
DE Sedan 4D		B26F	19294	**3975**	**4700**	**6275**	**8700**
ES Sedan 4D		B46F	20194	**4300**	**5100**	**6675**	**9150**
GALANT—V6—Equipment Schedule 4							
W.B. 108.3"; 3.8 Liter.							
LS Sedan 4D		B46S	22894	**5675**	**6625**	**8250**	**10950**
GTS Sedan 4D		B76S	26894	**6025**	**6975**	**8650**	**11350**

2006 MITSUBISHI — (J,4or6)(A3)A(J26E)-6-#

Body	Type	VIN	List	Trade-In Fair	Good	Pvt-Party Good	Retail Excellent
LANCER—4-Cyl.—Equipment Schedule 6							
W.B. 102.4"; 2.0 Liter, 2.4 Liter.							
ES Sedan 4D		J26E	15174	**4400**	**5200**	**6825**	**9375**
SE Sedan 4D		J26E	16704	**4400**	**5200**	**6825**	**9375**
OZ Rally Sedan 4D		J86E	17474	**5475**	**6350**	**8000**	**10700**
Ralliart Sedan 4D		J66F	19574	**6500**	**7475**	**9150**	**11900**
LANCER AWD—4-Cyl. Turbo—Equipment Schedule 4							
W.B. 103.3"; 2.0 Liter.							
Evolution RS Sedan 4D		H36C	29274	**14150**	**15925**	**17900**	**21700**
Evolution IX Sedan 4D		H86C	31994	**15525**	**17450**	**19400**	**23300**
Evolution MR Sedan 4D		H86C	35784	**16900**	**18975**	**21000**	**25200**
ECLIPSE—4-Cyl.—Equipment Schedule 4							
W.B. 101.4"; 2.4 Liter.							
GS Coupe 2D		K24F	19994	**6225**	**7200**	**8900**	**11650**
Auto Trans				**300**	**300**	**400**	**400**
ECLIPSE—V6—Equipment Schedule 4							
W.B. 101.4"; 3.8 Liter.							

Body	Type	VIN	List	Trade-In Fair	Good	Pvt-Party Good	Retail Excellent
	GT Coupe 2D	K34T	24294	8200	9375	11150	14200
	GT Special Ed Cpe 2D	K44T	26824	8700	9900	11700	14800
	Auto Trans			300	300	400	400
GALANT—4-Cyl.—Equipment Schedule 4							
W.B. 108.3"; 2.4 Liter.							
	DE Sedan 4D	B26F	19994	4625	5450	7050	9600
	ES Sedan 4D	B46F	20894	5025	5850	7500	10100
	SE Sedan 4D	B36F	22594	5475	6375	7975	10650
GALANT—V6—Equipment Schedule 4							
W.B. 108.3"; 3.8 Liter.							
	LS Sedan 4D	B46S	23594	6525	7525	9175	11900
	GTS Sedan 4D	B76S	27594	6875	7950	9600	12400

2007 MITSUBISHI — (Jor4)(A3)A(J26E)-7-#

Body	Type	VIN	List	Trade-In Fair	Good	Pvt-Party Good	Retail Excellent
LANCER—4-Cyl.—Equipment Schedule 4							
W.B. 102.4"; 2.0 Liter.							
	ES Sedan 4D	J26E	14599	5275	6150	7725	10250
ECLIPSE—4-Cyl.—Equipment Schedule 4							
W.B. 101.4"; 2.4 Liter.							
	GS Coupe 2D	K24F	21224	7125	8200	9800	12600
	GS Spyder Conv 2D	L25F	26914	8900	10150	11800	14850
	SE Coupe 2D	K64F	23024	7800	8925	10650	13500
ECLIPSE—V6—Equipment Schedule 4							
W.B. 101.4"; 3.8 Liter.							
	GT Coupe 2D	K34T	24924	9275	10575	12250	15350
	GT Spyder Conv 2D	L35T	29794	11475	12975	14700	18050
GALANT—4-Cyl.—Equipment Schedule 4							
W.B. 108.3"; 2.4 Liter.							
	DE Sedan 4D	B26F	20524	5500	6400	7925	10450
	ES Sedan 4D	B36F	21624	5925	6875	8400	11000
	SE Sedan 4D	B36F	23324	6400	7400	8950	11550
GALANT—V6—Equipment Schedule 4							
W.B. 108.3"; 3.8 Liter.							
	GTS Sedan 4D	B56S	25624	7950	9100	10750	13550
	Ralliart Sedan 4D	B76T	27624	8325	9525	11100	14000

2008 MITSUBISHI — (1,4orJ)A3—(U16U)-8-#

Body	Type	VIN	List	Trade-In Fair	Good	Pvt-Party Good	Retail Excellent
LANCER—4-Cyl.—Equipment Schedule 4							
W.B. 103.7"; 2.0 Liter.							
	DE Sedan 4D	U16U	14615	7400	8475	9900	12450
	ES Sedan 4D	U26U	16615	8200	9375	10900	13550
	GTS Sedan 4D	U86U	18115	9950	11275	12800	15750
LANCER—4-Cyl. Turbo—Equipment Schedule 4							
W.B. 104.3"; 2.0 Liter.							
	Evolution GSR Sedan	W86V	33615	20575	23025	24800	29000
	Evolution MR Sedan	W56V	38940				
ECLIPSE—4-Cyl.—Equipment Schedule 4							
W.B. 101.4"; 2.4 Liter.							
	GS Coupe 2D	K24F	21624	8500	9725	11300	14200
	GS Spyder Conv 2D	L25F	27324	10425	11800	13500	16600
	SE Coupe 2D	K64F	25424	9250	10525	12150	15150
ECLIPSE—V6—Equipment Schedule 4							
W.B. 101.4"; 3.8 Liter.							
	GT Coupe 2D	K34T	25124	10825	12300	13950	17150
	GT Spyder Conv 2D	L35T	30224	13225	14900	16550	20000
	SE Coupe 2D	K64T	29224	11800	13325	15050	18350
GALANT—4-Cyl.—Equipment Schedule 4							
W.B. 108.3"; 2.4 Liter.							
	DE Sedan 4D	B26F	20624	7400	8500	9950	12550
	ES Sedan 4D	B36F	21724	7875	9000	10500	13250
GALANT—V6—Equipment Schedule 4							
W.B. 108.3"; 3.8 Liter.							
	Ralliart Sedan 4D	B76T	27774	10475	11900	13400	16300

NISSAN

1994 NISSAN — (1N4orJN1)(EB32A)-R-#

Body	Type	VIN	List	Trade-In Fair	Good	Pvt-Party Good	Retail Excellent
SENTRA—4-Cyl.—Equipment Schedule 6							
W.B. 95.7"; 1.6 Liter, 2.0 Liter.							
	E Sedan 2D	EB32A	11924	525	700	1375	2475
	E Sedan 4D	EB31P	12474	525	700	1375	2475

1994 NISSAN

Body	Type	VIN	List	Trade-In Fair	Trade-In Good	Pvt-Party Good	Retail Excellent
	XE Sedan 2D	EB32A	12479	600	800	1575	2825
	XE Sedan 4D	EB31P	12679	600	800	1575	2825
	Limited Ed Sedan 2D	EB32A	13029	600	825	1625	2875
	Limited Ed Sedan 4D	EB31P	13249	625	850	1650	2925
	SE Sedan 2D	EB32A	13974	575	775	1550	2800
	SE-R Sedan 2D	GB32A	15174	775	1075	1975	3375
	GXE Sedan 4D	EB31C	15049	700	975	1825	3150
240SX—4-Cyl.—Equipment Schedule 5							
W.B. 97.4"; 2.4 Liter.							
	SE Convertible 2D	MS36A	25344	1850	2400	3650	5525
ALTIMA—4-Cyl.—Equipment Schedule 4							
W.B. 103.1"; 2.4 Liter.							
	XE Sedan 4D	BU31F	16904	625	900	1700	3000
	GXE Sedan 4D	BU31F	17264	650	925	1725	3050
	SE Sedan 4D	BU31F	19384	725	1025	1875	3250
	GLE Sedan 4D	BU31F	19559	900	1275	2225	3725
	Manual Trans			(200)	(200)	(265)	(265)
MAXIMA—V6—Equipment Schedule 4							
W.B. 104.3"; 3.0 Liter.							
	GXE Sedan 4D	HJ01F	22579	1125	1575	2725	4375
	SE Sedan 4D	EJ01F	24614	1125	1575	2725	4375
	Manual Trans			(200)	(200)	(265)	(265)
300ZX—V6—Equipment Schedule 3							
W.B. 96.5", 101.2" (2+2); 3.0 Liter.							
	Coupe 2D	RZ24D	34079	3750	4450	5950	8250
	2+2 Coupe 2D	RZ26D	36869	3950	4675	6175	8525
	Convertible 2D	RZ27D	41259	4575	5400	6950	9450
300ZX—V6 Turbo—Equipment Schedule 3							
W.B. 96.5"; 3.0 Liter.							
	Coupe 2D	CZ24D	40479	4575	5400	6975	9475

1995 NISSAN — (1N4orJN1)(AB41D)-S-#

Body	Type	VIN	List	Trade-In Fair	Trade-In Good	Pvt-Party Good	Retail Excellent
SENTRA—4-Cyl.—Equipment Schedule 6							
W.B. 99.8"; 1.6 Liter.							
	Sedan 4D	AB41D	11389	625	900	1725	3050
	XE Sedan 4D	AB41D	13139	700	1000	1875	3250
	GXE Sedan 4D	AB41D	13839	750	1075	1950	3375
	GLE Sedan 4D	AB41D	14839	900	1275	2325	3950
200SX—4-Cyl.—Equipment Schedule 6							
W.B. 99.8"; 1.6 Liter, 2.0 Liter.							
	Coupe 2D	AB42D	13874	725	1025	1875	3250
	SE Coupe 2D	AB42D	14674	750	1075	1925	3325
	SE-R Coupe 2D	BB42D	15674	875	1250	2200	3675
240SX—4-Cyl.—Equipment Schedule 5							
W.B. 99.4"; 2.4 Liter.							
	Coupe 2D	AS44D	19758	2000	2575	3850	5750
	SE Coupe 2D	AS44D	22439	2250	2825	4150	6100
ALTIMA—4-Cyl.—Equipment Schedule 4							
W.B. 103.1"; 2.4 Liter.							
	XE Sedan 4D	BU31D	17848	750	1050	1925	3325
	GXE Sedan 4D	BU31D	18218	750	1075	1950	3375
	SE Sedan 4D	BU31D	20089	850	1175	2125	3600
	GLE Sedan 4D	BU31D	20279	1050	1475	2575	4250
MAXIMA—V6—Equipment Schedule 4							
W.B. 106.3"; 3.0 Liter.							
	GXE Sedan 4D	CA21D	21989	1600	2100	3325	5125
	SE Sedan 4D	CA21D	22989	1600	2100	3325	5125
	GLE Sedan 4D	CA21D	25209	2075	2650	3900	5800
300ZX—V6—Equipment Schedule 3							
W.B. 96.5", 101.2" (2+2); 3.0 Liter.							
	Coupe 2D	RZ24D	35399	4275	5025	6600	9050
	2+2 Coupe 2D	RZ26D	38189	4475	5275	6850	9350
	Convertible 2D	RZ27D	42579	5175	6025	7775	10500
300ZX—V6 Turbo—Equipment Schedule 3							
W.B. 96.5"; 3.0 Liter.							
	Coupe 2D	CZ24D	41799	5200	6075	7825	10550

1996 NISSAN — (1N4or3N1)(AB41D)-T-#

Body	Type	VIN	List	Trade-In Fair	Trade-In Good	Pvt-Party Good	Retail Excellent
SENTRA—4-Cyl.—Equipment Schedule 6							
W.B. 99.8"; 1.6 Liter.							
	Sedan 4D	AB41D	11904	750	1050	1950	3375
	XE Sedan 4D	AB41D	13934	850	1175	2150	3650

Body	Type	VIN	List	Trade-In Fair	Trade-In Good	Pvt-Party Good	Retail Excellent
	GXE Sedan 4D	AB41D	14864	875	1250	2325	3950
	GLE Sedan 4D	AB41D	15634	1050	1500	2625	4300
200SX—4-Cyl.—Equipment Schedule 6							
W.B. 99.8"; 1.6 Liter, 2.0 Liter.							
	Coupe 2D	AB42D	14303	850	1200	2150	3650
	SE Coupe 2D	AB42D	15274	900	1275	2325	3950
	SE-R Coupe 2D	BB42D	16474	1050	1475	2575	4250
240SX—4-Cyl.—Equipment Schedule 5							
W.B. 99.4"; 2.4 Liter.							
	Coupe 2D	AS44D	20563	2400	3000	4300	6300
	SE Coupe 2D	AS44D	23454	2675	3275	4625	6700
ALTIMA—4-Cyl.—Equipment Schedule 4							
W.B. 103.1"; 2.4 Liter.							
	XE Sedan 4D	BU31D	18783	875	1225	2200	3725
	GXE Sedan 4D	BU31D	19533	900	1250	2325	3950
	SE Sedan 4D	BU31D	20534	975	1375	2500	4150
	GLE Sedan 4D	BU31D	21404	1225	1700	2875	4600
	Manual Trans			(200)	(200)	(265)	(265)
MAXIMA—V6—Equipment Schedule 4							
W.B. 106.3"; 3.0 Liter.							
	GXE Sedan 4D	CA21D	23084	1775	2275	3525	5400
	SE Sedan 4D	CA21D	24084	1850	2350	3625	5500
	GLE Sedan 4D	CA21D	26684	2350	2950	4250	6225
	Manual Trans			(200)	(200)	(265)	(265)
300ZX—V6—Equipment Schedule 3							
W.B. 96.5", 101.2" (2+2); 3.0 Liter.							
	Coupe 2D	RZ24D	37844	4850	5675	7300	9850
	2+2 Coupe 2D	RZ26D	40384	5100	5950	7650	10350
	Convertible 2D	RZ27D	45084	5875	6800	8575	11400
300ZX Turbo—V6 Turbo—Equipment Schedule 3							
W.B. 96.5"; 3.0 Liter.							
	Coupe 2D	CZ24D	44384	5925	6875	8675	11500

1997 NISSAN–(1N4or3N1)(AB41D)–V–

Body	Type	VIN	List	Trade-In Fair	Trade-In Good	Pvt-Party Good	Retail Excellent
SENTRA—4-Cyl.—Equipment Schedule 6							
W.B. 99.8"; 1.6 Liter.							
	Sedan 4D	AB41D	11919	875	1250	2325	3950
	XE Sedan 4D	AB41D	14069	975	1375	2475	4150
	GXE Sedan 4D	AB41D	15219	1050	1450	2600	4275
	GLE Sedan 4D	AB41D	16069	1225	1700	2900	4625
200SX—4-Cyl.—Equipment Schedule 6							
W.B. 99.8"; 1.6 Liter, 2.0 Liter.							
	Coupe 2D	AB42D	14418	1000	1400	2500	4175
	SE Coupe 2D	AB42D	15769	1050	1475	2625	4300
	SE-R Coupe 2D	BB42D	17169	1200	1675	2875	4600
240SX—4-Cyl.—Equipment Schedule 5							
W.B. 99.4"; 2.4 Liter.							
	Coupe 2D	AS44D	20628	2800	3425	4800	6850
	SE Coupe 2D	AS44D	23269	3125	3800	5200	7350
	LE Coupe 2D	AS44D	25719	3150	3825	5250	7400
ALTIMA—4-Cyl.—Equipment Schedule 4							
W.B. 103.1"; 2.4 Liter.							
	XE Sedan 4D	BU31D	18798	1050	1475	2600	4300
	GXE Sedan 4D	BU31D	19548	1075	1500	2675	4350
	SE Sedan 4D	BU31D	20549	1200	1675	2875	4600
	GLE Sedan 4D	BU31D	21419	1525	2000	3250	5050
	Manual Trans			(250)	(250)	(335)	(335)
MAXIMA—V6—Equipment Schedule 4							
W.B. 106.3"; 3.0 Liter.							
	GXE Sedan 4D	CA21D	23669	1975	2525	3800	5700
	SE Sedan 4D	CA21D	24719	2100	2675	3975	5875
	GLE Sedan 4D	CA21D	27319	2650	3250	4625	6675
	Manual Trans			(250)	(250)	(335)	(335)

1998 NISSAN — (1N4or3N1)(AB41D)–W–#

Body	Type	VIN	List	Trade-In Fair	Trade-In Good	Pvt-Party Good	Retail Excellent
SENTRA—4-Cyl.—Equipment Schedule 6							
W.B. 99.8"; 1.6 Liter, 2.0 Liter.							
	Sedan 4D	AB41D	11989	1050	1475	2625	4300
	XE Sedan 4D	AB41D	14189	1125	1575	2775	4475
	GXE Sedan 4D	AB41D	15389	1225	1700	2900	4650
	GLE Sedan 4D	AB41D	16239	1500	1975	3225	5050
	SE Sedan 4D	AB41D	17239	1625	2125	3375	5225

Body	Type	VIN	List	Trade-In Fair	Trade-In Good	Pvt-Party Good	Retail Excellent
200SX—4-Cyl.—Equipment Schedule 6							
W.B. 99.8"; 1.6 Liter, 2.0 Liter.							
Coupe 2D	AB42D	14638	**1150**	**1600**	**2775**	**4475**
SE Coupe 2D	AB42D	15889	**1225**	**1725**	**2925**	**4650**
SE-R Coupe 2D	BB42D	17239	**1475**	**1950**	**3175**	**4975**
240SX—4-Cyl.—Equipment Schedule 5							
W.B. 99.4"; 2.4 Liter.							
Coupe 2D	AS44D	20648	**3200**	**3900**	**5300**	**7450**
SE Coupe 2D	AS44D	23289	**3625**	**4325**	**5775**	**8025**
LE Coupe 2D	AS44D	25739	**3650**	**4350**	**5800**	**8050**
ALTIMA—4-Cyl.—Equipment Schedule 4							
W.B. 103.1"; 2.4 Liter.							
XE Sedan 4D	DL01D	18179	**1300**	**1800**	**3025**	**4775**
GXE Sedan 4D	DL01D	18480	**1375**	**1850**	**3075**	**4850**
SE Sedan 4D	DL01D	19780	**1575**	**2050**	**3300**	**5125**
GLE Sedan 4D	DL01D	20380	**1900**	**2450**	**3725**	**5600**
Manual Trans			**(300)**	**(300)**	**(400)**	**(400)**
MAXIMA—V6—Equipment Schedule 4							
W.B. 106.3"; 3.0 Liter.							
GXE Sedan 4D	CA21D	23739	**2250**	**2850**	**4150**	**6100**
SE Sedan 4D	CA21D	24989	**2450**	**3050**	**4350**	**6350**
GLE Sedan 4D	CA21D	27389	**3000**	**3625**	**5025**	**7125**
Manual Trans			**(300)**	**(300)**	**(400)**	**(400)**

1999 NISSAN — (1N4,JN1or3N1)(AB41D)-X-#

Body	Type	VIN	List	Trade-In Fair	Trade-In Good	Pvt-Party Good	Retail Excellent
SENTRA—4-Cyl.—Equipment Schedule 6							
W.B. 99.8"; 1.6 Liter, 2.0 Liter.							
XE Sedan 4D	AB41D	13319	**1400**	**1875**	**3100**	**4925**
GXE Sedan 4D	AB41D	14719	**1525**	**2025**	**3275**	**5125**
SE Sedan 4D	BB41D	15719	**1975**	**2525**	**3825**	**5725**
ALTIMA—4-Cyl.—Equipment Schedule 4							
W.B. 103.1"; 2.4 Liter.							
XE Sedan 4D	DL01D	18209	**1650**	**2125**	**3400**	**5275**
GXE Sedan 4D	DL01D	18510	**1700**	**2200**	**3475**	**5350**
SE Sedan 4D	DL01D	19810	**1925**	**2475**	**3775**	**5675**
GLE Sedan 4D	DL01D	20510	**2300**	**2900**	**4225**	**6175**
Manual Trans			**(350)**	**(350)**	**(465)**	**(465)**
MAXIMA—V6—Equipment Schedule 4							
W.B. 106.3"; 3.0 Liter.							
GXE Sedan 4D	CA21D	23769	**2600**	**3200**	**4525**	**6575**
SE Sedan 4D	CA21D	25019	**2800**	**3425**	**4775**	**6850**
GLE Sedan 4D	CA21D	27419	**3375**	**4075**	**5500**	**7675**
Manual Trans			**(350)**	**(350)**	**(465)**	**(465)**

2000 NISSAN — (1N4,JN1or3N1)(CB51D)-Y-#

Body	Type	VIN	List	Trade-In Fair	Trade-In Good	Pvt-Party Good	Retail Excellent
SENTRA—4-Cyl.—Equipment Schedule 6							
W.B. 99.8"; 1.8 Liter, 2.0 Liter.							
XE Sedan 4D	CB51D	12169	**1725**	**2225**	**3525**	**5400**
GXE Sedan 4D	CB51D	14019	**1875**	**2400**	**3700**	**5575**
CA Sedan 4D	DB51D	15319	**2100**	**2675**	**3975**	**5900**
SE Sedan 4D	BB51D	15419	**2375**	**2975**	**4300**	**6275**
ALTIMA—4-Cyl.—Equipment Schedule 4							
W.B. 103.1"; 2.4 Liter.							
XE Sedan 4D	DL01D	18459	**2025**	**2600**	**3900**	**5825**
GXE Sedan 4D	DL01D	18659	**2100**	**2675**	**3975**	**5900**
SE Sedan 4D	DL01D	19960	**2375**	**2975**	**4300**	**6300**
GLE Sedan 4D	DL01D	20910	**2775**	**3400**	**4750**	**6800**
Manual Trans			**(400)**	**(400)**	**(535)**	**(535)**
MAXIMA—V6—Equipment Schedule 4							
W.B. 108.3"; 3.0 Liter.							
GXE Sedan 4D	CA31A	23269	**3425**	**4150**	**5525**	**7725**
SE Sedan 4D	CA31A	24669	**3700**	**4400**	**5850**	**8075**
GLE Sedan 4D	CA31A	26769	**4300**	**5100**	**6575**	**8900**
Manual Trans			**(400)**	**(400)**	**(535)**	**(535)**

2001 NISSAN — (1N4,JN1or3N1)(CB51D)-1-#

Body	Type	VIN	List	Trade-In Fair	Trade-In Good	Pvt-Party Good	Retail Excellent
SENTRA—4-Cyl.—Equipment Schedule 6							
W.B. 99.8"; 1.8 Liter, 2.0 Liter.							
XE Sedan 4D	CB51D	13368	**2075**	**2650**	**3975**	**5900**
GXE Sedan 4D	CB51D	14019	**2275**	**2850**	**4175**	**6150**
CA Sedan 4D	DB51D	15319	**2500**	**3100**	**4425**	**6450**
SE Sedan 4D	BB51D	15419	**2800**	**3400**	**4775**	**6825**

2001 NISSAN

Body Type	VIN	List	Trade-In Fair	Trade-In Good	Pvt-Party Good	Retail Excellent
ALTIMA—4-Cyl.—Equipment Schedule 4						
W.B. 103.1"; 2.4 Liter.						
XE Sedan 4D	DL01D	18459	2525	3100	4450	6500
GXE Sedan 4D	DL01D	18659	2600	3175	4525	6575
SE Sedan 4D	DL01D	19960	2900	3525	4900	7000
GLE Sedan 4D	DL01D	20190	3275	3975	5375	7525
LE		-------	100	100	135	135
Manual Trans		-------	(425)	(425)	(565)	(565)
MAXIMA—V6—Equipment Schedule 4						
W.B. 108.3"; 3.0 Liter.						
GXE Sedan 4D	CA31D	23469	3900	4625	6050	8300
SE Sedan 4D	CA31D	24869	4200	4950	6400	8700
SE 20th Anniv Sed 4D	CA31A	28169	4775	5600	7150	9600
GLE Sedan 4D	CA31D	26969	4775	5600	7150	9600
Manual Trans		-------	(425)	(425)	(565)	(565)

2002 NISSAN — (1N4,JN1or3N1)(CB51D)-2-#

Body Type	VIN	List	Trade-In Fair	Trade-In Good	Pvt-Party Good	Retail Excellent
SENTRA—4-Cyl.—Equipment Schedule 6						
W.B. 99.8"; 1.8 Liter, 2.5 Liter.						
XE Sedan 4D	CB51D	13588	2450	3050	4550	6750
GXE Sedan 4D	CB51D	14289	2625	3225	4750	6975
CA Sedan 4D	DB51D	15439	2875	3500	5050	7325
SE-R Sedan 4D	AB51A	16539	3100	3750	5325	7650
SE-R Spec V Sedan 4D	AB51A	17539	3775	4500	6075	8500
ALTIMA—4-Cyl.—Equipment Schedule 4						
W.B. 110.2"; 2.5 Liter.						
2.5 Sedan 4D	AL11D	17869	3400	4100	5650	8025
2.5 S Sedan 4D	AL11D	19389	3575	4300	5850	8250
2.5 SL Sedan 4D	AL11D	23239	4075	4825	6425	8875
Manual Trans			(450)	(450)	(600)	(600)
ALTIMA—V6—Equipment Schedule 4						
W.B. 110.2"; 3.5 Liter.						
3.5 SE Sedan 4D	BL11D	23689	4575	5400	7050	9650
Manual Trans			(450)	(450)	(600)	(600)
MAXIMA—V6—Equipment Schedule 4						
W.B. 108.3"; 3.5 Liter.						
GXE Sedan 4D	CA31D	25239	4275	5050	6650	9150
SE Sedan 4D	CA31D	25989	4600	5425	7075	9675
GLE Sedan 4D	CA31D	27639	5225	6075	7800	10500

2003 NISSAN — (1N4,JN1or3N1)(CB51D)-3-#

Body Type	VIN	List	Trade-In Fair	Trade-In Good	Pvt-Party Good	Retail Excellent
SENTRA—4-Cyl.—Equipment Schedule 6						
W.B. 99.8"; 1.8 Liter, 2.5 Liter.						
XE Sedan 4D	CB51D	13888	2750	3375	4900	7175
GXE Sedan 4D	CB51D	14639	2925	3575	5125	7400
Limited Sedan 4D	AB51D	17139	3250	3925	5500	7825
SE-R Sedan 4D	AB51D	16739	3525	4250	5800	8175
SE-R Spec V Sed 4D	AB51D	17739	4300	5075	6700	9175
ALTIMA—4-Cyl.—Equipment Schedule 4						
W.B. 110.2"; 2.5 Liter.						
2.5 Sedan 4D	AL11D	17689	4125	4875	6500	8975
2.5 S Sedan 4D	AL11D	19539	4300	5050	6675	9175
2.5 SL Sedan 4D	AL11D	23539	4825	5650	7325	9950
Manual Trans			(500)	(500)	(665)	(665)
ALTIMA—V6—Equipment Schedule 4						
W.B. 110.2"; 3.5 Liter.						
3.5 SE Sedan 4D	BL11D	23689	5450	6325	8025	10750
Manual Trans			(500)	(500)	(665)	(665)
MAXIMA—V6—Equipment Schedule 4						
W.B. 108.3"; 3.5 Liter.						
GXE Sedan 4D	DA31D	25439	4675	5500	7150	9750
SE Sedan 4D	DA31D	26189	5150	6025	7700	10350
GLE Sedan 4D	DA31D	28089	5775	6725	8425	11150
350Z—V6—Equipment Schedule 3						
W.B. 104.3"; 3.5 Liter.						
Coupe 2D	AZ34D	26809	7575	8675	10550	13650
Enthusiast Coupe 2D	AZ34D	29759	7825	8975	10900	14000
Performance Cpe 2D	AZ34D	30969	7975	9125	11000	14150
Touring Coupe 2D	AZ34D	32129	8275	9475	11450	14750
Track Coupe 2D	AZ34D	34619	8725	9950	11950	15300

Body	Type	VIN	List	Trade-In Fair	Trade-In Good	Pvt-Party Good	Retail Excellent

2004 NISSAN—(1N4,JN1or3N1)(CB51D)–4–#

SENTRA—4-Cyl.—Equipment Schedule 6
W.B. 99.8"; 1.8 Liter, 2.5 Liter.

Body	Type	VIN	List	Fair	Good	Good	Excellent
Sedan 4D		CB51D	12740	3125	3800	5375	7725
1.8 S Sedan 4D		CB51D	14740	3325	4000	5550	7950
2.5 S Sedan 4D		AB51D	17360	3525	4250	5800	8200
SE-R Sedan 4D		AB51D	17640	4050	4800	6400	8850
SE-R Spec V Sed 4D		AB51D	17840	4875	5700	7375	10000

ALTIMA—4-Cyl.—Equipment Schedule 4
W.B. 110.2"; 2.5 Liter.

2.5 Sedan 4D		AL11D	17890	4975	5800	7500	10150
2.5 S Sedan 4D		AL11D	19740	5100	5950	7650	10300
2.5 SL Sedan 4D		AL11D	23740	5750	6675	8375	11100
Manual Trans				(525)	(525)	(700)	(700)

ALTIMA—V6—Equipment Schedule 4
W.B. 110.2"; 3.5 Liter.

3.5 SE Sedan 4D		BL11D	23790	6425	7425	9175	12000
Manual Trans				(525)	(525)	(700)	(700)

MAXIMA—V6—Equipment Schedule 4
W.B. 111.2"; 3.5 Liter.

SE Sedan 4D		BA41E	27490	7275	8350	10100	13050
SL Sedan 4D		BA41E	29440	8150	9325	11150	14250

350Z—V6—Equipment Schedule 3
W.B. 104.3"; 3.5 Liter.

Coupe 2D		AZ34D	26910	8425	9625	11550	14800
Enthusiast Coupe 2D		AZ34D	29860	8725	9950	11900	15200
Enthusiast Roadster		AZ36A	35360	10050	11425	13450	16900
Performance Cpe 2D		AZ34D	31070	8900	10150	12100	15450
Track Coupe 2D		AZ34D	34720	9750	11075	13100	16500
Touring Coupe 2D		AZ34D	33820	9275	10575	12550	15950
Touring Roadster 2D		AZ36A	37730	10425	11850	13850	17400

2005 NISSAN — (1N4,JN1or3N1)(CB51D)–5–#

SENTRA—4-Cyl.—Equipment Schedule 6
W.B. 99.8"; 1.8 Liter, 2.5 Liter.

Sedan 4D		CB51D	13280	3575	4300	5875	8275
S Sedan 4D		CB51D	15280	3750	4475	6075	8500
SE-R Sedan 4D		AB51D	18180	4550	5375	7025	9600
SE-R Spec V Sed 4D		AB51D	18380	5525	6400	8050	10750
Special Edition				100	100	135	135

ALTIMA—4-Cyl.—Equipment Schedule 4
W.B. 110.2"; 2.5 Liter.

2.5 Sedan 4D		AL11D	17760	5975	6925	8625	11350
2.5 S Sedan 4D		AL11D	20110	6075	7050	8750	11500
SL				900	900	1200	1200
Manual Trans				(550)	(550)	(735)	(735)

ALTIMA—V6—Equipment Schedule 4
W.B. 110.2"; 3.5 Liter.

3.5 SE Sedan 4D		BL11D	24310	7650	8750	10500	13450
3.5 SL Sedan 4D		BL11D	27460	8025	9200	11000	14000
3.5 SE-R Sedan 4D		BL11D	29760	9000	10250	12050	15250
5-Spd Manual Trans				(550)	(550)	(735)	(735)

MAXIMA—V6—Equipment Schedule 4
W.B. 111.2"; 3.5 Liter.

SE Sedan 4D		BA41E	27660	8200	9375	11150	14200
SL Sedan 4D		BA41E	29910	9175	10425	12200	15400

350Z—V6—Equipment Schedule 3
W.B. 104.3"; 3.5 Liter.

Coupe 2D		AZ35D	27060	9500	10825	12750	16100
Enthusiast Coupe 2D		AZ34D	30010	9850	11175	13150	16550
Enthusiast Roadster		AZ36A	34710	11325	12850	14800	18400
Performance Cpe 2D		AZ34D	31210	10000	11375	13350	16750
Touring Coupe 2D		AZ34D	32360	10425	11850	13800	17300
Touring Roadster 2D		AZ36A	38110	11850	13375	15400	19050
Track Coupe 2D		AZ34D	34860	11025	12500	14450	18050
35th Anniv Coupe 2D		AZ34D	37660	12300	13925	15900	19600
Grand Touring Rdstr		AZ36D	39780	12950	14250	16250	20000

2006 NISSAN — (1N4,JN1or3N1)(CB51D)–6–#

SENTRA—4-Cyl.—Equipment Schedule 6
W.B. 99.8"; 1.8 Liter, 2.5 Liter.

Body	Type	VIN	List	Trade-In Fair	Trade-In Good	Pvt-Party Good	Retail Excellent
Sedan 4D		CB51D	13680	**4050**	**4800**	**6425**	**8900**
S Sedan 4D		CB51D	15680	**4225**	**5000**	**6600**	**9100**
SE-R Sedan 4D		AB51D	16580	**5125**	**5975**	**7650**	**10300**
SE-R Spec V Sed 4D		AB51D	18780	**6150**	**7125**	**8800**	**11550**
Special Edition		------		**100**	**100**	**135**	**135**
ALTIMA—4-Cyl.—Equipment Schedule 4							
W.B. 110.2"; 2.5 Liter.							
2.5 Sedan 4D		AL11D	18230	**7150**	**8225**	**9900**	**12800**
2.5 S Sedan 4D		AL11D	20580	**7250**	**8300**	**10000**	**12900**
SL				**900**	**900**	**1200**	**1200**
5-Spd Manual Trans				**(575)**	**(575)**	**(765)**	**(765)**
ALTIMA—V6—Equipment Schedule 4							
W.B. 110.2"; 3.5 Liter.							
3.5 SE Sedan 4D		BL11D	24730	**8950**	**10200**	**12000**	**15150**
3.5 SL Sedan 4D		BL11D	27880	**9375**	**10675**	**12450**	**15650**
3.5 SE-R Sedan 4D		BL11D	30130	**10425**	**11800**	**13600**	**16900**
5-Spd Manual Trans				**(575)**	**(575)**	**(765)**	**(765)**
6-Spd Manual Trans		------		**0**	**0**	**0**	**0**
MAXIMA—V6—Equipment Schedule 4							
W.B. 111.2"; 3.5 Liter.							
SE Sedan 4D		BA41E	28330	**9250**	**10525**	**12300**	**15450**
SL Sedan 4D		BA41E	30580	**10250**	**11625**	**13400**	**16650**
350Z—V6—Equipment Schedule 3							
W.B. 104.3"; 3.5 Liter.							
Coupe 2D		AZ34D	28030	**10825**	**12300**	**14250**	**17800**
Enthusiast Coupe 2D		AZ34D	30730	**11225**	**12750**	**14650**	**18250**
Enthusiast Roadster		AZ36A	36430	**12875**	**14500**	**16500**	**20300**
Touring Coupe 2D		AZ34D	33330	**11850**	**13425**	**15400**	**19000**
Touring Roadster 2D		AZ36A	39030	**13425**	**15150**	**17150**	**21000**
Track Coupe 2D		AZ34D	34930	**12500**	**14100**	**16050**	**19800**
Grand Touring Cpe 2D		AZ34D	37230	**13425**	**15150**	**17150**	**21000**
Grand Touring Roadstr		AZ36D	41380	**14300**	**16075**	**18100**	**22000**

2007 NISSAN—(1N4,JN1or3N1)(BC11E)-7-#

Body	Type	VIN	List	Trade-In Fair	Trade-In Good	Pvt-Party Good	Retail Excellent
VERSA—4-Cyl.—Equipment Schedule 6							
W.B. 99.8", 102.4" (H'Back); 1.8 Liter.							
S Sedan 4D		BC11E	13165	**6450**	**7450**	**9100**	**11600**
S Hatchback 4D		BC13E	13065	**6375**	**7350**	**8900**	**11500**
SL Sedan 4D		BC11E	15165	**7050**	**8100**	**9650**	**12350**
SL Hatchback 4D		BC13E	15065	**6975**	**8000**	**9575**	**12250**
SENTRA—4-Cyl.—Equipment Schedule 6							
W.B. 105.7"; 2.0 Liter, 2.5 Liter.							
Sedan 4D		AB61E	15365	**6825**	**7875**	**9475**	**12200**
S Sedan 4D		AB61E	16265	**7100**	**8150**	**9750**	**12500**
SL Sedan 4D		AB61E	19015	**7300**	**8400**	**10000**	**12750**
SE-R Sedan 4D		BB61E	20015	**7975**	**9150**	**10850**	**13700**
SE-R Spec V Sed		CB61E	20315	**9175**	**10425**	**12100**	**15150**
ALTIMA—4-Cyl.—Equipment Schedule 4							
W.B. 109.3"; 2.5 Liter.							
2.5 Sedan 4D		AL21E	18565	**9525**	**10825**	**12500**	**15600**
2.5 S Sedan 4D		AL21E	20415	**10050**	**11425**	**13100**	**16200**
SL				**900**	**900**	**1200**	**1200**
ALTIMA—4-Cyl. Hybrid—Equipment Schedule 4							
W.B. 109.3"; 2.5 Liter.							
Sedan 4D		CL21E	25015	**12400**	**14025**	**15700**	**19050**
ALTIMA—V6—Equipment Schedule 4							
W.B. 109.3"; 3.5 Liter.							
3.5 SE Sedan 4D		BL21E	25115	**11950**	**13525**	**15200**	**18500**
3.5 SL Sedan 4D		BL21E	29015	**12400**	**14025**	**15700**	**19050**
MAXIMA—V6—Equipment Schedule 4							
W.B. 111.2"; 3.5 Liter.							
SE Sedan 4D		BA41E	28665	**10775**	**12200**	**13850**	**17000**
SL Sedan 4D		BA41E	30915	**11800**	**13325**	**15000**	**18250**
350Z—V6—Equipment Schedule 3							
W.B. 104.3"; 3.5 Liter.							
Coupe 2D		BZ34D	28515	**12500**	**14100**	**15950**	**19600**
Enthusiast Coupe 2D		BZ34D	30600	**12875**	**14500**	**16400**	**20100**
Enthusiast Roadster		BZ36A	36550	**14700**	**16525**	**18450**	**22300**
Touring Coupe 2D		BZ34D	33200	**13625**	**15325**	**17250**	**21000**
Touring Roadster 2D		BZ36A	38900	**15325**	**17250**	**19150**	**23100**
Grand Touring Cpe 2D		BZ34D	37100	**15325**	**17250**	**19150**	**23100**
Grand Touring Roadstr		BZ36A	41250	**16275**	**18275**	**20300**	**24300**
Nismo Coupe 2D		BZ34D	38695				

Body	Type	VIN	List	Trade-In Fair	Good	Pvt-Party Good	Retail Excellent

2008 NISSAN — (1N4,JN1or3N1)(BC11E)-8-#

VERSA—4-Cyl.—Equipment Schedule 6
W.B. 102.4"; 1.8 Liter.

S Sedan 4D		BC11E	13175	7525	8625	10050	12600
S Hatchback 4D		BC13E	13275	7425	8525	9950	12500
SL Sedan 4D		BC11E	15175	8150	9325	10850	13500
SL Hatchback 4D		BC13E	15275	8075	9225	10700	13400

SENTRA—4-Cyl.—Equipment Schedule 6
W.B. 105.7"; 2.0 Liter, 2.5 Liter.

Sedan 4D		AB61E	16375	7725	8850	10350	13000
S Sedan 4D		AB61E	16605	7975	9150	10650	13400
SL Sedan 4D		AB61E	19305	8200	9375	10900	13650
SE-R Sedan 4D		BB61E	20305	9000	10250	11800	14650
SE-R Spec V Sedan		CB61E	20805	10250	11625	13200	16200

ALTIMA—4-Cyl.—Equipment Schedule 4
W.B. 105.3", 109.3" (Sed); 2.5 Liter.

2.5 S Sedan 4D		AL21E	18855	11125	12600	14100	17200
2.5 S Sedan 4D		AL21E	21205	11700	13225	14800	17950
2.5 S Coupe 2D		AL24E	21615	12450	14075	15750	19100
SL				900	900	1200	1200

ALTIMA—4-Cyl. Hybrid—Equipment Schedule 4
W.B. 109.3"; 2.5 Liter.

Sedan 4D		CL21E	25695	14200	15975	17650	21100

ALTIMA—V6—Equipment Schedule 4
W.B. 105.3", 109.3" (Sed); 3.5 Liter.

3.5 SE Sedan 4D		BL21E	25205	13725	15475	17100	20500
3.5 SE Coupe 2D		BL24E	26015	14300	16075	17750	21300
3.5 SL Sedan 4D		BL21E	28905	14200	15975	17650	21100

MAXIMA—V6—Equipment Schedule 4
W.B. 111.2"; 3.5 Liter.

SE Sedan 4D		BA41E	28755	12925	14550	16100	19400
SL Sedan 4D		BA41E	31005	14025	15775	17350	20800

350Z—V6—Equipment Schedule 3
W.B. 104.3"; 3.5 Liter.

Coupe 2D		BZ34D	28605	14350	16125	18050	21900
Enthusiast Coupe 2D		BZ34D	31305	14750	16600	18500	22300
Enthusiast Roadster		BZ36A	37255	16750	18775	20800	24800
Touring Coupe 2D		BZ34D	33935	15525	17450	19350	23200
Touring Roadster 2D		BZ36A	39605	17450	19550	21500	25600
Grand Touring Cpe 2D		BZ34D	37835	17450	19550	21500	25600
Grand Touring Roadstr		BZ36A	41955	18525	20675	22600	26900
Nismo Coupe 2D		BZ34D	38775				

OLDSMOBILE

1994 OLDSMOBILE — (1or3)G3(NL553)-R-#

ACHIEVA—4-Cyl.—Equipment Schedule 5
W.B. 103.4"; 2.3 Liter.

S Sedan 4D		NL553	16045	250	350	875	1725
S Coupe 2D		NL153	15945	225	325	850	1675
SL Sedan 4D		NF55A	18715	300	425	1000	1875
SC Coupe 2D		NF15A	18715	300	425	1000	1875
V6 3.1 Liter		M		125	125	165	165

CIERA—V6—Equipment Schedule 4
W.B. 104.9"; 3.1 Liter.

S Sedan 4D		AG55M	17725	575	775	1550	2750
4-Cyl. 2.2 Liter		4		(150)	(150)	(200)	(200)

CUTLASS SUPREME—V6—Equipment Schedule 4
W.B. 107.5"; 3.1 Liter.

S Sedan 4D		WH55M	18827	650	925	1725	3050
S Coupe 2D		WH15M	18662	625	825	1625	2875
Convertible Cpe 2D		WT35M	25800	1175	1650	2800	4475
V6 3.4 Liter		X		150	150	200	200

CUTLASS CRUISER—V6—Equipment Schedule 4
W.B. 104.9"; 3.1 Liter.

S Wagon 4D		AJ85M	18757	625	850	1625	2875

EIGHTY EIGHT—V6—Equipment Schedule 4
W.B. 110.8"; 3.8 Liter.

Royale Sedan 4D		HN52L	22480	500	675	1350	2450
Royale LS Sedan 4D		HY52L	23450	525	725	1425	2525

Body	Type	VIN	List	Trade-In Fair	Good	Pvt-Party Good	Retail Excellent
LSS Pkg				50	50	65	65

NINETY EIGHT—V6—Equipment Schedule 4
W.B. 110.8"; 3.8 Liter.

	Regency Sedan 4D	CX52L	26695	800	1125	2000	3425
	Reg Elite Sed 4D	CW53L	28600	800	1125	2050	3475
	V6 3.8L Supercharged	1		150	150	200	200

1995 OLDSMOBILE — (1or2)G3(NL55D)–S–#

ACHIEVA—4-Cyl.—Equipment Schedule 5
W.B. 103.4"; 2.3 Liter.

	S Sedan 4D	NL55D	14750	350	475	1075	2000
	S Coupe 2D	NL15D	14750	325	450	1025	1950
	V6 3.1 Liter	M		125	125	165	165

CIERA—V6—Equipment Schedule 4
W.B. 104.9"; 3.1 Liter.

	SL Sedan 4D	AJ55M	16595	750	1075	1925	3325
	SL Wagon 4D	AJ85M	17595	775	1100	1975	3375
	4-Cyl. 2.2 Liter	4		(150)	(150)	(200)	(200)

CUTLASS SUPREME—V6—Equipment Schedule 4
W.B. 107.5"; 3.1 Liter.

	S Sedan 4D	WH52M	18995	750	1050	1900	3300
	S Coupe 2D	WH12M	18995	675	975	1825	3150
	Convertible 2D	WT32M	26531	1425	1875	3100	4875
	V6 3.4 Liter	X		150	150	200	200

EIGHTY EIGHT—V6—Equipment Schedule 4
W.B. 110.8"; 3.8 Liter.

	Royale Sedan 4D	HN52K	20995	600	800	1575	2825
	Royale LS Sedan 4D	HY52K	23295	625	875	1675	2975
	LSS Pkg			50	50	65	65
	V6 3.8L Supercharged	1		150	150	200	200

NINETY EIGHT—V6—Equipment Schedule 4
W.B. 110.7"; 3.8 Liter.

| | Reg Elite Sed 4D | CX52K | 26695 | 925 | 1325 | 2375 | 4000 |
| | V6 3.8L Supercharged | 1 | | 150 | 150 | 200 | 200 |

AURORA—V8—Equipment Schedule 2
W.B. 113.8"; 4.0 Liter.

| | Sedan 4D | GR52C | 31995 | 1150 | 1600 | 2750 | 4425 |

1996 OLDSMOBILE — (1or2)G3(NL52T)–T–#

ACHIEVA—4-Cyl.—Equipment Schedule 5
W.B. 103.4"; 2.4 Liter.

	SL Sedan 4D	NL52T	15790	425	575	1200	2225
	SC Coupe 2D	NL12T	15790	400	550	1175	2175
	V6 3.1 Liter	M		150	150	200	200

CIERA—V6—Equipment Schedule 4
W.B. 104.9"; 3.1 Liter.

	SL Sedan 4D	AJ55M	15305	800	1125	2025	3475
	SL Wagon 4D	AJ85M	17995	825	1150	2050	3500
	4-Cyl. 2.2 Liter	4		(175)	(175)	(235)	(235)

CUTLASS SUPREME—V6—Equipment Schedule 4
W.B. 107.5"; 3.1 Liter.

	SL Sedan 4D	WH52M	17995	825	1175	2125	3600
	SL Coupe 2D	WH12M	17995	775	1100	2025	3475
	V6 3.4 Liter	X		175	175	235	235

EIGHTY EIGHT—V6—Equipment Schedule 4
W.B. 110.8"; 3.8 Liter.

	Sedan 4D	HN52K	21370	700	975	1850	3200
	LS Sedan 4D	HN52K	23400	725	1025	1925	3325
	LSS Sedan 4D	HY52K	26600	1125	1575	2725	4400
	V6 3.8L Supercharged	1		200	200	265	265

NINETY EIGHT—V6—Equipment Schedule 4
W.B. 110.7"; 3.8 Liter.

| | Reg Elite Sed 4D | CX52K | 28800 | 1150 | 1625 | 2775 | 4475 |

AURORA—V8—Equipment Schedule 2
W.B. 113.8"; 4.0 Liter.

| | Sedan 4D | GR62C | 35000 | 1375 | 1850 | 3050 | 4800 |

1997 OLDSMOBILE — (1or2)G3(NL52T)–V–#

ACHIEVA—4-Cyl.—Equipment Schedule 5
W.B. 103.4"; 2.4 Liter.

| | SL Sedan 4D | NL52T | 15750 | 500 | 700 | 1400 | 2525 |
| | SC Coupe 2D | NL12T | 15950 | 475 | 650 | 1350 | 2450 |

1997 OLDSMOBILE

Body Type	VIN	List	Trade-In Fair	Good	Pvt-Party Good	Retail Excellent
V6 3.1 Liter	M	......	175	175	235	235
CUTLASS—V6—Equipment Schedule 4						
W.B. 107.0"; 3.1 Liter.						
Sedan 4D	WH52T	18170	775	1100	2025	3475
GLS Sedan 4D	WH52M	19225	975	1350	2475	4125
CUTLASS SUPREME—V6—Equipment Schedule 4						
W.B. 107.5"; 3.1 Liter.						
SL Sedan 4D	WH52M	19500	950	1325	2425	4075
SL Coupe 2D	WH12M	19500	875	1225	2325	3950
EIGHTY EIGHT—V6—Equipment Schedule 4						
W.B. 110.8"; 3.8 Liter.						
Sedan 4D	HN52K	23100	825	1150	2100	3600
LS Sedan 4D	HN52K	24400	875	1250	2325	3950
LSS—V6—Equipment Schedule 4						
W.B. 110.8"; 3.8 Liter.						
Sedan 4D	HY52K	28300	1375	1850	3075	4850
V6 3.8L Supercharged	1	......	250	250	335	335
REGENCY—V6—Equipment Schedule 4						
W.B. 110.8"; 3.8 Liter.						
Sedan 4D	HC52K	28600	1500	1975	3200	5000
AURORA—V8—Equipment Schedule 2						
W.B. 113.8"; 4.0 Liter.						
Sedan 4D	GR62C	36400	1325	1825	3025	4750

1998 OLDSMOBILE — (1or2)G3(NL52T)—W—#

Body Type	VIN	List	Trade-In Fair	Good	Pvt-Party Good	Retail Excellent
ACHIEVA—4-Cyl.—Equipment Schedule 5						
W.B. 103.4"; 2.4 Liter.						
SL Sedan 4D	NL52T	18340	725	1025	1950	3375
V6 3.1 Liter	M	......	200	200	265	265
CUTLASS—V6—Equipment Schedule 4						
W.B. 107.0"; 3.1 Liter.						
GL Sedan 4D	NB52M	18950	875	1225	2325	3950
GLS Sedan 4D	NG52M	19950	1100	1550	2700	4375
INTRIGUE—V6—Equipment Schedule 4						
W.B. 109.0"; 3.8 Liter.						
Sedan 4D	WH52K	21250	700	1000	1850	3250
GL Sedan 4D	WS52K	22650	800	1125	2050	3500
GLS Sedan 4D	WX52K	24660	950	1350	2425	4075
EIGHTY EIGHT—V6—Equipment Schedule 4						
W.B. 110.8"; 3.8 Liter.						
Sedan 4D	HN52K	23400	975	1375	2500	4175
LS Sedan 4D	HN52K	24800	1050	1475	2625	4300
LSS—V6—Equipment Schedule 4						
W.B. 110.8"; 3.8 Liter.						
Sedan 4D	HY52K	28700	1700	2200	3450	5300
V6 3.8L Supercharged	1	......	300	300	400	400
REGENCY—V6—Equipment Schedule 4						
W.B. 110.8"; 3.8 Liter.						
Sedan 4D	HC52K	29000	1825	2350	3600	5475
AURORA—V8—Equipment Schedule 2						
W.B. 113.8"; 4.0 Liter.						
Sedan 4D	GR62C	36625	1350	1850	3075	4825

1999 OLDSMOBILE — (1or2)G3(NK52T)—X—#

Body Type	VIN	List	Trade-In Fair	Good	Pvt-Party Good	Retail Excellent
ALERO—4-Cyl.—Equipment Schedule 5						
W.B. 107.0"; 2.4 Liter.						
GX Sedan 4D	NK52T	16850	850	1225	2300	3950
GX Coupe 2D	NK12T	16850	800	1125	2100	3600
GL Sedan 4D	NL52T	18745	975	1375	2500	4175
GL Coupe 2D	NL12T	19180	925	1300	2400	4075
V6 3.4 Liter	E	......	200	200	265	265
ALERO—V6—Equipment Schedule 4						
W.B. 107.0"; 3.4 Liter.						
GLS Sedan 4D	NF52E	21400	1450	1925	3125	4925
GLS Coupe 2D	NF12E	21400	1325	1825	3025	4775
CUTLASS—V6—Equipment Schedule 4						
W.B. 107.0"; 3.1 Liter.						
GL Sedan 4D	NB52M	19325	1000	1400	2550	4250
GLS Sedan 4D	NG52M	20250	1250	1725	2950	4700
INTRIGUE—V6—Equipment Schedule 4						
W.B. 109.0"; 3.5 Liter, 3.8 Liter.						
GX Sedan 4D	WH52K	21735	825	1175	2150	3675

Body	Type	VIN	List	Trade-In Fair	Trade-In Good	Pvt-Party Good	Retail Excellent
GL Sedan 4D		WS52K	23135	950	1350	2475	4150
GLS Sedan 4D		WX52H	25505	1150	1625	2800	4500

EIGHTY EIGHT—V6—Equipment Schedule 4
W.B. 110.8"; 3.8 Liter.

Body	Type	VIN	List	Fair	Good	Good	Excellent
Sedan 4D		HN52K	24170	1175	1625	2825	4550
LS Sedan 4D		HN52K	25720	1275	1750	2975	4725

LSS—V6—Equipment Schedule 4
W.B. 110.8"; 3.8 Liter.

Body	Type	VIN	List	Fair	Good	Good	Excellent
Sedan 4D		HY52K	29720	2025	2575	3875	5800
V6 3.8L Supercharged		1		325	325	435	435

AURORA—V8—Equipment Schedule 2
W.B. 113.8"; 4.0 Liter.

Body	Type	VIN	List	Fair	Good	Good	Excellent
Sedan 4D		GR62C	36899	1500	2000	3225	5050

2000 OLDSMOBILE — (1or2)G3(NK52T)-Y-#

ALERO—4-Cyl.—Equipment Schedule 5
W.B. 107.0"; 2.4 Liter.

Body	Type	VIN	List	Fair	Good	Good	Excellent
GX Sedan 4D		NK52T	16995	1075	1525	2675	4375
GX Coupe 2D		NK12T	16995	1025	1425	2575	4275
GL Sedan 4D		NL52T	18185	1175	1650	2850	4575
GL Coupe 2D		NL12T	18185	1125	1600	2775	4500
V6 3.4 Liter		E		200	200	265	265

ALERO—V6—Equipment Schedule 4
W.B. 107.0"; 3.4 Liter.

Body	Type	VIN	List	Fair	Good	Good	Excellent
GLS Sedan 4D		NF52E	21900	1875	2400	3675	5525
GLS Coupe 2D		NF12E	21900	1775	2300	3550	5400

INTRIGUE—V6—Equipment Schedule 4
W.B. 109.0"; 3.5 Liter.

Body	Type	VIN	List	Fair	Good	Good	Excellent
GX Sedan 4D		WH52H	22650	1000	1400	2525	4225
GL Sedan 4D		WS52H	24280	1125	1600	2775	4500
GLS Sedan 4D		WX52H	26280	1475	1950	3175	4975
Sterling Edition				50	50	65	65

2001 OLDSMOBILE — 1G3(NK52T)-1-#

ALERO—4-Cyl.—Equipment Schedule 5
W.B. 107.0"; 2.4 Liter.

Body	Type	VIN	List	Fair	Good	Good	Excellent
GX Sedan 4D		NK52T	17785	1300	1775	3000	4775
GX Coupe 2D		NK12T	17785	1200	1675	2925	4675
GL Sedan 4D		NL52T	19195	1450	1925	3175	5000
GL Coupe 2D		NL12T	19195	1375	1850	3100	4900
V6 3.4 Liter		E		200	200	265	265

ALERO—V6—Equipment Schedule 4
W.B. 107.0"; 3.4 Liter.

Body	Type	VIN	List	Fair	Good	Good	Excellent
GLS Sedan 4D		NF52E	22540	2275	2850	4150	6075
GLS Coupe 2D		NF12E	22765	2125	2700	4000	5900

INTRIGUE—V6—Equipment Schedule 4
W.B. 109.0"; 3.5 Liter.

Body	Type	VIN	List	Fair	Good	Good	Excellent
GX Sedan 4D		WH52H	22995	1175	1650	2850	4600
GL Sedan 4D		WS52H	24750	1450	1925	3150	4950
GLS Sedan 4D		WX52H	27115	1850	2375	3650	5525

AURORA—V6—Equipment Schedule 2
W.B. 112.2"; 3.5 Liter.

Body	Type	VIN	List	Fair	Good	Good	Excellent
Sedan 4D		GR64H	31579	1950	2500	3800	5700

AURORA—V8—Equipment Schedule 2
W.B. 112.2"; 4.0 Liter.

Body	Type	VIN	List	Fair	Good	Good	Excellent
Sedan 4D		GS64C	35314	2775	3400	4750	6800

2002 OLDSMOBILE — 1G3(NK52T)-2-#

ALERO—4-Cyl.—Equipment Schedule 5
W.B. 107.0"; 2.2 Liter.

Body	Type	VIN	List	Fair	Good	Good	Excellent
GX Sedan 4D		NK52T	18055	1550	2025	3450	5500
GX Coupe 2D		NK12T	18055	1450	1925	3350	5375
GL Sedan 4D		NL52T	20040	1700	2200	3625	5675
GL Coupe 2D		NL12T	20265	1625	2125	3550	5575
V6 3.4 Liter		E		200	200	265	265

ALERO—V6—Equipment Schedule 4
W.B. 107.0"; 3.4 Liter.

Body	Type	VIN	List	Fair	Good	Good	Excellent
GLS Sedan 4D		NF52E	22675	2650	3250	4725	6925
GLS Coupe 2D		NF12E	22900	2500	3075	4550	6750

INTRIGUE—V6—Equipment Schedule 2
W.B. 109.0"; 3.5 Liter.

Body	Type	VIN	List	Fair	Good	Good	Excellent
GX Sedan 4D		WH52H	23427	1375	1850	3225	5225

2002 OLDSMOBILE

Body	Type	VIN	List	Trade-In Fair	Good	Pvt-Party Good	Retail Excellent
GL Sedan 4D		WS52H	25012	1675	2175	3600	5600
GLS Sedan 4D		WX52H	28502	2150	2725	4150	6250

AURORA—V6—Equipment Schedule 2
W.B. 112.2"; 3.5 Liter.

| Sedan 4D | | GR64H | 31665 | 1975 | 2525 | 4000 | 6100 |

AURORA—V8—Equipment Schedule 2
W.B. 112.2"; 4.0 Liter.

| Sedan 4D | | GS64C | 35660 | 2850 | 3475 | 4975 | 7225 |

2003 OLDSMOBILE — 1G3(NK52F)-3-#

ALERO—4-Cyl.—Equipment Schedule 5
W.B. 107.0"; 2.2 Liter.

GX Sedan 4D		NK52F	18335	1850	2375	3825	5900
GX Coupe 2D		NK12F	18335	1750	2250	3700	5750
GL Sedan 4D		NL52F	20175	2050	2625	4075	6175
GL Coupe 2D		NL12F	20175	2000	2550	4000	6100
V6 3.4 Liter		E		250	250	335	335

ALERO—V6—Equipment Schedule 4
W.B. 107.0"; 3.4 Liter.

| GLS Sedan 4D | | NF52E | 22755 | 3100 | 3775 | 5300 | 7550 |
| GLS Coupe 2D | | NF12E | 23005 | 2950 | 3575 | 5100 | 7325 |

AURORA—V8—Equipment Schedule 2
W.B. 112.2"; 4.0 Liter.

| Sedan 4D | | GS64C | 34775 | 3350 | 4050 | 5575 | 7925 |

2004 OLDSMOBILE — 1G3(NK52F)-4-#

ALERO—4-Cyl.—Equipment Schedule 5
W.B. 107.0"; 2.2 Liter.

GX Sedan 4D		NK52F	18825	2225	2800	4275	6400
GX Coupe 2D		NK12F	18825	2075	2650	4125	6225
GL Sedan 4D		NL52F	20775	2500	3100	4575	6750
GL Coupe 2D		NL12F	20775	2450	3050	4500	6675
V6 3.4 Liter		E		275	275	365	365

ALERO—V6—Equipment Schedule 4
W.B. 107.0"; 3.4 Liter.

| GLS Sedan 4D | | NF52E | 23425 | 3675 | 4375 | 5875 | 8200 |
| GLS Coupe 2D | | NF12E | 23675 | 3475 | 4175 | 5650 | 7975 |

PLYMOUTH

1994 PLYMOUTH — (1,3,4orJ)P3-(A11A)-R-#

COLT—4-Cyl.—Equipment Schedule 6
W.B. 96.1", 98.4" (4D); 1.5 Liter, 1.8 Liter.

Sedan 2D		A11A	10779	450	625	1250	2275
Sedan 4D		A36C	13428	550	750	1500	2700
GL Sedan 2D		A21A	11400	500	675	1375	2450
GL Sedan 4D		A46C	13824	600	800	1575	2800

COLT VISTA—4-Cyl.—Equipment Schedule 6
W.B. 99.2"; 1.8 Liter, 2.4 Liter.

Wagon 3D		B30C	14565	1050	1475	2575	4225
SE Wagon 3D		B50G	16233	1125	1575	2675	4325
AWD Wagon 3D		C40G	16777	1225	1700	2875	4550

SUNDANCE—4-Cyl.—Equipment Schedule 5
W.B. 97.2"; 2.2 Liter, 2.5 Liter.

| Hatchback 2D | | P24D | 11052 | 275 | 375 | 900 | 1775 |
| Sedan 4D | | P28D | 11452 | 300 | 425 | 950 | 1850 |

SUNDANCE—V6—Equipment Schedule 5
W.B. 97.2"; 3.0 Liter.

Duster Hatchback 2D		P643	13008	400	550	1150	2100
Duster Sedan 4D		P683	13408	400	575	1150	2125
4-Cyl. 2.5 Liter		K		(100)	(100)	(135)	(135)

LASER—4-Cyl.—Equipment Schedule 4
W.B. 97.2"; 1.8 Liter, 2.0 Liter.

Hatchback 2D		F34B	14042	675	950	1775	3075
RS Hatchback 2D		F44E	16353	750	1050	1900	3300
Auto Trans				125	125	165	165

LASER—4-Cyl. Turbo—Equipment Schedule 4
W.B. 97.2"; 2.0 Liter.

RS Hatchback 2D		F44F	17887	800	1125	2050	3475
RS AWD H'Back 2D		G44F	20015	1075	1500	2625	4275
Auto Trans				125	125	165	165

Body	Type	VIN	List	Trade-In Fair	Trade-In Good	Pvt-Party Good	Retail Excellent
ACCLAIM—4-Cyl.—Equipment Schedule 5							
W.B. 103.5"; 2.5 Liter.							
Sedan 4D		A46K	14154	350	500	1100	2050
V6 3.0 Liter		3		150	150	200	200

1995 PLYMOUTH — (1,3,4orJ)P3–(S27C)–S–#

NEON—4-Cyl.—Equipment Schedule 6							
W.B. 104.0"; 2.0 Liter.							
Sedan 4D		S27C	12195	275	375	925	1800
Highline Sedan 4D		S47C	12443	350	475	1075	2000
Highline Coupe 2D		S41C	12443	300	425	1000	1925
Sport Sedan 4D		S67C	14393	450	600	1250	2275
Sport Coupe 2D		S61C	14693	525	700	1450	2625
ACCLAIM—4-Cyl.—Equipment Schedule 5							
W.B. 103.5"; 2.5 Liter.							
Sedan 4D		A46K	14828	450	625	1275	2350
V6 3.0 Liter		3		375	375	500	500

1996 PLYMOUTH — (1or3)P3–(S27C)–T–#

NEON—4-Cyl.—Equipment Schedule 6							
W.B. 104.0"; 2.0 Liter.							
Sedan 4D		S27C	11730	300	425	1000	1925
Coupe 2D		S22C	11230	300	400	975	1875
Highline Sedan 4D		S47C	12735	400	550	1175	2175
Highline Coupe 2D		S42C	12535	375	525	1125	2100
Sport Sedan 4D		S67C	14165	500	700	1375	2475
Sport Coupe 2D		S62C	13965	600	800	1575	2825
BREEZE—4-Cyl.—Equipment Schedule 5							
W.B. 108.0"; 2.0 Liter.							
Sedan 4D		J46C	15645	425	600	1250	2275

1997 PLYMOUTH — (1or3)P3–(S27C)–V–#

NEON—4-Cyl.—Equipment Schedule 6							
W.B. 104.0"; 2.0 Liter.							
Sedan 4D		S27C	12430	350	500	1125	2100
Coupe 2D		S22C	12230	350	475	1075	2050
Highline Sedan 4D		S47C	13170	475	625	1325	2400
Highline Coupe 2D		S42C	12970	425	600	1250	2300
BREEZE—4-Cyl.—Equipment Schedule 5							
W.B. 108.0"; 2.0 Liter.							
Sedan 4D		J46C	16380	425	600	1250	2300
PROWLER—V6—Equipment Schedule 1							
W.B. 113.0"; 3.5 Liter.							
Roadster 2D		W65F	39000	13025	14700	17300	21800

1998 PLYMOUTH — (1or3)P3–(S47C)–W–#

NEON—4-Cyl.—Equipment Schedule 6							
W.B. 104.0"; 2.0 Liter.							
Highline Sedan 4D		S47C	12855	550	750	1500	2700
Highline Coupe 2D		S42C	12655	525	700	1450	2625
Competition Sedan 4D		S27C	14660	800	1125	2075	3550
Competition Coupe 2D		S22C	14480	775	1100	2025	3500
BREEZE—4-Cyl.—Equipment Schedule 5							
W.B. 108.0"; 2.0 Liter, 2.4 Liter.							
Sedan 4D		J46C	16260	450	625	1300	2400

1999 PLYMOUTH — (1or3)P3(EorH)(S47C)–X–#

NEON—4-Cyl.—Equipment Schedule 6							
W.B. 104.0"; 2.0 Liter.							
Highline Sedan 4D		S47C	13320	650	925	1800	3150
Highline Coupe 2D		S42C	13120	625	875	1725	3075
Competition Sedan 4D		S27C	14985	950	1325	2450	4100
Competition Coupe 2D		S22C	14805	925	1300	2400	4050
BREEZE—4-Cyl.—Equipment Schedule 5							
W.B. 108.0"; 2.0 Liter, 2.4 Liter.							
Sedan 4D		J46C	16700	500	675	1425	2625
PROWLER—V6—Equipment Schedule 1							
W.B. 113.3"; 3.5 Liter.							
Roadster 2D		W65G	40000	15575	17500	20100	24800

Body	Type	VIN	List	Trade-In Fair	Trade-In Good	Pvt-Party Good	Retail Excellent

2000 PLYMOUTH — (1or3)P3(EorH)(S46C)–Y–#

NEON—4-Cyl.—Equipment Schedule 6
W.B. 105.0"; 2.0 Liter.

Highline Sedan 4D		S46C	13890	800	1100	2075	3600
LX Sedan 4D		S46C	14680	1075	1525	2700	4375

BREEZE—4-Cyl.—Equipment Schedule 5
W.B. 108.0"; 2.0 Liter, 2.4 Liter.

Sedan 4D		J46C	17525	600	800	1675	3050

PROWLER—V6—Equipment Schedule 1
W.B. 113.3"; 3.5 Liter.

Roadster 2D		W65G	43500	16950	19000	21700	26600

2001 PLYMOUTH — 1P3(EorH)(S46C)–1–#

NEON—4-Cyl.—Equipment Schedule 6
W.B. 105.0"; 2.0 Liter.

Highline Sedan 4D		S46C	14275	975	1375	2550	4250
LX Sedan 4D		S46C	15095	1325	1800	3050	4800

PONTIAC

1994 PONTIAC — (1G,JGorKL)2(JB54H)–R–#

SUNBIRD—4-Cyl.—Equipment Schedule 5
W.B. 101.3"; 2.0 Liter.

LE Sedan 4D		JB54H	11519	300	425	1000	1875
LE Coupe 2D		JB14H	11519	300	425	1000	1875
LE Convertible 2D		JB34H	17279	675	950	1750	3050
V6 3.1 Liter		T		100	100	135	135

SUNBIRD—V6—Equipment Schedule 5
W.B. 101.3"; 3.1 Liter.

SE Coupe 2D		JL14T	14179	375	525	1100	2050

GRAND AM—4-Cyl.—Equipment Schedule 5
W.B. 103.4"; 2.3 Liter.

SE Sedan 4D		NE553	14484	525	725	1450	2625
SE Coupe 2D		NE153	14384	525	725	1450	2625
GT Sedan 4D		NW55A	16354	600	825	1600	2825
GT Coupe 2D		NW15A	16254	575	775	1550	2750
Manual Trans				0	0	0	0
V6 3.1 Liter		M		125	125	165	165

FIREBIRD—V6—Equipment Schedule 4
W.B. 101.1"; 3.4 Liter.

Hatchback 2D		FS22S	16735	1500	1975	3200	4975
Convertible 2D		FS32S	22444	2325	2900	4225	6175
Manual Trans				(150)	(150)	(200)	(200)

FIREBIRD—V8—Equipment Schedule 4
W.B. 101.1"; 5.7 Liter.

Formula H'Back 2D		FV22P	19615	2025	2600	3875	5750
Formula Convertible 2D		FV32P	25544	2950	3575	4975	7075
Trans Am H'Back 2D		FV22P	21005	2375	2975	4300	6250
Trans Am GT H'Bk 2D		FV22P	22505	2525	3100	4425	6450
Trans Am GT Conv 2D		FV32P	27744	3600	4300	5750	8025

GRAND PRIX—V6—Equipment Schedule 4
W.B. 107.5"; 3.1 Liter.

SE Sedan 4D		WJ52M	17094	550	750	1500	2700
SE Coupe 2D		WJ16M	17295	475	650	1375	2525
GT/GTP Pkg				50	50	65	65
V6 3.4 Liter		X		150	150	200	200

BONNEVILLE—V6—Equipment Schedule 4
W.B. 110.8"; 3.8 Liter.

SE Sedan 4D		HX52L	21627	575	775	1500	2700
SSE Sedan 4D		HZ52L	26459	725	1025	1850	3200
SLE Pkg				75	75	100	100

BONNEVILLE—V6 Supercharged—Equipment Schedule 4
W.B. 110.8"; 3.8 Liter.

SSEi Sedan 4D		HZ521	29141	1100	1525	2625	4275

1995 PONTIAC — (1G,JGorKL)2(JB524)–S–#

SUNFIRE—4-Cyl.—Equipment Schedule 5
W.B. 104.1"; 2.2 Liter, 2.3 Liter.

SE Sedan 4D		JB524	12989	400	550	1150	2125

1995 PONTIAC

Body Type	VIN	List	Trade-In Fair	Trade-In Good	Pvt-Party Good	Retail Excellent
SE Coupe 2D	JB124	12839	350	500	1100	2050
SE Convertible 2D	JB324	18034	850	1175	2100	3550
GT Coupe 2D	JD12D	14824	525	725	1475	2650
GRAND AM—4-Cyl.—Equipment Schedule 5						
W.B. 103.4"; 2.3 Liter.						
SE Sedan 4D	NE55D	15084	625	850	1650	2925
SE Coupe 2D	NE15D	14984	625	850	1650	2925
GT Sedan 4D	NW55D	16204	700	975	1825	3150
GT Coupe 2D	NW15D	16104	675	950	1775	3075
Manual Trans			0	0	0	0
V6 3.1 Liter	M		125	125	165	165
FIREBIRD—V6—Equipment Schedule 4						
W.B. 101.1"; 3.4 Liter.						
Hatchback 2D	FS22S	17764	1575	2050	3250	5050
Convertible 2D	FS32S	23214	2425	3025	4325	6325
V6 3.8 Liter	K		100	100	135	135
FIREBIRD—V8—Equipment Schedule 4						
W.B. 101.1"; 5.7 Liter.						
Formula H'Back 2D	FV22P	21450	2100	2675	3950	5850
Formula Convertible 2D	FV22P	26404	3050	3700	5100	7225
Trans Am H'Back 2D	FV22P	22344	2475	3075	4375	6400
Trans Am Conv 2D	FV32P	28414	3725	4425	5925	8200
GRAND PRIX—V6—Equipment Schedule 4						
W.B. 107.5"; 3.1 Liter.						
SE Sedan 4D	WJ52M	17589	625	875	1675	2975
SE Coupe 2D	WJ16M	17919	575	775	1550	2800
GT/GTP Pkg			50	50	65	65
V6 3.4 Liter	X		150	150	200	200
BONNEVILLE—V6—Equipment Schedule 4						
W.B. 110.8"; 3.8 Liter.						
SE Sedan 4D	HX52K	21584	650	925	1725	3050
SSE Sedan 4D	HZ52K	26389	875	1250	2200	3675
SLE Pkg			75	75	100	100
V6 3.8L Supercharged (SE)	1		150	150	200	200
BONNEVILLE—V6 Supercharged—Equipment Schedule 4						
W.B. 110.8"; 3.8 Liter.						
SSEi Sedan 4D	HZ521	27556	1300	1775	2975	4675

1996 PONTIAC — (1,2,3or4)G2(JB524)-T-#

Body Type	VIN	List	Trade-In Fair	Trade-In Good	Pvt-Party Good	Retail Excellent
SUNFIRE—4-Cyl.—Equipment Schedule 5						
W.B. 104.1"; 2.2 Liter, 2.4 Liter.						
SE Sedan 4D	JB524	13514	475	650	1325	2400
SE Coupe 2D	JB124	13344	450	625	1250	2300
SE Convertible 2D	JB324	18229	1000	1425	2500	4150
GT Coupe 2D	JD12T	15299	625	875	1700	3000
GRAND AM—4-Cyl.—Equipment Schedule 5						
W.B. 103.4"; 2.4 Liter.						
SE Sedan 4D	NE52T	15624	725	1050	1900	3300
SE Coupe 2D	NE12T	15624	725	1050	1900	3300
GT Sedan 4D	NW52T	16794	850	1200	2125	3600
GT Coupe 2D	NW12T	16794	825	1150	2050	3500
Manual Trans			0	0	0	0
V6 3.1 Liter	M		150	150	200	200
FIREBIRD—V6—Equipment Schedule 4						
W.B. 101.1"; 3.8 Liter.						
Coupe 2D	FS22K	19408	1850	2400	3650	5525
Convertible 2D	FS32K	23739	2825	3450	4825	6900
Manual Trans			(200)	(200)	(265)	(265)
FIREBIRD—V8—Equipment Schedule 4						
W.B. 101.1"; 5.7 Liter.						
Formula Coupe 2D	FV22P	22363	2500	3075	4400	6425
Formula Conv 2D	FV32P	26579	3575	4300	5725	7975
Trans Am Coupe 2D	FV22P	22709	2900	3525	4900	7000
Trans Am Conv 2D	FV32P	28659	4325	5125	6650	9075
Ram Air Handling Pkg			575	575	765	765
GRAND PRIX—V6—Equipment Schedule 4						
W.B. 107.5"; 3.1 Liter.						
SE Sedan 4D	WJ52M	18049	700	975	1850	3200
SE Coupe 2D	WJ12M	18899	625	875	1675	3000
GT/GTP Pkg			75	75	100	100
V6 3.4 Liter	X		175	175	235	235
BONNEVILLE—V6—Equipment Schedule 4						
W.B. 110.8"; 3.8 Liter.						

Body	Type	VIN	List	Trade-In Fair	Trade-In Good	Pvt-Party Good	Retail Excellent
SE Sedan 4D		HX52K	22374	775	1100	2000	3425
SSE Sedan 4D		HZ52K	27149	1050	1475	2600	4250
SLE Pkg				100	100	135	135
V6 3.8L Supercharged (SE)		1		200	200	265	265

BONNEVILLE—V6 Supercharged—Equipment Schedule 4
W.B. 110.8"; 3.8 Liter.

Body	Type	VIN	List	Fair	Good	Good	Excellent
SSEi Sedan 4D		HZ521	28491	1650	2150	3350	5175

1997 PONTIAC — (1,2,3or4)G2(JB524)–V–#

SUNFIRE—4-Cyl.—Equipment Schedule 5
W.B. 104.1"; 2.2 Liter, 2.4 Liter.

Body	Type	VIN	List	Fair	Good	Good	Excellent
SE Sedan 4D		JB524	14079	600	800	1600	2875
SE Coupe 2D		JB124	13939	550	750	1550	2800
SE Convertible 2D		JB324	19399	1225	1700	2900	4600
GT Coupe 2D		JD12T	15859	750	1075	1950	3375

GRAND AM—4-Cyl.—Equipment Schedule 5
W.B. 103.4"; 2.4 Liter.

Body	Type	VIN	List	Fair	Good	Good	Excellent
SE Sedan 4D		NE52T	15969	900	1250	2325	3950
SE Coupe 2D		NE12T	15969	900	1250	2325	3950
GT Sedan 4D		NW52T	17209	1025	1425	2550	4200
GT Coupe 2D		NW12T	17209	975	1375	2475	4125
Manual Trans				0	0	0	0
V6 3.1 Liter		M		175	175	235	235

FIREBIRD—V6—Equipment Schedule 4
W.B. 101.1"; 3.8 Liter.

Body	Type	VIN	List	Fair	Good	Good	Excellent
Coupe 2D		FS22K	19209	1950	2500	3750	5625
Convertible 2D		FS32K	24374	3050	3675	5075	7175
Manual Trans				(250)	(250)	(335)	(335)

FIREBIRD—V8—Equipment Schedule 4
W.B. 101.1"; 5.7 Liter.

Body	Type	VIN	List	Fair	Good	Good	Excellent
Formula Coupe 2D		FV22P	21179	2800	3400	4750	6800
Formula Conv 2D		FV22P	26979	3900	4625	6100	8400
Trans Am Coupe 2D		FV22P	23339	3325	4025	5425	7600
Trans Am Conv 2D		FV32P	28899	4800	5625	7250	9800
Ram Air Handling Pkg				650	650	865	865

GRAND PRIX—V6—Equipment Schedule 4
W.B. 110.5"; 3.8 Liter.

Body	Type	VIN	List	Fair	Good	Good	Excellent
SE Sedan 4D		WJ52K	19249	775	1075	2000	3475
GT Sedan 4D		WP52K	20359	1075	1525	2675	4350
GT Coupe 2D		WP12K	20029	1000	1400	2525	4200
GTP Pkg				100	100	135	135
V6 3.1 Liter		M		(250)	(250)	(335)	(335)
V6 3.8L Supercharged		1		275	275	365	365

BONNEVILLE—V6—Equipment Schedule 4
W.B. 110.8"; 3.8 Liter.

Body	Type	VIN	List	Fair	Good	Good	Excellent
SE Sedan 4D		HX52K	22914	950	1325	2425	4075
SSE Sedan 4D		HZ52K	27769	1325	1800	3000	4750
SLE				125	125	165	165
V6 3.8L Superchrgd (SE)		1		250	250	335	335

BONNEVILLE—V6 Supercharged—Equipment Schedule 4
W.B. 110.8"; 3.8 Liter.

Body	Type	VIN	List	Fair	Good	Good	Excellent
SSEi Sedan 4D		HZ521	29111	2000	2550	3850	5725

1998 PONTIAC — (1,2,3or4)G2(JB524)–W–#

SUNFIRE—4-Cyl.—Equipment Schedule 5
W.B. 104.1"; 2.2 Liter, 2.4 Liter.

Body	Type	VIN	List	Fair	Good	Good	Excellent
SE Sedan 4D		JB524	14425	700	1000	1875	3300
SE Coupe 2D		JB124	14425	675	950	1825	3200
SE Convertible 2D		JB324	19995	1575	2050	3275	5100
GT Coupe 2D		JD12T	16805	900	1275	2375	4025

GRAND AM—4-Cyl.—Equipment Schedule 5
W.B. 103.4"; 2.4 Liter.

Body	Type	VIN	List	Fair	Good	Good	Excellent
SE Sedan 4D		NE52T	16359	1075	1525	2650	4325
SE Coupe 2D		NE12T	16209	1075	1525	2650	4325
GT Sedan 4D		NW52T	17809	1200	1675	2850	4575
GT Coupe 2D		NW12T	17659	1150	1600	2775	4475
Manual Trans				0	0	0	0
V6 3.1 Liter		M		200	200	265	265

FIREBIRD—V6—Equipment Schedule 4
W.B. 101.1"; 3.8 Liter.

Body	Type	VIN	List	Fair	Good	Good	Excellent
Coupe 2D		FS22K	20380	2075	2650	3950	5850
Convertible 2D		FS32K	25545	3250	3925	5325	7500

1998 PONTIAC

Body	Type	VIN	List	Trade-In Fair	Good	Pvt-Party Good	Retail Excellent
	T-Bar Roof	-------	-------	275 (300)	275 (300)	365 (400)	365 (400)
	Manual Trans	-------	-------				
FIREBIRD—V8—Equipment Schedule 4							
W.B. 101.1"; 5.7 Liter.							
	Formula Coupe 2D	FV22P	23290	3075	3750	5150	7275
	Trans Am Coupe 2D	FV22P	26400	3825	4525	6000	8275
	Trans Am Conv 2D	FV32P	30140	5300	6175	7825	10450
	T-Bar Roof	-------	-------	275	275	365	365
	Ram Air Handling Pkg	-------	-------	725	725	965	965
GRAND PRIX—V6—Equipment Schedule 4							
W.B. 110.5"; 3.8 Liter.							
	SE Sedan 4D	WJ52K	19885	800	1125	2100	3600
	GT Sedan 4D	WP52K	21215	1200	1675	2875	4600
	GT Coupe 2D	WP12K	20965	1075	1500	2650	4325
	GTP Pkg			100	100	135	135
	V6 3.1 Liter	M		(250)	(250)	(335)	(335)
	V6 3.8L Supercharged	1		300	300	400	400
BONNEVILLE—V6—Equipment Schedule 4							
W.B. 110.8"; 3.8 Liter.							
	SE Sedan 4D	HX52K	23215	1125	1575	2725	4425
	SSE Sedan 4D	HZ52K	29895	1675	2175	3400	5250
	SLE Pkg			150	150	200	200
BONNEVILLE—V6 Supercharged—Equipment Schedule 4							
W.B. 110.8"; 3.8 Liter.							
	SSEi Sedan 4D	HZ521	31165	2375	2975	4300	6250

1999 PONTIAC — (1,2,3or4)G2(JB524)-X-#

Body	Type	VIN	List	Trade-In Fair	Good	Pvt-Party Good	Retail Excellent
SUNFIRE—4-Cyl.—Equipment Schedule 5							
W.B. 104.1"; 2.2 Liter, 2.4 Liter.							
	SE Sedan 4D	JB524	14685	850	1225	2300	3950
	SE Coupe 2D	JB124	14685	825	1175	2150	3675
	GT Coupe 2D	JD12T	17065	1075	1525	2675	4350
	GT Convertible 2D	JB32T	21655	2025	2575	3850	5725
GRAND AM—4-Cyl.—Equipment Schedule 5							
W.B. 106.7"; 2.4 Liter.							
	SE Sedan 4D	NE52T	16995	1100	1550	2700	4375
	SE Coupe 2D	NE12T	16595	1100	1550	2700	4375
	V6 3.4 Liter	E		225	225	300	300
GRAND AM—V6—Equipment Schedule 5							
W.B. 106.7"; 3.4 Liter.							
	GT Sedan 4D	NW52E	19995	1550	2050	3275	5075
	GT Coupe 2D	NW12E	19595	1500	2000	3225	5025
FIREBIRD—V6—Equipment Schedule 4							
W.B. 101.1"; 3.8 Liter.							
	Coupe 2D	FS22K	20540	2300	2875	4175	6125
	Convertible 2D	FS32K	26465	3525	4250	5625	7850
	T-Bar Roof	-------	-------	300	300	400	400
	Manual Trans	-------	-------	(350)	(350)	(465)	(465)
FIREBIRD—V8—Equipment Schedule 4							
W.B. 101.1"; 5.7 Liter.							
	Formula Coupe 2D	FV22G	23930	3500	4200	5600	7800
	Trans Am Coupe 2D	FV22G	27040	4350	5150	6650	9000
	Trans Am Conv 2D	FV32G	31110	5875	6800	8475	11150
	T-Bar Roof	-------	-------	300	300	400	400
	Ram Air Handling Pkg	-------	-------	800	800	1065	1065
GRAND PRIX—V6—Equipment Schedule 4							
W.B. 110.5"; 3.8 Liter.							
	SE Sedan 4D	WJ52K	20210	875	1225	2350	4025
	GT Sedan 4D	WP52K	21705	1425	1900	3150	4975
	GT Coupe 2D	WP12K	21555	1150	1625	2825	4575
	V6 3.1 Liter	M		(250)	(250)	(335)	(335)
GRAND PRIX—V6 Supercharged—Equipment Schedule 4							
W.B. 110.5"; 3.8 Liter.							
	GTP Sedan 4D	WR521	24470	2200	2800	4100	6025
	GTP Coupe 2D	WR121	24320	2125	2700	3975	5900
BONNEVILLE—V6—Equipment Schedule 4							
W.B. 110.8"; 3.8 Liter.							
	SE Sedan 4D	HX52K	23715	1350	1850	3075	4850
	SSE Sedan 4D	HZ52K	30715	2050	2600	3900	5800
	SLE Pkg			150	150	200	200
BONNEVILLE—V6 Supercharged—Equipment Schedule 4							
W.B. 110.8"; 3.8 Liter.							
	SSEi Sedan 4D	HZ521	31665	2800	3425	4750	6800

2000 PONTIAC

Body	Type	VIN	List	Trade-In Fair	Good	Pvt-Party Good	Retail Excellent

2000 PONTIAC — (1,2,3or4)G2(JB524)-Y-#

SUNFIRE—4-Cyl.—Equipment Schedule 5
W.B. 104.1"; 2.2 Liter, 2.4 Liter.

SE Sedan 4D		JB524	15120	950	1350	2475	4175
SE Coupe 2D		JB124	15020	925	1300	2425	4100
GT Coupe 2D		JD12T	17530	1175	1650	2850	4575
GT Convertible 2D		JD32T	22120	2300	2875	4150	6075

GRAND AM—4-Cyl.—Equipment Schedule 5
W.B. 107.0"; 2.4 Liter.

SE Sedan 4D		NE52T	17540	1350	1850	3075	4850
SE Coupe 2D		NE12T	17240	1350	1850	3075	4850
V6 3.4 Liter		E		250	250	335	335

GRAND AM—V6—Equipment Schedule 5
W.B. 107.0"; 3.4 Liter.

GT Sedan 4D		NW52E	20385	1900	2425	3700	5575
GT Coupe 2D		NW12E	20085	1850	2375	3650	5525

FIREBIRD—V6—Equipment Schedule 4
W.B. 101.1"; 3.8 Liter.

Coupe 2D		FS22K	20535	2550	3150	4475	6500
Convertible 2D		FS32K	26460	3900	4625	6050	8300
T-Bar Roof				325	325	435	435
Manual Trans				(400)	(400)	(535)	(535)

FIREBIRD—V8—Equipment Schedule 4
W.B. 101.1"; 5.7 Liter.

Formula Coupe 2D		FV22G	24055	3925	4675	6100	8375
Trans Am Coupe 2D		FV22G	27165	4950	5800	7350	9850
Trans Am Conv 2D		FV32G	31235	6500	7500	9175	11950
T-Bar Roof				325	325	435	435
Ram Air Handling Pkg				875	875	1165	1165

GRAND PRIX—V6—Equipment Schedule 4
W.B. 110.5"; 3.8 Liter.

SE Sedan 4D		WJ52K	20610	975	1375	2575	4300
GT Sedan 4D		WP52K	22105	1725	2225	3500	5400
GT Coupe 2D		WP12K	21955	1350	1825	3075	4875
V6 3.1 Liter		J		(250)	(250)	(335)	(335)

GRAND PRIX—V6 Supercharged—Equipment Schedule 4
W.B. 110.5"; 3.8 Liter.

GTP Sedan 4D		WR521	24870	2500	3075	4425	6475
GTP Coupe 2D		WR121	24720	2375	2950	4300	6275

BONNEVILLE—V6—Equipment Schedule 4
W.B. 112.2"; 3.8 Liter.

SE Sedan 4D		HX52K	24295	1600	2100	3375	5225
SLE Sedan 4D		HY52K	27995	2300	2875	4200	6150
SSEi Sedan 4D		HZ52K	32250	3150	3825	5200	7325
V6 3.8L Supercharged		1		350	350	465	465

2001 PONTIAC — (1,2or3)G(2or7)(JB524)-1-#

SUNFIRE—4-Cyl.—Equipment Schedule 5
W.B. 104.1"; 2.2 Liter, 2.4 Liter.

SE Sedan 4D		JB524	15650	1125	1600	2800	4550
SE Coupe 2D		JB124	15395	1125	1575	2775	4500
GT Coupe 2D		JD12T	17625	1450	1925	3175	5000

GRAND AM—4-Cyl.—Equipment Schedule 5
W.B. 107.0"; 2.4 Liter.

SE Sedan 4D		NE52T	17800	1550	2050	3300	5125
SE Coupe 2D		NE12T	17500	1550	2050	3300	5125
V6 3.4 Liter		E		250	250	335	335

GRAND AM—V6—Equipment Schedule 5
W.B. 107.0"; 3.4 Liter.

GT Sedan 4D		NW52E	21110	2125	2700	4000	5900
GT Coupe 2D		NW12E	20810	2100	2650	3950	5850

FIREBIRD—V6—Equipment Schedule 4
W.B. 101.1"; 3.8 Liter.

Coupe 2D		FS22K	20810	2875	3500	4850	6925
Convertible 2D		FS32K	26735	4300	5100	6550	8850
T-Bar Roof				350	350	465	465
Manual Trans				(425)	(425)	(565)	(565)
25th Anniversary				375	375	500	500

FIREBIRD—V8—Equipment Schedule 4
W.B. 101.1"; 5.7 Liter.

Formula Coupe 2D		FV22G	24480	4425	5225	6700	9025

2001 PONTIAC

Body	Type	VIN	List	Trade-In Fair	Trade-In Good	Pvt-Party Good	Retail Excellent
Trans Am Coupe 2D		FV22G	27590	5600	6550	8100	10700
Trans Am Conv 2D		FV32G	31660	7200	8250	9950	12800
T-Bar Roof			------	350	350	465	465
Ram Air Handling Pkg			------	950	950	1265	1265
75th Anniversary			------	375	375	500	500
NHRA Pkg			------	200	200	265	265
GRAND PRIX—V6—Equipment Schedule 4							
W.B. 110.5"; 3.1 Liter, 3.8 Liter.							
SE Sedan 4D		WJ52J	21135	1125	1600	2850	4625
GT Sedan 4D		WP52K	22615	2025	2600	3925	5875
GT Coupe 2D		WP12K	22465	1600	2100	3400	5300
Special Edition			------	100	100	135	135
GRAND PRIX—V6 Supercharged—Equipment Schedule 4							
W.B. 110.5"; 3.8 Liter.							
GTP Sedan 4D		WR521	26135	2825	3450	4825	6900
GTP Coupe 2D		WR121	25935	2675	3275	4650	6725
Special Edition			------	100	100	135	135
BONNEVILLE—V6—Equipment Schedule 4							
W.B. 112.2"; 3.8 Liter.							
SE Sedan 4D		HX52K	25730	2000	2550	3825	5725
SLE Sedan 4D		HY52K	28700	2750	3350	4675	6725
BONNEVILLE—V6 Supercharged—Equipment Schedule 4							
W.B. 112.2"; 3.8 Liter.							
SSEi Sedan 4D		HZ521	33070	3675	4400	5775	7975

2002 PONTIAC — (1or2)G2(JB524)-2-#

Body	Type	VIN	List	Trade-In Fair	Trade-In Good	Pvt-Party Good	Retail Excellent
SUNFIRE—4-Cyl.—Equipment Schedule 5							
W.B. 104.1"; 2.2 Liter, 2.4 Liter.							
SE Sedan 4D		JB164	16545	1350	1825	3225	5225
SE Coupe 2D		JB124	16045	1300	1775	3175	5175
GT Coupe 2D		JD12T	18205	1675	2175	3600	5650
GRAND AM—4-Cyl.—Equipment Schedule 5							
W.B. 107.0"; 2.2 Liter.							
SE Sedan 4D		NE52T	18360	1825	2350	3800	5850
SE Coupe 2D		NE12T	18210	1825	2350	3800	5850
V6 3.4 Liter		E		250	250	335	335
GRAND AM—V6—Equipment Schedule 5							
W.B. 107.0"; 3.4 Liter.							
GT Sedan 4D		NW52E	21425	2450	3050	4500	6675
GT Coupe 2D		NW12E	21275	2375	2975	4425	6600
FIREBIRD—V6—Equipment Schedule 4							
W.B. 101.1"; 3.8 Liter.							
Coupe 2D		FS22K	21105	3125	3800	5400	7750
Convertible 2D		FS32K	27205	4650	5475	7175	9800
T-Bar Roof			------	400	400	535	535
GT Pkg			------	200	200	265	265
Manual Trans			------	(450)	(450)	(600)	(600)
FIREBIRD—V8—Equipment Schedule 4							
W.B. 101.1"; 5.7 Liter.							
Formula Coupe 2D		FV22G	26235	4875	5700	7425	10100
Trans Am Coupe 2D		FV22G	28265	6200	7175	8975	11850
Trans Am Conv 2D		FV32G	32335	7850	9000	10850	13950
Collector Ed Cpe 2D		FV22G	31265	7125	8175	10000	13050
Collector Ed Conv 2D		FV32G	35335	8875	10100	12100	15450
T-Bar Roof			------	400	400	535	535
NHRA Pkg			------	200	200	265	265
Ram Air Handling Pkg			------	1000	1000	1335	1335
GRAND PRIX—V6—Equipment Schedule 4							
W.B. 110.5"; 3.1 Liter, 3.8 Liter.							
SE Sedan 4D		WJ52J	21575	1275	1750	3200	5250
GT Sedan 4D		WP52K	23695	2325	2900	4400	6625
GT Coupe 2D		WP12K	23545	1825	2350	3825	5950
GRAND PRIX—V6 Supercharged—Equipment Schedule 4							
W.B. 110.5"; 3.8 Liter.							
GTP Sedan 4D		WR521	26415	3075	3750	5325	7650
GTP Coupe 2D		WR121	26235	2925	3550	5100	7400
BONNEVILLE—V6—Equipment Schedule 4							
W.B. 112.2"; 3.8 Liter.							
SE Sedan 4D		HX52K	26355	2325	2925	4400	6575
SLE Sedan 4D		HY52K	29545	3100	3775	5300	7575
BONNEVILLE—V6 Supercharged—Equipment Schedule 4							
W.B. 112.2"; 3.8 Liter.							
SSEi Sedan 4D		HZ521	33605	4175	4925	6500	8950

DEDUCT FOR RECONDITIONING 0709

Body	Type	VIN	List	Trade-In Fair	Good	Pvt-Party Good	Retail Excellent

SUNFIRE—4-Cyl.—Equipment Schedule 5
W.B. 104.1"; 2.2 Liter.

Coupe 2D		JB12F	15435	**1625**	**2100**	**3550**	**5575**

VIBE—4-Cyl.—Equipment Schedule 6
W.B. 102.4"; 1.8 Liter.

Sport Wagon 4D	SL628	16900	**3475**	**4200**	**5700**	**8025**
GT Sport Wagon	SN62L	19900	**3650**	**4350**	**5875**	**8225**
AWD Sport Wagon 4D	SM628	20100	**3850**	**4575**	**6150**	**8525**

GRAND AM—4-Cyl.—Equipment Schedule 5
W.B. 107.0"; 2.2 Liter.

SE Sedan 4D	NE52F	18465	**2200**	**2775**	**4225**	**6350**
V6 3.4 Liter	E		**300**	**300**	**400**	**400**

GRAND AM—V6—Equipment Schedule 5
W.B. 107.0"; 3.4 Liter.

GT Sedan 4D	NW52E	21640	**2950**	**3575**	**5100**	**7325**
GT Coupe 2D	NW12E	21640	**2900**	**3525**	**5000**	**7225**

GRAND PRIX—V6—Equipment Schedule 4
W.B. 110.5"; 3.1 Liter, 3.8 Liter.

SE Sedan 4D	WK52J	22140	**1675**	**2175**	**3700**	**5825**
GT Sedan 4D	WP52K	23990	**2950**	**3575**	**5175**	**7500**
Wide Track Sport Pkg			**400**	**400**	**535**	**535**

GRAND PRIX—V6 Supercharged—Equipment Schedule 4
W.B. 110.5"; 3.8 Liter.

GTP Sedan 4D	WR521	26800	**3725**	**4450**	**6050**	**8475**

BONNEVILLE—V6—Equipment Schedule 4
W.B. 112.2"; 3.8 Liter.

SE Sedan 4D	HX52K	26665	**2900**	**3525**	**5050**	**7300**
SLE Sedan 4D	HY52K	29855	**3800**	**4525**	**6075**	**8450**

BONNEVILLE—V6 Supercharged—Equipment Schedule 4
W.B. 112.2"; 3.8 Liter.

SSEi Sedan 4D	HZ541	34085	**5100**	**5950**	**7600**	**10200**

SUNFIRE—4-Cyl.—Equipment Schedule 5
W.B. 104.1"; 2.2 Liter.

Coupe 2D	JB12F	16695	**1975**	**2525**	**3975**	**6075**

VIBE—4-Cyl.—Equipment Schedule 6
W.B. 102.4"1.8 Liter.

Sport Wagon 4D	SL628	17045	**4225**	**4975**	**6550**	**8975**
GT Sport Wagon	SN62L	19995	**4525**	**5325**	**6925**	**9450**
AWD Sport Wagon 4D	SM628	20345	**4775**	**5600**	**7225**	**9775**

GRAND AM—4-Cyl.—Equipment Schedule 5
W.B. 107.0"; 2.2 Liter.

SE Sedan 4D	NE52F	18545	**2675**	**3275**	**4750**	**6950**
V6 3.4 Liter	E		**325**	**325**	**435**	**435**

GRAND AM—V6—Equipment Schedule 5
W.B. 107.0"; 3.4 Liter.

GT Sedan 4D	NW52E	22450	**3525**	**4250**	**5750**	**8075**
GT Coupe 2D	NW12E	22450	**3475**	**4175**	**5675**	**8000**

GRAND PRIX—V6—Equipment Schedule 4
W.B. 110.5"; 3.8 Liter.

GT Sedan 4D	WP522	22395	**4300**	**5050**	**6725**	**9275**

GRAND PRIX—V6 Supercharged—Equipment Schedule 4
W.B. 110.5"; 3.8 Liter.

GTP Sedan 4D	WR524	26495	**5000**	**5850**	**7550**	**10200**

BONNEVILLE—V6—Equipment Schedule 4
W.B. 112.2"; 3.8 Liter.

SE Sedan 4D	HX52K	27510	**3550**	**4250**	**5775**	**8125**
SLE Sedan 4D	HY52K	30420	**4550**	**5375**	**6975**	**9500**

BONNEVILLE—V8—Equipment Schedule 4
W.B. 112.2"; 4.6 Liter.

GXP Sedan 4D	HZ54Y	35995	**6125**	**7075**	**8750**	**11450**

GTO—V8—Equipment Schedule 2
W.B. 109.8"; 5.7 Liter.

Coupe 2D	VX13G	33495	**8475**	**9675**	**11550**	**14750**

SUNFIRE—4-Cyl.—Equipment Schedule 5
W.B. 104.1"; 2.2 Liter.

Coupe 2D	JB12F	15650	**2450**	**3050**	**4500**	**6675**

2005 PONTIAC

Body Type	VIN	List	Trade-In Fair	Good	Pvt-Party Good	Retail Excellent
VIBE—4-Cyl.—Equipment Schedule 6						
W.B. 102.4"; 1.8 Liter.						
Sport Wagon 4D	SL628	18735	5025	5875	7475	10050
GT Sport Wagon	SN62L	20535	5525	6400	8000	10650
AWD Sport Wagon 4D	SM628	20885	5800	6750	8350	11050
GRAND AM—4-Cyl.—Equipment Schedule 5						
W.B. 107.0"; 2.2 Liter.						
SE Sedan 4D	NE52F	20580	3150	3825	5350	7600
V6 3.4 Liter	E		350	350	465	465
GRAND AM—V6—Equipment Schedule 5						
W.B. 107.0"; 3.4 Liter.						
GT Coupe 2D	NW12E	22990	4125	4875	6425	8800
GRAND PRIX—V6—Equipment Schedule 4						
W.B. 110.5"; 3.8 Liter.						
Sedan 4D	WP522	23560	4775	5600	7275	9900
GT Sedan 4D	WS522	25460	5350	6225	7950	10650
GRAND PRIX—V6 Supercharged—Equipment Schedule 4						
W.B. 110.5"; 3.8 Liter.						
GTP Sedan 4D	WR524	27220	6100	7050	8775	11550
GRAND PRIX—V8—Equipment Schedule 4						
W.B. 110.5"; 5.3 Liter.						
GXP Sedan 4D	WC52C	29995	8425	9625	11400	14550
G6—V6—Equipment Schedule 4						
W.B. 112.3"; 3.5 Liter.						
Sedan 4D	ZG528	21700	5775	6725	8325	11000
GT Sedan 4D	ZH528	23925	5925	6875	8500	11150
BONNEVILLE—V6—Equipment Schedule 4						
W.B. 112.2"; 3.8 Liter.						
SE Sedan 4D	HX52K	28650	4325	5125	6700	9125
SLE Sedan 4D	HY52K	31035	5475	6375	7975	10600
BONNEVILLE—V8—Equipment Schedule 4						
W.B. 112.2"; 4.6 Liter.						
GXP Sedan 4D	HZ54Y	36120	7175	8250	9900	12750
GTO—V8—Equipment Schedule 2						
W.B. 109.8"; 6.0 Liter.						
Coupe 2D	VX12U	34295	10150	11525	13450	16850

2006 PONTIAC — (1,2,3,5or6)G2orY2(SL658)–6

Body Type	VIN	List	Trade-In Fair	Good	Pvt-Party Good	Retail Excellent
VIBE—4-Cyl.—Equipment Schedule 6						
W.B. 102.4"; 1.8 Liter.						
Sport Wagon 4D	SL658	16990	6000	6950	8575	11200
GT Sport Wagon 4D	SN65L	21015	6600	7625	9225	11950
AWD Sport Wagon 4D	SM658	20665	6950	7975	9625	12400
SOLSTICE—4-Cyl.—Equipment Schedule 6						
W.B. 95.1"; 2.4 Liter.						
Convertible 2D	MB35B	19995	9500	10775	12650	15950
GRAND PRIX—V6—Equipment Schedule 4						
W.B. 110.5"; 3.8 Liter.						
Sedan 4D	WP552	22990	5950	6900	8625	11400
GRAND PRIX—V6 Supercharged—Equipment Schedule 4						
W.B. 110.5"; 3.8 Liter.						
GT Sedan 4D	WR554	26745	6900	7975	9700	12600
GRAND PRIX—V8—Equipment Schedule 4						
W.B. 110.5"; 5.3 Liter.						
GXP Sedan 4D	WC55C	29395	10000	11375	13250	16500
G6—4-Cyl.—Equipment Schedule 4						
W.B. 112.3"; 2.4 Liter.						
Sedan 4D	ZF55B	18990	5875	6800	8425	11050
G6—V6—Equipment Schedule 4						
W.B. 112.3"; 3.5 Liter, 3.9 Liter.						
Sedan 4D	ZG558	20655	6600	7600	9225	11950
GT Sedan 4D	ZH558	23180	6750	7800	9400	12150
GT Coupe 2D	ZH158	22955	6975	8025	9675	12450
GT Hard Top Conv 2D	ZH358	28490	11275	12800	14500	17800
GTP Sedan 4D	ZM551	24835	7525	8625	10300	13150
GTP Coupe 2D	ZM151	24610	7700	8800	10450	13300
GTP Hard Top Conv 2D	ZM351	29990	11475	12925	14650	18000
GTO—V8—Equipment Schedule 2						
W.B. 109.8"; 6.0 Liter.						
Coupe 2D	VX12U	32995	11850	13375	15250	18750

194   DEDUCT FOR RECONDITIONING   0709

Body	Type	VIN	List	Trade-In Fair	Good	Pvt-Party Good	Retail Excellent

2007 PONTIAC — (1,2,3,5or6)G2orY2(SL658)–7

VIBE—4-Cyl.—Equipment Schedule 6
W.B. 102.4"; 1.8 Liter.
Sport Wagon 4D SL658 17215 **7125 8200 9700 12350**
SOLSTICE—4-Cyl.—Equipment Schedule 6
W.B. 95.1"; 2.4 Liter.
Convertible 2D.............. MB35B 22955 **10725 12150 13850 17150**
SOLSTICE—4-Cyl. Turbo—Equipment Schedule 6
W.B. 95.1"; 2.0 Liter.
GXP Convertible 2D.............. MG35X 27955 **12925 14600 16350 19900**
GRAND PRIX—V6—Equipment Schedule 4
W.B. 110.5"; 3.8 Liter.
Sedan 4D WP552 22315 **6625 7625 9250 12000**
GRAND PRIX—V6 Supercharged—Equipment Schedule 4
W.B. 110.5"; 3.8 Liter.
GT Sedan 4D WR554 25235 **7775 8900 10600 13500**
GRAND PRIX—V8—Equipment Schedule 4
W.B. 110.5"; 5.3 Liter.
GXP Sedan 4D WC55C 29315 **10625 12050 13750 17000**
G5—4-Cyl.—Equipment Schedule 4
W.B. 103.5"; 2.2 Liter, 2.4 Liter.
Coupe 2D AL15F 15845 **5975 6900 8400 10950**
GT Coupe 2D AN15B 18645 **7400 8475 10000 12650**
G6—4-Cyl.—Equipment Schedule 4
W.B. 112.3"; 2.4 Liter.
Sedan 4D ZG55B 19265 **6700 7725 9225 11850**
  Sport Pkg **350 350 465 465**
G6—V6—Equipment Schedule 4
W.B. 112.3"; 3.5 Liter, 3.6 Liter, 3.9 Liter.
GT Sedan 4D ZH55N 22845 **7700 8825 10350 13050**
GT Coupe 2D ZH15N 22615 **7900 9050 10650 13450**
GT Hard Top Conv 2D ZH35N 29215 **12600 14200 15850 19150**
GTP Sedan 4D ZM557 25115 **8500 9725 11300 14150**
GTP Coupe 2D ZM157 24915 **8650 9850 11400 14300**
  Sport Pkg **300 300 400 400**

2008 PONTIAC–(1,2,3or6G2,5Y2orKL2)(SL658)–8

VIBE—4-Cyl.—Equipment Schedule 6
W.B. 102.4"; 1.8 Liter.
Sport Wagon 4D SL658 17345 **8500 9725 11200 14000**
SOLSTICE—4-Cyl.—Equipment Schedule 6
W.B. 95.1"; 2.4 Liter.
Convertible 2D.............. MB35B 22295 **12400 14025 15650 18950**
SOLSTICE—4-Cyl. Turbo—Equipment Schedule 6
W.B. 95.1"; 2.0 Liter.
GXP Convertible 2D.............. MG35X 27895 **14800 16650 18400 22000**
GRAND PRIX—V6—Equipment Schedule 4
W.B. 110.5"; 3.8 Liter.
Sedan 4D WP552 22500 **8700 9900 11550 14550**
GRAND PRIX—V8—Equipment Schedule 4
W.B. 110.5"; 5.3 Liter.
GXP Sedan 4D WC55C 29500 **12350 13975 15700 19100**
G5—4-Cyl.—Equipment Schedule 4
W.B. 103.5"; 2.2 Liter, 2.4 Liter.
Coupe 2D AL15F 16450 **7425 8500 9850 12350**
GT Coupe 2D AN15B 20560 **8950 10200 11650 14400**
G6—4-Cyl.—Equipment Schedule 4
W.B. 112.3"; 2.4 Liter.
Sedan 4D ZG55B 19995 **8250 9425 10950 13650**
  Sport Pkg **375 375 500 500**
G6—V6—Equipment Schedule 4
W.B. 112.3"; 3.5 Liter, 3.6 Liter, 3.9 Liter.
GT Sedan 4D ZH55N 22995 **9275 10575 12100 15000**
GT Coupe 2D ZH15N 22995 **9550 10875 12400 15300**
GT Hard Top Conv 2D ZH35N 29995 **14600 16425 18050 21500**
GXP Sedan 4D ZM557 27310 **10200 11575 13150 16100**
GXP Coupe 2D ZM157 27105 **10300 11650 13250 16200**
  Sport Pkg **325 325 435 435**
G8—V6—Equipment Schedule 4
W.B. 114.8"; 3.6 Liter.
Sedan 4D EC557 27595 **15875 17825 19700 23600**

2008 PONTIAC

Body	Type	VIN	List	Trade-In Fair	Trade-In Good	Pvt-Party Good	Retail Excellent

G8—V8—Equipment Schedule 4
W.B. 114.8"; 6.0 Liter.
GT Sedan 4D ER55Y 29995 **17875 20000 22000 26100**

PORSCHE

1994 PORSCHE — WPO(AA296)–R–#

968—4-Cyl.—Equipment Schedule 1
W.B. 94.5"; 3.0 Liter.

Coupe 2D		AA296	43887	**6925**	**7975**	**9900**	**13050**
Cabriolet 2D		CA296	55530	**9950**	**11325**	**13650**	**17600**
Tiptronic Auto Trans				**300**	**300**	**400**	**400**

911 CARRERA 2—6-Cyl.—Equipment Schedule 1
W.B. 89.4"; 3.6 Liter.

RS America Coupe 2D		AB296	55525	**11525**	**13025**	**15600**	**19900**
Coupe 2D		AB296	65715	**11275**	**12750**	**15300**	**19550**
Targa 2D		BB296	66615	**11025**	**12450**	**15000**	**19150**
Cabriolet 2D		CB296	74915	**14800**	**16600**	**19700**	**24800**
Full Leather				**100**	**100**	**135**	**135**
Tiptronic Auto Trans				**300**	**300**	**400**	**400**

911 CARRERA 4 AWD—6-Cyl.—Equipment Schedule 1
W.B. 89.4"; 3.6 Liter.

Coupe 2D		AB296	81551	**12500**	**14100**	**16800**	**21400**
Full Leather				**100**	**100**	**135**	**135**

911 TURBO 3.6—6-Cyl. Turbo—Equipment Schedule 1
W.B. 89.4"; 3.6 Liter.

Coupe 2D		AC296	101825	**19800**	**22150**	**25900**	**32200**

928 GTS—V8—Equipment Schedule 1
W.B. 98.4"; 5.4 Liter.

Coupe 2D		AA292	85085	**17600**	**19700**	**23100**	**28900**

1995 PORSCHE — WPO(AA296)–S–#

968—4-Cyl.—Equipment Schedule 1
W.B. 94.5"; 3.0 Liter.

Coupe 2D		AA296	43887	**7700**	**8825**	**10900**	**14150**
Cabriolet 2D		CA296	55530	**10975**	**12450**	**14950**	**19100**
Tiptronic Auto Trans				**300**	**300**	**400**	**400**

911 CARRERA—6-Cyl.—Equipment Schedule 1
W.B. 89.4"; 3.6 Liter.

Coupe 2D		AA299	63055	**11900**	**13475**	**16100**	**20600**
Cabriolet 2D		CA299	71355	**15675**	**17600**	**20800**	**26200**
Full Leather				**100**	**100**	**135**	**135**
Hard Top (Cabriolet)				**300**	**300**	**400**	**400**
Aero Kit				**1200**	**1200**	**1600**	**1600**
Tiptronic Auto Trans				**300**	**300**	**400**	**400**

911 CARRERA 4 AWD—6-Cyl.—Equipment Schedule 1
W.B. 89.4"; 3.6 Liter.

Coupe 2D		AA299	70055	**13125**	**14800**	**17650**	**22300**
Cabriolet 2D		CA299	78355	**15875**	**17825**	**21100**	**26500**
Full Leather				**100**	**100**	**135**	**135**
Hard Top (Cabriolet)				**300**	**300**	**400**	**400**
Aero Kit				**1200**	**1200**	**1600**	**1600**

928 GTS—V8—Equipment Schedule 1
W.B. 98.4"; 5.4 Liter.

Coupe 2D		AA292	85085	**18625**	**20875**	**24400**	**30500**

1996 PORSCHE — WPO(AA299)–T–#

911 CARRERA—6-Cyl.—Equipment Schedule 1
W.B. 89.5"; 3.6 Liter.

Coupe 2D		AA299	67043	**12600**	**14200**	**16850**	**21400**
Targa 2D		DA299	74043	**13975**	**15725**	**18550**	**23400**
Cabriolet 2D		CA299	76293	**16525**	**18575**	**21800**	**27200**
Full Leather				**100**	**100**	**135**	**135**
Hard Top (Cabriolet)				**350**	**350**	**465**	**465**
Aero Kit				**1300**	**1300**	**1735**	**1735**
Tiptronic Auto Trans				**350**	**350**	**465**	**465**

911 CARRERA 4 AWD—6-Cyl.—Equipment Schedule 1
W.B. 89.5"; 3.6 Liter.

Coupe 2D		AA299	73393	**13875**	**15575**	**18400**	**23200**
4S Coupe 2D		AA299	76289	**24000**	**26750**	**30900**	**38100**
Cabriolet 2D		CA299	82643	**16800**	**18825**	**22100**	**27600**

1996 PORSCHE

Body	Type	VIN	List	Trade-In Fair	Good	Pvt-Party Good	Retail Excellent
	Full Leather			100	100	135	135
	Hard Top (Cabriolet)			350	350	465	465
	Aero Kit			1300	1300	1735	1735

911 TURBO—6-Cyl. Turbo—Equipment Schedule 1
W.B. 89.5"; 3.6 Liter.

Body	Type	VIN	List	Fair	Good	Pvt-Party Good	Retail Excellent
	Coupe 2D	AC299	115050	38525	42725	48400	58800

1997 PORSCHE — WPO(CA298)–V–#

BOXSTER—6-Cyl.—Equipment Schedule 1
W.B. 95.1"; 2.5 Liter.

Type	VIN	List	Fair	Good	Pvt-Party Good	Retail Excellent
Cabriolet 2D	CA298	43086	7450	8550	10550	13750
Full Leather			100	100	135	135
Hard Top			375	375	500	500
Aero Kit			1400	1400	1865	1865
Sport Touring Pkg			1150	1150	1535	1535
Tiptronic Auto Trans			400	400	535	535

911 CARRERA—6-Cyl.—Equipment Schedule 1
W.B. 89.5"; 3.6 Liter.

Type	VIN	List	Fair	Good	Pvt-Party Good	Retail Excellent
Coupe 2D	AA299	67063	13125	14800	17450	22000
S Coupe 2D	AA299	67063	13525	15250	17950	22500
Targa 2D	DA299	74063	15100	16950	19900	24900
Cabriolet 2D	CA299	76313	17250	19300	22400	27900
Full Leather			100	100	135	135
Hard Top (Cabriolet)			375	375	500	500
Aero Kit			1400	1400	1865	1865
Tiptronic Auto Trans			400	400	535	535

911 CARRERA 4 AWD—6-Cyl.—Equipment Schedule 1
W.B. 89.5"; 3.6 Liter.

Type	VIN	List	Fair	Good	Pvt-Party Good	Retail Excellent
4S Coupe 2D	AA299	76313	26450	29500	33600	41100
Cabriolet 2D	CA299	81663	18025	20200	23400	29000
Full Leather			100	100	135	135
Hard Top (Cabriolet)			375	375	500	500
Aero Kit			1400	1400	1865	1865

911 TURBO—6-Cyl. Turbo—Equipment Schedule 1
W.B. 89.5"; 3.6 Liter.

Type	VIN	List	Fair	Good	Pvt-Party Good	Retail Excellent
Coupe 2D	AC299	105765	42625	47325	53000	63900

1998 PORSCHE — WPO(CA298)–W–#

BOXSTER—6-Cyl.—Equipment Schedule 1
W.B. 95.2"; 2.5 Liter.

Type	VIN	List	Fair	Good	Pvt-Party Good	Retail Excellent
Cabriolet 2D	CA298	44316	7775	8900	10950	14250
Full Leather			100	100	135	135
Hard Top			400	400	535	535
Aero Kit			1500	1500	2000	2000
Sport Touring Pkg			1225	1225	1635	1635
Tiptronic Auto Trans			450	450	600	600

911 CARRERA—6-Cyl.—Equipment Schedule 1
W.B. 89.4"; 3.6 Liter.

Type	VIN	List	Fair	Good	Pvt-Party Good	Retail Excellent
S Coupe 2D	AA299	67461	14700	16525	19200	23900
Targa 2D	DA299	74461	16425	18425	21400	26500
Cabriolet 2D	CA299	76711	18075	20275	23300	28800
Full Leather			100	100	135	135
Hard Top (Cabriolet)			400	400	535	535
Aero Kit			1500	1500	2000	2000
Tiptronic Auto Trans			450	450	600	600

911 CARRERA 4 AWD—6-Cyl.—Equipment Schedule 1
W.B. 89.4"; 3.6 Liter.

Type	VIN	List	Fair	Good	Pvt-Party Good	Retail Excellent
4S Coupe 2D	AA299	76711	29000	32250	36400	44100
Cabriolet 2D	CA299	82061	19400	21750	24900	30700
Full Leather			100	100	135	135
Hard Top (Cabriolet)			400	400	535	535
Aero Kit			1500	1500	2000	2000

1999 PORSCHE — WPO(CA298)–X–#

BOXSTER—6-Cyl.—Equipment Schedule 1
W.B. 95.2"; 2.5 Liter.

Type	VIN	List	Fair	Good	Pvt-Party Good	Retail Excellent
Cabriolet 2D	CA298	44316	8325	9500	11550	15000
Full Leather			125	125	165	165
Hard Top			425	425	565	565
Aero Kit			1575	1575	2100	2100
Sport Design Pkg			500	500	665	665
Sport Touring Pkg			1300	1300	1735	1735

1999 PORSCHE

Body	Type	VIN	List	Trade-In Fair	Good	Pvt-Party Good	Retail Excellent
	Tiptronic Auto Trans			500	500	665	665
911 CARRERA—6-Cyl.—Equipment Schedule 1							
W.B. 92.6"; 3.4 Liter.							
	Coupe 2D	AA299	70815	16025	17975	20700	25500
	Cabriolet 2D	CA299	80245	19250	21550	24500	30000
	Full Leather			125	125	165	165
	Hard Top (Cabriolet)			425	425	565	565
	Aero Kit			1575	1575	2100	2100
	Tiptronic Auto Trans			500	500	665	665
911 CARRERA 4 AWD—6-Cyl.—Equipment Schedule 1							
W.B. 92.6"; 3.4 Liter.							
	Coupe 2D	AA299	75980	19050	21375	24300	29800
	Cabriolet 2D	CA299	85420	20875	23325	26500	32300
	Full Leather			125	125	165	165
	Hard Top (Cabriolet)			425	425	565	565
	Aero Kit			1575	1575	2100	2100
	Tiptronic Auto Trans			500	500	665	665

2000 PORSCHE — WPO(CA298)-Y-#

Body	Type	VIN	List	Trade-In Fair	Good	Pvt-Party Good	Retail Excellent
BOXSTER—6-Cyl.—Equipment Schedule 1							
W.B. 95.2"; 2.7 Liter, 3.2 Liter.							
	Cabriolet 2D	CA298	44745	9150	10425	12500	16000
	S Cabriolet 2D	CB298	53245	12100	13675	16000	20100
	Full Leather			150	150	200	200
	Hard Top			450	450	600	600
	Aero Kit			1650	1650	2200	2200
	Sport Design Pkg			500	500	665	665
	Sport Touring Pkg			1375	1375	1835	1835
	Tiptronic Auto Trans			550	550	735	735
911 CARRERA—6-Cyl.—Equipment Schedule 1							
W.B. 92.6"; 3.4 Liter.							
	Coupe 2D	AA299	71375	17650	19700	22400	27400
	Cabriolet 2D	CA299	80755	20575	22925	26000	31600
	Full Leather			150	150	200	200
	Hard Top (Cabriolet)			450	450	600	600
	Aero Kit			1650	1650	2200	2200
	Tiptronic Auto Trans			550	550	735	735
911 CARRERA 4 AWD—6-Cyl.—Equipment Schedule 1							
W.B. 92.6"; 3.4 Liter.							
	Coupe 2D	AA299	76805	20975	23425	26500	32100
	Cabriolet 2D	CA299	86185	22825	25475	28600	34600
	Full Leather			150	150	200	200
	Hard Top (Cabriolet)			450	450	600	600
	Aero Kit			1650	1650	2200	2200
	Millennium Pkg			3450	3450	4600	4600
	Tiptronic Auto Trans			550	550	735	735

2001 PORSCHE — WPO(CA298)-1-#

Body	Type	VIN	List	Trade-In Fair	Good	Pvt-Party Good	Retail Excellent
BOXSTER—6-Cyl.—Equipment Schedule 1							
W.B. 95.2"; 2.7 Liter, 3.2 Liter.							
	Cabriolet 2D	CA298	42865	10250	11650	13800	17550
	S Cabriolet 2D	CB298	50965	13525	15200	17600	21900
	Full Leather			175	175	235	235
	Hard Top			475	475	635	635
	Aero Kit			1725	1725	2300	2300
	Sport Design Pkg			500	500	665	665
	Sport Touring Pkg			1450	1450	1935	1935
	Tiptronic Auto Trans			575	575	765	765
911 CARRERA—6-Cyl.—Equipment Schedule 1							
W.B. 92.6"; 3.4 Liter.							
	Coupe 2D	AA299	70275	19500	21850	24600	29900
	Cabriolet 2D	CA299	79775	22250	24900	27800	33600
	Full Leather			175	175	235	235
	Hard Top (Cabriolet)			475	475	635	635
	Aero Kit			1725	1725	2300	2300
	Tiptronic Auto Trans			575	575	765	765
911 CARRERA 4 AWD—6-Cyl.—Equipment Schedule 1							
W.B. 92.6"; 3.4 Liter.							
	Coupe 2D	AA299	75320	23025	25775	28800	34700
	Cabriolet 2D	CA299	84820	24900	27725	30900	37100
	Full Leather			175	175	235	235
	Hard Top (Cabriolet)			475	475	635	635

2001 PORSCHE

Body	Type	VIN	List	Trade-In Fair	Trade-In Good	Pvt-Party Good	Retail Excellent
	Aero Kit		....	1725	1725	2300	2300
	Tiptronic Auto Trans		....	575	575	765	765

911 TURBO AWD—6-Cyl. Turbo—Equipment Schedule 1
W.B. 92.5"; 3.6 Liter.

Body	Type	VIN	List	Fair	Good	Good	Excellent
	Coupe 2D	AB299	111765	33700	37425	41200	48900
	Full Leather		....	175	175	235	235
	Aero Kit		....	1725	1725	2300	2300
	Tiptronic Auto Trans		....	575	575	765	765

2002 PORSCHE — WPO(CA298)-2-#

BOXSTER—6-Cyl.—Equipment Schedule 1
W.B. 95.2"; 2.7 Liter, 3.2 Liter.

Body	Type	VIN	List	Fair	Good	Good	Excellent
	Cabriolet 2D	CA298	43365	10425	11800	14100	18050
	S Cabriolet 2D	CB298	52365	13875	15625	18150	22500
	Full Leather		....	200	200	265	265
	Hard Top		....	500	500	665	665
	Aero Kit		....	1800	1800	2400	2400
	Sport Design Pkg		....	500	500	665	665
	Sport Touring Pkg		....	1500	1500	2000	2000
	Tiptronic Auto Trans		....	600	600	800	800

911 CARRERA—6-Cyl.—Equipment Schedule 1
W.B. 92.6"; 3.6 Liter.

Body	Type	VIN	List	Fair	Good	Good	Excellent
	Coupe 2D	AA299	73450	21650	24200	27100	32800
	Targa 2D	AA299	75965	24100	26950	30000	36100
	Cabriolet 2D	CA299	83150	24100	26950	30000	36100
	Full Leather		....	200	200	265	265
	Hard Top (Cabriolet)		....	500	500	665	665
	Aero Kit		....	1800	1800	2400	2400
	Tiptronic Auto Trans		....	600	600	800	800

911 CARRERA 4 AWD—6-Cyl.—Equipment Schedule 1
W.B. 92.5" (4S), 92.6"; 3.6 Liter.

Body	Type	VIN	List	Fair	Good	Good	Excellent
	4S Coupe 2D	AA299	80965	25475	28425	31600	37800
	Cabriolet 2D	CA299	88750	27250	30375	33600	40200
	Full Leather		....	200	200	265	265
	Hard Top (Cabriolet)		....	500	500	665	665
	Aero Kit		....	1800	1800	2400	2400
	Tiptronic Auto Trans		....	600	600	800	800

911 TURBO AWD—6-Cyl. Turbo—Equipment Schedule 1
W.B. 92.6"; 3.6 Liter.

Body	Type	VIN	List	Fair	Good	Good	Excellent
	Coupe 2D	AB299	115765	39400	43700	47600	56100
	Full Leather		....	200	200	265	265
	Aero Kit		....	1800	1800	2400	2400
	Tiptronic Auto Trans		....	600	600	800	800

911 TURBO—6-Cyl. Turbo—Equipment Schedule 1
W.B. 92.6"; 3.6 Liter.

Body	Type	VIN	List	Fair	Good	Good	Excellent
	GT2 Coupe 2D	AB299	180665	****	****	****	88900

2003 PORSCHE — WPO(CA298)-3-#

BOXSTER—6-Cyl.—Equipment Schedule 1
W.B. 95.1"; 2.7 Liter, 3.2 Liter.

Body	Type	VIN	List	Fair	Good	Good	Excellent
	Cabriolet 2D	CA298	45485	10975	12400	14750	18700
	S Cabriolet 2D	CB298	54485	14750	16600	19100	23600
	Full Leather		....	250	250	335	335
	Hard Top		....	550	550	735	735
	Aero Kit		....	1925	1925	2565	2565
	Sport Design Pkg		....	575	575	765	765
	Tiptronic Auto Trans		....	700	700	935	935

911 CARRERA—6-Cyl.—Equipment Schedule 1
W.B. 92.6"; 3.6 Liter.

Body	Type	VIN	List	Fair	Good	Good	Excellent
	Coupe 2D	AA299	72435	21750	24300	27100	32700
	Targa 2D	BA299	79835	24700	27550	30500	36500
	Cabriolet 2D	CA299	82235	24800	27625	30600	36600
	Full Leather		....	250	250	335	335
	Hard Top (Cabriolet)		....	550	550	735	735
	Aero Kit		....	1925	1925	2565	2565
	Tiptronic Auto Trans		....	700	700	935	935

911 CARRERA 4 AWD—6-Cyl.—Equipment Schedule 1
W.B. 92.6"; 3.6 Liter.

Body	Type	VIN	List	Fair	Good	Good	Excellent
	4S Coupe 2D	AA299	82565	26075	29000	32000	38300
	Cabriolet 2D	CA299	87835	28325	31550	34700	41300
	Full Leather		....	250	250	335	335
	Hard Top (Cabriolet)		....	550	550	735	735

Body	Type	VIN	List	Trade-In Fair	Good	Pvt-Party Good	Retail Excellent
	Aero Kit		------	1925	1925	2565	2565
	Tiptronic Auto Trans		------	700	700	935	935

911 TURBO AWD—6-Cyl. Turbo—Equipment Schedule 1
W.B. 92.6"; 3.6 Liter.

Body	Type	VIN	List	Fair	Good	Good	Excellent
	Coupe 2D	AB299	118265	42050	46650	50400	58900
	Full Leather		------	250	250	335	335
	Aero Kit		------	1925	1925	2565	2565
	Tiptronic Auto Trans		------	700	700	935	935

911 TURBO—6-Cyl. Turbo—Equipment Schedule 1
W.B. 92.6"; 3.6 Liter.

Body	Type	VIN	List	Fair	Good	Good	Excellent
	GT2 Coupe 2D	AB299	183765	****	****	****	96000

2004 PORSCHE — WPO(CA298)-4-#

BOXSTER—6-Cyl.—Equipment Schedule 1
W.B. 95.1"; 2.7 Liter, 3.2 Liter.

Body	Type	VIN	List	Fair	Good	Good	Excellent
	Cabriolet 2D	CA298	45485	12800	14400	16850	21100
	S Cabriolet 2D	CB298	54485	16900	18975	21600	26500
	Full Leather		------	300	300	400	400
	Hard Top		------	575	575	765	765
	Aero Kit		------	2050	2050	2735	2735
	Sport Design Pkg		------	650	650	865	865
	Special Edition		------	2000	2000	2665	2665
	Tiptronic Auto Trans		------	800	800	1065	1065

911 CARRERA—6-Cyl.—Equipment Schedule 1
W.B. 92.6"; 3.6 Liter.

Body	Type	VIN	List	Fair	Good	Good	Excellent
	Coupe 2D	AA299	72435	25100	28025	30900	36800
	Targa 2D	BA299	79835	28425	31650	34700	41100
	Cabriolet 2D	CA299	82235	28525	31750	34800	41200
	40th Anniversary Ed		------	5000	5000	6665	6665
	Full Leather		------	300	300	400	400
	Hard Top (Cabriolet)		------	575	575	765	765
	Aero Kit		------	2050	2050	2735	2735
	Tiptronic Auto Trans		------	800	800	1065	1065

911 CARRERA 4 AWD—6-Cyl.—Equipment Schedule 1
W.B. 92.5"; 3.6 Liter.

Body	Type	VIN	List	Fair	Good	Good	Excellent
	Cabriolet 2D	CA299	86285	32450	36075	39200	46100
	4S Coupe 2D	AA299	84165	29800	33125	36300	42800
	4S Cabriolet 2D	CA299	93965	35075	39000	42200	49500
	Full Leather		------	300	300	400	400
	Hard Top (Cabriolet)		------	575	575	765	765
	Aero Kit		------	2050	2050	2735	2735
	Tiptronic Auto Trans		------	800	800	1065	1065

911 TURBO AWD—6-Cyl. Turbo—Equipment Schedule 1
W.B. 92.5"; 3.6 Liter.

Body	Type	VIN	List	Fair	Good	Good	Excellent
	Coupe 2D	AB299	120465	47925	53125	56700	65800
	Cabriolet 2D	CB299	130265	51850	57425	61300	70800
	Full Leather		------	300	300	400	400
	Aero Kit		------	2050	2050	2735	2735
	Tiptronic Auto Trans		------	800	800	1065	1065

911 TURBO—6-Cyl. Turbo—Equipment Schedule 1
W.B. 92.7"; 3.6 Liter.

Body	Type	VIN	List	Fair	Good	Good	Excellent
	GT2 Coupe 2D	AB299	193765	****	****	****	106600

911—6-Cyl.—Equipment Schedule 1
W.B. 92.7"; 3.6 Liter.

Body	Type	VIN	List	Fair	Good	Good	Excellent
	GT3 Coupe 2D	AC299	101965	42250	46850	50300	58500

CARRERA GT—V10—Equipment Schedule 1
W.B. 107.5"; 5.7 Liter.

Body	Type	VIN	List	Fair	Good	Good	Excellent
	Roadster 2D	CA298	446165	****	****	****	297900

2005 PORSCHE — WPO(CA298)-5-#

BOXSTER—6-Cyl.—Equipment Schedule 1
W.B. 95.1"; 2.7 Liter, 3.2 Liter.

Body	Type	VIN	List	Fair	Good	Good	Excellent
	Cabriolet 2D	CA298	44595	15000	16850	19350	23900
	S Cabriolet 2D	CB298	53895	19450	21750	24400	29500
	Full Leather		------	350	350	465	465
	Hard Top		------	600	600	800	800
	Aero Kit		------	2175	2175	2900	2900
	Sport Pkg		------	725	725	965	965
	Tiptronic Auto Trans		------	875	875	1165	1165

911 CARRERA—6-Cyl.—Equipment Schedule 1
W.B. 92.5" (S), 92.6"; 3.6 Liter, 3.8 Liter.

Body	Type	VIN	List	Fair	Good	Good	Excellent
	Coupe 2D	AA299	73165	29100	32450	35300	41600

2005 PORSCHE

Body Type	VIN	List	Trade-In Fair	Trade-In Good	Pvt-Party Good	Retail Excellent
Targa 2D	BA299	79865	32725	36450	39400	46100
Cabriolet 2D	CA299	82965	32925	36650	39600	46400
S Coupe 2D	AB299	79895	31075	34500	37400	43900
S Cabriolet 2D	CB299	89695	35375	39300	42200	49300
Full Leather			350	350	465	465
Hard Top (Cabriolet)			600	600	800	800
Aero Kit			2175	2175	2900	2900
Tiptronic Auto Trans			875	875	1165	1165

911 CARRERA 4 AWD—6-Cyl.—Equipment Schedule 1
W.B. 92.5"; 3.6 Liter.

Body Type	VIN	List	Trade-In Fair	Trade-In Good	Pvt-Party Good	Retail Excellent
4S Coupe 2D	AA299	84195	34700	38525	41600	48500
4S Cabriolet 2D	CA299	93995	40575	45075	48100	55800
Full Leather			350	350	465	465
Hard Top (Cabriolet)			600	600	800	800
Aero Kit			2175	2175	2900	2900
Tiptronic Auto Trans			875	875	1165	1165

911 TURBO AWD—6-Cyl. Turbo—Equipment Schedule 1
W.B. 92.5"; 3.6 Liter.

Body Type	VIN	List	Trade-In Fair	Trade-In Good	Pvt-Party Good	Retail Excellent
Cabriolet 2D	CB299	130295	58800	65075	68700	78600
S Coupe 2D	AB299	133495	57425	63600	67100	76800
S Cabriolet 2D	CB299	143295	60575	67025	70700	80800
Full Leather			350	350	465	465
Aero Kit			2175	2175	2900	2900
Tiptronic Auto Trans			875	875	1165	1165

911 TURBO—6-Cyl. Turbo—Equipment Schedule 1
W.B. 92.7"; 3.6 Liter.

Body Type	VIN	List	Trade-In Fair	Trade-In Good	Pvt-Party Good	Retail Excellent
GT2 Coupe 2D	AB299	193795	****	****	****	118000

911—6-Cyl.—Equipment Schedule 1
W.B. 92.7"; 3.6 Liter.

Body Type	VIN	List	Trade-In Fair	Trade-In Good	Pvt-Party Good	Retail Excellent
GT3 Coupe 2D	AC299	101995	47925	53125	56400	65200

CARRERA GT—V10—Equipment Schedule 1
W.B. 107.5"; 5.7 Liter.

Body Type	VIN	List	Trade-In Fair	Trade-In Good	Pvt-Party Good	Retail Excellent
Roadster 2D	CA299	448400	****	****	****	326700

2006 PORSCHE — WPO(CA298)-6-#

BOXSTER—6-Cyl.—Equipment Schedule 1
W.B. 95.1"; 2.7 Liter, 3.2 Liter.

Body Type	VIN	List	Trade-In Fair	Trade-In Good	Pvt-Party Good	Retail Excellent
Cabriolet 2D	CA298	45795	17550	19700	22300	27200
S Cabriolet 2D	CB298	55495	22350	24900	27600	33100
Full Leather			400	400	535	535
Hard Top			625	625	835	835
Aero Kit			2300	2300	3065	3065
Sport Pkg			800	800	1065	1065
Tiptronic Auto Trans			950	950	1265	1265

CAYMAN—6-Cyl.—Equipment Schedule 1
W.B. 95.1"; 3.4 Liter.

Body Type	VIN	List	Trade-In Fair	Trade-In Good	Pvt-Party Good	Retail Excellent
S Coupe 2D	AB298	59695	25375	28325	31000	36800
Full Leather			625	625	835	835
Tiptronic Auto Trans			950	950	1265	1265

911 CARRERA—6-Cyl.—Equipment Schedule 1
W.B. 92.5"; 3.6 Liter, 3.8 Liter.

Body Type	VIN	List	Trade-In Fair	Trade-In Good	Pvt-Party Good	Retail Excellent
Coupe 2D	AA299	73615	33325	37050	39900	46600
Cabriolet 2D	CA299	83715	37525	41650	44600	51600
S Coupe 2D	AB299	83715	35375	39300	42100	49100
S Cabriolet 2D	CB299	93745	40175	44600	47500	54900
Full Leather			400	400	535	535
Hard Top (Cabriolet)			625	625	835	835
Aero Kit			2300	2300	3065	3065
Tiptronic Auto Trans			950	950	1265	1265

911 CARRERA 4 AWD—6-Cyl.—Equipment Schedule 1
W.B. 92.5"; 3.6 Liter, 3.8 Liter.

Body Type	VIN	List	Trade-In Fair	Trade-In Good	Pvt-Party Good	Retail Excellent
Coupe 2D	AA299	79415	34975	38900	41700	48600
Cabriolet 2D	CA299	89445	42150	46750	49700	57300
4S Coupe 2D	AB299	89415	39600	44000	46800	54200
4S Cabriolet 2D	CB299	99445	46150	51150	54200	62300
Full Leather			400	400	535	535
Hard Top (Cabriolet)			625	625	835	835
Aero Kit			2300	2300	3065	3065
Tiptronic Auto Trans			950	950	1265	1265

Body	Type	VIN	List	Trade-In Fair	Good	Pvt-Party Good	Retail Excellent

2007 PORSCHE — WPO(CA298)-7-#

BOXSTER—6-Cyl.—Equipment Schedule 1
W.B. 95.1"; 2.7 Liter, 3.4 Liter.

Cabriolet 2D		CA298	46395	20575	23025	25700	31000
S Cabriolet 2D		CB298	56295	25675	28625	31400	37200
Full Leather				450	450	600	600
Hard Top				650	650	865	865
Aero Kit				2400	2400	3200	3200
Sport Pkg				875	875	1165	1165
Tiptronic Auto Trans				1025	1025	1365	1365

CAYMAN—6-Cyl.—Equipment Schedule 1
W.B. 95.1"; 2.7 Liter, 3.4 Liter.

Coupe 2D		AA298	54955	24100	26950	29600	35300
S Coupe 2D		AB298	64455	29200	32450	35200	41400
Full Leather				650	650	865	865
Tiptronic Auto Trans				1025	1025	1365	1365

911 CARRERA—6-Cyl.—Equipment Schedule 1
W.B. 92.5"; 3.6 Liter, 3.8 Liter.

Coupe 2D		AA299	73195	37925	42050	44800	51700
Cabriolet 2D		CA299	83395	42525	47150	50000	57400
S Coupe 2D		AB299	83395	40175	44600	47300	54500
S Cabriolet 2D		CB299	93595	45275	50175	53000	60800
Full Leather				450	450	600	600
Hard Top (Cabriolet)				650	650	865	865
Aero Kit				2400	2400	3200	3200
Tiptronic Auto Trans				1025	1025	1365	1365

911 CARRERA 4 AWD—6-Cyl.—Equipment Schedule 1
W.B. 92.5"; 3.6 Liter, 3.8 Liter.

Coupe 2D		AA299	78995	39800	44200	46800	54000
Cabriolet 2D		CA299	89195	47525	52725	55600	63500
4S Coupe 2D		AB299	89195	44975	49775	52600	60000
4S Cabriolet 2D		CB299	99395	52225	57925	60700	69100
Full Leather				450	450	600	600
Hard Top (Cabriolet)				650	650	865	865
Aero Kit				2400	2400	3200	3200
Tiptronic Auto Trans				1025	1025	1365	1365

911 TARGA AWD—6-Cyl.—Equipment Schedule 1
W.B. 92.5"; 3.6 Liter, 3.8 Liter.

4 Coupe 2D		BA299	86495	40975	45475	48100	55400
4S Coupe 2D		BB299	96695	44600	49500	52200	60000
Full Leather				450	450	600	600
Tiptronic Auto Trans				1025	1025	1365	1365

911 GT3—6-Cyl.—Equipment Schedule 1
W.B. 92.7"; 3.6 Liter.

Coupe 2D		AC299	106795	75950	83900	86600	97200
Full Leather				450	450	600	600

911 TURBO AWD—6-Cyl. Turbo—Equipment Schedule 1
W.B. 92.5"; 3.6 Liter.

Coupe 2D		AD299	123695	76050	84075	86800	97400
Full Leather				450	450	600	600
Tiptronic Auto Trans				1025	1025	1365	1365

2008 PORSCHE — WPO(CA298)-8-#

BOXSTER—6-Cyl.—Equipment Schedule 1
W.B. 95.1"; 2.7 Liter, 3.4 Liter.

Cabriolet 2D		CA298	46660	24000	26750	29500	35100
Limited Ed Cabriolet		CA298	50760	27550	30675	33400	39400
S Cabriolet 2D		CB298	56560	29500	32725	35500	41700
S Limited Ed Cabriolet		CB298	60760	30975	34400	37000	43300
Full Leather				525	525	700	700
Hard Top				675	675	900	900
Aero Kit				2500	2500	3335	3335
Sport Pkg				950	950	1265	1265
Tiptronic Auto Trans				1100	1100	1465	1465

CAYMAN—6-Cyl.—Equipment Schedule 1
W.B. 95.1"; 2.7 Liter, 3.4 Liter.

Coupe 2D		AA298	53470	28025	31250	34000	40000
S Coupe 2D		AB298	63170	33525	37250	39900	46400
Full Leather				675	675	900	900
Design Edition 1				950	950	1265	1265
Tiptronic Auto Trans				1100	1100	1465	1465

Body	Type	VIN	List	Trade-In Fair	Good	Pvt-Party Good	Retail Excellent
911 CARRERA—6-Cyl.—Equipment Schedule 1							
W.B. 92.5"; 3.6 Liter, 3.8 Liter.							
Coupe 2D	AA299	74360	**42925**	**47625**	**50300**	**57700**
Cabriolet 2D	CA299	84660	**48025**	**53225**	**55800**	**63600**
S Coupe 2D	AB299	84660	**45375**	**50275**	**52900**	**60600**
S Cabriolet 2D	CB299	94960	**51050**	**56550**	**59100**	**67100**
Full Leather			**525**	**525**	**700**	**700**
Hard Top (Cabriolet)			**675**	**675**	**900**	**900**
Aero Kit			**2500**	**2500**	**3335**	**3335**
Tiptronic Auto Trans			**1100**	**1100**	**1465**	**1465**
911 CARRERA 4 AWD—6-Cyl.—Equipment Schedule 1							
W.B. 92.5"; 3.6 Liter, 3.8 Liter.							
Coupe 2D	AA299	80260	**44975**	**49775**	**52500**	**60100**
Cabriolet 2D	CA299	90560	**53500**	**59300**	**61800**	**70100**
4S Coupe 2D	AB299	90560	**50850**	**56350**	**58900**	**66900**
4S Cabriolet 2D	CB299	100860	**58900**	**65175**	**67700**	**76300**
Full Leather			**525**	**525**	**700**	**700**
Hard Top (Cabriolet)			**675**	**675**	**900**	**900**
Aero Kit			**2500**	**2500**	**3335**	**3335**
Tiptronic Auto Trans			**1100**	**1100**	**1465**	**1465**
911 TARGA AWD—6-Cyl.—Equipment Schedule 1							
W.B. 92.5"; 3.6 Liter, 3.8 Liter.							
4 Coupe 2D	BA299	87860	**46150**	**51150**	**53800**	**61400**
4S Coupe 2D	BB299	98160	**50375**	**55750**	**58400**	**66300**
Full Leather			**525**	**525**	**700**	**700**
Tiptronic Auto Trans			**1100**	**1100**	**1465**	**1465**
911 TURBO AWD—6-Cyl. Turbo—Equipment Schedule 1							
W.B. 92.5"; 3.6 Liter.							
Coupe 2D	AD299	127060				
Cabriolet 2D	CD299	137360				
Full Leather						
Tiptronic Auto Trans						

SAAB

1994 SAAB — YS3(DM35B)-R-#

Body	Type	VIN	List	Trade-In Fair	Good	Pvt-Party Good	Retail Excellent
900—4-Cyl.—Equipment Schedule 3							
W.B. 102.4"; 2.1 Liter, 2.3 Liter.							
S Coupe 2D	DM35B	22750	**350**	**500**	**1100**	**2050**
S Hatchback 4D	DM55B	21450	**350**	**475**	**1075**	**2000**
S Convertible 2D	AK75E	33735	**1550**	**2025**	**3225**	**5025**
V6 2.5 Liter	V		**200**	**200**	**265**	**265**
900—V6—Equipment Schedule 3							
W.B. 102.4"; 2.5 Liter.							
SE Hatchback 4D	DM55V	27450	**700**	**1000**	**1850**	**3200**
Auto Trans			**125**	**125**	**165**	**165**
900—4-Cyl. Turbo—Equipment Schedule 3							
W.B. 102.4"; 2.0 Liter.							
SE Coupe 2D	DN35L	27740	**750**	**1075**	**1925**	**3325**
Convertible 2D	AL75L	38875	**2275**	**2850**	**4150**	**6100**
Commem Ed Conv 2D	AL75T	40875	**2450**	**3050**	**4350**	**6350**
9000—4-Cyl.—Equipment Schedule 2							
W.B. 105.2"; 2.3 Liter.							
CS Hatchback 4D	CM68B	30670	**875**	**1225**	**2175**	**3650**
CD Sedan 4D	CM48B	32775	**800**	**1125**	**2050**	**3475**
CSE Hatchback 4D	CM68B	34450	**1000**	**1425**	**2525**	**4150**
CDE Sedan 4D	CM48B	34090	**1025**	**1450**	**2525**	**4175**
4-Cyl. 2.3 Liter Turbo	M		**700**	**700**	**935**	**935**
9000—4-Cyl. Turbo—Equipment Schedule 2							
W.B. 105.2"; 2.3 Liter.							
Aero Hatchback 4D	CN68M	39150	**1375**	**1850**	**3050**	**4775**
Traction Control			**100**	**100**	**135**	**135**

1995 SAAB — YS3(DD35B)-S-#

Body	Type	VIN	List	Trade-In Fair	Good	Pvt-Party Good	Retail Excellent
900—4-Cyl.—Equipment Schedule 3							
W.B. 102.4"; 2.3 Liter.							
S Coupe 2D	DD35B	24545	**425**	**600**	**1225**	**2275**
S Hatchback 4D	DD55B	24225	**400**	**575**	**1200**	**2225**
S Convertible 2D	DD75B	33465	**1575**	**2050**	**3275**	**5100**
Auto Trans			**125**	**125**	**165**	**165**

1995 SAAB

Body Type	VIN	List	Trade-In Fair	Good	Pvt-Party Good	Retail Excellent
900—V6—Equipment Schedule 3						
W.B. 102.4"; 2.5 Liter.						
SE Hatchback 4D	DF55V	29150	850	1175	2125	3600
Auto Trans			125	125	165	165
900—4-Cyl. Turbo—Equipment Schedule 3						
W.B. 102.4"; 2.0 Liter.						
SE Coupe 2D	DF35N	29460	875	1250	2225	3725
SE Convertible 2D	DF78N	39990	2200	2800	4100	6025
Auto Trans			125	125	165	165
V6 2.5 Liter	V		200	200	265	265
9000—4-Cyl. Light Pressure Turbo—Equipment Schedule 2						
W.B. 105.2"; 2.3 Liter.						
CS Hatchback 4D	CD68U	32695	1025	1450	2550	4225
9000—4-Cyl. Turbo—Equipment Schedule 2						
W.B. 105.2"; 2.3 Liter.						
Aero Hatchback 4D	CH68M,R	41770	1675	2175	3425	5250
9000—V6—Equipment Schedule 2						
W.B. 105.2"; 3.0 Liter.						
CSE Hatchback 4D	CF68W	39120	1300	1775	2975	4700
CDE Sedan 4D	CF48W	39465	1225	1725	2900	4600
4-Cyl. 2.3 Liter Turbo	M		0	0	0	0

1996 SAAB — YS3(DD35B)–T–#

Body Type	VIN	List	Trade-In Fair	Good	Pvt-Party Good	Retail Excellent
900—4-Cyl.—Equipment Schedule 3						
W.B. 102.4"; 2.3 Liter.						
S Coupe 2D	DD35B	24490	525	700	1475	2700
S Hatchback 4D	DD55B	25190	500	675	1400	2525
S Convertible 2D	DD75B	34490	1925	2475	3750	5625
Auto Trans			125	125	165	165
900—4-Cyl. Turbo—Equipment Schedule 3						
W.B. 102.4"; 2.0 Liter.						
SE Coupe 2D	DF35N	29490	1050	1500	2625	4300
SE Hatchback 4D	DF55N	30190	1075	1525	2650	4325
SE Convertible 2D	DF75N	40490	2700	3300	4675	6750
Auto Trans			125	125	165	165
V6 2.5 Liter	V		250	250	335	335
9000—4-Cyl. Light Pressure Turbo—Equipment Schedule 2						
W.B. 105.2"; 2.3 Liter.						
CS Hatchback 4D	CD68U	32695	1200	1675	2850	4575
Manual Trans	5		(225)	(225)	(300)	(300)
9000—4-Cyl. Turbo—Equipment Schedule 2						
W.B. 105.2"; 2.3 Liter.						
Aero Hatchback 4D	CH58M,R	42735	2025	2600	3875	5775
Manual Trans	5		(125)	(125)	(165)	(165)
9000—V6—Equipment Schedule 2						
W.B. 105.2"; 3.0 Liter.						
CSE Hatchback 4D	CF68W	40690	1625	2100	3350	5175
Manual Trans			(225)	(225)	(300)	(300)
4-Cyl. 2.3 Liter Turbo	M		0	0	0	0

1997 SAAB — YS3(DD35B)–V–#

Body Type	VIN	List	Trade-In Fair	Good	Pvt-Party Good	Retail Excellent
900—4-Cyl.—Equipment Schedule 3						
W.B. 102.4"; 2.3 Liter.						
S Coupe 2D	DD35B	25520	625	875	1750	3075
S Hatchback 4D	DD55B	26520	600	800	1650	2975
S Convertible 2D	DD75B	35520	2225	2825	4125	6075
Auto Trans			150	150	200	200
900—4-Cyl. Turbo—Equipment Schedule 3						
W.B. 102.4"; 2.0 Liter.						
S Coupe 2D	DF35N	30520	1250	1725	2925	4650
SE Hatchback 4D	DF55N	31520	1250	1725	2925	4650
SE Convertible 2D	DF75N	41520	3125	3800	5200	7350
Auto Trans			150	150	200	200
V6 2.5 Liter	V		275	275	365	365
9000—4-Cyl. Light Pressure Turbo—Equipment Schedule 2						
W.B. 105.2"; 2.3 Liter.						
CS Hatchback 4D	CD68U	35360	1550	2025	3275	5100
Manual Trans			(275)	(275)	(365)	(365)
9000—4-Cyl. Turbo—Equipment Schedule 2						
W.B. 105.2"; 2.3 Liter.						
Aero Hatchback 4D	CH68M	43065	2625	3225	4575	6625
Manual Trans			(150)	(150)	(200)	(200)

1997 SAAB

Body Type	VIN	List	Trade-In Fair	Good	Pvt-Party Good	Retail Excellent
9000—V6—Equipment Schedule 2						
W.B. 105.2"; 3.0 Liter.						
CSE Hatchback 4D	CF68W	41020	**2025**	**2575**	**3850**	**5750**
Manual Trans	5		**(275)**	**(275)**	**(365)**	**(365)**
4-Cyl. 2.3 Liter Turbo	U		**0**	**0**	**0**	**0**

1998 SAAB — YS3(DD55B)–W–#

Body Type	VIN	List	Trade-In Fair	Good	Pvt-Party Good	Retail Excellent
900—4-Cyl.—Equipment Schedule 3						
W.B. 102.4"; 2.3 Liter.						
S Hatchback 4D	DD55B	27505	**750**	**1050**	**2000**	**3475**
S Convertible 2D	DD75B	36945	**2625**	**3225**	**4575**	**6625**
Auto Trans			**175**	**175**	**235**	**235**
900—4-Cyl. Turbo—Equipment Schedule 3						
W.B. 102.4"; 2.0 Liter.						
S Coupe 2D	DD35N	25050	**975**	**1375**	**2500**	**4200**
SE Coupe 2D	DF35N	31545	**1575**	**2075**	**3325**	**5175**
SE Hatchback 4D	DF55N	32545	**1575**	**2050**	**3300**	**5125**
SE Convertible 2D	DF75N	42745	**3700**	**4400**	**5875**	**8125**
Auto Trans			**175**	**175**	**235**	**235**
9000—4-Cyl. Turbo—Equipment Schedule 2						
W.B. 105.2"; 2.3 Liter.						
CSE Hatchback 4D	CF68M	40175	**2525**	**3100**	**4450**	**6475**
Manual Trans	5		**(325)**	**(325)**	**(435)**	**(435)**

1999 SAAB — YS3(DD38N)–X–#

Body Type	VIN	List	Trade-In Fair	Good	Pvt-Party Good	Retail Excellent
9-3—4-Cyl. Turbo—Equipment Schedule 3						
W.B. 102.6"; 2.0 Liter.						
Hatchback 2D	DD38N	26225	**900**	**1275**	**2400**	**4075**
Hatchback 4D	DD58N	26725	**1025**	**1450**	**2600**	**4300**
Convertible 2D	DD78N	38725	**3425**	**4150**	**5525**	**7750**
SE Hatchback 4D	DF58N	33275	**1675**	**2175**	**3425**	**5300**
SE Convertible 2D	DF78N	44570	**3375**	**4075**	**5475**	**7650**
Auto Trans			**200**	**200**	**265**	**265**
4-Cyl. 2.0L HO Turbo	P		**225**	**225**	**300**	**300**
9-3—4-Cyl. HO Turbo—Equipment Schedule 3						
W.B. 102.6"; 2.3 Liter.						
Viggen Coupe 2D	DP35G	38325	**4325**	**5125**	**6600**	**8950**
9-5—V6 Turbo—Equipment Schedule 2						
W.B. 106.4"; 3.0 Liter.						
Sedan 4D	ED48Z	35640	**1375**	**1850**	**3050**	**4875**
Wagon 4D	ED58Z	37475	**1725**	**2225**	**3475**	**5350**
SE Sedan 4D	EF48Z	37825	**1925**	**2475**	**3750**	**5625**
Manual Trans			**(375)**	**(375)**	**(500)**	**(500)**
4-Cyl. 2.3L Turbo	E		**(800)**	**(800)**	**(1065)**	**(1065)**

2000 SAAB — YS3(DD35H)–Y–#

Body Type	VIN	List	Trade-In Fair	Good	Pvt-Party Good	Retail Excellent
9-3—4-Cyl. Turbo—Equipment Schedule 3						
W.B. 102.6"; 2.0 Liter.						
Hatchback 2D	DD35H	27675	**1175**	**1650**	**2875**	**4650**
Hatchback 4D	DD55H	28155	**1350**	**1825**	**3075**	**4875**
Convertible 2D	DD75H	41225	**4075**	**4825**	**6275**	**8575**
Auto Trans	8		**200**	**200**	**265**	**265**
9-3—4-Cyl. HO Turbo—Equipment Schedule 3						
W.B. 102.6"; 2.3 Liter.						
SE Hatchback 4D	DF55K	33670	**2125**	**2700**	**4000**	**5925**
SE Convertible 2D	DF75K	44770	**4025**	**4750**	**6200**	**8500**
Viggen Hatchback 2D	DP35G	38325	**5050**	**5875**	**7475**	**10000**
Viggen Hatchback 4D	DP55G	38325	**4300**	**5075**	**6550**	**8875**
Viggen Convertible 2D	DP75G	45570	**6675**	**7675**	**9375**	**12200**
Auto Trans	8		**200**	**200**	**265**	**265**
9-5—4-Cyl. Turbo—Equipment Schedule 2						
W.B. 106.4", 106.6" (Wagon); 2.3 Liter.						
Sedan 4D	ED48E	35300	**1775**	**2275**	**3550**	**5450**
Wagon 4D	ED58E	35300	**2150**	**2725**	**4025**	**5975**
Gary Fisher Edition			**550**	**550**	**735**	**735**
Manual Trans	5		**(425)**	**(425)**	**(565)**	**(565)**
9-5—4-Cyl. HO Turbo—Equipment Schedule 2						
W.B. 106.4", 106.6" (Wagon); 2.3 Liter.						
Aero Sedan 4D	EH48G	41550	**3250**	**3950**	**5350**	**7500**
Aero Wagon 4D	EH58G	44145	**3800**	**4500**	**5950**	**8200**
Manual Trans	5		**(425)**	**(425)**	**(565)**	**(565)**

Body	Type	VIN	List	Trade-In Fair	Trade-In Good	Pvt-Party Good	Retail Excellent
9-5—V6 Turbo—Equipment Schedule 2							
W.B. 106.4", 106.6" (Wagon); 3.0 Liter.							
SE Sedan 4D		EF48Z	38325	2375	2950	4300	6275
SE Wagon 4D		EF58Z	38325	2575	3175	4525	6575

2001 SAAB — YS3(DD35H)-1-#

Body	Type	VIN	List	Trade-In Fair	Trade-In Good	Pvt-Party Good	Retail Excellent
9-3—4-Cyl. Turbo—Equipment Schedule 3							
W.B. 102.6"; 2.0 Liter.							
Hatchback 2D		DD35H	27070	1700	2200	3500	5400
Hatchback 4D		DD55H	27570	1850	2400	3700	5600
Auto Trans				200	200	265	265
9-3—4-Cyl. HO Turbo—Equipment Schedule 3							
W.B. 102.6"; 2.0 Liter, 2.3 Liter.							
SE Hatchback 4D		DF55K	33170	2725	3325	4675	6750
SE Convertible 2D		DF75K	40570	4750	5550	7100	9575
Viggen Hatchback 2D		DP35G	38570	5875	6800	8425	11050
Viggen Hatchback 4D		DP55G	38570	5050	5900	7450	9950
Viggen Convertible 2D		DP75G	45570	7650	8750	10500	13450
Auto Trans				200	200	265	265
9-5—4-Cyl. Turbo—Equipment Schedule 2							
W.B. 106.4"; 2.3 Liter.							
Sedan 4D		ED48E	34570	2275	2850	4200	6175
Wagon 4D		ED58E	35270	2700	3300	4650	6725
Manual Trans				(475)	(475)	(635)	(635)
9-5—4-Cyl. HO Turbo—Equipment Schedule 2							
W.B. 106.4"; 2.3 Liter.							
Aero Sedan 4D		EH48G	40750	3900	4625	6075	8325
Aero Wagon 4D		EH58G	41450	4475	5300	6750	9125
Manual Trans				(475)	(475)	(635)	(635)
9-5—V6 Turbo—Equipment Schedule 2							
W.B. 106.4"; 3.0 Liter.							
SE Sedan 4D		EF48Z	39225	2925	3550	4925	7025
SE Wagon 4D		EF58Z	39925	3150	3825	5225	7350

2002 SAAB — YS3(DF55K)-2-#

Body	Type	VIN	List	Trade-In Fair	Trade-In Good	Pvt-Party Good	Retail Excellent
9-3—4-Cyl. Turbo—Equipment Schedule 3							
W.B. 102.6"; 2.0 Liter.							
SE Hatchback 4D		DF55K	29820	3300	3975	5650	8125
SE Convertible 2D		DF75K	41820	5525	6400	8250	11100
Auto Trans				200	200	265	265
9-3—4-Cyl. HO Turbo—Equipment Schedule 3							
W.B. 102.6"; 2.3 Liter.							
Viggen Hatchback 2D		DP35G	38720	6725	7750	9625	12700
Viggen Hatchback 4D		DP55G	38720	5850	6775	8650	11550
Viggen Convertible 2D		DP75G	45620	8600	9800	11850	15300
9-5—4-Cyl. Turbo—Equipment Schedule 2							
W.B. 106.4"; 2.3 Liter.							
Linear Sedan 4D		EB49E	35820	2825	3450	5100	7525
Linear Wagon 4D		EB59E	36520	3250	3925	5600	8075
Manual Trans		5		(500)	(500)	(665)	(665)
9-5—4-Cyl. HO Turbo—Equipment Schedule 2							
W.B. 106.4"; 2.3 Liter.							
Aero Sedan 4D		EH49G	40475	4550	5350	7125	9850
Aero Wagon 4D		EH59G	41175	5200	6075	7900	10750
Manual Trans		5		(500)	(500)	(665)	(665)
9-5—V6 Turbo—Equipment Schedule 2							
W.B. 106.4"; 3.0 Liter.							
Arc Sedan 4D		ED49Z	39275	3525	4225	5900	8425
Arc Wagon 4D		ED59Z	39975	3775	4500	6200	8775

2003 SAAB — YS3(FB45S)-3-#

Body	Type	VIN	List	Trade-In Fair	Trade-In Good	Pvt-Party Good	Retail Excellent
9-3—4-Cyl. Turbo—Equipment Schedule 3							
W.B. 105.3"; 2.0 Liter.							
Linear Sedan 4D		FB45S	26525	2775	3375	5100	7550
Auto Trans				225	225	300	300
9-3—4-Cyl. HO Turbo—Equipment Schedule 3							
W.B. 102.6", 105.3" (Sed); 2.0 Liter.							
Arc Sedan 4D		FD46Y	30620	4275	5050	6775	9450
Vector Sedan 4D		FF46Y	33120	5000	5825	7675	10500
SE Convertible 2D		DF75K	46020	6525	7525	9425	12500
Auto Trans				225	225	300	300

0709

2003 SAAB

Body	Type	VIN	List	Trade-In Fair	Trade-In Good	Pvt-Party Good	Retail Excellent
9-5—4-Cyl. Turbo—Equipment Schedule 2							
W.B. 106.4"; 2.3 Liter.							
Linear Sedan 4D	EB49E	35920	3425	4150	5850	8400
Linear Wagon 4D	EB59E	36620	3950	4675	6425	9050
Manual Trans			(550)	(550)	(735)	(735)
9-5—4-Cyl. HO Turbo—Equipment Schedule 2							
W.B. 106.4"; 2.3 Liter.							
Aero Sedan 4D	EH49G	40575	5450	6325	8175	11050
Aero Wagon 4D	EH59G	41275	6150	7125	9025	12000
Manual Trans			(550)	(550)	(735)	(735)
9-5—V6 Turbo—Equipment Schedule 2							
W.B. 106.4"; 3.0 Liter.							
Arc Sedan 4D	ED49Z	39275	4250	5025	6750	9425
Arc Wagon 4D	ED59Z	39975	4525	5350	7150	9900

2004 SAAB — YS3(FB45S)-4-#

Body	Type	VIN	List	Trade-In Fair	Trade-In Good	Pvt-Party Good	Retail Excellent
9-3—4-Cyl. Turbo—Equipment Schedule 3							
W.B. 105.3"; 2.0 Liter.							
Linear Sedan 4D	FB45S	26765	3525	4225	5975	8600
Auto Trans			250	250	335	335
9-3—4-Cyl. HO Turbo—Equipment Schedule 3							
W.B. 105.3"; 2.0 Liter.							
Arc Sedan 4D	FD46Y	30860	5200	6075	7950	10850
Arc Convertible 2D	FD75Y	40670	8550	9775	11800	15200
Aero Sedan 4D	FF45Y	34710	5750	6700	8575	11500
Aero Convertible 2D	FH76Y	43175	9475	10775	12850	16350
Auto Trans			250	250	335	335
9-5—4-Cyl. Turbo—Equipment Schedule 2							
W.B. 106.4"; 2.3 Liter.							
Linear Wagon 4D	EB59E	34225	4800	5625	7500	10350
Arc Sedan 4D	ED49G	36455	5175	6025	7900	10800
Arc Wagon 4D	ED59G	37165	5525	6425	8275	11200
Manual Trans			(600)	(600)	(800)	(800)
9-5—4-Cyl. HO Turbo—Equipment Schedule 2							
W.B. 106.4"; 2.3 Liter.							
Aero Sedan 4D	EH49G	41490	6500	7500	9400	12450
Aero Wagon 4D	EH59G	42195	7325	8400	10350	13500
Manual Trans			(600)	(600)	(800)	(800)

2005 SAAB — (YS3orJF4)(GG616)-5-#

Body	Type	VIN	List	Trade-In Fair	Trade-In Good	Pvt-Party Good	Retail Excellent
9-2X AWD—4-Cyl.—Equipment Schedule 3							
W.B. 99.4"; 2.5 Liter.							
Linear Wagon 4D	GG616	24935	5125	5975	7925	10850
9-2X AWD—4-Cyl. Turbo—Equipment Schedule 3							
W.B. 99.4"; 2.0 Liter.							
Aero Wagon 4D	GG226	28895	6525	7500	9450	12550
9-3—4-Cyl. Turbo—Equipment Schedule 3							
W.B. 105.3"; 2.0 Liter.							
Linear Sedan 4D	FB45S	28920	4450	5250	7150	10000
Linear Convertible 2D	FB75S	39170	8550	9775	11750	15150
Auto Trans			275	275	365	365
9-3—4-Cyl. HO Turbo—Equipment Schedule 3							
W.B. 105.3"; 2.0 Liter.							
Arc Sedan 4D	FD45Y	32320	6325	7325	9225	12300
Arc Convertible 2D	FD75Y	42170	10050	11425	13500	17050
Aero Sedan 4D	FF45Y	34920	6950	8000	9950	13100
Aero Convertible 2D	FH75Y	44670	11125	12600	14650	18350
Auto Trans			275	275	365	365
9-5—4-Cyl. Turbo—Equipment Schedule 2							
W.B. 106.4"; 2.3 Liter.							
Linear Wagon 4D	EB59E	34620	5875	6825	8750	11750
Arc Sedan 4D	ED49A	36970	6275	7250	9200	12250
Arc Wagon 4D	ED59A	37770	6650	7650	9575	12700
Manual Trans			(650)	(650)	(865)	(865)
9-5—4-Cyl. HO Turbo—Equipment Schedule 2							
W.B. 106.4"; 2.3 Liter.							
Aero Sedan 4D	EH49G	42020	8725	9950	12000	15400
Aero Wagon 4D	EH59G	42820	9575	10875	12950	16450
Manual Trans			(650)	(650)	(865)	(865)

Body	Type	VIN	List	Trade-In Fair	Trade-In Good	Pvt-Party Good	Retail Excellent
2006 SAAB — (YS3orJF4)(GG616)–6–#							
9-2X AWD—4-Cyl.—Equipment Schedule 3							
W.B. 99.4"; 2.5 Liter.							
2.5i Wagon 4D		GG616	24960	**6400**	**7375**	**9350**	**12500**
9-2X AWD—4-Cyl. Turbo—Equipment Schedule 3							
W.B. 99.4"; 2.5 Liter.							
Aero Wagon 4D		GG726	28920	**7900**	**9050**	**11100**	**14450**
9-3—4-Cyl. Turbo—Equipment Schedule 3							
W.B. 105.3"; 2.0 Liter.							
2.0T Sedan 4D		FD45Y	27970	**6625**	**7625**	**9600**	**12750**
2.0T Convertible 2D		FD75Y	38570	**11125**	**12600**	**14650**	**18350**
2.0T SportCombi Wag		FD55Y	28970	**8700**	**9900**	**11950**	**15400**
Auto Trans				**300**	**300**	**400**	**400**
9-3—6-Cyl. Turbo—Equipment Schedule 3							
W.B. 105.3"; 2.8 Liter.							
Aero Sedan 4D		FH41U	33970	**9325**	**10625**	**12700**	**16150**
Aero Convertible 2D		FH71U	43970	**13925**	**15675**	**17800**	**21800**
Aero SportCombi Wag		FH51U	34970	**11375**	**12850**	**14950**	**18650**
Aero 20th Anniv Conv		FH71U	44615	**15100**	**17000**	**19100**	**23200**
Auto Trans				**300**	**300**	**400**	**400**
9-5—4-Cyl. Turbo—Equipment Schedule 2							
W.B. 106.4"; 2.3 Liter.							
2.3T Sedan 4D		ED45G	36170	**10775**	**12200**	**14250**	**17950**
2.3T SportCombi Wag		ED56G	37170	**11750**	**13275**	**15400**	**19150**
Manual Trans				**(675)**	**(675)**	**(900)**	**(900)**
2007 SAAB — (YS3orJF4)(FD46Y)–7–#							
9-3—4-Cyl. Turbo—Equipment Schedule 3							
W.B. 105.3"; 2.0 Liter.							
2.0T Sedan 4D		FD46Y	28265	**8100**	**9275**	**11300**	**14650**
2.0T Convertible 2D		FD76Y	38865	**13025**	**14650**	**16750**	**20600**
2.0T SportCombi Wag		FD56Y	29265	**10400**	**11750**	**13800**	**17400**
Auto Trans		9		**300**	**300**	**400**	**400**
9-3—V6 Turbo—Equipment Schedule 3							
W.B. 105.3"; 2.8 Liter.							
Aero Sedan 4D		FH46U	34570	**11125**	**12600**	**14650**	**18300**
Aero Convertible 2D		FH76U	44470	**16075**	**18025**	**20200**	**24400**
Aero SportCombi Wag		FH56U	35470	**13275**	**15000**	**17050**	**21000**
Auto Trans		1		**300**	**300**	**400**	**400**
4-Cyl. 2.0L Turbo (Wag)		Y		**(1800)**	**(1800)**	**(2400)**	**(2400)**
9-5—4-Cyl. Turbo—Equipment Schedule 2							
W.B. 106.4"; 2.3 Liter.							
2.3T Sedan 4D		ED45G	36465	**12650**	**14300**	**16350**	**20200**
2.3T Aero Sedan 4D		EH49G	36535	**13275**	**15000**	**17050**	**21000**
2.3T SportCombi Wag		ED55G	37465	**13775**	**15525**	**17600**	**21600**
2.3T Aero SportCombi		EH59G	37535	**14450**	**16225**	**18350**	**22300**
Manual Trans				**(700)**	**(700)**	**(935)**	**(935)**
2008 SAAB — (YS3orJF4)(FD46Y)–8–#							
9-3—4-Cyl. Turbo—Equipment Schedule 3							
W.B. 105.3"; 2.0 Liter.							
2.0T Sedan 4D		FD46Y	29735	**9900**	**11225**	**13350**	**16950**
2.0T Convertible 2D		FD76Y	41060	**15150**	**17050**	**19100**	**23200**
2.0T SportCombi Wag		FD56Y	30980	**12300**	**13925**	**16000**	**19900**
Auto Trans		9		**300**	**300**	**400**	**400**
9-3—V6 Turbo—Equipment Schedule 3							
W.B. 105.3"; 2.8 Liter.							
Aero Sedan 4D		FH46U	36715	**13125**	**14800**	**16950**	**20900**
Aero Convertible 2D		FH76U	47015	**18525**	**20675**	**22800**	**27200**
Aero SportCombi Wag		FH56U	37615	**15475**	**17400**	**19550**	**23700**
AWD		2,7		**2000**	**2000**	**2665**	**2665**
Auto Trans		1,2		**300**	**300**	**400**	**400**
9-3 AWD—V6 Turbo—Equipment Schedule 3							
W.B. 105.3"; 2.8 Liter.							
Turbo X Sedan 4D		FM47R	43860				
Turbo X SportCombi		FM57U	44660				
Auto Trans		1					
9-5—4-Cyl. Turbo—Equipment Schedule 2							
W.B. 106.4"; 2.3 Liter.							
2.3T Sedan 4D		ED49G	37205	**14800**	**16650**	**18750**	**22800**
2.3T Aero Sedan 4D		EH49G	38300	**15525**	**17450**	**19600**	**23700**

Body	Type	VIN	List	Trade-In Fair	Trade-In Good	Pvt-Party Good	Retail Excellent
2.3T SportCombi Wag		ED59G	38455	16025	17975	20100	24300
2.3T Aero SportCombi		EH59G	39550	16750	18775	20900	25200
Manual Trans		5	....	**(725)**	**(725)**	**(965)**	**(965)**

SATURN

1994 SATURN — 1G8Z(F559)-R-#

SATURN—4-Cyl.—Equipment Schedule 6
W.B. 99.2", 102.4" (4D); 1.9 Liter.

SL Sedan 4D		F559	11210	375	525	1125	2100
SL1 Sedan 4D		G559	12010	500	675	1375	2450
SL2 Sedan 4D		J557	13010	625	850	1650	2925
SC1 Coupe 2D		E159	12910	525	725	1475	2650
SC2 Coupe 2D		G157	14110	650	900	1700	3000
SW1 Wagon 4D		G859	12910	575	800	1575	2800
SW2 Wagon 4D		J857	13810	650	925	1750	3050

1995 SATURN — 1G8Z(F528)-S-#

SATURN—4-Cyl.—Equipment Schedule 6
W.B. 99.2", 102.4" (4D); 1.9 Liter.

SL Sedan 4D		F528	11260	425	600	1250	2275
SL1 Sedan 4D		G528	12260	575	775	1550	2800
SL2 Sedan 4D		J527	13260	675	950	1800	3125
SC1 Coupe 2D		E128	13130	600	825	1600	2875
SC2 Coupe 2D		G127	14260	725	1025	1875	3250
SW1 Wagon 4D		G828	12960	625	875	1700	3000
SW2 Wagon 4D		J827	13960	750	1050	1900	3300

1996 SATURN — 1G8Z(F528)-T-#

SATURN—4-Cyl.—Equipment Schedule 6
W.B. 99.2", 102.4" (4D); 1.9 Liter.

SL Sedan 4D		F528	11805	450	625	1300	2350
SL1 Sedan 4D		G528	12705	625	850	1675	2975
SL2 Sedan 4D		J527	13605	775	1075	1975	3375
SC1 Coupe 2D		E128	13505	650	925	1775	3075
SC2 Coupe 2D		G127	14605	825	1150	2050	3500
SW1 Wagon 4D		G828	13305	700	1000	1850	3250
SW2 Wagon 4D		J827	14205	825	1175	2125	3600

1997 SATURN — 1G8Z(F528)-V-#

SATURN—4-Cyl.—Equipment Schedule 6
W.B. 102.4"; 1.9 Liter.

SL Sedan 4D		F528	11925	525	700	1475	2700
SL1 Sedan 4D		G528	12925	700	975	1850	3250
SL2 Sedan 4D		J527	13825	875	1225	2200	3725
SC1 Coupe 2D		E128	13825	750	1075	1975	3425
SC2 Coupe 2D		G127	15025	925	1325	2400	4050
SW1 Wagon 4D		G828	13525	800	1150	2075	3550
SW2 Wagon 4D		J827	14425	950	1350	2425	4075

1998 SATURN — 1G8Z(F528)-W-#

SATURN—4-Cyl.—Equipment Schedule 6
W.B. 102.4"; 1.9 Liter.

SL Sedan 4D		F528	11995	600	825	1650	2975
SL1 Sedan 4D		G528	12695	825	1150	2100	3600
SL2 Sedan 4D		J527	13195	1000	1425	2525	4200
SC1 Coupe 2D		E128	13825	900	1250	2350	3975
SC2 Coupe 2D		G127	15295	1075	1525	2675	4325
SW1 Wagon 4D		G828	13695	950	1325	2450	4100
SW2 Wagon 4D		J827	14695	1100	1550	2700	4400

1999 SATURN — 1G8Z(F528)-X-#

SATURN—4-Cyl.—Equipment Schedule 6
W.B. 102.4"; 1.9 Liter.

SL Sedan 4D		F528	11995	700	975	1900	3325
SL1 Sedan 4D		G528	12695	975	1350	2500	4175
SL2 Sedan 4D		J527	13195	1150	1625	2825	4550
SC1 Coupe 2D		E128	13345	1050	1500	2650	4325
SC1 Coupe 3D		E128	13845	1100	1525	2700	4375

1999 SATURN

Body	Type	VIN	List	Trade-In Fair	Good	Pvt-Party Good	Retail Excellent
SC2 Coupe 2D		G127	14945	**1275**	**1750**	**2975**	**4725**
SC2 Coupe 3D		G127	15445	**1325**	**1800**	**3025**	**4775**
SW1 Wagon 4D		G828	13695	**1100**	**1550**	**2750**	**4450**
SW2 Wagon 4D		J827	14695	**1300**	**1775**	**3025**	**4775**

2000 SATURN — 1G8(JorZ)(F528)-Y-#

SATURN—4-Cyl.—Equipment Schedule 6
W.B. 102.4"; 1.9 Liter.

Body	Type	VIN	List	Trade-In Fair	Good	Pvt-Party Good	Retail Excellent
SL Sedan 4D		F528	12085	**850**	**1200**	**2300**	**3975**
SL1 Sedan 4D		G528	12885	**1125**	**1600**	**2800**	**4525**
SL2 Sedan 4D		J527	13335	**1425**	**1900**	**3150**	**4950**
SC1 Coupe 3D		N128	12975	**1300**	**1775**	**3000**	**4775**
SC2 Coupe 3D		R127	15585	**1625**	**2125**	**3375**	**5225**
SW2 Wagon 4D		J827	14730	**1600**	**2100**	**3375**	**5225**

SATURN L-SERIES—4-Cyl.—Equipment Schedule 3
W.B. 106.5"; 2.2 Liter.

Body	Type	VIN	List	Trade-In Fair	Good	Pvt-Party Good	Retail Excellent
LS Sedan 4D		R52F	16700	**1075**	**1500**	**2725**	**4475**
LS1 Sedan 4D		T52F	18150	**1325**	**1800**	**3075**	**4875**
LW1 Wagon 4D		U82F	19375	**1575**	**2050**	**3325**	**5175**
Manual Trans				**(400)**	**(400)**	**(535)**	**(535)**

SATURN L-SERIES—V6—Equipment Schedule 3
W.B. 106.5"; 3.0 Liter.

Body	Type	VIN	List	Trade-In Fair	Good	Pvt-Party Good	Retail Excellent
LS2 Sedan 4D		W52R	20575	**2075**	**2650**	**3950**	**5875**
LW2 Wagon 4D		W82R	21800	**2325**	**2900**	**4225**	**6200**

2001 SATURN — 1G8(JorZ)(F528)-1-#

SATURN—4-Cyl.—Equipment Schedule 6
W.B. 102.4"; 1.9 Liter.

Body	Type	VIN	List	Trade-In Fair	Good	Pvt-Party Good	Retail Excellent
SL Sedan 4D		F528	11995	**1050**	**1475**	**2675**	**4375**
SL1 Sedan 4D		G528	12910	**1425**	**1900**	**3150**	**4950**
SL2 Sedan 4D		J527	13360	**1775**	**2275**	**3525**	**5400**
SC1 Coupe 3D		N128	13960	**1600**	**2100**	**3350**	**5200**
SC2 Coupe 3D		R127	16110	**1950**	**2525**	**3800**	**5675**
SW2 Wagon 4D		J527	14755	**1950**	**2500**	**3800**	**5700**

SATURN L-SERIES—4-Cyl.—Equipment Schedule 3
W.B. 106.5"; 2.2 Liter.

Body	Type	VIN	List	Trade-In Fair	Good	Pvt-Party Good	Retail Excellent
L100 Sedan 4D		R52F	16245	**1400**	**1850**	**3100**	**4900**
L200 Sedan 4D		T52F	18210	**1725**	**2225**	**3475**	**5350**
LW200 Wagon 4D		U82F	19335	**1975**	**2525**	**3800**	**5675**
Manual Trans				**(425)**	**(425)**	**(565)**	**(565)**

SATURN L-SERIES—V6—Equipment Schedule 3
W.B. 106.5"; 3.0 Liter.

Body	Type	VIN	List	Trade-In Fair	Good	Pvt-Party Good	Retail Excellent
L300 Sedan 4D		W52R	19995	**2550**	**3125**	**4425**	**6425**
LW300 Wagon 4D		W82R	21860	**2800**	**3400**	**4725**	**6750**

2002 SATURN — 1G8(JorZ)(F528)-2-#

SATURN—4-Cyl.—Equipment Schedule 6
W.B. 102.4"; 1.9 Liter.

Body	Type	VIN	List	Trade-In Fair	Good	Pvt-Party Good	Retail Excellent
SL Sedan 4D		F528	11995	**1225**	**1700**	**3100**	**5075**
SL1 Sedan 4D		G528	13275	**1700**	**2200**	**3625**	**5675**
SL2 Sedan 4D		J527	13800	**2025**	**2575**	**4025**	**6125**
SC1 Coupe 3D		N128	14325	**1850**	**2400**	**3825**	**5900**
SC2 Coupe 3D		R127	16545	**2275**	**2850**	**4300**	**6450**

SATURN L-SERIES—4-Cyl.—Equipment Schedule 3
W.B. 106.5"; 2.2 Liter.

Body	Type	VIN	List	Trade-In Fair	Good	Pvt-Party Good	Retail Excellent
L100 Sedan 4D		R52F	16870	**1750**	**2250**	**3675**	**5700**
L200 Sedan 4D		T52F	19070	**2075**	**2625**	**4075**	**6150**
LW200 Wagon 4D		U82F	20515	**2325**	**2925**	**4350**	**6500**
Manual Trans				**(450)**	**(450)**	**(600)**	**(600)**

SATURN L-SERIES—V6—Equipment Schedule 3
W.B. 106.5"; 3.0 Liter.

Body	Type	VIN	List	Trade-In Fair	Good	Pvt-Party Good	Retail Excellent
L300 Sedan 4D		W52R	20920	**2950**	**3575**	**5075**	**7300**
LW300 Wagon 4D		W82R	22850	**3175**	**3875**	**5375**	**7650**

2003 SATURN — 1G8(AF54F)-3-#

ION—4-Cyl.—Equipment Schedule 6
W.B. 103.2"; 2.2 Liter.

Body	Type	VIN	List	Trade-In Fair	Good	Pvt-Party Good	Retail Excellent
1 Sedan 4D		AF54F	12955	**2025**	**2575**	**4075**	**6200**
2 Sedan 4D		AZ52F	14075	**2375**	**2975**	**4450**	**6650**
3 Sedan 4D		AK52F	15575	**2675**	**3300**	**4800**	**7025**
2 Quad Coupe 2D		AM12F	14595	**2975**	**3625**	**5150**	**7425**
3 Quad Coupe 2D		AV12F	16095	**3300**	**3975**	**5525**	**7850**

2003 SATURN

Body	Type	VIN	List	Trade-In Fair	Good	Pvt-Party Good	Retail Excellent
SATURN L-SERIES—4-Cyl.—Equipment Schedule 3							
W.B. 106.5"; 2.2 Liter.							
L200 Sedan 4D		JT54F	19040	2400	3000	4425	6600
LW200 Wagon 4D		JU84F	20850	2700	3300	4775	6975
Manual Trans				(500)	(500)	(665)	(665)
SATURN L-SERIES—V6—Equipment Schedule 3							
W.B. 106.5"; 3.0 Liter.							
L300 Sedan 4D		JW54R	21255	3400	4100	5600	7925
LW300 Wagon 4D		JW84R	23185	3725	4450	5975	8325

2004 SATURN — 1G8(AF54F)-4-#

Body	Type	VIN	List	Trade-In Fair	Good	Pvt-Party Good	Retail Excellent
ION—4-Cyl.—Equipment Schedule 6							
W.B. 103.2"; 2.2 Liter.							
1 Sedan 4D		AF54F	10995	2450	3050	4550	6750
2 Sedan 4D		AZ52F	14750	2825	3450	4975	7250
3 Sedan 4D		AK52F	16275	3150	3825	5375	7700
2 Quad Coupe 2D		AM12F	14850	3500	4225	5775	8125
3 Quad Coupe 2D		AV12F	16800	3925	4675	6250	8650
ION—4-Cyl. Supercharged—Equipment Schedule 6							
W.B. 103.5"; 2.0 Liter.							
Red Line Quad Cpe 2D		AY12P	20950	6425	7425	9125	11900
SATURN L-SERIES—4-Cyl.—Equipment Schedule 3							
W.B. 106.5"; 2.2 Liter.							
L300 Sedan 4D		JC54F	16995	2825	3450	4950	7150
L300 Wagon 4D		JC84F	19045	3175	3850	5350	7600
SATURN L-SERIES—V6—Equipment Schedule 3							
W.B. 106.5"; 3.0 Liter.							
L300 Sedan 4D		JD54R	21410	4000	4750	6275	8625
L300 Wagon 4D		JD84R	23560	4375	5200	6725	9125

2005 SATURN — 1G8(AF52F)-5-#

Body	Type	VIN	List	Trade-In Fair	Good	Pvt-Party Good	Retail Excellent
ION—4-Cyl.—Equipment Schedule 6							
W.B. 103.2"; 2.2 Liter.							
1 Sedan 4D		AF52F	12955	2950	3575	5125	7425
2 Sedan 4D		AZ52F	14945	3375	4050	5600	7975
3 Sedan 4D		AK52F	16470	3775	4475	6050	8425
2 Quad Coupe 2D		AM12F	15495	4175	4925	6500	8925
3 Quad Coupe 2D		AV12F	17245	4600	5450	7050	9600
ION—4-Cyl. Supercharged—Equipment Schedule 6							
W.B. 103.2"; 2.0 Liter.							
Red Line Quad Cpe 2D		AY12P	21450	6900	7975	9625	12450
SATURN L-SERIES—V6—Equipment Schedule 3							
W.B. 106.5"; 3.0 Liter.							
L300 Sedan 4D		JD54R	21995	4725	5550	7125	9625

2006 SATURN — 1G8(AZ55F)-6-#

Body	Type	VIN	List	Trade-In Fair	Good	Pvt-Party Good	Retail Excellent
ION—4-Cyl.—Equipment Schedule 6							
W.B. 103.2"; 2.2 Liter, 2.4 Liter.							
2 Sedan 4D		AZ55F	13450	4075	4800	6400	8825
3 Sedan 4D		AK55F	14895	4475	5275	6875	9400
2 Quad Coupe 2D		AM15F	13490	4900	5725	7350	9900
3 Quad Coupe 2D		AV15F	16190	5475	6350	7975	10600
ION—4-Cyl. Supercharged—Equipment Schedule 6							
W.B. 103.2"; 2.0 Liter.							
Red Line Quad Cpe 2D		AY15P	19990	7525	8650	10300	13200

2007 SATURN — 1G8(AZ55F)-7-#

Body	Type	VIN	List	Trade-In Fair	Good	Pvt-Party Good	Retail Excellent
ION—4-Cyl.—Equipment Schedule 6							
W.B. 103.2"; 2.2 Liter, 2.4 Liter.							
2 Sedan 4D		AZ55F	13780	4850	5675	7225	9675
3 Sedan 4D		AK55F	15220	5350	6225	7750	10250
2 Quad Coupe 2D		AM15F	14780	5775	6700	8225	10800
3 Quad Coupe 2D		AV15F	16520	6400	7400	8950	11550
ION—4-Cyl. Supercharged—Equipment Schedule 6							
W.B. 103.2"; 2.0 Liter.							
Red Line Quad Cpe 2D		AY15P	20420	8250	9425	11050	13950
AURA—V6—Equipment Schedule 4							
W.B. 112.3"; 3.5 Liter, 3.6 Liter.							
XE Sedan 4D		ZS57N	20595	7900	9050	10700	13500
XR Sedan 4D		ZV577	24595	9425	10725	12350	15350
Panoramic Power Roof				475	475	635	635

EQUIPMENT & MILEAGE PAGE 9 TO 23

Body	Type	VIN	List	Trade-In Fair	Trade-In Good	Pvt-Party Good	Retail Excellent
SKY—4-Cyl.—Equipment Schedule 3							
W.B. 95.1"; 2.4 Liter.							
Roadster 2D		MB35B	26045	**11525**	**13025**	**14800**	**18200**
SKY—4-Cyl. Turbo—Equipment Schedule 3							
W.B. 95.1"; 2.0 Liter.							
Red Line Roadster 2D		MG35X	29745	**13775**	**15525**	**17350**	**21000**

2008 SATURN — 1G8(AR671)-8-#

Body	Type	VIN	List	Trade-In Fair	Trade-In Good	Pvt-Party Good	Retail Excellent
ASTRA—4-Cyl.—Equipment Schedule 4							
W.B. 102.9"; 1.8 Liter.							
XE Hatchback 4D		AR671	17718	**9125**	**10400**	**11850**	**14700**
XR Hatchback 2D		AT271	18870	**9550**	**10875**	**12350**	**15250**
XR Hatchback 4D		AT671	19115	**9675**	**10975**	**12500**	**15400**
AURA—4-Cyl. Hybrid—Equipment Schedule 4							
W.B. 112.3"; 2.4 Liter.							
Green Line Sedan 4D		ZR575	22790	**11375**	**12850**	**14400**	**17500**
AURA—V6—Equipment Schedule 4							
W.B. 112.3"; 3.5 Liter, 3.6 Liter.							
XE Sedan 4D		ZS57N	21495	**9325**	**10625**	**12100**	**14950**
XR Sedan 4D		ZV577	25495	**10975**	**12450**	**13950**	**17000**
4-Cyl. 2.4 Liter		B	------	**(400)**	**(400)**	**(535)**	**(535)**
SKY—4-Cyl.—Equipment Schedule 3							
W.B. 95.1"; 2.4 Liter.							
Roadster 2D		MB35B	26500	**13275**	**15000**	**16700**	**20200**
SKY—4-Cyl. Turbo—Equipment Schedule 3							
W.B. 95.1"; 2.0 Liter.							
Red Line Roadster 2D		MG35X	30700	**15725**	**17650**	**19450**	**23200**

SCION

2004 SCION — JT(KorL)(KT624)-4-#

Body	Type	VIN	List	Trade-In Fair	Trade-In Good	Pvt-Party Good	Retail Excellent
xA—4-Cyl.—Equipment Schedule 6							
W.B. 93.3"; 1.5 Liter.							
Hatchback 4D		KT624	12965	**4025**	**4775**	**6350**	**8800**
xB—4-Cyl.—Equipment Schedule 6							
W.B. 98.4"; 1.5 Liter.							
Sport Wagon 4D		KT324	14165	**5050**	**5900**	**7575**	**10200**

2005 SCION — JT(KorL)(KT624)-5-#

Body	Type	VIN	List	Trade-In Fair	Trade-In Good	Pvt-Party Good	Retail Excellent
xA—4-Cyl.—Equipment Schedule 6							
W.B. 93.3"; 1.5 Liter.							
Hatchback 4D		KT624	12995	**4475**	**5275**	**6900**	**9450**
Release Series 1.0			------	**800**	**800**	**1065**	**1065**
Release Series 2.0			------	**600**	**600**	**800**	**800**
xB—4-Cyl.—Equipment Schedule 6							
W.B. 98.4"; 1.5 Liter.							
Sport Wagon 4D		KT324	14195	**5625**	**6550**	**8200**	**10900**
Release Series 2.0			------	**600**	**600**	**800**	**800**
tC—4-Cyl.—Equipment Schedule 4							
W.B. 106.3"; 2.4 Liter.							
Hatchback Coupe 2D		DE177	17265	**6575**	**7575**	**9250**	**12050**

2006 SCION — JT(KorL)(KT624)-6-#

Body	Type	VIN	List	Trade-In Fair	Trade-In Good	Pvt-Party Good	Retail Excellent
xA—4-Cyl.—Equipment Schedule 6							
W.B. 93.3"; 1.5 Liter.							
Hatchback 4D		KT624	13245	**5000**	**5825**	**7500**	**10100**
Release Series 2.0			------	**600**	**600**	**800**	**800**
Release Series 3.0 or 4.0			------	**1000**	**1000**	**1335**	**1335**
xB—4-Cyl.—Equipment Schedule 6							
W.B. 98.4"; 1.5 Liter.							
Sport Wagon 4D		KT324	14395	**6250**	**7200**	**8875**	**11600**
Release Series 3.0			------	**600**	**600**	**800**	**800**
Release Series 3.0 or 4.0			------	**1000**	**1000**	**1335**	**1335**
tC—4-Cyl.—Equipment Schedule 4							
W.B. 106.3"; 2.4 Liter.							
Hatchback Coupe 2D		DE177	17515	**7275**	**8375**	**10050**	**12900**
Release Series 2.0			------	**900**	**900**	**1200**	**1200**
Special Edition			------	**2000**	**2000**	**2665**	**2665**

Body	Type	VIN	List	Trade-In Fair	Trade-In Good	Pvt-Party Good	Retail Excellent

2007 SCION — JT(KorL)(DE177)-7-#

tC—4-Cyl.—Equipment Schedule 4
W.B. 106.3"; 2.4 Liter.

Body	Type	VIN	List	Fair	Good	Good	Excellent
Spec H'Back Coupe 2D		DE177	16340	7275	8350	9900	12650
Hatchback Coupe 2D		DE177	17740	8025	9200	10850	13650
Release Series 3.0				900	900	1200	1200

2008 SCION — JT(KorL)(KU104)-8-#

xD—4-Cyl.—Equipment Schedule 4
W.B. 96.9"; 1.8 Liter.

Hatchback 4D		KU104	15970	9500	10825	12300	15200

xB—4-Cyl.—Equipment Schedule 6
W.B. 102.4"; 2.4 Liter.

Sport Wagon 4D		KE50E	16270	9675	10975	12500	15400

tC—4-Cyl.—Equipment Schedule 4
W.B. 106.3"; 2.4 Liter.

Spec H'Back Coupe 2D		DE167	16720	8200	9375	10900	13550
Hatchback Coupe 2D		DE167	18420	9050	10300	11800	14600

SUBARU

1994 SUBARU — (JF1,JF2,4S3or4S4)(KA722)-R-#

JUSTY—3-Cyl.—Equipment Schedule 6
W.B. 90.0"; 1.2 Liter.

DL Hatchback 2D		KA722	8194	300	425	975	1875
GL AWD Hatchback 5D		KD83A	10048	375	525	1100	2050

LOYALE AWD—4-Cyl.—Equipment Schedule 4
W.B. 96.9"; 1.8 Liter.

Wagon 4D		AN52B	13998	975	1375	2425	4050
Auto Trans				175	175	235	235

IMPREZA—4-Cyl.—Equipment Schedule 5
W.B. 99.2"; 1.8 Liter.

Sedan 4D		GC214	11645	575	775	1550	2800
L Sedan 4D		GC224	15195	625	900	1700	3000
L Wagon 4D		GF224	15595	775	1100	1975	3375
AWD				475	475	635	635

IMPREZA AWD—4-Cyl.—Equipment Schedule 5
W.B. 99.2"; 1.8 Liter.

LS Sedan 4D		GC255	18995	1075	1500	2625	4275
LS Wagon 4D		GF255	19395	1225	1725	2875	4575

LEGACY—4-Cyl.—Equipment Schedule 4
W.B. 101.6"; 2.2 Liter.

L Sedan 4D		BC633	17395	675	975	1800	3125
L Wagon 4D		BJ633	18695	825	1150	2075	3500
LS Sedan 4D		BC653	20145	750	1050	1925	3300
LS Wagon 4D		BJ653	20845	900	1250	2200	3675
AWD				475	475	635	635
Manual Trans				(200)	(200)	(265)	(265)

LEGACY AWD—4-Cyl.—Equipment Schedule 4
W.B. 101.6"; 2.2 Liter.

LSi Sedan 4D		BC653	22295	1100	1525	2650	4300
LSi Wagon 4D		BJ653	23295	1225	1725	2875	4575

LEGACY AWD—4-Cyl. Turbo—Equipment Schedule 4
W.B. 101.6"; 2.2 Liter.

Sport Sedan 4D		BC673	22595	1025	1450	2550	4175
Touring Wagon 4D		BJ673	23645	1150	1600	2750	4425
Manual Trans				(200)	(200)	(265)	(265)

SVX—6-Cyl.—Equipment Schedule 4
W.B. 102.8"; 3.3 Liter.

L Coupe 2D		CX323	24345	1625	2125	3350	5150
LS Coupe 2D		CX345	28995	1925	2475	3725	5575
LSi AWD Coupe 2D		CX355	34295	2425	3025	4325	6325

1995 SUBARU — 4S3orJF1(GC215)-S-#

IMPREZA—4-Cyl.—Equipment Schedule 5
W.B. 99.2"; 1.8 Liter, 2.2 Liter.

Sedan 4D		GC215	13420	650	925	1725	3050
Coupe 2D		GM215	13715	600	825	1625	2875
L Sedan 4D		GC235	15025	750	1050	1900	3300

Body	Type	VIN	List	Trade-In Fair	Good	Pvt-Party Good	Retail Excellent
L Coupe 2D		GM235	15025	675	950	1800	3125
AWD				500	500	665	665

IMPREZA AWD—4-Cyl.—Equipment Schedule 5
W.B. 99.2"; 1.8 Liter, 2.2 Liter.

L Wagon 4D		GF235	16425	1300	1775	2975	4675
LX Sedan 4D		GC655	17470	1275	1750	2950	4650
L Coupe 2D		GM655	17770	1175	1650	2800	4475
LX Wagon 4D		GF655	17870	1525	2000	3225	5000
Outback Wagon 4D		GF235	17225	1700	2200	3425	5250

LEGACY—4-Cyl.—Equipment Schedule 4
W.B. 103.5"; 2.2 Liter.

Sedan 4D		BD625	16517	925	1325	2400	4025
L Sedan 4D		BD635	18264	925	1325	2400	4025
L Wagon 4D		BK635	18964	1100	1525	2675	4325
AWD				500	500	665	665

LEGACY AWD—4-Cyl.—Equipment Schedule 4
W.B. 103.5"; 2.2 Liter.

Brighton Wagon 4D		BK625	17643	1300	1775	2975	4700
Outback Wagon 4D		BK635	21095	2025	2600	3875	5775
LS Sedan 4D		BD655	21595	1400	1850	3075	4825
LS Wagon 4D		BK655	22295	1575	2050	3275	5100
LSi Sedan 4D		BD655	24095	1550	2025	3250	5050
LSi Wagon 4D		BK655	24795	1825	2350	3600	5475

SVX—6-Cyl.—Equipment Schedule 4
W.B. 102.8"; 3.3 Liter.

L Coupe 2D		CX335	27275	1875	2425	3675	5550
L AWD Coupe 2D		CX335	28775	2275	2850	4175	6125
LSi Coupe 2D		CX355	34825	2800	3400	4775	6850

1996 SUBARU — JF1or4S3(GM225)-T-#

IMPREZA AWD—4-Cyl.—Equipment Schedule 5
W.B. 99.2"; 1.8 Liter, 2.2 Liter.

Brighton Coupe 2D		GM225	13990	1125	1575	2700	4375
L Sedan 4D		GC655	16890	1300	1800	3000	4725
L Coupe 2D		GM435	16890	1200	1675	2875	4575
L Wagon 4D		GF655	16490	1600	2100	3325	5150
LX Sedan 4D		GC455	18290	1575	2075	3300	5100
LX Coupe 2D		GM455	18590	1450	1925	3125	4925
LX Wagon 4D		GF455	18690	1850	2375	3650	5525
Outback Wagon 4D		GF485	18890	2050	2600	3875	5775
2WD				(575)	(575)	(765)	(765)

LEGACY—4-Cyl.—Equipment Schedule 4
W.B. 103.5"; 2.2 Liter.

L Sedan 4D		BD335	18775	1075	1525	2650	4325
L Wagon 4D		BK335	19475	1275	1750	2950	4675
AWD		4		575	575	765	765
Manual Trans (Sedan)				(200)	(200)	(265)	(265)

LEGACY AWD—4-Cyl.—Equipment Schedule 4
W.B. 103.5"; 2.2 Liter, 2.5 Liter.

Brighton Wagon 4D		BK425	18075	1575	2050	3300	5100
Outback Wagon 4D		BG685	22490	2425	3025	4325	6325
LS Sedan 4D		BD455	22590	1675	2175	3425	5275
LS Wagon 4D		BK655	23290	1850	2400	3675	5525
GT Sedan 4D		BD675	23790	1875	2425	3700	5575
GT Wagon 4D		BK675	23490	2150	2725	4025	5950
LSi Sedan 4D		BD665	25290	1850	2375	3650	5525
LSi Wagon 4D		BK665	25990	2150	2725	4025	5950
4-Cyl. 2.5L (Outback)		6		150	150	200	200

SVX AWD—6-Cyl.—Equipment Schedule 4
W.B. 102.8"; 3.3 Liter.

L Coupe 2D		CX835	30490	2675	3300	4650	6750
LSi Coupe 2D		CX865	35990	3225	3900	5325	7500

1997 SUBARU — JF1or4S3(GM425)-V-#

IMPREZA AWD—4-Cyl.—Equipment Schedule 5
W.B. 99.2"; 1.8 Liter, 2.2 Liter.

Brighton Coupe 2D		GM425	15290	1250	1750	2925	4650
L Sedan 4D		GC435	17190	1575	2050	3275	5100
L Coupe 2D		GM435	17190	1425	1900	3125	4900
L Sport Wagon 4D		GF435	17590	1850	2400	3650	5525
Outback Sport Wagon		GF485	19290	2375	2975	4275	6225

1997 SUBARU

Body Type	VIN	List	Trade-In Fair	Trade-In Good	Pvt-Party Good	Retail Excellent

LEGACY AWD—4-Cyl.—Equipment Schedule 4
W.B. 103.5"; 2.2 Liter, 2.5 Liter.

Body Type	VIN	List	Fair	Good	Good	Excellent
Brighton Wagon 4D	BK425	18490	2175	2750	4050	5975
L Sedan 4D	BD435	20490	2000	2550	3825	5725
L Wagon 4D	BK435	21190	2325	2900	4225	6200
Outback Wagon 4D	BG685	23790	3150	3825	5250	7400
Outback Ltd Wag 4D	BG685	25490	3250	3950	5375	7550
GT Sedan 4D	BD675	24090	2600	3200	4550	6600
GT Wagon 4D	BK675	24790	2900	3525	4925	7025
LSi Sedan 4D	BD665	25490	2600	3175	4525	6575
LSi Wagon 4D	BK665	26190	2850	3475	4850	6950
Manual Trans (Sedan)			(250)	(250)	(335)	(335)

SVX AWD—6-Cyl.—Equipment Schedule 4
W.B. 102.8"; 3.3 Liter.

Body Type	VIN	List	Fair	Good	Good	Excellent
L Coupe 2D	CX835	31120	3075	3750	5150	7300
LSi Coupe 2D	CX865	36740	3700	4400	5875	8150

1998 SUBARU — JF1or4S3(GC435)–W–#

IMPREZA AWD—4-Cyl.—Equipment Schedule 5
W.B. 99.2"; 2.2 Liter, 2.5 Liter.

Body Type	VIN	List	Fair	Good	Good	Excellent
L Sedan 4D	GC435	17190	1850	2375	3650	5525
L Coupe 2D	GM435	17190	1725	2225	3475	5325
L Sport Wagon 4D	GF435	17590	2175	2750	4050	5975
Outback Sport Wag 4D	GF485	19290	2725	3325	4675	6725
2.5RS Coupe 2D	GM675	20490	2900	3525	4900	6975

LEGACY AWD—4-Cyl.—Equipment Schedule 4
W.B. 103.5"; 2.2 Liter, 2.5 Liter.

Body Type	VIN	List	Fair	Good	Good	Excellent
Brighton Wagon 4D	BK425	18524	2550	3150	4475	6500
L Sedan 4D	BD435	20490	2350	2950	4250	6225
L Wagon 4D	BK435	21190	2725	3325	4675	6750
Outback Wagon 4D	BG685	23790	3650	4350	5800	8025
Outback Ltd Wag 4D	BG685	25890	3825	4550	6000	8275
GT Sedan 4D	BD675	24090	3050	3675	5075	7175
GT Limited Sedan 4D	BE656	25390	3175	3850	5250	7400
GT Wagon 4D	BK675	24790	3375	4075	5500	7675
Manual Trans (Sedan)			(300)	(300)	(400)	(400)
Dual Power Moon Roofs			100	100	135	135

1999 SUBARU — JF1or4S3(GC435)–X–#

IMPREZA AWD—4-Cyl.—Equipment Schedule 5
W.B. 99.2"; 2.2 Liter, 2.5 Liter.

Body Type	VIN	List	Fair	Good	Good	Excellent
L Sedan 4D	GC435	17190	2200	2775	4075	6000
L Coupe 2D	GM435	17190	2000	2575	3850	5750
L Sport Wagon 4D	GF435	17590	2550	3125	4450	6475
Outback Sport Wag 4D	GF485	19290	3075	3725	5100	7225
2.5RS Coupe 2D	GM675	20490	3275	3975	5375	7525

LEGACY AWD—4-Cyl.—Equipment Schedule 4
W.B. 103.5"; 2.2 Liter, 2.5 Liter.

Body Type	VIN	List	Fair	Good	Good	Excellent
Brighton Wagon 4D	BK425	18524	2975	3600	5000	7100
L Sedan 4D	BD435	20490	2775	3375	4750	6800
L Wagon 4D	BK435	21190	3150	3825	5225	7375
Outback Wagon 4D	BG686	23790	4200	4950	6450	8775
Outback Ltd Wag 4D	BG686	25890	4400	5200	6700	9075
GT Sedan 4D	BD675	24090	3525	4250	5650	7900
GT Limited Sedan 4D	BE656	25390	3700	4425	5850	8100
GT Wagon 4D	BK675	24790	3900	4650	6100	8375
Sport Util Sedan 4D	BD685	23890	3950	4700	6150	8450
Ltd Sport Util Sed 4D	BD685	26090	4300	5100	6600	8950
Dual Moon Roofs			125	125	165	165
Manual Trans (Sedan)			(350)	(350)	(465)	(465)

2000 SUBARU — JF1or4S3(GC435)–Y–#

IMPREZA AWD—4-Cyl.—Equipment Schedule 5
W.B. 99.2"; 2.2 Liter, 2.5 Liter.

Body Type	VIN	List	Fair	Good	Good	Excellent
L Sedan 4D	GC435	17190	2600	3200	4525	6575
L Coupe 2D	GM435	17190	2400	3000	4300	6300
L Sport Wagon 4D	GF435	17590	2975	3600	4975	7050
Outback Sport Wag 4D	GF485	19390	3525	4225	5625	7825
2.5RS Sedan 4D	GC675	20590	3650	4350	5775	7975
2.5RS Coupe 2D	GM675	20590	3775	4475	5900	8125

LEGACY AWD—4-Cyl.—Equipment Schedule 4
W.B. 104.3"; 2.5 Liter.

Body Type	VIN	List	Trade-In Fair	Good	Pvt-Party Good	Retail Excellent
Brighton Wagon 4D	BH625	19690	3050	3700	5075	7200
L Sedan 4D	BE635	20490	2825	3450	4800	6875
L Wagon 4D	BH635	21190	3225	3925	5325	7475
GT Sedan 4D	BE645	24090	3675	4375	5825	8050
GT Limited Sedan 4D	BE656	25590	3850	4575	6025	8275
GT Wagon 4D	BH645	24990	4075	4825	6275	8575
Dual Moon Roofs	------	------	150	150	200	200
Manual Trans (Sedan)	------	------	(400)	(400)	(535)	(535)

OUTBACK AWD—4-Cyl.—Equipment Schedule 4
W.B. 104.3"; 2.5 Liter.

Wagon 4D	BH666	23990	4250	5025	6500	8825
Limited Sedan 4D	BE686	26390	4400	5225	6700	9050
Limited Wagon 4D	BH686	27390	4500	5325	6775	9175
Dual Moon Roofs	------	------	150	150	200	200

2001 SUBARU — JF1or4S3(GC435)-1-#

IMPREZA AWD—4-Cyl.—Equipment Schedule 5
W.B. 99.2"; 2.2 Liter, 2.5 Liter.

L Sedan 4D	GC435	17290	3050	3700	5075	7175
L Coupe 2D	GM435	17290	2825	3450	4825	6875
L Sport Wagon 4D	GF435	17890	3425	4150	5525	7700
Outback Sport Wag 4D	GF485	19490	4025	4775	6200	8475
2.5RS Sedan 4D	GC675	20790	4175	4925	6375	8650
2.5RS Coupe 2D	GM675	20790	4300	5075	6525	8825

LEGACY AWD—4-Cyl.—Equipment Schedule 4
W.B. 104.3"; 2.5 Liter.

L Sedan 4D	BE635	20590	3350	4050	5450	7625
L Wagon 4D	BH635	21290	3825	4525	5975	8200
GT Sedan 4D	BE645	24190	4300	5100	6550	8875
GT Limited Sedan 4D	BE656	25690	4475	5300	6750	9125
GT Wagon 4D	BH645	25090	4700	5525	7050	9500
Dual Moon Roofs	------	------	175	175	235	235
Manual Trans (Sedan)	------	------	(425)	(425)	(565)	(565)

OUTBACK AWD—4-Cyl.—Equipment Schedule 4
W.B. 104.3"; 2.5 Liter.

Wagon 4D	BH665	24190	4900	5750	7300	9775
Limited Sedan 4D	BE686	26490	5100	5950	7525	10050
Limited Wagon 4D	BH686	27590	5225	6075	7650	10200
Dual Moon Roofs	------	------	175	175	235	235

OUTBACK AWD—H6—Equipment Schedule 4
W.B. 104.3"; 3.0 Liter.

L.L. Bean Wagon 4D	BH806	29990	5600	6525	8075	10700
VDC Wagon 4D	BH896	32390	6450	7425	9075	11800
Dual Moon Roofs	------	------	175	175	235	235

2002 SUBARU — JF1or4S3(GG655)-2-#

IMPREZA AWD—4-Cyl.—Equipment Schedule 5
W.B. 99.4"; 2.5 Liter.

2.5TS Sport Wagon 4D	GG655	18820	3900	4625	6225	8650
Outback Sport Wag 4D	GF485	20020	4475	5300	6950	9525
2.5RS Sedan 4D	GC675	20320	4600	5425	7100	9700

IMPREZA AWD—4-Cyl. Turbo—Equipment Schedule 4
W.B. 99.4"; 2.0 Liter.

WRX Sedan 4D	GD295	25520	6000	6950	8750	11600
WRX Sport Wagon 4D	GG295	25020	5775	6725	8500	11300

LEGACY AWD—4-Cyl.—Equipment Schedule 4
W.B. 104.3"; 2.5 Liter.

L Sedan 4D	BE635	20620	3875	4600	6200	8625
L Wagon 4D	BH635	21320	4350	5150	6750	9225
GT Sedan 4D	BE645	24220	4900	5725	7425	10050
GT Limited Sedan 4D	BE656	26020	5075	5925	7625	10300
GT Wagon 4D	BH645	25120	5350	6225	7925	10650
Dual Moon Roofs	------	------	200	200	265	265
Manual Trans (Sedan)	------	------	(450)	(450)	(600)	(600)

OUTBACK AWD—4-Cyl.—Equipment Schedule 4
W.B. 104.3"; 2.5 Liter.

Wagon 4D	BH665	24220	5525	6450	8125	10900
Limited Sedan 4D	BE686	26520	5775	6700	8425	11200
Limited Wagon 4D	BH686	27620	5900	6825	8575	11350
Dual Moon Roofs	------	------	200	200	265	265

OUTBACK AWD—H6—Equipment Schedule 4
W.B. 104.3"; 3.0 Liter.

Body	Type	VIN	List	Trade-In Fair	Trade-In Good	Pvt-Party Good	Retail Excellent
Sedan 4D		BE896	28520	5800	6750	8475	11250
L.L. Bean Wagon 4D		BH806	30020	6275	7250	9050	11900
VDC Sedan 4D		BH896	30920	6675	7700	9475	12400
VDC Wagon 4D		BH896	32420	7200	8250	10100	13100
Dual Moon Roofs				**200**	**200**	**265**	**265**

2003 SUBARU — JF1or4S3(GG655)-3-#

IMPREZA AWD—4-Cyl.—Equipment Schedule 5
W.B. 99.4"; 2.5 Liter.

Body	Type	VIN	List	Trade-In Fair	Trade-In Good	Pvt-Party Good	Retail Excellent
2.5TS Sport Wagon 4D		GG655	18920	4525	5325	6975	9550
Outback Sport Wag		GG685	20120	5225	6100	7775	10450
2.5RS Sedan 4D		GD675	20420	5325	6200	7875	10550

IMPREZA AWD—4-Cyl. Turbo—Equipment Schedule 4
W.B. 99.4"; 2.0 Liter.

Body	Type	VIN	List	Trade-In Fair	Trade-In Good	Pvt-Party Good	Retail Excellent
WRX Sedan 4D		GD296	25720	6975	8025	9850	12850
WRX Sport Wagon 4D		GG296	25220	6750	7750	9550	12500

LEGACY AWD—4-Cyl.—Equipment Schedule 4
W.B. 104.3"; 2.5 Liter.

Body	Type	VIN	List	Trade-In Fair	Trade-In Good	Pvt-Party Good	Retail Excellent
L Sedan 4D		BE635	20820	4450	5250	6900	9475
L Wagon 4D		BH635	21520	4975	5825	7500	10150
L Special Ed Sed 4D		BE635	21320	4550	5375	7025	9625
L Special Ed Wag 4D		BH635	22420	5125	5975	7675	10350
GT Sedan 4D		BE646	26320	5650	6575	8275	11050
GT Wagon 4D		BH646	27220	6150	7100	8850	11650
Dual Moon Roofs				**275**	**275**	**365**	**365**
Manual Trans (Sedan)				**(500)**	**(500)**	**(665)**	**(665)**

OUTBACK AWD—4-Cyl.—Equipment Schedule 4
W.B. 104.3"; 2.5 Liter.

Body	Type	VIN	List	Trade-In Fair	Trade-In Good	Pvt-Party Good	Retail Excellent
Wagon 4D		BH675	24370	6325	7300	9050	11900
Limited Sedan 4D		BE686	26820	6575	7600	9325	12200
Limited Wagon 4D		BH686	27920	6750	7750	9500	12400
Dual Moon Roofs				**275**	**275**	**365**	**365**

OUTBACK AWD—H6—Equipment Schedule 4
W.B. 104.3"; 3.0 Liter.

Body	Type	VIN	List	Trade-In Fair	Trade-In Good	Pvt-Party Good	Retail Excellent
Sedan 4D		BE896	29020	6625	7625	9400	12300
Wagon 4D		BH896	27520	6225	7200	8950	11750
L.L. Bean Wagon 4D		BH806	30520	7150	8225	10000	12950
VDC Sedan 4D		BE896	31420	7625	8750	10550	13550
VDC Wagon 4D		BH896	32920	8075	9375	11250	14450

2004 SUBARU — JF1or4S3(GG655)-4-#

IMPREZA AWD—4-Cyl.—Equipment Schedule 5
W.B. 99.4"; 2.5 Liter.

Body	Type	VIN	List	Trade-In Fair	Trade-In Good	Pvt-Party Good	Retail Excellent
2.5TS Sport Wagon 4D		GG655	19245	5250	6125	7800	10450
Outback Sport Wag		GG685	20445	6025	6975	8675	11400
2.5RS Sedan 4D		GD675	20745	6075	7025	8725	11450

IMPREZA AWD—4-Cyl. Turbo—Equipment Schedule 4
W.B. 99.4"; 2.0 Liter.

Body	Type	VIN	List	Trade-In Fair	Trade-In Good	Pvt-Party Good	Retail Excellent
WRX Sedan 4D		GD296	26045	8025	9200	11050	14200
WRX Sport Wagon 4D		GG296	25545	7750	8875	10700	13700

IMPREZA AWD—4-Cyl. HO Turbo—Equipment Schedule 4
W.B. 100.0"; 2.5 Liter.

Body	Type	VIN	List	Trade-In Fair	Trade-In Good	Pvt-Party Good	Retail Excellent
WRX STi Sedan 4D		GD706	31545	12200	13775	15800	19450

LEGACY AWD—4-Cyl.—Equipment Schedule 4
W.B. 104.3"; 2.5 Liter.

Body	Type	VIN	List	Trade-In Fair	Trade-In Good	Pvt-Party Good	Retail Excellent
L Sedan 4D		BE635	21245	5200	6075	7775	10450
L Wagon 4D		BH635	21945	5775	6700	8400	11150
GT Sedan 4D		BE646	26645	6550	7550	9275	12150
GT Wagon 4D		BH646	27545	7100	8150	9900	12850
Dual Moon Roofs				**350**	**350**	**465**	**465**
Manual Trans (Sedan)				**(525)**	**(525)**	**(700)**	**(700)**

OUTBACK AWD—4-Cyl.—Equipment Schedule 4
W.B. 104.3"; 2.5 Liter.

Body	Type	VIN	List	Trade-In Fair	Trade-In Good	Pvt-Party Good	Retail Excellent
Wagon 4D		BH675	24695	7225	8275	10050	12950
Limited Sedan 4D		BE686	27145	7525	8625	10400	13350
Limited Wagon 4D		BH686	28245	7700	8825	10600	13550
Dual Moon Roofs				**350**	**350**	**465**	**465**

OUTBACK AWD—H6—Equipment Schedule 4
W.B. 104.3"; 3.0 Liter.

Body	Type	VIN	List	Trade-In Fair	Trade-In Good	Pvt-Party Good	Retail Excellent
Sedan 4D		BE896	29345	7575	8675	10450	13400
35th Anniv Wagon 4D		BH815	27645	7125	8175	9950	12850
L.L. Bean Wagon 4D		BH806	30845	8150	9325	11150	14250

Body	Type	VIN	List	Trade-In Fair	Good	Pvt-Party Good	Retail Excellent
VDC Sedan 4D		BE896	31545	8700	9900	11750	14950
VDC Wagon 4D		BH896	33045	9325	10625	12500	15750

2005 SUBARU — (JF0r4S)(1,3or4)(GG675)–5–#

IMPREZA AWD—4-Cyl.—Equipment Schedule 5
W.B. 99.4"; 2.5 Liter.

Body	Type	VIN	List	Trade-In Fair	Good	Pvt-Party Good	Retail Excellent
2.5RS Sport Wagon 4D		GG675	19470	6050	7000	8675	11400
Outback Sport Wag		GG685	20370	6900	7975	9650	12500
Outback Spt Spcl Ed		GG685	20320	7050	8100	9800	12700
2.5RS Sedan 4D		GD675	19470	5975	6900	8600	11300

IMPREZA AWD—4-Cyl. Turbo—Equipment Schedule 4
W.B. 99.4"; 2.0 Liter.

Body	Type	VIN	List	Trade-In Fair	Good	Pvt-Party Good	Retail Excellent
WRX Sedan 4D		GD296	26470	9125	10400	12250	15550
WRX Sport Wagon 4D		GG296	25870	8775	10000	11850	15100

IMPREZA AWD—4-Cyl. HO Turbo—Equipment Schedule 4
W.B. 99.4"; 2.5 Liter.

Body	Type	VIN	List	Trade-In Fair	Good	Pvt-Party Good	Retail Excellent
WRX STi Sedan 4D		GD706	32770	13675	15425	17450	21300

LEGACY AWD—4-Cyl.—Equipment Schedule 4
W.B. 105.1"; 2.5 Liter.

Body	Type	VIN	List	Trade-In Fair	Good	Pvt-Party Good	Retail Excellent
2.5i Sedan 4D		BL616	22870	6425	7425	9150	11950
2.5i Wagon 4D		BP616	23870	7025	8075	9800	12700
2.5i Limited Sedan 4D		BL626	26120	7450	8550	10250	13200
2.5i Limited Wagon 4D		BP626	27320	7650	8750	10500	13450
Dual Moon Roofs		------	------	450	450	600	600
Manual Trans (Sedan)		------	------	(550)	(550)	(735)	(735)

LEGACY AWD—4-Cyl. Turbo—Equipment Schedule 4
W.B. 105.1"; 2.5 Liter.

Body	Type	VIN	List	Trade-In Fair	Good	Pvt-Party Good	Retail Excellent
2.5GT Sedan 4D		BL686	27870	7900	9050	10850	13850
2.5GT Wagon 4D		BP686	28870	8550	9775	11550	14700
2.5GT Limited Sed 4D		BL676	30370	10350	11700	13550	16900
2.5GT Limited Wag 4D		BP676	31570	10675	12100	13900	17300
Dual Moon Roofs		------	------	450	450	600	600
Manual Trans (Sedan)		------	------	(550)	(550)	(735)	(735)

OUTBACK AWD—4-Cyl.—Equipment Schedule 4
W.B. 105.1"; 2.5 Liter.

Body	Type	VIN	List	Trade-In Fair	Good	Pvt-Party Good	Retail Excellent
2.5i Wagon 4D		BP61C	25870	7575	8675	10400	13350
2.5i Limited Wagon		BP62C	28670	8275	9475	11250	14350
Dual Moon Roofs		------	------	450	450	600	600

OUTBACK AWD—4-Cyl. Turbo—Equipment Schedule 4
W.B. 105.1"; 2.5 Liter.

Body	Type	VIN	List	Trade-In Fair	Good	Pvt-Party Good	Retail Excellent
2.5XT Wagon 4D		BP68C	29870	8650	9850	11650	14800
2.5XT Limited Wag		BP67C	32570	8950	10200	12000	15150
Dual Moon Roofs		------	------	450	450	600	600

OUTBACK AWD—H6—Equipment Schedule 4
W.B. 105.1"; 3.0 Liter.

Body	Type	VIN	List	Trade-In Fair	Good	Pvt-Party Good	Retail Excellent
3.0R Sedan 4D		BL84C	31670	10200	11575	13400	16700
3.0R L.L. Bean Wagon		BP86C	32870	10825	12250	14100	17500
3.0R VDC Ltd Wagon		BP85C	34070	11700	13225	15100	18600
Dual Moon Roofs		------	------	450	450	600	600

2006 SUBARU — (JF0r4S)(1,3or4)(GG676)–6–#

IMPREZA AWD—4-Cyl.—Equipment Schedule 5
W.B. 99.4"; 2.5 Liter.

Body	Type	VIN	List	Trade-In Fair	Good	Pvt-Party Good	Retail Excellent
2.5i Sport Wagon		GG676	19720	6950	8000	9700	12550
2.5i Sedan 4D		GD676	19720	6875	7925	9600	12450
Outback Sport Wag		GG686	20620	7900	9050	10700	13550

IMPREZA AWD—4-Cyl. Turbo—Equipment Schedule 4
W.B. 99.4"; 2.5 Liter.

Body	Type	VIN	List	Trade-In Fair	Good	Pvt-Party Good	Retail Excellent
WRX TR Sedan 4D		GD796	24620	10200	11575	13450	16750
WRX Sedan 4D		GD796	26620	11225	12750	14600	18050
WRX Sport Wagon 4D		GG796	26120	10875	12350	14200	17600
WRX Limited Sedan		GD796	29120	12350	13975	15850	19400
WRX Limited Spt Wag		GG796	28620	12100	13675	15550	19100

IMPREZA AWD—4-Cyl. HO Turbo—Equipment Schedule 4
W.B. 100.0"; 2.5 Liter.

Body	Type	VIN	List	Trade-In Fair	Good	Pvt-Party Good	Retail Excellent
WRX STi Sedan 4D		GD706	33620	16275	18275	20200	24200

LEGACY AWD—4-Cyl.—Equipment Schedule 4
W.B. 105.1"; 2.5 Liter.

Body	Type	VIN	List	Trade-In Fair	Good	Pvt-Party Good	Retail Excellent
i Sedan 4D		BL616	23520	7500	8600	10300	13250
i Wagon 4D		BP616	24520	8100	9275	11050	14100
i Limited Sedan 4D		BL626	26120	8600	9800	11600	14700
i Limited Wagon 4D		BP626	27320	8900	10150	11950	15100

2006 SUBARU

Body Type	VIN	List	Trade-In Fair	Good	Pvt-Party Good	Retail Excellent
Dual Moon Roofs			550	550	735	735
Manual Trans (Sedan)			(575)	(575)	(765)	(765)
LEGACY AWD—4-Cyl. Turbo—Equipment Schedule 4						
W.B. 105.1"; 2.5 Liter.						
GT Limited Sed 4D	BL676	30620	11750	13275	15100	18550
GT Limited Wag 4D	BP676	31820	12150	13725	15550	19000
Manual Trans (Sedan)			(575)	(575)	(765)	(765)
OUTBACK AWD—4-Cyl.—Equipment Schedule 4						
W.B. 105.1"; 2.5 Liter.						
2.5i Wagon 4D	BP61C	26820	8825	10050	11800	14950
2.5i Limited Sedan 4D	BL62C	28020	9375	10675	12450	15650
2.5i Limited Wagon	BP62C	29220	9625	10925	12750	15950
Dual Moon Roofs			550	550	735	735
OUTBACK AWD—4-Cyl. Turbo—Equipment Schedule 4						
W.B. 105.1"; 2.5 Liter.						
2.5XT Wagon 4D	BP68C	29220	10000	11375	13200	16450
2.5XT Limited Wagon	BP67C	32820	10350	11700	13500	16800
Dual Moon Roofs			550	550	735	735
OUTBACK AWD—H6—Equipment Schedule 4						
W.B. 105.1"; 3.0 Liter.						
3.0R Wagon 4D	BP84C	29620	10350	11700	13500	16800
3.0R L.L. Bean Sed 4D	BL86C	31920	11700	13225	15050	18500
3.0R L.L. Bean Wagon	BP86C	33120	12400	14025	15850	19350
3.0R VDC Ltd Wagon	BP85C	36320	13375	15100	16950	20600
Dual Moon Roofs			550	550	735	735

2007 SUBARU — (JFor4S)(1,3or4)(GG616)-7-#

Body Type	VIN	List	Trade-In Fair	Good	Pvt-Party Good	Retail Excellent
IMPREZA AWD—4-Cyl.—Equipment Schedule 5						
W.B. 99.4"; 2.5 Liter.						
2.5i Sport Wagon	GG616	19420	7975	9150	10800	13650
2.5i Sedan 4D	GD616	19420	7900	9050	10700	13550
Outback Sport Wag	GG626	20620	9050	10300	11950	14950
IMPREZA AWD—4-Cyl. Turbo—Equipment Schedule 4						
W.B. 99.4"; 2.5 Liter.						
WRX Sedan 4D	GD746	25620	12400	14025	15850	19300
WRX Sport Wagon 4D	GG746	25120	12000	13575	15400	18800
WRX TR Sedan 4D	GD756	24620	11275	12800	14550	17950
WRX Limited Sedan	GD746	29120	13625	15325	17150	20800
WRX Limited Spt Wag	GG746	28620	13275	15000	16800	20400
IMPREZA AWD—4-Cyl. HO Turbo—Equipment Schedule 4						
W.B. 99.4"; 2.5 Liter.						
WRX STi Sedan 4D	GD766	34120	17875	20000	22000	26100
WRX STi Limited Sed	GD776	34120	18125	20275	22200	26400
LEGACY AWD—4-Cyl.—Equipment Schedule 4						
W.B. 105.1"; 2.5 Liter.						
i Sedan 4D	BL616	22120	8775	10000	11700	14700
i Wagon 4D	BP616	23620	9450	10725	12450	15550
i Limited Sedan 4D	BL626	24720	10000	11325	13050	16150
i Limited Wagon 4D	BP626	25920	10400	11750	13500	16650
Dual Moon Roofs			650	650	865	865
Manual Trans (Sedan)			(600)	(600)	(800)	(800)
LEGACY AWD—4-Cyl. Turbo—Equipment Schedule 4						
W.B. 105.1"; 2.5 Liter.						
GT Limited Sedan 4D	BL676	30120	13425	15150	16850	20400
GT Limited Wagon 4D	BP676	31520	13825	15575	17300	20900
GT spec.B Sedan 4D	BL696	34620	14950	16800	18550	22200
Manual Trans (Sedan)			(600)	(600)	(800)	(800)
OUTBACK AWD—4-Cyl.—Equipment Schedule 4						
W.B. 105.1"; 2.5 Liter.						
2.5i Basic Wagon 4D	BP61C	23620	10000	11375	13100	16200
2.5i Wagon 4D	BP61C	25220	10350	11700	13450	16600
2.5i Limited Sedan 4D	BL62C	27020	10925	12400	14100	17350
2.5i Limited Wagon 4D	BP62C	28020	11175	12650	14350	17650
Dual Moon Roofs			650	650	865	865
OUTBACK AWD—4-Cyl. Turbo—Equipment Schedule 4						
W.B. 105.1"; 2.5 Liter.						
2.5XT Limited Wagon	BP63C	32820	11950	13525	15250	18600
Dual Moon Roofs			650	650	865	865
OUTBACK AWD—H6 HO—Equipment Schedule 4						
W.B. 105.1"; 3.0 Liter.						
3.0R L.L. Bean Sedan	BL86C	30920	13425	15150	16850	20400
3.0R L.L. Bean Wagon	BP86C	32120	14200	15975	17750	21400
Dual Moon Roofs			650	650	865	865

2008 SUBARU

Body	Type	VIN	List	Trade-In Fair	Good	Pvt-Party Good	Retail Excellent

2008 SUBARU — (JFor4S)(1,3or4)(GE616)-8-#

IMPREZA AWD—4-Cyl.—Equipment Schedule 5
W.B. 103.1"; 2.5 Liter.

2.5i Sedan 4D		GE616	18640	9550	10875	12500	15500
2.5i Sport Wagon		GH616	19140	9850	11175	12800	15850
Outback Sport Wag		GG636	21640	10975	12450	14050	17250
Premium Pkg				200	200	265	265

IMPREZA AWD—4-Cyl. Turbo—Equipment Schedule 4
W.B. 103.1", 103.3" (STI); 2.5 Liter.

WRX Sedan 4D		GE756	25995	14400	16175	18000	21700
WRX Sport Wagon 4D		GH746	26495	14650	16475	18300	22000
WRX STI Sport Wag		GR796	35640	20100	22450	24200	28300
Premium Pkg				500	500	665	665

LEGACY AWD—4-Cyl.—Equipment Schedule 4
W.B. 105.1"; 2.5 Liter.

2.5i Sedan 4D		BL616	22140	10525	11950	13600	16750
2.5i Limited Sedan 4D		BL626	24740	11850	13375	15050	18400
Manual Trans				(625)	(625)	(835)	(835)

LEGACY AWD—4-Cyl. Turbo—Equipment Schedule 4
W.B. 105.1"; 2.5 Liter.

2.5GT Limited Sedan		BL676	30440	15575	17500	19200	22800
2.5GT spec.B Sedan		BL696	34640	17200	19250	21000	24800
Manual Trans				(625)	(625)	(835)	(835)

LEGACY AWD—6-Cyl.—Equipment Schedule 4
W.B. 105.1"; 3.0 Liter.

3.0R Limited Sedan 4D		BL856	31940	16025	17975	19700	23400

OUTBACK AWD—4-Cyl.—Equipment Schedule 4
W.B. 105.1"; 2.5 Liter.

Basic Wagon 4D		BP61C	23640	12250	13875	15550	18900
2.5i Wagon 4D		BP61C	25240	12650	14250	15950	19300
2.5i Limited Wagon 4D		BP62C	28040	13575	15300	16950	20400
Dual Moon Roofs				750	750	1000	1000

OUTBACK AWD—4-Cyl. Turbo—Equipment Schedule 4
W.B. 105.1"; 2.5 Liter.

2.5XT Ltd Wag 4D		BP63C	32840	14400	16175	17850	21400
Dual Moon Roofs				750	750	1000	1000

OUTBACK AWD—H6—Equipment Schedule 4
W.B. 105.1"; 3.0 Liter.

3.0R L.L. Bean Wag		BP86C	32140	16750	18775	20500	24300
Dual Moon Roofs				750	750	1000	1000

SUZUKI

1994 SUZUKI — (JSor2S)2(AE34S)-R-#

SWIFT—4-Cyl.—Equipment Schedule 6
W.B. 89.2", 93.1" (Sed); 1.3 Liter.

GA Sedan 4D		AE34S	8844	225	325	875	1725
GA Hatchback 2D		AC34S	7864	200	275	775	1600
GS Sedan 4D		AE34S	10344	325	450	1025	1950
GT Hatchback 2D		AC34S	10974	400	575	1175	2175

1995 SUZUKI — (JSor2S)2(AB21H)-S-#

SWIFT—4-Cyl.—Equipment Schedule 6
W.B. 93.1"; 1.3 Liter.

Hatchback 2D		AB21H	9029	225	325	875	1725

ESTEEM—4-Cyl.—Equipment Schedule 6
W.B. 97.6"; 1.6 Liter.

GL Sedan 4D		GB31S	11789	275	400	950	1850
GLX Sedan 4D		GB31S	14789	350	500	1100	2050

1996 SUZUKI — (JSor2S)2(AB21H)-T-#

SWIFT—4-Cyl.—Equipment Schedule 6
W.B. 93.1"; 1.3 Liter.

Hatchback 2D		AB21H	9359	275	375	950	1850

ESTEEM—4-Cyl.—Equipment Schedule 6
W.B. 97.6"; 1.6 Liter.

GL Sedan 4D		GB31S	11989	350	475	1075	2000
GLX Sedan 4D		GB31S	13289	425	600	1250	2275

Body	Type	VIN	List	Trade-In Fair	Trade-In Good	Pvt-Party Good	Retail Excellent

1997 SUZUKI — (JSor2S)2(AB21H)-V-#

SWIFT—4-Cyl.—Equipment Schedule 6
W.B. 93.1"; 1.3 Liter.

Hatchback 2D		AB21H	9359	325	450	1050	2000

ESTEEM—4-Cyl.—Equipment Schedule 6
W.B. 97.6"; 1.6 Liter.

GL Sedan 4D		GB31S	13319	400	575	1200	2225
GLX Sedan 4D		GB31S	14419	525	700	1400	2525

1998 SUZUKI — (JSor2S)2(AB21H)-W-#

SWIFT—4-Cyl.—Equipment Schedule 6
W.B. 93.1"; 1.3 Liter.

Hatchback 2D		AB21H	9479	375	525	1175	2225

ESTEEM—4-Cyl.—Equipment Schedule 6
W.B. 97.6"; 1.6 Liter.

GL Sedan 4D		GB31S	12429	500	650	1375	2475
GL Wagon 4D		GB31W	12929	600	825	1625	2925
GLX Sedan 4D		GB31S	13529	625	825	1650	2975
GLX Wagon 4D		GB31W	14029	650	925	1775	3125

1999 SUZUKI — (JSor2S)3(AB21H)-X-#

SWIFT—4-Cyl.—Equipment Schedule 6
W.B. 93.1"; 1.3 Liter.

Hatchback 2D		AB21H	9479	500	675	1400	2575

ESTEEM—4-Cyl.—Equipment Schedule 6
W.B. 97.6"; 1.6 Liter, 1.8 Liter.

GL Sedan 4D		GB31S	12629	600	825	1675	3000
GL Wagon 4D		GB31W	13129	700	1000	1900	3325
GLX Sedan 4D		GB31S	13729	725	1025	1925	3375
GLX Wagon 4D		GB31W	14229	775	1100	2050	3550

2000 SUZUKI — (JSor2S)3(AB21H)-Y-#

SWIFT—4-Cyl.—Equipment Schedule 6
W.B. 93.1"; 1.3 Liter.

GA Hatchback 2D		AB21H	9499	625	900	1800	3200
GL Hatchback 2D		AB21H	10499	725	1025	1975	3475

ESTEEM—4-Cyl.—Equipment Schedule 6
W.B. 97.6"; 1.6 Liter, 1.8 Liter.

GL Sedan 4D		GB31S	13349	750	1050	2000	3475
GL Wagon 4D		GB31W	13849	875	1225	2325	3975
GLX Sedan 4D		GB31S	14349	900	1250	2375	4050
GLX Wagon 4D		GB31W	14849	950	1350	2475	4175

2001 SUZUKI — (JSor2S)2(AB21H)-1-#

SWIFT—4-Cyl.—Equipment Schedule 6
W.B. 93.1"; 1.3 Liter.

GA Hatchback 2D		AB21H	9729	825	1175	2300	3975
GL Hatchback 2D		AB21H	10729	925	1300	2450	4150

ESTEEM—4-Cyl.—Equipment Schedule 6
W.B. 97.6"; 1.8 Liter.

GL Sedan 4D		GB41S	13679	950	1350	2500	4200
GL Wagon 4D		GB41W	14179	1075	1525	2700	4400
GLX Sedan 4D		GB41S	14479	1125	1575	2750	4450
GLX Wagon 4D		GB41W	14979	1175	1675	2875	4600

2002 SUZUKI — JS2(RA41S)-2-#

AERIO—4-Cyl.—Equipment Schedule 6
W.B. 97.6"; 2.0 Liter.

S Sedan 4D		RA41S	13999	1075	1500	2900	4875
GS Sedan 4D		RA41S	14999	1250	1725	3150	5175
SX Wagon 4D		RC41H	14999	1475	1950	3400	5450

ESTEEM—4-Cyl.—Equipment Schedule 6
W.B. 97.6"; 1.8 Liter.

GL Sedan 4D		GB41S	13999	1125	1600	2975	4900
GL Wagon 4D		GB41W	14299	1300	1775	3150	5150
GLX Sedan 4D		GB41S	14799	1350	1825	3200	5200
GLX Wagon 4D		GB41W	15299	1475	1950	3350	5375

2003 SUZUKI

Body	Type	VIN	List	Trade-In Fair	Trade-In Good	Pvt-Party Good	Retail Excellent

2003 SUZUKI — JS2(RA41S)-3-#

AERIO—4-Cyl.—Equipment Schedule 6
W.B. 97.6"; 2.0 Liter.

S Sedan 4D	RA41S	14094	1525	2000	3475	5525
GS Sedan 4D	RA41S	15294	1775	2300	3775	5875
SX Wagon 4D	RC41H	15594	2000	2550	4050	6175
AWD			350	350	465	465

2004 SUZUKI — JS2orKL5(RA61S)-4-#

AERIO—4-Cyl.—Equipment Schedule 6
W.B. 97.6"; 2.3 Liter.

S Sedan 4D	RA61S	13499	1825	2350	3850	5975
LX Sedan 4D	RA61S	15199	2125	2675	4200	6350
SX Wagon 4D	RC61H	15499	2375	2975	4475	6700
AWD			400	400	535	535

FORENZA—4-Cyl.—Equipment Schedule 3
W.B. 102.4"; 2.0 Liter.

S Sedan 4D	JD52Z	13799	1650	2150	3650	5750
LX Sedan 4D	JJ52Z	15699	1925	2475	4000	6150
EX Sedan 4D	JJ52Z	16499	2125	2675	4200	6350
Manual Trans			(525)	(525)	(700)	(700)

VERONA—6-Cyl.—Equipment Schedule 3
W.B. 106.3"; 2.5 Liter.

S Sedan 4D	VJ52L	16999	2575	3175	4650	6850
LX Sedan 4D	VJ52L	18299	2875	3500	5000	7225
EX Sedan 4D	VM52L	19999	3100	3775	5300	7575

2005 SUZUKI — JS2orKL5(RA62S)-5-#

AERIO—4-Cyl.—Equipment Schedule 6
W.B. 97.6"; 2.3 Liter.

S Sedan 4D	RA62S	13994	2575	3175	4700	6950
LX Sedan 4D	RA61S	15694	2925	3550	5100	7400
SX Wagon 4D	RC61H	15994	3175	3875	5425	7750
AWD	B,D		450	450	600	600

FORENZA—4-Cyl.—Equipment Schedule 3
W.B. 102.4"; 2.0 Liter.

S Sedan 4D	JD56Z	14794	2350	2925	4450	6675
S Wagon 4D	JD86Z	15294	2600	3200	4725	6975
LX Sedan 4D	JJ56Z	16694	2700	3300	4850	7100
LX Wagon 4D	JJ86Z	17194	2925	3550	5100	7400
EX Sedan 4D	JJ56Z	17494	2850	3475	5025	7300
EX Wagon 4D	JJ86Z	17994	3100	3775	5325	7650
Manual Trans			(550)	(550)	(735)	(735)

RENO—4-Cyl.—Equipment Schedule 4
W.B. 102.4"; 2.0 Liter.

S Hatchback 4D	JD66Z	14794	2300	2875	4400	6625
LX Hatchback 4D	JJ66Z	16694	3225	3925	5475	7800
EX Hatchback 4D	JJ66Z	17494	3550	4250	5800	8150
Manual Trans			(550)	(550)	(735)	(735)

VERONA—6-Cyl.—Equipment Schedule 3
W.B. 106.3"; 2.5 Liter.

S Sedan 4D	VJ56L	17994	3075	3725	5250	7525
LX Sedan 4D	VJ56L	19794	3400	4100	5625	7975
EX Sedan 4D	VM56L	20994	3700	4400	5950	8300

2006 SUZUKI — JS2orKL5(RA62S)-6-#

AERIO—4-Cyl.—Equipment Schedule 6
W.B. 97.6"; 2.3 Liter.

Sedan 4D	RA62S	14579	3525	4225	5800	8175
SX Wagon 4D	RC61H	15079	4225	5000	6575	9025
AWD	B,D		500	500	665	665

FORENZA—4-Cyl.—Equipment Schedule 3
W.B. 102.4"; 2.0 Liter.

Sedan 4D	JD56Z	15179	3200	3875	5475	7825
Wagon 4D	JD86Z	15879	3500	4200	5775	8150
Manual Trans			(575)	(575)	(765)	(765)

RENO—4-Cyl.—Equipment Schedule 4
W.B. 102.4"; 2.0 Liter.

| Hatchback 4D | JD66Z | 14679 | 3125 | 3800 | 5375 | 7700 |
| Manual Trans | | | (575) | (575) | (765) | (765) |

Body	Type	VIN	List	Trade-In Fair	Good	Pvt-Party Good	Retail Excellent

VERONA—6-Cyl.—Equipment Schedule 3
W.B. 106.3"; 2.5 Liter.

Sedan 4D		VJ56L	18879	**3675**	**4400**	**5925**	**8275**
Luxury Sedan 4D		VM56L	20879	**4075**	**4800**	**6350**	**8725**

2007 SUZUKI — JS2orKL5(RA62S)-7-#

AERIO—4-Cyl.—Equipment Schedule 6
W.B. 97.6"; 2.3 Liter.

Sedan 4D		RA62S	14894	**4500**	**5325**	**6825**	**9250**
AWD		B		**550**	**550**	**735**	**735**

SX4—4-Cyl.—Equipment Schedule 4
W.B. 98.4"; 2.0 Liter.

Hatchback Sedan 4D		YB413	16594	**6500**	**7500**	**9075**	**11700**
Sport H'Back Sed 4D		YB417	17994	**7000**	**8050**	**9625**	**12350**
Manual Trans				**(600)**	**(600)**	**(800)**	**(800)**

FORENZA—4-Cyl.—Equipment Schedule 3
W.B. 102.4"; 2.0 Liter.

Sedan 4D		JD56Z	15594	**4200**	**4950**	**6425**	**8750**
Wagon 4D		JD86Z	16294	**4450**	**5275**	**6775**	**9200**
Manual Trans				**(600)**	**(600)**	**(800)**	**(800)**

RENO—4-Cyl.—Equipment Schedule 4
W.B. 102.4"; 2.0 Liter.

Hatchback 4D		JD66Z	15094	**4025**	**4775**	**6250**	**8550**
Manual Trans				**(600)**	**(600)**	**(800)**	**(800)**

2008 SUZUKI — JS2orKL5(YC414)-8-#

SX4—4-Cyl.—Equipment Schedule 4
W.B. 98.4"; 2.0 Liter.

Sedan 4D		YC414	16495	**7250**	**8325**	**9800**	**12450**
Hatchback 4D		YA413	16495	**7250**	**8325**	**9800**	**12450**
AWD Hatchback 4D		YB413	16995	**7600**	**8700**	**10200**	**12850**
Manual Trans				**(625)**	**(625)**	**(835)**	**(835)**

FORENZA—4-Cyl.—Equipment Schedule 3
W.B. 102.4"; 2.0 Liter.

Sedan 4D		JD56Z	15974	**5150**	**6000**	**7375**	**9675**
Wagon 4D		JD86Z	16874	**5475**	**6375**	**7750**	**10100**
Manual Trans				**(625)**	**(625)**	**(835)**	**(835)**

RENO—4-Cyl.—Equipment Schedule 4
W.B. 102.4"; 2.0 Liter.

Hatchback 4D		JD66Z	15324	**4925**	**5775**	**7125**	**9400**
Manual Trans				**(625)**	**(625)**	**(835)**	**(835)**

TOYOTA

1994 TOYOTA — (1,4orJ)(NorT)(1,2orX)(EL46S)-R-#

TERCEL—4-Cyl.—Equipment Schedule 6
W.B. 93.7"; 1.5 Liter.

Sedan 2D		EL46S	10223	**625**	**850**	**1625**	**2875**
DX Sedan 2D		EL43S	12028	**725**	**1050**	**1875**	**3250**
DX Sedan 4D		EL43T	12028	**800**	**1125**	**2025**	**3425**

PASEO—4-Cyl.—Equipment Schedule 6
W.B. 93.7"; 1.5 Liter.

Coupe 2D		EL45U	13753	**875**	**1225**	**2175**	**3650**

COROLLA—4-Cyl.—Equipment Schedule 6
W.B. 97.0"; 1.6 Liter, 1.8 Liter.

Sedan 4D		AE04B	13308	**875**	**1225**	**2175**	**3650**
DX Sedan 4D		AE09B	14998	**900**	**1275**	**2225**	**3725**
DX Wagon 4D		AE09V	15553	**1075**	**1500**	**2625**	**4275**
LE Sedan 4D		AE00B	18113	**950**	**1325**	**2400**	**4025**

CAMRY—4-Cyl.—Equipment Schedule 6
W.B. 103.1"; 2.2 Liter.

DX Sedan 4D		SK11E	19293	**1150**	**1625**	**2775**	**4450**
DX Coupe 2D		SK11C	18963	**1025**	**1450**	**2550**	**4175**
DX Wagon 4D		SK11W	20703	**1325**	**1800**	**3000**	**4700**
LE Sedan 4D		SK12E	19613	**1200**	**1700**	**2850**	**4550**
LE Coupe 2D		SK12C	19323	**1100**	**1525**	**2650**	**4300**
LE Wagon 4D		SK12W	21003	**1400**	**1850**	**3075**	**4800**
XLE Sedan 4D		SK13E	21643	**1275**	**1750**	**2950**	**4650**
V6 3.0 Liter		G		**75**	**75**	**100**	**100**

CAMRY—V6—Equipment Schedule 4
W.B. 103.1"; 3.0 Liter.

Body	Type	VIN	List	Trade-In Fair	Good	Pvt-Party Good	Retail Excellent
SE Sedan 4D	GK14E	22913	1575	2050	3250	5050
SE Coupe 2D	GK14C	22623	1425	1900	3100	4875
MR2—4-Cyl.—Equipment Schedule 6							
W.B. 94.5"; 2.2 Liter.							
Coupe 2D	SW21M	23613	2175	2775	4050	5975
MR2—4-Cyl. Turbo—Equipment Schedule 6							
W.B. 94.5"; 2.0 Liter.							
Coupe 2D	SW22M	28663	3575	4275	5725	7975
CELICA—4-Cyl.—Equipment Schedule 4							
W.B. 99.9"; 1.8 Liter, 2.2 Liter.							
ST Sport Coupe 2D	AT00F	18628	1625	2125	3350	5150
ST Liftback 2D	AT00N	18968	1725	2225	3450	5275
GT Sport Coupe 2D	ST07F	20053	1725	2225	3450	5275
GT Liftback 2D	ST07N	20523	1800	2325	3575	5425
Auto Trans			125	125	165	165
SUPRA—6-Cyl.—Equipment Schedule 4							
W.B. 100.4"; 3.0 Liter.							
Liftback 2D	JA81L	36185	10525	11900	14350	18400
Sport Roof	J		200	200	265	265
Auto Trans			125	125	165	165
SUPRA—6-Cyl. Turbo—Equipment Schedule 4							
W.B. 100.4"; 3.0 Liter.							
Liftback 2D	JA82L	43185	16425	18425	21700	27000
Sport Roof	J		200	200	265	265
6-Spd Manual Trans			1500	1500	2000	2000

1995 TOYOTA — (1,4orJ)(NorT)(1,2,5orX)(EL55D)–S

Body	Type	VIN	List	Trade-In Fair	Good	Pvt-Party Good	Retail Excellent
TERCEL—4-Cyl.—Equipment Schedule 6							
W.B. 93.7"; 1.5 Liter.							
Sedan 2D	EL55D	11535	750	1075	1925	3325
DX Sedan 2D	EL56D	12685	925	1300	2350	3950
DX Sedan 4D	EL56E	13125	975	1375	2450	4075
PASEO—4-Cyl.—Equipment Schedule 6							
W.B. 93.7"; 1.5 Liter.							
Coupe 2D	EL45U	14725	1000	1400	2500	4150
COROLLA—4-Cyl.—Equipment Schedule 6							
W.B. 97.0"; 1.6 Liter, 1.8 Liter.							
Sedan 4D	AE04B	13782	1000	1425	2525	4175
DX Sedan 4D	AE09B	15552	1050	1475	2575	4250
DX Wagon 4D	AE09V	16527	1225	1725	2900	4600
LE Sedan 4D	AE00B	17075	1100	1525	2675	4325
CAMRY—4-Cyl.—Equipment Schedule 4							
W.B. 103.1"; 2.2 Liter.							
DX Sedan 4D	SK11E	19815	1400	1875	3075	4825
DX Coupe 2D	SK11C	19430	1175	1675	2825	4525
LE Sedan 4D	SK12E	19955	1475	1950	3175	4975
LE Coupe 2D	SK12C	19665	1275	1750	2950	4675
LE Wagon 4D	SK12W	21365	1675	2175	3425	5250
XLE Sedan 4D	SK13E	22015	1550	2025	3250	5050
V6 3.0 Liter	G		75	75	100	100
CAMRY—V6—Equipment Schedule 4							
W.B. 103.1"; 3.0 Liter.							
SE Sedan 4D	GK14E	23895	1850	2400	3675	5525
SE Coupe 2D	GK14C	23605	1725	2225	3475	5325
MR2—4-Cyl.—Equipment Schedule 6							
W.B. 94.5"; 2.2 Liter.							
Coupe 2D	SW21M	24655	2600	3200	4550	6625
MR2—4-Cyl. Turbo—Equipment Schedule 6							
W.B. 94.5"; 2.0 Liter.							
Coupe 2D	SW22M	29755	4000	4725	6250	8625
CELICA—4-Cyl.—Equipment Schedule 4							
W.B. 99.9"; 1.8 Liter, 2.2 Liter.							
ST Sport Coupe 2D	AT00F	19410	1975	2525	3775	5650
ST Liftback 2D	AT00N	19760	2075	2650	3900	5800
GT Sport Coupe 2D	ST07F	20925	2075	2650	3900	5800
GT Liftback 2D	ST07N	21415	2175	2750	4025	5950
GT Convertible 2D	ST07K	25635	3025	3675	5075	7200
Auto Trans			125	125	165	165
AVALON—V6—Equipment Schedule 4							
W.B. 107.1"; 3.0 Liter.							
XL Sedan 4D	GB10E	23155	1675	2175	3400	5225
XLS Sedan 4D	GB11E	27085	2375	2975	4300	6250

1995 TOYOTA

Body	Type	VIN	List	Trade-In Fair	Trade-In Good	Pvt-Party Good	Retail Excellent
SUPRA—6-Cyl.—Equipment Schedule 4							
W.B. 100.4"; 3.0 Liter.							
SE Liftback 2D		JA81L	31497	11225	12700	15450	19900
Liftback 2D		JA81L	37297	11650	13175	15750	20000
Sport Roof		J		200	200	265	265
Auto Trans				125	125	165	165
SUPRA—6-Cyl. Turbo—Equipment Schedule 4							
W.B. 100.4"; 3.0 Liter.							
Liftback 2D		JA82L	46997	18225	20375	24000	30200
Sport Roof		J		200	200	265	265
6-Spd Manual Trans				1500	1500	2000	2000

1996 TOYOTA — (4T,JTor1N)(1,2,5orX)(AC52L)-T-#

Body	Type	VIN	List	Trade-In Fair	Trade-In Good	Pvt-Party Good	Retail Excellent
TERCEL—4-Cyl.—Equipment Schedule 6							
W.B. 93.7"; 1.5 Liter.							
Sedan 2D		AC52L	11981	900	1250	2325	3950
DX Sedan 2D		AC52L	13458	1075	1525	2650	4325
DX Sedan 4D		BC52L	13768	1150	1600	2775	4475
PASEO—4-Cyl.—Equipment Schedule 6							
W.B. 93.7"; 1.5 Liter.							
Coupe 2D		CC52H	14383	1150	1625	2800	4475
COROLLA—4-Cyl.—Equipment Schedule 6							
W.B. 97.0"; 1.6 Liter, 1.8 Liter.							
Sedan 4D		BA02E	14538	1100	1550	2725	4400
DX Sedan 4D		BB02E	15448	1225	1700	2875	4600
DX Wagon 4D		EB02E	16598	1550	2025	3250	5075
CAMRY—4-Cyl.—Equipment Schedule 4							
W.B. 103.1"; 2.2 Liter.							
DX Sedan 4D		BG12K	19848	1675	2150	3400	5225
DX Coupe 2D		CG12K	19458	1400	1875	3075	4850
LE Sedan 4D		BG12K	20588	1750	2250	3525	5375
LE Coupe 2D		CG12K	20298	1525	2025	3250	5050
LE Wagon 4D		EG12K	22028	1950	2500	3775	5650
XLE Sedan 4D		BG12K	22698	1850	2350	3625	5500
Manual Trans				(200)	(200)	(265)	(265)
V6 3.0 Liter		F		125	125	165	165
CAMRY—V6—Equipment Schedule 4							
W.B. 103.1"; 3.0 Liter.							
SE Sedan 4D		BF12K	24528	2175	2750	4050	5975
SE Coupe 2D		CF12K	24248	2025	2575	3850	5750
CELICA—4-Cyl.—Equipment Schedule 4							
W.B. 99.9"; 1.8 Liter, 2.2 Liter.							
ST Sport Coupe 2D		CB02T	19638	2350	2950	4250	6225
ST Liftback 2D		DB02T	19998	2450	3075	4375	6400
GT Sport Coupe 2D		CG02T	21183	2475	3075	4400	6425
GT Liftback 2D		DG02T	21693	2575	3150	4500	6550
GT Convertible 2D		FG02T	25893	3575	4300	5750	8000
Auto Trans				125	125	165	165
AVALON—V6—Equipment Schedule 4							
W.B. 107.1"; 3.0 Liter.							
XL Sedan 4D		BF12B	23838	1900	2450	3725	5600
XLS Sedan 4D		BF12B	27868	2700	3300	4675	6750
SUPRA—6-Cyl.—Equipment Schedule 4							
W.B. 100.4"; 3.0 Liter.							
Liftback 2D		DD82A	39020	12800	14450	17300	22100
Sport Roof				250	250	335	335
Auto Trans				125	125	165	165
SUPRA—6-Cyl. Turbo—Equipment Schedule 4							
W.B. 100.4"; 3.0 Liter.							
Liftback 2D		DE82A	50820	19600	21950	25700	32000

1997 TOYOTA—(4T,JTor1N)(1,2,5orX)(AC52L)-V-#

Body	Type	VIN	List	Trade-In Fair	Trade-In Good	Pvt-Party Good	Retail Excellent
TERCEL—4-Cyl.—Equipment Schedule 6							
W.B. 93.7"; 1.5 Liter.							
CE Sedan 2D		AC52L	12508	1275	1775	2975	4725
CE Sedan 4D		BC52L	13968	1525	2025	3250	5050
Limited Edition				25	25	35	35
PASEO—4-Cyl.—Equipment Schedule 6							
W.B. 93.7"; 1.5 Liter.							
Coupe 2D		CC52H	14553	1375	1850	3075	4850
Convertible 2D		FC52H	18073	2100	2675	3975	5875

1997 TOYOTA

Body Type	VIN	List	Trade-In Fair	Good	Pvt-Party Good	Retail Excellent
COROLLA—4-Cyl.—Equipment Schedule 6						
W.B. 97.0"; 1.6 Liter, 1.8 Liter.						
Sedan 4D	BA02E	15028	1275	1750	2950	4675
CE Sedan 4D	BA02E	15063	1300	1775	2975	4725
DX Sedan 4D	BB02E	16445	1500	1975	3200	5000
CAMRY—4-Cyl.—Equipment Schedule 4						
W.B. 105.1"; 2.2 Liter.						
CE Sedan 4D	BG22K	19918	1625	2125	3375	5225
LE Sedan 4D	BG22K	20288	1750	2250	3500	5375
XLE Sedan 4D	BG22K	22228	1850	2375	3650	5525
Manual Trans			(250)	(250)	(335)	(335)
V6 3.0 Liter	F		175	175	235	235
CELICA—4-Cyl.—Equipment Schedule 4						
W.B. 99.9"; 1.8 Liter, 2.2 Liter.						
ST Sport Coupe 2D	CB02T	19703	2725	3325	4675	6750
ST Liftback 2D	DB02T	20063	2850	3450	4850	6925
GT Liftback 2D	DG02T	21893	2975	3600	5000	7100
GT Convertible 2D	FG02T	26093	4150	4900	6425	8775
Auto Trans			150	150	200	200
AVALON—V6—Equipment Schedule 4						
W.B. 107.1"; 3.0 Liter.						
XL Sedan 4D	BF12B	23958	2150	2725	4025	5950
XLS Sedan 4D	BF12B	27468	3075	3700	5100	7225
SUPRA—6-Cyl.—Equipment Schedule 4						
W.B. 100.4"; 3.0 Liter.						
Ltd Edition L'Back 2D	DD82A	30340	14075	15825	18750	23700
Sport Roof	P		275	275	365	365
Auto Trans			150	150	200	200
SUPRA—6-Cyl. Turbo—Equipment Schedule 4						
W.B. 100.4"; 3.0 Liter.						
Ltd Edition L'Back 2D	DE82A	39040	22050	24600	28400	35200
6-Spd Manual Trans			1650	1650	2200	2200

1998 TOYOTA–(4T,JTor1N)(1,2,5orX)(AC52L)–W–#

Body Type	VIN	List	Trade-In Fair	Good	Pvt-Party Good	Retail Excellent
TERCEL—4-Cyl.—Equipment Schedule 6						
W.B. 93.7"; 1.5 Liter.						
CE Sedan 2D	AC52L	13110	1550	2050	3275	5100
COROLLA—4-Cyl.—Equipment Schedule 6						
W.B. 97.0"; 1.8 Liter.						
VE Sedan 4D	BR12E	13443	1825	2350	3625	5500
CE Sedan 4D	BR12E	14208	1875	2425	3700	5575
LE Sedan 4D	BR12E	15218	2125	2700	3975	5900
CAMRY—4-Cyl.—Equipment Schedule 4						
W.B. 105.2"; 2.2 Liter.						
CE Sedan 4D	BG22K	20464	1925	2475	3750	5625
LE Sedan 4D	BG22K	20858	2050	2625	3925	5825
XLE Sedan 4D	BG22K	23279	2200	2775	4075	6000
Manual Trans			(300)	(300)	(400)	(400)
V6 3.0 Liter	F		225	225	300	300
CELICA—4-Cyl.—Equipment Schedule 4						
W.B. 99.9"; 2.2 Liter.						
GT Sport Coupe 2D	CG02T	20531	3150	3825	5225	7375
GT Liftback 2D	DG02T	21701	3400	4125	5525	7750
GT Convertible 2D	FG02T	24970	4700	5525	7100	9625
Auto Trans			175	175	235	235
AVALON—V6—Equipment Schedule 4						
W.B. 107.1"; 3.0 Liter.						
XL Sedan 4D	BF18B	24698	2475	3075	4400	6400
XLS Sedan 4D	BF18B	28548	3475	4175	5575	7800
SUPRA—6-Cyl.—Equipment Schedule 4						
W.B. 100.4"; 3.0 Liter.						
Liftback 2D	DD82A	31338	15375	17250	20200	25300
Sport Roof	P		300	300	400	400
SUPRA—6-Cyl. Turbo—Equipment Schedule 4						
W.B. 100.4"; 3.0 Liter.						
Liftback 2D	DE82A	40728	23725	26350	30200	37000
6-Spd Manual Trans			1725	1725	2300	2300

1999 TOYOTA–(J,1,2or4)(NorT)(X,1,2or5)(BR12E)–X

Body Type	VIN	List	Trade-In Fair	Good	Pvt-Party Good	Retail Excellent
COROLLA—4-Cyl.—Equipment Schedule 6						
W.B. 97.0"; 1.8 Liter.						
VE Sedan 4D	BR12E	13588	2125	2700	4000	5950

Body Type	VIN	List	Trade-In Fair	Trade-In Good	Pvt-Party Good	Retail Excellent
CE Sedan 4D	BR12E	14278	2225	2800	4100	6050
LE Sedan 4D	BR12E	15288	2500	3100	4425	6450
CAMRY—4-Cyl.—Equipment Schedule 4						
W.B. 105.2"; 2.2 Liter.						
CE Sedan 4D	BG22K	19444	2325	2925	4250	6225
LE Sedan 4D	BG22K	20218	2475	3075	4375	6400
XLE Sedan 4D	BG22K	23178	2625	3225	4550	6600
Manual Trans			(350)	(350)	(465)	(465)
V6 3.0 Liter	F		275	275	365	365
SOLARA—4-Cyl.—Equipment Schedule 4						
W.B. 105.1"; 2.2 Liter.						
SE Coupe 2D	CG22P	19858	2300	2900	4225	6175
Manual Trans			(350)	(350)	(465)	(465)
V6 3.0 Liter	F		275	275	365	365
SOLARA—V6—Equipment Schedule 4						
W.B. 105.1"; 3.0 Liter.						
SLE Coupe 2D	CF22P	25408	3250	3925	5350	7500
CELICA—4-Cyl.—Equipment Schedule 4						
W.B. 99.9"; 2.2 Liter.						
GT Liftback 2D	DG02T	22240	3925	4650	6100	8375
GT Convertible 2D	FG02T	25319	5350	6225	7850	10450
Auto Trans			200	200	265	265
AVALON—V6—Equipment Schedule 4						
W.B. 107.1"; 3.0 Liter.						
XL Sedan 4D	BF18B	24988	2850	3475	4850	6925
XLS Sedan 4D	BF18B	28998	3925	4675	6125	8400

2000 TOYOTA—(J,1,2or4)(NorT)(X,1,2or5)(BT123)—Y

Body Type	VIN	List	Trade-In Fair	Trade-In Good	Pvt-Party Good	Retail Excellent
ECHO—4-Cyl.—Equipment Schedule 6						
W.B. 93.3"; 1.5 Liter.						
Sedan 4D	BT123	11945	1625	2125	3375	5225
Coupe 2D	AT123	11645	1425	1900	3150	4950
COROLLA—4-Cyl.—Equipment Schedule 6						
W.B. 97.0"; 1.8 Liter.						
VE Sedan 4D	BR12E	13603	2475	3075	4400	6425
CE Sedan 4D	BR12E	14653	2600	3200	4525	6575
LE Sedan 4D	BR12E	15523	2925	3550	4925	7000
CAMRY—4-Cyl.—Equipment Schedule 4						
W.B. 105.2"; 2.2 Liter.						
CE Sedan 4D	BG22K	19820	2800	3425	4775	6850
LE Sedan 4D	BG22K	20743	2925	3550	4925	7025
XLE Sedan 4D	BG22K	24423	3075	3750	5125	7250
Manual Trans			(400)	(400)	(535)	(535)
V6 3.0 Liter	F		325	325	435	435
SOLARA—4-Cyl.—Equipment Schedule 4						
W.B. 105.1"; 2.2 Liter.						
SE Coupe 2D	CG22P	20193	2775	3375	4725	6775
SE Convertible 2D	FG22P	25523	4025	4775	6225	8525
Manual Trans			(400)	(400)	(535)	(535)
V6 3.0 Liter	F		325	325	435	435
SOLARA—V6—Equipment Schedule 4						
W.B. 105.1"; 3.0 Liter.						
SLE Coupe 2D	CF22P	26293	3800	4500	5950	8200
SLE Convertible 2D	FF22P	30943	5025	5875	7475	10000
MR2 SPYDER—4-Cyl.—Equipment Schedule 4						
W.B. 96.5"; 1.8 Liter.						
Convertible 2D	FG320	23553	4950	5800	7500	9850
CELICA—4-Cyl.—Equipment Schedule 4						
W.B. 102.3"; 1.8 Liter.						
GT Liftback 2D	DR32T	17970	3875	4600	6050	8300
GT-S Liftback 2D	DY32T	21620	4550	5375	6900	9325
Auto Trans			200	200	265	265
AVALON—V6—Equipment Schedule 4						
W.B. 107.1"; 3.0 Liter.						
XL Sedan 4D	BF28B	25650	4000	4725	6175	8450
XLS Sedan 4D	BF28B	30210	5150	6000	7600	10150

2001 TOYOTA—(J,1,2or4)(NorT)(D,X,1or2)(BT123)—1

Body Type	VIN	List	Trade-In Fair	Trade-In Good	Pvt-Party Good	Retail Excellent
ECHO—4-Cyl.—Equipment Schedule 6						
W.B. 93.3"; 1.5 Liter.						
Sedan 4D	BT123	11930	2000	2575	3850	5725
Coupe 2D	AT123	11400	1825	2350	3625	5500

Body	Type	VIN	List	Trade-In Fair	Good	Pvt-Party Good	Retail Excellent
COROLLA—4-Cyl.—Equipment Schedule 6							
W.B. 97.0"; 1.8 Liter.							
CE Sedan 4D		BR12E	13753	3000	3625	5025	7125
S Sedan 4D		BR12E	14343	3275	3950	5350	7500
LE Sedan 4D		BR12E	14863	3350	4050	5450	7625
PRIUS—4-Cyl. HYBRID—Equipment Schedule 3							
W.B. 100.4"; 1.5 Liter.							
Sedan 4D		BK12U	20450	5325	6200	7775	10350
CAMRY—4-Cyl.—Equipment Schedule 4							
W.B. 105.1"; 2.2 Liter.							
CE Sedan 4D		BG22K	19733	3325	4025	5425	7575
LE Sedan 4D		BG22K	20895	3450	4175	5550	7750
XLE Sedan 4D		BG22K	24575	3650	4350	5750	7975
Manual Trans				(425)	(425)	(565)	(565)
V6 3.0 Liter		F		375	375	500	500
SOLARA—4-Cyl.—Equipment Schedule 4							
W.B. 105.1"; 2.2 Liter.							
SE Coupe 2D		CG22P	20245	3250	3950	5350	7500
SE Convertible 2D		FG22P	25575	4650	5475	6975	9425
Manual Trans				(425)	(425)	(565)	(565)
V6 3.0 Liter		F		375	375	500	500
SOLARA—V6—Equipment Schedule 4							
W.B. 105.1"; 3.0 Liter.							
SLE Coupe 2D		CF22P	25645	4375	5175	6650	8975
SLE Convertible 2D		FF22P	30995	5750	6700	8275	10900
MR2 SPYDER—4-Cyl.—Equipment Schedule 4							
W.B. 96.5"; 1.8 Liter.							
Convertible 2D		FG320	24065	5600	6550	8100	10700
CELICA—4-Cyl.—Equipment Schedule 4							
W.B. 102.3"; 1.8 Liter.							
GT Liftback 2D		DR32T	18285	4425	5250	6750	9150
GT-S Liftback 2D		DY32T	21935	5200	6050	7600	10100
Auto Trans				200	200	265	265
AVALON—V6—Equipment Schedule 4							
W.B. 107.1"; 3.0 Liter.							
XL Sedan 4D		BF28B	26325	4500	5300	6750	9125
XLS Sedan 4D		BF28B	30885	5725	6675	8250	10900

2002 TOYOTA—(J,1,2or4)(NorT)(D,X,1or2)(BT123)—2

Body	Type	VIN	List	Trade-In Fair	Good	Pvt-Party Good	Retail Excellent
ECHO—4-Cyl.—Equipment Schedule 6							
W.B. 93.3"; 1.5 Liter.							
Sedan 4D		BT123	12265	2325	2925	4375	6525
Coupe 2D		AT123	11675	2125	2700	4175	6275
COROLLA—4-Cyl.—Equipment Schedule 6							
W.B. 97.0"; 1.8 Liter.							
CE Sedan 4D		BR12E	13533	3350	4050	5600	7975
S Sedan 4D		BR12E	14073	3675	4375	5975	8375
LE Sedan 4D		BR12E	14443	3750	4475	6050	8475
PRIUS—4-Cyl. HYBRID—Equipment Schedule 3							
W.B. 100.4"; 1.5 Liter.							
Sedan 4D		BK12U	20480	5825	6750	8525	11300
CAMRY—4-Cyl.—Equipment Schedule 4							
W.B. 107.1"; 2.4 Liter.							
LE Sedan 4D		BE32K	20285	3875	4600	6200	8625
SE Sedan 4D		BE32K	21625	4000	4750	6350	8800
XLE Sedan 4D		BF32K	22780	4175	4950	6550	9025
Manual Trans				(450)	(450)	(600)	(600)
V6 3.0 Liter		F		400	400	535	535
SOLARA—4-Cyl.—Equipment Schedule 4							
W.B. 105.1"; 2.4 Liter.							
SE Coupe 2D		CE22P	20650	3775	4475	6075	8475
SE Convertible 2D		FE22P	25980	5225	6100	7800	10500
Manual Trans				(450)	(450)	(600)	(600)
V6 3.0 Liter		F		400	400	535	535
SOLARA—V6—Equipment Schedule 4							
W.B. 105.1"; 3.0 Liter.							
SLE Coupe 2D		CF22P	25160	4925	5750	7450	10100
SLE Convertible 2D		FF22P	31010	6425	7400	9175	12050
MR2 SPYDER—4-Cyl.—Equipment Schedule 4							
W.B. 96.5"; 1.8 Liter.							
Convertible 2D		FR320	25000	6200	7175	8925	11750
CELICA—4-Cyl.—Equipment Schedule 4							
W.B. 102.4"; 1.8 Liter.							

Body	Type	VIN	List	Trade-In Fair	Trade-In Good	Pvt-Party Good	Retail Excellent
GT Liftback 2D		DR32T	18390	4950	5775	7500	10150
GT-S Liftback 2D		DY32T	22040	5725	6675	8375	11100
Auto Trans				200	200	265	265

AVALON—V6—Equipment Schedule 4
W.B. 107.1"; 3.0 Liter.

XL Sedan 4D		BF28B	26330	4925	5775	7450	10100
XLS Sedan 4D		BF28B	30890	6275	7225	9000	11850

2003 TOYOTA–J,1,2or4(NorT)D,X,1or2(BT123)–3

ECHO—4-Cyl.—Equipment Schedule 6
W.B. 93.3"; 1.5 Liter.

Sedan 4D		BT123	12375	2725	3350	4850	7050
Coupe 2D		AT123	11785	2500	3100	4575	6750

COROLLA—4-Cyl.—Equipment Schedule 6
W.B. 102.4"; 1.8 Liter.

CE Sedan 4D		BR32E	14055	4425	5225	6875	9425
S Sedan 4D		BR32E	15000	4775	5600	7275	9900
LE Sedan 4D		BR32E	15165	4875	5700	7375	10000
Sport Pkg				100	100	135	135
TRD Pkg				200	200	265	265

PRIUS—4-Cyl. Hybrid—Equipment Schedule 3
W.B. 100.4"; 1.5 Liter.

Sedan 4D		BK12U	20730	6700	7725	9475	12400

MATRIX—4-Cyl.—Equipment Schedule 6
W.B. 102.4"; 1.8 Liter.

Sport Wagon 4D		KR32E	15155	4300	5100	6650	9100
XR Sport Wagon 4D		KR32E	16665	4575	5400	7000	9550
XRS Sport Wagon 4D		KY32E	19235	5175	6025	7675	10300
4WD Sport Wagon 4D		LR32E	17600	4875	5725	7350	9950
4WD XR Sport Wag 4D		LR32E	18930	5000	5850	7500	10100
TRD Pkg				400	400	535	535

CAMRY—4-Cyl.—Equipment Schedule 4
W.B. 107.1"; 2.4 Liter.

LE Sedan 4D		BE30K	20285	4600	5425	7075	9675
SE Sedan 4D		BE30K	21625	4800	5625	7325	9950
XLE Sedan 4D		BF30K	22780	5025	5875	7550	10200
Manual Trans				(500)	(500)	(665)	(665)
V6 3.0 Liter		F		475	475	635	635

SOLARA—4-Cyl.—Equipment Schedule 4
W.B. 105.1"; 2.4 Liter.

SE Coupe 2D		CE22P	20650	4400	5200	6850	9425
SE Convertible 2D		FE22P	25980	6100	7075	8800	11600
Manual Trans				(500)	(500)	(665)	(665)
V6 3.0 Liter		F		475	475	635	635

SOLARA—V6—Equipment Schedule 4
W.B. 105.1"; 3.0 Liter.

SLE Coupe 2D		CF22P	25160	5750	6700	8400	11150
SLE Convertible 2D		FF22P	31010	7475	8575	10350	13350

MR2 SPYDER—4-Cyl.—Equipment Schedule 4
W.B. 96.5"; 1.8 Liter.

Convertible 2D		FR320	25055	7050	8125	9850	12800

CELICA—4-Cyl.—Equipment Schedule 4
W.B. 102.4"; 1.8 Liter.

GT Liftback 2D		DR32T	18610	5600	6550	8200	10950
GT-S Liftback 2D		DY32T	22455	6550	7550	9275	12150
Auto Trans				225	225	300	300

AVALON—V6—Equipment Schedule 4
W.B. 107.1"; 3.0 Liter.

XL Sedan 4D		BF28B	26330	5500	6400	8075	10800
XLS Sedan 4D		BF28B	27150	7025	8075	9850	12800

2004 TOYOTA–(J,1,2or4)(NorT)D,Xor1(BT123)–4–#

ECHO—4-Cyl.—Equipment Schedule 6
W.B. 93.3"; 1.5 Liter.

Sedan 4D		BT123	12215	3200	3875	5400	7675
Coupe 2D		AT123	11685	2950	3575	5100	7350

COROLLA—4-Cyl.—Equipment Schedule 6
W.B. 102.4"; 1.8 Liter.

CE Sedan 4D		BR32E	14085	5000	5850	7525	10150
S Sedan 4D		BR32E	15030	5400	6300	7975	10650
LE Sedan 4D		BR32E	15295	5500	6375	8075	10800

Body Type	VIN	List	Trade-In Fair	Good	Pvt-Party Good	Retail Excellent
PRIUS—4-Cyl. Hybrid—Equipment Schedule 3						
W.B. 106.3"; 1.5 Liter.						
Hatchback Sedan 4D	KB20U	20510	8900	10150	12000	15250
MATRIX—4-Cyl.—Equipment Schedule 6						
W.B. 102.4"; 1.8 Liter.						
Sport Wagon 4D	KR32E	15185	5025	5875	7500	10100
XR Sport Wagon 4D	KR32E	16695	5350	6225	7875	10500
XRS Sport Wagon 4D	KY32E	19265	5975	6925	8575	11250
4WD Sport Wagon 4D	LR32E	17630	5650	6575	8200	10900
4WD XR Sport Wag 4D	LR32E	18960	5800	6750	8375	11050
Sport Pkg			400	400	535	535
CAMRY—4-Cyl.—Equipment Schedule 4						
W.B. 107.1"; 2.4 Liter.						
Sedan 4D	BE32K	19390	5150	6000	7700	10350
LE Sedan 4D	BE32K	20390	5500	6400	8075	10800
SE Sedan 4D	BE32K	21220	5725	6650	8350	11050
XLE Sedan 4D	BE32K	22810	6000	6950	8675	11450
Manual Trans			(525)	(525)	(700)	(700)
V6 3.0/3.3 Liter	F,A		550	550	735	735
SOLARA—4-Cyl.—Equipment Schedule 4						
W.B. 107.2"; 2.4 Liter.						
SE Coupe 2D	CE38P	20465	5200	6075	7775	10450
SE Sport Coupe 2D	CE38P	21960	6075	7025	8750	11500
SLE Coupe 2D	CE38P	23510	6725	7750	9475	12350
Manual Trans			(525)	(525)	(700)	(700)
V6 3.3 Liter	A		550	550	735	735
SOLARA—V6—Equipment Schedule 4						
W.B 107.1"; 3.3 Liter.						
SE Convertible 2D	FA22P	26465	7100	8150	9900	12850
SLE Convertible 2D	FA22P	29965	8650	9850	11700	14900
MR2 SPYDER—4-Cyl.—Equipment Schedule 4						
W.B. 96.5"; 1.8 Liter.						
Convertible 2D	FR320	25410	7975	9150	11000	14050
CELICA—4-Cyl.—Equipment Schedule 4						
W.B. 102.4"; 1.8 Liter.						
GT Liftback 2D	DR32T	17905	6350	7325	9025	11800
GT-S Liftback 2D	DY32T	22570	7425	8525	10300	13250
Auto Trans			250	250	335	335
AVALON—V6—Equipment Schedule 4						
W.B. 107.1"; 3.0 Liter.						
XL Sedan 4D	BF28B	26560	6150	7100	8800	11550
XLS Sedan 4D	BF28B	31020	7875	9000	10800	13850

2005 TOYOTA—(J,1,2or4)(NorT)D,Xor1(BT123)—5

Body Type	VIN	List	Trade-In Fair	Good	Pvt-Party Good	Retail Excellent
ECHO—4-Cyl.—Equipment Schedule 6						
W.B. 93.3"; 1.5 Liter.						
Sedan 4D	BT123	12620	3775	4500	6025	8375
Coupe 2D	AT123	12090	3500	4200	5700	8025
COROLLA—4-Cyl.—Equipment Schedule 6						
W.B. 102.4"; 1.8 Liter.						
CE Sedan 4D	BR32E	14220	5600	6525	8175	10900
S Sedan 4D	BR32E	15265	6050	7000	8675	11400
LE Sedan 4D	BR32E	15430	6125	7100	8775	11500
XRS Sedan 4D	BY32E	17995	6575	7575	9250	12050
PRIUS—4-Cyl. Hybrid—Equipment Schedule 3						
W.B. 106.3"; 1.5 Liter.						
Hatchback Sedan 4D	KB22U	21515	10000	11325	13200	16500
MATRIX—4-Cyl.—Equipment Schedule 6						
W.B. 102.4"; 1.8 Liter.						
Sport Wagon 4D	KR32E	15300	5850	6775	8400	11050
XR Sport Wagon 4D	KR32E	16780	6150	7125	8775	11450
XRS Sport Wagon 4D	KY32E	19290	6875	7925	9550	12350
4WD Sport Wagon 4D	LR32E	17835	6550	7550	9200	11950
4WD XR Sport Wag 4D	LR32E	19175	6725	7725	9375	12150
CAMRY—4-Cyl.—Equipment Schedule 4						
W.B. 107.1"; 2.4 Liter.						
Sedan 4D	BE32K	19415	6100	7075	8750	11500
LE Sedan 4D	BE32K	20515	6525	7500	9200	12050
SE Sedan 4D	BE32K	21345	6775	7825	9525	12400
XLE Sedan 4D	BE32K	22935	7125	8200	9900	12800
Manual Trans			(550)	(550)	(735)	(735)
V6 3.0/3.3 Liter	F,A		600	600	800	800

2005 TOYOTA

Body	Type	VIN	List	Trade-In Fair	Trade-In Good	Pvt-Party Good	Retail Excellent
SOLARA—4-Cyl.—Equipment Schedule 4							
W.B. 107.1"; 2.4 Liter.							
SE Coupe 2D		CE38P	20590	6075	7050	8750	11500
SE Sport Coupe 2D		CE38P	22085	7025	8075	9800	12700
SLE Coupe 2D		CE38P	23635	7775	8900	10650	13600
Manual Trans				(550)	(550)	(735)	(735)
V6 3.3 Liter		A		600	600	800	800
SOLARA—V6—Equipment Schedule 4							
W.B. 107.1"; 3.3 Liter.							
SE Convertible 2D		FA38P	26920	8200	9375	11150	14250
SLE Convertible 2D		FA38P	30190	9900	11225	13100	16350
MR2 SPYDER—4-Cyl.—Equipment Schedule 4							
W.B. 96.5"; 1.8 Liter.							
Convertible 2D		FR320	26685	9050	10300	12100	15250
CELICA—4-Cyl.—Equipment Schedule 4							
W.B. 102.4"; 1.8 Liter.							
GT Liftback 2D		DR32T	19830	7175	8250	9950	12850
GT-S Liftback 2D		DY32T	23575	8425	9625	11350	14450
Auto Trans				275	275	365	365
AVALON—V6—Equipment Schedule 4							
W.B. 111.0"; 3.5 Liter.							
XL Sedan 4D		BK36B	26890	9250	10525	12300	15500
Touring Sedan 4D		BK36B	29140	10300	11650	13500	16750
XLS Sedan 4D		BK36B	31340	11175	12650	14450	17850
Limited Sedan 4D		BK36B	34080	11575	13075	14950	18400

2006 TOYOTA—(1,2,4orJ)(NorT)(1,DorX)(BR32E)—6

Body	Type	VIN	List	Trade-In Fair	Trade-In Good	Pvt-Party Good	Retail Excellent
COROLLA—4-Cyl.—Equipment Schedule 6							
W.B. 102.4"; 1.8 Liter.							
CE Sedan 4D		BR32E	14545	6275	7225	8950	11700
S Sedan 4D		BR32E	15590	6750	7775	9425	12250
LE Sedan 4D		BR32E	15755	6825	7875	9550	12400
XRS Sedan 4D		BY32E	18320	7300	8375	10100	12950
PRIUS—4-Cyl. Hybrid—Equipment Schedule 3							
W.B. 106.3"; 1.5 Liter.							
Hatchback Sedan 4D		KB22U	22305	11125	12600	14400	17850
MATRIX—4-Cyl.—Equipment Schedule 6							
W.B. 102.4"; 1.8 Liter.							
Sport Wagon 4D		KR32E	15650	6800	7850	9450	12200
XR Sport Wagon 4D		KR32E	17130	7150	8200	9850	12650
XRS Sport Wagon 4D		KY32E	19640	7900	9050	10750	13600
4WD Sport Wagon 4D		LR32E	18185	7575	8675	10300	13150
4WD XR Sport Wag 4D		LR32E	19525	7750	8875	10500	13350
CAMRY—4-Cyl.—Equipment Schedule 4							
W.B. 107.1"; 2.4 Liter.							
Sedan 4D		BE32K	18985	7250	8325	10000	12900
LE Sedan 4D		BE32K	20915	7700	8825	10550	13500
SE Sedan 4D		BE32K	21745	8025	9200	11000	14000
XLE Sedan 4D		BE32K	23335	8425	9625	11400	14500
Manual Trans				(575)	(575)	(765)	(765)
V6 3.0/3.3 Liter		F.A		650	650	865	865
SOLARA—4-Cyl.—Equipment Schedule 4							
W.B. 107.1"; 2.4 Liter.							
SE Coupe 2D		CE38P	20900	7125	8200	9900	12750
SE Sport Coupe 2D		CE38P	22395	8150	9325	11100	14150
SLE Coupe 2D		CE38P	23945	9000	10250	12050	15200
Manual Trans				(575)	(575)	(765)	(765)
V6 3.3 Liter		A		650	650	865	865
SOLARA—V6—Equipment Schedule 4							
W.B. 107.1"; 3.3 Liter.							
SE Convertible 2D		FA38P	27480	9475	10775	12600	15800
SLE Convertible 2D		FA38P	30750	11325	12800	14600	18050
AVALON—V6—Equipment Schedule 4							
W.B. 111.0"; 3.5 Liter.							
XL Sedan 4D		BK36B	27165	10425	11800	13550	16850
Touring Sedan 4D		BK36B	29415	11525	13025	14850	18250
XLS Sedan 4D		BK36B	31615	12500	14100	15950	19400
Limited Sedan 4D		BK36B	34355	12975	14600	16400	20000

2007 TOYOTA—(1,2,4orJ)(NorT)(1,DorX)(JT923)—7

YARIS—4-Cyl.—Equipment Schedule 6
W.B. 96.9", 100.4" (Sedan); 1.5 Liter.

2007 TOYOTA

Body	Type	VIN	List	Trade-In Fair	Good	Pvt-Party Good	Retail Excellent
Hatchback 2D		JT923	11630	5725	6650	8175	10750
Sedan 4D		BT923	12505	6325	7300	8850	11450
S Sedan 4D		BT923	14005	6925	7975	9525	12200
COROLLA—4-Cyl.—Equipment Schedule 6							
W.B. 102.4"; 1.8 Liter.							
CE Sedan 4D		BR32E	14785	6950	8000	9575	12300
S Sedan 4D		BR32E	15830	7500	8575	10200	12950
LE Sedan 4D		BR32E	15995	7575	8675	10250	13050
PRIUS—4-Cyl. Hybrid—Equipment Schedule 3							
W.B. 106.3"; 1.5 Liter.							
Hatchback Sedan 4D		KB20U	22755	12250	13825	15500	18850
Touring H'Back 4D		KB20U	23650	12650	14250	15950	19350
MATRIX—4-Cyl.—Equipment Schedule 6							
W.B. 102.4"; 1.8 Liter.							
Sport Wagon 4D		KR30E	15840	7900	9050	10600	13400
XR Sport Wagon 4D		KR30E	17320	8275	9475	11050	13850
CAMRY—4-Cyl. Hybrid—Equipment Schedule 4							
W.B. 109.3"; 2.4 Liter.							
Sedan 4D		BB46K	26480	13925	15675	17350	20900
CAMRY—4-Cyl.—Equipment Schedule 4							
W.B. 109.3"; 2.4 Liter.							
CE Sedan 4D		BE46K	19900	9475	10775	12450	15500
LE Sedan 4D		BE46K	21355	10000	11325	13000	16050
SE Sedan 4D		BE46K	22520	10675	12100	13750	16950
XLE Sedan 4D		BE46K	25280	10775	12200	13850	17050
Manual Trans				(600)	(600)	(800)	(800)
V6 3.5 Liter		K		700	700	935	935
SOLARA—4-Cyl.—Equipment Schedule 4							
W.B. 107.1"; 2.4 Liter.							
SE Coupe 2D		CE30P	21340	8550	9775	11400	14350
Sport Coupe 2D		CE30P	23610	9675	10975	12650	15750
SLE Coupe 2D		CE30P	24485	10575	12000	13650	16800
Manual Trans				(600)	(600)	(800)	(800)
V6 3.3 Liter		A		700	700	935	935
SOLARA—V6—Equipment Schedule 4							
W.B. 107.1"; 3.3 Liter.							
SE Convertible 2D		FA38P	27770	11125	12600	14250	17500
Sport Convertible 2D		FA38P	30040	12250	13875	15550	18900
SLE Convertible 2D		FA38P	31040	13125	14800	16500	20000
AVALON—V6—Equipment Schedule 4							
W.B. 111.0"; 3.5 Liter.							
XL Sedan 4D		BK36B	27455	12000	13575	15250	18500
Touring Sedan 4D		BK36B	29705	13225	14900	16550	20000
XLS Sedan 4D		BK36B	31905	14200	15975	17650	21200
Limited Sedan 4D		BK36B	34645	14750	16600	18300	21900

2008 TOYOTA—(1,2,4orJ)(NorT)(1,DorX)(JT923)–8

Body	Type	VIN	List	Trade-In Fair	Good	Pvt-Party Good	Retail Excellent
YARIS—4-Cyl.—Equipment Schedule 6							
W.B. 96.9", 100.4" (Sedan); 1.5 Liter.							
Hatchback 2D		JT923	11960	6750	7775	9150	11600
Sedan 4D		BT923	12835	7400	8475	9900	12450
S Hatchback 2D		JT923	13635	7475	8575	10000	12550
S Sedan 4D		BT923	14335	8025	9200	10650	13350
COROLLA—4-Cyl.—Equipment Schedule 6							
W.B. 102.4"; 1.8 Liter.							
CE Sedan 4D		BR32E	15065	7875	9000	10450	13150
S Sedan 4D		BR32E	16110	8425	9625	11050	13800
LE Sedan 4D		BR32E	16275	8500	9725	11150	13900
PRIUS—4-Cyl. Hybrid—Equipment Schedule 3							
W.B. 106.3"; 1.5 Liter.							
Hatchback Sedan 4D		KB20U	22985	13575	15300	16950	20400
Touring H'Back 4D		KB20U	23880	14025	15775	17400	20900
MATRIX—4-Cyl.—Equipment Schedule 6							
W.B. 102.4"; 1.8 Liter.							
Sport Wagon 4D		KR30E	16170	9275	10575	12050	14850
XR Sport Wagon 4D		KR30E	17650	9675	10975	12500	15350
CAMRY—4-Cyl. Hybrid—Equipment Schedule 4							
W.B. 109.3"; 2.4 Liter.							
Sedan 4D		BB46K	25860	15825	17750	19400	23000
CAMRY—4-Cyl.—Equipment Schedule 4							
W.B. 109.3"; 2.4 Liter.							
Sedan 4D		BE46K	20280	11025	12500	14000	17100
LE Sedan 4D		BE46K	21735	11525	13025	14600	17750

Body	Type	VIN	List	Trade-In Fair	Good	Pvt-Party Good	Retail Excellent
SE Sedan 4D		BE46K	22900	12300	13925	15500	18700
XLE Sedan 4D		BE46K	25660	12450	14075	15650	18850
Manual Trans		....	....	(625)	(625)	(835)	(835)
V6 3.5 Liter		K	....	750	750	1000	1000
SOLARA—4-Cyl.—Equipment Schedule 4							
W.B. 107.1"; 2.4 Liter.							
SE Coupe 2D		CE30P	21420				
SE Sport Coupe 2D		CE30P	23690				
SLE Coupe 2D		CE30P	24565				
Manual Trans		....	....				
V6 3.3 Liter		A	....				
SOLARA—V6—Equipment Schedule 4							
W.B. 107.1"; 3.3 Liter.							
SE Convertible 2D		FA38P	27850				
Sport Convertible 2D		FA38P	30120				
SLE Convertible 2D		FA38P	31120				
AVALON—V6—Equipment Schedule 4							
W.B. 111.0"; 3.5 Liter.							
XL Sedan 4D		BK36B	27735	14300	16075	17700	21100
Touring Sedan 4D		BK36B	29985	15575	17500	19150	22700
XLS Sedan 4D		BK36B	32035	16650	18725	20400	24100
Limited Sedan 4D		BK36B	35075	17300	19350	21000	24800

VOLKSWAGEN

1994 VOLKSWAGEN — (9orW)(BorV)W(BA81H)–R

Body	Type	VIN	List	Trade-In Fair	Good	Pvt-Party Good	Retail Excellent
GOLF III—4-Cyl.—Equipment Schedule 6							
W.B. 97.3"; 2.0 Liter.							
GL Hatchback 2D		BA81H	13565	750	1075	1975	3325
GL Hatchback 4D		FB21H	13140	775	1100	1975	3375
JETTA III—4-Cyl.—Equipment Schedule 6							
W.B. 97.3"; 2.0 Liter.							
GL Sedan 4D		RB21H	14365	850	1175	2100	3550
GLS Sedan 4D		SB81H	16090	925	1325	2375	4000
JETTA III—V6—Equipment Schedule 6							
W.B. 97.3"; 2.8 Liter.							
GLX Sedan 4D		TS81H	20365	1475	1950	3150	4925
PASSAT—V6—Equipment Schedule 4							
W.B. 103.3"; 2.8 Liter.							
GLX Sedan 4D		JF431	24340	1150	1625	2775	4450
GLX Wagon 4D		NF431	24765	1200	1700	2850	4550
CORRADO—V6—Equipment Schedule 3							
W.B. 97.2"; 2.8 Liter.							
SLC Coupe 2D		EF450	25540	2475	3075	4375	6400

1995 VOLKSWAGEN — (3VWorWVW)(JB81H)–S–#

Body	Type	VIN	List	Trade-In Fair	Good	Pvt-Party Good	Retail Excellent
GOLF III—4-Cyl.—Equipment Schedule 6							
W.B. 97.3"; 2.0 Liter.							
City Hatchback 4D		JB81H	11915	750	1075	1925	3325
Hatchback 4D		KA81H	12890	825	1150	2075	3500
GL Hatchback 2D		BA81H	14265	875	1250	2200	3675
GL Hatchback 4D		FA81H	14590	900	1275	2225	3725
Sport Hatchback 2D		BA81H	15640	1275	1750	2950	4650
GTI—V6—Equipment Schedule 6							
W.B. 97.3"; 2.8 Liter.							
Coupe 2D		HD81H	19265	2100	2675	3975	5875
JETTA III—4-Cyl.—Equipment Schedule 6							
W.B. 97.3"; 2.0 Liter.							
City Sedan 4D		VB81H	12915	925	1325	2375	4000
Sedan 4D		PB81H	13865	925	1325	2375	4000
GL Sedan 4D		RA81H	16065	1050	1500	2600	4250
GLS Sedan 4D		SB81H	17415	1175	1650	2800	4475
JETTA III—V6—Equipment Schedule 6							
W.B. 97.3"; 2.8 Liter.							
GLX Sedan 4D		TD81H	20365	1775	2275	3500	5350
CABRIO—4-Cyl.—Equipment Schedule 3							
W.B. 97.4"; 2.0 Liter.							
Convertible 2D		BC81E	21215	1250	1725	2900	4600
Manual Trans		....	....	(100)	(100)	(135)	(135)
PASSAT—4-Cyl.—Equipment Schedule 4							
W.B. 103.3"; 2.0 Liter.							

1995 VOLKSWAGEN

Body	Type	VIN	List	Trade-In Fair	Trade-In Good	Pvt-Party Good	Retail Excellent
GLS Sedan 4D		CC83A	19215	825	1175	2100	3550

PASSAT—V6—Equipment Schedule 4
W.B. 103.3"; 2.8 Liter.

| GLX Sedan 4D | | EE83A | 22080 | 1450 | 1925 | 3150 | 4925 |
| GLX Wagon 4D | | FE83A | 22510 | 1525 | 2000 | 3225 | 5025 |

1996 VOLKSWAGEN — (3VWorWVW)(FA81H)-T-#

GOLF—4-Cyl.—Equipment Schedule 6
W.B. 97.4"; 2.0 Liter.

| GL Hatchback 4D | | FA81H | 14435 | 1100 | 1550 | 2700 | 4375 |
| GTI Hatchback 2D | | DA81H | 16425 | 1525 | 2000 | 3250 | 5050 |

GOLF—4-Cyl. Turbo Diesel—Equipment Schedule 6
W.B. 97.4"; 1.9 Liter.

| TDI Hatchback 4D | | FF81H | 15660 | 1375 | 1850 | 3075 | 4825 |

GOLF GTI VR6—V6—Equipment Schedule 6
W.B. 97.4"; 2.8 Liter.

| Hatchback 2D | | HD81H | 20110 | 2450 | 3050 | 4375 | 6400 |

JETTA—4-Cyl.—Equipment Schedule 6
W.B. 97.4"; 2.0 Liter.

GL Sedan 4D		RA81H	15535	1175	1650	2825	4525
GLS Sedan 4D		SA81H	16725	1375	1850	3075	4825
Trek Edition		W	------	50	50	65	65
Wolfsburg Edition		P	------	50	50	65	65

JETTA—4-Cyl. Turbo Diesel—Equipment Schedule 6
W.B. 97.4"; 1.9 Liter.

| TDI Sedan 4D | | RF81H | 16760 | 1850 | 2400 | 3675 | 5525 |

JETTA—V6—Equipment Schedule 6
W.B. 97.4"; 2.8 Liter.

| GLX Sedan 4D | | TD81H | 21035 | 2200 | 2775 | 4075 | 6000 |

CABRIO—4-Cyl.—Equipment Schedule 3
W.B. 97.2"; 2.0 Liter.

| Convertible 2D | | BB81E | 21260 | 1525 | 2000 | 3225 | 5025 |
| Manual Trans | | | | (125) | (125) | (165) | (165) |

PASSAT—4-Cyl.—Equipment Schedule 4
W.B. 103.3"; 2.0 Liter.

| GLS Sedan 4D | | GC83A | 19715 | 975 | 1375 | 2475 | 4125 |
| Manual Trans | | | | (200) | (200) | (265) | (265) |

PASSAT—4-Cyl. Turbo Diesel—Equipment Schedule 4
W.B. 103.3"; 1.9 Liter.

| TDI Sedan 4D | | GG83A | 19905 | 2175 | 2750 | 4050 | 5975 |
| TDI Wagon 4D | | HG83A | 20335 | 2325 | 2925 | 4225 | 6200 |

PASSAT—V6—Equipment Schedule 4
W.B. 103.3"; 2.8 Liter.

GLX Sedan 4D		EE83A	23115	1750	2250	3525	5375
GLX Wagon 4D		FE83A	23545	1825	2325	3575	5450
Manual Trans				(200)	(200)	(265)	(265)

1997 VOLKSWAGEN — (3VWorWVW)(FA81H)-V-#

GOLF—4-Cyl.—Equipment Schedule 6
W.B. 97.4"; 2.0 Liter.

GL Hatchback 4D		FA81H	14830	1325	1800	3000	4750
GTI Hatchback 2D		DA81H	16820	1825	2350	3600	5475
Jazz Edition		M	------	50	50	65	65
Trek Edition		L	------	50	50	65	65
K2 Edition		K	------	50	50	65	65

GOLF GTI VR6—V6—Equipment Schedule 6
W.B. 97.4"; 2.8 Liter.

| Hatchback 2D | | HD81H | 20210 | 2900 | 3525 | 4900 | 6975 |

JETTA—4-Cyl.—Equipment Schedule 6
W.B. 97.4"; 2.0 Liter.

GL Sedan 4D		RA81H	15930	1425	1900	3125	4900
GT Sedan 4D		VA81H	16325	1650	2150	3400	5225
GLS Sedan 4D		SA81H	17420	1825	2350	3600	5475
Trek Edition		W	------	50	50	65	65

JETTA—4-Cyl. Turbo Diesel—Equipment Schedule 6
W.B. 97.4"; 1.9 Liter.

| TDI Sedan 4D | | RF81H | 17105 | 2175 | 2750 | 4050 | 5975 |

JETTA—V6—Equipment Schedule 6
W.B. 97.4"; 2.8 Liter.

| GLX Sedan 4D | | TD81H | 21055 | 2600 | 3200 | 4525 | 6575 |

CABRIO—4-Cyl.—Equipment Schedule 3
W.B. 97.4"; 2.0 Liter.

Body	Type	VIN	List	Trade-In Fair	Trade-In Good	Pvt-Party Good	Retail Excellent
Convertible 2D		AA81E	20785	1775	2300	3550	5400
Highline Conv 2D		BA81E	23050	1950	2525	3775	5650
Manual Trans				**(150)**	**(150)**	**(200)**	**(200)**

PASSAT—4-Cyl. Turbo Diesel—Equipment Schedule 4
W.B. 103.3"; 1.9 Liter.

Body	Type	VIN	List	Fair	Good	Good	Excellent
TDI Sedan 4D		GG83A	19930	2600	3200	4550	6600
TDI Wagon 4D		HG83A	20360	2800	3400	4775	6825

PASSAT—V6—Equipment Schedule 4
W.B. 103.3"; 2.8 Liter.

Body	Type	VIN	List	Fair	Good	Good	Excellent
GLX Sedan 4D		EE83A	23190	2150	2725	4025	5950
GLX Wagon 4D		FE83A	23620	2225	2825	4125	6075
Manual Trans				**(250)**	**(250)**	**(335)**	**(335)**

1998 VOLKSWAGEN—(3VWorWVW)(FA81H)–W–#

GOLF—4-Cyl.—Equipment Schedule 6
W.B. 97.4"; 2.0 Liter.

Body	Type	VIN	List	Fair	Good	Good	Excellent
GL Hatchback 4D		FA81H	14855	1625	2125	3375	5225
GTI Hatchback 2D		DA81H	17170	2175	2750	4050	5975
K2 Edition		K		50	50	65	65

GOLF GTI VR6—V6—Equipment Schedule 6
W.B. 97.4"; 2.8 Liter.

Body	Type	VIN	List	Fair	Good	Good	Excellent
Hatchback 2D		HD81H	20735	3375	4075	5500	7675

NEW BEETLE—4-Cyl.—Equipment Schedule 6
W.B. 98.9"; 2.0 Liter.

Body	Type	VIN	List	Fair	Good	Good	Excellent
Hatchback 2D		BB61C	15700	1800	2300	3575	5450

NEW BEETLE—4-Cyl. Turbo Diesel—Equipment Schedule 6
W.B. 98.9"; 1.9 Liter.

Body	Type	VIN	List	Fair	Good	Good	Excellent
TDI Hatchback 2D		BF61C	16975	3875	4600	6075	8350

JETTA—4-Cyl.—Equipment Schedule 6
W.B. 97.4"; 2.0 Liter.

Body	Type	VIN	List	Fair	Good	Good	Excellent
GL Sedan 4D		RA81H	15955	1725	2225	3475	5350
GT Sedan 4D		VA81H	16350	1950	2500	3775	5675
GLS Sedan 4D		SA81H	17445	2150	2725	4025	5950
K2 Edition		Y		50	50	65	65
Wolfsburg		P		50	50	65	65

JETTA—4-Cyl. Turbo Diesel—Equipment Schedule 6
W.B. 97.4"; 1.9 Liter.

Body	Type	VIN	List	Fair	Good	Good	Excellent
TDI Sedan 4D		RF81H	17130	2550	3125	4475	6500

JETTA—V6—Equipment Schedule 6
W.B. 97.4"; 2.8 Liter.

Body	Type	VIN	List	Fair	Good	Good	Excellent
GLX Sedan 4D		TD81H	21455	3050	3675	5075	7175

CABRIO—4-Cyl.—Equipment Schedule 3
W.B. 97.4"; 2.0 Liter.

Body	Type	VIN	List	Fair	Good	Good	Excellent
GL Convertible 2D		AA81E	20835	2050	2625	3900	5800
GLS Convertible 2D		BA81E	23665	2275	2875	4175	6100
Manual Trans				**(175)**	**(175)**	**(235)**	**(235)**

PASSAT—4-Cyl. Turbo—Equipment Schedule 4
W.B. 106.4"; 1.8 Liter.

Body	Type	VIN	List	Fair	Good	Good	Excellent
GLS Sedan 4D		MA63B	22325	1825	2325	3600	5475
GLS Wagon 4D		NA63B	22875	1875	2425	3700	5575
Manual Trans				**(300)**	**(300)**	**(400)**	**(400)**
V6 2.8 Liter		D		250	250	335	335

PASSAT—4-Cyl. Turbo Diesel—Equipment Schedule 4
W.B. 106.4"; 1.9 Liter.

Body	Type	VIN	List	Fair	Good	Good	Excellent
GLS TDI Sedan 4D		MG63B	22575	3900	4625	6100	8400
Manual Trans				**(300)**	**(300)**	**(400)**	**(400)**

PASSAT—V6—Equipment Schedule 4
W.B. 106.4"; 2.8 Liter.

Body	Type	VIN	List	Fair	Good	Good	Excellent
GLX Sedan 4D		PD63B	27825	2950	3575	4950	7050
Manual Trans				**(300)**	**(300)**	**(400)**	**(400)**

1999 VOLKSWAGEN — (3orW)VW(FB81H)–X–#

GOLF—4-Cyl.—Equipment Schedule 6
W.B. 97.4"; 2.0 Liter.

Body	Type	VIN	List	Fair	Good	Good	Excellent
GL Hatchback 4D		FB81H	14855	1975	2525	3800	5700
Wolfsburg		J		50	50	65	65

GOLF GTI VR6—V6—Equipment Schedule 6
W.B. 97.4"; 2.8 Liter.

Body	Type	VIN	List	Fair	Good	Good	Excellent
Hatchback 2D		HD81H	20735	3700	4425	5850	8075

NEW GOLF—4-Cyl.—Equipment Schedule 6
W.B. 98.9"; 2.0 Liter.

Body	Type	VIN	List	Fair	Good	Good	Excellent
GL Hatchback 2D		BC31J	15425	2425	3025	4300	6300

1999 VOLKSWAGEN

Body	Type	VIN	List	Trade-In Fair	Trade-In Good	Pvt-Party Good	Retail Excellent
GLS Hatchback 4D		GC31J	16875	2625	3225	4550	6575
NEW GOLF—4-Cyl. Turbo Diesel—Equipment Schedule 6							
W.B. 98.9"; 1.9 Liter.							
GL TDI H'Back 2D		BF31J	16720	**4500**	**5325**	**6800**	**9200**
GLS TDI H'Back 4D		GF31J	17925	**4625**	**5450**	**6975**	**9450**
NEW GTI—4-Cyl.—Equipment Schedule 6							
W.B. 98.9"; 2.0 Liter.							
GLS Hatchback 2D		DC31J	18025	**2925**	**3550**	**4950**	**7050**
NEW GTI—V6—Equipment Schedule 6							
W.B. 98.9"; 2.8 Liter.							
GLX Hatchback 2D		DE21J	22675	**4250**	**5000**	**6500**	**8825**
NEW BEETLE—4-Cyl.—Equipment Schedule 6							
W.B. 98.9"; 2.0 Liter.							
GL Hatchback 2D		BC21C	16425	**2075**	**2650**	**3950**	**5850**
GLS Hatchback 2D		CC21C	17375	**2350**	**2950**	**4250**	**6225**
NEW BEETLE—4-Cyl. Turbo—Equipment Schedule 6							
W.B. 98.9"; 1.8 Liter.							
GLS Hatchback 2D		CD21C	19525	**2500**	**3100**	**4425**	**6425**
GLX Hatchback 2D		DD21C	21425	**2650**	**3250**	**4600**	**6650**
NEW BEETLE—4-Cyl. Turbo Diesel—Equipment Schedule 6							
W.B. 98.9"; 1.9 Liter.							
GLS TDI H'Back 2D		CF21C	18425	**4450**	**5250**	**6725**	**9100**
JETTA—4-Cyl.—Equipment Schedule 6							
W.B. 97.4"; 2.0 Liter.							
GL Sedan 4D		RB81J	16205	**2050**	**2600**	**3900**	**5800**
Wolfsburg		P		**50**	**50**	**65**	**65**
JETTA—4-Cyl. Turbo Diesel—Equipment Schedule 6							
W.B. 97.4"; 1.9 Liter.							
TDI Sedan 4D		RF81H	17130	**2950**	**3575**	**4950**	**7050**
JETTA—V6—Equipment Schedule 6							
W.B. 97.4"; 2.8 Liter.							
GLX Sedan 4D		TD81H	21455	**3500**	**4225**	**5600**	**7825**
NEW JETTA—4-Cyl.—Equipment Schedule 6							
W.B. 98.9"; 2.0 Liter.							
GL Sedan 4D		RC29M	16400	**2250**	**2825**	**4125**	**6050**
GLS Sedan 4D		SC29M	16875	**2325**	**2925**	**4225**	**6175**
NEW JETTA—4-Cyl. Turbo Diesel—Equipment Schedule 6							
W.B. 98.9"; 1.9 Liter.							
GL TDI Sedan 4D		RF29M	17695	**4575**	**5400**	**6950**	**9400**
GLS TDI Sedan 4D		SF29M	17925	**4700**	**5525**	**7075**	**9550**
NEW JETTA VR6—V6—Equipment Schedule 6							
W.B. 98.9"; 2.8 Liter.							
GLS Sedan 4D		SE29M	20475	**3400**	**4100**	**5500**	**7675**
GLX Sedan 4D		TE29M	24025	**3850**	**4575**	**6000**	**8250**
CABRIO—4-Cyl.—Equipment Schedule 3							
W.B. 97.4"; 2.0 Liter.							
GL Convertible 2D		AB81E	20835	**2400**	**3000**	**4300**	**6275**
GLS Convertible 2D		BB81E	23665	**2650**	**3225**	**4575**	**6600**
Manual Trans				**(200)**	**(200)**	**(265)**	**(265)**
NEW CABRIO—4-Cyl.—Equipment Schedule 3							
W.B. 97.4"; 2.0 Liter.							
GL Convertible 2D		CB81E	22015	**2650**	**3250**	**4600**	**6650**
GLS Convertible 2D		DB81E	24700	**2900**	**3500**	**4875**	**6950**
Manual Trans				**(200)**	**(200)**	**(265)**	**(265)**
PASSAT—4-Cyl. Turbo—Equipment Schedule 4							
W.B. 106.4"; 1.8 Liter.							
GLS Sedan 4D		MA63B	22775	**2100**	**2675**	**3975**	**5900**
GLS Wagon 4D		NA63B	23325	**2225**	**2800**	**4100**	**6050**
Manual Trans				**(350)**	**(350)**	**(465)**	**(465)**
V6 2.8 Liter		D		**300**	**300**	**400**	**400**
PASSAT—V6—Equipment Schedule 4							
W.B. 106.4"; 2.8 Liter.							
GLX Sedan 4D		UD63B	30300	**3350**	**4050**	**5475**	**7650**

2000 VOLKSWAGEN — (3orW)VW(BC21J)-Y-#

Body	Type	VIN	List	Trade-In Fair	Trade-In Good	Pvt-Party Good	Retail Excellent
GOLF—4-Cyl.—Equipment Schedule 6							
W.B. 98.9"; 2.0 Liter.							
GL Hatchback 2D		BC21J	15425	**2825**	**3450**	**4800**	**6875**
GLS Hatchback 4D		GC21J	16875	**3025**	**3650**	**5050**	**7150**
GOLF—4-Cyl. Turbo—Equipment Schedule 6							
W.B. 98.9"; 1.8 Liter.							
GLS Hatchback 4D		GH21J	18425	**3300**	**3975**	**5375**	**7525**

2000 VOLKSWAGEN

Body	Type	VIN	List	Trade-In Fair	Good	Pvt-Party Good	Retail Excellent
GOLF—4-Cyl. Turbo Diesel—Equipment Schedule 6							
W.B. 98.9"; 1.9 Liter.							
GL TDI H'Back 2D		BF21J	16720	**5100**	**5950**	**7525**	**10050**
GLS TDI H'Back 4D		GF21J	17295	**5250**	**6125**	**7700**	**10250**
GTI—4-Cyl.—Equipment Schedule 6							
W.B. 98.9"; 2.0 Liter.							
GLS Hatchback 2D		DC21J	18200	**3375**	**4075**	**5475**	**7650**
GTI—4-Cyl. Turbo—Equipment Schedule 6							
W.B. 98.9"; 1.8 Liter.							
GLS Hatchback 2D		DH21J	19750	**4250**	**5000**	**6475**	**8775**
GTI—V6—Equipment Schedule 6							
W.B. 98.9"; 2.8 Liter.							
GLX Hatchback 2D		DE21J	23145	**4775**	**5600**	**7150**	**9625**
NEW BEETLE—4-Cyl.—Equipment Schedule 6							
W.B. 98.9"; 2.0 Liter.							
GL Hatchback 2D		BC21C	16425	**2475**	**3075**	**4375**	**6375**
GLS Hatchback 2D		CC21C	17375	**2725**	**3325**	**4675**	**6750**
NEW BEETLE—4-Cyl. Turbo—Equipment Schedule 6							
W.B. 98.9"; 1.8 Liter.							
GLS Hatchback 2D		CD21C	19525	**2900**	**3525**	**4875**	**6950**
GLX Hatchback 2D		DD21C	21600	**3075**	**3700**	**5100**	**7200**
NEW BEETLE—4-Cyl. Turbo Diesel—Equipment Schedule 6							
W.B. 98.9"; 1.9 Liter.							
GLS TDI H'Back 2D		CF21C	18425	**5050**	**5900**	**7475**	**10000**
JETTA—4-Cyl.—Equipment Schedule 6							
W.B. 98.9"; 2.0 Liter.							
GL Sedan 4D		RC29M	17225	**2650**	**3250**	**4575**	**6625**
GLS Sedan 4D		SC29M	18175	**2725**	**3325**	**4675**	**6750**
JETTA—4-Cyl. Turbo—Equipment Schedule 6							
W.B. 98.9"; 1.8 Liter.							
GLS Sedan 4D		SD29M	19725	**3075**	**3700**	**5100**	**7200**
JETTA—4-Cyl. Turbo Diesel—Equipment Schedule 6							
W.B. 98.9"; 1.9 Liter.							
GL TDI Sedan 4D		RF29M	18520	**5175**	**6050**	**7625**	**10150**
GLS TDI Sedan 4D		SF29M	19225	**5325**	**6200**	**7775**	**10350**
JETTA—V6—Equipment Schedule 6							
W.B. 98.9"; 2.8 Liter.							
GLS Sedan 4D		SE29M	20475	**3900**	**4650**	**6075**	**8350**
GLX Sedan 4D		TE29M	24695	**4350**	**5150**	**6625**	**8975**
CABRIO—4-Cyl.—Equipment Schedule 3							
W.B. 97.4"; 2.0 Liter.							
GL Convertible 2D		CC21V	22015	**3075**	**3725**	**5125**	**7225**
GLS Convertible 2D		DC21V	24700	**3325**	**4025**	**5425**	**7575**
Manual Trans				**(200)**	**(200)**	**(265)**	**(265)**
PASSAT—4-Cyl. Turbo—Equipment Schedule 4							
W.B. 106.4"; 1.8 Liter.							
GLS Sedan 4D		MA23B	22800	**2500**	**3075**	**4425**	**6450**
GLS Wagon 4D		NA23B	23600	**2625**	**3225**	**4575**	**6625**
Manual Trans				**(400)**	**(400)**	**(535)**	**(535)**
V6 2.8 Liter		D		**350**	**350**	**465**	**465**
PASSAT—V6—Equipment Schedule 4							
W.B. 106.4"; 2.8 Liter.							
GLX Sedan 4D		PD23B	29255	**3850**	**4575**	**6025**	**8275**
GLX Wagon 4D		VD23B	30055	**4025**	**4775**	**6225**	**8525**
Manual Trans				**(400)**	**(400)**	**(535)**	**(535)**
PASSAT 4MOTION AWD—V6—Equipment Schedule 4							
W.B. 106.4"; 2.8 Liter.							
GLS Sedan 4D		TH23B	27050	**4200**	**4975**	**6425**	**8750**
GLS Wagon 4D		RH23B	27850	**4350**	**5150**	**6625**	**8975**
GLX Sedan 4D		UH23B	30905	**4625**	**5475**	**7000**	**9450**
GLX Wagon 4D		WH23B	31705	**4725**	**5550**	**7100**	**9575**

2001 VOLKSWAGEN — (3orW)VW(BK21J)–1–#

Body	Type	VIN	List	Trade-In Fair	Good	Pvt-Party Good	Retail Excellent
GOLF—4-Cyl.—Equipment Schedule 6							
W.B. 98.9"; 2.0 Liter.							
GL Hatchback 2D		BK21J	15425	**3275**	**3950**	**5350**	**7500**
GLS Hatchback 4D		GK21J	16875	**3475**	**4175**	**5550**	**7750**
GOLF—4-Cyl. Turbo—Equipment Schedule 6							
W.B. 98.9"; 1.8 Liter.							
GLS Hatchback 4D		GC21J	18425	**3800**	**4525**	**5950**	**8175**
GOLF—4-Cyl. Turbo Diesel—Equipment Schedule 6							
W.B. 98.9"; 1.9 Liter.							
GL TDI H'Back 2D		BP21J	16720	**5725**	**6650**	**8225**	**10850**

2001 VOLKSWAGEN

Body	Type	VIN	List	Trade-In Fair	Good	Pvt-Party Good	Retail Excellent
	GLS TDI H'Back 4D	GP21J	17925	5900	6825	8425	11050
GTI—4-Cyl. Turbo—Equipment Schedule 6							
W.B. 98.9"; 1.8 Liter.							
	GLS Hatchback 2D	DC21J	19800	4775	5600	7150	9600
GTI—V6—Equipment Schedule 6							
W.B. 98.9"; 2.8 Liter.							
	GLX Hatchback 2D	PG21J	23425	5400	6275	7850	10400
NEW BEETLE—4-Cyl.—Equipment Schedule 6							
W.B. 98.7"; 2.0 Liter.							
	GL Hatchback 2D	BK21C	16425	2900	3525	4900	6975
	GLS Hatchback 2D	CK21C	17375	3300	3800	5200	7325
NEW BEETLE—4-Cyl. Turbo—Equipment Schedule 6							
W.B. 98.7"; 1.8 Liter.							
	GLS Hatchback 2D	CD21C	19525	3325	4025	5425	7575
	Sport Hatchback 2D	ED21C	21175	3375	4075	5475	7650
	GLX Hatchback 2D	DD21C	21700	3500	4225	5600	7825
NEW BEETLE—4-Cyl. Turbo Diesel—Equipment Schedule 6							
W.B. 98.7"; 1.9 Liter.							
	GLS TDI H'Back 2D	CP21C	18425	5700	6625	8200	10850
JETTA—4-Cyl.—Equipment Schedule 6							
W.B. 98.9", 99.0" (Wag); 2.0 Liter.							
	GL Sedan 4D	RK29M	17225	3075	3700	5100	7200
	GLS Sedan 4D	SK29M	18175	3125	3800	5200	7325
	GLS Wagon 4D	SK21J	19150	3375	4075	5475	7650
JETTA—4-Cyl. Turbo—Equipment Schedule 6							
W.B. 98.9"; 1.8 Liter.							
	GLS Sedan 4D	SD29M	19725	3500	4225	5600	7825
	Wolfsburg Edition			50	50	65	65
JETTA—4-Cyl. Turbo Diesel—Equipment Schedule 6							
W.B. 98.9"; 1.9 Liter.							
	GL TDI Sedan 4D	RP29M	18520	5800	6750	8325	10950
	GLS TDI Sedan 4D	SP29M	19225	5950	6900	8525	11150
JETTA—V6—Equipment Schedule 6							
W.B. 98.9", 99.0" (Wag); 2.8 Liter.							
	GLS Sedan 4D	SG29M	20475	4425	5225	6700	9025
	GLS Wagon 4D	SG21J	21450	4525	5350	6850	9275
	GLX Sedan 4D	TG29M	24825	4925	5750	7300	9775
	GLX Wagon 4D	TG21J	25950	5075	5925	7450	9950
CABRIO—4-Cyl.—Equipment Schedule 3							
W.B. 97.4"; 2.0 Liter.							
	GL Convertible 2D	BC21V	21625	3550	4275	5650	7850
	GLS Convertible 2D	CC21V	22000	3850	4575	5975	8200
	GLX Convertible 2D	DC21V	23700	4075	4825	6250	8500
	Manual Trans			(200)	(200)	(265)	(265)
PASSAT—4-Cyl. Turbo—Equipment Schedule 4							
W.B. 106.4"; 1.8 Liter.							
	GLS Sedan 4D	AD23B	23050	2950	3575	4950	7050
	GLS Wagon 4D	HD23B	23850	3075	3750	5125	7250
	Manual Trans			(425)	(425)	(565)	(565)
	V6 2.8 Liter	H		375	375	500	500
NEW PASSAT—4-Cyl. Turbo—Equipment Schedule 4							
W.B. 106.4"; 1.8 Liter.							
	GLS Sedan 4D	PD23B	23375	3100	3775	5175	7300
	GLS Wagon 4D	VD23B	24175	3250	3925	5325	7475
	Manual Trans			(425)	(425)	(565)	(565)
	V6 2.8 Liter	H		375	375	500	500
PASSAT—V6—Equipment Schedule 4							
W.B. 106.4"; 2.8 Liter.							
	GLX Sedan 4D	BH23B	29810	4425	5225	6675	9025
	GLX Wagon 4D	JH23B	30610	4575	5400	6900	9325
	Manual Trans			(425)	(425)	(565)	(565)
NEW PASSAT—V6—Equipment Schedule 4							
W.B. 106.4"; 2.8 Liter.							
	GLX Sedan 4D	RD23B	30375	3650	4375	5775	8000
	GLX Wagon 4D	WD23B	31175	4275	5050	6500	8825
	Manual Trans			(425)	(425)	(565)	(565)
PASSAT 4MOTION AWD—V6—Equipment Schedule 4							
W.B. 106.4"; 2.8 Liter.							
	GLS Sedan 4D	DH23B	27400	4750	5575	7125	9575
	GLS Wagon 4D	KH23B	28200	4900	5750	7300	9775
	GLX Sedan 4D	EH23B	31560	5250	6100	7675	10200
	GLX Wagon 4D	LH23B	32360	5325	6200	7800	10350

2001 VOLKSWAGEN

Body	Type	VIN	List	Trade-In Fair	Good	Pvt-Party Good	Retail Excellent
NEW PASSAT 4MOTION AWD—V6—Equipment Schedule 4							
W.B. 106.4"; 2.8 Liter.							
GLS Sedan 4D		SH23B	27625	3850	4575	6025	8275
GLS Wagon 4D		XH23B	28425	4200	4950	6400	8700
GLX Sedan 4D		TH23B	32125	4450	5275	6750	9100
GLX Wagon 4D		YH23B	32925	4775	5600	7150	9600

2002 VOLKSWAGEN–(3,9orW)(BorV)W(BK21J)–2

Body	Type	VIN	List	Trade-In Fair	Good	Pvt-Party Good	Retail Excellent
GOLF—4-Cyl.—Equipment Schedule 6							
W.B. 98.9"; 2.0 Liter.							
GL Hatchback 2D		BK21J	15600	3675	4375	5950	8325
GL Hatchback 4D		FK21J	15800	3750	4475	6050	8450
GLS Hatchback 4D		GK21J	17150	3875	4600	6175	8600
GOLF—4-Cyl. Turbo Diesel—Equipment Schedule 6							
W.B. 98.9"; 1.9 Liter.							
GL TDI H'Back 2D		BP21J	16895	6250	7225	8975	11800
GL TDI H'Back 4D		FP21J	17095	6200	7175	8925	11750
GLS TDI H'Back 4D		GP21J	18200	6425	7425	9200	12050
GTI—4-Cyl. Turbo—Equipment Schedule 6							
W.B. 98.9"; 1.8 Liter.							
Hatchback 2D		DE61J	19460	5300	6175	7875	10600
337 Edition H'Back 2D		DE61J	22775	5700	6625	8350	11100
GTI VR6—V6—Equipment Schedule 6							
W.B. 98.9"; 2.8 Liter.							
Hatchback 2D		DH61J	20845	5925	6875	8625	11400
NEW BEETLE—4-Cyl.—Equipment Schedule 6							
W.B. 98.7"; 2.0 Liter.							
GL Hatchback 2D		BK21C	16450	3225	3900	5450	7775
GLS Hatchback 2D		CK21C	17400	3500	4200	5750	8100
NEW BEETLE—4-Cyl. Turbo—Equipment Schedule 6							
W.B. 98.7"; 1.8 Liter.							
GLS Hatchback 2D		CD21C	19750	3700	4425	6000	8400
Sport Hatchback 2D		ED21C	20800	3750	4475	6050	8450
GLX Hatchback 2D		DD21C	22050	3900	4625	6200	8625
S Hatchback 2D		FE21C	23905	4625	5450	7100	9700
NEW BEETLE—4-Cyl. Turbo Diesel—Equipment Schedule 6							
W.B. 98.7"; 1.9 Liter.							
GLS TDI H'Back 2D		CP21C	18450	6250	7225	8975	11800
JETTA—4-Cyl.—Equipment Schedule 6							
W.B. 98.9", 99.0" (Wag); 2.0 Liter.							
GL Sedan 4D		RK69M	17400	3400	4100	5600	8000
GL Wagon 4D		RK61J	18200	3575	4300	5850	8225
GLS Sedan 4D		SK69M	18450	3500	4200	5750	8100
GLS Wagon 4D		SK21J	19250	3750	4475	6050	8450
JETTA—4-Cyl. Turbo—Equipment Schedule 6							
W.B. 98.9", 99.0" (Wag); 1.8 Liter.							
GLS Sedan 4D		SE69M	20100	3900	4625	6200	8625
GLS Wagon 4D		SE21J	20900	4150	4900	6500	8975
JETTA—4-Cyl. Turbo Diesel—Equipment Schedule 6							
W.B. 98.9", 99.0" (Wag); 1.9 Liter.							
GL TDI Sedan 4D		RP69M	18695	6350	7325	9100	11950
GL TDI Wagon 4D		RP69M	19495	6525	7525	9250	12150
GLS TDI Sedan 4D		SP69M	19500	6500	7500	9250	12150
GLS TDI Wagon 4D		SP69M	20300	6650	7675	9425	12350
JETTA—V6—Equipment Schedule 6							
W.B. 98.9", 99.0" (Wag); 2.8 Liter.							
GLS Sedan 4D		SH69M	20750	4850	5675	7375	10000
GLS Wagon 4D		SH61J	21550	5000	5850	7550	10200
GLI Sedan 4D		VH69M	23500	5850	6775	8500	11250
GLX Sedan 4D		TH69M	25250	5400	6275	7975	10700
GLX Wagon 4D		TH61J	26050	5550	6475	8175	10950
CABRIO—4-Cyl.—Equipment Schedule 3							
W.B. 97.4"; 2.0 Liter.							
GL Convertible 2D		BC21V	21025	3975	4725	6275	8700
GLS Convertible 2D		CC21V	22025	4300	5050	6650	9125
GLX Convertible 2D		DC21V	23725	4475	5275	6925	9475
Manual Trans				(200)	(200)	(265)	(265)
PASSAT—4-Cyl. Turbo—Equipment Schedule 4							
W.B. 106.4"; 1.8 Liter.							
GLS Sedan 4D		PD63B	23375	3550	4250	5825	8200
GLS Wagon 4D		VD63B	24175	3675	4375	5975	8375
Manual Trans				(450)	(450)	(600)	(600)
V6 2.8 Liter		H		400	400	535	535

2002 VOLKSWAGEN

Body	Type	VIN	List	Trade-In Fair	Good	Pvt-Party Good	Retail Excellent
PASSAT—V6—Equipment Schedule 4							
W.B. 106.4"; 2.8 Liter.							
GLX Sedan 4D		RH63B	30375	**4150**	**4900**	**6500**	**8975**
GLX Wagon 4D		WH63B	31175	**4775**	**5575**	**7275**	**9900**
Manual Trans				**(450)**	**(450)**	**(600)**	**(600)**
PASSAT 4MOTION AWD—V6—Equipment Schedule 4							
W.B. 106.4"; 2.8 Liter.							
GLS Sedan 4D		SH63B	27625	**4350**	**5150**	**6750**	**9225**
GLS Wagon 4D		XH63B	28425	**4675**	**5500**	**7175**	**9775**
GLX Sedan 4D		TH63B	32125	**5000**	**5825**	**7525**	**10200**
GLX Wagon 4D		YH63B	32925	**5350**	**6225**	**7925**	**10650**
PASSAT 4MOTION AWD—W8—Equipment Schedule 4							
W.B. 106.4"; 4.0 Liter.							
Sedan 4D		UH63B	38450	**6925**	**7975**	**9775**	**12750**
Wagon 4D		ZH63B	39250	**7100**	**8150**	**9950**	**12950**

2003 VOLKSWAGEN — (3,9orW)(BorV)W(BK21J)-3

Body	Type	VIN	List	Trade-In Fair	Good	Pvt-Party Good	Retail Excellent
GOLF—4-Cyl.—Equipment Schedule 6							
W.B. 98.9"; 2.0 Liter.							
GL Hatchback 2D		BK21J	15870	**4150**	**4900**	**6500**	**8975**
GL Hatchback 4D		FK21J	16070	**4275**	**5025**	**6625**	**9100**
GLS Hatchback 4D		JK21J	18095	**4375**	**5175**	**6750**	**9250**
GOLF—4-Cyl. Turbo Diesel—Equipment Schedule 6							
W.B. 98.9"; 1.9 Liter.							
GL TDI H'Back 2D		BP21J	17295	**7200**	**8275**	**10050**	**13000**
GL TDI H'Back 4D		FP21J	17495	**7200**	**8275**	**10050**	**13000**
GLS TDI H'Back 4D		GP21J	19285	**7425**	**8525**	**10300**	**13300**
GTI—4-Cyl. Turbo—Equipment Schedule 6							
W.B. 98.9"; 1.8 Liter.							
Hatchback 2D		DE61J	19640	**6000**	**6950**	**8650**	**11400**
20th Anniv H'Back 2D		DE61J	23800	**6575**	**7575**	**9275**	**12150**
GTI VR6—V6—Equipment Schedule 6							
W.B. 98.9"; 2.8 Liter.							
Hatchback 2D		DH61J	22570	**6750**	**7750**	**9500**	**12400**
NEW BEETLE—4-Cyl.—Equipment Schedule 6							
W.B. 98.7", 98.8" (Conv); 2.0 Liter.							
GL Hatchback 2D		BK21C	16525	**3700**	**4400**	**5975**	**8375**
GL Convertible 2D		BK21Y	21025	**5400**	**6300**	**7975**	**10700**
GLS Hatchback 2D		CK21C	18930	**3975**	**4725**	**6300**	**8750**
GLS Convertible 2D		CK21Y	22425	**5975**	**6925**	**8650**	**11400**
NEW BEETLE—4-Cyl. Turbo—Equipment Schedule 6							
W.B. 98.7", 98.8" (Conv); 1.8 Liter.							
GL Hatchback 2D		BD21C	19025	**4025**	**4775**	**6350**	**8800**
GLS Hatchback 2D		CD21C	20430	**4225**	**4975**	**6575**	**9050**
GLS Convertible 2D		CD21Y	24675	**6275**	**7250**	**9000**	**11800**
GLX Hatchback 2D		DE21C	22215	**4400**	**5200**	**6775**	**9275**
GLX Convertible 2D		DD21Y	26125	**7525**	**8625**	**10400**	**13400**
S Hatchback 2D		FE21C	24115	**5275**	**6150**	**7825**	**10500**
NEW BEETLE—4-Cyl. Turbo Diesel—Equipment Schedule 6							
W.B. 98.7"; 1.9 Liter.							
GL TDI H'Back 2D		BP21C	17770	**7100**	**8150**	**9900**	**12850**
GLS TDI H'Back 2D		CP21C	19570	**7200**	**8275**	**10050**	**13000**
JETTA—4-Cyl.—Equipment Schedule 6							
W.B. 98.9", 99.0" (Wag); 2.0 Liter.							
GL Sedan 4D		RK69M	17675	**3850**	**4575**	**6150**	**8575**
GL Wagon 4D		RK61J	18475	**4075**	**4825**	**6400**	**8850**
GLS Sedan 4D		SK69M	19365	**3950**	**4700**	**6275**	**8725**
GLS Wagon 4D		SK61J	20165	**4250**	**5000**	**6600**	**9075**
JETTA—4-Cyl. Turbo—Equipment Schedule 6							
W.B. 98.9", 99.0" (Wag); 1.8 Liter.							
GL Sedan 4D		RE69M	19325	**4150**	**4900**	**6500**	**8975**
GL Wagon 4D		RE61J	20125	**4400**	**5200**	**6850**	**9400**
Wolfsburg Sedan 4D		PE69M	20075	**4300**	**5075**	**6700**	**9175**
GLS Sedan 4D		SE29M	21015	**4400**	**5200**	**6775**	**9275**
GLS Wagon 4D		SE61J	21815	**4675**	**5500**	**7150**	**9750**
JETTA—4-Cyl. Turbo Diesel—Equipment Schedule 6							
W.B. 98.9"; (Wag); 1.9 Liter.							
GL TDI Sedan 4D		RP69M	19065	**7325**	**8400**	**10200**	**13150**
GL TDI Wagon 4D		RP61J	19865	**7500**	**8600**	**10350**	**13350**
GLS TDI Sedan 4D		SP69M	20545	**7475**	**8575**	**10350**	**13350**
GLS TDI Wagon 4D		SP61J	21345	**7625**	**8750**	**10550**	**13500**
JETTA—V6—Equipment Schedule 6							
W.B. 98.9"; 2.8 Liter.							

2003 VOLKSWAGEN

Body	Type	VIN	List	Trade-In Fair	Trade-In Good	Pvt-Party Good	Retail Excellent
GLI Sedan 4D		VH69M	23525	6650	7675	9400	12300
GLX Sedan 4D		TH69M	27515	6125	7100	8825	11600
PASSAT—4-Cyl. Turbo—Equipment Schedule 4							
W.B. 106.4"; 1.8 Liter.							
GL Sedan 4D		MD63B	23400	3225	3900	5475	7825
GL Wagon 4D		ND63B	24200	3575	4300	5850	8250
GLS Sedan 4D		PD63B	24535	4150	4900	6525	9000
GLS Wagon 4D		VD63B	27835	4300	5050	6675	9175
Manual Trans				(500)	(500)	(665)	(665)
V6 2.8 Liter		H		475	475	635	635
PASSAT—V6—Equipment Schedule 4							
W.B. 106.4"; 2.8 Liter.							
GLX Sedan 4D		RH63B	30400	4950	5800	7500	10150
GLX Wagon 4D		WH63B	31200	5700	6625	8325	11050
Manual Trans				(500)	(500)	(665)	(665)
PASSAT 4MOTION AWD—V6—Equipment Schedule 4							
W.B. 106.4"; 2.8 Liter.							
GLX Sedan 4D		TH63B	32150	5825	6750	8500	11250
GLX Wagon 4D		YH63B	32950	6200	7175	8925	11750
PASSAT 4MOTION AWD—W8—Equipment Schedule 4							
W.B. 106.4"; 4.0 Liter.							
Sedan 4D		UK63B	38475	8025	9200	11050	14200
Wagon 4D		ZK63B	39275	8425	9300	11300	14600

2004 VOLKSWAGEN–(W,3or9)(VorB)W(BK21J)–4–#

Body	Type	VIN	List	Trade-In Fair	Trade-In Good	Pvt-Party Good	Retail Excellent
GOLF—4-Cyl.—Equipment Schedule 6							
W.B. 98.9"; 2.0 Liter.							
GL Hatchback 2D		BK21J	16155	4650	5475	7125	9700
GL Hatchback 4D		FK21J	16355	4775	5600	7250	9850
GLS Hatchback 4D		GK21J	18715	4950	5775	7425	10050
GOLF—4-Cyl. Turbo Diesel—Equipment Schedule 6							
W.B. 98.9"; 1.9 Liter.							
GL TDI H'Back 4D		FP21J	17775	8250	9425	11200	14200
GLS TDI H'Back 4D		GP21J	19895	8475	9675	11500	14650
GTI—4-Cyl. Turbo—Equipment Schedule 6							
W.B. 98.9"; 1.8 Liter.							
Hatchback 2D		DE61J	19825	6750	7800	9500	12400
GTI VR6—V6—Equipment Schedule 6							
W.B. 98.9"; 2.8 Liter.							
Hatchback 2D		DH61J	22645	7575	8700	10450	13400
R32 AWD—V6—Equipment Schedule 3							
W.B. 99.1"; 3.2 Liter.							
Hatchback 2D		KG61J	29675	10825	12300	14200	17750
NEW BEETLE—4-Cyl.—Equipment Schedule 6							
W.B. 98.7", 98.8" (Conv); 2.0 Liter.							
GL Hatchback 2D		BK21C	16905	4200	4950	6550	9025
GL Convertible 2D		BK21Y	21475	6075	7025	8725	11450
GLS Hatchback 2D		CK21C	19095	4475	5275	6925	9475
GLS Convertible 2D		CK21Y	23215	6750	7775	9475	12350
NEW BEETLE—4-Cyl. Turbo—Equipment Schedule 6							
W.B. 98.7", 98.8 (Conv); 1.8 Liter.							
GLS Hatchback 2D		CD21C	21055	4750	5550	7200	9800
GLS Convertible 2D		CD21Y	25395	7075	8125	9900	12800
S Hatchback 2D		FE21C	24425	5950	6875	8575	11300
NEW BEETLE—4-Cyl. Turbo—Equipment Schedule 6							
W.B. 98.7"; 1.9 Liter.							
GL TDI H'Back 2D		BP21C	18205	8025	9200	11050	14100
GLS TDI H'Back 2D		CP21C	20335	8200	9375	11200	14300
JETTA—4-Cyl.—Equipment Schedule 6							
W.B. 98.9", 99.0 (Wag); 2.0 Liter.							
GL Sedan 4D		RK29M	18005	4300	5100	6725	9200
GL Wagon 4D		RK61J	19005	4550	5350	6975	9550
GLS Sedan 4D		SK29M	20035	4425	5225	6875	9425
GLS Wagon 4D		SK21J	21025	4725	5525	7200	9775
JETTA—4-Cyl. Turbo—Equipment Schedule 6							
W.B. 98.9", 99.0 (Wag); 1.8 Liter.							
GL Sedan 4D		SE69M	19485	4650	5475	7125	9700
GLS Sedan 4D		SE69M	21515	4950	5775	7425	10050
GLS Wagon 4D		SE61J	22515	5275	6150	7825	10500
GLI Sedan 4D		VE69M	24375	7525	8625	10400	13350
JETTA—4-Cyl. Turbo Diesel—Equipment Schedule 6							
W.B. 98.9", 99.0 (Wag); 1.9 Liter.							
GL TDI Sedan 4D		RP29M	19245	8325	9525	11350	14500

Body	Type	VIN	List	Trade-In Fair	Trade-In Good	Pvt-Party Good	Retail Excellent
GL TDI Wagon 4D		RP21J	20245	**8500**	**9725**	**11550**	**14700**
GLS TDI Sedan 4D		SP69M	21055	**8475**	**9675**	**11500**	**14650**
GLS TDI Wagon 4D		SP61J	22055	**8650**	**9850**	**11700**	**14900**

JETTA—V6—Equipment Schedule 6
W.B. 98.9"; 2.8 Liter.

Body	Type	VIN	List	Trade-In Fair	Trade-In Good	Pvt-Party Good	Retail Excellent
GLI Sedan 4D		VH69M	23785	**7475**	**8575**	**10350**	**13300**

PASSAT—4-Cyl. Turbo—Equipment Schedule 4
W.B. 106.4"; 1.8 Liter.

Body	Type	VIN	List	Trade-In Fair	Trade-In Good	Pvt-Party Good	Retail Excellent
GL Sedan 4D		MD63B	23430	**3850**	**4575**	**6175**	**8625**
GL Wagon 4D		ND63B	24430	**4250**	**5025**	**6625**	**9125**
GLS Sedan 4D		PD63B	25030	**4850**	**5675**	**7375**	**10000**
GLS Wagon 4D		VD63B	26030	**5000**	**5825**	**7500**	**10150**
Manual Trans				**(525)**	**(525)**	**(700)**	**(700)**

PASSAT 4MOTION AWD—4-Cyl. Turbo—Equipment Schedule 4
W.B. 106.4"; 1.8 Liter.

Body	Type	VIN	List	Trade-In Fair	Trade-In Good	Pvt-Party Good	Retail Excellent
GLS Sedan 4D		PD63B	26780	**5975**	**6900**	**8625**	**11400**
GLS Wagon 4D		VD63B	27780	**6400**	**7375**	**9125**	**11950**
Manual Trans				**(525)**	**(525)**	**(700)**	**(700)**

PASSAT—4-Cyl. Turbo Diesel—Equipment Schedule 4
W.B. 106.4"; 2.0 Liter.

Body	Type	VIN	List	Trade-In Fair	Trade-In Good	Pvt-Party Good	Retail Excellent
GL TDI Sedan 4D		ME63B	23635	**10425**	**11850**	**13750**	**17150**
GL TDI Wagon 4D		NE63B	24635	**10475**	**11900**	**13800**	**17250**
GLS TDI Sedan 4D		PE63B	25235	**11575**	**13075**	**15000**	**18550**
GLS TDI Wagon 4D		VE63B	26235	**11575**	**13075**	**15000**	**18550**
Manual Trans				**(525)**	**(525)**	**(700)**	**(700)**

PASSAT—V6—Equipment Schedule 4
W.B. 106.4"; 2.8 Liter.

Body	Type	VIN	List	Trade-In Fair	Trade-In Good	Pvt-Party Good	Retail Excellent
GLX Sedan 4D		RH63B	31430	**5925**	**6850**	**8575**	**11300**
GLX Wagon 4D		WH63B	32430	**6750**	**7775**	**9500**	**12400**
Manual Trans				**(525)**	**(525)**	**(700)**	**(700)**

PASSAT 4MOTION AWD—V6—Equipment Schedule 4
W.B. 106.4"; 2.8 Liter.

Body	Type	VIN	List	Trade-In Fair	Trade-In Good	Pvt-Party Good	Retail Excellent
GLX Sedan 4D		TH63B	33180	**6775**	**7825**	**9550**	**12450**
GLX Wagon 4D		YH63B	34180	**7225**	**8275**	**10050**	**12950**

PASSAT 4MOTION AWD—W8—Equipment Schedule 4
W.B. 106.4"; 4.0 Liter.

Body	Type	VIN	List	Trade-In Fair	Trade-In Good	Pvt-Party Good	Retail Excellent
Sedan 4D		UK63B	39235	**9275**	**10575**	**12450**	**15700**
Wagon 4D		ZK63B	40235	**9500**	**10825**	**12700**	**15950**
Sport Pkg				**275**	**275**	**365**	**365**

PHAETON AWD—V8—Equipment Schedule 1
W.B. 118.1"; 4.2 Liter.

Body	Type	VIN	List	Trade-In Fair	Trade-In Good	Pvt-Party Good	Retail Excellent
Sedan 4D		AF63D	65215	**11225**	**12750**	**14900**	**18700**
4-Seater Pkg				**650**	**650**	**865**	**865**

PHAETON AWD—W12—Equipment Schedule 1
W.B. 118.1"; 6.0 Liter.

Body	Type	VIN	List	Trade-In Fair	Trade-In Good	Pvt-Party Good	Retail Excellent
Sedan 4D		AH63D	80515	**17975**	**20100**	**22500**	**27300**
4-Seater Pkg				**650**	**650**	**865**	**865**

2005 VOLKSWAGEN—(W,3or9)(VorB)W(BL61J)-5-#

GOLF—4-Cyl.—Equipment Schedule 6
W.B. 98.9"; 2.0 Liter.

Body	Type	VIN	List	Trade-In Fair	Trade-In Good	Pvt-Party Good	Retail Excellent
GL Hatchback 2D		BL61J	15830	**5225**	**6100**	**7750**	**10400**
GL Hatchback 4D		FL61J	16050	**5375**	**6250**	**7925**	**10600**
GLS Hatchback 4D		GL61J	18390	**5525**	**6425**	**8075**	**10750**

GOLF—4-Cyl. Turbo Diesel—Equipment Schedule 6
W.B. 98.9"; 1.9 Liter.

Body	Type	VIN	List	Trade-In Fair	Trade-In Good	Pvt-Party Good	Retail Excellent
GL TDI H'Back 4D		FR61J	17450	**9575**	**10875**	**12700**	**15950**
GLS TDI H'Back 4D		GR61J	19580	**9800**	**11125**	**12950**	**16150**

GTI—4-Cyl. Turbo—Equipment Schedule 6
W.B. 98.9"; 1.8 Liter.

Body	Type	VIN	List	Trade-In Fair	Trade-In Good	Pvt-Party Good	Retail Excellent
Hatchback 2D		DE61J	19510	**7550**	**8675**	**10400**	**13350**

GTI VR6—V6—Equipment Schedule 6
W.B. 98.9"; 2.8 Liter.

Body	Type	VIN	List	Trade-In Fair	Trade-In Good	Pvt-Party Good	Retail Excellent
Hatchback 2D		DH61J	22330	**8475**	**9675**	**11450**	**14550**

NEW BEETLE—4-Cyl.—Equipment Schedule 6
W.B. 98.7", 98.8" (Conv); 2.0 Liter.

Body	Type	VIN	List	Trade-In Fair	Trade-In Good	Pvt-Party Good	Retail Excellent
GL Hatchback 2D		BK31X	17145	**4700**	**5525**	**7150**	**9725**
GL Convertible 2D		BM31Y	21865	**6750**	**7800**	**9475**	**12300**
GLS Hatchback 2D		CK31X	19345	**5050**	**5900**	**7550**	**10150**
GLS Convertible 2D		CM31Y	23615	**7550**	**8650**	**10350**	**13300**
Bi-Color H'Back 2D		CK31X	21360	**5575**	**6500**	**8150**	**10850**
Dark Flint Ed Conv		CM31Y	26405	**8150**	**9325**	**11100**	**14150**

Body Type	VIN	List	Trade-In Fair	Trade-In Good	Pvt-Party Good	Retail Excellent
NEW BEETLE—4-Cyl. Turbo—Equipment Schedule 6						
W.B. 98.7", 98.8" (Conv); 1.8 Liter.						
GLS Hatchback 2D	CD31C	21515	**5325**	**6200**	**7850**	**10500**
GLS Convertible 2D	CD31Y	26025	**7900**	**9050**	**10800**	**13800**
NEW BEETLE—4-Cyl. Turbo Diesel—Equipment Schedule 6						
W.B. 98.7"; 1.9 Liter.						
GLS TDI H'Back 2D	CR31C	20585	**9250**	**10525**	**12300**	**15500**
JETTA—4-Cyl.—Equipment Schedule 6						
W.B. 98.9", 99.0" (Wag); 2.0 Liter.						
GL Sedan 4D	RK69M	18255	**4825**	**5650**	**7300**	**9900**
GL Wagon 4D	RL61J	19255	**5100**	**5950**	**7600**	**10200**
GLS Sedan 4D	SK69M	20295	**4975**	**5825**	**7475**	**10100**
GLS Wagon 4D	SL61J	21295	**5275**	**6150**	**7800**	**10450**
JETTA—4-Cyl. Turbo—Equipment Schedule 6						
W.B. 98.9", 99.0" (Wag); 1.8 Liter.						
GLS Wagon 4D	SE61J	22775	**5900**	**6825**	**8500**	**11200**
GLI Sedan 4D	SE69M	24645	**8375**	**9575**	**11300**	**14400**
JETTA—4-Cyl. Turbo Diesel—Equipment Schedule 6						
W.B. 98.9", 99.0" (Wag); 1.9 Liter.						
GL TDI Wagon 4D	RR61J	20505	**9550**	**10875**	**12650**	**15900**
GLS TDI Sedan 4D	SR69M	21315	**9550**	**10875**	**12650**	**15900**
GLS TDI Wagon 4D	SR61J	22315	**9675**	**10975**	**12800**	**16000**
NEW JETTA—5-Cyl.—Equipment Schedule 6						
W.B. 101.5"; 2.5 Liter.						
Value Edition Sed 4D	PF71K	18515	**5325**	**6200**	**7850**	**10500**
2.5 Sedan 4D	SF71K	21005	**6150**	**7125**	**8825**	**11550**
Package #1			**450**	**450**	**600**	**600**
Package #2			**1000**	**1000**	**1335**	**1335**
NEW JETTA—4-Cyl. Turbo Diesel—Equipment Schedule 6						
W.B. 101.5"; 1.9 Liter.						
TDI Sedan 4D	RT71K	22000	**11225**	**12750**	**14550**	**18000**
Package #1			**450**	**450**	**600**	**600**
Package #2			**1000**	**1000**	**1335**	**1335**
PASSAT—4-Cyl. Turbo—Equipment Schedule 4						
W.B. 106.4"; 1.8 Liter.						
GL Sedan 4D	MD63B	23760	**4600**	**5425**	**7075**	**9675**
GL Wagon 4D	ND63B	24760	**5050**	**5900**	**7575**	**10200**
GLS Sedan 4D	AD63B	26030	**5725**	**6675**	**8350**	**11050**
GLS Wagon 4D	CD63B	27030	**5850**	**6775**	**8475**	**11200**
Manual Trans			**(550)**	**(550)**	**(735)**	**(735)**
PASSAT 4MOTION AWD—4-Cyl. Turbo—Equipment Schedule 4						
W.B. 106.4"; 1.8 Liter.						
GLS Sedan 4D	BD63B	27780	**6950**	**8000**	**9725**	**12600**
GLS Wagon 4D	DD63B	28780	**7475**	**8575**	**10300**	**13250**
Manual Trans			**(550)**	**(550)**	**(735)**	**(735)**
PASSAT—4-Cyl. Turbo Diesel—Equipment Schedule 4						
W.B. 106.4"; 2.0 Liter.						
GL TDI Sedan 4D	ME63B	23935	**11750**	**13275**	**15150**	**18650**
GL TDI Wagon 4D	NE63B	24935	**11950**	**13525**	**15400**	**18900**
GLS TDI Sedan 4D	AE63B	26235	**13025**	**14650**	**16550**	**20200**
GLS TDI Wagon 4D	CE63B	27235	**13175**	**14850**	**16750**	**20500**
PASSAT—V6—Equipment Schedule 4						
W.B. 106.4"; 2.8 Liter.						
GLX Sedan 4D	RU63B	31440	**7025**	**8075**	**9800**	**12700**
GLX Wagon 4D	WU63B	32440	**7950**	**9100**	**10900**	**13900**
Manual Trans			**(550)**	**(550)**	**(735)**	**(735)**
PASSAT 4MOTION AWD—V6—Equipment Schedule 4						
W.B. 106.4"; 2.8 Liter.						
GLX Sedan 4D	TU63B	33190	**7900**	**9050**	**10850**	**13850**
GLX Wagon 4D	YU63B	34190	**8375**	**9575**	**11350**	**14450**
PHAETON—V8—Equipment Schedule 1						
W.B. 118.1"; 4.2 Liter.						
Sedan 4D	AF93D	68865	**15325**	**17250**	**19500**	**23800**
4-Seater Pkg			**725**	**725**	**965**	**965**
PHAETON—W12—Equipment Schedule 1						
W.B. 118.1"; 6.0 Liter.						
Sedan 4D	AH93D	99715	**22825**	**25475**	**27900**	**33200**
4-Seater Pkg			**725**	**725**	**965**	**965**

2006 VOLKSWAGEN(W,3or9)(VorB)W(BR71K)–6–#

Body Type	VIN	List	Trade-In Fair	Trade-In Good	Pvt-Party Good	Retail Excellent
RABBIT—5-Cyl.—Equipment Schedule 6						
W.B. 101.5"; 2.5 Liter.						
Hatchback 2D	BR71K	15620	**6500**	**7500**	**9200**	**11950**

2006 VOLKSWAGEN

Body	Type	VIN	List	Trade-In Fair	Trade-In Good	Pvt-Party Good	Retail Excellent
Hatchback 4D		DR71K	17620	**6975**	**8025**	**9700**	**12550**
GOLF—4-Cyl.—Equipment Schedule 6							
W.B. 98.9"; 2.0 Liter.							
GL Hatchback 4D		FL61J	16645	**6000**	**6925**	**8600**	**11300**
GLS Hatchback 4D		GL61J	19005	**6125**	**7100**	**8775**	**11500**
GOLF—4-Cyl. Turbo Diesel—Equipment Schedule 6							
W.B. 98.9"; 1.9 Liter.							
GLS TDI H'Back 4D		GR61J	20195	**10925**	**12400**	**14150**	**17500**
GTI—4-Cyl. Turbo—Equipment Schedule 6							
W.B. 98.9", 101.5"; 1.8 Liter, 2.0 Liter.							
1.8T Hatchback 2D		DE61J	20955	**8100**	**9275**	**11050**	**14050**
2.0T Hatchback 2D		EV71K	22620	**9850**	**11175**	**12950**	**16150**
Package #2				**1000**	**1000**	**1335**	**1335**
NEW BEETLE—5-Cyl.—Equipment Schedule 6							
W.B. 98.7", 98.8" (Conv); 2.5 Liter.							
2.5 Hatchback 2D		PG31C	17795	**6525**	**7525**	**9200**	**11950**
2.5 Convertible 2D		PF31Y	22535	**8250**	**9425**	**11150**	**14200**
Package #1				**450**	**450**	**600**	**600**
Package #2				**1000**	**1000**	**1335**	**1335**
NEW BEETLE—4-Cyl. Turbo Diesel—Equipment Schedule 6							
W.B. 98.7"; 1.9 Liter.							
TDI Hatchback 2D		PR31C	19005	**10475**	**11900**	**13650**	**16950**
Package #1		R		**450**	**450**	**600**	**600**
Package #2		S		**1000**	**1000**	**1335**	**1335**
JETTA—5-Cyl.—Equipment Schedule 6							
W.B. 101.5"; 2.5 Liter.							
2.5 Value Edition Sed		PF71K	18515	**5925**	**6875**	**8525**	**11200**
2.5 Sedan 4D		RF71K	20905	**6850**	**7925**	**9600**	**12450**
Package #1		S		**500**	**500**	**665**	**665**
Package #2		D		**1000**	**1000**	**1335**	**1335**
JETTA—4-Cyl. Turbo—Equipment Schedule 6							
W.B. 101.5"; 2.0 Liter.							
2.0T Sedan 4D		AJ71K	24205	**7900**	**9050**	**10800**	**13800**
GLI Sedan 4D		TJ71K	24405	**9125**	**10400**	**12150**	**15300**
Package #1		K		**500**	**500**	**665**	**665**
Package #2		M		**1000**	**1000**	**1335**	**1335**
Package #3		N		**1600**	**1600**	**2135**	**2135**
JETTA—4-Cyl. Turbo Diesel—Equipment Schedule 6							
W.B. 101.5"; 1.9 Liter.							
TDI Sedan 4D		RT71K	21905	**12500**	**14100**	**15950**	**19400**
TDI Spcl Ed Sed		FT71K	24620	**13275**	**14950**	**16750**	**20400**
Package #1				**500**	**500**	**665**	**665**
Package #2				**1000**	**1000**	**1335**	**1335**
PASSAT—4-Cyl. Turbo—Equipment Schedule 4							
W.B. 106.7"; 2.0 Liter.							
2.0T Value Ed Sedan		AK73C	24640	**7050**	**8100**	**9800**	**12650**
2.0T Sedan 4D		AK73C	25590	**7125**	**8200**	**9900**	**12750**
Luxury Pkg				**1000**	**1000**	**1335**	**1335**
PASSAT—V6—Equipment Schedule 4							
W.B. 106.7"; 3.6 Liter.							
3.6 Sedan 4D		AU73C	30565	**9200**	**10475**	**12250**	**15450**
Luxury or Sport Pkg				**1000**	**1000**	**1335**	**1335**
PASSAT 4MOTION AWD—V6—Equipment Schedule 6							
W.B. 106.4"; 3.6 Liter.							
3.6 Sedan 4D		BU73C	32515	**9900**	**11225**	**13050**	**16250**
Luxury or Sport Pkg				**1000**	**1000**	**1335**	**1335**
PHAETON—V8—Equipment Schedule 1							
W.B. 118.1"; 4.2 Liter.							
Sedan 4D		AF03D	68655	**20275**	**22650**	**25000**	**29800**
4-Seater Pkg				**800**	**800**	**1065**	**1065**
PHAETON—W12—Equipment Schedule 1							
W.B. 118.1"; 6.0 Liter.							
Sedan 4D		AK03D	100255	**29800**	**33125**	**35700**	**41600**
4-Passenger				**800**	**800**	**1065**	**1065**

2007 VOLKSWAGEN—(W,3or9)(VorB)W(AR71K)-7

Body	Type	VIN	List	Trade-In Fair	Trade-In Good	Pvt-Party Good	Retail Excellent
RABBIT—5-Cyl.—Equipment Schedule 6							
W.B. 101.5"; 2.5 Liter.							
Hatchback 2D		AR71K	15620	**7200**	**8275**	**9800**	**12500**
Hatchback 4D		CR71K	17620	**7725**	**8850**	**10400**	**13150**
GTI—4-Cyl. Turbo—Equipment Schedule 6							
W.B. 101.5"; 2.0 Liter.							
2.0T Hatchback 2D		EV71K	22730	**10825**	**12300**	**13950**	**17150**

2007 VOLKSWAGEN

Body	Type	VIN	List	Trade-In Fair	Good	Pvt-Party Good	Retail Excellent
2.0T Hatchback 4D		GV71K	23230	11225	12750	14400	17650
Package #2				1000	1000	1335	1335
EOS—4-Cyl. Turbo—Equipment Schedule 3							
W.B. 101.5"; 2.0 Liter.							
Hardtop Conv 2D		AA71F	28620	14550	16375	18100	21700
2.0T Hardtop Conv 2D		CA71F	31695	15675	17600	19300	23000
EOS—V6—Equipment Schedule 3							
W.B. 101.5"; 3.2 Liter.							
3.2L Hardtop Conv 2D		DB71F	37480	18325	20475	22200	26300
NEW BEETLE—5-Cyl.—Equipment Schedule 6							
W.B. 98.7"; 98.8" (Conv); 2.5 Liter.							
2.5 Hatchback 2D		PF31C	17810	7225	8300	9850	12600
2.5 Convertible 2D		PF31Y	22750	9100	10350	12000	15000
Package #1				450	450	600	600
Package #2				1000	1000	1335	1335
JETTA—5-Cyl.—Equipment Schedule 6							
W.B. 101.5"; 2.5 Liter.							
Sedan 4D		GF71K	17120	6575	7575	9150	11800
2.5 Sedan 4D		PF71K	18620	7625	8725	10300	13100
Wolfsburg Ed Sedan		EF71K	19990	8425	9625	11250	14150
Package #1				500	500	665	665
Package #2				1000	1000	1335	1335
JETTA—4-Cyl. Turbo—Equipment Schedule 6							
W.B. 101.5"; 2.0 Liter.							
2.0T Sedan 4D		AJ71K	22620	8725	9950	11550	14500
GLI Sedan 4D		TJ71K	24620	10000	11375	13000	16050
Package #1				500	500	665	665
Package #2				1000	1000	1335	1335
PASSAT—4-Cyl. Turbo—Equipment Schedule 4							
W.B. 106.7"; 2.0 Liter.							
Sedan 4D		JK73C	24665	8950	10200	11850	14850
Wagon 4D		XK73C	26085	9275	10575	12250	15300
2.0T Sedan 4D		AK73C	25665	9175	10425	12100	15150
2.0T Value Ed Wag 4D		LK73C	25855	10000	11325	13000	16100
2.0T Wagon 4D		LK73C	26865	10000	11325	13000	16100
2.0T Wolfsburg Ed Sed		AK73C	27630	10725	12150	13850	17050
Luxury Pkg				1000	1000	1335	1335
Sport Pkg				1000	1000	1335	1335
PASSAT—V6—Equipment Schedule 4							
W.B. 106.7"; 3.6 Liter.							
3.6 Sedan 4D		AU73C	30590	11475	12925	14650	17950
3.6 Wagon 4D		LU73C	31790	12925	14550	16250	19700
Luxury Pkg				1000	1000	1335	1335
Sport Pkg				1000	1000	1335	1335
PASSAT 4MOTION AWD—V6—Equipment Schedule 4							
W.B. 106.7"; 3.6 Liter.							
3.6 Sedan 4D		BU73C	32540	12200	13775	15500	18800
3.6 Wagon 4D		MU73C	33740	14075	15825	17550	21100
Luxury Pkg				1000	1000	1335	1335
Sport Pkg				1000	1000	1335	1335

2008 VOLKSWAGEN—(W,3or9)(VorB)W(AA71K)–8

Body	Type	VIN	List	Trade-In Fair	Good	Pvt-Party Good	Retail Excellent
RABBIT—5-Cyl.—Equipment Schedule 6							
W.B. 101.5"; 2.5 Liter.							
Hatchback 2D		AA71K	16130	8100	9275	10800	13500
Hatchback 4D		CA71K	18125	8700	9900	11350	14150
GTI—4-Cyl. Turbo—Equipment Schedule 6							
W.B. 101.5"; 2.0 Liter.							
2.0T Hatchback 2D		EV71K	23370	12050	13625	15150	18350
2.0T Hatchback 4D		GV71K	23870	12500	14100	15650	18850
EOS—4-Cyl. Turbo—Equipment Schedule 3							
W.B. 101.5"; 2.0 Liter.							
Hardtop Conv 2D		AA71F	30630	16075	18025	19700	23300
Komfort HT Conv 2D		AA71F	32280	17300	19350	21100	24900
LUX Hardtop Conv 2D		FA71F	35630	17700	19900	21600	25400
EOS—V6—Equipment Schedule 3							
W.B. 101.5"; 3.2 Liter.							
VR6 Hardtop Conv 2D		DB71F	38630	20200	22550	24200	28200
NEW BEETLE—5-Cyl.—Equipment Schedule 6							
W.B. 98.8"; 2.5 Liter.							
S Hatchback 2D		PW31C	18005	8150	9325	10900	13600
S Convertible 2D		PF31Y	23765	10200	11575	13150	16150
SE Hatchback 2D		RW31C	21080	8725	9950	11450	14300

2008 VOLKSWAGEN

Body	Type	VIN	List	Trade-In Fair	Trade-In Good	Pvt-Party Good	Retail Excellent
SE Convertible 2D		RF31Y	26265	**10975**	**12450**	**14000**	**17150**
Package #1				**450**	**450**	**600**	**600**

GLI—4-Cyl. Turbo—Equipment Schedule 4
W.B. 101.5"; 2.0 Liter.

Body	Type	VIN	List	Fair	Good	Good	Excellent
2.0T Sedan 4D		BJ71K	25945	**11225**	**12700**	**14200**	**17250**

JETTA—5-Cyl.—Equipment Schedule 6
W.B. 101.5"; 2.5 Liter.

S Sedan 4D		JM71K	17630	**7450**	**8525**	**10000**	**12600**
SE Sedan 4D		RM71K	20400	**8550**	**9775**	**11300**	**14100**
SEL Sedan 4D		RM71K	23465	**9850**	**11175**	**12750**	**15750**

JETTA—4-Cyl. Turbo—Equipment Schedule 6
W.B. 101.5"; 2.0 Liter.

Wolfsburg Ed Sedan		RJ71K	21525	**9425**	**10725**	**12250**	**15200**

R32—V6—Equipment Schedule 3
W.B. 101.5"; 3.2 Liter.

Hatchback 2D		KC71K	33630	**16475**	**18475**	**20200**	**23900**

PASSAT—4-Cyl. Turbo—Equipment Schedule 4
W.B. 106.7"; 2.0 Liter.

Sedan 4D		JK73C	25630	**10425**	**11850**	**13450**	**16500**
Wagon 4D		XK73C	26830	**10825**	**12250**	**13850**	**16950**
Komfort Sedan 4D		AK73C	28430	**11575**	**13075**	**14800**	**18100**
Komfort Wagon 4D		LK73C	29630	**13175**	**14850**	**16550**	**20000**
LUX Sedan 4D		EK73C	30630	**12350**	**13975**	**15650**	**19000**
LUX Wagon 4D		TK73C	31830	**13975**	**15725**	**17400**	**20900**

PASSAT—V6—Equipment Schedule 3
W.B. 106.7"; 3.6 Liter.

VR6 Sedan 4D		CU73C	36630	**13175**	**14850**	**16500**	**19900**

PASSAT 4MOTION AWD—V6—Equipment Schedule 4
W.B. 106.7"; 3.6 Liter.

VR6 Sedan 4D		DU73C	38580	**13975**	**15725**	**17400**	**20900**
VR6 Wagon 4D		RU73C	39780	**15975**	**17925**	**19600**	**23200**

VOLVO

1994 VOLVO — YV1(LS551)–R–#

850—5-Cyl.—Equipment Schedule 3
W.B. 104.9"; 2.4 Liter.

Sedan 4D		LS551	24725	**1000**	**1400**	**2500**	**4150**
Wagon 4D		LW551	28120	**1525**	**2000**	**3225**	**5000**
Manual Trans							

850—5-Cyl. Turbo—Equipment Schedule 1
W.B. 104.9"; 2.3 Liter.

Sedan 4D		LS571	31900	**1800**	**2325**	**3575**	**5425**
Wagon 4D		LW571	32900	**2025**	**2600**	**3875**	**5750**

940—4-Cyl.—Equipment Schedule 3
W.B. 109.1"; 2.3 Liter.

Sedan 4D		JS881	23325	**1150**	**1625**	**2775**	**4450**
Wagon 4D		JW881	24425	**1200**	**1700**	**2850**	**4550**

940—4-Cyl. Turbo—Equipment Schedule 1
W.B. 109.1"; 2.3 Liter.

Sedan 4D		JS871	27220	**1450**	**1925**	**3125**	**4900**
Wagon 4D		JW871	28220	**1900**	**2450**	**3700**	**5550**

960—6-Cyl.—Equipment Schedule 1
W.B. 109.1"; 2.9 Liter.

Sedan 4D		KS951	33875	**1225**	**1725**	**2875**	**4575**
Wagon 4D		KW951	34875	**1500**	**1975**	**3200**	**4975**

1995 VOLVO — YV1(LS551)–S–#

850—5-Cyl.—Equipment Schedule 3
W.B. 104.9"; 2.4 Liter.

Sedan 4D		LS551	25540	**1175**	**1650**	**2825**	**4525**
Wagon 4D		LW551	26840	**1600**	**2075**	**3300**	**5125**
GLT Sedan 4D		LS551	27570	**1575**	**2050**	**3275**	**5100**
GLT Wagon 4D		LW551	28870	**1625**	**2125**	**3375**	**5200**
Manual Trans				**(125)**	**(125)**	**(165)**	**(165)**

850—5-Cyl. Turbo—Equipment Schedule 1
W.B. 104.9"; 2.3 Liter.

Sedan 4D		LS571	32000	**2175**	**2750**	**4050**	**5975**
Wagon 4D		LW571	33300	**2425**	**3025**	**4325**	**6350**
T-5 R Sedan 4D		LS581	36005	**2675**	**3275**	**4650**	**6725**
T-5 R Wagon 4D		LW581	37555	**2925**	**3550**	**4950**	**7075**

1995 VOLVO

Body	Type	VIN	List	Trade-In Fair	Trade-In Good	Pvt-Party Good	Retail Excellent
940—4-Cyl.—Equipment Schedule 3							
W.B. 109.1"; 2.3 Liter.							
Sedan 4D		JS831	24315	**1425**	**1900**	**3125**	**4900**
Wagon 4D		JW831	25615	**1525**	**2000**	**3225**	**5025**
GL Sedan 4D		JS831	25295	**1425**	**1900**	**3125**	**4900**
940—4-Cyl. Turbo—Equipment Schedule 1							
W.B. 109.1"; 2.3 Liter.							
Sedan 4D		JS861	24820	**1800**	**2300**	**3550**	**5425**
Wagon 4D		JW861	26120	**2300**	**2875**	**4200**	**6175**
960—6-Cyl.—Equipment Schedule 1							
W.B. 109.1"; 2.9 Liter.							
Sedan 4D		KS961	30360	**1550**	**2025**	**3250**	**5050**
Wagon 4D		KW961	31660	**1850**	**2375**	**3650**	**5525**

1996 VOLVO — YV1(LS554)–T–#

Body	Type	VIN	List	Trade-In Fair	Trade-In Good	Pvt-Party Good	Retail Excellent
850—5-Cyl.—Equipment Schedule 3							
W.B. 104.9"; 2.4 Liter.							
Sedan 4D		LS554	26620	**1475**	**1950**	**3175**	**4975**
Wagon 4D		LW554	27920	**1950**	**2500**	**3775**	**5650**
GLT Sedan 4D		LS554	29695	**1925**	**2475**	**3750**	**5625**
GLT Wagon 4D		LW554	30995	**2025**	**2575**	**3850**	**5750**
Manual Trans				**(125)**	**(125)**	**(165)**	**(165)**
850—5-Cyl. Turbo—Equipment Schedule 1							
W.B. 104.9"; 2.3 Liter.							
Sedan 4D		LS572	33145	**2650**	**3250**	**4600**	**6675**
Wagon 4D		LW572	34445	**2950**	**3575**	**4975**	**7100**
TLA Sedan 4D		LS572	37380	**3225**	**3900**	**5325**	**7500**
TLA Wagon 4D		LW572	38830	**3525**	**4250**	**5675**	**7950**
R Sedan 4D		LS572	38420	**3525**	**4250**	**5675**	**7950**
R Wagon 4D		LW572	39870	**4000**	**4725**	**6250**	**8600**
960—6-Cyl.—Equipment Schedule 1							
W.B. 109.1"; 2.9 Liter.							
Sedan 4D		KS960	34455	**1875**	**2425**	**3700**	**5575**
Wagon 4D		KW960	35755	**2225**	**2825**	**4125**	**6075**

1997 VOLVO — YV1(LS555)–V–#

Body	Type	VIN	List	Trade-In Fair	Trade-In Good	Pvt-Party Good	Retail Excellent
850—5-Cyl.—Equipment Schedule 3							
W.B. 104.9"; 2.4 Liter.							
Sedan 4D		LS555	28180	**1850**	**2400**	**3700**	**5575**
Wagon 4D		LW555	29480	**2400**	**3000**	**4300**	**6325**
Manual Trans				**(150)**	**(150)**	**(200)**	**(200)**
850—5-Cyl. Turbo—Equipment Schedule 1							
W.B. 104.9"; 2.3 Liter, 2.4 Liter.							
GLT Sedan 4D		LS564	33525	**3075**	**3700**	**5125**	**7275**
GLT Wagon 4D		LW564	34825	**2875**	**3475**	**4875**	**6975**
T-5 Sedan 4D		LS572	36190	**3250**	**3925**	**5350**	**7550**
T-5 Wagon 4D		LW572	37490	**3600**	**4300**	**5750**	**8025**
R Sedan 4D		LS582	39180	**3900**	**4625**	**6150**	**8475**
R Wagon 4D		LW582	40630	**4275**	**5025**	**6575**	**8975**
960—6-Cyl.—Equipment Schedule 1							
W.B. 109.1"; 2.9 Liter.							
Sedan 4D		KS960	34795	**2350**	**2950**	**4275**	**6250**
Wagon 4D		KW960	36345	**2800**	**3400**	**4775**	**6850**
90 SERIES—6-Cyl.—Equipment Schedule 1							
W.B. 109.1"; 2.9 Liter.							
S90 Sedan 4D		KS960	34875	**2625**	**3225**	**4600**	**6675**
V90 Wagon 4D		KW960	36425	**3200**	**3875**	**5300**	**7475**

1998 VOLVO — YV1(LS553)–W–#

Body	Type	VIN	List	Trade-In Fair	Trade-In Good	Pvt-Party Good	Retail Excellent
70 SERIES—5-Cyl.—Equipment Schedule 3							
W.B. 104.9"; 2.4 Liter.							
S70 Sedan 4D		LS553	28535	**1025**	**1450**	**2600**	**4300**
V70 Wagon 4D		LW553	29835	**1525**	**2000**	**3250**	**5100**
Manual Trans		4		**(175)**	**(175)**	**(235)**	**(235)**
70 SERIES—5-Cyl. Turbo—Equipment Schedule 1							
W.B. 104.9", 104.5" (AWD); 2.3 Liter, 2.4 Liter.							
C70 Coupe 2D		NK537	40545	**3450**	**4150**	**5475**	**7550**
C70 Convertible 2D		NC567	43570	**3025**	**3675**	**4950**	**6925**
S70 GLT Sedan 4D		LS564	33015	**2200**	**2775**	**4100**	**6075**
V70 GLT Wagon 4D		LW564	34315	**2225**	**2800**	**4125**	**6100**
S70 T-5 Sedan 4D		LS534	35560	**2575**	**3150**	**4500**	**6550**
V70 T-5 Wagon 4D		LW534	36860	**2950**	**3575**	**4975**	**7100**

0709   **EQUIPMENT & MILEAGE PAGE 9 TO 23**   **247**

Body	Type	VIN	List	Trade-In Fair	Good	Pvt-Party Good	Retail Excellent
V70 AWD Wagon 4D		LW564	36195	**3550**	**4250**	**5700**	**7950**
V70 XC AWD Wagon 4D		LZ564	38195	**3750**	**4450**	**5925**	**8200**
V70 R AWD Wagon 4D		LW524	41570	**4575**	**5400**	**6975**	**9475**

90 SERIES—6-Cyl.—Equipment Schedule 1
W.B. 109.1"; 2.9 Liter.

Body	Type	VIN	List	Fair	Good	Good	Excellent
S90 Sedan 4D		KS960	34875	**3175**	**3850**	**5275**	**7425**
V90 Wagon 4D		KW960	36425	**3825**	**4550**	**6025**	**8325**

1999 VOLVO — YV1(LS55A)–X–#

70 SERIES—5-Cyl.—Equipment Schedule 1
W.B. 104.9"; 2.4 Liter.

Body	Type	VIN	List	Fair	Good	Good	Excellent
S70 Sedan 4D		LS55A	28935	**1400**	**1850**	**3125**	**4975**
V70 Wagon 4D		LW55A	30235	**1975**	**2550**	**3850**	**5750**
Manual Trans			4	**(200)**	**(200)**	**(265)**	**(265)**

70 SERIES—5-Cyl. Turbo—Equipment Schedule 1
W.B. 104.5" (S70 AWD), 104.9" (C70, S70/V70 GLT, T-5 & R); 2.3 Liter, 2.4 Liter.

Body	Type	VIN	List	Fair	Good	Good	Excellent
C70 LT Coupe 2D		NK56D	37570	**3575**	**4275**	**5575**	**7675**
C70 HT Coupe 2D		NK53D	40945	**3900**	**4675**	**6150**	**8450**
C70 Convertible 2D		NC56D	43970	**3650**	**4350**	**5675**	**7800**
S70 GLT Sedan 4D		LS56A	35105	**2775**	**3400**	**4775**	**6850**
V70 GLT Wagon 4D		LW56A	36405	**2950**	**3575**	**4975**	**7075**
S70 T-5 Sedan 4D		LS53A	37155	**3200**	**3875**	**5300**	**7475**
V70 T-5 Wagon 4D		LW53A	38455	**3625**	**4325**	**5775**	**8025**
S70 AWD Sedan 4D		LT56A	36985	**3775**	**4475**	**5950**	**8225**
V70 AWD Wagon 4D		LV56A	38285	**4250**	**5025**	**6525**	**8875**
V70 XC AWD Wag 4D		LZ56A	39460	**4450**	**5275**	**6750**	**9175**
V70 R AWD Wagon 4D		LV52A	41970	**5400**	**6275**	**7925**	**10550**

80 SERIES—6-Cyl.—Equipment Schedule 1
W.B. 109.9"; 2.9 Liter.

Body	Type	VIN	List	Fair	Good	Good	Excellent
S80 2.9 Sedan 4D		TS97D	38790	**2575**	**3150**	**4525**	**6575**

80 SERIES—6-Cyl. Turbo—Equipment Schedule 1
W.B. 109.9"; 2.8 Liter.

Body	Type	VIN	List	Fair	Good	Good	Excellent
S80 T-6 Sedan 4D		TS90D	43755	**3750**	**4450**	**5925**	**8200**

2000 VOLVO — YV1(VS252)–Y–#

40 SERIES—4-Cyl. Turbo—Equipment Schedule 3
W.B. 100.3"; 1.9 Liter.

Body	Type	VIN	List	Fair	Good	Good	Excellent
S40 Sedan 4D		VS252	23475	**1350**	**1825**	**3075**	**4925**
V40 Wagon 4D		VW252	24475	**2175**	**2750**	**4075**	**6025**

70 SERIES—5-Cyl.—Equipment Schedule 3
W.B. 104.9"; 2.4 Liter.

Body	Type	VIN	List	Fair	Good	Good	Excellent
S70 Sedan 4D		LS61J	29075	**1925**	**2475**	**3800**	**5725**
S70 SE Sedan 4D		LS61J	30075	**2050**	**2625**	**3950**	**5900**
V70 Wagon 4D		LW61J	30375	**2575**	**3175**	**4550**	**6600**
V70 SE Wagon 4D		LW61J	31575	**2700**	**3300**	**4675**	**6750**
Manual Trans			4	**(200)**	**(200)**	**(265)**	**(265)**

70 SERIES—5-Cyl. Turbo—Equipment Schedule 3
W.B. 104.5", 104.9" (C70, S70 & V70 ex. AWD); 2.3 Liter, 2.4 Liter.

Body	Type	VIN	List	Fair	Good	Good	Excellent
C70 LT Coupe 2D		NK56D	36475	**4300**	**5075**	**6425**	**8625**
C70 LT Convertible 2D		NC56D	45675	**4350**	**5175**	**6525**	**8750**
C70 HT Coupe 2D		NK53D	40575	**4900**	**5725**	**7175**	**9550**
C70 HT Conv 2D		NC53D	47075	**4975**	**5825**	**7275**	**9650**
S70 GLT Sedan 4D		LS56D	34075	**3425**	**4150**	**5550**	**7800**
S70 GLT SE Sedan 4D		LS56D	33075	**3650**	**4350**	**5825**	**8075**
V70 GLT Wagon 4D		LW56D	35975	**3775**	**4475**	**5950**	**8200**
S70 T-5 Sedan 4D		LS53D	37275	**3975**	**4700**	**6175**	**8500**
S70 AWD Sedan 4D		LT56D	36575	**4525**	**5350**	**6825**	**9250**
V70 XC AWD Wag 4D		LZ56D	39075	**5275**	**6150**	**7775**	**10350**
V70 XC AWD SE Wag		LZ56D	37575	**4850**	**5675**	**7275**	**9775**
V70 R AWD Wagon 4D		LV60D	42075	**6275**	**7250**	**8950**	**11700**

80 SERIES—6-Cyl.—Equipment Schedule 1
W.B. 109.9"; 2.9 Liter.

Body	Type	VIN	List	Fair	Good	Good	Excellent
S80 2.9 Sedan 4D		TS94D	37775	**3150**	**3825**	**5250**	**7425**

80 SERIES—6-Cyl. Turbo—Equipment Schedule 1
W.B. 109.9"; 2.8 Liter.

Body	Type	VIN	List	Fair	Good	Good	Excellent
S80 T-6 Sedan 4D		TS90D	42275	**4450**	**5275**	**6775**	**9200**

2001 VOLVO — YV1(VS295)–1–#

40 SERIES—4-Cyl. Turbo—Equipment Schedule 3
W.B. 100.3"; 1.9 Liter.

Body	Type	VIN	List	Fair	Good	Good	Excellent
S40 Sedan 4D		VS295	24075	**1950**	**2525**	**3850**	**5775**

2001 VOLVO

Body	Type	VIN	List	Trade-In Fair	Trade-In Good	Pvt-Party Good	Retail Excellent
S40 SE Sedan 4D		VS295	28025	**2800**	**3425**	**4800**	**6875**
V40 Wagon 4D		VW295	25075	**2850**	**3475**	**4875**	**6975**
V40 SE Wagon 4D		VW295	29025	**3375**	**4075**	**5475**	**7675**
60 SERIES—5-Cyl.—Equipment Schedule 3							
W.B. 106.9"; 2.4 Liter.							
S60 2.4 Sedan 4D		RS61N	27075	**2800**	**3425**	**4800**	**6875**
60 SERIES—5-Cyl. Turbo—Equipment Schedule 3							
W.B. 106.9"; 2.3 Liter, 2.4 Liter.							
S60 2.4T Sedan 4D		RS58D	30375	**3600**	**4300**	**5725**	**7975**
S60 T5 Sedan 4D		RS53D	32375	**4575**	**5400**	**6900**	**9350**
70 SERIES—5-Cyl.—Equipment Schedule 3							
W.B. 108.5"; 2.4 Liter.							
V70 Wagon 4D		SW61N	30075	**4500**	**5300**	**6775**	**9175**
70 SERIES—5-Cyl. Turbo—Equipment Schedule 1							
W.B. 104.9", 108.5" (V70 ex XC), 108.8" (XC); 2.3 Liter, 2.4 Liter.							
C70 LT Convertible 2D		NC56D	44075	**5225**	**6100**	**7550**	**9950**
C70 HT Coupe 2D		NK53D	38475	**5775**	**6725**	**8175**	**10700**
C70 HT Conv 2D		NC53D	47075	**5900**	**6825**	**8325**	**10850**
V70 2.4T Wagon 4D		SW58D	35375	**5425**	**6300**	**7875**	**10450**
V70 T5 Wagon 4D		SW53D	36675	**5800**	**6750**	**8375**	**11050**
V70 XC AWD Wag 4D		SZ58D	37975	**6375**	**7350**	**9025**	**11750**
80 SERIES—6-Cyl.—Equipment Schedule 3							
W.B. 109.9"; 2.9 Liter.							
S80 2.9 Sedan 4D		TS94D	38675	**3900**	**4625**	**6100**	**8400**
80 SERIES—6-Cyl. Turbo—Equipment Schedule 1							
W.B. 109.9"; 2.8 Liter.							
S80 T-6A Executive 4D		TS90D	42675	**5300**	**6175**	**7800**	**10400**
S80 T-6 Executive 4D		TS90D	48075	**5525**	**6425**	**8025**	**10700**

2002 VOLVO — YV1(VS295)-2-#

Body	Type	VIN	List	Trade-In Fair	Trade-In Good	Pvt-Party Good	Retail Excellent
40 SERIES—4-Cyl. Turbo—Equipment Schedule 3							
W.B. 100.9"; 1.9 Liter.							
S40 Sedan 4D		VS295	24525	**2625**	**3225**	**4775**	**7025**
V40 Wagon 4D		VW295	25525	**3550**	**4275**	**5850**	**8275**
60 SERIES—5-Cyl.—Equipment Schedule 3							
W.B. 106.9"; 2.4 Liter.							
S60 2.4 Sedan 4D		RS61N	27750	**3475**	**4175**	**5750**	**8150**
60 SERIES—5-Cyl. Turbo—Equipment Schedule 3							
W.B. 106.9"; 2.3 Liter, 2.4 Liter.							
S60 2.4T Sedan 4D		RS58D	32250	**4325**	**5125**	**6750**	**9300**
S60 T5 Sedan 4D		RS53D	34650	**5425**	**6325**	**8050**	**10850**
S60 2.4T AWD Sed 4D		RH58D	34000	**4725**	**5525**	**7250**	**9900**
70 SERIES—5-Cyl.—Equipment Schedule 3							
W.B. 108.5"; 2.4 Liter.							
V70 Wagon 4D		SW61N	30650	**5325**	**6200**	**7950**	**10700**
70 SERIES—5-Cyl. Turbo—Equipment Schedule 1							
W.B. 104.9", 108.5" (V70 ex XC), 108.8" (XC); 2.3 Liter, 2.4 Liter.							
C70 LT Convertible 2D		NC56D	44750	**6225**	**7175**	**8775**	**11400**
C70 HT Coupe 2D		NK53D	38150	**6825**	**7875**	**9450**	**12200**
C70 HT Convertible		NC53D	46750	**6950**	**8000**	**9600**	**12350**
V70 2.4T Wagon 4D		SW58D	36150	**6300**	**7275**	**9075**	**11950**
V70 2.4T AWD Wag 4D		SJ58D	37900	**7300**	**8375**	**10250**	**13300**
V70 T5 Wagon 4D		SW53D	38350	**6750**	**7750**	**9575**	**12550**
V70 XC AWD Wag 4D		SZ58D	38425	**7350**	**8425**	**10300**	**13350**
80 SERIES—6-Cyl.—Equipment Schedule 1							
W.B. 109.9"; 2.9 Liter.							
S80 2.9 Sedan 4D		TS94D	38775	**4625**	**5450**	**7175**	**9850**
80 SERIES—6-Cyl. Turbo—Equipment Schedule 1							
W.B. 109.9"; 2.9 Liter.							
S80 T-6 Sedan 4D		TS90D	42775	**6150**	**7100**	**8925**	**11800**
S80 T-6 Executive 4D		TS90D	50575	**6375**	**7350**	**9175**	**12100**

2003 VOLVO — YV1(VS275)-3-#

Body	Type	VIN	List	Trade-In Fair	Trade-In Good	Pvt-Party Good	Retail Excellent
40 SERIES—4-Cyl. Turbo—Equipment Schedule 3							
W.B. 100.9"; 1.9 Liter.							
S40 Sedan 4D		VS275	24560	**3250**	**3950**	**5525**	**7950**
V40 Wagon 4D		VW275	25560	**4375**	**5175**	**6800**	**9350**
60 SERIES—5-Cyl.—Equipment Schedule 3							
W.B. 107.0"; 2.4 Liter.							
S60 2.4 Sedan 4D		RS61T	28030	**4225**	**5000**	**6650**	**9175**
60 SERIES—5-Cyl. Turbo—Equipment Schedule 3							
W.B. 107.0"; 2.3 Liter, 2.4 Liter, 2.5 Liter.							

2003 VOLVO

Body	Type	VIN	List	Trade-In Fair	Good	Pvt-Party Good	Retail Excellent
S60 2.4T Sedan 4D		RS58D	31085	**5300**	**6175**	**7925**	**10650**
S60 2.5T AWD Sed 4D		RH59H	32835	**5775**	**6725**	**8450**	**11250**
S60 T5 Sedan 4D		RS53D	34685	**6450**	**7425**	**9200**	**12100**
70 SERIES—5-Cyl.—Equipment Schedule 3							
W.B. 108.5"; 2.4 Liter.							
V70 Wagon 4D		SW61T	29530	**6350**	**7325**	**9125**	**12000**
70 SERIES—5-Cyl. Turbo—Equipment Schedule 1							
W.B. 104.9", 108.5" (V70), 108.8" (XC70); 2.3 Liter, 2.4 Liter,							
2.5 Liter.							
C70 LT Convertible 2D		NC63D	44785	**7350**	**8450**	**10050**	**12850**
C70 HT Conv 2D		NC62D	47785	**8175**	**9350**	**11050**	**13900**
V70 2.4T Wagon 4D		SW58D	31530	**7475**	**8575**	**10400**	**13450**
V70 2.5T AWD Wag 4D		SJ59H	33280	**8650**	**9850**	**11750**	**15050**
V70 T5 Wagon 4D		SW53D	35730	**8075**	**9225**	**11150**	**14350**
XC70 AWD Wagon 4D		SZ59H	34530	**8700**	**9900**	**11850**	**15150**
80 SERIES—6-Cyl.—Equipment Schedule 1							
W.B. 109.9"; 2.9 Liter.							
S80 2.9 Sedan 4D		TS92D	39110	**5525**	**6450**	**8175**	**11000**
80 SERIES—6-Cyl. Turbo—Equipment Schedule 1							
W.B. 109.9"; 2.9 Liter.							
S80 T6 Sedan 4D		TS91D	44595	**7250**	**8325**	**10200**	**13250**
S80 T6 Elite Sedan 4D		TS91Z	48880	**7525**	**8625**	**10500**	**13550**

2004 VOLVO — YV1(VS275)-4-#

Body	Type	VIN	List	Trade-In Fair	Good	Pvt-Party Good	Retail Excellent
40 SERIES—4-Cyl. Turbo—Equipment Schedule 3							
W.B. 101.0"; 1.9 Liter.							
S40 Sedan 4D		VS275	25385	**4150**	**4900**	**6525**	**9050**
S40 LSE Sedan 4D		VS275	29530	**5075**	**5925**	**7650**	**10350**
V40 Wagon 4D		VW275	26685	**5375**	**6275**	**7975**	**10750**
V40 LSE Wagon 4D		VW275	30530	**6225**	**7200**	**8975**	**11800**
40 SERIES—5-Cyl.—Equipment Schedule 3							
W.B. 103.9"; 2.4 Liter.							
S40 2.4i Sedan 4D		MS382	27170	**5250**	**6125**	**7850**	**10550**
40 SERIES—5-Cyl. Turbo—Equipment Schedule 3							
W.B. 103.9"; 2.5 Liter.							
S40 T5 Sedan 4D		MS682	29970	**6375**	**7350**	**9100**	**11950**
60 SERIES—5-Cyl.—Equipment Schedule 3							
W.B. 106.9" 2.4 Liter.							
S60 2.4 Sedan 4D		RS61T	28645	**5175**	**6025**	**7750**	**10450**
60 SERIES—5-Cyl. Turbo—Equipment Schedule 3							
W.B. 106.9", 107.0" (R); 2.3 Liter, 2.5 Liter.							
S60 2.5T Sedan 4D		RS59V	30295	**6450**	**7450**	**9200**	**12100**
S60 2.5T AWD Sed 4D		RH59H	32070	**7000**	**8050**	**9850**	**12800**
S60 T5 Sedan 4D		RS53D	35170	**7675**	**8800**	**10600**	**13600**
S60 R AWD Sedan 4D		RH52Y	39185	**9475**	**10775**	**12700**	**16000**
70 SERIES—5-Cyl.—Equipment Schedule 3							
W.B. 108.5"; 2.4 Liter.							
V70 Wagon 4D		SW61T	30145	**7625**	**8750**	**10550**	**13550**
70 SERIES—5-Cyl. Turbo—Equipment Schedule 1							
W.B. 104.9", 108.5" (V70), 108.8" (XC70); 2.3L, 2.4L, 2.5L.							
C70 LT Convertible 2D		NC63D	40565	**8725**	**9950**	**11600**	**14600**
C70 HT Conv 2D		NC62D	43565	**9625**	**10925**	**12650**	**15750**
V70 2.5T Wagon 4D		SW59V	35070	**8875**	**10100**	**12000**	**15250**
V70 2.5T AWD Wag 4D		SJ59H	36895	**10150**	**11525**	**13500**	**16900**
V70 T5 Wagon 4D		SW53D	38145	**9575**	**10875**	**12850**	**16150**
V70 R AWD Wagon 4D		SJ52Y	40635	**11475**	**12975**	**14950**	**18550**
XC70 AWD Wagon 4D		SZ59H	38145	**10200**	**11575**	**13500**	**16950**
80 SERIES—6-Cyl.—Equipment Schedule 1							
W.B. 109.9"; 2.9 Liter.							
S80 2.9 Sedan 4D		TS92D	39725	**6625**	**7650**	**9450**	**12400**
80 SERIES—5-Cyl. Turbo—Equipment Schedule 1							
W.B. 109.9"; 2.5 Liter.							
S80 2.5T Sedan 4D		TR59V	38630	**7100**	**8150**	**10000**	**13050**
S80 2.5T AWD Sed 4D		TH59H	40380	**7725**	**8850**	**10700**	**13750**
80 SERIES—6-Cyl. Twin Turbo—Equipment Schedule 1							
W.B. 109.9"; 2.9 Liter.							
S80 T6 Sedan 4D		TS91Z	45210	**8550**	**9775**	**11700**	**15000**
S80 T6 Premier Sed 4D		TS91Z	49200	**8950**	**10200**	**12150**	**15500**

2005 VOLVO — YV1(MS382)-5-#

40 SERIES—5-Cyl.—Equipment Schedule 3
W.B. 103.9"; 2.4 Liter.

2005 VOLVO

Body Type	VIN	List	Trade-In Fair	Good	Pvt-Party Good	Retail Excellent
S40 2.4i Sedan 4D	MS382	25145	**6425**	**7425**	**9175**	**12000**
40 SERIES—5-Cyl. Turbo—Equipment Schedule 3						
W.B. 103.9"; 2.5 Liter.						
S40 T5 Sedan 4D	MS682	27945	**7700**	**8800**	**10600**	**13600**
S40 T5 AWD Sedan 4D	MH682	29595	**8275**	**9475**	**11300**	**14450**
50 SERIES—5-Cyl.—Equipment Schedule 3						
W.B. 103.9"; 2.4 Liter.						
2.4i Sport Wagon 4D	MW382	28640	**7675**	**8775**	**10600**	**13550**
50 SERIES—5-Cyl. Turbo—Equipment Schedule 3						
W.B. 103.9"; 2.5 Liter.						
T5 Sport Wagon 4D	MW682	30159	**9475**	**10775**	**12650**	**15950**
T5 AWD Sport Wag 4D	MJ682	31809	**10150**	**11525**	**13400**	**16750**
60 SERIES—5-Cyl.—Equipment Schedule 3						
W.B. 106.9"; 2.4 Liter.						
S60 2.4 Sedan 4D	RS612	28920	**6300**	**7275**	**9025**	**11850**
60 SERIES—5-Cyl. Turbo—Equipment Schedule 3						
W.B. 106.9"; 2.4 Liter, 2.5 Liter.						
S60 2.5T Sedan 4D	RS592	30420	**7825**	**8950**	**10750**	**13750**
S60 2.5T AWD Sed 4D	RH592	32020	**8475**	**9675**	**11500**	**14700**
S60 T5 Sedan 4D	RS547	35170	**9100**	**10350**	**12200**	**15450**
S60 R AWD Sedan 4D	RH527	37935	**11125**	**12600**	**14500**	**18000**
70 SERIES—5-Cyl.—Equipment Schedule 3						
W.B. 108.5"; 2.4 Liter.						
V70 Wagon 4D	SW612	30445	**9100**	**10350**	**12200**	**15450**
70 SERIES—5-Cyl. Turbo—Equipment Schedule 1						
W.B. 103.9", 108.8" (XC70); 2.4 Liter, 2.5 Liter.						
V70 2.5T Wagon 4D	SW592	36895	**10425**	**11850**	**13750**	**17150**
V70 T5 Wagon 4D	SW547	39345	**11375**	**12850**	**14750**	**18300**
V70 R AWD Wagon 4D	SJ527	40635	**13375**	**15100**	**17050**	**20800**
XC70 AWD Wagon 4D	SZ592	38145	**11950**	**13525**	**15450**	**19050**
80 SERIES—5-Cyl. Turbo—Equipment Schedule 1						
W.B. 109.9"; 2.5 Liter.						
S80 2.5T Sedan 4D	TS592	39185	**8425**	**9625**	**11500**	**14750**
S80 2.5T AWD Sedan 4D	TH592	40835	**9125**	**10400**	**12300**	**15600**
80 SERIES—6-Cyl. Twin Turbo—Equipment Schedule 1						
W.B. 109.9"; 2.9 Liter.						
S80 T6 Sedan 4D	TS911	45210	**10050**	**11425**	**13350**	**16750**
S80 T6 Premier Sed 4D	TR911	49240	**10475**	**11900**	**13800**	**17300**

2006 VOLVO — YV1(MS382)-6-#

Body Type	VIN	List	Trade-In Fair	Good	Pvt-Party Good	Retail Excellent
40 SERIES—5-Cyl.—Equipment Schedule 3						
W.B. 103.9"; 2.4 Liter.						
S40 2.4i Sedan 4D	MS382	25650	**7825**	**8975**	**10750**	**13700**
40 SERIES—5-Cyl. Turbo—Equipment Schedule 3						
W.B. 103.9"; 2.5 Liter.						
S40 T5 Sedan 4D	MS682	28510	**9175**	**10425**	**12250**	**15500**
S40 T5 AWD Sedan 4D	MH682	30285	**9850**	**11175**	**13050**	**16300**
50 SERIES—5-Cyl.—Equipment Schedule 3						
W.B. 103.9"; 2.4 Liter.						
2.4i Sport Wagon 4D	MW382	26900	**9175**	**10425**	**12250**	**15500**
50 SERIES—5-Cyl. Turbo—Equipment Schedule 3						
W.B. 103.9"; 2.5 Liter.						
T5 Sport Wagon 4D	MW682	29735	**11175**	**12650**	**14500**	**17950**
T5 AWD Sport Wag 4D	MJ682	31510	**11900**	**13475**	**15350**	**18850**
60 SERIES—5-Cyl. Turbo—Equipment Schedule 3						
W.B. 106.9"; 2.4 Liter, 2.5 Liter.						
S60 2.5T Sedan 4D	RS592	30965	**9375**	**10675**	**12550**	**15800**
S60 2.5T AWD Sed 4D	RH592	32740	**10100**	**11475**	**13350**	**16650**
S60 T5 Sedan 4D	RS547	33940	**10725**	**12150**	**14000**	**17400**
S60 R AWD Sedan 4D	RH527	39865	**12925**	**14550**	**16450**	**20100**
70 SERIES—5-Cyl.—Equipment Schedule 3						
W.B. 108.5"; 2.4 Liter.						
V70 2.4 Wagon 4D	SW612	31140	**10725**	**12150**	**14000**	**17400**
70 SERIES—5-Cyl. Turbo—Equipment Schedule 1						
W.B. 103.9" (C70), 108.5" (V70), 108.8" (XC70); 2.5 Liter.						
C70 T5 Convertible 2D	MC682	38710	**18875**	**21175**	**22800**	**26900**
V70 2.5T Wagon 4D	SW592	36445	**12250**	**13875**	**15750**	**19300**
V70 R AWD Wagon 4D	SJ527	42640	**15475**	**17350**	**19250**	**23100**
XC70 AWD Wagon 4D	SZ592	39390	**13925**	**15675**	**17550**	**21300**
XC70 Ocean Race Wag	SZ592	41430	**15200**	**17100**	**19000**	**22900**
80 SERIES—5-Cyl. Turbo—Equipment Schedule 1						
W.B. 109.9"; 2.5 Liter.						
S80 2.5T Sedan 4D	TS592	38280	**10000**	**11325**	**13250**	**16600**

2006 VOLVO

Body	Type	VIN	List	Trade-In Fair	Good	Pvt-Party Good	Retail Excellent
S80 2.5T AWD Sed 4D		TH592	40055	**10775**	**12200**	**14100**	**17550**

2007 VOLVO — YV1(MS382)-7-#

40 SERIES—5-Cyl.—Equipment Schedule 3
W.B. 103.9"; 2.4 Liter.
| S40 2.4i Sedan 4D | | MS382 | 26185 | **9475** | **10775** | **12550** | **15700** |

40 SERIES—5-Cyl. Turbo—Equipment Schedule 3
W.B. 103.9"; 2.5 Liter.
| S40 T5 Sedan 4D | | MS682 | 29085 | **10925** | **12400** | **14150** | **17500** |
| S40 T5 AWD Sedan 4D | | MH682 | 30935 | **11650** | **13175** | **15000** | **18400** |

50 SERIES—5-Cyl.—Equipment Schedule 3
W.B. 103.9"; 2.4 Liter.
| V50 2.4i Sport Wagon | | MW382 | 27385 | **10925** | **12400** | **14150** | **17500** |

50 SERIES—5-Cyl. Turbo—Equipment Schedule 3
W.B. 103.9"; 2.5 Liter.
| V50 T5 Sport Wag 4D | | MW682 | 30285 | **13075** | **14750** | **16600** | **20200** |
| V50 T5 AWD Spt Wag | | MJ682 | 32135 | **13925** | **15675** | **17500** | **21200** |

60 SERIES—5-Cyl. Turbo—Equipment Schedule 3
W.B. 106.9"; 2.4 Liter, 2.5 Liter.
S60 2.5T Sedan 4D		RS592	31580	**11225**	**12700**	**14450**	**17850**
S60 2.5T AWD Sed 4D		RH592	33430	**12000**	**13575**	**15400**	**18800**
S60 T5 Sedan 4D		RS547	34680	**12600**	**14200**	**15950**	**19500**
S60 R AWD Sedan 4D		RH527	40930	**15000**	**16850**	**18650**	**22400**

70 SERIES—5-Cyl.—Equipment Schedule 3
W.B. 108.5"; 2.4 Liter.
| V70 2.4 Wagon 4D | | SW612 | 31740 | **12650** | **14250** | **16000** | **19500** |

70 SERIES—5-Cyl. Turbo—Equipment Schedule 1
W.B. 103.9" (C70), 108.5" (V70), 108.8" (XC70); 2.5 Liter.
C70 T5 Convertible 2D		MC682	42430	**21550**	**24100**	**25800**	**29900**
V70 2.5T Wagon 4D		SW592	37120	**14300**	**16075**	**17950**	**21700**
V70 R AWD Wagon 4D		SJ527	45285	**17775**	**20000**	**21900**	**26000**
XC70 AWD Wagon 4D		SZ592	40110	**16125**	**18075**	**19900**	**23700**

80 SERIES—6-Cyl.—Equipment Schedule 1
W.B. 111.6"; 3.2 Liter.
| S80 Sedan 4D | | AS982 | 39400 | **15375** | **17300** | **19200** | **23100** |
| Sport Pkg | | | | **350** | **350** | **465** | **465** |

80 SERIES—V8—Equipment Schedule 1
W.B. 111.6"; 4.4 Liter.
| S80 Sedan 4D | | AH852 | 48045 | **18875** | **21075** | **23000** | **27300** |
| Sport Pkg | | | | **350** | **350** | **465** | **465** |

2008 VOLVO — YV1(MK672)-8-#

30 SERIES—5-Cyl. Turbo—Equipment Schedule 3
W.B. 103.9"; 2.5 Liter.
C30 T5 1.0 H'Back 2D		MK672	23695	**12850**	**14450**	**16400**	**20100**
C30 T5 2.0 H'Back 2D		MK672	26445	**14075**	**15825**	**17750**	**21600**
T5 2.0 R-Design H'Back		MK672	26445				

40 SERIES—5-Cyl.—Equipment Schedule 3
W.B. 103.9"; 2.4 Liter.
| S40 2.4i Sedan 4D | | MS382 | 26360 | **12000** | **13575** | **15350** | **18700** |

40 SERIES—5-Cyl. Turbo—Equipment Schedule 3
W.B. 103.9"; 2.5 Liter.
| S40 T5 Sedan 4D | | MS672 | 29260 | **13625** | **15325** | **17050** | **20600** |
| S40 T5 AWD Sedan 4D | | MH672 | 31110 | **14400** | **16175** | **17950** | **21600** |

50 SERIES—5-Cyl.—Equipment Schedule 3
W.B. 103.9"; 2.4 Liter.
| V50 2.4i Sport Wagon | | MW382 | 27560 | **12975** | **14600** | **16400** | **19900** |

50 SERIES—5-Cyl. Turbo—Equipment Schedule 3
W.B. 103.9"; 2.5 Liter.
| V50 T5 Sport Wag 4D | | MW672 | 30460 | **15300** | **17200** | **18900** | **22600** |
| V50 T5 AWD Spt Wag | | MJ672 | 32310 | **16225** | **18175** | **19900** | **23700** |

60 SERIES—5-Cyl. Turbo—Equipment Schedule 3
W.B. 106.9"; 2.4 Liter, 2.5 Liter.
S60 2.5T Sedan 4D		RS592	31630	**13225**	**14900**	**16650**	**20200**
S60 2.5T AWD Sed 4D		RH592	33480	**14100**	**15875**	**17650**	**21300**
S60 T5 Sedan 4D		RS547	34730	**14650**	**16475**	**18250**	**21900**

70 SERIES—5-Cyl. Turbo—Equipment Schedule 3
W.B. 103.9"; 2.5 Liter.
| C70 T5 Convertible 2D | | MC672 | 42230 | **25975** | **28900** | **30400** | **34800** |

70 SERIES—6-Cyl.—Equipment Schedule 3
W.B. 110.9"; 3.2 Liter.
| V70 3.2 Wagon 4D | | SW612 | 33210 | **16275** | **18225** | **20000** | **23800** |

Body	Type	VIN	List	Trade-In Fair	Good	Pvt-Party Good	Retail Excellent
70 SERIES AWD—6-Cyl.—Equipment Schedule 1							
W.B. 110.8"; 3.2 Liter.							
XC70 3.2 AWD Wagon 4D		BZ982	37520	20100	22450	24200	28300
80 SERIES—6-Cyl.—Equipment Schedule 1							
W.B. 111.6"; 3.2 Liter.							
S80 Sedan 4D		AS982	39450	17775	20000	21900	26000
Sport Pkg				375	375	500	500
80 SERIES AWD—6-Cyl. Turbo—Equipment Schedule 1							
W.B. 111.6"; 3.0 Liter.							
S80 T6 Sedan 4D		AH992	42790	19550	21850	23700	27900
Sport Pkg				375	375	500	500
80 SERIES AWD—V8—Equipment Schedule 1							
W.B. 111.6"; 4.4 Liter.							
S80 Sedan 4D		AH852	49955	21550	24000	25900	30300
Sport Pkg				375	375	500	500

Body	Type	VIN	List	Trade-In Fair	Good	Pvt-Party Good	Retail Excellent

Truck & Van Section

ACURA

1996 ACURA — JAE(DJ58V)-T-#

SLX 4WD—V6—Truck Equipment Schedule T3
Sport Utility 4D .... DJ58V 38420 — 1250 — 1725 — 2975 — 4725

1997 ACURA — JAE(DJ58V)-V-#

SLX 4WD—V6—Truck Equipment Schedule T3
Sport Utility 4D .... DJ58V 38735 — 1300 — 1775 — 3050 — 4850

1998 ACURA — JAE(DJ58X)-W-#

SLX 4WD—V6—Truck Equipment Schedule T3
Sport Utility 4D .... DJ58X 36735 — 1425 — 1900 — 3200 — 5050

1999 ACURA — JAE(DJ58X)-X-#

SLX 4WD—V6—Truck Equipment Schedule T3
Sport Utility 4D .... DJ58X 36755 — 1725 — 2225 — 3550 — 5500

2000 ACURA — No Production

2001 ACURA — 2HN(YD182)-1-#

MDX 4WD—V6—Truck Equipment Schedule T3
Sport Utility 4D .... YD182 34850 — 5750 — 6700 — 8350 — 11050
Touring Spt Util 4D .... YD186 37450 — 6675 — 7675 — 9375 — 12200

2002 ACURA — 2HN(YD182)-2-#

MDX 4WD—V6—Truck Equipment Schedule T3
Sport Utility 4D .... YD182 35180 — 6750 — 7775 — 9700 — 12800
Touring Spt Util 4D .... YD186 37780 — 7725 — 8825 — 10800 — 14000

2003 ACURA — 2HN(YD182)-3-#

MDX 4WD—V6—Truck Equipment Schedule T3
Sport Utility 4D .... YD182 36200 — 7750 — 8875 — 10850 — 14000
Touring Spt Util 4D .... YD186 38800 — 8875 — 10100 — 12150 — 15600

2004 ACURA — 2NH(YD182)-4-#

MDX 4WD—V6—Truck Equipment Schedule T3
Sport Utility 4D .... YD182 36945 — 9475 — 10775 — 12800 — 16200
Touring Spt Util 4D .... YD186 39545 — 10725 — 12150 — 14200 — 17850

2005 ACURA — 2HN(YD182)-5-#

MDX 4WD—V6—Truck Equipment Schedule T3
Sport Utility 4D .... YD182 37270 — 11425 — 12875 — 14900 — 18550
Touring Spt Util 4D .... YD186 40095 — 12800 — 14450 — 16450 — 20300

2006 ACURA — 2HN(YD182)-6-#

MDX 4WD—V6—Truck Equipment Schedule T3
Sport Utility 4D .... YD182 37740 — 13575 — 15300 — 17250 — 21100
Touring Spt Util 4D .... YD186 40565 — 15100 — 16950 — 18950 — 22900

2007 ACURA — 2HN(TB182)-7-#

RDX AWD—4-Cyl. Turbo—Truck Equipment Schedule T3
Sport Utility 4D .... TB182 33610 — 17200 — 19250 — 21200 — 25300
MDX AWD—V6—Truck Equipment Schedule T3
Sport Utility 4D .... YD282 40665 — 23825 — 26550 — 28500 — 33300

2008 ACURA — 2HNor5J8(TB182)-8-#

RDX AWD—4-Cyl. Turbo—Truck Equipment Schedule T3
Sport Utility 4D .... TB182 33910 — 19800 — 22150 — 23900 — 28000
MDX AWD—V6—Truck Equipment Schedule T3
Sport Utility 4D .... YD282 40910 — 26550 — 29600 — 31500 — 36400

Body	Type	VIN	List	Trade-In Fair	Trade-In Good	Pvt-Party Good	Retail Excellent

TRUCKS & VANS

BMW

2003 BMW — 5UX(FA535)-3-#

X5 AWD—6-Cyl.—Truck Equipment Schedule T3
3.0i Sport Utility 4D	FA535	42920	**11850**	**13425**	**15650**	**19550**
Sport Pkg			**250**	**250**	**335**	**335**

X5 AWD—V8—Truck Equipment Schedule T3
4.4i Sport Utility 4D	FB335	50645	**12250**	**13875**	**16100**	**20100**
4.6is Sport Utility 4D	FB935	67495	**18075**	**20200**	**22700**	**27600**
Sport Pkg			**250**	**250**	**335**	**335**

2004 BMW — WBXor5UX(PA734)-4-#

X3 AWD—6-Cyl.—Truck Equipment Schedule T3
2.5i Sport Utility 4D	PA734	33740	**10150**	**11525**	**13550**	**17740**
3.0i Sport Utility 4D	PA934	38270	**10975**	**12450**	**14550**	**18250**
Sport Pkg			**275**	**275**	**365**	**365**
Premium Pkg			**1000**	**1000**	**1335**	**1335**

X5 AWD—6-Cyl.—Truck Equipment Schedule T3
3.0i Sport Utility 4D	FA135	40995	**13725**	**15475**	**17750**	**21900**
Sport Pkg			**275**	**275**	**365**	**365**

X5 AWD—V8—Truck Equipment Schedule T3
4.4i Sport Utility 4D	FB535	52195	**14350**	**16125**	**18400**	**22600**
4.8is Sport Utility 4D	FA935	70495	**20100**	**22450**	**24900**	**29900**
Sport Pkg			**275**	**275**	**365**	**365**

2005 BMW — WBXor5UX(PA734)-5-#

X3 AWD—6-Cyl.—Truck Equipment Schedule T3
2.5i Sport Utility 4D	PA734	34715	**11625**	**13125**	**15200**	**18850**
3.0i Sport Utility 4D	PA934	38445	**12650**	**14250**	**16250**	**20100**
Sport Pkg			**300**	**300**	**400**	**400**
Premium Pkg			**1000**	**1000**	**1335**	**1335**

X5 AWD—6-Cyl.—Truck Equipment Schedule T3
3.0i Sport Utility 4D	FA135	45120	**15775**	**17700**	**19900**	**24100**
Sport Pkg			**300**	**300**	**400**	**400**

X5 AWD—V8—Truck Equipment Schedule T3
4.4i Sport Utility 4D	FB535	53495	**16550**	**18625**	**20900**	**25400**
4.8is Sport Utility 4D	FA935	70795	**23125**	**25775**	**28200**	**33400**
Sport Pkg			**300**	**300**	**400**	**400**

2006 BMW — WBXor5UX(PA934)-6-#

X3 AWD—6-Cyl.—Truck Equipment Schedule T3
3.0i Sport Utility 4D	PA934	38945	**14700**	**16550**	**18550**	**22500**
Sport Pkg			**325**	**325**	**435**	**435**
Premium Pkg			**1000**	**1000**	**1335**	**1335**

X5 AWD—6-Cyl.—Truck Equipment Schedule T3
3.0i Sport Utility 4D	FA135	45920	**18075**	**20200**	**22400**	**27000**
Sport Pkg			**325**	**325**	**435**	**435**

X5 AWD—V8—Truck Equipment Schedule T3
4.4i Sport Utility 4D	FB535	54295	**19300**	**21550**	**23800**	**28400**
4.8is Sport Utility 4D	FA935	71795	**26350**	**29400**	**31800**	**37200**
Sport Pkg			**325**	**325**	**435**	**435**

2007 BMW — WBXor5UX(PC934)-7-#

X3 AWD—6-Cyl.—Truck Equipment Schedule T3
3.0si Sport Utility 4D	PC934	41145	**19800**	**22150**	**24200**	**28600**
Sport Pkg			**350**	**350**	**465**	**465**
Premium Pkg			**1000**	**1000**	**1335**	**1335**

X5 AWD—6-Cyl.—Truck Equipment Schedule T3
3.0si Sport Utility 4D	FE435	48045	**31550**	**35075**	**37200**	**42900**
Sport Pkg			**350**	**350**	**465**	**465**
Third Seat			**700**	**700**	**935**	**935**
Adaptive Cruise			**475**	**475**	**635**	**635**

X5 AWD—V8—Truck Equipment Schedule T3
4.8i Sport Utility 4D	FE834	55195	**34100**	**37925**	**40100**	**46100**
Sport Pkg			**350**	**350**	**465**	**465**
Third Seat			**700**	**700**	**935**	**935**
Adaptive Cruise			**475**	**475**	**635**	**635**

2008 BMW

Body	Type	VIN	List	Trade-In Fair	Good	Pvt-Party Good	Retail Excellent

2008 BMW — WBXor5UX(PC934)-8-#

X3 AWD—6-Cyl.—Truck Equipment Schedule T3
3.0si Sport Utility 4D	PC934	40225	28725	31950	33800	38900
Sport Pkg			375	375	500	500
Premium Pkg			1000	1000	1335	1335

X5 AWD—6-Cyl.—Truck Equipment Schedule T3
3.0si Sport Utility 4D	FE435	46675	34900	38800	40700	46400
Sport Pkg			375	375	500	500
Third Row			750	750	1000	1000
Adaptive Cruise Control			500	500	665	665

X5 AWD—V8—Truck Equipment Schedule T3
4.8i Sport Utility 4D	FE835	55275	41350	45875	47700	53900
Sport Pkg			375	375	500	500
Third Row			750	750	1000	1000
Adaptive Cruise Control			500	500	665	665

X6 AWD—V6 Twin Turbo—Truck Equipment Schedule T3
35i Sport Utility 4D	FG435	53275				
Sport Pkg						
Adaptive Cruise Control						

X6 AWD—V8 Twin Turbo—Truck Equipment Schedule T3
50i Sport Utility 4D	FG835	63775				
Sport Pkg						
Adaptive Cruise Control						

BUICK

2003 BUICK — 3G5-(A03E)-3-#

RENDEZVOUS—V6—Truck Equipment Schedule T3
CX Sport Utility 4D	A03E	26975	3800	4525	6200	8750
CXL Sport Utility 4D	B03E	30200	4300	5075	6775	9375
Third Seat			300	300	400	400
AWD	B		650	650	865	865

2004 BUICK — (3G5or5GA)-(A03E)-4-#

RENDEZVOUS—V6—Truck Equipment Schedule T3
CX Sport Utility 4D	A03E	26545	4825	5650	7425	10150
CXL Sport Utility 4D	A03E	31410	5400	6275	8050	10850
Third Seat	B		350	350	465	465
AWD	7		725	725	965	965
V6 3.6 Liter			400	400	535	535

RENDEZVOUS AWD—V6—Truck Equipment Schedule T3
| Ultra Sport Utility 4D | B037 | 39695 | 6525 | 7525 | 9300 | 12250 |
| Third Seat | | | 350 | 350 | 465 | 465 |

RAINIER AWD—6-Cyl.—Truck Equipment Schedule T1
CXL Sport Utility 4D	T13S	37895	6375	7350	9175	12100
2WD	S		(650)	(650)	(865)	(865)
V8 5.3 Liter	P		350	350	465	465

2005 BUICK — (3G5or5GA)-(V23L)-5-#

TERRAZA—V6—Truck Equipment Schedule T3
CX Minivan 4D	V23L	28825	5000	5825	7525	10200
CX AWD Minivan 4D	X23L	31705	5475	6375	8075	10850
CXL Minivan 4D	V33L	31885	6000	6950	8675	11450
CXL AWD Minivan	X33L	34570	6500	7500	9225	12100

RENDEZVOUS—V6—Truck Equipment Schedule T3
CX Sport Utility 4D	A04E	27270	6025	6975	8775	11600
CXL Sport Utility 4D	A03E	31600	6675	7675	9450	12400
Ultra Sport Utility 4D	A03E	36840	7825	8950	10800	13900
Third Seat	B		400	400	535	535
AWD	7		800	800	1065	1065
V6 3.6 Liter			400	400	535	535

RAINIER AWD—6-Cyl.—Truck Equipment Schedule T1
CXL Sport Utility 4D	T13S	37590	7575	8700	10550	13550
2WD	S		(725)	(725)	(965)	(965)
V8 5.3 Liter	M		375	375	500	500

2006 BUICK — (3G5or5GA)-(V23L)-6-#

TERRAZA—V6—Truck Equipment Schedule T3
| CX Minivan 4D | V23L | 28530 | 6425 | 7400 | 9150 | 11950 |

Body	Type	VIN	List	Trade-In Fair	Trade-In Good	Pvt-Party Good	Retail Excellent
CX AWD Minivan 4D		X23L	30990	6925	7975	9700	12600
CXL Minivan 4D		V33L	31930	7550	8650	10400	13300
CXL AWD Minivan		X33L	33990	8075	9225	11050	14050
RENDEZVOUS—V6—Truck Equipment Schedule T3							
CX Sport Utility 4D		A03L	27305	7400	8500	10300	13300
CXL Sport Utility 4D		A03L	30955	8075	9225	11050	14200
Third Seat		B		425	425	565	565
AWD		B		875	875	1165	1165
V6 3.6 Liter		7		400	400	535	535
RAINIER AWD—6-Cyl.—Truck Equipment Schedule T1							
CXL Sport Utility 4D		T13S	35785	9000	10250	12100	15350
2WD		S		(800)	(800)	(1065)	(1065)
V8 5.3 Liter		M		400	400	535	535

Body	Type	VIN	List	Trade-In Fair	Trade-In Good	Pvt-Party Good	Retail Excellent
TERRAZA—V6—Truck Equipment Schedule T3							
CX Minivan 4D		V231	27275	8325	9525	11200	14150
CX Plus Minivan 4D		V231	28615	8600	9800	11500	14500
CXL Minivan 4D		V331	31395	9575	10875	12600	15700
RENDEZVOUS—V6—Truck Equipment Schedule T3							
CX Sport Utility 4D		A03L	25795	9000	10250	12000	15150
CXL Sport Utility 4D		A03L	29370	9750	11075	12900	16050
Third Seat				450	450	600	600
RAINIER AWD—6-Cyl.—Truck Equipment Schedule T1							
CXL Sport Utility 4D		T13S	34140	10675	12100	13850	17200
2WD		S		(875)	(875)	(1165)	(1165)
V8 5.3 Liter		M		400	400	535	535

Body	Type	VIN	List	Trade-In Fair	Trade-In Good	Pvt-Party Good	Retail Excellent
ENCLAVE—V6—Truck Equipment Schedule T3							
CX Sport Utility 4D		R137	34760	20375	22825	24700	29000
CXL Sport Utility 4D		R237	36990	23325	25975	27800	32300
AWD		V		1025	1025	1365	1365

CADILLAC

Body	Type	VIN	List	Trade-In Fair	Trade-In Good	Pvt-Party Good	Retail Excellent
ESCALADE AWD—V8—Truck Equipment Schedule T3							
Sport Utility 4D		K13R	46525	5100	5950	7600	10250

Body	Type	VIN	List	Trade-In Fair	Trade-In Good	Pvt-Party Good	Retail Excellent
ESCALADE AWD—V8—Truck Equipment Schedule T3							
Sport Utility 4D		K13R	46875	5325	6200	7875	10550

Body	Type	VIN	List	Trade-In Fair	Trade-In Good	Pvt-Party Good	Retail Excellent
ESCALADE AWD—V8—Truck Equipment Schedule T3							
Sport Utility 4D		K63N	51980	8025	9200	11250	14650
2WD		C		(500)	(500)	(665)	(665)
V8 5.3 Liter		T		(300)	(300)	(400)	(400)
ESCALADE EXT AWD—V8—Truck Equipment Schedule T3							
Sport Util Pickup 4D		K13N	49990	10675	12100	14400	18300

Body	Type	VIN	List	Trade-In Fair	Trade-In Good	Pvt-Party Good	Retail Excellent
ESCALADE AWD—V8—Truck Equipment Schedule T3							
Sport Utility 4D		K63N	53975	9900	11225	13350	16950
2WD		C		(575)	(575)	(765)	(765)
V8 5.3 Liter		T		(350)	(350)	(465)	(465)
ESCALADE EXT AWD—V8—Truck Equipment Schedule T3							
Sport Util Pickup 4D		K63N	51215	12400	14025	16300	20400
ESCALADE ESV AWD—V8—Truck Equipment Schedule T3							
Sport Utility 4D		K66N	56160	10925	12400	14550	18300

Body	Type	VIN	List	Trade-In Fair	Trade-In Good	Pvt-Party Good	Retail Excellent
SRX—V8—Truck Equipment Schedule T3							
Sport Utility 4D		E63A	46995	9325	10625	12600	16000
Third Seat				800	800	1065	1065
Luxury Performance				1650	1650	2200	2200

TRUCKS & VANS

TRUCKS & VANS

Body Type	VIN	List	Trade-In Fair	Good	Pvt-Party Good	Retail Excellent
AWD			725	725	965	965
V6 3.6 Liter	7		(400)	(400)	(535)	(535)
ESCALADE AWD—V8—Truck Equipment Schedule T3						
Sport Utility 4D	K63N	55695	11900	13475	15650	19450
2WD	C		(650)	(650)	(865)	(865)
V8 5.3 Liter	C		(375)	(375)	(500)	(500)
ESCALADE EXT AWD—V8—Truck Equipment Schedule T3						
Sport Util Pickup 4D	K63N	52975	14100	15875	18300	22500
ESCALADE ESV AWD—V8—Truck Equipment Schedule T3						
Sport Utility 4D	K66N	58095	13225	14900	17050	21100
Platinum Utility 4D	K66N	69730	15875	17825	20100	24500

2005 CADILLAC — (1or3)GY-(E63A)-5-#

SRX—V8—Truck Equipment Schedule T3						
Sport Utility 4D	E63A	50830	10875	12350	14300	17850
Third Seat			800	800	1065	1065
Luxury Performance			1725	1725	2300	2300
AWD			800	800	1065	1065
V6 3.6 Liter	7		(450)	(450)	(600)	(600)
ESCALADE AWD—V8—Truck Equipment Schedule T3						
Sport Utility 4D	K63N	56615	14150	15925	18100	22100
2WD	C		(725)	(725)	(965)	(965)
V8 5.3 Liter	T		(400)	(400)	(535)	(535)
ESCALADE EXT AWD—V8—Truck Equipment Schedule T3						
Sport Util Pickup 4D	K62N	53895	15875	17775	20200	24600
ESCALADE ESV AWD—V8—Truck Equipment Schedule T3						
Sport Utility 4D	K66N	59015	15825	17750	19900	24100
Platinum Sport Util	K66N	70385	18775	20975	23300	27900

2006 CADILLAC — (1or3)GY-(E63A)-6-#

SRX—V8—Truck Equipment Schedule T3						
Sport Utility 4D	E63A	47995	12650	14300	16200	19900
Third Seat			800	800	1065	1065
AWD			875	875	1165	1165
V6 3.6 Liter	7		(500)	(500)	(665)	(665)
ESCALADE AWD—V8—Truck Equipment Schedule T3						
Sport Utility 4D	K63N	57280	16550	18625	20800	25100
2WD	C		(800)	(800)	(1065)	(1065)
ESCALADE EXT AWD—V8—Truck Equipment Schedule T3						
Sport Util Pickup 4D	K62N	54210	17650	19800	22100	26800
ESCALADE ESV AWD—V8—Truck Equipment Schedule T3						
Sport Utility 4D	K66N	59680	18875	21075	23300	27800
Platinum Sport Util	K66N	71050	22050	24600	26900	31800

2007 CADILLAC — (1or3)GY-(E63A)-7-#

SRX—V8—Truck Equipment Schedule T3						
Sport Utility 4D	E63A	43870	14650	16475	18400	22100
Third Seat			800	800	1065	1065
4-AWD			950	950	1265	1265
V6 3.6 Liter	7		(550)	(550)	(735)	(735)
ESCALADE AWD—V8—Truck Equipment Schedule T3						
Sport Utility 4D	K638	57675	28225	31450	33500	38900
2WD	C		(875)	(875)	(1165)	(1165)
ESCALADE EXT AWD—V8—Truck Equipment Schedule T3						
Sport Util Pickup 4D	K628	54605	28325	31550	33900	39500
ESCALADE ESV AWD—V8—Truck Equipment Schedule T3						
Sport Utility 4D	K668	60075	29500	32825	35000	40700

2008 CADILLAC — (1or3)GY-(E23A)-8-#

SRX—V8—Truck Equipment Schedule T3						
Sport Utility 4D	E23A	44670	18575	20775	22600	26800
Third Row			800	800	1065	1065
4-AWD	4,5		1025	1025	1365	1365
V6 3.6 Liter	7		(575)	(575)	(765)	(765)
ESCALADE AWD—V8—Truck Equipment Schedule T3						
Sport Utility 4D	K638	58195	31850	35375	37200	42600
2WD	C		(950)	(950)	(1265)	(1265)
ESCALADE EXT AWD—V8—Truck Equipment Schedule T3						
Sport Util Pickup 4D	K628	55115	32050	35675	37800	43500
ESCALADE ESV AWD—V8—Truck Equipment Schedule T3						
Sport Utility 4D	K668	60610	34700	38525	40400	46000
2WD			(950)	(950)	(1265)	(1265)

Body	Type	VIN	List	Trade-In Fair	Good	Pvt-Party Good	Retail Excellent

TRUCKS & VANS

CHEVROLET/GMC

1994 CHEVY/GMC — 1G(C,T,NorB)-(T18Z)-R-#

S10 BLAZER/JIMMY 4WD—V6—Truck Equipment Sch T1
Sport Utility 2D	T18Z	19649		600	825	1650	2975
Sport Utility 4D	T13Z	21377		825	1150	2100	3600
2WD	S			(125)	(125)	(165)	(165)
V6 4.3L High Output	W			100	100	135	135

BLAZER/YUKON 4WD—V8—Truck Equipment Schedule T1
Sport Utility 2D	K18K	23460		1425	1900	3125	4900
V8 6.5L Turbo Diesel	S			275	275	365	365

SUBURBAN—V8—Truck Equipment Schedule T1
C1500 Sport Utility	C16K	21651		1175	1650	2850	4550
C2500 Sport Utility	C26K	22883		1300	1800	3000	4750
w/o Third Seat				(200)	(200)	(265)	(265)
4WD	K			500	500	665	665
V8 454/7.4 Liter	N			150	150	200	200
V8 6.5L Turbo Diesel	F			275	275	365	365

LUMINA—V6—Truck Equipment Schedule T2
Cargo	U06D	16015		250	350	900	1800

LUMINA—V6—Truck Equipment Schedule T1
Passenger	U06D	18175		300	425	1000	1925
5 Passenger				(200)	(200)	(265)	(265)
V6 3.8 Liter	L			50	50	65	65

ASTRO/SAFARI—V6—Truck Equipment Schedule T2
Cargo Minivan	M15Z	15985		475	625	1325	2400
Extended Cargo	M19Z	16458		475	625	1325	2400
AWD	L			250	250	335	335
V6 4.3L High Output	W			100	100	135	135

ASTRO/SAFARI—V6—Truck Equipment Schedule T1
Minivan	M15Z	17819		575	775	1575	2825
Extended Minivan	M19Z	18121		625	875	1725	3050
5 Passenger				(200)	(200)	(265)	(265)
AWD	L			250	250	335	335
V6 4.3L High Output	W			100	100	135	135

SPORTVAN/RALLY WAGON—V8—Truck Equipment Sch T1
G20 Passenger Van	G25H	20344		775	1100	2025	3475
G30 Passenger Van	G35K	21696		825	1150	2075	3550
5 Passenger				(200)	(200)	(265)	(265)
146" W.B.	9			50	50	65	65
V6 4.3 Liter	Z			(200)	(200)	(265)	(265)
V8 454/7.4 Liter	N			100	100	135	135
V8 6.5 Liter Diesel	P			(100)	(100)	(135)	(135)

G-SERIES/VANDURA—V6—Truck Equipment Schedule T1
G10 Cargo Van	G15Z	17544		725	1025	1900	3300
G20 Cargo Van	G25Z	17534		775	1100	2025	3475
G30 Cargo Van	G35Z	17661		825	1150	2075	3550
146" W.B.	9			50	50	65	65
V8 5.0, 5.7 Liter	H,K			100	100	135	135
V8 454/7.4 Liter	N			200	200	265	265
V8 6.5 Liter Diesel	P			(75)	(75)	(100)	(100)

S10/SONOMA PICKUP—4-Cyl.—Truck Equipment Schedule T2
Short Bed	S144	10201		400	550	1175	2175
Long Bed	S144	10501		300	425	1025	1950
Extended Cab	S194	12260		600	825	1625	2925
4WD	T			400	400	535	535
V6 4.3 Liter	Z			150	150	200	200
V6 4.3L High Output	W			200	200	265	265

REGULAR CAB PICKUP—V8—Truck Equipment Schedule T1
1500 Short Bed	C14H	16322		1550	2025	3275	5100
1500 Long Bed	C14H	16602		1450	1925	3175	4975
2500 Long Bed	C24H	17579		1275	1750	2975	4700
3500 Long Bed	C34H	19313		1325	1800	3025	4775
Work Truck/Special				(250)	(250)	(335)	(335)
4WD	K			500	500	665	665
V6 4.3 Liter	Z			(350)	(350)	(465)	(465)
V8 5.7 Liter	K			75	75	100	100
V8 454/7.4 Liter	N			150	150	200	200
V8 6.5 Liter Diesel	P,Y			(100)	(100)	(135)	(135)
V8 6.5L Turbo Diesel	F,S			275	275	365	365

TRUCKS & VANS

Body	Type	VIN	List	Trade-In Fair	Trade-In Good	Pvt-Party Good	Retail Excellent
EXTENDED CAB PICKUP—V8—Truck Equipment Schedule T1							
1500 Short Bed		C19H	18319	1800	2325	3600	5475
1500 Long Bed		C19H	19162	1750	2250	3500	5375
2500 Short Bed		C29H	20107	1950	2500	3775	5675
2500 Long Bed		C29K	20995	1800	2325	3600	5475
3500 Long Bed		C39K	22547	1850	2375	3650	5525
4WD		K		500	500	665	665
V6 4.3 Liter		Z		(350)	(350)	(465)	(465)
V8 5.7 Liter		K		75	75	100	100
V8 454/7.4 Liter		N		150	150	200	200
V8 6.5 Liter Diesel		P,Y		(100)	(100)	(135)	(135)
V8 6.5L Turbo Diesel		F,S		275	275	365	365
CREW CAB PICKUP—V8—Truck Equipment Schedule T1							
3500 Long Bed		C33K	21652	2325	2900	4250	6225
4WD		K		500	500	665	665
V8 454/7.4 Liter		N		150	150	200	200
V8 6.5L Turbo Diesel		S		275	275	365	365

Body	Type	VIN	List	Trade-In Fair	Trade-In Good	Pvt-Party Good	Retail Excellent
BLAZER/JIMMY 4WD—V6—Truck Equipment Schedule T1							
Sport Utility 2D		T18W	20390	725	1025	1900	3325
Sport Utility 4D		T13W	22438	975	1375	2500	4150
2WD		S		(125)	(125)	(165)	(165)
TAHOE/YUKON 4WD—V8—Truck Equipment Schedule T1							
Sport Utility 2D		K18K	24215	1025	1450	2600	4300
Sport Utility 4D		K13K	29195	1675	2175	3450	5325
2WD		C		(125)	(125)	(165)	(165)
V8 6.5L Turbo Diesel		S		275	275	365	365
SUBURBAN—V8—Truck Equipment Schedule T1							
C1500 Sport Utility		C16K	24264	1325	1800	3025	4800
C2500 Sport Utility		C26K	25497	1450	1925	3175	5000
4WD		K		(200)	(200)	(265)	(265)
w/o Third Seat				500	500	665	665
V8 454/7.4 Liter		N		150	150	200	200
V8 6.5L Turbo Diesel		F		275	275	365	365
LUMINA—V6—Truck Equipment Schedule T2							
Cargo		U06D	16775	275	400	1000	1925
LUMINA—V6—Truck Equipment Schedule T1							
Passenger		U06D	19625	350	475	1100	2100
5 Passenger				(200)	(200)	(265)	(265)
V6 3.8 Liter		L		50	50	65	65
ASTRO/SAFARI—V6—Truck Equipment Schedule T2							
Cargo Minivan		M19W	18340	550	750	1550	2800
Dutch Doors				50	50	65	65
AWD		L		250	250	335	335
ASTRO/SAFARI—V6—Truck Equipment Schedule T1							
Minivan		M19W	19886	725	1000	1900	3300
5 Passenger				(200)	(200)	(265)	(265)
Dutch Doors				50	50	65	65
AWD		L		250	250	335	335
SPORTVAN/RALLY WAGON—V8—Truck Equipment Sch T1							
G20 Passenger Van		G25H	21776	925	1300	2375	4025
G30 Passenger Van		G35K	22595	950	1325	2425	4075
5 Passenger				(200)	(200)	(265)	(265)
146" W.B.		9		50	50	65	65
V6 4.3 Liter		Z		(200)	(200)	(265)	(265)
V8 454/7.4 Liter		N		100	100	135	135
V8 6.5 Liter Diesel		Y		(100)	(100)	(135)	(135)
G-SERIES/VANDURA—V6—Truck Equipment Schedule T1							
G10 Cargo Van		G15Z	18588	825	1175	2150	3650
G20 Cargo Van		G25Z	18578	900	1250	2350	4000
G30 Cargo Van		G35Z	18732	925	1300	2400	4050
146" W.B.				50	50	65	65
V8 5.0, 5.7 Liter		H,K		100	100	135	135
V8 454/7.4 Liter		N		200	200	265	265
V8 6.5 Liter Diesel		Y		(75)	(75)	(100)	(100)
S10/SONOMA PICKUP—4-Cyl.—Truck Equipment Schedule T2							
Short Bed		S144	10820	475	625	1350	2450
Long Bed		S144	11130	350	500	1125	2125
Extended Cab		S194	12990	700	975	1850	3250
4WD		T		400	400	535	535
V6 4.3 Liter		Z		150	150	200	200
V6 4.3L High Output		W		200	200	265	265

1995 CHEVROLET/GMC

Body	Type	VIN	List	Trade-In Fair	Trade-In Good	Pvt-Party Good	Retail Excellent
REGULAR CAB PICKUP—V8—Truck Equipment Schedule T1							
1500 Short Bed		C14H	17217	1800	2325	3625	5525
1500 Long Bed		C14H	17497	1725	2225	3500	5375
2500 Short Bed		C24H	18679	1525	2000	3250	5100
3500 HD Long Bed		C34K	19803	1575	2075	3350	5200
Work Truck/Special				(250)	(250)	(335)	(335)
4WD		K		500	500	665	665
V6 4.3 Liter		Z		(350)	(350)	(465)	(465)
V8 5.7 Liter		K		75	75	100	100
V8 454/7.4 Liter		N		150	150	200	200
V8 6.5 Liter Diesel		P		(100)	(100)	(135)	(135)
V8 6.5L Turbo Diesel		S		275	275	365	365
EXTENDED CAB PICKUP—V8—Truck Equipment Schedule T1							
1500 Short Bed		C19H	19177	2050	2625	3925	5875
1500 Long Bed		C19H	19545	1975	2550	3850	5775
2500 Short Bed		C29H	21115	2250	2825	4175	6175
2500 Long Bed		C29H	21172	2225	2800	4150	6125
3500 HD Long Bed		C39K	23129	2125	2675	4025	5975
4WD		K		500	500	665	665
V6 4.3 Liter		Z		(350)	(350)	(465)	(465)
V8 5.7 Liter		K		75	75	100	100
V8 454/7.4 Liter		N		150	150	200	200
V8 6.5 Liter Diesel		P		(100)	(100)	(135)	(135)
V8 6.5L Turbo Diesel		S		275	275	365	365
CREW CAB PICKUP—V8—Truck Equipment Schedule T1							
3500 Long Bed		C33K	22389	2700	3300	4700	6775
4WD		K		500	500	665	665
V8 454/7.4 Liter		N		150	150	200	200
V8 6.5L Turbo Diesel		F,S		275	275	365	365

1996 CHEVY/GMC — 1G(C,K,NorT)–(T18W)–T–#

Body	Type	VIN	List	Trade-In Fair	Trade-In Good	Pvt-Party Good	Retail Excellent
BLAZER/JIMMY 4WD—V6—Truck Equipment Schedule T1							
Sport Utility 2D		T18W	21694	800	1125	2100	3600
Sport Utility 4D		T13W	23742	1100	1550	2725	4400
2WD		S		(200)	(200)	(265)	(265)
TAHOE/YUKON 4WD—V8—Truck Equipment Schedule T1							
Sport Utility 2D		K18R	26596	1200	1675	2875	4625
Sport Utility 4D		K13R	31079	1975	2525	3825	5750
2WD		C		(200)	(200)	(265)	(265)
V8 6.5L Turbo Diesel		S		325	325	435	435
SUBURBAN—V8—Truck Equipment Schedule T1							
C1500 Sport Utility		C16R	26709	1625	2100	3375	5225
C2500 Sport Utility		C26R	27942	1750	2250	3525	5425
w/o Third Seat				(250)	(250)	(335)	(335)
4WD		K		600	600	800	800
V8 454/7.4 Liter		J		175	175	235	235
V8 6.5L Turbo Diesel		F		325	325	435	435
LUMINA—V6—Truck Equipment Schedule T2							
Cargo		U06E	18415	275	375	975	1925
LUMINA—V6—Truck Equipment Schedule T1							
Passenger		U06E	20435	375	525	1175	2225
5 Passenger				(250)	(250)	(335)	(335)
ASTRO/SAFARI—V6—Truck Equipment Schedule T2							
Cargo/SL Cargo		M19W	19152	600	825	1650	2975
Dutch Doors				75	75	100	100
AWD		L		300	300	400	400
ASTRO/SAFARI—V6—Truck Equipment Schedule T1							
Minivan/SL Minivan		M19W	19736	775	1100	2025	3500
5 Passenger				(250)	(250)	(335)	(335)
Dutch Doors				75	75	100	100
AWD		L		300	300	400	400
EXPRESS/SAVANA—V8—Truck Equipment Schedule T1							
1500 Passenger Van		G15W	23342	975	1350	2475	4150
2500 Passenger Van		G25R	25767	1000	1400	2550	4250
3500 Passenger Van		G35R	25927	1050	1475	2625	4325
5 Passenger				(250)	(250)	(335)	(335)
155" W.B.		9		75	75	100	100
V6 4.3 Liter		W		(250)	(250)	(335)	(335)
V8 454/7.4 Liter		J		125	125	165	165
V8 6.5L Turbo Diesel		F		125	125	165	165
SPORTVAN/RALLY WAGON—V8—Truck Equipment Sch T1							
G30 Passenger Van		G35K	23451	875	1250	2350	4000
146" W.B.				75	75	100	100

TRUCKS & VANS

TRUCKS & VANS

Body Type	VIN	List	Trade-In Fair	Trade-In Good	Pvt-Party Good	Retail Excellent
V8 454/7.4 Liter	N	------	125	125	165	165
V8 6.5 Liter Diesel	Y	------	(125)	(125)	(165)	(165)
G-SERIES/SAVANA—V6—Truck Equip Schedule T1						
1500 Cargo Van	G15W	20214	950	1350	2450	4125
2500 Cargo Van	G25W	20639	1000	1400	2525	4200
3500 Cargo Van	G35R	22019	1050	1475	2600	4300
155" W.B.	9	------	100	100	100	100
V8 5.0, 5.7 Liter	M,R	------	125	125	165	165
V8 454/7.4 Liter	J	------	250	250	335	335
V8 6.5L Turbo Diesel	F	------	200	200	265	265
G-SERIES/VANDURA—V8—Truck Equipment Schedule T1						
G30 Classic	G39K	20469	1000	1400	2525	4200
146" W.B.		------	75	75	100	100
V6 4.3 Liter	Z	------	(250)	(250)	(335)	(335)
V8 454/7.4 Liter	N	------	125	125	165	165
V8 6.5 Liter Diesel	Y	------	(100)	(100)	(135)	(135)
S10/SONOMA PICKUP—4-Cyl.—Truck Equipment Schedule T2						
Short Bed	S144	11755	525	725	1525	2800
Long Bed	S144	12065	425	600	1275	2350
Extended Cab	S194	14470	800	1125	2075	3550
Third Door		------	150	150	200	200
4WD	T	------	525	525	700	700
V6 4.3 Liter	X	------	200	200	265	265
V6 4.3L High Output	W	------	250	250	335	335
REGULAR CAB PICKUP—V8—Truck Equipment Schedule T1						
1500 Short Bed	C14M	18311	1825	2350	3650	5525
1500 Long Bed	C14M	18591	1725	2225	3500	5400
2500 Long Bed	C24M	19273	1625	2125	3400	5275
3500 Long Bed	C34R	20477	1725	2225	3500	5400
Work Truck/Special		------	(300)	(300)	(400)	(400)
4WD	K	------	600	600	800	800
V6 4.3 Liter	W	------	(375)	(375)	(500)	(500)
V8 5.7 Liter	R	------	125	125	165	165
V8 454/7.4 Liter	J	------	175	175	235	235
V8 6.5L Turbo Diesel	F,S	------	325	325	435	435
EXTENDED CAB PICKUP—V8—Truck Equipment Schedule T1						
1500 Short Bed	C19M	20371	2225	2825	4150	6125
1500 Long Bed	C19M	20819	2125	2700	4025	5975
2500 Short Bed	C29M	21889	2525	3100	4475	6550
2500 HD Long Bed	C29M	21946	2450	3050	4400	6450
3500 Long Bed	C39R	23903	2350	2950	4300	6300
Third Door		------	125	125	165	165
4WD	K	------	600	600	800	800
V6 4.3 Liter	W	------	(375)	(375)	(500)	(500)
V8 5.7 Liter	R	------	125	125	165	165
V8 454/7.4 Liter	J	------	175	175	235	235
V8 6.5L Turbo Diesel	F,S	------	325	325	435	435
CREW CAB PICKUP—V8—Truck Equipment Schedule T1						
3500 Long Bed	C33R	23611	3000	3625	5075	7225
4WD	K	------	600	600	800	800
V8 454/7.4 Liter	J	------	175	175	235	235
V8 6.5L Turbo Diesel	F	------	325	325	435	435

1997 CHEVY/GMC — 1G(C,K,NorT)–T18W–V–#

Body Type	VIN	List	Trade-In Fair	Trade-In Good	Pvt-Party Good	Retail Excellent
BLAZER/JIMMY 4WD—V6—Truck Equipment Schedule T1						
Sport Utility 2D	T18W	22631	900	1250	2375	4050
Sport Utility 4D	T13W	24631	1250	1725	2950	4725
2WD	S	------	(250)	(250)	(335)	(335)
TAHOE/YUKON 4WD—V6—Truck Equipment Schedule T1						
Sport Utility 2D	K18R	27642	1425	1875	3150	4975
Sport Utility 4D	K13R	32125	2300	2900	4225	6225
2WD	C	------	(400)	(400)	(535)	(535)
V8 6.5L Turbo Diesel	S	------	375	375	500	500
SUBURBAN—V8—Truck Equipment Schedule T1						
C1500 Sport Utility	C16R	27350	1900	2450	3750	5650
C2500 Sport Utility	C26R	28583	2025	2600	3900	5850
w/o Third Seat		------	(275)	(275)	(365)	(365)
4WD	K	------	700	700	935	935
V8 454/7.4 Liter	J	------	200	200	265	265
V8 6.5L Turbo Diesel	F	------	375	375	500	500
VENTURE—V6—Truck Equipment Schedule T1						
Minivan	U03E	20495	475	650	1375	2525
Extended Minivan	X06E	21660	675	950	1850	3250

Body Type	VIN	List	Trade-In Fair	Good	Pvt-Party Good	Retail Excellent
w/o 2nd Sliding Door			(50)	(50)	(65)	(65)
ASTRO/SAFARI—V6—Truck Equipment Schedule T2						
Cargo/SL Cargo	M19W	19583	625	850	1700	3050
Dutch Doors			100	100	135	135
AWD	L		350	350	465	465
ASTRO/SAFARI—V6—Truck Equipment Schedule T1						
Base/SLX Minivan	M19W	20167	850	1175	2150	3675
5 Passenger			(275)	(275)	(365)	(365)
Dutch Doors			100	100	135	135
AWD	L		350	350	465	465
EXPRESS/SAVANA—V8—Truck Equipment Schedule T1						
1500 Passenger Van	G15M	23380	1125	1575	2750	4475
2500 Passenger Van	G25R	25411	1175	1650	2875	4600
3500 Passenger Van	G35R	25571	1250	1725	2925	4675
5 Passenger			(275)	(275)	(365)	(365)
155" W.B.	9		100	100	135	135
V6 4.3 Liter	W		(275)	(275)	(365)	(365)
V8 454/7.4 Liter	J		150	150	200	200
V8 6.5L Turbo Diesel	F		150	150	200	200
G-SERIES/SAVANA—V6—Truck Equipment Schedule T1						
1500 Cargo Van	G15W	20662	1050	1475	2625	4300
2500 Cargo Van	G25W	21087	1100	1550	2700	4400
3500 Cargo Van	G35R	22467	1125	1600	2775	4500
155" W.B.	9		100	100	135	135
V8 5.0, 5.7 Liter	M,R		150	150	200	200
V8 454/7.4 Liter	J		275	275	365	365
V8 6.5L Turbo Diesel	F		250	250	335	335
S10/SONOMA PICKUP—4-Cyl.—Truck Equipment Schedule T2						
Short Bed	S144	12008	625	850	1725	3075
Long Bed	S144	12308	500	675	1500	2750
Extended Cab	S194	14863	925	1300	2400	4075
Third Door			175	175	235	235
4WD	T		650	650	865	865
V6 4.3 Liter	W		225	225	300	300
V6 4.3L High Output	X		275	275	365	365
REGULAR CAB PICKUP—V8—Truck Equipment Schedule T1						
1500 Short Bed	C14M	18837	1875	2425	3725	5625
1500 Long Bed	C14M	19137	1775	2275	3575	5475
2500 Long Bed	C24M	19819	1800	2300	3600	5500
3500 Long Bed	C34R	20807	1875	2425	3725	5625
Work Truck/Special			(350)	(350)	(465)	(465)
4WD	K		700	700	935	935
V6 4.3 Liter	W		(400)	(400)	(535)	(535)
V8 5.7 Liter	R		175	175	235	235
V8 454/7.4 Liter	J		200	200	265	265
V8 6.5L Turbo Diesel	F,S		375	375	500	500
EXTENDED CAB PICKUP—V8—Truck Equipment Schedule T1						
1500 Short Bed	C19M	20917	2450	3050	4400	6450
1500 Long Bed	C19M	21417	2325	2900	4250	6250
2500 Short Bed	C29M	22435	2800	3425	4825	6925
2500 HD Long Bed	C29M	22272	2725	3325	4725	6800
3500 Long Bed	C39R	24229	2600	3200	4575	6675
Third Door			150	150	200	200
4WD	K		700	700	935	935
V6 4.3 Liter	W		(400)	(400)	(535)	(535)
V8 5.7 Liter	R		175	175	235	235
V8 454/7.4 Liter	J		200	200	265	265
V8 6.5L Turbo Diesel	F,S		375	375	500	500
CREW CAB PICKUP—V8—Truck Equipment Schedule T1						
3500 Long Bed	C33R	23937	3325	4025	5475	7700
4WD	K		700	700	935	935
V8 454/7.4 Liter	J		200	200	265	265
V8 6.5L Turbo Diesel	F		375	375	500	500

1998 CHEVY/GMC—1G(C,K,NorT)—J186—W—#

Body Type	VIN	List	Trade-In Fair	Good	Pvt-Party Good	Retail Excellent
TRACKER 4WD—4-Cyl.—Truck Equipment Schedule T2						
Sport Util Conv 2D	J186	15301	400	575	1250	2350
Sport Utility 4D	J136	16251	750	1075	2025	3500
2WD	E		(300)	(300)	(400)	(400)
BLAZER/JIMMY 4WD—V6—Truck Equipment Schedule T1						
Sport Utility 2D	T18W	24166	1000	1400	2575	4300
Sport Utility 4D	T13W	25691	1450	1925	3200	5050
2WD	S		(300)	(300)	(400)	(400)

TRUCKS & VANS

Body	Type	VIN	List	Trade-In Fair	Trade-In Good	Pvt-Party Good	Retail Excellent
ENVOY 4WD—V6—Truck Equipment Schedule T3							
Sport Utility 4D		K13W	34650	2275	2875	4200	6200
TAHOE/YUKON 4WD—V8—Truck Equipment Schedule T1							
Sport Utility 2D		K18R	27670	1675	2175	3450	5350
Sport Utility 4D		K13R	32625	2675	3275	4650	6750
2WD		C	------	(425)	(425)	(565)	(565)
V8 6.5L Turbo Diesel		S	------	425	425	565	565
SUBURBAN—V8—Truck Equipment Schedule T1							
C1500 Sport Utility		C16R	27767	2250	2825	4175	6150
C2500 Sport Utility		C26R	29351	2375	2975	4300	6350
w/o Third Seat			------	(300)	(300)	(400)	(400)
4WD		K	------	800	800	1065	1065
V8 454/7.4 Liter		J	------	225	225	300	300
V8 6.5L Turbo Diesel		F	------	425	425	565	565
VENTURE—V6—Truck Equipment Schedule T2							
Cargo Minivan		G05E	21329	425	600	1275	2400
w/o 2nd Sliding Door			------	(50)	(50)	(65)	(65)
VENTURE—V6—Truck Equipment Schedule T1							
Minivan		U05E	21999	550	750	1575	2875
Extended Minivan		X09E	22829	775	1100	2050	3550
w/o 2nd Sliding Door			------	(50)	(50)	(65)	(65)
ASTRO/SAFARI—V6—Truck Equipment Schedule T2							
Cargo/SL Cargo		M19W	19925	650	925	1825	3200
Dutch Doors			------	100	100	135	135
AWD		L	------	400	400	535	535
ASTRO/SAFARI—V6—Truck Equipment Schedule T1							
Base/SLX Minivan		M19W	21628	925	1300	2400	4075
5 Passenger			------	(300)	(300)	(400)	(400)
Dutch Doors			------	100	100	135	135
AWD		L	------	400	400	535	535
EXPRESS/SAVANA—V8—Truck Equipment Schedule T1							
1500 Passenger Van		G15M	23871	1375	1850	3075	4900
2500 Passenger Van		G25R	25876	1475	1950	3200	5050
3500 Passenger Van		G35R	26165	1550	2025	3275	5125
5 Passenger			------	(300)	(300)	(400)	(400)
155" W.B.		9	------	100	100	135	135
V6 4.3 Liter		W	------	(300)	(300)	(400)	(400)
V8 454/7.4 Liter		J	------	175	175	235	235
V8 6.5L Turbo Diesel		F	------	175	175	235	235
G-SERIES/SAVANA—V6—Truck Equipment Schedule T1							
1500 Cargo Van		G15W	21102	1175	1650	2850	4600
2500 Cargo Van		G25W	21527	1225	1700	2950	4700
3500 Cargo Van		G35R	23061	1300	1775	3025	4800
155" W.B.		9	------	100	100	135	135
V8 5.0, 5.7 Liter		M,R	------	175	175	235	235
V8 454/7.4 Liter		J	------	300	300	400	400
V8 6.5L Turbo Diesel		F	------	300	300	400	400
S10/SONOMA PICKUP—4-Cyl.—Truck Equipment Schedule T2							
Short Bed		S144	12508	725	1025	1975	3475
Long Bed		S144	13172	600	825	1700	3075
Extended Cab		S194	15740	1075	1500	2675	4400
Third Door			------	200	200	265	265
4WD		T	------	775	775	1035	1035
V6 4.3 Liter		X	------	250	250	335	335
V6 4.3L High Output		W	------	300	300	400	400
REGULAR CAB PICKUP—V8—Truck Equipment Schedule T1							
1500 Short Bed		C14M	19250	1975	2525	3825	5750
1500 Long Bed		C14M	19550	1850	2350	3650	5550
2500 Long Bed		C24M	20232	1950	2500	3800	5725
3500 Long Bed		C34R	21419	2075	2625	3950	5875
Work Truck/Special			------	(400)	(400)	(535)	(535)
4WD		K	------	800	800	1065	1065
V6 4.3 Liter		W	------	(425)	(425)	(565)	(565)
V8 5.7 Liter		R	------	200	200	265	265
V8 454/7.4 Liter		J	------	225	225	300	300
V8 6.5L Turbo Diesel		F,S	------	425	425	565	565
EXTENDED CAB PICKUP—V8—Truck Equipment Schedule T1							
1500 Short Bed		C19M	21250	2700	3300	4675	6750
1500 Long Bed		C19M	22045	2525	3125	4475	6525
2500 Short Bed		C29M	22848	3075	3725	5150	7300
2500 HD Long Bed		C29M	22884	2975	3625	5025	7150
3500 Long Bed		C39R	24842	2875	3500	4900	7000
Third Door			------	175	175	235	235

1998 CHEVROLET/GMC

Body	Type	VIN	List	Trade-In Fair	Trade-In Good	Pvt-Party Good	Retail Excellent
4WD		K		800	800	1065	1065
V6 4.3 Liter		W		(425)	(425)	(565)	(565)
V8 5.7 Liter		R		200	200	265	265
V8 454/7.4 Liter		J		225	225	300	300
V8 6.5L Turbo Diesel		F,S		425	425	565	565
CREW CAB PICKUP—V8—Truck Equipment Schedule T1							
3500 Long Bed		C33R	24549	3700	4400	5875	8150
4WD		K		800	800	1065	1065
V8 454/7.4 Liter		J		225	225	300	300
V8 6.5L Turbo Diesel		F		425	425	565	565

1999 CHEVY/GMC–(1,2or3)(CorG)(A,CorN)–J186–X

Body	Type	VIN	List	Trade-In Fair	Trade-In Good	Pvt-Party Good	Retail Excellent
TRACKER 4WD—4-Cyl.—Truck Equipment Schedule T2							
Sport Util Conv 2D		J186	12995	525	700	1525	2825
Sport Utility 4D		J136	16295	900	1275	2400	4075
2WD		E		(350)	(350)	(465)	(465)
BLAZER/JIMMY 4WD—V6—Truck Equipment Schedule T1							
Sport Utility 2D		T18W	22995	1125	1600	2825	4575
Sport Utility 4D		T13W	25945	1725	2225	3525	5425
2WD		S		(350)	(350)	(465)	(465)
ENVOY 4WD—V6—Truck Equipment Schedule T3							
Sport Utility 4D		K13W	34125	2675	3300	4650	6725
TAHOE/YUKON 4WD—V8—Truck Equipment Schedule T1							
Sport Utility 2D		K18R	27995	1950	2500	3825	5750
Sport Utility 4D		K13R	32950	3075	3700	5125	7275
2WD		C		(450)	(450)	(600)	(600)
V8 6.5L Turbo Diesel		F		475	475	635	635
YUKON DENALI 4WD—V8—Truck Equipment Schedule T3							
Sport Utility 4D		K13R	43505	4325	5125	6700	9150
SUBURBAN—V8—Truck Equipment Schedule T1							
C1500 Sport Utility		C16R	28267	2625	3200	4600	6675
C2500 Sport Utility		C26R	29851	2725	3325	4725	6825
w/o Third Seat				(325)	(325)	(435)	(435)
4WD		K		900	900	1200	1200
V8 454/7.4 Liter		J		250	250	335	335
V8 6.5L Turbo Diesel		F		475	475	635	635
VENTURE—V6—Truck Equipment Schedule T2							
Cargo Minivan 4D		G05E	22025	525	700	1475	2700
VENTURE—V6—Truck Equipment Schedule T1							
Minivan 4D		U05E	22625	650	925	1850	3250
Extended Minivan		X09E	23625	925	1300	2425	4100
w/o 2nd Sliding Door				(50)	(50)	(65)	(65)
ASTRO/SAFARI—V6—Truck Equipment Schedule T2							
Cargo/SL Cargo		M19W	20268	725	1025	1975	3475
Dutch Doors				100	100	135	135
AWD		L		450	450	600	600
ASTRO/SAFARI—V6—Truck Equipment Schedule T1							
Minivan/SL Minivan		M19W	21547	1025	1450	2600	4300
Dutch Doors				100	100	135	135
AWD		L		450	450	600	600
EXPRESS/SAVANA—V8—Truck Equipment Schedule T1							
1500 Passenger Van		G15M	24100	1700	2200	3475	5350
2500 Passenger Van		G25R	26105	1800	2325	3600	5500
3500 Passenger Van		G35R	26394	1875	2425	3700	5600
5 Passenger				(325)	(325)	(435)	(435)
155" W.B.		9		100	100	135	135
V6 4.3 Liter		W		(325)	(325)	(435)	(435)
V8 454/7.4 Liter		J		200	200	265	265
V8 6.5L Turbo Diesel		F,S		200	200	265	265
EXPRESS/SAVANA—V6—Truck Equipment Schedule T1							
1500 Cargo Van		G15W	21505	1400	1875	3125	4975
2500 Cargo Van		G25W	21955	1475	1950	3200	5050
3500 Cargo Van		G35R	23489	1525	2025	3300	5150
155" W.B.		9		100	100	135	135
V8 5.0, 5.7 Liter		M,R		200	200	265	265
V8 454/7.4 Liter		J		325	325	435	435
V8 6.5L Turbo Diesel		F,S		325	325	435	435
S10/SONOMA PICKUP—4-Cyl.—Truck Equipment Schedule T2							
Short Bed		S144	12658	875	1250	2375	4075
Long Bed		S144	13322	725	1025	2000	3500
Extended Cab		S194	15890	1275	1750	3000	4775
Third Door				200	200	265	265
4WD		T		900	900	1200	1200

1999 CHEVROLET/GMC

Body	Type	VIN	List	Trade-In Fair	Trade-In Good	Pvt-Party Good	Retail Excellent
	V6 4.3 Liter	X		275	275	365	365
	V6 4.3L High Output	W		325	325	435	435
SILVERADO/SIERRA REGULAR CAB—V8 (New)—Truck Sch T1							
1500	Short Bed	C14V	18390	2725	3325	4725	6800
1500	Long Bed	C14V	18690	2525	3100	4475	6550
2500	Long Bed	C24T	21601	2850	3475	4875	7000
2500 HD	Long Bed	C24T	22445	3175	3850	5275	7475
	4WD	K		900	900	1200	1200
	V6 4.3 Liter	W		(450)	(450)	(600)	(600)
	V8 5.3 Liter	T		225	225	300	300
	V8 6.0 Liter	U		250	250	335	335
	V8 6.5L Turbo Diesel	F,S		475	475	635	635
SILVERADO/SIERRA EXTENDED CAB—V8 (New)—Truck Sch T1							
1500	Short Bed	C19V	22635	3925	4650	6150	8475
1500	Long Bed	C19V	22935	3650	4350	5825	8100
2500	Short Bed	C29T	24051	4350	5150	6675	9075
2500 HD	Short Bed	K29T	27995	4625	5450	7050	9575
2500 HD	Long Bed	C29T	25195	4225	5000	6525	8900
	4WD	K		900	900	1200	1200
	V6 4.3 Liter	W		(450)	(450)	(600)	(600)
	V8 5.3 Liter	T		225	225	300	300
	V8 6.0 Liter	U		250	250	335	335
	V8 6.5L Turbo Diesel	F,S		475	475	635	635
REGULAR CAB PICKUP—V8—Truck Equipment Schedule T1							
2500 HD	Long Bed	C24R	21558	2350	2950	4300	6300
3500	Long Bed	C34R	21856	2275	2850	4200	6175
	4WD	K		900	900	1200	1200
	V8 454/7.4 Liter	J		250	250	335	335
	V8 6.5L Turbo Diesel	F,S		475	475	635	635
EXTENDED CAB PICKUP—V8—Truck Equipment Schedule T1							
1500	Short Bed	C19M	23366	2925	3550	4950	7075
2500 HD	Short Bed	K29M	26268	3550	4250	5675	7950
2500 HD	Long Bed	C29M	23162	3250	3950	5375	7550
3500	Long Bed	C39R	25282	3150	3825	5225	7400
	4WD	K		900	900	1200	1200
	V8 5.7 Liter	R		225	225	300	300
	V8 454/7.4 Liter	J		250	250	335	335
	V8 6.5L Turbo Diesel	F,S		475	475	635	635
CREW CAB PICKUP—V8—Truck Equipment Schedule T1							
2500	Short Bed	C23R	24547	3575	4275	5700	7975
3500	Short Bed	C33J	26466	4275	5050	6550	8925
3500	Long Bed	C33R	24986	4075	4825	6325	8650
	4WD	K		900	900	1200	1200
	V8 454/7.4 Liter	J		250	250	335	335
	V8 6.5L Turbo Diesel	F,S		475	475	635	635

2000 CHEVY/GMC—(1,2or3)(CorG)(1,CorN)—J186—Y

Body	Type	VIN	List	Trade-In Fair	Trade-In Good	Pvt-Party Good	Retail Excellent
TRACKER 4WD—4-Cyl.—Truck Equipment Schedule T2							
Sport Util Conv 2D		J186	15425	650	925	1850	3325
Sport Utility 4D		J13C	16650	1100	1550	2750	4475
2WD		E		(400)	(400)	(535)	(535)
BLAZER/JIMMY 4WD—V6—Truck Equipment Schedule T1							
Sport Utility 2D		T18W	23495	1375	1850	3125	4975
Sport Utility 4D		T13W	26995	2025	2600	3925	5875
2WD		S		(400)	(400)	(535)	(535)
ENVOY 4WD—V6—Truck Equipment Schedule T3							
Sport Utility 4D		T13W	34695	3100	3775	5200	7350
TAHOE 4WD—V8 4.8L Engine (New)—Truck Equipment Schedule T1							
Sport Utility 4D		K13V	29441	3500	4225	5650	7925
w/o Third Seat				(350)	(350)	(465)	(465)
2WD		C		(475)	(475)	(635)	(635)
V8 5.3 Liter		T		250	250	335	335
TAHOE 4WD—V8 5.7L Engine—Truck Equipment Schedule T1							
Sport Utility 4D		K13R	39544	3000	3625	5050	7200
2WD		C		(475)	(475)	(635)	(635)
YUKON 4WD—V8 (New)—Truck Equipment Schedule T1							
SLE Sport Utility 4D		K13V	35835	3600	4300	5750	8000
w/o Third Seat				(350)	(350)	(465)	(465)
2WD		C		(475)	(475)	(635)	(635)
V8 5.3 Liter		T		250	250	335	335
YUKON DENALI 4WD—V8—Truck Equipment Schedule T3							
Sport Utility 4D		K13R	44185	4875	5700	7350	9950

2000 CHEVROLET/GMC

Body Type	VIN	List	Trade-In Fair	Trade-In Good	Pvt-Party Good	Retail Excellent
SUBURBAN—V8—Truck Equipment Schedule T1						
C1500 Sport Utility	C16T	27651	3025	3650	5075	7225
C2500 Sport Utility	C26U	29535	3125	3800	5225	7400
w/o Third Seat			(350)	(350)	(465)	(465)
4WD	K		1000	1000	1335	1335
YUKON XL—V8—Truck Equipment Schedule T1						
1500 Sport Utility	C13T	35178	3075	3750	5175	7325
2500 Sport Utility	C23U	36696	3250	3925	5350	7525
w/o Third Seat			(350)	(350)	(465)	(465)
4WD	K		1000	1000	1335	1335
VENTURE—V6—Truck Equipment Schedule T2						
Cargo Minivan 4D	U05E	22330	625	875	1800	3200
VENTURE—V6—Truck Equipment Schedule T1						
Minivan 4D	U05E	21230	800	1125	2150	3725
Extended Minivan	X09EA	24930	1100	1525	2725	4450
ASTRO/SAFARI—V6—Truck Equipment Schedule T2						
Cargo/SL Cargo	M19W	20635	850	1200	2325	4025
Dutch Doors			100	100	135	135
AWD	L		500	500	665	665
ASTRO/SAFARI—V6—Truck Equipment Schedule T1						
Minivan/SL Minivan	M19W	21982	1175	1650	2875	4625
Dutch Doors			100	100	135	135
AWD	L		500	500	665	665
EXPRESS/SAVANA—V8—Truck Equipment Schedule T1						
1500 Passenger Van	G15M	24240	2075	2650	3950	5875
2500 Passenger Van	G25R	26245	2175	2750	4075	6025
3500 Passenger Van	G35R	26534	2300	2875	4200	6175
5 Passenger	9		(350)	(350)	(465)	(465)
155" W.B.			100	100	135	135
V6 4.3 Liter	W		(350)	(350)	(465)	(465)
V8 454/7.4 Liter	J		200	200	265	265
V8 6.5L Turbo Diesel	F		225	225	300	300
EXPRESS/SAVANA—V6—Truck Equipment Schedule T1						
1500 Cargo Van	G15W	21910	1675	2175	3475	5375
2500 Cargo Van	G25W	22360	1750	2250	3550	5450
3500 Cargo Van	G35R	23894	1825	2325	3625	5525
155" W.B.			100	100	135	135
V8 5.0, 5.7 Liter	M,R		200	200	265	265
V8 454/7.4 Liter	J		350	350	465	465
V8 6.5L Turbo Diesel	F		350	350	465	465
S10/SONOMA PICKUP—4-Cyl.—Truck Equipment Schedule T2						
Short Bed	S144	12610	1075	1525	2725	4475
Long Bed	S144	12661	925	1300	2475	4200
Extended Cab	S194	15309	1600	2075	3375	5250
Third Door			200	200	265	265
4WD	T		1025	1025	1365	1365
V6 4.3 Liter	W		350	350	465	465
SILVERADO/SIERRA REGULAR CAB—V8 (New)—Truck Schedule T1						
1500 Short Bed	C14V	18510	3050	3700	5125	7275
1500 Long Bed	C14V	18810	2825	3450	4875	7000
2500 Long Bed	C24T	21950	3200	3875	5325	7525
2500 HD Long Bed	C24T	23074	3550	4275	5725	7975
4WD	K		1000	1000	1335	1335
V6 4.3 Liter	W		(450)	(450)	(600)	(600)
V8 5.3 Liter	T		250	250	335	335
V8 6.0 Liter	U		275	275	365	365
SILVERADO/SIERRA EXTENDED CAB—V8 (New)—Truck Schedule T1						
1500 Short Bed	C19V	22884	4350	5150	6675	9075
1500 Long Bed	C19V	23184	4100	4850	6350	8700
2500 Short Bed	C29T	24400	4800	5625	7225	9775
2500 HD Short Bed	C29T	28324	5125	5975	7600	10200
2500 HD Long Bed	C29T	25524	4950	5775	7400	9950
4WD	K		1000	1000	1335	1335
Fourth Door			200	200	265	265
V6 4.3 Liter	W		(450)	(450)	(600)	(600)
V8 5.3 Liter	T		250	250	335	335
V8 6.0 Liter	U		275	275	365	365
REGULAR CAB PICKUP—V8—Truck Equipment Schedule T1						
2500 HD Long Bed	C24R	21837	2625	3225	4600	6675
3500 Long Bed	C34R	22435	2500	3100	4475	6525
4WD	K		1000	1000	1335	1335
V8 454/7.4 Liter	J		275	275	365	365
V8 6.5L Turbo Diesel	F		525	525	700	700

Body Type	VIN	List	Trade-In Fair	Good	Pvt-Party Good	Retail Excellent
EXTENDED CAB PICKUP—V8—Truck Equipment Schedule T1						
2500 HD Short Bed	K29R	26547	3925	4650	6125	8425
2500 HD Long Bed	C29R	23441	3550	4275	5700	7975
3500 Long Bed	C39R	25861	3450	4150	5575	7825
4WD	K		1000	1000	1335	1335
V8 454/7.4 Liter	J		275	275	365	365
V8 6.5L Turbo Diesel	F		525	525	700	700
CREW CAB PICKUP—V8—Truck Equipment Schedule T1						
2500 Short Bed	C23R	24826	3925	4650	6125	8425
3500 Short Bed	C33R	27045	4675	5500	7075	9575
3500 Long Bed	C33R	25565	4475	5275	6775	9200
4WD	K		1000	1000	1335	1335
V8 454/7.4 Liter	J		275	275	365	365
V8 6.5L Turbo Diesel	F		525	525	700	700

2001 CHEVY/GMC–(1,2or3)(CorG)(A,CorN)–J186–1

Body Type	VIN	List	Trade-In Fair	Good	Pvt-Party Good	Retail Excellent
TRACKER 4WD—4-Cyl.—Truck Equipment Schedule T2						
Sport Util Conv 2D	J186	16760	875	1250	2400	4125
Sport Utility 4D	J13C	17380	1400	1875	3150	5000
ZR2 Spt Utl Conv 2D	J78C	18835	1175	1650	2900	4675
ZR2 Sport Utility 4D	J734	19250	1950	2500	3825	5725
LT Sport Utility 4D	J634	21880	2375	2975	4300	6275
2WD	E		(450)	(450)	(600)	(600)
V6 2.5 Liter	4		375	375	500	500
BLAZER/JIMMY 4WD—V6—Truck Equipment Schedule T1						
Sport Utility 2D	T18W	23745	1700	2200	3500	5425
Sport Utility 4D	T13W	27345	2425	3025	4350	6400
2WD	S		(450)	(450)	(600)	(600)
TAHOE 4WD—V8—Truck Equipment Schedule T1						
Sport Utility 4D	K13V	31021	4050	4775	6275	8625
w/o Third Seat	C		(375)	(375)	(500)	(500)
2WD	C		(500)	(500)	(665)	(665)
V8 5.3 Liter	T		275	275	365	365
YUKON 4WD—V8—Truck Equipment Schedule T1						
SLE Sport Utility 4D	K13T	36128	4125	4875	6375	8725
w/o Third Seat	C		(375)	(375)	(500)	(500)
2WD	C		(500)	(500)	(665)	(665)
V8 5.3 Liter	T,Z		275	275	365	365
YUKON DENALI AWD—V8—Truck Equipment Schedule T3						
Sport Utility 4D	K13U	46680	5100	5950	7600	10250
SUBURBAN—V8—Truck Equipment Schedule T1						
C1500 Sport Utility	C16T	29428	3475	4175	5600	7875
C2500 Sport Utility	C26U	31287	3600	4300	5775	8025
w/o Third Seat			(375)	(375)	(500)	(500)
4WD	K		1100	1100	1465	1465
V8 8.1 Liter	G		275	275	365	365
YUKON XL—V8—Truck Equipment Schedule T1						
1500 Sport Utility	C13T	36287	3550	4275	5700	7975
2500 Sport Utility	C23U	37659	3725	4450	5900	8175
4WD	K		1100	1100	1465	1465
V8 8.1 Liter	G		275	275	365	365
YUKON XL DENALI AWD—V8—Truck Equipment Schedule T3						
1500 Sport Utility 4D	K16U	48185	6300	7275	9000	11800
VENTURE—V6—Truck Equipment Schedule T1						
Minivan 4D	U05E	21605	1000	1425	2625	4350
Extended Minivan	X09E	26085	1350	1825	3075	4900
ASTRO/SAFARI—V6—Truck Equipment Schedule T2						
Cargo/SL Cargo	M19W	21238	1025	1450	2650	4375
Dutch Doors			100	100	135	135
AWD	L		525	525	700	700
ASTRO/SAFARI—V6—Truck Equipment Schedule T1						
Minivan 3D	M19W	23886	1450	1925	3200	5050
Dutch Doors			100	100	135	135
AWD	L		525	525	700	700
EXPRESS/SAVANA VAN—V8—Truck Equipment Schedule T1						
1500 Passenger Van	G15M	24730	2550	3150	4500	6550
2500 Passenger Van	G25R	26735	2650	3250	4625	6700
3500 Passenger Van	G35R	27024	2800	3400	4775	6850
155" W.B.			100	100	135	135
V6 4.3 Liter	W		(375)	(375)	(500)	(500)
V8 8.1 Liter	G		200	200	265	265
V8 6.5L Turbo Diesel	F		250	250	335	335

Body Type	VIN	List	Trade-In Fair	Trade-In Good	Pvt-Party Good	Retail Excellent
EXPRESS/SAVANA VAN—V8—Truck Equipment Schedule T1						
1500 Cargo Van	G15W	22520	2025	2575	3900	5825
2500 Cargo Van	G25W	22650	2075	2650	3950	5900
3500 Cargo Van	G35R	24929	2150	2725	4050	6000
155" W.B.			100	100	135	135
V6 4.3 Liter	W		(200)	(200)	(265)	(265)
V8 8.1 Liter	G		375	375	500	500
V8 6.5L Turbo Diesel	F		375	375	500	500
S10/SONOMA PICKUP—4-Cyl. Flex Fuel—Truck Equip Schedule T2						
Short Bed	S145	12859	1350	1850	3100	4950
Long Bed	S145	13210	1150	1625	2875	4675
Extended Cab	S195	16203	1950	2500	3825	5750
Third Door			200	200	265	265
4WD	T		1150	1150	1535	1535
V6 4.3 Liter	W		375	375	500	500
S10/SONOMA CREW CAB 4WD—V6—Truck Equip Schedule T1						
LS/SLS Short Bed	T13W	23569	3575	4300	5700	7925
SILVERADO/SIERRA REGULAR CAB—V8—Truck Equip Schedule T1						
1500 Short Bed	C14V	19145	3400	4100	5525	7750
1500 Long Bed	C14V	19485	3150	3825	5250	7425
2500 Long Bed	C24U	23689	3600	4300	5750	8000
2500 HD Long Bed	C24U	24109	3975	4700	6175	8500
3500 Long Bed	C34U	25361	4000	4750	6225	8550
4WD	K		1100	1100	1465	1465
V6 4.3 Liter	W		(450)	(450)	(600)	(600)
V8 5.3 Liter	T		275	275	365	365
V8 8.1 Liter	G		275	275	365	365
V8 6.6L Turbo Diesel	1		4100	4100	5465	5465
SILVERADO/SIERRA EXTENDED CAB—V8—Truck Equip Schedule T1						
1500 Short Bed	C19V	23589	4825	5625	7225	9750
1500 Long Bed	C19V	23889	4525	5350	6825	9250
2500 Short Bed	K29U	29039	5300	6175	7800	10400
2500 HD Short Bed	C29U	26614	5600	6525	8125	10800
2500 HD Long Bed	C29U	26859	5450	6350	7975	10600
3500 Long Bed	C39U	28141	5575	6500	8100	10750
4WD	K		1100	1100	1465	1465
V6 4.3 Liter	W		(450)	(450)	(600)	(600)
V8 5.3 Liter	T		275	275	365	365
V8 8.1 Liter	G		275	275	365	365
V8 6.6L Turbo Diesel	1		4100	4100	5465	5465
SIERRA EXTENDED CAB PICKUP AWD—V8—Truck Equip Schedule T1						
1500 C3 Short Bed	C19U	38995	8075	9250	11100	14250
SILVERADO/SIERRA CREW CAB—V8—Truck Equipment Schedule T1						
1500 HD Short Bed	C13U	28912	5575	6500	8100	10750
2500 HD Short Bed	C23U	27984	5925	6850	8525	11200
2500 HD Long Bed	C23U	28284	5825	6775	8400	11050
3500 Long Bed	C33U	30766	6000	6925	8600	11300
4WD	K		1100	1100	1465	1465
V8 8.1 Liter	G		275	275	365	365
V8 6.6L Turbo Diesel	1		4100	4100	5465	5465

2002 CHEVY/GMC—1,2or3(CorG)A,CorN—(J18C)—2

Body Type	VIN	List	Trade-In Fair	Trade-In Good	Pvt-Party Good	Retail Excellent
TRACKER 4WD—4-Cyl.—Truck Equipment Schedule T2						
Sport Util Conv 2D	J18C	17415	1025	1425	2900	4950
Sport Utility 4D	J13C	18105	1650	2150	3700	5850
ZR2 Spt Utl Conv 2D	J78C	19395	1400	1850	3375	5525
ZR2 Sport Utility 4D	J734	21845	2250	2850	4375	6650
LT Sport Utility 4D	J634	22270	2675	3275	4875	7200
2WD	E		(500)	(500)	(665)	(665)
V6 2.5 Liter	4		400	400	535	535
BLAZER 4WD—V6—Truck Equipment Schedule T1						
Sport Utility 2D	T18W	23895	1925	2475	4050	6300
Sport Utility 4D	T13W	26130	2700	3300	4950	7325
2WD	S		(500)	(500)	(665)	(665)
TRAILBLAZER 4WD—6-Cyl.—Truck Equipment Schedule T1						
Sport Utility 4D	T1S3	28130	3025	3650	5300	7725
Extended Spt Util 4D	T16S	33610	3600	4300	6000	8500
2WD	S		(500)	(500)	(665)	(665)
ENVOY 4WD—6-Cyl.—Truck Equipment Schedule T1						
Sport Utility 4D	T13S	31770	3800	4500	6200	8750
2WD	S		(500)	(500)	(665)	(665)
ENVOY XL 4WD—6-Cyl.—Truck Equipment Schedule T1						
Sport Utility 4D	T16S	33820	3600	4300	6000	8500

TRUCKS & VANS

Body	Type	VIN	List	Trade-In Fair	Good	Pvt-Party Good	Retail Excellent
2WD 4WD		S		(500)	(500)	(665)	(665)
TAHOE 4WD—V8—Truck Equipment Schedule T1							
Sport Utility 4D		K13V	36345	4425	5225	6950	9600
w/o Third Seat				(400)	(400)	(535)	(535)
2WD		C		(500)	(500)	(665)	(665)
V8 5.3 Liter		T,Z		300	300	400	400
YUKON 4WD—V8—Truck Equipment Schedule T1							
Sport Utility 4D		K13V	37000	4475	5300	7075	9800
w/o Third Seat				(400)	(400)	(535)	(535)
2WD		C		(500)	(500)	(665)	(665)
V8 5.3 Liter		T,Z		300	300	400	400
YUKON DENALI 4WD—V8—Truck Equipment Schedule T3							
Sport Utility 4D		K13U	47355	5500	6400	8300	11250
SUBURBAN—Truck Equipment Schedule T1							
C1500 Sport Utility		C16T	35988	3825	4525	6250	8825
C2500 Sport Utility		C26U	37601	3950	4675	6400	9000
4WD		K		1200	1200	1600	1600
V8 8.1 Liter		G		300	300	400	400
YUKON XL—V8—Truck Equipment Schedule T1							
1500 Sport Utility		C13T	37047	3900	4625	6350	8925
2500 Sport Utility		C23U	38419	4075	4825	6550	9150
4WD		K		1200	1200	1600	1600
V8 8.1 Liter		G		300	300	400	400
YUKON XL DENALI AWD—V8—Truck Equipment Schedule T3							
1500 Sport Utility 4D		K16U	48890	7050	8100	10100	13300
VENTURE—V6—Truck Equipment Schedule T2							
Cargo Minivan 4D		U05E	24697	875	1250	2650	4650
VENTURE—V6—Truck Equipment Schedule T1							
Minivan 4D		U03E	22035	1125	1575	3075	5125
Extended Minivan 4D		X03E	26255	1550	2025	3550	5675
5 Passenger				(400)	(400)	(535)	(535)
AWD				550	550	735	735
ASTRO/SAFARI—V6—Truck Equipment Schedule T2							
Cargo/SL Cargo		M19W	21768	1125	1575	3075	5125
Dutch Doors				100	100	135	135
AWD		L		550	550	735	735
ASTRO/SAFARI—V6—Truck Equipment Schedule T1							
Minivan 3D		M19W	24416	1625	2125	3650	5775
Dutch Doors				100	100	135	135
AWD		L		550	550	735	735
EXPRESS/SAVANA VAN—V8—Truck Equipment Schedule T1							
1500 Passenger Van		G15M	25287	2950	3575	5200	7575
2500 Passenger Van		G25R	27292	3050	3700	5325	7725
3500 Passenger Van		G35R	27581	3175	3850	5500	7925
155" W.B.				100	100	135	135
V6 4.3 Liter		W		(400)	(400)	(535)	(535)
V8 8.1 Liter		G		200	200	265	265
V8 6.5L Turbo Diesel		F		250	250	335	335
EXPRESS/SAVANA VAN—V8—Truck Equipment Schedule T1							
1500 Cargo Van		G15W	22948	2275	2850	4400	6700
2500 Cargo Van		G25W	23078	2325	2925	4500	6775
3500 Cargo Van		G35R	25357	2400	3000	4575	6850
155" W.B.				100	100	135	135
V6 4.3 Liter		W		(200)	(200)	(265)	(265)
V8 8.1 Liter		G		400	400	535	535
V8 6.5L Turbo Diesel		F		400	400	535	535
S10/SONOMA PICKUP—4-Cyl. Flex Fuel—Truck Equipment Schedule T2							
Short Bed		S145	14327	1575	2075	3625	5775
Long Bed		S145	15772	1350	1850	3375	5525
Extended Cab		S195	16309	2225	2800	4350	6650
4WD		T		1250	1250	1665	1665
V6 4.3 Liter		W		400	400	535	535
S10/SONOMA CREW CAB PICKUP 4WD—V6—Truck Equipment Schedule T1							
LS/SLS Short Bed		T13W	24584	3950	4700	6375	8925
AVALANCHE 4WD—V8—Truck Equipment Schedule T1							
1500 Spt Util Pickup		C13T	33965	6175	7150	9175	12300
2500 Spt Util Pickup		C23G	35865	7325	8400	10500	13750
2WD				(500)	(500)	(665)	(665)
NorthFace Edition				600	600	800	800
SILVERADO/SIERRA REGULAR CAB—V8—Truck Equipment Schedule T1							
1500 Short Bed		C14V	20028	3550	4275	5950	8500
1500 Long Bed		C14V	20328	3300	3975	5650	8150
2500 Long Bed		C24U	24182	3775	4500	6225	8800

TRUCKS & VANS

Body	Type	VIN	List	Trade-In Fair	Trade-In Good	Pvt-Party Good	Retail Excellent
2500 HD Long Bed		C24U	24672	4175	4925	6675	9300
3500 Long Bed		C34U	29017	4225	4975	6725	9350
4WD		K		1200	1200	1600	1600
V6 4.3 Liter		W,X		(450)	(450)	(600)	(600)
V8 5.3 Liter		T		300	300	400	400
V8 8.1 Liter		G		300	300	400	400
V8 6.6L Turbo Diesel		1		4250	4250	5665	5665
SILVERADO/SIERRA EXTENDED CAB—V8—Truck Equipment Schedule T1							
1500 Short Bed		C19V	23952	5075	5925	7775	10600
1500 Long Bed		C19V	25052	4750	5575	7400	10200
2500 Short Bed		K29U	29407	5575	6500	8350	11250
2500 HD Short Bed		K29U	27177	5900	6825	8700	11650
2500 HD Long Bed		C29U	27452	5750	6700	8550	11450
3500 Long Bed		C39U	28734	5925	6875	8750	11700
Quadrasteer				525	525	700	700
4WD		K		1200	1200	1600	1600
V6 4.3 Liter		W,X		(450)	(450)	(600)	(600)
V8 5.3 Liter		T		300	300	400	400
V8 8.1 Liter		G		300	300	400	400
V8 6.6L Turbo Diesel		1		4250	4250	5665	5665
SIERRA DENALI EXT CAB PICKUP AWD—V8—Truck Equipment Schedule T3							
1500 Short Bed		K69U	44105	9525	10825	13000	16550
SILVERADO/SIERRA CREW CAB PICKUP—V8—Truck Equipment Schedule T1							
1500 Short Bed		C13U	29425	5900	6825	8700	11650
2500 HD Short Bed		C23U	28577	6225	7200	9100	12100
2500 HD Long Bed		C23U	28877	6150	7100	9000	12000
3500 Long Bed		C33U	30159	6325	7300	9200	12200
4WD		K		1200	1200	1600	1600
V8 8.1 Liter		G		300	300	400	400
V8 6.6L Turbo Diesel		1		4250	4250	5665	5665

2003 CHEV/GMC—1,2or3(CorG)A,CorN—(J18C)—3

Body	Type	VIN	List	Trade-In Fair	Trade-In Good	Pvt-Party Good	Retail Excellent
TRACKER 4WD—4-Cyl.—Truck Equipment Schedule T2							
Sport Util Conv 2D		J18C	17815	1400	1875	3425	5550
Sport Utility 4D		J13C	18505	2225	2800	4350	6625
ZR2 Spt Utl Conv 2D		J78C	19675	1900	2450	4000	6200
ZR2 Sport Utility 4D		J734	22125	2900	3525	5150	7500
LT Sport Utility 4D		J634	22550	3400	4100	5700	8125
2WD		E		(575)	(575)	(765)	(765)
V6 2.5 Liter		4		475	475	635	635
BLAZER 4WD—V6—Truck Equipment Schedule T1							
Sport Utility 2D		T18X	24705	2100	2675	4300	6575
Sport Utility 4D		T13X	26585	3025	3650	5325	7750
2WD		S		(575)	(575)	(765)	(765)
TRAILBLAZER 4WD—6-Cyl.—Truck Equipment Schedule T1							
Sport Utility 4D		T13S	28800	3625	4325	6000	8525
Extended Spt Util 4D		T16S	33510	4175	4925	6650	9200
2WD		S		(575)	(575)	(765)	(765)
V8 5.3 Liter		P		325	325	435	435
ENVOY 4WD—6-Cyl.—Truck Equipment Schedule T1							
Sport Utility 4D		T13S	30820	4425	5225	6975	9650
2WD		S		(575)	(575)	(765)	(765)
ENVOY XL 4WD—6-Cyl.—Truck Equipment Schedule T1							
Sport Utility 4D		T16S	33220	5000	5850	7625	10400
2WD		S		(575)	(575)	(765)	(765)
V8 5.3 Liter		P		325	325	435	435
TAHOE 4WD—V8—Truck Equipment Schedule T1							
Sport Utility 4D		K13V	37387	5575	6500	8300	11150
w/o Third Seat				(475)	(475)	(635)	(635)
2WD		C		(575)	(575)	(765)	(765)
V8 5.3 Liter		T,Z		325	325	435	435
YUKON 4WD—V8—Truck Equipment Schedule T1							
Sport Utility 4D		K13V	37920	5650	6575	8425	11300
w/o Third Seat				(475)	(475)	(635)	(635)
2WD		C		(575)	(575)	(765)	(765)
V8 5.3 Liter		T,Z		325	325	435	435
YUKON DENALI 4WD—V8—Truck Equipment Schedule T3							
Sport Utility 4D		K13U	49195	7550	8650	10700	13950
SUBURBAN—V8—Truck Equipment Schedule T1							
C1500 Sport Utility		C16T	37030	5125	5975	7800	10600
C2500 Sport Utility		C26U	38643	5350	6225	8025	10900
Quadrasteer				600	600	800	800
4WD		K		1375	1375	1835	1835

TRUCKS & VANS

Body	Type	VIN	List	Trade-In Fair	Trade-In Good	Pvt-Party Good	Retail Excellent
V8 8.1 Liter		G		350	350	465	465
YUKON XL—V8—Truck Equipment Schedule T1							
1500 Sport Utility		C13T	37967	5225	6100	7900	10700
2500 Sport Utility		C23U	39435	5450	6350	8125	11000
Quadrasteer				600	600	800	800
4WD		K		1375	1375	1835	1835
V8 8.1 Liter		G		350	350	465	465
YUKON XL DENALI AWD—V8—Truck Equipment Schedule T3							
1500 Sport Utility 4D		K16U	50859	8700	9900	12000	15500
VENTURE—V6—Truck Equipment Schedule T1							
Cargo Minivan 4D		U03E	22925	1125	1600	3075	5175
VENTURE—V6—Truck Equipment Schedule T2							
Minivan 4D		U03E	23139	1550	2050	3575	5725
Extended Minivan 4D		X03E	24509	2050	2600	4175	6375
5 Passenger				(475)	(475)	(635)	(635)
AWD		V		650	650	865	865
ASTRO/SAFARI—V6—Truck Equipment Schedule T2							
Cargo/SL Cargo 3D		M19X	21952	1200	1675	3175	5300
Dutch Doors				150	150	200	200
AWD		L		650	650	865	865
ASTRO/SAFARI—V6—Truck Equipment Schedule T1							
Minivan 3D		M19X	23801	1925	2475	4000	6200
Dutch Doors				150	150	200	200
AWD		L		650	650	865	865
EXPRESS/SAVANA VAN—V8—Truck Equipment Schedule T2							
1500 Passenger Van		G15X	27005	3700	4400	6050	8550
2500 Passenger Van		G25U	28000	3850	4575	6225	8750
3500 Passenger Van		G35U	28504	4025	4775	6450	8975
155" W.B.				150	150	200	200
AWD		H		650	650	865	865
V6 4.3 Liter		X		(475)	(475)	(635)	(635)
EXPRESS/SAVANA VAN—V8—Truck Equipment Schedule T1							
1500 Cargo Van		G15X	23265	2975	3600	5225	7600
2500 Cargo Van		G25X	23415	3050	3700	5325	7725
3500 Cargo Van		G35U	25969	3150	3825	5450	7850
155" W.B.				150	150	200	200
V6 4.3 Liter		X		(250)	(250)	(335)	(335)
V8 6.0 Liter		U		450	450	600	600
S10/SONOMA PICKUP—4-Cyl.—Truck Equipment Schedule T2							
Short Bed		S14H	14771	1975	2525	4125	6350
Long Bed		S14H	16216	1750	2275	3825	6025
Extended Cab		S19H	16593	2750	3350	4975	7325
4WD		T		1425	1425	1900	1900
V6 4.3 Liter		X		475	475	635	635
S10/SONOMA CREW CAB PICKUP 4WD—V6—Truck Equipment Schedule T1							
LS/SLS Short Bed		T13X	24404	5025	5875	7625	10350
SSR REGULAR CAB PICKUP—V8—Truck Equipment Schedule T3							
LS Convertible 2D		S14P	41995	13675	15425	17650	21800
AVALANCHE 4WD—V8—Truck Equipment Schedule T1							
1500 Spt Util Pickup		K13T	35139	7200	8275	10350	13600
2500 Spt Util Pickup		K23G	37039	8425	9625	11800	15350
2WD		C		(575)	(575)	(765)	(765)
North Face Edition				675	675	900	900
SILVERADO/SIERRA REGULAR CAB PICKUP—V8—Truck Equipment Sched T1							
1500 Short Bed		C14V	20726	4025	4750	6500	9100
1500 Long Bed		C14V	21026	3725	4425	6175	8750
2500 Long Bed		C24U	23627	4275	5050	6775	9425
2500 HD Long Bed		C24U	23877	4675	5525	7325	10100
3500 Long Bed		K34U	29317	4750	5575	7375	10150
Work Truck				(650)	(650)	(865)	(865)
4WD				1375	1375	1835	1835
V6 4.3 Liter		X		(525)	(525)	(700)	(700)
V8 5.3 Liter				325	325	435	435
V8 8.1 Liter		G		350	350	465	465
V8 6.6L Turbo Diesel		1		4475	4475	5965	5965
SILVERADO/SIERRA EXT CAB PICKUP—V8—Truck Equipment Schedule T1							
1500 Short Bed		C19V	24465	5750	6700	8525	11400
1500 Long Bed		C19V	25565	5400	6275	8100	11000
2500 Short Bed		K29U	29822	6300	7300	9175	12150
2500 HD Short Bed		K29U	26557	6825	7875	9775	12850
2500 HD Long Bed		C29U	26532	6725	7750	9625	12700
3500 Long Bed		C39U	28909	6875	7950	9800	12900
Quadrasteer				600	600	800	800

TRUCKS & VANS

Body	Type	VIN	List	Trade-In Fair	Trade-In Good	Pvt-Party Good	Retail Excellent
Work Truck				(650)	(650)	(865)	(865)
4WD	K			1375	1375	1835	1835
V6 4.3 Liter	X			(525)	(525)	(700)	(700)
V8 5.3 Liter	T			325	325	435	435
V8 8.1 Liter	G			350	350	465	465
V8 6.6L Turbo Diesel	1			4475	4475	5965	5965
SILVERADO SS EXT CAB PICKUP AWD—V8—Truck Equipment Schedule T3							
1500 Short Bed	K19U	39995	11125	12600	14700	18450
SIERRA DENALI EXT CAB PICKUP AWD—V8—Truck Equipment Schedule T3							
1500 Short Bed	K19U	44995	11025	12500	14600	18350
SILVERADO/SIERRA CREW CAB PICKUP—V8—Truck Equipment Schedule T1							
1500 HD Short Bed	C13U	30442	6700	7725	9625	12700
2500 HD Short Bed	C23U	29277	7500	8575	10500	13650
2500 HD Long Bed	C23U	29577	7400	8500	10450	13550
3500 Long Bed	C33U	30714	7575	8675	10600	13750
Quadrasteer				600	600	800	800
4WD	K			1375	1375	1835	1835
V8 8.1 Liter	G			350	350	465	465
V8 6.6L Turbo Diesel	1			4475	4475	5965	5965

Body	Type	VIN	List	Trade-In Fair	Trade-In Good	Pvt-Party Good	Retail Excellent
TRACKER 4WD—V6—Truck Equipment Schedule T2							
Sport Utility 4D	J134	21355	2925	3575	5175	7550
ZR2 Sport Utility 4D	J734	22705	3700	4400	6025	8500
LT Sport Utility 4D	J634	23105	4275	5025	6700	9200
2WD	E			(650)	(650)	(865)	(865)
BLAZER 4WD—V6—Truck Equipment Schedule T1							
Sport Utility 2D	T18X	25395	2525	3100	4750	7100
Sport Utility 4D	T13X	27345	3525	4225	5875	8375
2WD	S			(650)	(650)	(865)	(865)
TRAILBLAZER 4WD—6-Cyl.—Truck Equipment Schedule T1							
Sport Utility 4D	T13S	30045	4400	5225	6950	9600
Extended Spt Util 4D	T16S	32595	4925	5750	7525	10250
2WD	S			(650)	(650)	(865)	(865)
V8 5.3 Liter	P			350	350	465	465
ENVOY 4WD—6-Cyl.—Truck Equipment Schedule T1							
Sport Utility 4D	T13S	31745	5300	6175	7950	10750
2WD	S			(650)	(650)	(865)	(865)
ENVOY XL 4WD—6-Cyl.—Truck Equipment Schedule T1							
Sport Utility 4D	T16S	33845	5875	6800	8600	11450
2WD	S			(650)	(650)	(865)	(865)
V8 5.3 Liter	P			350	350	465	465
ENVOY XUV 4WD—6-Cyl.—Truck Equipment Schedule T1							
Sport Utility 4D	T12S	34115	6675	7700	9500	12450
2WD	S			(650)	(650)	(865)	(865)
V8 5.3 Liter	P			350	350	465	465
TAHOE 4WD—V8—Truck Equipment Schedule T1							
Sport Utility 4D	K13V	38425	6950	8000	9900	12950
w/o Third Seat	C			(550)	(550)	(735)	(735)
2WD	C			(650)	(650)	(865)	(865)
V8 5.3 Liter	T,Z			350	350	465	465
YUKON 4WD—V8—Truck Equipment Schedule T1							
Sport Utility 4D	K13V	38785	7050	8100	10000	13100
w/o Third Seat	C			(550)	(550)	(735)	(735)
2WD	C			(650)	(650)	(865)	(865)
V8 5.3 Liter	T			350	350	465	465
YUKON DENALI AWD—V8—Truck Equipment Schedule T3							
Sport Utility 4D	K13U	50125	9800	11125	13300	16900
SUBURBAN—V8—Truck Equipment Schedule T1							
C1500 Sport Utility	C16T	37865	6550	7575	9400	12400
C2500 Sport Utility	C26U	39465	6825	7875	9750	12800
Quadrasteer				675	675	900	900
4WD	K			1550	1550	2065	2065
V8 8.1 Liter	G			400	400	535	535
YUKON XL—V8—Truck Equipment Schedule T1							
1500 Sport Utility	C13T	38775	6700	7700	9525	12500
2500 Sport Utility	C23U	40275	6925	7975	9850	12850
Quadrasteer				675	675	900	900
4WD	K			1550	1550	2065	2065
V8 8.1 Liter	G			400	400	535	535
YUKON XL DENALI AWD—V8—Truck Equipment Schedule T3							
1500 Sport Utility	K16U	51775	10425	11850	13950	17650

TRUCKS & VANS

Body / Type	VIN	List	Trade-In Fair	Trade-In Good	Pvt-Party Good	Retail Excellent
VENTURE—V6—Truck Equipment Schedule T2						
Cargo Minivan 4D	U03E	23120	1650	2125	3675	5825
VENTURE—V6—Truck Equipment Schedule T1						
Minivan 4D	U03E	21995	2150	2725	4275	6500
Extended Minivan 4D	X09E	23570	2700	3325	4900	7200
5 Passenger			(550)	(550)	(735)	(735)
AWD	V		725	725	965	965
ASTRO/SAFARI—V6—Truck Equipment Schedule T2						
Cargo 3D	M19X	22965	1475	1950	3475	5600
Dutch Doors			200	200	265	265
AWD	L		725	725	965	965
ASTRO/SAFARI—V6—Truck Equipment Schedule T1						
Minivan 3D	M19X	24395	2350	2950	4475	6750
Dutch Doors			200	200	265	265
AWD	L		725	725	965	965
EXPRESS/SAVANA VAN—V8—Truck Equipment Schedule T1						
1500 Passenger Van	G15T	27280	4600	5425	7125	9775
2500 Passenger Van	G25U	28685	4800	5625	7350	10050
3500 Passenger Van	G35U	29089	5000	5850	7575	10300
155" W.B.			175	175	235	235
AWD	H		650	650	865	865
V6 4.3 Liter	X		(550)	(550)	(735)	(735)
EXPRESS/SAVANA VAN—V8—Truck Equipment Schedule T1						
1500 Cargo Van	G15X	23185	3750	4475	6125	8600
2500 Cargo Van	G25X	23965	3875	4600	6250	8750
3500 Cargo Van	G35U	27194	4025	4750	6425	8950
3500 Van Cab-Ch	G35U		3850	4575	6225	8725
155" W.B.			175	175	235	235
AWD			650	650	865	865
V6 4.3 Liter	X		(275)	(275)	(365)	(365)
V8 6.0 Liter	U		475	475	635	635
S10/SONOMA CREW CAB PICKUP 4WD—V6—Truck Equipment Schedule T1						
LS/SLS Short Bed	T13X	25095	6250	7225	9000	11850
COLORADO/CANYON PICKUP—4-Cyl.—Truck Equipment Schedule T2						
Regular Cab	S148	16200	2575	3175	4775	7100
Extended Cab	S198	18545	3500	4225	5850	8300
Crew Cab	S138	20670	4450	5250	6950	9575
4WD	T		1600	1600	2135	2135
5-Cyl. 3.5 Liter	6		200	200	265	265
SSR REGULAR CAB PICKUP—V8—Truck Equipment Schedule T3						
Convertible 2D	S14P	41995	15925	17875	20100	24400
AVALANCHE 4WD—V8—Truck Equipment Schedule T1						
1500 Spt Util Pickup	K12T	36100	8200	9375	11550	15050
2500 Spt Util Pickup	K22G	37935	9525	10825	13050	16700
2WD	C		(650)	(650)	(865)	(865)
SILVERADO/SIERRA REGULAR CAB PICKUP—V8—Truck Equipment Sched T1						
1500 Short Bed	C14V	23400	4425	5250	7025	9750
1500 Long Bed	C14V	23700	4175	4925	6675	9275
2500 Long Bed	C24U	26660	4750	5550	7375	10150
2500 HD Long Bed	C24U	26910	5225	6100	7925	10750
3500 Long Bed	K34U	30940	5325	6200	8000	10850
Work Truck			(800)	(800)	(1065)	(1065)
4WD	K		1550	1550	2065	2065
V6 4.3 Liter	X		(600)	(600)	(800)	(800)
V8 5.3 Liter	T		350	350	465	465
V8 8.1 Liter	G		400	400	535	535
V8 6.6L Turbo Diesel	1,2		4700	4700	6265	6265
SILVERADO/SIERRA EXT CAB PICKUP—V8—Truck Equipment Schedule T1						
1500 Short Bed	C19V	26260	6425	7425	9275	12250
1500 Long Bed	C19V	26815	6000	6950	8800	11700
2500 Short Bed	K29U	31615	7025	8075	10000	13100
2500 HD Short Bed	C29U	29160	7800	8925	10850	14000
2500 HD Long Bed	C29U	29460	7700	8825	10750	13850
3500 Long Bed	C39U	30400	7875	9000	11000	14200
Work Truck			(800)	(800)	(1065)	(1065)
Quadrasteer			675	675	900	900
4WD	K		1550	1550	2065	2065
V6 4.3 Liter	X		(600)	(600)	(800)	(800)
V8 5.3 Liter	T		350	350	465	465
V8 6.0 Liter (1500)	U		550	550	735	735
V8 8.1 Liter	G		400	400	535	535
V8 6.6L Turbo Diesel	1,2		4700	4700	6265	6265

Body	Type	VIN	List	Trade-In Fair	Good	Pvt-Party Good	Retail Excellent
SILVERADO SS EXT CAB PICKUP AWD—V8—Truck Equipment Schedule T3							
1500 Short Bed		K19N	40195	12400	14025	16100	20000
SIERRA DENALI EXT CAB PICKUP AWD—V8—Truck Equipment Schedule T3							
1500 Short Bed		K19U	41995	12450	14075	16150	20000
SILVERADO/SIERRA CREW CAB PICKUP—V8—Truck Equipment Schedule T1							
1500 Short Bed		C13T	31020	7500	8600	10500	13600
2500 Short Bed		C23U	31540	8250	9425	11400	14700
2500 HD Short Bed		C23U	31460	8700	9900	11900	15250
2500 HD Long Bed		C23U	31160	8600	9800	11800	15150
3500 Long Bed		C33U	32400	8825	10050	12250	15450
Work Truck				(800)	(800)	(1065)	(1065)
Quadrasteer				675	675	900	900
4WD		K		1550	1550	2065	2065
V8 8.1 Liter		G		400	400	535	535
V8 6.6L Turbo Diesel		1,2		4700	4700	6265	6265

2005 CHEVY/GMC—(1,2or3)(CorG)(A,CorN)—T18X–5

Body	Type	VIN	List	Trade-In Fair	Good	Pvt-Party Good	Retail Excellent
BLAZER 4WD—V6—Truck Equipment Schedule T1							
Sport Utility 2D		T18X	25850	3075	3725	5400	7850
Sport Utility 4D		T13X	28025	4225	4975	6675	9225
2WD		S		(725)	(725)	(965)	(965)
EQUINOX—V6—Truck Equipment Schedule T1							
LS Sport Utility 4D		L13F	21660	5250	6125	7900	10650
LT Sport Utility 4D		L63F	23600	5725	6675	8400	11200
AWD		2,7		800	800	1065	1065
TRAILBLAZER 4WD—6-Cyl.—Truck Equipment Schedule T1							
Sport Utility 4D		T13S	30655	5425	6300	8050	10850
Extended Spt Util 4D		T16S	32775	5875	6800	8575	11400
2WD		S		(725)	(725)	(965)	(965)
V8 5.3 Liter		M		375	375	500	500
ENVOY 4WD—6-Cyl.—Truck Equipment Schedule T1							
Sport Utility 4D		T13S	32685	6325	7300	9075	11950
2WD		S		(725)	(725)	(965)	(965)
ENVOY DENALI 4WD—V8—Truck Equipment Schedule T3							
Sport Utility 4D		T63M	39640	10925	12400	14300	17800
2WD		S		(725)	(725)	(965)	(965)
ENVOY XL 4WD—6-Cyl.—Truck Equipment Schedule T1							
Sport Utility 4D		T16S	34355	6925	7975	9775	12750
2WD		S		(725)	(725)	(965)	(965)
V8 5.3 Liter		M		375	375	500	500
ENVOY XL DENALI 4WD—V8—Truck Equipment Schedule T3							
Sport Utility 4D		T16M	40920	10875	12350	14250	17750
2WD		S		(725)	(725)	(965)	(965)
ENVOY XUV 4WD—6-Cyl.—Truck Equipment Schedule T1							
Sport Utility 4D		T12S	34440	7900	9050	10900	14000
2WD		S		(725)	(725)	(965)	(965)
V8 5.3 Liter		M		375	375	500	500
TAHOE 4WD—V8—Truck Equipment Schedule T1							
Sport Utility 4D		K13V	39185	8700	9900	11850	15150
w/o Third Seat				(600)	(600)	(800)	(800)
2WD		C		(725)	(725)	(965)	(965)
V8 5.3 Liter		T		375	375	500	500
YUKON 4WD—V8—Truck Equipment Schedule T1							
Sport Utility 4D		K13V	39545	8775	10000	11950	15300
w/o Third Seat				(600)	(600)	(800)	(800)
2WD		C		(725)	(725)	(965)	(965)
V8 5.3 Liter		T		375	375	500	500
YUKON DENALI AWD—V8—Truck Equipment Schedule T3							
Sport Utility 4D		K63U	50885	12400	14025	16150	20100
SUBURBAN—V8—Truck Equipment Schedule T1							
C1500 Sport Utility		C16Z	38875	8275	9475	11400	14700
C2500 Sport Utility		C26U	40475	8650	9850	11800	15100
Quadrasteer				750	750	1000	1000
4WD		K		1725	1725	2300	2300
V8 8.1 Liter		G		450	450	600	600
YUKON XL—V8—Truck Equipment Schedule T1							
1500 Sport Utility		C16Z	39535	8475	9675	11550	14800
2500 Sport Utility		C26U	41035	8775	10000	11900	15150
Quadrasteer				750	750	1000	1000
4WD		K		1725	1725	2300	2300
V8 8.1 Liter		G		450	450	600	600
YUKON XL DENALI AWD—V8—Truck Equipment Schedule T3							
1500 Sport Utility 4D		K66U	52535	12550	14150	16250	20200

2005 CHEVROLET/GMC

TRUCKS & VANS

Body Type	VIN	List	Trade-In Fair	Good	Pvt-Party Good	Retail Excellent
VENTURE—V6—Truck Equipment Schedule T2						
Cargo Minivan 4D	V03E	23880	2350	2950	4500	6750
VENTURE—V6—Truck Equipment Schedule T1						
Extended Minivan 4D	V09E	24080	3600	4300	5875	8300
5 Passenger			(600)	(600)	(800)	(800)
ASTRO/SAFARI—V6—Truck Equipment Schedule T2						
Cargo 3D	M19X	23540	1950	2500	4050	6275
Dutch Doors			250	250	335	335
AWD	L		800	800	1065	1065
ASTRO/SAFARI—V6—Truck Equipment Schedule T1						
Minivan 3D	M19X	25040	3000	3650	5225	7575
Dutch Doors			250	250	335	335
AWD	L		800	800	1065	1065
UPLANDER—V6—Truck Equipment Schedule T2						
Cargo Minivan 4D	V13L	21415	1500	1975	3575	5775
UPLANDER—V6—Truck Equipment Schedule T1						
Extended Minivan 4D	V03L	24350	1925	2475	4075	6325
LS Extended Minivan	V23L	26955	2275	2850	4425	6750
LT Extended Minivan	V33L	29385	2550	3125	4725	7050
LT AWD Ext Minivan	X33L	32100	3175	3850	5475	7875
EXPRESS/SAVANA VAN—V8—Truck Equipment Schedule T1						
1500 Passenger Van	G15T	26305	5750	6675	8400	11150
2500 Passenger Van	G25V	29405	5975	6900	8625	11400
3500 Passenger Van	G35U	30009	6200	7150	8900	11700
155" W.B.			200	200	265	265
AWD	H		725	725	965	965
V6 4.3 Liter	X		(600)	(600)	(800)	(800)
EXPRESS/SAVANA VAN—V8—Truck Equipment Schedule T1						
1500 Cargo Van	G15T	23575	4700	5525	7225	9850
2500 Cargo Van	G25V	24275	4825	5650	7375	10050
3500 Cargo Van	G35U	26809	5025	5875	7600	10300
155" W.B.			200	200	265	265
AWD	H		725	725	965	965
V6 4.3 Liter	X		(300)	(300)	(400)	(400)
V8 6.0 Liter	U		500	500	665	665
COLORADO/CANYON PICKUP—4-Cyl.—Truck Equipment Schedule T2						
Regular Cab	S148	16430	3050	3700	5325	7725
Extended Cab	S198	18775	4125	4875	6525	9050
Crew Cab	S138	21920	5175	6025	7750	10450
4WD	T		1775	1775	2365	2365
5-Cyl. 3.5 Liter	6		200	200	265	265
SSR REGULAR CAB PICKUP—V8—Truck Equipment Schedule T3						
Convertible 2D	S14H	40555	18325	20475	22700	27200
AVALANCHE 4WD—V8—Truck Equipment Schedule T1						
1500 Spt Util Pickup	K12T	37170	9200	10475	12700	16300
2500 Spt Util Pickup	K22G	39005	10675	12100	14300	18150
2WD	C		(725)	(725)	(965)	(965)
SILVERADO/SIERRA REGULAR CAB PICKUP—V8—Truck Equipment Sched T1						
1500 Short Bed	C14V	23635	4950	5775	7600	10400
1500 Long Bed	C14V	23935	4575	5400	7200	9950
2500 HD Long Bed	C24U	27700	5800	6750	8575	11450
3500 Long Bed	K34U	31730	5900	6825	8675	11550
Work Truck			(950)	(950)	(1265)	(1265)
4WD	K		1725	1725	2300	2300
V6 4.3 Liter	X		(675)	(675)	(900)	(900)
V8 5.3 Liter	T,Z		375	375	500	500
V8 8.1 Liter	G		450	450	600	600
V8 6.6L Turbo Diesel	2		4900	4900	6530	6530
SILVERADO/SIERRA EXT CAB—V8 Hybrid—Truck Equipment Schedule T1						
1500 LS/SLE Short	C19T	28845	11025	12500	14500	18100
4WD	K		1725	1725	2300	2300
SILVERADO/SIERRA EXT CAB PICKUP—V8—Truck Equipment Schedule T1						
1500 Short Bed	C19V	27295	7150	8200	10100	13150
1500 Long Bed	C19V	28295	6650	7675	9500	12500
2500 HD Short Bed	C29U	30000	8725	9950	11900	15250
2500 HD Long Bed	C29U	30300	8650	9850	11800	15100
3500 Long Bed	C39U	31240	8875	10100	12050	15400
Work Truck			(950)	(950)	(1265)	(1265)
Quadrasteer			750	750	1000	1000
4WD	K		1725	1725	2300	2300
V6 4.3 Liter	X		(675)	(675)	(900)	(900)
V8 5.3 Liter	B,T,Z		375	375	500	500
V8 6.0 Liter (1500)	U		550	550	735	735

276   DEDUCT FOR RECONDITIONING

0709

Body	Type	VIN	List	Trade-In Fair	Trade-In Good	Pvt-Party Good	Retail Excellent
V8 8.1 Liter		G		450	450	600	600
V8 6.6L Turbo Diesel		2		4900	4900	6530	6530
SILVERADO SS EXT CAB PICKUP—V8—Truck Equipment Schedule T3							
1500 Short Bed		K19N	36440	13025	14700	16750	20600
AWD				1725	1725	2300	2300
SILVERADO/SIERRA CREW CAB PICKUP—V8—Truck Equipment Schedule T1							
1500 Short Bed		C13T,V	30875	8275	9475	11400	14700
1500 HD Short Bed		C13U	32480	9175	10425	12400	15800
2500 HD Short Bed		C23U	32100	9950	11275	13300	16700
2500 HD Long Bed		C23U	32400	9850	11175	13200	16600
3500 Long Bed		C33U	33340	10050	11425	13450	16900
Work Truck				(950)	(950)	(1265)	(1265)
Quadrasteer				750	750	1000	1000
4WD		K		1725	1725	2300	2300
V8 8.1 Liter		G		450	450	600	600
V8 6.6L Turbo Diesel		2		4900	4900	6530	6530
SIERRA DENALI CREW CAB PICKUP AWD—V8—Truck Equipment Schedule T3							
1500 Short Bed		K63N	42585	15375	17300	19400	23500

2006 CHEVY—(1,2or3)(CorG)(A,CorN)–(L13F)–6–#

Body	Type	VIN	List	Trade-In Fair	Trade-In Good	Pvt-Party Good	Retail Excellent
EQUINOX—V6—Truck Equipment Schedule T1							
LS Sport Utility 4D		L13F	22345	6400	7375	9175	12050
LT Sport Utility 4D		L63F	22990	6900	7950	9725	12650
AWD		2,7		875	875	1165	1165
TRAILBLAZER 4WD—6-Cyl.—Truck Equipment Schedule T1							
Sport Utility 4D		T13S	29660	6625	7650	9400	12300
Extended Spt Util 4D		T16S	31280	7025	8075	9850	12800
2WD		S		(800)	(800)	(1065)	(1065)
V8 5.3 Liter		M		400	400	535	535
TRAILBLAZER 4WD—V8—Truck Equipment Schedule T1							
SS Sport Utility 4D		T13H	33505	12050	13625	15550	19100
2WD		S		(800)	(800)	(1065)	(1065)
ENVOY 4WD—6-Cyl.—Truck Equipment Schedule T1							
Sport Utility 4D		T13S	31550	7600	8700	10500	13500
2WD		S		(800)	(800)	(1065)	(1065)
ENVOY DENALI 4WD—V8—Truck Equipment Schedule T3							
Sport Utility 4D		T63M	39395	13125	14800	16700	20400
2WD		S		(800)	(800)	(1065)	(1065)
ENVOY XL 4WD—6-Cyl.—Truck Equipment Schedule T1							
Sport Utility 4D		T16S	32880	8200	9375	11200	14400
2WD		S		(800)	(800)	(1065)	(1065)
V8 5.3 Liter		M		400	400	535	535
ENVOY XL DENALI 4WD—V8—Truck Equipment Schedule T3							
Sport Utility 4D		T66M	40825	12850	14450	16350	20000
2WD		S		(800)	(800)	(1065)	(1065)
TAHOE 4WD—V8—Truck Equipment Schedule T1							
Sport Utility 4D		K13T	40750	10825	12250	14150	17650
w/o Third Seat				(650)	(650)	(865)	(865)
2WD		C		(800)	(800)	(1065)	(1065)
V8 5.3 Liter		T		400	400	535	535
YUKON 4WD—V8—Truck Equipment Schedule T1							
Sport Utility 4D		K13V	37640	10875	12350	14300	17850
w/o Third Seat				(650)	(650)	(865)	(865)
2WD		C		(800)	(800)	(1065)	(1065)
V8 5.3 Liter		T		400	400	535	535
YUKON DENALI AWD—V8—Truck Equipment Schedule T3							
Sport Utility 4D		K63U	51160	15375	17300	19500	23700
SUBURBAN—V8—Truck Equipment Schedule T1							
C1500 Sport Utility		C16Z	39640	10475	11900	13800	17300
C2500 Sport Utility		C26U	40815	10875	12350	14250	17800
4WD		K		1900	1900	2535	2535
V8 8.1 Liter		G		500	500	665	665
YUKON XL—V8—Truck Equipment Schedule T1							
1500 Sport Utility		C16Z	38730	10675	12100	14000	17450
2500 Sport Utility		C26U	41405	10975	12450	14350	17850
4WD		K		1900	1900	2535	2535
V8 8.1 Liter		G		500	500	665	665
YUKON XL DENALI—V8—Truck Equipment Schedule T1							
1500 Sport Utility 4D		K66U	52810	15000	16850	19000	23100
UPLANDER—V6—Truck Equipment Schedule T2							
Cargo Minivan 4D		V13L	21640	2600	3175	4825	7200
UPLANDER—V6—Truck Equipment Schedule T1							
LS Minivan 4D		U23L	21990	2625	3200	4850	7225

TRUCKS & VANS

TRUCKS & VANS

Body Type	VIN	List	Trade-In Fair	Trade-In Good	Pvt-Party Good	Retail Excellent
LS Extended Minivan	V23L	24575	3425	4125	5750	8200
LT Extended Minivan	V33L	28385	3775	4475	6125	8625
LT AWD Ext Minivan	X33L	34535	4425	5225	6900	9525
EXPRESS/SAVANA VAN—V8—Truck Equipment Schedule T1						
1500 Passenger Van	G15T	26770	7125	8200	9900	12800
2500 Passenger Van	G25V	28625	7375	8450	10200	13150
3500 Passenger Van	G35U	30704	7650	8750	10500	13450
155" W.B.			225	225	300	300
AWD	H		800	800	1065	1065
V6 4.3 Liter	X		(650)	(650)	(865)	(865)
EXPRESS/SAVANA VAN—V8—Truck Equipment Schedule T1						
1500 Cargo Van	G15X	23980	5900	6825	8525	11250
2500 Cargo Van	G25V	25750	6050	7000	8700	11450
3500 Cargo Van	G35U	27434	6275	7250	8975	11750
155" W.B.			225	225	300	300
AWD	H		800	800	1065	1065
V6 4.3 Liter	X		(325)	(325)	(435)	(435)
V8 6.0 Liter	U		525	525	700	700
V8 6.6L Turbo Diesel	2		5100	5100	6800	6800
COLORADO/CANYON PICKUP—4-Cyl.—Truck Equipment Schedule T2						
Regular Cab	S148	15990	3700	4400	6050	8525
Extended Cab	S198	18365	4850	5675	7400	10050
Crew Cab	S138	22995	6025	6975	8700	11450
4WD	T		1950	1950	2600	2600
5-Cyl. 3.5 Liter	6		200	200	265	265
SSR REGULAR CAB PICKUP—V8—Truck Equipment Schedule T3						
Convertible 2D	S14H	39990	20875	23325	25400	30000
AVALANCHE 4WD—V8—Truck Equipment Schedule T1						
1500 Spt Util Pickup	K12Z	37885	10250	11625	13850	17650
2500 Spt Util Pickup	K22G	39295	11850	13375	15650	19600
2WD			(800)	(800)	(1065)	(1065)
SILVERADO/SIERRA REGULAR CAB PICKUP—V8—Truck Equipment Sched T1						
1500 Short Bed	C14V	24390	5475	6350	8150	11050
1500 Long Bed	C14V	24690	5050	5900	7725	10550
2500 HD Long Bed	C24U	27295	6400	7375	9225	12200
3500 Long Bed	C34U	30275	6500	7475	9325	12300
Work Truck			(1100)	(1100)	(1465)	(1465)
4WD	K		1900	1900	2535	2535
V6 4.3 Liter	X		(750)	(750)	(1000)	(1000)
V8 5.3 Liter	T		400	400	535	535
V8 8.1 Liter	G		500	500	665	665
V8 6.6L Turbo Diesel	2		5100	5100	6800	6800
SILVERADO/SIERRA EXT CAB—V8 Hybrid—Truck Equipment Schedule T1						
1500 LT/SLE Short	C19T	26485	12150	13725	15700	19350
4WD	K		1900	1900	2535	2535
SILVERADO/SIERRA EXT CAB PICKUP—V8—Truck Equipment Schedule T1						
1500 LT 5 3/4'	C19T	30130	8325	9525	11450	14700
1500 6 1/2'	C19V	27195	7875	9000	10950	14100
1500 Long Bed	C19T	28125	7325	8425	10300	13350
2500 HD Short Bed	C29U	29570	9725	11025	13000	16400
2500 HD Long Bed	C29U	29860	9625	10925	12900	16250
3500 Long Bed	C39U	32790	9850	11175	13150	16550
Work Truck			(1100)	(1100)	(1465)	(1465)
4WD	K		1900	1900	2535	2535
V6 4.3 Liter	X		(750)	(750)	(1000)	(1000)
V8 5.3 Liter	T		400	400	535	535
V8 6.0 Liter (1500)	U		550	550	735	735
V8 8.1 Liter	G		500	500	665	665
V8 6.6L Turbo Diesel	2,D		5100	5100	6800	6800
SILVERADO SS EXTENDED CAB PICKUP—V8—Truck Equipment Schedule T3						
1500 Short Bed	C19N	36625	14400	16175	18250	22100
SILVERADO/SIERRA CREW CAB PICKUP—V8—Truck Equipment Schedule T1						
1500 Short Bed	C13V	27990	9175	10425	12400	15750
1500 HD Short Bed	C13U	32855	10100	11475	13450	16850
2500 HD Short Bed	C23U	31540	11225	12700	14650	18250
2500 HD Long Bed	C23U	31830	11175	12650	14600	18150
3500 Long Bed	C33U	35005	11375	12850	14850	18400
Work Truck			(1100)	(1100)	(1465)	(1465)
4WD	K		1900	1900	2535	2535
V8 6.0 Liter (1500 ex HD)	U		550	550	735	735
V8 8.1 Liter	G		500	500	665	665
V8 6.6L Turbo Diesel	2,D		5100	5100	6800	6800

Body	Type	VIN	List	Trade-In Fair	Trade-In Good	Pvt-Party Good	Retail Excellent

SIERRA DENALI CREW CAB PICKUP AWD—V8—Truck Equipment Schedule T3

Body/Type	VIN	List	Fair	Good	Pvt Good	Retail Exc
1500 Short Bed	K63N	42610	17100	19150	21300	25500

2007 CHEVY—(1,2or3)(CorG)(A,CorN)—(L13F)—7—#

EQUINOX—V6—Truck Equipment Schedule T1

Body/Type	VIN	List	Fair	Good	Pvt Good	Retail Exc
LS Sport Utility 4D	L13F	22680	7725	8850	10550	13450
LT Sport Utility 4D	L63F	23655	8275	9475	11200	14250
AWD	2,7		950	950	1265	1265

TRAILBLAZER 4WD—6-Cyl.—Truck Equipment Schedule T1

Body/Type	VIN	List	Fair	Good	Pvt Good	Retail Exc
Sport Utility 4D	T13S	27735	8075	9225	11000	14000
2WD	S		(875)	(875)	(1165)	(1165)
V8 5.3 Liter	M		400	400	535	535

TRAILBLAZER AWD—V8—Truck Equipment Schedule T1

Body/Type	VIN	List	Fair	Good	Pvt Good	Retail Exc
SS Sport Utility 4D	T13H	34015	14075	15825	17600	21300
2WD	S		(875)	(875)	(1165)	(1165)

ENVOY 4WD—6-Cyl.—Truck Equipment Schedule T1

Body/Type	VIN	List	Fair	Good	Pvt Good	Retail Exc
Sport Utility 4D	T13S	29330	9100	10350	12100	15250
2WD	S		(875)	(875)	(1165)	(1165)

ENVOY DENALI 4WD—V8—Truck Equipment Schedule T3

Body/Type	VIN	List	Fair	Good	Pvt Good	Retail Exc
Sport Utility 4D	T63M	37570	15575	17500	19300	23100
2WD	S		(875)	(875)	(1165)	(1165)

ACADIA—V6—Truck Equipment Schedule T1

Body/Type	VIN	List	Fair	Good	Pvt Good	Retail Exc
Sport Utility 4D	R137	29990	15425	17350	19200	23100
AWD	V		950	950	1265	1265

TAHOE 4WD—V8—Truck Equipment Schedule T1

Body/Type	VIN	List	Fair	Good	Pvt Good	Retail Exc
LS Sport Utility 4D	K130	38170	18075	20200	22100	26400
w/o Third Seat			(700)	(700)	(935)	(935)
2WD	C		(875)	(875)	(1165)	(1165)
V8 5.3 Liter	J		400	400	535	535

YUKON 4WD—V8—Truck Equipment Schedule T1

Body/Type	VIN	List	Fair	Good	Pvt Good	Retail Exc
Sport Utility 4D	K130	38865	18125	20275	22300	26600
w/o Third Seat			(700)	(700)	(935)	(935)
2WD	C		(875)	(875)	(1165)	(1165)
V8 5.3 Liter	J		400	400	535	535

YUKON DENALI AWD—V8—Truck Equipment Schedule T3

Body/Type	VIN	List	Fair	Good	Pvt Good	Retail Exc
Sport Utility 4D	K638	48370	24500	27350	29500	34600

SUBURBAN—V8—Truck Equipment Schedule T1

Body/Type	VIN	List	Fair	Good	Pvt Good	Retail Exc
C1500 Sport Utility	C16J	37365	16175	18125	20000	23900
C2500 Sport Utility	C26K	38550	16625	18625	20600	24600
4WD	K		2075	2075	2765	2765
V8 6.0 Liter (1500)	Y		550	550	735	735

YUKON XL—V8—Truck Equipment Schedule T1

Body/Type	VIN	List	Fair	Good	Pvt Good	Retail Exc
1500 Sport Utility	C16J	40970	16175	18125	20000	23900
2500 Sport Utility	C26K	42170	16650	18725	20700	24700
4WD	K		2075	2075	2765	2765
V8 6.0 Liter (1500)	Y		550	550	735	735

YUKON XL DENALI AWD—V8—Truck Equipment Schedule T3

Body/Type	VIN	List	Fair	Good	Pvt Good	Retail Exc
1500 Sport Utility 4D	K168	50870	26350	29400	31600	36800

UPLANDER—V6—Truck Equipment Schedule T2

Body/Type	VIN	List	Fair	Good	Pvt Good	Retail Exc
Cargo Minivan 4D	V131	22670	4225	4975	6525	8950

UPLANDER—V6—Truck Equipment Schedule T1

Body/Type	VIN	List	Fair	Good	Pvt Good	Retail Exc
LS Minivan 4D	U231	20770	4225	4975	6525	8950
LS Extended Minivan	V231	23845	5075	5925	7500	10050
LT Extended Minivan	V331	27970	5500	6400	7975	10600

EXPRESS/SAVANA VAN—V8—Truck Equipment Schedule T1

Body/Type	VIN	List	Fair	Good	Pvt Good	Retail Exc
1500 Passenger Van	G15T	26460	8875	10100	11750	14800
2500 Passenger Van	G25V	27265	9125	10400	12100	15150
3500 Passenger Van	G35U	29299	9425	10725	12400	15500
155" W.B.			250	250	335	335
AWD	H		875	875	1165	1165

EXPRESS/SAVANA VAN—V8—Truck Equipment Schedule T1

Body/Type	VIN	List	Fair	Good	Pvt Good	Retail Exc
1500 Cargo Van	G15X	22720	7350	8450	10050	12850
2500 Cargo Van	G25V	23495	7500	8600	10250	13050
3500 Cargo Van	G35V	26099	7775	8900	10600	13500
155" W.B.			250	250	335	335
AWD	H		875	875	1165	1165
V6 4.3 Liter	X		(350)	(350)	(465)	(465)
V8 6.0 Liter	U		550	550	735	735
V8 6.6L Turbo Diesel	2		5300	5300	7065	7065

COLORADO/CANYON PICKUP—4-Cyl.—Truck Equipment Schedule T2

Body/Type	VIN	List	Fair	Good	Pvt Good	Retail Exc
Regular Cab	S149	14495	4475	5300	6875	9350
Extended Cab	S199	16845	5775	6725	8300	10950
Crew Cab	S139	20895	7050	8100	9700	12450

TRUCKS & VANS

2007 CHEVROLET/GMC

Body Type	VIN	List	Trade-In Fair	Good	Pvt-Party Good	Retail Excellent
4WD	T		2125	2125	2835	2835
5-Cyl. 3.7 Liter	E		200	200	265	265
AVALANCHE 4WD—V8—Truck Equipment Schedule T1						
Sport Util Pickup 4D	K123	35865	16650	18725	21000	25500
2WD	C		(875)	(875)	(1165)	(1165)
SILVERADO/SIERRA CLASSIC REGULAR CAB—V8—Truck Equipment Schedule T1						
1500 Short Bed	C14V	23015	6625	7625	9375	12300
1500 Long Bed	C14V	23455	6175	7125	8925	11750
2500 HD Long Bed	C24U	24915	7675	8775	10550	13550
3500 Long Bed	C34U	25410	7750	8875	10650	13650
Work Truck			(1250)	(1250)	(1665)	(1665)
4WD	K		2075	2075	2765	2765
V6 4.3 Liter	X		(800)	(800)	(1065)	(1065)
V8 5.3 Liter	T		400	400	535	535
V8 8.1 Liter	N		550	550	735	735
V8 6.6L Turbo Diesel	D		5300	5300	7065	7065
SILVERADO/SIERRA CLASSIC EXT—V8 Hybrid—Truck Equipment Schedule T1						
1500 LT/SLE Short	C19T	29000	13925	15675	17600	21400
4WD	K		2075	2075	2765	2765
SILVERADO/SIERRA CLASSIC EXT CAB—V8—Truck Equipment Schedule T1						
1500 5 3/4'	C19T	27830	9750	11075	12950	16250
1500 6 1/2'	C19V	25785	9250	10525	12400	15650
1500 Long Bed	C19T	26815	8700	9900	11750	14950
2500 HD Short Bed	C29U	28310	11375	12850	14750	18250
2500 HD Long Bed	C29U	28605	11275	12750	14650	18150
3500 Long Bed	C39U	29520	11525	13025	14950	18450
Work Truck			(1250)	(1250)	(1665)	(1665)
4WD	K		2075	2075	2765	2765
V6 4.3 Liter	X		(800)	(800)	(1065)	(1065)
V8 5.3 Liter	T		400	400	535	535
V8 6.0 Liter (1500)	N		550	550	735	735
V8 8.1 Liter	N		550	550	735	735
V8 6.6L Turbo Diesel	D		5300	5300	7065	7065
SILVERADO SS CLASSIC EXT CAB—V8—Truck Equipment Schedule T3						
1500 Short Bed	C19N	34180	16375	18375	20300	24300
SILVERADO/SIERRA CLASSIC CREW CAB—V8—Truck Equipment Schedule T1						
1500 Short Bed	C13V	25595	10625	12050	13900	17350
1500 HD Short Bed	C13U	30545	11700	13225	15150	18650
2500 HD Short Bed	C23U	30295	13125	14800	16700	20400
2500 HD Long Bed	C23U	30595	13025	14700	16600	20300
3500 Long Bed	C33U	31515	13275	14950	16850	20600
Work Truck			(1250)	(1250)	(1665)	(1665)
4WD	K		2075	2075	2765	2765
V8 6.0 Liter (1500 ex HD)	N		550	550	735	735
V8 8.1 Liter	N		550	550	735	735
V8 6.6L Turbo Diesel	D		5300	5300	7065	7065
SIERRA DENALI CLASSIC CREW CAB AWD—V8—Truck Schedule T3						
1500 Short Bed	K63N	40025	19450	21750	23700	28100
SILVERADO/SIERRA REGULAR CAB—V8—Truck Equipment Schedule T1						
1500 Short Bed	C14C	24410	9000	10250	12100	15350
1500 Long Bed	C14C	24705	8550	9775	11600	14800
2500 HD Long Bed	C24U	24575	9175	10425	12300	15550
3500 Long Bed	C34U	28060	9250	10525	12400	15650
Work Truck			(1250)	(1250)	(1665)	(1665)
4WD	K		2075	2075	2765	2765
V6 4.3 Liter	X		(800)	(800)	(1065)	(1065)
V8 5.3 Liter	J		400	400	535	535
V8 6.6L Turbo Diesel	6		5300	5300	7065	7065
SILVERADO/SIERRA EXT CAB PICKUP—V8—Truck Equipment Schedule T1						
1500 5 3/4'	C19C	26565	11275	12750	14650	18150
1500 6 1/2'	C19C	26880	11125	12600	14450	17950
1500 Long Bed	C19J	28205	10350	11700	13550	16950
2500 HD Short Bed	C29K	30470	13375	15100	17000	20700
2500 HD Long Bed	C29K	30765	13225	14900	16800	20500
3500 Long Bed	C39K	31790	13625	15325	17250	21000
Work Truck			(1250)	(1250)	(1665)	(1665)
4WD	K		2075	2075	2765	2765
V6 4.3 Liter	X		(800)	(800)	(1065)	(1065)
V8 5.3 Liter	J		400	400	535	535
V8 6.0 Liter (1500)	Y		550	550	735	735
V8 6.6L Turbo Diesel	6		5300	5300	7065	7065
SILVERADO/SIERRA CREW CAB PICKUP—V8—Truck Equipment Schedule T1						
1500 Short Bed	C13C	29415	12925	14550	16500	20200

280   DEDUCT FOR RECONDITIONING

0709

TRUCKS & VANS

Body	Type	VIN	List	Trade-In Fair	Trade-In Good	Pvt-Party Good	Retail Excellent
2500 HD Short Bed		C23K	32545	15250	17150	19050	22900
2500 HD Long Bed		C23K	32840	15100	16950	18850	22350
3500 Long Bed		C33K	34000	15725	17650	19600	23500
Work Truck				(1250)	(1250)	(1665)	(1665)
4WD		K		2075	2075	2765	2765
V8 6.0 Liter (1500)		Y		550	550	735	735
V8 6.6L Turbo Diesel		6		5300	5300	7065	7065
SIERRA DENALI CREW CAB PICKUP AWD—V8—Truck Schedule T3							
1500 Short Bed		K63N	42095	22150	24700	26800	31400
2WD				(875)	(875)	(1165)	(1165)

2008 CHEVY—(1,2or3)(CorG)(A,CorN)—(L13F)—8—#

Body	Type	VIN	List	Trade-In Fair	Trade-In Good	Pvt-Party Good	Retail Excellent
EQUINOX—V6—Truck Equipment Schedule T1							
LS Sport Utility 4D		L13F	22995	9525	10825	12550	15700
LT Sport Utility 4D		L33F	23855	10200	11575	13350	16500
LTZ Sport Utility 4D		L73F	27995	11800	13325	15100	18450
Sport SUV 4D		L937	27995	12350	13975	15750	19150
AWD		2,4,6,8,0		1025	1025	1365	1365
TRAILBLAZER 4WD—6-Cyl.—Truck Equipment Schedule T1							
Sport Utility 4D		T13S	29650	11175	12650	14350	17700
2WD		S		(950)	(950)	(1265)	(1265)
V8 5.3 Liter		M		400	400	535	535
TRAILBLAZER AWD—V8—Truck Equipment Schedule T1							
SS Sport Utility 4D		T33H	33990	17650	19800	21500	25400
2WD		S		(950)	(950)	(1265)	(1265)
ENVOY 4WD—6-Cyl.—Truck Equipment Schedule T1							
Sport Utility 4D		T23S	29850	11575	13075	14850	18250
2WD		S		(950)	(950)	(1265)	(1265)
ENVOY DENALI 4WD—V8—Truck Equipment Schedule T3							
Sport Utility 4D		T43M	36730	19700	22050	23700	27800
2WD		S		(950)	(950)	(1265)	(1265)
ACADIA—V6—Truck Equipment Schedule T1							
SLE Sport Utility 4D		R137	29845	17875	20000	22000	26100
SLT Sport Utility 4D		T13S	35410	21550	24000	25900	30300
AWD		V		1025	1025	1365	1365
TAHOE 4WD—V8 Hybrid—Truck Equipment Schedule T1							
Sport Utility 4D		K135	53295	30475	33900	35700	40800
w/o Third Row				(750)	(750)	(1000)	(1000)
2WD		C		(950)	(950)	(1265)	(1265)
TAHOE 4WD—V8—Truck Equipment Schedule T1							
LS Sport Utility 4D		K130	38795	22450	25000	26900	31300
w/o Third Row				(750)	(750)	(1000)	(1000)
2WD		C		(950)	(950)	(1265)	(1265)
V8 5.3 Liter		J		400	400	535	535
YUKON 4WD—V8 Hybrid—Truck Equipment Schedule T1							
Sport Utility 4D		K135	53755	30475	33900	35700	40800
w/o Third Row				(750)	(750)	(1000)	(1000)
2WD		C		(950)	(950)	(1265)	(1265)
YUKON 4WD—V8—Truck Equipment Schedule T1							
Sport Utility 4D		K230	39490	22550	25100	27000	31500
w/o Third Row				(750)	(750)	(1000)	(1000)
2WD		C		(950)	(950)	(1265)	(1265)
V8 5.3 Liter		J		400	400	535	535
YUKON DENALI AWD—V8—Truck Equipment Schedule T3							
Sport Utility 4D		K038	49420	29700	33025	35100	40600
2WD		C		(950)	(950)	(1265)	(1265)
SUBURBAN—V8—Truck Equipment Schedule T1							
C1500 Sport Utility		C16J	38185	20200	22550	24400	28600
C2500 Sport Utility		C46K	39570	20675	23125	24900	29200
4WD		K		2250	2250	3000	3000
V8 6.0 Liter (1500)		Y		550	550	735	735
YUKON XL—V8—Truck Equipment Schedule T1							
1500 Sport Utility		C26J	41790	20275	22650	24400	28600
2500 Sport Utility		C56K	43190	20775	23225	25000	29200
4WD		K		2250	2250	3000	3000
V8 6.0 Liter (1500)		Y		550	550	735	735
YUKON XL DENALI AWD—V8—Truck Equipment Schedule T3							
1500 Sport Utility 4D		K068	51980	31450	34975	36900	42400
2WD		C		(950)	(950)	(1265)	(1265)
UPLANDER—V6—Truck Equipment Schedule T2							
Cargo Minivan 4D		V131	23385	5875	6825	8275	10750
UPLANDER—V6—Truck Equipment Schedule T1							
LS Minivan 4D		U231	21870	5875	6825	8275	10750

Body	Type	VIN	List	Trade-In Fair	Trade-In Good	Pvt-Party Good	Retail Excellent
LS Extended Minivan		V231	24540	6775	7825	9300	11900
LT Extended Minivan		V331	29540	7300	8375	9900	12600
EXPRESS/SAVANA VAN—V8—Truck Equipment Schedule T1							
1500 Passenger Van		G154	26710	11125	12600	14250	17500
2500 Passenger Van		G25K	28195	11425	12875	14600	17850
3500 Passenger Van		G35K	29914	11700	13225	14950	18250
155" W.B.		H		275	275	365	365
AWD				950	950	1265	1265
EXPRESS/SAVANA VAN—V8—Truck Equipment Schedule T1							
1500 Cargo Van		G154	23130	10050	11425	13100	16150
2500 Cargo Van		G25C	24205	10250	11625	13300	16350
3500 Cargo Van		G35C	26809	10525	11950	13600	16750
3500 Van Cab-Ch		G31K		10350	11700	13400	16500
155" W.B.		H		275	275	365	365
AWD				950	950	1265	1265
V6 4.3 Liter		X		(375)	(375)	(500)	(500)
V8 6.0 Liter		K		575	575	765	765
V8 6.6L Turbo Diesel		6		5500	5500	7330	7330
COLORADO/CANYON PICKUP—4-Cyl.—Truck Equipment Schedule T2							
Regular Cab		S149	15470	5850	6775	8200	10650
Extended Cab		S199	17760	7225	8300	9750	12350
Crew Cab		S139	21600	8600	9800	11350	14200
Work Truck (Canyon)				(400)	(400)	(535)	(535)
4WD		T		2300	2300	3065	3065
5-Cyl. 3.7 Liter		E		200	200	265	265
AVALANCHE 4WD—V8—Truck Equipment Schedule T1							
Sport Util Pickup 4D		K123	36610	19350	21650	24000	28700
2WD		C		(950)	(950)	(1265)	(1265)
SILVERADO/SIERRA REGULAR CAB PICKUP—V8—Truck Schedule T1							
1500 Short Bed		C24C	24955	11025	12500	14300	17750
1500 Long Bed		C24C	27880	10475	11900	13750	17100
2500 HD Long Bed		C54K	28400	11225	12700	14550	18000
3500 Long Bed		C84K	28340	11275	12750	14600	18100
Work Truck				(1375)	(1375)	(1835)	(1835)
4WD		K		2250	2250	3000	3000
V6 4.3 Liter		X		(850)	(850)	(1135)	(1135)
V8 5.3 Liter		J		400	400	535	535
V8 6.6L Turbo Diesel		6		5500	5500	7330	7330
SILVERADO/SIERRA EXT CAB PICKUP—V8—Truck Equipment Schedule T1							
1500 5 3/4'		C29C	26935	13475	15200	17050	20700
1500 6 1/2'		C29C	30035	13275	14950	16750	20400
1500 Long Bed		C29J	28125	12450	14075	15950	19450
2500 HD Short Bed		C59K	30750	15775	17700	19550	23400
2500 HD Long Bed		C59K	31045	15575	17500	19300	23100
3500 Long Bed		C89K	32345	15975	17925	19800	23700
Work Truck				(1375)	(1375)	(1835)	(1835)
4WD		K		2250	2250	3000	3000
V6 4.3 Liter		X		(850)	(850)	(1135)	(1135)
V8 5.3 Liter		J		400	400	535	535
V8 6.0 Liter (1500)		Y		550	550	735	735
V8 6.6L Turbo Diesel		6		5500	5500	7330	7330
SILVERADO/SIERRA CREW CAB PICKUP—V8—Truck Schedule T1							
1500 Short Bed		C23C	29785	15250	17150	18950	22700
2500 HD Short Bed		C53K	32825	17775	20000	21900	26000
2500 HD Long Bed		C53K	33120	17650	19800	21700	25700
3500 Long Bed		C83K	34555	18325	20475	22400	26600
Work Truck				(1375)	(1375)	(1835)	(1835)
4WD		K		2250	2250	3000	3000
V8 6.0 Liter (1500)		Y		550	550	735	735
V8 6.6L Turbo Diesel		6		5500	5500	7330	7330
SIERRA DENALI CREW CAB PICKUP AWD—V8—Truck Schedule T3							
1500 Short Bed		K638	42120	25275	28125	30000	34800
2WD		C		(950)	(950)	(1265)	(1265)

CHRYSLER

1994 CHRYSLER — (1or3)C4–(H54L)–R–#

Body	Type	VIN	List	Trade-In Fair	Trade-In Good	Pvt-Party Good	Retail Excellent
TOWN & COUNTRY—V6—Truck Equipment Schedule T3							
Minivan		H54L	27844	925	1275	2375	4025
5 Passenger				(200)	(200)	(265)	(265)
w/o Rear Air Conditioning				(100)	(100)	(135)	(135)

1994 CHRYSLER

TRUCKS & VANS

Body	Type	VIN	List	Trade-In Fair	Trade-In Good	Pvt-Party Good	Retail Excellent
AWD		K		250	250	335	335

1995 CHRYSLER — (1or3)C4–(H54L)–S–#

TOWN & COUNTRY—V6—Truck Equipment Schedule T3

Type	VIN	List	Fair	Good	Pvt Good	Retail
Minivan	H54L	28240	1025	1450	2600	4275
5 Passenger			(200)	(200)	(265)	(265)
w/o Rear Air Conditioning			(100)	(100)	(135)	(135)
AWD	K		250	250	335	335

1996 CHRYSLER — 1C4–(P55R)–T–#

TOWN & COUNTRY—V6—Truck Equipment Schedule T3

Type	VIN	List	Fair	Good	Pvt Good	Retail
LX Minivan	P55R	25850	1200	1675	2875	4600
Minivan	P54R	25865	1275	1750	2950	4700
LXi Minivan	P64L	30605	1400	1875	3075	4875
5 Passenger			(250)	(250)	(335)	(335)
w/o Quad Seating			(125)	(125)	(165)	(165)
w/o 2nd Sliding Door			(50)	(50)	(65)	(65)
w/o Rear Air Conditioning			(125)	(125)	(165)	(165)

1997 CHRYSLER — 1C4–(P55R)–V–#

TOWN & COUNTRY—V6—Truck Equipment Schedule T3

Type	VIN	List	Fair	Good	Pvt Good	Retail
SX Minivan	P55R	28070	1425	1900	3150	4975
LX Minivan	P54R	28285	1550	2025	3275	5125
LXi Minivan	P64L	32045	1700	2200	3475	5350
5 Passenger			(275)	(275)	(365)	(365)
w/o Quad Seating			(150)	(150)	(200)	(200)
w/o Rear Air Conditioning			(150)	(150)	(200)	(200)
AWD	T		350	350	465	465

1998 CHRYSLER — 1C4–(P55R)–W–#

TOWN & COUNTRY—V6—Truck Equipment Schedule T3

Type	VIN	List	Fair	Good	Pvt Good	Retail
SX Minivan	P55R	28150	1700	2200	3475	5350
LX Minivan	P54R	28605	1850	2375	3675	5550
LXi Minivan	P64L	32300	2000	2575	3875	5800
w/o Quad Seating			(150)	(150)	(200)	(200)
w/o Rear Air Conditioning			(175)	(175)	(235)	(235)
AWD	T		400	400	535	535

1999 CHRYSLER — 1C4–(P55R)–X–#

TOWN & COUNTRY—V6—Truck Equipment Schedule T3

Type	VIN	List	Fair	Good	Pvt Good	Retail
SX Minivan	P55R	28855	2000	2575	3875	5800
LX Minivan	P54R	29130	2200	2775	4100	6050
LXi Minivan	P64L	31955	2400	2975	4300	6325
Limited Minivan	P64L	34345	3100	3775	5175	7325
w/o Rear Air Conditioning			(200)	(200)	(265)	(265)
AWD	T		450	450	600	600

2000 CHRYSLER — 1C4–(J253)–Y–#

VOYAGER—V6—Truck Equipment Schedule T1

Type	VIN	List	Fair	Good	Pvt Good	Retail
Minivan 4D	J253	20895	925	1300	2475	4225
SE Minivan 4D	J453	23840	1000	1400	2600	4350
Grand Minivan 4D	J243	22545	1100	1525	2775	4525
SE Grand Minivan 4D	J443	24835	1150	1625	2875	4650
5 Passenger			(350)	(350)	(465)	(465)
w/o 2nd Sliding Door			(50)	(50)	(65)	(65)
4-Cyl. 2.4 Liter	B		(650)	(650)	(865)	(865)

TOWN & COUNTRY—V6—Truck Equipment Schedule T3

Type	VIN	List	Fair	Good	Pvt Good	Retail
LX Minivan	P44R	26950	2625	3200	4575	6650
LXi Minivan	P54L	31530	2825	3450	4825	6925
Limited Minivan	P64L	34855	3650	4350	5800	8050
w/o Rear Air Conditioning			(225)	(225)	(300)	(300)
AWD	T		500	500	665	665

2001 CHRYSLER — 1C(4or8)–(J24G)–1–#

VOYAGER—V6—Truck Equipment Schedule T1

Type	VIN	List	Fair	Good	Pvt Good	Retail
Minivan	J24G	20770	1125	1575	2825	4600
LX Minivan	J54G	24165	1200	1700	2950	4750
5 Passenger			(375)	(375)	(500)	(500)
4-Cyl. 2.4 Liter	B		(700)	(700)	(935)	(935)

2001 CHRYSLER

Body	Type	VIN	List	Trade-In Fair	Trade-In Good	Pvt-Party Good	Retail Excellent
TOWN & COUNTRY—V6—Truck Equipment Schedule T3							
LX Minivan		P44G	26155	3075	3750	5125	7250
EX Minivan		P54L	26830	3175	3850	5250	7375
LXi Minivan		P64G	30705	3325	4025	5425	7575
Limited Minivan		P64L	35490	4250	5025	6525	8900
w/o Quad Seating		....	....	(150)	(150)	(200)	(200)
w/o Rear Air Conditioning		....	....	(250)	(250)	(335)	(335)
AWD		T	....	525	525	700	700

2002 CHRYSLER — 1C(4or8)–(J15B)–2–#

Body	Type	VIN	List	Trade-In Fair	Trade-In Good	Pvt-Party Good	Retail Excellent
VOYAGER—V6—Truck Equipment Schedule T1							
eC Minivan		J15B	16995	1050	1500	2975	5050
Minivan		J253	19995	1275	1750	3275	5400
Minivan		J453	24060	1375	1850	3400	5525
5 Passenger		....	....	(400)	(400)	(535)	(535)
4-Cyl. 2.4 Liter		....	....	(750)	(750)	(1000)	(1000)
TOWN & COUNTRY—V6—Truck Equipment Schedule T3							
eL Minivan		P343	24330	2375	2950	4525	6825
LX Minivan		P443	27065	3450	4150	5800	8250
EX Minivan		P74L	26830	3550	4250	5900	8375
LXi Minivan		P543	30970	3725	4425	6100	8600
Limited Minivan		P64L	35990	4750	5550	7325	10050
w/o Quad Seating		....	....	(150)	(150)	(200)	(200)
w/o Rear Air Conditioning		....	....	(250)	(250)	(335)	(335)
AWD		T	....	550	550	735	735

2003 CHRYSLER — 1C(4or8)–(J453)–3–#

Body	Type	VIN	List	Trade-In Fair	Trade-In Good	Pvt-Party Good	Retail Excellent
VOYAGER—V6—Truck Equipment Schedule T1							
LX Minivan		J453	24025	1775	2300	3875	6075
5 Passenger		....	....	(475)	(475)	(635)	(635)
4-Cyl. 2.4 Liter		B	....	(875)	(875)	(1165)	(1165)
TOWN & COUNTRY—V6—Truck Equipment Schedule T3							
Minivan		P24R	25975	2825	3450	5075	7425
eL Minivan		P343	24830	2725	3325	4950	7300
LX Minivan		P443	27010	4000	4750	6425	8950
EX Minivan		P74L	27235	4250	5025	6700	9225
LXi Minivan		P54L	34080	4425	5250	6950	9600
Limited Minivan		P64L	36535	5775	6700	8475	11300
w/o Quad Seating		....	....	(200)	(200)	(265)	(265)
w/o Rear Air Conditioning		....	....	(300)	(300)	(400)	(400)
AWD		T	....	650	650	865	865

2004 CHRYSLER — (1or2)C(4or8)–(P45R)–4–#

Body	Type	VIN	List	Trade-In Fair	Trade-In Good	Pvt-Party Good	Retail Excellent
TOWN & COUNTRY—V6—Truck Equipment Schedule T3							
Minivan		P45R	23520	3075	3725	5350	7750
LX Minivan		P44R	27490	4425	5225	6875	9450
eX Minivan		P74L	30110	4800	5625	7350	10050
Touring Minivan		P54L	33245	5075	5925	7650	10350
Limited Minivan		P64L	38380	6675	7675	9450	12400
w/o Quad Seating		....	....	(250)	(250)	(335)	(335)
w/o Rear Air Conditioning		....	....	(350)	(350)	(465)	(465)
AWD		T	....	725	725	965	965
PACIFICA—V6—Truck Equipment Schedule T3							
Minivan		M684	30410	5825	6750	8550	11400
AWD		F	....	725	725	965	965

2005 CHRYSLER — (1or2)C(4or8)–(P45R)–5

Body	Type	VIN	List	Trade-In Fair	Trade-In Good	Pvt-Party Good	Retail Excellent
TOWN & COUNTRY—V6—Truck Equipment Schedule T3							
Minivan		P45R	21185	3600	4300	5925	8375
LX Minivan		P44R	25640	5075	5925	7650	10350
Touring Minivan		P54L	27940	5950	6875	8625	11400
Limited Minivan		P64L	35940	7775	8900	10750	13800
w/o Quad Seating		....	....	(300)	(300)	(400)	(400)
w/o Rear Air Conditioning		....	....	(400)	(400)	(535)	(535)
Signature Series		....	....	500	500	665	665
PACIFICA—V6—Truck Equipment Schedule T3							
Minivan		M48L	24995	5500	6400	8150	10950
Touring Minivan		M684	28525	6975	8025	9800	12800
AWD		F	....	800	800	1065	1065
PACIFICA AWD—V6—Truck Equipment Schedule T3							
Limited Minivan		F784	36995	9125	10400	12250	15550

Body	Type	VIN	List	Trade-In Fair	Trade-In Good	Pvt-Party Good	Retail Excellent

TRUCKS & VANS

2006 CHRYSLER — (1or2)C(4or8)–(P45R)–6

TOWN & COUNTRY—V6—Truck Equipment Schedule T3

Body	Type	VIN	List	Fair	Good	Pvt Good	Excellent
Minivan		P45R	21735	4425	5225	6900	9525
LX Minivan		P44R	26100	6075	7025	8750	11500
Touring Minivan		P54L	28590	7150	8225	9950	12850
Limited Minivan		P64L	36465	9275	10575	12350	15550
w/o Quad Seating				(325)	(325)	(435)	(435)
w/o Rear Air Conditioning				(425)	(425)	(565)	(565)
Signature Series				500	500	665	665

PACIFICA—V6—Truck Equipment Schedule T3

Minivan		M484	25895	6675	7675	9425	12350
Touring Minivan		M684	29095	8275	9475	11300	14500
Limited Minivan		M784	35540	10675	12100	13950	17400
Signature Series				500	500	665	665
AWD		F		875	875	1165	1165

2007 CHRYSLER–(1or2)C(4or8)–(W58N)–7–#

ASPEN 4WD—V8—Truck Equipment Schedule T1

Limited Spt Util 4D		W58N	34265	12300	13925	15750	19200
2WD		X		(875)	(875)	(1165)	(1165)
V8 5.7 Liter HEMI		2		1050	1050	1400	1400

TOWN & COUNTRY—V6—Truck Equipment Schedule T3

Minivan		P45R	21985	5775	6725	8300	10950
LX Minivan		P44R	26350	7575	8675	10350	13200
Touring Minivan		P54L	28790	8875	10100	11750	14800
Limited Minivan		P64L	36860	11225	12700	14400	17700
w/o Quad Seating				(350)	(350)	(465)	(465)
w/o Rear Air Conditioning				(450)	(450)	(600)	(600)
Signature Series				500	500	665	665

PACIFICA—V6—Truck Equipment Schedule T3

Minivan		M48L	24890	8075	9225	11000	14000
Touring Minivan		M68X	27980	9850	11175	12950	16150
Limited Minivan		M78X	34155	12450	14075	15900	19350
Signature Series				500	500	665	665
AWD		F		950	950	1265	1265

2008 CHRYSLER–(1or2)C(4or8)–(W58N)–8–#

ASPEN 4WD—V8—Truck Equipment Schedule T1

Limited Spt Util 4D		W58N	35625	14500	16325	18100	21700
2WD		X		(950)	(950)	(1265)	(1265)
V8 5.7 Liter HEMI		2		1125	1125	1500	1500

TOWN & COUNTRY—V6—Truck Equipment Schedule T3

LX Minivan		R44H	23190	10775	12200	13850	17050
Touring Minivan		R54P	28430	12250	13875	15550	18900
Limited Minivan		R64X	36400	14900	16750	18400	22000
w/o Quad Seating				(375)	(375)	(500)	(500)
w/o Rear Air Conditioning				(475)	(475)	(635)	(635)

PACIFICA—V6—Truck Equipment Schedule T3

Minivan		M48L	27310	9950	11275	13000	16150
Touring Minivan		M68X	30435	11850	13425	15200	18550
Limited Minivan		M78X	34880	14700	16525	18250	21900
Signature Series				500	500	665	665
AWD		F		1025	1025	1365	1365

DODGE/PLYMOUTH

1994 DODGE/PLYM — (1orJ)BorP(4or7)–(H11K)–R

CARAVAN C/V—4-Cyl.—Truck Equipment Schedule T2

Cargo Minivan		H11K	14972	225	325	875	1775
V6 3.0 Liter		3		200	200	265	265

CARAVAN C/V—V6—Truck Equipment Schedule T2

Extended Minivan		H14R	17426	250	350	975	1925

CARAVAN/VOYAGER—4-Cyl.—Truck Equipment Schedule T1

Minivan		H25K	17135	375	550	1225	2300
5 Passenger				(200)	(200)	(265)	(265)
V6 3.0 Liter		3		200	200	265	265

CARAVAN/VOYAGER—V6—Truck Equipment Schedule T1

SE Minivan		H453	19113	475	625	1375	2525
LE Minivan		H553	22523	550	750	1550	2800

Body Type	VIN	List	Trade-In Fair	Trade-In Good	Pvt-Party Good	Retail Excellent
ES/LX Minivan	H553	23230	575	775	1575	2825
Grand Minivan	H243	19595	475	625	1375	2525
SE Grand Minivan	H44R	20278	550	725	1525	2750
LE Grand Minivan	H54R	23443	575	775	1575	2825
ES Grand Minivan	H54R	23952	625	850	1675	3000
5 Passenger			(200)	(200)	(265)	(265)
AWD	K		250	250	335	335
V6 3.8 Liter	L		50	50	65	65
RAM WAGON—V8—Truck Equipment Schedule T1						
B150 Passenger Van	B15Y	16643	725	1025	1900	3300
B250 Passenger Van	B25Y	20412	775	1100	2000	3425
B350 Passenger Van	B35Y	21113	875	1250	2225	3725
5 Passenger			(200)	(200)	(265)	(265)
Maxi-Wagon	4		50	50	65	65
V6 3.9 Liter	X		(200)	(200)	(265)	(265)
V8 5.9 Liter	Z		50	50	65	65
RAM VAN—V6—Truck Equipment Schedule T1						
B150 Cargo Van	B11X	17431	625	875	1700	3000
B250 Cargo Van	B21X	17844	675	950	1825	3150
Maxi-Van	4		50	50	65	65
V8 5.2 Liter	Y		100	100	135	135
V8 5.9 Liter	Z		200	200	265	265
RAM VAN—V8—Truck Equipment Schedule T1						
B350 Cargo Van	B31Y	19124	775	1100	2000	3425
Maxi-Van	4		50	50	65	65
V8 5.9 Liter	Z		50	50	65	65
DAKOTA PICKUP—4-Cyl.—Truck Equipment Schedule T2						
WS Short Bed	L26G	10249	275	400	975	1875
WS Long Bed	L26G	11774	325	450	1075	2050
Sport Short Bed	L26G	11237	325	450	1075	2050
Short Bed	L26G	11927	375	525	1150	2175
Long Bed	L26G	12777	300	425	1000	1950
4WD	G		400	400	535	535
V6 3.9 Liter	X		125	125	165	165
V8 5.2 Liter	Y		150	150	200	200
DAKOTA PICKUP—V6—Truck Equipment Schedule T2						
Sport Club Cab	L23X	14537	775	1100	2025	3475
Club Cab	L23X	14794	825	1150	2100	3600
4WD	G		400	400	535	535
V8 5.2 Liter	Y		100	100	135	135
RAM REGULAR CAB PICKUP—V8—Truck Equipment Schedule T1						
1500 Short Bed	C16Y	17265	775	1100	2025	3475
1500 Long Bed	C16Y	17537	650	925	1775	3125
2500 Long Bed	C26Y	18205	900	1275	2350	4000
3500 Long Bed	C36Z	20706	1000	1400	2525	4175
Work Special			(250)	(250)	(335)	(335)
4WD	FM		500	500	665	665
V6 3.9 Liter	X		(350)	(350)	(465)	(465)
6-Cyl. 5.9L Turbo Dsl	C		1475	1475	1965	1965
V8 5.9 Liter	Z		75	75	100	100
V10 8.0 Liter	W		100	100	135	135

1995 DODGE/PLYM — (1orJ)BorP(4or7)—(H11K)–S

Body Type	VIN	List	Trade-In Fair	Trade-In Good	Pvt-Party Good	Retail Excellent
CARAVAN C/V—4-Cyl.—Truck Equipment Schedule T2						
Cargo Minivan	H11K	16705	275	375	950	1875
V6 3.0 Liter	3		200	200	265	265
CARAVAN C/V—V6—Truck Equipment Schedule T2						
Extended Minivan	H14R	18245	275	400	1050	2050
CARAVAN/VOYAGER—4-Cyl.—Truck Equipment Schedule T1						
Minivan	H25K	17930	450	625	1325	2475
5 Passenger			(200)	(200)	(265)	(265)
V6 3.0 Liter	3		200	200	265	265
CARAVAN/VOYAGER—V6—Truck Equipment Schedule T1						
SE Minivan	H453	20275	525	700	1475	2700
LE Minivan	H553	23940	625	850	1675	3000
ES Minivan	H553	24895	625	875	1725	3050
Grand Minivan	H243	20025	525	725	1500	2750
SE Grand Minivan	H44R	20375	625	850	1650	2975
LE Grand Minivan	H54R	24240	625	850	1700	3050
ES Grand Minivan	H54R	25095	725	1000	1900	3325
5 Passenger			(200)	(200)	(265)	(265)
AWD	K		250	250	335	335
V6 3.8 Liter	L		50	50	65	65

TRUCKS & VANS

Body	Type	VIN	List	Trade-In Fair	Trade-In Good	Pvt-Party Good	Retail Excellent
RAM WAGON—V8—Truck Equipment Schedule T1							
1500 Passenger Van	B15Y	17951	850	1175	2150	3650
2500 Passenger Van	B25Y	21627	900	1275	2350	4000
3500 Passenger Van	B35Y	22627	1025	1425	2575	4250
5 Passenger			(200)	(200)	(265)	(265)
Maxi-Wagon	4		50	50	65	65
V6 3.9 Liter	X		(200)	(200)	(265)	(265)
V8 5.9 Liter	Z		50	50	65	65
RAM VAN—V6—Truck Equipment Schedule T1							
1500 Cargo Van	B11X	18605	725	1025	1900	3325
2500 Cargo Van	B21X	18743	800	1125	2050	3500
Maxi-Van	4		50	50	65	65
V8 5.2 Liter	Y		100	100	135	135
V8 5.9 Liter	Z		200	200	265	265
RAM VAN—V8—Truck Equipment Schedule T1							
3500 Cargo Van	B31Y	20673	900	1275	2350	4000
Maxi-Van	4		50	50	65	65
V8 5.9 Liter	Z		50	50	65	65
DAKOTA PICKUP—4-Cyl.—Truck Equipment Schedule T2							
WS Short Bed	L26G	10975	350	475	1100	2100
WS Long Bed	L26G	12291	400	550	1200	2225
Sport Short Bed	L26G	11489	400	550	1200	2225
Short Bed	L26G	12710	450	625	1350	2525
Long Bed	L26G	13921	350	500	1125	2125
4WD	G		400	400	535	535
V6 3.9 Liter	X		125	125	165	165
V8 5.2 Liter	Y		50	150	200	200
DAKOTA PICKUP—V6—Truck Equipment Schedule T2							
Sport Club Cab	L23X	14722	900	1275	2350	4000
Club Cab	L23X	16006	975	1350	2475	4125
4WD	G		400	400	535	535
V8 5.2 Liter	Y		100	100	135	135
RAM REGULAR CAB PICKUP—V8—Truck Equipment Schedule T1							
1500 Short Bed	C16Y	17594	875	1250	2350	4000
1500 Long Bed	C16Y	17878	750	1050	1975	3425
2500 Long Bed	C26Y	18851	1050	1475	2600	4300
3500 Long Bed	C36Z	21468	1125	1575	2750	4475
Work Special			(250)	(250)	(335)	(335)
4WD	F		500	500	665	665
V6 3.9 Liter	X		(350)	(350)	(465)	(465)
6-Cyl. 5.9L Turbo Dsl	C		1500	1500	2000	2000
V8 5.9 Liter	Z		75	75	100	100
V10 8.0 Liter	W		100	100	135	135
RAM CLUB CAB PICKUP—V8—Truck Equipment Schedule T1							
1500 Short Bed	C13Y	20040	1400	1875	3125	4925
1500 Long Bed	C13Y	20321	1225	1700	2925	4675
2500 Short Bed	C23Z	21840	1750	2250	3525	5425
2500 Long Bed	C23Z	22046	1625	2125	3400	5250
3500 Long Bed	C33Z	23667	1750	2250	3525	5425
4WD	F		500	500	665	665
6-Cyl. 5.9L Turbo Dsl	C		1500	1500	2000	2000
V8 5.9 Liter	Z		75	75	100	100
V10 8.0 Liter	W		100	100	135	135

1996 DODGE/PLYM–(1,2or3)BorP(4or7)–(P253)–T

Body	Type	VIN	List	Trade-In Fair	Trade-In Good	Pvt-Party Good	Retail Excellent
CARAVAN/VOYAGER—V6—Truck Equipment Schedule T1							
Minivan	P253	18510	500	675	1475	2700
SE Minivan	P453	21070	625	825	1675	3000
LE Minivan	P55R	24180	650	925	1800	3150
ES Minivan	P55R	25605	725	1050	1975	3425
Grand Minivan	P243	19410	625	825	1675	3000
SE Grand Minivan	P443	21810	625	875	1750	3075
LE Grand Minivan	P54R	24670	725	1050	1975	3425
ES Grand Minivan	P54R	26595	875	1250	2350	4000
5 Passenger			(250)	(250)	(335)	(335)
w/o 2nd Sliding Door			(50)	(50)	(65)	(65)
4-Cyl. 2.4 Liter	B		(375)	(375)	(500)	(500)
V6 3.8 Liter	L		75	75	100	100
RAM WAGON—V8—Truck Equipment Schedule T1							
1500 Passenger Van	B15Y	19965	975	1350	2475	4150
2500 Passenger Van	B24Y	21374	1025	1425	2575	4275
3500 Passenger Van	B34Y	22575	1150	1625	2825	4525
Maxi-Wagon			75	75	100	100

1996 DODGE/PLYMOUTH

TRUCKS & VANS

Body Type	VIN	List	Trade-In Fair	Good	Pvt-Party Good	Retail Excellent
V6 3.9 Liter	X		(250)	(250)	(335)	(335)
V8 5.9 Liter	Z		50	50	65	65
RAM VAN—V6—Truck Equipment Schedule T1						
1500 Cargo Van	B11X	18460	850	1200	2200	3725
2500 Cargo Van	B21X	18563	925	1325	2425	4075
Maxi-Van			75	75	100	100
V8 5.2 Liter	Y		125	125	165	165
V8 5.9 Liter	Z		250	250	335	335
RAM VAN—V8—Truck Equipment Schedule T1						
3500 Cargo Van	B31Y	21075	1075	1500	2650	4350
Maxi-Van			75	75	100	100
V8 5.9 Liter	Z		50	50	65	65
DAKOTA PICKUP—4-Cyl.—Truck Equipment Schedule T2						
WS Short Bed	L26G	11764	350	500	1150	2175
WS Long Bed	L26G	12380	400	575	1225	2300
Sport Short Bed	L26G	12440	400	575	1225	2300
Short Bed	L26G	13665	475	625	1425	2625
Long Bed	L26X	14176	375	525	1175	2225
4WD	G		525	525	700	700
V6 3.9 Liter	X		150	150	200	200
V8 5.2 Liter	Y		200	200	265	265
DAKOTA PICKUP—V6—Truck Equipment Schedule T2						
Sport Club Cab	L23X	15616	950	1325	2450	4125
Club Cab	L23X	16746	1025	1425	2550	4250
4WD	G		525	525	700	700
V8 5.2 Liter	Y		125	125	165	165
RAM REGULAR CAB PICKUP—V8—Truck Equipment Schedule T1						
1500 Short Bed	C16Y	18032	950	1325	2475	4150
1500 Long Bed	C16Y	18316	800	1125	2100	3600
2500 Short Bed	C26Y	19569	1100	1550	2750	4475
3500 Long Bed	C365	22286	1225	1725	2950	4700
Work Special			(300)	(300)	(400)	(400)
4WD	F		600	600	800	800
V6 3.9 Liter	X		(375)	(375)	(500)	(500)
6-Cyl. 5.9L Turbo Diesel	C		1875	1875	2500	2500
V8 5.9 Liter	Z		125	125	165	165
V10 8.0 Liter	W		125	125	165	165
RAM CLUB CAB PICKUP—V8—Truck Equipment Schedule T1						
1500 Short Bed	C13Y	20190	1600	2075	3350	5200
1500 Long Bed	C13Y	20471	1400	1850	3100	4925
2500 Short Bed	C23Z	22958	1975	2525	3825	5750
2500 Long Bed	C23Z	23164	1850	2375	3675	5575
3500 Long Bed	C33Z	24685	1975	2525	3825	5750
4WD	F		600	600	800	800
6-Cyl. 5.9L Turbo Diesel	C		1875	1875	2500	2500
V8 5.9 Liter	Z,5		125	125	165	165
V10 8.0 Liter	W		125	125	165	165

1997 DODGE/PLYM—1(BorP)4—(P253)—V—#

Body Type	VIN	List	Trade-In Fair	Good	Pvt-Party Good	Retail Excellent
CARAVAN/VOYAGER—V6—Truck Equipment Schedule T1						
Minivan	P253	19570	575	775	1625	2975
SE Minivan	P453	22495	650	925	1825	3200
LE Minivan	P55R	25715	725	1000	1925	3375
ES Minivan	P55R	27055	850	1175	2300	3950
Grand Minivan	P243	20565	675	950	1875	3300
SE Grand Minivan	P443	23325	700	1000	1925	3375
LE Grand Minivan	P54R	26405	875	1225	2350	4025
ES Grand Minivan	P54R	26995	1025	1425	2575	4300
5 Passenger			(275)	(275)	(365)	(365)
w/o 2nd Sliding Door			(50)	(50)	(65)	(65)
AWD	T		350	350	465	465
4-Cyl. 2.4 Liter	B		(450)	(450)	(600)	(600)
V6 3.8 Liter	L		100	100	135	135
RAM WAGON—V8—Truck Equipment Schedule T1						
1500 Passenger Van	B15Y	21192	1025	1450	2600	4300
2500 Passenger Van	B25Y	22555	1100	1550	2725	4425
3500 Passenger Van	B25Y	23755	1300	1775	3000	4750
Maxi-Wagon			100	100	135	135
V6 3.9 Liter	X		(275)	(275)	(365)	(365)
V8 5.9 Liter	Z		50	50	65	65
RAM VAN—V6—Truck Equipment Schedule T1						
1500 Cargo Van	B11X	19090	925	1300	2425	4075
2500 Cargo Van	B21X	19295	1000	1425	2575	4275

288   DEDUCT FOR RECONDITIONING   0709

1997 DODGE/PLYMOUTH

Body Type	VIN	List	Trade-In Fair	Good	Pvt-Party Good	Retail Excellent
Maxi-Van			100	100	135	135
V8 5.2 Liter	Y		150	150	200	200
V8 5.9 Liter			275	275	365	365
RAM VAN—V8—Truck Equipment Schedule T1						
3500 Cargo Van	B31Y	21885	1175	1650	2825	4550
Maxi-Van			100	100	135	135
V8 5.9 Liter	Z		50	50	65	65
DAKOTA PICKUP—4-Cyl.—Truck Equipment Schedule T1						
Short Bed	L26P	14959	525	700	1525	2800
Long Bed	L26P	15419	425	600	1300	2400
4WD	G		650	650	865	865
V6 3.9 Liter	X		175	175	235	235
V8 5.2 Liter	Y		250	250	335	335
DAKOTA PICKUP—V6—Truck Equipment Schedule T1						
Club Cab	L23X	18654	1125	1575	2775	4500
4WD	G		650	650	865	865
V8 5.2 Liter	Y		150	150	200	200
RAM REGULAR CAB PICKUP—V8—Truck Equipment Schedule T1						
1500 Short Bed	C16Y	13881	1050	1500	2675	4375
1500 Long Bed	C16Y	19118	875	1250	2375	4050
2500 Long Bed	C26Z	21134	1250	1725	2975	4750
3500 Long Bed	C36Z	22619	1425	1900	3175	5000
Work Special			(350)	(350)	(465)	(465)
4WD	F		700	700	935	935
V6 3.9 Liter	X		(400)	(400)	(535)	(535)
6-Cyl. 5.9L Turbo Diesel			2250	2250	3000	3000
V8 5.9 Liter	5,Z		175	175	235	235
V10 8.0 Liter			150	150	200	200
RAM CLUB CAB PICKUP—V8—Truck Equipment Schedule T1						
1500 Short Bed	C13Y	20914	1825	2350	3650	5525
1500 Long Bed	C13Y	21194	1600	2100	3375	5250
2500 Short Bed	C23Z	23139	2250	2825	4175	6175
2500 Long Bed	C23Z	23344	2125	2700	4025	5975
3500 Long Bed	C33Z	24964	2250	2825	4175	6175
4WD	F		700	700	935	935
6-Cyl. 5.9L Turbo Diesel			2250	2250	3000	3000
V8 5.9 Liter	5,Z		175	175	235	235
V10 8.0 Liter	W		150	150	200	200

1998 DODGE/PLYM—1(BorP)4—(S28Y)—W—#

Body Type	VIN	List	Trade-In Fair	Good	Pvt-Party Good	Retail Excellent
DURANGO 4WD—V8—Truck Equipment Schedule T1						
SLT Sport Utility 4D	S28Y	28575	2225	2825	4150	6125
w/o Third Seat			(350)	(350)	(465)	(465)
V6 3.9 Liter	X		(350)	(350)	(465)	(465)
V8 5.9 Liter	Y		175	175	235	235
CARAVAN/VOYAGER—V6—Truck Equipment Schedule T1						
Minivan	P253	20535	650	925	1850	3250
SE Minivan	P453	22065	725	1025	1975	3475
LE Minivan	P55R	25610	800	1125	2100	3650
Grand Minivan	P243	20730	800	1125	2100	3650
SE Grand Minivan	P443	23060	800	1150	2150	3725
LE Grand Minivan	P54R	26605	1025	1450	2625	4325
ES Grand Minivan	P54R	27760	1175	1650	2850	4600
5 Passenger			(300)	(300)	(400)	(400)
w/o 2nd Sliding Door			(50)	(50)	(65)	(65)
AWD	T		400	400	535	535
4-Cyl. 2.4 Liter	B		(525)	(525)	(700)	(700)
V6 3.8 Liter	L		100	100	135	135
RAM WAGON—V8—Truck Equipment Schedule T1						
1500 Passenger Van	B15Y	21655	1125	1575	2775	4475
2500 Passenger Van	B25Y	23480	1225	1700	2925	4675
3500 Maxi Passenger	B35Y	26185	1475	1950	3200	5000
V6 3.9 Liter	X		(300)	(300)	(400)	(400)
V8 5.9 Liter			50	50	65	65
RAM VAN—V6—Truck Equipment Schedule T1						
1500 Cargo Van	B11X	19440	1025	1425	2575	4300
Maxi-Van			100	100	135	135
V8 5.2 Liter	Y		175	175	235	235
V8 5.9 Liter	Z		300	300	400	400
RAM VAN—V8—Truck Equipment Schedule T1						
2500 Cargo Van	B21Y	21375	1300	1775	3000	4775
3500 Cargo Van	B31Y	22545	1350	1825	3050	4825
Maxi-Van			100	100	135	135

TRUCKS & VANS

0709

SEE BACK PAGES FOR TRUCK EQUIPMENT

289

TRUCKS & VANS

Body	Type	VIN	List	Trade-In Fair	Trade-In Good	Pvt-Party Good	Retail Excellent
	V8 5.9 Liter	Z		50	50	65	65
DAKOTA PICKUP—4-Cyl.—Truck Equipment Schedule T1							
Short Bed		L26P	15235	600	800	1675	3050
R/T Short Bed		L26P	19205	900	1275	2425	4100
Long Bed		L26P	15695	500	675	1500	2800
4WD		G		775	775	1035	1035
V6 3.9 Liter		X		200	200	265	265
V8 5.2 Liter		Y		300	300	400	400
V8 5.9 Liter (ex R/T)		Z		400	400	535	535
DAKOTA PICKUP—V6—Truck Equipment Schedule T1							
Club Cab		L22X	18430	1325	1800	3050	4825
R/T Club Cab		L22Z	21360	1750	2275	3550	5450
4WD		G		775	775	1035	1035
4-Cyl. 2.5 Liter		P		(200)	(200)	(265)	(265)
V8 5.2 Liter		Y		175	175	235	235
V8 5.9 Liter (ex R/T)		Z		300	300	400	400
RAM REGULAR CAB PICKUP—V8—Truck Equipment Schedule T1							
1500 Short Bed		C16Y	19240	1175	1625	2875	4650
1500 Long Bed		C16Y	19525	1000	1425	2575	4300
2500 Long Bed		C26Z	21900	1450	1925	3200	5050
3500 Long Bed		C36Z	23190	1650	2150	3425	5325
Work Special				(400)	(400)	(535)	(535)
4WD		F		800	800	1065	1065
V6 3.9 Liter		X		(425)	(425)	(565)	(565)
6-Cyl. 5.9L Turbo Dsl		6,D		2600	2600	3465	3465
V8 5.9 Liter		5,Z		200	200	265	265
V10 8.0 Liter		W		175	175	235	235
RAM CLUB CAB PICKUP—V8—Truck Equipment Schedule T1							
1500 Short Bed		C12Y	21365	2075	2625	3950	5900
1500 Long Bed		C12Y	21645	1850	2350	3675	5575
2500 Short Bed		C22Z	23680	2550	3150	4525	6600
2500 Long Bed		C22Z	23870	2425	3025	4350	6400
4WD		F		800	800	1065	1065
6-Cyl. 5.9L Turbo Dsl		6,D		2600	2600	3465	3465
V8 5.9 Liter		Z		200	200	265	265
V10 8.0 Liter		W		175	175	235	235
RAM QUAD CAB PICKUP—V8—Truck Equipment Schedule T1							
1500 Short Bed		C13Y	22115	2325	2925	4275	6275
1500 Long Bed		C13Y	22395	2150	2725	4050	6025
2500 Short Bed		C23Z	24430	2825	3450	4850	6975
2500 Long Bed		C23Z	24620	2700	3300	4675	6750
3500 Long Bed		C33Z	26325	2850	3475	4875	7000
4WD		F		800	800	1065	1065
6-Cyl. 5.9L Turbo Dsl		6,D		2600	2600	3465	3465
V8 5.9 Liter		5,Z		200	200	265	265
V10 8.0 Liter		W		175	175	235	235

1999 DODGE/PLYM—(1,2,3or4)B4—(S28Y)—X—#

Body	Type	VIN	List	Trade-In Fair	Trade-In Good	Pvt-Party Good	Retail Excellent
DURANGO 4WD—V8—Truck Equipment Schedule T1							
SLT Sport Utility 4D		S28Y	29030	2475	3075	4400	6425
w/o Third Seat				(400)	(400)	(535)	(535)
2WD		R		(350)	(350)	(465)	(465)
V6 3.9 Liter		X		(400)	(400)	(535)	(535)
V8 5.9 Liter		Z		200	200	265	265
CARAVAN/VOYAGER—V6—Truck Equipment Schedule T1							
Minivan 4D		P25S	21185	775	1100	2100	3650
SE Minivan 4D		P45S	22460	850	1200	2325	4025
LE Minivan 4D		P55R	28280	900	1275	2425	4150
Grand Minivan 4D		P24S	22580	925	1300	2450	4175
SE Grand Minivan 4D		P44S	23455	975	1350	2525	4250
LE Grand Minivan 4D		P54R	27275	1225	1700	2950	4725
ES Grand Minivan 4D		P54L	29485	1450	1925	3200	5025
5 Passenger				(325)	(325)	(435)	(435)
w/o 2nd Sliding Door				(50)	(50)	(65)	(65)
AWD		T		450	450	600	600
4-Cyl. 2.4 Liter		B		(600)	(600)	(800)	(800)
V6 3.8 Liter		L		100	100	135	135
RAM WAGON—V8—Truck Equipment Schedule T1							
1500 Passenger Van		B15Y	22000	1300	1775	3025	4800
2500 Passenger Van		B25Y	23725	1450	1925	3175	5025
3500 Maxi Passenger		B35Y	26430	1725	2225	3500	5400
V6 3.9 Liter		X		(325)	(325)	(435)	(435)
V8 5.9 Liter		Z		50	50	65	65

1999 DODGE/PLYMOUTH

Body Type	VIN	List	Trade-In Fair	Trade-In Good	Pvt-Party Good	Retail Excellent
RAM VAN—V6—Truck Equipment Schedule T1						
1500 Cargo Van	B11X	19685	1150	1600	2825	4575
Maxi-Van			100	100	135	135
V8 5.2 Liter	Y		200	200	265	265
V8 5.9 Liter	Z		325	325	435	435
RAM VAN—V8—Truck Equipment Schedule T1						
2500 Cargo Van	B21Y	21620	1525	2025	3275	5125
3500 Cargo Van	B31Y	22790	1575	2050	3325	5175
Maxi-Van			100	100	135	135
V8 5.9 Liter	Z		50	50	65	65
DAKOTA PICKUP—4-Cyl.—Truck Equipment Schedule T1						
Short Bed	L26P	15545	675	925	1850	3325
Long Bed	L26P	16005	600	800	1700	3075
R/T Short Bed	L26Z	19745	1050	1475	2650	4350
4WD	G		900	900	1200	1200
V6 3.9 Liter	X		225	225	300	300
V8 5.2 Liter	Y		325	325	435	435
V8 5.9 Liter (ex R/T)	Z		450	450	600	600
DAKOTA PICKUP—V6—Truck Equipment Schedule T1						
Club Cab	L22X	18740	1575	2050	3325	5175
R/T Club Cab	L22Z	20215	2000	2575	3875	5800
4WD	G		900	900	1200	1200
4-Cyl. 2.5 Liter	P		(225)	(225)	(300)	(300)
V8 5.2 Liter	Y		200	200	265	265
V8 5.9 Liter (ex R/T)	Z		325	325	435	435
RAM REGULAR CAB PICKUP—V8—Truck Equipment Schedule T1						
1500 Short Bed	C16Y	19485	1350	1825	3075	4925
1500 Long Bed	C16Y	19770	1100	1550	2775	4550
2500 Long Bed	C26Z	22145	1650	2150	3450	5350
3500 Long Bed	C36Z	23935	1850	2400	3700	5625
Work Special			(425)	(425)	(565)	(565)
4WD	F		900	900	1200	1200
V6 3.9 Liter	X		(450)	(450)	(600)	(600)
6-Cyl. 5.9L Turbo Diesel	6		2950	2950	3930	3930
V8 5.9 Liter	5,Z		225	225	300	300
V10 8.0 Liter	W		200	200	265	265
RAM CLUB CAB PICKUP—V8—Truck Equipment Schedule T1						
1500 Short Bed	C12Y	21515	2350	2925	4300	6300
1500 Long Bed	C12Y	21795	2075	2625	3975	5950
2500 Short Bed	C22Z	23330	2850	3475	4875	7000
2500 Long Bed	C22Z	23520	2725	3325	4725	6800
4WD	F		900	900	1200	1200
6-Cyl. 5.9L Turbo Diesel	6		2950	2950	3930	3930
V8 5.9 Liter	Z		225	225	300	300
V10 8.0 Liter	W		200	200	265	265
RAM QUAD CAB PICKUP—V8—Truck Equipment Schedule T1						
1500 Short Bed	C13Y	22310	2625	3225	4600	6700
1500 Long Bed	C13Y	22590	2425	3025	4375	6425
2500 Short Bed	C23Z	24125	3175	3850	5275	7475
2500 Long Bed	C23Z	24315	3000	3650	5075	7225
3500 Long Bed	C33Z	26915	3175	3875	5300	7500
4WD	F		900	900	1200	1200
6-Cyl. 5.9L Turbo Dsl	6		2950	2950	3930	3930
V8 5.9 Liter	5,Z		225	225	300	300
V10 8.0 Liter	W		200	200	265	265

2000 DODGE/PLYM—(1,2,3or4)B4—(S28N)—Y—#

Body Type	VIN	List	Trade-In Fair	Trade-In Good	Pvt-Party Good	Retail Excellent
DURANGO 4WD—V8—Truck Equipment Schedule T1						
SLT Sport Utility 4D	S28N	29060	2750	3350	4725	6800
R/T Sport Utility 4D	S28Z	33810	3100	3775	5200	7350
w/o Third Seat			(450)	(450)	(600)	(600)
2WD	R		(400)	(400)	(535)	(535)
V8 5.9 Liter (ex R/T)	Z		225	225	300	300
CARAVAN/VOYAGER—V6—Truck Equipment Schedule T1						
Minivan 4D	P243	21905	925	1300	2475	4225
SE Minivan 4D	P443	23675	1000	1400	2600	4350
Grand Minivan 4D	P243	22380	1100	1525	2775	4525
SE Grand Minivan 4D	P443	24670	1150	1625	2875	4650
LE Grand Minivan 4D	P54R	27785	1550	2025	3300	5175
ES Grand Minivan 4D	P54L	29995	1800	2300	3600	5525
5 Passenger			(350)	(350)	(465)	(465)
w/o 2nd Sliding Door			(50)	(50)	(65)	(65)
AWD	T		500	500	665	665

TRUCKS & VANS

TRUCKS & VANS

Body	Type	VIN	List	Trade-In Fair	Trade-In Good	Pvt-Party Good	Retail Excellent
4-Cyl. 2.4 Liter		B		**(650)**	**(650)**	**(865)**	**(865)**
V6 3.8 Liter		L		**100**	**100**	**135**	**135**
GRAND CARAVAN AWD—V6—Truck Equipment Schedule T1							
Sport Minivan 4D		T44L	28670	**1625**	**2125**	**3425**	**5300**
5 Passenger				**(350)**	**(350)**	**(465)**	**(465)**
RAM WAGON—V8—Truck Equipment Schedule T1							
1500 Passenger Van		B15Y	22245	**1575**	**2075**	**3350**	**5225**
2500 Passenger Van		B25Y	23670	**1775**	**2275**	**3550**	**5450**
3500 Maxi Passenger		B35Y	26675	**2025**	**2600**	**3900**	**5825**
V6 3.9 Liter		X		**(350)**	**(350)**	**(465)**	**(465)**
V8 5.9 Liter		Z		**50**	**50**	**65**	**65**
RAM VAN—V6—Truck Equipment Schedule T1							
1500 Cargo Van		B11X	19575	**1375**	**1850**	**3100**	**4925**
Maxi-Van				**100**	**100**	**135**	**135**
V8 5.2 Liter		T,Y		**200**	**200**	**265**	**265**
V8 5.9 Liter		Z		**350**	**350**	**465**	**465**
RAM VAN—V8—Truck Equipment Schedule T1							
2500 Cargo Van		B21Y	21075	**1825**	**2325**	**3625**	**5525**
3500 Cargo Van		B31Y	23260	**1850**	**2375**	**3675**	**5550**
Maxi-Van				**100**	**100**	**135**	**135**
V8 5.9 Liter		Z		**50**	**50**	**65**	**65**
DAKOTA PICKUP—4-Cyl.—Truck Equipment Schedule T1							
Short Bed		L26P	15850	**800**	**1125**	**2300**	**4025**
R/T Short Bed		L26Z	20090	**1200**	**1675**	**2950**	**4775**
4WD		G		**1025**	**1025**	**1365**	**1365**
V6 3.9 Liter		X		**250**	**250**	**335**	**335**
V8 4.7 Liter		Y		**350**	**350**	**465**	**465**
V8 5.9 Liter (ex R/T)		Z		**500**	**500**	**665**	**665**
DAKOTA PICKUP—V6—Truck Equipment Schedule T1							
Club Cab		L22X	19045	**1850**	**2375**	**3675**	**5575**
R/T Club Cab		L22Z	22340	**2325**	**2925**	**4275**	**6300**
Quad Cab		L2AX	20290	**2150**	**2725**	**4050**	**6000**
4WD				**1025**	**1025**	**1365**	**1365**
4-Cyl. 2.5 Liter		P		**(250)**	**(250)**	**(335)**	**(335)**
V8 4.7 Liter		N		**200**	**200**	**265**	**265**
V8 5.9 Liter (ex R/T)		Z		**350**	**350**	**465**	**465**
RAM REGULAR CAB PICKUP—V8—Truck Equipment Schedule T1							
1500 Short Bed		C16Y	19695	**1525**	**2025**	**3350**	**5250**
1500 Long Bed		C16Y	19980	**1250**	**1725**	**3025**	**4850**
2500 Long Bed		C26Z	22570	**1850**	**2375**	**3725**	**5675**
3500 Long Bed		C36Z	24330	**2100**	**2650**	**4025**	**6000**
Work Special				**(450)**	**(450)**	**(600)**	**(600)**
4WD		F		**1000**	**1000**	**1335**	**1335**
V6 3.9 Liter		X		**(450)**	**(450)**	**(600)**	**(600)**
6-Cyl. 5.9L Turbo Diesel		6		**3300**	**3300**	**4400**	**4400**
V8 5.9 Liter		Z,5		**250**	**250**	**335**	**335**
V10 8.0 Liter		W		**225**	**225**	**300**	**300**
RAM CLUB CAB PICKUP—V8—Truck Equipment Schedule T1							
1500 Short Bed		C12Y	21890	**2625**	**3225**	**4625**	**6725**
4WD		F		**1000**	**1000**	**1335**	**1335**
V8 5.9 Liter		Z		**250**	**250**	**335**	**335**
RAM QUAD CAB PICKUP—V8—Truck Equipment Schedule T1							
1500 Short Bed		C13Y	22750	**2925**	**3550**	**4950**	**7100**
1500 Long Bed		C13Y	23030	**2725**	**3325**	**4700**	**6800**
2500 Short Bed		C23Z	24335	**3525**	**4225**	**5675**	**7950**
2500 Long Bed		C23Z	24525	**3325**	**4025**	**5475**	**7700**
3500 Long Bed		C33Z	27125	**3550**	**4275**	**5725**	**7975**
4WD		F		**1000**	**1000**	**1335**	**1335**
6-Cyl. 5.9L Turbo Dsl		6		**3300**	**3300**	**4400**	**4400**
V8 5.9 Liter		Z,5		**250**	**250**	**335**	**335**
V10 8.0 Liter		W		**225**	**225**	**300**	**300**

2001 DODGE—(1or2)B(4,7or8)-(S28N)-1

Body	Type	VIN	List	Trade-In Fair	Trade-In Good	Pvt-Party Good	Retail Excellent
DURANGO 4WD—V8—Truck Equipment Schedule T1							
SLT Sport Utility 4D		S28N	30740	**3075**	**3750**	**5150**	**7300**
R/T Sport Utility 4D		S28Z	30990	**3500**	**4200**	**5625**	**7850**
w/o Third Seat				**(475)**	**(475)**	**(635)**	**(635)**
2WD		R		**(450)**	**(450)**	**(600)**	**(600)**
V8 5.9 Liter (ex R/T)		Z		**250**	**250**	**335**	**335**
CARAVAN—V6—Truck Equipment Schedule T1							
SE Minivan 4D		P44B	19800	**1125**	**1575**	**2825**	**4600**
Sport Minivan 4D		P64G	24165	**1200**	**1700**	**2950**	**4750**
SE Grand Minivan 4D		P44G	22440	**1200**	**1675**	**2925**	**4725**

TRUCKS & VANS

Body	Type	VIN	List	Trade-In Fair	Good	Pvt-Party Good	Retail Excellent
Sport Grand 4D		P64G	24915	1475	1950	3225	5100
EX Grand Minivan 4D		P44L	26725	1425	1900	3200	5050
ES Grand Minivan 4D		P54L	29750	2175	2750	4075	6025
5 Passenger				(375)	(375)	(500)	(500)
AWD		T		525	525	700	700
4-Cyl. 2.4 Liter		B		(700)	(700)	(935)	(935)
V6 3.8 Liter		L		475	475	635	635
RAM WAGON—V8—Truck Equipment Schedule T1							
1500 Passenger Van		B15Y	22615	1950	2500	3800	5700
2500 Passenger Van		B25Y	24040	2125	2675	4000	5925
3500 Maxi Passenger		B35Y	27055	2425	3025	4325	6350
V6 3.9 Liter		X		(375)	(375)	(500)	(500)
V8 5.9 Liter		Z		50	50	65	65
RAM VAN—V6—Truck Equipment Schedule T1							
1500 Cargo Van		B11X	19890	1700	2200	3500	5375
2500 Cargo Van		B21X	21390	1850	2350	3650	5525
Maxi-Van				100	100	135	135
V8 5.2 Liter		Y		200	200	265	265
V8 5.9 Liter		Z		375	375	500	500
RAM VAN—V8—Truck Equipment Schedule T1							
3500 Cargo Van		B31Y	23575	2225	2800	4100	6050
Maxi-Van				100	100	135	135
V8 5.9 Liter		Z		50	50	65	65
DAKOTA PICKUP—4-Cyl.—Truck Equipment Schedule T1							
Short Bed		L26P	16255	975	1375	2625	4400
R/T Short Bed		L26Z	20505	1500	1975	3300	5225
4WD		G		1150	1150	1535	1535
V6 3.9 Liter		X		250	250	335	335
V8 4.7 Liter		N		375	375	500	500
V8 5.9 Liter (ex R/T)		5		550	550	735	735
DAKOTA PICKUP—V6—Truck Equipment Schedule T1							
Club Cab		L22X	19580	2200	2775	4150	6175
R/T Club Cab		L22Z	22885	2725	3325	4725	6825
Quad Cab		L23X	21950	2525	3100	4475	6575
4WD		G		1150	1150	1535	1535
4-Cyl. 2.5 Liter		P		(275)	(275)	(365)	(365)
V8 4.7 Liter		N		200	200	265	265
V8 5.6 Liter (ex R/T)		5		375	375	500	500
RAM REGULAR CAB PICKUP—V8—Truck Equipment Schedule T1							
1500 Short Bed		C16Y	20145	1775	2275	3625	5550
1500 Long Bed		C16Y	20430	1450	1925	3250	5175
2500 Long Bed		C26Z	23475	2075	2650	4000	6000
3500 Long Bed		C36Z	25360	2350	2925	4300	6350
Work Special				(475)	(475)	(635)	(635)
4WD		F		1100	1100	1465	1465
V6 3.9 Liter		X		(450)	(450)	(600)	(600)
6-Cyl. 5.9L Turbo Diesel		6		3650	3650	4865	4865
6-Cyl. 5.9L HO Turbo Dsl		7		4300	4300	5730	5730
V8 5.9 Liter		Z		275	275	365	365
V10 8.0 Liter		W		225	225	300	300
RAM CLUB CAB PICKUP—V8—Truck Equipment Schedule T1							
1500 Short Bed		C12Y	21465	2900	3525	4950	7075
4WD		F		1100	1100	1465	1465
V8 5.9 Liter		Z		275	275	365	365
RAM QUAD CAB PICKUP—V8—Truck Equipment Schedule T1							
1500 Short Bed		C13Y	23575	3200	3900	5325	7525
1500 Long Bed		C13Y	23655	3000	3625	5050	7200
2500 Short Bed		C23Z	25440	3875	4600	6075	8375
2500 Long Bed		C23Z	25630	3700	4400	5875	8150
3500 Long Bed		C33Z	28155	3950	4675	6150	8475
4WD		F		1100	1100	1465	1465
6-Cyl. 5.9L Turbo Dsl		6		3650	3650	4865	4865
6-Cyl. 5.9L HO Turbo Dsl		7		4300	4300	5730	5730
V8 5.9 Liter		Z		275	275	365	365
V10 8.0 Liter		W		225	225	300	300

2002 DODGE — 1B(4,7or8)-(S38N)-2-#

Body	Type	VIN	List	Trade-In Fair	Good	Pvt-Party Good	Retail Excellent
DURANGO 4WD—V8—Truck Equipment Schedule T1							
Sport Utility 4D		S38N	27595	3350	4050	5675	8150
R/T Sport Utility 4D		S78Z	37010	4275	5050	6750	9350
w/o Third Seat				(500)	(500)	(665)	(665)
2WD		R		(500)	(500)	(665)	(665)
V8 5.9 Liter (ex R/T)		Z		250	250	335	335

TRUCKS & VANS

Body	Type	VIN	List	Trade-In Fair	Trade-In Good	Pvt-Party Good	Retail Excellent
CARAVAN—V6—Truck Equipment Schedule T1							
eC Minivan 4D	P15B	16995	1050	1500	2975	5050
SE Minivan 4D	P44B	19795	1275	1750	3275	5400
Sport Minivan 4D	P64G	24060	1375	1850	3400	5525
SE Grand Minivan 4D	P44G	22440	1375	1850	3400	5525
eL Grand Minivan 4D	P343	24175	1575	2050	3600	5750
Sport Grand 4D	P64G	24930	1675	2175	3725	5900
EX Grand Minivan 4D	P44L	26725	1650	2150	3700	5875
ES Grand Minivan 4D	P54L	30135	2400	3000	4575	6875
5 Passenger			(400)	(400)	(535)	(535)
AWD	T		550	550	735	735
4-Cyl. 2.4 Liter	B		(750)	(750)	(1000)	(1000)
V6 3.8 Liter	L		500	500	665	665
RAM WAGON—V8—Truck Equipment Schedule T1							
1500 Passenger Van	B15Y	22035	2225	2800	4350	6625
2500 Passenger Van	B25Y	24050	2400	3000	4550	6825
3500 Maxi Passenger	B35Y	27055	2725	3325	4925	7250
V6 3.9 Liter	X		(400)	(400)	(535)	(535)
V8 5.9 Liter	Z		50	50	65	65
RAM VAN—V6—Truck Equipment Schedule T1							
1500 Cargo Van	B11X	20050	1900	2425	3975	6150
2500 Cargo Van	B21X	21595	2025	2575	4125	6325
Maxi-Van			100	100	135	135
V8 5.2 Liter	Y		200	200	265	265
V8 5.9 Liter	Z		400	400	535	535
RAM VAN—V8—Truck Equipment Schedule T1							
3500 Cargo Van	B31Y	23780	2450	3050	4600	6875
Maxi-Van			100	100	135	135
V8 5.9 Liter	Z		50	50	65	65
DAKOTA PICKUP—4-Cyl.—Truck Equipment Schedule T1							
Short Bed	L26P	16370	1050	1475	3025	5150
R/T Short Bed	L26Z	21290	1675	2150	3750	5975
4WD	G		1250	1250	1665	1665
V6 3.9 Liter	X		250	250	335	335
V8 4.7 Liter	N		400	400	535	535
V8 5.9 Liter (ex R/T)	Z		600	600	800	800
DAKOTA PICKUP—V6—Truck Equipment Schedule T1							
Club Cab	L22X	19695	2450	3050	4650	7000
R/T Club Cab	L22Z	23585	2950	3575	5275	7700
Quad Cab	L23X	21985	2725	3350	5000	7400
4WD	G		1250	1250	1665	1665
4-Cyl. 2.5 Liter	P		(300)	(300)	(400)	(400)
V8 4.7 Liter	N		200	200	265	265
V8 5.9 Liter (ex R/T)	Z		400	400	535	535
RAM REGULAR CAB PICKUP—V8—Truck Equipment Schedule T1							
1500 Short Bed	C16Y	19620	2475	3075	4725	7100
1500 Long Bed	C16Y	19905	2225	2800	4425	6750
2500 HD Long Bed	C26Z	23490	2100	2675	4300	6625
3500 Long Bed	C36Z	25375	2400	3000	4625	6975
4WD	F		1200	1200	1600	1600
V6 3.7 Liter	K		(450)	(450)	(600)	(600)
6-Cyl. 5.9L Turbo Diesel	6		4000	4000	5330	5330
6-Cyl. 5.9L HO Turbo Dsl	7		4500	4500	6000	6000
V8 5.9 Liter	Z		300	300	400	400
V10 8.0 Liter	W		225	225	300	300
RAM QUAD CAB PICKUP—V8—Truck Equipment Schedule T1							
1500 Short Bed	C13Y	23840	4125	4850	6600	9200
1500 Long Bed	C13Y	24120	3875	4600	6325	8925
2500 Short Bed	C23Z	25455	4050	4800	6525	9150
2500 Long Bed	C23Z	25645	3875	4600	6325	8925
3500 Long Bed	C33Z	28170	4125	4875	6625	9225
4WD	F		1200	1200	1600	1600
6-Cyl. 5.9L Turbo Dsl	6		4000	4000	5330	5330
6-Cyl. 5.9L HO Turbo Dsl	7		4500	4500	6000	6000
V8 5.9 Liter	Z		300	300	400	400
V10 8.0 Liter	W		225	225	300	300

2003 DODGE — (1,2or3)D(3,4,7or8)-(S38N)-3

Body	Type	VIN	List	Trade-In Fair	Trade-In Good	Pvt-Party Good	Retail Excellent
DURANGO 4WD—V8—Truck Equipment Schedule T1							
Sport Utility 4D	S38N	28875	3900	4650	6325	8875
R/T Sport Utility 4D	S78Z	38670	4950	5775	7550	10300
w/o Third Seat			(475)	(475)	(635)	(635)
2WD	R		(575)	(575)	(765)	(765)

TRUCKS & VANS

Body	Type	VIN	List	Trade-In Fair	Trade-In Good	Pvt-Party Good	Retail Excellent
	V8 5.9 Liter (ex R/T)	Z		300	300	400	400
CARAVAN—V6—Truck Equipment Schedule T2							
Cargo Minivan		P253	21965	775	1075	2525	4550
Grand Cargo Minivan		P253	22850	975	1375	2875	4950
CARAVAN—V6—Truck Equipment Schedule T1							
SE Minivan 4D		P25B	21440	1775	2300	3875	6075
Sport Minivan 4D		P453	25110	1850	2400	3950	6175
SE Grand Minivan 4D		P24R	22890	1800	2325	3900	6100
eL Grand Minivan 4D		P343	24425	1975	2525	4125	6350
Sport Grand 4D		P44R	28040	2125	2700	4300	6550
EX Grand Minivan 4D		P74L	26400	2100	2650	4250	6500
ES Grand Minivan 4D		P54L	33335	2950	3575	5200	7575
5 Passenger				(475)	(475)	(635)	(635)
AWD		T		650	650	865	865
4-Cyl. 2.4 Liter		B		(875)	(875)	(1165)	(1165)
V6 3.8 Liter		L		575	575	765	765
RAM VAN—V6—Truck Equipment Schedule T1							
1500 Cargo Van		B11X	20685	2650	3250	4850	7150
2500 Cargo Van		B21X	21640	2825	3425	5025	7350
Maxi-Van				150	150	200	200
V8 5.2 Liter		Y		250	250	335	335
V8 5.9 Liter		Z		450	450	600	600
RAM VAN—V8—Truck Equipment Schedule T1							
3500 Cargo Van		B31Y	24415	3300	4000	5575	7975
Maxi-Van				150	150	200	200
V8 5.9 Liter		Z		100	100	135	135
DAKOTA PICKUP—V6—Truck Equipment Schedule T1							
Short Bed		L16X	17680	1375	1850	3450	5675
R/T Short Bed		L76Z	22800	2125	2700	4325	6650
Club Cab		L22X	19375	2950	3600	5275	7725
R/T Club Cab		L22Z	25100	3600	4300	6000	8550
Quad Cab		L23X	22550	3350	4050	5725	8225
4WD		G		1425	1425	1900	1900
V8 4.7 Liter		N		250	250	335	335
V8 5.9 Liter (ex R/T)		Z		475	475	635	635
RAM REGULAR CAB PICKUP—V8—Truck Equipment Schedule T1							
1500 Short Bed		A16N	20225	3425	4125	5825	8350
1500 Long Bed		A16N	20510	3075	3725	5450	7925
4WD		U		1375	1375	1835	1835
V6 3.7 Liter		K		(525)	(525)	(700)	(700)
V8 5.7 Liter HEMI		D		875	875	1165	1165
V8 5.9 Liter		Z,5		250	250	335	335
RAM REGULAR CAB PICKUP—V8 HEMI—Truck Equipment Schedule T1							
2500 Long Bed		A26D	24255	3900	4625	6375	8975
3500 Long Bed		A36D	26140	4225	4975	6725	9350
4WD		U		1375	1375	1835	1835
6-Cyl. 5.9L Turbo Diesel		6		4150	4150	5530	5530
6-Cyl. 5.9L HO Turbo Dsl		C		4725	4725	6300	6300
V10 8.0 Liter		W		250	250	335	335
RAM QUAD CAB PICKUP—V8—Truck Equipment Schedule T1							
1500 Short Bed		A18N	24960	5125	5975	7825	10650
1500 Long Bed		A18N	25240	4825	5650	7475	10250
4WD		U		1375	1375	1835	1835
V6 3.7 Liter		K		(525)	(525)	(700)	(700)
V8 5.7 Liter HEMI		D		875	875	1165	1165
V8 5.9 Liter		Z,5		250	250	335	335
RAM QUAD CAB PICKUP—V8 HEMI—Truck Equipment Schedule T1							
2500 Short Bed		A28D	26600	5900	6850	8700	11600
2500 Long Bed		A28D	26790	5625	6550	8375	11250
3500 Short Bed		A386	32455	6075	7025	8900	11800
3500 Long Bed		A38D	29315	5950	6900	8775	11700
4WD		U		1375	1375	1835	1835
6-Cyl. 5.9L Turbo Dsl		6		4150	4150	5530	5530
6-Cyl. 5.9L HO Turbo Dsl		C		4725	4725	6300	6300
V10 8.0 Liter		W		250	250	335	335

2004 DODGE–(1,3orW)D(2,3,4,5,7or8)–(S38N)–4

Body	Type	VIN	List	Trade-In Fair	Trade-In Good	Pvt-Party Good	Retail Excellent
DURANGO 4WD—V8—Truck Equipment Schedule T1							
Sport Utility 4D		S38N	29350	4925	5750	7525	10250
w/o Third Seat				(550)	(550)	(735)	(735)
2WD		R		(650)	(650)	(865)	(865)
V6 3.7 Liter		K		(800)	(800)	(1065)	(1065)
V8 5.7 Liter		D		800	800	1065	1065

Body	Type	VIN	List	Trade-In Fair	Good	Pvt-Party Good	Retail Excellent
CARAVAN—V6—Truck Equipment Schedule T2							
Cargo Minivan	P21R	22585		825	1175	2650	4700
Grand Cargo Minivan	P23R	23455		1075	1525	3050	5175
CARAVAN—V6—Truck Equipment Schedule T1							
SE Minivan 4D	P25B	21795		2050	2600	4200	6450
SXT Minivan 4D	P45R	24850		2125	2700	4300	6550
SE Grand Minivan 4D	P24R	24975		2075	2650	4250	6500
EX Grand Minivan 4D	P74L	27225		2450	3050	4625	6925
SXT Grand Minivan	P44L	30335		3075	3725	5350	7750
5 Passenger	T			(550)	(550)	(735)	(735)
AWD	T			725	725	965	965
4-Cyl. 2.4 Liter	B			(1000)	(1000)	(1335)	(1335)
V6 3.8 Liter	L			650	650	865	865
DAKOTA PICKUP—V6—Truck Equipment Schedule T1							
Short Bed	L16X	18725		1875	2400	4050	6350
Club Cab	L22X	21395		3600	4300	6000	8550
Quad Cab	L23X	23595		4125	4875	6625	9200
4WD	G			1600	1600	2135	2135
V8 4.7 Liter	N			550	550	735	735
RAM REGULAR CAB PICKUP—V8—Truck Equipment Schedule T1							
1500 Short Bed	A16N	21900		3975	4700	6450	9050
1500 Long Bed	A16N	22185		3575	4300	6025	8575
4WD	U			1550	1550	2065	2065
V6 3.7 Liter	K			(600)	(600)	(800)	(800)
V8 5.7 Liter HEMI	D			950	950	1265	1265
RAM REGULAR CAB PICKUP—V8 HEMI—Truck Equipment Schedule T1							
2500 Long Bed	A26D	25695		4575	5400	7175	9900
3500 Long Bed	A36D	27715		4900	5725	7550	10350
4WD	U			1550	1550	2065	2065
6-Cyl. 5.9L Turbo Diesel	6			4300	4300	5730	5730
6-Cyl. 5.9L HO Turbo Dsl	C			4950	4950	6600	6600
RAM REGULAR CAB PICKUP—V10—Truck Equipment Schedule T1							
SRT-10 1500 Short	A16H	45795		13725	15475	17650	21700
6-Spd Manual Trans				0	0	0	0
RAM QUAD CAB PICKUP—V8—Truck Equipment Schedule T1							
1500 Short Bed	A18N	26060		5975	6925	8775	11700
1500 Long Bed	A18N	26415		5625	6575	8375	11250
4WD	U			1550	1550	2065	2065
V6 3.7 Liter	K			(600)	(600)	(800)	(800)
V8 5.7 Liter HEMI	D			950	950	1265	1265
RAM QUAD CAB PICKUP—V8 HEMI—Truck Equipment Schedule T1							
2500 Short Bed	A28D	28150		6975	8025	9900	12950
2500 Long Bed	A28D	28340		6625	7625	9475	12500
3500 Short Bed	A386	34530		7150	8200	10100	13200
3500 Long Bed	A38D	30790		7000	8050	9950	13050
4WD	U			1550	1550	2065	2065
6-Cyl. 5.9L Turbo Dsl	6			4300	4300	5730	5730
6-Cyl. 5.9L HO Turbo Dsl	C			4950	4950	6600	6600

2005 DODGE — (1,3orW)D(2,3,4,5,7or8)–(B38N)–5

Body	Type	VIN	List	Trade-In Fair	Good	Pvt-Party Good	Retail Excellent
DURANGO 4WD—V8—Truck Equipment Schedule T1							
Sport Utility 4D	B38N	30360		5875	6800	8575	11400
w/o Third Seat				(600)	(600)	(800)	(800)
2WD	D			(725)	(725)	(965)	(965)
V6 3.7 Liter	K			(900)	(900)	(1200)	(1200)
V8 5.7 Liter HEMI	D			900	900	1200	1200
CARAVAN—V6—Truck Equipment Schedule T1							
Cargo Minivan	P21R	20185		1050	1500	3050	5200
Grand Cargo Minivan	P23R	20885		1450	1925	3525	5725
CARAVAN—V6—Truck Equipment Schedule T1							
Minivan 4D	P25B	18995		2575	3175	4800	7125
SXT Minivan 4D	P45R	22485		2650	3250	4875	7225
Grand Minivan 4D	P24R	22185		2625	3225	4850	7200
SXT Grand Minivan	P44L	27185		3650	4350	6000	8475
5 Passenger				(600)	(600)	(800)	(800)
4-Cyl. 2.4 Liter	B			(1100)	(1100)	(1465)	(1465)
DAKOTA PICKUP—V6—Truck Equipment Schedule T1							
Club Cab	E22K	20305		3750	4475	6225	8800
Quad Cab	E28K	22514		4375	5175	6950	9650
4WD	W			1775	1775	2365	2365
V8 4.7 Liter/V8 4.7L HO	N,J			625	625	835	835
RAM REGULAR CAB PICKUP—V8—Truck Equipment Schedule T1							
1500 Short Bed	A16N	22910		4500	5325	7100	9850

Body	Type	VIN	List	Trade-In Fair	Trade-In Good	Pvt-Party Good	Retail Excellent
1500 Long Bed		A16N	23195	4150	4900	6650	9275
4WD		U		1729	1725	2300	2300
V6 3.7 Liter		K		(675)	(675)	(900)	(900)
V8 5.7 Liter HEMI		D		1025	1025	1365	1365
RAM REGULAR CAB PICKUP—V8 HEMI—Truck Equipment Schedule T1							
2500 Long Bed		R26D	26510	5300	6175	7975	10850
3500 Long Bed		R36D	28395	5625	6550	8350	11200
4WD		S		1725	1725	2300	2300
6-Cyl. 5.9L HO Turbo Dsl		C		5175	5175	6900	6900
RAM REGULAR CAB PICKUP 4WD—V8 HEMI—Truck Equipment Schedule T1							
2500 Power Wagon		S26D	36660	10425	11850	13850	17400
RAM REGULAR CAB PICKUP—V10—Truck Equipment Schedule T1							
SRT-10 1500 Short		A16H	45850	15475	17350	19500	23600
6-Spd Manual Trans				0	0	0	0
RAM QUAD CAB PICKUP—V8—Truck Equipment Schedule T1							
1500 Short Bed		A18N	26920	6825	7900	9725	12750
1500 Long Bed		A18N	27275	6475	7475	9300	12300
4WD		S		1725	1725	2300	2300
V6 3.7 Liter		K		(675)	(675)	(900)	(900)
V8 5.7 Liter HEMI		D		1025	1025	1365	1365
RAM QUAD CAB PICKUP—V10—Truck Equipment Schedule T1							
SRT-10 1500 Short		A18H	50850	17875	20000	22200	26800
RAM QUAD CAB PICKUP 4WD—V8 HEMI—Truck Equipment Schedule T1							
2500 Power Wagon		R28D	41040	12650	14250	16250	20100
RAM QUAD CAB PICKUP—V8 HEMI—Truck Equipment Schedule T1							
2500 Short Bed		R28D	28890	8025	9200	11100	14350
2500 Long Bed		R28D	29080	7625	8750	10650	13700
3500 Short Bed		R48D	35480	8250	9425	11350	14650
3500 Long Bed		R48D	31605	8100	9275	11200	14450
4WD		S		1725	1725	2300	2300
6-Cyl. 5.9L HO Turbo Dsl		C		5175	5175	6900	6900

2006 DODGE — (1,3orW)D(2,3,4,5,7or8)–(B38N)–6

Body	Type	VIN	List	Trade-In Fair	Trade-In Good	Pvt-Party Good	Retail Excellent
DURANGO 4WD—V8—Truck Equipment Schedule T1							
Sport Utility 4D		B38N	31825	7025	8075	9850	12800
w/o Third Seat				(650)	(650)	(865)	(865)
2WD		D		(800)	(800)	(1065)	(1065)
V6 3.7 Liter		K		(1000)	(1000)	(1335)	(1335)
V8 5.7 Liter HEMI		2		975	975	1300	1300
CARAVAN—V6—Truck Equipment Schedule T2							
Cargo Minivan		P21R	20645	1700	2200	3825	6075
Grand Cargo Minivan		P23R	21345	2200	2800	4400	6725
CARAVAN—V6—Truck Equipment Schedule T1							
SE Minivan 4D		P25R	19095	3425	4125	5750	8200
SXT Minivan 4D		P45R	23035	3500	4225	5850	8300
Grand Minivan 4D		P24R	23745	3525	4250	5875	8325
SXT Grand Minivan		P44L	27830	4550	5375	7050	9675
5 Passenger				(650)	(650)	(865)	(865)
4-Cyl. 2.4 Liter		B		(1200)	(1200)	(1600)	(1600)
DAKOTA PICKUP—V6—Truck Equipment Schedule T1							
Club Cab		E22K	21750	4600	5425	7200	9950
Quad Cab		E28K	23150	5375	6250	8050	10900
4WD		W		1950	1950	2600	2600
V8 4.7L/V8 4.7L HO		N,J		700	700	935	935
RAM REGULAR CAB PICKUP—V8—Truck Equipment Schedule T1							
1500 Short Bed		A16N	23580	5125	5975	7825	10650
1500 Long Bed		A16N	23865	4675	5525	7325	10100
4WD		U		1900	1900	2535	2535
V6 3.7 Liter		K		(750)	(750)	(1000)	(1000)
V8 5.7 Liter HEMI		2		1100	1100	1465	1465
RAM REGULAR CAB PICKUP—V8 HEMI—Truck Equipment Schedule T1							
Long Bed		R26D	27180	6050	6975	8850	11750
3500 Long Bed		L36D	29065	6400	7375	9225	12200
4WD		S,X		1900	1900	2535	2535
6-Cyl. 5.9L HO Turbo Dsl		C		5400	5400	7200	7200
RAM REGULAR CAB PICKUP 4WD—V8 HEMI—Truck Equipment Schedule T1							
2500 Power Wagon		S26D	38645	11850	13425	15400	19000
RAM REGULAR CAB PICKUP—V10—Truck Equipment Schedule T1							
SRT-10 1500 Short		A16H	48505	17200	19250	21400	25600
6-Spd Manual Trans				0	0	0	0
RAM QUAD CAB PICKUP—V8—Truck Equipment Schedule T1							
1500 Short Bed		A18N	27650	7750	8875	10750	13850
1500 Long Bed		A18N	28005	7350	8425	10300	13400

TRUCKS & VANS

2006 DODGE

Body Type	VIN	List	Trade-In Fair	Trade-In Good	Pvt-Party Good	Retail Excellent
4WD	U		1900	1900	2535	2535
V6 3.7 Liter	K		(750)	(750)	(1000)	(1000)
V8 5.7 Liter HEMI	2		1100	1100	1465	1465
RAM QUAD CAB PICKUP 4WD—V8 HEMI—Truck Equipment Schedule T1						
2500 Power Wagon	R28D	41475	14250	16025	18050	22000
RAM QUAD CAB PICKUP—V10—Truck Equipment Schedule T1						
SRT-10 1500 Short	A18H	52710	20000	22350	24500	29000
RAM QUAD CAB PICKUP—V8 HEMI—Truck Equipment Schedule T1						
2500 Short Bed	R28D	30055	9175	10425	12400	15750
2500 Long Bed	R28D	30245	8700	9900	11850	15150
3500 Short Bed	L38C	37065	9375	10675	12600	15950
3500 Long Bed	L48D	32695	9250	10525	12500	15850
4WD	S,X		1900	1900	2535	2535
6-Cyl. 5.9L HO Turbo Dsl	C		5400	5400	7200	7200
RAM MEGA CAB PICKUP—V8 HEMI—Truck Equipment Schedule T1						
1500 Short Bed	R19D	32760	10425	11850	13800	17300
2500 Short Bed	R29D	35065	12250	13875	15850	19500
4WD	A,S		1900	1900	2535	2535
6-Cyl. 5.9L HO Turbo Dsl	C		5400	5400	7200	7200
RAM MEGA CAB PICKUP—6-Cyl. HO Turbo Diesel—Truck Schedule T1						
3500 Short Bed	L39C	41505	17000	19050	21200	25400
4WD	U		1900	1900	2535	2535

2007 DODGE — (1,2or3)D(2,3,4,5,7or8)–(U28K)–7

Body Type	VIN	List	Trade-In Fair	Trade-In Good	Pvt-Party Good	Retail Excellent
NITRO 4WD—V6—Truck Equipment Schedule T1						
SXT Sport Utility 4D	U28K	21545	6750	7775	9400	12200
SLT Sport Utility 4D	U58K	24805	7950	9100	10850	13750
R/T Sport Utility 4D	U586	25795	10100	11475	13250	16400
2WD	T		(875)	(875)	(1165)	(1165)
DURANGO 4WD—V8—Truck Equipment Schedule T1						
Sport Utility 4D	B38N	29855	9275	10575	12350	15500
w/o Third Seat			(700)	(700)	(935)	(935)
2WD	D		(875)	(875)	(1165)	(1165)
V6 3.7 Liter	K		(1100)	(1100)	(1465)	(1465)
V8 5.7 Liter HEMI	2		1050	1050	1400	1400
CARAVAN—V6—Truck Equipment Schedule T2						
Cargo Minivan	P21N	20845	2875	3475	5025	7300
Grand Cargo Minivan	P23R	21545	3475	4175	5700	8025
CARAVAN—V6—Truck Equipment Schedule T1						
Minivan 4D	P25R	19345	4750	5575	7175	9700
SXT Minivan 4D	P45R	23235	4850	5675	7275	9800
Grand Minivan 4D	P24R	23995	4900	5725	7325	9850
SXT Grand Minivan	P44L	28030	5975	6925	8525	11150
5 Passenger			(700)	(700)	(935)	(935)
4-Cyl. 2.4 Liter	B		(1300)	(1300)	(1735)	(1735)
DAKOTA PICKUP—V6—Truck Equipment Schedule T1						
Club Cab	E22K	20840	5275	6125	7850	10550
Quad Cab	E28K	23540	6500	7475	9200	12000
4WD	W		2125	2125	2835	2835
V8 4.7 Liter/V8 4.7L HO	N,J		750	750	1000	1000
RAM REGULAR CAB PICKUP—V8—Truck Equipment Schedule T1						
1500 Short Bed	A16N	23940	5750	6700	8425	11200
1500 Long Bed	A16N	24225	5275	6150	7900	10650
4WD	U		2075	2075	2765	2765
V6 3.7 Liter	K		(800)	(800)	(1065)	(1065)
V8 5.7 Liter HEMI	2		1175	1175	1565	1565
RAM REGULAR CAB PICKUP—V8 HEMI—Truck Equipment Schedule T1						
2500 Long Bed	R26D	27540	6775	7825	9600	12550
3500 Long Bed	L36D	29425	7175	8250	10050	13000
4WD	S,X		2075	2075	2765	2765
6-Cyl. 5.9L HO Turbo Dsl	C		5600	5600	7465	7465
6-Cyl. 6.7L Turbo Dsl	C		5900	5900	7865	7865
RAM REGULAR CAB PICKUP 4WD—V8 HEMI—Truck Equipment Schedule T1						
2500 Power Wagon	S26D	37955	13275	14950	16850	20600
RAM QUAD CAB PICKUP—V8—Truck Equipment Schedule T1						
1500 Short Bed	A18N	28010	8650	9850	11700	14900
1500 Long Bed	A18N	28365	8200	9375	11200	14350
4WD	U		2075	2075	2765	2765
V6 3.7 Liter	K		(800)	(800)	(1065)	(1065)
V8 5.7 Liter HEMI	2		1175	1175	1565	1565
RAM QUAD CAB PICKUP—V8 HEMI—Truck Equipment Schedule T1						
2500 Short Bed	R28D	30340	10300	11650	13500	16900
2500 Long Bed	R28D	30530	9725	11025	12900	16200

Body Type	VIN	List	Trade-In Fair	Trade-In Good	Pvt-Party Good	Retail Excellent
3500 Short Bed	L38A	37425	10525	11950	13800	17250
3500 Long Bed	L48D	33055	10400	11750	13600	17000
4WD	S,X		2075	2075	2765	2765
6-Cyl. 5.9L HO Turbo Dsl	C		5600	5600	7465	7465
6-Cyl. 6.7L Turbo Diesel	A		5900	5900	7865	7865
RAM QUAD CAB PICKUP 4WD—V8 HEMI—Truck Equipment Schedule T1						
2500 Power Wagon	S28D	40890	15875	17775	19700	23600
RAM MEGA CAB PICKUP—V8 HEMI—Truck Equipment Schedule T1						
1500 Short Bed	A19D	33095	11575	13075	15000	18500
2500 Short Bed	R29D	35400	13625	15325	17250	21000
4WD	S,U		2075	2075	2765	2765
6-Cyl. 5.9L HO Turbo Dsl	C		5600	5600	7465	7465
6-Cyl. 6.7L Turbo Diesel	A		5900	5900	7865	7865
RAM MEGA CAB PICKUP—6-Cyl. HO Turbo Diesel—Truck Schedule T1						
3500 Short Bed	L39C	43155	18775	20975	22900	27200
4WD	X		2075	2075	2765	2765

2008 DODGE — (1,3orW)D(2,3,4,5,7or8)—(U28K)—8

Body Type	VIN	List	Trade-In Fair	Trade-In Good	Pvt-Party Good	Retail Excellent
NITRO 4WD—V6—Truck Equipment Schedule T1						
SXT Sport Utility 4D	U28K	21915	7950	9100	10700	13500
SLT Sport Utility 4D	U58K	25325	9050	10525	12150	15100
R/T Sport Utility 4D	U586	28500	11575	13075	14750	18000
2WD	T		(950)	(950)	(1265)	(1265)
DURANGO 4WD—V8—Truck Equipment Schedule T1						
Sport Utility 4D	B38N	30480	11225	12700	14450	17800
w/o Third Row			(750)	(750)	(1000)	(1000)
2WD	D		(950)	(950)	(1265)	(1265)
V6 3.7 Liter	K		(1200)	(1200)	(1600)	(1600)
V8 5.7 Liter HEMI			1125	1125	1500	1500
CARAVAN—V6—Truck Equipment Schedule T2						
Grand Cargo Minivan	N11H	22470	6400	7375	8875	11400
V6 3.3L Flex Fuel	E		0	0	0	0
CARAVAN—V6—Truck Equipment Schedule T1						
SE Grand Minivan	N44H	22470	7950	9100	10700	13500
SXT Grand Minivan	N54P	27535	9050	10300	11900	14850
5 Passenger Seating			(750)	(750)	(1000)	(1000)
DAKOTA PICKUP—V6—Truck Equipment Schedule T1						
Extended Cab	E32X	21215	6800	7850	9425	12150
Crew Cab	E38X	23915	8900	10150	11850	14900
4WD	W		2300	2300	3065	3065
V8 4.7L Flex Fuel	N		800	800	1065	1065
RAM REGULAR CAB PICKUP—V8—Truck Equipment Schedule T1						
1500 Short Bed	A16N	23150	7725	8850	10600	13500
1500 Long Bed	A16N	23435	7200	8275	9950	12850
4WD	U		2250	2250	3000	3000
V6 3.7 Liter	K		(850)	(850)	(1135)	(1135)
V8 5.7 Liter HEMI	2		1250	1250	1665	1665
RAM REGULAR CAB PICKUP—V8 HEMI—Truck Equipment Schedule T1						
2500 Long Bed	R26D	27750	8900	10150	11950	15100
3500 Long Bed	L36D	29685	9275	10575	12400	15600
4WD	S,X		2250	2250	3000	3000
6-Cyl. 5.9L HO Turbo Dsl	C		5800	5800	7730	7730
6-Cyl. 6.7L Turbo Dsl	A		6100	6100	8130	8130
RAM REGULAR CAB PICKUP 4WD—V8 HEMI—Truck Equipment Schedule T1						
2500 Power Wagon	S26D	40020	16025	17975	19800	23700
6-Cyl. 6.7 Turbo Diesel	A		6100	6100	8130	8130
RAM QUAD CAB PICKUP—V8—Truck Equipment Schedule T1						
1500 Short Bed	A18N	27320	10875	12350	14200	17600
1500 Long Bed	A18N	29755	10425	11800	13650	17000
4WD	U		2250	2250	3000	3000
V6 3.7 Liter	K		(850)	(850)	(1135)	(1135)
V8 5.7 Liter HEMI	2		1250	1250	1665	1665
RAM QUAD CAB PICKUP—V8 HEMI—Truck Equipment Schedule T1						
2500 Short Bed	R28D	30475	12750	14400	16200	19800
2500 Long Bed	R28D	30740	12475	13725	15600	19100
3500 Long Bed	L48D	33315	12850	14450	16300	19900
4WD	S,X		2250	2250	3000	3000
6-Cyl. 6.7L Turbo Diesel	A		6100	6100	8130	8130
6-Cyl. 5.9L HO Turbo Dsl	C		5800	5800	7730	7730
RAM QUAD CAB PICKUP—6-Cyl. Turbo Diesel—Truck Schedule T1						
3500 Short Bed	L38A	38105	12975	14650	16500	20100
4WD	S,X		2250	2250	3000	3000

TRUCKS & VANS

Body	Type	VIN	List	Trade-In Fair	Trade-In Good	Pvt-Party Good	Retail Excellent
RAM QUAD CAB PICKUP 4WD—V8 HEMI—Truck Equipment Schedule T1							
2500 Power Wagon		S28D	43180	18875	21075	22900	27100
6-Cyl. 6.7 Turbo Diesel		A		6100	6100	8130	8130
RAM MEGA CAB PICKUP—V8 HEMI—Truck Equipment Schedule T1							
1500 Short Bed		A19D	33635	14075	15875	17700	21400
2500 Short Bed		R29D	35880	16275	18225	20100	24000
4WD		S,U		2250	2250	3000	3000
6-Cyl. 6.7 Turbo Diesel		A		6100	6100	8130	8130
RAM MEGA CAB PICKUP—6-Cyl. Turbo Diesel—Truck Equip Sch T1							
3500 Short Bed		L39A	44660	21750	24300	26200	30600
4WD		X		2250	2250	3000	3000

FORD

1994 FORD — 1F(MorT)–(U24X)–R–#

Body	Type	VIN	List	Trade-In Fair	Trade-In Good	Pvt-Party Good	Retail Excellent
EXPLORER 4WD—V6—Truck Equipment Schedule T1							
Sport Utility 2D		U24X	21145	625	875	1700	3050
Sport Utility 4D		U34X	22055	925	1300	2375	4025
2WD		2		(125)	(125)	(165)	(165)
BRONCO 4WD—V8—Truck Equipment Schedule T1							
Sport Utility 2D		U15N	24036	1925	2475	3750	5650
V8 5.8 Liter		H		75	75	100	100
AEROSTAR—V6—Truck Equipment Schedule T2							
Cargo Minivan		A14U	15796	125	175	700	1500
Extended Cargo		A34U	16346	175	225	775	1600
Window Minivan		A15U	16091	150	200	725	1550
Extended Window		A35U	16641	175	250	775	1625
4WD		2,4		250	250	335	335
V6 4.0 Liter		X		50	50	65	65
AEROSTAR—V6—Truck Equipment Schedule T1							
Minivan		A11U	16302	200	275	825	1675
Extended Minivan		A31U	17747	250	350	925	1850
5 Passenger				(200)	(200)	(265)	(265)
4WD		2,4		250	250	335	335
V6 4.0 Liter		X		50	50	65	65
CLUB WAGON—V8—Truck Equipment Schedule T1							
Passenger Van		E11N	19790	850	1175	2125	3600
Heavy Duty Van		E31H	21739	875	1250	2225	3725
Super Passenger Van		S31H	22925	925	1325	2400	4025
5 Passenger				(200)	(200)	(265)	(265)
6-Cyl. 4.9 Liter		Y		(200)	(200)	(265)	(265)
V8 460/7.5 Liter		G		100	100	135	135
V8 7.3 Liter Diesel		M		(100)	(100)	(135)	(135)
ECONOLINE—6-Cyl.—Truck Equipment Schedule T1							
E150 Cargo Van		E14Y	16923	625	875	1725	3050
E250 Cargo Van		E24Y	17635	675	950	1825	3150
E250 Extended Cargo		E24Y	18434	875	1225	2175	3675
E350 Cargo Van		E34Y	18416	750	1050	1950	3375
E350 Extended Cargo		E34Y	19385	975	1350	2450	4075
V8 5.0, 5.8 Liter		N,H		100	100	135	135
V8 460/7.5 Liter		G		200	200	265	265
V8 7.3 Liter Diesel		M		200	200	265	265
RANGER PICKUP—4-Cyl.—Truck Equipment Schedule T2							
Short Bed		R10A	9826	300	425	1000	1925
Long Bed		R10A	10200	225	300	875	1775
Super Cab		R14A	12469	525	725	1500	2750
Splash Short Bed		R10A	13305	450	600	1250	2300
Splash Super Cab		R14A	14774	625	900	1725	3050
4WD		1,5		400	400	535	535
V6 3.0 Liter		U		125	125	165	165
V6 4.0 Liter		X		150	150	200	200
REGULAR CAB PICKUP—V8—Truck Equipment Schedule T1							
F150 Short Bed		F15N	16434	775	1100	2025	3475
F150 Lightning		F15R	23127	1800	2325	3600	5475
F150 Long Bed		F15N	16658	675	950	1850	3200
F250 Long Bed		F25H	17480	1100	1525	2725	4425
F350 Long Bed		F35H	20088	1100	1550	2725	4425
Special				(250)	(250)	(335)	(335)
4WD		4,6		500	500	665	665
6-Cyl. 4.9 Liter		Y		(350)	(350)	(465)	(465)
V8 5.8 Liter		H,R		75	75	100	100

1994 FORD

Body Type	VIN	List	Trade-In Fair	Trade-In Good	Pvt-Party Good	Retail Excellent
V8 460/7.5 Liter	G		150	150	200	200
V8 7.3 Liter Diesel	M		200	200	265	265
V8 7.3L Diesel	K		600	600	800	800
V8 7.3L Power Stroke	F		1600	1600	2135	2135
SUPER CAB PICKUP—V8—Truck Equipment Schedule T1						
F150 Short Bed	X15N	18040	1400	1875	3100	4900
F150 Long Bed	X15N	18283	1375	1850	3075	4825
F250 Long Bed	X25H	20578	1650	2150	3425	5275
F350 Long Bed	X35G	22410	1725	2225	3475	5350
Special			(250)	(250)	(335)	(335)
4WD	4,6		500	500	665	665
6-Cyl. 4.9 Liter	Y		(350)	(350)	(465)	(465)
V8 5.8 Liter	H		75	75	100	100
V8 460/7.5 Liter	G		150	150	200	200
V8 7.3 Liter Diesel	M		200	200	265	265
V8 7.3L Turbo Diesel	K		600	600	800	800
V8 7.3L Power Stroke	F		1600	1600	2135	2135
CREW CAB PICKUP—V8—Truck Equipment Schedule T1						
F350 Long Bed	W35H	21591	1775	2275	3550	5425
4WD	6		500	500	665	665
V8 460/7.5 Liter	G		150	150	200	200
V8 7.3 Liter Diesel	M		200	200	265	265
V8 7.3L Turbo Diesel	K		600	600	800	800
V8 7.3L Power Stroke	F		1600	1600	2135	2135

1995 FORD—(1or2)F(B,MorT)–(U24X)–S–#

Body Type	VIN	List	Trade-In Fair	Trade-In Good	Pvt-Party Good	Retail Excellent
EXPLORER 4WD—V6—Truck Equipment Schedule T1						
Sport Utility 2D	U24X	22380	675	950	1800	3150
Sport Utility 4D	U34X	23735	1000	1400	2525	4175
2WD	2		(125)	(125)	(165)	(165)
BRONCO 4WD—V8—Truck Equipment Schedule T1						
Sport Utility 2D	U15N	24305	2250	2825	4150	6125
V8 5.8 Liter	H		75	75	100	100
AEROSTAR—V6—Truck Equipment Schedule T2						
Cargo Minivan	A14U	17486	175	250	775	1625
AEROSTAR—V6—Truck Equipment Schedule T1						
Minivan	A11U	17895	350	475	1100	2100
Extended Minivan	A31U	22261	375	525	1150	2175
5 Passenger			(200)	(200)	(265)	(265)
4WD	4		250	250	335	335
V6 4.0 Liter	X		50	50	65	65
WINDSTAR—V6—Truck Equipment Schedule T2						
Cargo Minivan	A544	18655	325	450	1050	2000
WINDSTAR—V6—Truck Equipment Schedule T1						
GL Minivan	A514	19995	450	625	1275	2350
LX Minivan	A514	24080	525	725	1500	2750
CLUB WAGON—V8—Truck Equipment Schedule T1						
Passenger Van	E11N	21286	975	1350	2475	4125
Heavy Duty Van	E31H	22967	1025	1450	2575	4250
Super Passenger Van	S31H	24780	1075	1525	2675	4350
6-Cyl. 4.9 Liter	Y		(200)	(200)	(265)	(265)
V8 460/7.5 Liter	G		100	100	135	135
V8 7.3L Turbo Diesel	F		1125	1125	1500	1500
ECONOLINE—6-Cyl.—Truck Equipment Schedule T1						
E150 Cargo Van	E14Y	17675	725	1050	1950	3375
E250 Cargo Van	E24Y	18514	775	1100	2025	3500
E250 Extended Cargo	E24Y	19328	1000	1425	2550	4225
E350 Cargo Van	E34Y	19723	875	1225	2200	3725
E350 Extended Cargo	E34Y	20707	1125	1575	2750	4425
V8 5.0, 5.8 Liter	N,H		100	100	135	135
V8 460/7.5 Liter	G		200	200	265	265
V8 7.3L Turbo Diesel	F		1300	1300	1735	1735
RANGER PICKUP—4-Cyl.—Truck Equipment Schedule T2						
Short Bed	R10A	10746	350	500	1125	2125
Long Bed	R10A	11130	275	375	975	1925
Super Cab	R14A	13298	600	800	1625	2925
Splash Short Bed	R10A	13825	525	700	1475	2700
Splash Super Cab	R14A	15400	725	1025	1900	3325
4WD	1,5		400	400	535	535
V6 3.0 Liter	U		125	125	165	165
V6 4.0 Liter	X		150	150	200	200
REGULAR CAB PICKUP—V8—Truck Equipment Schedule T1						
F150 Short Bed	F15N	17418	875	1250	2350	4000

Body	Type	VIN	List	Trade-In Fair	Trade-In Good	Pvt-Party Good	Retail Excellent
F150 Lightning		F15R	......	**2100**	**2675**	**4000**	**5950**
F150 Long Bed		F15N	17642	**800**	**1100**	**2075**	**3550**
F250 Long Bed		F25H	18264	**1325**	**1800**	**3050**	**4825**
F350 Long Bed		F35H	20236	**1350**	**1825**	**3050**	**4825**
Special				**(250)**	**(250)**	**(335)**	**(335)**
4WD		4,6	......	**500**	**500**	**665**	**665**
6-Cyl. 4.9 Liter		Y,Z	......	**(350)**	**(350)**	**(465)**	**(465)**
V8 5.8 Liter		H,R	......	**75**	**75**	**100**	**100**
V8 460/7.5 Liter		G	......	**150**	**150**	**200**	**200**
V8 7.3L Turbo Diesel		F	......	**1600**	**1600**	**2135**	**2135**
SUPER CAB PICKUP—V8—Truck Equipment Schedule T1							
F150 Short Bed		X15N	19297	**1675**	**2175**	**3450**	**5325**
F150 Long Bed		X15N	19540	**1625**	**2125**	**3400**	**5250**
F250 Long Bed		X25H	20670	**1950**	**2525**	**3825**	**5750**
F350 Long Bed		X35G	22730	**2025**	**2600**	**3900**	**5850**
Special				**(250)**	**(250)**	**(335)**	**(335)**
4WD		4,6	......	**500**	**500**	**665**	**665**
6-Cyl. 4.9 Liter		Y	......	**(350)**	**(350)**	**(465)**	**(465)**
V8 5.8 Liter		H	......	**75**	**75**	**100**	**100**
V8 460/7.5 Liter		G	......	**150**	**150**	**200**	**200**
V8 7.3L Turbo Diesel		F	......	**1600**	**1600**	**2135**	**2135**
CREW CAB PICKUP—V8—Truck Equipment Schedule T1							
F350 Long Bed		W35H	21938	**2100**	**2675**	**4000**	**5950**
4WD		6	......	**500**	**500**	**665**	**665**
V8 460/7.5 Liter		G	......	**150**	**150**	**200**	**200**
V8 7.3L Turbo Diesel		F	......	**1600**	**1600**	**2135**	**2135**

1996 FORD–(1or2)F(B,MorT)–(U24X)–T–#

Body	Type	VIN	List	Trade-In Fair	Trade-In Good	Pvt-Party Good	Retail Excellent
EXPLORER 4WD—V6—Truck Equipment Schedule T1							
Sport Utility 2D		U24X	22980	**750**	**1050**	**1975**	**3425**
XL Sport Utility 4D		U34X	24335	**1100**	**1550**	**2725**	**4400**
2WD		2	......	**(200)**	**(200)**	**(265)**	**(265)**
AWD		5	......	**0**	**0**	**0**	**0**
V8 5.0 Liter		P	......	**125**	**125**	**165**	**165**
BRONCO 4WD—V8—Truck Equipment Schedule T1							
XL Sport Utility 2D		U15N	25375	**2650**	**3250**	**4625**	**6700**
V8 5.8 Liter		H	......	**125**	**125**	**165**	**165**
AEROSTAR—V6—Truck Equipment Schedule T1							
Cargo Minivan		A14U	17966	**200**	**275**	**825**	**1725**
AEROSTAR—V6—Truck Equipment Schedule T1							
XLT Minivan		A11U	18375	**375**	**525**	**1175**	**2225**
XLT Extended		A31U	22840	**425**	**600**	**1275**	**2350**
5 Passenger				**(250)**	**(250)**	**(335)**	**(335)**
4WD		4	......	**300**	**300**	**400**	**400**
V6 4.0 Liter		X	......	**75**	**75**	**100**	**100**
WINDSTAR—V6—Truck Equipment Schedule T2							
Cargo Minivan		A544	18825	**350**	**500**	**1125**	**2125**
V6 3.0 Liter		U	......	**(125)**	**(125)**	**(165)**	**(165)**
WINDSTAR—V6—Truck Equipment Schedule T1							
GL Minivan		A514	20785	**500**	**650**	**1375**	**2525**
LX Minivan		A514	25340	**600**	**825**	**1650**	**2975**
V6 3.0 Liter		U	......	**(125)**	**(125)**	**(165)**	**(165)**
CLUB WAGON—V8—Truck Equipment Schedule T1							
XL Passenger Van		E11N	22224	**1025**	**1425**	**2550**	**4250**
XL Heavy Duty Van		E31H	23925	**1075**	**1500**	**2650**	**4350**
XL Super Pass Van		S31H	25764	**1125**	**1575**	**2775**	**4475**
6-Cyl. 4.9 Liter		Y	......	**(250)**	**(250)**	**(335)**	**(335)**
V8 460/7.5 Liter		G	......	**125**	**125**	**165**	**165**
V8 7.3L Turbo Diesel		F	......	**1300**	**1300**	**1735**	**1735**
ECONOLINE—6-Cyl.—Truck Equipment Schedule T1							
E150 Cargo Van		E14Y	18255	**800**	**1150**	**2100**	**3600**
E250 Cargo Van		E24Y	18680	**875**	**1225**	**2325**	**3950**
E250 Extended Cargo		E24Y	19400	**1100**	**1550**	**2725**	**4400**
E350 Cargo Van		E34Y	20305	**975**	**1350**	**2475**	**4150**
E350 Extended Cargo		E34Y	21290	**1225**	**1700**	**2900**	**4625**
V8 5.0, 5.8 Liter		N,H	......	**125**	**125**	**165**	**165**
V8 460/7.5 Liter		G	......	**250**	**250**	**335**	**335**
V8 7.3L Turbo Diesel		F	......	**1475**	**1475**	**1965**	**1965**
RANGER PICKUP—4-Cyl.—Truck Equipment Schedule T2							
Short Bed		R10A	11087	**425**	**600**	**1275**	**2350**
Long Bed		R10A	11472	**325**	**450**	**1100**	**2100**
Super Cab		R14A	14217	**675**	**975**	**1850**	**3250**
Splash Short Bed		R10A	14645	**625**	**825**	**1675**	**3000**

Body	Type	VIN	List	Trade-In Fair	Trade-In Good	Pvt-Party Good	Retail Excellent
Splash Super Cab		R14U	16305	850	1200	2200	3725
4WD		1,5		525	525	700	700
V6 3.0 Liter		U		150	150	200	200
V6 4.0 Liter		X		200	200	265	265
REGULAR CAB PICKUP—V8—Truck Equipment Schedule T1							
F150 Short Bed		F15N	18327	1025	1425	2575	4275
F150 Long Bed		F15N	18552	900	1275	2375	4050
F250 Long Bed		F25H	19017	1475	1950	3225	5050
F350 Long Bed		F35H	20157	1550	2025	3300	5150
Special				(300)	(300)	(400)	(400)
4WD		4,6		600	600	800	800
6-Cyl. 4.9 Liter		Y		(375)	(375)	(500)	(500)
V8 5.8 Liter		H		125	125	165	165
V8 460/7.5 Liter		G		175	175	235	235
V8 7.3L Turbo Diesel		F		1925	1925	2565	2565
SUPER CAB PICKUP—V8—Truck Equipment Schedule T1							
F150 Short Bed		X15N	20352	1850	2400	3700	5600
F150 Long Bed		X15N	20597	1825	2325	3625	5525
F250 Short Bed		X25H	21667	2350	2950	4300	6300
F250 Long Bed		X25H	21487	2250	2850	4175	6175
F350 Long Bed		X35G	23485	2375	2950	4300	6325
Special				(300)	(300)	(400)	(400)
4WD		4,6		600	600	800	800
6-Cyl. 4.9 Liter		Y		(375)	(375)	(500)	(500)
V8 5.8 Liter		H		125	125	165	165
V8 460/7.5 Liter		G		175	175	235	235
V8 7.3L Turbo Diesel		F		1925	1925	2565	2565
CREW CAB PICKUP—V8—Truck Equipment Schedule T1							
F250 Short Bed		W25G	23422	2725	3325	4725	6800
F350 Long Bed		W35H	23482	2425	3025	4375	6425
4WD		6		600	600	800	800
V8 460/7.5 Liter		G		175	175	235	235
V8 7.3L Turbo Diesel		F		1925	1925	2565	2565

1997 FORD—(1or2)F(B,M,orT)—(U24X)—V—#

Body	Type	VIN	List	Trade-In Fair	Trade-In Good	Pvt-Party Good	Retail Excellent
EXPLORER 4WD—V6—Truck Equipment Schedule T1							
Sport Utility 2D		U24X	24065	850	1175	2300	3950
XL Sport Utility 4D		U34X	25420	1250	1725	2950	4725
2WD		2		(250)	(250)	(335)	(335)
AWD		5		0	0	0	0
V6 4.0 Liter SOHC		P		150	150	200	200
V8 5.0 Liter				150	150	200	200
EXPEDITION 4WD—V8—Truck Equipment Schedule T1							
XLT Sport Utility 4D		U18W	30510	1625	2100	3375	5250
w/o Third Seat				(350)	(350)	(465)	(465)
2WD		7		(400)	(400)	(535)	(535)
V8 5.4 Liter		L		175	175	235	235
AEROSTAR—V6—Truck Equipment Schedule T2							
Cargo Minivan		A14U	17995	225	300	900	1850
AEROSTAR—V6—Truck Equipment Schedule T1							
XLT Minivan		A11U	18405	450	600	1325	2450
XLT Extended		A31U	21170	475	650	1400	2575
5 Passenger				(275)	(275)	(365)	(365)
4WD		4		350	350	465	465
V6 4.0 Liter		X		100	100	135	135
WINDSTAR—V6—Truck Equipment Schedule T2							
Cargo Minivan		A544	19600	375	525	1175	2225
V6 3.0 Liter		U		(150)	(150)	(200)	(200)
WINDSTAR—V6—Truck Equipment Schedule T1							
Minivan		A514	19995	525	700	1500	2750
GL Minivan		A514	23070	525	725	1525	2800
LX Minivan		A514	26195	625	900	1775	3125
V6 3.0 Liter		U		(150)	(150)	(200)	(200)
CLUB WAGON—V8—Truck Equipment Schedule T1							
XL Passenger Van		E11N	23210	1075	1500	2675	4375
XL Heavy Duty Van		E31L	25255	1150	1625	2800	4525
XL Super Pass Van		S31L	27135	1250	1725	2925	4675
V6 4.2 Liter		2		(275)	(275)	(365)	(365)
V8 7.3L Turbo Diesel		F		1475	1475	1965	1965
V10 6.8 Liter		S		350	350	465	465
ECONOLINE—V6—Truck Equipment Schedule T1							
E150 Cargo Van		E142	19370	925	1300	2425	4075
E250 Cargo Van		E242	20090	1000	1400	2525	4200

Body Type	VIN	List	Trade-In Fair	Good	Pvt-Party Good	Retail Excellent
E250 Extended Cargo	E242	20905	1300	1775	3000	4750
E350 Cargo Van	E34L	22430	1100	1550	2700	4400
E350 Extended Cargo	E34L	23415	1450	1925	3150	4975
V8 4.6, 5.4 Liter	6,L		150	150	200	200
V8 7.3L Turbo Diesel	F		1650	1650	2200	2200
V10 6.8 Liter	S		300	300	400	400
RANGER PICKUP—4-Cyl.—Truck Equipment Schedule T2						
Short Bed	R10A	11060	525	700	1525	2800
Long Bed	R10A	11445	400	575	1250	2350
Super Cab	R14A	14905	825	1150	2150	3675
Splash Short Bed	R10A	15385	750	1050	2000	3475
Splash Super Cab	R14U	17010	1025	1450	2600	4300
4WD	1,5		650	650	865	865
V6 3.0 Liter	U		175	175	235	235
V6 4.0 Liter	X		225	225	300	300
REGULAR CAB PICKUP—V8—Truck Equipment Schedule T1						
F150 Short Bed	F176,W	17480	1250	1725	2975	4750
F150 Long Bed	F176,W	17750	1100	1525	2725	4425
F250 Short Bed	F276,W	18770	1600	2100	3375	5250
F250 H.D. Long Bed	F25H	20265	2025	2600	3900	5850
F350 Long Bed	F35H	20775	2050	2625	3925	5875
Standard (Work Truck)			(350)	(350)	(465)	(465)
4WD	6,8		700	700	935	935
V6 4.2 Liter	2		(400)	(400)	(535)	(535)
V8 5.4 Liter	L		175	175	235	235
V8 460/7.5 Liter	G		200	200	265	265
V8 7.3L Turbo Diesel	F		2250	2250	3000	3000
SUPER CAB PICKUP—V8—Truck Equipment Schedule T1						
F150 Short Bed	X176,W	19635	2200	2775	4125	6100
F150 Long Bed	X176,W	19920	2025	2600	3900	5850
F250 Short Bed	X276,W	20620	2750	3350	4750	6825
F250 H.D. Short Bed	X25H	22285	2250	2825	4175	6175
F250 H.D. Long Bed	X25H	22105	2150	2725	4050	6000
F350 Long Bed	X35G	23875	2550	3125	4500	6575
Standard (Work Truck)			(350)	(350)	(465)	(465)
4WD	6,8		700	700	935	935
V6 4.2 Liter	2		(400)	(400)	(535)	(535)
V8 5.4 Liter	L		175	175	235	235
V8 460/7.5 Liter	G		200	200	265	265
V8 7.3L Turbo Diesel	F		2250	2250	3000	3000
CREW CAB PICKUP—V8—Truck Equipment Schedule T1						
F250 Short Bed	W25G	24160	3100	3775	5225	7400
F350 Long Bed	W35H	24220	2825	3425	4825	6950
4WD	6		700	700	935	935
V8 460/7.5 Liter	G		200	200	265	265
V8 7.3L Turbo Diesel	F		2250	2250	3000	3000

1998 FORD –(1or2)F(B,MorT)–(U24X)–W–#

Body Type	VIN	List	Trade-In Fair	Good	Pvt-Party Good	Retail Excellent
EXPLORER 4WD—V6—Truck Equipment Schedule T1						
Sport Utility 2D	U24X	24315	975	1375	2525	4225
XL Sport Utility 4D	U34X	24995	1450	1925	3200	5050
2WD	2		(300)	(300)	(400)	(400)
AWD	5		0	0	0	0
V6 4.0 Liter SOHC	E		150	150	200	200
V8 5.0 Liter	P		175	175	235	235
EXPEDITION 4WD—V8—Truck Equipment Schedule T1						
XLT Sport Utility 4D	U18W	31225	1850	2375	3675	5575
w/o Third Seat			(400)	(400)	(535)	(535)
2WD	7		(425)	(425)	(565)	(565)
V8 5.4 Liter	L		200	200	265	265
WINDSTAR—V6—Truck Equipment Schedule T2						
Cargo Minivan	A544	18590	425	600	1275	2400
V6 3.0 Liter	U		(175)	(175)	(235)	(235)
WINDSTAR—V6—Truck Equipment Schedule T1						
Minivan	A514	20970	575	775	1625	2975
GL Minivan	A514	24025	600	800	1650	3000
LX Minivan	A514	28365	725	1000	1925	3375
Limited Minivan	A514	30085	850	1200	2300	3950
V6 3.0 Liter	U		(175)	(175)	(235)	(235)
CLUB WAGON—V8—Truck Equipment Schedule T1						
XL Passenger Van	E11N	23090	1175	1675	2900	4650
XL Heavy Duty Van	E31L	25255	1325	1800	3050	4825
XL Super Pass Van	S31L	26970	1450	1925	3175	5000

Body	Type	VIN	List	Trade-In Fair	Good	Pvt-Party Good	Retail Excellent
V6 4.2 Liter		2		(300)	(300)	(400)	(400)
V8 7.3L Turbo Diesel		F		1650	1650	2200	2200
V10 6.8 Liter		S		400	400	535	535

ECONOLINE—V6—Truck Equipment Schedule T1

Body	Type	VIN	List	Trade-In Fair	Good	Pvt-Party Good	Retail Excellent
E150 Cargo Van		E142	19885	1075	1500	2675	4375
E250 Cargo Van		E242	20210	1125	1600	2775	4475
E250 Extended Cargo		E242	20910	1550	2025	3275	5100
E350 Cargo Van		E34L	22870	1275	1750	2975	4725
E350 Extended Cargo		E34L	23850	1725	2225	3475	5350
V8 4.6, 5.4 Liter		6,L		175	175	235	235
V8 7.3L Turbo Diesel		F		1800	1800	2400	2400
V10 6.8 Liter		S		350	350	465	465

RANGER PICKUP—4-Cyl.—Truck Equipment Schedule T2

Body	Type	VIN	List	Trade-In Fair	Good	Pvt-Party Good	Retail Excellent
XL Short Bed		R10C	11575	600	800	1675	3050
XL Long Bed		R10C	12045	475	625	1375	2575
Splash Short Bed		R10C	15195	875	1250	2375	4050
Super Cab 2D		R14C	15625	950	1325	2475	4175
Super Cab 4D		R14C	15625	1525	2025	3275	5125
Splash Super Cab 2D		R14U	16825	1175	1650	2900	4650
Splash Super Cab 4D		R14U	17420	1525	2025	3275	5125
4WD		1,5		775	775	1035	1035
V6 3.0 Liter		U		200	200	265	265
V6 4.0 Liter		X		250	250	335	335

REGULAR CAB PICKUP—V8—Truck Equipment Schedule T1

Body	Type	VIN	List	Trade-In Fair	Good	Pvt-Party Good	Retail Excellent
F150 Short Bed		F176,W	18815	1500	2000	3275	5125
F150 Long Bed		F176,W	19115	1250	1725	2975	4775
F250 Long Bed		F276,W	20225	1850	2375	3700	5600
Standard (Work Truck)				(400)	(400)	(535)	(535)
4WD		6,8		800	800	1065	1065
V6 4.2 Liter		2		(425)	(425)	(565)	(565)
V8 5.4 Liter		L		200	200	265	265

SUPER CAB PICKUP—V8—Truck Equipment Schedule T1

Body	Type	VIN	List	Trade-In Fair	Good	Pvt-Party Good	Retail Excellent
F150 Short Bed		X176,W	21255	2525	3125	4475	6550
F150 Long Bed		X176,W	21555	2325	2925	4275	6275
F250 Short Bed		X276,W	22300	3100	3750	5200	7375
Standard (Work Truck)				(400)	(400)	(535)	(535)
4WD		6,8		800	800	1065	1065
V6 4.2 Liter		2		(425)	(425)	(565)	(565)
V8 5.4 Liter		L		200	200	265	265

EXPLORER 4WD—V6—Truck Equipment Schedule T1

Body	Type	VIN	List	Trade-In Fair	Good	Pvt-Party Good	Retail Excellent
Sport Utility 2D		U24X	24545	1125	1575	2800	4550
XL Sport Utility 4D		U34X	25310	1725	2225	3525	5425
2WD		2		(350)	(350)	(465)	(465)
AWD		8		0	0	0	0
V6 4.0 Liter SOHC		E		150	150	200	200
V8 5.0 Liter		P		200	200	265	265

EXPEDITION 4WD—V8—Truck Equipment Schedule T1

Body	Type	VIN	List	Trade-In Fair	Good	Pvt-Party Good	Retail Excellent
XLT Sport Utility 4D		U18W	32610	2100	2675	4000	5975
w/o Third Seat				(450)	(450)	(600)	(600)
2WD		7		(450)	(450)	(600)	(600)
V8 5.4 Liter		L		225	225	300	300

WINDSTAR—V6—Truck Equipment Schedule T2

Body	Type	VIN	List	Trade-In Fair	Good	Pvt-Party Good	Retail Excellent
Cargo Minivan		A544	18955	500	675	1500	2800
V6 3.0 Liter		U		(200)	(200)	(265)	(265)

WINDSTAR—V6—Truck Equipment Schedule T1

Body	Type	VIN	List	Trade-In Fair	Good	Pvt-Party Good	Retail Excellent
Minivan		A51U	21300	650	925	1850	3250
LX Minivan		A514	24590	675	925	1850	3300
SE Minivan		A524	28075	825	1150	2175	3725
SEL Minivan		A534	30995	975	1375	2525	4225
w/o 2nd Sliding Door				(50)	(50)	(65)	(65)

ECONOLINE WAGON—V8—Truck Equipment Schedule T1

Body	Type	VIN	List	Trade-In Fair	Good	Pvt-Party Good	Retail Excellent
E150 XL Passenger		E112	22710	1400	1875	3150	4975
E350 XL Super Duty		S31L	25595	1575	2050	3325	5175
E350 XL S.D. Ext		S31L	27285	1700	2200	3475	5350
V6 4.2 Liter		2		(325)	(325)	(435)	(435)
V8 7.3L Turbo Diesel		F		1800	1800	2400	2400
V10 6.8 Liter		S		450	450	600	600

ECONOLINE VAN—V6—Truck Equipment Schedule T1

Body	Type	VIN	List	Trade-In Fair	Good	Pvt-Party Good	Retail Excellent
E150 Cargo Van		E142	20270	1275	1750	2975	4750
E250 Cargo Van		E24L	20350	1350	1850	3075	4875
E250 Extended Cargo		S24L	21050	1850	2350	3650	5525

TRUCKS & VANS

Body Type	VIN	List	Trade-In Fair	Trade-In Good	Pvt-Party Good	Retail Excellent
E350 Super Cargo	E34L	23300	1550	2025	3300	5150
E350 Ext SD Cargo	S34L		2025	2575	3875	5800
V8 4.6, 5.4 Liter	W,L		200	200	265	265
V8 7.3L Turbo Diesel	F		1950	1950	2600	2600
V10 6.8 Liter	S		400	400	535	535
RANGER PICKUP—4-Cyl.—Truck Equipment Schedule T2						
Short Bed	R10C	11795	650	925	1850	3300
Long Bed	R10C	12265	525	725	1575	2925
Super Cab 2D	R14C	15250	1075	1500	2700	4425
Super Cab 4D	R14X	15910	1775	2275	3550	5450
4WD	1,5		900	900	1200	1200
V6 3.0L Flex Fuel	V		225	225	300	300
V6 4.0 Liter	X		275	275	365	365
REGULAR CAB PICKUP—V8—Truck Equipment Schedule T1						
F150 Short Bed	F17W	19205	1775	2300	3600	5525
F150 Long Bed	F17W	19505	1500	1975	3275	5150
F250 Long Bed	F276,W	20575	2150	2700	4050	6025
Work Truck			(425)	(425)	(565)	(565)
4WD	6,8		900	900	1200	1200
V6 4.2 Liter	2		(450)	(450)	(600)	(600)
V8 5.4 Liter	L		225	225	300	300
REGULAR CAB PICKUP—V8 Supercharged—Truck Schedule T1						
F150 Lightning	F073	29355	6000	6925	8650	11400
SUPER CAB PICKUP—V8—Truck Equipment Schedule T1						
F150 Short Bed	X17W	21985	2850	3475	4875	7000
F150 Long Bed	X17W	22285	2675	3275	4650	6750
F250 Long Bed	X276,W	23355	3500	4200	5650	7925
Work Truck			(425)	(425)	(565)	(565)
4WD	6,8		900	900	1200	1200
V6 4.2 Liter	2		(450)	(450)	(600)	(600)
V8 5.4 Liter	L		225	225	300	300
SUPER DUTY REGULAR CAB—V8—Truck Equipment Schedule T1						
F250 Long Bed	F20L	21505	3175	3875	5300	7500
F350 Long Bed	F30L	22150	3325	4025	5450	7675
4WD	1		900	900	1200	1200
V10 6.8 Liter	S		400	400	535	535
V8 7.3L Turbo Diesel	F		2900	2900	3865	3865
SUPER DUTY SUPER CAB—V8—Truck Equipment Schedule T1						
F250 Short Bed	X20L	23260	4350	5175	6700	9100
F250 Long Bed	X20L	23460	4175	4950	6450	8825
F350 Short Bed	X30L	24245	4550	5375	6950	9450
F350 Long Bed	X30L	24445	4450	5250	6775	9200
4WD	1		900	900	1200	1200
V8 7.3L Turbo Diesel	F		2900	2900	3865	3865
V10 6.8 Liter	S		400	400	535	535
SUPER DUTY CREW CAB—V8—Truck Equipment Schedule T1						
F250 Short Bed	W20L	24985	5050	5900	7550	10150
F250 Long Bed	W20L	25185	4875	5700	7325	9900
F350 Short Bed	W30L	25835	5250	6125	7775	10400
F350 Long Bed	W30L	26035	5150	6000	7650	10250
4WD	1		900	900	1200	1200
V8 7.3L Turbo Diesel	F		2900	2900	3865	3865
V10 6.8 Liter	S		400	400	535	535

2000 FORD–(1,2or3)F(B,MorT)–(U70X)–Y–

Body Type	VIN	List	Trade-In Fair	Trade-In Good	Pvt-Party Good	Retail Excellent
EXPLORER SPORT 4WD—V6—Truck Equipment Schedule T1						
Utility 2D	U70X	24690	1400	1875	3125	4975
2WD	6		(400)	(400)	(535)	(535)
V6 4.0 Liter SOHC	E		150	150	200	200
EXPLORER 4WD—V6—Truck Equipment Schedule T1						
XL Sport Utility 4D	U72X	26790	2025	2600	3925	5875
Eddie Bauer Spt Util	U74P	34470	2750	3350	4725	6800
2WD	6		(400)	(400)	(535)	(535)
AWD	8		0	0	0	0
V6 4.0 Liter SOHC	E		150	150	200	200
V8 5.0 Liter	P		200	200	265	265
EXPEDITION 4WD—V8—Truck Equipment Schedule T1						
XLT Sport Utility 4D	U166	33165	2425	3050	4375	6425
Eddie Bauer Spt Util	U18L	40575	3175	3850	5275	7425
w/o Third Seat			(500)	(500)	(665)	(665)
2WD	5,7		(475)	(475)	(635)	(635)
V8 5.4 Liter	L		250	250	335	335

Body Type	VIN	List	Trade-In Fair	Trade-In Good	Pvt-Party Good	Retail Excellent
EXCURSION 4WD—V10—Truck Equipment Schedule T1						
XLT Sport Utility 4D	U41S	38090	2775	3375	4775	6875
w/o Third Seat			(500)	(500)	(665)	(665)
2WD			(475)	(475)	(635)	(635)
V8 5.4 Liter	L		(450)	(450)	(600)	(600)
V8 7.3L Turbo Diesel	F		3200	3200	4265	4265
WINDSTAR—V6—Truck Equipment Schedule T2						
Cargo Minivan	A544	20395	600	825	1725	3125
WINDSTAR—V6—Truck Equipment Schedule T1						
Minivan	A504	23080	775	1100	2100	3650
LX Minivan	A514	25045	800	1125	2125	3675
SE Minivan	A524	28195	975	1350	2500	4225
SEL Minivan	A534	30535	1100	1550	2775	4500
Limited Minivan	A534	33990	1200	1700	2925	4675
w/o 2nd Sliding Door	0		(50)	(50)	(65)	(65)
V6 3.0 Liter	U		(225)	(225)	(300)	(300)
ECONOLINE WAGON—V8—Truck Equipment Schedule T1						
E150 Passenger Van	E112	23810	1700	2200	3475	5375
E350 Super Duty Van	E31L	25900	1850	2400	3675	5575
E350 Super Duty Ext	S31L	27570	1975	2550	3850	5750
V6 4.2 Liter	2		(350)	(350)	(465)	(465)
V8 7.3L Turbo Diesel	F		1950	1950	2600	2600
V10 6.8 Liter	S		500	500	665	665
ECONOLINE VAN—V6—Truck Equipment Schedule T1						
E150 Cargo Van	E142	20950	1575	2050	3325	5175
E250 Cargo Van	E24L	22055	1675	2150	3425	5300
E250 Extended Cargo	E24L	22900	2175	2750	4050	6000
E350 Super Cargo	E34L	24500	1850	2400	3700	5575
E350 Ext SD Cargo	S34L	25475	2400	3000	4300	6300
V8 4.6, 5.4 Liter	W,L		200	200	265	265
V8 7.3L Turbo Diesel	F		2100	2100	2800	2800
V10 6.8 Liter	S		450	450	600	600
RANGER PICKUP—4-Cyl.—Truck Equipment Schedule T2						
Short Bed	R10C	11995	775	1075	2100	3675
Long Bed	R10C	12465	625	850	1800	3250
Super Cab 2D	R14C	15655	1250	1725	2975	4775
Super Cab 4D	R14C	16230	1800	2300	3600	5525
4WD	1,5		1025	1025	1365	1365
V6 3.0L Flex Fuel	X		250	250	335	335
V6 4.0 Liter	X		300	300	400	400
REGULAR CAB PICKUP—V8—Truck Equipment Schedule T1						
F150 Short Bed	F17W	19510	2050	2600	3950	5925
F150 Long Bed	F17W	19810	1750	2275	3600	5525
4WD	6,8		1000	1000	1335	1335
Work Truck			(450)	(450)	(600)	(600)
V6 4.2 Liter	2		(450)	(450)	(600)	(600)
V8 5.4 Liter	L		250	250	335	335
REGULAR CAB—V8 Supercharged—Truck Equip Schedule T1						
F150 Lightning	F073	30895	6675	7700	9425	12300
SUPER CAB PICKUP—V8—Truck Equipment Schedule T1						
F150 Short Bed	X17W	22195	3200	3875	5325	7525
F150 Harley Davidson	X17L	33800	5800	6750	8400	11100
F150 Long Bed	X17W	22495	3000	3650	5075	7225
4WD	6,8		1000	1000	1335	1335
Work Truck			(450)	(450)	(600)	(600)
V6 4.2 Liter	2		(450)	(450)	(600)	(600)
V8 5.4 Liter	L		250	250	335	335
SUPER DUTY REGULAR CAB PICKUP—V8—Truck Equip Schedule T1						
F250 Long Bed	F20L	22450	3675	4375	5850	8125
F350 Long Bed	F30L	23175	3825	4550	6050	8350
4WD	1		1000	1000	1335	1335
V8 7.3L Turbo Diesel	F		3200	3200	4265	4265
V10 6.8 Liter	S		450	450	600	600
SUPER DUTY SUPER CAB PICKUP—V8—Truck Equip Schedule T1						
F250 Short Bed	X20L	24620	4950	5775	7400	9950
F250 Long Bed	X20L	24820	4725	5525	7125	9650
F350 Short Bed	X30L	25410	5175	6025	7650	10250
F350 Long Bed	X30L	25610	5025	5875	7500	10100
4WD	1		1000	1000	1335	1335
V8 7.3L Turbo Diesel	F		3200	3200	4265	4265
V10 6.8 Liter	S		450	450	600	600
SUPER DUTY CREW CAB PICKUP—V8—Truck Equipment Schedule T1						
F250 Short Bed	W20L	25930	5700	6625	8275	11000

TRUCKS & VANS

Body Type	VIN	List	Trade-In Fair	Trade-In Good	Pvt-Party Good	Retail Excellent
F250 Long Bed	W20L	26130	5525	6425	8050	10750
F350 Short Bed	W30L	26590	5900	6825	8500	11200
F350 Long Bed	W30L	26790	5800	6750	8400	11100
4WD	1		1000	1000	1335	1335
V8 7.3L Turbo Diesel	F		3200	3200	4265	4265
V10 6.8 Liter			450	450	600	600

2001 FORD — (1or2)F(B,MorT)–(U021)–1–#

Body Type	VIN	List	Trade-In Fair	Trade-In Good	Pvt-Party Good	Retail Excellent
ESCAPE 4WD—V6—Truck Equipment Schedule T1						
XLS Sport Utility 4D	U021	21185	3025	3650	5075	7200
XLT Sport Utility 4D	U041	22815	3450	4150	5550	7800
2WD	2		(500)	(500)	(665)	(665)
4-Cyl. 2.0 Liter	B		(475)	(475)	(635)	(635)
EXPLORER SPORT 4WD—V6—Truck Equipment Schedule T1						
Sport Utility 2D	U70E	24435	1775	2300	3600	5525
2WD	6		(450)	(450)	(600)	(600)
EXPLORER 4WD—V6—Truck Equipment Schedule T1						
XLS Sport Utility 4D	U71E	27570	2450	3050	4375	6425
Eddie Bauer Spt Util	U74E	34590	3125	3800	5200	7350
2WD	6		(450)	(450)	(600)	(600)
AWD	7		0	0	0	0
V8 5.0 Liter	P		200	200	265	265
EXPLORER SPORT TRAC 4WD—V6—Truck Equipment Sch T1						
Utility Pickup 4D	U77E	25010	3100	3775	5175	7325
2WD	6		(450)	(450)	(600)	(600)
EXPEDITION 4WD—V8—Truck Equipment Schedule T1						
XLT Sport Utility 4D	U16W	33405	2825	3425	4850	6975
Eddie Bauer Spt Util	U18L	41410	3650	4350	5800	8050
w/o Third Seat			(550)	(550)	(735)	(735)
2WD	5		(500)	(500)	(665)	(665)
V8 5.4 Liter	L		275	275	365	365
EXCURSION 4WD—V10—Truck Equipment Schedule T1						
XLT Sport Utility 4D	U41S	38925	3200	3875	5325	7525
w/o Third Seat			(550)	(550)	(735)	(735)
2WD	0,2		(500)	(500)	(665)	(665)
V8 5.4 Liter	L		(475)	(475)	(635)	(635)
V8 7.3L Turbo Diesel	F		3500	3500	4665	4665
WINDSTAR—V6—Truck Equipment Schedule T2						
Cargo Minivan	A544	20540	750	1075	2100	3675
WINDSTAR—V6—Truck Equipment Schedule T1						
LX Minivan	A514	25320	975	1375	2550	4300
SE Sport Minivan	A574	27755	1150	1600	2825	4600
SE Minivan	A524	28915	1150	1625	2850	4625
SEL Minivan	A534	31435	1375	1850	3100	4925
Limited Minivan	A584	34085	1525	2000	3275	5125
w/o 2nd Sliding Door	0		—	—	(50)	(50)
ECONOLINE WAGON—V8—Truck Equipment Schedule T1						
E150 Passenger Van	E11W	24060	2050	2625	3925	5850
E350 Super Duty	E31L	26350	2250	2825	4150	6100
E350 Super Duty Ext	S31L	27970	2375	2975	4300	6275
V6 4.2 Liter	2		(375)	(375)	(500)	(500)
V8 7.3L Turbo Diesel	F		2100	2100	2800	2800
V10 6.8 Liter	S		550	550	735	735
ECONOLINE VAN—V6—Truck Equipment Schedule T1						
E150 Cargo Van	E142	21445	1925	2475	3775	5700
E250 Cargo Van	E24L	22565	2025	2575	3900	5825
E250 Extended Cargo	S24L	23410	2600	3175	4525	6575
E350 Super Cargo	E34L	24995	2250	2850	4175	6150
E350 Ext SD Cargo	S34L	25970	2825	3450	4825	6875
Crew Van Pkg			200	200	265	265
V8 4.6, 5.4 Liter	W,L		200	200	265	265
V8 7.3L Turbo Diesel	F		2250	2250	3000	3000
V10 6.8 Liter	S		475	475	635	635
RANGER PICKUP—4-Cyl.—Truck Equipment Schedule T2						
Short Bed	R10C	12400	925	1300	2500	4250
Long Bed	R10C	13515	775	1075	2225	3950
Super Cab 2D	R14C	16465	1525	2000	3300	5175
Super Cab 4D	R14C	20960	2125	2675	4025	5975
4WD	1,5		1150	1150	1535	1535
V6 3.0 Liter	U		250	250	335	335
V6 4.0 Liter	E		325	325	435	435
REGULAR CAB PICKUP—V8—Truck Equipment Schedule T1						
F150 Short Bed	F17W	20170	2350	2925	4375	6525

Body	Type	VIN	List	Trade-In Fair	Trade-In Good	Pvt-Party Good	Retail Excellent
F150 Long Bed		F17W	20470	2000	2575	4000	6075
Work Truck				(475)	(475)	(635)	(635)
4WD		6,8		1100	1100	1465	1465
V6 4.2 Liter		2		(450)	(450)	(600)	(600)
V8 5.4 Liter		L,Z		275	275	365	365
REGULAR CAB PICKUP—V8 Supercharged—Truck Schedule T1							
F150 Lightning		F073	32460	7375	8450	10300	13350
SUPER CAB PICKUP—V8—Truck Equipment Schedule T1							
F150 Short Bed		X17W	22855	3600	4300	5825	8175
F150 Long Bed		X17W	23155	3350	4050	5550	7875
Work Truck				(475)	(475)	(635)	(635)
4WD		6,8		1100	1100	1465	1465
V6 4.2 Liter		2		(450)	(450)	(600)	(600)
V8 5.4 Liter		L,Z		275	275	365	365
SUPERCREW PICKUP—V8—Truck Equipment Schedule T1							
F150 Short Bed 4D		W07W	26940	4775	5575	7250	9850
F150 King Ranch		W07W	31455	6150	7100	8775	11500
F150 HarleyDavidson		W07L	34495	8625	9850	11700	14950
4WD		8		1100	1100	1465	1465
V8 5.4 Liter		L		275	275	365	365
SUPER DUTY REGULAR CAB—V8—Truck Equipment Schedule T1							
F250 Long Bed		F20L	23155	4150	4900	6400	8775
F350 Long Bed		F30L	23580	4300	5100	6600	9000
4WD		1		1100	1100	1465	1465
V8 7.3L Turbo Diesel		F		3500	3500	4665	4665
V10 6.8 Liter		S		475	475	635	635
SUPER DUTY SUPER CAB—V8—Truck Equipment Schedule T1							
F250 Short Bed		X20L	25295	5525	6425	8025	10700
F250 Long Bed		X20L	25495	5300	6175	7800	10400
F350 Short Bed		X30L	26085	5725	6675	8300	11000
F350 Long Bed		X30L	26285	5600	6525	8150	10850
4WD		1		1100	1100	1465	1465
V8 7.3L Turbo Diesel		F		3500	3500	4665	4665
V10 6.8 Liter		S		475	475	635	635
SUPER DUTY CREW CAB—V8—Truck Equipment Schedule T1							
F250 Short Bed		W20L	25295	6325	7300	9025	11800
F250 Long Bed		W20L	25495	6125	7075	8775	11500
F350 Short Bed		W30L	27265	6525	7525	9225	12050
F350 Long Bed		W30L	27465	6450	7450	9150	11950
Platinum Edition				100	100	135	135
4WD		1		1100	1100	1465	1465
V8 7.3L Turbo Diesel		F		3500	3500	4665	4665
V10 6.8 Liter		S		475	475	635	635

2002 FORD — (1or2)F(B,MorT)—(U021)—2—#

Body	Type	VIN	List	Trade-In Fair	Trade-In Good	Pvt-Party Good	Retail Excellent
ESCAPE 4WD—V6—Truck Equipment Schedule T1							
XLS Sport Utility 4D		U021	21910	3450	4150	5800	8275
XLT Sport Utility 4D		U041	23935	3925	4675	6375	8925
2WD				(500)	(500)	(665)	(665)
4-Cyl. 2.0 Liter		B		(500)	(500)	(665)	(665)
EXPLORER 4WD—V6—Truck Equipment Schedule T1							
Sport Utility 2D		U70E	24785	1950	2525	4075	6300
2WD		6		(500)	(500)	(665)	(665)
EXPLORER 4WD—V6—Truck Equipment Schedule T1							
XLS Sport Utility 4D		U72E	27775	2650	3250	4900	7250
Eddie Bauer Spt Util		U74K	35135	3350	4050	5675	8150
Third Seat				400	400	535	535
2WD		6		(500)	(500)	(665)	(665)
V8 4.6 Liter		W		200	200	265	265
EXPLORER SPORT TRAC 4WD—V6—Truck Equipment Schedule T1							
Utility Pickup 4D		U77E	25410	3350	4050	5675	8150
2WD		6		(500)	(500)	(665)	(665)
EXPEDITION 4WD—V8—Truck Equipment Schedule T1							
XLT Sport Utility 4D		U16W	33810	3075	3725	5400	7850
Eddie Bauer Spt Util		U18L	41825	3950	4675	6400	8975
w/o Third Seat				(600)	(600)	(800)	(800)
2WD		5,7		(500)	(500)	(665)	(665)
V8 5.4 Liter		L		300	300	400	400
EXCURSION 4WD—V10—Truck Equipment Schedule T1							
XLT Sport Utility 4D		U41S	38985	3550	4275	5950	8475
w/o Third Seat				(600)	(600)	(800)	(800)
2WD				(500)	(500)	(665)	(665)
V8 5.4 Liter		L		(500)	(500)	(665)	(665)

TRUCKS & VANS

Body	Type	VIN	List	Trade-In Fair	Trade-In Good	Pvt-Party Good	Retail Excellent
V8 7.3L Turbo Diesel		F		3800	3800	5065	5065
WINDSTAR—V6—Truck Equipment Schedule T2							
Cargo Minivan		A544	20905	850	1200	2600	4600
WINDSTAR—V6—Truck Equipment Schedule T1							
LX Minivan		A514	22995	1075	1500	2975	5025
SE Minivan		A524	29280	1325	1800	3300	5400
SEL Minivan		A534	31950	1550	2025	3550	5675
Limited Minivan		A584	34360	1725	2225	3750	5900
w/o 2nd Sliding Door		0		(50)	(50)	(65)	(65)
ECONOLINE WAGON—V6—Truck Equipment Schedule T1							
E150 Passenger Van		E11W	24660	2325	2925	4475	6750
V8 4.6, 5.4 Liter		W		200	200	265	265
ECONOLINE WAGON—V8—Truck Equipment Schedule T1							
E350 Super Duty		E31L	26950	2525	3125	4700	7000
E350 Super Duty Ext.		S31L	28370	2675	3275	4875	7200
V8 7.3L Turbo Diesel		F		2250	2250	3000	3000
V10 6.8 Liter		S		600	600	800	800
ECONOLINE VAN—V6—Truck Equipment Schedule T1							
E150 Cargo Van		E142	21880	2175	2750	4300	6575
E250 Cargo Van		E242	22750	2275	2850	4400	6675
E250 Ext Cargo		E242	23960	2875	3500	5125	7475
E350 Super Cargo		E34L	25230	2525	3125	4700	7000
E350 Ext SD Cargo		E34L	26520	3125	3800	5400	7800
Crew Van Pkg				200	200	265	265
V8 4.6/5.4 Liter		W,L		200	200	265	265
V8 7.3L Turbo Diesel		F		2400	2400	3200	3200
V10 6.8 Liter		S		500	500	665	665
RANGER PICKUP—4-Cyl.—Truck Equipment Schedule T2							
Short Bed		R10C	12725	1000	1400	2875	4950
Long Bed		R10C	13655	850	1200	2625	4650
Super Cab 2D		R14C	16400	1675	2150	3725	5900
Super Cab 4D		R14C	18075	2300	2900	4475	6750
4WD		1,5		1250	1250	1665	1665
V6 3.0 Liter		U		250	250	335	335
V6 3.0L Flex Fuel		V		250	250	335	335
V6 4.0 Liter		E		350	350	465	465
REGULAR CAB PICKUP—V8—Truck Equipment Schedule T1							
F150 Short Bed		F17W	20640	2450	3050	4750	7225
F150 Long Bed		F17W	20940	2075	2650	4350	6775
Work Truck				(500)	(500)	(665)	(665)
4WD		6,8		1200	1200	1600	1600
V6 4.2 Liter		2		(450)	(450)	(600)	(600)
V8 5.4 Liter		L,Z		300	300	400	400
V8 5.4L Bi-Fuel		M		300	300	400	400
REGULAR CAB PICKUP—V8 Supercharged—Truck Equipment Schedule T1							
F150 Lightning		F073	32490	7875	9000	11100	14550
SUPER CAB PICKUP—V8—Truck Equipment Schedule T1							
F150 Short Bed		X17W	23290	3775	4500	6325	9000
F150 Long Bed		X17W	22840	3500	4225	6000	8650
F150 King Ranch		X17W	29735	5125	5975	7900	10850
4WD		6,8		1200	1200	1600	1600
Work Truck				(500)	(500)	(665)	(665)
V6 4.2 Liter		2		(450)	(450)	(600)	(600)
V8 5.4 Liter		L,Z		300	300	400	400
SUPERCREW PICKUP—V8—Truck Equipment Schedule T1							
F150 Short Bed 4D		W07W	27660	5025	5875	7800	10750
F150 King Ranch 4D		W07W	32135	6500	7500	9475	12650
4WD		8		1200	1200	1600	1600
V8 5.4 Liter		L		300	300	400	400
SUPERCREW PICKUP—V8 Supercharged—Truck Equipment Schedule T1							
F150 HarleyDavidson		W073	36520	9200	10475	12700	16300
SUPER DUTY REGULAR CAB PICKUP—V8—Truck Equipment Schedule T1							
F250 Long Bed		F20L	22725	4400	5200	7075	9900
F350 Long Bed		F30L	23985	4575	5400	7300	10150
4WD		1		1200	1200	1600	1600
V8 7.3L Turbo Diesel		F		3800	3800	5065	5065
V10 6.8 Liter		S		500	500	665	665
SUPER DUTY SUPER CAB PICKUP—V8—Truck Equipment Schedule T1							
F250 Short Bed		X20L	25715	5900	6825	8775	11800
F250 Long Bed		X20L	25915	5675	6600	8550	11550
F350 Short Bed		X30L	26505	6100	7050	9025	12100
F350 Long Bed		X30L	26705	5975	6925	8900	11950
4WD		1		1200	1200	1600	1600

Body Type	VIN	List	Trade-In Fair	Trade-In Good	Pvt-Party Good	Retail Excellent
V8 7.3L Turbo Diesel	F		3800	3800	5065	5065
V10 6.8 Liter	S		500	500	665	665
SUPER DUTY CREW CAB PICKUP—V8—Truck Equipment Schedule T1						
F250 Short Bed	W20L	27025	6750	7775	9775	12950
F250 Long Bed	W20L	27225	6550	7550	9525	12700
F350 Short Bed	W30L	27685	6950	8000	10050	13300
F350 Long Bed	W30L	27885	6925	7975	10000	13250
4WD	1		1200	1200	1600	1600
V8 7.3L Turbo Diesel	F		3800	3800	5065	5065
V10 6.8 Liter	S		500	500	665	665

2003 FORD — (1or2)F(B,MorT)—(U921)-3-#

Body Type	VIN	List	Trade-In Fair	Trade-In Good	Pvt-Party Good	Retail Excellent
ESCAPE 4WD—V6—Truck Equipment Schedule T1						
XLS Sport Utility 4D	U921	22550	4000	4725	6425	9000
XLT Sport Utility 4D	U931	25475	4475	5275	7025	9700
Limited Sport Util 4D	U941	27475	4800	5625	7400	10150
2WD	0		(575)	(575)	(765)	(765)
4-Cyl. 2.0 Liter	B		(600)	(600)	(800)	(800)
EXPLORER SPORT 4WD—V6—Truck Equipment Schedule T1						
XLS Sport Util 2D	U70E	25825	2925	3575	5200	7575
2WD	6		(575)	(575)	(765)	(765)
EXPLORER 4WD—V6 Flex Fuel—Truck Equipment Schedule T1						
XLS Sport Utility 4D	U72K	23845	3850	4575	6250	8800
Eddie Bauer Spt Util	U74K	35970	4725	5550	7325	10050
Third Seat			475	475	635	635
2WD	6		(575)	(575)	(765)	(765)
AWD	8		0	0	0	0
V8 4.6 Liter	W		250	250	335	335
EXPLORER SPORT TRAC 4WD—V6—Truck Equipment Schedule T1						
XLS Util Pickup 4D	U77E	26185	4725	5525	7325	10050
2WD	6		(575)	(575)	(765)	(765)
EXPEDITION 4WD—V8—Truck Equipment Schedule T1						
XLT Sport Utility 4D	U16W	34165	4150	4925	6625	9200
Eddie Bauer Spt Util	U18L	39140	5325	6200	7975	10800
w/o Third Seat			(700)	(700)	(935)	(935)
2WD	5,7		(575)	(575)	(765)	(765)
V8 5.4 Liter	L		325	325	435	435
EXCURSION 4WD—V10—Truck Equipment Schedule T1						
XLT Sport Utility 4D	U41S	39635	4525	5350	7125	9850
Eddie Bauer Spt Util	U45S	44405	5650	6575	8425	11300
w/o Third Seat			(475)	(475)	(635)	(635)
2WD	0,2,4		(575)	(575)	(765)	(765)
V8 5.4 Liter	L		(500)	(500)	(665)	(665)
V8 6.0L Turbo Diesel	P		4225	4225	5630	5630
V8 7.3L Turbo Diesel	F		3925	3925	5230	5230
WINDSTAR—V6—Truck Equipment Schedule T2						
Cargo Minivan	A544	21360	1300	1775	3275	5400
WINDSTAR—V6—Truck Equipment Schedule T1						
LX Minivan	A514	23365	1675	2175	3725	5875
SE Minivan	A524	29675	1975	2525	4100	6300
SEL Minivan	A534	32405	2225	2800	4350	6600
Limited Minivan	A584	35110	2425	3025	4575	6825
w/o 2nd Sliding Door	0		(175)	(175)	(235)	(235)
ECONOLINE WAGON—V6—Truck Equipment Schedule T1						
E150 Passenger Van	E11W	25250	2900	3525	5125	7500
V8 4.6, 5.4 Liter	W		250	250	335	335
ECONOLINE WAGON—V8—Truck Equipment Schedule T1						
E350 Super Duty	E31L	24790	3100	3775	5400	7800
E350 Super Duty Ext	S31L	28910	3550	4275	5900	8350
V8 7.3L Turbo Diesel	F		2500	2500	3335	3335
V10 6.8 Liter	S		650	650	865	865
ECONOLINE VAN—V6—Truck Equipment Schedule T1						
E150 Super Cargo	E142	22420	2775	3375	5000	7325
E250 Super Cargo	E242	23290	2875	3500	5100	7450
E250 Ext SD Cargo	E242	24200	3575	4300	5900	8350
E350 Super Cargo	E34L	25770	3175	3850	5475	7850
E350 Ext SD Cargo	E34L	26760	3875	4600	6250	8750
Crew Van Pkg.			250	250	335	335
V8 4.6, 5.4 Liter	W,L		250	250	335	335
V8 7.3L Turbo Diesel	F		2750	2750	3665	3665
V10 6.8 Liter	S		550	550	735	735
RANGER PICKUP—4-Cyl.—Truck Equipment Schedule T2						
Short Bed	R10D	13620	1450	1925	3475	5625

TRUCKS & VANS

Body	Type	VIN	List	Trade-In Fair	Trade-In Good	Pvt-Party Good	Retail Excellent
Long Bed		R10D	14370	1175	1650	3175	5325
Super Cab 2D		R14U	17320	2350	2950	4525	6800
Super Cab 4D		R44E	18605	3075	3750	5375	7775
4WD		1,5	------	1425	1425	1900	1900
V6 3.0 Liter		U	------	300	300	400	400
V6 3.0L Flex Fuel		V	------	300	300	400	400
V6 4.0 Liter		E	------	425	425	565	565
REGULAR CAB PICKUP—V8—Truck Equipment Schedule T1							
F150 Short Bed		F17W	21300	2625	3225	4900	7325
F150 Long Bed		F17W	21600	2250	2850	4475	6825
Work Truck			------	(650)	(650)	(865)	(865)
4WD		6,8	------	1375	1375	1835	1835
V6 4.2 Liter		2	------	(525)	(525)	(700)	(700)
V8 5.4 Liter		L,Z	------	325	325	435	435
V8 5.4L Bi-Fuel		M	------	325	325	435	435
REGULAR CAB PICKUP—V8 Supercharged—Truck Equipment Schedule T1							
F150 Lightning		F073	33255	8900	10150	12200	15650
SUPER CAB PICKUP—V8—Truck Equipment Schedule T1							
F150 Short Bed		X17W	23950	4125	4875	6625	9225
F150 Long Bed		X17W	24250	3850	4575	6325	8925
F150 King Ranch 4D		X17W	31660	5650	6600	8425	11300
Work Truck			------	(650)	(650)	(865)	(865)
4WD		6,8	------	1375	1375	1835	1835
V6 4.2 Liter		2	------	(525)	(525)	(700)	(700)
V8 5.4 Liter		L,Z	------	325	325	435	435
SUPERCREW PICKUP—V8—Truck Equipment Schedule T1							
F150 Short Bed 4D		W07W	28320	5625	6550	8375	11250
F150 King Ranch 4D		W07W	33115	7525	8625	10550	13700
4WD		8	------	1375	1375	1835	1835
V8 5.4 Liter		L	------	325	325	435	435
SUPERCREW PICKUP—V8 Supercharged—Truck Equipment Schedule T1							
F150 HarleyDavidson		W073	37295	10475	11900	14000	17700
SUPER DUTY REGULAR CAB PICKUP—V8—Truck Equipment Schedule T1							
F250 Long Bed		F20L	23760	5100	5950	7900	10850
F350 Long Bed		F30L	24215	5300	6175	8100	11050
4WD		1	------	1375	1375	1835	1835
V8 6.0L Turbo Diesel		P	------	4225	4225	5630	5630
V8 7.3L Turbo Diesel		F	------	3925	3925	5230	5230
V10 6.8 Liter		S	------	550	550	735	735
SUPER DUTY SUPER CAB PICKUP—V8—Truck Equipment Schedule T1							
F250 Short Bed		X20L	25945	6775	7825	9800	13000
F250 Long Bed		X20L	26145	6525	7525	9525	12700
F350 Short Bed		X30L	26735	7050	8100	10100	13350
F350 Long Bed		X30L	26935	6875	7950	9950	13200
4WD		1	------	1375	1375	1835	1835
V8 6.0L Turbo Diesel		P	------	4225	4225	5630	5630
V8 7.3L Turbo Diesel		F	------	3925	3925	5230	5230
V10 6.8 Liter		S	------	550	550	735	735
SUPER DUTY CREW CAB PICKUP—V8—Truck Equipment Schedule T1							
F250 Short Bed		W20L	27355	7775	8900	11050	14400
F250 King Ranch 6'		W20L	36460	8700	9900	12050	15600
F250 Long Bed		W20L	27555	7550	8650	10700	14000
F250 King Ranch 8'		W20L	36660	8375	9575	11700	15200
F350 Short Bed		W30L	28015	8025	9200	11300	14750
F350 King Ranch 6'		W30L	37325	9000	10250	12400	15950
F350 Long Bed		W30L	28215	7950	9100	11150	14600
F350 King Ranch 8'		W30L	37525	8700	9900	12050	15600
4WD		1	------	1375	1375	1835	1835
V8 6.0L Turbo Diesel		P	------	4225	4225	5630	5630
V8 7.3L Turbo Diesel		F	------	3925	3925	5230	5230
V10 6.8 Liter		S	------	550	550	735	735

2004 FORD—(1or2)F(B,MorT)—(U921)-4-#

Body	Type	VIN	List	Trade-In Fair	Trade-In Good	Pvt-Party Good	Retail Excellent
ESCAPE 4WD—V6—Truck Equipment Schedule T1							
XLS Sport Utility 4D		U921	22515	4650	5475	7200	9900
XLT Sport Utility 4D		U931	24770	5175	6050	7825	10600
Limited Sport Util 4D		U941	26830	5600	6500	8300	11100
2WD		0	------	(650)	(650)	(865)	(865)
4-Cyl. 2.0 Liter		B	------	(700)	(700)	(935)	(935)
EXPLORER 4WD—V6 Flex Fuel—Truck Equipment Schedule T1							
XLS Sport Utility 4D		U72K	29155	5200	6050	7825	10600
Eddie Bauer Spt Util		U74K	36435	6325	7300	9100	12000
Third Seat			------	550	550	735	735

2004 FORD

Body	Type	VIN	List	Trade-In Fair	Good	Pvt-Party Good	Retail Excellent
2WD		6		(650)	(650)	(865)	(865)
AWD		8		0	0	0	0
V8 4.6 Liter		W		300	300	400	400
EXPLORER SPORT TRAC 4WD—V6 Flex Fuel—Truck Equipment Schedule T1							
XLS Utility Pickup		U77K	26460	6275	7250	9075	11950
2WD		6		(650)	(650)	(865)	(865)
EXPEDITION 4WD—V8—Truck Equipment Schedule T1							
XLS Sport Utility 4D		U16W	33505	5350	6225	8000	10850
Eddie Bauer Spt Util		U18L	42790	6800	7850	9675	12700
w/o Third Seat				(800)	(800)	(1065)	(1065)
2WD		3,5,7		(650)	(650)	(865)	(865)
V8 5.4 Liter		L		350	350	465	465
EXCURSION 4WD—V10—Truck Equipment Schedule T1							
XLS Sport Utility 4D		U41S	40485	5650	6575	8400	11250
Eddie Bauer Spt Util		U45S	44985	6875	7925	9800	12850
w/o Third Seat				(800)	(800)	(1065)	(1065)
2WD		0,2,4		(650)	(650)	(865)	(865)
V8 5.4 Liter		L		(500)	(500)	(665)	(665)
V8 6.0L Turbo Diesel		P		4450	4450	5930	5930
FREESTAR—V6—Truck Equipment Schedule T2							
Cargo Minivan		A546	22070	625	875	2300	4325
FREESTAR—V6—Truck Equipment Schedule T1							
S Minivan		A546	24460	1350	1850	3375	5525
SE Minivan		A526	26930	1575	2050	3625	5800
SES Minivan		A576	28750	1850	2350	3925	6150
SEL Minivan		A532	29995	2025	2575	4150	6400
Limited Minivan		A582	33630	2400	3000	4550	6850
ECONOLINE WAGON—V8—Truck Equipment Schedule T1							
E150 Passenger Van		E11W	25255	3625	4325	5925	8375
E350 Super Duty		E31L	27995	3900	4625	6275	8750
E350 Super Duty Ext		S31L	29415	4600	5425	7100	9725
V8 5.4 Liter (E150)				275	275	365	365
V6 6.0L Turbo Diesel		P		2750	2750	3665	3665
V10 6.8 Liter		S		675	675	900	900
ECONOLINE VAN—V8—Truck Equipment Schedule T1							
E150 Super Cargo		E14W	23060	3475	4175	5775	8200
E250 Super Cargo		E24W	24105	3600	4300	5925	8375
E250 Ext SD Cargo		E24W	25220	4350	5150	6850	9450
E350 Super Cargo		E34L	26110	3950	4700	6325	8825
E350 Ext SD Cargo		E34L	27705	4725	5525	7250	9900
Crew Van Pkg				275	275	365	365
V8 5.4 Liter		L		275	275	365	365
V8 6.0L Turbo Diesel		P		3100	3100	4130	4130
V10 6.8 Liter		S		575	575	765	765
RANGER PICKUP—4-Cyl.—Truck Equipment Schedule T2							
Short Bed		R10D	14385	2075	2650	4250	6500
Long Bed		R10D	15135	1800	2300	3900	6100
Super Cab 2D		R14U	18120	3150	3825	5475	7875
Super Cab 4D		R44E	19405	4000	4750	6400	8900
4WD		1,5		1600	1600	2135	2135
V6 3.0 Liter		U		350	350	465	465
V6 4.0 Liter		E		500	500	665	665
HERITAGE REGULAR CAB PICKUP—V8—Truck Equipment Sch T1							
F150 Short Bed		F17W	21765	4650	5475	7275	10050
F150 Long Bed		F17W	22065	4275	5050	6775	9425
Work Truck				(800)	(800)	(1065)	(1065)
4WD		6,8		1550	1550	2065	2065
V6 4.2 Liter		2		(600)	(600)	(800)	(800)
V8 5.4L Bi-Fuel		3		350	350	465	465
REGULAR CAB PICKUP—V8 Supercharged—Truck Equipment Schedule T1							
F150 Lightning		F073	33560	11650	13175	15300	19000
HERITAGE SUPER CAB PICKUP—V8—Truck Equipment Schedule T1							
F150 Short Bed		X17W	24415	6225	7200	9050	12000
F150 Long Bed		X17W	24715	6025	6975	8825	11750
Work Truck				(800)	(800)	(1065)	(1065)
4WD		8		1550	1550	2065	2065
V6 4.2 Liter		2		(600)	(600)	(800)	(800)
V8 5.4L Bi-Fuel		Z		350	350	465	465
REGULAR CAB PICKUP—V8—Truck Equipment Schedule T1							
F150 Short Bed		F12W	22010	4775	5575	7400	10150
F150 Long Bed		F12W	22310	4375	5175	6950	9675
4WD		4		1550	1550	2065	2065
V8 5.4 Liter		5		350	350	465	465

0709 **SEE BACK PAGES FOR TRUCK EQUIPMENT** 313

Body Type	VIN	List	Trade-In Fair	Good	Pvt-Party Good	Retail Excellent

SUPER CAB PICKUP—V8—Truck Equipment Schedule T1
F150 5 1/2'	X12W	25010	6325	7300	9175	12150
F150 6 1/2'	X12W	24660	6375	7350	9200	12200
F150 8'	X12W	24960	6100	7050	8925	11850
4WD	4		1550	1550	2065	2065
V8 5.4 Liter	5		350	350	465	465

SUPERCREW PICKUP—V8—Truck Equipment Schedule T1
F150 Short Bed 4D	W12W	29815	7950	9100	11050	14300
4WD	4		1550	1550	2065	2065
V8 5.4 Liter	5		350	350	465	465

SUPER DUTY REGULAR CAB PICKUP—V8—Truck Equipment Schedule T1
F250 Long Bed	F20L	24430	5775	6725	8700	11750
F350 Long Bed	F30L	24885	6000	6950	8950	12000
4WD	1		1550	1550	2065	2065
V8 6.0L Turbo Diesel	P		4450	4450	5930	5930
V10 6.8 Liter	S		575	575	765	765

SUPER DUTY SUPER CAB PICKUP—V8—Truck Equipment Schedule T1
F250 Short Bed	X20L	26615	7700	8825	10850	14150
F250 Long Bed	X20L	26815	7400	8475	10500	13750
F350 Short Bed	X30L	27405	7975	9150	11200	14650
F350 Long Bed	X30L	27605	7825	8950	11050	14450
4WD	1		1550	1550	2065	2065
V8 6.0L Turbo Diesel	P		4450	4450	5930	5930
V10 6.8 Liter	S		575	575	765	765

SUPER DUTY SUPER CAB PICKUP 4WD—V8 Turbo Diesel—Truck Schedule T1
F250 Harley 6'	X20S	39890	13525	15250	17550	21800
F250 Harley 8'	X20S	40090	13275	14950	17250	21400
F350 Harley 6'	X31S	40895	13725	15475	17800	22000
F350 Harley 8'	X31S	41095	13475	15200	17450	21600
V10 6.8 Liter			(650)	(650)	(865)	(865)

SUPER DUTY CREW CAB PICKUP—V8—Truck Equipment Schedule T1
F250 Short Bed	W20L	28025	8825	10050	12200	15750
F250 King Ranch 6'	W20L	37350	9800	11125	13350	17000
F250 Long Bed	W20L	28225	8550	9775	11900	15450
F250 King Ranch 8'	W20L	37550	9475	10775	12950	16500
F350 Short Bed	W30L	28685	9100	10350	12500	16000
F350 King Ranch 6'	W30L	38215	10150	11525	13650	17400
F350 Long Bed	W30L	28885	8950	10200	12350	15900
F350 King Ranch 8'	W30L	38415	9800	11125	13300	16950
4WD	1		1550	1550	2065	2065
V8 6.0L Turbo Diesel	P		4450	4450	5930	5930
V10 6.8 Liter	S		575	575	765	765

SUPER DUTY CREW CAB PICKUP 4WD—V8 Turbo Diesel—Truck Schedule T1
F250 Harley 6'	W21S	42385	15875	17825	20200	24600
F250 Harley 8'	W21S	42585	15675	17600	20000	24400
F350 Harley 6'	W35S	43000	15975	17925	20300	24700
F350 Harley 8'	W35S	43200	15825	17750	20100	24500
V10 6.8 Liter			(650)	(650)	(865)	(865)

2005 FORD—(1or2)F(B,MorT)—(U96H)—5—#

ESCAPE 4WD—4-Cyl. Hybrid—Truck Equipment Schedule T1
| Sport Utility 4D | U96H | 28595 | 9625 | 10925 | 12850 | 16150 |
| 2WD | 0 | | (725) | (725) | (965) | (965) |

ESCAPE 4WD—V6—Truck Equipment Schedule T1
XLS Sport Utility 4D	U92Z	22045	5500	6400	8150	10950
XLT Utility 4D	U931	25545	6050	7000	8800	11650
Limited Sport Util 4D	U941	27145	6575	7575	9350	12300
2WD	0		(725)	(725)	(965)	(965)
4-Cyl. 2.3 Liter			(800)	(800)	(1065)	(1065)

FREESTYLE AWD—V6—Truck Equipment Schedule T1
SE Sport Utility 4D	K041	27295	5200	6050	7825	10600
SEL Sport Utility 4D	K051	28695	5525	6450	8175	11000
Limited Sport Utility	K061	30895	6025	6950	8725	11550
2WD			(725)	(725)	(965)	(965)

EXPLORER 4WD—V6 Flex Fuel—Truck Equipment Schedule T1
XLS Sport Utility 4D	U72K	29880	6725	7725	9500	12450
Eddie Bauer Spt Util	U74K	36995	8075	9225	11100	14250
Third Seat			600	600	800	800
2WD	6		(725)	(725)	(965)	(965)
V8 4.6 Liter	W		350	350	465	465

EXPLORER SPORT TRAC 4WD—V6 Flex Fuel—Truck Equipment Schedule T1
| XLS Utility Pickup | U77K | 27125 | 7975 | 9150 | 11050 | 14150 |
| 2WD | 6 | | (725) | (725) | (965) | (965) |

2005 FORD

Body Type	VIN	List	Trade-In Fair	Good	Pvt-Party Good	Retail Excellent
EXPEDITION 4WD—V8—Truck Equipment Schedule T1						
XLS Sport Utility 4D	U145	35935	6850	7900	9700	12700
Eddie Bauer Spt Util	U185	43725	8650	9850	11750	15000
King Ranch Sport Util	U185	46560	9675	10975	12950	16300
w/o Third Seat			(900)	(900)	(1200)	(1200)
2WD	3,5,7,9		(725)	(725)	(965)	(965)
EXCURSION 4WD—V10—Truck Equipment Schedule T1						
XLS Sport Utility 4D	U41S	41065	7075	8125	10000	13050
Eddie Bauer Spt Util	U45S	46145	8425	9625	11550	14850
w/o Third Seat			(900)	(900)	(1200)	(1200)
2WD	0,2,4		(725)	(725)	(965)	(965)
V8 5.4 Liter	L		(500)	(500)	(665)	(665)
V8 6.0L Turbo Diesel	P		4675	4675	6230	6230
FREESTAR—V6—Truck Equipment Schedule T2						
Cargo Minivan	A546	22295	1075	1500	3075	5200
FREESTAR—V6—Truck Equipment Schedule T1						
S Minivan	A506	24595	2100	2675	4250	6500
SE Minivan	A516	27195	2325	2900	4475	6750
SES Minivan	A576	28695	2600	3200	4800	7125
SEL Minivan	A522	29605	2800	3425	5050	7400
Limited Minivan	A582	33395	3200	3900	5525	7925
ECONOLINE WAGON—V8—Truck Equipment Schedule T1						
E150 Super Duty	E11W	25525	4575	5400	7050	9675
E350 Super Duty	E31L	28265	4900	5725	7450	10100
E350 Super Duty Ext	S31L	30865	5900	6825	8550	11300
V8 5.4 Liter (E150)			300	300	400	400
V8 6.0L Turbo Diesel	P		3000	3000	4000	4000
V10 6.8 Liter	S		700	700	935	935
ECONOLINE VAN—V8—Truck Equipment Schedule T1						
E150 Super Cargo	E14W	23330	4350	5125	6750	9300
E250 Super Cargo	E24W	24375	4450	5275	6925	9525
E250 Ext SD Cargo	E24W	25695	5375	6250	7950	10650
E350 Super Cargo	E34L	27160	4850	5675	7400	10050
E350 Ext SD Cargo	E34L	28295	5725	6650	8350	11100
Crew Van Pkg			300	300	400	400
V8 5.4 Liter	L		300	300	400	400
V8 6.0L Turbo Diesel	P		3450	3450	4600	4600
V10 6.8 Liter	S		600	600	800	800
RANGER PICKUP—4-Cyl.—Truck Equipment Schedule T2						
Short Bed	R10D	14985	2825	3450	5075	7450
Long Bed	R10D	17865	2500	3075	4675	7000
Super Cab 2D	R14U	17685	4100	4850	6500	9025
Super Cab 4D	R44U	20250	4975	5825	7525	10200
4WD	1,5		1775	1775	2365	2365
V6 3.0 Liter	U		400	400	535	535
V6 4.0 Liter	E		550	550	735	735
REGULAR CAB PICKUP—V8—Truck Equipment Schedule T1						
F150 Short Bed	F12W	21436	5425	6325	8125	11000
F150 Long Bed	F12W	21736	5000	5850	7650	10450
4WD	4		1725	1725	2300	2300
V6 4.2 Liter	2		(675)	(675)	(900)	(900)
V8 5.4 Liter	5		375	375	500	500
SUPER CAB PICKUP—V8—Truck Equipment Schedule T1						
F150 5 1/2'	X12W	25430	7125	8175	10050	13150
F150 6 1/2'	X12W	25080	7175	8225	10100	13200
F150 8'	X125	26580	6900	7975	9800	12850
4WD	4		1725	1725	2300	2300
V8 5.4 Liter	5		375	375	500	500
SUPERCREW PICKUP—V8—Truck Equipment Schedule T1						
F150 Short Bed 4D	W12W	30185	9000	10250	12200	15550
F150 King Ranch	W125	36325	11750	13275	15300	18950
4WD	4		1725	1725	2300	2300
V8 5.4 Liter	5		375	375	500	500
SUPER DUTY REGULAR CAB PICKUP—V8—Truck Equipment Schedule T1						
F250 Long Bed	F205	25525	6475	7475	9500	12700
F350 Long Bed	F305	26270	6725	7750	9750	12950
4WD	1		1725	1725	2300	2300
V8 6.0L Turbo Diesel	P		4675	4675	6230	6230
V10 6.8 Liter	Y		600	600	800	800
SUPER DUTY SUPER CAB PICKUP—V8—Truck Equipment Schedule T1						
F250 Short Bed	X205	27710	8600	9800	11950	15450
F250 Long Bed	X205	27910	8250	9425	11550	15000
F350 Short Bed	X305	28790	8950	10200	12350	15900

TRUCKS & VANS

Body	Type	VIN	List	Trade-In Fair	Trade-In Good	Pvt-Party Good	Retail Excellent
F350 Long Bed		X305	28990	8775	10000	12100	15650
4WD		1		1725	1725	2300	2300
V8 6.0L Turbo Diesel		P		4675	4675	6230	6230
V10 6.8 Liter		Y		600	600	800	800
SUPER DUTY CREW CAB PICKUP—V8—Truck Equipment Schedule T1							
F250 Short Bed		W205	29120	9850	11175	13350	17000
F250 King Ranch 6'		W205	37105	10975	12450	14600	18400
F250 King Ranch 8'		W205	29320	9525	10825	13000	16600
F250 King Ranch 8'		W205	37305	10575	12000	14150	17900
F350 Short Bed		W305	30070	10150	11525	13650	17400
F350 King Ranch 6'		W305	38450	11375	12850	15050	18850
F350 Long Bed		W305	30270	10000	11325	13500	17150
F350 King Ranch 8'		W305	38650	10975	12450	14600	18400
4WD		1		1725	1725	2300	2300
V8 6.0L Turbo Diesel		P		4675	4675	6230	6230
V10 6.8 Liter		Y		600	600	800	800
SUPER DUTY CREW CAB PICKUP 4WD—V8 Turbo Diesel—Truck Schedule T1							
F250 Harley 6'		W215	41835	17700	19900	22200	27000
F250 Harley 8'		W215	42035	17450	19550	22000	26700
F350 Harley 6'		W315	42610	17875	20000	22400	27000
F350 Harley 8'		W315	42810	17650	19800	22100	26800
V10 6.8 Liter (F250)		Y		(725)	(725)	(965)	(965)

2006 FORD — (1,2or3)F(D,MorT)—(U96H)—6

Body	Type	VIN	List	Trade-In Fair	Trade-In Good	Pvt-Party Good	Retail Excellent
ESCAPE 4WD—4-Cyl. Hybrid—Truck Equipment Schedule T1							
Sport Utility 4D		U96H	29140	11125	12600	14450	17950
2WD		0		(800)	(800)	(1065)	(1065)
ESCAPE 4WD—V6—Truck Equipment Schedule T1							
XLS Sport Utility 4D		U92Z	22435	6500	7500	9250	12150
XLT Utility 4D		U931	25755	7100	8150	9950	12900
Limited Sport Util 4D		U941	27295	7725	8850	10650	13600
2WD		0		(800)	(800)	(1065)	(1065)
4-Cyl. 2.3 Liter		Z		(900)	(900)	(1200)	(1200)
FREESTYLE AWD—V6—Truck Equipment Schedule T1							
SE Sport Utility 4D		K041	27655	6150	7100	8900	11750
SEL Sport Utility 4D		K051	29055	6525	7525	9275	12200
Limited Sport Utility		K061	31280	7100	8150	9950	12900
2WD		1,2,3		(800)	(800)	(1065)	(1065)
EXPLORER 4WD—V6—Truck Equipment Schedule T1							
XLS Sport Utility 4D		U72E	29400	8475	9675	11500	14700
Eddie Bauer Spt Util		U74E	33070	10050	11425	13350	16650
Third Seat				650	650	865	865
2WD		6		(800)	(800)	(1065)	(1065)
V8 4.6 Liter		8		400	400	535	535
EXPEDITION 4WD—V8—Truck Equipment Schedule T1							
XLS Sport Utility 4D		U145	36010	8825	10050	11950	15200
Eddie Bauer Spt Util		U185	42710	10875	12350	14250	17700
King Ranch Sport Util		U185	46060	11850	13375	15300	18850
w/o Third Seat				(975)	(975)	(1300)	(1300)
2WD		3,5,7,9		(800)	(800)	(1065)	(1065)
FREESTAR—V6—Truck Equipment Schedule T2							
Cargo Minivan		A546	20380	2000	2575	4175	6425
FREESTAR—V6—Truck Equipment Schedule T1							
SE Minivan		A516	24385	3375	4075	5675	8075
SEL Minivan		A522	27345	3950	4675	6300	8775
Limited Minivan		A582	30475	4305	5175	6825	9400
ECONOLINE WAGON—V8—Truck Equipment Schedule T1							
E150 Super Duty		E11W	26170	5825	6750	8450	11150
E350 Super Duty		E31L	28610	6175	7150	8850	11600
E350 Super Duty Ext		S31L	30600	7475	8550	10300	13200
V8 5.4 Liter (E150)		L		325	325	435	435
V8 6.0L Turbo Diesel		P		3250	3250	4330	4330
V10 6.8 Liter		S		725	725	965	965
ECONOLINE VAN—V8—Truck Equipment Schedule T1							
E150 Super Cargo		E14W	23975	5450	6325	8000	10700
E250 Super Cargo		E24W	24590	5550	6475	8125	10850
E250 Ext SD Cargo		E24W	25740	6550	7550	9225	12050
E350 Super Cargo		E34L	27380	6000	6950	8625	11350
E350 Ext SD Cargo		E34L	28310	6925	7975	9700	12550
E350 Cab-Ch/DRW		E39L		5225	6075	7775	10450
Crew Van Pkg				325	325	435	435
V8 5.4 Liter (E150/E250)		L		325	325	435	435
V8 6.0L Turbo Diesel		P		3800	3800	5065	5065

Body	Type	VIN	List	Trade-In Fair	Trade-In Good	Pvt-Party Good	Retail Excellent
	V10 6.8 Liter	........................S		625	625	835	835

RANGER PICKUP—4-Cyl.—Truck Equipment Schedule T2

Body	Type	VIN	List	Fair	Good	Good	Excellent
	Short Bed	R10D	15085	3725	4425	6075	8550
	Long Bed	R10D	16190	3325	4025	5650	8075
	Super Cab 2D	R14D	16795	5150	6000	7700	10400
	Super Cab 4D	R44U	19850	6100	7050	8775	11550
	4WD	1,5		1950	1950	2600	2600
	V6 3.0 Liter	U		450	450	600	600
	V6 4.0 Liter	E		600	600	800	800

REGULAR CAB PICKUP—V8—Truck Equipment Schedule T1

Body	Type	VIN	List	Fair	Good	Good	Excellent
	F150 Short Bed	F12W	21650	6075	7050	8875	11800
	F150 Long Bed	F12W	21945	5650	6600	8400	11250
	4WD	4		1900	1900	2535	2535
	V6 4.2 Liter	2		(750)	(750)	(1000)	(1000)
	V8 5.4 Liter	5		400	400	535	535

SUPER CAB PICKUP—V8—Truck Equipment Schedule T1

Body	Type	VIN	List	Fair	Good	Good	Excellent
	F150 5 1/2'	X12W	26300	7950	9100	11050	14200
	F150 6 1/2'	X12W	24985	7975	9150	11050	14250
	F150 Harley 6'	X125	35645	12700	14350	16300	20000
	F150 8'	X125	25280	7750	8875	10750	13850
	4WD	4		1900	1900	2535	2535
	V8 5.4 Liter	5		400	400	535	535

SUPERCREW PICKUP—V8—Truck Equipment Schedule T1

Body	Type	VIN	List	Fair	Good	Good	Excellent
	F150 5 1/2'	W12W	31035	10000	11375	13350	16750
	F150 6 1/2'	W12W	31335	9850	11175	13150	16550
	F150 King Ranch 5'	W125	37180	13275	14950	16900	20700
	F150 King Ranch 6'	W125	37480	13175	14850	16800	20600
	4WD	4		1900	1900	2535	2535
	V8 5.4 Liter	5		400	400	535	535

SUPER DUTY REGULAR CAB PICKUP—V8—Truck Equipment Schedule T1

Body	Type	VIN	List	Fair	Good	Good	Excellent
	F250 Long Bed	F205	24835	7250	8325	10400	13700
	F350 Long Bed	F305	25565	7525	8625	10700	14000
	4WD	1		1900	1900	2535	2535
	V8 6.0L Turbo Diesel	P		4900	4900	6530	6530
	V10 6.8 Liter	Y		625	625	835	835

SUPER DUTY SUPER CAB PICKUP—V8—Truck Equipment Schedule T1

Body	Type	VIN	List	Fair	Good	Good	Excellent
	F250 Short Bed	X205	26965	9575	10875	13050	16650
	F250 Long Bed	X205	27165	9250	10525	12650	16200
	F350 Short Bed	X305	28875	10000	11325	13500	17150
	F350 Long Bed	X305	29065	9750	11075	13250	16850
	4WD	1		1900	1900	2535	2535
	V8 6.0L Turbo Diesel	P		4900	4900	6530	6530
	V10 6.8 Liter	Y		625	625	835	835

SUPER DUTY CREW CAB PICKUP—V8—Truck Equipment Schedule T1

Body	Type	VIN	List	Fair	Good	Good	Excellent
	F250 Short Bed	W205	28345	10975	12450	14600	18350
	F250 King Ranch 6'	W205	39950	12200	13775	15950	19800
	F250 Long Bed	W205	28540	10625	12050	14200	17950
	F250 King Ranch 8'	W205	40145	11800	13325	15500	19350
	F350 Short Bed	W305	29275	11325	12800	14950	18750
	F350 King Ranch 6'	W305	41110	12650	14250	16440	20400
	F350 Long Bed	W305	29475	11075	12550	14700	18450
	F350 King Ranch 8'	W305	41305	12200	13775	15950	19800
	4WD	1		1900	1900	2535	2535
	V8 6.0L Turbo Diesel	P		4900	4900	6530	6530
	V10 6.8 Liter	Y		625	625	835	835

SUPER DUTY CREW CAB PICKUP 4WD—V8 Turbo Diesel—Schedule T1

Body	Type	VIN	List	Fair	Good	Good	Excellent
	F250 Harley 6 3/4'	W215	50780	19600	21950	24300	29100
	F250 Harley 8'	W215	50985	19350	21650	24000	28700
	F350 Harley 6 3/4'	W315	51555	19900	22250	24600	29400
	F350 Harley 8'	W315	51760	19550	21850	24200	29000

2007 FORD—(1,2or3)F(D,MorT)—(U59H)-7

ESCAPE 4WD—4-Cyl. Hybrid—Truck Equipment Schedule T1

Body	Type	VIN	List	Fair	Good	Good	Excellent
	Sport Utility 4D	U59H	27925	12750	14400	16150	19700
	2WD	0		(875)	(875)	(1165)	(1165)

ESCAPE 4WD—V6—Truck Equipment Schedule T1

Body	Type	VIN	List	Fair	Good	Good	Excellent
	XLS Sport Utility 4D	U921	22515	7700	8825	10550	13450
	XLT Sport Utility 4D	U931	25525	8325	9525	11250	14300
	Limited Sport Util 4D	U941	27045	9050	10300	12050	15200
	2WD	0		(875)	(875)	(1165)	(1165)
	4-Cyl. 2.3 Liter	Z		(1000)	(1000)	(1335)	(1335)

EDGE—V6—Truck Equipment Schedule T1

Body	Type	VIN	List	Fair	Good	Good	Excellent
	SE Sport Utility 4D	K36C	25995	10050	11425	13200	16400

TRUCKS & VANS

Body Type	VIN	List	Trade-In Fair	Trade-In Good	Pvt-Party Good	Retail Excellent
SEL Sport Utility 4D	K38C	27990	11275	12750	14550	17900
SEL Plus Spt Util 4D	K39C	29745	13275	14950	16700	20300
AWD		4	950	950	1265	1265
FREESTYLE AWD—V6—Truck Equipment Schedule T1						
SEL Sport Utility 4D	K051	28120	7725	8850	10550	13450
Limited Sport Utility	K061	31405	8375	9575	11300	14350
2WD		2,3	(875)	(875)	(1165)	(1165)
EXPLORER 4WD—V6—Truck Equipment Schedule T1						
XLT Sport Utility 4D	U73E	28290	10425	11850	13600	16900
Eddie Bauer Spt Util	U74E	31290	12250	13875	15650	19100
Third Seat			700	700	935	935
2WD		6	(875)	(875)	(1165)	(1165)
V8 4.6 Liter		8	450	450	600	600
EXPLORER SPORT TRAC 4WD—V6—Truck Equipment Schedule T1						
XLT Utility Pickup	U51K	27475	12150	13725	15500	18950
2WD		3	(875)	(875)	(1165)	(1165)
V8 4.6 Liter		8	450	450	600	600
EXPEDITION 4WD—V8—Truck Equipment Schedule T1						
XLT Sport Utility 4D	U165	32895	12500	14100	15950	19400
Eddie Bauer Spt Util	U185	39295	14400	16175	18050	21800
w/o Third Seat			(1050)	(1050)	(1400)	(1400)
2WD		3,5,7,9	(875)	(875)	(1165)	(1165)
EXPEDITION EL 4WD—V8—Truck Equipment Schedule T1						
XLT Sport Utility 4D	K165	37345	12550	14150	15950	19450
Eddie Bauer Spt Util	K185	41945	15200	17100	18900	22700
w/o Third Seat			(1050)	(1050)	(1400)	(1400)
2WD		5,7,9	(875)	(875)	(1165)	(1165)
FREESTAR—V6—Truck Equipment Schedule T2						
Cargo Minivan	A542	20480	3475	4200	5675	7975
FREESTAR—V6—Truck Equipment Schedule T1						
SE Minivan	A512	24485	4925	5775	7350	9850
SEL Minivan	A522	27445	5550	6475	8025	10600
Limited Minivan	A582	30355	6050	7000	8575	11200
ECONOLINE WAGON—V8—Truck Equipment Schedule T1						
E150 Super Duty	E11W	26460	7425	8500	10100	12850
E350 Super Duty	E31L	28485	7825	8950	10600	13500
E350 Super Duty Ext	S31L	31190	9375	10675	12350	15400
V8 5.4 Liter (E150)	L		350	350	465	465
V8 6.0L Turbo Diesel	P		3500	3500	4665	4665
ECONOLINE VAN—V8—Truck Equipment Schedule T1						
E150 Super Cargo	E14W	24250	6800	7850	9425	12150
E250 Super Cargo	E24W	24865	6925	7975	9575	12300
E250 Ext SD Cargo	E24W	26550	8025	9200	10850	13700
E350 Super Cargo	E34L	27745	7425	8525	10100	12900
E350 Ext SD Cargo	E34L	29120	8475	9675	11300	14250
E350 Cab-Ch/DR	E39L		6300	7275	8850	11500
Crew Van Pkg			350	350	465	465
V8 5.4 Liter (E150/E250)	L		350	350	465	465
V8 6.0L Turbo Diesel	P		4150	4150	5530	5530
V10 6.8 Liter	S		650	650	865	865
RANGER PICKUP—4-Cyl.—Truck Equipment Schedule T2						
Short Bed	R10D	14495	4750	5575	7175	9700
Long Bed	R10D	15700	4350	5150	6750	9200
Super Cab 2D	R14D	15905	6350	7325	8975	11650
Super Cab 4D	R44D	18520	7400	8500	10100	12900
4WD		1,5	2125	2125	2835	2835
V6 3.0 Liter	U		500	500	665	665
V6 4.0 Liter	E		650	650	865	865
REGULAR CAB PICKUP—V8—Truck Equipment Schedule T1						
F150 Short Bed	F12W	21840	6750	7800	9575	12500
F150 Long Bed	F12W	24485	6300	7275	9050	11900
4WD		4	2075	2075	2765	2765
V6 4.2 Liter	2		(800)	(800)	(1065)	(1065)
V8 5.4 Liter	5		400	400	535	535
SUPER CAB PICKUP—V8—Truck Equipment Schedule T1						
F150 5 1/2'	X12W	25790	8775	10000	11850	15050
F150 6 1/2'	X12W	24240	8825	10050	11900	15150
F150 8'	X125	24540	8550	9775	11600	14800
4WD		4	2075	2075	2765	2765
V8 5.4 Liter	5		400	400	535	535
SUPERCREW PICKUP—V8—Truck Equipment Schedule T1						
F150 5 1/2'	W12W	30490	11075	12550	14400	17900
F150 6 1/2'	W12W	30790	10825	12300	14150	17600

TRUCKS & VANS

Body	Type	VIN	List	Trade-In Fair	Trade-In Good	Pvt-Party Good	Retail Excellent
F150	KingRanch 5 1/2	W125	36290	14750	16600	18550	22400
F150	KingRanch 6 1/2	W125	36590	14650	16475	18400	22200
F150	Harley Davidson	W125	37150	16025	17975	19900	23800
4WD		4		2075	2075	2765	2765
V8 5.4 Liter		5		400	400	535	535
SUPER DUTY REGULAR CAB PICKUP—V8—Truck Equipment Schedule T1							
F250	Long Bed	F205	25795	7975	9150	11200	14650
F350	Long Bed	F305	26525	8275	9475	11550	15000
4WD		1		2075	2075	2765	2765
V8 6.0L Turbo Diesel		P		5100	5100	6800	6800
V10 6.8 Liter		Y		650	650	865	865
SUPER DUTY SUPER CAB PICKUP—V8—Truck Equipment Schedule T1							
F250	Short Bed	X205	27925	10525	11950	14100	17800
F250	Long Bed	X205	28125	10150	11525	13650	17300
F350	Short Bed	X305	28985	10925	12400	14500	18250
F350	Long Bed	X305	29175	10725	12150	14250	18000
4WD		1		2075	2075	2765	2765
V8 6.0L Turbo Diesel		P		5100	5100	6800	6800
V10 6.8 Liter		Y		650	650	865	865
SUPER DUTY CREW CAB PICKUP—V8—Truck Equipment Schedule T1							
F250	Short Bed	W205	29305	12050	13625	15800	19600
F250	King Ranch 6 3/4	W205	40060	13375	15100	17250	21300
F250	Long Bed	W20P	29500	11650	13175	15350	19150
F250	King Ranch 8'	W205	40255	12925	14550	16700	20700
F350	Short Bed	W305	30235	12400	14025	16100	20000
F350	King Ranch 6 3/4	W305	41220	13825	15575	17750	21800
F350	Long Bed	W305	30435	12100	13675	15850	19700
F350	King Ranch 8'	W305	41415	13375	15100	17250	21300
4WD				2075	2075	2765	2765
V8 6.0L Turbo Diesel		P		5100	5100	6800	6800
V10 6.8 Liter		Y		650	650	865	865
SUPER DUTY CREW CAB PICKUP 4WD—V8 Turbo Diesel—Schedule T1							
F250	Harley 6 3/4	W21P	50890	21550	24000	26300	31100
F250	Harley 8'	W21P	51095	21175	23725	25900	30700
F350	Harley 6 3/4	W31P	51665	21850	24400	26700	31600
F350	Harley 8'	W31P	51870	21375	23825	26100	30900

2008 FORD (1,2or3)F(D,MorT)—U59H—8

Body	Type	VIN	List	Fair	Good	Pvt Good	Excellent
ESCAPE 4WD—4-Cyl. Hybrid—Truck Equipment Schedule T1							
Sport Utility 4D		U59H	27680	16375	18375	20100	23900
2WD		0,4		(950)	(950)	(1265)	(1265)
ESCAPE 4WD—V6—Truck Equipment Schedule T1							
XLS Sport Utility 4D		U92Z	22175	10875	12350	14050	17350
XLT Sport Utility 4D		U931	24485	11575	13075	14850	18250
Limited Sport Util 4D		U941	26185	12350	13975	15750	19150
2WD		0,4		(950)	(950)	(1265)	(1265)
4-Cyl. 2.3 Liter		Z		(1100)	(1100)	(1465)	(1465)
EDGE—V6—Truck Equipment Schedule T1							
SE Sport Utility 4D		K36C	26025	12000	13575	15300	18600
SEL Sport Utility 4D		K38C	28020	13275	15000	16750	20300
Limited Sport Util 4D		K39C	29775	15475	17400	19150	22800
AWD		4		1025	1025	1365	1365
TAURUS X AWD—V6—Truck Equipment Schedule T1							
SEL Sport Utility 4D		K05W	29215	11575	13075	14850	18250
Eddie Bauer Spt Util		K08W	31955	12700	14350	16050	19550
Limited Sport Util		K06W	32935	13075	14750	16500	20000
2WD		2,3,7		(950)	(950)	(1265)	(1265)
EXPLORER 4WD—V6—Truck Equipment Schedule T1							
XLT Sport Utility 4D		U73E	28805	12750	14400	16100	19600
Eddie Bauer Spt Util		U74E	31525	14750	16600	18350	22000
Third Row				750	750	1000	1000
2WD		6		(950)	(950)	(1265)	(1265)
AWD		8		0	0	0	0
V8 4.6 Liter		8		475	475	635	635
EXPLORER SPORT TRAC 4WD—V6—Truck Equipment Schedule T1							
XLT Utility Pickup		U51K	27930	14600	16425	18150	21800
2WD		3		(950)	(950)	(1265)	(1265)
AWD				0	0	0	0
V8 4.6 Liter		8		475	475	635	635
EXPEDITION 4WD—V8—Truck Equipment Schedule T1							
XLT Sport Utility 4D		U165	34420	16525	18525	20300	24200
Eddie Bauer Spt Util		U185	39665	18575	20775	22600	26700
King Ranch Spt Util		U185	43765	19100	21375	23100	27200

Body	Type	VIN	List	Trade-In Fair	Trade-In Good	Pvt-Party Good	Retail Excellent
w/o **Third Row**		....	....	(1125)	(1125)	(1500)	(1500)
2WD		5,7,9	....	(950)	(950)	(1265)	(1265)

EXPEDITION EL 4WD—V8—Truck Equipment Schedule T1

Body	Type	VIN	List	Fair	Good	Good	Excellent
XLT Sport Utility 4D		K165	37945	16375	18375	20200	24000
Eddie Bauer Spt Util		K185	42315	19350	21650	23400	27500
King Ranch Spt Util		K185	46415	20200	22550	24300	28400
w/o **Third Row**		....	....	(1125)	(1125)	(1500)	(1500)
2WD		5,7,9	....	(950)	(950)	(1265)	(1265)

ECONOLINE WAGON—V8—Truck Equipment Schedule T1

Body	Type	VIN	List	Fair	Good	Good	Excellent
E150 Super Duty		E11W	26790	9475	10775	12350	15300
E350 Super Duty		E31L	30320	9900	11225	12850	15850
E350 Super Duty Ext		S31L	32710	11750	13275	14950	18200
V8 5.4 Liter (E150)		L	....	375	375	500	500
V8 6.0L Turbo Diesel		P	....	3750	3750	5000	5000

ECONOLINE VAN—V8—Truck Equipment Schedule T1

Body	Type	VIN	List	Fair	Good	Good	Excellent
E150 Cargo Van		E14W	24595	9425	10725	12300	15250
E150 Extended Cargo		S14W	25595	9750	11075	12700	15700
E250 Cargo Van		E24W	25925	9525	10825	12450	15400
E250 Extended Cargo		E24W	27075	10725	12150	13750	16850
E350 Super Cargo		E34L	28715	10050	11425	13050	16050
E350 Ext SD Cargo		E34L	29645	11225	12700	14300	17500
E350 Cab-Ch/DR		E39L	....	8825	10050	11600	14500
Crew Van Pkg			....	375	375	500	500
V8 5.4 Liter (E150/E250)		L	....	375	375	500	500
V8 6.0L Turbo Diesel		P	....	4475	4475	5965	5965
V10 6.8 Liter		S	....	675	675	900	900

RANGER PICKUP—4-Cyl.—Truck Equipment Schedule T2

Body	Type	VIN	List	Fair	Good	Good	Excellent
Short Bed		R10D	14655	6325	7325	8800	11300
Long Bed		R10D	15925	5925	6875	8325	10800
Super Cab 2D		R14D	16130	8075	9225	10850	13650
Super Cab 4D		R44U	19825	9200	10475	12100	15100
4WD		1,5	....	2300	2300	3065	3065
V6 3.0 Liter		U	....	525	525	700	700
V6 4.0 Liter		E	....	700	700	935	935

REGULAR CAB PICKUP—V8—Truck Equipment Schedule T1

Body	Type	VIN	List	Fair	Good	Good	Excellent
F150 Short Bed		F12W	20215	8725	9950	11700	14850
F150 Long Bed		F12W	20215	8250	9425	11200	14250
4WD		4	....	2250	2250	3000	3000
V6 4.2 Liter		2	....	(850)	(850)	(1135)	(1135)
V8 5.4 Liter		5	....	400	400	535	535

SUPER CAB PICKUP—V8—Truck Equipment Schedule T1

Body	Type	VIN	List	Fair	Good	Good	Excellent
F150 5 1/2'		X12W	25920	10875	12350	14200	17600
F150 6 1/2'		X12W	24645	10925	12400	14250	17650
F150 8'		X125	24665	10675	12100	13900	17300
4WD		4	....	2250	2250	3000	3000
V8 5.4 Liter		5	....	400	400	535	535

SUPERCREW PICKUP—V8—Truck Equipment Schedule T1

Body	Type	VIN	List	Fair	Good	Good	Excellent
F150 5 1/2'		W12W	27820	13375	15100	16950	20600
F150 6 1/2'		W12W	28120	13175	14850	16650	20300
F150 KingRanch 5 1/2'		W125	36420	17550	19700	21600	25600
F150 KingRanch 6 1/2'		W125	36720	17350	19450	21400	25400
4WD		4	....	2250	2250	3000	3000
V8 5.4 Liter		5	....	400	400	535	535

SUPERCREW PICKUP AWD—V8—Truck Equipment Schedule T1

Body	Type	VIN	List	Fair	Good	Good	Excellent
F150 Harley Davidson		W145	37425	18775	20975	22800	27000
2WD			....	(950)	(950)	(1265)	(1265)

SUPER DUTY REGULAR CAB PICKUP—V8—Truck Equipment Schedule T1

Body	Type	VIN	List	Fair	Good	Good	Excellent
F250 Long Bed		F205	25655	12000	13575	15800	19700
F350 Long Bed		F305	26375	12300	13925	16050	20000
4WD		1,3	....	2250	2250	3000	3000
V8 6.4L Turbo Diesel		R	....	5300	5300	7065	7065
V10 6.8 Liter		Y	....	675	675	900	900

SUPER DUTY SUPER CAB PICKUP—V8—Truck Equipment Schedule T1

Body	Type	VIN	List	Fair	Good	Good	Excellent
F250 Short Bed		X205	27780	14700	16550	18700	22800
F250 Long Bed		X205	27975	14350	16125	18300	22300
F350 Short Bed		X305	28825	15150	17050	19200	23400
F350 Long Bed		X305	29015	14900	16750	18900	23000
4WD		1,3	....	2250	2250	3000	3000
V8 6.4L Turbo Diesel		R	....	5300	5300	7065	7065
V10 6.8 Liter		Y	....	675	675	900	900

SUPER DUTY CREW CAB PICKUP—V8—Truck Equipment Schedule T1

Body	Type	VIN	List	Fair	Good	Good	Excellent
F250 Short Bed		W205	29140	16375	18375	20500	24800
F250 Long Bed		W205	29335	15925	17875	20100	24300

TRUCKS & VANS

Body	Type	VIN	List	Trade-In Fair	Trade-In Good	Pvt-Party Good	Retail Excellent
F250 King Ranch 6'		W205	40395	17775	20000	22100	26600
F250 King Ranch 8'		W205	40585	17300	19350	21600	26000
F350 Short Bed		W305	30060	16750	18775	21000	25300
F350 Long Bed		W305	30260	16375	18375	20500	24800
F350 King Ranch 6'		W305	41475	18325	20475	22600	27100
F350 King Ranch 8'		W305	41475	17775	20000	22100	26600
4WD		1,3		2250	2250	3000	3000
V8 6.4L Turbo Diesel		R		5300	5300	7065	7065
V10 6.8 Liter		Y		675	675	900	900
SUPER DUTY CREW CAB 4WD—V8 Turbo Diesel—Truck Schedule T1							
F250 Harley Short		W21R	52425	26650	29700	31900	37000
F250 Harley Long		W21R	52620	26275	29200	31400	36600
F350 Harley Short		W31R	53075	27150	30175	32300	37500
F350 Harley Long		W31R	53270	26450	29500	31700	36800
V10 6.8 Liter		Y		(950)	(950)	(1265)	(1265)
SUPER DUTY CREW CAB—V8 Turbo Diesel—Truck Equipment Schedule T1							
F450 Long Bed		W42R	42470	19750	21850	24000	28600
F450 King Ranch 8'		W42R	53715	22925	25575	27700	32500
4WD		1,3		2250	2250	3000	3000

GMC — See CHEVROLET TRUCKS

GEO

1994 GEO — 2CC–(J18U)–R–#

TRACKER 4WD—4-Cyl.—Truck Equipment Schedule T2

Body Type	VIN	List	Fair	Good	Good	Excellent
Sport Utility 2D	J18U	12901	225	300	850	1725
Spt Utility Conv 2D	J18U	12741	200	275	825	1675
LSi Sport Utility 2D	J18U	14065	275	400	975	1875
LSi Spt Util Conv 2D	J18U	13800	250	350	900	1800
2WD	E		(125)	(125)	(165)	(165)

1995 GEO — 2C(CorN)–(J186)–S–#

TRACKER 4WD—4-Cyl.—Truck Equipment Schedule T2

Body Type	VIN	List	Fair	Good	Good	Excellent
Sport Utility 2D	J186	13631	275	375	950	1875
Spt Utility Conv 2D	J186	13551	250	350	925	1850
LSi Sport Utility 2D	J186	14795	350	475	1100	2100
LSi Spt Util Conv 2D	J186	14615	300	425	1050	2000
2WD	E		(125)	(125)	(165)	(165)

1996 GEO — 2C(CorN)–(J186)–T–#

TRACKER 4WD—4-Cyl.—Truck Equipment Schedule T2

Body Type	VIN	List	Fair	Good	Good	Excellent
Spt Utility Conv 2D	J186	15071	275	375	975	1925
Sport Utility 4D	J136	15941	475	650	1350	2475
LSi Spt Util Conv 2D	J186	15501	325	475	1100	2100
LSi Sport Utility 4D	J136	16331	625	875	1750	3075
2WD	E		(200)	(200)	(265)	(265)

1997 GEO — 2C(CorN)–(J186)–V–#

TRACKER 4WD—4-Cyl.—Truck Equipment Schedule T2

Body Type	VIN	List	Fair	Good	Good	Excellent
Spt Utility Conv 2D	J186	15096	325	475	1100	2125
Sport Utility 4D	J136	15966	525	725	1550	2825
LSi Sport Utility 4D	J186	16356	725	1000	1925	3375
2WD	E		(250)	(250)	(335)	(335)

HONDA

1994 HONDA — 4S6(CG58E)–R–#

PASSPORT—4-Cyl.—Truck Equipment Schedule T1

Body Type	VIN	List	Fair	Good	Good	Excellent
DX Sport Utility 4D	CG58E	16035	625	850	1675	2975
Manual Trans			(125)	(125)	(165)	(165)
PASSPORT 4WD—V6—Truck Equipment Schedule T1						
LX Sport Utility 4D	CY58V	22825	1000	1425	2525	4175
EX Sport Utility 4D	CY58V	25375	1200	1700	2875	4575
2WD	G		(125)	(125)	(165)	(165)

TRUCKS & VANS

TRUCKS & VANS

Body	Type	VIN	List	Trade-In Fair	Good	Pvt-Party Good	Retail Excellent
1995 HONDA — (JHMor4S6)(CG58E)–S–#							
PASSPORT—4-Cyl.—Truck Equipment Schedule T1							
DX Sport Utility 4D	CG58E	16610	**750**	**1050**	**1950**	**3375**
Dual Air Bags			**0**	**0**	**0**	**0**
Manual Trans			**(125)**	**(125)**	**(165)**	**(165)**
PASSPORT 4WD—V6—Truck Equipment Schedule T1							
LX Sport Utility 4D	CY58V	23830	**1125**	**1575**	**2750**	**4425**
EX Sport Utility 4D	CY58V	26930	**1400**	**1850**	**3075**	**4875**
2WD	G		**(125)**	**(125)**	**(165)**	**(165)**
Dual Air Bags			**0**	**0**	**0**	**0**
ODYSSEY—4-Cyl.—Truck Equipment Schedule T1							
LX Minivan 4D	RA184	23380	**1200**	**1675**	**2850**	**4575**
EX Minivan 4D	RA187	25390	**1325**	**1800**	**3025**	**4775**
1996 HONDA — (JHMor4S6)(CK58E)–T–#							
PASSPORT—4-Cyl.—Truck Equipment Schedule T1							
DX Sport Utility 4D	CK58E	18385	**900**	**1275**	**2375**	**4025**
Manual Trans			**(125)**	**(125)**	**(165)**	**(165)**
PASSPORT 4WD—V6—Truck Equipment Schedule T1							
LX Sport Utility 4D	CM58V	25895	**1275**	**1750**	**2975**	**4725**
EX Sport Utility 4D	CM58V	29425	**1625**	**2125**	**3375**	**5225**
2WD	G		**(200)**	**(200)**	**(265)**	**(265)**
ODYSSEY—4-Cyl.—Truck Equipment Schedule T1							
LX Minivan 4D	RA184	23955	**1450**	**1925**	**3150**	**4975**
EX Minivan 4D	RA187	25945	**1575**	**2075**	**3325**	**5175**
1997 HONDA–(JHL,JHMor4S6)(RD184)–V–#							
CR-V 4WD—4-Cyl.—Truck Equipment Schedule T2							
Sport Utility 4D	RD184	19695	**2150**	**2725**	**4050**	**6000**
PASSPORT 4WD—V6—Truck Equipment Schedule T1							
LX Sport Utility 4D	CM58V	25895	**1450**	**1925**	**3175**	**5000**
EX Sport Utility 4D	CM58V	29425	**1850**	**2375**	**3650**	**5525**
2WD	G		**(250)**	**(250)**	**(335)**	**(335)**
ODYSSEY—4-Cyl.—Truck Equipment Schedule T1							
LX Minivan 4D	RA184	23955	**1700**	**2200**	**3475**	**5350**
EX Minivan 4D	RA187	25945	**1850**	**2375**	**3650**	**5525**
1998 HONDA–(JHL,JHMor4S6)(RD174)–W–#							
CR-V 4WD—4-Cyl.—Truck Equipment Schedule T2							
LX Sport Utility 4D	RD174	19145	**2500**	**3075**	**4450**	**6500**
EX Sport Utility 4D	RD176	20645	**2925**	**3550**	**4975**	**7100**
2WD	2		**(300)**	**(300)**	**(400)**	**(400)**
PASSPORT 4WD—V6—Truck Equipment Schedule T1							
LX Sport Utility 4D	CM58W	26995	**1675**	**2175**	**3450**	**5325**
EX Sport Utility 4D	CM58W	29345	**2100**	**2675**	**3975**	**5900**
2WD	K		**(300)**	**(300)**	**(400)**	**(400)**
ODYSSEY—4-Cyl.—Truck Equipment Schedule T1							
LX Minivan 4D	RA386	24205	**1975**	**2525**	**3825**	**5725**
EX Minivan 4D	RA387	26195	**2150**	**2725**	**4025**	**5975**
1999 HONDA–(JHL,2HKor4S6)(RD174)–X–#							
CR-V 4WD—4-Cyl.—Truck Equipment Schedule T2							
LX Sport Utility 4D	RD174	19365	**2900**	**3525**	**4925**	**7050**
EX Sport Utility 4D	RD176	20865	**3400**	**4100**	**5525**	**7750**
2WD	2		**(350)**	**(350)**	**(465)**	**(465)**
PASSPORT 4WD—V6—Truck Equipment Schedule T1							
LX Sport Utility 4D	CM58W	27015	**1925**	**2475**	**3775**	**5700**
EX Sport Utility 4D	CM58W	29365	**2425**	**3025**	**4350**	**6375**
2WD	K		**(350)**	**(350)**	**(465)**	**(465)**
ODYSSEY—V6—Truck Equipment Schedule T1							
LX Minivan 4D	RL184	23615	**2525**	**3100**	**4475**	**6525**
EX Minivan 4D	RL186	26215	**3000**	**3625**	**5025**	**7150**
2000 HONDA–(JHL,2HKor4S6)(RD174)–Y–#							
CR-V 4WD—4-Cyl.—Truck Equipment Schedule T2							
LX Sport Utility 4D	RD174	19465	**3400**	**4100**	**5525**	**7725**
EX Sport Utility 4D	RD176	20965	**3975**	**4700**	**6175**	**8500**
SE Sport Utility 4D	RD187	23015	**4050**	**4800**	**6275**	**8600**
2WD	2		**(400)**	**(400)**	**(535)**	**(535)**

Body	Type	VIN	List	Trade-In Fair	Trade-In Good	Pvt-Party Good	Retail Excellent
PASSPORT 4WD—V6—Truck Equipment Schedule T1							
LX Sport Utility 4D		CM58V	27515	**2250**	**2850**	**4175**	**6150**
EX Sport Utility 4D		CM58V	29465	**2800**	**3400**	**4775**	**6850**
2WD		K		**(400)**	**(400)**	**(535)**	**(535)**
ODYSSEY—V6—Truck Equipment Schedule T1							
LX Minivan 4D		RL185	23815	**2775**	**3375**	**4750**	**6800**
EX Minivan 4D		RL186	26415	**3250**	**3950**	**5350**	**7525**

2001 HONDA–(JHL,2HKor4S6)(RD174)–1–#

Body	Type	VIN	List	Trade-In Fair	Trade-In Good	Pvt-Party Good	Retail Excellent
CR-V 4WD—4-Cyl.—Truck Equipment Schedule T2							
LX Sport Utility 4D		RD174	19590	**4000**	**4725**	**6200**	**8500**
EX Sport Utility 4D		RD176	21190	**4625**	**5450**	**6925**	**9325**
SE Sport Utility 4D		RD187	23240	**4725**	**5550**	**7125**	**9600**
2WD		2		**(450)**	**(450)**	**(600)**	**(600)**
PASSPORT 4WD—V6—Truck Equipment Schedule T1							
LX Sport Utility 4D		CM58W	27740	**2650**	**3250**	**4600**	**6675**
EX Sport Utility 4D		CM58W	29690	**3175**	**3875**	**5250**	**7400**
2WD		K		**(450)**	**(450)**	**(600)**	**(600)**
ODYSSEY—V6—Truck Equipment Schedule T1							
LX Minivan 4D		RL185	24340	**3050**	**3700**	**5100**	**7225**
EX Minivan 4D		RL186	26840	**3600**	**4300**	**5750**	**7975**

2002 HONDA–(JHL,2HKor4S6)(RD784)–2–#

Body	Type	VIN	List	Trade-In Fair	Trade-In Good	Pvt-Party Good	Retail Excellent
CR-V 4WD—4-Cyl.—Truck Equipment Schedule T2							
LX Sport Utility 4D		RD784	19760	**4475**	**5275**	**7025**	**9725**
EX Sport Utility 4D		RD788	21940	**5175**	**6050**	**7850**	**10650**
2WD		2		**(500)**	**(500)**	**(665)**	**(665)**
PASSPORT 4WD—V6—Truck Equipment Schedule T1							
LX Sport Utility 4D		CM58W	28040	**2925**	**3550**	**5175**	**7550**
EX Sport Utility 4D		CM58W	29990	**3525**	**4225**	**5850**	**8325**
2WD		K		**(500)**	**(500)**	**(665)**	**(665)**
ODYSSEY—V6—Truck Equipment Schedule T1							
LX Minivan 4D		RL185	24690	**3225**	**3925**	**5550**	**8000**
EX Minivan 4D		RL186	27190	**3800**	**4575**	**6275**	**8800**

2003 HONDA–(Jor5)HorJ(L,Kor6)(YH282)–3

Body	Type	VIN	List	Trade-In Fair	Trade-In Good	Pvt-Party Good	Retail Excellent
ELEMENT 4WD—4-Cyl.—Truck Equipment Schedule T2							
DX Sport Utility 4D		YH282	18760	**4300**	**5100**	**6850**	**9525**
EX Sport Utility 4D		YH285	21310	**5100**	**5950**	**7725**	**10500**
2WD				**(575)**	**(575)**	**(765)**	**(765)**
CR-V 4WD—4-Cyl.—Truck Equipment Schedule T2							
LX Sport Utility 4D		RD774	19760	**5300**	**6150**	**7950**	**10750**
EX Sport Utility 4D		RD778	22060	**6075**	**7025**	**8850**	**11750**
2WD		2		**(575)**	**(575)**	**(765)**	**(765)**
PILOT 4WD—V6—Truck Equipment Schedule T1							
LX Sport Utility 4D		YF181	27360	**5150**	**6000**	**7775**	**10550**
EX Sport Utility 4D		YF184	29730	**6000**	**6950**	**8775**	**11650**
ODYSSEY—V6—Truck Equipment Schedule T1							
LX Minivan 4D		RL185	24860	**3900**	**4625**	**6300**	**8825**
EX Minivan 4D		RL186	27360	**4575**	**5375**	**7125**	**9800**

2004 HONDA–(J,2or5)F,HorJ(K,L,Nor6)(YH282)–4

Body	Type	VIN	List	Trade-In Fair	Trade-In Good	Pvt-Party Good	Retail Excellent
ELEMENT 4WD—4-Cyl.—Truck Equipment Schedule T2							
DX Sport Utility 4D		YH282	17990	**5100**	**5950**	**7725**	**10500**
LX Sport Utility 4D		YH273	18990	**5650**	**6575**	**8350**	**11150**
EX Sport Utility 4D		YH285	20790	**5950**	**6900**	**8700**	**11550**
2WD		1		**(650)**	**(650)**	**(865)**	**(865)**
CR-V 4WD—4-Cyl.—Truck Equipment Schedule T2							
LX Sport Utility 4D		RD774	19890	**6200**	**7175**	**9000**	**11900**
EX Sport Utility 4D		RD778	22240	**7125**	**8175**	**10000**	**13050**
2WD		2		**(650)**	**(650)**	**(865)**	**(865)**
PILOT 4WD—V6—Truck Equipment Schedule T1							
LX Sport Utility 4D		YF181	27590	**6225**	**7200**	**9025**	**11900**
EX Sport Utility 4D		YF184	29960	**7225**	**8300**	**10150**	**13200**
ODYSSEY—V6—Truck Equipment Schedule T1							
LX Minivan 4D		RL185	24980	**4675**	**5500**	**7225**	**9900**
EX Minivan 4D		RL186	27480	**5475**	**6350**	**8100**	**10900**

2005 HONDA–(J,2or5)F,HorJ(K,L,Nor6)(YH273)–5

Body	Type	VIN	List	Trade-In Fair	Trade-In Good	Pvt-Party Good	Retail Excellent
ELEMENT 4WD—4-Cyl.—Truck Equipment Schedule T2							
LX Sport Utility 4D		YH273	18990	**6650**	**7650**	**9425**	**12350**

Body Type	VIN	List	Trade-In Fair	Trade-In Good	Pvt-Party Good	Retail Excellent
EX Sport Utility 4D	YH276	20790	**6975**	**8025**	**9800**	**12800**
2WD	1		**(725)**	**(725)**	**(965)**	**(965)**

CR-V 4WD—4-Cyl.—Truck Equipment Schedule T2

LX Sport Utility 4D	RD774	21710	**7300**	**8375**	**10200**	**13200**
EX Sport Utility 4D	RD778	22965	**8275**	**9475**	**11300**	**14500**
SE Sport Utility 4D	RD779	25565	**8950**	**10200**	**12100**	**15350**
2WD	6		**(725)**	**(725)**	**(965)**	**(965)**

PILOT 4WD—V6—Truck Equipment Schedule T1

LX Sport Utility 4D	YF181	27865	**7525**	**8625**	**10400**	**13450**
EX Sport Utility 4D	YF184	30435	**8650**	**9850**	**11700**	**14950**

ODYSSEY—V6—Truck Equipment Schedule T1

LX Minivan 4D	RL185	25510	**7050**	**8125**	**9900**	**12850**
EX Minivan 4D	RL186	28510	**8025**	**9200**	**11050**	**14200**
Touring Minivan 4D	RL188	35010	**9625**	**10925**	**12850**	**16150**

2006 HONDA–(J,2or5)(F,HorJ)(J,K,L,Nor6)YH273–6

ELEMENT 4WD—4-Cyl.—Truck Equipment Schedule T2

LX Sport Utility 4D	YH273	19700	**7775**	**8900**	**10800**	**13850**
EX Sport Utility 4D	YH276	21575	**8150**	**9325**	**11150**	**14300**
EX-P Sport Util 4D	YH277	22920	**8325**	**9525**	**11350**	**14550**
2WD	1		**(800)**	**(800)**	**(1065)**	**(1065)**

CR-V 4WD—4-Cyl.—Truck Equipment Schedule T2

LX Sport Utility 4D	RD774	22145	**8550**	**9775**	**11600**	**14800**
EX Sport Utility 4D	RD778	24300	**9675**	**10975**	**12900**	**16150**
SE Sport Utility 4D	RD779	26000	**10425**	**11850**	**13750**	**17150**
2WD	6		**(800)**	**(800)**	**(1065)**	**(1065)**

PILOT 4WD—V6—Truck Equipment Schedule T1

LX Sport Utility 4D	YF181	28745	**11175**	**12650**	**14500**	**18000**
EX Sport Utility 4D	YF184	31295	**12400**	**14025**	**15900**	**19500**
2WD	2		**(800)**	**(800)**	**(1065)**	**(1065)**

ODYSSEY—V6—Truck Equipment Schedule T1

LX Minivan 4D	RL185	25895	**8900**	**10150**	**11950**	**15150**
EX Minivan 4D	RL186	28945	**10000**	**11375**	**13250**	**16500**
Touring Minivan 4D	RL188	37145	**11750**	**13275**	**15150**	**18600**

RIDGELINE 4WD—V6—Truck Equipment Schedule T1

RT Short Bed	YK162	28250	**10250**	**11625**	**13650**	**17250**
RTS Short Bed	YK164	30625	**11475**	**12925**	**15000**	**18700**
RTL Short Bed	YK165	32040	**12550**	**14150**	**16200**	**20000**

2007 HONDA–(J,2or5)(F,HorJ)(J,K,L,Nor6)YH273–7

ELEMENT 4WD—4-Cyl.—Truck Equipment Schedule T2

LX Sport Utility 4D	YH273	21695	**9175**	**10425**	**12200**	**15300**
EX Sport Utility 4D	YH277	23705	**9525**	**10825**	**12600**	**15800**
2WD	1		**(875)**	**(875)**	**(1165)**	**(1165)**

ELEMENT—4-Cyl.—Truck Equipment Schedule T2

SC Sport Utility 4D	YH179	24090	**9725**	**11025**	**12800**	**15950**

CR-V 4WD—4-Cyl.—Truck Equipment Schedule T2

LX Sport Utility 4D	RE483	22395	**10925**	**12400**	**14150**	**17450**
EX Sport Utility 4D	RE485	24645	**12150**	**13725**	**15500**	**18900**
2WD	3		**(875)**	**(875)**	**(1165)**	**(1165)**

PILOT 4WD—V6—Truck Equipment Schedule T1

LX Sport Utility 4D	YF181	28990	**13225**	**14900**	**16700**	**20300**
EX Sport Utility 4D	YF184	31540	**14600**	**16425**	**18200**	**21900**
2WD	2		**(875)**	**(875)**	**(1165)**	**(1165)**

ODYSSEY—V6—Truck Equipment Schedule T1

LX Minivan 4D	RL382	26240	**11225**	**12700**	**14400**	**17700**
EX Minivan 4D	RL384	29290	**12400**	**14025**	**15750**	**19150**
Touring Minivan 4D	RL388	37490	**14350**	**16125**	**17950**	**21600**

RIDGELINE 4WD—V6—Truck Equipment Schedule T1

RT Short Bed	YK162	28395	**11225**	**12700**	**14700**	**18350**
RTX Short Bed	YK163	28895	**11900**	**13475**	**15500**	**19200**
RTS Short Bed	YK164	30870	**12550**	**14150**	**16150**	**19900**
RTL Short Bed	YK165	33535	**13675**	**15425**	**17500**	**21400**

2008 HONDA–(J,2or5)(F,HorJ)(J,K,L,Nor6)YH273–8

ELEMENT 4WD—4-Cyl.—Truck Equipment Schedule T2

LX Sport Utility 4D	YH273	21015	**11075**	**12550**	**14200**	**17450**
EX Sport Utility 4D	YH277	23025	**11475**	**12975**	**14700**	**18000**
2WD	1		**(950)**	**(950)**	**(1265)**	**(1265)**

ELEMENT—4-Cyl.—Truck Equipment Schedule T2

SC Sport Utility 4D	YH179	23410	**11700**	**13225**	**14950**	**18300**

TRUCKS & VANS

Body	Type	VIN	List	Trade-In Fair	Trade-In Good	Pvt-Party Good	Retail Excellent

CR-V 4WD—4-Cyl.—Truck Equipment Schedule T2

Body	Type	VIN	List	Fair	Good	Good	Excellent
LX Sport Utility 4D		RE483	22535	12550	14150	15900	19300
EX Sport Utility 4D		RE485	24785	13825	15575	17300	20900
2WD		3		(950)	(950)	(1265)	(1265)

PILOT 4WD—V6—Truck Equipment Schedule T1

VP Sport Utility 4D		YF182	29630	15525	17450	19150	22800
EX Sport Utility 4D		YF184	31100	17100	19150	20900	24800
SE Sport Utility 4D		YF183	33630	17975	20100	21900	25800
2WD		2		(950)	(950)	(1265)	(1265)

ODYSSEY—V6—Truck Equipment Schedule T1

LX Minivan 4D		RL382	26495	14150	15925	17600	21100
EX Minivan 4D		RL384	29595	15475	17400	19100	22700
Touring Minivan 4D		RL388	40645	17650	19800	21500	25450

RIDGELINE 4WD—V6—Truck Equipment Schedule T1

RT Short Bed		YK162	28635	13525	15250	17300	21200
RTX Short Bed		YK163	29135	14250	16025	18050	22000
RTS Short Bed		YK164	31060	14950	16800	18750	22700
RTL Short Bed		YK165	33725	16225	18175	20200	24300

HUMMER

1994 HUMMER—137(YA82)--R-#

H1 4WD—V8 DIESEL—Truck Equipment Schedule T3

Body	Type	VIN	List	Fair	Good	Good	Excellent
Hard Top 2D		YA82	42706	17825	20000	23400	29300
Open Top 4D		YA85	47440	18725	20975	24500	30600
Hard Top 4D		YA83	53960	19100	21375	25000	31300
Wagon 4D		YA84	57019	19700	21950	25700	31900
GA Pkg				1000	1000	1335	1335
GC Pkg				1500	1500	2000	2000
Winch				400	400	535	535

1995 HUMMER—137(YA82)--S-#

H1 4WD—V8 DIESEL—Truck Equipment Schedule T3

Hard Top 2D		YA82	43265	19500	21750	25500	31800
HardTop Enlarged 2D		YA82	46970	19900	22250	26000	32300
OpenTop Recruit 4D		YA85	50317	20475	22825	26700	33100
Open Top 4D		YA85	53239	20475	22825	26700	33100
Hard Top 4D		YA83	57652	20875	23325	27100	33700
Wagon 4D		YA84	60858	21450	24000	27800	34600
GA Pkg				1000	1000	1335	1335
GC Pkg				1500	1500	2000	2000
Winch				400	400	535	535
V8 5.7 Liter		D		(1000)	(1000)	(1335)	(1335)

1996 HUMMER — 137(YA82)--T-#

H1 4WD—V8 DIESEL—Truck Equipment Schedule T3

Hard Top 2D		YA82	46765	20375	22725	26400	32600
HardTop Enlarged 2D		YA82	50649	20775	23225	26900	33200
OpenTop Recruit 4D		YA85	54230	21275	23825	27500	34000
Open Top 4D		YA85	57346	21275	23825	27500	34000
Hard Top 4D		YA83	62037	21850	24400	28100	34800
Wagon 4D		YA84	65421	22450	25000	28900	35700
GA Pkg				1150	1150	1535	1535
GC Pkg				1750	1750	2335	2335
Winch				475	475	635	635
V8 5.7 Liter		D		(1075)	(1075)	(1435)	(1435)
V8 6.5L Turbo Diesel		Z		875	875	1165	1165

1997 HUMMER — 137(YA82)--V-#

H1 4WD—V8 DIESEL—Truck Equipment Schedule T3

Hard Top 2D		YA82	55749	21550	24100	27600	34000
Open Top 4D		YA85	61954	22150	24800	28400	34900
Hard Top 4D		YA83	67330	22825	25475	29200	35900
Wagon 4D		YA84	70614	23525	26175	30000	36800
GA Pkg				1300	1300	1735	1735
GC Pkg				1975	1975	2635	2635
Winch				550	550	735	735
V8 6.5L Turbo Diesel		Z		1000	1000	1335	1335

TRUCKS & VANS

1998 HUMMER

Body	Type	VIN	List	Trade-In Fair	Good	Pvt-Party Good	Retail Excellent
1998 HUMMER — 137(YA82)--W-#							
H1 4WD—V8 DIESEL—Truck Equipment Schedule T3							
Hard Top 2D		YA82	57859	22450	25000	28500	34900
Open Top 4D		YA85	64451	23225	25875	29500	36000
Hard Top 4D		YA83	70174	23900	26650	30300	36900
Wagon 4D		YA84	73605	24600	27450	31200	37900
GA Pkg				1450	1450	1935	1935
GC Pkg				2200	2200	2935	2935
Winch				600	600	800	800
V8 6.5L Turbo Diesel		Z		1100	1100	1465	1465
1999 HUMMER — 137(YA82)--X-#							
H1 4WD—V8 DIESEL—Truck Equipment Schedule T3							
Hard Top 2D		YA82	66522	23525	26175	29500	35900
Open Top 4D		YA85	73580	24300	27150	30600	37000
Hard Top 4D		YA83	79677	25100	28025	31500	38100
Wagon 4D		YA84	83211	25875	28800	32400	39300
GA Pkg				1600	1600	2135	2135
GC Pkg				2425	2425	3235	3235
Winch				650	650	865	865
2000 HUMMER — 137(ZA89)--Y-#							
H1 4WD—V8 Turbo Diesel—Truck Equipment Sch T3							
Hard Top 2D		ZA89	70819	26850	29900	33300	40100
Open Top 4D		ZA90	80499	27825	30975	34500	41500
Hard Top 4D		ZA83	87058	28725	31950	35600	42600
Wagon 4D		ZA84	90844	29600	32925	36600	43800
Slantback 4D		ZA91	93197	29800	33225	36800	44100
GA Pkg				1750	1750	2335	2335
GC Pkg				2650	2650	3530	3530
Winch				700	700	935	935
2001 HUMMER — 137(ZA82)--1-#							
H1 4WD—V8 Turbo Diesel—Truck Equipment Sch T3							
Hard Top 2D		ZA82	76862	29700	33025	36400	43300
Open Top 4D		ZA85	84608	30675	34100	37600	44700
Hard Top 4D		ZA83	91553	31750	35275	38800	46100
Wagon 4D		ZA84	95404	32625	36250	39800	47200
GA Pkg				1875	1875	2500	2500
GC Pkg				2875	2875	3830	3830
Winch				750	750	1000	1000
2002 HUMMER — 137(ZA85)--2-#							
H1 4WD—V8 Turbo Diesel—Truck Equipment Schedule T3							
Open Top 4D		ZA85	98681	34300	38125	41700	49500
Enclosed Wagon 4D		ZA84	109834	36350	40375	44100	52100
Winch				800	800	1065	1065
2003 HUMMER — 5GR-(N23U)-3-#							
H2 4WD—V8—Truck Equipment Schedule T3							
Sport Utility 4D		N23U	50200	12150	13725	16000	20100
Third Seat				475	475	635	635
Adventure Pkg				300	300	400	400
Lux Pkg				300	300	400	400
Air Suspension				400	400	535	535
H1 4WD—V8 Turbo Diesel—Truck Equipment Schedule T3							
Open Top 4D		A903	106185	38025	42250	45800	53600
Wagon 4D		A843	117508	40675	45175	48700	56900
Winch				925	925	1235	1235
2004 HUMMER — 5GR-(N23U)-4-#							
H2 4WD—V8—Truck Equipment Schedule T3							
Sport Utility 4D		N23U	51395	14300	16075	18400	22700
Limited Ed Spt Util		N23U	59840	14950	16800	19200	23600
Third Seat				550	550	735	735
Adventure Pkg				350	350	465	465
Lux Pkg				350	350	465	465
Air Suspension				400	400	535	535

2004 HUMMER

Body	Type	VIN	List	Trade-In Fair	Trade-In Good	Pvt-Party Good	Retail Excellent
H1 4WD—V8 Turbo Diesel—Truck Equipment Schedule T3							
Open Top 4D		A903	106185	42725	47425	50900	59200
Wagon 4D		ZA84	117508	45875	50850	54500	63200
Winch				1050	1050	1400	1400
Adventure Pkg				350	350	465	465

2005 HUMMER — 5GR(N23U)-5-#

Body	Type	VIN	List	Trade-In Fair	Trade-In Good	Pvt-Party Good	Retail Excellent
H2 4WD—V8—Truck Equipment Schedule T3							
Sport Utility 4D		N23U	52000	16850	18875	21300	25900
Third Seat				600	600	800	800
Adventure Pkg				400	400	535	535
Lux Pkg				400	400	535	535
Air Suspension				400	400	535	535
H2 SUT 4WD—V8—Truck Equipment Schedule T3							
Sport Utility Pickup		N22U	53055	19100	21375	23800	28700
Adventure Pkg				400	400	535	535
Victory Red Ltd Ed				400	400	535	535
Lux Pkg				400	400	535	535
Air Suspension				400	400	535	535

2006 HUMMER — 5G(RorT)-(N136)-6-#

Body	Type	VIN	List	Trade-In Fair	Trade-In Good	Pvt-Party Good	Retail Excellent
H3 4WD—5-Cyl.—Truck Equipment Schedule T3							
Sport Utility 4D		N136	31195	12925	14600	16500	20200
Adventure Pkg				425	425	565	565
Luxury Pkg				425	425	565	565
Off-Road Suspension				400	400	535	535
H2 4WD—V8—Truck Equipment Schedule T3							
Sport Utility 4D		N23U	53855	19700	22050	24400	29300
Third Seat				650	650	865	865
Adventure Pkg				425	425	565	565
Limited Edition				425	425	565	565
Luxury Pkg				425	425	565	565
Air Suspension				400	400	535	535
H2 SUT 4WD—V8—Truck Equipment Schedule T3							
Sport Utility Pickup		N22U	53910	21075	23625	26000	31000
Adventure Pkg				425	425	565	565
Limited Edition				425	425	565	565
Luxury Pkg				425	425	565	565
Air Suspension				400	400	535	535
H1 4WD—V8 Turbo Diesel—Truck Equipment Schedule T3							
Open Top 4D		PH90	129399	67825	74975	78000	88200
Wagon 4D		PH84	140796	72025	79575	82600	93200
Winch				1300	1300	1735	1735
Adventure Pkg				425	425	565	565

2007 HUMMER — 5G(RorT)-(N13E)-7-#

Body	Type	VIN	List	Trade-In Fair	Trade-In Good	Pvt-Party Good	Retail Excellent
H3 4WD—5-Cyl.—Truck Equipment Schedule T3							
Sport Utility 4D		N13E	31690	15150	17050	18850	22600
Adventure Pkg				450	450	600	600
Luxury Pkg				450	450	600	600
H3X				450	450	600	600
Off-Road Suspension				400	400	535	535
H2 4WD—V8—Truck Equipment Schedule T3							
Sport Utility 4D		N23U	54255	26550	29600	31900	37400
Third Seat				700	700	935	935
Adventure Pkg				450	450	600	600
Luxury Pkg				450	450	600	600
Special Edition				450	450	600	600
Air Suspension				400	400	535	535
H2 SUT 4WD—V8—Truck Equipment Schedule T3							
Sport Utility Pickup		N22U	54300	25175	28025	30400	35800
Adventure Pkg				450	450	600	600
Luxury Pkg				450	450	600	600
Special Edition				450	450	600	600
Air Suspension				400	400	535	535

2008 HUMMER — 5G(RorT)-(N13E)-8-#

Body	Type	VIN	List	Trade-In Fair	Trade-In Good	Pvt-Party Good	Retail Excellent
H3 4WD—5-Cyl.—Truck Equipment Schedule T3							
Sport Utility 4D		N13E	32390	17650	19800	21500	25400
Adventure Pkg			3	475	475	635	635
Luxury Pkg			4	475	475	635	635
Off-Road Suspension				400	400	535	535

SEE BACK PAGES FOR TRUCK EQUIPMENT

TRUCKS & VANS

Body	Type	VIN	List	Trade-In Fair	Good	Pvt-Party Good	Retail Excellent
H3x 4WD—5-Cyl.—Truck Equipment Schedule T3							
Sport Utility 4D		N53E	40685	18675	20875	22600	26700
Luxury Pkg		4	------	475	475	635	635
H3 ALPHA 4WD—V8—Truck Equipment Schedule T3							
Sport Utility 4D		N63L	39260	18875	21075	22800	26900
Luxury Pkg		4	------	475	475	635	635
Off-Road Suspension			------	400	400	535	535
H2 4WD—V8—Truck Equipment Schedule T3							
Sport Utility 4D		N238	56410	33325	37050	39100	45000
Third Row			------	750	750	1000	1000
Adventure Pkg		7	------	475	475	635	635
Luxury Pkg		8	------	475	475	635	635
Air Suspension			------	400	400	535	535
H2 SUT 4WD—V8—Truck Equipment Schedule T3							
Sport Utility Pickup		N928	56455	31850	35375	37500	43200
Adventure Pkg			------	475	475	635	635
Luxury Pkg		0	------	475	475	635	635
Air Suspension			------	400	400	535	535

HYUNDAI

2003 HYUNDAI — KM8S(B82B)-3-#

Body Type	VIN	List	Fair	Good	Good	Excellent
SANTA FE—4-Cyl.—Truck Equipment Schedule T2						
Sport Utility 4D	B82B	17894	1800	2300	3875	6100
SANTA FE 4WD—V6—Truck Equipment Schedule T2						
GLS Sport Utility 4D	C72D	21894	2475	3075	4675	6975
LX Sport Utility 4D	C72D	24394	3025	3675	5325	7725
2WD	8	------	(575)	(575)	(765)	(765)
V6 3.5 Liter	E	------	500	500	665	665

2004 HYUNDAI — KM8S(B82B)-4-#

Body Type	VIN	List	Fair	Good	Good	Excellent
SANTA FE—4-Cyl.—Truck Equipment Schedule T2						
Sport Utility 4D	B82B	18589	2375	2975	4575	6900
SANTA FE 4WD—V6—Truck Equipment Schedule T2						
GLS Sport Utility 4D	C72D	23089	3175	3850	5525	7950
LX Sport Utility 4D	C72E	26089	3850	4575	6250	8775
2WD	8	------	(650)	(650)	(865)	(865)
V6 3.5 Liter	E	------	500	500	665	665

2005 HYUNDAI — KM8(SC73D)-5-#

Body Type	VIN	List	Fair	Good	Good	Excellent
SANTA FE 4WD—V6—Truck Equipment Schedule T2						
GLS Sport Util 4D	SC73D	23594	4050	4775	6450	8975
LX Sport Utility 4D	SC73E	26594	4750	5575	7300	10000
2WD	1	------	(725)	(725)	(965)	(965)
V6 3.5 Liter (GLS)	E	------	500	500	665	665
TUCSON 4WD—4-Cyl.—Truck Equipment Schedule T1						
GL Sport Utility 4D	JM72B	19594	2850	3450	5100	7500
2WD	1	------	(725)	(725)	(965)	(965)
TUCSON 4WD—V6—Truck Equipment Schedule T1						
GLS Sport Util 4D	JN72D	22094	3800	4500	6175	8675
LX Sport Utility 4D	JN72D	23344	4900	5750	7475	10150
2WD	1	------	(725)	(725)	(965)	(965)

2006 HYUNDAI — KM8(SC73D)-6-#

Body Type	VIN	List	Fair	Good	Good	Excellent
SANTA FE 4WD—V6—Truck Equipment Schedule T2						
GLS Sport Util 4D	SC73D	23795	4950	5800	7525	10200
Limited Sport Util	SC73E	26495	5800	6750	8450	11200
2WD	1	------	(800)	(800)	(1065)	(1065)
V6 3.5 Liter (GLS)	E	------	500	500	665	665
TUCSON 4WD—4-Cyl.—Truck Equipment Schedule T1						
GL Sport Utility 4D	JM72B	19595	3700	4425	6100	8600
2WD	1	------	(800)	(800)	(1065)	(1065)
TUCSON 4WD—V6—Truck Equipment Schedule T1						
GLS Sport Utility 4D	JN72D	22495	4725	5550	7275	9950
Limited Sport Util	JN72D	23795	6050	7000	8725	11500
2WD	1	------	(800)	(800)	(1065)	(1065)

2007 HYUNDAI — KM8(SG73D)7-#

Body Type	VIN	List	Fair	Good	Good	Excellent
SANTA FE AWD—V6—Truck Equipment Schedule T2						
GLS Sport Util 4D	SG73D	23595	7300	8375	10000	12850

2007 HYUNDAI

Body	Type	VIN	List	Trade-In Fair	Good	Pvt-Party Good	Retail Excellent
SE Sport Utility 4D		SH73E	26295	7650	8750	10400	13300
Limited Sport Util		SH73E	28595	8250	9425	11150	14150
Third Seat				450	450	600	600
2WD			1	(875)	(875)	(1165)	(1165)
TUCSON 4WD—4-Cyl.—Truck Equipment Schedule T1							
GLS Sport Util 4D		JM72B	18995	5600	6525	8150	10850
2WD			1	(875)	(875)	(1165)	(1165)
TUCSON 4WD—V6—Truck Equipment Schedule T1							
SE Sport Utility 4D		JN72D	22995	6725	7750	9375	12150
Limited Sport Util		JN72D	24345	8150	9325	11050	14050
2WD			1	(875)	(875)	(1165)	(1165)
VERACRUZ—V6—Truck Equipment Schedule T1							
GLS Sport Utility 4D		NU13C	28695	13175	14850	16650	20200
SE Sport Utility 4D		NU13C	30395	13875	15625	17450	21100
Limited Sport Util		NU73C	34695	15475	17400	19200	23000
AWD			7	950	950	1265	1265
ENTOURAGE—V6—Truck Equipment Schedule T1							
GLS Minivan		MC233	24495	5900	6850	8425	11050
SE Minivan		MC233	26995	6425	7425	9000	11650
Limited Minivan		MC233	29495	7425	8525	10100	12900

2008 HYUNDAI — KM8(SG73D)–8–#

Body	Type	VIN	List	Trade-In Fair	Good	Pvt-Party Good	Retail Excellent
SANTA FE AWD—V6—Truck Equipment Schedule T2							
GLS Sport Utility 4D		SG73D	24690	8550	9775	11350	14300
SE Sport Utility 4D		SH73E	26495	8900	10150	11750	14750
Limited Sport Util		SH73E	30295	9575	10875	12550	15650
Third Row				475	475	635	635
2WD			1	(950)	(950)	(1265)	(1265)
TUCSON—4-Cyl.—Truck Equipment Schedule T1							
GLS Sport Util 4D		JM12B	20195	6725	7750	9250	11900
Limited Sport Util		JN12B	22895	7550	8650	10200	12950
TUCSON 4WD—V6—Truck Equipment Schedule T1							
SE Sport Utility 4D		JN72D	23645	7900	9050	10700	13500
Limited Sport Util		JN72D	25445	9475	10775	12450	15500
2WD			1	(950)	(950)	(1265)	(1265)
VERACRUZ—V6—Truck Equipment Schedule T1							
GLS Sport Utility 4D		NU13C	27595	17450	19550	21300	25200
SE Sport Utility 4D		NU13C	29295	18225	20375	22100	26200
Limited Sport Util		NU13C	34745	20000	22350	24000	28100
AWD			7	1025	1025	1365	1365
ENTOURAGE—V6—Truck Equipment Schedule T1							
GLS Minivan		MC233	24595	10150	11525	13150	16150
Limited Minivan		MC233	30495	11800	13325	15000	18250

INFINITI

1997 INFINITI — JN6(AR05Y)–V–#

Body	Type	VIN	List	Trade-In Fair	Good	Pvt-Party Good	Retail Excellent
QX4 4WD—V6—Truck Equipment Schedule T3							
Sport Utility 4D		AR05Y	36045	3525	4250	5700	7975

1998 INFINITI — JN6(AR05Y)–W–#

| **QX4 4WD—V6—Truck Equipment Schedule T3** | | | | | | | |
| Sport Utility 4D | | AR05Y | 36045 | 3975 | 4700 | 6225 | 8550 |

1999 INFINITI — JN6(AR05Y)–X–#

| **QX4 4WD—V6—Truck Equipment Schedule T3** | | | | | | | |
| Sport Utility 4D | | AR05Y | 36075 | 4450 | 5250 | 6750 | 9175 |

2000 INFINITI — JNR(AR05Y)–Y–#

| **QX4 4WD—V6—Truck Equipment Schedule T3** | | | | | | | |
| Sport Utility 4D | | AR05Y | 36075 | 4975 | 5825 | 7400 | 9950 |

2001 INFINITI — JNR(DR07Y)–1–#

QX4 4WD—V6—Truck Equipment Schedule T3							
Sport Utility 4D		DR07Y	36075	6000	6950	8600	11250
2WD			X	(450)	(450)	(600)	(600)

Body	Type	VIN	List	Trade-In Fair	Good	Pvt-Party Good	Retail Excellent

TRUCKS & VANS

2002 INFINITI — JNR(DR07Y)-2-#

QX4 4WD—V6—Truck Equipment Schedule T3
| Sport Utility 4D | DR07Y | 36095 | 6550 | 7550 | 9425 | 12450 |
| 2WD | X | | (500) | (500) | (665) | (665) |

2003 INFINITI — JNR(AS08W)-3-#

FX35 AWD—V6—Truck Equipment Schedule T3
Sport Utility 4D	AS08W	36245	11475	12925	15100	18850
Intelligent Cruise Cntrl			375	375	500	500
Sport Pkg			1000	1000	1335	1335
2WD	U		(575)	(575)	(765)	(765)

FX45 AWD—V8—Truck Equipment Schedule T3
| Sport Utility 4D | BS08W | 44770 | 12925 | 14550 | 16750 | 20800 |
| Intelligent Cruise Cntrl | | | 375 | 375 | 500 | 500 |

QX4 4WD—V6—Truck Equipment Schedule T3
| Sport Utility 4D | DR09Y | 36695 | 7625 | 8750 | 10600 | 13700 |
| 2WD | X | | (575) | (575) | (765) | (765) |

2004 INFINITI — JNR(AS08W)-4-#

FX35 AWD—V6—Truck Equipment Schedule T3
Sport Utility 4D	AS08W	36395	12925	14600	16700	20600
Intelligent Cruise Cntrl			400	400	535	535
Sport Pkg			1000	1000	1335	1335
2WD	U		(650)	(650)	(865)	(865)

FX45 AWD—V8—Truck Equipment Schedule T3
| Sport Utility 4D | BS08W | 44920 | 14800 | 16650 | 18800 | 22900 |
| Intelligent Cruise Cntrl | | | 400 | 400 | 535 | 535 |

QX56 4WD—V8—Truck Equipment Schedule T3
Sport Utility 4D	AA08C	51080	14100	15875	18150	22200
Intelligent Cruise Cntrl			400	400	535	535
2WD			(650)	(65Q)	(865)	(865)

2005 INFINITI — JNR(AS08W)-5-#

FX35 AWD—V6—Truck Equipment Schedule T3
Sport Utility 4D	AS08W	37060	14700	16525	18600	22600
Adaptive Cruise Control			425	425	565	565
Sport Pkg			1000	1000	1335	1335
2WD	U		(725)	(725)	(965)	(965)

FX45 AWD—V8—Truck Equipment Schedule T3
| Sport Utility 4D | BS08W | 46060 | 16900 | 18975 | 21200 | 25600 |
| Adaptive Cruise Control | | | 425 | 425 | 565 | 565 |

QX56 4WD—V8—Truck Equipment Schedule T3
Sport Utility 4D	AA08C	51700	16525	18525	20800	25100
Adaptive Cruise Control			425	425	565	565
2WD			(725)	(725)	(965)	(965)

2006 INFINITI — JNR(AS08W)-6-#

FX35 AWD—V6—Truck Equipment Schedule T3
Sport Utility 4D	AS08W	40050	16650	18725	20800	25000
Adaptive Cruise Control			450	450	600	600
Sport Pkg			1000	1000	1335	1335
2WD	U		(800)	(800)	(1065)	(1065)

FX45 AWD—V8—Truck Equipment Schedule T3
| Sport Utility 4D | BS08W | 50500 | 19350 | 21650 | 23700 | 28200 |
| Adaptive Cruise Control | | | 450 | 450 | 600 | 600 |

QX56 4WD—V8—Truck Equipment Schedule T3
Sport Utility 4D	AA08C	53250	19100	21375	23500	28100
Adaptive Cruise Control			450	450	600	600
2WD	A		(800)	(800)	(1065)	(1065)

2007 INFINITI — JNR(AS08W)-7-#

FX35 AWD—V6—Truck Equipment Schedule T3
Sport Utility 4D	AS08W	40000	18775	20975	22900	27100
Adaptive Cruise Control			475	475	635	635
Sport Pkg			1000	1000	1335	1335
2WD	U		(875)	(875)	(1165)	(1165)

FX45 AWD—V8—Truck Equipment Schedule T3
| Sport Utility 4D | BS08W | 50550 | 21850 | 24400 | 26400 | 30900 |
| Adaptive Cruise Control | | | 475 | 475 | 635 | 635 |

Body	Type	VIN	List	Trade-In Fair	Good	Pvt-Party Good	Retail Excellent
QX56 4WD—V8—Truck Equipment Schedule T3							
Sport Utility 4D		AA08C	53850	**21850**	**24400**	**26600**	**31300**
Adaptive Cruise Control				475	475	635	635
2WD		A		(875)	(875)	(1165)	(1165)

2008 INFINITI — JNR(AJ09F)-8-#

Body	Type	VIN	List	Trade-In Fair	Good	Pvt-Party Good	Retail Excellent
EX35 AWD—V6—Truck Equipment Schedule T3							
Sport Utility 4D		AJ09F	33415	**23425**	**26175**	**27900**	**32300**
Journey Sport Util		AJ09F	36965	**25100**	**27925**	**29700**	**34400**
Adaptive Cruise Control				500	500	665	665
2WD				(950)	(950)	(1265)	(1265)
FX35 AWD—V6—Truck Equipment Schedule T3							
Sport Utility 4D		AS08W	40365	**21075**	**23625**	**25400**	**29700**
Adaptive Cruise Control				500	500	665	665
Sport Pkg				1000	1000	1335	1335
2WD		U		(950)	(950)	(1265)	(1265)
FX45 AWD—V8—Truck Equipment Schedule T3							
Sport Utility 4D		BS08W	50915	**25475**	**28425**	**30300**	**35000**
Adaptive Cruise Control				500	500	665	665
QX56 4WD—V8—Truck Equipment Schedule T3							
Sport Utility 4D		AA08C	56165	**31850**	**35375**	**37200**	**42600**
Adaptive Cruise Control				500	500	665	665
		D		(950)	(950)	(1265)	(1265)

ISUZU

1994 ISUZU — (JAA,4S1or4S2)-(Y07E)-R

Body	Type	VIN	List	Trade-In Fair	Good	Pvt-Party Good	Retail Excellent
AMIGO 4WD—4-Cyl.—Truck Equipment Schedule T2							
S Sport Utility 2D		Y07E	17149	**275**	**375**	**950**	**1875**
XS Sport Utility 2D		Y07E	17549	**300**	**425**	**1050**	**2000**
2WD		G		(125)	(125)	(165)	(165)
RODEO 4WD—V6—Truck Equipment Schedule T1							
S Sport Utility 4D		Y58V	21574	**850**	**1200**	**2150**	**3650**
LS Sport Utility 4D		Y58V	25274	**1100**	**1525**	**2675**	**4325**
2WD				(125)	(125)	(165)	(165)
4-Cyl. 2.6 Liter		E		(300)	(300)	(400)	(400)
TROOPER 4WD—V6—Truck Equipment Schedule T1							
S Sport Utility 4D		H58V	23700	**1025**	**1450**	**2550**	**4225**
RS Sport Utility 2D		H57W	25550	**1075**	**1500**	**2625**	**4300**
LS Sport Utility 4D		H58W	28400	**1400**	**1875**	**3100**	**4875**
SE Sport Utility 4D		H58W	33200	**1800**	**2300**	**3550**	**5425**
PICKUP—4-Cyl.—Truck Equipment Schedule T2							
S Short Bed		L11E	12349	**300**	**425**	**1000**	**1925**
S Long Bed		L14E	11159	**325**	**450**	**1050**	**2000**
S Spacecab		L16E	13059	**525**	**725**	**1475**	**2700**
4WD		R		400	400	535	535
4-Cyl. 2.3 Liter		L		(100)	(100)	(135)	(135)
V6 3.1 Liter		Z		100	100	135	135

1995 ISUZU — (JAA,JACor4S2)-(Y58V)-S

Body	Type	VIN	List	Trade-In Fair	Good	Pvt-Party Good	Retail Excellent
RODEO 4WD—V6—Truck Equipment Schedule T1							
S Sport Utility 4D		Y58V	22750	**975**	**1350**	**2475**	**4125**
LS Sport Utility 4D		Y58V	26670	**1225**	**1725**	**2925**	**4650**
2WD		G,K		(125)	(125)	(165)	(165)
4-Cyl. 2.6 Liter		E		(300)	(300)	(400)	(400)
TROOPER 4WD—V6—Truck Equipment Schedule T1							
S Sport Utility 4D		J58V	26270	**1225**	**1700**	**2900**	**4600**
RS Sport Utility 2D		J57W	29220	**1300**	**1775**	**3000**	**4750**
LS Sport Utility 4D		J58V	30400	**1775**	**2275**	**3550**	**5425**
SE Sport Utility 4D		J58V	34445	**2175**	**2750**	**4050**	**6000**
Ltd Sport Utility 4D		J58W	37220	**2375**	**2975**	**4300**	**6325**
PICKUP—4-Cyl.—Truck Equipment Schedule T2							
S Short Bed		L11L	10399	**350**	**500**	**1125**	**2125**
S Long Bed		L14L	11809	**375**	**525**	**1200**	**2300**
PICKUP 4WD—4-Cyl.—Truck Equipment Schedule T2							
S Short Bed		R11E	14519	**975**	**1350**	**2475**	**4150**

1996 ISUZU—(JR2,1GG,4S2orJAC)-(M58V)-T

Body	Type	VIN	List	Trade-In Fair	Good	Pvt-Party Good	Retail Excellent
RODEO 4WD—V6—Truck Equipment Schedule T1							
S Sport Utility 4D		M58V	25085	**1100**	**1550**	**2725**	**4400**

Body	Type	VIN	List	Trade-In Fair	Trade-In Good	Pvt-Party Good	Retail Excellent
LS Sport Utility 4D		M58V	28705	1475	1950	3200	5025
2WD		K		(200)	(200)	(265)	(265)
4-Cyl. 2.6 Liter		E		(350)	(350)	(465)	(465)
OASIS—4-Cyl.—Truck Equipment Schedule T1							
S Minivan 4D		J184	23940	1025	1450	2600	4275
LS Minivan 4D		J187	26435	1175	1650	2850	4575
TROOPER 4WD—V6—Truck Equipment Schedule T1							
S Sport Utility 4D		J58V	28585	1275	1750	2975	4725
LS Sport Utility 4D		J58V	32015	1850	2375	3650	5525
Ltd Sport Utility 4D		J58V	38435	2500	3075	4425	6475
SE Sport Utility 4D		J58V	38945	2275	2850	4200	6175
HOMBRE—4-Cyl.—Truck Equipment Schedule T2							
S Short Bed		S144	11719	400	575	1300	2450
XS Short Bed		S144	12548	450	625	1350	2525

1997 ISUZU—(JR2,1GG,4S2orJAC)—(M58V)—V

Body	Type	VIN	List	Trade-In Fair	Trade-In Good	Pvt-Party Good	Retail Excellent
RODEO 4WD—V6—Truck Equipment Schedule T1							
S Sport Utility 4D		M58V	25235	1275	1775	3000	4750
LS Sport Utility 4D		M58V	28855	1775	2275	3550	5425
2WD		K		(250)	(250)	(335)	(335)
4-Cyl. 2.6 Liter		E		(375)	(375)	(500)	(500)
OASIS—4-Cyl.—Truck Equipment Schedule T1							
S Minivan 4D		J184	24175	1150	1625	2825	4550
LS Minivan 4D		J187	26435	1400	1850	3100	4900
TROOPER 4WD—V6—Truck Equipment Schedule T1							
S Sport Utility 4D		J58V	28245	1375	1850	3075	4875
LS Sport Utility 4D		J58V	32715	2000	2550	3850	5750
Ltd Sport Utility 4D		J58V	38435	2775	3375	4750	6825
HOMBRE—4-Cyl.—Truck Equipment Schedule T2							
S Short Bed		S144	11992	500	650	1450	2700
XS Short Bed		S144	12419	525	700	1525	2800
XS Spacecab		S194	14774	875	1225	2325	4000
V6 4.3 Liter		X		175	175	235	235

1998 ISUZU—(JR2,1GG,4S2orJAC)—(M57D)—W

Body	Type	VIN	List	Trade-In Fair	Trade-In Good	Pvt-Party Good	Retail Excellent
AMIGO 4WD—4-Cyl.—Truck Equipment Schedule T2							
S Sport Utility 2D		M57D	17945	925	1300	2450	4150
2WD		K		(300)	(300)	(400)	(400)
V6 3.2 Liter		W		450	450	600	600
RODEO 4WD—V6—Truck Equipment Schedule T1							
S Sport Utility 4D		M58W	25635	1600	2075	3350	5200
LS Sport Utility 4D		M58W	29355	2125	2700	4000	5950
2WD		K		(300)	(300)	(400)	(400)
4-Cyl. 2.2 Liter		D		(400)	(400)	(535)	(535)
OASIS—4-Cyl.—Truck Equipment Schedule T1							
S Minivan 4D		J286	23977	1375	1850	3075	4900
LS Minivan 4D		J287	26247	1625	2125	3400	5250
TROOPER 4WD—V6—Truck Equipment Schedule T1							
S Sport Utility 4D		J58X	28245	1500	1975	3250	5075
HOMBRE—4-Cyl.—Truck Equipment Schedule T2							
S Short Bed		S144	12169	600	800	1675	3050
XS Short Bed		S144	12704	625	850	1750	3125
XS Spacecab		S194	15650	1000	1425	2600	4300
4WD		T		775	775	1035	1035
V6 4.3 Liter		X		200	200	265	265

1999 ISUZU—(JAC,JR2,4S2or1GG)—(M57D)—X—

Body	Type	VIN	List	Trade-In Fair	Trade-In Good	Pvt-Party Good	Retail Excellent
AMIGO 4WD—4-Cyl.—Truck Equipment Schedule T2							
S Sport Utility 2D		M57D	18825	1100	1550	2750	4475
2WD		K		(350)	(350)	(465)	(465)
Hard Top				100	100	135	135
V6 3.2 Liter		W		500	500	665	665
RODEO 4WD—V6—Truck Equipment Schedule T1							
S Sport Utility 4D		M58W	26135	1725	2225	3525	5425
LS Sport Utility 4D		M58W	27985	2325	2925	4250	6250
LSE Sport Utility 4D		M58W	31145	2800	3400	4775	6850
2WD		K		(350)	(350)	(465)	(465)
4-Cyl. 2.2 Liter		D		(425)	(425)	(565)	(565)
VEHICROSS 4WD—V6—Truck Equipment Schedule T1							
Sport Utility 2D		N57X	29595	3525	4250	5675	7925
OASIS—4-Cyl.—Truck Equipment Schedule T1							
S Minivan 4D		J286	24175	1625	2125	3400	5275

TRUCKS & VANS

Body	Type	VIN	List	Trade-In Fair	Good	Pvt-Party Good	Retail Excellent
TROOPER 4WD—V6—Truck Equipment Schedule T1							
S Sport Utility 4D		J58X	27595	**1700**	**2175**	**3475**	**5350**
Performance Pkg				200	200	265	265
HOMBRE—4-Cyl.—Truck Equipment Schedule T2							
S Short Bed		S144	12040	**700**	**1000**	**1975**	**3475**
XS Short Bed		S144	12575	**750**	**1050**	**2025**	**3550**
XS Spacecab		S194	15695	**1200**	**1700**	**2925**	**4700**
Third Door				200	200	265	265
4WD		T		900	900	1200	1200
V6 4.3 Liter		X		225	225	300	300

2000 ISUZU — (JAC,4S2or1GG)–(M57D)–Y–#

Body	Type	VIN	List	Trade-In Fair	Good	Pvt-Party Good	Retail Excellent
AMIGO 4WD—4-Cyl.—Truck Equipment Schedule T2							
S Sport Utility 2D		M57D	20190	**1350**	**1850**	**3100**	**4925**
2WD		K		(400)	(400)	(535)	(535)
Hard Top				100	100	135	135
V6 3.2 Liter		W		550	550	735	735
RODEO 4WD—V6—Truck Equipment Schedule T1							
S Sport Utility 4D		M58W	24935	**1900**	**2450**	**3750**	**5675**
LS Sport Utility 4D		M58W	27615	**2600**	**3175**	**4550**	**6600**
LSE Sport Utility 4D		M58W	31760	**3075**	**3700**	**5100**	**7225**
2WD		K		(400)	(400)	(535)	(535)
4-Cyl. 2.2 Liter		D		(450)	(450)	(600)	(600)
VEHICROSS 4WD—V6—Truck Equipment Schedule T1							
Sport Utility 2D		N57X	31045	**4100**	**4850**	**6350**	**8675**
TROOPER 4WD—V6—Truck Equipment Schedule T1							
S Sport Utility 4D		J58X	29445	**1900**	**2450**	**3750**	**5675**
LS Sport Utility 4D		J58X	31145	**2750**	**3350**	**4725**	**6775**
Limited Sport Util 4D		J58X	35193	**3775**	**4500**	**5950**	**8200**
2WD				(650)	(650)	(865)	(865)
HOMBRE—4-Cyl.—Truck Equipment Schedule T2							
S Short Bed		S144	11855	**900**	**1250**	**2400**	**4125**
XS Short Bed		S144	13355	**900**	**1275**	**2450**	**4200**
S Spacecab		S194	14180	**1325**	**1825**	**3075**	**4875**
XS Spacecab		S194	16005	**1525**	**2025**	**3300**	**5150**
Third Door				200	200	265	265
4WD		T		1025	1025	1365	1365
V6 4.3 Liter		W		250	250	335	335

2001 ISUZU — (JACor4S2)–(M57W)–1–#

Body	Type	VIN	List	Trade-In Fair	Good	Pvt-Party Good	Retail Excellent
RODEO SPORT 4WD—V6—Truck Equipment Schedule T2							
Soft Top 2D		M57W	20270	**1725**	**2250**	**3525**	**5425**
Hard Top 2D		M57W	20880	**1825**	**2350**	**3625**	**5525**
2WD		K		(450)	(450)	(600)	(600)
4-Cyl. 2.2 Liter		D		(475)	(475)	(635)	(635)
RODEO 4WD—V6—Truck Equipment Schedule T1							
S Sport Utility 4D		M58W	26025	**2200**	**2775**	**4100**	**6075**
LS Sport Utility 4D		M58W	27480	**2950**	**3575**	**4950**	**7050**
LSE Sport Utility 4D		M58W	31950	**3425**	**4125**	**5525**	**7725**
2WD		K		(450)	(450)	(600)	(600)
4-Cyl. 2.2 Liter		D		(475)	(475)	(635)	(635)
VEHICROSS 4WD—V6—Truck Equipment Schedule T1							
Sport Utility 2D		N57X	31045	**4750**	**5575**	**7150**	**9625**
TROOPER 4WD—V6—Truck Equipment Schedule T1							
S Sport Utility 4D		J58X	29690	**2250**	**2825**	**4175**	**6150**
LS Sport Utility 4D		J58X	31285	**3125**	**3800**	**5200**	**7325**
Limited Sport Util 4D		J58X	35333	**4275**	**5050**	**6500**	**8825**
2WD				(725)	(725)	(965)	(965)

2002 ISUZU — (JACor4S2)–(M57W)–2–#

Body	Type	VIN	List	Trade-In Fair	Good	Pvt-Party Good	Retail Excellent
RODEO SPORT 4WD—V6—Truck Equipment Schedule T2							
Soft Top 2D		M57W	22655	**2000**	**2550**	**4100**	**6300**
Hard Top 2D		M57W	22380	**2075**	**2650**	**4200**	**6425**
2WD		K		(500)	(500)	(665)	(665)
4-Cyl. 2.2 Liter		D		(500)	(500)	(665)	(665)
RODEO 4WD—V6—Truck Equipment Schedule T1							
S Sport Utility 4D		M58W	25305	**2400**	**3000**	**4575**	**6850**
LS Sport Utility 4D		M58W	28355	**3175**	**3850**	**5475**	**7900**
LSE Sport Utility 4D		M58W	32340	**3725**	**4425**	**6100**	**8600**
2WD		K		(500)	(500)	(665)	(665)
4-Cyl. 2.2 Liter		D		(500)	(500)	(665)	(665)

TRUCKS & VANS

Body	Type	VIN	List	Trade-In Fair	Trade-In Good	Pvt-Party Good	Retail Excellent
AXIOM 4WD—V6—Truck Equipment Schedule T1							
Sport Utility 4D		F58X	29625	2325	2925	4500	6775
XS Sport Utility 4D		F58X	31945	2500	3100	4700	7000
2WD				(500)	(500)	(665)	(665)
TROOPER 4WD—V6—Truck Equipment Schedule T1							
S Sport Utility 4D		J58X	30015	2500	3075	4675	6975
LS Sport Utility 4D		J58X	33300	3425	4150	5775	8225
Limited Sport Util 4D		J58X	37270	4625	5475	7200	9900
2WD				(800)	(800)	(1065)	(1065)

2003 ISUZU — (4NUor4S2)–(K57D)–3–#

Body	Type	VIN	List	Trade-In Fair	Trade-In Good	Pvt-Party Good	Retail Excellent
RODEO SPORT—4-Cyl.—Truck Equipment Schedule T2							
S Soft Top 2D		K57D	14624	1450	1925	3475	5600
RODEO SPORT 4WD—V6—Truck Equipment Schedule T2							
S Hard Top 2D		M57W	20040	2500	3075	4675	6950
2WD		K		(575)	(575)	(765)	(765)
4-Cyl. 2.2 Liter		D		(575)	(575)	(765)	(765)
RODEO 4WD—V6—Truck Equipment Schedule T1							
S Sport Utility 4D		M58W	22004	2925	3550	5175	7550
2WD		K		(575)	(575)	(765)	(765)
4-Cyl. 2.2 Liter		D		(575)	(575)	(765)	(765)
AXIOM 4WD—V6—Truck Equipment Schedule T1							
S Sport Utility 4D		F58X	27620	2950	3575	5225	7600
XS Sport Utility 4D		F58X	30620	3150	3825	5475	7875
2WD		E		(575)	(575)	(765)	(765)
ASCENDER 4WD—6-Cyl.—Truck Equipment Schedule T1							
S Sport Utility 4D		T16S	31974	3200	3875	5525	7975
LS				500	500	665	665
Limited				900	900	1200	1200
2WD		S		(575)	(575)	(765)	(765)
V8 5.3 Liter		T		350	350	465	465

2004 ISUZU — (4NUor4S2)–(M58W)–4–#

Body	Type	VIN	List	Trade-In Fair	Trade-In Good	Pvt-Party Good	Retail Excellent
RODEO 4WD—V6—Truck Equipment Schedule T1							
S Sport Utility 4D		M58W	23479	3600	4300	5950	8400
2WD		K		(650)	(650)	(865)	(865)
V6 3.5 Liter		Y		500	500	665	665
AXIOM 4WD—V6—Truck Equipment Schedule T1							
S Sport Utility 4D		F58X	28149	3700	4425	6075	8550
XS Sport Utility 4D		F58X	31149	3950	4700	6350	8850
2WD		E		(650)	(650)	(865)	(865)
ASCENDER 4WD—6-Cyl.—Truck Equipment Schedule T1							
S Sport Utility 4D		T16S	31849	3875	4600	6275	8825
w/o Third Seat		3		(900)	(900)	(1200)	(1200)
LS				500	500	665	665
Limited				900	900	1200	1200
2WD		S		(650)	(650)	(865)	(865)
V8 5.3 Liter		P		400	400	535	535

2005 ISUZU — 4NU–(T16S)–5–#

Body	Type	VIN	List	Trade-In Fair	Trade-In Good	Pvt-Party Good	Retail Excellent
ASCENDER 4WD—6-Cyl.—Truck Equipment Schedule T1							
S Sport Utility 4D		T16S	32083	4700	5525	7250	9950
w/o Third Seat		3		(900)	(900)	(1200)	(1200)
LS				500	500	665	665
Limited				900	900	1200	1200
2WD		S		(725)	(725)	(965)	(965)
V8 5.3 Liter		M		450	450	600	600

2006 ISUZU — (1GGor4NU)–(S198)–6–#

Body	Type	VIN	List	Trade-In Fair	Trade-In Good	Pvt-Party Good	Retail Excellent
i280 EXTENDED CAB PICKUP—4-Cyl.—Truck Equipment Schedule T2							
S Short Bed		S198	17649	4525	5325	6975	9525
LS Short Bed		S198	19649	4725	5525	7175	9750
i350 CREW CAB PICKUP 4WD—5-Cyl.—Truck Equipment Schedule T2							
LS Short Bed		T136	28018	5950	6900	8575	11250
ASCENDER 4WD—6-Cyl.—Truck Equipment Schedule T1							
S Sport Utility 4D		T16S	31878	5775	6700	8450	11250
w/o Third Seat		3		(900)	(900)	(1200)	(1200)
LS				500	500	665	665
Limited				900	900	1200	1200
2WD		S		(800)	(800)	(1065)	(1065)
V8 5.3 Liter		M		500	500	665	665

Body	Type	VIN	List	Trade-In Fair	Trade-In Good	Pvt-Party Good	Retail Excellent

2007 ISUZU — (1GGor4NU)–(S199)–7–#

i290 EXTENDED CAB PICKUP—4-Cyl.—Truck Equipment Schedule T2

Body	Type	VIN	List	Fair	Good	Good	Excellent
S Short Bed		S199	17674	5425	6300	7850	10350
LS Short Bed		S199	20613	5625	6550	8075	10650

i370 EXTENDED CAB PICKUP—5-Cyl.—Truck Equipment Schedule T2

| LS Short Bed | | S19E | 21763 | 6450 | 7425 | 9000 | 11600 |

i370 CREW CAB PICKUP—5-Cyl.—Truck Equipment Schedule T2

| LS Short Bed | | S13E | 28043 | 6950 | 8000 | 9550 | 12250 |
| 4WD | | T | | 2125 | 2125 | 2835 | 2835 |

ASCENDER 4WD—6-Cyl.—Truck Equipment Schedule T1

S Sport Utility 4D		T13S	28694	7100	8175	9850	12700
LS				500	500	665	665
2WD		S		(875)	(875)	(1165)	(1165)

2008 ISUZU — (1GGor4NU)–(S199)–8–#

i290 EXTENDED CAB PICKUP—4-Cyl.—Truck Equipment Schedule T2

| S Short Bed | | S199 | 18084 | 6800 | 7850 | 9250 | 11750 |

i370 EXTENDED CAB PICKUP—5-Cyl.—Truck Equipment Schedule T2

| LS Short Bed | | S19E | 23084 | 7950 | 9100 | 10600 | 13300 |

i370 CREW CAB PICKUP—5-Cyl.—Truck Equipment Schedule T2

| LS Short Bed | | S13E | 25214 | 8500 | 9725 | 11200 | 14000 |
| 4WD | | T | | 2300 | 2300 | 3065 | 3065 |

ASCENDER 4WD—6-Cyl.—Truck Equipment Schedule T1

S Sport Utility 4D		T13S	29884	8700	9900	11600	14600
LS				500	500	665	665
2WD		S		(950)	(950)	(1265)	(1265)

JEEP

1994 JEEP — 1J4–(Y19P)–R–#

WRANGLER 4WD—4-Cyl.—Truck Equipment Schedule T2

S Sport Utility 2D		Y19P	12610	1525	2000	3225	5050
w/o Rear Seat				(50)	(50)	(65)	(65)
Hard Top				250	250	335	335

WRANGLER 4WD—6-Cyl.—Truck Equipment Schedule T2

SE Sport Utility 2D		Y29S	14949	2225	2825	4125	6100
Sahara Spt Util 2D		Y49S	17372	2325	2900	4250	6225
Renegade Spt Util 2D		Y69S	19201	2350	2925	4275	6250
w/o Rear Seat				(50)	(50)	(65)	(65)
Hard Top				250	250	335	335

CHEROKEE 4WD—6-Cyl.—Truck Equipment Schedule T1

SE Sport Utility 2D		J27S	17402	700	1000	1900	3300
SE Sport Utility 4D		J28S	18412	850	1175	2150	3650
Sport 2D		J67S	18947	700	975	1850	3250
Sport 4D		J68S	19957	850	1175	2150	3650
Country Sport Util 2D		J77S	20584	700	1000	1900	3300
Country Sport Util 4D		J78S	21594	850	1175	2150	3650
2WD		T		(125)	(125)	(165)	(165)
4-Cyl. 2.5 Liter		P		(300)	(300)	(400)	(400)

GRAND CHEROKEE 4WD—6-Cyl.—Truck Equipment Sch T1

SE Sport Utility 4D		Z68S	23488	925	1325	2400	4050
Laredo Sport Util 4D		Z58S	23627	1100	1550	2725	4425
2WD		X		(125)	(125)	(165)	(165)
V8 5.2 Liter		Y		150	150	200	200

GRAND CHEROKEE 4WD—V8—Truck Equipment Schedule T3

| Limited Sport Util 4D | | Z78Y | 30113 | 2075 | 2650 | 3950 | 5875 |
| 6-Cyl. 4.0 Liter | | S | | (150) | (150) | (200) | (200) |

1995 JEEP — 1J4–(Y19P)–S–#

WRANGLER 4WD—4-Cyl.—Truck Equipment Schedule T2

S Sport Utility 2D		Y19P	13038	1725	2225	3475	5350
w/o Rear Seat				(50)	(50)	(65)	(65)
Rio Grande Pkg				250	250	335	335
Hard Top				250	250	335	335

WRANGLER 4WD—6-Cyl.—Truck Equipment Schedule T2

SE Sport Utility 2D		Y29S	15932	2500	3075	4425	6475
Sahara Spt Util 2D		Y49S	17957	2575	3175	4550	6625
w/o Rear Seat				(50)	(50)	(65)	(65)
Hard Top				250	250	335	335

Body	Type	VIN	List	Trade-In Fair	Trade-In Good	Pvt-Party Good	Retail Excellent
CHEROKEE 4WD—6-Cyl.—Truck Equipment Schedule T1							
SE Sport Utility 2D	J27S	18194	**800**	**1125**	**2050**	**3500**
SE Sport Utility 4D	J28S	19228	**925**	**1300**	**2375**	**4025**
Sport 2D	J67S	19800	**775**	**1100**	**2025**	**3475**
Sport 4D	J68S	20834	**925**	**1325**	**2400**	**4050**
Country Sport Util 4D	J78S	22398	**925**	**1300**	**2375**	**4025**
2WD	T	-------	**(125)**	**(125)**	**(165)**	**(165)**
4-Cyl. 2.5 Liter	P	-------	**(300)**	**(300)**	**(400)**	**(400)**
GRAND CHEROKEE 4WD—6-Cyl.—Truck Equipment Sch T1							
SE Sport Utility 4D	Z68S	25075	**1025**	**1450**	**2575**	**4250**
Laredo Sport Util 4D	Z58S	25706	**1225**	**1725**	**2925**	**4650**
2WD	X	-------	**(125)**	**(125)**	**(165)**	**(165)**
V8 5.2 Liter	Y	-------	**150**	**150**	**200**	**200**
GRAND CHEROKEE 4WD—V8—Truck Equipment Schedule T3							
Limited/Orvis 4D	Z78Y	31182	**2300**	**2875**	**4225**	**6200**
2WD	X	-------	**(125)**	**(125)**	**(165)**	**(165)**
6-Cyl. 4.0 Liter	S	-------	**(150)**	**(150)**	**(200)**	**(200)**

1996 JEEP — 1J4–(J27S)–T–#

Body	Type	VIN	List	Trade-In Fair	Trade-In Good	Pvt-Party Good	Retail Excellent
CHEROKEE 4WD—6-Cyl.—Truck Equipment Schedule T1							
SE Sport Utility 2D	J27S	18369	**900**	**1275**	**2375**	**4025**
SE Sport Utility 4D	J28S	19403	**1050**	**1475**	**2600**	**4300**
Sport 2D	J67S	19908	**875**	**1250**	**2350**	**4000**
Sport 4D	J68S	20942	**1050**	**1475**	**2650**	**4325**
Country Sport Util 4D	J78S	22476	**1050**	**1475**	**2600**	**4300**
2WD	T	-------	**(200)**	**(200)**	**(265)**	**(265)**
4-Cyl. 2.5 Liter	P	-------	**(350)**	**(350)**	**(465)**	**(465)**
GRAND CHEROKEE 4WD—6-Cyl.—Truck Equipment Sch T1							
Laredo Sport Util 4D	Z58S	27071	**1450**	**1925**	**3175**	**4975**
2WD	X	-------	**(200)**	**(200)**	**(265)**	**(265)**
V8 5.2 Liter	Y	-------	**225**	**225**	**300**	**300**
GRAND CHEROKEE 4WD—V8—Truck Equipment Schedule T3							
Limited/Orvis 4D	Z78Y	33406	**2650**	**3250**	**4625**	**6700**
2WD	X	-------	**(200)**	**(200)**	**(265)**	**(265)**
6-Cyl. 4.0 Liter	S	-------	**(225)**	**(225)**	**(300)**	**(300)**

1997 JEEP — 1J4–(Y29P)–V–#

Body	Type	VIN	List	Trade-In Fair	Trade-In Good	Pvt-Party Good	Retail Excellent
WRANGLER 4WD—4-Cyl.—Truck Equipment Schedule T2							
SE Sport Utility 2D	Y29P	14857	**2475**	**3075**	**4400**	**6450**
w/o Rear Seat		-------	**(100)**	**(100)**	**(135)**	**(135)**
Hard Top		-------	**300**	**300**	**400**	**400**
WRANGLER 4WD—6-Cyl.—Truck Equipment Schedule T2							
Sport Utility 2D	Y19S	17665	**3150**	**3825**	**5250**	**7425**
Sahara Spt Util 2D	Y49S	19363	**3175**	**3850**	**5275**	**7450**
w/o Rear Seat		-------	**(100)**	**(100)**	**(135)**	**(135)**
Hard Top		-------	**300**	**300**	**400**	**400**
CHEROKEE 4WD—6-Cyl.—Truck Equipment Schedule T1							
SE Sport Utility 2D	J27S	19280	**1025**	**1425**	**2575**	**4300**
SE Sport Utility 4D	J28S	20315	**1150**	**1625**	**2850**	**4600**
Sport 2D	J67S	20895	**1000**	**1400**	**2575**	**4275**
Sport 4D	J68S	21930	**1200**	**1675**	**2900**	**4650**
Country Sport Util 4D	J78S	23945	**1150**	**1625**	**2850**	**4600**
2WD	T	-------	**(250)**	**(250)**	**(335)**	**(335)**
4-Cyl. 2.5 Liter	P	-------	**(375)**	**(375)**	**(500)**	**(500)**
GRAND CHEROKEE 4WD—6-Cyl.—Truck Equipment Sch T1							
Laredo Sport Util 4D	Z58S	28040	**1625**	**2100**	**3375**	**5250**
TSi Sport Util 4D	Z58Y	30190	**1800**	**2300**	**3600**	**5500**
2WD	X	-------	**(250)**	**(250)**	**(335)**	**(335)**
V8 5.2 Liter	Y	-------	**300**	**300**	**400**	**400**
GRAND CHEROKEE 4WD—V8—Truck Equipment Schedule T3							
Limited/Orvis 4D	Z78Y	34315	**2900**	**3525**	**4950**	**7075**
2WD	X	-------	**(250)**	**(250)**	**(335)**	**(335)**
6-Cyl. 4.0 Liter	S	-------	**(300)**	**(300)**	**(400)**	**(400)**

1998 JEEP — 1J4–(Y29P)–W–#

Body	Type	VIN	List	Trade-In Fair	Trade-In Good	Pvt-Party Good	Retail Excellent
WRANGLER 4WD—4-Cyl.—Truck Equipment Schedule T2							
SE Sport Utility 2D	Y29P	15480	**2800**	**3425**	**4800**	**6900**
w/o Rear Seat		-------	**(100)**	**(100)**	**(135)**	**(135)**
Hard Top		-------	**325**	**325**	**435**	**435**
WRANGLER 4WD—6-Cyl.—Truck Equipment Schedule T2							
Sport Utility 2D	Y19S	18030	**3600**	**4300**	**5750**	**8000**
Sahara Spt Util 2D	Y49S	20140	**3600**	**4300**	**5775**	**8025**

TRUCKS & VANS

1998 JEEP

Body	Type	VIN	List	Trade-In Fair	Trade-In Good	Pvt-Party Good	Retail Excellent
	w/o Rear Seat			(100)	(100)	(135)	(135)
	Hard Top			325	325	435	435
CHEROKEE 4WD—6-Cyl.—Truck Equipment Schedule T1							
	SE Sport Utility 2D	J27S	20270	1150	1625	2825	4575
	SE Sport Utility 4D	J28S	21305	1400	1875	3125	4950
	Sport 2D	J67S	21885	1150	1600	2800	4550
	Sport 4D	J68S	22920	1450	1925	3175	5000
	Classic Sport Util 4D	J68S	23370	1400	1875	3125	4950
	Limited Sport Util 4D	J78S	24885	2350	2950	4275	6275
	2WD	T		(300)	(300)	(400)	(400)
	4-Cyl. 2.5 Liter	P		(400)	(400)	(535)	(535)
GRAND CHEROKEE 4WD—6-Cyl.—Truck Equipment Sch T1							
	Laredo Sport Util 4D	Z58S	28340	1825	2325	3625	5525
	Special Ed Sport Util	Z48S	30040	1850	2400	3700	5600
	TSi Sport Utility 4D	Z58S	30490	2000	2550	3875	5800
	2WD	X		(300)	(300)	(400)	(400)
	V8 5.2 Liter	Y		350	350	465	465
GRAND CHEROKEE 4WD—V8—Truck Equipment Schedule T3							
	Limited Sport Util 4D	Z78Y	35195	3175	3850	5275	7450
	5.9 Limited Sport Util	Z88Z	38700	3850	4575	6050	8350
	2WD	X		(300)	(300)	(400)	(400)
	6-Cyl. 4.0 Liter	S		(350)	(350)	(465)	(465)

1999 JEEP — 1J4–(Y29P)–X–#

Body	Type	VIN	List	Trade-In Fair	Trade-In Good	Pvt-Party Good	Retail Excellent
WRANGLER 4WD—4-Cyl.—Truck Equipment Schedule T2							
	SE Sport Utility 2D	Y29P	15670	3175	3875	5275	7425
	w/o Rear Seat			(100)	(100)	(135)	(135)
	Hard Top			350	350	465	465
WRANGLER 4WD—6-Cyl.—Truck Equipment Schedule T2							
	Sport Utility 2D	Y19S	18335	4050	4800	6275	8600
	Sahara Spt Util 2D	Y49S	20495	4100	4850	6325	8650
	w/o Rear Seat			(100)	(100)	(135)	(135)
	Hard Top			350	350	465	465
CHEROKEE 4WD—6-Cyl.—Truck Equipment Schedule T1							
	SE Sport Utility 2D	F27P	20815	1400	1875	3125	4975
	SE Sport Utility 4D	F28P	21850	1700	2175	3475	5350
	Sport 2D	F67S	22540	1350	1850	3075	4900
	Sport 4D	F68S	23575	1725	2225	3525	5425
	Classic Sport Util 4D	F68S	23945	1700	2175	3475	5350
	Limited Sport Util 4D	F78S	25505	2725	3325	4700	6775
	2WD	T		(350)	(350)	(465)	(465)
	4-Cyl. 2.5 Liter	P		(425)	(425)	(565)	(565)
GRAND CHEROKEE 4WD—6-Cyl.—Truck Equipment Sch T1							
	Laredo Sport Util 4D	W58S	28225	2050	2600	3925	5850
	2WD	2		(350)	(350)	(465)	(465)
	V8 4.7 Liter	N		400	400	535	535
GRAND CHEROKEE 4WD—V8—Truck Equipment Schedule T3							
	Limited Sport Util	W68N	35480	3500	4225	5650	7900
	2WD	2		(350)	(350)	(465)	(465)
	6-Cyl. 4.0 Liter	S		(400)	(400)	(535)	(535)

2000 JEEP — 1J4–(A29P)–Y–#

Body	Type	VIN	List	Trade-In Fair	Trade-In Good	Pvt-Party Good	Retail Excellent
WRANGLER 4WD—4-Cyl.—Truck Equipment Schedule T2							
	SE Sport Utility 2D	A29P	16305	3650	4350	5800	8050
	w/o Rear Seat			(100)	(100)	(135)	(135)
	Hard Top			375	375	500	500
WRANGLER 4WD—6-Cyl.—Truck Equipment Schedule T2							
	Sport Utility 2D	A49S	18995	4550	5350	6900	9350
	Sahara Spt Util 2D	A59S	20925	4575	5400	6950	9425
	w/o Rear Seat			(100)	(100)	(135)	(135)
	Hard Top			375	375	500	500
CHEROKEE 4WD—6-Cyl.—Truck Equipment Schedule T1							
	SE Sport Utility 2D	F27P	21285	1725	2225	3525	5450
	SE Sport Utility 4D	F28P	22320	2025	2575	3900	5850
	Sport 2D	F47S	21860	1650	2150	3475	5375
	Sport 4D	F48S	22895	2050	2625	3950	5900
	Classic Sport Util 4D	F58S	23420	2025	2575	3900	5850
	Limited Sport Util 4D	F68S	25745	3125	3800	5225	7375
	2WD	T		(400)	(400)	(535)	(535)
	4-Cyl. 2.5 Liter	P		(450)	(450)	(600)	(600)
GRAND CHEROKEE 4WD—6-Cyl.—Truck Equipment Sch T1							
	Laredo Sport Util 4D	W48S	29075	2350	2950	4300	6300

Body	Type	VIN	List	Trade-In Fair	Good	Pvt-Party Good	Retail Excellent
	2WD	X		(400)	(400)	(535)	(535)
	V8 4.7 Liter	N		450	450	600	600
GRAND CHEROKEE 4WD—V8—Truck Equipment Schedule T3							
Limited Spt Util 4D		258N	35950	3900	4625	6100	8400
	2WD	X		(400)	(400)	(535)	(535)
	6-Cyl. 4.0 Liter	S		(450)	(450)	(600)	(600)

2001 JEEP — 1J4–(A29P)–1–#

Body	Type	VIN	List	Trade-In Fair	Good	Pvt-Party Good	Retail Excellent
WRANGLER 4WD—4-Cyl.—Truck Equipment Schedule T2							
SE Sport Utility 2D		A29P	16095	4175	4950	6400	8725
w/o Rear Seat				(100)	(100)	(135)	(135)
Hard Top				400	400	535	535
WRANGLER 4WD—6-Cyl.—Truck Equipment Schedule T2							
Sport Utility 2D		A49S	19815	5150	6000	7575	10100
Sahara Spt Util 2D		A59S	22895	5175	6050	7650	10200
Hard Top				400	400	535	535
CHEROKEE 4WD—6-Cyl.—Truck Equipment Schedule T1							
SE Sport Utility 2D		F27S	21780	2125	2675	4025	6000
SE Sport Utility 4D		F28S	22815	2450	3050	4375	6425
Sport Utility 2D		F47S	22410	2050	2600	3950	5900
Sport Utility 4D		F48S	23445	2500	3075	4450	6500
Classic Sport Util 4D		F58S	23835	2450	3050	4375	6425
Limited Sport Util 4D		F68S	23970	3650	4350	5800	8025
	2WD	T		(450)	(450)	(600)	(600)
GRAND CHEROKEE 4WD—6-Cyl.—Truck Equipment Sch T1							
Laredo Sport Util 4D		W48S	29855	2725	3350	4725	6800
	2WD	X		(450)	(450)	(600)	(600)
	V8 4.7 Liter	N		500	500	665	665
GRAND CHEROKEE 4WD—V8—Truck Equipment Schedule T3							
Limited Spt Util 4D		W58N	35870	4350	5150	6650	9000
	2WD	X		(450)	(450)	(600)	(600)
	6-Cyl. 4.0 Liter	S		(500)	(500)	(665)	(665)

2002 JEEP — 1J(4or8)–(A29P)–2–#

Body	Type	VIN	List	Trade-In Fair	Good	Pvt-Party Good	Retail Excellent
WRANGLER 4WD—4-Cyl.—Truck Equipment Schedule T2							
SE Sport Utility 2D		A29P	16410	4575	5400	7150	9850
w/o Rear Seat				(100)	(100)	(135)	(135)
Hard Top				400	400	535	535
WRANGLER 4WD—6-Cyl.—Truck Equipment Schedule T2							
X Sport Utility 2D		A49S	18995	4850	5675	7450	10200
Sport Utility 2D		A49S	20665	5625	6550	8350	11200
Sahara Spt Util 2D		A59S	24035	5650	6600	8400	11250
Hard Top				400	400	535	535
LIBERTY 4WD—V6—Truck Equipment Schedule T1							
Sport Utility 4D		L48K	21070	4150	4900	6600	9200
Limited Utility 4D		L58K	23305	4550	5375	7125	9850
Renegade Utility 4D		L38K	23855	4725	5550	7325	10050
	2WD	K		(500)	(500)	(665)	(665)
	4-Cyl. 2.4 Liter	1		(500)	(500)	(665)	(665)
GRAND CHEROKEE 4WD—6-Cyl.—Truck Equipment Schedule T1							
Laredo Sport Util 4D		W48S	27995	3025	3650	5300	7725
Sport Utility 4D		W38S	29140	3125	3800	5450	7900
	2WD	X		(500)	(500)	(665)	(665)
	V8 4.7 Liter	N		550	550	735	735
GRAND CHEROKEE 4WD—V8—Truck Equipment Schedule T3							
Limited Spt Util 4D		W58N	33300	4725	5550	7325	10050
Overland Spt Utl 4D		W68N	37430	6025	6975	8825	11750
	2WD	X		(500)	(500)	(665)	(665)
	6-Cyl. 4.0 Liter	S		(550)	(550)	(735)	(735)

2003 JEEP — 1J(4or8)–(A291)–3–#

Body	Type	VIN	List	Trade-In Fair	Good	Pvt-Party Good	Retail Excellent
WRANGLER 4WD—4-Cyl.—Truck Equipment Schedule T2							
SE Sport Utility 2D		A291	16910	4975	5800	7575	10300
w/o Rear Seat				(150)	(150)	(200)	(200)
Hard Top				475	475	635	635
WRANGLER 4WD—6-Cyl.—Truck Equipment Schedule T2							
X Sport Utility 2D		A39S	19295	5325	6200	7975	10750
Sport Utility 2D		A49S	21105	6150	7100	8925	11800
Sahara Spt Util 2D		A59S	24695	6275	7225	9050	11950
Rubicon Spt Utl 2D		A59S	24995	6750	7800	9600	12600
Hard Top				475	475	635	635

2003 JEEP

Body	Type	VIN	List	Trade-In Fair	Trade-In Good	Pvt-Party Good	Retail Excellent
LIBERTY 4WD—V6—Truck Equipment Schedule T1							
Sport Utility 4D	L48K	21880	**4425**	**5225**	**6975**	**9650**
Limited Utility 4D	L58K	24045	**5075**	**5925**	**7725**	**10500**
Renegade Utility 4D	L38K	24630	**5250**	**6125**	**7900**	**10700**
2WD		K		**(575)**	**(575)**	**(765)**	**(765)**
4-Cyl. 2.4 Liter		1		**(600)**	**(600)**	**(800)**	**(800)**
GRAND CHEROKEE 4WD—6-Cyl.—Truck Equipment Schedule T1							
Laredo Sport Util 4D	W48S	28640	**3675**	**4375**	**6050**	**8575**
2WD		X		**(575)**	**(575)**	**(765)**	**(765)**
V8 4.7 Liter		N		**650**	**650**	**865**	**865**
GRAND CHEROKEE 4WD—V8—Truck Equipment Schedule T3							
Limited Spt Util 4D	W58N	34920	**5725**	**6675**	**8475**	**11300**
Overland Spt Util 4D	W68J	37975	**7125**	**8175**	**10050**	**13150**
2WD		X		**(575)**	**(575)**	**(765)**	**(765)**
6-Cyl. 4.0 Liter		S		**(675)**	**(675)**	**(900)**	**(900)**

2004 JEEP — 1J(4or8)-(A291)-4-#

Body	Type	VIN	List	Trade-In Fair	Trade-In Good	Pvt-Party Good	Retail Excellent
WRANGLER 4WD—4-Cyl.—Truck Equipment Schedule T2							
SE Sport Utility 2D	A291	17515	**5525**	**6400**	**8175**	**11000**
w/o Rear Seat				**(175)**	**(175)**	**(235)**	**(235)**
Hard Top				**550**	**550**	**735**	**735**
WRANGLER 4WD—6-Cyl.—Truck Equipment Schedule T2							
X Sport Utility 2D	A49S	19945	**5925**	**6850**	**8625**	**11450**
Sport Utility 2D	A49S	21930	**6825**	**7875**	**9675**	**12650**
Unlimited Util LWB	A49S	24995	**6375**	**7350**	**9150**	**12050**
Sahara Spt Util 2D	A59S	25520	**7000**	**8050**	**9850**	**12950**
Rubicon Spt Util 2D	A59S	25695	**7550**	**8650**	**10500**	**13500**
Hard Top				**550**	**550**	**735**	**735**
LIBERTY 4WD—V6—Truck Equipment Schedule T1							
Sport Utility 4D	L48K	21855	**4950**	**5775**	**7550**	**10300**
Limited Utility 4D	L58K	24870	**5775**	**6700**	**8475**	**11300**
Renegade Utility 4D	L38K	25455	**5950**	**6875**	**8675**	**11500**
2WD		K		**(650)**	**(650)**	**(865)**	**(865)**
4-Cyl. 2.4 Liter		1		**(700)**	**(700)**	**(935)**	**(935)**
GRAND CHEROKEE 4WD—6-Cyl.—Truck Equipment Schedule T1							
Laredo Sport Util 4D	W48S	29875	**4500**	**5325**	**7050**	**9725**
2WD		X		**(650)**	**(650)**	**(865)**	**(865)**
V8 4.7 Liter		N,J		**725**	**725**	**965**	**965**
GRAND CHEROKEE 4WD—V8—Truck Equipment Schedule T3							
Limited Spt Util 4D	W58N	35655	**6925**	**7975**	**9800**	**12800**
Overland Spt Util 4D	W68J	39920	**8375**	**9575**	**11500**	**14750**
2WD		X		**(650)**	**(650)**	**(865)**	**(865)**
6-Cyl. 4.0 Liter		S		**(800)**	**(800)**	**(1065)**	**(1065)**

2005 JEEP — 1J(4or8)-(A291)-5-#

Body	Type	VIN	List	Trade-In Fair	Trade-In Good	Pvt-Party Good	Retail Excellent
WRANGLER 4WD—4-Cyl.—Truck Equipment Schedule T2							
SE Sport Utility 2D	A291	18510	**6125**	**7100**	**8875**	**11700**
w/o Rear Seat				**(200)**	**(200)**	**(265)**	**(265)**
6-Cyl. 4.0 Liter		S		**1000**	**1000**	**1335**	**1335**
WRANGLER 4WD—6-Cyl.—Truck Equipment Schedule T2							
X Sport Utility 2D	A39S	20820	**6625**	**7625**	**9375**	**12300**
Sport Utility 2D	A49S	23600	**7650**	**8750**	**10550**	**13550**
Unlimited Util LWB	A44S	24355	**7075**	**8150**	**9950**	**12900**
Rubicon Spt Util 2D	A69S	27825	**8375**	**9575**	**11450**	**14650**
Rubicon LWB Util 2D	A69S	28825	**8025**	**9200**	**11050**	**14200**
Unltd Rubicon LWB	A69S	29195	**8650**	**9850**	**11700**	**14950**
Hard Top				**600**	**600**	**800**	**800**
LIBERTY 4WD—V6—Truck Equipment Schedule T1							
Sport Utility 4D	L48K	22985	**5625**	**6550**	**8300**	**11100**
Limited Utility 4D	L58K	25645	**6650**	**7650**	**9425**	**12350**
Renegade Utility 4D	L38K	24920	**6800**	**7850**	**9650**	**12600**
2WD		K		**(725)**	**(725)**	**(965)**	**(965)**
4-Cyl. 2.4 Liter		1		**(800)**	**(800)**	**(1065)**	**(1065)**
4-Cyl. 2.8L Turbo Diesel		5		**2000**	**2000**	**2665**	**2665**
GRAND CHEROKEE 4WD—6-Cyl.—Truck Equipment Schedule T1							
Laredo Sport Util 4D	R48K	28745	**6475**	**7475**	**9225**	**12150**
2WD		S		**(725)**	**(725)**	**(965)**	**(965)**
V8 4.7 Liter		N		**800**	**800**	**1065**	**1065**
GRAND CHEROKEE 4WD—V8—Truck Equipment Schedule T3							
Limited Spt Util 4D	R58N	34690	**9250**	**10525**	**12400**	**15700**
2WD		S		**(725)**	**(725)**	**(965)**	**(965)**
V8 5.7 Liter HEMI		2		**800**	**800**	**1065**	**1065**

gn="vertical">TRUCKS & VANS

2006 JEEP

Body	Type	VIN	List	Trade-In Fair	Good	Pvt-Party Good	Retail Excellent
2006 JEEP — 1J(4or8)-(A291)-6-#							
WRANGLER 4WD—4-Cyl.—Truck Equipment Schedule T2							
SE Sport Utility 2D		A291	18730	6900	7950	9675	12600
w/o Rear Seat				(225)	(225)	(300)	(300)
6-Cyl. 4.0 Liter		S		1000	1000	1335	1335
WRANGLER 4WD—6-Cyl.—Truck Equipment Schedule T2							
X Sport Utility 2D		A39S	21040	7450	8550	10300	13300
Sport Utility 2D		A49S	23900	8550	9775	11550	14700
Unlimited LWB Util		A44S	24655	7950	9100	10900	13950
Rubicon Spt Utl 2D		A69S	28125	9375	10675	12500	15750
Unltd Rubicon LWB		A69S	29125	9625	10925	12800	16000
Hard Top				650	650	865	865
LIBERTY 4WD—V6—Truck Equipment Schedule T1							
Sport Utility 4D		L48K	23965	6550	7550	9300	12200
Renegade Utility 4D		L38K	25855	7900	9050	10900	14000
Limited Sport Utl		L58K	27405	7775	8900	10700	13700
2WD		K		(800)	(800)	(1065)	(1065)
4-Cyl. 2.8L Turbo Diesel		K		2000	2000	2665	2665
COMMANDER 4WD—V8—Truck Equipment Schedule T1							
Sport Utility 4D		G48N	29985	8950	10200	12050	15300
Limited Sport Util 4D		G58N	38900	10350	11700	13550	16950
2WD		H		(800)	(800)	(1065)	(1065)
V6 3.7 Liter		K		(1000)	(1000)	(1335)	(1335)
V8 5.7 Liter HEMI		2		875	875	1165	1165
GRAND CHEROKEE 4WD—V6—Truck Equipment Schedule T1							
Laredo Sport Util 4D		R48K	29830	8100	9275	11100	14250
2WD		S		(800)	(800)	(1065)	(1065)
V8 4.7 Liter		N		875	875	1165	1165
GRAND CHEROKEE 4WD—V8—Truck Equipment Schedule T3							
Limited Spt Utl 4D		R58N	36700	11225	12700	14600	18100
2WD		S		(800)	(800)	(1065)	(1065)
V8 5.7 Liter HEMI		2		875	875	1165	1165
GRAND CHEROKEE 4WD—V8 HEMI—Truck Equipment Schedule T1							
SRT8 Sport Utl 4D		R783	39995	19700	22050	24100	28500
Overland Sport Utl 4D		R682	42925	12875	14500	16400	20100
2WD		S		(800)	(800)	(1065)	(1065)
2007 JEEP — 1J(4or8)-(F28W)-7-#							
PATRIOT 4WD—4-Cyl.—Truck Equipment Schedule T1							
Sport Utility 4D		F28W	16735	6650	7650	9250	12000
Limited Sport Util 4D		F48W	21735	8150	9325	11050	14000
2WD		T		(875)	(875)	(1165)	(1165)
COMPASS 4WD—4-Cyl.—Truck Equipment Schedule T1							
Sport SUV 4D		F47W	17585	6800	7850	9475	12250
Limited Sport Util 4D		F57W	21740	7575	8675	10350	13200
2WD		T		(875)	(875)	(1165)	(1165)
WRANGLER 4WD—V6—Truck Equipment Schedule T2							
X Sport Utility 2D		A241	18765	9175	10425	12150	15250
Unlimited X Spt Util		A391	22410	10925	12400	14100	17400
Sahara Spt Utl 2D		A541	23530	11225	12700	14400	17750
Unltd Sahara Util 4D		A591	26735	13125	14800	16550	20100
Rubicon Spt Utl 2D		A641	26750	12850	14450	16200	19700
Unltd Rubicon 4D		A691	28895	14450	16275	18100	21800
Hard Top				700	700	935	935
2WD		B		(875)	(875)	(1165)	(1165)
LIBERTY 4WD—V6—Truck Equipment Schedule T1							
Sport Utility 4D		L48K	23460	7775	8900	10600	13500
Limited Utility 4D		L58K	27045	9125	10400	12150	15250
2WD		K		(875)	(875)	(1165)	(1165)
COMMANDER 4WD—V8—Truck Equipment Schedule T1							
Sport Utility 4D		G48N	30485	10725	12150	13900	17250
Limited Sport Util		G58N	39215	12250	13825	15600	19050
2WD		H		(875)	(875)	(1165)	(1165)
V6 3.7 Liter		H		(1100)	(1100)	(1465)	(1465)
V8 5.7 Liter HEMI		2		950	950	1265	1265
COMMANDER 4WD—V8 HEMI—Truck Equipment Schedule T1							
Overland Sport Util		G682	44545	16650	18725	20600	24600
2WD		H		(875)	(875)	(1165)	(1165)
GRAND CHEROKEE 4WD—V6—Truck Equipment Schedule T1							
Laredo Sport Util 4D		R48K	30205	10000	11375	13150	16350
2WD		S		(875)	(875)	(1165)	(1165)

340 DEDUCT FOR RECONDITIONING

0709

Body	Type	VIN	List	Trade-In Fair	Trade-In Good	Pvt-Party Good	Retail Excellent
V8 4.7 Liter		N		950	950	1265	1265
GRAND CHEROKEE 4WD—V8—Truck Equipment Schedule T3							
Limited Spt Util 4D		R58N	37890	13475	15200	17000	20600
2WD		S		(875)	(875)	(1165)	(1165)
V6 3.0L Turbo Diesel		M		2500	2500	3335	3335
V8 5.7 Liter HEMI		2		950	950	1265	1265
GRAND CHEROKEE 4WD—V8 HEMI—Truck Equipment Schedule T3							
SRT8 Sport Util 4D		R783	40675	22650	25275	27100	31800
Overland Sport Utl 4D		R682	43260	15200	17100	18900	22700
2WD		S		(875)	(875)	(1165)	(1165)
V6 3.0L Turbo Diesel		M		2500	2500	3335	3335

2008 JEEP — 1J(4or8)–(F28W)–8–#

Body	Type	VIN	List	Trade-In Fair	Trade-In Good	Pvt-Party Good	Retail Excellent
PATRIOT 4WD—4-Cyl.—Truck Equipment Schedule T1							
Sport SUV 4D		F28W	18885	7875	9000	10550	13350
Limited Sport Util 4D		F48W	23605	9500	10775	12400	15400
2WD		T		(950)	(950)	(1265)	(1265)
COMPASS 4WD—4-Cyl.—Truck Equipment Schedule T1							
Sport SUV 4D		F47W	19885	8025	9200	10800	13550
Limited Sport Util 4D		F57W	23915	8875	10100	11700	14600
2WD		T		(950)	(950)	(1265)	(1265)
WRANGLER 4WD—V6—Truck Equipment Schedule T2							
X Sport Utility 2D		A241	19320	10575	12000	13600	16750
Unlimited X Spt Util		A391	23340	12500	14100	15800	19100
Sahara Spt Util 2D		A541	24775	12800	14450	16100	19500
Unltd Sahara Util 4D		A591	28150	14850	16700	18400	22000
Rubicon Spt Utl 2D		A641	27880	14550	16375	18100	21700
Unltd Rubicon Util 4D		A691	30195	16325	18325	20100	23800
Hard Top		B		750	750	1000	1000
2WD		B		(950)	(950)	(1265)	(1265)
LIBERTY 4WD—V6—Truck Equipment Schedule T1							
Sport Utility 4D		N28K	22495	9850	11175	12950	16050
Limited Utility 4D		N58K	26785	11425	12875	14600	17900
2WD		P		(950)	(950)	(1265)	(1265)
COMMANDER 4WD—V8—Truck Equipment Schedule T1							
Sport Utility 4D		G48N	30110	12750	14400	16100	19600
Limited Sport Util		G58N	39620	14400	16175	17950	21600
2WD		H		(950)	(950)	(1265)	(1265)
V6 3.7 Liter		K		(1200)	(1200)	(1600)	(1600)
V8 5.7 Liter HEMI		2		1025	1025	1365	1365
COMMANDER 4WD—V8 HEMI—Truck Equipment Schedule T1							
Overland Sport Util		G682	44545	19200	21450	23200	27200
2WD		H		(950)	(950)	(1265)	(1265)
GRAND CHEROKEE 4WD—V6—Truck Equipment Schedule T1							
Laredo Sport Util 4D		R48K	31085	12200	13775	15550	18950
2WD		S		(950)	(950)	(1265)	(1265)
V6 3.0L Turbo Diesel		M		2500	2500	3335	3335
V8 4.7L Flex Fuel		N		1025	1025	1365	1365
GRAND CHEROKEE 4WD—V8—Truck Equipment Schedule T3							
Limited Spt Util 4D		R58N	39250	15975	17925	19700	23400
2WD		S		(950)	(950)	(1265)	(1265)
V6 3.0L Turbo Diesel		M		2500	2500	3335	3335
V8 5.7 Liter HEMI		2		1025	1025	1365	1365
GRAND CHEROKEE 4WD—V8 HEMI—Truck Equipment Schedule T3							
SRT8 Sport Util 4D		R783	41220	25875	28800	30600	35200
Overland Sport Utl 4D		R682	44135	17775	20000	21700	25600
2WD		S		(950)	(950)	(1265)	(1265)
V6 3.0L Turbo Diesel		M		2500	2500	3335	3335

KIA

1995 KIA — KND(JA721)–S–#

Body	Type	VIN	List	Trade-In Fair	Trade-In Good	Pvt-Party Good	Retail Excellent
SPORTAGE 4WD—4-Cyl.—Truck Equipment Schedule T2							
Sport Utility 4D		JA721	14895	425	600	1250	2300
EX Sport Utility 4D		JA721	15895	525	700	1475	2700
2WD		3		(125)	(125)	(165)	(165)
4-Cyl. 2.0L DOHC		3		50	50	65	65

1996 KIA — KND(JA723)–T–#

Body	Type	VIN	List	Trade-In Fair	Trade-In Good	Pvt-Party Good	Retail Excellent
SPORTAGE 4WD—4-Cyl.—Truck Equipment Schedule T2							
Sport Utility 4D		JA723	15720	500	675	1400	2575

TRUCKS & VANS

TRUCKS & VANS

Body	Type	VIN	List	Trade-In Fair	Good	Pvt-Party Good	Retail Excellent
EX Sport Utility 4D		JA723	16420	600	825	1650	3000
2WD		B		(200)	(200)	(265)	(265)

1997 KIA — KND(JA723)–V–#

SPORTAGE 4WD—4-Cyl.—Truck Equipment Schedule T2
Sport Utility 4D		JA723	16420	575	800	1625	2975
EX Sport Utility 4D		JA723	17040	700	1000	1900	3325
2WD		B		(250)	(250)	(335)	(335)

1998 KIA — KND(JA723)–W–#

SPORTAGE 4WD—4-Cyl.—Truck Equipment Schedule T2
Sport Utility 4D		JA723	17845	675	950	1875	3325
EX Sport Utility 4D		JA723	18945	825	1175	2275	3950
2WD		B		(300)	(300)	(400)	(400)

1999 KIA — KNM(JA623)–X–#

SPORTAGE 4WD—4-Cyl.—Truck Equipment Schedule T2
Sport Util Conv 2D		JA623	14945	625	900	1825	3250
Sport Utility 4D		JA723	16745	825	1175	2300	3975
EX Sport Utility 4D		JA723	19045	1000	1425	2600	4300
2WD		B		(350)	(350)	(465)	(465)

2000 KIA — KNM(JA623)–Y–#

SPORTAGE 4WD—4-Cyl.—Truck Equipment Schedule T2
Sport Util Conv 2D		JA623	14945	825	1175	2325	4050
Sport Utility 4D		JA723	16745	1050	1475	2700	4450
EX Sport Utility 4D		JA723	19045	1250	1725	3000	4800
2WD		B		(400)	(400)	(535)	(535)

2001 KIA — KND(JB623)–1–#

SPORTAGE 4WD—4-Cyl.—Truck Equipment Schedule T2
Sport Util Conv 2D		JB623	15345	1075	1525	2775	4550
Sport Utility 4D		JB723	17245	1350	1850	3125	5000
EX Sport Utility 4D		JB723	19545	1650	2150	3450	5375
Limited Spt Util 4D		JB723	20090	2000	2550	3900	5850
2WD		B		(450)	(450)	(600)	(600)

2002 KIA — KND(JA623)–2–#

SPORTAGE 4WD—4-Cyl.—Truck Equipment Schedule T2
Sport Util Conv 2D		JA623	15640	1275	1750	3275	5425
Sport Utility 4D		JA723	18715	1625	2125	3700	5875
2WD		B		(500)	(500)	(665)	(665)

SEDONA—V6—Truck Equipment Schedule T1
LX Minivan		UP131	19590	700	1000	2400	4375
EX Minivan		UP131	21590	1000	1425	2900	4950

2003 KIA — KND(UP131)–3–#

SEDONA—V6—Truck Equipment Schedule T1
LX Minivan		UP131	19965	975	1350	2825	4900
EX Minivan		UP131	22180	1375	1850	3400	5525

SORENTO 4WD—V6—Truck Equipment Schedule T1
LX Sport Utility 4D		JC733	21795	2675	3300	4950	7325
EX Sport Utility 4D		JC733	24595	3800	4525	6200	8750
2WD				(575)	(575)	(765)	(765)

2004 KIA — KND(UP131)–4–#

SEDONA—V6—Truck Equipment Schedule T1
LX Minivan		UP131	20615	1425	1900	3450	5600
EX Minivan		UP131	22725	1975	2525	4100	6325

SORENTO 4WD—V6—Truck Equipment Schedule T1
LX Sport Utility 4D		JC733	23290	3475	4175	5825	8325
EX Sport Utility 4D		JC733	25490	4575	5400	7150	9850
2WD		D		(650)	(650)	(865)	(865)

2005 KIA — KND(JE723)–5–#

SPORTAGE 4WD—V6—Truck Equipment Schedule T2
LX Sport Utility 4D		JE723	20290	3350	4050	5675	8125
EX Sport Utility 4D		JE723	21990	4175	4925	6600	9150
2WD		F		(725)	(725)	(965)	(965)

2005 KIA

Body	Type	VIN	List	Trade-In Fair	Trade-In Good	Pvt-Party Good	Retail Excellent
	4-Cyl. 2.0 Liter	4		**(600)**	**(600)**	**(800)**	**(800)**

SEDONA—V6—Truck Equipment Schedule T1
LX Minivan		UP131	20840	**2175**	**2750**	**4325**	**6625**
EX Minivan		UP131	23240	**2800**	**3425**	**5050**	**7400**

SORENTO 4WD—V6—Truck Equipment Schedule T1
LX Sport Utility 4D		JC733	23840	**4400**	**5200**	**6925**	**9600**
EX Sport Utility 4D		JC733	26140	**5525**	**6450**	**8175**	**11000**
2WD		D		**(725)**	**(725)**	**(965)**	**(965)**

2006 KIA — KND(JE723)–6–#

SPORTAGE 4WD—V6—Truck Equipment Schedule T2
LX Sport Utility 4D		JE723	20890	**4350**	**5150**	**6850**	**9500**
EX Sport Utility 4D		JE723	22590	**5275**	**6125**	**7875**	**10600**
2WD		F		**(800)**	**(800)**	**(1065)**	**(1065)**
4-Cyl. 2.0 Liter		4		**(650)**	**(650)**	**(865)**	**(865)**

SEDONA—V6—Truck Equipment Schedule T1
LX Minivan		MB233	23665	**3750**	**4450**	**6100**	**8550**
EX Minivan		MB233	26265	**4425**	**5225**	**6875**	**9450**

SORENTO 4WD—V6—Truck Equipment Schedule T1
LX Sport Utility 4D		JC733	24470	**5525**	**6450**	**8175**	**11000**
EX Sport Utility 4D		JC733	26770	**6650**	**7675**	**9425**	**12350**
2WD		D		**(800)**	**(800)**	**(1065)**	**(1065)**

2007 KIA — KND(JE723)–7–#

SPORTAGE 4WD—V6—Truck Equipment Schedule T2
LX Sport Utility 4D		JE723	21790	**5525**	**6425**	**8050**	**10700**
EX Sport Utility 4D		JE723	23490	**6475**	**7475**	**9125**	**11850**
2WD		F		**(875)**	**(875)**	**(1165)**	**(1165)**
4-Cyl. 2.0 Liter		4		**(700)**	**(700)**	**(935)**	**(935)**

SEDONA—V6—Truck Equipment Schedule T1
Minivan 4D		MB133	21195	**4950**	**5800**	**7350**	**9850**
LX Minivan 4D		MB233	24295	**5350**	**6225**	**7800**	**10350**
EX Minivan 4D		MB233	26895	**6100**	**7050**	**8625**	**11250**

SORENTO 2WD—V6—Truck Equipment Schedule T1
Sport Utility 4D		JD736	20665	**6025**	**6975**	**8650**	**11350**

SORENTO 4WD—V6—Truck Equipment Schedule T1
LX Sport Utility 4D		JC736	25265	**6825**	**7900**	**9550**	**12350**
EX Sport Utility 4D		JC736	26865	**7950**	**9100**	**10850**	**13850**
2WD		D		**(875)**	**(875)**	**(1165)**	**(1165)**

2008 KIA — KND(JE723)–8–#

SPORTAGE 4WD—V6—Truck Equipment Schedule T2
LX Sport Utility 4D		JE723	21970	**6800**	**7850**	**9375**	**12050**
EX Sport Utility 4D		JE723	23520	**7825**	**8950**	**10550**	**13400**
2WD		F		**(950)**	**(950)**	**(1265)**	**(1265)**
4-Cyl. 2.0 Liter		4		**(750)**	**(750)**	**(1000)**	**(1000)**

SEDONA—V6—Truck Equipment Schedule T1
Minivan 4D		MB133	21420	**7175**	**8250**	**9700**	**12300**
LX Minivan 4D		MB233	24320	**7600**	**8700**	**10200**	**12850**
EX Minivan 4D		MB233	26920	**8425**	**9625**	**11150**	**14000**

SORENTO—V6—Truck Equipment Schedule T1
Sport Utility 4D		JD735	21695	**7825**	**8950**	**10650**	**13500**

SORENTO 4WD—V6—Truck Equipment Schedule T1
LX Sport Utility 4D		JC735	24895	**8700**	**9900**	**11600**	**14600**
EX Sport Utility 4D		JC736	26895	**9800**	**11125**	**12900**	**16000**
2WD		D		**(950)**	**(950)**	**(1265)**	**(1265)**

LAND ROVER

1994 LAND ROVER — SAL(DV228)–R–#

DEFENDER 90 4WD—V8—Truck Equipment Schedule T2
Sport Utility 2D		DV228	28495	********	********	********	**25800**

DISCOVERY 4WD—V8—Truck Equipment Schedule T3
Sport Utility 4D		JY124	30725	**875**	**1250**	**2325**	**3950**
Dual Moon Roofs				**475**	**475**	**635**	**635**
Rear Jump Seats				**200**	**200**	**265**	**265**
Manual Trans				**(250)**	**(250)**	**(335)**	**(335)**
Rear Air Conditioning				**100**	**100**	**135**	**135**

RANGE ROVER 4WD—V8—Truck Equipment Schedule T3
County Sport Utl 4D		HV124	47525	**1600**	**2075**	**3350**	**5200**

1994 LAND ROVER

TRUCKS & VANS

Body Type	VIN	List	Trade-In Fair	Good	Pvt-Party Good[a]	Retail Excellent
County LWB 4D	HC134	50825	1475	1950	3200	5025

1995 LAND ROVER — SAL(DV228)–S–#

DEFENDER 90 4WD—V8—Truck Equipment Schedule T2
Soft Top Spt Util 2D	DV228	29275	****	****	****	29200
Hard Top Spt Utl 2D	DV228		****	****	****	29600

DISCOVERY 4WD—V8—Truck Equipment Schedule T3
Sport Utility 4D	JY124	32375	1025	1450	2575	4275
Dual Moon Roofs			500	500	665	665
Rear Jump Seats			200	200	265	265
Rear Air Conditioning			100	100	135	135
Manual Trans			(250)	(250)	(335)	(335)

RANGE ROVER 4WD—V8—Truck Equipment Schedule T3
County Classic 4D	HV124	45625	1575	2050	3325	5200
County LWB 4D	HC134	53125	1650	2150	3425	5325
4.0 SE Sport Util 4D	PV124	54625	3100	3775	5250	7450

1996 LAND ROVER — SAL(JY124)–T–#

DISCOVERY 4WD—V8—Truck Equipment Schedule T3
SD Sport Utility 4D	JY124	32975	1175	1650	2875	4600
SE Sport Utility 4D	JY124	35975	1825	2350	3625	5525
SE7 Sport Utility 4D	JY124	38550	2000	2575	3875	5825
Rear Jump Seats (Ex SE7)			250	250	335	335
Dual Moon Roofs			550	550	735	735
Manual Trans		8	(250)	(250)	(335)	(335)

RANGE ROVER 4WD—V8—Truck Equipment Schedule T3
4.0 SE Spt Util 4D	PV124	55625	3650	4350	5875	8225
4.6 HSE Spt Util 4D	PV144	62625	5225	6100	7850	10600

1997 LAND ROVER — SAL(DV224)–V–#

DEFENDER 90 4WD—V8—Truck Equipment Schedule T2
Soft Top Spt Util 2D	DV224	32625	****	****	****	34200
Hard Top Spt Utl 2D	DV324	34625	****	****	****	34900

DISCOVERY 4WD—V8—Truck Equipment Schedule T3
SD Sport Utility 4D	JY124	34625	1350	1825	3075	4900
XD Sport Utility 4D	JY124	36125	1975	2525	3875	5825
SE Sport Utility 4D	JY124	36625	2025	2575	3925	5875
SE7 Sport Utility 4D	JY124	39125	2250	2825	4200	6200
Rear Jump Seats (Ex SE7)			275	275	365	365
Dual Moon Roofs			575	575	765	765
Manual Trans		8	(275)	(275)	(365)	(365)

RANGE ROVER 4WD—V8—Truck Equipment Schedule T3
4.0 SE Spt Util 4D	PV124	56125	3900	4625	6175	8550
4.6 HSE Spt Util 4D	PV144	63625	5375	6250	7975	10750

1998 LAND ROVER — SAL(JY124)–W–#

DISCOVERY 4WD—V8—Truck Equipment Schedule T3
LE Sport Utility 4D	JY124	35125	2375	2950	4300	6350
LSE Sport Utility 4D	JY124	38625	2600	3200	4575	6675
Rear Jump Seats			300	300	400	400
Rear Air Conditioning			175	175	235	235
Dual Moon Roofs			600	600	800	800

RANGE ROVER 4WD—V8—Truck Equipment Schedule T3
4.0 SE Spt Util 4D	PV124	56625	4225	5000	6575	9000
4.6 HSE Spt Util 4D	PV144	64125	5600	6525	8250	11050

1999 LAND ROVER — SAL(JY124)–X–#

DISCOVERY 4WD—V8—Truck Equipment Schedule T3
SD Sport Utility 4D	JY124	33625	1925	2475	3825	5800
Rear Jump Seats			325	325	435	435
Dual Moon Roofs			625	625	835	835

DISCOVERY SERIES II 4WD—V8—Truck Equipment Schedule T3
Sport Utility 4D	TY124	36725	2650	3250	4675	6775
Rear Jump Seats			325	325	435	435
Rear Air Conditioning			200	200	265	265
Dual Moon Roofs			625	625	835	835
Performance Pkg			500	500	665	665

RANGE ROVER 4WD—V8—Truck Equipment Schedule T3
4.0 Sport Utility 4D	PA124	57625	4450	5250	6825	9300
4.0 S Sport Utility 4D	PA124	57625	4300	5075	6625	9075
4.0 SE Sport Util 4D	PV124	58625	4675	5525	7100	9625

1999 LAND ROVER

Body	Type	VIN	List	Trade-In Fair	Trade-In Good	Pvt-Party Good	Retail Excellent
4.6 HSE Sport Utl 4D		PV144	66625	5950	6900	8650	11450

2000 LAND ROVER — SAL(TY124)-Y-#

DISCOVERY SERIES II 4WD—V8—Truck Equipment Schedule T3

Body/Type	VIN	List	Fair	Good	Pvt Good	Retail
SD Sport Utility 4D	TY124	33975	2275	2875	4250	6300
SD7 Sport Utility 4D	TY124	35725	2825	3450	4875	7025
Sport Utility 4D	TY124	36725	3225	3900	5350	7550
Rear Jump Seats			350	350	465	465
Rear Air Conditioning			225	225	300	300
Dual Moon Roofs			650	650	865	865
Performance Pkg			550	550	735	735

RANGE ROVER 4WD—V8—Truck Equipment Schedule T3

Body/Type	VIN	List	Fair	Good	Pvt Good	Retail
County Sport Util 4D	PA124	58925	4225	4975	6550	9000
4.0 Sport Util 4D	PA124	59625	4675	5525	7100	9625
4.0 SE Sport Util 4D	PV124	59625	5300	6150	7850	10550
4.6 HSK Spt Util 4D	PF164	67625	6375	7350	9150	12000
4.6 HSE Spt Util 4D	PV144	67925	6450	7425	9200	12100
4.6 Vitesse Util 4D	PF164	68625	7400	8500	10350	13450
4.6 Holland Holland	PV164	79625	9750	11075	13200	16700

2001 LAND ROVER — SAL(TY124)-1-#

DISCOVERY SERIES II 4WD—V8—Truck Equipment Schedule T3

Body/Type	VIN	List	Fair	Good	Pvt Good	Retail
SD Sport Utility 4D	TY124	33975	2950	3575	5025	7200
SD7 Sport Utility 4D	TY124	35725	3550	4250	5725	8000
LE Sport Utility 4D	TY124	34975	4050	4800	6300	8675
LE7 Sport Utility 4D	TY124	36725	4225	5000	6525	8900
SE Sport Utility 4D	TY124	36975	4275	5025	6575	8975
SE7 Sport Utility 4D	TY124	38725	4575	5400	6925	9375
Rear Jump Seats			375	375	500	500
Rear Air Conditioning			250	250	335	335
Dual Moon Roofs			675	675	900	900
Performance Pkg			575	575	765	765

RANGE ROVER 4WD—V8—Truck Equipment Schedule T3

Body/Type	VIN	List	Fair	Good	Pvt Good	Retail
4.6 SE Sport Util 4D	PV164	62625	5675	6600	8325	11050
4.6 HSE Sport Util	PV164	68625	7100	8150	10000	13000

2002 LAND ROVER — SAL(NM222)-2-#

FREELANDER AWD—V6—Truck Equipment Schedule T3

Body/Type	VIN	List	Fair	Good	Pvt Good	Retail
S Sport Utility 4D	NM222	25600	2075	2625	4225	6500
SE Sport Utility 4D	NY222	28400	2925	3575	5225	7650
HSE Sport Util 4D	NE222	32200	3800	4525	6225	8775

DISCOVERY SERIES II 4WD—V8—Truck Equipment Schedule T3

Body/Type	VIN	List	Fair	Good	Pvt Good	Retail
SD Sport Utility 4D	TL144	33995	2900	3525	5250	7725
SD7 Sport Utility 4D	TK144	34995	3550	4275	6000	8575
SE Sport Utility 4D	TY124	37795	4300	5075	6825	9525
SE7 Sport Utility 4D	TW124	38875	4625	5450	7275	10050
Rear Jump Seats			400	400	535	535
Rear Air Conditioning			250	250	335	335
Dual Moon Roofs			700	700	935	935
Performance Pkg			600	600	800	800

RANGE ROVER 4WD—V8—Truck Equipment Schedule T3

Body/Type	VIN	List	Fair	Good	Pvt Good	Retail
4.6 HSE Sport Util	PL162	68665	7750	8875	11100	14650

2003 LAND ROVER — SAL(NM222)-3-#

FREELANDER AWD—V6—Truck Equipment Schedule T3

Body/Type	VIN	List	Fair	Good	Pvt Good	Retail
S Sport Utility 4D	NM222	25600	2475	3075	4700	7050
SE3 Sport Utility 2D	NY122	26995	3475	4175	5850	8350
SE Sport Utility 4D	NY222	28400	3475	4175	5850	8350
HSE Sport Util 4D	NE222	32200	4450	5250	7000	9700

DISCOVERY 4WD—V8—Truck Equipment Schedule T3

Body/Type	VIN	List	Fair	Good	Pvt Good	Retail
S Sport Utility 4D	TL144	34995	3150	3825	5550	8100
SE Sport Utility 4D	TY144	38995	4825	5650	7525	10350
SE7 Sport Utility 4D	TW144	39995	5150	6025	7875	10750
HSE Sport Utility 4D	TP144	40995	6225	7200	9125	12150
HSE7 Sport Util 4D	TR144	41995	6350	7325	9225	12300
Rear Jump Seats			475	475	635	635
Rear Air Conditioning			300	300	400	400
Dual Moon Roofs			750	750	1000	1000
Suspension Pkg			700	700	935	935

RANGE ROVER 4WD—V8—Truck Equipment Schedule T3

Body/Type	VIN	List	Fair	Good	Pvt Good	Retail
HSE Sport Util 4D	MB114	71865	11125	12600	15000	19100

TRUCKS & VANS

Body	Type	VIN	List	Trade-In Fair	Good	Pvt-Party Good	Retail Excellent
2004 LAND ROVER — SAL(NY222)-4-#							
FREELANDER AWD—V6—Truck Equipment Schedule T3							
SE Sport Utility 4D		NY222	25995	4175	4925	6650	9225
SE3 Sport Utility 2D		NY222	28195	4175	4925	6650	9225
HSE Sport Util 4D		NE222	28995	5300	6175	7950	10750
DISCOVERY 4WD—V8—Truck Equipment Schedule T3							
S Sport Utility 4D		TL194	34995	3650	4350	6150	8775
SE Sport Utility 4D		TY194	39250	5600	6525	8375	11300
SE7 Sport Utility 4D		TW194	40350	5900	6825	8750	11700
HSE Sport Utility 4D		TP194	41250	7100	8150	10100	13250
HSE7 Sport Util 4D		TR194	42250	7225	8300	10250	13400
G4 Sport Utility 4D		TL194	39995	6275	7250	9175	12200
Rear Jump Seats				550	550	735	735
Rear Air Conditioning				350	350	465	465
Dual Moon Roofs				775	775	1035	1035
Suspension Pkg				800	800	1065	1065
RANGE ROVER 4WD—V8—Truck Equipment Schedule T3							
HSE Sport Util 4D		ME114	72250	14150	15925	18550	23100
Westminster Util		MH114	84700	18575	20775	23600	28800
2005 LAND ROVER — SAL(NY222)-5-#							
FREELANDER AWD—V6—Truck Equipment Schedule T3							
SE Sport Utility 4D		NY222	27495	5025	5850	7650	10400
SE3 Sport Utility 2D		NM212	27495	5025	5850	7650	10400
LR3 4WD—V6—Truck Equipment Schedule T3							
Sport Utility 4D		AB244	38950	11325	12800	15150	19150
SE Sport Utility 4D		AD244	41950	12250	13875	16150	20300
Third Seat				600	600	800	800
LR3 4WD—V8—Truck Equipment Schedule T3							
SE Sport Utility 4D		AD254	44995	13225	14900	17300	21600
HSE Sport Utility 4D		AF254	49995	15375	17300	19700	24100
Third Seat				600	600	800	800
RANGE ROVER 4WD—V8—Truck Equipment Schedule T3							
HSE Sport Util 4D		ME114	73750	17450	19550	22200	27200
Westminster Util		MH114	86000	22450	25000	27800	33400
2006 LAND ROVER — SAL(AB244)-6-#							
LR3 4WD—V6—Truck Equipment Schedule T3							
Sport Utility 4D		AB244	38950	12925	14550	16950	21200
SE Sport Utility 4D		AD244	41950	13925	15675	18050	22300
Third Seat		C,E		650	650	865	865
LR3 4WD—V8—Truck Equipment Schedule T3							
SE Sport Utility 4D		AD254	45450	15000	16850	19250	23700
HSE Sport Util 4D		AG254	53450	17350	19450	22000	26700
Third Seat		G		650	650	865	865
RANGE ROVER SPORT 4WD—V8—Truck Equipment Schedule T3							
HSE Sport Util 4D		SF254	56750	24200	27050	29400	34700
RANGE ROVER SPORT 4WD—V8 Supercharged—Truck Equipment Sch T3							
Sport Utility 4D		SD234	69750	29200	32450	35000	40800
Adaptive Cruise				450	450	600	600
RANGE ROVER 4WD—V8—Truck Equipment Schedule T3							
HSE Sport Util 4D		ME154	74950	25975	28900	31900	37800
RANGE ROVER 4WD—V8 Supercharged—Truck Equipment Sch T3							
Sport Utility 4D		MF134	89950	35975	39975	42900	50000
2007 LAND ROVER — SAL(AD244)-7-#							
LR3 4WD—V6—Truck Equipment Schedule T3							
SE Sport Utility 4D		AD244	42150	16225	18175	20600	25200
Third Seat				700	700	935	935
LR3 4WD—V8—Truck Equipment Schedule T3							
SE Sport Utility 4D		AE254	48950	18525	20675	23200	28000
HSE Sport Util 4D		AG254	53950	21075	23625	26000	31100
Third Seat				700	700	935	935
RANGE ROVER SPORT 4WD—V8—Truck Equipment Schedule T3							
HSE Sport Util 4D		SF254	57950	29500	32825	35200	40900
RANGE ROVER SPORT 4WD—V8 Supercharged—Truck Equipment Sch T3							
Sport Utility 4D		SD234	71250	34900	38800	41200	47300
Adaptive Cruise				475	475	635	635
RANGE ROVER 4WD—V8—Truck Equipment Schedule T3							
HSE Sport Util 4D		ME154	77250	31450	34975	37800	44300

Body	Type	VIN	List	Trade-In Fair	Good	Pvt-Party Good	Retail Excellent
RANGE ROVER 4WD—V8 Supercharged—Truck Equipment Schedule T3							
Sport Utility 4D		MF134	92750	43225	47925	50900	58500

TRUCKS & VANS

2008 LAND ROVER — SAL(FP24N)-8-#

LR2 AWD—6-Cyl.—Truck Equipment Schedule T3							
SE Sport Utility 4D		FP24N	34700	20200	22550	24300	28400
HSE Sport Utility 4D		FR24N	36150	21750	24300	26100	30400
LR3 4WD—V8—Truck Equipment Schedule T3							
SE Sport Utility 4D		AE254	49300	26275	29200	31700	37200
HSE Sport Util 4D		AG254	54800	29000	32350	34700	40500
Third Row				750	750	1000	1000
RANGE ROVER SPORT 4WD—V8—Truck Equipment Schedule T3							
HSE Sport Utility 4D		SF254	58500	36650	40775	42700	48800
RANGE ROVER SPORT 4WD—V8 Supercharged—Truck Equipment Sch T3							
Sport Utility 4D		SH234	71950	43900	48700	50800	57600
Adaptive Cruise Control				500	500	665	665
RANGE ROVER 4WD—V8—Truck Equipment Schedule T3							
HSE Sport Util 4D		ME154	77950	41850	46350	49000	56300
RANGE ROVER 4WD—V8 Supercharged—Truck Equipment Schedule T3							
Sport Utility 4D		MF134	93600	54675	60575	63200	71600

LEXUS

1996 LEXUS — JT6(HJ88J)-T-#

LX 450 4WD—6-Cyl.—Truck Equipment Schedule T3							
Sport Utility 4D		HJ88J	47995	6800	7850	9750	12850

1997 LEXUS — JT6(HJ88J)-V-#

LX 450 4WD—6-Cyl.—Truck Equipment Schedule T3							
Sport Utility 4D		HJ88J	48945	7825	8975	10950	14150

1998 LEXUS — JT6(HT00W)-W-#

LX 470 4WD—V8—Truck Equipment Schedule T3							
Sport Utility 4D		HT00W	55445	10725	12150	14450	18350

1999 LEXUS — JT6(HF10U)-X-#

RX 300 4WD—V6—Truck Equipment Schedule T3							
Sport Utility 4D		HF10U	34980	5850	6775	8475	11200
2WD		G		(550)	(550)	(735)	(735)
LX 470 4WD—V8—Truck Equipment Schedule T3							
Sport Utility 4D		HT00W	56400	12000	13525	15900	19900

2000 LEXUS — JT6(HF10U)-Y-#

RX 300 4WD—V6—Truck Equipment Schedule T3							
Sport Utility 4D		HF10U	35680	6575	7575	9275	12100
2WD				(475)	(475)	(635)	(635)
LX 470 4WD—V8—Truck Equipment Schedule T3							
Sport Utility 4D		HT00W	59500	13375	15100	17400	21600

2001 LEXUS — JTJ(HF10U)-1-#

RX 300 4WD—V6—Truck Equipment Schedule T3							
Sport Utility 4D		HF10U	37430	7500	8600	10350	13300
Silversport Edition				200	200	265	265
2WD				(500)	(500)	(665)	(665)
LX 470 4WD—V8—Truck Equipment Schedule T3							
Sport Utility 4D		HT00W	61950	14950	16800	19100	23400

2002 LEXUS — JTJ(HF10U)-2-#

RX 300 4WD—V6—Truck Equipment Schedule T3							
Sport Utility 4D		HF10U	37580	8375	9575	11600	15000
Coach Edition				250	250	335	335
2WD		G		(500)	(500)	(665)	(665)
LX 470 4WD—V8—Truck Equipment Schedule T3							
Sport Utility 4D		HT00W	63051	16525	18525	21100	25800

2003 LEXUS — JTJ(HF10U)-3-#

RX 300 4WD—V6—Truck Equipment Schedule T3							
Sport Utility 4D		HF10U	38800	9100	10350	12350	15800

Body	Type	VIN	List	Trade-In Fair	Trade-In Good	Pvt-Party Good	Retail Excellent
2WD		G		(575)	(575)	(765)	(765)
GX 470 4WD—V8—Truck Equipment Schedule T3							
Sport Utility 4D		BT20X	45500	12050	13625	15800	19700
Third Row Seat				800	800	1065	1065
LX 470 4WD—V8—Truck Equipment Schedule T3							
Sport Utility 4D		HT00W	63700	18775	20975	23500	28500

2004 LEXUS — JTJ(HA31U)-4-#

Body	Type	VIN	List	Trade-In Fair	Trade-In Good	Pvt-Party Good	Retail Excellent
RX 330 AWD—V6—Truck Equipment Schedule T3							
Sport Utility 4D		HA31U	39195	12500	14100	16150	20000
Dynamic Cruise Control				400	400	535	535
Performance Pkg				2500	2500	3335	3335
2WD		G		(650)	(650)	(865)	(865)
GX 470 4WD—V8—Truck Equipment Schedule T3							
Sport Utility 4D		BT20X	45780	14550	16375	18550	22700
Third Row Seat				800	800	1065	1065
LX 470 4WD—V8—Truck Equipment Schedule T3							
Sport Utility 4D		HT00W	64800	21750	24200	26800	31900

2005 LEXUS — JTJ(HA31U)-5-#

Body	Type	VIN	List	Trade-In Fair	Trade-In Good	Pvt-Party Good	Retail Excellent
RX 330 AWD—V6—Truck Equipment Schedule T3							
Sport Utility 4D		HA31U	37800	14350	16125	18200	22100
Dynamic Cruise Control				425	425	565	565
Performance Pkg				2500	2500	3335	3335
2WD		G		(725)	(725)	(965)	(965)
GX 470 4WD—V8—Truck Equipment Schedule T3							
Sport Utility 4D		BT20X	46425	17300	19350	21600	26000
Third Row Seat				800	800	1065	1065
LX 470 4WD—V8—Truck Equipment Schedule T3							
Sport Utility 4D		HT00W	65400	24700	27550	29900	35300

2006 LEXUS — JTJ(HA31U)-6-#

Body	Type	VIN	List	Trade-In Fair	Trade-In Good	Pvt-Party Good	Retail Excellent
RX 330 AWD—V6—Truck Equipment Schedule T3							
Sport Utility 4D		HA31U	38420	16375	18375	20400	24400
Dynamic Cruise Control				450	450	600	600
Performance Pkg				2500	2500	3335	3335
2WD		G		(800)	(800)	(1065)	(1065)
RX 400h AWD—V6 Hybrid—Truck Equipment Schedule T3							
Sport Utility 4D		HW31U	49060	22350	24900	27000	31800
Dynamic Cruise Control				450	450	600	600
2WD		G		(800)	(800)	(1065)	(1065)
GX 470 4WD—V8—Truck Equipment Schedule T3							
Sport Utility 4D		BT20X	47185	20200	22550	24700	29300
Third Row Seat				800	800	1065	1065
LX 470 4WD—V8—Truck Equipment Schedule T3							
Sport Utility 4D		HT00W	67945	27925	31175	33400	39000

2007 LEXUS — JTJ-(HK31U)-7-#

Body	Type	VIN	List	Trade-In Fair	Trade-In Good	Pvt-Party Good	Retail Excellent
RX 350 AWD—V6—Truck Equipment Schedule T3							
Sport Utility 4D		HK31U	39495	21175	23725	25600	30100
Dynamic Cruise Control				475	475	635	635
Performance Pkg				2500	2500	3335	3335
2WD		G		(875)	(875)	(1165)	(1165)
RX 400h AWD—V6 Hybrid—Truck Equipment Schedule T3							
Sport Utility 4D		HW31U	43275	24900	27825	29700	34500
Dynamic Cruise Control				475	475	635	635
2WD		G		(875)	(875)	(1165)	(1165)
GX 470 4WD—V8—Truck Equipment Schedule T3							
Sport Utility 4D		BT20X	47330	24900	27825	29800	34600
Third Row Seat				800	800	1065	1065
LX 470 4WD—V8—Truck Equipment Schedule T3							
Sport Utility 4D		HT00W	68090	34500	38325	40500	46400

2008 LEXUS — JTJ-(HK31U)-8-#

Body	Type	VIN	List	Trade-In Fair	Trade-In Good	Pvt-Party Good	Retail Excellent
RX 350 AWD—V6—Truck Equipment Schedule T3							
Sport Utility 4D		HK31U	39565	23725	26450	28100	32600
Dynamic Cruise Control				500	500	665	665
Performance Pkg				2500	2500	3335	3335
2WD				(1500)	(1500)	(2000)	(2000)
RX 400h AWD—V6 Hybrid—Truck Equipment Schedule T3							
Sport Utility 4D		HW31U	43345	29000	32350	34000	39000

Body	Type	VIN	List	Trade-In Fair	Trade-In Good	Pvt-Party Good	Retail Excellent
	Dynamic Cruise Control			500	500	665	665
	2WD	G		(950)	(950)	(1265)	(1265)
	GX 470 4WD—V8—Truck Equipment Schedule T3						
	Sport Utility 4D	BT20X	47580	31175	34700	36500	41700
	Third Row			800	800	1065	1065
	LX 570 4WD—V8—Truck Equipment Schedule T3						
	Sport Utility 4D	HY00W	74565				

LINCOLN

1998 LINCOLN — 5LM–(U28L)–W–#

NAVIGATOR 4WD—V8—Truck Equipment Schedule T3

Body	Type	VIN	List	Fair	Good	Good	Excellent
	Sport Utility 4D	U28L	43300	3200	3900	5350	7550
	w/o Rear Air Conditioning			(175)	(175)	(235)	(235)
	2WD	7		(425)	(425)	(565)	(565)

1999 LINCOLN — 5LM–(U28L)–X–#

NAVIGATOR 4WD—V8—Truck Equipment Schedule T3

	Sport Utility 4D	U28L	43800	3725	4450	5950	8250
	w/o Rear Air Conditioning			(200)	(200)	(265)	(265)
	2WD	7		(450)	(450)	(600)	(600)

2000 LINCOLN — 5LM–(U28A)–Y–#

NAVIGATOR 4WD—V8—Truck Equipment Schedule T3

	Sport Utility 4D	U28A	46500	4375	5175	6725	9150
	w/o Rear Air Conditioning			(225)	(225)	(300)	(300)
	2WD	7		(475)	(475)	(635)	(635)

2001 LINCOLN — 5LM–(U28A,R)–1–#

NAVIGATOR 4WD—V8—Truck Equipment Schedule T3

	Sport Utility 4D	U28A,R	48085	5175	6025	7650	10250
	2WD			(500)	(500)	(665)	(665)

2002 LINCOLN — 5LM–(U28R)–2–#

NAVIGATOR 4WD—V8—Truck Equipment Schedule T3

	Sport Utility 4D	U28R	48680	5925	6875	8775	11750
	2WD	7		(500)	(500)	(665)	(665)

BLACKWOOD—V8—Truck Equipment Schedule T3

	Sport Util Pickup 4D	W05A	52500	8550	9775	11800	15200

2003 LINCOLN — 5LM–(U88H)–3–#

AVIATOR AWD—V8—Truck Equipment Schedule T3

	Sport Utility 4D	U88H	42945	6575	7575	9400	12400
	2WD	6		(575)	(575)	(765)	(765)

NAVIGATOR 4WD—V8—Truck Equipment Schedule T3

	Sport Utility 4D	U28R	52425	8550	9775	11800	15250
	2WD			(575)	(575)	(765)	(765)

2004 LINCOLN — 5LM–(U88H)–4–#

AVIATOR AWD—V8—Truck Equipment Schedule T3

	Sport Utility 4D	U88H	43400	7375	8450	10300	13350
	2WD	6		(650)	(650)	(865)	(865)

NAVIGATOR 4WD—V8—Truck Equipment Schedule T3

	Sport Utility 4D	U28R	52775	10625	12050	14150	17850
	2WD	7		(650)	(650)	(865)	(865)

2005 LINCOLN — 5LM–(U88H)–5–#

AVIATOR AWD—V8—Truck Equipment Schedule T3

	Sport Utility 4D	U88H	44150	8325	9525	11350	14550
	2WD	6		(725)	(725)	(965)	(965)

NAVIGATOR 4WD—V8—Truck Equipment Schedule T3

	Sport Utility 4D	U285	53985	12925	14550	16700	20600
	2WD	7		(725)	(725)	(965)	(965)

2006 LINCOLN — 5L(MorT)–(W165)–6–#

MARK LT—V8—Truck Equipment Schedule T3

	Super Crew Pickup	W165	39995	13625	15325	17300	21100
	4WD	8		1900	1900	2535	2535

TRUCKS & VANS

Body	Type	VIN	List	Trade-In Fair	Good	Pvt-Party Good	Retail Excellent
NAVIGATOR 4WD—V8—Truck Equipment Schedule T3							
Sport Utility 4D		U285	53075	**15425**	**17350**	**19400**	**23500**
Limited Edition			------	400	400	535	535
2WD		7	------	(800)	(800)	(1065)	(1065)

2007 LINCOLN — 5L(MorT)–(U68C)–7–#

Body	Type	VIN	List	Trade-In Fair	Good	Pvt-Party Good	Retail Excellent
MKX—V6—Truck Equipment Schedule T3							
Sport Utility 4D		U68C	34795	**18225**	**20375**	**22300**	**26500**
Elite Pkg			------	400	400	535	535
AWD		8	------	950	950	1265	1265
MARK LT—V8—Truck Equipment Schedule T3							
Super Crew 5 1/2'		W165	42095	**15475**	**17350**	**19250**	**23100**
Super Crew 6 1/2'		W165	42395	**15300**	**17200**	**19050**	**22900**
4WD		8	------	2075	2075	2765	2765
NAVIGATOR 4WD—V8—Truck Equipment Schedule T3							
Sport Utility 4D		U285	49475	**23325**	**25975**	**28000**	**32800**
Elite Pkg			------	400	400	535	535
2WD		7	------	(875)	(875)	(1165)	(1165)
NAVIGATOR L 4WD—V8—Truck Equipment Schedule T3							
Sport Utility 4D		L285	52475	**25000**	**27925**	**30000**	**35000**
Elite Pkg			------	400	400	535	535
2WD		7	------	(875)	(875)	(1165)	(1165)

2008 LINCOLN — 5L(MorT)–(U68C)–8–#

Body	Type	VIN	List	Trade-In Fair	Good	Pvt-Party Good	Retail Excellent
MKX—V6—Truck Equipment Schedule T3							
Sport Utility 4D		U68C	36095	**20475**	**22925**	**24600**	**28800**
Limited Edition			------	400	400	535	535
AWD		8	------	1025	1025	1365	1365
MARK LT—V8—Truck Equipment Schedule T3							
Super Crew 5 1/2'		W165	39265				
Super Crew 6 1/2'		W165	39565				
4WD		8	------				
NAVIGATOR 4WD—V8—Truck Equipment Schedule T3							
Sport Utility 4D		U285	51555	**26075**	**29000**	**31000**	**35900**
Elite Pkg			------	400	400	535	535
2WD		7	------	(950)	(950)	(1265)	(1265)
NAVIGATOR L 4WD—V8—Truck Equipment Schedule T3							
Sport Utility 4D		L285	54555	**27725**	**30875**	**32700**	**37800**
Elite Pkg			------	400	400	535	535
2WD		7	------	(950)	(950)	(1265)	(1265)

MAZDA

1994 MAZDA — (JMor4F)(2or3)–(V521)–R

Body	Type	VIN	List	Trade-In Fair	Good	Pvt-Party Good	Retail Excellent
MPV—4-Cyl.—Truck Equipment Schedule T1							
Minivan		V521	20900	**500**	**675**	**1425**	**2625**
V6 3.0 Liter		U	------	**200**	**200**	**265**	**265**
MPV 4WD—V6—Truck Equipment Schedule T1							
Minivan		V523	24700	**800**	**1125**	**2050**	**3500**
NAVAJO 4WD—V6—Truck Equipment Schedule T1							
DX Sport Utility 2D		U44X	20350	**550**	**750**	**1475**	**2650**
LX Sport Utility 2D		U44X	23260	**625**	**900**	**1750**	**3075**
2WD		2	------	(125)	(125)	(165)	(165)
B2300 PICKUP—4-Cyl.—Truck Equipment Schedule T2							
Short Bed		R12A	10025	**375**	**525**	**1150**	**2125**
Cab Plus		R16A	12480	**625**	**850**	**1675**	**2975**
SE Short Bed		R12A	11670	**450**	**600**	**1325**	**2450**
B3000 PICKUP—V6—Truck Equipment Schedule T2							
SE Short Bed		R12U	12140	**525**	**700**	**1450**	**2650**
SE Long Bed		R21U	12785	**550**	**750**	**1525**	**2750**
Cab Plus		R16U	12950	**700**	**975**	**1850**	**3200**
SE Cab Plus		R16U	13630	**750**	**1075**	**1950**	**3375**
B3000 PICKUP 4WD—V6—Truck Equipment Schedule T2							
Short Bed		R13U	14895	**650**	**925**	**1750**	**3075**
Cab Plus		R17U	15955	**900**	**1275**	**2325**	**3950**
B4000 PICKUP—V6—Truck Equipment Schedule T2							
SE Long Bed		R21X	12960	**550**	**750**	**1525**	**2750**
LE Cab Plus		R16X	15815	**650**	**925**	**1750**	**3075**
B4000 PICKUP 4WD—V6—Truck Equipment Schedule T2							
SE Short Bed		R13X	16885	**675**	**950**	**1825**	**3150**
SE Cab Plus		R17X	17755	**925**	**1300**	**2375**	**4000**

Body	Type	VIN	List	Trade-In Fair	Trade-In Good	Pvt-Party Good	Retail Excellent
LE Cab Plus		R17X	19960	1000	1400	2525	4175

1995 MAZDA — (JM3or4F4)–(V522)–S–#

MPV—V6—Truck Equipment Schedule T1
L Minivan		V522	22505	575	775	1550	2825
LX Minivan		V522	23155	625	875	1700	3050
LXE Minivan		V522	24845	725	1025	1900	3325
4WD		3		250	250	335	335

B2300 PICKUP—4-Cyl.—Truck Equipment Schedule T2
Short Bed		R12A	10765	450	625	1350	2525
Long Bed		R12A	11155	475	625	1400	2575
Cab Plus		R16A	13485	700	975	1850	3250
SE Short Bed		R12A	12485	525	700	1475	2700
SE Cab Plus		R16A	14185	825	1150	2100	3600
4WD		3		400	400	535	535

B3000 PICKUP—V6—Truck Equipment Schedule T2
| SE Short Bed | | R12U | 13155 | 600 | 825 | 1650 | 2975 |
| SE Cab Plus | | R16U | 14855 | 875 | 1250 | 2325 | 3950 |

B3000 PICKUP 4WD—V6—Truck Equipment Schedule T2
| Cab Plus | | R17U | 17715 | 1025 | 1450 | 2575 | 4275 |

B4000 PICKUP—V6—Truck Equipment Schedule T2
| SE Cab Plus | | R16X | 15400 | 750 | 1050 | 1950 | 3375 |
| LE Cab Plus | | R16X | 16925 | 775 | 1100 | 2025 | 3475 |

B4000 PICKUP 4WD—V6—Truck Equipment Schedule T2
SE Short Bed		R13X	18360	800	1125	2050	3500
SE Cab Plus		R17X	19485	1050	1475	2600	4300
LE Cab Plus		R17X	20975	1150	1625	2800	4525

1996 MAZDA — (JM3or4F4)(LV522)–T–#

MPV—V6—Truck Equipment Schedule T1
DX Minivan		LV522	22845	650	925	1800	3150
LX Minivan		LV522	22735	725	1025	1950	3375
ES Minivan		LV522	25135	875	1225	2325	3950
4WD		3		300	300	400	400

B2300 PICKUP—4-Cyl.—Truck Equipment Schedule T2
Short Bed		R12A	10600	550	750	1550	2825
Long Bed		R12A	10985	575	775	1625	2925
Cab Plus		R16A	13720	850	1200	2200	3725
SE Short Bed		R12A	12545	625	850	1700	3050
SE Cab Plus		R16A	14840	975	1375	2525	4200
4WD		3,7		525	525	700	700

B3000 PICKUP—V6—Truck Equipment Schedule T2
| SE Cab Plus | | R16U | 15675 | 1075 | 1500 | 2650 | 4350 |

B3000 PICKUP 4WD—V6—Truck Equipment Schedule T2
| Cab Plus | | R17U | 18170 | 1275 | 1750 | 2975 | 4725 |

B4000 PICKUP—V6—Truck Equipment Schedule T2
| LE Cab Plus | | R16X | 17845 | 925 | 1325 | 2425 | 4075 |

B4000 PICKUP 4WD—V6—Truck Equipment Schedule T2
SE Short Bed		R13X	18810	975	1350	2475	4150
SE Cab Plus		R17X	20065	1300	1775	3000	4750
LE Cab Plus		R17X	22140	1475	1950	3200	5025

1997 MAZDA — (JM3or4F4)(LV522)–V–#

MPV—V6—Truck Equipment Schedule T1
LX Minivan		LV522	24370	875	1225	2300	3950
ES Minivan		LV522	28270	1025	1450	2575	4275
4WD		3		350	350	465	465

B2300 PICKUP—4-Cyl.—Truck Equipment Schedule T2
Short Bed		R12A	11060	650	925	1825	3200
SE Short Bed		R13225		750	1050	2000	3475
SE Cab Plus		R16A	15480	1175	1650	2850	4600

B4000 PICKUP—V6—Truck Equipment Schedule T2
| SE Cab Plus | | R16X | 16225 | 1425 | 1875 | 3125 | 4925 |

B4000 PICKUP 4WD—V6—Truck Equipment Schedule T2
Short Bed		R13X	16775	1150	1600	2800	4525
Cab Plus		R17X	18660	1575	2050	3300	5150
SE Cab Plus		R17X	20275	1625	2100	3375	5225

1998 MAZDA — (JM3or4F4)(LV522)–W–#

MPV—V6—Truck Equipment Schedule T1
| LX Minivan | | LV522 | 24370 | 1025 | 1450 | 2600 | 4300 |
| ES Minivan | | LV522 | 28270 | 1200 | 1675 | 2875 | 4600 |

TRUCKS & VANS

Body	Type	VIN	List	Trade-In Fair	Trade-In Good	Pvt-Party Good	Retail Excellent
4WD		3	....	400	400	535	535
B2500 PICKUP—4-Cyl.—Truck Equipment Schedule T2							
SX Short Bed		R12C	11575	700	1000	1950	3425
SE Short Bed		R12C	13215	825	1150	2175	3725
SE Cab Plus 2D		R16C	15355	1125	1575	2775	4525
SE Cab Plus 4D		R16C	15950	1525	2000	3250	5100
B3000 PICKUP—V6—Truck Equipment Schedule T2							
SE Cab Plus 2D		R16U	16305	1325	1825	3075	4850
SE Cab Plus 4D		R14U	16900	1525	2025	3275	5125
B3000 PICKUP 4WD—V6—Truck Equipment Schedule T2							
SX Short Bed		R13U	15925	1100	1550	2725	4450
SE Short Bed		R13U	17455	1250	1725	2950	4725
SE Cab Plus 2D		R17U	18940	1850	2375	3650	5550
SE Cab Plus 4D		R15U	19535	2075	2625	3950	5875
B4000 PICKUP—V6—Truck Equipment Schedule T2							
SE Cab Plus 2D		R16X	17155	1625	2125	3375	5250
SE Cab Plus 4D		R14X	17750	1750	2275	3550	5450
B4000 PICKUP 4WD—V6—Truck Equipment Schedule T2							
SE Cab Plus 2D		R17X	19840	1825	2350	3625	5525
SE Cab Plus 4D		R15X	20435	2150	2725	4050	6000

Body	Type	VIN	List	Trade-In Fair	Trade-In Good	Pvt-Party Good	Retail Excellent
B2500 PICKUP—4-Cyl.—Truck Equipment Schedule T2							
SX Short Bed		R12C	11795	825	1150	2275	3950
SE Short Bed		R12C	14170	950	1325	2500	4200
Troy Lee Short Bed		R12C	15130	1050	1475	2675	4375
SE Cab Plus 2D		R16C	16225	1300	1775	3025	4800
SE Cab Plus 4D		R15X	16885	1775	2300	3575	5475
B3000 PICKUP—V6—Truck Equipment Schedule T2							
SE Cab Plus 2D		R16U	16800	1575	2075	3350	5200
SE Cab Plus 4D		R16U	17460	1800	2325	3600	5500
Troy Lee Cab Plus 4D		R16U	18955	2000	2575	3875	5800
B3000 PICKUP 4WD—V6—Truck Equipment Schedule T2							
SE Short Bed		R13U	18060	1475	1950	3200	5050
SE Cab Plus 2D		R17U	19715	2150	2725	4025	5975
SE Cab Plus 4D		R17U	20375	2400	3000	4300	6325
B4000 PICKUP—V6—Truck Equipment Schedule T2							
SE Short Bed		R12X	18090	1150	1625	2850	4600
SE Cab Plus 2D		R16X	20145	1875	2425	3700	5600
SE Cab Plus 4D		R16X	20805	2050	2625	3925	5850
B4000 PICKUP 4WD—V6—Truck Equipment Schedule T2							
SE Cab Plus 2D		R17X	22140	2100	2675	3975	5900
SE Cab Plus 4D		R17X	22800	2500	3075	4425	6450
Troy Lee Cab Plus 4D		R17X	23995	2775	3375	4750	6800

Body	Type	VIN	List	Trade-In Fair	Trade-In Good	Pvt-Party Good	Retail Excellent
MPV—V6—Truck Equipment Schedule T1							
DX Minivan 4D		LW28	20475	1275	1750	3000	4775
LX Minivan 4D		LW28	22530	1450	1925	3175	5000
ES Minivan 4D		LW28	26030	1775	2275	3550	5425
B2500 PICKUP—4-Cyl.—Truck Equipment Schedule T2							
SX Short Bed		R12C	12005	975	1375	2550	4275
SE Short Bed		R12C	14315	1100	1550	2750	4500
SE Cab Plus 2D		R16C	16505	1550	2050	3300	5175
B3000 PICKUP—V6—Truck Equipment Schedule T2							
SX Short Bed		R12V	12400	1175	1650	2900	4675
SE Short Bed		R12V	14710	1300	1800	3050	4850
SE Cab Plus 2D		R16V	16975	1850	2400	3700	5600
SE Cab Plus 4D		R16V	17715	2100	2675	4000	5925
Troy Lee Cab Plus 4D		R16V	19120	2350	2950	4275	6275
B3000 PICKUP 4WD—V6—Truck Equipment Schedule T2							
SE Short Bed		R13V	18235	1750	2250	3550	5450
SE Cab Plus 4D		R17V	20720	2800	3400	4775	6850
B4000 PICKUP—V6—Truck Equipment Schedule T2							
SE Cab Plus 4D		R16X	21140	2425	3025	4325	6350
B4000 PICKUP 4WD—V6—Truck Equipment Schedule T2							
SE Cab Plus 4D		R17X	23050	2875	3500	4875	6950
Troy Lee Cab Plus 4D		R17X	24150	3125	3825	5225	7375

Body	Type	VIN	List	Trade-In Fair	Trade-In Good	Pvt-Party Good	Retail Excellent
TRIBUTE 4WD—V6—Truck Equipment Schedule T1							
DX Sport Utility 4D		U06B	21055	2200	2775	4125	6100

2001 MAZDA

Body	Type	VIN	List	Trade-In Fair	Trade-In Good	Pvt-Party Good	Retail Excellent
LX Sport Utility 4D		U08B	22535	2875	3500	4900	7025
ES Sport Utility 4D		U081	23540	3225	3900	5325	7500
2WD				(500)	(500)	(665)	(665)
4-Cyl. 2.0 Liter		B		(475)	(475)	(635)	(635)
MPV—V6—Truck Equipment Schedule T1							
DX Minivan 4D		LW28	21155	1600	2100	3375	5250
LX Minivan 4D		LW28	23280	1800	2300	3600	5500
ES Minivan 4D		LW28	26760	2100	2675	3975	5900
B2300 PICKUP—4-Cyl.—Truck Equipment Schedule T2							
SX Short Bed		R12D	12930	1175	1650	2925	4725
SE Short Bed		R12D	15130	1425	1900	3175	5050
B2500 PICKUP—4-Cyl.—Truck Equipment Schedule T2							
SX Short Bed		R12C	12785	1150	1625	2875	4675
SE Short Bed		R12C	14985	1325	1800	3075	4900
B3000 PICKUP—V6—Truck Equipment Schedule T2							
SE Short Bed		R12V	15280	1600	2100	3375	5275
Dual Short Bed		R12V	15315	1650	2150	3450	5350
SE Cab Plus 2D		R16V	17515	2225	2800	4125	6100
SE Cab Plus 4D		R16V	18180	2500	3075	4425	6450
Dual Sport Cab + 2D		R16V	17735	2600	3200	4550	6600
B3000 PICKUP 4WD—V6—Truck Equipment Schedule T2							
SE Short Bed		R13V	18810	2075	2625	3950	5900
SE Cab Plus 2D		R13V	20480	2900	3525	4900	7000
B4000 PICKUP—V6—Truck Equipment Schedule T2							
Dual Sport Cab + 4D		R17X	19935	2800	3425	4800	6875
B4000 PICKUP 4WD—V6—Truck Equipment Schedule T2							
SE Cab Plus 4D		R17X	22780	3300	3975	5400	7550

2001 MAZDA—(JM3,4F2or4F4)—(U06B)—2

Body	Type	VIN	List	Trade-In Fair	Trade-In Good	Pvt-Party Good	Retail Excellent
TRIBUTE 4WD—V6—Truck Equipment Schedule T1							
DX Sport Utility 4D		U06B	22575	2600	3200	4800	7150
LX Sport Utility 4D		U08B	23225	3300	4000	5650	8100
ES Sport Utility 4D		U081	24455	3675	4375	6050	8575
2WD				(500)	(500)	(665)	(665)
4-Cyl. 2.0 Liter		B		(500)	(500)	(665)	(665)
MPV—V6—Truck Equipment Schedule T1							
LX Minivan 4D		LW28	22770	1975	2550	4075	6275
ES Minivan 4D		LW28	27712	2350	2925	4475	6750
B2300 PICKUP—4-Cyl.—Truck Equipment Schedule T2							
Short Bed		R12D	13240	1350	1850	3375	5525
SE Cab Plus		R16D		2050	2600	4175	6425
B3000 PICKUP—V6—Truck Equipment Schedule T2							
Dual Sport Short Bed		R12V	15870	1850	2350	3925	6125
Dual Sport Cab + 2D		R16V	18290	2875	3500	5125	7500
B3000 PICKUP 4WD—V6—Truck Equipment Schedule T2							
Cab Plus 2D		R13V	20775	3175	3850	5500	7925
B4000 PICKUP—V6—Truck Equipment Schedule T2							
Dual Sport Cab + 4D		R17X	20085	3100	3750	5400	7800
B4000 PICKUP 4WD—V6—Truck Equipment Schedule T2							
Cab Plus 4D		R17X	22830	3650	4350	6000	8500

2003 MAZDA—(JM3,4F2or4F4)—(Z92B)—3

Body	Type	VIN	List	Trade-In Fair	Trade-In Good	Pvt-Party Good	Retail Excellent
TRIBUTE 4WD—4-Cyl.—Truck Equipment Schedule T1							
DX Sport Utility 4D		Z92B	20440	2925	3550	5225	7625
2WD		0		(575)	(575)	(765)	(765)
Manual Trans		0		0	0	0	0
TRIBUTE 4WD—V6—Truck Equipment Schedule T1							
LX Sport Utility 4D		Z941	22125	3875	4600	6300	8850
ES Sport Utility 4D		Z961	24885	4300	5075	6775	9375
2WD		0		(575)	(575)	(765)	(765)
MPV—V6—Truck Equipment Schedule T1							
LX S-V Minivan 4D		LW28A	21895	1975	2525	4100	6300
LX Minivan 4D		LW28A	23120	2475	3075	4625	6900
ES Minivan 4D		LW28A	26520	2850	3475	5075	7400
B2300 PICKUP—4-Cyl.—Truck Equipment Schedule T2							
Short Bed		R12D	13740	1850	2375	3950	6150
SE Cab Plus		R16D	17960	2600	3200	4825	7150
B3000 PICKUP—V6—Truck Equipment Schedule T2							
Dual Sport Short Bed		R12U	16590	2375	2975	4550	6825
Dual Sport Cab + 2D		R16V	18700	3550	4250	5875	8350
SE Cab Plus 4D		R46V	18935	3500	4200	5825	8300

TRUCKS & VANS

Body	Type	VIN	List	Trade-In Fair	Good	Pvt-Party Good	Retail Excellent
B4000 PICKUP—V6—Truck Equipment Schedule T2							
Dual Sport Cab + 4D		R17E	20495	**3825**	**4550**	**6225**	**8725**
B4000 PICKUP 4WD—V6—Truck Equipment Schedule T2							
Cab Plus 2D		R17X	20260	**3750**	**4475**	**6125**	**8625**
SE Cab Plus 2D		R17X	21705	**4275**	**5025**	**6725**	**9250**
SE Cab Plus 4D		R17X	23240	**4450**	**5250**	**6975**	**9625**

2004 MAZDA–(JM3,4F2or4F4)–(Z92B)–4

Body	Type	VIN	List	Trade-In Fair	Good	Pvt-Party Good	Retail Excellent
TRIBUTE 4WD—4-Cyl.—Truck Equipment Schedule T1							
DX Sport Utility 4D		Z92B	21087	**3575**	**4300**	**5975**	**8475**
2WD		0		**(650)**	**(650)**	**(865)**	**(865)**
Manual Trans				**0**	**0**	**0**	**0**
TRIBUTE 4WD—V6—Truck Equipment Schedule T1							
LX Sport Utility 4D		Z941	23972	**4550**	**5375**	**7125**	**9800**
ES Sport Utility 4D		Z961	25562	**5050**	**5900**	**7650**	**10400**
2WD		0		**(650)**	**(650)**	**(865)**	**(865)**
MPV—V6—Truck Equipment Schedule T1							
LX Minivan 4D		W28A	23780	**3075**	**3700**	**5300**	**7650**
ES Minivan 4D		W28A	28750	**3500**	**4225**	**5800**	**8200**
B2300 PICKUP—4-Cyl.—Truck Equipment Schedule T2							
Short Bed		R12D	14840	**2450**	**3050**	**4625**	**6925**
SE Cab Plus		R16D	18980	**3300**	**3975**	**5600**	**8025**
B3000 PICKUP—V6—Truck Equipment Schedule T2							
Dual Sport Short Bed		R12U	17915	**3050**	**3675**	**5300**	**7700**
Dual Sport Cab + 2D		R16V	19871	**4325**	**5100**	**6800**	**9425**
SE Cab Plus 4D		R46V	20140	**4300**	**5075**	**6750**	**9275**
B4000 PICKUP—V6—Truck Equipment Schedule T2							
Dual Sport Cab + 4D		R17E	21865	**4650**	**5475**	**7175**	**9850**
B4000 PICKUP 4WD—V6—Truck Equipment Schedule T2							
Cab Plus 2D		R17X	20850	**4575**	**5400**	**7100**	**9750**
SE Cab Plus 2D		R17X	22350	**5150**	**6025**	**7775**	**10500**
SE Cab Plus 4D		R17X	24090	**5425**	**6300**	**8025**	**10800**

2005 MAZDA–(JM3,4F2or4F4)–(Z92Z)–5

Body	Type	VIN	List	Trade-In Fair	Good	Pvt-Party Good	Retail Excellent
TRIBUTE 4WD—4-Cyl.—Truck Equipment Schedule T1							
i Sport Utility 4D		Z92Z	22325	**4375**	**5175**	**6900**	**9575**
2WD		0		**(725)**	**(725)**	**(965)**	**(965)**
TRIBUTE 4WD—V6—Truck Equipment Schedule T1							
s Sport Utility 4D		Z941	24980	**5450**	**6325**	**8075**	**10900**
2WD		0		**(725)**	**(725)**	**(965)**	**(965)**
MPV—V6—Truck Equipment Schedule T1							
LX-SV Minivan 4D		W28A	22665	**3300**	**4000**	**5575**	**7975**
LX Minivan 4D		W28A	23485	**3925**	**4650**	**6250**	**8700**
ES Minivan 4D		W28J	29050	**4400**	**5225**	**6850**	**9425**
B2300 PICKUP—4-Cyl.—Truck Equipment Schedule T2							
Short Bed		R12D	15935	**3125**	**3800**	**5425**	**7825**
B3000 PICKUP—V6—Truck Equipment Schedule T2							
Extended Cab 4D		R46U	19480	**5200**	**6075**	**7800**	**10500**
Dual Sport Short Bed		R12U	20120	**3825**	**4550**	**6200**	**8675**
Dual Sport Ext 4D		R46U	21870	**5250**	**6125**	**7850**	**10550**
B4000 PICKUP 4WD—V6—Truck Equipment Schedule T2							
Extended Cab 4D		R47E	22220	**5550**	**6475**	**8175**	**10950**
SE Extended Cab 4D		R47E	26765	**6475**	**7475**	**9200**	**12050**

2006 MAZDA–(JM1or3,4F2or4)(CR293)–6–#

Body	Type	VIN	List	Trade-In Fair	Good	Pvt-Party Good	Retail Excellent
MAZDA5—4-Cyl.—Truck Equipment Schedule T1							
Sport Minivan 4D		CR293	18895	**5000**	**5825**	**7525**	**10150**
Touring Minivan 4D		CR193	20410	**5650**	**6575**	**8225**	**10950**
TRIBUTE 4WD—4-Cyl.—Truck Equipment Schedule T1							
i Sport Utility 4D		Z92Z	23025	**5375**	**6275**	**8000**	**10800**
2WD		0		**(800)**	**(800)**	**(1065)**	**(1065)**
TRIBUTE 4WD—V6—Truck Equipment Schedule T1							
s Sport Utility 4D		Z941	25290	**6450**	**7450**	**9200**	**12100**
2WD		0		**(800)**	**(800)**	**(1065)**	**(1065)**
MPV—V6—Truck Equipment Schedule T1							
LX-SV Minivan 4D		W28A	22675	**4450**	**5250**	**6875**	**9425**
LX Minivan 4D		W28A	23510	**5100**	**5950**	**7625**	**10250**
ES Minivan 4D		W28J	29075	**5650**	**6600**	**8225**	**10950**
B2300 PICKUP—4-Cyl.—Truck Equipment Schedule T2							
Short Bed		R12D	15690	**4000**	**4750**	**6400**	**8900**
B3000 PICKUP—V6—Truck Equipment Schedule T2							
Extended Cab 4D		R46U	19510	**6275**	**7250**	**8975**	**11750**

Body	Type	VIN	List	Trade-In Fair	Trade-In Good	Pvt-Party Good	Retail Excellent
Dual Sport Short Bed		R12U	20145	4750	5550	7250	9900
Dual Sport Ext 4D		R46U	21900	6325	7300	9025	11800
B4000 PICKUP 4WD—V6—Truck Equipment Schedule T2							
Extended Cab 4D		R47E	22515	6650	7675	9350	12200
SE Extended Cab 4D		R47E	27060	7725	8850	10600	13500

2007 MAZDA–(JM1or3,4F2or4)(CR193)-7-#

Body	Type	VIN	List	Trade-In Fair	Trade-In Good	Pvt-Party Good	Retail Excellent
MAZDA5—4-Cyl.—Truck Equipment Schedule T1							
Sport Minivan 4D		CR193	19130	6825	7875	9450	12150
Touring Minivan 4D		CR193	20645	7525	8650	10200	13000
Grand Touring 4D		CR193	21895	8150	9325	11000	13900
CX-7—4-Cyl. Turbo—Truck Equipment Schedule T1							
Sport Utility 4D		ER293	26010	8425	9625	11350	14450
Touring Sport Util		ER293	27760	9425	10725	12500	15650
Grand Touring Util		ER293	28560	10050	11425	13250	16450
AWD				950	950	1265	1265
CX-9—V6—Truck Equipment Schedule T1							
Sport Utility 4D		TB28Y	30830	12250	13875	15700	19150
Touring Sport Util		TB28Y	32930	13025	14700	16500	20100
Grand Touring Util		TB28Y	34470	13625	15325	17150	20800
AWD		3		950	950	1265	1265
B2300 PICKUP—4-Cyl.—Truck Equipment Schedule T2							
Short Bed		R12D	16170	5025	5875	7450	10000
B3000 PICKUP—V6—Truck Equipment Schedule T2							
Extended Cab 4D		R46U	19675	7525	8625	10250	13050
Dual Sport Short Bed		R12U	20310	5850	6775	8375	11050
Dual Sport Ext 4D		R46U	22065	7575	8675	10300	13150
B4000 PICKUP 4WD—V6—Truck Equipment Schedule T2							
Extended Cab 4D		R47E	22680	7900	9050	10750	13600
SE Extended Cab 4D		R47E	27225	9125	10400	12100	15150

2008 MAZDA–(JM1or3,4F2or4)(CR293)-8-#

Body	Type	VIN	List	Trade-In Fair	Trade-In Good	Pvt-Party Good	Retail Excellent
MAZDA5—4-Cyl.—Truck Equipment Schedule T1							
Sport Minivan 4D		CR293	19580	9325	10625	12200	15150
Touring Minivan 4D		CR293	21245	10050	11425	13050	16050
Grand Touring 4D		CR293	23000	10825	12250	13850	17000
TRIBUTE 4WD—4-Cyl.—Truck Equipment Schedule T1							
i Sport Utility 4D		Z92Z	22660	9725	11025	12750	15900
i Touring Spt Util		Z92Z	23435	10775	12200	13850	17050
i Grand Touring Util		Z92Z	25625	11650	13175	14900	18250
HEV Tour Spt Util 4D		Z59H					
HEV Grand Tour Util		Z59H					
2WD		0		(950)	(950)	(1265)	(1265)
TRIBUTE 4WD—V6—Truck Equipment Schedule T1							
s Sport Utility 4D		Z961	23900	10875	12350	14050	17350
s Touring Spt Util		Z961	24675	11175	12650	14300	17550
s Grand Touring Util		Z961	26865	12050	13625	15350	18650
2WD		0		(950)	(950)	(1265)	(1265)
CX-7—4-Cyl. Turbo—Truck Equipment Schedule T1							
Sport Utility 4D		ER293	24345	10200	11575	13350	16500
Touring Sport Util		ER293	26095	11275	12750	14500	17850
Grand Touring Util		ER293	26895	11950	13525	15300	18650
AWD				1025	1025	1365	1365
CX-9—V6—Truck Equipment Schedule T1							
Sport Utility 4D		TB28A	29995	14450	16225	18050	21700
Touring Sport Util		TB28A	32210	15250	17150	18900	22600
Grand Touring Util		TB28A	33950	15875	17825	19600	23400
AWD		3		1025	1025	1365	1365
B2300 PICKUP—4-Cyl.—Truck Equipment Schedule T2							
Short Bed		R12D	16170	6575	7575	9075	11600
B4000 PICKUP 4WD—V6—Truck Equipment Schedule T2							
Extended Cab 4D		R47E	22680	9725	11025	12700	15750
SE Extended Cab 4D		R47E	27225	11025	12500	14150	17350

MERCEDES-BENZ

1998 MERCEDES-BENZ — 4JG(AB54E)-W-#

Body	Type	VIN	List	Trade-In Fair	Trade-In Good	Pvt-Party Good	Retail Excellent
ML-CLASS 4WD—V6—Truck Equipment Schedule T3							
ML320 Sport Utl 4D		AB54E	38590	3775	4475	5975	8275
Third Seat				225	225	300	300

SEE BACK PAGES FOR TRUCK EQUIPMENT

TRUCKS & VANS

1999 MERCEDES-BENZ

Body	Type	VIN	List	Trade-In Fair	Good	Pvt-Party Good	Retail Excellent
1999 MERCEDES-BENZ — 4JG(AB54E)–X–#							
ML-CLASS 4WD—V6—Truck Equipment Schedule T3							
ML320 Sport Utl 4D	AB54E	39590	**4300**	5100	6625	9025
Third Seat			**250**	250	335	335
ML-CLASS 4WD—V8—Truck Equipment Schedule T3							
ML430 Sport Utl 4D	AB72E	44345	**5325**	6200	7850	10500
Third Seat			**250**	250	335	335
2000 MERCEDES-BENZ — 4JG(AB54E)–Y–#							
ML-CLASS 4WD—V6—Truck Equipment Schedule T3							
ML320 Sport Utl 4D	AB54E	36895	**5025**	5875	7475	10050
Third Seat			**275**	275	365	365
ML-CLASS 4WD—V8—Truck Equipment Schedule T3							
ML430 Sport Utl 4D	AB72E	44345	**6150**	7125	8800	11550
ML55 Sport Utl 4D	AB74E	65495	**11225**	12700	14850	18550
Third Seat			**275**	275	365	365
2001 MERCEDES-BENZ — 4JG(AB54E)–1–#							
ML-CLASS 4WD—V6—Truck Equipment Schedule T3							
ML320 Sport Utl 4D	AB54E	38045	**5900**	6825	8475	11150
Sport Pkg			**650**	650	865	865
Third Seat			**300**	300	400	400
designo Edition			**750**	750	1000	1000
ML-CLASS 4WD—V8—Truck Equipment Schedule T3							
ML430 Sport Utl 4D	AB72E	44845	**7100**	8150	9900	12800
ML55 Sport Utl 4D	AB74E	66545	**12550**	14150	16300	20200
Sport Pkg			**650**	650	865	865
Third Seat			**300**	300	400	400
designo Edition			**750**	750	1000	1000
2002 MERCEDES-BENZ — WDCor4JG(AB54E)–2–#							
ML-CLASS 4WD—V6—Truck Equipment Schedule T3							
ML320 Sport Utl 4D	AB54E	36945	**6750**	7775	9675	12750
designo Edition			**800**	800	1065	1065
Third Seat			**300**	300	400	400
Sport Pkg			**700**	700	935	935
ML-CLASS 4WD—V8—Truck Equipment Schedule T3							
ML500 Sport Utl 4D	AB75E	45595	**7500**	8600	10550	13700
ML55 Sport Utl 4D	AB74E	66545	**13725**	15475	17850	22100
Sport Pkg			**700**	700	935	935
Third Seat			**300**	300	400	400
designo Edition			**800**	800	1065	1065
G-CLASS 4WD—V8—Truck Equipment Schedule T3							
G500 Sport Utl 4D	YR49E	73145	**22725**	25375	28400	34200
designo Edition			**800**	800	1065	1065
2003 MERCEDES-BENZ — WDCor4JG(AB54E)–3–#							
ML-CLASS 4WD—V6—Truck Equipment Schedule T3							
ML320 Sport Utl 4D	AB54E	40315	**7675**	8800	10700	13800
ML350 Sport Utl 4D	AB57E	40665	**8075**	9225	11200	14500
Sport Pkg			**700**	700	935	935
Inspiration Edition			**650**	650	865	865
designo Edition			**825**	825	1100	1100
Third Seat			**350**	350	465	465
ML-CLASS 4WD—V8—Truck Equipment Schedule T3							
ML500 Sport Utl 4D	AB75E	46015	**8475**	9675	11650	15000
ML55 Sport Utl 4D	AB74E	66565	**15575**	17500	19800	24200
Sport Pkg			**700**	700	935	935
Inspiration Edition			**650**	650	865	865
designo Edition			**825**	825	1100	1100
Third Seat			**350**	350	465	465
G-CLASS 4WD—V8—Truck Equipment Schedule T3							
G500 Sport Utility 4D	YR49	74265	**26550**	29600	32600	38800
G55 Sport Utility 4D	YR46	90565	**32250**	35875	39100	46100
designo Edition			**825**	825	1100	1100
2004 MERCEDES-BENZ — WDCor4JG(AB57E)–4–#							
ML-CLASS 4WD—V6—Truck Equipment Schedule T3							
ML350 Sport Utl 4D	AB57E	39720	**9125**	10400	12350	15750
Inspiration Edition			**675**	675	900	900

Body	Type	VIN	List	Trade-In Fair	Trade-In Good	Pvt-Party Good	Retail Excellent
	designo Edition			850	850	1135	1135
	Third Seat			400	400	535	535
ML-CLASS 4WD—V8—Truck Equipment Schedule T3							
ML500 Sport Utl 4D		AB75E	46470	9675	10975	13000	16450
	Inspiration Edition			675	675	900	900
	designo Edition			850	850	1135	1135
	Third Seat			400	400	535	535
G-CLASS 4WD—V8—Truck Equipment Schedule T3							
G500 Sport Utility 4D		YR49	76870	30575	34000	36900	43400
G55 Sport Utility 4D		YR46	93420	37150	41150	44300	51600
	designo Edition			850	850	1135	1135

2005 MERCEDES-BENZ — WDCor4JG(AB57E)-5-#

Body	Type	VIN	List	Trade-In Fair	Trade-In Good	Pvt-Party Good	Retail Excellent
ML-CLASS 4WD—V6—Truck Equipment Schedule T3							
ML350 Sport Utl 4D		AB57E	40370	10400	11750	13700	17200
	Special Edition			700	700	935	935
	designo Edition			875	875	1165	1165
	Third Seat			450	450	600	600
ML-CLASS 4WD—V8—Truck Equipment Schedule T3							
ML500 Sport Utl 4D		AB75E	47120	11125	12600	14550	18150
	Special Edition			700	700	935	935
	designo Edition			875	875	1165	1165
	Third Seat			450	450	600	600
G-CLASS 4WD—V8—Truck Equipment Schedule T3							
G500 Sport Utl 4D		YR49E	78420	34800	38600	41400	48100
G500 Grand Ed Util		YR49C	80420	36150	40175	42900	49900
	designo Edition			875	875	1165	1165
G-CLASS 4WD—V8 Supercharged—Truck Equipment Sch T3							
G55 Sport Utility 4D		YR46E	100620	42050	46650	49600	57200
G55 Grand Ed Util		YR46C	103720	43425	48125	51200	59000

2006 MERCEDES-BENZ — 4JG(BB86E)-6-#

Body	Type	VIN	List	Trade-In Fair	Trade-In Good	Pvt-Party Good	Retail Excellent
ML-CLASS 4WD—V6—Truck Equipment Schedule T3							
ML350 Sport Utl 4D		BB86E	40525	19600	21950	24000	28500
	Premium Pkg			900	900	1200	1200
	Sport Pkg			700	700	935	935
ML-CLASS 4WD—V8—Truck Equipment Schedule T3							
ML500 Sport Utl 4D		BB75E	49275	20575	23025	25100	29700
	Premium Pkg			900	900	1200	1200
	Sport Pkg			700	700	935	935
G-CLASS 4WD—V8—Truck Equipment Schedule T3							
G500 Sport Utl 4D		YR49E	78420	39100	43425	46000	52800
G-CLASS 4WD—V8 Supercharged—Truck Equipment Sch T3							
G55 Sport Utility 4D		YR71E	100620	47225	52325	55100	62900
R-CLASS AWD—V6—Truck Equipment Schedule T3							
R350 Sport Wagon		CB65E	48775	16850	18875	21300	25800
	Premium Pkg			900	900	1200	1200
	Sport Pkg			700	700	935	935
R-CLASS AWD—V8—Truck Equipment Schedule T3							
R500 Sport Wagon		CB75E	56275	18575	20775	23200	27900
	Premium Pkg			900	900	1200	1200
	Sport Pkg			700	700	935	935

2007 MERCEDES-BENZ — 4JG(BB22E)-7-#

Body	Type	VIN	List	Trade-In Fair	Trade-In Good	Pvt-Party Good	Retail Excellent
ML-CLASS 4WD—V6—Truck Equipment Schedule T3							
ML320 CDI Spt Util		BB22E	44455	30275	33700	35700	41100
ML350 Sport Utl 4D		BB86E	43455	21950	24500	26500	31000
	Premium Pkg			900	900	1200	1200
	Sport Pkg			700	700	935	935
	Adaptive Cruise			475	475	635	635
ML-CLASS 4WD—V8—Truck Equipment Schedule T3							
ML500 Sport Utl 4D		BB75E	49975	23025	25675	27600	32200
ML63 Sport Utl 4D		BB77E	86275	43225	47925	50100	56800
	Premium Pkg			900	900	1200	1200
	Sport Pkg			700	700	935	935
	Adaptive Cruise			475	475	635	635
G-CLASS 4WD—V8—Truck Equipment Schedule T3							
G500 Sport Utl 4D		YR49E	81675	47150	52225	54600	62000
G-CLASS 4WD—V8 Supercharged—Truck Equipment Sch T3							
G55 Sport Utility 4D		YR71E	105275	56150	62225	64600	72800
GL-CLASS 4WD—V6 Turbo Diesel—Truck Equip Sch T3							
GL320 CDI Spt Util		BF22E	53175	36250	40275	42500	48900

2007 MERCEDES-BENZ

Body	Type	VIN	List	Trade-In Fair	Trade-In Good	Pvt-Party Good	Retail Excellent
Premium Pkg				350	350	465	465
Adaptive Cruise				475	475	635	635
GL-CLASS 4WD—V8—Truck Equipment Schedule T3							
GL450 Sport Util 4D		BF71E	55675	31550	35075	37300	43200
Premium Pkg				350	350	465	465
Adaptive Cruise				475	475	635	635
R-CLASS 4WD—V6 Turbo Diesel—Truck Equipment Schedule T3							
R320 CDI Sport Wag		CB22E	44775	22350	24900	27200	32200
Premium Pkg				900	900	1200	1200
Adaptive Cruise				475	475	635	635
R-CLASS 4WD—V6—Truck Equipment Schedule T3							
R350 Sport Wagon		CB65E	43775	19100	21375	23700	28400
Premium Pkg				900	900	1200	1200
Sport Pkg				700	700	935	935
Adaptive Cruise				475	475	635	635
R-CLASS 4WD—V8—Truck Equipment Schedule T3							
R500 Sport Wagon		CB75E	51275	20975	23525	25800	30700
R63 Sport Wagon		CB77E	88175				
Premium Pkg				900	900	1200	1200
Sport Pkg				700	700	935	935
Adaptive Cruise				475	475	635	635

2008 MERCEDES-BENZ — 4JG(BB22E)-8-#

Body	Type	VIN	List	Trade-In Fair	Trade-In Good	Pvt-Party Good	Retail Excellent
ML-CLASS 4WD—V6 Turbo Diesel—Truck Equipment Schedule T3							
ML320 CDI Spt Util		BB22E	45425	33025	36750	38400	43700
Premium Pkg				700	700	935	935
Adaptive Cruise Control				500	500	665	665
ML-CLASS 4WD—V6—Truck Equipment Schedule T3							
ML350 Sport Util 4D		BB86E	44425	27825	30975	32700	37600
ML350 Edition Util		BB86E	52705	28625	31850	33500	38500
Premium Pkg				700	700	935	935
Adaptive Cruise Control				500	500	665	665
ML-CLASS 4WD—V8—Truck Equipment Schedule T3							
ML550 Sport Util 4D		BB72E	53175	38325	42525	44200	50000
ML63 Sport Util 4D		BB77E	87425	51150	56650	58300	65400
Premium Pkg				900	900	1200	1200
Adaptive Cruise Control				500	500	665	665
G-CLASS 4WD—V8—Truck Equipment Schedule T3							
G500 Sport Util 4D		YR49E	86975				
designo Edition							
G-CLASS 4WD—V8 Supercharged—Truck Equipment Sch T3							
G55 Sport Utility 4D		YR71E	110675				
GL-CLASS 4WD—V6 Turbo Diesel—Truck Equipment Schedule T3							
GL320 CDI Spt Utl		BF22E	53775	43425	48225	50400	57100
Premium Pkg				375	375	500	500
Adaptive Cruise Control				500	500	665	665
GL-CLASS 4WD—V8—Truck Equipment Schedule T3							
GL450 Sport Util 4D		BF71E	56275	41550	46050	48100	54600
GL550 Sport Util 4D		BF86E	77750	53500	59300	61300	68800
Premium Pkg				375	375	500	500
Adaptive Cruise Control				500	500	665	665
R-CLASS 4WD—V6 Turbo Diesel—Truck Equipment Schedule T3							
R320 CDI Sport Wag		CB22E	46175				
Premium Pkg							
Distronic Cruise Control							
R-CLASS 4WD—V6—Truck Equipment Schedule T3							
R350 Sport Wagon		CB65E	45175	30475	33900	36100	41700
Premium Pkg				900	900	1200	1200
Distronic Cruise				500	500	665	665
2WD				(950)	(950)	(1265)	(1265)

MERCURY

1994 MERCURY — 4M2-(V11W)-R-#

Body	Type	VIN	List	Trade-In Fair	Trade-In Good	Pvt-Party Good	Retail Excellent
VILLAGER—V6—Truck Equipment Schedule T1							
GS Minivan		V11W	19292	275	375	950	1850
LS Minivan		V11W	22975	500	675	1375	2475
Nautica Minivan		V11W	26218	600	825	1625	2925
5 Passenger				(200)	(200)	(265)	(265)

1995 MERCURY

Body	Type	VIN	List	Trade-In Fair	Trade-In Good	Pvt-Party Good	Retail Excellent
1995 MERCURY — 4M2-(V11W)-S-#							
VILLAGER—V6—Truck Equipment Schedule T1							
GS Minivan		V11W	21090	275	375	950	1875
LS Minivan		V11W	24650	525	700	1475	2700
Nautica Minivan		V11W	27535	625	850	1675	3000
5 Passenger				(200)	(200)	(265)	(265)
1996 MERCURY — 4M2-(V11W)-T-#							
VILLAGER—V6—Truck Equipment Schedule T1							
GS Minivan		V11W	21745	325	475	1100	2100
LS Minivan		V11W	25595	625	825	1675	3000
Nautica Minivan		V11W	28375	725	1025	1950	3375
5 Passenger				(250)	(250)	(335)	(335)
1997 MERCURY — 4M(2or4)-(U55P)-V-#							
MOUNTAINEER AWD—V8—Truck Equipment Schedule T1							
Sport Utility 4D		U55P	29995	1350	1850	3075	4875
2WD		2		(250)	(250)	(335)	(335)
VILLAGER—V6—Truck Equipment Schedule T1							
GS Minivan		V111	22395	400	575	1225	2300
LS Minivan		V111	27595	700	975	1875	3300
Nautica Minivan		V111	28995	875	1225	2300	3950
5 Passenger				(275)	(275)	(365)	(365)
1998 MERCURY — 4M(2or4)-(U55P)-W-#							
MOUNTAINEER AWD—V8—Truck Equipment Schedule T1							
Sport Utility 4D		U55P	29785	1575	2050	3325	5200
2WD		2		(300)	(300)	(400)	(400)
4WD		4		0	0	0	0
V6 4.0 Liter		E		(200)	(200)	(265)	(265)
VILLAGER—V6—Truck Equipment Schedule T1							
GS Minivan		V111	22885	500	675	1475	2750
LS Minivan		V111	27485	825	1150	2150	3675
Nautica Minivan		V111	28885	1025	1425	2575	4275
5 Passenger				(300)	(300)	(400)	(400)
1999 MERCURY — 4M2-(U55P)-X-#							
MOUNTAINEER AWD—V8—Truck Equipment Schedule T1							
Sport Utility 4D		U55P	30015	1850	2350	3650	5550
2WD		2		(350)	(350)	(465)	(465)
4WD		4		0	0	0	0
V6 4.0 Liter		E		(225)	(225)	(300)	(300)
VILLAGER—V6—Truck Equipment Schedule T1							
Minivan 4D		V11T	22995	625	850	1750	3125
Sport Minivan 4D		V11T	25595	1175	1650	2850	4600
Estate Minivan 4D		V11T	25595	1200	1700	2900	4650
2000 MERCURY — 4M2-(U86P)-Y-#							
MOUNTAINEER AWD—V8—Truck Equipment Schedule T1							
Sport Utility 4D		U86P	30360	2150	2725	4050	6025
Premier				550	550	735	735
2WD		6		(400)	(400)	(535)	(535)
4WD		7		0	0	0	0
V6 4.0 Liter		E		(250)	(250)	(335)	(335)
VILLAGER—V6—Truck Equipment Schedule T1							
Minivan 4D		V11T	22995	750	1075	2075	3600
Sport Minivan 4D		V12T	25995	1450	1925	3175	5000
Estate Minivan 4D		V14T	27695	1550	2025	3275	5125
2001 MERCURY — 4M2-(U86P)-1-#							
MOUNTAINEER AWD—V8—Truck Equipment Schedule T1							
Sport Utility 4D		U86P	30695	2550	3150	4500	6575
Premier				625	625	835	835
2WD		6		(450)	(450)	(600)	(600)
4WD		7		0	0	0	0
V6 4.0 Liter		E		(275)	(275)	(365)	(365)
VILLAGER—V6—Truck Equipment Schedule T1							
Minivan 4D		V11T	23140	975	1350	2525	4275
Sport Minivan 4D		V12T	26365	1800	2325	3625	5525

Body	Type	VIN	List	Trade-In Fair	Good	Pvt-Party Good	Retail Excellent
Estate Minivan 4D		V14T	27840	**1875**	**2425**	**3700**	**5600**

TRUCKS & VANS

2002 MERCURY — 4M2-(U86W)-2-#

MOUNTAINEER AWD—V8—Truck Equipment Schedule T1
Sport Utility 4D		U86W	31310	**3075**	**3750**	**5400**	**7850**
Premier			------	**700**	**700**	**935**	**935**
w/o Third Seat			------	**(800)**	**(800)**	**(1065)**	**(1065)**
2WD		6	------	**(500)**	**(500)**	**(665)**	**(665)**
V6 4.0 Liter		E	------	**(300)**	**(300)**	**(400)**	**(400)**

VILLAGER—V6—Truck Equipment Schedule T1
Minivan 4D		V11T	19995	**1100**	**1525**	**3000**	**5050**
Sport Minivan 4D		V12T	24995	**2050**	**2625**	**4150**	**6350**
Estate Minivan 4D		V14T	26995	**2150**	**2700**	**4250**	**6475**

2003 MERCURY — 4M2-(U86W)-3-#

MOUNTAINEER AWD—V8—Truck Equipment Schedule T1
Sport Utility 4D		U86W	32605	**4525**	**5325**	**7075**	**9775**
Premier			------	**800**	**800**	**1065**	**1065**
w/o Third Seat			------	**(800)**	**(800)**	**(1065)**	**(1065)**
2WD		6	------	**(575)**	**(575)**	**(765)**	**(765)**
V6 4.0L Flex Fuel		K	------	**(350)**	**(350)**	**(465)**	**(465)**

2004 MERCURY — (2MRor4M2)-(A202)-4-#

MONTEREY—V6—Truck Equipment Schedule T1
Minivan		A202	29995	**1350**	**1850**	**3375**	**5525**
Premier			------	**550**	**550**	**735**	**735**

MOUNTAINEER AWD—V8—Truck Equipment Schedule T1
Sport Utility 4D		U86W	32855	**6150**	**7100**	**8925**	**11800**
Premier			------	**900**	**900**	**1200**	**1200**
w/o Third Seat			------	**(800)**	**(800)**	**(1065)**	**(1065)**
2WD		6	------	**(650)**	**(650)**	**(865)**	**(865)**
V6 4.0L Flex Fuel		K	------	**(400)**	**(400)**	**(535)**	**(535)**

2005 MERCURY — (2MRor4M2)-(A222)-5

MONTEREY—V6—Truck Equipment Schedule T1
Minivan		A222	29695	**2100**	**2675**	**4250**	**6500**
Premier			------	**625**	**625**	**835**	**835**

MARINER 4WD—V6—Truck Equipment Schedule T1
Sport Utility 4D		U571	25245	**6250**	**7200**	**9025**	**11900**
2WD		6	------	**(725)**	**(725)**	**(965)**	**(965)**
4-Cyl. 2.3 Liter		Z	------	**(800)**	**(800)**	**(1065)**	**(1065)**

MOUNTAINEER AWD—V8—Truck Equipment Schedule T1
Sport Utility 4D		U86W	33505	**7950**	**9100**	**11000**	**14100**
Premier			------	**1000**	**1000**	**1335**	**1335**
w/o Third Seat			------	**(800)**	**(800)**	**(1065)**	**(1065)**
2WD		6	------	**(725)**	**(725)**	**(965)**	**(965)**
V6 4.0 Liter		E,K	------	**(450)**	**(450)**	**(600)**	**(600)**

2006 MERCURY — (2MRor4M2)-(A222)-6

MONTEREY—V6—Truck Equipment Schedule T1
Minivan		A222	29325	**3175**	**3850**	**5475**	**7875**

MARINER 4WD—4-Cyl. Hybrid—Truck Equipment Schedule T1
Sport Utility 4D		U98H	29840	**11125**	**12600**	**14450**	**17950**

MARINER 4WD—V6—Truck Equipment Schedule T1
Sport Utility 4D		U571	25650	**7375**	**8450**	**10250**	**13250**
Premier			------	**200**	**200**	**265**	**265**
2WD		6	------	**(800)**	**(800)**	**(1065)**	**(1065)**
4-Cyl. 2.3 Liter		Z	------	**(900)**	**(900)**	**(1200)**	**(1200)**

MOUNTAINEER AWD—V8—Truck Equipment Schedule T1
Sport Utility 4D		U468	35195	**10000**	**11325**	**13250**	**16550**
Premier			------	**875**	**875**	**1165**	**1165**
w/o Third Seat			------	**(800)**	**(800)**	**(1065)**	**(1065)**
2WD		3	------	**(800)**	**(800)**	**(1065)**	**(1065)**
V6 4.0 Liter		E	------	**(500)**	**(500)**	**(665)**	**(665)**

2007 MERCURY — (2MRor4M2)-(A222)-7

MONTEREY—V6—Truck Equipment Schedule T1
Minivan		A222	29350	**4750**	**5575**	**7150**	**9625**

MARINER 4WD—4-Cyl. Hybrid—Truck Equipment Schedule T1
Sport Utility 4D		U39H	28615	**12750**	**14400**	**16150**	**19700**

Body	Type	VIN	List	Trade-In Fair	Good	Pvt-Party Good	Retail Excellent
MARINER 4WD—V6—Truck Equipment Schedule T1							
Sport Utility 4D		U901	25420	8700	9900	11650	14750
Premier				200	200	265	265
2WD		8		(875)	(875)	(1165)	(1165)
4-Cyl. 2.3 Liter		Z		(1000)	(1000)	(1335)	(1335)
MOUNTAINEER AWD—V8—Truck Equipment Schedule T1							
Sport Utility 4D		U47E	30270	12250	13875	15700	19150
Premier				950	950	1265	1265
w/o Third Seat				(800)	(800)	(1065)	(1065)
2WD		3		(875)	(875)	(1165)	(1165)
V6 4.0 Liter		E		(550)	(550)	(735)	(735)

2008 MERCURY — (2MRor4M2)–(U39H)–8

Body	Type	VIN	List	Trade-In Fair	Good	Pvt-Party Good	Retail Excellent
MARINER 4WD—4-Cyl. Hybrid—Truck Equipment Schedule T1							
Sport Utility 4D		U39H	28370	16375	18375	20100	23900
2WD		2		(950)	(950)	(1265)	(1265)
MARINER 4WD—V6—Truck Equipment Schedule T1							
Sport Utility 4D		U911	24335	11950	13525	15300	18650
Premier Spt Util 4D		U971	26235	12800	14450	16150	19600
2WD		8		(950)	(950)	(1265)	(1265)
4-Cyl. 2.3 Liter		Z		(1100)	(1100)	(1465)	(1465)
MOUNTAINEER AWD—V8—Truck Equipment Schedule T1							
Sport Utility 4D		U478	32850	14800	16650	18400	22100
Premier		8		1025	1025	1365	1365
w/o Third Row				(800)	(800)	(1065)	(1065)
2WD		3		(950)	(950)	(1265)	(1265)
V6 4.0 Liter		E		(575)	(575)	(765)	(765)

MITSUBISHI

1994 MITSUBISHI–JA(4or7)–(R41H)–R–#

Body	Type	VIN	List	Trade-In Fair	Good	Pvt-Party Good	Retail Excellent
MONTERO 4WD—V6—Truck Equipment Schedule T1							
LS Sport Utility 4D		R41H	26024	1775	2275	3550	5425
SR Sport Utility 4D		R51M	31920	2400	3000	4325	6350
MIGHTY MAX PICKUP—4-Cyl.—Truck Equipment Schedule T2							
Short Bed		S21G	10170	300	425	1000	1925
Macro Cab Short Bed		S23G	11640	625	850	1675	2975
MIGHTY MAX PICKUP 4WD—V6—Truck Equipment Sch T2							
Short Bed		T21H	14639	550	750	1525	2750

1995 MITSUBISHI–JA(4or7)–(R41H)–S–#

Body	Type	VIN	List	Trade-In Fair	Good	Pvt-Party Good	Retail Excellent
MONTERO 4WD—V6—Truck Equipment Schedule T1							
LS Sport Utility 4D		R41H	28920	2075	2650	3950	5875
SR Sport Utility 4D		R51M	35070	2825	3425	4825	6950
MIGHTY MAX PICKUP—4-Cyl.—Truck Equipment Schedule T2							
Short Bed		S21G	10779	350	500	1200	2275

1996 MITSUBISHI — JA4–(R41H)–T–#

Body	Type	VIN	List	Trade-In Fair	Good	Pvt-Party Good	Retail Excellent
MONTERO 4WD—V6—Truck Equipment Schedule T1							
LS Sport Utility 4D		R41H	31458	2325	2900	4250	6225
SR Sport Utility 4D		R51M	38200	3100	3775	5200	7375
MIGHTY MAX PICKUP—4-Cyl.—Truck Equipment Schedule T2							
Short Bed		S21G	11590	400	550	1275	2400

1997 MITSUBISHI — JA4–(S21G)–V–#

Body	Type	VIN	List	Trade-In Fair	Good	Pvt-Party Good	Retail Excellent
MONTERO SPORT 2WD—4-Cyl.—Truck Equipment Schedule T1							
ES Utility 4D		S21G	18980	800	1125	2100	3600
MONTERO SPORT 4WD—V6—Truck Equipment Schedule T1							
LS Utility 4D		T31P	25452	1650	2125	3400	5250
XLS Utility 4D		T41P	31555	1775	2275	3550	5425
2WD		S		(250)	(250)	(335)	(335)
MONTERO 4WD—V6—Truck Equipment Schedule T1							
LS Sport Util 4D		R41R	31040	2600	3175	4550	6625
SR Sport Util 4D		R51R	38827	3475	4200	5650	7925

1998 MITSUBISHI — JA4–(S21G)–W–#

Body	Type	VIN	List	Trade-In Fair	Good	Pvt-Party Good	Retail Excellent
MONTERO SPORT 2WD—4-Cyl.—Truck Equipment Schedule T1							
ES Utility 4D		S21G	19390	800	1150	2150	3675

TRUCKS & VANS

1998 MITSUBISHI

Body	Type	VIN	List	Trade-In Fair	Trade-In Good	Pvt-Party Good	Retail Excellent
MONTERO SPORT 4WD—V6—Truck Equipment Schedule T1							
LS Utility 4D		T31P	26140	**1725**	**2225**	**3500**	**5375**
XLS Utility 4D		T41P	32695	1850	2400	3700	5575
2WD		S		(300)	(300)	(400)	(400)
MONTERO 4WD—V6—Truck Equipment Schedule T1							
Sport Utility 4D		R51R	33975	2875	3500	4900	7025

1999 MITSUBISHI — JA4–(S21G)–X–#

MONTERO SPORT 2WD—4-Cyl.—Truck Equipment Schedule T1							
ES Utility 4D		S21G	19680	**850**	**1200**	**2350**	**4050**
MONTERO SPORT 4WD—V6—Truck Equipment Schedule T1							
LS Utility 4D		T31H	27445	1850	2375	3675	5575
XLS Utility 4D		T31H	29355	2025	2575	3900	5825
Limited Utility 4D		T41R	33085	2625	3225	4575	6650
2WD		S		(350)	(350)	(465)	(465)
MONTERO 4WD—V6—Truck Equipment Schedule T1							
Sport Utility 4D		R51R	31825	3225	3900	5325	7500

2000 MITSUBISHI — JA4–(S21H)–Y–#

MONTERO SPORT 2WD—V6—Truck Equipment Schedule T1							
ES Utility 4D		S21H	22982	**950**	**1350**	**2525**	**4250**
MONTERO SPORT 4WD—V6—Truck Equipment Schedule T1							
LS Utility 4D		T31H	27262	2025	2600	3925	5850
XLS Utility 4D		T31H	29782	2225	2800	4125	6075
Limited Utility 4D		T41R	31812	2875	3475	4875	6950
2WD		S		(400)	(400)	(535)	(535)
MONTERO 4WD—V6—Truck Equipment Schedule T1							
Sport Utility 4D		R51R	32262	3650	4350	5800	8050
Endeavor Pkg				200	200	265	265

2001 MITSUBISHI — JA4–(T21H)–1–#

MONTERO SPORT 4WD—V6—Truck Equipment Schedule T1							
ES Utility 4D		T21H	25467	**1725**	**2225**	**3525**	**5425**
LS Utility 4D		T31H	28177	2325	2900	4250	6225
XS Sport Utility 4D		T31H	29187	2400	3000	4325	6350
XLS Utility 4D		T31H	29827	2500	3075	4425	6450
Limited Utility 4D		T41R	33297	3175	3875	5250	7400
2WD		S		(450)	(450)	(600)	(600)
MONTERO 4WD—V6—Truck Equipment Schedule T1							
XLS Sport Utility 4D		W31R	31817	4275	5050	6525	8850
Limited Spt Util 4D		W51R	35817	4750	5550	7125	9600

2002 MITSUBISHI — JA4–(T21H)–2–#

MONTERO SPORT 4WD—V6—Truck Equipment Schedule T1							
ES Utility 4D		T21H	25647	**1850**	**2375**	**3925**	**6125**
LS Utility 4D		T31H	28337	2500	3075	4675	6975
XLS Utility 4D		T31H	30187	2650	3250	4875	7200
Limited Utility 4D		T41R	33447	3425	4150	5775	8225
2WD		S		(500)	(500)	(665)	(665)
MONTERO 4WD—V6—Truck Equipment Schedule T1							
XLS Sport Utility 4D		W31R	32247	4725	5550	7325	10050
Limited Spt Util 4D		W51R	36357	5250	6125	7925	10750

2003 MITSUBISHI — JA4–(Z31G)–3–#

OUTLANDER AWD—4-Cyl.—Truck Equipment Schedule T1							
LS Sport Utility 4D		Z31G	19877	**3075**	**3725**	**5400**	**7825**
XLS Sport Utility 4D		Z41G	21370	3575	4300	5950	8450
2WD				(575)	(575)	(765)	(765)
MONTERO SPORT 4WD—V6—Truck Equipment Schedule T1							
ES Utility 4D		T21H	25802	2275	2875	4450	6750
LS Utility 4D		T31H	28362	3050	3675	5325	7725
XLS Utility 4D		T31H	30212	3250	3925	5550	7975
Limited Utility 4D		T41R	33472	4150	4900	6600	9150
2WD		S		(575)	(575)	(765)	(765)
MONTERO 4WD—V6—Truck Equipment Schedule T1							
XLS Sport Utility 4D		W31S	33072	5975	6925	8725	11600
Limited Spt Util 4D		W51S	37182	6575	7600	9425	12400

2004 MITSUBISHI — (Jor4)A4–(Z31G)–4–#

OUTLANDER AWD—4-Cyl.—Truck Equipment Schedule T1							
LS Sport Utility 4D		Z31G	20692	**3625**	**4325**	**6000**	**8525**

Body	Type	VIN	List	Trade-In Fair	Trade-In Good	Pvt-Party Good	Retail Excellent
	XLS Sport Utility 4D	Z41G	22792	4200	4950	6675	9225
	2WD	X		(650)	(650)	(865)	(865)
MONTERO SPORT 4WD—V6—Truck Equipment Schedule T1							
	LS Utility 4D	T31R	26392	3800	4525	6175	8650
	XLS Utility 4D	T31R	28592	4050	4800	6450	8975
	2WD	S		(650)	(650)	(865)	(865)
ENDEAVOR AWD—V6—Truck Equipment Schedule T1							
	LS Sport Utility 4D	N21S	28192	3825	4550	6250	8775
	XLS Sport Utility 4D	N31S	30492	4775	5575	7350	10050
	Limited Sport Util 4D	N41S	33792	5400	6275	8025	10850
	2WD	M		(650)	(650)	(865)	(865)
MONTERO 4WD—V6—Truck Equipment Schedule T1							
	Limited Spt Util 4D	W51S	35624	8075	9225	11150	14350

2005 MITSUBISHI — (Jor4)A4(LZ31F)-5

Body	Type	VIN	List	Trade-In Fair	Trade-In Good	Pvt-Party Good	Retail Excellent
OUTLANDER AWD—4-Cyl.—Truck Equipment Schedule T1							
	LS Sport Utility 4D	LZ31F	21244	4325	5125	6800	9400
	XLS Sport Utility 4D	LZ41F	23724	4950	5775	7550	10300
	Limited Sport Util	LZ81F	25774	5625	6575	8325	11100
	2WD	X		(725)	(725)	(965)	(965)
ENDEAVOR AWD—V6—Truck Equipment Schedule T1							
	LS Sport Utility 4D	MN21S	28294	4725	5550	7300	10000
	XLS Sport Util 4D	MN31S	30894	5825	6750	8525	11350
	Limited Sport Util	MN41S	33794	6425	7425	9200	12100
	2WD	X		(725)	(725)	(965)	(965)
MONTERO 4WD—V6—Truck Equipment Schedule T1							
	Limited Spt Util 4D	NW51S	36424	10150	11525	13450	16850

2006 MITSUBISHI — (Jor4)A(3,4or7)(LZ31F)-6

Body	Type	VIN	List	Trade-In Fair	Trade-In Good	Pvt-Party Good	Retail Excellent
OUTLANDER AWD—4-Cyl.—Truck Equipment Schedule T1							
	LS Sport Utility 4D	LZ31F	22094	5225	6100	7850	10600
	SE Sport Utility 4D	LZ41F	23994	5925	6850	8625	11450
	Limited Sport Util	LZ81F	26544	6700	7725	9475	12400
	2WD	X		(800)	(800)	(1065)	(1065)
ENDEAVOR AWD—V6—Truck Equipment Schedule T1							
	LS Sport Utility 4D	MN21S	28294	5900	6825	8600	11400
	Limited Sport Util	MN41S	32894	7725	8850	10650	13600
	2WD	M		(800)	(800)	(1065)	(1065)
MONTERO 4WD—V6—Truck Equipment Schedule T1							
	Limited Sport Util 4D	MW51S	36784	11700	13225	15150	18650
RAIDER EXTENDED CAB—V6—Truck Equipment Schedule T1							
	LS Short Bed	HC22K	22400	4600	5425	7150	9800
	DuroCross Short	HC32K	24085	5325	6200	7950	10700
	4WD	T		1950	1950	2600	2600
	V8 4.7 Liter	N		700	700	935	935
RAIDER DOUBLE CAB—V6—Truck Equipment Schedule T1							
	LS Short Bed	HC28K	24325	6200	7175	8925	11750
	DuroCross Short	HC38K	26010	6325	7300	9050	11900
	4WD	T		1950	1950	2600	2600
	V8 4.7 Liter	N		700	700	935	935
RAIDER DOUBLE CAB—V8—Truck Equipment Schedule T1							
	XLS Short Bed	HC48K	31320	7475	8575	10350	13300
	AWD			1950	1950	2600	2600

2007 MITSUBISHI — (Jor4)A(3,4or7)(MS31X)-7

Body	Type	VIN	List	Trade-In Fair	Trade-In Good	Pvt-Party Good	Retail Excellent
OUTLANDER—V6—Truck Equipment Schedule T1							
	ES Sport Utility 4D	MS31X	21995	7050	8100	9800	12650
	Third Seat			450	450	600	600
OUTLANDER 4WD—V6—Truck Equipment Schedule T1							
	LS Sport Utility 4D	MT31X	23033	8550	9775	11500	14600
	XLS Sport Util 4D	MT41X	25635	9325	10625	12400	15550
	Third Seat			450	450	600	600
	2WD	X		(875)	(875)	(1165)	(1165)
ENDEAVOR AWD—V6—Truck Equipment Schedule T1							
	LS Sport Utility 4D	MN21S	29624	7325	8400	10100	12950
	SE Sport Utility 4D	MN31S	31374	9250	10525	12250	15400
	2WD	M		(875)	(875)	(1165)	(1165)
RAIDER EXTENDED CAB—V6—Truck Equipment Schedule T1							
	LS Short Bed	HC22K	23665	5650	6600	8225	10900
RAIDER DOUBLE CAB—V6—Truck Equipment Schedule T1							
	LS Short Bed	HC28K	24650	7400	8500	10150	13000
	DuroCross Short	HC38K	27395	7525	8625	10300	13200

TRUCKS & VANS

Body	Type	VIN	List	Trade-In Fair	Trade-In Good	Pvt-Party Good	Retail Excellent
4WD		T		2125	2125	2835	2835
V8 4.7 Liter		N		750	750	1000	1000
RAIDER DOUBLE CAB—V8—Truck Equipment Schedule T1							
SE Short Bed		HC28N	27355	8025	9200	10950	13900

2008 MITSUBISHI—(Jor4)A(3,4or7)–(MT31W)–8

Body	Type	VIN	List	Trade-In Fair	Trade-In Good	Pvt-Party Good	Retail Excellent
OUTLANDER 4WD—4-Cyl.—Truck Equipment Schedule T1							
ES Sport Utility 4D		MT31W	22000	12000	13575	15350	18700
SE Sport Utility 4D		MS31W	25240	14450	16225	18000	21600
Third Row				475	475	635	635
2WD		S		(950)	(950)	(1265)	(1265)
OUTLANDER 4WD—V6—Truck Equipment Schedule T1							
LS Sport Utility 4D		MT31X	24520	13625	15325	17050	20600
XLS Sport Util 4D		MT41X	25760	15375	17300	18950	22600
Third Row				475	475	635	635
2WD		S		(950)	(950)	(1265)	(1265)
ENDEAVOR AWD—V6—Truck Equipment Schedule T1							
LS Sport Utility 4D		MN21S	29724	9000	10250	11950	15000
SE Sport Utility 4D		MN31S	31524	11075	12550	14200	17450
2WD		M		(950)	(950)	(1265)	(1265)
RAIDER EXTENDED CAB—V6—Truck Equipment Schedule T1							
LS Short Bed		HC22K	23735	7250	8325	9900	12600
RAIDER DOUBLE CAB—V6—Truck Equipment Schedule T1							
LS Short Bed		HC28K	25795	9125	10400	12050	15050
4WD		T		2300	2300	3065	3065

NISSAN

1994 NISSAN — (JN8or1N6)(HD17Y)–R–#

Body	Type	VIN	List	Trade-In Fair	Trade-In Good	Pvt-Party Good	Retail Excellent
PATHFINDER 4WD—V6—Truck Equipment Schedule T1							
XE Sport Utility 4D		HD17Y	23844	975	1350	2475	4125
SE Sport Utility 4D		HD17Y	27484	1450	1925	3175	4975
LE Sport Utility 4D		HD17Y	29379	1775	2275	3550	5425
2WD		S		(125)	(125)	(165)	(165)
QUEST—V6—Truck Equipment Schedule T1							
XE Minivan		DN11W	18909	450	600	1250	2300
GXE Minivan		DN11W	23419	625	900	1725	3050
PICKUP—4-Cyl.—Truck Equipment Schedule T2							
Short Bed		SD11S	9739	425	600	1300	2450
XE Short Bed		SD11S	10509	425	600	1275	2400
XE King Cab		SD16S	12059	725	1000	1900	3300
4WD		Y		400	400	535	535
V6 3.0 Liter		H		125	125	165	165
PICKUP—V6—Truck Equipment Schedule T2							
Long Bed		HD12S	11569	500	675	1425	2625
SE King Cab		HD16S	14659	775	1100	2000	3425
4WD		Y		400	400	535	535

1995 NISSAN — (JN8or4N2)(HD17Y)–S–#

Body	Type	VIN	List	Trade-In Fair	Trade-In Good	Pvt-Party Good	Retail Excellent
PATHFINDER 4WD—V6—Truck Equipment Schedule T1							
XE Sport Utility 4D		HD17Y	24988	1100	1525	2700	4375
SE Sport Utility 4D		HD17Y	29028	1725	2225	3475	5350
LE Sport Utility 4D		HD17Y	30749	2025	2600	3900	5800
2WD		S		(125)	(125)	(165)	(165)
QUEST—V6—Truck Equipment Schedule T1							
XE Minivan		DN11W	20229	450	625	1300	2400
GXE Minivan		DN11W	24999	650	925	1775	3125
PICKUP—4-Cyl.—Truck Equipment Schedule T2							
Short Bed		SD11S	10319	500	675	1450	2650
XE Short Bed		SD11S	11399	475	650	1425	2625
XE King Cab		SD16S	13079	825	1150	2100	3600
4WD		Y		400	400	535	535
V6 3.0 Liter		H		125	125	165	165
PICKUP—V6—Truck Equipment Schedule T2							
Long Bed		HD11S	12479	575	775	1600	2875
4WD		Y		400	400	535	535
PICKUP 4WD—V6—Truck Equipment Schedule T2							
SE King Cab		HD16Y	20989	1300	1775	3000	4750

Body	Type	VIN	List	Trade-In Fair	Good	Pvt-Party Good	Retail Excellent

TRUCKS & VANS

1996 NISSAN — (JN8or4N2)(AR05Y)–T–#

PATHFINDER 4WD—V6—Truck Equipment Schedule T1

Body	Type	VIN	List	Fair	Good	Good	Excellent
XE Sport Utility 4D		AR05Y	26803	1225	1700	2925	4675
SE Sport Utility 4D		AR05Y	29748	1950	2500	3800	5700
LE Sport Utility 4D		AR05Y	32129	2325	2900	4250	6225
2WD		S		(200)	(200)	(265)	(265)

QUEST—V6—Truck Equipment Schedule T1

| XE Minivan | | DN11W | 21304 | 550 | 750 | 1550 | 2825 |
| GXE Minivan | | DN11W | 26104 | 775 | 1100 | 2025 | 3500 |

PICKUP—4-Cyl.—Truck Equipment Schedule T2

Short Bed		SD11S	11404	550	750	1550	2825
XE Short Bed		SD11S	13469	625	825	1675	3000
XE King Cab		SD16S	14554	975	1375	2500	4175
SE King Cab		SD16S	17004	1050	1475	2625	4325
4WD		Y		525	525	700	700

1997 NISSAN — (JN8,1N6or4N2)(AR05Y)–V–#

PATHFINDER 4WD—V6—Truck Equipment Schedule T1

XE Sport Utility 4D		AR05Y	27318	1600	2075	3350	5225
SE Sport Utility 4D		AR05Y	30568	2250	2850	4175	6175
LE Sport Utility 4D		AR05Y	32719	2650	3225	4625	6700
2WD		S		(250)	(250)	(335)	(335)

QUEST—V6—Truck Equipment Schedule T1

| XE Minivan | | DN111 | 21669 | 625 | 900 | 1775 | 3150 |
| GXE Minivan | | DN111 | 26469 | 925 | 1300 | 2400 | 4075 |

PICKUP—4-Cyl.—Truck Equipment Schedule T2

Short Bed		SD11S	11469	625	850	1725	3075
XE Short Bed		SD11S	13469	675	975	1875	3300
XE King Cab		SD16S	15119	1150	1625	2825	4550
SE King Cab		SD16S	17519	1350	1825	3075	4850
4WD		Y		650	650	865	865

1998 NISSAN — (JN8,4N2or1N6)(AR05Y)–W–#

PATHFINDER 4WD—V6—Truck Equipment Schedule T1

XE Sport Utility 4D		AR05Y	27489	1975	2525	3825	5750
SE Sport Utility 4D		AR05Y	30589	2625	3200	4575	6650
LE Sport Utility 4D		AR05Y	33339	2975	3600	5025	7150
2WD		S		(300)	(300)	(400)	(400)

QUEST—V6—Truck Equipment Schedule T1

XE Minivan		DN111	23589	750	1075	2050	3550
GXE Minivan		DN111	26539	1075	1500	2700	4400
GLE Minivan		DN111	27838	1200	1700	2925	4675

FRONTIER PICKUP—4-Cyl.—Truck Equipment Schedule T2

Short Bed		DD21S	12480	800	1125	2125	3675
XE Short Bed		DD21S	13680	875	1250	2375	4050
XE King Cab		DD26S	15130	1525	2025	3275	5125
SE King Cab		DD26S	18480	1850	2375	3650	5550
4WD		Y		775	775	1035	1035

1999 NISSAN — (1N6,4N2orJN8)(AR05Y)–X

PATHFINDER 4WD—V6—Truck Equipment Schedule T1

XE Sport Utility 4D		AR05Y	27669	2425	3025	4350	6375
SE Sport Utility 4D		AR05Y	30769	3000	3625	5025	7150
LE Sport Utility 4D		AR05Y	33469	3325	4025	5450	7650
2WD		S		(350)	(350)	(465)	(465)

PATHFINDER 4WD (1999.5)—V6—Truck Equip Schedule T1

XE Sport Utility 4D		AR07Y	28819	2500	3100	4425	6475
SE Sport Utility 4D		AR07Y	30769	3100	3750	5175	7325
LE Sport Utility 4D		AR07Y	31719	3675	4375	5825	8075
2WD		S		(350)	(350)	(465)	(465)

QUEST—V6—Truck Equipment Schedule T1

GXE Minivan		XN11T	22679	925	1300	2450	4150
SE Minivan		XN11T	24419	1275	1750	3000	4775
GLE Minivan		XN11T	26819	1500	1975	3225	5075

FRONTIER—4-Cyl.—Truck Equipment Schedule T2

XE Short Bed		DD21S	12010	975	1375	2550	4300
XE King Cab		DD26S	14010	1775	2300	3600	5500
SE King Cab		DD26S	15510	2175	2750	4100	6050
4WD		Y		900	900	1200	1200
V6 3.3 Liter		E		225	225	300	300

Body	Type	VIN	List	Trade-In Fair	Trade-In Good	Pvt-Party Good	Retail Excellent

TRUCKS & VANS

2000 NISSAN—(1N6,4N2,5N1orJN8)(ED28Y)–Y–#

XTERRA 4WD—V6—Truck Equipment Schedule T1
XE Sport Utility 4D	ED28Y	22019	**2500**	**3100**	**4450**	**6500**
SE Sport Utility 4D	ED28Y	26069	**2925**	**3575**	**4950**	**7075**
2WD	T		**(400)**	**(400)**	**(535)**	**(535)**
4-Cyl. 2.4 Liter	D		**(350)**	**(350)**	**(465)**	**(465)**

PATHFINDER 4WD—V6—Truck Equipment Schedule T1
XE Sport Utility 4D	AR05Y	28919	**2900**	**3525**	**4925**	**7050**
SE Sport Utility 4D	AR05Y	30869	**3450**	**4150**	**5550**	**7800**
LE Sport Utility 4D	AR05Y	31819	**3775**	**4500**	**5950**	**8225**
2WD	S		**(400)**	**(400)**	**(535)**	**(535)**

QUEST—V6—Truck Equipment Schedule T1
GXE Minivan	XN11T	22779	**1100**	**1525**	**2775**	**4525**
SE Minivan	XN11T	24919	**1600**	**2075**	**3375**	**5250**
GLE Minivan	XN11T	26919	**1800**	**2325**	**3625**	**5525**

FRONTIER—4-Cyl.—Truck Equipment Schedule T2
XE Short Bed	DD21S	12110	**1100**	**1550**	**2775**	**4550**
XE King Cab	DD26S	14060	**2050**	**2625**	**3950**	**5900**
4WD	Y		**1025**	**1025**	**1365**	**1365**
V6 3.3 Liter	E		**250**	**250**	**335**	**335**

FRONTIER—V6—Truck Equipment Schedule T2
Desrt Rnr XE King	ED26S	16260	**2400**	**3000**	**4325**	**6350**
Desrt Rnr SE King	ED26S	18410	**2525**	**3125**	**4475**	**6525**
SE King Cab	DD26Y	21010	**2475**	**3075**	**4425**	**6475**
XE Crew Cab 4D	ED27S	17810	**2800**	**3425**	**4800**	**6900**
SE Crew Cab 4D	ED27S	19110	**3025**	**3650**	**5075**	**7200**
4WD	Y		**1025**	**1025**	**1365**	**1365**

2001 NISSAN—(1N6,4N2,5N1orJN8)(ED28Y)–1–#

XTERRA 4WD—V6—Truck Equipment Schedule T1
XE Sport Utility 4D	ED28Y	22569	**2975**	**3600**	**5000**	**7125**
SE Sport Utility 4D	ED28Y	26619	**3400**	**4100**	**5525**	**7725**
2WD	T		**(450)**	**(450)**	**(600)**	**(600)**
4-Cyl. 2.4 Liter	D		**(375)**	**(375)**	**(500)**	**(500)**

PATHFINDER 4WD—V6—Truck Equipment Schedule T1
XE Sport Utility 4D	DR07Y	30169	**3475**	**4175**	**5600**	**7825**
SE Sport Utility 4D	DR07Y	30869	**3975**	**4725**	**6175**	**8475**
LE Sport Utility 4D	DR07Y	31819	**4300**	**5075**	**6550**	**8875**
2WD	X		**(450)**	**(450)**	**(600)**	**(600)**
AWD	Y		**0**	**0**	**0**	**0**

QUEST—V6—Truck Equipment Schedule T1
GXE Minivan	ZN15T	22959	**1375**	**1850**	**3100**	**4950**
SE Minivan	ZN16T	24919	**1925**	**2475**	**3775**	**5700**
GLE Minivan	ZN17T	27569	**2175**	**2750**	**4075**	**6025**

FRONTIER—4-Cyl.—Truck Equipment Schedule T2
XE Short Bed	DD21S	12219	**1325**	**1800**	**3075**	**4925**
XE King Cab	DD26S	14169	**2425**	**3025**	**4350**	**6400**
4WD	Y		**1150**	**1150**	**1535**	**1535**
V6 3.3 Liter	E		**250**	**250**	**335**	**335**

FRONTIER—V6—Truck Equipment Schedule T2
Desrt Rnr XE King	ED26T	16469	**2800**	**3425**	**4800**	**6875**
Desrt Rnr SE King	ED26T	18619	**2950**	**3575**	**4975**	**7075**
SE King Cab	ED26Y	21219	**2900**	**3525**	**4925**	**7025**
XE Crew Cab 4D	ED27T	18569	**3225**	**3900**	**5325**	**7500**
SE Crew Cab 4D	ED27T	20719	**3450**	**4150**	**5575**	**7800**
4WD	Y		**1150**	**1150**	**1535**	**1535**

FRONTIER—V6 Supercharged—Truck Equipment Schedule T2
King Cab	MD26T	20519	**2775**	**3400**	**4775**	**6850**
Crew Cab 4D	MD27T	21969	**3350**	**4050**	**5475**	**7675**
4WD	Y		**1150**	**1150**	**1535**	**1535**

2002 NISSAN—(1N6,5N1orJN8)(ED28Y)–2–#

XTERRA 4WD—V6—Truck Equipment Schedule T1
XE Sport Utility 4D	ED28Y	22739	**3300**	**4000**	**5625**	**8075**
SE Sport Utility 4D	ED28Y	26739	**3800**	**4500**	**6175**	**8700**
2WD	T		**(500)**	**(500)**	**(665)**	**(665)**
4-Cyl. 2.4 Liter	D		**(400)**	**(400)**	**(535)**	**(535)**

XTERRA 4WD—V6 Supercharged—Truck Equipment Schedule T1
XE S/C Spt Util 4D	MD28T	26239	**3575**	**4300**	**5925**	**8425**
SE S/C Spt Util 4D	MD28T	28039	**4425**	**5225**	**6975**	**9650**
2WD	T		**(500)**	**(500)**	**(665)**	**(665)**

Body　Type	VIN	List	Trade-In Fair	Trade-In Good	Pvt-Party Good	Retail Excellent
PATHFINDER 4WD—V6—Truck Equipment Schedule T1						
SE Sport Utility 4D	DR07Y	29189	4375	5175	6925	9600
LE Sport Utility 4D	DR07Y	32039	4675	5525	7275	10000
2WD	X	....	(500)	(500)	(665)	(665)
QUEST—V6—Truck Equipment Schedule T1						
GXE Minivan	ZN15T	23279	1575	2075	3625	5775
SE Minivan	ZN16T	25039	2175	2750	4325	6600
GLE Minivan	ZN17T	27689	2450	3050	4625	6925
FRONTIER KING CAB—4-Cyl.—Truck Equipment Schedule T2						
Short Bed	ED27S	13339	2650	3250	4850	7200
XE Short Bed	DD26S	14339	2650	3250	4850	7200
4WD	Y	....	1250	1250	1665	1665
V6 3.3 Liter	E	....	250	250	335	335
FRONTIER KING CAB—V6—Truck Equipment Schedule T2						
Desert Runner XE	ED26T	16539	3075	3700	5350	7750
Desert Runner SE	ED26T	19739	3225	3900	5525	7975
SE Short Bed	ED26Y	22339	3175	3850	5500	7925
4WD	Y	....	1250	1250	1665	1665
FRONTIER CREW CAB—V6—Truck Equipment Schedule T2						
XE Short Bed	ED27T	18739	3550	4275	5925	8400
XE Long Bed	ED27T	19299	3425	4125	5750	8225
SE Short Bed	ED27T	22239	3775	4500	6175	8675
SE Long Bed	ED27T	22799	3600	4300	5975	8450
4WD	Y	....	1250	1250	1665	1665
FRONTIER KING CAB—V6 Supercharged—Truck Equipment Schedule T2						
Short Bed	MD26T	20889	3050	3675	5325	7725
4WD	Y	....	1250	1250	1665	1665
FRONTIER CREW CAB—V6 Supercharged—Truck Equipment Schedule T2						
Short Bed	MD27T	23739	3700	4400	6075	8575
Long Bed	MD27T	24299	3500	4225	5850	8325
4WD	Y	....	1250	1250	1665	1665
2003 NISSAN–(1N6,5N1orJN8)(ED28Y)-3-#						
XTERRA 4WD—V6—Truck Equipment Schedule T1						
XE Sport Utility 4D	ED28Y	23939	4250	5025	6700	9250
SE Sport Utility 4D	ED28Y	27239	4775	5600	7350	10050
2WD	T	....	(575)	(575)	(765)	(765)
4-Cyl. 2.4 Liter	D	....	(475)	(475)	(635)	(635)
XTERRA 4WD—V6 Supercharged—Truck Equipment Schedule T1						
SE S/C Spt Util 4D	MD28T	28539	5525	6450	8200	11050
2WD	T	....	(575)	(575)	(765)	(765)
MURANO AWD—V6—Truck Equipment Schedule T1						
SL Sport Utility 4D	AZ08W	30339	7775	8900	10800	13950
SE Sport Utility 4D	AZ08W	31139	7875	9000	10950	14150
2WD		....	(575)	(575)	(765)	(765)
PATHFINDER 4WD—V6—Truck Equipment Schedule T1						
SE Sport Utility 4D	DR09Y	29339	5150	6000	7775	10550
LE Sport Utility 4D	DR09Y	34339	5550	6475	8275	11100
2WD	X	....	(575)	(575)	(765)	(765)
FRONTIER KING CAB—4-Cyl.—Truck Equipment Schedule T2						
Short Bed	ED27S	13529	3175	3850	5525	7950
XE Short Bed	DD26S	14579	3325	4025	5675	8125
4WD	Y	....	1425	1425	1900	1900
V6 3.3 Liter	E	....	300	300	400	400
FRONTIER KING CAB—V6—Truck Equipment Schedule T2						
Desert Runner XE	ED26T	16709	3750	4450	6125	8625
Desert Runner SE	ED26T	21109	3975	4725	6400	8950
FRONTIER KING CAB 4WD—V6—Truck Equipment Schedule T2						
SE Short Bed	ED26Y	23709	3975	4725	6400	8950
FRONTIER CREW CAB—V6—Truck Equipment Schedule T2						
XE Short Bed	ED27T	18979	4325	5125	6825	9475
XE Long Bed	ED27T	19529	4250	5025	6700	9250
SE Short Bed	ED27T	22829	4625	5450	7200	9900
SE Long Bed	ED27T	23379	4500	5300	7025	9700
4WD	E	....	1425	1425	1900	1900
FRONTIER KING CAB—V6 Supercharged—Truck Equipment Schedule T2						
Short Bed	MD26T	21359	3950	4675	6350	8875
4WD	Y	....	1425	1425	1900	1900
FRONTIER CREW CAB—V6 Supercharged—Truck Equipment Schedule T2						
Short Bed	MD27T	24329	4675	5500	7250	9950
Long Bed	MD27T	24879	4575	5375	7125	9800
4WD	Y	....	1425	1425	1900	1900

TRUCKS & VANS

TRUCKS & VANS

Body	Type	VIN	List	Trade-In Fair	Trade-In Good	Pvt-Party Good	Retail Excellent
2004 NISSAN—(1N6,5N1orJN8)(ED28Y)—4—#								
XTERRA 4WD—V6—Truck Equipment Schedule T1								
XE Sport Utility 4D	ED28Y	22940	5325	6200	7975	10750
SE Sport Utility 4D	ED28Y	27240	5925	6850	8625	11450
2WD	T		(650)	(650)	(865)	(865)
4-Cyl. 2.4 Liter	D		(550)	(550)	(735)	(735)
XTERRA 4WD—V6 Supercharged—Truck Equipment Schedule T1								
SE S/C Spt Util 4D	MD28T	28540	6750	7800	9625	12600
2WD	T		(650)	(650)	(865)	(865)
MURANO AWD—V6—Truck Equipment Schedule T1								
SL Sport Utility 4D	AZ08B	30340	9125	10400	12350	15700
SE Sport Utility 4D	AZ08B	31290	9250	10525	12500	15900
2WD	T		(650)	(650)	(865)	(865)
QUEST—V6—Truck Equipment Schedule T1								
S Minivan	BV28U	24780	3775	4500	6150	8625
SL Minivan	BV28U	27280	4300	5100	6800	9425
SE Minivan	BV28U	32780	4450	5250	6950	9575
PATHFINDER 4WD—V6—Truck Equipment Schedule T1								
SE Sport Utility 4D	DR09Y	29440	6050	7000	8825	11700
LE Sport Utility 4D	DR09Y	34590	6625	7650	9450	12400
2WD	X		(650)	(650)	(865)	(865)
PATHFINDER ARMADA 4WD—V8—Truck Equipment Schedule T1								
SE Sport Utility 4D	AA08B	36750	7200	8275	10100	13150
SE Off-Road Spt Utl	AA08B	39900	8275	9475	11400	14650
LE Sport Utility 4D	AA08B	41250	8825	10050	12000	15300
2WD	A		(650)	(650)	(865)	(865)
FRONTIER KING CAB—4-Cyl.—Truck Equipment Schedule T2								
Short Bed	ED27S	13830	3875	4600	6275	8800
XE Short Bed	DD26S	14880	4175	4925	6625	9200
4WD	Y		1600	1600	2135	2135
V6 3.3 Liter	E		350	350	465	465
FRONTIER KING CAB—V6—Truck Equipment Schedule T2								
Desert Runner XE	ED26T	17030	4500	5300	7025	9700
FRONTIER KING CAB 4WD—V6 Supercharged—Truck Equip Sched T2								
Short Bed	MD26T	25430	4925	5775	7525	10250
FRONTIER CREW CAB—V6—Truck Equipment Schedule T2								
XE Short Bed	ED27T	19360	5250	6125	7875	10650
XE Long Bed	ED27T	19910	5150	6025	7800	10550
LE Short Bed	ED27T	24900	5750	6700	8450	11250
LE Long Bed	ED27T	25450	5525	6400	8175	11000
4WD	Y		1600	1600	2135	2135
FRONTIER CREW CAB—V6 Supercharged—Truck Equipment Schedule T2								
Short Bed	MD27T	24810	5800	6750	8500	11300
Long Bed	MD27T	25360	5750	6700	8450	11250
4WD	Y		1600	1600	2135	2135
TITAN KING CAB—V8—Truck Equipment Schedule T1								
XE Short Bed	AA06A	23050	5175	6025	7925	10850
SE Short Bed	AA06A	25050	5850	6775	8725	11700
LE Short Bed	AA06A	29450	6050	7000	8975	12000
4WD	B		1550	1550	2065	2065
TITAN CREW CAB—V8—Truck Equipment Schedule T1								
XE Short Bed	AA07A	25750	6550	7550	9475	12600
SE Short Bed	AA07A	27350	7275	8350	10350	13550
LE Short Bed	AA07A	31750	7725	8850	10850	14100
4WD	B		1550	1550	2065	2065
2005 NISSAN—(1N6,5N1orJN8)(AN08W)—5—#								
XTERRA 4WD—V6—Truck Equipment Schedule T1								
S Sport Utility 4D	AN08W	24280	6500	7475	9225	12100
Off-Road Sport Util	AN08W	27280	6750	7800	9575	12500
SE Sport Utility 4D	AN08W	27880	7150	8225	10000	12950
2WD	T		(725)	(725)	(965)	(965)
MURANO AWD—V6—Truck Equipment Schedule T1								
S Sport Utility 4D	AZ08W	29180	9575	10875	12800	16100
SL Sport Utility 4D	AZ08W	30680	10625	12050	13950	17450
SE Sport Utility 4D	AZ08W	31630	10725	12150	14050	17550
2WD	T		(725)	(725)	(965)	(965)
QUEST—V6—Truck Equipment Schedule T1								
Minivan	BV28U	23910	4050	4800	6450	8950
S Minivan	BV28U	25110	4900	5725	7450	10100
SL Minivan	BV28U	26810	5525	6450	8150	10900

Body	Type	VIN	List	Trade-In Fair	Trade-In Good	Pvt-Party Good	Retail Excellent
SE Minivan		BV28U	32810	5950	6875	8625	11400
PATHFINDER 4WD—V6—Truck Equipment Schedule T1							
XE Sport Utility 4D		AR19W	27300	7450	8525	10350	13350
SE Sport Utility 4D		AR18W	28500	8600	9800	11650	14900
SE Off-Road Util		AR18W	31280	8650	9850	11700	14950
LE Sport Utility 4D		AR18W	35400	9250	10525	12400	15700
2WD		U		(725)	(725)	(965)	(965)
ARMADA 4WD—V8—Truck Equipment Schedule T1							
SE Sport Utility 4D		AA08B	37050	8250	9425	11300	14500
SE Off-Road Spt Utl		AA08B	40420	9475	10775	12700	16000
LE Sport Utility 4D		AA08B	42150	10150	11525	13500	16900
2WD		A		(725)	(725)	(965)	(965)
FRONTIER KING CAB—4-Cyl.—Truck Equipment Schedule T1							
XE Short Bed		BD06T	16080	4600	5425	7150	9800
FRONTIER KING CAB—V6—Truck Equipment Schedule T2							
SE Short Bed		AD06T	18980	5075	5925	7675	10400
LE Short Bed		AD06T	22780	6275	7250	9050	11900
Nismo Short Bed		AD06U	22580	6450	7450	9200	12100
4WD		Y		1775	1775	2365	2365
FRONTIER CREW CAB—V6—Truck Equipment Schedule T2							
SE Short Bed		AD07T	21130	6400	7375	9150	12000
LE Short Bed		AD07T	24480	6850	7925	9700	12650
Nismo Short Bed		AD07U	24630	7600	8700	10500	13500
4WD		Y		1775	1775	2365	2365
TITAN KING CAB—V8—Truck Equipment Schedule T1							
XE Short Bed		AA06A	23300	5800	6750	8700	11700
SE Short Bed		AA06A	25450	6600	7600	9550	12700
LE Short Bed		AA06A	29900	6825	7900	9850	13050
4WD		B		1725	1725	2300	2300
TITAN CREW CAB—V8—Truck Equipment Schedule T1							
XE Short Bed		AA07A	26150	7375	8450	10450	13650
SE Short Bed		AA07A	27950	8150	9325	11350	14750
LE Short Bed		AA07A	32700	8775	10000	12050	15500
4WD		B		1725	1725	2300	2300

2006 NISSAN—(1N6,5N1orJN8)(AN08W)-6-#

Body	Type	VIN	List	Trade-In Fair	Trade-In Good	Pvt-Party Good	Retail Excellent
XTERRA 4WD—V6—Truck Equipment Schedule T1							
X Sport Utility 4D		AN08W	23330	6725	7725	9450	12350
S Sport Utility 4D		AN08W	25530	7775	8900	10650	13600
Off-Road Spt Util		AN08W	27630	8075	9225	11050	14100
SE Sport Utility 4D		AN08W	28230	8500	9725	11500	14650
2WD		U		(800)	(800)	(1065)	(1065)
MURANO AWD—V6—Truck Equipment Schedule T1							
S Sport Utility 4D		AZ08W	29805	11175	12650	14500	18000
SL Sport Utility 4D		AZ08W	31355	12250	13875	15800	19350
SE Sport Utility 4D		AZ08W	32305	12400	14025	15900	19500
2WD		T		(800)	(800)	(1065)	(1065)
QUEST—V6—Truck Equipment Schedule T1							
Minivan		BV28U	24580	5450	6325	8000	10750
S Special Edition		BV28U	25880	6200	7175	8900	11700
SL Minivan		BV28U	27480	7075	8125	9850	12750
SE Minivan		BV28U	34000	7775	8900	10650	13550
PATHFINDER 4WD—V6—Truck Equipment Schedule T1							
S Sport Utility 4D		AR19W	27830	8600	9800	11650	14850
SE Sport Utility 4D		AR18W	29080	10000	11325	13250	16550
SE Off-Road Util		AR18W	31880	10000	11325	13250	16550
LE Sport Utility 4D		AR18W	36130	10775	12200	14050	17500
2WD		U		(800)	(800)	(1065)	(1065)
ARMADA 4WD—V8—Truck Equipment Schedule T1							
SE Sport Utility 4D		AA08W	37970	9725	11025	12950	16250
SE Off-Road Util		AA08W	41505	11075	12550	14450	17950
LE Sport Utility 4D		AA08W	43270	11900	13475	15400	18950
2WD		A		(800)	(800)	(1065)	(1065)
FRONTIER KING CAB—4-Cyl.—Truck Equipment Schedule T2							
XE Short Bed		BD06T	16480	5525	6425	8150	10950
FRONTIER KING CAB—V6—Truck Equipment Schedule T2							
SE Short Bed		AD06T	19680	6100	7050	8800	11600
LE Short Bed		AD06T	23230	7400	8500	10250	13250
Nismo Short Bed		AD06U	23030	7600	8725	10450	13450
4WD		Y		1950	1950	2600	2600
FRONTIER CREW CAB—V6—Truck Equipment Schedule T2							
SE Short Bed		AD07T	21530	7575	8675	10450	13400
LE Short Bed		AD07T	24930	8100	9275	11050	14150

TRUCKS & VANS

Body	Type	VIN	List	Trade-In Fair	Trade-In Good	Pvt-Party Good	Retail Excellent
Nismo Short Bed		AD07U	25080	8875	10100	11900	15100
4WD		Y		1950	1950	2600	2600
TITAN KING CAB—V8—Truck Equipment Schedule T1							
XE Short Bed		AA06A	23920	6500	7475	9450	12600
SE Short Bed		AA06A	26070	7325	8425	10400	13600
LE Short Bed		AA06A	30870	7675	8775	10800	14000
4WD		B		1900	1900	2535	2535
TITAN CREW CAB—V8—Truck Equipment Schedule T1							
XE Short Bed		AA07A	26770	8200	9375	11400	14800
SE Short Bed		AA07A	28570	9100	10350	12400	15900
LE Short Bed		AA07A	33370	9850	11175	13250	16800
4WD		B		1900	1900	2535	2535

2007 NISSAN—(1N6,5N1orJN8)(AN08W)—7—#

Body	Type	VIN	List	Trade-In Fair	Trade-In Good	Pvt-Party Good	Retail Excellent
XTERRA 4WD—V6—Truck Equipment Schedule T1							
X Sport Utility 4D		AN08W	23505	8025	9200	10950	13900
S Sport Utility 4D		AN08W	25755	9175	10425	12200	15300
Off-Road Sport Util		AN08W	27805	9525	10825	12600	15750
SE Sport Utility 4D		AN08W	28555	10000	11325	13100	16250
2WD		U		(875)	(875)	(1165)	(1165)
MURANO AWD—V6—Truck Equipment Schedule T1							
S Sport Utility 4D		AZ08W	30000	12875	14500	16300	19800
SL Sport Utility 4D		AZ08W	31550	14075	15875	17650	21300
SE Sport Utility 4D		AZ08W	32500	14200	15975	17800	21500
2WD		T		(875)	(875)	(1165)	(1165)
QUEST—V6—Truck Equipment Schedule T1							
Minivan		BV28U	25350	7300	8375	10000	12800
S Minivan		BV28U	26300	8150	9325	11050	13950
SL Minivan		BV28U	28500	9125	10400	12100	15150
SE Minivan		BV28U	35300	10050	11425	13150	16250
PATHFINDER 4WD—V6—Truck Equipment Schedule T1							
S Sport Utility 4D		AR18W	28250	10050	11425	13200	16400
SE Sport Utility 4D		AR18W	29500	11700	13225	15000	18400
SE Off-Road Util		AR18W	32300	11625	13125	14900	18300
LE Sport Utility 4D		AR18W	36650	12600	14200	15950	19450
2WD		U		(875)	(875)	(1165)	(1165)
ARMADA 4WD—V8—Truck Equipment Schedule T1							
SE Sport Utility 4D		AA08B	38485	12050	13625	15450	18850
LE Sport Utility 4D		AA08B	43785	14500	16325	18150	21900
2WD		A		(875)	(875)	(1165)	(1165)
FRONTIER KING CAB—4-Cyl.—Truck Equipment Schedule T2							
XE Short Bed		BD06T	16700	6575	7575	9200	11900
FRONTIER KING CAB—V6—Truck Equipment Schedule T2							
SE Short Bed		AD06U	19600	7300	8400	10050	12850
LE Short Bed		AD06U	23550	8700	9900	11600	14600
Nismo Short Bed		AD06U	23250	8900	10150	11850	14900
4WD		W		2125	2125	2835	2835
FRONTIER CREW CAB—V6—Truck Equipment Schedule T2							
SE Short Bed		AD07U	21450	8875	10100	11800	14850
SE Long Bed		AD09U	22250	8775	10000	11700	14750
LE Short Bed		AD07U	25250	9500	10775	12500	15650
LE Long Bed		AD09U	25750	9500	10775	12500	15650
Nismo Short Bed		AD07U	25300	10300	11650	13400	16550
4WD		W		2125	2125	2835	2835
TITAN KING CAB—V8—Truck Equipment Schedule T1							
XE Short Bed		AA06A	24435	7200	8275	10200	13350
SE Short Bed		AA06A	26585	8075	9225	11200	14550
LE Short Bed		AA06A	31385	8475	9675	11650	15050
4WD		B		2075	2075	2765	2765
TITAN CREW CAB—V8—Truck Equipment Schedule T1							
XE Short Bed		AA07A	27285	9100	10350	12350	15800
SE Short Bed		AA07A	29085	10000	11375	13400	16900
LE Short Bed		AA07A	33885	10975	12450	14450	18100
4WD		B		2075	2075	2765	2765

2008 NISSAN—(J,1or5)N(1,6or8)(AS58V)—8—#

Body	Type	VIN	List	Trade-In Fair	Trade-In Good	Pvt-Party Good	Retail Excellent
ROGUE AWD—4-Cyl.—Truck Equipment Schedule T1							
S Sport Utility 4D		AS58V	21195	12200	13775	15550	18950
SL Sport Utility 4D		AS58V	22615	12850	14450	16200	19700
2WD		T		(950)	(950)	(1265)	(1265)
XTERRA 4WD—V6—Truck Equipment Schedule T1							
X Sport Utility 4D		AN08W	24725	9425	10725	12350	15400

2008 NISSAN

Body	Type	VIN	List	Trade-In Fair	Good	Pvt-Party Good	Retail Excellent
	S Sport Utility 4D	AN08W	26425	10675	12100	13800	17000
	Off-Road Sport Util	AN08W	27075	11075	12550	14250	17500
	SE Sport Utility 4D	AN08W	29375	11525	13025	14750	18100
	2WD	U		(950)	(950)	(1265)	(1265)
QUEST—V6—Truck Equipment Schedule T1							
	Minivan	BV28U	25725	9850	11175	12850	15900
	S Minivan	BV28U	28415	10825	12250	13900	17100
	SL Minivan	BV28U	30325	11800	13325	15050	18350
	SE Minivan	BV28U	35825	13025	14700	16350	19800
PATHFINDER 4WD—V6—Truck Equipment Schedule T1							
	S Sport Utility 4D	AR18B	28405	13575	15300	17050	20600
	SE Sport Utility 4D	AR18B	31705	15425	17350	19050	22700
	SE Off-Road Util	AR18B	34605	15300	17200	18850	22500
	LE Sport Utility 4D	AR18B	37705	16425	18425	20200	24000
	2WD	A		(950)	(950)	(1265)	(1265)
	V8 5.6 Liter	B		475	475	635	635
ARMADA 4WD—V8—Truck Equipment Schedule T1							
	SE Sport Utility 4D	AA08C	38795	15575	17500	19250	23000
	LE Sport Utility 4D	AA08C	45295	18325	20475	22300	26400
	2WD	D		(950)	(950)	(1265)	(1265)
FRONTIER KING CAB—4-Cyl.—Truck Equipment Schedule T2							
	XE Short Bed	BD06T	16895	8150	9325	10900	13600
FRONTIER KING CAB—V6—Truck Equipment Schedule T2							
	SE Short Bed	AD06U	19795	9050	10300	11800	14700
	LE Short Bed	AD06U	24095	10475	11900	13500	16500
	Nismo Short Bed	AD06U	24145	10775	12200	13750	16800
	4WD	W		2300	2300	3065	3065
	4-Cyl. 2.5 Liter	B		(300)	(300)	(400)	(400)
FRONTIER CREW CAB—V6—Truck Equipment Schedule T2							
	SE Short Bed	AD07U	21645	10725	12150	13700	16750
	SE Long Bed	AD09U	22445	10575	12000	13550	16600
	LE Short Bed	AD07U	25795	11475	12925	14550	17700
	LE Long Bed	AD09U	26295	11375	12850	14450	17600
	Nismo Short Bed	AD07U	25495	12250	13825	15450	18650
	4WD	W		2300	2300	3065	3065
TITAN KING CAB—V8—Truck Equipment Schedule T1							
	XE Short Bed	AA06A	25135	9175	10425	12400	15800
	XE Long Bed	AA06E	25545	9050	10300	12250	15650
	SE Short Bed	AA06A	27395	10150	11525	13500	17000
	SE Long Bed	AA06E	27805	9575	10875	12900	16300
	LE Short Bed	AA06A	33365	10575	12000	14000	17550
	LE Long Bed	AA06E	33775	10475	11900	13900	17450
	4WD	C,F		2250	2250	3000	3000
TITAN KING CAB 4WD—V8—Truck Equipment Schedule T1							
	Pro-4X Short Bed	AA06C	32725	12650	14250	16250	20100
TITAN CREW CAB—V8—Truck Equipment Schedule T1							
	XE Short Bed	AA07D	28065	11225	12700	14750	18400
	XE Long Bed	AA07G	28475	11225	12700	14700	18350
	SE Short Bed	AA07D	29965	12250	13825	15850	19600
	SE Long Bed	AA07G	30385	11700	13225	15300	18950
	LE Short Bed	AA07D	35935	13325	15050	17100	21000
	LE Long Bed	AA07G	36345	12650	14250	16250	20100
	4WD	C,F		2250	2250	3000	3000
TITAN CREW CAB 4WD—V8—Truck Equipment Schedule T1							
	Pro-4X Short Bed	AA07C	34925	15200	17100	19100	23100
	Pro-4X Long Bed	AA07F	37260	15050	16900	18900	22900

OLDSMOBILE

1994 OLDSMOBILE — 1GH–(U06D)–R–#

Body	Type	VIN	List	Fair	Good	Good	Excellent
SILHOUETTE—V6—Truck Equipment Schedule T1							
	Minivan	U06D	20625	525	725	1475	2700
	V6 3.8 Liter	L		50	50	65	65
BRAVADA AWD—V6—Truck Equipment Schedule T3							
	Sport Utility 4D	T13W	27120	1100	1550	2700	4375

1995 OLDSMOBILE — 1GH–(U06L)–S–#

Body	Type	VIN	List	Fair	Good	Good	Excellent
SILHOUETTE—V6—Truck Equipment Schedule T1							
	Minivan	U06L	20795	600	825	1650	2975

TRUCKS & VANS

Body	Type	VIN	List	Trade-In Fair	Trade-In Good	Pvt-Party Good	Retail Excellent
1996 OLDSMOBILE — 1GH–(U06E)–T–#							
SILHOUETTE—V6—Truck Equipment Schedule T1							
Minivan		U06E	21900	650	925	1800	3150
BRAVADA AWD—V6—Truck Equipment Schedule T3							
Sport Utility 4D		T13W	29995	1575	2050	3300	5150
1997 OLDSMOBILE — 1GH–(U06E)–V–#							
SILHOUETTE—V6—Truck Equipment Schedule T1							
Minivan		U06E	22245	625	850	1700	3050
Extended Minivan		X06E	23075	825	1150	2125	3650
GL Extended		X06E	25145	925	1300	2400	4050
GLS Extended		X06E	26805	950	1325	2450	4125
w/o 2nd Sliding Door				(50)	(50)	(65)	(65)
BRAVADA AWD—V6—Truck Equipment Schedule T3							
Sport Utility 4D		T13W	30800	1825	2325	3600	5500
1998 OLDSMOBILE — 1GH–(U03E)–W–#							
SILHOUETTE—V6—Truck Equipment Schedule T1							
GS Minivan		U03E	25000	675	950	1875	3300
GL Extended		X03E	24535	1050	1475	2625	4300
GLS Extended		X03E	27735	1075	1500	2675	4375
BRAVADA AWD—V6—Truck Equipment Schedule T3							
Sport Utility 4D		T13W	31160	2075	2650	3950	5875
1999 OLDSMOBILE — 1GH–(U03E)–X–#							
SILHOUETTE—V6—Truck Equipment Schedule T1							
GS Minivan		U03E	25370	825	1150	2175	3725
GL Extended		X03E	24990	1200	1700	2900	4650
GLS Extended		X03E	28665	1250	1725	2975	4725
Premiere Extended		X03E	31580	1800	2325	3600	5475
BRAVADA AWD—V6—Truck Equipment Schedule T3							
Sport Utility 4D		T13W	31568	2425	3025	4350	6375
2000 OLDSMOBILE — 1GH–(X03E)–Y–#							
SILHOUETTE—V6—Truck Equipment Schedule T1							
GL Extended		X03E	25530	1475	1950	3200	5025
GLS Extended		X03E	29220	1550	2025	3275	5125
Premiere Extended		X03E	32130	2125	2700	3975	5900
BRAVADA AWD—V6—Truck Equipment Schedule T3							
Sport Utility 4D		T13W	31923	2800	3400	4800	6875
2001 OLDSMOBILE — 1GH–(X03E)–1–#							
SILHOUETTE—V6—Truck Equipment Schedule T1							
GL Extended		X03E	26920	1800	2325	3625	5525
GLS Extended		X03E	31055	1875	2425	3700	5600
Premiere Extended		X03E	33855	2525	3100	4425	6450
BRAVADA AWD—V6—Truck Equipment Schedule T3							
Sport Utility 4D		T13W	32335	3225	3925	5325	7475
2002 OLDSMOBILE — 1GH–(X23E)–2–#							
SILHOUETTE—V6—Truck Equipment Schedule T1							
GL Extended		X23E	27560	2000	2575	4100	6300
GLS Extended		X03E	31635	2100	2650	4225	6425
Premiere Extended		X13E	33535	2800	3400	5000	7325
AWD		V		550	550	735	735
BRAVADA AWD—6-Cyl.—Truck Equipment Schedule T3							
Sport Utility 4D		T13W	34967	3975	4700	6375	8925
2WD		S		(500)	(500)	(665)	(665)
2003 OLDSMOBILE — 1GH–(X23E)–3–#							
SILHOUETTE—V6—Truck Equipment Schedule T1							
GL Extended		X23E	28510	2600	3200	4800	7100
GLS Extended		X03E	32175	2700	3300	4900	7200
Premiere Extended		X13E	34225	3500	4200	5800	8225
AWD		V		650	650	865	865
BRAVADA AWD—6-Cyl.—Truck Equipment Schedule T3							
Sport Utility 4D		T13S	35145	4725	5525	7275	9950
2WD		S		(575)	(575)	(765)	(765)

Body	Type	VIN	List	Trade-In Fair	Trade-In Good	Pvt-Party Good	Retail Excellent

2004 OLDSMOBILE — 1GH–(X23E)–4–#

SILHOUETTE—V6—Truck Equipment Schedule T1

Body	Type	VIN	List	Fair	Good	Good	Excellent
GL Extended		X23E	28790	3325	4025	5600	8000
GLS Extended		X03E	32450	3450	4150	5725	8125
Premiere Extended		X13E	34510	4325	5125	6775	9350
AWD		V		725	725	965	965

BRAVADA AWD—6-Cyl.—Truck Equipment Schedule T3

Sport Utility 4D		T13S	36245	5675	6600	8350	11100
2WD		S		(650)	(650)	(865)	(865)

PLYMOUTH — See DODGE TRUCKS

PONTIAC

1994 PONTIAC — 1G(YorM)–(U06D)–R–#

TRANS SPORT—V6—Truck Equipment Schedule T1

SE Minivan		U06D	18279	450	600	1250	2300
5 Passenger				(200)	(200)	(265)	(265)
V6 3.8 Liter		L		50	50	65	65

1995 PONTIAC — 1G(YorM)–(U06D)–S–#

TRANS SPORT—V6—Truck Equipment Schedule T1

SE Minivan		U06D	19964	500	675	1450	2650
5 Passenger				(200)	(200)	(265)	(265)
V6 3.8 Liter		L		50	50	65	65

1996 PONTIAC — 1GM–(U06E)–T–#

TRANS SPORT—V6—Truck Equipment Schedule T1

SE Minivan		U06E	21595	550	750	1550	2825
5 Passenger				(250)	(250)	(335)	(335)

1997 PONTIAC — 1GM–(U06E)–V–#

TRANS SPORT—V6—Truck Equipment Schedule T1

SE Minivan		U06E	21049	675	950	1875	3300
SE Extended Minivan		X09E	23939	1050	1500	2650	4350
Montana				650	650	865	865
w/o 2nd Sliding Door				(50)	(50)	(65)	(65)

1998 PONTIAC — 1GM–(U03E)–W–#

TRANS SPORT—V6—Truck Equipment Schedule T1

Minivan		U03E	22950	775	1100	2075	3600
Extended Minivan		X03E	23660	1200	1675	2900	4650
Montana				75	75	100	100
w/o 2nd Sliding Door				(50)	(50)	(65)	(65)

1999 PONTIAC — 1GM–(U03E)–X–#

MONTANA—V6—Truck Equipment Schedule T1

Minivan		U03E	23455	925	1300	2425	4100
Extended Minivan		X03E	24455	1450	1925	3175	5000
w/o 2nd Sliding Door				(50)	(50)	(65)	(65)

2000 PONTIAC — 1GM–(U03E)–Y–#

MONTANA—V6—Truck Equipment Schedule T1

Minivan		U03E	24255	1100	1525	2725	4450
Extended Minivan		X03E	25365	1750	2250	3525	5400

2001 PONTIAC — (1GMor3G7)–(A03E)–1–#

AZTEK—V6—Truck Equipment Schedule T1

Sport Utility 4D		A03E	21995	1050	1475	2675	4425
GT Sport Utility 4D		A03E	24995	1475	1950	3250	5100
AWD		B		525	525	700	700

MONTANA—V6—Truck Equipment Schedule T1

Minivan 4D		U03E	24810	1350	1825	3075	4900
Extended Minivan 4D		X03E	27150	2075	2650	3950	5875

2002 PONTIAC

Body	Type	VIN	List	Trade-In Fair	Trade-In Good	Pvt-Party Good	Retail Excellent

2002 PONTIAC — (1GMor3G7)–(A03E)–2–#

AZTEK—V6—Truck Equipment Schedule T1
| Sport Utility 4D | | A03E | 20545 | 1275 | 1775 | 3275 | 5425 |
| AWD | | B | | 550 | 550 | 735 | 735 |

MONTANA—V6—Truck Equipment Schedule T1
| Minivan 4D | | U03E | 24990 | 1550 | 2025 | 3550 | 5675 |
| Extended Minivan 4D | | X03E | 27390 | 2325 | 2900 | 4450 | 6700 |

2003 PONTIAC — (1GMor3G7)–(A03E)–3–#

AZTEK—V6—Truck Equipment Schedule T1
| Sport Utility 4D | | A03E | 20870 | 1425 | 1900 | 3450 | 5600 |
| AWD | | B | | 650 | 650 | 865 | 865 |

MONTANA—V6—Truck Equipment Schedule T1
Minivan 4D		U03E	24845	2050	2600	4175	6375
Extended Minivan 4D		X03E	26645	2975	3600	5200	7550
AWD		V		1000	1000	1335	1335

2004 PONTIAC — (1GMor3G7)–(A03E)–4–#

AZTEK—V6—Truck Equipment Schedule T1
| Sport Utility 4D | | A03E | 21595 | 1850 | 2375 | 3975 | 6200 |
| AWD | | B | | 725 | 725 | 965 | 965 |

MONTANA—V6—Truck Equipment Schedule T1
Minivan 4D		U03E	23845	2700	3325	4900	7200
Extended Minivan 4D		X03E	26220	3725	4450	6050	8500
AWD		V		1000	1000	1335	1335

2005 PONTIAC — (1GMor3G7)–(A03E)–5–#

AZTEK—V6—Truck Equipment Schedule T1
| Sport Utility 4D | | A03E | 22060 | 2450 | 3050 | 4650 | 6975 |
| AWD | | B | | 800 | 800 | 1065 | 1065 |

MONTANA—V6—Truck Equipment Schedule T1
| Extended Minivan 4D | | V23E | 26755 | 4700 | 5525 | 7175 | 9775 |

MONTANA SV6—V6—Truck Equipment Schedule T1
Minivan 4D		V03L	25235	2000	2575	4125	6350
5 Passenger				(600)	(600)	(800)	(800)
AWD		X		1000	1000	1335	1335

2006 PONTIAC — (1GMor3G7)–(L63F)–6

TORRENT—V6—Truck Equipment Schedule T1
| Sport Utility 4D | | L63F | 22990 | 7250 | 8325 | 10100 | 13100 |
| AWD | | 7 | | 875 | 875 | 1165 | 1165 |

MONTANA SV6—V6—Truck Equipment Schedule T1
Minivan 4D		V03L	25580	3125	3800	5400	7750
4/5 Passenger				(650)	(650)	(865)	(865)
AWD		X		875	875	1165	1165

2007 PONTIAC — (1GMor3G7)–(L63F)–7

TORRENT—V6—Truck Equipment Schedule T1
| Sport Utility 4D | | L63F | 24395 | 8650 | 9850 | 11600 | 14700 |
| AWD | | 7 | | 950 | 950 | 1265 | 1265 |

2008 PONTIAC — (1GMor3G7)–(L33F)–8

TORRENT—V6—Truck Equipment Schedule T1
Sport Utility 4D		L33F	23470	10575	12000	13750	17000
GXP Sport Utility 4D		L537	27995	12350	13975	15750	19150
AWD		4,7		1025	1025	1365	1365

PORSCHE

2003 PORSCHE — WP1–(AB29P)–3–#

CAYENNE AWD—V8—Truck Equipment Schedule T3
| S Sport Utility 4D | | AB29P | 56665 | 15775 | 17700 | 20100 | 24600 |

CAYENNE AWD—V8 Turbo—Truck Equipment Schedule T3
| Sport Utility 4D | | AC29P | 89665 | 20475 | 22925 | 25600 | 30800 |

TRUCKS & VANS

2004 PORSCHE

Body	Type	VIN	List	Trade-In Fair	Trade-In 'Good	Pvt-Party Good	Retail Excellent

2004 PORSCHE — WP1-(AA29P)-4-#

CAYENNE AWD—V6—Truck Equipment Schedule T3
Sport Utility 4D AA29P 43665 **15300 17200 19450 23700**
CAYENNE AWD—V8—Truck Equipment Schedule T3
S Sport Utility 4D AB29P 56665 **17875 20000 22400 27100**
CAYENNE AWD—V8 Twin Turbo—Truck Equipment Schedule T3
Sport Utility 4D AC29P 89665 **24100 26950 29500 35000**

2005 PORSCHE — WP1-(AA29P)-5-#

CAYENNE AWD—V6—Truck Equipment Schedule T3
Sport Utility 4D AA29P 44995 **17350 19450 21800 26300**
CAYENNE AWD—V8—Truck Equipment Schedule T3
S Sport Utility 4D AB29P 57195 **20275 22725 25100 30000**
CAYENNE AWD—V8 Twin Turbo—Truck Equipment Schedule T3
Sport Utility 4D AC29P 90195 **28025 31250 33800 39700**

2006 PORSCHE — WP1-(AA29P)-6-#

CAYENNE AWD—V6—Truck Equipment Schedule T3
Sport Utility 4D AA29P 46015 **19550 21850 24100 28700**
   SportDesign **1500 1500 2000 2000**
   Off-Road Tech **1500 1500 2000 2000**
   Off-Road Design **1500 1500 2000 2000**
CAYENNE AWD—V8—Truck Equipment Schedule T3
S Sport Utility 4D AB29P 58015 **22725 25375 27600 32600**
S Titanium Spt Util AB29P 65715 **28225 31450 33800 39400**
   SportDesign **1500 1500 2000 2000**
   Off-Road Tech **1500 1500 2000 2000**
   Off-Road Design **1500 1500 2000 2000**
CAYENNE AWD—V8 Twin Turbo—Truck Equipment Schedule T3
Sport Utility 4D AC29P 91015 **32050 35675 38000 44100**
S Sport Utility 4D AC29P 112415 **37625 41750 44200 50900**
   SportDesign **1500 1500 2000 2000**
   Off-Road Tech **1500 1500 2000 2000**
   Off-Road Design **1500 1500 2000 2000**

2007 PORSCHE — No Production

2008 PORSCHE — WP1(AA29P)-8-#

CAYENNE AWD—V6—Truck Equipment Schedule T3
Sport Utility 4D AA29P 47295 **30575 34000 36000 41300**
   SportDesign Pkg **1500 1500 2000 2000**
   Off-Road Tech **1500 1500 2000 2000**
CAYENNE AWD—V8—Truck Equipment Schedule T3
S Sport Utility 4D AB29P 58795 **37925 42050 43900 49900**
   SportDesign Pkg **1500 1500 2000 2000**
   Off-Road Tech **1500 1500 2000 2000**
CAYENNE AWD—V8 Twin Turbo—Truck Equipment Schedule T3
Sport Utility 4D AC29P 94595 **59975 66350 68000 76000**
   SportDesign **1500 1500 2000 2000**
   Off-Road Tech **1500 1500 2000 2000**

SAAB

2005 SAAB — 5S3E(T13S)-5-#

9-7X AWD—6-Cyl.—Truck Equipment Schedule T3
Linear Sport Util 4D T13S 38990 **7775 8900 11050 14400**
9-7X AWD—V8—Truck Equipment Schedule T3
Arc Sport Utility 4D T13M 40990 **9050 10300 12450 15950**

2006 SAAB — 5S3-(T13S)-6-#

9-7X AWD—6-Cyl.—Truck Equipment Schedule T3
4.2i Sport Utility 4D T13S 39240 **9375 10675 12850 16450**
9-7X AWD—V8—Truck Equipment Schedule T3
5.3i Sport Utility 4D T13M 41240 **10775 12200 14350 18150**

2007 SAAB — 5S3-(T13S)-7-#

9-7X AWD—6-Cyl.—Truck Equipment Schedule T3
4.2i Sport Utility 4D T13S 39735 **11175 12650 14800 18550**

Body Type	VIN	List	Trade-In Fair	Good	Pvt-Party Good	Retail Excellent

9-7X AWD—V8—Truck Equipment Schedule T3
| 5.3i Sport Utility 4D | T13M | 41735 | 12650 | 14300 | 16450 | 20400 |

2008 SAAB — 5S3–(T13S)–8–#

9-7X AWD—6-Cyl.—Truck Equipment Schedule T3
| 4.2i Sport Utility 4D | T13S | 39935 | | | | |
9-7X AWD—V8—Truck Equipment Schedule T3
| 5.3i Sport Utility 4D | T13M | 42035 | | | | |
| Aero Sport Utility 4D | T23H | 45750 | | | | |

SATURN

2003 SATURN — 5GZ–(Z23D)–3–#

VUE—4-Cyl.—Truck Equipment Schedule T1
Sport Utility 4D	Z23D	18295	3375	4075	5725	8200
AWD	4,6		650	650	865	865
V6 3.0 Liter	B		475	475	635	635

2004 SATURN — 5GZ–(Z23D)–4–#

VUE—4-Cyl.—Truck Equipment Schedule T1
Sport Utility 4D	Z23D	19135	4175	4925	6650	9200
AWD	4,6		725	725	965	965
V6 3.5 Liter	B		550	550	735	735

2005 SATURN — 5GZ–(Z23D)–5–#

VUE—4-Cyl.—Truck Equipment Schedule T1
Sport Utility 4D	Z23D	21190	5100	5950	7725	10450
AWD	4,6		800	800	1065	1065
V6 3.5 Liter	4		600	600	800	800
RELAY—V6—Truck Equipment Schedule T1
2 Minivan	V03L	24485	2700	3300	4900	7200
3 Minivan	V23L	27580	3325	4025	5600	7975
AWD	X		800	800	1065	1065

2006 SATURN — 5GZ–(Z23D)–6–#

VUE—4-Cyl.—Truck Equipment Schedule T1
Sport Utility 4D	Z23D	19345	6200	7175	8950	11800
AWD	4,6		875	875	1165	1165
V6 3.5 Liter	4		650	650	865	865
RELAY—V6—Truck Equipment Schedule T1
2 Minivan	V03L	23590	3850	4575	6175	8625
3 Minivan	V23L	27490	4525	5350	6975	9550
AWD	X		875	875	1165	1165

2007 SATURN — 5GZ–(Z33Z)–7–#

VUE—4-Cyl. Hybrid—Truck Equipment Schedule T1
| Sport Utility 4D | Z33Z | 22995 | 10625 | 12050 | 13800 | 17100 |
VUE—4-Cyl.—Truck Equipment Schedule T1
Sport Utility 4D	Z23D	19770	7550	8650	10300	13200
AWD	4,6		950	950	1265	1265
V6 3.5 Liter	L		700	700	935	935
RELAY—V6—Truck Equipment Schedule T1
Minivan	V531	22210	5500	6400	7950	10500
2 Minivan	V031	24540	6250	7225	8775	11350
3 Minivan	V231	28625	7750	8875	10450	13250
OUTLOOK—V6—Truck Equipment Schedule T1
XE Sport Utility 4D	R137	27990	13925	15675	17550	21300
XR Sport Utility 4D	R237	30290	15050	16900	18750	22600
AWD	V		950	950	1265	1265

2008 SATURN — 5GZor3GS(L03Z)–8–#

VUE—4-Cyl. Hybrid—Truck Equipment Schedule T1
| Green Line Sport Util | L03Z | 24795 | | | | |
VUE—4-Cyl.—Truck Equipment Schedule T1
XE Sport Utility 4D	L33P	21395	9375	10675	12300	15350
AWD	4,7		1025	1025	1365	1365
V6 3.5 Liter	N		750	750	1000	1000
VUE—V6—Truck Equipment Schedule T1
| XR Sport Utility 4D | L537 | 24895 | 10825 | 12300 | 13950 | 17200 |

Body	Type	VIN	List	Trade-In Fair	Good	Pvt-Party Good	Retail Excellent
Red Line Sport Utility		L937	27395	14800	16650	18400	22100
AWD		4,7		1025	1025	1365	1365
OUTLOOK—V6—Truck Equipment Schedule T1							
XE Sport Utility 4D		R137	28340	16275	18225	20100	24000
XR Sport Utility 4D		R237	30640	17450	19550	21500	25500
AWD		V		1025	1025	1365	1365

SUBARU

1998 SUBARU — JF1(SF615)–W–#

FORESTER AWD—4-Cyl.—Truck Equipment Schedule T1
Sport Utility 4D		SF615	19190	2350	2925	4275	6275
L Sport Utility 4D		SF635	21290	2700	3300	4675	6750
S Sport Utility 4D		SF655	23490	2975	3600	5025	7150

1999 SUBARU — JF1(SF615)–X–#

FORESTER AWD—4-Cyl.—Truck Equipment Schedule T1
Sport Utility 4D		SF615	19190	2775	3375	4750	6825
L Sport Utility 4D		SF635	21290	3100	3775	5200	7350
S Sport Utility 4D		SF655	23790	3425	4150	5550	7800

2000 SUBARU — JF1(SF635)–Y–#

FORESTER AWD—4-Cyl.—Truck Equipment Schedule T1
L Sport Utility 4D		SF635	21390	3975	4700	6175	8500
S Sport Utility 4D		SF655	23890	4325	5125	6625	9000

2001 SUBARU — JF1(SF635)–1–#

FORESTER AWD—4-Cyl.—Truck Equipment Schedule T1
L Sport Utility 4D		SF635	21590	4450	5275	6750	9150
S Sport Utility 4D		SF655	24190	4875	5700	7275	9775

2002 SUBARU — JF1(SF635)–2–#

FORESTER AWD—4-Cyl.—Truck Equipment Schedule T1
L Sport Utility 4D		SF635	21590	4875	5700	7500	10250
S Sport Utility 4D		SF655	24220	5325	6200	8000	10850

2003 SUBARU –(JF1or4S4)(BorS)(G636)–3

FORESTER AWD—4-Cyl.—Truck Equipment Schedule T1
X Sport Utility 4D		G636	21870	5525	6450	8225	11050
XS Sport Utility 4D		G656	24220	6050	7000	8825	11700

BAJA AWD—4-Cyl.—Truck Equipment Schedule T1
Sport Util Pickup 4D		T61C	24520	5525	6450	8175	11000

2004 SUBARU –(JF1or4S4)(BorS)(G636)–4

FORESTER AWD—4-Cyl.—Truck Equipment Schedule T1
X Sport Utility 4D		G636	22245	6350	7325	9150	12050
XS Sport Utility 4D		G656	24495	6900	7950	9750	12750

FORESTER AWD—4-Cyl. Turbo—Truck Equipment Schedule T1
XT Sport Utility 4D		G696	26320	7575	8700	10550	13600

BAJA AWD—4-Cyl.—Truck Equipment Schedule T1
Sport Util Pickup 4D		T61C	22545	6875	7925	9700	12650

BAJA AWD—4-Cyl. Turbo—Truck Equipment Schedule T1
Sport Util Pickup 4D		T63C	24545	7750	8800	10600	13650

2005 SUBARU –(JF1or4S4)(BorS)(G636)–5

FORESTER AWD—4-Cyl.—Truck Equipment Schedule T1
X Sport Utility 4D		G636	22670	7300	8375	10200	13200
XS Sport Utility 4D		G656	25070	7900	9050	10900	14000
XS LL Bean Spt Util		G676	26970	8550	9775	11650	14850

FORESTER AWD—4-Cyl. Turbo—Truck Equipment Schedule T1
XT Sport Utility 4D		G696	27070	8650	9850	11700	14950

BAJA AWD—4-Cyl.—Truck Equipment Schedule T1
Sport Util Pickup 4D		T62C	22770	8325	9525	11350	14500

BAJA AWD—4-Cyl. Turbo—Truck Equipment Schedule T1
Sport Util Pickup 4D		T63C	24770	9275	10575	12450	15700

TRUCKS & VANS

Body	Type	VIN	List	Trade-In Fair	Good	Pvt-Party Good	Retail Excellent

2006 SUBARU—(JF1or4S4)(B,SorW)(G636)—6

FORESTER AWD—4-Cyl.—Truck Equipment Schedule T1
X Sport Utility 4D		G636	23220	**8425**	9625	11450	14650
X LL Bean Spt Util		G676	27521	**9800**	11125	13000	16300

FORESTER AWD—4-Cyl. Turbo—Truck Equipment Schedule T1
XT Limited Spt Util		G696	29320	**9950**	11275	13200	16500

BAJA AWD—4-Cyl.—Truck Equipment Schedule T1
Sport Util Pickup 4D		T62C	23920	**10000**	11325	13150	16400

BAJA AWD—4-Cyl. Turbo—Truck Equipment Schedule T1
Sport Util Pickup 4D		T63C	26220	**11075**	12550	14300	17700

B9 TRIBECA AWD—H6—Truck Equipment Schedule T1
Sport Utility 4D		X82D	31320	**10000**	11325	13250	16600
Limited Sport Utility		X82D	32910	**11375**	12850	14750	18300
Third Seat				425	425	565	565

2007 SUBARU—(JF1or4S4)(B,SorW)(G636)—7

FORESTER AWD—4-Cyl.—Truck Equipment Schedule T1
X Sport Utility 4D		G636	22620	**9800**	11125	12900	16100
Sports X Spt Util		G636	22320	**9950**	11275	13050	16250
X LL Bean Spt Util		G676	27320	**11275**	12750	14550	17950

FORESTER AWD—4-Cyl. Turbo—Truck Equipment Schedule T1
Sports XT Spt Util		G636	26620	**10975**	12450	14200	17550
XT Limited Spt Util		G696	29320	**11425**	12875	14650	18050

B9 TRIBECA AWD—H6—Truck Equipment Schedule T1
Sport Utility 4D		X82D	30620	**11525**	13025	14850	18250
Limited Sport Utility		X82D	33120	**13025**	14700	16500	20100
Third Seat				450	450	600	600

2008 SUBARU—(JF1or4S4)(B,SorW)(G636)—8

FORESTER AWD—4-Cyl.—Truck Equipment Schedule T1
X Sport Utility 4D		G636	22640	**11650**	13175	14950	18350
Sports X Spt Util		G666	23140	**11850**	13375	15150	18500
X LL Bean Spt Util		G676	27340	**13275**	14950	16700	20200

FORESTER AWD—4-Cyl. Turbo—Truck Equipment Schedule T1
Sports XT Spt Util		G696	28640	**12925**	14600	16350	19900
XT Limited Spt Util		G696	29540	**13425**	15150	16850	20400

TRIBECA AWD—H6—Truck Equipment Schedule T1
Sport Utility 4D		X91D	30640	**13625**	15325	17100	20700
Limited Sport Utility		X92D	33240	**15250**	17150	18900	22600
Third Row				475	475	635	635

SUZUKI

1994 SUZUKI — (JSor2S)(3or4)(JC31C)—R

SAMURAI 4WD—4-Cyl.—Truck Equipment Schedule T2
JL Convertible		JC31C	9799	**200**	275	825	1675
Fiberglass Hard Top				50	50	65	65

SIDEKICK—4-Cyl.—Truck Equipment Schedule T2
JS Convertible 2D		TC01C	11779	**200**	275	825	1675
JS Sport Utility 4D		TE01C	13199	**225**	300	850	1725

SIDEKICK 4WD—4-Cyl.—Truck Equipment Schedule T2
JX Convertible 2D		TA01C	13179	**125**	175	675	1450
JX Sport Utility 4D		TD01V	14429	**400**	550	1175	2175
JLX Sport Util 4D		TD01V	15779	**500**	675	1375	2475

1995 SUZUKI — (JS3,JS4or2S3)(JC31C)—S

SAMURAI 4WD—4-Cyl.—Truck Equipment Schedule T2
JL Convertible		JC31C	10234	**250**	375	950	1875
Fiberglass Hard Top				50	50	65	65

SIDEKICK—4-Cyl.—Truck Equipment Schedule T2
JS Convertible 2D		TC01C	12344	**250**	350	925	1850
JS Sport Utility 4D		TE02V	13869	**250**	375	950	1875
Limited				50	50	65	65

SIDEKICK 4WD—4-Cyl.—Truck Equipment Schedule T2
JX Convertible 2D		TA02C	13844	**175**	225	775	1625
JX Sport Utility 4D		TD03V	15179	**450**	625	1300	2400
JLX Sport Util 4D		TD03V	16689	**575**	775	1600	2875
Limited				50	50	65	65

0709

TRUCKS & VANS (side tab)

Body Type	VIN	List	Trade-In Fair	Trade-In Good	Pvt-Party Good	Retail Excellent
1996 SUZUKI — (2SorJS)3(TC02C)–T–#						
SIDEKICK—4-Cyl.—Truck Equipment Schedule T2						
JS Convertible 2D	TC02C	13274	250	350	950	1875
JS Utility 4D	TE02V	14789	300	425	1050	2050
SIDEKICK 4WD—4-Cyl.—Truck Equipment Schedule T2						
JX Convertible 2D	TA02C	15044	200	300	875	1800
JX Utility 4D	TD03V	16389	500	700	1500	2750
Sport JX Utility 4D	TD21V	18389	850	1200	2200	3725
Sport JLX Util 4D	TD21V	19389	875	1250	2350	4000
X-90 4WD—4-Cyl.—Truck Equipment Schedule T2						
Sport Utility 2D	LB11S	15389	250	350	1025	2050
2WD	A		(200)	(200)	(265)	(265)
1997 SUZUKI — (2SorJS)3(TC02C)–V–#						
SIDEKICK—4-Cyl.—Truck Equipment Schedule T2						
JS Convertible 2D	TC02C	13299	250	350	975	1925
JS Utility 4D	TE02V	14819	375	500	1175	2225
Sport JS Utility 4D	TE21V	17119	400	550	1225	2300
SIDEKICK 4WD—4-Cyl.—Truck Equipment Schedule T2						
JX Convertible 2D	TA02C	15069	275	375	1000	1950
JX Utility 4D	TD03V	16419	575	775	1600	2925
Sport JX Utility 4D	TD21V	18119	975	1375	2500	4175
Sport JLX Util 4D	TD21V	19619	1000	1400	2550	4250
X-90 4WD—4-Cyl.—Truck Equipment Schedule T2						
Sport Utility 2D	LB11S	15019	325	450	1150	2225
2WD	A		(250)	(250)	(335)	(335)
1998 SUZUKI — (2SorJS)3(TC02C)–W–#						
SIDEKICK—4-Cyl.—Truck Equipment Schedule T2						
JS Convertible 2D	TC02C	13519	300	425	1100	2125
JS Utility 4D	TE02V	14829	425	600	1325	2475
Sport JS Utility 4D	TE02V	17329	475	625	1400	2575
SIDEKICK 4WD—4-Cyl.—Truck Equipment Schedule T2						
JX Convertible 2D	TA02C	15289	350	500	1200	2275
JX Utility 4D	TD03V	16429	625	900	1800	3200
Sport JX Utility 4D	TD21V	18329	1100	1550	2750	4475
Sport JLX Util 4D	TD21V	19829	1150	1600	2800	4550
X-90 4WD—4-Cyl.—Truck Equipment Schedule T2						
Sport Utility 2D	LB11S	15229	400	575	1325	2525
2WD	A		(300)	(300)	(400)	(400)
1999 SUZUKI — (Jor2)S3(TC52C)–X–#						
VITARA—4-Cyl.—Truck Equipment Schedule T2						
JS Convertible 2D	TC52C	14719	400	575	1300	2450
JS Hard Top 4D	TE52V	15829	550	725	1600	2975
4-Cyl. 1.6 Liter			(200)	(200)	(265)	(265)
VITARA 4WD—4-Cyl.—Truck Equipment Schedule T2						
JX Convertible 2D	TA52C	16519	300	425	1125	2175
JX Hard Top 4D	TD52V	17429	675	950	1900	3375
4-Cyl. 1.6 Liter			(200)	(200)	(265)	(265)
GRAND VITARA—V6—Truck Equipment Schedule T1						
JS Utility 4D	TE62V	18429	725	1000	1975	3500
GRAND VITARA 4WD—V6—Truck Equipment Schedule T1						
JLX Utility 4D	TD62V	19429	950	1325	2500	4225
2000 SUZUKI — (Jor2)S3(TC03C)–Y–#						
VITARA—4-Cyl.—Truck Equipment Schedule T2						
JS Convertible 2D	TC03C	13939	550	750	1625	2975
JS Hard Top 4D	TE52V	15949	700	975	1975	3500
JLS Convertible 2D	TC52C	15439	525	700	1600	3000
JLS Hard Top 4D	TE52V	16749	825	1150	2300	4025
VITARA 4WD—4-Cyl.—Truck Equipment Schedule T2						
JX Convertible 2D	TA03C	15739	450	625	1450	2700
JX Hard Top 4D	TD52V	17549	850	1225	2375	4100
JLX Convertible 2D	TA52C	17239	1200	1675	2925	4725
JLX Hard Top 4D	TD52V	18349	1400	1875	3150	5000
GRAND VITARA—V6—Truck Equipment Schedule T1						
JLS Hard Top 4D	TE62V	19749	925	1300	2475	4225
Ltd Hard Top 4D	TE62V	22149	1075	1500	2725	4500

Body	Type	VIN	List	Trade-In Fair	Trade-In Good	Pvt-Party Good	Retail Excellent
GRAND VITARA 4WD—V6—Truck Equipment Schedule T1							
JLX Hard Top 4D		TD62V	20749	1175	1650	2900	4700
Ltd Hard Top 4D		TD62V	23149	1225	1700	2975	4800

2001 SUZUKI — (Jor2)S3(TC03C)–1–#

Body	Type	VIN	List	Fair	Good	Good	Excellent
VITARA—4-Cyl.—Truck Equipment Schedule T2							
JS Convertible 2D		TC03C	14369	625	850	1775	3200
JS Hard Top 4D		TE52V	16079	900	1275	2475	4250
JLS Convertible 2D		TC52C	15869	725	1025	2075	3675
JLS Hard Top 2D		TE52V	16869	975	1375	2600	4350
JLS Hard Top 4D		TE52V	17079	1050	1450	2675	4450
VITARA 4WD—4-Cyl.—Truck Equipment Schedule T2							
JX Convertible 2D		TA03C	15969	650	900	1925	3475
JX Hard Top 4D		TD52V	17579	1100	1550	2800	4575
JLX Convertible 2D		TA52C	17469	1575	2075	3375	5275
JLX Hard Top 2D		TD52V	18469	1875	2425	3750	5675
JLX Hard Top 4D		TD52V	18579	1775	2300	3600	5525
GRAND VITARA—V6—Truck Equipment Schedule T1							
JLS Hard Top 4D		TE62V	19879	1175	1650	2925	4750
Ltd Hard Top 4D		TE62V	22279	1425	1875	3200	5075
GRAND VITARA 4WD—V6—Truck Equipment Schedule T1							
JLX Hard Top 4D		TD62V	21079	1600	2075	3400	5300
Ltd Hard Top 4D		TD62V	23479	1650	2150	3475	5400
XL-7 4WD—V6—Truck Equipment Schedule T1							
Sport Utility 4D		TX92V	21499	1725	2225	3525	5450
Plus Sport Util 4D		TX92V	23999	1875	2425	3750	5675
Touring Spt Utl 4D		TX92V	24999	1925	2475	3800	5725
Limited Spt Utl 4D		TX92V	26499	2025	2575	3925	5875
2WD		Y		(450)	(450)	(600)	(600)

2002 SUZUKI — (Jor2)S3(TC52C)–2–#

Body	Type	VIN	List	Fair	Good	Good	Excellent
VITARA—4-Cyl.—Truck Equipment Schedule T2							
JLS Convertible 2D		TC52C	16089	875	1225	2675	4700
JLS Hard Top 4D		TE52V	17299	1175	1650	3150	5300
VITARA 4WD—4-Cyl.—Truck Equipment Schedule T2							
JLX Convertible 2D		TA52C	17489	1825	2350	3925	6125
JLX Hard Top 4D		TD52V	18699	2025	2600	4175	6425
GRAND VITARA—V6—Truck Equipment Schedule T1							
JLS Hard Top 4D		TE62V	19099	1475	1950	3500	5675
Ltd Hard Top 4D		TE62V	22299	1725	2225	3825	6025
GRAND VITARA 4WD—V6—Truck Equipment Schedule T1							
JLX Hard Top 4D		TD62V	20299	1875	2425	4025	6250
Ltd Hard Top 4D		TD62V	23499	1975	2525	4125	6350
XL-7 4WD—V6—Truck Equipment Schedule T1							
Sport Utility 4D		TX92V	22319	1950	2525	4100	6350
Plus Spt Util 4D		TX92V	23819	2150	2725	4300	6600
Touring Spt Utl 4D		TX92V	25319	2175	2750	4350	6650
Limited Spt Utl 4D		TX92V	26519	2325	2900	4500	6800
2WD		Y		(500)	(500)	(665)	(665)

2003 SUZUKI — (Jor2)S3(TA52C)–3–#

Body	Type	VIN	List	Fair	Good	Good	Excellent
VITARA 4WD—4-Cyl.—Truck Equipment Schedule T2							
Convertible 2D		TA52C	17509	2400	3000	4600	6900
Hard Top 4D		TD52V	18719	2650	3250	4875	7225
2WD		C,E		(575)	(575)	(765)	(765)
GRAND VITARA 4WD—V6—Truck Equipment Schedule T1							
Hard Top 4D		TD62V	20319	2225	2825	4425	6750
2WD		E		(575)	(575)	(765)	(765)
XL-7 4WD—V6—Truck Equipment Schedule T1							
Touring Spt Utl 4D		TX92V	22339	2675	3275	4925	7300
Limited Spt Utl 4D		TX92V	25399	2825	3450	5100	7500
w/o Third Seat				(350)	(350)	(465)	(465)
2WD		Y		(575)	(575)	(765)	(765)

2004 SUZUKI — (Jor2)S3(TD52V)–4–#

Body	Type	VIN	List	Fair	Good	Good	Excellent
VITARA 4WD—V6—Truck Equipment Schedule T2							
LX Hard Top 4D		TD52V	17999	3400	4100	5750	8200
2WD		E		(650)	(650)	(865)	(865)
GRAND VITARA 4WD—V6—Truck Equipment Schedule T1							
LX Hard Top 4D		TD62V	19499	2725	3325	4975	7375
EX Hard Top 4D		TD62V	22499	2975	3625	5275	7700
2WD		E		(650)	(650)	(865)	(865)

Body	Type	VIN	List	Trade-In Fair	Good	Pvt-Party Good	Retail Excellent
XL-7 4WD—V6—Truck Equipment Schedule T1							
LX Sport Utility 4D		TX92V	22899	3350	4025	5675	8150
EX Sport Utility 4D		TX92V	25399	3525	4225	5875	8375
w/o Third Seat				(550)	(550)	(735)	(735)
2WD				(650)	(650)	(865)	(865)

2005 SUZUKI — JS3(TD62V)–5–#

Body	Type	VIN	List	Trade-In Fair	Good	Pvt-Party Good	Retail Excellent
GRAND VITARA 4WD—V6—Truck Equipment Schedule T1							
LX Hard Top 4D		TD62V	21694	3375	4075	5725	8225
EX Hard Top 4D		TD62V	23194	3625	4325	6025	8550
2WD		E		(725)	(725)	(965)	(965)
XL-7 4WD—V6—Truck Equipment Schedule T1							
LX Sport Utility 4D		TX92V	25394	4250	5000	6700	9275
EX Sport Utility 4D		TX92V	28394	4375	5175	6900	9575
w/o Third Seat				(600)	(600)	(800)	(800)
2WD		Y		(725)	(725)	(965)	(965)

2006 SUZUKI — JS3(TD941)–6–#

Body	Type	VIN	List	Trade-In Fair	Good	Pvt-Party Good	Retail Excellent
GRAND VITARA 4WD—V6—Truck Equipment Schedule T1							
Sport Utility 4D		TD941	21794	5450	6350	8100	10900
2WD		E		(800)	(800)	(1065)	(1065)
XL-7 4WD—V6—Truck Equipment Schedule T1							
Sport Utility 4D		TX92V	25494	5325	6200	7975	10750
w/o Third Seat				(650)	(650)	(865)	(865)
2WD		Y		(800)	(800)	(1065)	(1065)

2007 SUZUKI — (2orJ)S3(TD941)–7–#

Body	Type	VIN	List	Trade-In Fair	Good	Pvt-Party Good	Retail Excellent
GRAND VITARA 4WD—V6—Truck Equipment Schedule T1							
Sport Utility 4D		TD941	22519	6625	7650	9300	12100
2WD		E		(875)	(875)	(1165)	(1165)
XL7 4WD—V6—Truck Equipment Schedule T1							
Sport Utility 4D		DA217	26584	6975	8025	9700	12550
w/o Third Seat				(700)	(700)	(935)	(935)
2WD		B		(875)	(875)	(1165)	(1165)

2008 SUZUKI — (2orJ)S3(TD941)–8–#

Body	Type	VIN	List	Trade-In Fair	Good	Pvt-Party Good	Retail Excellent
GRAND VITARA 4WD—V6—Truck Equipment Schedule T1							
Sport Utility 4D		TD941	22769	8325	9525	11200	14150
2WD		E		(950)	(950)	(1265)	(1265)
XL7 4WD—V6—Truck Equipment Schedule T1							
Sport Utility 4D		DA217	25499	8700	9900	11600	14600
w/o Third Row				(750)	(750)	(1000)	(1000)
2WD		B		(950)	(950)	(1265)	(1265)

TOYOTA

1994 TOYOTA — (JT3orR1N4)(RN37W)–R–#

Body	Type	VIN	List	Trade-In Fair	Good	Pvt-Party Good	Retail Excellent
4RUNNER 4WD—4-Cyl.—Truck Equipment Schedule T1							
SR5 Spt Utility 4D		RN37W	21338	2050	2625	3925	5850
2WD		2		(125)	(125)	(165)	(165)
V6 3.0 Liter		V		150	150	200	200
LAND CRUISER 4WD—6-Cyl.—Truck Equipment Schedule T1							
Sport Utility 4D		DJ81W	34653	4750	5575	7275	9900
Third Seat Pkg				200	200	265	265
PREVIA—4-Cyl.—Truck Equipment Schedule T1							
DX Minivan		AC11R	24218	625	900	1725	3050
LE Minivan		AC12R	26183	850	1200	2150	3650
All-Trac AWD		2		250	250	335	335
PREVIA—4-Cyl. Supercharged—Truck Equipment Schedule T1							
LE S/C Minivan		AC14R	28543	1050	1500	2625	4300
All-Trac AWD		2		250	250	335	335
PICKUP—4-Cyl.—Truck Equipment Schedule T1							
Short Bed		RN81A	10443	700	1000	1875	3250
DX Short Bed		RN81P	11533	750	1050	1950	3375
DX Xtra Cab		RN93P	13083	1100	1550	2700	4375
4WD		0,1		400	400	535	535
V6 3.0 Liter		V		100	100	135	135
PICKUP—V6—Truck Equipment Schedule T2							
SR5 Xtra Cab		VN93G	15943	1375	1850	3050	4800
4WD		1		400	400	535	535

TRUCKS & VANS

Body Type	VIN	List	Trade-In Fair	Good	Pvt-Party Good	Retail Excellent
T100 PICKUP—4-Cyl.—Truck Equipment Schedule T2						
Long Bed	UD10D	13623	875	1225	2175	3675
T100 PICKUP—V6—Truck Equipment Schedule T2						
DX Long Bed	VD10A	15323	975	1375	2500	4150
DX 1 Ton Long Bed	VD10B	16063	1175	1650	2825	4550
SR5 Long Bed	VD10C	17153	1125	1575	2750	4425
4WD	2		500	500	665	665

1995 TOYOTA–(JT3,JT4or4TA)(RN37W)–S–#

Body Type	VIN	List	Trade-In Fair	Good	Pvt-Party Good	Retail Excellent
4RUNNER 4WD—4-Cyl.—Truck Equipment Schedule T1						
SR5 Spt Utility 4D	RN37W	22450	2375	2950	4300	6300
Limited			200	200	265	265
2WD	2		(125)	(125)	(165)	(165)
V6 3.0 Liter	V		150	150	200	200
LAND CRUISER 4WD—6-Cyl.—Truck Equipment Schedule T1						
Sport Utility 4D	DJ81W	39085	5475	6375	8150	11000
Third Seat Pkg			200	200	265	265
PREVIA—4-Cyl.—Truck Equipment Schedule T1						
DX Minivan	AC11R	24400	800	1125	2050	3500
LE Minivan	AC12R	26975	1025	1450	2575	4250
All-Trac AWD			250	250	335	335
PREVIA—4-Cyl. Supercharged—Truck Equipment Schedule T1						
DX S/C Minivan	AC13R	24900	1050	1500	2625	4300
LE S/C Minivan	AC14R	27475	1350	1825	3050	4800
All-Trac AWD			250	250	335	335
PICKUP—4-Cyl.—Truck Equipment Schedule T2						
Short Bed	RN81A	10985	800	1125	2075	3550
DX Short Bed	RN81P	11885	825	1175	2150	3650
DX Xtra Cab	RN93P	13495	1250	1725	2950	4675
4WD	0,1		400	400	535	535
V6 3.0 Liter	V		100	100	135	135
PICKUP—V6—Truck Equipment Schedule T2						
SR5 Xtra Cab	VN93G	16455	1575	2050	3300	5125
4WD	1		400	400	535	535
TACOMA—4-Cyl.—Truck Equipment Sch T2						
Short Bed	UN41B	12435	850	1200	2200	3725
Xtra Cab	UN53B	14545	1100	1525	2725	4425
4WD	6,7		400	400	535	535
V6 3.4 Liter	V		100	100	135	135
TACOMA 4WD—V6—Truck Equipment Sch T2						
SR5 Xtra Cab	VN73K	21715	2100	2675	4000	5950
T100 PICKUP—V6—Truck Equipment Schedule T2						
Long Bed	VD10D	15135	1000	1400	2550	4225
DX Long Bed	VD11E	16155	1150	1600	2775	4475
DX 1 Ton Long Bed	VD11G	16935	1400	1875	3100	4900
DX Xtra Cab	VD12E	18000	1850	2375	3675	5550
SR5 Xtra Cab	VD12F	19275	2200	2775	4100	6075
4WD	2		400	400	535	535
4-Cyl. 2.7 Liter	U		(100)	(100)	(135)	(135)

1996 TOYOTA–(JT3,JT4or4TA)(YP10V)–T–#

Body Type	VIN	List	Trade-In Fair	Good	Pvt-Party Good	Retail Excellent
RAV4 4WD—4-Cyl.—Truck Equipment Schedule T2						
Sport Utility 2D	YP10V	17058	1775	2275	3550	5450
Sport Utility 4D	HP10V	17758	2075	2625	3950	5875
2WD	G,X		(200)	(200)	(265)	(265)
Dual Sun Roofs			50	50	65	65
4RUNNER 4WD—4-Cyl.—Truck Equipment Schedule T1						
Sport Utility 4D	HM84R	23853	2500	3075	4425	6475
2WD	G		(200)	(200)	(265)	(265)
4RUNNER 4WD—V6—Truck Equipment Schedule T1						
SR5 Spt Utility 4D	HN86R	27453	2675	3275	4650	6750
Limited Spt Util 4D	HN87R	33408	3475	4175	5650	7925
2WD	G		(200)	(200)	(265)	(265)
LAND CRUISER 4WD—6-Cyl.—Truck Equipment Schedule T3						
Sport Utility 4D	HJ85J	45483	6300	7275	9150	12100
Third Seat Pkg			250	250	335	335
PREVIA—4-Cyl. Supercharged—Truck Equipment Schedule T1						
DX S/C Minivan	GK12M	26473	1225	1700	2900	4625
LE S/C Minivan	GK13M	29278	1625	2100	3350	5200
AWD			300	300	400	400
TACOMA—4-Cyl.—Truck Equipment Schedule T2						
Short Bed	NL42M	12643	975	1350	2500	4175

TRUCKS & VANS

Body Type	VIN	List	Trade-In Fair	Trade-In Good	Pvt-Party Good	Retail Excellent
Xtra Cab	VL52M	14793	1300	1775	3025	4800
4WD	6,7		525	525	700	700
V6 3.4 Liter	N		175	175	235	235
TACOMA 4WD—V6—Truck Equipment Schedule T2						
SR5 Xtra Cab	WN74N	22648	2600	3200	4575	6675
T100 PICKUP—4-Cyl.—Truck Equipment Schedule T2						
Long Bed	JM11D	15113	1175	1650	2850	4575
T100 PICKUP—V6—Truck Equipment Schedule T2						
Xtra Cab	TN12D	18683	2200	2800	4125	6075
SR5 Xtra Cab	UN14D	20158	2625	3200	4600	6675
4WD	2		600	600	800	800

1997 TOYOTA—(JT3,JT4or4TA)(YP10V)—V

Body Type	VIN	List	Trade-In Fair	Trade-In Good	Pvt-Party Good	Retail Excellent
RAV4 4WD—4-Cyl.—Truck Equipment Schedule T2						
Sport Utility 2D	YP10V	17128	1800	2300	3600	5500
Sport Utility 4D	HP10V	17828	2125	2700	4025	5975
2WD	G,X		(250)	(250)	(335)	(335)
Dual Sun Roofs			50	50	65	65
4RUNNER 4WD—4-Cyl.—Truck Equipment Schedule T1						
Sport Utility 4D	HM84R	24293	2700	3300	4700	6775
2WD	G		(250)	(250)	(335)	(335)
4RUNNER 4WD—V6—Truck Equipment Schedule T1						
SR5 Sport Util 4D	HN86R	27983	3000	3625	5050	7200
Limited Spt Util 4D	HN87R	34158	3925	4650	6175	8525
2WD	G		(250)	(250)	(335)	(335)
LAND CRUISER 4WD—6-Cyl.—Truck Equipment Schedule T3						
Sport Utility 4D	HJ85J	46293	7250	8325	10300	13450
Third Seat Pkg			350	350	465	465
PREVIA—4-Cyl. Supercharged—Truck Equipment Schedule T1						
DX S/C Minivan	GK12M	26963	1500	1975	3225	5050
LE S/C Minivan	GK13M	29858	1925	2475	3750	5650
All-Trac AWD	2		350	350	465	465
TACOMA—4-Cyl.—Truck Equipment Schedule T2						
Short Bed	NL42N	12813	1100	1550	2750	4475
Xtra Cab	VL52N	14983	1600	2075	3350	5225
4WD			650	650	865	865
V6 3.4 Liter	N		250	250	335	335
TACOMA—V6—Truck Equipment Schedule T2						
SR5 Xtra Cab	WN74N	22868	3125	3800	5250	7425
T100—4-Cyl.—Truck Equipment Schedule T2						
Long Bed	JM11D	15303	1450	1925	3175	5000
T100—V6—Truck Equipment Schedule T2						
DX Xtra Cab	TN12D	19213	2625	3200	4575	6625
SR5 Xtra Cab	UN14D	20428	3075	3725	5150	7300
4WD			700	700	935	935

1998 TOYOTA—(JT3,JT4or4TA)(YP10V)—W

Body Type	VIN	List	Trade-In Fair	Trade-In Good	Pvt-Party Good	Retail Excellent
RAV4 4WD—4-Cyl.—Truck Equipment Schedule T2						
Sport Util Conv 2D	YP10V	17218	1900	2450	3750	5675
Sport Utility 2D	YP10V	17218	1850	2400	3700	5600
Sport Utility 4D	HP10V	18078	2250	2825	4175	6150
2WD	G,X		(300)	(300)	(400)	(400)
4RUNNER 4WD—4-Cyl.—Truck Equipment Schedule T1						
Sport Utility 4D	HM84R	25013	2925	3550	4975	7100
2WD	G		(300)	(300)	(400)	(400)
4RUNNER 4WD—V6—Truck Equipment Schedule T1						
SR5 Sport Util 4D	HN86R	28573	3350	4050	5500	7700
Limited Spt Util 4D	HN87R	35038	4400	5200	6750	9175
2WD	G		(300)	(300)	(400)	(400)
LAND CRUISER 4WD—V8—Truck Equipment Schedule T3						
Sport Utility 4D	HT05J	46413	8850	10100	12200	15700
Third Seat Pkg			400	400	535	535
SIENNA—V6—Truck Equipment Schedule T1						
CE Minivan	GF19C	21560	1775	2275	3550	5450
LE Minivan	ZF13C	24395	2125	2700	4000	5950
XLE Minivan	ZF13C	27520	2525	3100	4450	6500
w/o 2nd Sliding Door			(50)	(50)	(65)	(65)
TACOMA—4-Cyl.—Truck Equipment Schedule T2						
Short Bed	NL42N	13228	1300	1775	3025	4825
Xtra Cab	VL52N	15128	1875	2400	3725	5625
PreRunner Xtra	SM92N	17658	2425	3025	4350	6400
4WD	6,7		775	775	1035	1035

1998 TOYOTA

TRUCKS & VANS

Body	Type	VIN	List	Trade-In Fair	Trade-In Good	Pvt-Party Good	Retail Excellent
V6 3.4 Liter		N		325	325	435	435
TACOMA 4WD—V6—Truck Equipment Schedule T2							
Limited Xtra Cab		WN74N	24448	3325	4025	5475	7700
T100—4-Cyl.—Truck Equipment Schedule T2							
Long Bed		JM11D	15248	1775	2300	3575	5475
T100—V6—Truck Equipment Schedule T2							
DX Xtra Cab		TN12D	19218	3025	3675	5075	7225
SR5 Xtra Cab		TN14D	20848	3550	4275	5700	7975
4WD		2		800	800	1065	1065

1999 TOYOTA–(4,5orJ)T(3,AorB)(YP10V)–X

Body	Type	VIN	List	Trade-In Fair	Trade-In Good	Pvt-Party Good	Retail Excellent
RAV4 4WD—4-Cyl.—Truck Equipment Schedule T2							
Sport Utility Conv 2D		YP10V	17508	2550	3125	4500	6550
Sport Utility 4D		HP10V	18198	2450	3050	4375	6425
2WD		G,X		(350)	(350)	(465)	(465)
4RUNNER 4WD—4-Cyl.—Truck Equipment Schedule T1							
Sport Utility 4D		HM84R	25443	3200	3875	5300	7475
2WD		G		(350)	(350)	(465)	(465)
4RUNNER 4WD—V6—Truck Equipment Schedule T1							
SR5 Sport Util 4D		HN86R	28773	3775	4500	5950	8225
Limited Spt Util 4D		HN87R	36088	4900	5725	7350	9900
2WD		G		(350)	(350)	(465)	(465)
LAND CRUISER 4WD—V8—Truck Equipment Schedule T3							
Sport Utility 4D		HT05J	48718	9950	11275	13400	17000
Third Seat Pkg				425	425	565	565
SIENNA—V6—Truck Equipment Schedule T1							
CE Minivan		GF19C	22738	1825	2350	3650	5550
LE Minivan		ZF13C	24778	2225	2800	4150	6125
XLE Minivan		ZF13C	28099	2675	3275	4650	6725
w/o 2nd Sliding Door				(50)	(50)	(65)	(65)
TACOMA—4-Cyl.—Truck Equipment Schedule T2							
Short Bed		NL42N	13388	1575	2050	3350	5225
Xtra Cab		VL52N	15288	2200	2775	4125	6125
PreRunner Short		NM92N	15188	2175	2725	4075	6050
PreRunner Xtra		SM92N	18028	2850	3475	4875	7000
4WD		6,7		900	900	1200	1200
V6 3.4 Liter				400	400	535	535
TACOMA 4WD—V6—Truck Equipment Schedule T2							
Limited Xtra Cab		WN74N	25108	3975	4700	6200	8525

2000 TOYOTA–(4,5orJ)T(3,AorB)(HP10V)–Y

Body	Type	VIN	List	Trade-In Fair	Trade-In Good	Pvt-Party Good	Retail Excellent
RAV4 4WD—4-Cyl.—Truck Equipment Schedule T1							
Sport Utility 4D		HP10V	18558	2775	3375	4775	6850
2WD		G,X		(475)	(475)	(635)	(635)
4RUNNER 4WD—4-Cyl.—Truck Equipment Schedule T1							
Sport Utility 4D		HM84R	26046	3550	4275	5700	7950
2WD		G		(400)	(400)	(535)	(535)
4RUNNER 4WD—V6—Truck Equipment Schedule T1							
SR5 Sport Util 4D		HN86R	29786	4275	5025	6525	8875
Limited Spt Util 4D		HN87R	36948	5475	6350	7975	10600
2WD		G		(400)	(400)	(535)	(535)
LAND CRUISER 4WD—V8—Truck Equipment Schedule T3							
Sport Utility 4D		HT05J	51308	11125	12600	14750	18500
Third Seat Pkg				450	450	600	600
SIENNA—V6—Truck Equipment Schedule T1							
CE Minivan		ZF19C	23338	1925	2475	3775	5700
LE Minivan		ZF13C	25378	2375	2975	4300	6325
XLE Minivan		ZF13C	27414	2850	3475	4850	6950
w/o 2nd Sliding Door				(50)	(50)	(65)	(65)
TACOMA—4-Cyl.—Truck Equipment Schedule T2							
Short Bed		NL42N	12208	1875	2425	3750	5700
Xtra Cab		VL52N	14458	2600	3200	4575	6650
PreRunner Short		NM92N	14298	2550	3150	4525	6600
PreRunner Xtra		SM92N	17418	3325	4025	5475	7675
4WD				1025	1025	1365	1365
V6 3.4 Liter		N		475	475	635	635
TACOMA 4WD—V6—Truck Equipment Schedule T2							
Limited Xtra Cab		WN74N	24758	4575	5400	6950	9450
TUNDRA—V6—Truck Equipment Schedule T2							
Long Bed		JN321	15475	1600	2100	3450	5425
TUNDRA 4WD—V8—Truck Equipment Schedule T2							
SR5 Long Bed		KT441	23190	2450	3050	4450	6575

Body	Type	VIN	List	Trade-In Fair	Good	Pvt-Party Good	Retail Excellent
V6 3.4 Liter		N		(450)	(450)	(600)	(600)
TUNDRA—V8—Truck Equipment Schedule T2							
SR5 Access Cab 4D		RT341	22730	2875	3500	4950	7150
Ltd Access Cab 4D		RT381	24975	3125	3800	5275	7500
4WD		4		1000	1000	1335	1335
V6 3.4 Liter		N		(450)	(450)	(600)	(600)

2001 TOYOTA–(4,5orJ)T(3,B,DorE)(HH20V)–1

Body	Type	VIN	List	Trade-In Fair	Good	Pvt-Party Good	Retail Excellent
RAV4 4WD—4-Cyl.—Truck Equipment Schedule T2							
Sport Utility 4D		HH20V	18095	4950	5800	7375	9900
2WD		G,Z		(500)	(500)	(665)	(665)
HIGHLANDER 4WD—V6—Truck Equipment Schedule T1							
Sport Utility 4D		HF21A	26950	5475	6375	7950	10550
Limited Spt Util 4D		HF21A	30445	6075	7025	8675	11350
2WD				(450)	(450)	(600)	(600)
4-Cyl. 2.4 Liter		D		(475)	(475)	(635)	(635)
4RUNNER 4WD—V6—Truck Equipment Schedule T1							
SR5 Sport Util 4D		HN86R	29375	4775	5600	7175	9650
Limited Sport Util 4D		HN87R	38085	6100	7050	8675	11350
2WD		G		(450)	(450)	(600)	(600)
SEQUOIA 4WD—V8—Truck Equipment Schedule T1							
SR5 Spt Util 4D		BT44A	34825	5575	6500	8175	10950
Limited Spt Util 4D		BT48A	42755	7200	8250	10100	13100
2WD				(450)	(450)	(600)	(600)
LAND CRUISER 4WD—V8—Truck Equipment Schedule T3							
Sport Utility 4D		HT05J	53375	12500	14100	16250	20200
Third Seat Pkg				475	475	635	635
SIENNA—V6—Truck Equipment Schedule T1							
CE Minivan		ZF19C	24385	2100	2675	4000	5975
LE Minivan		ZF13C	26235	2600	3200	4575	6650
XLE Minivan		ZF13C	28916	3075	3750	5150	7300
TACOMA—4-Cyl.—Truck Equipment Schedule T2							
Short Bed		NL42N	12325	2300	2875	4250	6275
Xtra Cab		VL52N	14965	3025	3675	5100	7250
PreRunner Short		NM92N	14215	2975	3625	5050	7200
PreRunner Xtra		SM92N	16815	3900	4625	6100	8400
PreRunner 4D		GM92N	18335	4575	5375	6950	9425
PreRunner Ltd 4D		GM92N	22690	5025	5875	7475	10050
4WD				1150	1150	1535	1535
V6 3.4 Liter		N		550	550	735	735
TACOMA—V6—Truck Equipment Schedule T2							
S-Runner Xtra Cab		VN52N	18385	3400	4100	5550	7800
TACOMA 4WD—V6—Truck Equipment Schedule T2							
Limited Xtra Cab		WN72N	24895	5300	6175	7800	10400
Double Cab		HN72N	22345	5475	6375	7975	10600
Ltd Double Cab 4D		HN72N	25840	5400	6300	7925	10550
4-Cyl. 2.7 Liter		M		(475)	(475)	(635)	(635)
TUNDRA—V6—Truck Equipment Schedule T2							
Long Bed		JN321	16085	1750	2250	3650	5650
TUNDRA 4WD—V8—Truck Equipment Schedule T2							
SR5 Long Bed		KT441	23885	2650	3250	4700	6850
TUNDRA—V8—Truck Equipment Schedule T2							
SR5 Access Cab 4D		RT341	23455	3100	3775	5250	7500
Ltd Access Cab 4D		RT381	26205	3375	4075	5550	7850
4WD		4		1100	1100	1465	1465
V6 3.4 Liter		N		(475)	(475)	(635)	(635)

2002 TOYOTA–(4,5orJ)T(3,B,DorE)(HH20V)–2

Body	Type	VIN	List	Trade-In Fair	Good	Pvt-Party Good	Retail Excellent
RAV4 4WD—4-Cyl.—Truck Equipment Schedule T2							
Sport Utility 4D		HH20V	18435	5600	6525	8350	11200
2WD		G		(500)	(500)	(665)	(665)
HIGHLANDER 4WD—V6—Truck Equipment Schedule T1							
Sport Utility 4D		HF21A	27370	6050	7025	8875	11800
Limited Spt Util 4D		HF21A	31305	6725	7750	9625	12700
2WD		G		(500)	(500)	(665)	(665)
4-Cyl. 2.4 Liter		D		(500)	(500)	(665)	(665)
4RUNNER 4WD—V6—Truck Equipment Schedule T1							
SR5 Sport Util 4D		HN86R	29385	5250	6125	7925	10750
Limited Spt Util 4D		HN87R	36615	6650	7650	9525	12550
2WD		G		(500)	(500)	(665)	(665)
SEQUOIA 4WD—V8—Truck Equipment Schedule T1							
SR5 Spt Util 4D		BT44A	35305	6200	7150	9150	12250

TRUCKS & VANS

Body	Type	VIN	List	Trade-In Fair	Trade-In Good	Pvt-Party Good	Retail Excellent
Limited Spt Util 4D		BT48A	43235	7900	9050	11150	14650
2WD		Z		(500)	(500)	(665)	(665)
LAND CRUISER 4WD—V8—Truck Equipment Schedule T3							
Sport Utility 4D		HT05J	53105	13925	15675	18050	22300
SIENNA—V6—Truck Equipment Schedule T1							
CE Minivan		ZF19C	24415	2150	2725	4300	6600
LE Minivan		ZF13C	26265	2700	3300	4925	7300
XLE Minivan		ZF13C	28522	3200	3900	5525	7975
TACOMA—4-Cyl.—Truck Equipment Schedule T2							
Short Bed		NL42N	12410	2575	3175	4800	7175
Xtra Cab		VL52N	15050	3325	4025	5700	8200
PreRunner Short		NM92N	14400	3300	3975	5650	8125
PreRunner Xtra		SM92N	17000	4300	5075	6800	9450
PreRunner 4D		GM92N	18620	5025	5875	7700	10500
4WD				1250	1250	1665	1665
V6 3.4 Liter		N		600	600	800	800
TACOMA 4WD—Truck Equipment Schedule T2							
S-Runner Xtra Cab		VN52N	18570	3775	4500	6200	8775
PreRunner Ltd 4D		GM92N	23000	5550	6475	8325	11200
TACOMA 4WD—V6—Truck Equipment Schedule T2							
Limited Xtra Cab		WN72N	23655	5875	6800	8675	11600
Double Cab 4D		HN72N	22630	5975	6925	8800	11750
Ltd Double Cab 4D		HN72N	26150	5925	6850	8725	11650
TUNDRA—V6—Truck Equipment Schedule T2							
Long Bed		JN321	16115	1700	2200	3875	6200
TUNDRA 4WD—V8—Truck Equipment Schedule T2							
SR5 Long Bed		KT441	23915	2650	3250	4975	7425
TUNDRA—V8—Truck Equipment Schedule T2							
SR5 Access Cab 4D		RT341	23485	3150	3825	5550	8100
Ltd Access Cab 4D		RT381	27230	3425	4125	5875	8450
4WD		4		1200	1200	1600	1600
V6 3.4 Liter		N		(500)	(500)	(665)	(665)

2003 TOYOTA-(4,5orJ)T(B,DorE)(HH20V)-3

Body	Type	VIN	List	Trade-In Fair	Trade-In Good	Pvt-Party Good	Retail Excellent
RAV4 4WD—4-Cyl.—Truck Equipment Schedule T2							
Sport Utility 4D		HH20V	18435	6125	7100	8950	11850
2WD		G,Z		(575)	(575)	(765)	(765)
HIGHLANDER 4WD—V6—Truck Equipment Schedule T1							
Sport Utility 4D		HF21A	25790	6750	7750	9600	12600
Limited Spt Utl 4D		HF21A	31305	7700	8825	10700	13800
2WD		D		(575)	(575)	(765)	(765)
4-Cyl. 2.4 Liter		D		(600)	(600)	(800)	(800)
4RUNNER 4WD—V6—Truck Equipment Schedule T1							
SR5 Sport Util 4D		BU14R	29990	7325	8400	10250	13350
Sport Util Utl 4D		BU14R	31785	7975	9150	11100	14350
Limited Spt Utl 4D		BU17R	36190	8950	10200	12200	15600
2WD		Z		(575)	(575)	(765)	(765)
V8 4.7 Liter		T		300	300	400	400
SEQUOIA 4WD—V8—Truck Equipment Schedule T1							
SR5 Spt Util 4D		BT44A	35565	7550	8650	10700	14000
Limited Spt Util 4D		BT48A	44030	9475	10775	12950	16550
2WD				(575)	(575)	(765)	(765)
LAND CRUISER 4WD—V8—Truck Equipment Schedule T3							
Sport Utility 4D		HT05J	53915	15475	17350	19800	24200
SIENNA—V6—Truck Equipment Schedule T1							
CE Minivan		ZF19C	24415	3075	3725	5350	7775
LE Minivan		ZF13C	26265	3700	4400	6075	8575
XLE Minivan		ZF13C	28522	4375	5200	6925	9575
TACOMA—4-Cyl.—Truck Equipment Schedule T2							
Short Bed		NL42N	12610	3175	3850	5525	8000
Xtra Cab		VL52N	15250	4125	4875	6600	9200
PreRunner Short		NM92N	14525	4075	4825	6550	9150
PreRunner Xtra		SM92N	17200	5175	6025	7850	10650
PreRunner 4D		GM92N	18820	6050	7000	8850	11750
4WD				1425	1425	1900	1900
V6 3.4 Liter		N		700	700	935	935
TACOMA—V6—Truck Equipment Schedule T2							
PreRunner Ltd 4D		GN92N	23430	6650	7675	9525	12550
TACOMA 4WD—V6—Truck Equipment Schedule T2							
Limited Xtra Cab		WN72N	24085	7125	8175	10100	13200
Double Cab 4D		HN72N	22830	7100	8150	10100	13200
Ltd Double Cab 4D		HN72N	26580	7275	8350	10250	13400

TRUCKS & VANS

Body	Type	VIN	List	Trade-In Fair	Trade-In Good	Pvt-Party Good	Retail Excellent
TUNDRA—V6—Truck Equipment Schedule T2							
Long Bed		JN321	16465	2175	2750	4450	6875
TUNDRA 4WD—V8—Truck Equipment Schedule T2							
SR5 Long Bed		KT441	24265	3450	4175	5925	8550
TUNDRA—V8—Truck Equipment Schedule T2							
SR5 Access Cab 4D		RT341	23835	4125	4875	6700	9375
Ltd Access Cab 4D		RT381	27465	4425	5225	7075	9900
4WD		4		1375	1375	1835	1835
V6 3.4 Liter		N		(575)	(575)	(765)	(765)

2004 TOYOTA—(5orJ)T(B,DorE)(HD20V)—4—#

Body	Type	VIN	List	Trade-In Fair	Trade-In Good	Pvt-Party Good	Retail Excellent
RAV4 4WD—4-Cyl.—Truck Equipment Schedule T2							
Sport Utility 4D		HD20V	20290	6825	7875	9700	12700
2WD		G		(650)	(650)	(865)	(865)
HIGHLANDER 4WD—V6—Truck Equipment Schedule T1							
Sport Utility 4D		HD21A	27930	7600	8700	10550	13600
Limited Spt Utl 4D		HF21A	31920	8825	10050	12000	15300
Third Seat				550	550	735	735
2WD				(650)	(650)	(865)	(865)
4-Cyl. 2.4 Liter		D		(700)	(700)	(935)	(935)
4RUNNER 4WD—V6—Truck Equipment Schedule T2							
SR5 Sport Util 4D		BU14R	29985	8600	9800	11750	15050
Sport Utility 4D		BU14R	31225	9375	10675	12650	16000
Limited Spt Util 4D		BU17R	36260	10475	11900	13900	17450
Third Seat				350	350	465	465
2WD		Z		(650)	(650)	(865)	(865)
V8 4.7 Liter		T		350	350	465	465
SEQUOIA 4WD—V8—Truck Equipment Schedule T1							
SR5 Spt Util 4D		BT44A	35695	9050	10300	12450	16000
Limited Spt Util 4D		BT48A	44760	11175	12650	14850	18700
2WD		Z		(650)	(650)	(865)	(865)
LAND CRUISER 4WD—V8—Truck Equipment Schedule T3							
Sport Utility 4D		HT05J	54765	17700	19900	22200	27000
SIENNA—V6—Truck Equipment Schedule T2							
CE Minivan		ZA23C	23495	4000	4725	6425	8950
LE Minivan		ZA23C	24800	4700	5525	7225	9900
XLE Minivan		ZA22C	28800	5600	6525	8275	11050
XLE Limited		ZA22C	35020	6350	7350	9125	12000
AWD		B		725	725	965	965
TACOMA PICKUP—4-Cyl.—Truck Equipment Schedule T2							
Short Bed		NL42N	12800	3950	4700	6425	9000
Xtra Cab		VL52N	15460	4975	5825	7625	10400
PreRunner Short		NM92N	14715	4925	5775	7575	10350
PreRunner Xtra		SM92N	17410	6150	7100	8950	11850
PreRunner 4D		GM92N	19030	7175	8250	10150	13200
4WD		W,H		1600	1600	2135	2135
V6 3.4 Liter		N		800	800	1065	1065
TACOMA PICKUP—V6—Truck Equipment Schedule T2							
S-Runner Xtra Cab		VN52N	20700	5975	6925	8750	11650
PreRunner Ltd 4D		GN92N	23640	7875	9000	10950	14150
TACOMA PICKUP 4WD—V6—Truck Equipment Schedule T2							
Limited Xtra Cab		WN72N	24295	8500	9725	11650	15000
Double Cab 4D		HN72N	23040	8325	9525	11450	14750
Ltd Double Cab 4D		HN72N	26790	8775	10000	11950	15300
TUNDRA—V6—Truck Equipment Schedule T2							
Long Bed		JN321	16495	2625	3225	5025	7575
TUNDRA 4WD—V8—Truck Equipment Schedule T2							
SR5 Long Bed		KT441	24415	4300	5075	6875	9650
TUNDRA—V8—Truck Equipment Schedule T2							
SR5 Access Cab 4D		RN341	23985	5050	5900	7825	10750
Ltd Access Cab 4D		RT381	27615	5425	6325	8225	11150
SR5 Double Cab 4D		ET341	26185	6975	8025	10000	13200
Ltd Double Cab 4D		ET381	29810	7625	8750	10750	14000
4WD		4		1550	1550	2065	2065
V6 3.4 Liter		N		(650)	(650)	(865)	(865)

2005 TOYOTA—(5orJ)T(B,DorE)(HD20V)—5—#

Body	Type	VIN	List	Trade-In Fair	Trade-In Good	Pvt-Party Good	Retail Excellent
RAV4 4WD—4-Cyl.—Truck Equipment Schedule T2							
Sport Utility 4D		HD20V	20515	7700	8825	10650	13650
2WD		G		(725)	(725)	(965)	(965)
HIGHLANDER 4WD—V6—Truck Equipment Schedule T1							
Sport Utility 4D		HD21A	27955	8600	9800	11650	14900

TRUCKS & VANS

Body Type	VIN	List	Trade-In Fair	Good	Pvt-Party Good	Retail Excellent
Limited Spt Util 4D EP21A	31945	**10150**	**11525**	**13450**	**16850**
Third Seat			**600**	**600**	**800**	**800**
2WD .... E,G			**(725)**	**(725)**	**(965)**	**(965)**
4-Cyl. 2.4 Liter .... D			**(800)**	**(800)**	**(1065)**	**(1065)**
4RUNNER 4WD—V6—Truck Equipment Schedule T1						
SR5 Sport Util 4D BU14R	30335	**10100**	**11475**	**13400**	**16750**
Sport Utility 4D BU14R	31605	**10975**	**12450**	**14350**	**17850**
Limited Spt Util 4D BU17R	36610	**12250**	**13875**	**15850**	**19450**
Third Seat			**400**	**400**	**535**	**535**
2WD .... Z			**(725)**	**(725)**	**(965)**	**(965)**
V8 4.7 Liter .... T			**400**	**400**	**535**	**535**
SEQUOIA 4WD—V8—Truck Equipment Schedule T1						
SR5 Spt Util 4D BT44A	36520	**10725**	**12150**	**14300**	**18100**
Limited Spt Util 4D BT48A	45525	**13025**	**14700**	**16950**	**21000**
2WD			**(725)**	**(725)**	**(965)**	**(965)**
LAND CRUISER 4WD—V8—Truck Equipment Schedule T3						
Sport Utility 4D HT05J	55590	**20100**	**22450**	**24700**	**29500**
SIENNA—V6—Truck Equipment Schedule T1						
CE Minivan ZA23C	23790	**5150**	**6000**	**7725**	**10450**
LE Minivan ZA23C	25295	**5925**	**6850**	**8625**	**11400**
XLE Minivan ZA22C	29590	**7025**	**8100**	**9900**	**12850**
XLE Limited ZA22C	35860	**7875**	**9000**	**10850**	**13950**
AWD .... B			**800**	**800**	**1065**	**1065**
TACOMA PICKUP—4-Cyl.—Truck Equipment Schedule T2						
Short Bed NX22N	13980	**4300**	**5100**	**6800**	**9450**
Access Cab TX22N	17395	**5575**	**6525**	**8325**	**11150**
PreRunner Short NX62N	14850	**4700**	**5525**	**7300**	**10050**
4WD 4,5			**1775**	**1775**	**2365**	**2365**
V6 4.0 Liter .... U			**900**	**900**	**1200**	**1200**
TACOMA PICKUP—4-Cyl.—Truck Equipment Schedule T2						
PreRunner Access TX62N	18155	**6450**	**7450**	**9275**	**12250**
TACOMA PICKUP—V6—Truck Equipment Schedule T2						
X-Runner Access TU22N	23650	**9375**	**10675**	**12600**	**15950**
PreRunner Access TU62N	19610	**7525**	**8625**	**10500**	**13550**
PreRunner Dbl 5' JU62N	22240	**9125**	**10400**	**12300**	**15650**
PreRunner Dbl 6' KU72N	22740	**9100**	**10350**	**12250**	**15600**
TACOMA PICKUP 4WD—V6—Truck Equipment Schedule T2						
Double Cab 5' LU42N	24435	**9950**	**11275**	**13250**	**16650**
Double Cab 6' MU52N	25815	**9900**	**11225**	**13200**	**16600**
TUNDRA—V6—Truck Equipment Schedule T2						
Long Bed JU321	16520	**3125**	**3800**	**5625**	**8300**
TUNDRA—V8—Truck Equipment Schedule T2						
Work Truck Long JT321	18995	**3950**	**4675**	**6550**	**9300**
SR5 Access Cab 4D RT341	24700	**6025**	**6975**	**8950**	**12000**
Ltd Access Cab 4D RT381	27640	**6425**	**7425**	**9375**	**12500**
SR5 Double Cab 4D ET341	26685	**7950**	**9100**	**11100**	**14450**
Ltd Double Cab 4D ET381	30310	**8700**	**9900**	**11950**	**15400**
4WD 4			**1725**	**1725**	**2300**	**2300**
V6 4.0 Liter .... U			**(725)**	**(725)**	**(965)**	**(965)**

2006 TOYOTA—(3,5orJ)T(B,D,EorM)(BD33V)-6

Body Type	VIN	List	Trade-In Fair	Good	Pvt-Party Good	Retail Excellent
RAV4 4WD—4-Cyl.—Truck Equipment Schedule T2						
Sport Utility 4D BD33V	22305	**8825**	**10050**	**11900**	**15150**
Sport SUV 4D BD32V	23880	**9500**	**10775**	**12700**	**15950**
Limited SUV 4D BD31V	24560	**10350**	**11700**	**13550**	**16950**
Third Seat			**425**	**425**	**565**	**565**
2WD .... Z			**(800)**	**(800)**	**(1065)**	**(1065)**
V6 3.5 Liter .... K			**800**	**800**	**1065**	**1065**
HIGHLANDER 4WD—V6 Hybrid—Truck Equipment Sch T1						
Sport Utility 4D EW21A	34995	**15325**	**17250**	**19150**	**23000**
Limited Utility 4D EW21A	39855	**16750**	**18775**	**20800**	**25000**
Third Seat			**650**	**650**	**865**	**865**
2WD .... D,G			**(800)**	**(800)**	**(1065)**	**(1065)**
HIGHLANDER 4WD—V6—Truck Equipment Schedule T1						
Sport Utility 4D HD21A	27595	**9900**	**11225**	**13150**	**16450**
Sport SUV 4D HD21A	29840	**10775**	**12200**	**14050**	**17500**
Limited Spt Utl 4D EP21A	32425	**11750**	**13275**	**15200**	**18700**
Third Seat			**650**	**650**	**865**	**865**
2WD .... D,G			**(800)**	**(800)**	**(1065)**	**(1065)**
4-Cyl. 2.4 Liter .... D			**(900)**	**(900)**	**(1200)**	**(1200)**
4RUNNER 4WD—V6—Truck Equipment Schedule T1						
SR5 Sport Util 4D BU14R	30475	**11800**	**13325**	**15250**	**18750**
Sport Utility 4D BU14R	32815	**12750**	**14400**	**16250**	**19900**

TRUCKS & VANS

Body Type	VIN	List	Trade-In Fair	Trade-In Good	Pvt-Party Good	Retail Excellent
Limited Spt Util 4D	BU17R	37190	14150	15925	17900	21700
Third Seat			425	425	565	565
2WD	Z		(800)	(800)	(1065)	(1065)
V8 4.7 Liter	T		425	425	565	565
SEQUOIA 4WD—V8—Truck Equipment Schedule T1						
SR5 Spt Util 4D	BT44A	36870	12650	14250	16400	20400
Limited Spt Util 4D	BT48A	45875	15100	17000	19250	23500
2WD	Z		(800)	(800)	(1065)	(1065)
LAND CRUISER AWD—V8—Truck Equipment Schedule T3						
Sport Utility 4D	HT05J	56680	22650	25275	27500	32400
SIENNA—V6—Truck Equipment Schedule T1						
CE Minivan	ZA23C	24190	6650	7650	9375	12250
LE Minivan	ZA23C	25695	7475	8575	10350	13350
XLE Minivan	ZA22C	29990	8825	10050	11850	15000
XLE Limited	ZA22C	36445	9725	11025	12900	16100
AWD	B		875	875	1165	1165
TACOMA PICKUP—4-Cyl.—Truck Equipment Schedule T1						
Short Bed	NX22N	14345	5125	5975	7800	10600
Access Cab	TX22N	17785	6550	7550	9350	12300
PreRunner Short	NX62N	15215	5600	6525	8325	11150
PreRunner Access	TX62N	18545	7500	8600	10450	13500
4WD	4,5		1950	1950	2600	2600
V6 4.0 Liter	U		1000	1000	1335	1335
TACOMA PICKUP—V6—Truck Equipment Schedule T2						
X-Runner Access	TU22N	24110	10775	12200	14100	17600
PreRunner Dbl 5'	JU62N	22605	10425	11850	13750	17250
PreRunner Dbl 6'	KU72N	23105	10425	11800	13750	17200
TACOMA PICKUP 4WD—V6—Truck Equipment Schedule T2						
Double Cab 5'	LU42N	24800	11425	12875	14850	18400
Double Cab 6'	MU52N	26180	11375	12850	14800	18350
TUNDRA—V6—Truck Equipment Schedule T2						
Long Bed	JU321	16720	3650	4350	6275	9075
TUNDRA—V8—Truck Equipment Schedule T2						
Work Truck Long	JT321	19195	4525	5350	7300	10250
SR5 Access Cab 4D	RT341	24880	7025	8075	10100	13300
Ltd Access Cab 4D	RT381	27820	7475	8575	10600	13800
SR5 Double Cab 4D	ET341	27185	8950	10200	12250	15750
Ltd Double Cab 4D	ET381	30810	9750	11075	13200	16700
4WD	4		1900	1900	2535	2535
V6 4.0 Liter	U		(800)	(800)	(1065)	(1065)

Body Type	VIN	List	Trade-In Fair	Trade-In Good	Pvt-Party Good	Retail Excellent
RAV4 4WD—4-Cyl.—Truck Equipment Schedule T2						
Sport Utility 4D	BD33V	22855	10350	11700	13500	16700
Sport SUV 4D	BD32V	22470	11125	12600	14350	17700
Limited SUV 4D	BD31V	25110	11950	13525	15350	18750
Third Seat			450	450	600	600
2WD	Z		(875)	(875)	(1165)	(1165)
V6 3.5 Liter	K		800	800	1065	1065
FJ CRUISER 4WD—V6—Truck Equipment Schedule T1						
Sport Utility 2D	BU11F	24105	13925	15675	17450	21100
TRD Special Edition			1500	1500	2000	2000
2WD			(875)	(875)	(1165)	(1165)
HIGHLANDER 4WD—V6 Hybrid—Truck Equipment Schedule T1						
Sport Utility 4D	EW21A	34495	17450	19550	21500	25500
Limited Utility 4D	EW21A	36615	19000	21275	23100	27300
Third Seat			700	700	935	935
2WD			(875)	(875)	(1165)	(1165)
HIGHLANDER 4WD—V6—Truck Equipment Schedule T1						
Sport Utility 4D	HD21A	27945	11525	13025	14800	18200
Sport SUV 4D	HD21A	30190	12450	14075	15850	19300
Limited Spt Utl 4D	EP21A	32815	13675	15425	17250	20900
Third Seat			700	700	935	935
2WD	D,G		(875)	(875)	(1165)	(1165)
4-Cyl. 2.4 Liter	D		(1000)	(1000)	(1335)	(1335)
4RUNNER 4WD—V6—Truck Equipment Schedule T1						
SR5 Sport Util 4D	BU14R	30515	13775	15525	17350	21000
Sport Utility 4D	BU14R	32855	14750	16600	18400	22100
Limited Spt Util 4D	BU17R	37230	16375	18375	20200	24000
Third Seat			450	450	600	600
2WD	Z		(875)	(875)	(1165)	(1165)
V8 4.7 Liter	T		450	450	600	600

TRUCKS & VANS

Body Type	VIN	List	Trade-In Fair	Trade-In Good	Pvt-Party Good	Retail Excellent
SEQUOIA 4WD—V8—Truck Equipment Schedule T1						
SR5 Spt Util 4D	BT44A	37250	15300	17200	19400	23600
Limited Spt Util 4D	BT48A	46265	18325	20475	22700	27300
2WD	Z		(875)	(875)	(1165)	(1165)
LAND CRUISER AWD—V8—Truck Equipment Schedule T3						
Sport Utility 4D	HT05J	56820	28525	31750	33800	39200
SIENNA—V6—Truck Equipment Schedule T1						
CE Minivan	ZK23C	24800	8650	9850	11550	14600
LE Minivan	ZK23C	26325	9525	10825	12600	15750
XLE Minivan	ZK22C	30770	11125	12600	14300	17600
XLE Limited	ZK22C	36110	12050	13625	15400	18800
AWD	B		950	950	1265	1265
TACOMA PICKUP—4-Cyl.—Truck Equipment Schedule T2						
Short Bed	TX22N	14885	6100	7050	8775	11550
Access Cab	TX22N	18125	7675	8775	10500	13450
PreRunner Short	NX62N	15555	6675	7675	9375	12200
PreRunner Access	TX62N	18885	8700	9900	11700	14800
4WD	4,5		2125	2125	2835	2835
V6 4.0 Liter	U		1100	1100	1465	1465
TACOMA PICKUP—V6—Truck Equipment Schedule T2						
X-Runner Access	TU22N	24450	12250	13875	15700	19150
PreRunner Dbl 5'	JU62N	22945	11950	13525	15350	18750
PreRunner Dbl 6'	KU72N	23445	11900	13475	15300	18700
TACOMA PICKUP 4WD—V6—Truck Equipment Schedule T2						
Double Cab 5'	LU42N	25140	13025	14700	16500	20100
Double Cab 6'	MU52N	26520	12925	14600	16400	20000
TUNDRA PICKUP—V8—Equipment Schedule T1						
Short Bed	JT521	24075	9575	10875	12950	16400
Long Bed	LT521	24405	9375	10675	12700	16100
SR5 Double 6 1/2'	RT541	27495	12000	13575	15650	19350
SR5 Double 8'	ST541	27825	11525	13025	15100	18750
Ltd Double Cab 4D	RT581	34885	15375	17300	19350	23400
SR5 CrewMax 4D	ET541	30320	13075	14750	16800	20700
Limited CrewMax 4D	ET581	38185	17550	19700	21800	26200
4WD	M		2075	2075	2765	2765
V6 4.0 Liter	U		(875)	(875)	(1165)	(1165)
V8 4.7 Liter	T		(500)	(500)	(665)	(665)

Body Type	VIN	List	Trade-In Fair	Trade-In Good	Pvt-Party Good	Retail Excellent
RAV4 4WD—4-Cyl.—Truck Equipment Schedule T2						
Sport Utility 4D	BD33V	23185	12350	13975	15700	19050
Sport SUV 4D	BD32V	24760	13175	14850	16600	20100
Limited SUV 4D	BD31V	25440	14100	15875	17650	21300
Third Row			475	475	635	635
2WD	Z		(950)	(950)	(1265)	(1265)
V6 3.5 Liter	K		800	800	1065	1065
FJ CRUISER 4WD—V6—Truck Equipment Schedule T1						
Sport Utility 2D	BU11F	23230	16275	18225	20000	23700
2WD	Z		(950)	(950)	(1265)	(1265)
HIGHLANDER 4WD—V6 Hybrid—Truck Equipment Schedule T1						
Sport Utility 4D	EW41A	34885	21550	24000	25800	30000
Limited Utility 4D	EW44A	40635	24400	27250	28900	33300
Third Row			750	750	1000	1000
HIGHLANDER 4WD—V6—Truck Equipment Schedule T1						
Sport Utility 4D	ES41A	29435	16325	18325	20100	23800
Sport SUV 4D	ES43A	32085	17300	19350	21100	25000
Limited Spt Util 4D	ES42A	34835	19550	21850	23600	27600
Third Row			750	750	1000	1000
2WD	D		(950)	(950)	(1265)	(1265)
4RUNNER 4WD—V6—Truck Equipment Schedule T1						
SR5 Sport Util 4D	BU14R	30975	17100	19150	20900	24800
Sport SUV 4D	BU14R	31010	18125	20275	22100	26100
Limited Spt Util 4D	BU17R	35385	19900	22250	23900	28000
Third Row			475	475	635	635
2WD	Z		(950)	(950)	(1265)	(1265)
V8 4.7 Liter	T		475	475	635	635
SEQUOIA 4WD—V8—Truck Equipment Schedule T1						
SR5 Spt Util 4D	BT44A	39185	22825	25475	27600	32500
Limited Spt Util 4D	BY68A	49135	26075	29000	31300	36600
Platinum Spt Util	BY67A	56285	27825	30975	33100	38400
2WD	Z		(950)	(950)	(1265)	(1265)
LAND CRUISER 4WD—V8—Truck Equipment Schedule T3						
Sport Utility 4D	HY05J	63885				

TRUCKS & VANS

Body	Type	VIN	List	Trade-In Fair	Good	Pvt-Party Good	Retail Excellent
SIENNA—V6—Truck Equipment Schedule T1							
CE Minivan	ZK23C	25025	11275	12750	14400	17600
LE Minivan	ZK23C	26550	12250	13875	15550	18850
XLE Minivan	ZK22C	30210	14075	15825	17550	21100
XLE Limited	ZK22C	36150	16525	18525	20300	24100
4WD	B	------	1025	1025	1365	1365
TACOMA PICKUP—4-Cyl.—Truck Equipment Schedule T2							
Short Bed	TX22N	14985	7650	8750	10350	13100
Access Cab	TX22N	18405	9325	10625	12300	15350
PreRunner Short	NX62N	15835	8250	9425	11050	14000
PreRunner Access	TX62N	19165	10425	11850	13500	16700
4WD	P,U	------	2300	2300	3065	3065
V6 4.0 Liter	U	------	1200	1200	1600	1600
TACOMA PICKUP—V6—Truck Equipment Schedule T2							
X-Runner Access	TU22N	24730	14350	16125	17950	21600
PreRunner Dbl 5'	JU62N	23225	14075	15825	17600	21200
PreRunner Dbl 6'	KU72N	23725	13975	15725	17500	21100
TACOMA PICKUP 4WD—V6—Truck Equipment Schedule T2							
Double Cab 5'	LU42N	25420	15200	17100	18850	22600
Double Cab 6'	MU52N	26800	15100	17000	18750	22500
TUNDRA PICKUP—V8—Truck Equipment Schedule T1							
Short Bed	JT521	24115	11625	13125	15200	18850
Long Bed	LT521	24445	11425	12875	14900	18550
Double 6 1/2'	RU541	25545	13075	14750	16800	20700
Double 8'	ST541	26475	12800	14450	16450	20300
SR5 Double 6 1/2'	RT541	27535	14200	15975	18050	22000
SR5 Double 8'	ST541	27885	13725	15475	17550	21500
Ltd Double Cab 4D	ET581	35145	17875	20000	22100	26500
CrewMax 4D	ET541	28370	14700	16525	18550	22500
SR5 CrewMax 4D	ET541	30360	15425	17350	19400	23500
Limited CrewMax	ET581	38445	20275	22650	24700	29200
4WD	K,M	------	2250	2250	3000	3000
V6 4.0 Liter	U	------	(950)	(950)	(1265)	(1265)
V8 4.7 Liter	T	------	(500)	(500)	(665)	(665)

VOLKSWAGEN

1994 - 1998 VOLKSWAGEN — Not Imported

1999 VOLKSWAGEN — WV2(KH270)-X-#

Body	Type	VIN	List	Trade-In Fair	Good	Pvt-Party Good	Retail Excellent
EUROVAN—V6—Truck Equipment Schedule T1							
GLS Minivan	KH270	30465	4650	5500	7050	9550
MV Minivan	MH270	31965	5050	5900	7525	10100
Weekender Pkg		------	7000	7000	9330	9330

2000 VOLKSWAGEN — WV2(KH270)-Y-#

Body	Type	VIN	List	Trade-In Fair	Good	Pvt-Party Good	Retail Excellent
EUROVAN—V6—Truck Equipment Schedule T1							
GLS Minivan	KH270	31890	5725	6675	8275	10950
MV Minivan	MH270	33390	6175	7125	8800	11500
Weekender Pkg		------	7000	7000	9330	9330

2001 VOLKSWAGEN — WV2(KH470)-1-#

Body	Type	VIN	List	Trade-In Fair	Good	Pvt-Party Good	Retail Excellent
EUROVAN—V6—Truck Equipment Schedule T1							
Minivan	KH470	26815	6850	7925	9575	12400
MV Minivan	MH470	28315	7325	8400	10100	13000
Weekender Pkg		------	7000	7000	9330	9330

2002 VOLKSWAGEN — WV2(KB470)-2-#

Body	Type	VIN	List	Trade-In Fair	Good	Pvt-Party Good	Retail Excellent
EUROVAN—V6—Truck Equipment Schedule T1							
GLS Minivan	KB470	26815	7900	9050	11050	14300
MV Minivan	MB470	28315	8375	9575	11550	14900
Weekender Pkg		------	7000	7000	9330	9330

2003 VOLKSWAGEN — WV2(KB470)-3-#

Body	Type	VIN	List	Trade-In Fair	Good	Pvt-Party Good	Retail Excellent
EUROVAN—V6—Truck Equipment Schedule T1							
GLS Minivan	KB470	26815	9275	10575	12550	15950
MV Minivan	MB470	28315	9850	11175	13200	16650
Weekender Pkg		------	7000	7000	9330	9330

2004 VOLKSWAGEN

Body	Type	VIN	List	Trade-In Fair	Good	Pvt-Party Good	Retail Excellent
2004 VOLKSWAGEN — WVG(BC67L)-4-#							
TOUAREG 4WD—V6—Truck Equipment Schedule T3							
Sport Utility 4D		BC67L	35515	9725	11025	13100	16550
4 Corner Air Suspension				2000	2000	2665	2665
TOUAREG 4WD—V8—Truck Equipment Schedule T3							
Sport Utility 4D		GM67L	43255	11275	12750	14850	18500
4 Corner Air Suspension				2000	2000	2665	2665
TOUAREG 4WD—V10 Turbo Diesel—Truck Equipment Schedule T3							
TDI Sport Util 4D		GH67L	58415	26450	29500	32100	38000
2005 VOLKSWAGEN — WVG(BG77L)-5-#							
TOUAREG 4WD—V6—Truck Equipment Schedule T3							
Sport Utility 4D		BG77L	37755	11075	12550	14550	18200
4 Corner Air Suspension				2000	2000	2665	2665
TOUAREG 4WD—V8—Truck Equipment Schedule T3							
Sport Utility 4D		GM67L	44915	12925	14600	16700	20600
4 Corner Air Suspension				2000	2000	2665	2665
2006 VOLKSWAGEN — WVG(BG67L)-6-#							
TOUAREG 4WD—V6—Truck Equipment Schedule T3							
Sport Utility 4D		BG67L	37975	12600	14200	16150	19900
4 Corner Air Suspension				2000	2000	2665	2665
TOUAREG 4WD—V8—Truck Equipment Schedule T3							
Sport Utility 4D		GM67L	45420	14800	16650	18650	22600
4 Corner Air Suspension				2000	2000	2665	2665
TOUAREG 4WD—V10—Truck Equipment Schedule T3							
TDI Sport Utility 4D		PT77L	68420	31075	34500	36800	42600
2007 VOLKSWAGEN — WVG(BE77L)-7-#							
TOUAREG 4WD—V6—Truck Equipment Schedule T3							
Sport Utility 4D		BE77L	38660	14250	16025	18000	21800
4 Corner Air Suspension				2000	2000	2665	2665
TOUAREG 4WD—V8—Truck Equipment Schedule T3							
Sport Utility 4D		CB77L	43660	16850	18875	20900	24900
4 Corner Air Suspension				2000	2000	2665	2665
TOUAREG 4WD—V10 Turbo Diesel—Truck Equipment Schedule T3							
TDI Sport Utility 4D		PT77L	59690	34100	37925	40000	45800
2008 VOLKSWAGEN — WVG(BE77L)-8-#							
TOUAREG 2 4WD—V6—Truck Equipment Schedule T3							
Sport Utility 4D		BE77L	40000	24000	26750	28500	33100
4 Corner Air Suspension				2000	2000	2665	2665
TOUAREG 2 4WD—V8—Truck Equipment Schedule T3							
Sport Utility 4D		CB77L	49000	26950	30000	31900	36800
4 Corner Air Suspension				2000	2000	2665	2665
TOUAREG 2 4WD—V10 Turbo Diesel—Truck Equipment Schedule T3							
TDI Sport Utility 4D		PT77L	69000				

VOLVO

2003 VOLVO — YV1(CN59H)-3-#							
XC90—5-Cyl. Turbo—Truck Equipment Schedule T3							
Sport Utility 4D		CN59H	36610	6625	7650	9600	12750
Third Row Seat				350	350	465	465
AWD				1200	1200	1600	1600
XC90 AWD—6-Cyl. Twin Turbo—Truck Equipment Schedule T3							
T6 Sport Utility 4D		CM91H	40660	8200	9375	11450	14900
Third Row Seat				350	350	465	465
2004 VOLVO — YV1(CN59V)-4-#							
XC90—5-Cyl. Turbo—Truck Equipment Schedule T3							
Sport Utility 4D		CN59V	35475	7975	9150	11200	14600
Third Row Seat				400	400	535	535
AWD				1200	1200	1600	1600
XC90 AWD—6-Cyl. Twin Turbo—Truck Equipment Schedule T3							
T6 Sport Utility 4D		CM91H	41650	9750	11075	13250	16850
Third Row Seat				400	400	535	535

392   DEDUCT FOR RECONDITIONING   0709

2005 VOLVO

Body	Type	VIN	List	Trade-In Fair	Trade-In Good	Pvt-Party Good	Retail Excellent
2005 VOLVO — YV1(CN592)-5-#							
XC90—5-Cyl. Turbo—Truck Equipment Schedule T3							
Sport Utility 4D		CN592	35525	9525	10825	12950	16500
Third Row Seat		Y		450	450	600	600
AWD		M		1200	1200	1600	1600
XC90 AWD—6-Cyl. Twin Turbo—Truck Equipment Schedule T3							
T6 Sport Utility 4D		CM911	41700	11525	13025	15200	18950
Third Row Seat		Y		450	450	600	600
XC90 AWD—V8—Truck Equipment Schedule T3							
Sport Utility 4D		CM852	46080	12750	14400	16550	20500
Third Row Seat		Z		450	450	600	600
2006 VOLVO — YV1(CN592)-6-#							
XC90—5-Cyl. Turbo—Truck Equipment Schedule T3							
2.5T Sport Utility 4D		CN592	36335	11325	12800	14900	18650
Third Row Seat		Y		500	500	665	665
AWD		M		1200	1200	1600	1600
XC90 AWD—V8—Truck Equipment Schedule T3							
Sport Utility 4D		CM852	46535	14800	16650	18800	22900
Ocean Race Spt Utl		CM852	50555	16900	18975	21300	25700
Third Row Seat		Z		500	500	665	665
2007 VOLVO — YV1(CN982)-7-#							
XC90—6-Cyl.—Truck Equipment Schedule T3							
3.2 Sport Utility 4D		CN982	36830	15525	17450	19600	23700
Third Row Seat		Y,Z		550	550	735	735
AWD				550	550	735	735
XC90 AWD—V8—Truck Equipment Schedule T3							
Sport Utility 4D		CT852	47120	19450	21750	23900	28500
Sport SUV 4D		CZ852	49995	21375	23825	26100	30800
Third Row Seat		T,Z		550	550	735	735
2008 VOLVO — YV4(CN982)-8-#							
XC90—6-Cyl.—Truck Equipment Schedule T3							
3.2 Sport Utility 4D		CN982	36955	20875	23425	25500	30100
Third Row		Y,Z		575	575	765	765
XC90 AWD—V8—Truck Equipment Schedule T3							
Sport Utility 4D		CZ852	49250	25100	27925	30100	35100
Sport SUV 4D		CT852	50615	27150	30275	32300	37500
Third Row		T,Z		575	575	765	765

TRUCKS & VANS

Equipment	94-95	96	97	98	99	00	01

MODEL PACKAGES (Truck Schedules T1 & T2)
(Add Only If Not Listed on Individual Vehicle Listing)

CHEVROLET/GMC:

	94-95	96	97	98	99	00	01
LT (Astro)/SLT (Safari)	100	100	100	100	125	150	175

FORD:

	94-95	96	97	98	99	00	01
Limited, Chateau	100	150	225	300	375	450	525
Eddie Bauer	600	625	650	675	700	—	—

ALL MAKES:
(All Other Model Packages Not Listed)

	94-95	96	97	98	99	00	01
	75	75	75	75	75	75	100

TRUCK SCHEDULE T1 (Deduct For)

	94-95	96	97	98	99	00	01
Manual Trans	(250)	(250)	(275)	(300)	(325)	(350)	(375)
w/o Pwr Steering	(125)	(125)	(150)	(150)	(150)	(150)	(150)
w/o Air Cond	(175)	(175)	(200)	(225)	(250)	(250)	(250)

TRUCK SCHEDULE T2 (Add For)

	94-95	96	97	98	99	00	01
Auto Trans	200	200	225	250	275	300	325
Power Steering	75	75	75	75	75	75	75
Air Cond	175	175	200	200	200	200	200
TOTAL	450	450	500	525	550	575	600

TRUCK SCHEDULE T3 (See Page 395)

OTHER OPTIONS (Truck Schedules T1 & T2)

	94-95	96	97	98	99	00	01
Cassette	25	25	25	25	25	50	75
Power Windows	75	75	100	100	100	100	100
Pwr Door Locks	50	50	50	50	50	50	50
Tilt Wheel	50	50	75	75	75	75	75
Cruise Control	25	25	25	25	25	25	25
TOTAL	225	225	275	275	275	300	325

	94-95	96	97	98	99	00	01
w/o AM/FM	(50)	(50)	(50)	(50)	(50)	(50)	(50)
CD (Single Disc)	100	100	100	100	125	150	175
CD (Multi Disc)	200	200	200	200	225	250	275
Premium Sound	50	50	50	50	50	50	50
Air Cond, Rear	125	125	150	175	200	225	250
Leather	50	50	75	100	125	150	175
Quad Seating (4 Buckets)	125	125	150	150	150	150	150

1994 –2001 TRUCK FACTORY EQUIPMENT

Equipment	94-95	96	97	98	99	00	01
Van Seating Pkgs							
(11/12 Pass)	275	275	300	325	350	375	400
(15 Passenger)	525	525	550	575	600	625	650
Privacy Glass (Vans/Wagons/Sport Utilities)							
	50	50	50	50	50	50	50
Sliding Rear Window (Pickups)							
	25	25	25	25	25	25	25
Roof Rack	25	25	25	25	25	25	25
Sun Roof or Moon Roof							
(Sliding)	150	150	175	200	225	250	275
Pickup Shell/Cap	75	75	100	100	100	100	100
Bed Liner	50	50	50	50	50	50	75
Grille Guard	50	50	50	50	50	50	50
Winch	50	50	50	50	75	100	125
Custom Bumper	50	50	50	50	50	50	50
Stepside							
(Short Bed PU)	50	50	75	100	125	150	150
(Long Bed PU)	(250)	(250)	(250)	(250)	(250)	(250)	(250)
Running Boards	200	200	200	200	200	200	200
Alloy Wheels	75	75	100	125	150	150	150
Premium Wheels	150	150	175	200	225	250	275
Wide Tires or Oversize Off-Road Tires							
	50	50	50	50	50	50	75
ABS (4-Wheel)	75	75	100	125	150	150	150
Opt Fuel Tank	50	50	50	50	—	—	—
Towing Pkg	125	125	150	175	200	200	200
Dual Rear Wheels (Add Only on Models Not Listed as DR)							
	600	600	650	700	725	750	775

TRUCK SCHEDULE T3 (This Equipment Only)

	94-95	96	97	98	99	00	01
CD (Single Disc)	100	100	100	100	125	150	175
CD (Multi Disc)	200	200	200	200	225	250	275
Premium Sound	75	75	100	125	150	150	150
Sun/Moon Roof	150	150	175	200	225	250	275
Grille Guard	50	50	50	50	50	50	50
Running Boards	200	200	200	200	200	200	200
Premium Wheels	150	150	175	200	225	250	275
Towing Pkg	125	125	150	175	200	200	200
w/o Leather	(25)	(25)	(50)	(75)	(100)	(125)	(150)

TRUCKS & VANS

FOR MILEAGE ADJUSTMENT — SEE PAGE 9

SEE PAGE 9 FOR PVT PARTY & RETAIL EQUIPMENT 395

TRUCKS & VANS

Equipment	02	03	04	05	06	07	08

MODEL & TRIM PACKAGES (Truck Schedules T1 & T2)
(Add Only If Not Listed on Individual Vehicle Listing)

CHEVROLET/GMC:

LS, LT, LTZ, TrailBlazer, Xtreme, SLE (Full-Size), SLT, Diamond, Warner Bros Ed

	02	03	04	05	06	07	08
	125	450	500	550	600	650	725
SLE (Sonoma/Canyon/Safari), LS (S10/Colorado), ZR2 Suspension	125	275	300	325	375	425	475
SLS	125	225	—	—	—	—	—
SL, Z66, Z71	125	125	125	125	150	175	200

DODGE:

SLT, SXT, Laramie, Limited, Rumble Bee, Adventurer

	02	03	04	05	06	07	08
	125	325	375	425	475	525	575
ST, Sport, Off-Road, TRX, Night Runner, Big Horn, Lone Star	125	125	125	125	150	175	200

FORD:

	02	03	04	05	06	07	08
Limited, Chateau, Amarillo	600	925	1050	1200	1350	1500	1650
Lariat	600	650	725	800	875	950	1025
XLT, XLT Sport, XLT NBX, FX4, Edge Plus, Adrenaline	125	450	500	550	600	—	725
STX, XLS, Edge	125	275	300	325	375	425	475
XL, Sport, Off-Road, Tremor, LE, NBX	125	125	125	125	150	175	200

ALL MAKES: (All Other Model Pkgs Not Listed)

	02	03	04	05	06	07	08
	125	125	125	125	150	175	200

TRUCK SCHEDULE T1 (Deduct For)

	02	03	04	05	06	07	08
5-Spd Manual	(400)	(475)	(550)	(600)	(650)	(700)	(750)
6-Spd Manual	(400)	(300)	(350)	(400)	(425)	(450)	(475)
w/o Pwr Steering	(150)	(175)	(200)	(225)	(250)	(275)	(300)
w/o Air Cond	(250)	(300)	(350)	(400)	(450)	(500)	(550)

TRUCK SCHEDULE T2 (Add For)

	02	03	04	05	06	07	08
Auto Trans	350	400	450	500	550	600	650
Power Steering	75	100	125	150	150	150	150
Air Cond	200	250	300	350	400	450	475
TOTAL	625	750	875	1000	1100	1200	1275

TRUCK SCHEDULE T3 (See Page 398)

2002–2008 TRUCK FACTORY EQUIPMENT

Equipment	02	03	04	05	06	07	08
OTHER OPTIONS (Truck Schedules T1 & T2)							
Cassette	100	100	100	100	100	125	150
Power Windows	100	125	150	175	200	225	250
Pwr Door Locks	50	75	100	125	150	175	175
Tilt Wheel	75	100	125	150	175	200	200
Cruise Control	25	50	75	100	125	150	150
TOTAL	350	450	550	650	750	875	925
w/o AM/FM	(50)	(75)	(100)	(100)	(100)	(100)	(100)
CD (Single Disc)	200	200	200	200	200	200	200
CD (Multi Disc)	300	300	300	300	300	300	300
MP3 (Single CD)	300	300	300	300	300	300	300
MP3 (Multi CD)	400	400	400	400	400	400	400
Premium Sound	50	100	125	150	175	200	225
Video/DVD	200	250	275	300	325	350	375
NavigationSystm	400	450	475	500	525	550	575
Air Cond, Rear	250	300	350	400	425	450	475
Leather	200	250	275	300	325	350	375
Power Seat	25	25	25	50	75	100	125
Dual Pwr Seats	75	100	125	150	175	200	225
Quad Seating							
(4 Buckets)	150	200	250	300	325	350	375
Van Seating Packages							
(11/12 Pass)	400	450	500	550	600	650	700
(14/15 Pass)	650	800	950	1100	1225	1350	1475
Power Sliding Doors (Minivans)							
Single	25	25	25	25	25	50	75
Dual	50	50	75	100	125	150	175
Privacy Glass (Vans/Wagons/Sport Utilities)							
	50	75	100	100	100	100	100
Sliding Rear Window (Pickups)							
	25	50	75	75	75	75	75
Roof Rack	25	50	75	100	100	100	100
Sun/Moon Roof	300	350	400	450	500	550	575
Pickup Shell/Cap	100	150	175	200	225	250	275
Hard Tonneau	50	100	125	150	175	200	225
Bed Liner	100	100	100	100	125	150	175
Grille Guard	50	75	75	75	75	75	75
Winch	150	150	175	200	225	250	275
Custom Bumper	50	75	100	100	100	100	100
Parking Sensors	50	50	75	100	125	150	175
Custom Paint	25	25	25	50	75	100	125
Two-Tone Paint	25	25	25	50	75	100	125
Stepside Bed	150	200	250	300	325	350	375
Running Boards	200	200	200	200	200	200	200
Alloy Wheels	150	175	200	225	250	275	300
Premium Wheels	300	350	375	400	425	450	475

SEE PAGE 9 FOR PVT PARTY & RETAIL EQUIPMENT **397**

TRUCKS & VANS

Equipment	02	03	04	05	06	07	08
Oversize Premium Wheels (20" Plus)							
	450	525	600	675	750	800	850
Wide Tires or Oversize Off-Road Tires							
	100	100	100	100	125	150	175
ABS (4 Wheel)	150	175	200	200	200	200	200
Towing Pkg	200	225	250	275	300	300	300
Dual Rear Wheels (Add Only on Models Not Listed as DR)							
	800	925	1050	1175	1300	1425	1550

TRUCK SCHEDULE T3 (This Equipment Only)

Equipment	02	03	04	05	06	07	08
CD (Single Disc)	200	200	200	200	200	200	200
CD (Multi Disc)	300	300	300	300	300	300	300
MP3 (Single CD)	300	300	300	300	300	300	300
MP3 (Multi CD)	400	400	400	400	400	400	400
Premium Sound	150	200	250	300	325	350	375
Video/DVD	200	250	275	300	325	350	375
NavigationSystm	400	450	475	500	525	550	575
Sun/Moon Roof	300	350	400	450	500	550	575
Premium Wheels	300	350	375	400	425	450	475
Oversize Premium Wheels (20" Plus)							
	450	525	600	675	750	800	850
Grille Guard	50	75	75	75	75	75	75
Parking Sensors	50	50	75	100	125	150	175
Running Boards	200	200	200	200	200	200	200
Power Sliding Doors (Minivans)							
Single	—	25	25	25	25	50	75
Dual	—	50	75	100	125	150	175
Towing Pkg	200	225	250	275	300	300	300
w/o Leather	(200)	(250)	(300)	(350)	(400)	(450)	(525)

FOR MILEAGE ADJUSTMENT — SEE PAGE 9

NOTES

NOTES

NOTES

LIFE CREATES CAR SHOPPERS.
WE HELP CREATE CAR BUYERS.

Life Happens. From a job promotion to a new addition in the family, life events occur that leave millions of consumers in need of a new vehicle. And when that need occurs, Kelley Blue Book, *The Trusted Resource*®, is there.

Kbb.com has it covered:

- New Car Blue Book® Values
- Perfect Car Finder® Tool
- Side-by-Side Comparison Tool
- Video Reviews
- Advice Articles
- Vehicle Buying Guides
- Incentives & Rebates
- Safety Information
- Financing & Insurance
  And more...

Visit **www.kbb.com** today!

From new-car pricing to trade-in values, Kelley Blue Book provides information essential to the purchase of a new vehicle.